CURRENT MOLECULAR TARGETS OF HETEROCYCLIC COMPOUNDS FOR CANCER THERAPY

CURRENT MOLECULAR TARGETS OF HETEROCYCLIC COMPOUNDS FOR CANCER THERAPY

Edited by

VIVEK ASATI

Department of Pharmaceutical Chemistry, ISF College of Pharmacy, Moga, Punjab, India

ANKUR VAIDYA

Faculty of Pharmacy, Uttar Pradesh University of Medical Sciences, Saifai, Uttar Pradesh, India

ELSEVIER

ACADEMIC PRESS

An imprint of Elsevier

Academic Press is an imprint of Elsevier
125 London Wall, London EC2Y 5AS, United Kingdom
525 B Street, Suite 1650, San Diego, CA 92101, United States
50 Hampshire Street, 5th Floor, Cambridge, MA 02139, United States

Notices

Knowledge and best practice in this field are constantly changing. As new research and experience broaden our understanding, changes in research methods, professional practices, or medical treatment may become necessary.

Practitioners and researchers must always rely on their own experience and knowledge in evaluating and using any information, methods, compounds, or experiments described herein. In using such information or methods they should be mindful of their own safety and the safety of others, including parties for whom they have a professional responsibility.

To the fullest extent of the law, neither the Publisher nor the authors, contributors, or editors, assume any liability for any injury and/or damage to persons or property as a matter of products liability, negligence or otherwise, or from any use or operation of any methods, products, instructions, or ideas contained in the material herein.

ISBN: 978-0-323-96121-9

For information on all Academic Press publications visit our website at
https://www.elsevier.com/books-and-journals

Publisher: Stacy Masucci
Acquisitions Editor: Linda Bushman
Editorial Project Manager: Tracy Tufaga
Production Project Manager: Swapna Srinivasan
Cover Designer: Christian Bilbow

Typeset by TNQ Technologies

Working together
to grow libraries in
developing countries

www.elsevier.com • www.bookaid.org

Dedication

Dr. Hari Singh Gour

This book is dedicated to the late Dr. Hari Singh Gour, the founder of Dr. Harisingh Gour Vishwavidyalaya Sagar, M.P., India. Dr. Gour is one of those remarkable persons who lived such a life as to become the perennial fountain of inspiration to all the succeeding generations. The story of his life, career, and achievements sounds like a heroic romance bubbling with the dynamism of his colorful and many-sided personality. A man from a humble background who rises to the greatest possible heights in life with nothing but his own brilliance, firmness of purpose, and a never say die spirit. Great Savant Dr. Gour was veritably a pioneer in many walks of life and commanded great admiration and respect from all ranks of the Indian community. Made of stern metal, he disdained luxury.

Dr. Sir Hari Singh Gour was born in Sanichari Tauri Ward, Saugar, Madhya Pradesh, India, on the 26th of November 1870. Dr. Gour got his early education from the Government High School, Saugar. Later on, for higher education, Dr. Gour joined the Hislop College at Nagpur. He had passed his entrance and intermediate examinations in first class, standing first in the Province and sweeping all the prizes available to such students. In 1889, Dr. Gour proceeded to Cambridge to complete his studies, where he resided for 3 years and took Honors in the Moral Science Tripos Law (1892). He was a frequent speaker at the Union Debates, where he was spoken of as one of the orators of the day. As a worthy student of the university, he represented his university in the interuniversity education committees. His name was well known in literary circles by his two volumes of verse, "*The Stepping Westward*" and "*Random Rhymes*," and he was acclaimed by the journals of the day as a poet of great promise. The author was also the recipient of delicate compliments from men like Lord Tennyson and W. B. Gladstone. During the vacations, he used to go on lecture tours, and during his last years' residence at the university, he was a strong champion of Dadabhai Nawroji's candidature for the membership of the British Parliament.

Dr. Gour was a man of letters. While yet a student, articles from his pen began to find a place in some of the leading magazines, such as the '*National Review*.' His earliest effort at writing poetry *'Stepping Westward'* and other poems made him famous in the literary world, and he was elected a member of the Royal Society of Literature, a society founded in 1820, with the patronage of King George IV, to "reward literary merit and excite literary talent." He also became a member of the Writers' Forum due to his participation in the debates and a member of the National Liberal Club. He was a student's special testimonial, and his parting gift to his *alma mater* was a short drama acted in a suburban theatre.

He wrote three novels, *His Only Love* (1929) being one of them. Random Rhymes (1892), Stepping Westward and Other Poems, were his collections of poems, his essays and articles were compiled in his book entitled Facts and Fancies (1948), Seven Lives (1944) his autobiography. The Spirit of Buddhism (1929), a serious and elemental study of Buddhist philosophy, contained his ideas on religion. Lost Soul, Passing Clouds, and Letters from Heaven were his other works.

It is a convincing proof of his sincerity for the cause of the promotion of education that despite the very hard pressure on his valuable time, he accepted the honorary office of Vice Chancellor of Delhi University. He successfully organized the university in an incredibly short time, and his great services were rightly acknowledged by those in authority. The Chancellor referred to them in his successive convocation addresses. In recognition of his eminent public services, more particularly those in the field of education, he was knighted on January 1, 1925, and it was acclaimed all over the country as a fit tribute to his public service.

From such distinguished service in the fields of law, education, and progressive thoughts, Dr. Harisingh Gour slowly rose to the status of an All-India figure. He built his career on the rock of industrious habits, and by his crystal-clear insight in men and moments, he built for himself a reputation that a few of his generation could aspire. He offered his services as the vice chancellor of the University of Nagpur, India, for two successive terms and, starting from scratch, transformed it into a prestigious university. In the evening of his life, as shadows lengthened to his native town of Saugar, and through his prince's donation of about a crore of rupees (roughly 800 million today), laid the foundation of the University of Saugar, now known as Dr. Hari Singh Gour Vishwavidyalaya, Sagar, strong and true. The University was inaugurated on the 18th of July 1946, and although Dr. Gour himself was away at Nagpur on this auspicious day, holding important conversations with the authorities at Nagpur, the institution has, from its very initiation, breathed his noble spirit and aspired to live up to his great ideals. For two and a half years, he nurtured the babe, and when he passed away on the 25th of December 1949, he had the satisfaction that he had vouchsafed his spirit of truth and tolerance and the great love of life to the institution he founded and loved as his own. The trust placed in the University of Saugar is a challenge and a beacon-light to us, and shall never fail the Great Spirit that launched forth a hundred dreams of great beauty. His massive intellect and mighty spirit shall ever guide us to better modes of learning and thought.

Contents

Contributors xi
Preface xiii
Acknowledgments xv

1. Activin receptor-like kinase-2 inhibitors

Shelly Pathania and Pankaj Kumar Singh

1. Introduction 1
2. Structure and types of ALK2 1
3. ALK2 signal transduction 2
4. Physiological role of ALK2 3
5. Disorders associated with ALK2 3
6. ALK2 inhibitors 4
7. Conclusions 14
References 14

2. Ataxia telangiectasia and Rad3-related protein inhibitors

Adarsh Sahu, Preeti Sahu, Vivek Asati, Sanjeev Kumar Sahu and Jyotika Mishra

1. Introduction 17
2. ATM and ATR in relation to DNA damage response 18
3. Structure of the ataxia telangiectasia-mutated and Rad3-related checkpoints 18
4. Etiological association of ATM and ATR in precipitating cancer in at patients 23
5. Heterocyclics used for inhibiting ATM and ATR 23
6. ATM and ATR inhibitors currently under clinical trial 28
7. Closing statement 32
References 33
Further reading 36

3. Breakpoint cluster region Abelson kinase inhibitors

Sushanta Bhattacharya, Vivek Asati and Amena Ali

1. Introduction 37
2. BCR-AbL 37
3. Conclusions 42
Declaration of interests 42
References 42

4. Casein kinase (CK) inhibitors

Xin Zhai

1. Introduction 45
2. Protein kinase CK1 45
3. Protein kinase CK2 56
4. Protein kinase Fam20C 70
5. Conclusions 72
Declaration of interests 73
References 73

5. Recent updates on c-Src kinase and Src-Abl nonreceptor tyrosine kinases inhibitors

Navneesh, Shivanshu Pandey, Ruchi Shakya, Sumit Pasricha, Balak Das Kurmi and Preeti Patel

1. Introduction 83
2. Phosphorylation and dephosphorylation: Regulation of c-Src kinase activity 87
3. Src-Abl: Fusion protein and leukemia connection 90
References 109

6. Cyclin-dependent kinase 4 and 6 in cancer: Exploration of CDK4/6 inhibitors as anticancer agents

Nilay Kumar Nandi, Chahat, Rohit Bhatia, Gaurav Chauhan, Sourav Kalra and Bhupinder Kumar

1. Introduction   115
2. Different types of CDKs   117
3. Regulation by CDKs in cancer   119
4. Structure—activity relationship for the already reported CDK 4/6 inhibitors   122
References   133

7. Impact of epidermal growth factor receptors as a key clinical target against cancer

Ankush Kumar, Raj Kumar Narang and Rohit Kumar Bhatia

1. Introduction   139
2. Conclusion   156
References   157

8. Cancer and insulin-like growth factor inhibitors: Recent advancements and SAR analysis

Diksha Choudhary, Bhupinder Kumar and Amandeep Thakur

1. Introduction   161
2. Insulin-like growth factors   162
3. Involvement of IGFs/IGFR in various diseases   164
4. Role of IGF in cancer   164
5. Clinical developments for IGFs   167
6. Recent development targeting IGFR   168
7. Conclusion   176
References   177

9. Mitotic kinesin spindle protein (KSP/Eg5 ATPase) inhibitors

Ravindra Kumar Chourasiya, Wafa Hourani, Pran Kishore Deb and Katharigatta N. Venugopala

1. Introduction   183
2. Kinesin spindle protein inhibitors   186
3. Conclusion   196
4. Summary and future outlook   196
Abbreviation   197
References   197

10. p21-Activated kinase 1 inhibitors

Ravichandran Veerasamy and Rohini Karunakaran

1. Introduction   201
2. PAK1 structure and regulation   203
3. PAK1 role in cancer   203
4. PAK1 inhibitors   204
5. Conclusion   212
References   213

11. p38 mitogen-activated protein kinase inhibitors

Ashraf K. El-Damasy, Mohamed S.H. Salem, Mahmoud M. Sebaiy and Mohamed Saleh Elgawish

1. Introduction   219
2. MAPK types and signal transduction   221
3. FDA-approved MAPK inhibitors   222
4. Mechanisms of resistance   235
5. Therapeutic strategies to overcome MAPK resistance   237
6. The future of MAPK inhibitors therapeutics   239
7. Summary and future outlook   245
References   246

12. Proviral integration site for Moloney murine leukemia virus-1 (PIM-1) kinase inhibitors

Vinod Kumar Gurjar, Vivek Shrivastava, Shweta Jain, Rakesh Chawla and Ankur Vaidya

1. Introduction   255
2. Structure of PIM-1   256
3. Physiological functions of PIM-1   257
4. Functional relevance of PIM-1 in carcinomas   258
5. PIM-1 kinase inhibitors   260
6. Summary   316
References   316

13. Rearranged during transfection (RET) inhibitors

Vivek Shrivastava, Vinod Kumar Gurjar, Shweta Jain, Ankur Vaidya and Ankur Sharma

1. Introduction   323
2. Aberrant activation of RET in cancer and other diseases   327

3. Classes of RET inhibitors 340
4. Mechanisms of action 356
5. Therapeutic applications of RET inhibitors 356
6. Resistance mechanisms and overcoming resistance to RET inhibitors 357
7. Future perspectives and challenges of RET inhibitors 359
8. Conclusion 361
References 361

14. Serine/threonine-protein kinase B-Raf inhibitors

Rohini Karunakaran, Ravindra Kumar Chourasiya, Ankur Vaidya and Ravichandran Veerasamy

1. Introduction 377
2. Mitogen-activated protein kinases 378
3. RAF—RAS—MEK—ERK (MAP kinase) signaling paths 378
4. BRAF as therapeutic target 381
5. B-RAF inhibitors 381
6. MEK inhibitors 383
7. Conclusion 389
8. Summary and future outlook 390
Abbreviation 390
References 390

15. Tubulin polymerization inhibitors

Sanjeev Kumar Sahu, Manish Chaudhary, Shweta Jain and Kuldeep Kumar Bansal

1. Introduction 395
2. Induction of tubulin assembly—binding at taxoid and laulimalide site 397
3. Inhibition of tubulin assembly via β-tubulin alkylation or binding with colchicine or vinca domains 398
4. Recent developments in tubulin polymerization inhibitors 406
5. Summary and future outlook 413
References 413

16. Tumor necrosis factor receptor—associated protein 1 (TRAP1) inhibitors

Sanjeev Kumar Sahu, Charanjit Kaur, Shweta Jain, Pushpendra Kumar and Ankur Vaidya

1. Introduction 419
2. Role of TRAP1 in cancers 420
3. TNF-α and cancer 424
4. TRAP1 as a target of oncotherapy 425
5. TRAP1 inhibitors 425
6. Conclusion and future prospects 438
References 439

17. Vascular endothelial growth factor receptors (VEGFR/PDGFR) inhibitors

Mohamed Saleh Elgawish and Eman Abdeldayem

1. Introduction 443
2. Molecular mechanisms and clinical applications of angiogenesis 444
3. Inhibition of VEGFR and PDGFR signaling by small molecule drugs 447
4. The physicochemical properties of orally effective drugs 450
5. Adverse effect of VEGFR/PDGFR TKIs 453
6. FDA-approved VEGFR/PDGFR TKIs 453
7. Summary and future outlook 469
References 472

Index 477

Contributors

Eman Abdeldayem Department of Chemistry, Korea University, Seoul, Republic of Korea

Amena Ali Department of Pharmaceutical Chemistry, College of Pharmacy, Taif University, Taif, Saudi Arabia

Vivek Asati ISF College of Pharmacy, Moga, Punjab, India

Kuldeep Kumar Bansal Pharmaceutical Sciences Laboratory, Faculty of Science and Engineering Abo Akademi University, Turku, Finland

Rohit Kumar Bhatia Department of Pharmaceutical Chemistry, ISF College of Pharmacy, Moga, Punjab, India

Rohit Bhatia Department of Pharmaceutical Chemistry, ISF College of Pharmacy Moga, Moga, Punjab, India

Sushanta Bhattacharya Gupta College of Technological Sciences, Pharmaceutical Chemistry, Asansol, West Bengal, India

Chahat Department of Pharmaceutical Chemistry, ISF College of Pharmacy Moga, Moga, Punjab, India; Department of Pharmaceutical Sciences, HNB Garhwal University, Srinagar, Uttarakhand, India

Manish Chaudhary School of Pharmaceutical Sciences, Lovely Professional University, Phagwara, Punjab, India

Gaurav Chauhan School of Engineering and Sciences, Tecnologico de Monterrey, Monterrey, Nuevo León, Mexico

Rakesh Chawla University Institute of Pharmaceutical Sciences & Research, Baba Farid University of Health Sciences, Faridkot, Punjab, India

Diksha Choudhary Chitkara College of Pharmacy, Chitkara University, Rajpura, Punjab, India

Ravindra Kumar Chourasiya SVN Institute of Pharmaceutical Sciences, Swami Vivekanand University, Sagar, Madhya Pradesh, India

Pran Kishore Deb Department of Pharmaceutical Sciences and Technology, Birla Institute of Technology (BIT), Mesra, Jharkhand, India

Ashraf K. El-Damasy Department of Medicinal Chemistry, Faculty of Pharmacy, Mansoura University, Mansoura, Egypt; Brain Science Institute, Korea Institute of Science and Technology (KIST), Seoul, Republic of Korea

Mohamed Saleh Elgawish Department of Medicinal Chemistry, Faculty of Pharmacy, Suez Canal University, Ismailia, Egypt; Department of Chemistry, Korea University, Seoul, Republic of Korea

Vinod Kumar Gurjar School of Pharmacy, Faculty of Pharmacy, Parul University, Vadodara, Gujarat, India

Wafa Hourani Department of Pharmaceutical Sciences, Faculty of Pharmacy, Philadelphia University, Amman, Jordan

Shweta Jain Sir Madanlal Institute of Pharmacy, Etawah, Uttar Pradesh, India

Sourav Kalra School of Pharmacy, Chitkara University, Himachal Pradesh, India

Rohini Karunakaran Unit of Biochemistry, Faculty of Medicine, AIMST University, Semeling, Bedong, Kedah, Malaysia

Charanjit Kaur School of Pharmaceutical Sciences, Lovely Professional University, Phagwara, Punjab, India

Ankush Kumar Institute of Pharmaceutical Sciences, IET Bhaddal Technical Campus, Ropar, Punjab, India

Pushpendra Kumar Faculty of Pharmacy, Uttar Pradesh University of Medical Sciences, Saifai, Uttar Pradesh, India

Bhupinder Kumar Department of Pharmaceutical Sciences, HNB Garhwal University, Srinagar, Uttarakhand, India

Balak Das Kurmi Department of Pharmaceutics, ISF College of Pharmacy, Moga, Punjab, India

Jyotika Mishra Dr Harisingh Gour Vishwavidyalaya, Department of Pharmaceutical Sciences, Sagar, Madhya Pradesh, India

Nilay Kumar Nandi Meerut Institute of Engineering and Technology, Department of Pharmaceutical Technology, Meerut, Uttar Pradesh, India

Raj Kumar Narang Department of Pharmaceutics, ISF College of Pharmacy, Moga, Punjab, India

Navneesh Department of Pharmaceutical Analysis, ISF College of Pharmacy, Moga, Punjab, India

Shivanshu Pandey Department of Pharmaceutical Analysis, ISF College of Pharmacy, Moga, Punjab, India

Sumit Pasricha Department of Pharmaceutical Analysis, ISF College of Pharmacy, Moga, Punjab, India

Preeti Patel Department of Pharmaceutical Chemistry, ISF College of Pharmacy, Moga, Punjab, India

Shelly Pathania Integrative Physiology and Pharmacology, Institute of Biomedicine, Faculty of Medicine, University of Turku, Turku, Finland

Adarsh Sahu Dr Harisingh Gour Vishwavidyalaya, Department of Pharmaceutical Sciences, Sagar, Madhya Pradesh, India; School of Pharmaceutical Sciences, Lovely Professional University, Phagwara, Punjab, India; Amity Institute of Pharmacy, Amity University Rajasthan, Jaipur, Rajasthan, India

Sanjeev Kumar Sahu School of Pharmaceutical Sciences, Lovely Professional University, Phagwara, Punjab, India

Preeti Sahu Department of Chemistry, Central University of Kerala, Kasaragod, Kerala, India

Mohamed S.H. Salem SANKEN (The Institute of Scientific and Industrial Research), Osaka University, Osaka, Japan; Pharmaceutical Organic Chemistry Department, Faculty of Pharmacy, Suez Canal University, Ismailia, Egypt

Mahmoud M. Sebaiy Medicinal Chemistry Department, Faculty of Pharmacy, Zagazig University, Sharkia, Egypt

Ruchi Shakya Department of Pharmaceutical Chemistry, ISF College of Pharmacy, Moga, Punjab, India

Ankur Sharma Department of Medicine and Rheumatology, The University of Oklahoma Health Sciences Centre, Oklahoma City, OK, United States

Vivek Shrivastava School of Pharmacy, Faculty of Pharmacy, Parul University, Vadodara, Gujarat, India

Pankaj Kumar Singh Integrative Physiology and Pharmacology, Institute of Biomedicine, Faculty of Medicine, University of Turku, Turku, Finland

Amandeep Thakur School of Pharmacy, College of Pharmacy, Taipei Medical University, Taipei, Taiwan

Ankur Vaidya Pharmacy College, Uttar Pradesh University of Medical Sciences, Etawah, Uttar Pradesh, India; Faculty of Pharmacy, Uttar Pradesh University of Medical Sciences, Saifai, Uttar Pradesh, India

Ravichandran Veerasamy Pharmaceutical Chemistry Unit, Faculty of Pharmacy, AIMST University, Semeling, Bedong, Kedah, Malaysia

Katharigatta N. Venugopala Department of Biotechnology and Food Science, Faculty of Applied Sciences, Durban University of Technology, Durban, South Africa; Department of Pharmaceutical Sciences, College of Clinical Pharmacy, King Faisal University, Al-Ahsa, Saudi Arabia

Xin Zhai Shenyang Pharmaceutical University, Shenyang, China

Preface

Cancer is a nontreatable disease and some treatments are available that are only used to slow down the progression of the disease. The last 100 years have been a milestone for the development of treatments for this disease. Over this time frame, targeted therapies have been conceived and validated which have resulted in significant increases in 5-year survival rates, and in some forms of cancer now being considered essentially curable (early-stage prostate, thyroid, testicular, melanoma, breast). Furthermore, still some types of cancers have become a concern for humans particularly those in advanced stages, remaining challenging to treat. Traditionally, chemotherapy and radiation are the standard of care used to treat these advanced cancers, with significantly reduced 5-year survival rates. Targeted therapy is a type of cancer treatment that targets proteins that control how cancer cells grow, divide, and spread. It is the foundation of precision medicine. As researchers learn more about the DNA changes and proteins that drive cancer, they are better able to design treatments that target these proteins. Targeted drugs can be roughly classified into two categories: small molecules and macromolecules (e.g., monoclonal antibodies, polypeptides, antibody–drug conjugates, and nucleic acids). Compared with macromolecule drugs, small-molecule targeted drugs have advantages in some aspects such as the pharmacokinetic (PK) properties, costs, patient compliance, and drug storage and transportation. Despite challenged by macromolecule drugs represented by monoclonal antibodies in recent years, small-molecule targeted drugs still gain great development.

This book includes the development of small molecular inhibitors including a total of 17 chapters that are selected on the basis of different target. The name of chapter includes 1. Activin receptor-like kinase-2 (ALK2) inhibitors, 2. Ataxia telangiectasia and Rad3-related protein (ATR) inhibitors, 3. Breakpoint cluster region Abelson kinase (BCR-AbL) inhibitors, 4. Casein kinase (CK) inhibitors, 5. Recent updates on c-Src kinase and Src-Abl nonreceptor tyrosine kinases inhibitors, 6. Cyclin-dependent kinase 4 and 6 inhibitors as anticancer agents, 7. Impact of epidermal growth factor receptors as a key clinical target against cancer, 8. Insulin-like growth factor (IGF) inhibitors, 9. Mitotic kinesin spindle protein (KSP/Eg5 ATPase) inhibitors, 10. p21-activated kinase 1 (PAK1) inhibitors, 11. p38 mitogen-activated protein (MAP) kinase inhibitors, 12. Proviral integration site for Moloney murine leukemia virus-1 (PIM-1) kinase inhibitors, 13. Rearranged during transfection (RET) inhibitors, 14. Serine/threonine-protein kinase B-Raf inhibitors, 15. Tubulin polymerization inhibitors, 16. Tumor necrosis factor receptor-associated protein 1 (TRAP1) inhibitors, 17. Vascular endothelial growth factor receptors (VEGFR/PDGFR) inhibitors.

I have made every effort to avoid printing errors. However, despite best efforts, some might have crept in inadvertently. I shall be obliged if these are brought to my notice. Constructive suggestions, comments, and criticism on the subject matter of the book will be gratefully acknowledged, as they will certainly help to improve the future editions of the book. It is hoped that this book will be received favorably as an effective text book by medical scientists, students, and teachers of pharmacy and science.

Vivek Asati

Ankur Vaidya

Acknowledgments

To begin with, we owe everything to our parents for bestowing upon us wisdom, inspiration, zeal, and light for undertaking this task and providing us with the strength to enable its completion. Without their support and encouragement, our work would not have been imaginable.

First and foremost, we would like to thank the "ALMIGHTY GOD" for showering blessings of life and wisdom over us and for never forsaking us, even when we have forgotten, at too many occasions, to pray and thank him for all the blessings that he bestows on us.

We would like to thank Dr. Vinod Kumar Dixit for his years of guidance and support in writing this book. Without him, this book wouldn't have been possible.

We would like to thank Dr. G.D. Gupta for his valuable suggestions and expert advice throughout all the stages of the work.

We would like to thank Dr. Prabhat Kumar Singh for his support and encouragement while writing this book. He has been a constant source of inspiration.

We would also like to thank my friends who assisted us in one way or another through the writing of this book, especially Pushpendra Kumar, Mudit Kumar, Pankaj Kumar Jain, Balak Das Kurmi, Kuldeep Patel, Mithun Bhowmick, Pankaj Singhai, and Chakresh Jain, for their endless support in every aspect.

We would like to thank our many colleagues and friends who have helped me in the preparation of this book.

We are grateful to the contributors to this book especially the authors and reviewers of chapters; without their input, the book cannot be published.

We would also like to thank the Elsevier Inc. for providing this project. Tracy Tufaga, Editorial Project Manager from Elsevier, has guided the project from start to finish. We are indebted to her for her commitment to this book.

Finally, we would also like to thank Shweta Jain and Shiva Asati for their constant help while we were writing this book.

1

Activin receptor-like kinase-2 inhibitors

Shelly Pathania and Pankaj Kumar Singh

Integrative Physiology and Pharmacology, Institute of Biomedicine, Faculty of Medicine, University of Turku, Turku, Finland

1. Introduction

Activin receptor-like kinase 2 (ALK2) is a type I bone morphogenetic protein (BMP) receptor and member of the TGFβ family subgroup (Katagiri et al., 2021). It is involved in the canonical SMAD1/5/8 BMP signaling pathway by forming tetrameric complexes with BMPRII and ACVRIIA (activin receptor type-2A) and also in noncanonical signaling through p38MAPK (Maruyama et al., 2022). It plays a key role in the growth and differentiation of bone, heart, nervous, and reproductive systems. Single point mutations (gain of function) in ALK2 are very commonly observed in the two untreatable rare diseases, that is, fibrodysplasia ossificans progressiva (FOP) and diffuse intrinsic pontine glioma (DIPG) (Taylor, Mackay, et al., 2014; Taylor, Vinci, et al., 2014). In both diseases, there is a need for the discovery of ALK2-targeted agents. Some of the drug discovery efforts have been successful resulting in the development of dorsomorphin, LDN193189, K02288, and LDN214117 (Fig. 1.1) (Dinter et al., 2019).

2. Structure and types of ALK2

ALK2, a transmembrane protein, serves as a receptor for members of the transforming growth factor-β (TGF-β) family, especially for members inducing osteogenic signaling, such as bone morphogenetic proteins (BMPs) (Katagiri et al., 2021). It consists of 509 amino acids that can be divided into multiple domains: a signal peptide (amino acids 1–20), an extramembrane ligand-binding domain (amino acids 21–123), a transmembrane domain (amino acids 124–146), an intracellular region containing the glycine/serine (GS) domain (amino acids 178–207), and the serine/threonine kinase (amino acids 208–502) (Gipson et al., 2020). The human ALK2 proteins show 99.8% homology with mouse in its amino

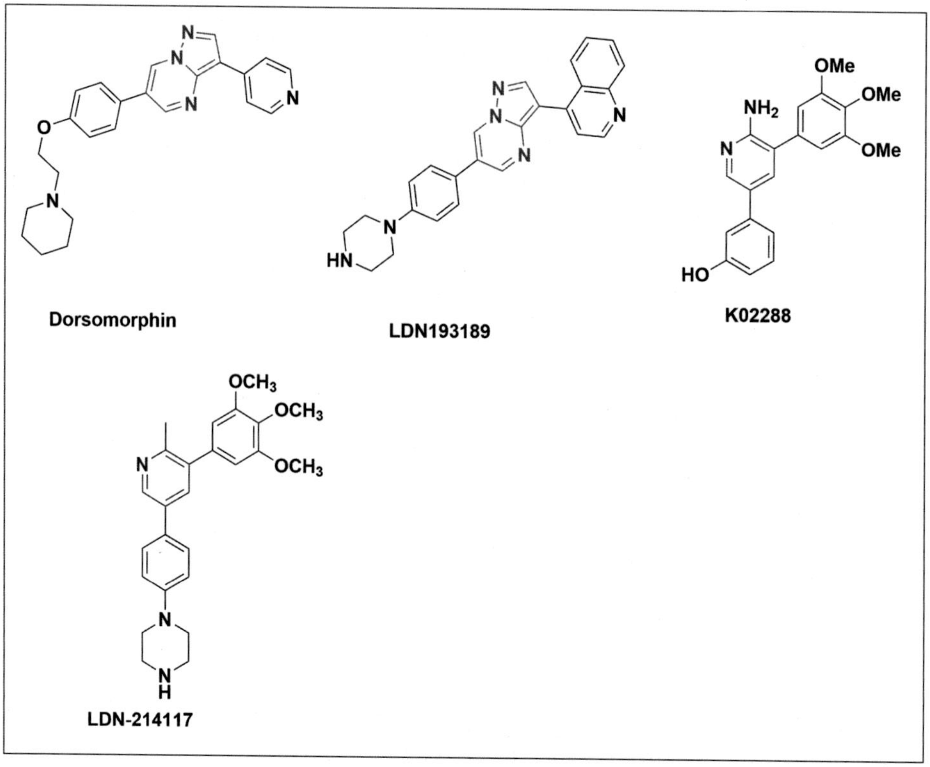

FIGURE 1.1   Some reported ALK2 inhibitors.

acid sequences. In humans, seven subtypes of ALK (ALK1 to ALK7) transmembrane kinase proteins are reported, which act as a binding site to the TGF-β family ligands (Khodr et al., 2020). They are classified as type I receptors due to the presence of a characteristic stretch of the GS domain in the cytoplasmic juxta-membrane domain. Type I receptor kinases are activated by phosphorylation of their GS domain by the type II receptor kinases within the tetrameric complexes (Agnew et al., 2021). Recent crystallography studies of ALK2 cytoplasmic region have indicated that the kinase domain has a typical bilobal architecture and the GS domain extends from the N-lobe into a helix-loop-helix motif that can bind the endogenous inhibitor FKBP12 (Shi et al., 2019). In the inactive conformation of ALK2 kinase, the activation region remains folded toward the solvent-exposed region preventing ATP binding (Sekimata et al., 2020). Almost all the ALK2 inhibitors bind in the ATP pocket, interacting with His286, Lys235, and Glu248 (Williams & Bullock, 2018).

3. ALK2 signal transduction

ALKs are type I receptors responsible for growth factor-β (TGFβ) superfamily signal transduction (Ahmadi et al., 2019). Out of all the ALKs, ALK1/2/3/6 form bone morphogenetic protein (BMP) type I receptors, while ALK4/5/7 are TGFβ type I receptors (Choi et al., 2021). Therefore, various BMP ligands can bind to ALK2, which can trigger the release of FKBP12 and the phosphorylation of the GS domain (Sekimata et al., 2020). This is followed by the phosphorylation of SMAD1/5/8, which forms heteromeric complexes with Co-SMAD (SMAD4) (Sanchez-Duffhues et al., 2020). These SMAD4-containing transcriptional complexes then translocate to the nucleus where they regulate the expression of the inhibitor of DNA binding/differentiation genes (Ullah et al., 2018).

4. Physiological role of ALK2

ALK2 plays a pivotal role in multiple physiological functions including embryonic development, tissue maintenance and regeneration, and cell death. Osteogenic ligands such as BMP2, BMP4, BMP7, and BMP9 bind to ALK2 inducing phosphorylation of the transcription factors, Smad1 and Smad5 (Mostafa et al., 2019).

5. Disorders associated with ALK2

5.1 Fibrodysplasia ossificans progressiva

FOP involves abnormal heterotopic ossification in skeletal muscle, tendons, and ligaments in childhood (Pignolo et al., 2020). Although the ossification process in FOP is similar to normal bone development, in more than 90% of patients with FOP, R206H mutation of ALK2 has been reported (Williams et al., 2021). This mutation occurs in the GS domain close to the juxta-membrane region and induces phosphorylation of Smad1/5 and BMP signaling. Additionally, 12 mutations such as L196P have also been reported in atypical FOP (Ohte et al., 2011). Interestingly, all mutations associated with FOP are observed in the intracellular, GS, or kinase domains. Overexpression of FOP-associated ALK2 mutants activates intracellular signaling suggesting them to be gain-of-function mutations (Katagiri et al., 2018).

5.2 Diffuse intrinsic pontine glioma

DIPG in simple terms represents a type of pediatric brain tumor that does not have any effective treatment (Biswas, 2022). In 2014, a study established DIPG as one of the ALK2-related disorders (Jones & Baker, 2014). Genome sequencing of patients with DIPG disclosed that some harbor additional mutations such as R206H, R258G, and G356D in ALK2/ACVR1. Among them, G328V is only observed in DIPG (Cao et al., 2020). Out of different ALK2 mutations related to DIPG, the G328V variant shows the highest in vitro and in vivo kinase activity. Studies suggest that DIPG is caused by hyperactivation of BMP signaling through gain-of-function mutations in ALK2 (Khuong-Quang et al., 2012).

5.3 Diffuse idiopathic skeletal hyperostosis

Diffuse idiopathic skeletal hyperostosis (DISH) is a disease involving calcification and ossification of spinal ligaments (Mader et al., 2013). In 2019, a study identified K400E mutant

ALK2 in a patient suffering from DISH (Tsukamoto et al., 2020). Another in vitro study reported that hyperactivation of intracellular signaling by BMP ligands occurs upon overexpression of K400E mutant ALK2. Although similar to FOP, DISH is also a skeletal disorder involving activation of ALK2/ACVR1, it does not show any heterotopic ossification of skeletal muscle tissues, which could be explained by the failure of K400E variant to be activated by Activin A (Licini et al., 2020).

6. ALK2 inhibitors

Dorsomorphin (Fig. 1.1) is one of the earliest inhibitors of ALK2, identified via an in vivo high-throughput screening (HTS) screening of a chemical library aimed to identify molecules with the ability to dorsalize developing zebrafish embryos. Dorsomorphin showed significant off-target kinase activity and lacked metabolic stability. Further development of dorsomorphin involving expansion of 4-pyridyl ring to a 4-quinoline and replacement of ether with piperazine resulted in LDN-193189 with improved potency and metabolic stability. Another HTS effort involving in vitro screening resulted in K02288. However, it showed poor solubility, and several modifications, such as the replacement of the 3-phenol with the 4-phenylpiperazine, were performed to yield LDN-214117. Some of the more recent efforts to identify ALK2 inhibitors are discussed here.

In 2022, Ullrich et al. reported a new series of 2-aminopyrazine-3-carboxamide derivatives as ALK2 inhibitors for the treatment of FOP. The derivatives were synthesized via three three-component Suzuki cross-coupling/N-alkylation reactions. Among the series, compound **1** was found as most active compound with IC$_{50}$ of 0.008 μM against ALK2^{R206H}. Activity against HEK293 cells also suggested a high cellular potency of **1** with IC$_{50}$ of 0.044 μM. The binding affinity of compound **1** was assessed against 450 kinases, which recommended that **1** possessed excellent selectivity toward ALK2. SAR displayed the importance of bicyclo [2.2.2]octanol moiety which is bridged in cyclohexane ring from 1 to 4 position (Fig. 1.2). Docking analysis also showed that bicyclo[2.2.2]octanol moiety sits well under the P loop of the receptor and forms an H-bond with ASN341(Ullrich et al., 2022).

In 2022, Witten et al. designed a new scaffold containing bicyclic lactam moiety via modification of previously reported aminopyrimidine ALK2 inhibitor **2**. They transformed the open amide group into lactam to see the change in potency and selectivity. This resulted in new 6,6 and 6,5-lactam scaffolds, which were put forward for the synthesis. Three series of different derivatives were prepared and tested. In one series, derivatives were synthesized using enantiopure (R)-2-methylpyrrolidine on the right side of the molecule along with cyclohexylamines on the left side. The molecules were evaluated as a mixture of cis/trans isomers but showed 63 times less potency than **2**. Through modeling study, it was established that weaker activity was due to less binding of the diastereomeric mixture. Further, they developed another series with pyrazole moiety on the right side, which resulted in the same potency. Then, a third series of derivatives was prepared by introducing N-methyl substituents on the pyrazole moiety. Compound **3** with methyl-capped tertiary amine was found to exhibit single-digit nanomolar activity toward ALK2 (IC$_{50}$ = 2.9 nM). The left side of the scaffold was also optimized with different substituents and resulted in compound 3a bearing cyclobutylamide with IC$_{50}$ value of 11 nM (Fig. 1.3). Overall, the authors

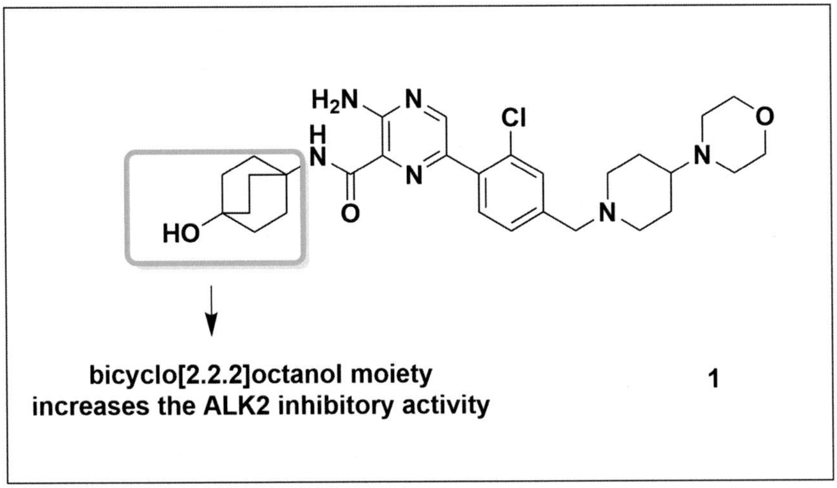

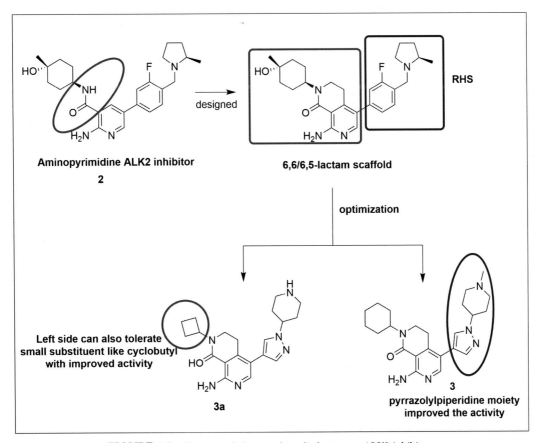

FIGURE 1.2   2-aminopyrazine-3-carboxamide derivatives as ALK2 inhibitor for the treatment of FOP.

FIGURE 1.3   Compounds bearing bicyclic lactam as ALK2 inhibitors.

optimized the right and left side substituent of the inhibitor to a pyrrazolylpiperidine and cyclobutyl, respectively with improved activity (Witten et al., 2022).

In 2021, Asati et al. reported the virtual screening exercise to design putative ALK2 inhibitors. They followed 3D-QSAR, pharmacophore model, and molecular docking experiments to determine the putative hits against ALK2. The validated pharmacophore hypothesis showed four features including an H-bond acceptor and aromatic ring. The followed-up 3D-QSAR study revealed the map of different features required for the inhibitory activity. This information was utilized to virtually screen the molecules from the ZINC database. The top screened molecules were subjected to molecular docking and dynamics study, which resulted in the identification of four (ZINC66091638, ZINC43524105, ZINC19458227, and ZINC72441013) putative ALK2 inhibitors having the fused pyrazole heterocyclic core (Asati et al., 2021).

In 2021, Yamamoto et al. reported novel bicyclic pyrazoles as potent ALK2 (R206H) inhibitors for the treatment of FOP. In their study, they identified a series of novel bicyclic pyrazole ALK2 (R206H) inhibitors by chemical modification of RK-59638. Among all the derivatives, compound 4 exhibited potent ALK2 (R206H) inhibitory activity with an IC_{50} value of 18.2 nM. SAR analysis showed that in the solvent region, para-substituted derivatives exhibited significant activity while ortho- and meta-substituted derivatives showed a reduction in the activity. Saturated heterocyclic derivatives containing oxygen or nitrogen at the end of the structure were found to be significantly potent, while the N-methoxyethyl group containing derivative showed the highest enzyme inhibitory activity, significant permeability, and acceptable P-gp-mediated efflux (Fig. 1.4). X-ray crystallographic analysis showed that these pyrazole derivatives formed two H-bonds with the main chain amine and carbonyl of the His286 in the hinge region (Yamamoto et al., 2021).

In 2020, Ensan et al. reported an orally bioavailable inhibitor of ALK2 by doing modification in LDN-214117, a well-known inhibitor of ALK2. Various analogs were prepared by swapping the methyl group from C2 to C4 of the pyridyl moiety of LDN-214117. This modification resulted in an active compound M4K2009 with an IC_{50} value of 13 nM against ALK2.

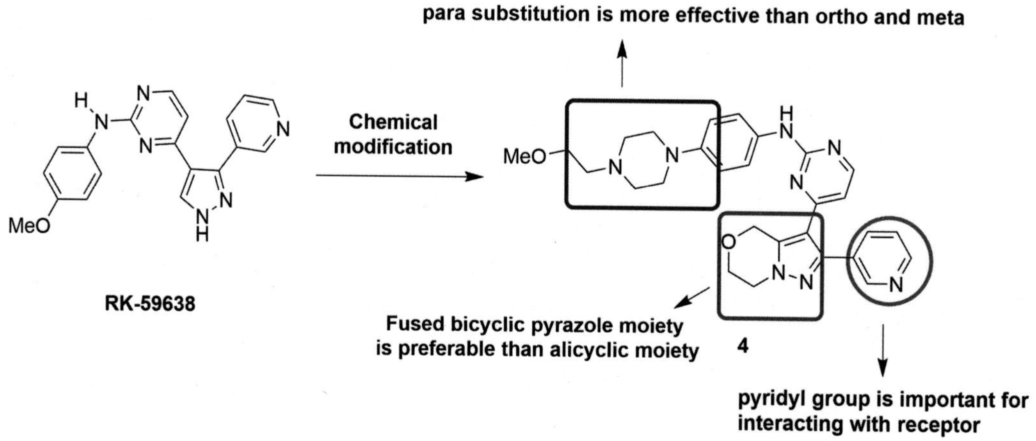

FIGURE 1.4   Novel bicyclic pyrazoles as potent ALK2 (R206H) inhibitors.

Although the compound was potent, in vivo study against hERG ($IC_{50} = 8$ μM) suggested the risk of arrhythmia. Later, the trimethoxyphenyl moiety of M4K2009 was modified to the benzamide group, which resulted in M4K2149 with significant ALK2 inhibitory activity ($IC_{50} = 17$ nM) and IC_{50} of >50 μM against hERG. Docking studies showed that the benzamide moiety of M4K2149 occupied properly in the hydrophobic pocket of ALK2 and also formed H-bonds with H286 and K235. SAR study highlights the significance of the methoxy group as if it is removed from the compound, there is a 28 times reduction in ALK2 inhibition. Analog 5 containing electron withdrawing groups like fluorine and electron donating groups like trimethoxy at the ortho position of the amide group also showed good ALK2 inhibition but possessed poor selectivity (Fig. 1.5). Further, more analogs substituted with alkyl groups at piperazine moiety were prepared to improve the permeability and selectivity, resulting in 2-fluoro-6-methoxybenzamide derivatives with kinome-wide selectivity and improved pharmacokinetic parameters (Ensan et al., 2020).

In 2020, Engers et al. reported the discovery of 7-aryl-imidazo[1,2-*a*]pyridine-3-ylquinolines as ALK inhibitors. They reviewed the heterocyclic cores reported for ALK2 inhibitory activity and selected imidazo[1,2-*a*]pyridine scaffold to explore their ALK2 inhibitory potential. They explored the different sites of the imidazo[1,2-*a*]pyridine core to identify potent inhibitors. Overall, lead optimization and SAR analysis identified three compounds (**6a-c**) having a piperazine moiety with 2-methyl-fluorinated quinoline (Fig. 1.6). These compounds showed potent ALK2 inhibitory potential and selectivity against other related receptors. Further profiling showed that these compounds have a balanced in vivo pharmacokinetic profile, amenable to further advancement into IND-enabling studies (Engers et al., 2020).

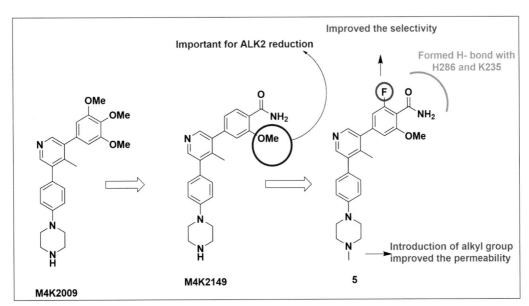

FIGURE 1.5 2-Fluoro-6-methoxybenzamide derivative as selective ALK2 inhibitor with improved pharmacokinetics.

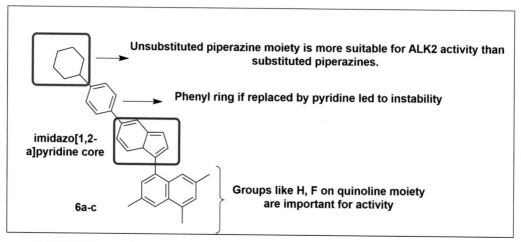

FIGURE 1.6   7-aryl-imidazo[1,2-*a*]pyridine-3-ylquinolines with selective ALK2 inhibitory activity.

In 2020, Sato et al. reported the identification and structural basis of bis-heteroaryl pyrazole-based ALK2 (R206H) inhibitors for the treatment of FOP via integrated ligand-based and structure-based drug design approaches. They started by using a similarity search on 142,785 compounds in the Drug Discovery Initiative compound library at The University of Tokyo. As query compounds, they used 16 ALK2 inhibitors and 220 inhibitors of other ALK family proteins (ALK1, ALK3, ALK4, ALK5, and ALK6) derived from the ChEMBL database. Using four structural fingerprints, they selected 976 compounds for the initial ALK2 (R206H) kinase assay. In parallel, they screened the Drug Discovery Initiative compound library via molecular docking analysis, as a structure-based approach, resulting in 1428 compounds for the initial kinase assay. After kinase assay, they found 6-(1*H*-pyrazol-5- yl)pyrimidine scaffold to be present in multiple potent hits. On the basis of high potency, patentability, and synthetic feasibility, RK-59638 was selected as the seed compound for further development. They further synthesized derivatives of RK-59638 by the addition of a hydrophilic chemical group and an alkyl chain. Out of all, RK-71807 (**7**) with ethyl group on N1 of pyrazole and piperazine group in place of methoxy resulted in the most potent derivative (Fig. 1.7). X-ray complexes of RK-71807 and ALK2 showed piperazine to be located near Asp293 (4.02 Å). The *N*-ethyl group is located near Tyr219 (3.69 Å) (Sato et al., 2020).

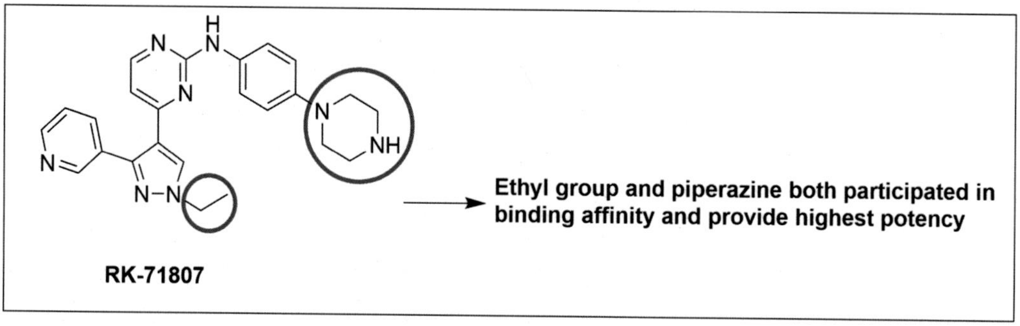

FIGURE 1.7   Bis-heteroaryl pyrazole-based inhibitors for the treatment of FOP.

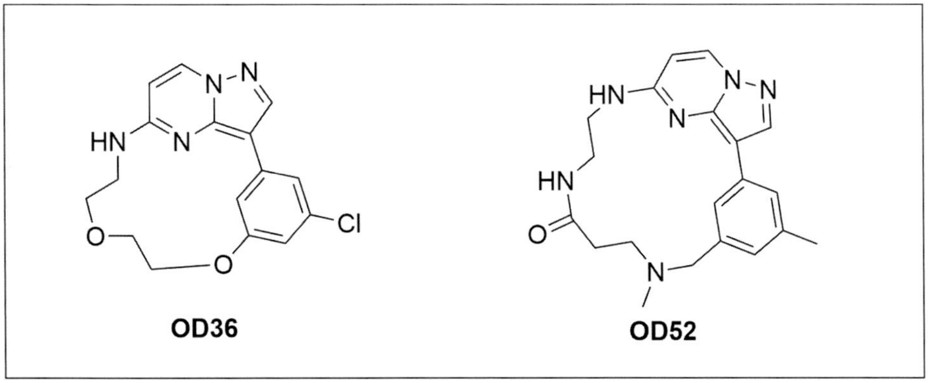

FIGURE 1.8 Two novel macrocyclic inhibitors OD36 and OD52 with potent binding to the ALK2 kinase ATP pocket.

In 2019, Sánchez-Duffhues et al. reported the discovery of macrocyclic ALK2 inhibitors. In the study, they first characterized an in vitro model for FOP, followed by the identification of novel macrocycles with putative ALK2 inhibitory potential. Briefly, they first identified OD36 (**8**) as having high affinity against ALK2, then as the first round of optimization, the linker was modified to improve the selectivity, which led to OD52 (**9**) (Fig. 1.8). Molecular modeling analysis revealed that OD36 and OD52 interact with His286 in the binding pocket of ALK2. In comparison to LDN-193189, OD36 and OD52 occupy more space in the ATP pocket due to their macrocycle linkers (Sánchez-Duffhues et al., 2019).

In 2019, Sekimata et al. reported the identification of bis-heteroaryl pyrazoles-based inhibitors of ALK2 (R206H). They followed their previous study whereby they identified several ALK2 (R206H) inhibitors via in silico and in vitro screening experiments. Taking forward, they selected crystal structures of one of the previously identified inhibitors (**10**) bound to ALK2 (R206H) and utilized the interaction pattern to design derivatives of this inhibitor and to study their SAR. Briefly, SAR analysis showed that the 3-pyridyl ring is vital for the H-bond within the binding pocket. Alkyl substitution on the N2 of the pyrazole was found to impart improved cell permeability and efflux (Fig. 1.9). Overall, compound **11** with morpholine in place of the methoxy group resulted in a most potent compound that can be considered for further study (Sekimata et al., 2020).

In 2018, Kuasar and Nayeem reported virtual screening of ALK2 inhibitors employing DFT (density functional theory) and MD simulations analysis. They screened a library of 23,050 molecules from PubChem via molecular docking exercise using UCSF-DOCK, which yielded five lead molecules. Analysis showed that the screened hits possess similar interactions within the binding pocket as defined in the crystal structure. Physicochemical results suggested that the identified lead molecules were having with drug-likeness properties. Further, they investigated the stability of the complexes of all the five hits via MD simulation and calculated relative binding free energy via MM/PBSA, which showed that selected hits possessed better binding affinity in comparison to the control (Kausar & Nayeem, 2018).

In 2018, Hudson et al. reported structure—activity relationship and kinase profiling of novel quinazolinone inhibitors of ALK2. They first identified a 6-pyrazole quinazolinone-based

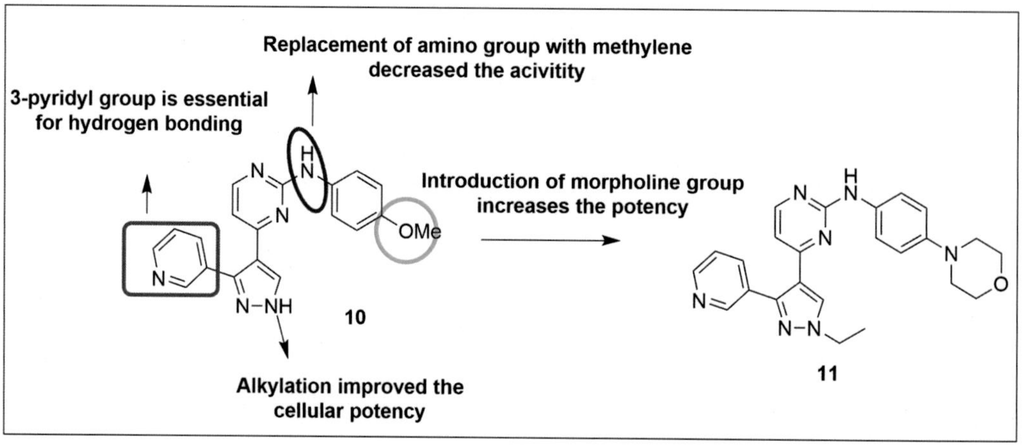

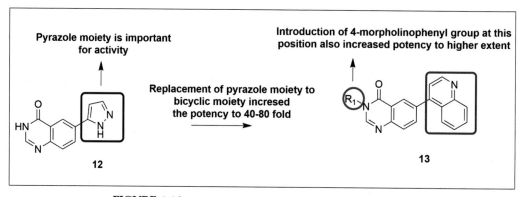

FIGURE 1.9   Bis-heteroaryl pyrazole-based ALK2 inhibitors.

compound, **12**, as an ALK2 inhibitor (IC$_{50}$ = 8.2 μM). Followed by the modification at the pyr-azole ring on the sixth position of quinazoline, exploration of further substitutions at the third position of quinazolinone was carried out, along with the incorporation of solvent channel groups. SAR analysis revealed that the replacement of the 6-pyrazole of **12** with bicyclic groups improves potency. Further, the introduction of a 4-morpholinophenyl as the solvent channel resulted in the most potent compound, **13** (Fig. 1.10). Binding mode analysis of **13** revealed that quinazolinone N-1 forms an H-bond with His286 (Hudson et al., 2018).

Jiang et al. (2018), reported the identification of 3-(4-sulfamoylnaphthyl) substituted pyra-zolo[1,5-a]pyrimidines as selective ALK2 inhibitors. Taking a cue from the binding pattern of LDN-193189 in the pocket of ALK2, they envisaged substituting the quinoline ring group with the other aromatic rings at the 3-position of the pyrazolo[1,5-*a*]pyrimidine core to explore selectivity between ALK2 and ALK3 and sterically hinder the solvent-exposed piper-azine ring. SAR suggested that replacing the quinoline ring with 4-(methylsulfonyl)phenyl and 4-(sulfamoyl)phenyl improved potency. Also, moving the sulfamoyl group from the fourth to the fifth position resulted in decreased potency and selectivity. Out of all the

FIGURE 1.10   Novel quinazolinone-based inhibitors of ALK2.

compounds, they found **14** ($IC_{50} = 19$ nM) as a potent and highly selective ALK2 inhibitor. The binding interaction model of **7** showed that the 4-sulfamoyl group forms H-bond interactions with Lys235 and Asp354. Although compound 7 possessed good potency and selectivity for ALK2, further SAR study was performed to see the outcome of substitutions on the sixth position of the scaffold (Fig. 1.11). Compound **15** ($IC_{50} = 9$ nM) emerged as more potent and selective than compound 7 (Jiang et al., 2018).

In 2017, Kim et al. reported the discovery of ALK2 inhibitors via a high-throughput screen. Upon establishing the role of abnormal activation of ALK2 in cancer cell proliferation, they performed HTS to discover inhibitors for ALK2. Out of the 71 compounds showing more than 80% inhibition at 1 mM, two compounds, KRC203 (**16**) and KRC360 (**17**) having similar 5-[1- (piperidin-4-yl)-1H-pyrazol-4-yl]pyridine-2-amine scaffold, showed nanomolar range inhibitory potential (Fig. 1.12). During further study, both the compounds were found to

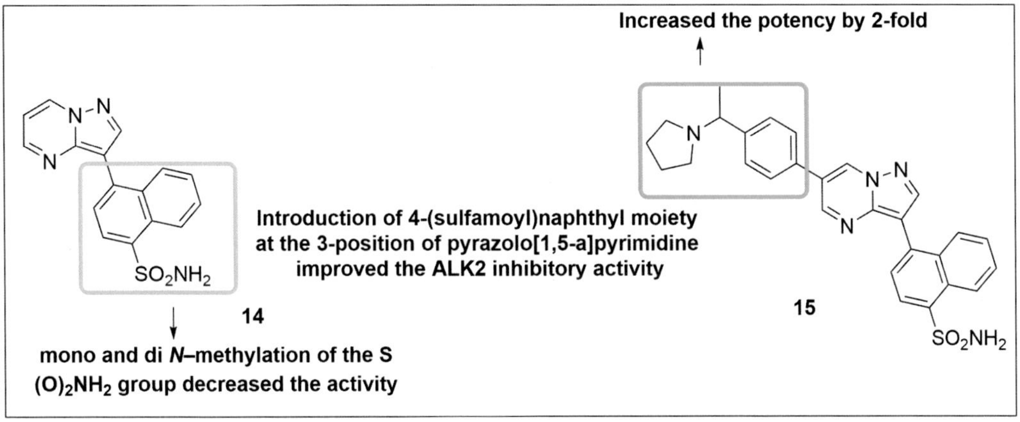

FIGURE 1.11 3-(4-Sulfamoylnaphthyl)pyrazolo[1,5-a]pyrimidine derivatives as potent and selective ALK2 inhibitors.

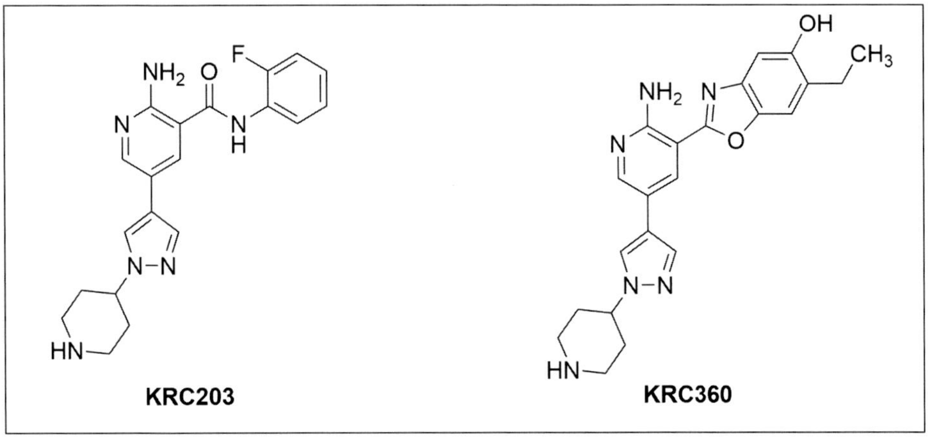

FIGURE 1.12 5-[1- (Piperidin-4-yl)-1H-pyrazol-4-yl]pyridine-2-amine-based ALK2 inhibitors.

exhibit more specific inhibitory potential against ALK1 and ALK2, particularly ALK2, in comparison to reference, LDN193189 (Kim et al., 2017).

In 2014, Mohedas et al. reported SAR of 3,5-diaryl-2-aminopyridine-based ALK2 inhibitors. They followed their previous work whereby they reported **K02288 (18)**, a BMP inhibitor having a 2-aminopyridine core, which possesses more selectivity than LDN-193189. In the current work, they described SAR of **18** as an ALK2 inhibitor. Overall, they found that the 3-phenol group resulted in its low cellular activity as compared to the enzymatic assay. Substituting 3-phenol with 4-phenol or 4-phenylpiperazine improved cellular potency. On the trimethoxy ring, 4-methoxy was dispensable, while 3- or 5-methoxy was important (Fig. 1.13). Also, the substitution of primary amine with a nonpolar methyl group on the 2-aminopyridine core shifted potency from TGF-β to BMP selective, resulting in a more selective compound **19 (LDN-214117)**. Binding mode analysis of 10 in ALK2 showed the presence of an ATP-mimetic H-bond with H286 (Mohedas et al., 2014).

Mohedas et al., in 2013, reported the identification of selective ALK2 inhibitors. They followed their previous work involving the discovery of dorsomorphin and LDN-193189 as highly potent as a BMP inhibitor. In the current work, they reported the discovery of LDN-212854 (**20**), a selective BMP and ALK2 inhibitor. Briefly, they synthesized and evaluated quinoline-coupled pyrazolo[1,5-*a*]pyrimidine derivatives. SAR analysis showed that quinoline substitution on the third, eighth, and sixth position of the core resulted in a loss of activity against BMP receptors. However, quinoline substitution in the fifth position resulted in a potent and selective BMP inhibitor. Further, incorporating the phenyl-piperazine group on the 5-quinoline moiety resulted in a more potent and selective compound, LDN-212854 (Fig. 1.14). Finally, a complex of ALK2 with LDN-212,854 suggested that the 5-quinoline group forms an H-bond with K235 in the catalytic domain (Mohedas et al., 2013).

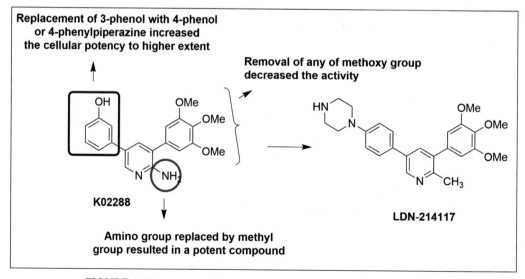

FIGURE 1.13   SAR analysis of 3,5-diaryl-2-aminopyridine ALK2 inhibitors.

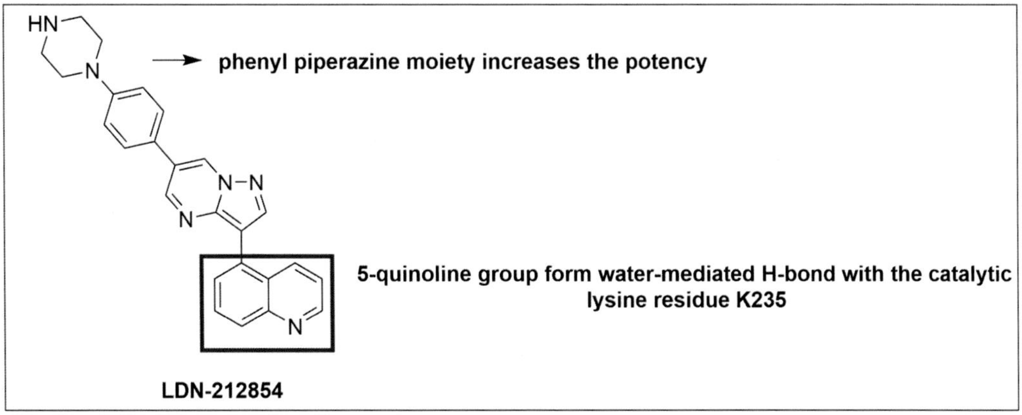

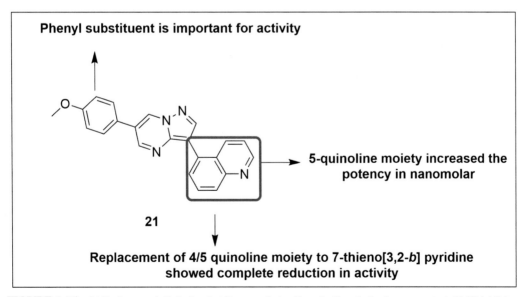

FIGURE 1.14   SAR of quinoline fused pyrazolo[1,5-*a*]pyrimidine derivatives as ALK2-biased kinase inhibitor.

Engers et al., in 2013, discussed the structure–activity relationships of pyrazolo[1.5-a]py-rimidine scaffold-based selective ALK2 inhibitor. Considering the structure of dorsomorphin and LDN-193189, they selected the pyrazolo[1.5-*a*]pyrimidine core to develop more selective ALK2 inhibitors leading to the discovery of ML347. In SAR, they retained the 6-(4-methoxyphenyl) group and varied the third position substituent disclosing that 4-nitrogen heterocycles were optimal (Fig. 1.15). Interestingly, they found 5-quinoline containing deriv-ative (**21**), without 4-nitrogen heterocycle, showed nanomolar potency. Overall, the deriva-tive with 4-quinoline substituent showed the most potency in the BMP4 cell assay. Further

FIGURE 1.15   SAR of pyrazolo[1.5-a]pyrimidine coupled with quinoline derivatives as potent ALK2 inhibitor.

evaluation of potent inhibitors for kinase selectivity revealed that compounds containing a 5-quinoline displayed selectivity against ALK3 (BMPR1A) (Engers et al., 2013).

7. Conclusions

ALK2 kinase has been one of the up-and-coming anticancer targets. Interestingly though, the amount of work done on exploring this kinase target is still limited. In the recent past, there have been sincere efforts to develop and study different chemical frameworks as ALK2 inhibitors, improving the potency and selectivity of the previous classes. Some of such recently developed compounds have also been reported to demonstrate high selectivity across the kinome, especially against similar BMP and TGF-β receptors. More importantly, some of these ALK2 inhibitors are reported to demonstrate efficacy in in vivo models of DIPG and FOP. With such ALK2 inhibitors entering clinical trials, a better understanding is needed to determine how we can scale up research and development of ALK2-targeted therapeutic agents.

References

Agnew, C., Ayaz, P., Kashima, R., Loving, H. S., Ghatpande, P., Kung, J. E., Underbakke, E. S., Shan, Y., Shaw, D. E., Hata, A., & Jura, N. (2021). Structural basis for ALK2/BMPR2 receptor complex signaling through kinase domain oligomerization. *Nature Communications, 12*(1). https://doi.org/10.1038/s41467-021-25248-5

Ahmadi, A., Najafi, M., Farhood, B., & Mortezaee, K. (2019). Transforming growth factor-β signaling: Tumorigenesis and targeting for cancer therapy. *Journal of Cellular Physiology, 234*(8), 12173−12187. https://doi.org/10.1002/jcp.27955

Asati, V., Bharti, S. K., Das, R., Kashaw, V., & Kashaw, S. K. (2021). Discovery of novel ALK2 inhibitors of pyrazolo-pyrimidines: A computational study. *Journal of Biomolecular Structure and Dynamics*, 10422−10436. https://doi.org/10.1080/07391102.2021.1944320

Biswas, A. (2022). Clinicopathology & molecular analysis of diffuse intrinsic pontine glioma (DIPG) in children— insights from past, present, and future directions. *Journal for Research in Applied Sciences and Biotechnology, 1*(4), 63−70. https://doi.org/10.55544/jrasb.1.4.8

Cao, H., Jin, M., Gao, M., Zhou, H., Tao, Y. J., & Skolnick, J. (2020). Differential kinase activity of ACVR1 G328V and R206H mutations with implications to possible TβRI cross-talk in diffuse intrinsic pontine glioma. *Scientific Reports, 10*(1). https://doi.org/10.1038/s41598-020-63061-0

Choi, W., Lee, H. W., Pak, B., Han, O., Kim, M., & Jin, S. W. (2021). Transcriptomic analysis identifies novel targets for individual bone morphogenetic protein type 1 receptors in endothelial cells. *Federation of American Societies for Experimental Biology Journal, 35*(3). https://doi.org/10.1096/fj.202002071R

Dinter, T., Bocobo, G. A., & Yu, P. B. (2019). Pharmacologic strategies for assaying BMP signaling function. *Methods in Molecular Biology, 1891*, 221−233. https://doi.org/10.1007/978-1-4939-8904-1_16

Engers, D. W., Bollinger, S. R., Felts, A. S., Vadukoot, A. K., Williams, C. H., Blobaum, A. L., Lindsley, C. W., Hong, C. C., & Hopkins, C. R. (2020). Discovery, synthesis and characterization of a series of 7-aryl-imidazo [1,2-a]pyridine-3-ylquinolines as activin-like kinase (ALK) inhibitors. *Bioorganic & Medicinal Chemistry Letters, 30*(18). https://doi.org/10.1016/j.bmcl.2020.127418

Engers, D. W., Frist, A. Y., Lindsley, C. W., Hong, C. C., & Hopkins, C. R. (2013). Synthesis and structure-activity relationships of a novel and selective bone morphogenetic protein receptor (BMP) inhibitor derived from the pyrazolo[1.5-a]pyrimidine scaffold of Dorsomorphin: The discovery of ML347 as an ALK2 versus ALK3 selective MLPCN probe. *Bioorganic & Medicinal Chemistry Letters, 23*(11), 3248−3252. https://doi.org/10.1016/j.bmcl.2013.03.113

Ensan, D., Smil, D., Zepeda-Velázquez, C. A., Panagopoulos, D., Wong, J. F., Williams, E. P., Adamson, R., Bullock, A. N., Kiyota, T., Aman, A., Roberts, O. G., Edwards, A. M., O'meara, J. A., Isaac, M. B., & Al-Awar, R. (2020). Targeting ALK2: An open science approach to developing therapeutics for the treatment of diffuse intrinsic pontine glioma. *Journal of Medicinal Chemistry, 63*(9), 4978−4996. https://doi.org/10.1021/acs.jmedchem.0c00395

Gipson, G. R., Goebel, E. J., Hart, K. N., Kappes, E. C., Kattamuri, C., McCoy, J. C., & Thompson, T. B. (2020). Structural perspective of BMP ligands and signaling. *Bone, 140.* https://doi.org/10.1016/j.bone.2020.115549

Hudson, L., Mui, J., Vázquez, S., Carvalho, D. M., Williams, E., Jones, C., Bullock, A. N., & Hoelder, S. (2018). Novel quinazolinone inhibitors of ALK2 flip between alternate binding modes: Structure-activity relationship, structural characterization, kinase profiling, and cellular proof of concept. *Journal of Medicinal Chemistry, 61*(16), 7261−7272. https://doi.org/10.1021/acs.jmedchem.8b00782

Jiang, J.k., Huang, X., Shamim, K., Patel, P. R., Lee, A., Wang, A. Q., Nguyen, K., Tawa, G., Cuny, G. D., Yu, P. B., Zheng, W., Xu, X., Sanderson, P., & Huang, W. (2018). Discovery of 3-(4-sulfamoylnaphthyl)pyrazolo[1,5-a]pyrimidines as potent and selective ALK2 inhibitors. *Bioorganic & Medicinal Chemistry Letters, 28*(20), 3356−3362. https://doi.org/10.1016/j.bmcl.2018.09.006

Jones, C., & Baker, S. J. (2014). Unique genetic and epigenetic mechanisms driving paediatric diffuse high-grade glioma. *Nature Reviews Cancer, 14*(10), 651−661. https://doi.org/10.1038/nrc3811

Katagiri, T., Tsukamoto, S., & Kuratani, M. (2021). Accumulated knowledge of activin receptor-like kinase 2 (ALK2)/activin a receptor, type 1 (ACVR1) as a target for human disorders. *Biomedicines, 9*(7). https://doi.org/10.3390/biomedicines9070736

Katagiri, T., Tsukamoto, S., Nakachi, Y., & Kuratani, M. (2018). Recent topics in fibrodysplasia ossificans progressiva. *Endocrinology and Metabolism, 33*(3), 331−338. https://doi.org/10.3803/EnM.2018.33.3.331

Kausar, T., & Nayeem, S. M. (2018). Identification of small molecule inhibitors of ALK2: A virtual screening, density functional theory, and molecular dynamics simulations study. *Journal of Molecular Modeling, 24*(9). https://doi.org/10.1007/s00894-018-3789-2

Khodr, V., Machillot, P., Migliorini, E., Reiser, J. B., & Picart, C. (2020). High throughput measurements of BMP/BMP receptors interactions using bio-layer interferometry. *bioRxiv.* https://doi.org/10.1101/2020.10.20.348060

Khuong-Quang, D. A., Buczkowicz, P., Rakopoulos, P., Liu, X. Y., Fontebasso, A. M., Bouffet, E., Bartels, U., Albrecht, S., Schwartzentruber, J., Letourneau, L., Bourgey, M., Bourque, G., Montpetit, A., Bourret, G., Lepage, P., Fleming, A., Lichter, P., Kool, M., Von Deimling, A., … Hawkins, C. (2012). K27M mutation in histone H3.3 defines clinically and biologically distinct subgroups of pediatric diffuse intrinsic pontine gliomas. *Acta Neuropathologica, 124*(3), 439−447. https://doi.org/10.1007/s00401-012-0998-0

Kim, M., Choi, O., Pyo, S., Choi, S. U., & Park, C. H. (2017). Identification of novel ALK2 inhibitors and their effect on cancer cells. *Biochemical and Biophysical Research Communications, 492*(1), 121−127. https://doi.org/10.1016/j.bbrc.2017.08.016

Licini, C., Farinelli, L., Cerqueni, G., Hosein, A., Marchi, S., Gigante, A., & Mattioli-Belmonte, M. (2020). Heterotopic ossification in a patient with diffuse idiopathic skeletal hyperostosis: Input from histological findings. *European Journal of Histochemistry, 64*(4), 317−322. https://doi.org/10.4081/ejh.2020.3176

Mader, R., Verlaan, J. J., & Buskila, D. (2013). Diffuse idiopathic skeletal hyperostosis: Clinical features and pathogenic mechanisms. *Nature Reviews Rheumatology, 9*(12), 741−750. https://doi.org/10.1038/nrrheum.2013.165

Maruyama, H., Sakai, S., & Ieda, M. (2022). Endothelin-1 alters BMP signaling to promote proliferation of pulmonary artery smooth muscle cells. *Canadian Journal of Physiology and Pharmacology, 100*(10), 1018−1027. https://doi.org/10.1139/cjpp-2022-0104

Mohedas, A. H., Wang, Y., Sanvitale, C. E., Canning, P., Choi, S., Xing, X., Bullock, A. N., Cuny, G. D., & Yu, P. B. (2014). Structure-activity relationship of 3,5-diaryl-2-aminopyridine ALK2 inhibitors reveals unaltered binding affinity for fibrodysplasia ossificans progressiva causing mutants. *Journal of Medicinal Chemistry, 57*(19), 7900−7915. https://doi.org/10.1021/jm501177w

Mohedas, A. H., Xing, X., Armstrong, K. A., Bullock, A. N., Cuny, G. D., & Yu, P. B. (2013). Development of an ALK2-biased BMP type i receptor kinase inhibitor. *ACS Chemical Biology, 8*(6), 1291−1302. https://doi.org/10.1021/cb300655w

Mostafa, S., Pakvasa, M., Coalson, E., Zhu, A., Alverdy, A., Castillo, H., Fan, J., Li, A., Feng, Y., Wu, D., Bishop, E., Du, S., Spezia, M., Li, A., Hagag, O., Deng, A., Liu, W., Li, M., Ho, S. S., … Reid, R. R. (2019). The wonders of BMP9: From mesenchymal stem cell differentiation, angiogenesis, neurogenesis, tumorigenesis, and metabolism to regenerative medicine. *Genes and Diseases, 6*(3), 201−223. https://doi.org/10.1016/j.gendis.2019.07.003

Ohte, S., Shin, M., Sasanuma, H., Yoneyama, K., Akita, M., Ikebuchi, K., Jimi, E., Maruki, Y., Matsuoka, M., Namba, A., Tomoda, H., Okazaki, Y., Ohtake, A., Oda, H., Owan, I., Yoda, T., Furuya, H., Kamizono, J., Kitoh, H., … Katagiri, T. (2011). A novel mutation of ALK2, L196P, found in the most benign case of fibrodysplasia ossificans progressiva activates BMP-specific intracellular signaling equivalent to a typical mutation, R206H. *Biochemical and Biophysical Research Communications, 407*(1), 213–218. https://doi.org/10.1016/j.bbrc.2011.03.001

Pignolo, R. J., Wang, H., & Kaplan, F. S. (2020). Fibrodysplasia ossificans progressiva (FOP): A segmental progeroid syndrome. *Frontiers in Endocrinology, 10*. https://doi.org/10.3389/fendo.2019.00908

Sanchez-Duffhues, G., Williams, E., Goumans, M. J., Heldin, C. H., & ten Dijke, P. (2020). Bone morphogenetic protein receptors: Structure, function and targeting by selective small molecule kinase inhibitors. *Bone, 138*. https://doi.org/10.1016/j.bone.2020.115472

Sato, T., Sekimata, K., Sakai, N., Watanabe, H., Mishima-Tsumagari, C., Taguri, T., Matsumoto, T., Fujii, Y., Handa, N., Tanaka, A., Shirouzu, M., Yokoyama, S., Hashizume, Y., Miyazono, K., Koyama, H., & Honma, T. (2020). Structural basis of activin receptor-like kinase 2 (R206H) inhibition by bis-heteroaryl pyrazole-based inhibitors for the treatment of fibrodysplasia ossificans progressiva identified by the integration of ligand-based and structure-based drug design approaches. *ACS Omega, 5*(20), 11411–11423. https://doi.org/10.1021/acsomega.9b04245

Sekimata, K., Sato, T., & Sakai, N. (2020). ALK2: A therapeutic target for fibrodysplasia ossificans progressiva and diffuse intrinsic pontine glioma. *Chemical and Pharmaceutical Bulletin, 68*(3), 194–200. https://doi.org/10.1248/cpb.c19-00882

Sánchez-Duffhues, G., Williams, E., Benderitter, P., Orlova, V., van Wijhe, M., Garcia de Vinuesa, A., Kerr, G., Caradec, J., Lodder, K., de Boer, H. C., Goumans, M. J., Eekhoff, E. M. W., Morales-Piga, A., Bachiller-Corral, J., Koolwijk, P., Bullock, A. N., Hoflack, J., & ten Dijke, P. (2019). Development of macrocycle kinase inhibitors for ALK2 using fibrodysplasia ossificans progressiva-derived endothelial cells. *JBMR Plus, 3*(11). https://doi.org/10.1002/jbm4.10230

Shi, F., Gao, J., Zou, J., Ying, Y., & Lin, H. (2019). Targeting heterotopic ossification by inhibiting activin receptor-like kinase 2 function (Review). *Molecular Medicine Reports, 20*(4), 2979–2989. https://doi.org/10.3892/mmr.2019.10556

Taylor, K. R., Mackay, A., Truffaux, N., Butterfield, Y. S., Morozova, O., Philippe, C., Castel, D., Grasso, C. S., Vinci, M., Carvalho, D., Carcaboso, A. M., De Torres, C., Cruz, O., Mora, J., Entz-Werle, N., Ingram, W. J., Monje, M., Hargrave, D., Bullock, A. N., … Grill, J. (2014). Recurrent activating ACVR1 mutations in diffuse intrinsic pontine glioma. *Nature Genetics, 46*(5), 457–461. https://doi.org/10.1038/ng.2925

Taylor, K. R., Vinci, M., Bullock, A. N., & Jones, C. (2014). ACVR1 mutations in DIPG: Lessons learned from FOP. *Cancer Research, 74*(17), 4565–4570. https://doi.org/10.1158/0008-5472.CAN-14-1298

Tsukamoto, S., Kuratani, M., & Katagiri, T. (2020). Functional characterization of a unique mutant of ALK2, p.K400E, that is associated with a skeletal disorder, diffuse idiopathic skeletal hyperostosis. *Bone, 137*, 115410. https://doi.org/10.1016/j.bone.2020.115410

Ullah, I., Sun, W., Tang, L., & Feng, J. (2018). Roles of SmAds family and alternative splicing variants of Smad4 in different cancers. *Journal of Cancer, 9*(21), 4018–4028. https://doi.org/10.7150/jca.20906

Ullrich, T., Arista, L., Weiler, S., Teixeira-Fouchard, S., Broennimann, V., Stiefl, N., Head, V., Kramer, I., & Guth, S. (2022). Discovery of a novel 2-aminopyrazine-3-carboxamide as a potent and selective inhibitor of activin receptor-like kinase-2 (ALK2) for the treatment of fibrodysplasia ossificans progressiva. *Bioorganic & Medicinal Chemistry Letters, 64*, 128667. https://doi.org/10.1016/j.bmcl.2022.128667

Williams, E., Bagarova, J., Kerr, G., Xia, D. D., Place, E. S., Dey, D., Shen, Y., Bocobo, G. A., Mohedas, A. H., Huang, X., Sanderson, P. E., Lee, A., Zheng, W., Economides, A. N., Smith, J. C., Yu, P. B., & Bullock, A. N. (2021). Saracatinib is an efficacious clinical candidate for fibrodysplasia ossificans progressiva. *JCI Insight, 6*(8). https://doi.org/10.1172/jci.insight.95042

Williams, E., & Bullock, A. N. (2018). Structural basis for the potent and selective binding of LDN-212854 to the BMP receptor kinase ALK2. *Bone, 109*, 251–258. https://doi.org/10.1016/j.bone.2017.09.004

Witten, M. R., Wu, L., Lai, C. T., Kapilashrami, K., Pusey, M., Gallagher, K., Chen, Y., & Yao, W. (2022). Inhibition of ALK2 with bicyclic pyridyllactams. *Bioorganic & Medicinal Chemistry Letters, 55*. https://doi.org/10.1016/j.bmcl.2021.128452

Yamamoto, H., Sakai, N., Ohte, S., Sato, T., Sekimata, K., Matsumoto, T., Nakamura, K., Watanabe, H., Mishima-Tsumagari, C., Tanaka, A., Hashizume, Y., Honma, T., Katagiri, T., Miyazono, K., Tomoda, H., Shirouzu, M., & Koyama, H. (2021). Novel bicyclic pyrazoles as potent ALK2 (R206H) inhibitors for the treatment of fibrodysplasia ossificans progressiva. *Bioorganic & Medicinal Chemistry Letters, 38*, 127858. https://doi.org/10.1016/j.bmcl.2021.127858

2

Ataxia telangiectasia and Rad3-related protein inhibitors

Adarsh Sahu[1,3,4], Preeti Sahu[2], Vivek Asati[5], Sanjeev Kumar Sahu[3] and Jyotika Mishra[1]

[1]Dr Harisingh Gour Vishwavidyalaya, Department of Pharmaceutical Sciences, Sagar, Madhya Pradesh, India; [2]Department of Chemistry, Central University of Kerala, Kasaragod, Kerala, India; [3]School of Pharmaceutical Sciences, Lovely Professional University, Phagwara, Punjab, India; [4]Amity Institute of Pharmacy, Amity University Rajasthan, Jaipur, Rajasthan, India; [5]ISF College of Pharmacy, Moga, Punjab, India

1. Introduction

Ataxia telangiectasia (AT), also known as Louis—Bar Syndrome is a rare autosomal recessive genetic disorder characterized by progressive neurologic problems that lead to ataxia or difficulty walking and an increased risk of developing various types of cancer (Panteliadis & Benjamin, 2022). The disease is also characterized by the appearance of small clusters of enlarged blood vessels or telangiectasia in the eye or on the surface of the skin. AT is an early-onset disease. By the age of 5, patients develop slurred speech and difficulty in walking and may require wheelchair assistance by the time they reach adolescence (Levy & Lang, 2018). Apart from ataxia and telangiectasia, other symptoms of AT include neuropathy, oculomotor apraxia, chorea, and myoclonic twitches (Teive et al., 2018).

AT came to light in 1941 Madame Louise Bar, a Belgian neurologist was the pioneer to report the manifestations of AT. In her case study, Madame Bar discussed the prognosis of progressive cerebellar ataxia and extensive cutaneous telangiectasia in a nine-year-old boy (Coon & Benarroch, 2018). The genetic predisposition of the disease was mapped in 1988. The international consortium of scientists allocated the gene responsible for AT (ATM) located on the long arm (q) of chromosome 11 (11q22. 3) (Lavin & Shiloh, 1997). Although AT dispassionately afflicts all races and ethnicities, incidences of AT are found to be relatively higher in populations with exorbitant rates of consanguineous marriages (Ghiasy et al., 2017).

The management of patients with AT involves addressing the specific symptoms of the disease, and while significant improvement has been made in the field, a specific treatment to cure this disease is yet to be available. In recent years with advancements in heterocyclic chemistry, several potent and selective inhibitors of ATR have been developed demonstrating efficacy in preclinical studies (Bin et al., 2022). In this chapter, we provide an overview of the various candidate molecules envisaged for the treatment of AT by inhibiting ATR.

2. ATM and ATR in relation to DNA damage response

AT is a hereditary disorder. The etiology of AT involves mutations in the ataxia telangiectasia (ATM) gene located on chromosome 11. These mutations can be of nonsense, frameshift, missense, and insertion-deletion type (Li & Swift, 2000). In human physiology, any form of genetic mutation or chromosomal aberration activates the DDR or DNA damage response task force (Podhorecka et al., 2010). DDR is a complex network of interconnected signaling pathways that is essential to defend the integrity of the human genome against both exogenous and endogenous genotoxic insults, such as ultraviolet radiation, ionizing radiation, or reactive oxygen species (Nastasi et al., 2020). Ataxia telangiectasia-mutated (ATM) checkpoint kinase 2 (CHK2) and Rad3-related (ATR) checkpoint kinase 1 (CHK1) signals are two key pathways to initiate DDR (Mu et al., 2007). DNA is the key component of genetic heredity. It gets constantly exposed to damaging agents such as free radicals, irradiations, and carcinogens. Damaged DNA can cause disruption in hemostasis leading to a myriad of disease states such as cancer. DNA damage manifests either as double-strand breaks (DSB) or single-strand breaks (SSB) (Zou, 2007). Fig. 2.1 enumerates the various components of DDR. Based on the type of DNA damage, these components collaborate as a complex network of interconnected pathways to initiate either cell cycle arrest or DNA repair processes or apoptosis (Kuczler et al., 2021).

DSB activates the ternary Mre11–Rad50–NBS1 (MNR) complex. Activated MNR interacts with chromatin to autophosphorylate ataxia telangiectasia mutated (ATM) kinase. The activated ATM communicates with several transducer enzymes, including checkpoint kinase 2 (CHK2) and the transcription factor p53. In case, DNA encounters an SSB the Rad9–Hus1–Rad1 complex comes into play. This complex, in association with Rad17, Rfc2, Rfc3, Rfc4, and Rfc5 activates ataxia telangiectasia and Rad3-related kinase (ATR). The latter enzyme is directed by its subunit ATR interacting protein (ATRIP) to replication protein A (RPA)-coated single-stranded DNA. Following this sensing step, Rad9 binds its partner protein TopBP1, which results in the stimulation of ATR-mediated CHK1 phosphorylation. CHK1 and CHK2 amplify the signals from the sensors, phosphorylating a variety of effectors. In the context of both DSB as well as SSB, cells either transiently arrest cell cycle progression or induce apoptosis depending on the severity of the encountered damage (Lee & Paull, 2005).

3. Structure of the ataxia telangiectasia-mutated and Rad3-related checkpoints

ATM and ATR are serine/threonine protein kinases that function as key factors in maintaining genome stability. ATM and ATR are serine/threonine protein kinases that function as key factors in maintaining genome stability. Fig. 2.3 describes the structure of ATM protein

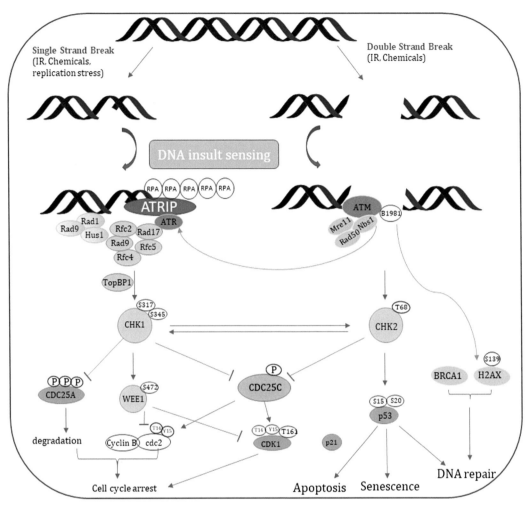

FIGURE 2.1   Components of the DNA damage response pathways modulated by ATM and ATR (Ronco et al., 2017).

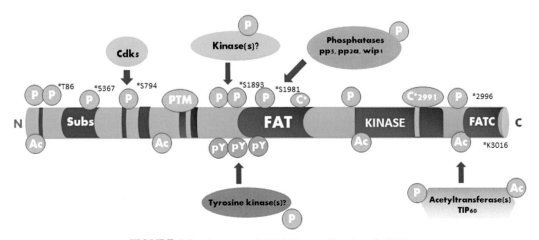

FIGURE 2.2   Structure of ATM kinases (Bhatti et al., 2011).

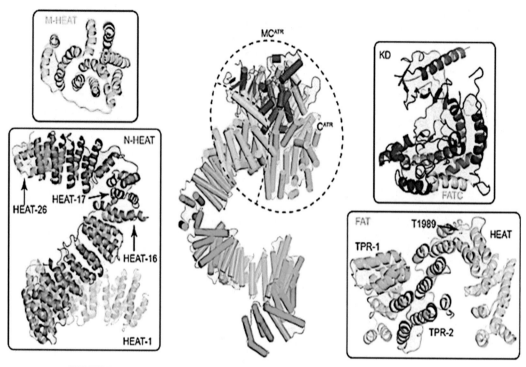

FIGURE 2.3   Cryo-EM structure of human ATR-ATRIP complex (Rao et al., 2018).

kinase. Kinase, FAT, FATC, and PRD (yellow) domains are shown in the C-terminus; HEAT (Huntingtin, Elongation factor 3, alpha subunit of PP2A and TOR1), TPR (tetratricopeptide), ARM (Armadillo), and PFT (protein farnesyl transferase) repeats are shown in the N-terminus schematically in dark green and magenta. Protein interaction motifs of ATM are also shown: TAN (Tel1/ATM N-terminal) motif (dark blue), N-terminal substrate-binding site (Subs); putative leucine zipper (red). Protein interaction motifs of ATM are also shown: TAN (Tel1/ATM N-terminal) motif (dark blue), N-terminal substrate-binding site (Subs); putative leucine zipper (red) and proline-rich motif (dark purple). Fig. 2.3 also demonstrates the posttranslational modifications of ATM. Accordingly, the figure identifies sites for ATM autophosphorylation and phosphorylation (P), Acetylation (Ac), and cysteine modification (C*). These sites interact to ensure activation of the ATM kinase. Despite significant research, the exact number of phosphotyrosine (pY) sites or the identities of tyrosine kinases capable of phosphorylating these sites in ATM remain elusive. However, in Fig. 2.2, the authors have also identified sites for possible but yet unidentified posttranslational modifications (PTM) of ATM kinase (Bhatti et al., 2011).

ATR consists of a 2644-amino acid residue phosphatidylinositol 3-kinase-related family member with overlapping sequence and functional homologies to the DNA-dependent and ATM protein kinases (Harnor et al., 2017). Fig. 2.3 defines the cryo-EM structure of the human ATR-ATRIP (ATR interacting protein) complex. In the figure, the ATR domains namely N-HEAT, M-HEAT, FAT, and kinase domain (containing FATC) have been demonstrated in

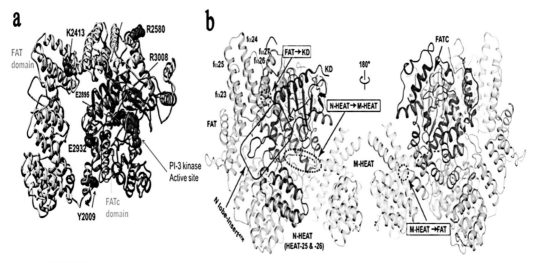

FIGURE 2.4   Structure of ATM (A) Pourahmadiyan et al. (2019) and ATR (B) Rao et al. (2018).

ribbon representations. The cryo-electron microscopy (EM) structure of the human ATR-ATRIP complex was observed at 4.7 Å resolution. The complex adopts a hollow "heart" shape. The conformational flexibility of ATR monomers allows ATRIP to properly lock the N-termini of the two ATR monomers to favor ATR-ATRIP complex formation and functional diversity (Rao et al., 2018).

Fig. 2.4 compares the structures of both ATM and ATR genes. While both ATM and ATR share high sequence homology and functional similarity, ATM primarily responds to DNA double-strand breaks (DSBs), whereas ATR is activated by a broader spectrum of DNA damage, including DSBs, cross-links, and DNA replication stress (Scott & Pandita, 2006).

In Fig. 2.5, we have summarized the ATM signaling network. ATM is associated with the prognosis of significant pathological malfunctions such as AT and tissue-specific processes such as apoptosis, CNS development, immunity, and angiogenesis. ATM phosphorylates proteins to control signal transduction in conditions akin to cellular stresses, such as DNA damage and reactive oxygen species (ROS)-mediated oxidative stress. Apart from AT, ATM is also implicated in impaired central nervous system (CNS) development, exhibiting either neurodegeneration or microcephaly, and displays varying degrees of immunodeficiency. In addition, ATM is often associated with cancer predisposition, and in certain cases, problems related to fertility and metabolism have also been cited (Zaki-Dizaji et al., 2017).

ATR was first identified as an indispensable component of embryonic development. It also gets activated by hypoxia, cellular mechanical, and oxidative stressors. Fig. 2.6 exhibits the schematics of ATR signaling pathways. Principally ATR is responsible for safeguarding replication S-phase fork integrity, regulating cell cycle progression, and initiating cell cycle checkpoints in case of genotoxic insults. In associating with centromeres, ATR encourages effective chromosomal segregation during mitosis. Most importantly, ATR is responsible for apprehending damaged or stalled DNA replication folks by recognizing Replication Protein A-coated single-stranded DNA (ssDNA). A significant number of studies have documented

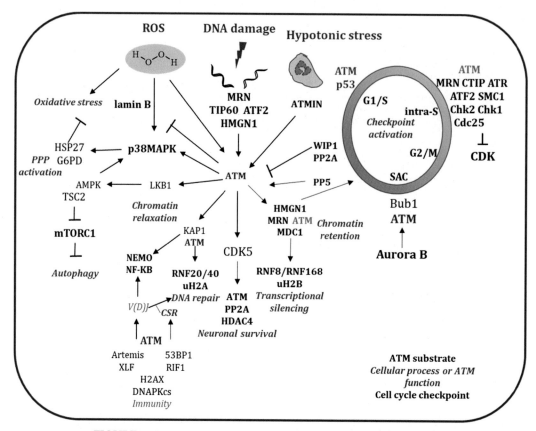

FIGURE 2.5 Schematic of ATM signaling pathways (Stracker et al., 2013).

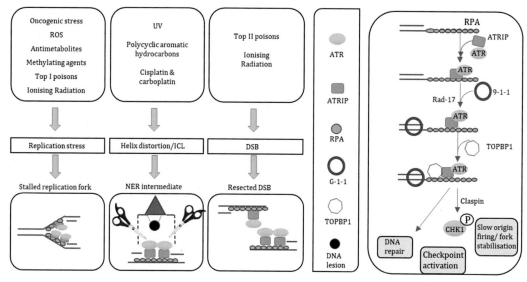

FIGURE 2.6 Schematic of ATR signaling pathways (Stracker et al., 2013).

the predisposition of Seckel syndrome type 1 in patients with hypomorphic ATR mutations. Consequently, ATR mutations often get implicated in primordial dwarfism, avian faces, accelerated aging, micrognathia, microcephaly, growth retardation, intellectual disability, and defects in the DDR. Complete ablation of ATR functions results in rapid cell death.

4. Etiological association of ATM and ATR in precipitating cancer in at patients

The pathological hallmark of cancer is uncontrolled proliferation attributed to chromosomal aberration of DNA damage (Macheret & Halazonetis, 2015). ATM and ATR are two distinct signaling cascades responsible for triggering the cellular response to DNA damage. ATM is required both for ATR-Chk1 activation and to initiate DNA repair by promoting the formation of single-stranded DNA at sites of damage through nucleolytic resection. On the other hand, the ATR-Chk1 pathway is the foremost effector of DNA damage and replication checkpoints and, hence, is essential for the survival of many, cell types. Although cells can persist even with mutations in ATM and ATR, the cost of survival includes genomic instability and cancer predisposition in the now-mutated organisms. Therefore, inhibitors of ATM and ATR protein kinases can enhance the sensitivity of tumor cells for diverse anticancer agents. As a proof of concept scientists have developed a number of synthetic inhibitor compounds with the propensity to encumber ATM and ATR. In the course of this chapter, we will be discussing about various anticancer heterocyclics that have been documented to inhibit ATM and ATR protein kinases (Takeuchi et al., 2019).

5. Heterocyclics used for inhibiting ATM and ATR

Heterocyclics target damaged DNA in cancer cells. However, DDR negates the efficacy as drugs by recognizing and repairing damaged DNA. ATM and ATR are major regulators of the DDR and hence form attractive targets for anticancer therapy (Cheng et al., 2022). Fig. 2.7 describes the timeline of the discovery of various synthetic heterocyclics. In this section, we have described the attributes of some popular heterocyclics used as ATM and ATR inhibitors.

5.1 Caffeine

Caffeine (1) is a purine alkaloid that is found as a constituent of tea and coffee (Fig. 2.8). Initially, it was observed that drinking coffee exerts anticarcinogenic efficacy in skin cancer patients. However, the consumption of decaffeinated coffee had no such effect. These and many studies citing the anticancer properties of tea and coffee brought caffeine into the research preview. A significant number of studies proclaim that decaffeinated is popularly employed to study ATM and ATR signaling. The molecular structure of caffeine (1) restrains these kinases in vitro and overcomes cell cycle checkpoint reactions in vivo (Cortez, 2003). Caffeine improves apoptosis and disposal of precancerous cells. Also, several studies have documented that caffeine-mediated apoptosis occurs via both p53-dependent and p53-independent mechanisms. Investigations of the p53-independent impact of caffeine led to the

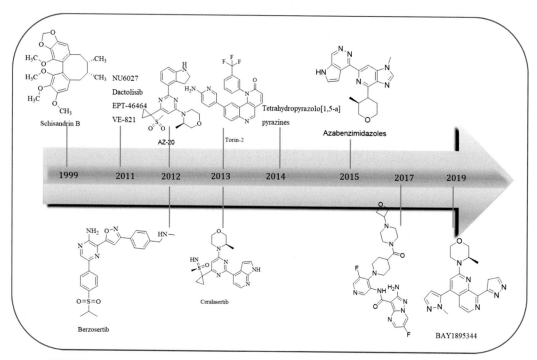

FIGURE 2.7 Timeline for synthesis of various ATM and ATR inhibitors (Barnieh et al., 2021).

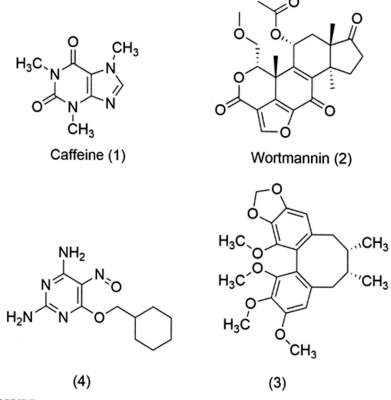

FIGURE 2.8 Structure of caffeine (1), wortmannin (2), schisandrin (3), and NU6027 (4).

conclusion that caffeine causes an increment in the ATR-mediated arrangement of phospho-Chk1 (Ser345) and subsequently increases apoptosis (Matt & Hofmann, 2016).

5.2 Wortmannin

Wortmannin (2) is a fungal metabolite. It was initially identified as a strong enzyme inhibitor. It binds to the ATP location of regulatory kinases such as PI-3 kinase and Polo-like kinase. Subsequent studies have indicated wortmannin to bind covalently forming ATP-site adducts with DNA-PK, ATM, and ATR. However, the efficacy of wortmannin is limited as a relatively high concentration of the drug is required to induce ATR inhibition (Angira et al., 2020).

5.3 Schisandrin B

Schisandrin B or Sch B (3) is a dibenzocyclooctadiene derivative. It is naturally found in the fruits of *Schisandra chinensis* also known as the Mongolian berry (Todorova et al., 2021). The molecular structure of Schisandrin B is described in Fig. 2.8. Sch B is known for its hepatoprotective, antioxidant, antiaging, antianxiety, and anticancer properties (Nasser et al., 2020). It is also acknowledged as the first ever small molecule to be reported for its ATR inhibitory potential (ATR IC50 = 7.25 μM) (Bradbury et al., 2020). In the cell-based assay, it was observed that Sch B increases the sensitivity of cancer cells to UV treatment by inhibiting the UV-activated G2/M and S-phase checkpoints and by obstructing the UV-induced ATR-dependent signaling pathway (Nishida et al., 2009). However, Sch B is limited by weak ATR potency. For the cancer cells to be sensitized to UV treatment extremely high concentration (≥30 μM) of Sch B was required. At such high concentrations, Sch B induces off-target inhibition and systemic toxicity (Veuger & Curtin, 2014).

5.4 NU6027

NU6027 (4) is a potent inhibitor of cellular ATR activity with IC50 of 6.7 μM in MCF7 cells and 2.8 μM in GM847KD cells. The molecular structure of NU6027 is described in Fig. 2.8. Mechanistically similar to Sch B, NU6027 also acts on the G2/M checkpoints and inhibits RAD51 focus formation, thereby increasing the sensitivity of ovarian and breast cancer cells toward cytotoxic agents having DNA damaging mechanism of action (Gralewska et al., 2020). However, unlike SCh B, NU6027 was identified as a low micromolar inhibitor of ATR activity in cancer cells (IC50 = 6.7 μM). This cellular inhibition of ATR by NU6027 was observed to sensitize ovarian and breast cancer cells to various DNA-damaging anticancer therapeutics although this was more profound with cisplatin (twofold increase in potency) and hydroxyurea (3.2-fold increase). Literary evidence also suggests that in a contest of single-stranded DNA break caused either through poly(ADP-ribose) polymerase (PARP) inhibition or defects in XRCC1, NU6027 exerts extra aggressive lethality. Furthermore, it was also observed that treatment with NU6027 increased cisplatin sensitivity in cancer cells with functional p53 and mismatch repair (MMR), and sensitization to temozolomide was greatest in p53 mutant cells with functional MMR (Peasland et al., 2011).

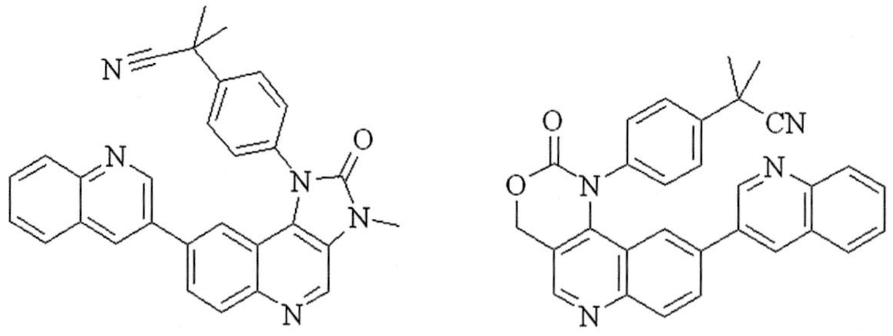

NVP-BEZ235 (5)   ETP-46464 (6)

FIGURE 2.9   Structure of NVP-BEZ235 and ETP-46464.

5.5 NVP-BEZ235 and ETP-46464

NVP-BEZ235 and ETP-46464 are ATM/ATR/mTOR inhibitors that exert activity in the nanomolar concentration. IC50 of ETP-46,464 was found to be 25 nM and that of NVP-BEZ235 was found to be 100 nM (Huang et al., 2021). The molecular structure of both NVP-BEZ235 and ETP-46464 are described in Fig. 2.9. While ETP-46464 is developed based on a quinoline core, the development of NVP-BEZ235 was based on an imidazo[4,5-c]quino-lone core (Salazar et al., 2018). Also, while ETP-46464 was a novel compound, NVP-BEZ235 was already in phase I/II clinical trials for advanced solid tumors (NCT00620594; NCT01508104; NCT01658436: NCT01756118; NCT01658436) at the time of its identification as a potent ATR inhibitor. Additionally, NVP-BEZ235 was reported to be highly active against DNA-PK (IC50 = 5 nM) and hence NVP-BEZ235 is often referred to as an inhibitor of DDR, rather than an inhibitor of ATR alone (Toledo et al., 2011).

5.6 Torin-2

Torin-2 is a highly potent second-generation ATP competitive mTOR kinase inhibitor (EC50 = 250 pmol/L). It also exhibits significant biochemical and cellular activity against both ATM (EC50 = 28 nmol/L) and ATR (EC50 = 35 nmol/L) kinases in the low nanomo-lar range (IC50 < 10 nM) (Shaik et al., 2018). The molecular structure of Torin-2 is described in Fig. 2.10. Treatment with Torin-2 increased the sensitivity of cancer cell mass to irradiation. It has also been observed that 24 h treatment with Torin-2 causes a pro-longed block in the negative feedback and T308 phosphorylation on Akt inducing strong growth inhibition in vitro cancer cell lines. In the context of in vivo treatment, mono Torin-2 therapy does not yield significant efficacy against KRAS-driven lung tumors; however, in conjugation with mitogen-activated protein/extracellular signal-regulated kinase (MEK) inhibitor AZD6244, Torin-2 induced a significant in vivo growth inhibition (Fig. 2.10) (Liu et al., 2013).

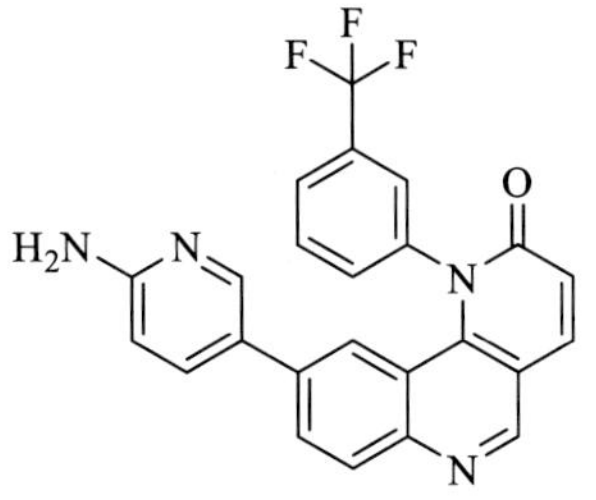

Torin-2 (7)

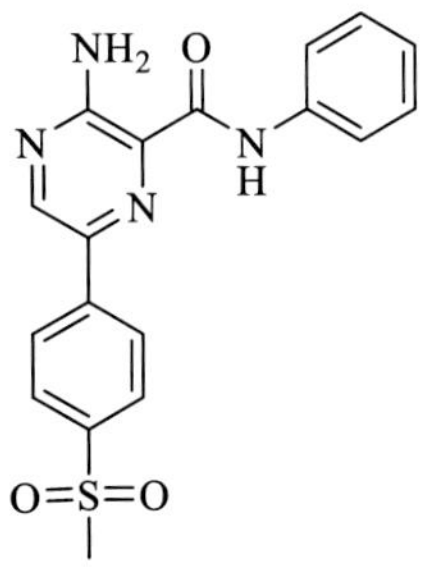

VE 821
ATR Ki = 26 nM
cell IC$_{50}$= 800 nM

FIGURE 2.10   Structure of torin and VE821.

5.7 VE-821

VE-821 is a potent and selective ATP competitive inhibitor of ATR with Ki/IC50 of 13 nM/26 nM in cell-free assays (Barnieh et al., 2021). In conjugation with genotoxic chemotherapeutics such as gemcitabine, camptothecin, etoposide, cisplatin, and carboplatin, VE 821 exerts marked antiproliferative synergy. The mechanism of action of VE 821 was found to be strong inhibition of the H2AX and CHK1 phosphorylation (Rundle et al., 2017). In single-cell assays combined with DNA fiber analysis, VE-821 abolishes the S-phase replication elongation checkpoint along with the replication origin-firing checkpoint induced by genotoxic anticancer agents and LMP-400. Furthermore, the clinical derivative of VE-821, VX-970, enhanced the in vivo tumor response to irinotecan without additional toxicity (Fig. 2.10) (Jossé et al., 2014).

5.8 AZ20

AZ20, chemically recognized as 4-[4-[(3R)-3-methyl-4-morpholinyl]-6-[1-(methylsulfonyl) cyclopropyl]-2-pyrimidinyl]-1H-indole, is a potent ATR inhibitor (ATR IC50 = 5 nM) (Foote et al., 2013). Studies documented that AZ20 decreases pChk1 Ser345, pChk1 Ser317, and pChk1 Ser296 levels in a concentration-dependent manner (Velic et al., 2015). Furthermore, prolonged exposure to AZ20 increases replication stress and S-phase arrest in targeted cells. Synergistically, in conjugation with selective ATM inhibitor KU-60019, the cytotoxic efficacy of AZ20 to induce growth inhibition and apoptosis gets markedly enhanced. Last but not least AZ20 is associated with a promising therapeutic index indicated by a transient increase in mouse bone marrow at therapeutic doses (Fig. 2.11) (Jacq et al., 2012; Foote et al., 2013).

5.9 Azabenzimidazole

Azabenzimidazole compounds were developed by HTS and derived from the virtual screening hits to create a series of ATR-selective and pharmacologically suitable inhibitors. Azabenzimidazole derivatives (Fig. 2.12) are devoid of any CYP3A4 and hERG liabilities.

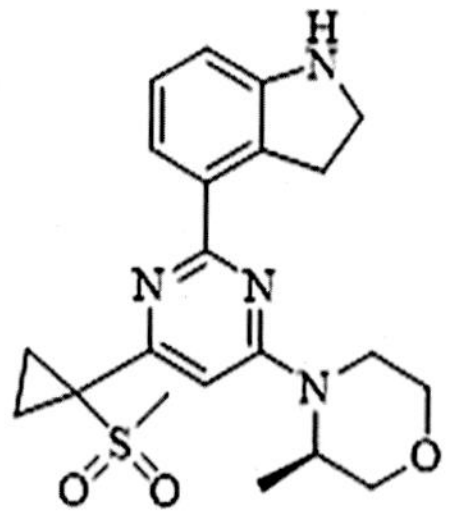

AZ-20

FIGURE 2.11   Structure of AZ-20.

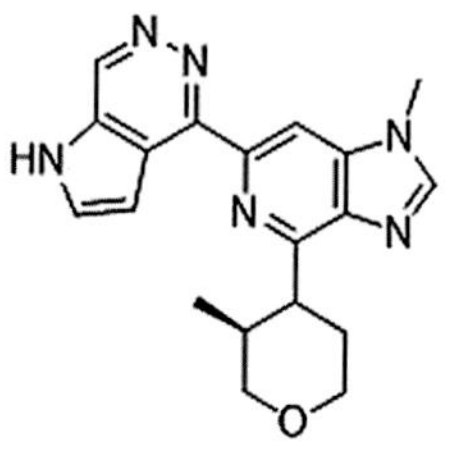

Azabenzimidazoles

FIGURE 2.12   Structure of Azabenzimidazoles.

This agent was reportedly discovered through modification of the core of a morpholino-imidazopyrimidine hit identified through a combined virtual screening and HTS campaign using a diverse subset of a Novartis compound collection. However, despite the potency of this morpholino-imidazopyrimidine hit against ATR (IC50 = 96 nM) and selectivity (>1000-fold) over ATR homologs, it harbored some pharmacokinetics and CYP3A4 concerns (Barsanti et al., 2015; Velic et al., 2015).

6. ATM and ATR inhibitors currently under clinical trial

6.1 Berzosertib

Berzosertib is the first ATR inhibitor to be evaluated in humans, with the first participant enrolled in a clinical study on December 10, 2012 (NCT02157792), about 13 years after the first selective ATR inhibitor was reported. Initially discovered and developed by Vertex Pharmaceuticals as VE-822 (VX-970), an improved analog of VE-821 (a potent and selective ATR inhibitor, which lacked the drug-like properties required for its progression as a clinical

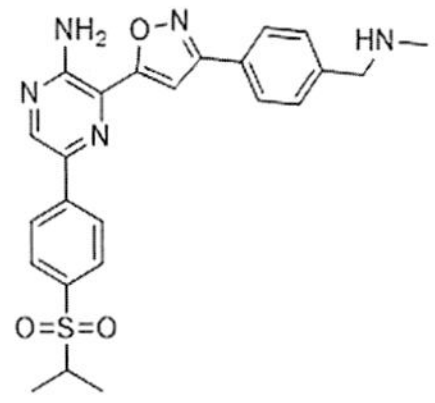

Berzosertib (11)

FIGURE 2.13 Structure of Berzosertib.

candidate), this agent has now been acquired by Merck KGaA, Germany, for further clinical development after exhibiting some preliminary clinical potential in a phase I trial (NCT02487095) (Fig. 2.13) (Thomas et al., 2021).

6.2 M6620 (VX-970)

M6620 is a highly potent and selective ATR inhibitor, inhibiting ATR activity both in cell-free assays (ATR IC50 = 0.2 nM) and in cellular assays (ATR IC50 = 19 nM) with over >100-fold selectivity over DNA-PK, ATM, and other PI3Kα kinases, in addition to its improved solubility (aqueous solubility of 52 μM) and pharmacokinetic properties compared to its precursor, VE-821 (13) (Yap et al., 2020). VX-970 was observed to significantly regress and delay tumor growth in six of these models in combination with cisplatin, even at VX-970 doses known to lack efficacy as a monotherapy, and in tumor models shown to be nonresponsive to cisplatin monotherapy. Again, in another study, VX-970 was demonstrated to be highly synergistic with cisplatin and etoposide in treatment-resistant SCLC models, such that VE-VX-790 in combination with cisplatin was more efficacious than a combination of cisplatin with etoposide both in vitro and in vivo. Strikingly, the combination of VX-790 and cisplatin was reported to not only profoundly inhibit tumor growth in these SCLC mouse models but also improve the survival of these mice. These data were a strong pointer toward possible clinical success as a chemo-sensitizer of DNA-damaging agents in lung cancer patients (Gorecki et al., 2020).

M4344 (14), formerly known as VX-803, is another orally bioactive ATR inhibitor that was originally developed by Vertex Pharmaceuticals but has now been acquired by Merck KGaA, Germany (in addition to M6620) for further development. M4344 is by far the most potent ATR inhibitor reported, strongly inhibiting ATR activity both in cell-free assays (ATR IC50 = 0.15 nM) and in cellular assays (ATR IC50 = 8 nM), with over 100-fold selectivity against a panel of 308 kinases, including ATR homologs and PI3K kinases (Zenke et al., 2019). Preclinical data of M4344 has not been extensively reported (Zenke et al., 2019) which was further reported to exhibit synergy with several DNA-damaging chemotherapeutics, PARP and CHK1 inhibitors in a panel of 92 cancer cell lines. It has also demonstrated tumor regression in tumor models in vivo. While M4344 has entered two phase I clinical trials as a monotherapy or in combination with carboplatin and cisplatin for advanced solid tumors (NCT02278250), and in combination with niraparib (a PARP inhibitor) against PARP-resistant recurrent ovarian cancer (NCT04149145), at the time of writing, no clinical data have been reported (Fig. 2.14) (Jo et al., 2021).

6.3 Ceralasertib

Ceralasertib also known as AZD6738 was developed by AstraZeneca, as an improved sulfoximine morpholinopyrimidine analog of AZ20 (Banerjee et al., 2021). AZD6738 has been extensively studied and is still being studied, in various tumor models both as a single agent and in combination with DNA damaging agents (including cisplatin and cyclophosphamide), PARP inhibitors (olaparib), antimetabolites (gemcitabine), radiotherapy, and even immunotherapy (Chen et al., 2022). It has been documented as a highly potent against ATR activity both in cell-free assays (ATR IC50 = 4 nM) and in cellular assays (ATR IC50 = 74 nM) with improved selectivity (300-fold) over ATR homologs DNA-PK, ATM, mTOR, and other PI3Kα kinases. More importantly, AZD6738 monotherapy induces potent tumor growth inhibition in ATM- and p53-deficient cells, both in vitro and in xenograft models in vivo. AZD6738 was also observed to increase the accumulation of high volumes of unrepaired DNA damage in these ATM-deficient cells, leading to cell death due to mitotic catastrophe. Moreover, AZD6738 exhibits profound ATR inhibition as a single agent across different panels of cancer cell lines in vitro. In a LoVo xenograft model (ATM-deficient) in vivo, AZD6738 achieved near complete tumor growth inhibition at well-tolerated doses, although this observation was absent in an HT29 xenograft model (ATM-proficient) despite the sensitivity of these cells to the drug in vitro. Based on very promising preclinical data, AZD6738 was first admitted to a clinical trial in 2013 (NCT01955668), and is currently being assessed in various phase I and II clinical trials (Fig. 2.15) (Yap et al., 2021).

6.4 BAY1895344

BAY1895344 is the most recently reported potent ATR inhibitor to have begun evaluation in the clinic (NCT03188965) (Fig. 2.15). It is a potent and selective orally administered ATR inhibitor developed by Bayer AG (Germany) as an optimized version of BAY-937 (structure not disclosed). BAY-937 showed promising ATR inhibition both in cell-free (IC50 = 78 nM) and cellular (IC50 = 360 nM) assays, with antitumor activity demonstrated both in vitro and in vivo as either a single agent or in combination with cisplatin (Luecking et al., 2017). Issues of low aqueous solubility, low bioavailability (rat), and more critically hERG inhibition observed with BAY-937 hindered further development, however. Hence the development of BAY1895344, an improved analog with enhanced aqueous solubility, bioavailability across species, and with an absence of significant hERG liabilities (Wengner et al., 2020). In vitro, BAY1895344 has proved to be a highly potent ATR inhibitor both in cell-free (IC50 = 7 nM) and cellular (IC50 = 36 nM) assays with selectivity over ATR homologs; ATM (>200-fold), DNA-PK (>40-fold), mTOR (≥6-fold), and PI3K (>400-fold) (De Bono et al., 2019).

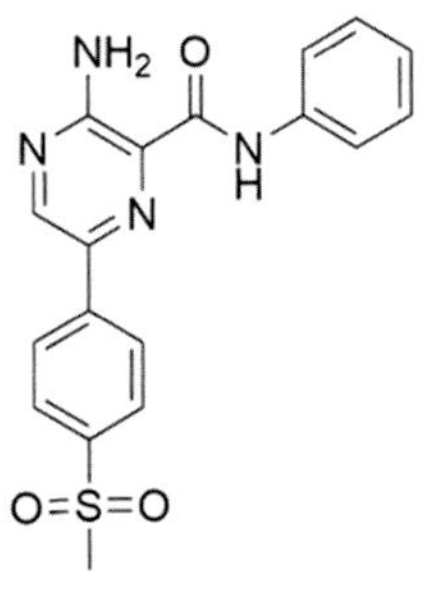

VE 821 (13)
ATR Ki = 26 nM
cell IC$_{50}$= 800 nM

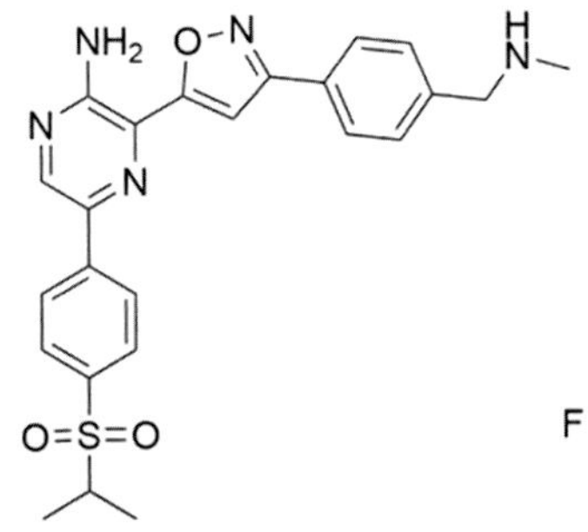

VX 970/VE 822/M6620 (12)
berzosertib
ATR Ki < 0.2 nM
cell IC$_{50}$ = 19 nM

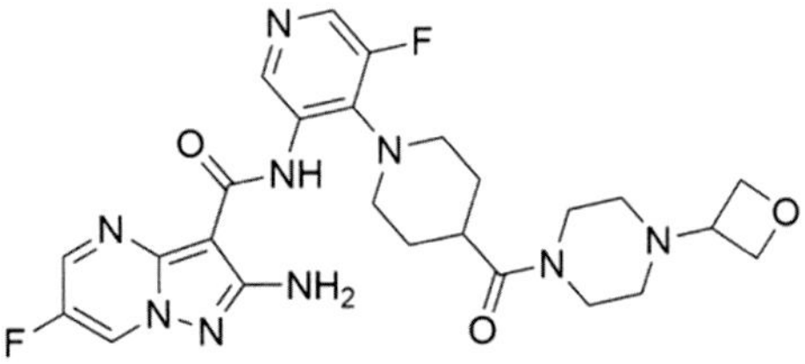

VX-803/M4344 (14)
ATR Ki < 0.2 nM
cell IC$_{50}$= 8 nM

FIGURE 2.14   Structure of VX970 (12), VE821 (13), and VX-803 (14).

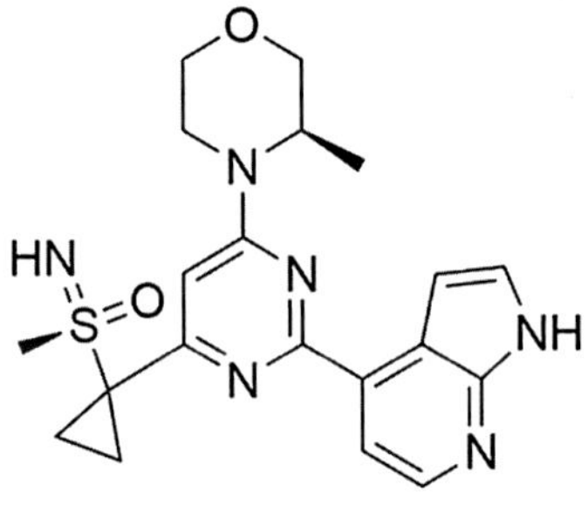

Ceralasertib (15) 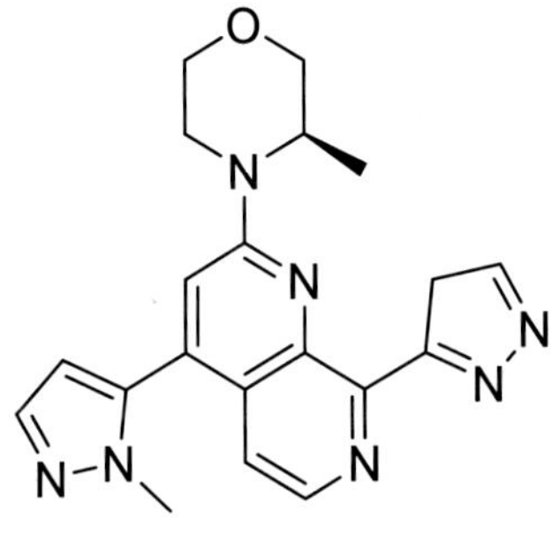   BAY1895344 (16) 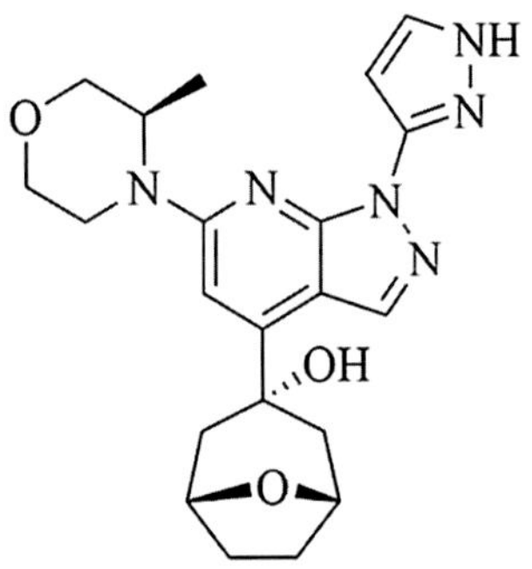   Camnosertib (17)

FIGURE 2.15   Structure of Ceralasertib (15), BAY1895344 (16), Camnosertib (17).

6.5 Camnosertib

Camnosertib or RP-3500 is a potent and selective oral small molecule inhibitor of ATR that is being developed for the treatment of tumors with mutations in ATM (Fig. 2.15). It possesses over 2000-fold selectivity over ataxia telangiectasia mutated (ATM), DNA-dependent protein kinase (DNA-PK), and phosphatidylinositol 3-kinase alpha (PI3Kα) kinases. It has been found that, treatment with RP-3500 results in potent tumor regression at minimum effective doses (MED) of 5−7 mg/kg od. From a pharmacodynamic viewpoint, RP-3500 induces dose-proportional tumor inhibition of phosphorylated checkpoint kinase 1 (pCHK1) (IC80 = 18.6 nmol/L) and induction of phosphorylated H2A.X variant histone (γH2AX), phosphorylated DNA-PK catalytic subunit (pDNA-PKcs), and phosphorylated KRAB-associated protein 1 (pKAP1). Furthermore, RP-3500 monotherapy or in combination with reduced doses of olaparib or niraparib, have shown to enhance tumor antiproliferation while it minimized the impact on red blood cell depletion. Thus, RP-3500 can reverse erythroid toxicity demonstrating inordinately better efficacy compared with sequential treatment with other anticancer agents (Roulston et al., 2022). Currently, camonsertib is being investigated in the phase I/IIa TRESR trial (NCT04497116) in patients with solid tumors and ATR inhibitor-sensitizing mutations. Following on from last year's preliminary findings of antitumor activity in the phase I part of the trial, results from dose-scheduling and pharmacokinetic (PK) analyses presented at the ESMO Targeted Anticancer Therapies Congress 2022 give further insights into the clinical potential of this agent (Berberabe, 2022).

7. Closing statement

DDR pathways, especially ATR-CHK1, have been illustrated over later decades to play basic parts in both the improvement of cancers, and their reactions to classical cancer medications, such as cytotoxic chemotherapy, radiotherapy, and immunotherapy (Sun et al., 2018). The hunt for a powerful and specific ATR inhibitor for cancer treatment has accelerated in recent times with an increasing number of novel ATR inhibitors being assessed in different clinical trials. In view of the promising preclinical information for these agents, there remains significant positive thinking for successful clinical results in these trials. Despite this good faith, there also remains a considerable cause for caution. Whereas the outcomes of these clinical trials are enthusiastically anticipated, preliminary investigations have raised a few prior concerns about toxicities raised with ATR inhibitors as a cancer treatment (Karnitz & Zou, 2015).

Despite this optimism, there is also cause for caution. While the results of these clinical trials are eagerly awaited, preliminary data seem to validate some earlier concerns of toxicities raised with ATR inhibition as a cancer treatment (Karnitz & Zou, 2015). Despite some promising responses, including complete responses observed with some ATR inhibitors currently being investigated in the clinic (Krebs et al., 2018), the occurrence of dose-limiting hematological toxicities, and treatment-emergent adverse events seem to be a common observation with these agents, particularly when in combination with cytotoxic chemotherapy (perhaps the most likely clinical scenario) although these agents are well-tolerated as monotherapies, with no dose-limiting toxicities.

Interestingly, some of these toxicities had been earlier observed in various preclinical settings. For example, the dosing of carboplatin the administration of AZD6738 was not tolerated, leading to drastic weight loss in rats, while the reverse dosing sequence was tolerated (Clack et al., 2015). Also, several dose-limiting toxicities were reported to be observed with AZD6738 dosing, including changes in food consumption and body weight in dogs, rats, and mice, in addition to bone marrow toxicity, hypocellularity in multiple lymphoid tissues, and an increase in alveolar macrophages, although recovery from these toxicities was observed after the termination of dosing.

Again, the combination of BAY1895344 with carboplatin was observed to produce dose-dependent toxicity, which limited the potential therapeutic value of this combination, and potentially with other Pt-based chemotherapies (Wengner et al., 2020). It is therefore of no surprise that safety and tolerability of different dosing schedules are now the key emphasis for new entry ATR inhibitors (M4334 and BAY1895344) under clinical investigation, perhaps to avoid or minimize toxicities which may likely undermine the clinical potential of these promising ATR inhibitors.

ATR is an established essential protein whose functions are known to be critical for both the viability and survival of cells, although these functions are even more critical in many tumors for survival and growth (Brown & Baltimore, 2000), hence the rationale for ATR targeting as an anticancer therapy. However, considering the essentiality of the ATR kinase and its ATR-CHK1 pathway, the "nonselective" targeting of ATR may still hold the possibility to be lethal to normal cells, leading to serious toxicity, particularly in combination with other cytotoxic chemotherapeutics. It is worth stating that despite the selectivity, potency, and promising preclinical data for this generation of ATR inhibitors, the clinical success of these agents particularly in combination with chemotherapy, radiotherapy, and immunotherapy will rely on smart dosing strategies that limit the occurrence of hematological and other toxicities. Failing that, specific targeting of these agents (e.g., as tumor-targeted prodrugs (Barnieh et al., 2021)) may be necessary and could provide a significant opportunity to circumvent the issues of systemic toxicity.

With the observed preliminary clinical responses reported in various ongoing clinical investigations, particularly in patients with ATM and HR defective tumors, the completion of these trials is likely to open multiple insights in the field of ATR and DDR in general.

References

Angira, D., Shaik, A., & Thiruvenkatam, V. (2020). Structural and strategic landscape of PIKK protein family and their inhibitors: An overview. *Frontiers in Bioscience-Landmark, 25*(8), 1538−1567.

Banerjee, S., Stewart, J., Porta, N., Toms, C., Leary, A., Lheureux, S., Khalique, S., Tai, J., Attygalle, A., Vroobel, K., & Lord, C. J. (2021). ATARI trial: ATR inhibitor in combination with olaparib in gynecological cancers with ARID1A loss or no loss (ENGOT/GYN1/NCRI). *International Journal of Gynecological Cancer, 31*(11).

Barnieh, F. M., Loadman, P. M., & Falconer, R. A. (2021). Progress towards a clinically-successful ATR inhibitor for cancer therapy. *Current Research in Pharmacology and Drug Discovery, 2*, Article 100017.

Barsanti, P. A., Pan, Y., Lu, Y., Jain, R., Cox, M., Aversa, R. J., Dillon, M. P., Elling, R., Hu, C., Jin, X., & Knapp, M. (2015). Structure-based drug design of novel, potent, and selective azabenzimidazoles (ABI) as ATR inhibitors. *ACS Medicinal Chemistry Letters, 6*(1), 42−46.

Berberabe, A. (2022). TRESR study identifies tolerable dosing schedule for ATR inhibitor RP-3500. *Targeted Therapies in Oncology, 6*.

Bhatti, S., Kozlov, S., Farooqi, A. A., Naqi, A., Lavin, M., & Khanna, K. K. (2011). ATM protein kinase: The linchpin of cellular defenses to stress. *Cellular and Molecular Life Sciences, 68*(18), 2977−3006.

Bin, H., Chen, P., Wu, M., Wang, F., Lin, G., Pan, S., Liu, J., Mu, B., Nan, J., Huang, Q., & Li, L. (2022). Discovery of a potent and highly selective inhibitor of ataxia telangiectasia mutated and Rad3-Related (ATR) kinase: Structural activity relationship and antitumor activity both in vitro and in vivo. *European Journal of Medicinal Chemistry, 232*, Article 114187.

Bradbury, A., Hall, S., Curtin, N., & Drew, Y. (2020). Targeting ATR as cancer therapy: A new era for synthetic lethality and synergistic combinations? *Pharmacology & Therapeutics, 207*, Article 107450.

Brown, E. J., & Baltimore, D. (2000). ATR disruption leads to chromosomal fragmentation and early embryonic lethality. *Genes & Development, 14*(4), 397−402.

Chen, T., Tongpeng, S., Lu, Z., Topatana, W., Juengpanich, S., Li, S., Hu, J., Cao, J., Lee, C., Tian, Y., & Chen, M. (2022). DNA damage response inhibition-based combination therapies in cancer treatment: Recent advances and future directions. *Aging and Cancer, 3*(1), 44−67.

Cheng, B., Pan, W., Xing, Y., Xiao, Y., Chen, J., & Xu, Z. (2022). Recent advances in DDR (DNA damage response) inhibitors for cancer therapy. *European Journal of Medicinal Chemistry*, Article 114109.

Clack, G., Lau, A., Pierce, A., Smith, S., & Stephens, C. (2015). ATR inhibitor AZD6738. *Annals of Oncology, 26*, ii8.

Coon, E. A., & Benarroch, E. E. (2018). DNA damage response: Selected review and neurologic implications. *Neurology, 90*(8), 367−376.

Cortez, D. (2003). Caffeine inhibits checkpoint responses without inhibiting the ataxia-telangiectasia-mutated (ATM) and ATM-and Rad3-related (ATR) protein kinases. *Journal of Biological Chemistry, 278*(39), 37139−37145.

De Bono, J. S., Tan, D. S. P., Caldwell, R., Terbuch, A., Goh, B. C., Heong, V., Haris, N. M., Bashir, S., Hong, D. S., Meric-Bernstam, F., & Bordia, S. (2019). *First-in-human trial of the oral ataxia telangiectasia and Rad3-related (ATR) inhibitor BAY 1895344 in patients (pts) with advanced solid tumors.*

Foote, K. M., Blades, K., Cronin, A., Fillery, S., Guichard, S. S., Hassall, L., Hickson, I., Jacq, X., Jewsbury, P. J., McGuire, T. M., & Nissink, J. W. M. (2013). Discovery of 4-{4-[(3 R)-3-Methylmorpholin-4-yl]-6-[1-(methylsulfonyl) cyclopropyl] pyrimidin-2-yl}-1 H-indole (AZ20): A potent and selective inhibitor of ATR protein kinase with monotherapy in vivo antitumor activity. *Journal of Medicinal Chemistry, 56*(5), 2125–2138.

Ghiasy, S., Parvaneh, L., Azizi, G., Sadri, G., Zaki dizaji, M., Abolhassani, H., & Aghamohammadi, A. (2017). The clinical significance of complete class switching defect in Ataxia telangiectasia patients. *Expert Review of Clinical Immunology, 13*(5), 499–505.

Gorecki, L., Andrs, M., Rezacova, M., & Korabecny, J. (2020). Discovery of ATR kinase inhibitor berzosertib (VX-970, M6620): Clinical candidate for cancer therapy. *Pharmacology & Therapeutics, 210*, Article 107518.

Gralewska, P., Gajek, A., Marczak, A., & Rogalska, A. (2020). Participation of the ATR/CHK1 pathway in replicative stress targeted therapy of high-grade ovarian cancer. *Journal of Hematology and Oncology, 13*(1), 1–16.

Harnor, S., Pickles, J., & Cano, C. (2017). *Modulation of the DNA-damage response by inhibitors of the phosphatidylinositol 3-kinase related kinase (PIKK) family.* Cancer II, 189-189.

Huang, C., Filippone, N. R., Reiner, T., & Roberts, S. (2021). Sensors and inhibitors for the detection of ataxia telangiectasia mutated (ATM) protein kinase. *Molecular Pharmaceutics, 18*(7), 2470–2481.

Jacq, X., Smith, L., Brown, E., Hughes, A., Odedra, R., Heathcote, D., Barnes, J., Powell, S., Maguire, S., Pearson, V., & Boros, J. (2012). AZ20, a novel potent and selective inhibitor of ATR kinase with in vivo antitumour activity. *Cancer Research, 72*(8), 1823-1823.

Jo, U., Senatorov, I., Zimmermann, A., Saha, L. K., Murai, Y., Kim, S. H., Rajapakse, V. N., Elloumi, F., Takahashi, N., Schultz, C., & Thomas, A. (2021). Novel and highly potent ATR inhibitor M4344 kills cancer cells with replication stress and enhances the chemotherapeutic activity of widely used DNA damaging agents. *Cancer Research, 81*(13), 1055-1055.

Jossé, R., Martin, S. E., Guha, R., Ormanoglu, P., Pfister, T. D., Reaper, P. M., Barnes, C. S., Jones, J., Charlton, P., Pollard, J. R., & Morris, J. (2014). ATR inhibitors VE-821 and VX-970 sensitize cancer cells to topoisomerase i inhibitors by disabling DNA replication initiation and fork elongation responses. *Cancer Research, 74*(23), 6968–6979.

Karnitz, L. M., & Zou, L. (2015). Molecular pathways: Targeting ATR in cancer TherapyTargeting ATR in cancer therapy. *Clinical Cancer Research, 21*(21), 4780–4785.

Krebs, M. G., Lopez, J., El-Khoueiry, A., Bang, Y. J., Postel-Vinay, S., Abida, W., Carter, L., Xu, W., Im, S. A., Pierce, A., & Frewer, P. (2018). Abstract CT026: Phase I study of AZD6738, an inhibitor of ataxia telangiectasia Rad3-related (ATR), in combination with olaparib or durvalumab in patients (pts) with advanced solid cancers. *Cancer Research, 78*(13). CT026-CT026.

Kuczler, M. D., Olseen, A. M., Pienta, K. J., & Amend, S. R. (2021). ROS-induced cell cycle arrest as a mechanism of resistance in polyaneuploid cancer cells (PACCs). *Progress in Biophysics and Molecular Biology, 165*, 3–7.

Lavin, M. F., & Shiloh, Y. (1997). The genetic defect in ataxia-telangiectasia. *Annual Review of Immunology, 15*, 177.

Lee, J. H., & Paull, T. T. (2005). ATM activation by DNA double-strand breaks through the Mre11-Rad50-Nbs1 complex. *Science, 308*(5721), 551–554.

Levy, A., & Lang, A. E. (2018). Ataxia-telangiectasia: A review of movement disorders, clinical features, and genotype correlations. *Movement Disorders, 33*(8), 1238–1247.

Li, A., & Swift, M. (2000). Mutations at the ataxia-telangiectasia locus and clinical phenotypes of A–T patients. *American Journal of Medical Genetics, 92*(3), 170–177.

Liu, Q., Xu, C., Kirubakaran, S., Zhang, X., Hur, W., Liu, Y., Kwiatkowski, N. P., Wang, J., Westover, K. D., Gao, P., & Ercan, D. (2013). Characterization of Torin2, an ATP-competitive inhibitor of mTOR, ATM, and ATRPIKK inhibitor Torin2 with antitumor activity. *Cancer Research, 73*(8), 2574–2586.

Luecking, U. T., Lefranc, J., Wengner, A., Wortmann, L., Schick, H., Briem, H., Siemeister, G., Lienau, P., Schatz, C., Bader, B., & Deeg, G. (2017). Identification of potent, highly selective and orally available ATR inhibitor BAY 1895344 with favorable PK properties and promising efficacy in monotherapy and combination in preclinical tumor models. *Cancer Research, 77*(13), 983-983.

Macheret, M., & Halazonetis, T. D. (2015). DNA replication stress as a hallmark of cancer. *Annual Review of Pathology: Mechanisms of Disease, 10*(1), 425–448.

Matt, S., & Hofmann, T. G. (2016). The DNA damage-induced cell death response: A roadmap to kill cancer cells. *Cellular and Molecular Life Sciences, 73*(15), 2829–2850.

Mu, J. J., Wang, Y., Luo, H., Leng, M., Zhang, J., Yang, T., Besusso, D., Jung, S. Y., & Qin, J. (2007). A proteomic analysis of ataxia telangiectasia-mutated (ATM)/ATM-Rad3-related (ATR) substrates identifies the ubiquitin-proteasome system as a regulator for DNA damage checkpoints. *Journal of Biological Chemistry, 282*(24), 17330–17334.

Nasser, M. I., Zhu, S., Chen, C., Zhao, M., Huang, H., & Zhu, P. (2020). A comprehensive review on schisandrin B and its biological properties. *Oxidative Medicine and Cellular Longevity, 2020.*

Nastasi, C., Mannarino, L., & D'Incalci, M. (2020). DNA damage response and immune defense. *International Journal of Molecular Sciences, 21*(20), 7504.

Nishida, H., Tatewaki, N., Nakajima, Y., Magara, T., Ko, K. M., Hamamori, Y., & Konishi, T. (2009). Inhibition of ATR protein kinase activity by schisandrin B in DNA damage response. *Nucleic Acids Research, 37*(17), 5678–5689.

Panteliadis, C. P., & Benjamin, R. (2022). Ataxia-telangiectasia (Louis-Bar syndrome). In *Neurocutaneous disorders* (pp. 97–104). Cham: Springer.

Peasland, A., Wang, L. Z., Rowling, E., Kyle, S., Chen, T., Hopkins, A., Cliby, W. A., Sarkaria, J., Beale, G., Edmondson, R. J., & Curtin, N. J. (2011). Identification and evaluation of a potent novel ATR inhibitor, NU6027, in breast and ovarian cancer cell lines. *British Journal of Cancer, 105*(3), 372–381.

Podhorecka, M., Skladanowski, A., & Bozko, P. (2010). H2AX phosphorylation: Its role in DNA damage response and cancer therapy. *Journal of Nucleic Acids, 2010.*

Pourahmadiyan, A., Alipour, P., Fattahi, N., Kasiri, M., Rezaeian, F., Taghipour-Sheshdeh, A., Mohammadi-Asl, J., Tabatabaiefar, M. A., & Hashemzadeh Chaleshtori, M. (2019). A pathogenic variant in SLC26A4 is associated with Pendred syndrome in a consanguineous Iranian family. *International Journal of Audiology, 58*(10), 628–634.

Rao, Q., Liu, M., Tian, Y., Wu, Z., Hao, Y., Song, L., Qin, Z., Ding, C., Wang, H. W., Wang, J., & Xu, Y. (2018). Cryo-EM structure of human ATR-ATRIP complex. *Cell Research, 28*(2), 143–156.

Ronco, C., Martin, A. R., Demange, L., & Benhida, R. (2017). ATM, ATR, CHK1, CHK2 and WEE1 inhibitors in cancer and cancer stem cells. *MedChemComm, 8*(2), 295–319.

Roulston, A., Zimmermann, M., Papp, R., Skeldon, A., Pellerin, C., Dumas-Bérube, É., Dumais, V., Dorich, S., Fader, L. D., Fournier, S., & Li, L. (2022). RP-3500: A novel, potent, and selective ATR inhibitor that is effective in preclinical models as a monotherapy and in combination with PARP inhibitors. *Molecular Cancer Therapeutics, 21*(2), 245–256.

Rundle, S., Bradbury, A., Drew, Y., & Curtin, N. J. (2017). Targeting the ATR-CHK1 axis in cancer therapy. *Cancers, 9*(5), 41.

Salazar, R., Garcia-Carbonero, R., Libutti, S. K., Hendifar, A. E., Custodio, A., Guimbaud, R., Lombard-Bohas, C., Ricci, S., Klümpen, H. J., Capdevila, J., & Reed, N. (2018). Phase II study of BEZ235 versus everolimus in patients with mammalian target of rapamycin inhibitor-naïve advanced pancreatic neuroendocrine tumors. *The Oncologist, 23*(7), 766.

Scott, S. P., & Pandita, T. K. (2006). The cellular control of DNA double-strand breaks. *Journal of Cellular Biochemistry, 99*(6), 1463–1475.

Shaik, A., Bhakuni, R., & Kirubakaran, S. (2018). Design, synthesis, and docking studies of new Torin2 analogs as potential ATR/mTOR kinase inhibitors. *Molecules, 23*(5), 992.

Stracker, T. H., Roig, I., Knobel, P. A., & Marjanović, M. (2013). The ATM signaling network in development and disease. *Frontiers in Genetics, 4*, 37.

Sun, L. L., Yang, R. Y., Li, C. W., Chen, M. K., Shao, B., Hsu, J. M., Chan, L. C., Yang, Y., Hsu, J. L., Lai, Y. J., & Hung, M. C. (2018). Inhibition of ATR downregulates PD-L1 and sensitizes tumor cells to T cell-mediated killing. *American Journal of Cancer Research, 8*(7), 1307.

Takeuchi, M., Tanikawa, M., Nagasaka, K., Oda, K., Kawata, Y., Oki, S., Agapiti, C., Sone, K., Miyagawa, Y., Hiraike, H., & Wada-Hiraike, O. (2019). Anti-tumor effect of inhibition of DNA damage response proteins, ATM and ATR, in endometrial cancer cells. *Cancers, 11*(12), 1913.

Teive, H. A. G., Camargo, C. H. F., & Munhoz, R. P. (2018). More than ataxia—movement disorders in ataxia-telangiectasia. *Parkinsonism and Related Disorders, 46*, 3–8.

Thomas, A., Cappuzzo, F., Ying, C., Yamamoto, N., Chen, Y., Cortot, A. B., Berghmans, T., Aransay, N. R., Shibata, Y., Jianying, Z., & Yoshida, T. (2021). 1666TiP phase II study of berzosertib (M6620)+ topotecan in patients with relapsed platinum-resistant SCLC: DDRiver SCLC 250. *Annals of Oncology, 32*, S1171.

Todorova, V., Ivanov, K., Delattre, C., Nalbantova, V., Karcheva-Bahchevanska, D., & Ivanova, S. (2021). Plant adaptogens—history and future perspectives. *Nutrients, 13*(8), 2861.

Toledo, L. I., Murga, M., Zur, R., Soria, R., Rodriguez, A., Martinez, S., Oyarzabal, J., Pastor, J., Bischoff, J. R., & Fernandez-Capetillo, O. (2011). A cell-based screen identifies ATR inhibitors with synthetic lethal properties for cancer-associated mutations. *Nature Structural & Molecular Biology, 18*(6), 721—727.

Velic, D., Couturier, A. M., Ferreira, M. T., Rodrigue, A., Poirier, G. G., Fleury, F., & Masson, J. Y. (2015). DNA damage signalling and repair inhibitors: The long-sought-after achilles' heel of cancer. *Biomolecules, 5*(4), 3204—3259.

Veuger, S., & Curtin, N. J. (2014). Inhibition of DNA repair as a therapeutic target. In *Cancer drug design and discovery* (2nd ed., pp. 193—237).

Wengner, A. M., Siemeister, G., Lücking, U., Lefranc, J., Wortmann, L., Lienau, P., Bader, B., Bömer, U., Moosmayer, D., Eberspächer, U., & Golfier, S. (2020). The novel ATR inhibitor BAY 1895344 is efficacious as monotherapy and combined with DNA damage—inducing or repair—compromising therapies in preclinical cancer ModelsAntitumor effects of ATR inhibition. *Molecular Cancer Therapeutics, 19*(1), 26—38.

Yap, T. A., Krebs, M. G., Postel-Vinay, S., El-Khouiery, A., Soria, J. C., Lopez, J., Berges, A., Cheung, S. A., Irurzun-Arana, I., Goldwin, A., & Felicetti, B. (2021). Ceralasertib (AZD6738), an oral ATR kinase inhibitor, in combination with carboplatin in patients with advanced solid tumors: A phase I study. *Clinical Cancer Research, 27*(19), 5213—5224.

Yap, T. A., O'Carrigan, B., Penney, M. S., Lim, J. S., Brown, J. S., de Miguel Luken, M. J., Tunariu, N., Perez-Lopez, R., Rodrigues, D. N., Riisnaes, R., & Figueiredo, I. (2020). Phase I trial of first-in-class ATR inhibitor M6620 (VX-970) as monotherapy or in combination with carboplatin in patients with advanced solid tumors. *Journal of Clinical Oncology, 38*(27), 3195.

Zaki-Dizaji, M., Akrami, S. M., Abolhassani, H., Rezaei, N., & Aghamohammadi, A. (2017). Ataxia telangiectasia syndrome: Moonlighting ATM. *Expert Review of Clinical Immunology, 13*(12), 1155—1172.

Zenke, Frank T., Zimmermann, Astrid, Dahmen, Heike, Elenbaas, Brian, Pollard, John, Reaper, Philip, Bagrodia, S., Spilker, M. E., Amendt, C., & Blaukat, Andree (2019). Antitumor activity of M4344, a potent and selective ATR inhibitor, in monotherapy and combination therapy. *Cancer Research, 79*(13_Suppl. ment), 369-369.

Zou, L. (2007). Single-and double-stranded DNA: Building a trigger of ATR-mediated DNA damage response. *Genes & Development, 21*(8), 879—885.

Further reading

Ball, H. L., Ehrhardt, M. R., Mordes, D. A., Glick, G. G., Chazin, W. J., & Cortez, D. (2007). Function of a conserved checkpoint recruitment domain in ATRIP proteins. *Molecular and Cellular Biology, 27*(9), 3367—3377.

Löffler, H., Bochtler, T., Fritz, B., Tews, B., Ho, A. D., Lukas, J., Bartek, J., & Krämer, A. (2007). DNA damage-induced accumulation of centrosomal Chk1 contributes to its checkpoint function. *Cell Cycle, 6*(20), 2541—2548.

MacDougall, C. A., Byun, T. S., Van, C., Yee, M. C., & Cimprich, K. A. (2007). The structural determinants of checkpoint activation. *Genes & Development, 21*(8), 898—903.

Mokrani-Benhelli, H., Gaillard, L., Biasutto, P., Le Guen, T., Touzot, F., Vasquez, N., Komatsu, J., Conseiller, E., Pïcard, C., Gluckman, E., & Francannet, C. (2013). Primary microcephaly, impaired DNA replication, and genomic instability caused by compound heterozygous ATR mutations. *Human Mutation, 34*(2), 374—384.

Smith, J., Tho, L. M., Xu, N., & Gillespie, D. A. (2010). The ATM—Chk2 and ATR—Chk1 pathways in DNA damage signaling and cancer. *Advances in Cancer Research, 108*, 73—112.

Topatana, W., Juengpanich, S., Li, S., Cao, J., Hu, J., Lee, J., Suliyanto, K., Ma, D., Zhang, B., Chen, M., & Cai, X. (2020). Advances in synthetic lethality for cancer therapy: Cellular mechanism and clinical translation. *Journal of Hematology and Oncology, 13*(1), 1—22.

3

Breakpoint cluster region Abelson kinase inhibitors

Sushanta Bhattacharya[1], Vivek Asati[2] and Amena Ali[3]

[1]Gupta College of Technological Sciences, Pharmaceutical Chemistry, Asansol, West Bengal, India; [2]ISF College of Pharmacy, Moga, Punjab, India; [3]Department of Pharmaceutical Chemistry, College of Pharmacy, Taif University, Taif, Saudi Arabia

1. Introduction

Breakpoint cluster region-Abelson (BCR-AbL) is a fusion protein that triggers the development of chronic myeloid leukemia (CML) and acute lymphocytic leukemia (ALL) (Iqbal, 2014). Leukemia can be effectively treated with BCR-AbL inhibitors; however, a gatekeeper mutation (T315I) in BCR-AbL causes resistance to these inhibitors, which significantly reduces their efficacy (Sun et al., 2017). Numerous studies have demonstrated that it has been challenging to find medications that maintain significant efficacy over an extended length of time due to aberrant mutations. Point mutations and gene amplification are the main causes of the BCR-AbL protein's resistance to pharmacotherapy, along with a number of BCR-AbL-independent processes (Carrà et al., 2016; Loscocco et al., 2019). Imatinib is one tyrosine kinase inhibitor (TKI) that has been shown to be highly effective in treating some CML patients (Pophali & Patnaik, 2016). However, the emergence of the "T315I" mutation in the BCR-AbL protein's gatekeeper region markedly reduced or eliminated the therapeutic efficacy of some TKIs (Liu et al., 2021). In this chapter, we go over the structure, function, the most common resistance mechanisms that occur in the BCR-AbL protein in CML patients and the approaches that have been developed over the last 2 decades to inhibit the function of the BCR-AbL protein.

2. BCR-AbL

2.1 Structure and function

Many different types of human leukemias, including the majority of chronic myeloid leukemia with the Philadelphia chromosome positive, are caused by the oncoprotein Bcr-Abl.

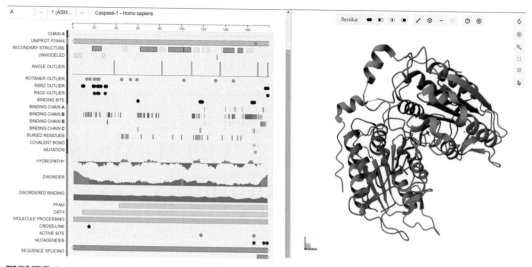

FIGURE 3.1   Crystal structure of BCR-AbL. The crystal structure of BCR-AbL was deduced from XRD with a resolution of 2.20 Å.

Bcr-Abl oligomerization is necessary for oncogenicity (Kang et al., 2016). Dimerization occurs by switching the N-terminal helices on two N-shaped monomers and creating an antiparallel coil between their C-terminal helices. To create a tetramer, two dimers are then stacked on top of one another. By interfering with Bcr-Abl oligomerization, the Bcr1-72 structure provides a framework for the design of inhibitors of Bcr-Abl transforming action (Zhao et al., 2002). The crystal structure of BCR-AbL was deduced from XRD with a resolution of 2.20 Å (Fig. 3.1), total structure weight: 69.68 kDa (https://www.rcsb.org/structure/1K1F).

2.2 Inhibitors of BCR-AbL

2.2.1 First-generation inhibitor; Imatinib

Imatinib (Fig. 3.2) was the first tyrosine kinase inhibitor discovered with high specificity for Bcr-Abl protein. A number of Bcr-Abl-dependent and Bcr-Abl-independent mechanisms of resistance to imatinib have emerged since it became the first-line therapy for the treatment of CML, despite the drug's explicit targeting of that oncoprotein. The selectivity for Bcr-Abl was improved by the orthopositional insertion of a methyl group into the amino

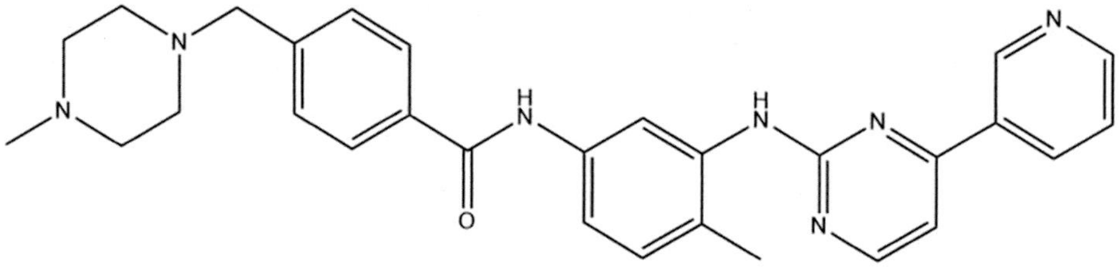

FIGURE 3.2   2-Phenyl amino pyrimidine analog: imatinib.

group. The addition of an N-methylpiperazine group significantly increased the molecule's oral bioavailability and water solubility, which were initially low in the final product. The N-methylpiperazine addition would have resulted in an aniline moiety in the structure notwithstanding the aforementioned advantages and the higher affinity of the resultant molecule for its target. The amide group and a linker benzene ring were added to the compound to abolish its mutagenic potential (Rana et al., 2015).

2.2.1.1 Mechanisms of resistance to imatinib

About one-third of patients receiving imatinib experience therapeutic failure. Bcr-Abl-dependent and Bcr-Abl-independent mechanisms are the two categories into which underlying mechanisms of resistance are traditionally classified. The latter consists primarily of alternate onco-pathways being activated, as well as enhanced drug efflux and decreased absorption. However, a small percentage of Bcr-Abl-dependent resistances are also caused by gene amplification or hyperexpression. The former, on the other hand, are primarily caused by point mutations in Bcr-Abl that modify inhibitor binding or conformational alterations. As point mutations account for the great majority of instances, new inhibitors have been created using a rational drug design strategy with the goal of overcoming resistances by easing conformational and binding constraints without sacrificing selectivity. With the exception of T315I, second-generation inhibitors can almost eliminate all mutations. By breaking an H-b and significantly stabilizing the active DFG-in conformation, the replacement of the gatekeeper residue blocks the effects of inhibitors. Only third-generation inhibitors have been able to get through this persistent barrier (Patel et al., 2017).

2.2.2 Second-generation inhibitors

2.2.2.1 Phenylamino-pyrimidine derivative: Nilotinib (Fig. 3.3)

It is a Bcr-Abl tyrosine kinase inhibitor with anticancer efficacy that is orally accessible and derived from aminopyrimidines. This drug was developed to overcome imatinib resistance, binds to and stabilizes the inactive conformation of the kinase domain of the Abl protein of the Bcr-Abl fusion protein, which prevents Bcr-Abl from mediating the proliferation of CML cells with the Philadelphia chromosome (Ph+). Additionally, the drug blocks the receptor tyrosine kinases platelet-derived growth factor receptor (PDGF-R) and c-kit, a mutant and constitutively active receptor tyrosine kinase seen in the majority of gastrointestinal stromal tumors (GISTs). The drug has been demonstrated to have an approximately 20-fold higher

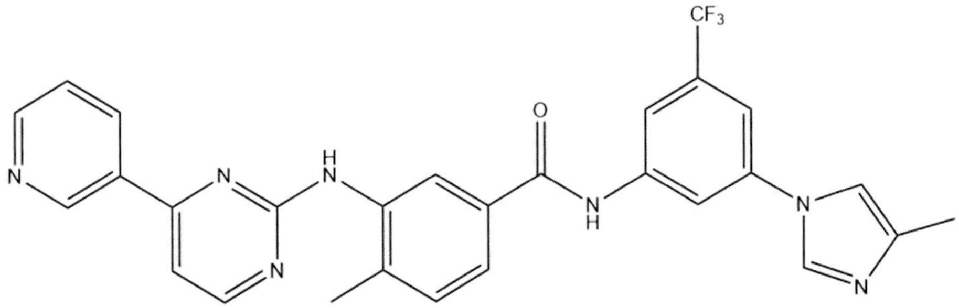

FIGURE 3.3 Phenylamino-pyrimidine derivative: nilotinib.

efficacy in kinase and proliferation assays compared to imatinib due to a binding mechanism that is energetically more favorable (Du & Lovly, 2018).

2.2.2.2 Thiazole carboximide derivative: Dasatinib

It is also a protein tyrosine kinase SRC-family orally accessible synthetic small molecule inhibitor. It binds to these kinases and prevents them from stimulating growth. Dasatinib (Fig. 3.4) has been demonstrated to overcome the resistance to imatinib of CML cells with BCR-ABL kinase domain point mutations. This appears to be because dasatinib has a less strict binding affinity for the BCR-ABL kinase. Tyrosine kinases from the SRC family interact with a variety of cell surface receptors and are involved in intracellular signal transduction pathways; tumorigenic forms can develop as a result of altered endogenous protein production or regulation as well as through virally encoded kinase genes (Soverini et al., 2018).

2.2.2.3 Quinolone derivative: Bosutinib

It is a dual kinase inhibitor and synthetic quinolone derivative that has the potential to have anticancer effects. It targets both Abl and Src kinases. Bosutinib (Fig. 3.5), in contrast to imatinib, prevents both Abl and Src kinases from autophosphorylating, which reduces

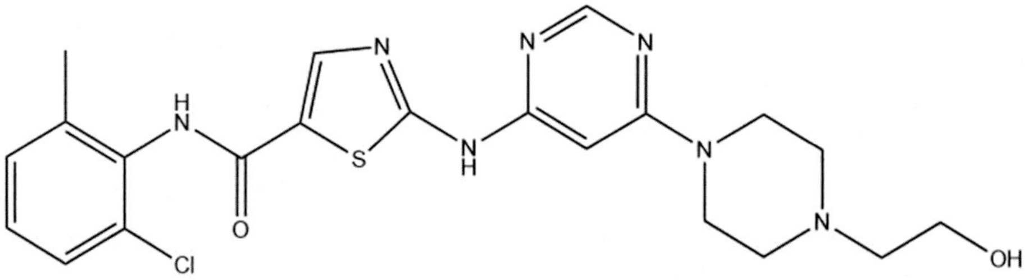

FIGURE 3.4   Thiazole carboximide derivative: dasatinib.

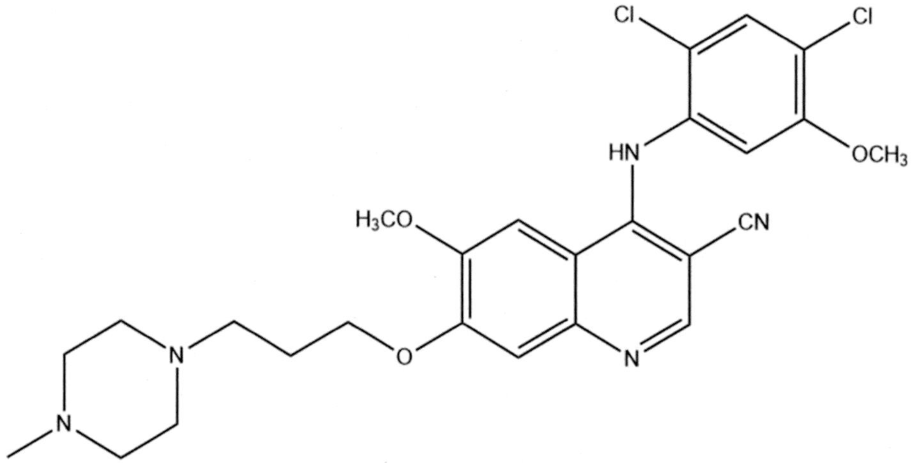

FIGURE 3.5   Quinolone derivative: bosutinib.

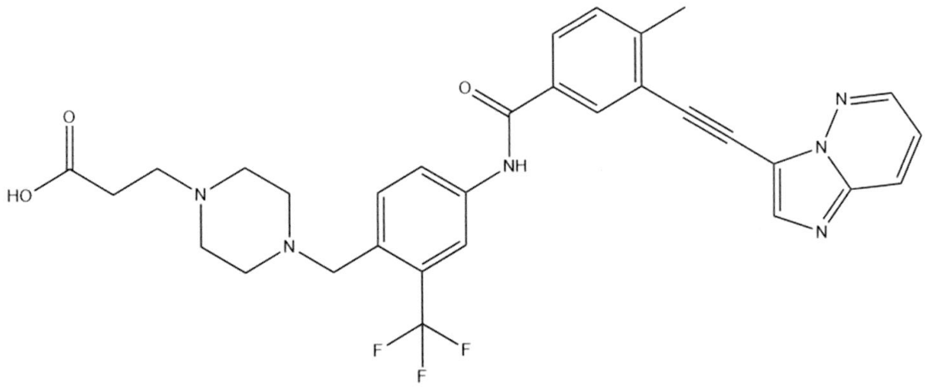

FIGURE 3.6   Imidazo-benzamide derivative: ponatinib.

cell proliferation and death. Due to its two mechanisms of action, this drug may be effective against solid tumors, other myeloid malignancies, and resistant CML. The aberrant Bcr-abl fusion protein, which is frequently linked to chronic myeloid leukemia, induces an increase in the activity of the enzyme abl kinase (CML). The phenotype of imatinib-resistant CML is also linked to the overexpression of particular Src kinases (Bieerkehazhi et al., 2017).

2.2.3 Third generation inhibitors

2.2.3.1 Imidazo-benzamide derivative: Ponatinib

It is a multitargeted RTK inhibitor that is orally accessible and has the potential to have antiangiogenic and anticancer effects. Ponatinib (Fig. 3.6) suppresses Bcr-Abl in all of its mutant forms, including the extremely drug-resistant missense mutation T315I. Additionally, this drug inhibits the tyrosine kinase receptors TIE2 and FMS-related tyrosine kinase receptor-3, as well as those linked to fibroblast growth factor receptors (FGFRs) and vascular endothelial growth factor receptors (VEGFRs) (Flt3). Ponatinib's RTK inhibition may prevent angiogenesis and cellular growth, as well as cause cell death. A fusion tyrosine kinase called Bcr-Abl is encoded by the Philadelphia chromosome (Garner et al., 2014).

2.2.3.2 Pyrazo-pyrimidine derivative: Asciminib

It is an allosteric Bcr-Abl1 tyrosine kinase inhibitor with anticancer action that is ingested. Asciminib (Fig. 3.7) inhibits the activity of both wild-type and some mutation forms of Bcr-Abl, including the T315I mutation, by locating and binding to the myristoyl pocket of the Bcr-Abl1 fusion protein, which is separate from the ATP-binding domain, upon administration. Because of this binding, hematological malignancies with the Philadelphia chromosome (Ph+) are less likely to proliferate and are more likely to undergo apoptosis. An aberrant enzyme made by leukemia cells with the Philadelphia chromosome is called the Bcr-Abl1 fusion protein tyrosine kinase (Schoepfer et al., 2018).

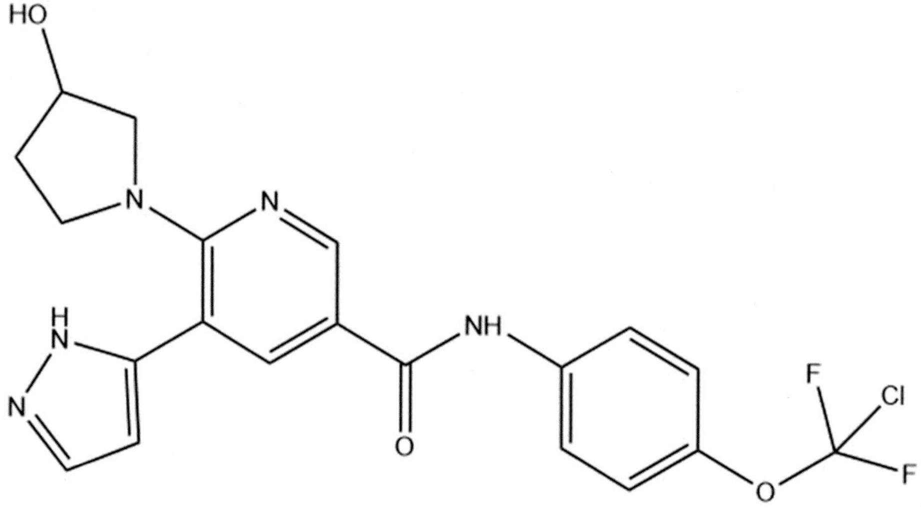

FIGURE 3.7   Pyrazo-pyrimidine derivative: asciminib.

3. Conclusions

Bcr-Abl is a hot target for leukemia, especially chronic myeloid and acute lymphatic type. Many inhibitors of this target have been developed to treat the leukemia. Imatinib is the prototype of this category and is regarded as first generation drug. It experienced resistance due to mutation. To minimize the resistance of first-generation drugs, new chemical entities such as nilotinib, dasatinib, and bosutinib were explored. These drugs are categorized as second-generation drugs. After that, the latest chemical agents, ponatinib and asciminib, exhibited better results and were classified as third-generation drugs.

Declaration of interests

The authors have no relevant affiliations or financial involvement with any organization or entity with a financial interest in or financial conflict with the subject matter or materials discussed in the manuscript. This includes employment, consultancies, honoraria, stock ownership or options, expert testimony, grants or patents received or pending, or royalties.

Reviewer disclosures

Peer reviewers on this manuscript have no relevant financial or other relationships to disclose.

References

Bieerkehazhi, S., Chen, Z., Zhao, Y., Yu, Y., Zhang, H., Vasudevan, S. A., Woodfield, S. E., Tao, L., Joanna, S. Y., Muscal, J. A., & Pang, J. C. (January 1, 2017). Novel Src/Abl tyrosine kinase inhibitor bosutinib suppresses neuroblastoma growth via inhibiting Src/Abl signaling. *Oncotarget, 8*(1), 1469.

Carrà, G., Torti, D., Crivellaro, S., Panuzzo, C., Taulli, R., Cilloni, D., Guerrasio, A., Saglio, G., & Morotti, A. (October 4, 2016). The BCR-ABL/NF-κB signal transduction network: A long lasting relationship in Philadelphia positive leukemias. *Oncotarget, 7*(40), Article 66287.

Du, Z., & Lovly, C. M. (December 2018). Mechanisms of receptor tyrosine kinase activation in cancer. *Molecular Cancer, 17,* 1–3.

Garner, A. P., Gozgit, J. M., Anjum, R., Vodala, S., Schrock, A., Zhou, T., Serrano, C., Eilers, G., Zhu, M., Ketzer, J., & Wardwell, S. (November 15, 2014). Ponatinib inhibits polyclonal drug-resistant KIT oncoproteins and shows therapeutic potential in heavily pretreated gastrointestinal stromal tumor (GIST) patients. *Clinical Cancer Research, 20*(22), 5745–5755.

Iqbal, Z. (January 2014). A comprehensive analysis of breakpoint cluster region-Abelson fusion oncogene splice variants in chronic myeloid leukemia and their correlation with disease biology. *Indian Journal of Human Genetics, 20*(1), 64.

Kang, Z. J., Liu, Y. F., Xu, L. Z., Long, Z. J., Huang, D., Yang, Y., Liu, B., Feng, J. X., Pan, Y. J., Yan, J. S., & Liu, Q. (December 2016). The Philadelphia chromosome in leukemogenesis. *Chinese Journal of Cancer, 35*(1), 1–5.

Liu, J., Zhang, Y., Huang, H., Lei, X., Tang, G., Cao, X., & Peng, J. (March 2021). Recent advances in Bcr-Abl tyrosine kinase inhibitors for overriding T315I mutation. *Chemical Biology and Drug Design, 97*(3), 649–664.

Loscocco, F., Visani, G., Galimberti, S., Curti, A., & Isidori, A. (September 24, 2019). BCR-ABL independent mechanisms of resistance in chronic myeloid leukemia. *Frontiers in Oncology, 9,* 939.

Patel, A. B., O'Hare, T., & Deininger, M. W. (August 1, 2017). Mechanisms of resistance to ABL kinase inhibition in chronic myeloid leukemia and the development of next generation ABL kinase inhibitors. *Hematology/Oncology Clinics, 31*(4), 589–612.

Pophali, P. A., & Patnaik, M. M. (January 2016). The role of new tyrosine kinase inhibitors in chronic myeloid leukemia. *Cancer Journal, 22*(1), 40.

Rana, R., Das, S., Swami, A., Pon, D., Ramesh, S., & Kumar, S. D. (2015). Strategic therapeutic approaches to overcome emerging dual SRC/ABL kinase inhibitors resistances in chronic phase Ph positive chronic myeloid leukemia. *Asian Journal of Medical Sciences, 6*(1), 8–15.

Schoepfer, J., Jahnke, W., Berellini, G., Buonamici, S., Cotesta, S., Cowan-Jacob, S. W., Dodd, S., Drueckes, P., Fabbro, D., Gabriel, T., & Groell, J. M. (2018). Discovery of asciminib (ABL001), an allosteric inhibitor of the tyrosine kinase activity of BCR-ABL1. *Journal of Medicinal Chemistry, 61*(18), 8120–8135.

Soverini, S., Mancini, M., Bavaro, L., Cavo, M., & Martinelli, G. (December 2018). Chronic myeloid leukemia: The paradigm of targeting oncogenic tyrosine kinase signaling and counteracting resistance for successful cancer therapy. *Molecular Cancer, 17*(1), 1–5.

Sun, Y., Zhao, N., Wang, H., Wu, Q., Han, Y., Liu, Q., Wu, M., Liu, Y., Kong, F., Wang, H., & Sun, Y. (2017). CT-721, a potent Bcr-Abl inhibitor, exhibits excellent in vitro and in vivo efficacy in the treatment of chronic myeloid leukemia. *Journal of Cancer, 8*(14), 2774.

Zhao, X., Ghaffari, S., Lodish, H., Malashkevich, V. N., & Kim, P. S. (February 2002). Structure of the Bcr-Abl oncoprotein oligomerization domain. *Nature Structural Biology, 9*(2), 117–120.

4

Casein kinase (CK) inhibitors

Xin Zhai

Shenyang Pharmaceutical University, Shenyang, China

1. Introduction

Protein kinases represent a large family of more than 500 members with vital roles in the regulation of many biological processes, and their dysfunction has been implicated in a variety of human diseases including multiple malignant tumors. Casein kinase (CK) is one of core members in protein kinases family which phosphorylates many important proteins in a variety of signaling pathways (Dar & Shokat, 2011). Casein kinase denotes three classes of kinases, namely protein kinase CK1, protein kinase CK2, and Golgi CK (also termed Fam20C). Interestingly, protein kinase CK1 and CK2 are physiologically unrelated to casein because they are mainly cytosolic and nuclear proteins that barely encounter casein in the secretory pathway (Allende & Allende, 1995). Contrastively, only Golgi CK is the bona fide casein kinase that phosphorylates secreted proteins within S-x-E/pS motifs (Ser-x-Glu/phosphor-Ser, where x is any amino acid), including casein, fibroblast growth factor 23 (FGF23), and small integrin-binding ligand N-linked glycoproteins (SIBLINGs) (Ishikawa et al., 2012; Tagliabracci et al., 2014). In the following chapters, the three classes of CKs along with representative inhibitors will be introduced individually.

2. Protein kinase CK1

2.1 Structures and function

Protein kinase CK1 is a unique family within the superfamily of Ser/Thr-specific protein kinases that is ubiquitously expressed in eukaryotic organisms (Peters et al., 1999). To date, seven CK1 isoforms (α, β, $\gamma1$, $\gamma2$, $\gamma3$, δ, and ε) have been characterized in mammals and described as monomeric, constitutively active kinases (Knippschild, Gocht, et al., 2005). All CK1 isoforms are highly conserved within kinase domains but remarkably differed in the length and primary structure of N-terminal (8—44 aa) and C-terminal noncatalytic domains (55—134 aa) (Gross & Anderson, 1998). Structurally, CK1 presents a typical bilobal structure which is constituted of a smaller N-lobe and a larger α-helical C-lobe, and a cleft is formed between the two fragments for binding ATP (Longenecker et al., 1996; Xu et al., 1995). In detail, the ATP-binding site of CK1 can be divided into five binding regions: adenine region, ribose region, phosphate-binding region, a deep hydrophobic selectivity pocket controlled by gatekeeper residue Met82, and a second spacious hydrophobic region adjacent to the hinge region (Fig. 4.1) (Rodrigues & Silva, 2017).

Substantial evidences link the overexpression of CK1 to a variety of cancers closely, including kidney cancer (CK1γ3) (Masuda et al., 2003), leukemia (CK1ε) (Seok & Stockwell, 2008), B-cell lymphomas (CK1δ) (Maritzen et al., 2003), lung cancer (CK1ε), breast cancer (CK1ε) (Shin et al., 2014), pancreatic cancer (CK1δ/ε) (Brockschmidt et al., 2008), and ovarian

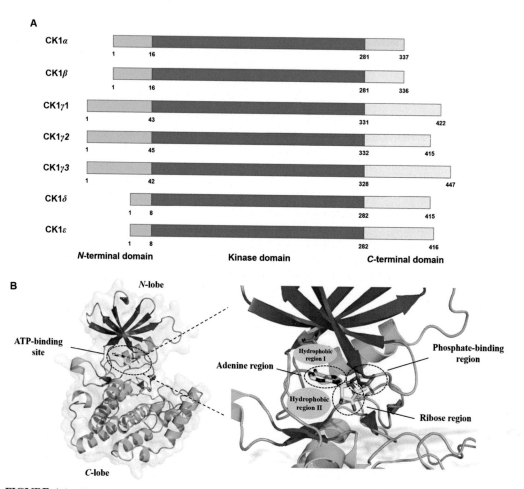

FIGURE 4.1   The CK1 family. (A) Sequence alignment of seven CK1 isoforms, protein sequences were obtained from the NCBI database: Human CK1α (GI:49457406), bovine CK1β (GI:126717449), human CK1γ1 (GI:18202957), human CK1γ2 (GI:22450768), human CK1γ3 (GI:47117932), human CK1δ (GI:881619), human CK1ε (GI:23199991). (B) The cocrystal structure of CK1δ in complex with ADP (PDB ID: 5X17).

cancer (CK1ε) (Rodriguez et al., 2012). The upregulated CK1 contributes to the phosphorylation of tumor suppressor p53, resulting in uncontrolled growth of cancer cells (Knippschild, Wolff, et al., 2005). It has also been reported that CK1 is involved in several signaling pathways responsible for cell proliferation and survival, such as Wnt/β-catenin (Klaus & Birchmeier, 2008), Hedgehog (Rubin & de Sauvage, 2006), and Hippo pathways (Bao et al., 2011; Pan, 2010). Moreover, CK1-mediated phosphorylation of p75 tumor necrosis factor receptor and caspase 8 trigger the suppression of apoptosis (Beyaert et al., 1995; Desagher et al., 2001). Accordingly, targeting CK1 provides a promising strategy for cancer therapy. Despite the challenge in isoform selectivity, a large number of CK1 inhibitors with different scaffolds have been developed successively in the past decades.

2.2 Inhibitors of protein kinase CK1

2.2.1 Bicyclic scaffold inhibitors

2.2.1.1 Isoquinoline and indolinone derivatives

Chijiwa et al. (1989) disclosed the first CK1 inhibitor. The ATP-competitive isoquinoline derivative1 (CKI-7) displayed moderate inhibitory activity against CK1 (K$_i$ = 8.5 μM) and poor selectivity between different CK1 isoforms (Fig. 4.2). The co-crystal structure of CK1 in complex with compound 1 (PDB ID: 2CSN) indicated that isoquinoline core occupied the adenine region and 2-nitrogen atom formed a hydrogen bond with residue Leu88 (Xu et al., 1996). Additionally, 5-Cl substituent and 8-ethylamine sulfonamide chain of 1 made several polar interactions with residues Tyr59, Ser91, and Asp94. Regardless of the unsatisfactory activity and selectivity, compound 1 provided a useful tool in the identification of CK1 family members (Fish et al., 1995).

In 2000, the first CK1 inhibitor endowed with isoform selectivity has been developed through high throughput screening (HTS). The indolinone compound 2 (IC261) inhibited CK1 isoforms α, δ, and ε with IC$_{50}$ values of 16, 1, and 1 μM, respectively (Mashhoon et al., 2000), and caused a near-total growth arrest of multiple human cancer cell lines at 0.1 μM (Cheong et al., 2011). Notably, further in vivo studies demonstrated that 2 could inhibit tumor growth at 20.5 mg/kg dose in PancTu-1 xenograft models of pancreatic cancer (Brockschmidt et al., 2008). Cocrystal structure (PDB ID: 1EH4) confirmed that the indolinone scaffold of 2 bound to CK1 in a similar manner to compound 1 and formed two hydrogen bonds with residues Lue88 and Asp86. The trimethoxy phenyl moiety located at the rear of ATP-binding pocket and was involved in a hydrogen bonding network with residues Lys41, Ser22, and Asp154 (Mashhoon et al., 2000).

2.2.1.2 Benzimidazole and indazole derivatives

Based on an HTS of the Amgen compound library, a series of benzimidazole derivatives were identified as potent inhibitors of CK1γ (Hua et al., 2012). Compound 3 showed good inhibition against CK1γ (IC$_{50}$ = 0.14 μM) along with favorable selectivity over other CK1 isoforms (CK1δ IC$_{50}$ = 5.8 μM; CK1α IC$_{50}$ = 12.1 μM) and a panel of 399 kinases. The cocrystal structure of 3 in complex with CK1γ3 (PDB ID: 4G16) revealed that benzimidazole core bound deeply into the ATP-binding pocket and 6-cyano substituent was involved in water-mediated hydrogen bond interactions with residues Tyr90 and Glu86. Moreover, 2-

Year	Chemical structure	Binding site	Biological data	PDB ID
1989	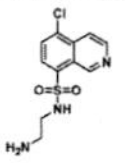 Compound 1 (CKI-7)	ATP-binding site	K_i = 8.5 μM	2CSN
2000	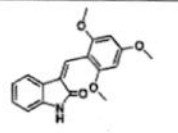 Compound 2 (IC261)	ATP-binding site	CK1α IC$_{50}$= 16 μM CK1δ IC$_{50}$= 1 μM CK1ε IC$_{50}$= 1 μM	1EH4
2012	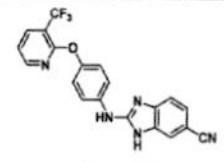 Compound 3	ATP-binding site	CK1γ IC$_{50}$= 0.14 μM CK1δ IC$_{50}$= 5.8 μM CK1α IC$_{50}$= 12.1 μM	4G16
2012	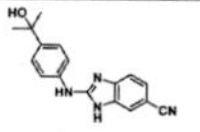 Compound 4	ATP-binding site	CK1γ IC50= 18 nM CK1δ IC$_{50}$= 9.2 μM CK1α IC$_{50}$= 2.3 μM	N/A
2012	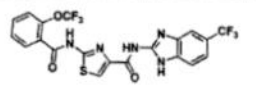 Compound 5 (Bischof-6)	ATP-binding site	CK1δ IC$_{50}$= 40 nM CK1ε IC$_{50}$= 199 nM	4TWC
2014	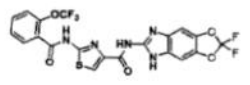 Compound 6	ATP-binding site	CK1δ IC$_{50}$= 20 nM CK1ε IC$_{50}$= 210 nM	4TW9
2019	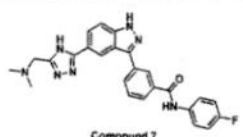 Compound 7	ATP-binding site	CK1δ IC$_{50}$= 132 nM	N/A
2018	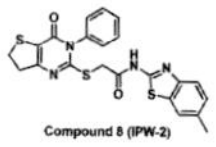 Compound 8 (PW-2)	ATP-binding site	^{wt}CK1δ (IC$_{50}$= 0.93 μM) ^{wt}CK1ε (IC$_{50}$= 4.03 μM) ^{M82F}CK1δ (IC$_{50}$= 0.04 μM)	5OKT
2014	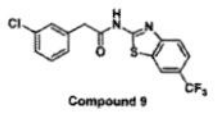 Compound 9	ATP-binding site	CK1δ IC$_{50}$= 23 nM	N/A
2018	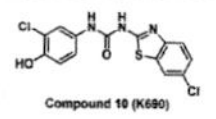 Compound 10 (K680)	ATP-binding site	CK1δ IC$_{50}$= 0.84 μM ABAD IC$_{50}$= 1.89 μM	N/A
2008	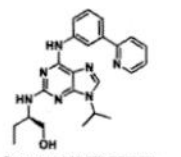 Compound 11 ((R)-DRF053)	ATP-binding site	CK1 IC$_{50}$= 14 nM CDK1 IC$_{50}$= 220 nM CDK5 IC$_{50}$= 80 nM	N/A
2013	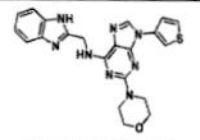 Compound 12 (SR-653234)	ATP-binding site	CK1δ IC$_{50}$= 0.16 μM CK1ε IC$_{50}$= 0.54 μM	N/A
2013	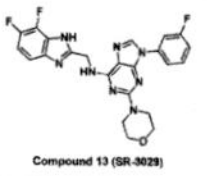 Compound 13 (SR-3029)	ATP-binding site	CK1δ IC$_{50}$= 44 nM CK1ε IC$_{50}$= 260 nM	6RCG
2018	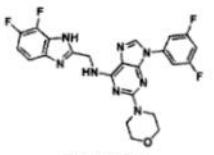 Compound 14	ATP-binding site	CK1δ IC$_{50}$= 53 nM CK1ε IC$_{50}$= 145 nM	N/A
2021	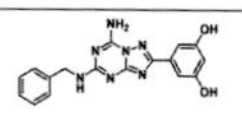 Compound 15	ATP-binding site	CK1δ IC$_{50}$= 0.18 μM	N/A
2009	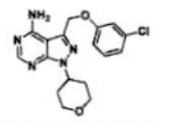 Compound 16 (PF-4800567)	ATP-binding site	CK1ε IC$_{50}$= 32 nM CK1δ IC$_{50}$= 711 nM	N/A
2012	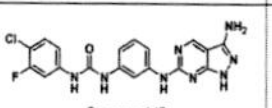 Compound 17	ATP-binding site	CK1ε IC$_{50}$= 78 nM	N/A

FIGURE 4.2 Bicyclic scaffold inhibitors of CK1. The chemical structures and biological data of bicyclic scaffold inhibitors of CK1.

amino-imidazole portion formed another two hydrogen bonds with residue Leu119. Regrettably, inhibitor **3** demonstrated only modest potency in the LRP6 phosphorylation cell assay ($IC_{50} = 6.56\ \mu M$) and poor pharmaceutical properties (high metabolic clearance and low solubility). Further structural optimization afforded analog **4** which exhibited excellent potency (CK1γ $IC_{50} = 18\ nM$), isoforms selectivity (CK1δ $IC_{50} = 9.2\ \mu M$, CK1α $IC_{50} = 2.3\ \mu M$), and cellular efficacy ($IC_{50} = 0.7\ \mu M$) (Hua et al., 2012).

Apart from CK1γ inhibitor, benzimidazole derivatives were reported as CK1δ/ε inhibitor, either. Through structural modification of NF-κB inhibitors, **5** (Bischof-5) was identified as CK1 inhibitor with fivefold higher affinity toward CK1δ ($IC_{50} = 40\ nM$) than CK1ε ($IC_{50} = 199\ nM$) (Bischof et al., 2012). However, only Frwt648 and mKSA cells were highly sensitive to the treatment with $4\ \mu M$ of compound **5** in a panel of cell lines. Another benzimidazole **6** (CK1δ $IC_{50} = 20\ nM$, CK1ε $IC_{50} = 210\ nM$) optimized from **5** presented obviously increased intracellular availability in several cancer cell lines, such as BxPC3 ($EC_{50} = 0.83\ \mu M$), HT29 ($EC_{50} = 1.27\ \mu M$), and AC1M88 ($EC_{50} = 1.41\ \mu M$) (Richter et al., 2014). Cocrystal structure of CK1δ-**6** complex (PDB ID: 4TW9) suggested that the hinge residues Glu83 and Leu85 formed hydrogen bonded to the benzimidazole core, the nitrogen of the amide moiety, and aromatic hydrogen of the thiazole ring. Furthermore, the difluorobenzodioxolane portion reduced distance from fluorine atom to Tyr56-oxygen and highly improved hydrogen bond geometry, accounting for the enhanced potency of **6** (Fig. 4.3).

Indazole-based compounds were another class of CK1δ inhibitors which were obtained by molecular dynamics (MD)-integrated virtual screening, and the most potent inhibitor **7** showed an IC_{50} of 134 nM (Sciabola et al., 2019). Molecular docking study indicated that indazole core formed bidentate hydrogen bonds with residues Leu85 and Glu86, meanwhile, the triazole fragment formed hydrogen bond with Ile15 either. The hydrophobic fluoro-

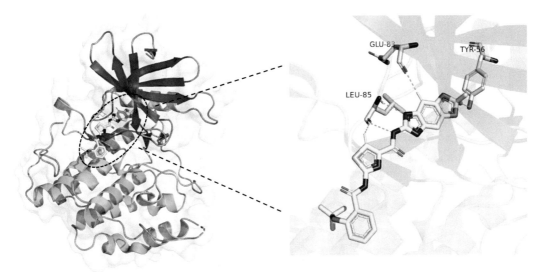

FIGURE 4.3 The cocrystal structure of CK1δ in complex with compound 6 (PDB ID: 4TW9). **6** is colored yellow and the hydrogen bonds are shown as *green dashed lines*.

phenyl group was buried in the hydrophobic region lined by Tyr56, Ile68, Met80, and Met82. On the opposite side, the basic dimethyl-amine moiety pointed toward the solvent boundary. In brief, compound **7** bound to CK1δ in a similar way to benzimidazoles **5** and **6**.

2.2.1.3 Benzothiazole derivatives

Inhibitors of Wnt production (IWPs) are known antagonists of the Wnt pathway, targeting the membrane-bound O-acyltransferase porcupine. Since the structural similarities between IWPs and benzimidazole-based CK1 inhibitors, Knippschild's team has developed a novel class of IWP-derived CK1 inhibitors successfully (García-Reyes et al., 2018). Through an ATP-competitive manner, the benzothiazoles **8** (IPW-2) inhibited not only wild type ^{wt}CK1δ (IC$_{50}$ = 0.93 μM) and ^{wt}CK1ε (IC$_{50}$ = 4.03 μM) but also the gatekeeper mutant ^{M82F}CK1δ (IC$_{50}$ = 0.04 μM). In cell assay, **8** strongly inhibited the proliferation of various cancer cell lines within single digit micromolar range. In addition, it was observed that compound **8** possessed significant selectivity for CK1δ in a panel of 320 protein kinases. Cocrystal structure (PDB ID: 5OKT) of CK1δ in complex with **8** validated that 2-aminobenzothiazole scaffold formed two key hydrogen bond interactions with hinge residue Leu85. Noteworthy, benzothiazole core induced a significant rearrangement of Met82 and a rotation of Ile68 side chain by 180 degrees, contributing to the isoform selectivity of **8**.

Another class of benzothiazole derivatives was developed as CK1δ inhibitors for the treatment of amyotrophic lateral sclerosis (Salado et al., 2014). Based on library screening and hit-to-lead optimization, compound **9** was identified as the most potent inhibitor with IC$_{50}$ value of 23 nM and selectivity on a 456 kinases panel. Due to its satisfactory permeability in favor to crossing the blood–brain barrier, **9** was used to evaluate therapeutic potential in vivo. In a new transgenic *Drosophila* model of TDP-43 proteinopathies, compound **9** obviously extended fly lifespan (mean lifespan = 37.84 days) at a dose of 100 nM compared with control group (mean lifespan = 33.17 days).

Owing to the structural similarities shared by compound **9** and amyloid-beta–binding alcohol dehydrogenase (ABAD) inhibitors, a class of dual CK1δ and ABAD inhibitors with benzothiazole scaffold have been developed through replacing amide group of **9** with urea group (Benek et al., 2018). Compound **10** (K690) showed only acceptable potency against CK1δ (IC$_{50}$ = 0.84 μM) and ABAD (IC$_{50}$ = 1.89 μM) but improved permeability (Pe = 13.2) compared with **9** (Pe = 11.2), offering a potential molecule for the treatment of neurodegenerative disorders.

2.2.1.4 Purine and purine-like derivatives

Purines represent a large family of biologically active molecules and constitute the scaffold of a wide variety of promising drugs, including kinase inhibitors (Legraverend & Grierson, 2006). Aiming to discover dual CK1 and CDK inhibitors contributing to the potential therapeutic applications in Alzheimer's disease (AD) field, a class of purine derivatives has been developed by Oumata et al. (2008). Derivative **11** ((R)-DRF053) as the most potent compound remarkably inhibited CK1 (IC$_{50}$ = 14 nM), CDK1 (IC$_{50}$ = 220 nM), and CDK5 (IC$_{50}$ = 80 nM). Docking study of **11** in CK1δ illustrated that the purine core formed bidentate hydrogen bonds with residue Leu85, and the pyridine fragment was involved in a mixed hydrogen bond stacking interaction with residue Arg13, resulting in favorable affinity of **11** with respect to CK1.

Starting from a purine-based lead **12** (SR-653234, CK1δ IC$_{50}$ = 0.16 μM, CK1ε IC$_{50}$ = 0.54 μM) identified through HTS, Roush's team developed another series of potent CK1 inhibitors (Bibian et al., 2013). Compound **13** (SR-3029) presented powerful inhibitory activity for CK1δ (IC$_{50}$ = 44 nM) and CK1ε (IC$_{50}$ = 260 nM). Furthermore, **13** tremendously inhibited proliferation of breast cancer MDA-MB-231 cell (EC$_{50}$ = 26 nM) and melanoma A375 cell (EC$_{50}$ = 86 nM). However, six off-target kinases were detected in kinase selectivity analysis of derivative **13**. Replacing 3-fluorophenyl group of **13** with 3,5-difluorophenyl afforded analog **14** (CK1δ IC$_{50}$ = 53 nM, CK1ε IC$_{50}$ = 145 nM, MDA-MB-231 cell EC$_{50}$ = 68 nM) with improved selectivity (Monastyrskyi et al., 2018). In a panel of 97 kinases, only CK1δ was inhibited by **14** more than 90 % at 10 μM, and fibromyalgia syndrome–related tyrosine kinase 3 (FLT3) as the only off-target kinase was unrelated to the antiproliferative activity. Similarly, docking analysis of this class of inhibitors uncovered that purine core bound to hinge region and formed hydrogen bonds with residue Leu85. Benzimidazole fragment pointed to solvent boundary and formed additional hydrogen bond with residue Leu85, while the fluorophenyl ring was located at hydrophobic region I (Fig. 4.4).

In addition, several compounds with purine-like core were also disclosed as ATP-competitive inhibitors of CK1, including triazolo[1,5-α][1,3,5]triazines **15** (CK1δ IC$_{50}$ = 0.18 μM) (Grieco et al., 2021), pyrazolopyrimidines **16** (PF-4800567, CK1ε IC$_{50}$ = 32 nM, CK1δ IC$_{50}$ = 711 nM) (Walton et al., 2009) and **17** (CK1 IC$_{50}$ = 78 nM) (Yang et al., 2012). Regretfully, none of their anticancer evaluation data are available.

2.2.2 Monocyclic scaffold inhibitors

2.2.2.1 Imidazole and isoxazole derivatives

Imidazole derivative **18** (D4476), originally an ALK5 inhibitor, was discovered to inhibit CK1δ with an IC$_{50}$ value of 0.3 μM (Fig. 4.5). After a selectivity profiling on a panel of 30

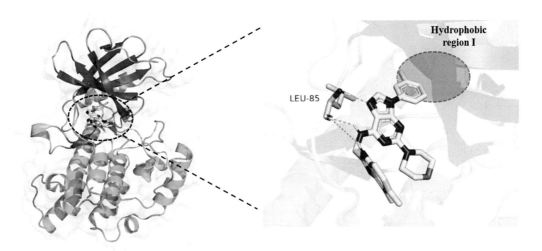

FIGURE 4.4 The cocrystal structure of CK1δ in complex with compound 13 (PDB ID: 6RCG). **13** is displayed as yellow sticks and the hydrogen bonds are shown as *green dashed lines*.

Year	Chemical structure	Binding site	Biological data	PDB ID
2004	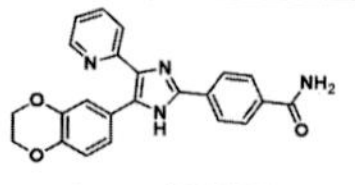 Compound 18 (D4476)	ATP-binding site	CK1δ IC$_{50}$= 0.3 μM	N/A
2009	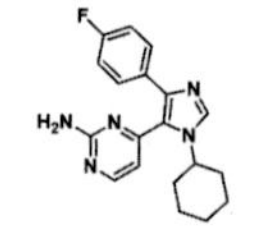 Compound 19 (PF-670462)	ATP-binding site	CK1δ IC$_{50}$= 13 nM CK1ε IC$_{50}$= 80 nM	3UZP
2009	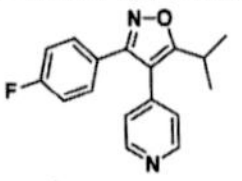 Compound 20	ATP-binding site	CK1δ IC$_{50}$= 0.23 μM p38α MAPK IC$_{50}$= 0.45 μM	4G16
2009	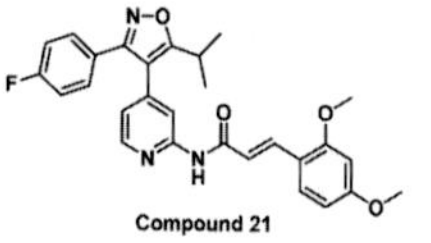 Compound 21	ATP-binding site	CK1δ IC$_{50}$= 47 nM p38α MAPK IC$_{50}$= 2.52 μM	N/A
2009	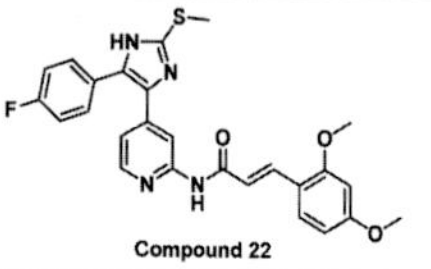 Compound 22	ATP-binding site	CK1δ IC$_{50}$= 5 nM CK1ε IC$_{50}$= 73 nM p38α MAPK IC$_{50}$= 19 nM	N/A
2017	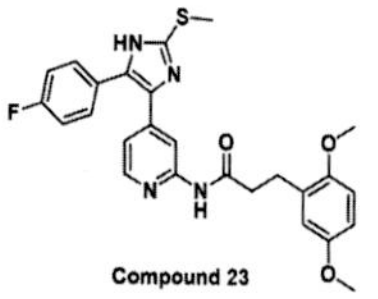 Compound 23	ATP-binding site	CK1δ IC$_{50}$= 4 nM CK1ε IC$_{50}$= 25 nM p38α MAPK IC$_{50}$= 10 nM	N/A
2019	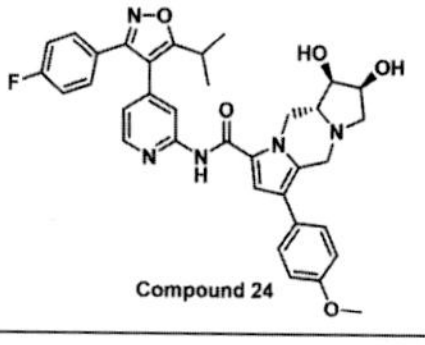 Compound 24	ATP-binding site	CK1δ IC$_{50}$= 11 nM CK1ε IC$_{50}$= 56 nM	N/A
2013	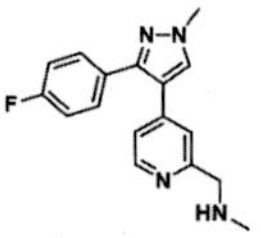 Compound 25	ATP-binding site	CK1δ IC$_{50}$= 12.9 nM CK1ε IC$_{50}$= 67.2 nM p38α MAPK IC$_{50}$= 3040 nM	4KB8
2017	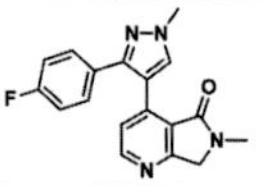 Compound 26 (PF-5236216)	ATP-binding site	CK1δ IC$_{50}$= 8 nM CK1ε IC$_{50}$= 36 nM p38α MAPK IC$_{50}$= 861 nM	5W4W
2015	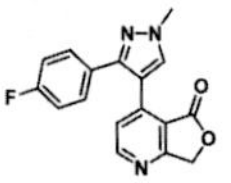 Compound 27 (BIIB-118)	ATP-binding site (Speculation)	N/A	N/A

FIGURE 4.5 Monocyclic scaffold inhibitors of CK1 The chemical structures and biological data of monocyclic scaffold inhibitors of CK1.

protein kinases, **18** was demonstrated to inhibit CK1δ 20~30-fold more potent than protein kinase D1 (PKD1) or p38α mitogen-activated protein kinase (MAPK) (Bain et al., 2007; Rena et al., 2004). In particular, **18** showed favorable inhibition on acute myeloid leukemia and multiple myeloma cells (Hu et al., 2015; Järås et al., 2014). Pfizer also disclosed an imidazole-based compound **19** (PF-670462) as an ATP-competitive inhibitor of CK1δ/ε (CK1δ IC$_{50}$ = 13 nM, CK1ε IC$_{50}$ = 80 nM) (Walton et al., 2009). Despite excellent potency, **19** manifested poor selectivity for several kinases including protein kinase A, protein kinase C, and glycogen synthase kinase 3β.

In 2009, isoxazoles **20** as a p38α MAPK inhibitor (IC$_{50}$ = 0.45 μM) was uncovered to inhibit CK1δ with an IC$_{50}$ value of 0.23 μM. Based on the sufficient analysis of the binding modes of lead **20** in the ATP-binding pocket, isoxazole **21** (CK1δ IC$_{50}$ = 47 nM, p38α MAPK IC$_{50}$ = 2.52 μM) and imidazole **22** (CK1δ IC$_{50}$ = 5 nM, CK1ε IC$_{50}$ = 73 nM, p38α MAPK IC$_{50}$ = 19 nM) were developed as dual CK1δ and p38α MAPK inhibitor by Peifer et al. (2009). Especially, **22** exhibited favorable selectivity in a panel of 76 kinases and obvious pro-apoptosis effect in AC1-M88 cell. Molecular modeling of **22** suggested that imidazole scaffold dictated an ideal angle for positioning of the vicinal aryl moieties within the ATP-binding pocket of CK1 and was involved in water-mediated hydrogen bond interactions with core catalytic residues Lys38 and Asp149. The 2-amino-pyridine fragment formed bidentate hydrogen bonds with residue Leu85, while 4-fluorophenyl group induced a rotation of gatekeeper residue Met82 toward Pro66 by 180 degrees, thereby accessing to hydrophobic region I. Moreover, the 2,4-dimethoxyphenyl portion was accommodated by hydrophobic region II toward the solvent boundary of the ATP-binding site.

In spite of powerful potency of **22**, further studies in vivo were limited by the instability of acrylamide Michael acceptor moiety and E/Z-isomerization. To enhance chemical stability and selectivity, a variety of imidazole-based inhibitors of CK1 were developed by the same team derived from compound **22** (Halekotte et al., 2017). The structure—activity relationships (SARs) investigations indicated that the olefin could be reduced without changing potency, while the reduction of carbonyl group abolished the CK1 inhibition. Furthermore, oxidation of 2-thioether of imidazole core was tolerated, barely affecting isoform selectivity and potency. In addition, 2,4-dimethoxyphenyl and 2,5-dimethoxyphenyl substituted patterns were optimal. Consequently, analogue **23** was determined as the most potent inhibitor (CK1δ IC$_{50}$ = 4 nM, CK1ε IC$_{50}$ = 25 nM, p38α MAPK IC$_{50}$ = 10 nM). Of note, **23** remarkably inhibited proliferation of pancreatic cancer Colo357 (EC$_{50}$ = 3.5 μM) and Panc89 cell (EC$_{50}$ = 1.5 μM).

Molecular docking of isoxazoles **21** in CK1δ clarified that **21** only occupied the adenine region of ATP-binding site, leaving polar ribose region unexploited (Luxenburger et al., 2019). Therefore, Peifer et al. developed another class of isoxazole-based CK1 inhibitor featured by chiral pyrrolidine fragment to mimic ribose. The most powerful inhibitor **24** presented excellent enzymatic activity against CK1δ/ε (CK1δ IC$_{50}$ = 11 nM, CK1ε IC$_{50}$ = 56 nM) along with antiproliferation effect in breast cancer MCF-7 cell (EC$_{50}$ = 1.3 μM) and colon cancer HT-29 cell (EC$_{50}$ = 1.1 μM).

2.2.2.2 Pyrazole derivatives

In 2013, Pfizer discovered several pyrazole scaffold compounds endowed with CK1δ/ε inhibition through HTS effort. Inhibitor **25** showed high potency against CK1δ/ε (CK1δ

$IC_{50} = 12.9$ nM, CK1ε $IC_{50} = 67.2$ nM), favorable selectivity for p38 MAPK ($IC_{50} = 3040$ nM), and good brain exposure (7.5 µM) (Mente et al., 2013). However, the imine basic center was found to increase hERG liability ($IC_{50} = 3.99$ µM). Hence, further structural optimization was carried out on the basis of lead **25**. Through rigidifying the molecule and locking it into a bioactive conformation, pyrazoles **26** was obtained as the most potent compound with powerful CK1δ/ε inhibitory activity in enzymatic assay (CK1δ $IC_{50} = 8$ nM, CK1ε $IC_{50} = 36$ nM) and in cell assay (CK1δ $EC_{50} = 58$ nM, CK1ε $EC_{50} = 318$ nM) (Wager et al., 2017). Cocrystal structure (PDB ID: 5W4W) authenticated that **26** bound to CK1δ in a similar binding mode with imidazole inhibitor **22**. The pyrazole core formed a water-mediated hydrogen bond with residue Lys38, while the pyridine ring was involved in a hydrogen bond interaction with hinge residue Leu85. In addition, the 4-fluorophenyl group poked into hydrophobic region I and formed a favorable stacking interaction with residue Met82 (Fig. 4.6).

Excitingly, compound **27** (BIIB-118 or PF-05251749) as an oral-available, brain-penetrable CK1δ/ε inhibitor has been enrolled in phase I clinical evaluation. Despite the unpublished biological data in vitro and in vivo, **27** is speculated to possess excellent efficacy and selectivity based on the structural similarity to **26**. Originally, **27** developed by Pfizer entered phase I clinical trial for the treatment of AD in 2015. However, it was discontinued because Pfizer terminated its neurological research and development in 2018. Until 2020, **27** was acquired by Biogen Inc. and reentered phase I clinical trials to evaluate the therapeutic effect on irregular sleep wake rhythm disorder in Parkinson's disease (PD) and sundown syndrome in AD (NCT02443740 and NCT02691702).

2.2.3 Tricyclic scaffold inhibitors and others

Utilizing a structure-based virtual screening of 4 million synthetic and natural compounds, Cozza et al. (2008) identified two anthraquinones as novel CK1 inhibitors (Fig. 4.7). Compound **28** selectively inhibited δ isoform with an IC_{50} value at sub-micromolar range

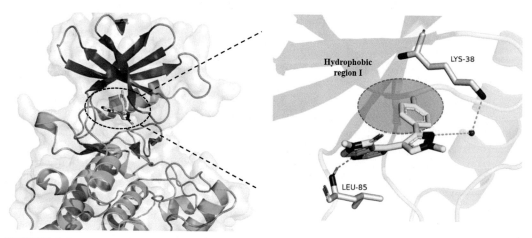

FIGURE 4.6 The cocrystal structure of CK1δ in complex with compound 26 (PDB ID: 5W4W). **26** is colored yellow and the hydrogen bonds are shown as *green dashed lines*.

Year	Chemical structure	Binding site	Biological data	PDB ID
2008	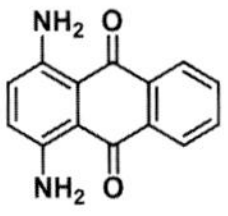 Compound 28	ATP-binding site	CK1δ IC$_{50}$= 0.3 µM	N/A
2020	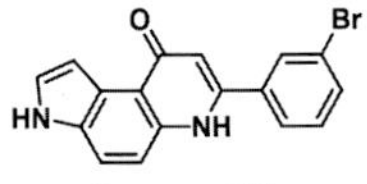 Compound 29	ATP-binding site	CK1δ IC$_{50}$= 15.22 µM	N/A
2014	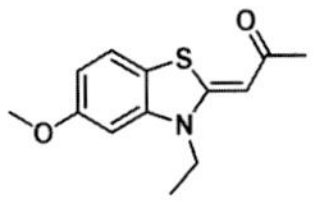 Compound 30 (TG003)	ATP-binding site	CK1α IC$_{50}$= 0.33 µM CK1δ IC$_{50}$= 0.34 µM CK1ε IC$_{50}$= 1.4 µM CK1γ1 IC$_{50}$= 1.5 µM CK1γ2 IC$_{50}$= 0.93 µM CK1γ3 IC$_{50}$= 0.88 µM	N/A
2016	Compound 31	ATP-binding site	CK1δ/ε IC$_{50}$= 0.78 µM	N/A
2015	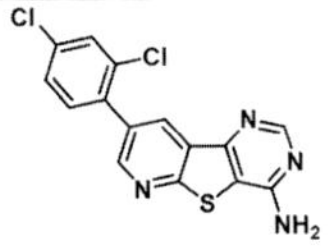 Compound 32	ATP-binding site	CK1δ/ε IC$_{50}$= 0.22 µM	N/A
2004	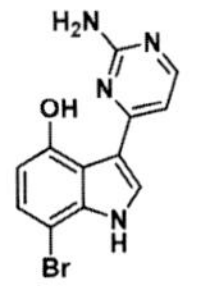 Compound 33 (meriadinin E)	ATP-binding site	CK1 IC$_{50}$= 0.4 µM	N/A
2008	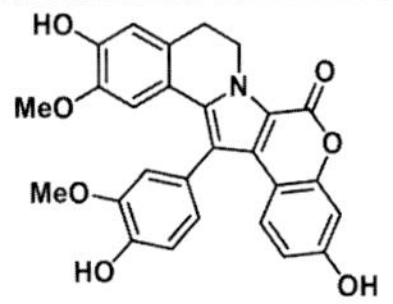 Compound 34 (lamellarin 3)	ATP-binding site	CK1 IC$_{50}$= 0.41 µM	N/A
2016	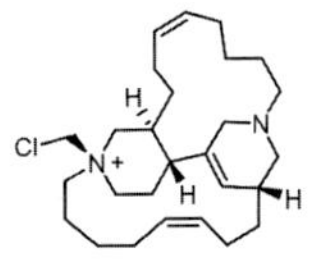 Compound 35 (chloromethylhalicyclamine B)	ATP-binding site	CK1δ/ε IC$_{50}$= 6 µM	N/A

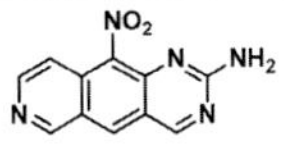

FIGURE 4.7 Tricyclic scaffold inhibitors and others. The chemical structures and biological data of tricyclic scaffold inhibitors and others.

(IC$_{50}$ = 0.33 μM). Molecular docking suggested that amino group at the 1-position and 4-position formed hydrogen bonds with hinge residues Glu83 and Asp149, respectively. Moreover, one of the carbonyl groups was involved in hydrogen bond interaction with the residue Leu85. Similarly, another pyrrolo[3,2-*f*]quinolinone derivative **29** (IC$_{50}$ = 15.22 μM) was discovered as CK1δ inhibitor by virtual screening, either (Cescon et al., 2020). The carbonyl oxygen of the pyrrolo-quinolinone core hydrogen bonded to hinge region residue Leu85, while the 3-bromophenyl group filled the hydrophobic pocket composed of residues Lys38, Met80, and the gatekeeper residue Met82.

In addition, various molecules as multi-kinases inhibitors were reported to inhibit CK1. For instance, compound **30** (TG003) originally identified as a CDC2-like kinase inhibitor exerted ubiquitously inhibitory effects on multiple isoforms of CK1 (Kurihara et al., 2014). Pyridoquinazoline derivative **31** and pyridothienopyrimidin derivative **32** were CMGC kinase family (CDK, MAPK, GSK3, and CLK families) inhibitors with good CK1δ/ε inhibition (Esvan et al., 2016; Loidreau et al., 2015). A variety of natural products have also been demonstrated to be potent inhibitors of CK1, such as compound **33** (meriadinin E) (Gompel et al., 2004), **34** (lamellarin 3) (Baunbæk et al., 2008), and **35** (chloromethylhalicyclamine B) (Esposito et al., 2016).

3. Protein kinase CK2

3.1 Structures and function

Protein kinase CK2 is a constitutively active Ser/Thr kinase belonging to CMGC kinase group (Kobe et al., 2005). Structurally, CK2 is present as a tetramer consisted of two catalytic subunits α/α′ and two regulatory subunits β. The two catalytic subunits α/α′ share 85% sequence identity and assemble in any combination to form tetrameric holoenzyme, such as αα′ββ, ααββ, and α′α′ββ (Lozeman et al., 1990). CK2α subunit is widely expressed while the CK2α′ is only found in the brain and testis (Guerra et al., 1999). The regulatory subunit CK2β as the central component of tetramer affects activity and stability of holoenzyme as well as controls CK2β-dependent substrate specificity (Filhol et al., 2015).

The ATP-binding site located in CK2α can be divided into three areas roughly: a basic region where residue Lys68 holds the ATP β-phosphate; a hinge region, on the opposite side, connecting the N-lobe and C-lobe (residues Glu114~Asp120); a hydrophobic area between the two previous regions sandwiches the adenosine moiety of ATP (residues Val53, Val66, Ile95, Phe113, Met163, and Ile174) (Dalle Vedove et al., 2020). Beside of ATP-binding site, two allosteric sites have been identified within CK2α along with corresponding inhibitors. Allosteric site I locates at the α/β interface and consists of residues Tyr39, Val67, Val112, and Val101 (Raaf et al., 2008), while allosteric site II (also termed αD pocket) sits in the vicinity of ATP-binding site and is composed of residues Phe121, Tyr125, Leu128, Pro159, Val162, and Met225 (Brear et al., 2016) (Fig. 4.8).

CK2 as one of the most pleiotropic kinases phosphorylates over 300 substrates (Salvi et al., 2009), some of which are vital components in various signaling cascades. On the one side, CK2 promotes cellular proliferation and survival through several signaling pathways including PI3K/Akt pathway (Ruzzene et al., 2017), IKK/NF-κB pathway (Dominguez

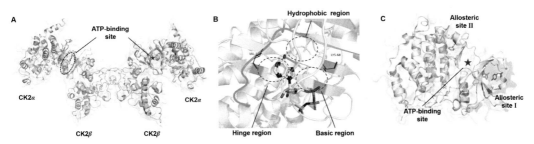

FIGURE 4.8   The cocrystal structure of CK2 tetramer. (A) Overall structure of CK2 complex (PDB ID: 1JWH), cofactor ANP is shown in yellow. (B) Details of ATP-binding site in CK2α. (C) Two allosteric sites of CK2α.

et al., 2009), JAK2/STAT3 pathway (Zheng et al., 2011), and Wnt/β-catenin pathway. On the other side, CK2 has a prominent antiapoptotic role by counteracting the action of caspases (Duncan et al., 2010). Therefore, the overexpression of CK2 has been observed in a wide range of hematological malignancies and solid tumors. Moreover, CK2 contributes to malignancies also by reducing the amount and the activity of tumor suppressor proteins and potentiating the multidrug resistance phenotype (Borgo & Ruzzene, 2019; Cox & Meek, 2010). Given its implication in several dysregulated pathways in human pathologies, CK2 is considered as a promising drug target, which in turn drives the design of inhibitors with diverse modes of action.

3.2 Inhibitors of protein kinase CK2

3.2.1 Bicyclic scaffold inhibitors

3.2.1.1 Polyhalogenated benzimidazole and benzotriazole derivatives

In 1986, an ATP mimetic molecule **36** (DRB) was identified as the first CK2 inhibitor (Fig. 4.9), exerting efficacy through ATP-competitive manner ($K_i = 29.2\ \mu M$) (Zandomeni et al., 1986). Interestingly, subsequent studies (PDB ID: 3H30) confirmed that **36** could also bind to the allosteric site I between CK2α/β interface and disrupt the assembly of CK2α and CK2β subunits (noncompetitive $K_i = 39.7\ \mu M$) (Raaf et al., 2008). Nevertheless, **36** was an orthosteric inhibitor of CK2 for that the binding at allosteric site I did not cause any conformational changes of CK2α. Despite its low potency and selectivity, **36** represented a good lead for further optimization (Fig. 4.10).

Removing the ribose ring of **36** and replacing the chloride atoms with bulky bromine gave rise to other two CK2 inhibitors **37** (TBB) and **38** (DMAT) (Pagano, Meggio, et al., 2004; Szyszka et al., 1995). In spite of simplified structure, both benzotriazoles **37** ($K_i = 0.4\ \mu M$) and benzimidazoles **38** ($K_i = 0.04\ \mu M$) displayed improved inhibitory activity. Notably, **38** was reported to inhibit the growth of prostate and liver cancer at a dose of 500 μg/kg in mouse xenograft models (Sass et al., 2011; Trembley et al., 2014). Cocrystal structure of **38** in complex with CK2α (PDB ID: 1ZOE) revealed that bromine atoms at 5-position and 6-position formed halogen bonds with hinge residues Glu114 and Val116, while two N-methyl groups interacted with several hydrophobic residues (Val53, Ile66, Lys68, Phe113, Val95, and Ile174) through apolar contacts (Battistutta et al., 2005; Pagano, Andrzejewska, et al., 2004).

Year	Chemical structure	Binding site	Biological data	PDB ID
1986	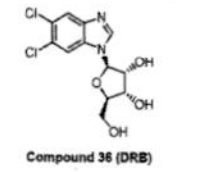 Compound 36 (DRB)	ATP-binding site and allosteric site I	competitive K_i= 29.2 μM noncompetitive K_i= 39.7 μM	3H30
1995	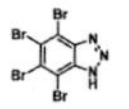 Compound 37 (TBB)	ATP-binding site	K_i= 0.4 μM	1J91
2004	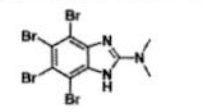 Compound 38 (DMAT)	ATP-binding site	K_i= 0.04 μM	1ZOE
2013	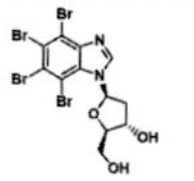 Compound 39 (TDB)	ATP-binding site	CK2 IC_{50}= 32 nM PIM-1 IC_{50}= 86 nM	4KWP
2021	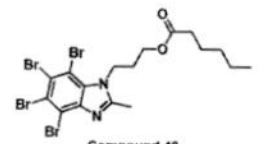 Compound 40	ATP-binding site	MCF-7 EC_{50}= 18.31 μM MDA-MB-231 EC_{50}= 22.06 μM	N/A
2021	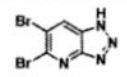 Compound 41	ATP-binding site	IC_{50}= 2.56 μM	7A4B
2007	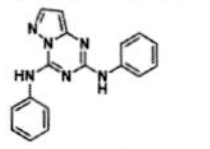 Compound 42	ATP-binding site	K_i= 0.26 μM	2PVH
2007	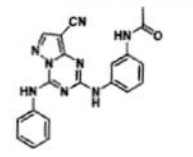 Compound 43	ATP-binding site	K_i= 0.35 nM HCT116 IC_{50}= 0.99 μM	2PVN
2008	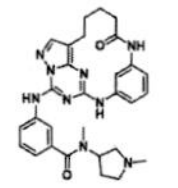 Compound 44	ATP-binding site	K_i= 2 nM HCT116 IC_{50}= 0.083 μM PC3 IC_{50}= 0.12 μM	N/A
2008	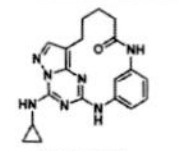 Compound 45	ATP-binding site	K_i= 24 nM HCT116 IC_{50}= 0.29 μM PC3 IC_{50}= 0.88 μM	3BE9
2016	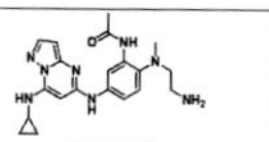 Compound 46	ATP-binding site	CK2α Kd= 6.33 pM HTC116 GI_{50}= 10 nM DLD1 GI_{50}= 50 nM SW620 GI_{50}= 5 nM	5H8E
2011	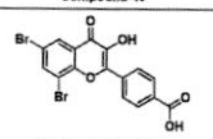 Compound 47 (FLC26)	ATP-binding site	IC_{50}= 9 nM	4UBA and 4UB7
2013	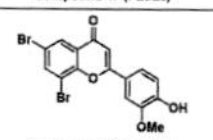 Compound 48 (FNH79)	ATP-binding site	IC_{50}= 4 nM	N/A
2020	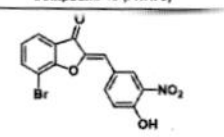 Compound 49 (BF013)	ATP-binding site	IC_{50}= 3.6 nM	N/A
2016	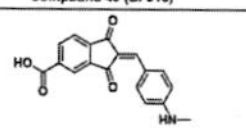 Compound 50 (SL-15)	ATP-binding site	IC_{50}= 0.85 μM	N/A
2021	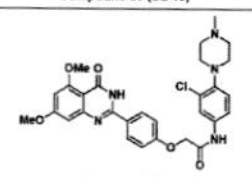 Compound 51	ATP-binding site	CK2 IC_{50}= 230 nM BRD4 IC_{50}= 180 nM	N/A

FIGURE 4.9 Bicyclic scaffold inhibitors of CK2. The chemical structures and biological data of bicyclic scaffold inhibitors of CK2.

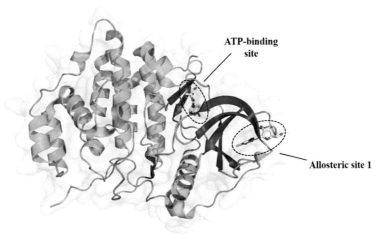

FIGURE 4.10   The cocrystal structure of CK2α in complex with compound 36 (PDB ID: 3H30). Two molecules of **36** are found attached to the enzyme.

However, **37** and **38** were demonstrated to be less selective after a selectivity profile against 70 protein kinases, among which seven kinases were inhibited more strongly than CK2 itself (Pagano et al., 2008).

In order to improve selectivity and potency, the TBB scaffold was further modified through reintroducing a deoxyribose moiety. Compound **39** (TDB) emerged as a cell permeable dual inhibitors of CK2 (IC$_{50}$ = 32 nM) and PIM1 (IC$_{50}$ = 86 nM) (Cozza et al., 2013, 2014). In a panel of 124 kinases, only CDC-like kinase 2 (CLK2) and dual-specificity tyrosine-phosphorylated and regulated kinase 1A (DYRK1A) are inhibited by **39** as drastically as CK2 and PIM-1. Cell testing demonstrated that the antiproliferative effect of **39** was mainly attributed to pro-apoptosis, hence, cancer cells CEM (DC$_{50}$ = 2.51 µM) and HeLa (DC$_{50}$ = 2.45 µM) were affected more drastically than nontumor cell lines. Cocrystal analysis (PDB ID: 4KWP) validated that two halogen bonds were formed between 6,7-bromine atoms and residues Val116 and Glu114, respectively. A weaker halogen bond was formed between 5-bromine atoms and a water molecule, bridging it to the side chain of Asp175. The deoxyribofuranosyl moiety protruded from the ATP-binding pocket toward the solvent, hydrogen bonding with residue Asn118 (Fig. 4.11).

Most recently, a novel class of TBB-based CK2 inhibitors with pro-apoptotic properties were claimed by Chojnacki et al. Compound **40** powerfully decreased the viability of both MCF-7 and MDA-MB-231 cells with EC$_{50}$ values of 18.31 and 22.06 µM, respectively (Chojnacki, Wińska, et al., 2021). Meanwhile, **40** acted on MCF-7 and MDA-MB-231 cells as an effective inducer of apoptosis with amounts of apoptotic cells equal to 57.5% and 49%, respectively. Furthermore, another series of TBB analogs with pyridine nitrogen atom instead of bromine atom in the C4 position were designed by the same team (Chojnacki, Lindenblatt, et al., 2021). Although analog **41** displayed favorable CK2 inhibition (IC$_{50}$ = 2.56 µM), little antiproliferative activity was observed in MCF-7 and CCRF-CEM cell at 50 µM.

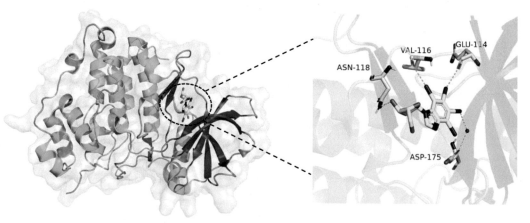

FIGURE 4.11   Binding mode of compound 39 with CK2α (PDB ID: 4KWP). **39** is colored yellow and the hydrogen bonds are shown as *green dashed lines*.

3.2.1.2 Pyrazolo-triazine and pyrazolo-pyrimidine derivatives

Based on a protein structure specific library screening, followed by de novo rational design, pyrazolo-triazines **42** was identified as a lead compound with a good affinity for CK2 ($K_i = 0.26\ \mu M$) (Nie et al., 2007). The cocrystal structure (PDB ID: 2PVH) suggested that the pyrazolo-triazine core of **42** occupied the adenine-binding region and formed two crucial hydrogen bonds with hinge residue Val116, thereby anchoring the molecule in ATP-binding site. The two phenyl groups adopted a folded conformation owing to the intramolecular stacking interactions, among which 2-anilino moiety extended toward the substrate-binding crevice between the phosphate-binding loop (Gly46 and Arg47) and the catalytic loop. In pursuit of occupying the underfilled ATP-binding cavity adequately, further structural modifications were carried out based on **42**. Introducing a cyano-group at the 8-position of pyrazolo-triazine core resulted in a 10-fold improvement of potency. Meanwhile, introducing an acetamido group at 2-anilino moiety afforded a potent CK2 inhibitor **43** with sub-nanomolar affinity ($K_i = 0.35\ nM$). Cocrystal structure of **43** in complex with CK2 (PDB ID: 2PVN) indicated that the improved inhibitory effect was mainly attributed to the acetamido group, occupying the back pocket and forming three hydrogen bonds with Asp175, Lys68, and a buried water molecule (Fig. 4.12). Notably, a big discrepancy was observed on compound **43** between its enzymatic potency and cell growth inhibition (HCT116 $IC_{50} = 0.99\ \mu M$), probably ascribing to its low aqueous solubility and poor cell membrane permeability.

Aiming to improve membrane permeability in favor to cellular activity, a novel class of macrocyclic pyrazolo-triazine derivatives have been designed and synthesized subsequently (Nie et al., 2008). Compound **44** showed improved growth inhibition of colon cancer HCT116 cell ($IC_{50} = 83\ nM$) in spite of decreased enzymic activity ($K_i = 2\ nM$). Furthermore, **44** effectively inhibited proliferation of prostate cancer PC3 cell with an IC_{50} value of 120 nM. Cocrystal structure of analogue **45** in complex with CK2 (PDB ID: 3BE9) illustrated that the alkyl linker reduced planarity of molecule, thereby increasing the membrane permeability as expected.

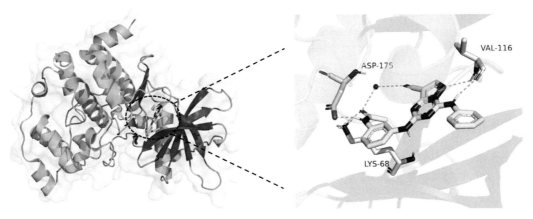

FIGURE 4.12   Details of internal pocket in CK2α and binding mode of 43 (PDB ID: 2PVN). **43** is colored yellow and the hydrogen bonds are shown as *green dashed lines*.

Employing a kinase-focused subset screening followed by SARs studies, a similar class of pyrazolo-pyrimidine derivatives were identified as CK2 inhibitors (Dowling et al., 2012, 2016). Compound **46** exhibited excellent enzymatic (CK2α K_d = 6:33 pM), cellular activity (HTC116 GI_{50} = 10 nM, DLD1 GI_{50} = 50 nM, SW620 GI_{50} = 5 nM), and good safety (hERG IC_{50} > 100 μM). Kinase selectivity profiling of **46** at a concentration of 0.1 μM against a panel of 402 kinases revealed a high degree of selectivity. The limited off-target activity (12 kinases with >50% inhibition) was restricted to members of the CMGC family. In vivo studies demonstrated **46** inhibited tumor growth in a dose-dependent manner, achieving 94% TGI (tumor growth inhibition) in HCT-116 (β-catenin mutant) models and 74% TGI in SW620 (APC mutant) models at a 30 mg/kg dose. Cocrystal structure (PDB ID: 5H8E) revealed that **46** adopted a similar binding mode with compound **43**. The pyrazolo-pyrimidine core formed bidentate hydrogen bonds with residue Val116, while imine at 5-position formed a hydrogen bond interaction with an ordered water molecule. Moreover, the cyano-group and acetamide group were involved in water-mediated hydrogen bonds with Asp175, and the terminal unsubstituted amino group of side chain was able to directly coordinate an ordered water and the residue Asn161.

3.2.1.3 Flavonoid derivatives

Many natural compounds, such as flavonoids, have been identified as CK2 inhibitors. Despite their promising activity on CK2, the family of flavonoids displays a high promiscuity across the human kinases. Subsequently, a variety of synthetic flavonoid derivatives were disclosed with improved potency and selectivity. Compound **47** (FLC26) and compound **48** (FNH79) were representative molecules which extremely inhibited CK2 with IC_{50} values of 9 and 4 nM, respectively (Golub et al., 2011, 2013). Preliminary selectivity testing in a panel of 8 kinases indicated considerable cross reactivity for **47** and acceptable selectivity for **48**. Since the number of kinases used in the assay is limited, additional tests were required to draw final conclusions on the selectivity issues. Docking studies of **48** revealed that one hydrogen bond formed between hydroxyl or methoxy group of the inhibitor and positively charged residue Lys68. Another hydrogen bond was formed between carbonyl group and hinge region residue Val116. Furthermore, stacking-like interaction of the phenyl group with residue Phe113 played a vital role in anchoring the inhibitor at the ATP-binding site.

Inspired by flavonoid, Protopopov et al. (2020) developed a class of aurones derivatives that inhibited CK2 with IC_{50} values in the nanomolar range. Compound **49** (BF013, $IC_{50} = 3.6$ nM) shared a similar binding mode with **47** in the ATP-binding site of CK2. In addition, 1,3-dioxo-2,3-dihydro-1H-indenes **50** (SL-15) was also claimed as CK2 inhibitor ($IC_{50} = 0.85$ μM) (Liu et al., 2016). Interestingly, molecular modeling predicted that **50** bound to ATP-binding site in an opposite orientation to **49**, perhaps accounting for the reduced potency. The carboxyl group of **50** formed hydrogen bonds with residues Lys68 and Asp175, while the imine group contacted with the backbone of Leu45 mediated by a water molecule. Regrettably, none of the selectivity data of these compounds are available.

In 2021, a novel series of quinazoline derivatives was reported as dual CK2 and BRD4 inhibitors for the treatment of triple-negative breast cancer (Zhang et al., 2021). Based on rational drug design followed by SARs investigations, inhibitor **51** was identified to possess potent and balanced activities against CK2 ($IC_{50} = 230$ nM) and BRD4 ($IC_{50} = 180$ nM) along with outstanding selectivity on a panel of 412 kinases. In vitro experiments showed that **51** could inhibit the proliferation of MDA-MB-231 ($IC_{50} = 2.66$ μM) and MDA-MB-468 cells ($IC_{50} = 3.52$ μM) as well as induce apoptosis and autophagy-associated cell death. In the MDA-MB-231 xenograft tumor models, **51** displayed pronounced tumor growth inhibition (TGI = 63.8%) after intragastric administration at 50 mg/kg dose for consecutive 19 days, without obvious toxicities. Molecular docking analysis revealed the binding modes of **51** in the ATP-binding site of CK2. The quinazoline core was deeply inserted into the hydrophobic pocket, forming hydrogen bonds with residues Lys77, Lys158, and Asn161. A hydrogen bond formed between the amide group and residue Leu45 was responsible for fixing the position and conformation of **51** in CK2. Moreover, the N-methylpiperazine fragment interacted with hinge region residues Asn118 and Asp120 through hydrogen bonds, enhancing the binding stability.

3.2.2 Tricyclic scaffold inhibitors

3.2.2.1 Benzonaphthyridine derivatives

Since the structural similarity between CK2 inhibitors and PARP inhibitors, a class of benzonaphthyridine derivatives have been developed as CK2 inhibitors based on the structural modification of PARP inhibitors (Pierre et al., 2011) (Fig. 4.13). Resultantly, compound **52** (CX-4945) was obtained as the most potent inhibitor of CK2 ($K_i = 0.38$ nM, $IC_{50} = 1$ nM). In a panel of 238 kinases, **52** displayed an excellent selectivity profile which was even more remarkable when considering the low molecular weight (349.8 g/mol) (Battistutta et al., 2011). Furthermore, **52** powerfully inhibited the proliferation of various cancer cell lines in the low micromolar range, including prostate, pancreatic, lung, breast, colorectal, melanotic cancer, and leukemia (Siddiqui-Jain et al., 2010). As an orally bioavailable ATP-competitive CK2 inhibitor, **52** was demonstrated to effectively inhibit tumor growth (TGI = 86%) in prostate cancer PC3 xenograft models at a dose of 75 mg/kg. Cocrystal structure (PDB ID: 3PE1 and 3NGA) confirmed that the benzonaphthyridine core formed direct hydrogen bond with residue Val116 and water-mediated hydrogen bond with His160, while

Year	Chemical structure	Binding site	Biological data	PDB ID
2009	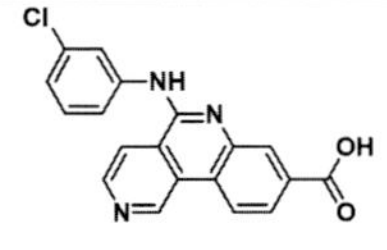 Compound 52 (CX-4945)	ATP-binding site	K_i= 0.38 nM IC_{50}= 1 nM	3PE1 and 3NGA
2021	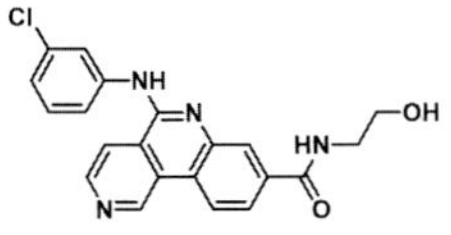 Compound 53	ATP-binding site	IC_{50}= 0.66 nM	N/A
2012	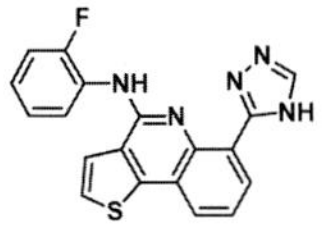 Compound 54	ATP-binding site	CK2 IC_{50}= 4 nM Pim-1 IC_{50}= 2 nM Pim-2 IC_{50}= 2 nM	N/A
2009	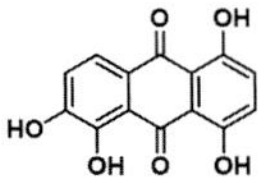 Compound 55 (quinalizarin)	ATP-binding site	K_i= 52 nM	3FL5, 3Q9Y, 3Q9Z
2004	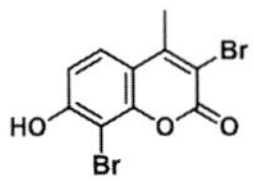 Compound 56 (DBC)	ATP-binding site	IC_{50}= 0.1 μM	2QC6
2006	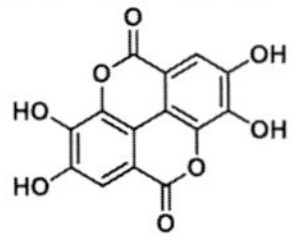 Compound 57 (ellagic acid)	ATP-binding site	IC_{50}= 0.04 μM	2ZJW
2010	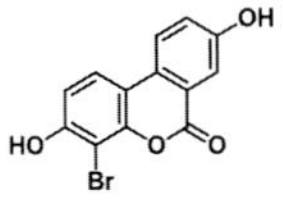 Compound 58	ATP-binding site	IC_{50}= 15 nM	N/A

FIGURE 4.13 Tricyclic scaffold inhibitors of CK2. The chemical structures and biological data of tricyclic scaffold inhibitors of CK2.

the 3-chlorophenylamino portion was hydrogen bonded to Asn118 via a water molecule as well (Ferguson et al., 2011). The carboxylate group were involved in hydrogen bonding interactions with residue Lys68, Asp175, and an ordered water molecule, playing an important role in improving potency. Collectively, extensive direct and water-mediated hydrogen bonds as well as large surface hydrophobic interaction contributed to the potent activity of **52** (Fig. 4.14).

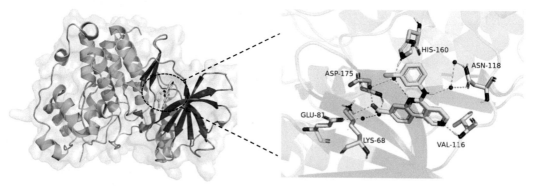

FIGURE 4.14   Key interactions between 52 and CK2α (PDB ID: 3PE1). 52 is colored yellow and the hydrogen bonds are displayed as *green dashed lines*.

Owing to its favorable pharmacokinetic properties and safety, **52** as the first small-molecular candidate targeting CK2 has entered clinical studies for the treatment of multiple cancers, including metastatic basal cell carcinoma (NCT03897036), medulloblastoma (NCT03904862), cholangiocarcinoma (NCT02128282), multiple myeloma (NCT01199718), and advanced solid tumors (NCT00891280). Especially, two phase II trials are in progress to evaluate the efficacy of **52** for the treatment of severe acute respiratory syndrome coronavirus 2 (SARS-CoV-2) infection (NCT04668209 and NCT04663737).

Despite good selectivity, **52** possessed powerful inhibition against CLK2 ($IC_{50} = 3.8$ nM by Kim et al., 2014) which was even stronger than its inhibition against CK2 ($IC_{50} = 14.7$ nM by Kim et al., 2014). Based on reasonable structural modification of **52**, another series of benzo-naphthyridine analogs were obtained with increasing anticancer activity and CK2 selectivity (Wang et al., 2021). Compared with **52**, compound **53** exhibited stronger CK2 inhibitory activity ($IC_{50} = 0.66$ nM) and higher CLK2/CK2 selectivity. In HCT-116 xenograft mouse models, **53** markedly inhibited tumor growth (TGI = 59%) at dose of 60 mg/kg which was 3.9 times higher than that of **52** (TGI = 15%). In addition, a novel family of potent dual inhibitors of CK2 and the Pim kinases were discovered by scaffold hopping strategy (Pierre et al., 2012). Analogue **54** was active at single digit nanomolar IC_{50} values against CK2 ($IC_{50} = 4$ nM) and the Pim isoforms Pim-1 ($IC_{50} = 2$ nM) and Pim-2 ($IC_{50} = 2$ nM).

3.2.2.2 Anthraquinone and coumarin derivatives

Anthraquinone and coumarin are other two families of natural molecules active as inhibitors of CK2. The most promising anthraquinone derivative is undoubtedly compound **55** (quinalizarin, $K_i = 52$ nM) discovered by computer-aided virtual screening (Cozza et al., 2009). The main advantage of **55** is the outstanding selectivity as judged by profiling it on a large panel of 140 protein kinases (Cozza et al., 2015). Cocrystal structure (PDB ID: 3FL5) illustrated that 2-hydroxy group made hydrogen bonding interactions with residue Lys68 and a water molecule, while 5-hydroxy group interacted with residue Val116 through another water molecule. Meanwhile, 8-hydroxy formed two hydrogen bonds with residue His160 and Arg47, stabilizing the kinase into a close conformation which entrapped the inhibitor inside the pocket.

The coumarin derivatives identified in early stage are represented by molecules **56** (DBC, $IC_{50} = 0.1\ \mu M$) and **57** (ellagic acid, $IC_{50} = 0.04\ \mu M$) (Cozza et al., 2006; Meggio et al., 2004). Based on the meticulous analysis of the co-crystal structure of CK2 in complex with **56** and **57**, a urolithin derivative **58** was designed and synthesized as CK2 inhibitors with improved target affinity ($IC_{50} = 15\ nM$) (Cozza et al., 2011). Preliminary selectivity study verified that **58** was quite specific for CK2 in a panel of 8 kinases. Unfortunately, limited antitumor effects of **58** were observed in KARPAS-299 and MOLT-4 cells. Overall, researches about anthraquinone and coumarin derivatives are relatively less in the last decade.

3.2.3 Monocyclic scaffold inhibitors

3.2.3.1 2-Amino aromatic heterocyclic derivatives

Using a virtual ligand screening campaign targeting the α/β interface of CK2, a novel class of 2-aminothiazole derivatives were identified as CK2 inhibitors (Bestgen, Krimm, et al., 2019) (Fig. 4.15). Analogs **59** ($IC_{50} = 14\ \mu M$) and **60** ($IC_{50} = 0.6\ \mu M$) exhibited favorable inhibitory activity and selectivity against CK2 (Bestgen, Kufareva, et al., 2019). Furthermore, **60** induced apoptosis in 786-O cells ($EC_{50} = 5\ \mu M$) and inhibited STAT3 activation even more potently than candidate **52** (EC_{50} values of 1.6 vs. 5.3 μM). Interestingly, this class of inhibitors were originally speculated to bind to an allosteric site based on STD NMR and circular dichroism spectroscopy analysis. Until 2020, the solved cocrystal structure (PDB ID: 6TEI and 6TEW) corroborated that they were orthosteric inhibitor occupying the ATP cavity (Lindenblatt et al., 2020). The carboxylate group of **59** formed salt bridges with residues Lys68 as well as hydrogen bonds with Asp175 and a water molecule (Fig. 4.16).

Since a natural product isoliquiritigenin was discovered to inhibit CK2 with an IC_{50} value of 17.3 μM, a series of CK2 inhibitor endowed with propenone scaffold have been developed on the basis of isoliquiritigenin (Qi et al., 2019). Compound **61** was found to be the most potent molecule ($IC_{50} = 0.6\ \mu M$) with the antiproliferative activity on HepG2 cancer cells ($IC_{50} = 14\ \mu M$). Similarly, the carboxylate group of **61** interacted with residue Lys86 by hydrogen bonds and salt bridge, while the amide moiety hydrogen bonded to residue Val116.

Recently, several thiadiazole analogs were reported as CK2 inhibitors featured by remarkable selectivity on a panel of 320 kinases (Dalle Vedove et al., 2020). The high selectivity attributed to the thiadiazoles were only compatible with the open conformation of the hinge/αD region of CK2. This was unambiguously confirmed by cocrystal structure of CK2 with **62** (PDB ID: 6RFE), in which the guaiacol moiety formed hydrogen bonds with residues Lys68, Asp175, and a conserved water molecule, anchoring **62** in the ATP-binding site. The central 2-cyano-2-propenamide fragment contacted the hinge region through a water-mediated hydrogen bond between the propenamide carbonyl oxygen and residue Val116, meanwhile the sulfur atom of thiadiazole core also established an interaction with residue Val116. As the most potent compound of this series, **62** significantly reduced cell viability in leukemia Jurkat cells with a DC_{50} value of 12.80 μM.

3.2.3.2 Phenyl-based derivatives

Polyhalogenated phenyl carboxylic acids are a class of CK2 inhibitors derived from polyhalogenated benzimidazoles. The representative compound **63** (TBCA) displayed favorable CK2 inhibition ($IC_{50} = 0.11\ \mu M$) and selectivity (Pagano et al., 2007). Crucially, the potency

Year	Chemical structure	Binding site	Biological data	PDB ID
2019	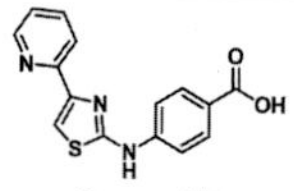 Compound 59	ATP-binding site	IC$_{50}$= 14 μM	6TEI and 6TE2
2019	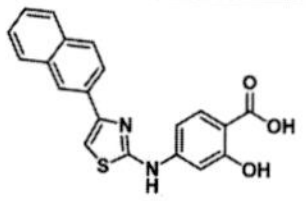 Compound 60	ATP-binding site	IC$_{50}$= 0.6 μM	6TEW
2019	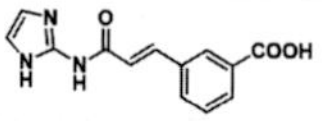 Compound 61	ATP-binding site	IC$_{50}$= 0.6 μM	N/A
2020	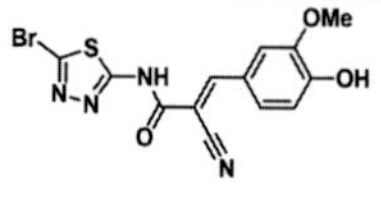 Compound 62	ATP-binding site	IC$_{50}$= 0.28 μM	6RFE
2007	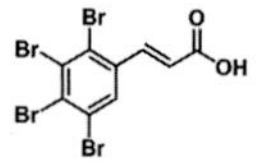 Compound 63 (TBCA)	ATP-binding site	IC$_{50}$= 0.11 μM	N/A
2018	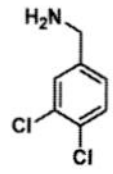 Compound 64 (NMR154)	ATP-binding site, allosteric site I and allosteric site II	IC$_{50}$= 900 μM	N/A
2018	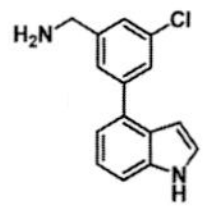 Compound 65 (CAM187)	Allosteric site I	IC$_{50}$= 44 μM	6GIH
2019	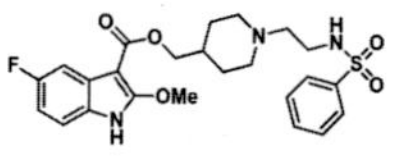 Compound 66	Allosteric site I	IC$_{50}$= 22 μM	6FVG
2016	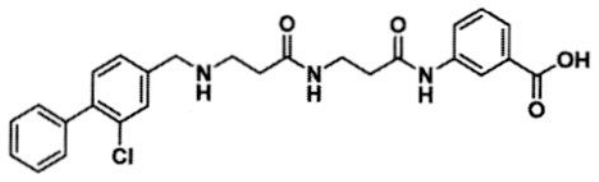 Compound 67 (CAM4066)	ATP-binding site and allosteric site II	IC$_{50}$= 0.37 μM	5CU3 and 5CU4
2018	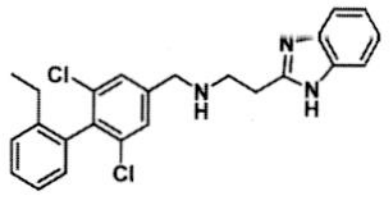 Compound 68 (CAM4712)	Allosteric site II	IC$_{50}$= 7 μM	5OTY
2020	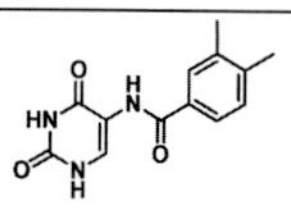 Compound 69	Allosteric site II	IC$_{50}$= 13.0 μM	N/A

FIGURE 4.15 Monocyclic scaffold inhibitors of CK2. The chemical structures and biological data of monocyclic scaffold inhibitors of CK2.

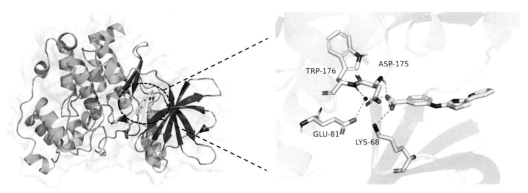

FIGURE 4.16   The cocrystal structure of CK2α in complex with 59 confirmed that 59 was an ATP-competitive inhibitor (PDB ID: 6TEI). **59** is colored yellow and the hydrogen bonds are shown as *green dashed lines*.

of **63** depended on the carboxylate side chain interacting with Lys68, as illustrated by the loss of inhibitory activity experienced by methylation of its carboxyl group or by alteration of steric conformation from *trans-* to *cis*-configuration.

Utilizing a fragment-based screening campaign, compound **64** (NMR154) was uncovered as a lead to bind in the ATP site, allosteric site I and allosteric site II of CK2 simultaneously (IC$_{50}$ = 900 μM) (Brear et al., 2018). Through elaborate iterations, analog **65** (CAM187) was achieved with improved inhibitory activity (IC$_{50}$ = 44 μM) and selectivity toward allosteric site I. This was affirmed by cocrystal structure (PDB ID: 6GIH) of **65**-CK2α, in which the amino group formed a water-mediated hydrogen bond with Asp37. The indole ring sat under the β4β5 loop and the nitrogen of the indole interacts with the residue Thr108. Due to its fragment-like properties, **65** leaves room for further development (Fig. 4.17).

In parallel, another series of molecules targeting allosteric site I were discovered by Kufareva et al. (2019) through virtual screening. Compound **66** (IC$_{50}$ = 22 μM) exhibited significant selectivity for CK2 with a Gini coefficient of 0.81, higher than that of candidate **52** (0.62). In triple-negative breast cancer MBA-MB-231 cells, **66** effectively inhibited cell growth,

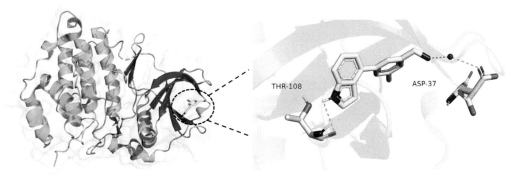

FIGURE 4.17   Closeup view of 65 in the allosteric site I of CK2 (PDB ID: 6GIH). **65** is colored yellow and the hydrogen bonds are shown as *green dashed lines*.

migration, and triggered apoptosis. Cocrystal structure (PDB ID: 6FVG) demonstrated that **66** bound at the CK2α/β interface and thus blocked the assembly of holoenzyme, accounting for the specific inhibition of CK2β-dependent substrates. Moreover, the binding of **66** also caused the transition of the αD loop from the open to the closed conformation, thereby partially destabilizing ATP in hinge region. The sulfonamide group hydrogen bonded to residues Ser106 and Thr108 of the β4β5 loop, and the piperidine ring made a salt bridge interaction with Asp103. The indole moiety was buried in the hydrophobic pocket and interacted with polar residue Gln36 and Tyr39.

In 2016, the first generation of inhibitors targeting allosteric site II of CK2 were developed by Spring's team (Brear et al., 2016). The representative molecule **67** (CAM4066) possessed powerful inhibition against CK2 (IC$_{50}$ = 0.37 μM) and prominent selectivity in a panel of 52 kinases. Cocrystal structure (PDB ID: 5CU3 and 5CU4) revealed that **67** induced the rearrangement of Tyr125 and releases the αD helix from the C-lobe, thereby opening the αD pocket. The benzoic acid portion of **67** located in ATP-binding site and formed salt bridge and hydrogen bond with Lys68, while the diphenyl moiety inserted into the αD pocket and formed multiple hydrophobic interactions. The long-chain linker occupied a shallow groove and was involved in an elaborate network of hydrogen bonds (Fig. 4.18). In spite of satisfied enzymatic activity, **67** suffered from poor cellular permeability, resulting in no effect in cellular testing. Moreover, **67** was also limited by other adverse properties which were usually associated with poor oral bioavailability, including a long flexible linker, a zwitterionic nature, amide bonds and a high molecular weight.

Aiming to overcome the defects of **67**, the second generation of inhibitors were designed by the same team (Iegre et al., 2018). Apart from potency, compound **68** (CAM4712) was endowed with numerous advantages over **67**, such as a reduction in the number of rotatable bonds and the absence of amide groups susceptible to the action of proteases. Notably, good cellular permeability of **68** led to its similar efficacy in inhibiting kinase (IC$_{50}$ = 7 μM) and cell proliferation (GI$_{50}$ = 10 μM). Cocrystal structure (PDB ID: 5OTY) authenticated that **68** occupied the allosteric site II and induced the flipping of the Met163, thereby blocking access to the ATP-binding site (Fig. 4.12). The benzimidazole fragment of **68** sandwiched between His160 and Met163 formed low-energy hydrophobic π-π interaction, accounting for the loss of binding affinity and potency compared with **67**. Besides, pyrimidinedione derivative

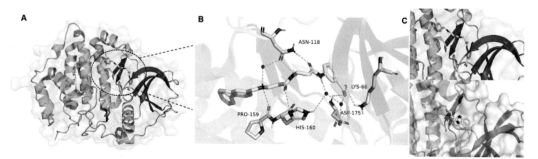

FIGURE 4.18   Cocrystal structures of CK2α in complex with 67 and 68. (A) Overall structure of CK2α in complex with **67** (*ligand yellow*, PDB ID 5CU3). (B) Binding site interactions of **67**. (C) Comparison of the binding modes of **67** (*up*) and **68** (*down*, PDB ID: 5OTY) with CK2α.

69 were also reported as inhibitors of allosteric site II ($IC_{50} = 13.0 \, \mu M$) with the antiproliferative activity in A549 cells ($IC_{50} = 23.1 \, \mu M$), either (Li et al., 2020).

3.2.4 Tetracyclic scaffold inhibitors and others

Based on a natural product library screening, compound **70** was identified as a novel CK2 inhibitor with an IC_{50} value of 0.55 μM (Hung et al., 2009) (Fig. 4.19). Different from other natural products, **70** (hematein) was highly selective for CK2 in a panel of 48 kinases. In a xenograft nude mouse model of lung cancer, **70** significantly inhibited tumor growth at a dose of 50 mg/kg (Hung et al., 2013). Interestingly, molecular modeling elucidated that **70** bound to both ATP-binding site and allosteric site I. Additionally, diazodinaphthalene **71** ($IC_{50} = 0.4 \, \mu M$) (Moucadel et al., 2011) and furocarbazole **72** (W16, $IC_{50} = 20 \, \mu M$) (Kröger et al., 2020; Laudet et al., 2008) were reported as CK2 inhibitors binding at allosteric site I although their crystal structures were unpublished.

Indenoindole derivatives were additional class of ATP-competitive inhibitors of CK2 (Hundsdörfer, Hemmerling, Götz, et al., 2012; Hundsdörfer, Hemmerling, Hamberger, et al., 2012). The most potent analog **73** could powerfully inhibit CK2 with an IC_{50} value at nanomolar range ($IC_{50} = 25 \, nM$) (Jabor Gozzi et al., 2015). Dose-dependent and strong antiproliferative effects were induced by **73** in different types of cancer cells known to be overexpressing CK2 (A431 $EC_{50} = 8.4 \, \mu M$, A549 $EC_{50} = 18.2 \, \mu M$ and LNCaP $EC_{50} = 11.4 \, \mu M$) (El-Awaad et al., 2021). Of note, cocrystal structures of **73** with CK2α (PDB ID: 5ONI)

Year	Chemical structure	Binding site	Biological data	PDB ID
2009	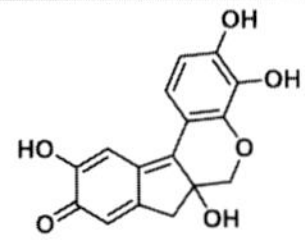 Compound 70 (hematein)	ATP-binding site and allosteric site I	$IC_{50} = 0.55 \, \mu M$	N/A
2011	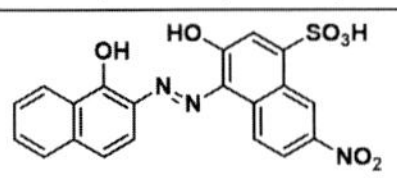 Compound 71	Allosteric site I	$IC_{50} = 0.4 \, \mu M$	N/A
2008	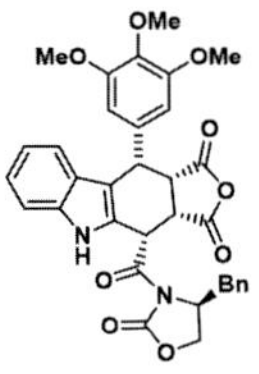 Compound 72 (W16)	Allosteric site I	$IC_{50} = 20 \, \mu M$	N/A
2015	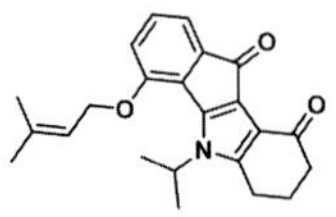 Compound 73	ATP-binding site	$IC_{50} = 25 \, nM$	5OMY, 5ONI and 5OOI

FIGURE 4.19 Tetracyclic scaffold inhibitors and others. The chemical structures and biological data of tricyclic scaffold inhibitors and others.

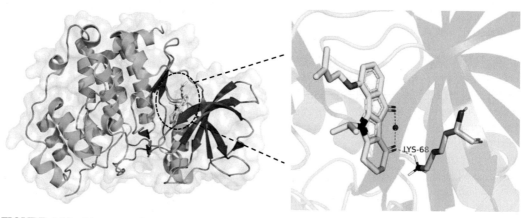

FIGURE 4.20 The cocrystal structure of CK2α in complex with compound 73 (PDB ID: 5ONI). **73** is colored yellow and the hydrogen bonds are shown as *green dashed lines*.

revealed an unusual "hydrophobic-out/oxygen-in" binding mode mainly mediated by the hydrophobic interactions (Hochscherf et al., 2017). The indenoindole core and two hydrophobic side chains were involved in extensive hydrophobic interactions with numerous residues, while two carbonyl group formed hydrogen bonds with Lys68 and a conserved water, determining binding orientation of **73** within ATP-binding site (Fig. 4.20). Unfortunately, **73** was reported with poor metabolic stability, posing a challenge to improve the drug-like properties of this series of derivatives.

4. Protein kinase Fam20C

4.1 Structures and function

Fam20C is an atypical kinase functions in the secretory pathway to phosphorylate proteins within S-x-E/pS motifs (Tagliabracci et al., 2012; Zhang et al., 2018). More than 100 proteins have been identified as substrates of Fam20C with extensive roles in physiologies processes, such as biomineralization, wound healing, cell adhesion, and migration (Tagliabracci et al., 2015). Furthermore, Fam20C is active in multiple tissues including mammary gland, liver, spleen, brain, and kidney (Lasa et al., 1997). Given these premises, it is not surprising that dysregulation of Fam20C is associated with a variety of pathologies, including cancers. It has been validated that knockout of Fam20C could inhibit proliferation, migration, and invasion of triple-negative breast cancer MDA-MB-468 cells (Tagliabracci et al., 2015; Zhao et al., 2021). In addition, numerous Fam20C substrates are involved in the apoptosis and metastasis of tumor cells, authorizing Fam20C a promising anticancer target (Qin et al., 2016).

Unfortunately, Fam20C is insensitive to promiscuous protein kinase inhibitors reported previously, such as staurosporine, flavonoids, and heparin (Lasa et al., 1997; Lolli et al., 2012). This should not be surprising for that Fam20C contains distinctly different residues in the ATP-binding site compared to other protein kinases. Delightfully, the crystal structure of the *Caenorhabditis elegans* homolog of human Fam20C (PDB ID: 4KQB) was solved in 2013

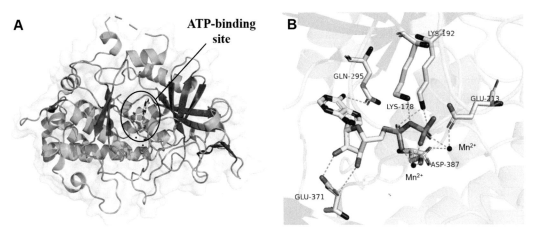

FIGURE 4.21 The cocrystal structure of Fam20C in complex with ADP. (A) Overall structure of the Fam20C in complex with ADP (PDB ID: 4KQB), cofactor ADP is shown in *yellow*. (B) The interactions between ADP and Fam20C.

(Xiao et al., 2013). Structurally, Fam20 displays a relatively large kinase domain and its core consists of *N*-lobe and *C*-lobe. The ATP-binding site is located at the cleft between the *N*-lobe and *C*-lobe, and substantial residues participate in a hydrogen bond network with ADP, including Lys178, Lys192, Glu213, Gln295, Glu371, and Asp387 (Fig. 4.21). Recently, the structural characteristics of human Fam20C were also identified (PDB ID: 5YH3) (Zhang et al., 2018), these architectures of Fam20C have provided a remarkable rationale for the development of selective inhibitors.

4.2 Inhibitors of protein kinase Fam20C

In 2016, the first Fam20C inhibitor **74** (FL-1607) was discovered based on virtual screening and molecular dynamics simulation (Qin et al., 2016) (Fig. 4.22). Docking studies found that **74** formed one conventional hydrogen bond with residue Arg400 and four nonconventional

Year	Chemical structure	Binding site	Biological data	PDB ID
2016	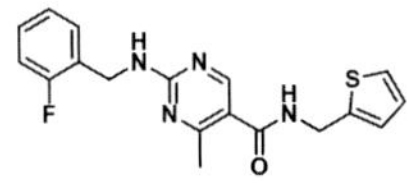 Compound 74 (FL-1607)	ATP-binding site	MDA-MB-468 IC$_{50}$= 7.89 μM	N/A
2021	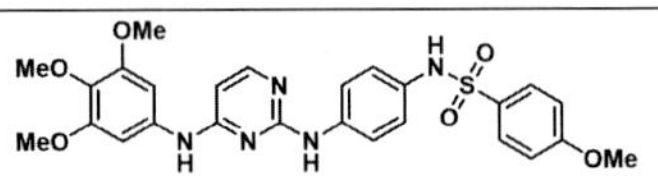 Compound 75	ATP-binding site	IC$_{50}$= 6.24 μM	N/A

FIGURE 4.22 Inhibitors of protein kinase Fam20C. The chemical structures and biological data of Fam20C inhibitors.

hydrogen bonds with residues Phe391 and Asp478. Noteworthy, previous study confirmed that Asp478 as a metal-binding residue was critical for Fam20C kinase activity (Cui et al., 2015). As a consequence, **74** strongly inhibited proliferation of MDA-MB-468 cell with an IC_{50} value of 7.89 μM. Meanwhile, it has also been reported that **74** could induce apoptosis and inhibit cell migration in MDA-MB-468 cell. The discovery of **74** provided a new clue to the development of Fam20C inhibitors for cancer therapy.

Combining in silico HTS with SARs studies, another Fam20C inhibitor **75** was obtained with an IC_{50} value of 6.24 μM (Zhao et al., 2021). In MDA-MB-231 cell, **75** was demonstrated to effectively induce apoptosis via the mitochondrial pathway and inhibit cell migration. Especially, **75** exhibited significant tumor growth inhibition in MDA-MB-231 xenograft models along with favorable safety. Molecular modeling suggested that trimethoxy phenyl portion formed two hydrogen bonds with residue Lys271, while sulfonamide group formed another two with residues Lys264 and Arg400. In addition, multiple hydrophobic interactions were formed between **75** and residues Leu477, Leu283, and Phe391.

5. Conclusions

CK1, CK2, and Fam20C belong to different kinase families and have no functional relatedness with each other, but all of them are implicated in a plethora of human diseases. Apart from Fam20C, a considerable amount of CK1 and CK2 inhibitors have been developed in the past decades. However, many molecules encounter the problem of selectivity, cell permeability, metabolic stability, physicochemical property, and safety in spite of excellent potency in vitro, leading to less quantity of candidates in clinical trials to date. Indeed, the improved selectivity has become the primary factor restricting the development of CK1 inhibitors for that the seven isoforms of CK1 possess similar, distinct or opposite physiological and pathological implications. Hence, isoform-specific inhibitors of CK1 should be designed based on indications, such as neurodegenerative diseases (CK1δ/ε), inflammatory disorders (CK1α/δ/ε) and cancer (CK1α/δ/ε/γ). Nevertheless, this obstacle is difficult to completely overcome by ATP-competitive inhibitors due to the highly conserved kinase domains shared by seven isoforms. As an alternative, novel compounds targeting the evolutionarily less conserved allosteric sites offer a promising strategy to address this quandary. Regrettably, none of allosteric inhibitors or allosteric sites of CK1 have been reported to date, requiring further exploration.

Due to the smaller ATP-binding pocket, ATP-competitive inhibitors of CK2 present favorable selectivity against CMGC kinase family. Even though a fully selective ATP-competitive probe for CK2 has yet to be discovered, persistent optimization of existing inhibitors and the identification of novel scaffolds will alter this situation. Moreover, two allosteric sites in CK2α have been reported along with highly selective allosteric inhibitors, while another three allosteric sites were predicted in CK2α based on computational detection (Jiang et al., 2017). Fam20C inhibitors are currently in their infancy and only two series of compounds have been claimed. The discovery of these molecules provides a chemical probe to shed light on the potential mechanisms regulated by Fam20C in cancer cells and offers inspiration for the subsequent development of Fam20C inhibitors.

Overall, casein kinases (CKs) turn out to be a class of promising targets for the treatment of many human malignancies and other disorders, including AD, PD, and COVID-19. In addition to small-molecule inhibitors CX-4945 and BIIB-118, a synthetic peptide CIGB-300 that inhibits CK2-mediated phosphorylation has also entered phase II clinical trials to treat cervix cancer (NCT01639625). Besides, targeted protein degradation strategy provides another powerful tool for CKs drug design. A proteolysis targeting chimera (PROTAC) degrader targeting CK2 were disclosed with similar anticancer effect to CX-4945, whereas mechanism is quite distinct (Chen et al., 2018). The continuous advancement of drug design strategy and in-depth insight of protein structure would further facilitate the discovery of CKs candidates, providing more drugs for cancer therapy.

Declaration of interests

The authors have no relevant affiliations or financial involvement with any organization or entity with a financial interest in or financial conflict with the subject matter or materials discussed in the manuscript. This includes employment, consultancies, honoraria, stock ownership or options, expert testimony, grants or patents received or pending, or royalties.

Reviewer disclosures

Peer reviewers on this manuscript have no relevant financial or other relationships to disclose.

References

Allende, J. E., & Allende, C. C. (1995). Protein kinase CK2: An enzyme with multiple substrates and a puzzling regulation. *Federation of American Societies for Experimental Biology Journal, 9*(5), 313–323. https://doi.org/10.1096/fasebj.9.5.7896000

Bain, J., Plater, L., Elliott, M., Shpiro, N., Hastie, C. J., Mclauchlan, H., Klevernic, I., Arthur, J. S. C., Alessi, D. R., & Cohen, P. (2007). The selectivity of protein kinase inhibitors: A further update. *Biochemical Journal, 408*(3), 297–315. https://doi.org/10.1042/BJ20070797

Bao, Y., Hata, Y., Ikeda, M., & Withanage, K. (2011). Mammalian Hippo pathway: From development to cancer and beyond. *Journal of Biochemistry, 149*(4), 361–379. https://doi.org/10.1093/jb/mvr021

Battistutta, R., Cozza, G., Pierre, F., Papinutto, E., Lolli, G., Sarno, S., Obrien, S. E., Siddiqui-Jain, A., Haddach, M., Anderes, K., Ryckman, D. M., Meggio, F., & Pinna, L. A. (2011). Unprecedented selectivity and structural determinants of a new class of protein kinase CK2 inhibitors in clinical trials for the treatment of cancer. *Biochemistry, 50*(39), 8478–8488. https://doi.org/10.1021/bi2008382

Battistutta, R., Mazzorana, M., Sarno, S., Kazimierczuk, Z., Zanotti, G., & Pinna, L. A. (2005). Inspecting the structure-activity relationship of protein kinase CK2 inhibitors derived from tetrabromo-benzimidazole. *Chemistry & Biology, 12*(11), 1211–1219. https://doi.org/10.1016/j.chembiol.2005.08.015

Baunbæk, D., Trinkler, N., Ferandin, Y., Lozach, O., Ploypradith, P., Rucirawat, S., Ishibashi, F., Iwao, M., & Meijer, L. (2008). Anticancer alkaloid lamellarins inhibit protein kinases. *Marine Drugs, 6*(4), 514–527. https://doi.org/10.3390/md20080026

Benek, O., Hroch, L., Aitken, L., Gunn-Moore, F., Vinklarova, L., Kuca, K., Perez, D. I., Perez, C., Martinez, A., Fisar, Z., & Musilek, K. (2018). 1-(Benzo[d]thiazol-2-yl)-3-phenylureas as dual inhibitors of casein kinase 1 and ABAD enzymes for treatment of neurodegenerative disorders. *Journal of Enzyme Inhibition and Medicinal Chemistry, 33*(1), 665–670. https://doi.org/10.1080/14756366.2018.1445736

Bestgen, B., Krimm, I., Kufareva, I., Kamal, A. A. M., Seetoh, W. G., Abell, C., Hartmann, R. W., Abagyan, R., Cochet, C., Le Borgne, M., Engel, M., & Lomberget, T. (2019). 2-Aminothiazole derivatives as selective allosteric modulators of the protein kinase CK2. 1. Identification of an allosteric binding site. *Journal of Medicinal Chemistry, 62*(4), 1803–1816. https://doi.org/10.1021/acs.jmedchem.8b01766

Bestgen, B., Kufareva, I., Seetoh, W., Abell, C., Hartmann, R. W., Abagyan, R., Le Borgne, M., Filhol, O., Cochet, C., Lomberget, T., & Engel, M. (2019). 2-Aminothiazole derivatives as selective allosteric modulators of the protein kinase CK2. 2. Structure-based optimization and investigation of effects specific to the allosteric mode of action. *Journal of Medicinal Chemistry, 62*(4), 1817−1836. https://doi.org/10.1021/acs.jmedchem.8b01765

Beyaert, R., Vanhaesebroeck, B., Declercq, W., Van Lint, J., Vandenabeele, P., Agostinis, P., Vandenheede, J. R., & Fiers, W. (1995). Casein kinase-1 phosphorylates the p75 tumor necrosis factor receptor and negatively regulates tumor necrosis factor signaling for apoptosis. *Journal of Biological Chemistry, 270*(40), 23293−23299. https://doi.org/10.1074/jbc.270.40.23293

Bibian, M., Rahaim, R. J., Choi, J. Y., Noguchi, Y., Schürer, S., Chen, W., Nakanishi, S., Licht, K., Rosenberg, L. H., Li, L., Feng, Y., Cameron, M. D., Duckett, D. R., Cleveland, J. L., & Roush, W. R. (2013). Development of highly selective casein kinase 1δ/1ε (CK1δ/ε) inhibitors with potent antiproliferative properties. *Bioorganic & Medicinal Chemistry Letters, 23*(15), 4374−4380. https://doi.org/10.1016/j.bmcl.2013.05.075

Bischof, J., Leban, J., Zaja, M., Grothey, A., Radunsky, B., Othersen, O., Strobl, S., Vitt, D., & Knippschild, U. (2012). 2-Benzamido-N-(1H-benzo[d]imidazole-2-yl)thiazole-4-carboxamide derivatives as potent inhibitors of CK1δ/ε. *Amino Acids, 43*(4), 1577−1591. https://doi.org/10.1007/s00726-012-1234-x

Borgo, C., & Ruzzene, M. (2019). Role of protein kinase CK2 in antitumor drug resistance. *Journal of Experimental & Clinical Cancer Research, 38*(1). https://doi.org/10.1186/s13046-019-1292-y

Brear, P., De Fusco, C., Hadje Georgiou, K., Francis-Newton, N. J., Stubbs, C. J., Sore, H. F., Venkitaraman, A. R., Abell, C., Spring, D. R., & Hyvönen, M. (2016). Specific inhibition of CK2α from an anchor outside the active site. *Chemical Science, 7*(11), 6839−6845. https://doi.org/10.1039/c6sc02335e

Brear, P., North, A., Iegre, J., Hadje Georgiou, K., Lubin, A., Carro, L., Green, W., Sore, H. F., Hyvönen, M., & Spring, D. R. (2018). Novel non-ATP competitive small molecules targeting the CK2 α/β interface. *Bioorganic & Medicinal Chemistry, 26*(11), 3016−3020. https://doi.org/10.1016/j.bmc.2018.05.011

Brockschmidt, C., Hirner, H., Huber, N., Eismann, T., Hillenbrand, A., Giamas, G., Radunsky, B., Ammerpohl, O., Bohm, B., Henne-Bruns, D., Kalthoff, H., Leithäuser, F., Trauzold, A., & Knippschild, U. (2008). Anti-apoptotic and growth-stimulatory functions of CK1 delta and epsilon in ductal adenocarcinoma of the pancreas are inhibited by IC261 in vitro and in vivo. *Gut, 57*(6), 799−806. https://doi.org/10.1136/gut.2007.123695

Cescon, E., Cescon, E., Bolcato, G., Federico, S., Bissaro, M., Valentini, A., Ferlin, M. G., Spalluto, G., Sturlese, M., & Moro, S. (2020). Scaffold repurposing of in-house chemical library toward the identification of new casein kinase 1 δinhibitors. *ACS Medicinal Chemistry Letters, 11*(6), 1168−1174. https://doi.org/10.1021/acsmedchemlett.0c00028

Chen, H., Chen, F., Liu, N., Wang, X., & Gou, S. (2018). Chemically induced degradation of CK2 by proteolysis targeting chimeras based on a ubiquitin−proteasome pathway. *Bioorganic Chemistry, 81*, 536−544. https://doi.org/10.1016/j.bioorg.2018.09.005

Cheong, J. K., Hung, N. T., Wang, H., Tan, P., Voorhoeve, P. M., Lee, S. H., & Virshup, D. M. (2011). IC261 induces cell cycle arrest and apoptosis of human cancer cells via CK1δ/ε and Wnt/B-catenin independent inhibition of mitotic spindle formation. *Oncogene, 30*(22), 2558−2569. https://doi.org/10.1038/onc.2010.627

Chijiwa, T., Hagiwara, M., & Hidaka, H. (1989). A newly synthesized selective casein kinase I inhibitor, N-(2-aminoethyl)-5-chloroisoquinoline-8-sulfonamide, and affinity purification of casein kinase I from bovine testis. *Journal of Biological Chemistry, 264*(9), 4924−4927.

Chojnacki, K., Lindenblatt, D., Wińska, P., Wielechowska, M., Toelzer, C., Niefind, K., & Bretner, M. (2021). Synthesis, biological properties and structural study of new halogenated azolo[4,5-b]pyridines as inhibitors of CK2 kinase. *Bioorganic Chemistry, 106*, 104502. https://doi.org/10.1016/j.bioorg.2020.104502

Chojnacki, K., Wińska, P., Karatsai, O., Koronkiewicz, M., Milner-Krawczyk, M., Wielechowska, M., Redowicz, M. J., Bretner, M., & Borowiecki, P. (2021). Synthesis of novel acyl derivatives of 3-(4,5,6,7-tetrabromo-1H-benzimidazol-1-yl)propan-1-ols—intracellular TBBi-based CK2 inhibitors with proapoptotic properties. *International Journal of Molecular Sciences, 22*(12), 6261. https://doi.org/10.3390/ijms22126261

Cox, M. L., & Meek, D. W. (2010). Phosphorylation of serine 392 in p53 is a common and integral event during p53 induction by diverse stimuli. *Cellular Signalling, 22*(3), 564−571. https://doi.org/10.1016/j.cellsig.2009.11.014

Cozza, G., Bonvini, P., Zorzi, E., Poletto, G., Pagano, M. A., Sarno, S., Donella-Deana, A., Zagotto, G., Rosolen, A., Pinna, L. A., Meggio, F., & Moro, S. (2006). Identification of ellagic acid as potent inhibitor of protein kinase CK2: A successful example of a virtual screening application. *Journal of Medicinal Chemistry, 49*(8), 2363−2366. https://doi.org/10.1021/jm060112m

Cozza, G., Gianoncelli, A., Bonvini, P., Zorzi, E., Pasquale, R., Rosolen, A., Pinna, L. A., Meggio, F., Zagotto, G., & Moro, S. (2011). Urolithin as a converging scaffold linking ellagic acid and coumarin analogues: Design of potent protein kinase CK2 inhibitors. *ChemMedChem, 6*(12), 2273−2286. https://doi.org/10.1002/cmdc.201100338

Cozza, G., Gianoncelli, A., Montopoli, M., Caparrotta, L., Venerando, A., Meggio, F., Pinna, L. A., Zagotto, G., & Moro, S. (2008). Identification of novel protein kinase CK1 delta (CK1δ) inhibitors through structure-based virtual screening. *Bioorganic & Medicinal Chemistry Letters, 18*(20), 5672−5675. https://doi.org/10.1016/j.bmcl.2008.08.072

Cozza, G., Girardi, C., Ranchio, A., Lolli, G., Sarno, S., Orzeszko, A., Kazimierczuk, Z., Battistutta, R., Ruzzene, M., & Pinna, L. A. (2014). Cell-permeable dual inhibitors of protein kinases CK2 and PIM-1: Structural features and pharmacological potential. *Cellular and Molecular Life Sciences, 71*(16), 3173−3185. https://doi.org/10.1007/s00018-013-1552-5

Cozza, G., Mazzorana, M., Papinutto, E., Bain, J., Elliott, M., Di Maira, G., Gianoncelli, A., Pagano, M. A., Sarno, S., Ruzzene, M., Battistutta, R., Meggio, F., Moro, S., Zagotto, G., & Pinna, L. A. (2009). Quinalizarin as a potent, selective and cell-permeable inhibitor of protein kinase CK2. *Biochemical Journal, 421*(3), 387−395. https://doi.org/10.1042/BJ20090069

Cozza, G., Sarno, S., Ruzzene, M., Girardi, C., Orzeszko, A., Kazimierczuk, Z., Zagotto, G., Bonaiuto, E., Di Paolo, M. L., & Pinna, L. A. (2013). Exploiting the repertoire of CK2 inhibitors to target DYRK and PIM kinases. *Biochimica et Biophysica Acta - Proteins and Proteomics, 1834*(7), 1402−1409. https://doi.org/10.1016/j.bbapap.2013.01.018

Cozza, G., Venerando, A., Sarno, S., & Pinna, L. A. (2015). The selectivity of CK2 inhibitor quinalizarin: A reevaluation. *BioMed Research International, 2015.* https://doi.org/10.1155/2015/734127

Cui, J., Xiao, J., Tagliabracci, V. S., Wen, J., Rahdar, M., & Dixon, J. E. (2015). A secretory kinase complex regulates extracellular protein phosphorylation. *Elife, 2015*(4). https://doi.org/10.7554/eLife.06120

Dalle Vedove, A., Zonta, F., Zanforlin, E., Demitri, N., Ribaudo, G., Cazzanelli, G., Ongaro, A., Sarno, S., Zagotto, G., Battistutta, R., Ruzzene, M., & Lolli, G. (2020). A novel class of selective CK2 inhibitors targeting its open hinge conformation. *European Journal of Medicinal Chemistry, 195,* 112267. https://doi.org/10.1016/j.ejmech.2020.112267

Dar, A. C., & Shokat, K. M. (2011). The evolution of protein kinase inhibitors from antagonists to agonists of cellular signaling. *Annual Review of Biochemistry, 80,* 769−795. https://doi.org/10.1146/annurev-biochem-090308-173656

Desagher, S., Osen-Sand, A., Montessuit, S., Magnenat, E., Vilbois, F., Hochmann, A., Journot, L., Antonsson, B., & Martinou, J. C. (2001). Phosphorylation of Bid by casein kinases I and II regulates its cleavage by caspase 8. *Molecular Cell, 8*(3), 601−611. https://doi.org/10.1016/S1097-2765(01)00335-5

Dominguez, I., Sonenshein, G. E., & Seldin, D. C. (2009). CK2 and its role in Wnt and NF-κB signaling: Linking development and cancer. *Cellular and Molecular Life Sciences, 66*(11−12), 1850−1857. https://doi.org/10.1007/s00018-009-9153-z

Dowling, J. E., Alimzhanov, M., Bao, L., Chuaqui, C., Denz, C. R., Jenkins, E., Larsen, N. A., Lyne, P. D., Pontz, T., Ye, Q., Holdgate, G. A., Snow, L., O'Connell, N., & Ferguson, A. D. (2016). Potent and selective CK2 kinase inhibitors with effects on Wnt pathway signaling in vivo. *ACS Medicinal Chemistry Letters, 7*(3), 300−305. https://doi.org/10.1021/acsmedchemlett.5b00452

Dowling, J. E., Chuaqui, C., Pontz, T. W., Lyne, P. D., Larsen, N. A., Block, M. H., Chen, H., Su, N., Wu, A., Russell, D., Pollard, H., Lee, J. W., Peng, B., Thakur, K., Ye, Q., Zhang, T., Brassil, P., Racicot, V., Bao, L., Denz, C. R., & Cooke, E. (2012). Potent and selective inhibitors of CK2 kinase identified through structure-guided hybridization. *ACS Medicinal Chemistry Letters, 3*(4), 278−283. https://doi.org/10.1021/ml200257n

Duncan, J. S., Turowec, J. P., Vilk, G., Li, S. S. C., Gloor, G. B., & Litchfield, D. W. (2010). Regulation of cell proliferation and survival: Convergence of protein kinases and caspases. *Biochimica et Biophysica Acta - Proteins and Proteomics, 1804*(3), 505−510. https://doi.org/10.1016/j.bbapap.2009.11.001

El-Awaad, E., Birus, R., Marminon, C., Bouaziz, Z., Ballentin, L., Aichele, D., Le Borgne, M., & Jose, J. (2021). Broad-spectrum anticancer activity and pharmacokinetic properties of a prenyloxy-substituted indeno[1,2-b]indole derivative, discovered as CK2 inhibitor. *Pharmaceuticals, 14*(6), 542. https://doi.org/10.3390/ph14060542

Esposito, G., Bourguet-Kondracki, M. L., Mai, L. H., Longeon, A., Teta, R., Meijer, L., Van Soest, R., Mangoni, A., & Costantino, V. (2016). Chloromethylhalicyclamine B, a marine-derived protein kinase CK1δ/inhibitor. *Journal of Natural Products, 79*(11), 2953−2960. https://doi.org/10.1021/acs.jnatprod.6b00939

Esvan, Y. J., Zeinyeh, W., Boibessot, T., Nauton, L., Théry, V., Knapp, S., Chaikuad, A., Loaëc, N., Meijer, L., Anizon, F., Giraud, F., & Moreau, P. (2016). Discovery of pyrido[3,4-g]quinazoline derivatives as CMGC family protein kinase inhibitors: Design, synthesis, inhibitory potency and X-ray co-crystal structure. *European Journal of Medicinal Chemistry, 118,* 170−177. https://doi.org/10.1016/j.ejmech.2016.04.004

Ferguson, A. D., Sheth, P. R., Basso, A. D., Paliwal, S., Gray, K., Fischmann, T. O., & Le, H. V. (2011). Structural basis of CX-4945 binding to human protein kinase CK2. *FEBS Letters, 585*(1), 104–110. https://doi.org/10.1016/j.febslet.2010.11.019

Filhol, O., Giacosa, S., Wallez, Y., & Cochet, C. (2015). Protein kinase CK2 in breast cancer: The CK2β regulatory subunit takes center stage in epithelial plasticity. *Cellular and Molecular Life Sciences, 72*(17), 3305–3322. https://doi.org/10.1007/s00018-015-1929-8

Fish, K. J., Cegielska, A., Getman, M. E., Landes, G. M., & Virshup, D. M. (1995). Isolation and characterization of human casein kinase Iε (CKI), a novel member of the CKI gene family. *Journal of Biological Chemistry, 270*(25), 14875–14883. https://doi.org/10.1074/jbc.270.25.14875

García-Reyes, B., Witt, L., Jansen, B., Karasu, E., Gehring, T., Leban, J., Henne-Bruns, D., Pichlo, C., Brunstein, E., Baumann, U., Wesseler, F., Rathmer, B., Schade, D., Peifer, C., & Knippschild, U. (2018). Discovery of inhibitor of Wnt production 2 (IWP-2) and related compounds as selective ATP-competitive inhibitors of casein kinase 1 (CK1) δ/ε. *Journal of Medicinal Chemistry, 61*(9), 4087–4102. https://doi.org/10.1021/acs.jmedchem.8b00095

Golub, A. G., Bdzhola, V. G., Kyshenia, Y. V., Sapelkin, V. M., Prykhod'ko, A. O., Kukharenko, O. P., Ostrynska, O. V., & Yarmoluk, S. M. (2011). Structure-based discovery of novel flavonol inhibitors of human protein kinase CK2. *Molecular and Cellular Biochemistry, 356*(1–2), 107–115. https://doi.org/10.1007/s11010-011-0945-8

Golub, A. G., Bdzhola, V. G., Ostrynska, O. V., Kyshenia, I. V., Sapelkin, V. M., Prykhod'Ko, A. O., Kukharenko, O. P., & Yarmoluk, S. M. (2013). Discovery and characterization of synthetic 4'-hydroxyflavones - new CK2 inhibitors from flavone family. *Bioorganic & Medicinal Chemistry, 21*(21), 6681–6689. https://doi.org/10.1016/j.bmc.2013.08.013

Gompel, M., Leost, M., De Kier Joffe, E. B., Puricelli, L., Franco, L. H., Palermo, J., & Meijer, L. (2004). Meridianins, a new family of protein kinase inhibitors isolated from the Ascidian Aplidium meridianum. *Bioorganic & Medicinal Chemistry Letters, 14*(7), 1703–1707. https://doi.org/10.1016/j.bmcl.2004.01.050

Grieco, I., Bissaro, M., Tiz, D. B., Perez, D. I., Perez, C., Martinez, A., Redenti, S., Mariotto, E., Bortolozzi, R., Viola, G., Cozza, G., Spalluto, G., Moro, S., & Federico, S. (2021). Developing novel classes of protein kinase CK1δ inhibitors by fusing [1,2,4]triazole with different bicyclic heteroaromatic systems. *European Journal of Medicinal Chemistry, 216*. https://doi.org/10.1016/j.ejmech.2021.113331

Gross, S. D., & Anderson, R. A. (1998). Casein kinase I: Spatial organization and positioning of a multifunctional protein kinase family. *Cellular Signalling, 10*(10), 699–711. https://doi.org/10.1016/S0898-6568(98)00042-4

Guerra, B., Siemer, S., Boldyreff, B., & Issinger, O. G. (1999). Protein kinase CK2: Evidence for a protein kinase CK2β subunit fraction, devoid of the catalytic CK2α subunit, in mouse brain and testicles. *FEBS Letters, 462*(3), 353–357. https://doi.org/10.1016/S0014-5793(99)01553-7

Halekotte, J., Witt, l., & Ianes, C. (2017). 5-diarylimidazoles as potent/selective inhibitors of protein kinase CK1 delta and their structural relation to p38 alpha MAPK. *Molecules, 4*.

Hochscherf, J., Lindenblatt, D., Witulski, B., Birus, R., Aichele, D., Marminon, C., Bouaziz, Z., Le Borgne, M., Jose, J., & Niefind, K. (2017). Unexpected binding mode of a potent indeno[1,2-b]indole-type inhibitor of protein kinase CK2 revealed by complex structures with the catalytic subunit CK2α and its paralog CK2α'. *Pharmaceuticals, 10*(4). https://doi.org/10.3390/ph10040098

Hu, Y., Song, W., Cirstea, D., Lu, D., Munshi, N. C., & Anderson, K. C. (2015). CSNK1α1 mediates malignant plasma cell survival. *Leukemia, 29*(2), 474–482. https://doi.org/10.1038/leu.2014.202

Hua, Z., Huang, X., Bregman, H., Chakka, N., Dimauro, E. F., Doherty, E. M., Goldstein, J., Gunaydin, H., Huang, H., Mercede, S., Newcomb, J., Patel, V. F., Turci, S. M., Yan, J., Wilson, C., & Martin, M. W. (2012). 2-Phenylamino-6-cyano-1H-benzimidazole-based isoform selective casein kinase 1 gamma (CK1γ) inhibitors. *Bioorganic & Medicinal Chemistry Letters, 22*(17), 5392–5395. https://doi.org/10.1016/j.bmcl.2012.07.046

Hundsdörfer, C., Hemmerling, H. J., Götz, C., Totzke, F., Bednarski, P., Le Borgne, M., & Jose, J. (2012). Indeno[1,2-b]indole derivatives as a novel class of potent human protein kinase CK2 inhibitors. *Bioorganic & Medicinal Chemistry, 20*(7), 2282–2289. https://doi.org/10.1016/j.bmc.2012.02.017

Hundsdörfer, C., Hemmerling, H. J., Hamberger, J., Le Borgne, M., Bednarski, P., Götz, C., Totzke, F., & Jose, J. (2012). Novel indeno[1,2-b]indoloquinones as inhibitors of the human protein kinase CK2 with antiproliferative activity towards a broad panel of cancer cell lines. *Biochemical and Biophysical Research Communications, 424*(1), 71–75. https://doi.org/10.1016/j.bbrc.2012.06.068

Hung, M. S., Xu, Z., Chen, Y., Smith, E., Mao, J. H., Hsieh, D., Lin, Y. C., Yang, C. T., Jablons, D. M., & You, L. (2013). Hematein, a casein kinase II inhibitor, inhibits lung cancer tumor growth in a murine xenograft model. *International Journal of Oncology, 43*(5), 1517−1522. https://doi.org/10.3892/ijo.2013.2087

Hung, M. S., Xu, Z., Lin, Y. C., Mao, J. H., Yang, C. T., Chang, P. J., Jablons, D. M., & You, L. (2009). Identification of hematein as a novel inhibitor of protein kinase CK2 from a natural product library. *BMC Cancer, 9.* https://doi.org/10.1186/1471-2407-9-135

Iegre, J., Brear, P., De Fusco, C., Yoshida, M., Mitchell, S. L., Rossmann, M., Carro, L., Sore, H. F., Hyvönen, M., & Spring, D. R. (2018). Second-generation CK2α inhibitors targeting the αd pocket. *Chemical Science, 9*(11), 3041−3049. https://doi.org/10.1039/c7sc05122k

Ishikawa, H. O., Xu, A., Ogura, E., Manning, G., & Irvine, K. D. (2012). The raine syndrome protein FAM20C is a golgi kinase that phosphorylates bio-mineralization proteins. *PLoS One, 7*(8). https://doi.org/10.1371/journal.pone.0042988

Jabor Gozzi, G., Bouaziz, Z., Winter, E., Daflon-Yunes, N., Aichele, D., Nacereddine, A., Marminon, C., Valdameri, G., Zeinyeh, W., Bollacke, A., Guillon, J., Lacoudre, A., Pinaud, N., Cadena, S. M., Jose, J., Le Borgne, M., & Di Pietro, A. (2015). Converting potent indeno[1,2- b]indole inhibitors of protein kinase CK2 into selective inhibitors of the breast cancer resistance protein ABCG2. *Journal of Medicinal Chemistry, 58*(1), 265−277. https://doi.org/10.1021/jm500943z

Jiang, H. M., Dong, J. K., Song, K., Wang, T. D., Huang, W. K., Zhang, J. M., Yang, X. Y., Shen, Y., & Zhang, J. (2017). A novel allosteric site in casein kinase 2α discovered using combining bioinformatics and biochemistry methods. *Acta Pharmacologica Sinica, 38*(12), 1691−1698. https://doi.org/10.1038/aps.2017.55

Järås, M., Miller, P. G., Chu, L. P., Puram, R. V., Fink, E. C., Schneider, R. K., Al-Shahrour, F., Peña, P., Breyfogle, L. J., Hartwell, K. A., McConkey, M. E., Cowley, G. S., Root, D. E., Kharas, M. G., Mullally, A., & Ebert, B. L. (2014). Csnk1a1 inhibition has p53-dependent therapeutic efficacy in acute myeloid leukemia. *Journal of Experimental Medicine, 211*(4), 605−612. https://doi.org/10.1084/jem.20131033

Kim, H., Choi, K., Kang, H., Lee, S. Y., Chi, S. W., Lee, M. S., Song, J., Im, D., Choi, Y., & Cho, S. (2014). Identification of a novel function of CX-4945 as a splicing regulator. *PLoS One, 9*(4). https://doi.org/10.1371/journal.pone.0094978

Klaus, A., & Birchmeier, W. (2008). Wnt signalling and its impact on development and cancer. *Nature Reviews Cancer, 8*(5), 387−398. https://doi.org/10.1038/nrc2389

Knippschild, U., Gocht, A., Wolff, S., Huber, N., Löhler, J., & Stöter, M. (2005). The casein kinase 1 family: Participation in multiple cellular processes in eukaryotes. *Cellular Signalling, 17*(6), 675−689. https://doi.org/10.1016/j.cellsig.2004.12.011

Knippschild, U., Wolff, S., Giamas, G., Brockschmidt, C., Wittau, M., Würl, P. U., Eismann, T., & Stöter, M. (2005). The role of the casein kinase 1 (CK1) family in different signaling pathways linked to cancer development. *Onkologie, 28*(10), 508−514. https://doi.org/10.1159/000087137

Kobe, B., Kampmann, T., Forwood, J. K., Listwan, P., & Brinkworth, R. I. (2005). Substrate specificity of protein kinases and computational prediction of substrates. *Biochimica et Biophysica Acta - Proteins and Proteomics, 1754*(1−2), 200−209. https://doi.org/10.1016/j.bbapap.2005.07.036

Kröger, L., Daniliuc, C. G., Ensan, D., Borgert, S., Nienberg, C., Lauwers, M., Steinkrüger, M., Jose, J., Pietsch, M., & Wünsch, B. (2020). Synthesis and SAR of tetracyclic inhibitors of protein kinase CK2 derived from furocarbazole W16. *ChemMedChem, 15*(10), 871−881. https://doi.org/10.1002/cmdc.202000040

Kufareva, I., Bestgen, B., Brear, P., Prudent, R., Laudet, B., Moucadel, V., Ettaoussi, M., Sautel, C. F., Krimm, I., Engel, M., Filhol, O., Borgne, M. L., Lomberget, T., Cochet, C., & Abagyan, R. (2019). Discovery of holoenzyme-disrupting chemicals as substrate-selective CK2 inhibitors. *Scientific Reports, 9*(1). https://doi.org/10.1038/s41598-019-52141-5

Kurihara, T., Sakurai, E., Toyomoto, M., Kii, I., Kawamoto, D., Asada, T., Tanabe, T., Yoshimura, M., Hagiwara, M., & Miyata, A. (2014). Alleviation of behavioral hypersensitivity in mouse models of inflammatory pain with two structurally different casein kinase 1 (CK1) inhibitors. *Molecular Pain, 10*(1). https://doi.org/10.1186/1744-8069-10-17

Lasa, M., Marin, O., & Pinna, L. A. (1997). Rat liver Golgi apparatus contains a protein kinase similar to the casein kinase of lactating mammary gland. *European Journal of Biochemistry, 243*(3), 719−725. https://doi.org/10.1111/j.1432-1033.1997.00719.x

Laudet, B., Moucadel, V., Prudent, R., Filhol, O., Wong, Y. S., Royer, D., & Cochet, C. (2008). Identification of chemical inhibitors of protein-kinase CK2 subunit interaction. *Molecular and Cellular Biochemistry, 316*(1−2), 63−69. https://doi.org/10.1007/s11010-008-9821-6

Legraverend, M., & Grierson, D. S. (2006). The purines: Potent and versatile small molecule inhibitors and modulators of key biological targets. *Bioorganic & Medicinal Chemistry, 14*(12), 3987−4006. https://doi.org/10.1016/j.bmc.2005.12.060

Li, C., Zhang, X., Zhang, N., Zhou, Y., Sun, G., Zhao, L., & Zhong, R. (2020). Identification and biological evaluation of CK2 allosteric fragments through structure-based virtual screening. *Molecules, 25*(1), 237. https://doi.org/10.3390/molecules25010237

Lindenblatt, D., Nickelsen, A., Applegate, V. M., Jose, J., & Niefind, K. (2020). Structural and mechanistic basis of the inhibitory potency of selected 2-aminothiazole compounds on protein kinase CK2. *Journal of Medicinal Chemistry, 63*(14), 7766−7772. https://doi.org/10.1021/acs.jmedchem.0c00587

Liu, Z.-L., Zhang, R.-M., Meng, Q.-G., Zhang, X.-C., & Sun, Y. (2016). Discovery of new protein kinase CK2 inhibitors with 1,3-dioxo-2,3-dihydro-1H-indene core. *MedChemComm, 7*(7), 1352−1355. https://doi.org/10.1039/C6MD00189K

Loidreau, Y., Deau, E., Marchand, P., Nourrisson, M. R., Logé, C., Coadou, G., Loaëc, N., Meijer, L., & Besson, T. (2015). Synthesis and molecular modelling studies of 8-arylpyrido[30,20:4,5] thieno[3,2-d]pyrimidin-4-amines as multitarget Ser/Thr kinases inhibitors. *European Journal of Medicinal Chemistry, 92*, 124−134. https://doi.org/10.1016/j.ejmech.2014.12.038

Lolli, G., Cozza, G., Mazzorana, M., Tibaldi, E., Cesaro, L., Donella-Deana, A., Meggio, F., Venerando, A., Franchin, C., Sarno, S., Battistutta, R., & Pinna, L. A. (2012). Inhibition of protein kinase CK2 by flavonoids and tyrphostins. a structural insight. *Biochemistry, 51*(31), 6097−6107. https://doi.org/10.1021/bi300531c

Longenecker, K. L., Roach, P. J., & Hurley, T. D. (1996). Three-dimensional structure of mammalian casein kinase I: Molecular basis for phosphate recognition. *Journal of Molecular Biology, 257*(3), 618−631. https://doi.org/10.1006/jmbi.1996.0189

Lozeman, F. J., Litchfield, D. W., Piening, C., Krebs, E. G., Takio, K., Walsh, K. A., Krebs, E. G., Lozeman, F. J., Litchfield, D. W., Krebs, E. G., Lozeman, F. J., & Litchfield, D. W. (1990). Isolation and characterization of human cDNA clones encoding the α and the α′ subunits of casein kinase II. *Biochemistry, 29*(36), 8436−8447. https://doi.org/10.1021/bi00488a034

Luxenburger, A., Schmidt, D., Ianes, C., Pichlo, C., Krüger, M., von Drathen, T., Brunstein, E., Gainsford, G., Baumann, U., Knippschild, U., & Peifer, C. (2019). Design, synthesis and biological evaluation of isoxazole-based CK1 inhibitors modified with chiral pyrrolidine scaffolds. *Molecules, 24*(5), 873. https://doi.org/10.3390/molecules24050873

Maritzen, T., Löhler, J., Deppert, W., & Knippschild, U. (2003). Casein kinase I delta (CKIδ) is involved in lymphocyte physiology. *European Journal of Cell Biology, 82*(7), 369−378. https://doi.org/10.1078/0171-9335-00323

Mashhoon, N., DeMaggio, A. J., Tereshko, V., Bergmeier, S. C., Egli, M., Hoekstra, M. F., & Kuret, J. (2000). Crystal structure of a conformation-selective casein kinase-1 inhibitor. *Journal of Biological Chemistry, 275*(26), 20052−20060. https://doi.org/10.1074/jbc.M001713200

Masuda, K., Ono, M., Okamoto, M., Morikawa, W., Otsubo, M., Migita, T., Tsuneyosh, M., Okuda, H., Shuin, T., Naito, S., & Kuwano, M. (2003). Downregulation of Cap43 gene by von Hippel-Lindau tumor suppressor protein in human renal cancer cells. *International Journal of Cancer, 105*(6), 803−810. https://doi.org/10.1002/ijc.11152

Meggio, F., Pagano, M. A., Moro, S., Zagotto, G., Ruzzene, M., Sarno, S., Cozza, G., Bain, J., Elliott, M., Deana, A. D., Brunati, A. M., & Pinna, L. A. (2004). Inhibition of protein kinase CK2 by condensed polyphenolic derivatives. An in vitro and in vivo study. *Biochemistry, 43*(40), 12931−12936. https://doi.org/10.1021/bi048999g

Mente, S., Arnold, E., Butler, T., Chakrapani, S., Chandrasekaran, R., Cherry, K., Dirico, K., Doran, A., Fisher, K., Galatsis, P., Green, M., Hayward, M., Humphrey, J., Knafels, J., Li, J., Liu, S., Marconi, M., McDonald, S., Ohren, J., … Wager, T. (2013). Ligand-protein interactions of selective casein kinase 1δ inhibitors. *Journal of Medicinal Chemistry, 56*(17), 6819−6828. https://doi.org/10.1021/jm4006324

Monastyrskyi, A., Nilchan, N., Quereda, V., Noguchi, Y., Ruiz, C., Grant, W., Cameron, M., Duckett, D., & Roush, W. (2018). Development of dual casein kinase 1δ/1ε (CK1δ/ε) inhibitors for treatment of breast cancer. *Bioorganic & Medicinal Chemistry, 26*(3), 590−602. https://doi.org/10.1016/j.bmc.2017.12.020

Moucadel, V., Prudent, R., Sautel, C. F., Teillet, F., Barette, C., Lafanechere, L., Receveur-Brechot, V., & Cochet, C. (2011). Antitumoral activity of allosteric inhibitors of protein kinase CK2. *Oncotarget, 2*(12), 997–1010. https://doi.org/10.18632/oncotarget.361

Nie, Z., Perretta, C., Erickson, P., Margosiak, S., Almassy, R., Lu, J., Averill, A., Yager, K. M., & Chu, S. (2007). Structure-based design, synthesis, and study of pyrazolo[1,5-a][1,3,5]triazine derivatives as potent inhibitors of protein kinase CK2. *Bioorganic & Medicinal Chemistry Letters, 17*(15), 4191–4195. https://doi.org/10.1016/j.bmcl.2007.05.041

Nie, Z., Perretta, C., Erickson, P., Margosiak, S., Lu, J., Averill, A., Almassy, R., & Chu, S. (2008). Structure-based design and synthesis of novel macrocyclic pyrazolo[1,5-a] [1,3,5]triazine compounds as potent inhibitors of protein kinase CK2 and their anticancer activities. *Bioorganic & Medicinal Chemistry Letters, 18*(2), 619–623. https://doi.org/10.1016/j.bmcl.2007.11.074

Oumata, N., Bettayeb, K., Ferandin, Y., Demange, L., Lopez-Giral, A., Goddard, M. L., Myrianthopoulos, V., Mikros, E., Flajolet, M., Greengard, P., Meijer, L., & Galons, H. (2008). Roscovitine-derived, dual-specificity inhibitors of cyclin-dependent kinases and casein kinases 1. *Journal of Medicinal Chemistry, 51*(17), 5229–5242. https://doi.org/10.1021/jm800109e

Pagano, M. A., Andrzejewska, M., Ruzzene, M., Sarno, S., Cesaro, L., Bain, J., Elliott, M., Meggio, F., Kazimierczuk, Z., & Pinna, L. A. (2004). Optimization of protein kinase CK2 inhibitors derived from 4,5,6,7-tetrabromobenzimidazole. *Journal of Medicinal Chemistry, 47*(25), 6239–6247. https://doi.org/10.1021/jm049854a

Pagano, M. A., Bain, J., Kazimierczuk, Z., Sarno, S., Ruzzene, M., Di Maira, G., Elliott, M., Orzeszko, A., Cozza, G., Meggio, F., & Pinna, L. A. (2008). The selectivity of inhibitors of protein kinase CK2: An update. *Biochemical Journal, 415*(3), 353–365. https://doi.org/10.1042/BJ20080309

Pagano, M. A., Meggio, F., Ruzzene, M., Andrzejewska, M., Kazimierczuk, Z., & Pinna, L. A. (2004). 2-Dimethylamino-4,5,6,7-tetrabromo-1H-benzimidazole: A novel powerful and selective inhibitor of protein kinase CK2. *Biochemical and Biophysical Research Communications, 321*(4), 1040–1044. https://doi.org/10.1016/j.bbrc.2004.07.067

Pagano, M. A., Poletto, G., Di Maira, G., Cozza, G., Ruzzene, M., Sarno, S., Bain, J., Elliott, M., Moro, S., Zagotto, G., Meggio, F., & Pinna, L. A. (2007). Tetrabromocinnamic acid (TBCA) and related compounds represent a new class of specific protein kinase CK2 inhibitors. *ChemBioChem, 8*(1), 129–139. https://doi.org/10.1002/cbic.200600293

Pan, D. (2010). The hippo signaling pathway in development and cancer. *Developmental Cell, 19*(4), 491–505. https://doi.org/10.1016/j.devcel.2010.09.011

Peifer, C., Abadleh, M., Bischof, J., Hauser, D., Schattel, V., Hirner, H., Knippschild, U., & Laufer, S. (2009). 3,4-Diaryl-isoxazoles and -imidazoles as potent dual inhibitors of p38α mitogen activated protein kinase and casein kinase 1δ. *Journal of Medicinal Chemistry, 52*(23), 7618–7630. https://doi.org/10.1021/jm9005127

Peters, J. M., McKay, R. M., McKay, J. P., & Graff, J. M. (1999). Casein kinase I transduces Wnt signals. *Nature, 401*(6751), 345–350. https://doi.org/10.1038/43830

Pierre, F., Chua, P. C., Obrien, S. E., Siddiqui-Jain, A., Bourbon, P., Haddach, M., Michaux, J., Nagasawa, J., Schwaebe, M. K., Stefan, E., Vialettes, A., Whitten, J. P., Chen, T. K., Darjania, L., Stansfield, R., Anderes, K., Bliesath, J., Drygin, D., Ho, C., … Ryckman, D. M. (2011). Discovery and SAR of 5-(3-Chlorophenylamino) benzo[c][2,6]naphthyridine-8- carboxylic Acid (CX-4945), the first clinical stage inhibitor of protein kinase CK2 for the treatment of cancer. *Journal of Medicinal Chemistry, 54*(2), 635–654. https://doi.org/10.1021/jm101251q

Pierre, F., Regan, C. F., Chevrel, M. C., Siddiqui-Jain, A., MacAlino, D., Streiner, N., Drygin, D., Haddach, M., O'Brien, S. E., Rice, W. G., & Ryckman, D. M. (2012). Novel potent dual inhibitors of CK2 and Pim kinases with antiproliferative activity against cancer cells. *Bioorganic & Medicinal Chemistry Letters, 22*(9), 3327–3331. https://doi.org/10.1016/j.bmcl.2012.02.099

Protopopov, M. V., Vdovin, V. S., Starosyla, S. A., Borysenko, I. P., Prykhod'ko, A. O., Lukashov, S. S., Bilokin, Y. V., Bdzhola, V. G., & Yarmoluk, S. M. (2020). Flavone inspired discovery of benzylidenebenzofuran-3(2H)-ones (aurones) as potent inhibitors of human protein kinase CK2. *Bioorganic Chemistry, 102*, 104062. https://doi.org/10.1016/j.bioorg.2020.104062

Qi, X., Zhang, N., Zhao, L., Hu, L., Cortopassi, W. A., Jacobson, M. P., Li, X., & Zhong, R. (2019). Structure-based identification of novel CK2 inhibitors with a linear 2-propenone scaffold as anti-cancer agents. *Biochemical and Biophysical Research Communications, 512*(2), 208–212. https://doi.org/10.1016/j.bbrc.2019.03.016

Qin, Z., Wang, P., Li, X., Zhang, S., Tian, M., Dai, Y., & Fu, L. (2016). Systematic network-based discovery of a Fam20C inhibitor (FL-1607) with apoptosis modulation in triple-negative breast cancer. *Molecular BioSystems, 12*(7), 2108–2118. https://doi.org/10.1039/c6mb00111d

Raaf, J., Brunstein, E., Issinger, O. G., & Niefind, K. (2008). The CK2α/CK2β interface of human protein kinase CK2 harbors a binding pocket for small molecules. *Chemistry & Biology, 15*(2), 111–117. https://doi.org/10.1016/j.chembiol.2007.12.012

Rena, G., Bain, J., Elliott, M., & Cohen, P. (2004). D4476, a cell-permeant inhibitor of CK1, suppresses the site-specific phosphorylation and nuclear exclusion of FOXO1a. *EMBO Reports, 5*(1), 60–65. https://doi.org/10.1038/sj.embor.7400048

Richter, J., Bischof, J., Zaja, M., Kohlhof, H., Othersen, O., Vitt, D., Alscher, V., Pospiech, I., García-Reyes, B., Berg, S., Leban, J., & Knippschild, U. (2014). Difluoro-dioxolo-benzoimidazol-benzamides as potent inhibitors of CK1δ and ε with nanomolar inhibitory activity on cancer cell proliferation. *Journal of Medicinal Chemistry, 57*(19), 7933–7946. https://doi.org/10.1021/jm500600b

Rodrigues, R. P., & Silva, C. H. T. P. (2017). Discovery of potential neurodegenerative inhibitors in Alzheimer's disease by casein kinase 1 structure-based virtual screening. *Medicinal Chemistry Research, 26*(12), 3274–3285. https://doi.org/10.1007/s00044-017-2020-9

Rodriguez, N., Yang, J., Hasselblatt, K., Liu, S., Zhou, Y., Rauh-Hain, J. A., Ng, S.-K., Choi, P.-W., Fong, W.-P., Agar, N. Y. R., Welch, W. R., Berkowitz, R. S., & Ng, S.-W. (2012). Casein kinase I epsilon interacts with mitochondrial proteins for the growth and survival of human ovarian cancer cells. *EMBO Molecular Medicine, 4*(9), 952–963. https://doi.org/10.1002/emmm.201101094

Rubin, L. L., & de Sauvage, F. J. (2006). Targeting the hedgehog pathway in cancer. *Nature Reviews Drug Discovery, 5*(12), 1026–1033. https://doi.org/10.1038/nrd2086

Ruzzene, M., Bertacchini, J., Toker, A., & Marmiroli, S. (2017). Cross-talk between the CK2 and AKT signaling pathways in cancer. *Advances in Biological Regulation, 64*, 1–8. https://doi.org/10.1016/j.jbior.2017.03.002

Salado, I. G., Redondo, M., Bello, M. L., Perez, C., Liachko, N. F., Kraemer, B. C., Miguel, L., Lecourtois, M., Gil, C., Martinez, A., & Perez, D. I. (2014). Protein kinase CK-1 inhibitors as new potential drugs for amyotrophic lateral sclerosis. *Journal of Medicinal Chemistry, 57*(6), 2755–2772. https://doi.org/10.1021/jm500065f

Salvi, M., Sarno, S., Cesaro, L., Nakamura, H., & Pinna, L. A. (2009). Extraordinary pleiotropy of protein kinase CK2 revealed by weblogo phosphoproteome analysis. *Biochimica et Biophysica Acta - Molecular Cell Research, 1793*(5), 847–859. https://doi.org/10.1016/j.bbamcr.2009.01.013

Sass, G., Klinger, N., Sirma, H., Hashemolhosseini, S., Hellerbrand, C., Neureiter, D., Wege, H., Ocker, M., & Tiegs, G. (2011). Inhibition of experimental HCC growth in mice by use of the kinase inhibitor DMAT. *International Journal of Oncology, 39*(2), 433–442. https://doi.org/10.3892/ijo.2011.1037

Sciabola, S., Benedetti, P., D'Arrigo, G., Torella, R., Baroni, M., Cruciani, G., & Spyrakis, F. (2019). Discovering new casein kinase 1d inhibitors with an innovative molecular dynamics enabled virtual screening workflow. *ACS Medicinal Chemistry Letters, 10*(4), 487–492. https://doi.org/10.1021/acsmedchemlett.8b00523

Seok, W. S., & Stockwell, B. R. (2008). Inhibition of casein kinase 1-epsilon induces cancer-cell-selective, PERIOD2-dependent growth arrest. *Genome Biology, 9*(6). https://doi.org/10.1186/gb-2008-9-6-r92

Shin, S., Wolgamott, L., Roux, P. P., & Yoon, S. O. (2014). Casein kinase 1ε promotes cell proliferation by regulating mRNA translation. *Cancer Research, 74*(1), 201–211. https://doi.org/10.1158/0008-5472.CAN-13-1175

Siddiqui-Jain, A., Drygin, D., Streiner, N., Chua, P., Pierre, F., O'Brien, S. E., Bliesath, J., Omori, M., Huser, N., Ho, C., Proffitt, C., Schwaebe, M. K., Ryckman, D. M., Rice, W. G., & Anderes, K. (2010). CX-4945, an orally bioavailable selective inhibitor of protein kinase CK2, inhibits prosurvival and angiogenic signaling and exhibits antitumor efficacy. *Cancer Research, 70*(24), 10288–10298. https://doi.org/10.1158/0008-5472.can-10-1893

Szyszka, R., Grankowski, N., Felczak, K., & Shugar, D. (1995). Halogenated benzimidazoles and benzotriazoles as selective inhibitors of protein kinases CK-I and CK-II from Saccharomyces cerevisiae and other sources. *Biochemical and Biophysical Research Communications, 208*(1), 418–424. https://doi.org/10.1006/bbrc.1995.1354

Tagliabracci, V. S., Engel, J. L., Wen, J., Wiley, S. E., Worby, C. A., Kinch, L. N., Xiao, J., Grishin, N. V., & Dixon, J. E. (2012). Secreted kinase phosphorylates extracellular proteins that regulate biomineralization. *Science, 336*(6085), 1150–1153. https://doi.org/10.1126/science.1217817

Tagliabracci, V. S., Engel, J. L., Wiley, S. E., Xiao, J., Gonzalez, D. J., Appaiah, H. N., Koller, A., Nizet, V., White, K. E., & Dixon, J. E. (2014). Dynamic regulation of FGF23 by Fam20C phosphorylation, GalNAc-T3 glycosylation, and furin proteolysis. *Proceedings of the National Academy of Sciences of the United States of America, 111*(15), 5520–5525. https://doi.org/10.1073/pnas.1402218111

Tagliabracci, V. S., Wiley, S. E., Guo, X., Kinch, L. N., Durrant, E., Wen, J., Xiao, J., Cui, J., Nguyen, K. B., Engel, J. L., Coon, J. J., Grishin, N., Pinna, L. A., Pagliarini, D. J., & Dixon, J. E. (2015). A single kinase generates the majority of the secreted phosphoproteome. *Cell, 161*(7), 1619–1632. https://doi.org/10.1016/j.cell.2015.05.028

Trembley, J. H., Unger, G. M., Gomez, O. C., Abedin, M. J., Korman, V. L., Vogel, R. I., Niehans, G., Kren, B. T., & Ahmed, K. (2014). Tenfibgen-DMAT nanocapsule delivers CK2 inhibitor DMAT to prostate cancer xenograft tumors causing inhibition of cell proliferation. *Molecular and Cellular Pharmacology, 6*(2), 15–25. https://doi.org/10.4255/mcpharmacol.14.02

Wager, T. T., Galatsis, P., Chandrasekaran, R. Y., Butler, T. W., Li, J., Zhang, L., Mente, S., Subramanyam, C., Liu, S., Doran, A. C., Chang, C., Fisher, K., Grimwood, S., Hedde, J. R., Marconi, M., & Schildknegt, K. (2017). Identification and profiling of a selective and brain penetrant radioligand for in vivo target occupancy measurement of casein kinase 1 (CK1) inhibitors. *ACS Chemical Neuroscience, 8*(9), 1995–2004. https://doi.org/10.1021/acschemneuro.7b00155

Walton, K. M., Fisher, K., Rubitski, D., Marconi, M., Meng, Q. J., Sládek, M., Adams, J., Bass, M., Chandrasekaran, R., Butler, T., Griffor, M., Rajamohan, F., Serpa, M., Chen, Y., Claffey, M., Hastings, M., Loudon, A., Maywood, E., Ohren, J., Doran, A., & Wager, T. T. (2009). Selective inhibition of casein kinase 1ε minimally alters circadian clock period. *Journal of Pharmacology and Experimental Therapeutics, 330*(2), 430–439. https://doi.org/10.1124/jpet.109.151415

Wang, Y., Lv, Z., Chen, F., Wang, X., & Gou, S. (2021). Discovery of 5-(3-Chlorophenylamino)benzo[c][2,6]naphthyridine derivatives as highly selective CK2 inhibitors with potent cancer cell stemness inhibition. *Journal of Medicinal Chemistry, 64*(8), 5082–5098. https://doi.org/10.1021/acs.jmedchem.1c00131

Xiao, J., Tagliabracci, V. S., Wen, J., Kim, S. A., & Dixon, J. E. (2013). Crystal structure of the golgi casein kinase. *Proceedings of the National Academy of Sciences of the United States of America, 110*(26), 10574–10579. https://doi.org/10.1073/pnas.1309211110

Xu, R. M., Carmel, G., Kuret, J., & Cheng, X. (1996). Structural basis for selectivity of the isoquinoline sulfonamide family of protein kinase inhibitors. *Proceedings of the National Academy of Sciences of the United States of America, 93*(13), 6308–6313. https://doi.org/10.1073/pnas.93.13.6308

Xu, R. M., Carmel, G., Sweet, R. M., Kuret, J., & Cheng, X. (1995). Crystal structure of casein kinase-1, a phosphate-directed protein kinase. *EMBO Journal, 14*(5), 1015–1023. https://doi.org/10.1002/j.1460-2075.1995.tb07082.x

Yang, L. L., Li, G. B., Yan, H. X., Sun, Q. Z., Ma, S., Ji, P., Wang, Z. R., Feng, S., Zou, J., & Yang, S. Y. (2012). Discovery of N6-phenyl-1H-pyrazolo[3,4-d]pyrimidine-3,6-diamine derivatives as novel CK1 inhibitors using common-feature pharmacophore model based virtual screening and hit-to-lead optimization. *European Journal of Medicinal Chemistry, 56*, 30–38. https://doi.org/10.1016/j.ejmech.2012.08.007

Zandomeni, R., Zandomeni, M. C., Shugar, D., & Weinmann, R. (1986). Casein kinase type II is involved in the inhibition by 5,6-dichloro-1-beta-D-ribofuranosylbenzimidazole of specific RNA polymerase II transcription. *Journal of Biological Chemistry, 261*(7), 3414–3419. https://doi.org/10.1016/s0021-9258(17)35799-x

Zhang, H., Zhu, Q., Cui, J., Wang, Y., Chen, M. J., Guo, X., Tagliabracci, V. S., Dixon, J. E., & Xiao, J. (2018). Structure and evolution of the Fam20 kinases. *Nature Communications, 9*(1). https://doi.org/10.1038/s41467-018-03615-z

Zhang, J., Tang, P., Zou, L., Zhang, J., Chen, J., Yang, C., He, G., Liu, B., Liu, J., Chiang, C. M., Wang, G., Ye, T., & Ouyang, L. (2021). Discovery of novel dual-target inhibitor of bromodomain-containing protein 4/casein kinase 2 inducing apoptosis and autophagy-associated cell death for triple-negative breast cancer therapy. *Journal of Medicinal Chemistry, 64*(24), 18025–18053. https://doi.org/10.1021/acs.jmedchem.1c01382

Zhao, R., Fu, L., Yuan, Z., Liu, Y., Zhang, K., Chen, Y., Wang, L., Sun, D., Chen, L., Liu, B., & Zhang, L. (2021). Discovery of a novel small-molecule inhibitor of Fam20C that induces apoptosis and inhibits migration in triple negative breast cancer. *European Journal of Medicinal Chemistry, 210*, 113088. https://doi.org/10.1016/j.ejmech.2020.113088

Zheng, Y., Qin, H., Frank, S. J., Deng, L., Litchfield, D. W., Tefferi, A., Pardanani, A., Lin, F. T., Li, J., Sha, B., & Benveniste, E. N. (2011). ACK2-dependent mechanism for activation of the JAK-STAT signaling pathway. *Blood, 118*(1), 156–166. https://doi.org/10.1182/blood-2010-01-266320

Recent updates on c-Src kinase and Src-Abl nonreceptor tyrosine kinases inhibitors

Navneesh[1], Shivanshu Pandey[1], Ruchi Shakya[2], Sumit Pasricha[1], Balak Das Kurmi[3] and Preeti Patel[2]

[1]Department of Pharmaceutical Analysis, ISF College of Pharmacy, Moga, Punjab, India;
[2]Department of Pharmaceutical Chemistry, ISF College of Pharmacy, Moga, Punjab, India;
[3]Department of Pharmaceutics, ISF College of Pharmacy, Moga, Punjab, India

1. Introduction

c-Src kinase and Src-Abl are two nonreceptor tyrosine kinases belonging to the Src family. They possess a conserved domain structure and play a crucial role in signal transduction (Kruewel et al., 2010). Tyrosine kinases, as enzymes, facilitate the transfer of phosphate groups from ATP to tyrosine residues on target proteins, thereby regulating their activity and interactions (Decourtye-Espiard & Guilford, 2023). Both c-Src kinase and Src-Abl share a similar domain structure comprising an N-terminal myristoylation site, an SH3 domain, an SH2 domain, and a tyrosine kinase domain. The myristoylation site allows covalent attachment of a fatty acid chain, anchoring the proteins to the plasma membrane, where they engage in interactions with various signaling molecules. The SH3 and SH2 domains, which are modular domains, facilitate protein—protein interactions by recognizing proline-rich motifs and phosphorylated tyrosines, respectively. The tyrosine kinase domain serves as the catalytic domain housing the ATP-binding site and the substrate-binding site (Brandvold et al., 2012; Mingione et al., 2023). While c-Src kinase and Src-Abl exhibit similarities in their domain structure, they differ in terms of regulation and function. c-Src kinase normally remains inactive due to an intramolecular interaction between the SH2 domain and a phosphorylated tyrosine at the C-terminus. This interaction can be disrupted by dephosphorylation or by ligand binding to the SH2 or SH3 domains, consequently leading to the activation of c-Src kinase. On the other hand, Src-Abl is a fusion protein of c-Src kinase and c-Abl, another nonreceptor tyrosine kinase associated with leukemia. Src-Abl emerges from a chromosomal translocation that fuses the BCR gene with the ABL1 gene. It remains constitutively active due to the loss of the C-terminal regulatory region and the presence of the BCR coiled-coil domain, which induces dimerization and transphosphorylation. Notably, Src-Abl exhibits resistance to several inhibitors targeting c-Src kinase or c-Abl, such as imatinib (Leak et al., 2023; Shaul, 2000).

1.1 Structural features of c-Src kinase and Src-Abl

c-Src kinase and Src-Abl share significant structural features that are essential for their respective functions and regulation. These structural elements provide valuable insights into their molecular properties and interactions within cellular signaling pathways. Here are the key structural characteristics of c-Src kinase and Src-Abl.

1.1.1 Conserved domain structure

The conserved domain structure is a significant characteristic shared by c-Src kinase and Src-Abl, which contributes to their functional properties and involvement in cellular signaling pathways. This conserved domain structure comprises specific domains arranged in a particular sequence. Here are the key domains within the conserved domain structure of c-Src kinase and Src-Abl.

1. N-terminal Myristoylation Site: The N-terminal myristoylation site is present in both c-Src kinase and Src-Abl. This site facilitates the attachment of a fatty acid chain called myristate to the N-terminus of the kinases. This lipid modification plays a crucial role in anchoring the kinases to the plasma membrane, facilitating their interaction with various signaling molecules and promoting their localization to specific cellular compartments.
2. SH3 Domain (Src Homology 3): Both c-Src kinase and Src-Abl contain an SH3 domain within their conserved domain structure. The SH3 domain is a modular protein domain involved in protein—protein interactions. It recognizes and binds to short peptide motifs rich in proline residues found in target proteins. Through these interactions, the SH3 domain mediates the assembly of protein complexes, contributing to the regulation of cellular signaling pathways and the formation of protein networks.
3. SH2 Domain (Src Homology 2): The conserved domain structure of c-Src kinase and Src-Abl includes an SH2 domain. The SH2 domain is another modular protein domain involved in protein-protein interactions. It specifically recognizes and binds to phosphorylated tyrosine residues in target proteins. By binding to phosphorylated tyrosines, the SH2 domain enables the kinases to interact with other signaling molecules and participate in downstream signaling events. This domain plays a critical role in signal transduction and the regulation of cellular processes.
4. Tyrosine Kinase Domain: The tyrosine kinase domain is a fundamental component within the conserved domain structure of both c-Src kinase and Src-Abl. This domain is responsible for the catalytic activity of the kinases. It possesses an ATP-binding site where adenosine triphosphate (ATP) is bound and subsequently hydrolyzed to provide energy for phosphorylation reactions. Additionally, the tyrosine kinase domain includes

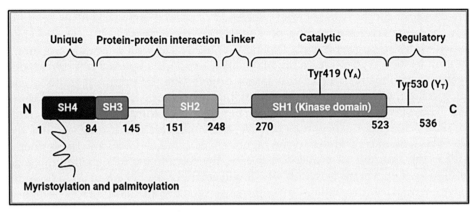

FIGURE 5.1   Domain structure of c-Src.

a substrate-binding site that recognizes and phosphorylates specific tyrosine residues on target proteins, modulating their activity and interactions within cellular signaling pathways (Panjarian et al., 2013; Roskoski, 2015; Seeliger et al., 2009) (Fig. 5.1).

1.1.2 N-terminal myristoylation site: Covalent attachment and membrane anchoring

The N-terminal myristoylation site is an important structural element shared by c-Src kinase and Src-Abl. This site plays a vital role in the attachment of a fatty acid chain called myristate to the kinases' N-terminus (Yuan et al., 2020). This covalent modification enables the kinases to anchor themselves to the plasma membrane, facilitating their interaction with various signaling molecules and promoting their localization to specific cellular compartments. The process of myristoylation involves the enzymatic transfer of myristate from myristoyl-CoA to the N-terminal glycine residue of the kinases. This attachment occurs during or immediately after protein synthesis. Once myristoylation takes place, the myristate moiety acts as a hydrophobic anchor that inserts itself into the lipid bilayer of the plasma membrane. By being anchored to the membrane, c-Src kinase and Src-Abl are strategically positioned to interact with other proteins and participate in cellular signaling pathways (McClendon & Miller, 2020). The myristoylation-mediated membrane anchoring allows these kinases to transduce signals across the plasma membrane and regulate various cellular processes such as cell proliferation, differentiation, and survival. Understanding the importance of the N-terminal myristoylation site provides valuable insights into the regulation and functional significance of c-Src kinase and Src-Abl. Their association with the plasma membrane through myristoylation is essential for their proper localization and efficient participation in cellular signaling networks (Patwardhan & Resh, 2010).

1.1.3 SH3 domain: Mediating protein–protein interactions through proline recognition

The SH3 domain, which is present in both c-Src kinase and Src-Abl, plays a significant role in facilitating protein–protein interactions. This domain acts as a modular protein structure and is involved in recognizing and binding to short peptide motifs that are rich in proline residues, which are commonly found in target proteins. The SH3 domain possesses a distinct structure characterized by a beta-barrel composed of several antiparallel beta strands. This unique architecture creates a binding pocket or groove that specifically accommodates the proline-rich motifs in target proteins. Proline, an amino acid with a unique structure, introduces a kink in the polypeptide chain, allowing it to adopt a specific conformation. Upon encountering a proline-rich motif in a target protein, the SH3 domain forms a complex through specific interactions between its binding pocket and the proline residues within the motif. These interactions involve various amino acid residues, including those adjacent to the proline-rich motif. By mediating protein–protein interactions through proline recognition, the SH3 domain contributes to the regulation of cellular processes. These interactions can result in the assembly of protein complexes, the recruitment of signaling molecules, or the modulation of enzymatic activities. The involvement of the SH3 domain in these interactions plays a crucial role in cellular signaling, cytoskeletal organization, and the establishment of protein networks (Brasher et al., 2001).

1.1.4 SH2 domain: Facilitating protein–protein interactions via phosphotyrosine recognition

The SH2 domain, which is present in both c-Src kinase and Src-Abl, plays a crucial role in facilitating protein–protein interactions through the recognition of phosphorylated tyrosine residues in target proteins. The SH2 domain possesses a conserved structural motif that enables it to bind specifically to phosphorylated tyrosine residues. Within the domain, there is a binding pocket that accommodates the phosphorylated tyrosine and establishes interactions with surrounding amino acid residues. The recognition of the phosphorylated tyrosine occurs through hydrogen bonding and electrostatic interactions between the SH2 domain and the phosphate group attached to the tyrosine residue. When the SH2 domain encounters a phosphorylated tyrosine residue in a target protein, it forms a stable complex through these specific interactions. This interaction between the SH2 domain and the phosphorylated tyrosine residue allows the kinases to engage with other signaling molecules and participate in downstream signaling events (Hantschel & Superti-Furga, 2004). By facilitating protein–protein interactions through phosphotyrosine recognition, the SH2 domain plays a critical role in regulating various cellular processes. These interactions can lead to the formation of protein complexes, the recruitment of signaling molecules, or the modulation of enzymatic activities. The involvement of the SH2 domain in these interactions is essential for effective signal transduction and the proper functioning of cellular signaling networks. Understanding the significance of the SH2 domain in facilitating protein–protein interactions via phosphotyrosine recognition provides valuable insights into the activity and regulation of c-Src kinase and Src-Abl. It enhances our understanding of their roles in cellular processes and opens up potential therapeutic opportunities by targeting these interactions for drug development (Dölker et al., 2014).

1.1.5 Tyrosine kinase domain: Catalytic activity and substrate binding

The tyrosine kinase domain is a pivotal component found in both c-Src kinase and Src-Abl. This domain plays a critical role in their catalytic activity by facilitating the transfer of phosphate groups from ATP to tyrosine residues on target proteins. The tyrosine kinase domain possesses distinctive structural features that enable its catalytic function. It includes an ATP-binding site, allowing it to bind and utilize ATP as a phosphate donor (Levinson et al., 2006).

ATP binding is crucial for the subsequent transfer of the phosphate group to the target protein. Additionally, the tyrosine kinase domain comprises a substrate-binding site that specifically recognizes and binds to tyrosine residues on target proteins. The catalytic activity of the tyrosine kinase domain involves a series of steps. Initially, ATP binds to the ATP-binding site, followed by the interaction between the target protein and the substrate-binding site. This brings the tyrosine residue of the target protein in close proximity to the phosphate group of ++ATPS. Through a process known as phosphoryl transfer, the phosphate group is transferred from ATP to the tyrosine residue, leading to the phosphorylation of the target protein. Phosphorylation, catalyzed by the tyrosine kinase domain, plays a regulatory role in modulating the activity and interactions of target proteins within cellular signaling pathways. It can induce conformational changes, facilitate the recruitment of signaling molecules, trigger downstream signaling cascades, or affect protein–protein interactions (Karuppagounder et al., 2023).

2. Phosphorylation and dephosphorylation: Regulation of c-Src kinase activity

The activity of c-Src kinase, a nonreceptor tyrosine kinase, is intricately regulated through phosphorylation and dephosphorylation events, which play a vital role in modulating its functional state and activity level. In its inactive state, c-Src kinase is maintained by an intramolecular interaction between its SH2 domain and a phosphorylated tyrosine residue located at the C-terminus (Cipak, 2022). This interaction prevents the activation of c-Src kinase by stabilizing its inactive conformation. Phosphorylation and dephosphorylation events serve as key regulatory mechanisms for controlling c-Src kinase activity. Dephosphorylation of the C-terminal tyrosine residue disrupts the intramolecular interaction between the SH2 domain and the phosphorylated tyrosine, resulting in the activation of c-Src kinase. This dephosphorylation event is mediated by specific protein tyrosine phosphatases. Furthermore, ligands binding to the SH2 or SH3 domains of c-Src kinase can induce a conformational change that disrupts the intramolecular interaction and triggers the activation of the kinase. Ligand binding occurs through various cellular signaling processes, enabling external stimuli to activate c-Src kinase (Roskoski, 2005). Upon activation, c-Src kinase transitions into an active state, allowing it to phosphorylate its target proteins and initiate signaling cascades. These phosphorylation events regulate the activity and interactions of downstream signaling molecules, thereby influencing various cellular processes (Ferrero et al., 2012).

2.1 Intramolecular interaction between SH2 domain and C-terminal phosphorylated tyrosine

The intramolecular interaction between the SH2 domain and a phosphorylated tyrosine residue at the C-terminus is a pivotal regulatory mechanism that governs the activity of c-Src kinase. In its inactive state, c-Src kinase is maintained through a noncovalent interaction between the SH2 domain and the phosphorylated tyrosine residue located at the C-terminus. This interaction stabilizes the kinase in an inactive conformation, preventing its activation (Te Boekhorst & Friedl, 2016). The SH2 domain, which is a modular domain present in c-Src kinase, specifically recognizes and binds to phosphorylated tyrosine residues. The SH2 domain contains a binding pocket that accommodates the phosphorylated tyrosine and establishes specific interactions with surrounding amino acid residues. The recognition of the phosphorylated tyrosine occurs through hydrogen bonding and electrostatic interactions between the SH2 domain and the phosphate group attached to the tyrosine residue (Poulin et al., 2005). By binding to the phosphorylated tyrosine residue at the C-terminus, the SH2 domain restricts the access of substrates to the active site of c-Src kinase, thus inhibiting its catalytic activity. This intramolecular interaction masks the activation loop of the kinase, maintaining it in an inactive conformation. The release of the SH2 domain from the phosphorylated tyrosine residue is crucial for the activation of c-Src kinase. Several mechanisms can disrupt this intramolecular interaction, including dephosphorylation events or binding of ligands to the SH2 domain or other regulatory domains of c-Src kinase. Once released, the kinase undergoes conformational changes, exposing its active site and enabling it to phosphorylate target proteins (Young et al., 2001).

2.2 Disruption of the inactive state: Dephosphorylation and ligand binding

The inactive state of c-Src kinase, a nonreceptor tyrosine kinase, can be disrupted through two important processes: dephosphorylation and ligand binding. These mechanisms play crucial roles in regulating the activation of c-Src kinase and modulating its cellular functions. Dephosphorylation involves the removal of phosphate groups from specific amino acid residues, particularly the tyrosine residues within c-Src kinase. In the inactive state, c-Src kinase is stabilized by an intramolecular interaction between its SH2 domain and a phosphorylated tyrosine residue located at the C-terminus (Gul et al., 2023). Dephosphorylation of this tyrosine residue disrupts the interaction, inducing a conformational change that releases c-Src kinase from its inactive state and allows it to transition into an active form. Ligand binding is another mechanism that can disrupt the inactive state of c-Src kinase. Ligands, which can be small molecules or proteins, bind to specific domains of c-Src kinase, such as the SH2 or SH3 domains. This binding event triggers conformational changes that allosterically regulate the kinase's activity. Depending on the nature of the ligand and its interaction with the kinase, ligand binding can either promote or inhibit the activation of c-Src kinase. Both dephosphorylation and ligand binding contribute to the activation of c-Src kinase, enabling it to phosphorylate target proteins and initiate downstream signaling cascades. These processes provide precise control over the kinase's activity, ensuring accurate regulation of cellular signaling pathways (Gilburt et al., 2019; Gul et al., 2023).

2.3 Activation mechanisms and implications for cellular signaling

The activation mechanisms of c-Src kinase, a nonreceptor tyrosine kinase, are intricate and have significant implications for cellular signaling pathways. A comprehensive understanding of these mechanisms is essential for unraveling the functional roles of c-Src kinase and its impact on various cellular processes. The activation of c-Src kinase involves multiple processes, including dephosphorylation and ligand binding, which collectively regulate its catalytic activity and signaling potential (Boczek et al., 2019). Dephosphorylation of the inhibitory tyrosine residue located at the C-terminus disrupts the intramolecular interaction with the

SH2 domain, leading to a conformational change that releases c-Src kinase from its inactive state. This conformational transition enables c-Src kinase to adopt an active conformation and phosphorylate its target proteins. Ligand binding to specific domains of c-Src kinase, such as the SH2 or SH3 domains, plays a critical role in its activation. The binding of ligands induces allosteric changes in the kinase, exposing its active site and facilitating substrate binding. Ligands can include proteins involved in signaling pathways or small molecules that modulate the kinase's activity (Boczek et al., 2019). The binding of these ligands allosterically regulates c-Src kinase, either enhancing or inhibiting its catalytic activity. The activation of c-Src kinase has profound implications for cellular signaling. As a pivotal regulator of multiple downstream signaling pathways, activated c-Src kinase phosphorylates various target proteins involved in essential cellular processes such as proliferation, survival, migration, and differentiation. These phosphorylation events initiate intricate signaling cascades that modulate gene expression, cytoskeletal dynamics, and cell adhesion, among other critical functions (Daday et al., 2022). Dysregulation of c-Src kinase activation and signaling can contribute to the development and progression of diseases, particularly cancer. Aberrant activation of c-Src kinase has been associated with promoting cell transformation, metastasis, and drug resistance. Therefore, gaining a comprehensive understanding of the mechanisms underlying c-Src kinase activation and identifying potential therapeutic targets within its signaling network hold tremendous promise for the development of targeted therapies to combat cancer and related disorders (Jin, 2020; Li et al., 2019) (Fig. 5.2).

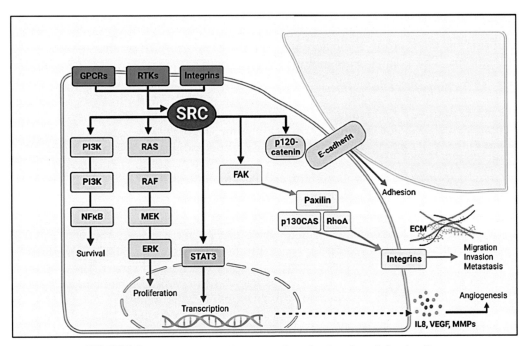

FIGURE 5.2   Activation mechanisms and implications for cellular signaling.

3. Src-Abl: Fusion protein and leukemia connection

Src-Abl is a fusion protein that is closely associated with specific types of leukemia and arises from a chromosomal translocation event. This fusion occurs between the BCR (Breakpoint Cluster Region) gene and the ABL1 (Abelson) gene, resulting in the formation of a hybrid gene called BCR-ABL1 (Chatain et al., 2013). The fusion of the BCR and ABL1 genes leads to the production of the Src-Abl fusion protein, which possesses unique properties compared to its individual components, c-Src kinase and c-Abl. Src-Abl displays constitutive activity, meaning it remains active regardless of external signals or regulatory mechanisms. This constitutive activation is primarily attributed to the loss of the C-terminal regulatory region and the presence of the BCR coiled-coil domain plays a critical role in the activation and signaling of the Src-Abl fusion protein (Greuber et al., 2013). Derived from the BCR gene, this domain facilitates dimerization and transphosphorylation events, which are key steps in Src-Abl activation. This signaling pathway play a role in the development of leukemia, particularly chronic myeloid leukemia (CML) and a subset of acute lymphoblastic leukemia (Panjarian et al., 2013). The continuous kinase activity of Src-Abl contributes to abnormal proliferation and survival of leukemic cells, disruption of normal hematopoiesis, and inhibition of apoptosis. Moreover, the presence of Src-Abl in leukemia cells confers resistance to many inhibitors that target c-Src kinase or c-Abl, such as imatinib. This resistance poses significant challenges in the treatment of leukemia and emphasizes the need for alternative therapeutic strategies and the development of novel drugs specifically designed to target Src-Abl (Musumeci et al., 2012).

3.1 There are various chemical categories of inhibitors that target c-Src kinase and Src-Abl, modulating their activity and showing promise in therapeutic applications. These categories include

3.1.1 ATP-competitive inhibitors

- Compete with ATP for binding to the kinase domain of c-Src kinase.
- Compete with ATP for binding to the ATP-binding site of c-Abl kinase.
- Bind to the ATP-binding pocket, blocking ATP from binding and inhibiting kinase activity.
- Examples include Dasatinib, Bosutinib, and Ponatinib (Brandvold et al., 2012; Kasahara et al., 2021; Kruewel et al., 2010).

Shumei Kato et al. explored the potential of combined inhibition of MET and c-SRC for the treatment of cancer. The critical roles of these molecules in cancer progression and their established cross talk have been well-documented. Preclinical studies have shown promising results for MET and c-SRC inhibitor combinations in various types of cancer. The researchers conducted a concurrent phase I study to assess the safety and efficacy of administering dasatinib (a c-SRC inhibitor) in combination with crizotinib (a MET inhibitor). A total of 61 patients were enrolled, with Arm A receiving fixed doses of crizotinib (250 mg twice daily) and escalating doses of dasatinib, and Arm B receiving fixed dasatinib (140 mg daily) with escalating doses of crizotinib. Both arms experienced dose-limiting toxicities, and the recommended phase II dose was determined to be arm A, DL1 (250 mg crizotinib orally twice per day plus 50 mg dasatinib orally daily). Although adverse events limited tolerability, the combination was considered safe for administration. The study reported modest responses, including partial response and durable stable disease, indicating potential therapeutic benefits. However, the observed toxicity associated with this specific combination presents challenges for further precision therapy approaches. Future investigations are warranted to explore alternative strategies that optimize the therapeutic potential of MET and c-SRC inhibition while minimizing toxicity in cancer patients (Kato et al., 2018).

Patrick G. Morris et al. conducted a phase II trial by the combination of the Src inhibitor dasatinib with weekly paclitaxel was evaluated in HER2-negative metastatic breast cancer patients. The study enrolled 40 patients but was terminated early due to slow accrual. Results showed an overall response rate of 23%, with a median progression-free survival of 5.2 months and a median overall survival of 20.6 months. Common side effects included fatigue, neuropathy, and diarrhea, while no significant predictive biomarkers were identified. Although the trial demonstrated clinical activity, further investigation in larger cohorts is necessary to validate the efficacy of dasatinib and paclitaxel in metastatic breast cancer (Morris et al., 2018).

Laura C. Kennedy and Vijayakrishna Gadi investigated the potential of the Src inhibitor dasatinib in breast cancer treatment. Src, a nonreceptor tyrosine kinase, has been implicated in breast carcinogenesis and bone metastases. The study focused on a phase II clinical trial that evaluated the combination of dasatinib and paclitaxel in HER2-negative metastatic breast cancer patients. Although the trial was terminated prematurely due to slow accrual, the combination therapy exhibited activity in select patients, with an overall response rate of 23% and a clinical benefit rate of 43%. The findings underscored the potential of Src inhibition in breast cancer, particularly in cases involving bone metastases and triple-negative breast cancer. However, the lack of predictive biomarkers and the broader kinase inhibition profile of dasatinib raised questions regarding its specific mechanisms of action and optimal patient selection. Further investigations, such as personalized testing using organoids or patient-derived xenografts, may offer insights into identifying breast cancer tumors that are most likely to respond effectively to dasatinib (Kennedy & Gadi, 2018).

Francisco Hermida-Prado et al. investigated the role of the SRC inhibitor dasatinib in head and neck squamous cell carcinomas (HNSCC) and the potential counteractive effects of the mithramycin analog EC-8042. While the monotherapy with dasatinib and saracatinib showed limited efficacy in HNSCC patients, this research revealed that these inhibitors exhibited undesirable properties by promoting stem cell characteristics. These findings highlight the need for a deeper understanding of the mechanistic actions of these drugs to enhance clinical outcomes and develop more effective combination strategies. However, when dasatinib was combined with EC-8042, it resulted in complementary antiinvasive, antiproliferative, and anticancer stem cell effects, effectively countering the stemness-promoting effects of dasatinib. This combination therapy demonstrated promising results in vitro and in vivo, suggesting its potential as a novel therapeutic approach for HNSCC patients. The study suggests that exploring combinational strategies involving EC-8042 could improve treatment efficacy and long-term clinical outcomes in HNSCC, warranting further investigation (Hermida-Prado et al., 2019).

Tanya B. Dorff et al. conducted a randomized phase II trial and investigated the impact of adding dasatinib, a Src inhibitor, to abiraterone in men with metastatic castration-resistant prostate cancer (mCRPC). The study aimed to determine if the combination could delay prostate cancer progression compared to abiraterone alone. Although the addition of dasatinib did not significantly extend progression-free survival (PFS) compared to abiraterone alone, there were notable complete responses observed. Circulating tumor cell kinetics, including a "flare" phenomenon, were also observed. Despite the early termination of the study and limitations in power, the combination treatment demonstrated robust objective responses. Further research is needed to explore the potential of dasatinib in combination therapies for mCRPC patients (Dorff et al., 2019).

Keiji Mashimo et al. conducted a study that aimed to gain a better understanding of the mechanisms involved in drug resistance in multiple myeloma (MM) cells triggered by receptor activator of NF-κB ligand (RANKL). It was observed that RANKL contributed to drug resistance by activating c-Src and downstream signaling molecules, including Akt, mTOR, STAT3, JNK, and NF-κB, while suppressing the expression of Bim, a pro-apoptotic protein. However, treatment with dasatinib, a c-Src inhibitor, effectively overcame RANKL-induced drug resistance by inhibiting the activation of these signaling pathways and enhancing Bim expression. These findings highlight the potential of c-Src inhibition as a promising therapeutic strategy to overcome drug resistance in MM patients influenced by RANKL. Further research is warranted to explore the clinical implications of targeting c-Src in MM treatment (Mashimo et al., 2019).

Austin et al. performed a study to explore the potential of Src kinase inhibition in reversing the downregulation of E-cadherin expression in pancreatic ductal adenocarcinoma (PDAC). Their findings revealed an inverse relationship between Src activation and E-cadherin levels in human PDAC samples, indicating the involvement of Src in promoting epithelial-to-mesenchymal transition (EMT) and suppressing E-cadherin. Through the administration of dasatinib, a Src inhibitor, the researchers observed a decrease in Slug, a transcriptional repressor of E-cadherin, leading to enhanced E-cadherin transcription. Additionally, dasatinib treatment resulted in increased levels of total and membranous E-cadherin/β-catenin in drug-sensitive PDAC cells. In vivo xenograft models demonstrated the restoration of E-cadherin levels specifically in BxPC3 xenograft tumors upon dasatinib treatment. These findings highlight the therapeutic potential of Src kinase inhibition in reversing EMT and restoring E-cadherin expression in drug-sensitive PDAC cells, underscoring the significance of E-cadherin as a potential biomarker for assessing the response to dasatinib treatment. This study significantly contributes to the understanding of the molecular mechanisms underlying PDAC progression and provides a strong rationale for targeting Src kinase to combat EMT and metastasis in PDAC patients (Dosch et al., 2019).

Xiao-Long Qian et al. conducted a study on Triple-Negative Breast Cancer (TNBC) cells to investigate the efficacy of dasatinib, an inhibitor of c-src phosphorylation. They discovered that Syndecan-Binding Protein (SDCBP) overexpression promoted TNBC cell proliferation by enhancing c-src phosphorylation, which was effectively inhibited by dasatinib. SDCBP expression correlated with p-c-src-Y419 levels in TNBC tissues. The findings suggest that SDCBP could serve as a potential marker for identifying TNBC cases suitable for dasatinib therap (Qian et al., 2017).

Nagla Abdel Karim et al. conducted a phase I clinical study by exploring the potential synergy between Bosutinib, a Src kinase inhibitor, and the antifolate drug pemetrexed in patients with advanced metastatic solid tumors, including nonsmall cell lung cancer (NSCLC). The study enrolled 14 patients who had experienced disease progression after standard chemotherapy. The primary objective of the study was to determine the maximum tolerated dose (MTD) of Bosutinib in combination with pemetrexed and assess the safety profile of the treatment. Patients received oral Bosutinib once daily, starting at a dose of 200 mg, and intravenous pemetrexed at a dose of 500 mg/m^2 on a 3-week schedule. The MTD for Bosutinib in this combination was established as 300 mg daily. Out of the evaluable patients, two individuals (17%) achieved a partial response (PR), while seven patients (58%) exhibited stable disease (SD) as the best response after four treatment cycles. Immunohistochemical staining demonstrated Src overexpression in the two responders and two patients with prolonged stable disease, indicating its potential role in treatment response. The median progression-free survival (PFS) was measured as 6.89 months, and the median overall survival (OS) was 11.7 months. Despite the limitations inherent to Phase I studies, these findings suggest promising efficacy of the Bosutinib-pemetrexed combination in previously treated patients (Karim et al., 2022).

A study conducted by Adil I. Daud et al. evaluated the safety, tolerability, and preliminary efficacy of bosutinib, an ATP-competitive inhibitor of Src/Abl kinases, in patients with advanced solid tumor malignancies. The trial consisted of dose escalation (part 1) and dose expansion (part 2). The recommended phase II dose (RP2D) of bosutinib was established as 400 mg/day due to dose-limiting toxicities observed at higher doses. The most common adverse events were nausea, diarrhea, vomiting, fatigue, and anorexia. While partial responses in breast cancer and an unconfirmed complete response in pancreatic cancer were observed, the primary efficacy endpoints for refractory colorectal, pancreatic, and nonsmall cell lung cancers were not met in part 2 of the study. Overall, the study provided valuable insights into the use of bosutinib in advanced solid tumor malignancies (Daud et al., 2012).

3.1.2 Allosteric inhibitors

- Target allosteric sites on c-Src kinase, distinct from the ATP-binding pocket.
- Bind to a site on c-Abl kinase other than the active site.
- Binding to allosteric sites induces conformational changes in the kinase domain, leading to kinase inhibition.
- Saracatinib, GNF-2, GNF-5 are the examples of an allosteric inhibitor of c-Src and c-abl kinase.

In a phase II trial led by Ailsa J. Oswald et al., the efficacy of saracatinib (AZD0530), an oral Src kinase inhibitor, was investigated in postmenopausal women with hormone receptor-positive metastatic breast cancer. The study aimed to assess whether the addition of saracatinib to aromatase inhibitors could address estrogen resistance and reduce osteoclast activity. However, the results revealed no significant improvement in progression-free survival or reduction in bony progression when using saracatinib. Furthermore, no benefits were observed in terms of overall survival or objective response rate. These findings suggest that saracatinib did not exhibit efficacy as an adjunct therapy for hormone receptor—positive metastatic breast cancer, providing insights into its limitations in this patient population (Oswald et al., 2023).

Sarah Danson et al. conducted an exploratory phase II randomized controlled trial to evaluate the effectiveness of saracatinib, an orally available Src inhibitor, as an analgesic for cancer patients with painful bone metastases. Persistent pain is a challenging symptom in advanced cancer, and N-methyl-D-aspartate (NMDA) glutamate receptors are thought to contribute to enhanced sensory processing. Src kinase, which regulates NMDA receptor activity, is implicated in persistent pain. Animal studies have shown promising results for saracatinib as an analgesic. The trial included 12 patients, with 6 receiving saracatinib (125 mg/day for 28 days) and 6 receiving a placebo. Pharmacokinetic measurements confirmed appropriate drug levels in the saracatinib-treated group, and clinical evidence of Src inhibition was observed through a significant reduction in a bone resorption biomarker. However, there were no clinically significant differences in self-reported pain scores between the saracatinib and placebo groups after 4 weeks of treatment. Consumption of maintenance analgesia remained unchanged in the saracatinib group, and Quality-of-Life scores did not show improvement. Based on the data obtained, the trial did not demonstrate the effectiveness of saracatinib as an analgesic. Nevertheless, saracatinib may hold potential as an antibone resorptive agent. The findings emphasize the importance of further research to explore alternative strategies for effectively managing cancer-induced bone pain (Danson et al., 2019).

In a study by Ling-Yen Chiu et al., titled "Combination treatment of saracatinib, a Src inhibitor, with GMI, a Ganoderma microsporum immunomodulatory protein, induces synthetic lethality via autophagy and apoptosis in lung cancer cells," the authors investigated the cytotoxic effects of combining saracatinib and GMI on parental and pemetrexed-resistant lung cancer cells. The study aimed to evaluate the efficacy of combining saracatinib and GMI in lung cancer treatment. The results showed that the combination treatment exhibited synergistic and additive cytotoxic effects in A549 and A400 lung cancer cells. Saracatinib and GMI together induced caspase-7 activation in A549 cells and increased LC3B-II, indicating enhanced autophagy, in A400 cells. Silencing ATG5, a regulator of autophagy, reduced cell death in A549 cells after the cotreatment. This study proposes a novel approach to treating lung cancer, both with and without drug resistance, by combining saracatinib and GMI. The synergistic induction of autophagy and apoptosis contributes to the cytotoxic effects observed in the combination therapy (Lang et al., 2019).

A study conducted by Fei-Teng Lu et al., titled "SRC inhibitor saracatinib enhances efficacy of PD-1/PD-L1 immune checkpoint blockade in non-small cell lung cancer," investigated the potential of saracatinib as an enhancer of antitumor immunity in nonsmall lung cancer. The study aimed to address the limitations of immune checkpoint inhibitors (ICI) in achieving therapeutic responses. The authors focused on SRC family kinases as a target for combination therapy and found that saracatinib effectively reduced PD-L1 expression in cancer cells and enhanced T-cell—mediated killing of tumor cells in vitro and in vivo. The combination therapy also resulted in prolonged survival in animal models. These findings suggest that saracatinib has the potential to enhance the effectiveness of immunotherapy in nonsmall cell lung cancer by boosting antitumor immune responses (Lu et al., 2022).

In the study titled "Saracatinib (AZD0530) and docetaxel in metastatic, castrate-refractory prostate cancer (mCRPC)—A phase I/randomized phase II study" by Robert J. Jones et al., the authors investigated the efficacy of combining saracatinib, an inhibitor of Abl and Src family members, with docetaxel for the treatment of mCRPC. The study involved 152 patients and aimed to evaluate progression-free survival (PFS), overall survival (OS), and safety. However, the results showed that the addition of saracatinib did not improve PFS or OS compared to docetaxel alone. Although there were no significant drug interactions or dose-limiting toxicities, the combination therapy led to increased treatment-related toxicities. Based on these findings, the authors concluded that further development of this combination therapy for mCRPC should not be pursued (Jones et al., 2021).

3.1.3 Peptide substrate–based inhibitors

- Designed based on the substrate sequence recognized by c-Src kinase.
- Mimic the substrate and bind to the kinase domain, blocking substrate binding and inhibiting kinase activity.
- Peptide-based inhibitors are often modified for stability and specificity.
- Examples include PP1 and PP2, peptide analogs derived from the c-Src/abl kinase substrate.

The article titled "Modulation of serine/threonine-protein phosphatase 1 (PP1) complexes: A promising approach in cancer treatment" by Bárbara Matos et al. explores the potential of targeting PP1 and its complexes as a viable therapeutic strategy for cancer. Despite the existence of various treatment options, cancer remains a leading cause of death worldwide due to challenges like tumor heterogeneity and chemoresistance. Therefore, finding effective therapies is crucial. PP1 and its complexes have been identified as potential drug targets, and researchers have developed diverse chemical compounds to disrupt or stabilize these complexes in different cancer types, aiming to hinder disease progression. Encouraging results have been observed in in vitro studies, necessitating further validation through preclinical and clinical trials. However, the specific roles of PP1 complexes in tumorigenesis are still not fully understood, and the characterization of only a fraction of these complexes in cancer models limits the approach. Despite challenges, the modulation of PP1 complexes presents a promising therapeutic strategy in cancer treatment, which requires continued research and validation to fully exploit its potential (Matos et al., 2021).

Head and neck squamous cell carcinoma (HNSCC) are a common and deadly cancer. Treatment outcomes for HNSCC have not significantly improved, and c-Src inhibitors have shown limited clinical efficacy. In a study by SunYoung Lee et al., they investigated the effectiveness of the c-Src inhibitor PP2 on HNSCC. PP2 inhibited tumor cell growth, promoted apoptosis, and prevented metastasis in both cell lines and mice. It achieved these effects by regulating the epithelial–mesenchymal transition (EMT) pathway downstream of c-Src. These findings suggest that PP2 could be a potential therapeutic option for HNSCC by targeting the EMT pathway (Lee et al., 2022).

3.1.4 Covalent inhibitors

- Form a covalent bond with a specific amino acid residue in the kinase domain of c-Src kinase.
- This irreversible binding permanently prevents kinase activity.
- Covalent inhibitors are less common for c-Src kinase compared to other kinases.

• Examples of covalent inhibitors targeting other kinases include Ibrutinib and Afatinib.

Chronic lymphocytic leukemia (CLL) is a prevalent type of leukemia characterized by the clonal expansion of B-cells. Bruton's tyrosine kinase (BTK) inhibitors, such as ibrutinib and acalabrutinib, have shown efficacy in treating CLL but are associated with an increased risk of bleeding in patients. A recent study by Elaskalani et al. investigated the potential role of adenosine in amplifying the antiplatelet effects of BTK inhibitors and contributing to the bleeding risk observed in CLL patients. In this study, researchers examined plasma samples from both CLL patients and healthy individuals to assess soluble CD73 levels and activity. They conducted platelet activation assays using various agonists and BTK inhibitors to investigate the impact of adenosine on platelet function. The findings revealed that adenosine enhanced the antiplatelet effect of ibrutinib and acalabrutinib, with ibrutinib exhibiting a more pronounced effect. This combined treatment reduced platelet aggregation induced by collagen and influenced the phosphorylation of downstream kinases involved in platelet activation. These findings suggest that the increased bleeding risk observed in CLL patients receiving BTK inhibitors may result from the synergistic interaction between the inhibitors and elevated adenosine levels within the CLL microenvironment. Further research should focus on elucidating the relationship between adenosine levels, CD73 expression, and platelet activation in CLL patients. This knowledge could enhance the development of improved management strategies and personalized treatment approaches for CLL patients undergoing BTK inhibitor therapy (Elaskalani et al., 2022) (Fig. 5.3).

3.2 Miscellaneous

Dottorando et al. explored the synthesis and evaluation of a series of pyrazolo[3,4-d]pyrimidine derivatives as potential anticancer agents. The researchers employed an easy and versatile synthetic approach, leading to the identification of significant structure–activity relationships (SARs). Several compounds in this new family, such as 8a, 8j, and 8k, exhibited high inhibition of c-Src/Abl kinase activity and K562 cell viability in chronic myeloid leukemia (CML) studies. Molecular modeling studies utilizing docking and molecular dynamics techniques provided insights into the behavior of these inhibitors within the Abl enzymatic pocket. Additionally, compounds 22a and 22b demonstrated inhibitory activity against mutated Abl (T315I), but the most potent compound was found to be Compound 1 with IC_{50} of 0.053 and 3.7 µM for Abl and c-Src, respectively (Dottorando & Di Maria).

Eman K.A. Abdelall et al. designed and synthesized novel heterocyclic compounds based on a 4-aryl-4H-chromene scaffold as potential anticancer agents. The study encompasses the characterization of three sets of derivatives (4a–c, 6a–d, and 7a–c) through elemental analyses and spectral data. These compounds were then assessed for their antiproliferative activity against HCT-116, HepG-2, and MCF-7 cell lines, comparing them to reference drugs vinblastine and staurosporine. Notably, compounds 4b, 4c, and 6d demonstrated notable cytotoxicity against the respective cell lines, surpassing the reference drugs in some cases. The compound 2 was most potent with IC_{50} of 0.07 µM for c-Src inhibition (Abdelall et al., 2022).

Mohamed Ramadan et al. synthesized and developed novel 2'-aminospiro[pyrano[3,2–c]quinoline]-3'-carbonitrile derivatives as non-ATP competitive Src kinase inhibitors to suppress breast cancer cell migration and proliferation. The compounds showed potent

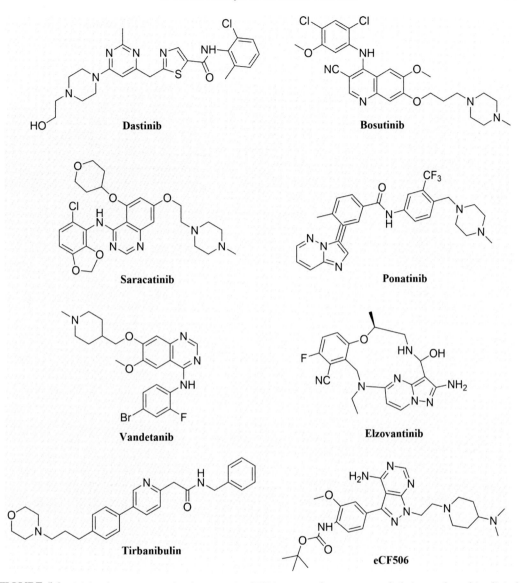

FIGURE 5.3 Molecular structures that have received FDA approval or are currently being evaluated in clinical trials as inhibitors of the Src family.

inhibition of Src kinase activity, selectively targeting it without affecting other kinases. The lead compound 3 demonstrated significant suppression of Src ($IC_{50} = 0.87$ µM), Fak, and paxillin phosphorylation in breast cancer cell lines, resulting in cell growth suppression and apoptosis induction. These findings suggest the potential of these derivatives as targeted therapeutic agents for breast cancer by specifically inhibiting Src kinase activity (Ramadan et al., 2021).

Yuting Zhou et al. aimed to discover potent kinase inhibitors for the treatment of colorectal cancer. They designed and synthesized a novel series of quinoline analogs containing thiazolidinones, based on their previous research. The most promising compound, 4, displayed potent inhibitory activity against c-Met and Ron kinases. It also exhibited moderate inhibitory effects on PDGFRa, c-Src, and AXL kinases. In vitro antitumor assays demonstrated that compound 4 had significant cytotoxicity and antiproliferative effects on HT-29 colorectal cancer cells, surpassing the potency of Regorafenib and Cabozantinib. Cellular assays further confirmed its ability to induce apoptosis and cause slight cell cycle arrest in HT-29 cells. Notably, compound 4 exhibited selectivity toward cancer cells while sparing normal colorectal cells. These findings suggest that compound 4 holds promise as a lead compound for the development of potent anticancer agents targeting colorectal cancer, warranting further structural optimization (Zhou et al., 2020).

In the study conducted by S. Bapat et al. the authors focused on the synthesis, biological evaluation, and molecular modeling studies of novel chromone/aza-chromone fused—aminophosphonates as Src kinase inhibitors. The compounds were successfully synthesized using silica chloride as a catalyst, and their inhibitory activity against c-Src kinase was tested. Among the synthesized compounds, a specific azachromone derivative demonstrated, i.e., Compound 5 which possess significant inhibition of Src kinase with an IC_{50} value of 15.8 μM. Molecular docking and dynamics simulations were employed to investigate the detailed interactions between the compounds and both phosphorylated and unphosphorylated forms of the Src kinase protein. The findings indicated that the compound exhibited stronger affinity toward the phosphorylated form of Src kinase. Overall, this study contributes to the advancement of chromone/aza-chromone-aminophosphonate conjugates as potential inhibitors of Src kinase, offering valuable information on their binding sites and potential implications in drug design (Bapat et al., 2019).

Bhupender et al. synthesized novel derivatives and evaluated their inhibitory effects on tyrosine kinases. Compound 10 showed significant antiproliferative activity against HT-29 and SK-OV-3 cells, with modest inhibitory effects on c-Src, Btk, and Lck but the lead compound to inhibit the activity of c-Src was compound 6 which is 3-(4-Amino-3-phenyl-1H-pyrazolo[3,4-d]pyrimidin-1-yl)-4-(4-methoxyphenyl)but-3-en-2-one with IC_{50} value of 21.7 μM. Molecular simulations supported the observed selectivity, providing insights into the interaction patterns. These findings contribute to the development of selective protein kinase inhibitors (Chhikara et al., 2020).

Jian Peng et al. developed a series of N-benzyl-2-(5-phenylpyridin-2-yl) acetamide-based derivatives that were successfully designed and synthesized as anticancer agents. Among these derivatives, Compound 7 was identified as a potential lead compound 7 exhibiting dual mechanisms of action, targeting both Src signaling and tubulin polymerization. Compound 7 demonstrated remarkable inhibitory effects on the proliferation of various cancer cell lines, particularly small-cell lung cancer (SCLC) cells, with IC_{50} values ranging from 5 to 188 nM. Furthermore, in an SCLC xenograft model using H446 cells, compound 7 displayed significant therapeutic efficacy by reducing tumor volume without causing noticeable toxicity. Mechanistically, compound 7 inhibited tubulin polymerization in vitro, induced G2/M cell cycle arrest, and interacted with the kinase catalytic domain of Src, resulting in reduced Src phosphorylation. These findings highlight the potential of compound 7 as a lead compound for further development of novel antitumor drugs specifically targeting SCLC (Peng et al., 2022).

Lun Wang et al. focused on the development of effective inhibitors targeting tubulin and Src protein. They investigated Klisyri (KX01), a dual tubulin/Src inhibitor, which showed promise in preclinical tumor models but failed to demonstrate efficacy in a phase II clinical trial for bone-metastatic castration-resistant prostate cancer. By analyzing the crystal structure and binding interactions of KX01, the authors hypothesized that enhancing its interaction with α-tubulin could enhance its tubulin inhibitory activity. Through rational design and synthesis guided by docking studies, a series of KX01 derivatives were developed, with compound 8 showing over 10-fold increased antiproliferative activity compared to KX01 in multiple tumor cell lines. Furthermore, 8a exhibited significantly improved in vivo antitumor effects. X-ray crystal structure analysis revealed that 8a bound to the colchicine site of tubulin and formed potent interactions within α-tubulin, representing a novel binding mode. The findings of this study identified compound 8 as a potential clinical candidate for cancer therapy because it was seen with high potency (IC_{50}- ranges from 0.2 to 1.8 nM) which target dual inhibitors of Tubulin as well as Src kinase (Wang et al., 2021) (Fig. 5.4).

Guangyan Du et al. aimed to develop a highly specific inhibitor for SRC kinase, a critical regulator in cancer development. Unlike existing inhibitors, the researchers focused on targeting cysteine 277 on the SRC P-loop. Through their efforts, they successfully designed covalent inhibitor Compound 9 i.e., 4-((2-Acrylamidophenyl)amino)-N-(2-chloro-6-methylphenyl)-2-((4-(4methylpiperazin1yl)phenyl) amino)pyrimidine-5-carboxamide and Src $IC_{50} = 3$ nM, which exhibited selective inhibition of SRC signaling both in vitro and in vivo. Notably, Compound 9 demonstrated sustained activity and displayed significant antiproliferative effects in nonsmall cell lung cancer cell lines with activated SRC. These results indicate the promising potential of this approach for future drug development targeting SRC in cancer treatment (Du et al., 2020).

Ali Rafinejad et al. synthesized 2-amino-4-aryl-4H-benzo[h or f]chromene-3-carbonitrile derivatives as Src kinase inhibitors and their antiproliferative activities in breast carcinoma (BT-20) cell lines. The derivatives were synthesized through a one-pot, three-component reaction using α or β-naphthol, malonitrile, and an aromatic aldehyde. Among the tested compounds, the unsubstituted 4-phenyl analog Compound 10 exhibited the most potent Src kinase inhibitory effect, with an IC50 value of 28.1 µM. Additionally, some derivatives, such as 3-nitro-phenyl 4e and 3-pyridinyl 4h, showed significant inhibition of cell proliferation in BT-20 cells, surpassing the efficacy of doxorubicin. The study highlights the potential of the 4-aryl-4H-naphthopyrans scaffold for the design of more potent Src kinase inhibitors and/or anticancer lead compounds. The incorporation of less bulky groups, such as unsubstituted phenyl, at the aryl position demonstrated preferable and well-tolerated Src inhibitory activity. These findings provide valuable insights into the structural requirements for further optimization of chromene-carbonitrile derivatives, paving the way for the development of more potent and selective Src kinase inhibitors and/or anticancer agents (Rafinejad et al., 2012).

Dalip Kumar et al. carried out synthesis of two classes of 1,4-disubstituted 1,2,3-triazoles using a click chemistry approach. These triazoles were synthesized through the reaction of a-tosyloxy ketones/a-halo ketones, sodium azide, and terminal alkynes in the presence of aqueous polyethylene glycol (PEG). The synthesized compounds were then evaluated for their inhibitory activity against Src kinase. The researchers conducted structure—activity relationship analysis and found that the insertion of C6H5- and 4-CH3C6H4- groups at position

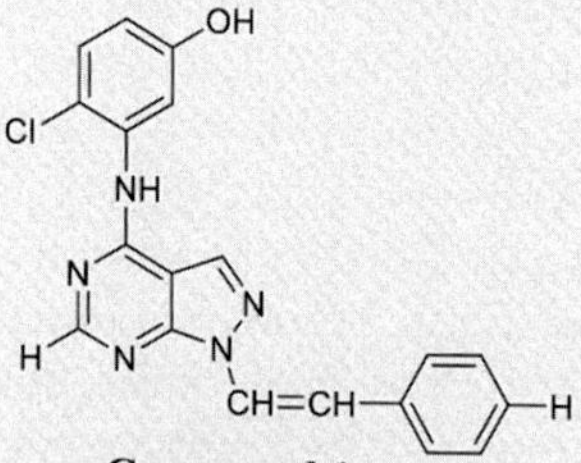

Compound 1
IC_{50} = 0.053 μM for Abl
IC_{50} = 3.7 μM for c-Src

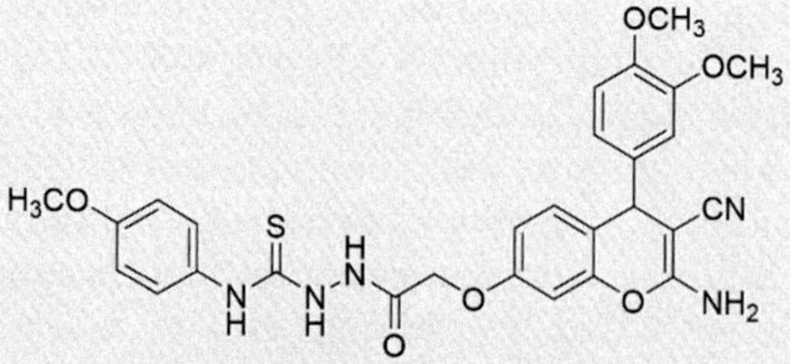

Compound 2
IC_{50} = 0.07 μM for c-Src

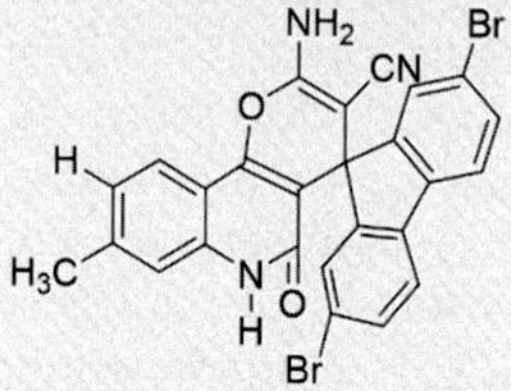

Compound 3
IC_{50} = 0.87 μM for c-Src

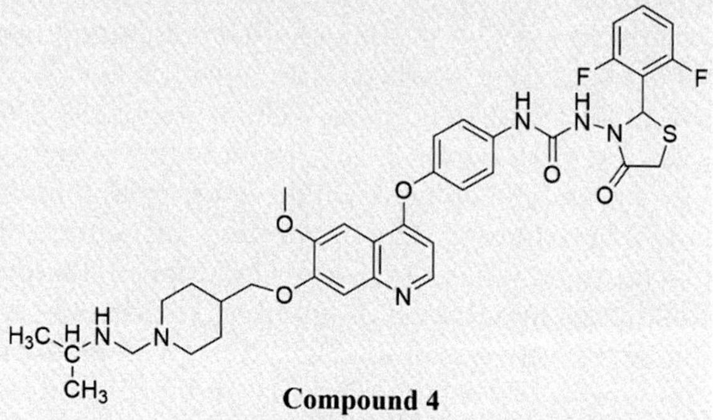

Compound 4
IC_{50} = 0.122-0.382 μM for c-Src

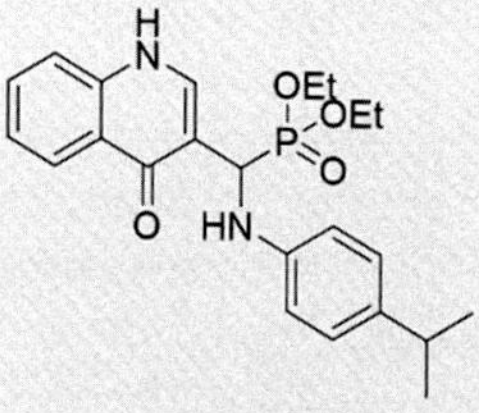

Compound 5
IC_{50} = 15.8 μM for c-Src

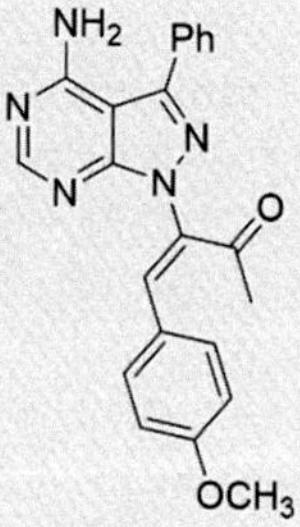

Compound 6
IC_{50} = 21.7 μM for c-Src

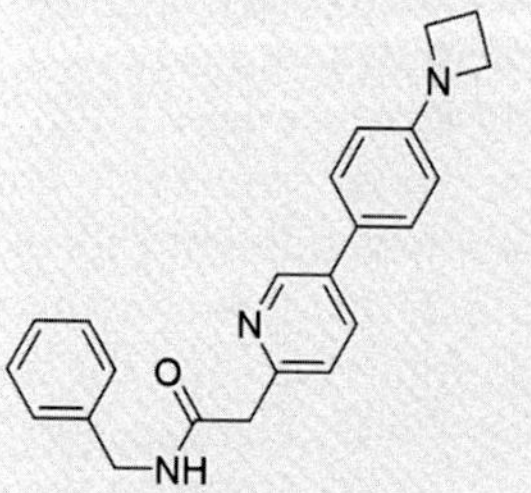

Compound 7
IC_{50} = 5-188 nM for dual tubulin and c-Src

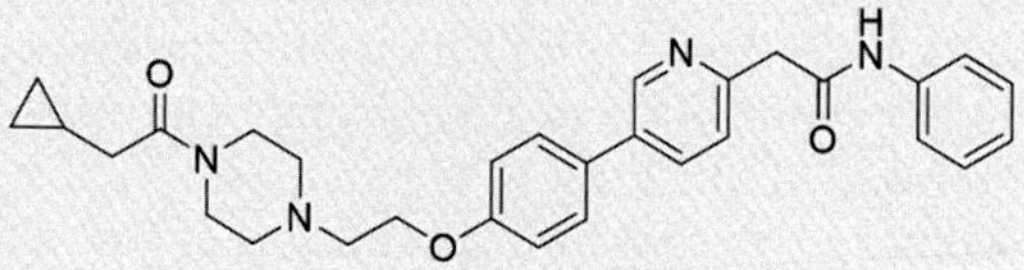

Compound 8
IC_{50} = 0.2-1.8 μM for dual tubulin and c-Src

FIGURE 5.4 Compounds 1–8 showing anticancer activity by inhibiting c-Src/Abl kinase inhibitor.

four in both classes, as well as the presence of a less bulky aromatic group at position 1 in class 1, played a crucial role in achieving modest Src inhibition activity. The 1,4-disubstituted 1,2,3-triazoles exhibited an IC_{50} range of 32–43 µM against Src kinase. But, the most potent compound found was compound 11 with IC_{50} value of 32.5 which having high potency to inhibit c-Src kinase enzyme (Kumar et al., 2011).

Asal Fallah-Tafti et al. investigates the evaluation of 4-aryl substituted derivatives of 2-amino-7-dimethylamino-4H-chromene-3-carbonitrile as Src kinase inhibitors and their potential anticancer activities. Src kinase mutations and overexpression have been associated with various human cancers, making the development of potent and selective Src kinase inhibitors a significant area of interest. The researchers employed a one-pot reaction using appropriate substituted aromatic aldehydes, malononitrile, and 3-(dimethylamino)phenol in the presence of piperidine to synthesize the derivatives. A total of 23 compounds were assessed for their inhibitory effects against Src kinase and their impact on cell proliferation in human colon adenocarcinoma (HT-29) and leukemia (CCRF-CEM) cell lines. Among the compounds tested, 2-chlorophenyl (4c), substituted chromenes exhibited inhibitory effects on Src kinase with IC_{50} value 11.1 µM. Compound 12 demonstrated relative selectivity against Src kinase compared to other selected kinases such as epidermal growth factor receptor (EGFR), C-terminal Src kinase (Csk), and lymphocyte-specific protein tyrosine kinase (Lck) (Fallah-Tafti et al., 2011).

Tintori et al. worked on the optimization of pyrazolo[3,4-d]pyrimidines as potent c-Src inhibitors active against neuroblastoma. c-Src, a member of the Src-family kinases, is known to be overexpressed and hyperactivated in various cancer cells, making it an attractive target for solid tumor therapy. The study employs a multidisciplinary drug discovery approach to enhance the lead compound 3, a dual c-Src/Abl inhibitor. By utilizing the X-ray crystal structure of c-Src in complex with compound 3, Monte Carlo free energy perturbation calculations guide the design of improved c-Src inhibitors. Computational analysis suggests that the addition of a meta hydroxyl group on the C4 anilino ring would be highly beneficial, leading to enhanced activity. Based on these findings, a series of inhibitors incorporating the recommended structural modification are synthesized. The synthesized inhibitors exhibit increased potency compared to the lead compound 3. Notably, the most promising compound was Compound 13 which having high potency to inhibit bot c-Src as well as Abl with IC_{50} of 0.01 and 0.12 µM, respectively (Tintori et al., 2015).

Jin-gui Ma et al. focused on the identification and evaluation of Compound 14, a potential inhibitor of Src kinase, for the treatment of human breast cancer. Src kinase plays a critical role in tumor progression and metastasis, making it an attractive target for breast cancer therapy. Through a comprehensive approach involving combinatorial library design, virtual screening, chemical synthesis, and high-throughput screening, the researchers developed compound 14, a novel inhibitor based on a 6-hydrazinopurine scaffold. Compound 14 exhibited selective inhibition of c-Src kinase, specifically targeting its ATP-binding site. Effect of compound 14 on the activity of a panel of tyrosine kinases with IC_{50} was 0.38 and 1.98 µM for c-Src and Abl, respectively (Ma et al., 2011).

Laurent F. Hennequin et al. investigated a novel and highly selective dual-specific c-Src/Abl kinase inhibitor, named AZD0530. The study focused on a subseries of C-5-substituted anilinoquinazolines that demonstrated high affinity and specificity for the tyrosine kinase domain of c-Src and Abl enzymes. The compounds displayed remarkable selectivity for

Src family kinases (SFKs) and exhibited favorable pharmacokinetics. AZD0530 which is compound number 15 was effectively inhibited tumor growth in preclinical models with enzyme inhibition activity of IC_{50} was 0.0027 µM showed promising results in an aggressive orthotopic model of human pancreatic cancer. These findings highlight the potential of AZD0530 as a valuable therapeutic option for targeting c-Src and Abl kinases in cancer treatment (Hennequin et al., 2006) (Fig. 5.5).

Alessio Molinari et al. conducted an efficient optimization study to develop pyrazolopyrimidine derivatives as inhibitors of c-Src kinase for the treatment of neuroblastoma. The proto-oncogene c-Src is a nonreceptor tyrosine kinase that plays a crucial role in regulating cellular processes such as adhesion, differentiation, and survival. Aberrant activation of c-Src has been observed in various tumors, including neuroblastoma, a leading cause of infant neoplasia-related mortality. Previous work by the authors identified a significant group of pyrazolopyrimidines that showed inhibitory activity against c-Src. Notably, some of these derivatives also demonstrated efficacy against the SH-SY5Y neuroblastoma cell line. Building upon their prior findings, the researchers performed Free Energy Perturbation/Monte Carlo calculations and conducted an optimization study, leading to the identification of a novel series of derivatives. Compound 16 exhibited nanomolar Ki values against c-Src, demonstrated antiproliferative activity against SH-SY5Y cells, and possessed favorable absorption, distribution, metabolism, and excretion (ADME) profiles (Molinari et al., 2018).

Leo Widler et al. focused on the synthesis and characterization of a novel class of inhibitors targeting the tyrosine kinase pp60c-Src. The researchers prepared compound 17 using a-bromoacetophenones as starting materials. These compounds demonstrated potent inhibitory activity against the tyrosine kinase c-Src, while exhibiting good specificity toward other tyrosine kinases, including EGF-R and v-Abl. The findings suggest that these compounds have the potential to serve as effective and selective inhibitors of c-Src, offering promising prospects for further development in the field of targeted cancer therapy (Missbach et al., 2000).

Hyun-Jin Nam et al. performed a study by investigating the potential of saracatinib, a c-Src/Abl kinase inhibitor, in the treatment of gastric cancer. Their research focuses on evaluating the inhibitory effects of saracatinib on the growth and migration of gastric cancer cell lines. Through blocking multiple signaling pathways associated with tumorigenesis, saracatinib demonstrates specific inhibition of Src kinase activity. The treatment induces G1 cell cycle arrest and apoptosis, with the proapoptotic protein Bim playing a crucial role. The study also explores the synergistic effects of saracatinib in combination with other targeted agents and chemotherapeutic drugs. In a xenograft model, saracatinib combined with compound 18 exhibits enhanced antitumor activity. These findings highlight the potential of saracatinib as a promising therapeutic strategy for gastric cancer, specifically targeting Src kinase activity (Nam et al., 2013).

Martin Missbach explored a novel class of inhibitors called Ð5,7-Diphenyl-pyrrolopyrimidines and their efficacy as potent inhibitors of the tyrosine kinase c-Src. The researchers discovered that these inhibitors demonstrate high potency (IC50 < 50 nM) and selectivity against a range of tyrosine kinases. The substitution pattern on the phenyl rings plays a crucial role in determining both potency and specificity, offering a means to modulate cellular activity. Through an optimization strategy, the study successfully developed highly potent and remarkably selective inhibitors of c-Src kinase in vitro. These inhibitors effectively block

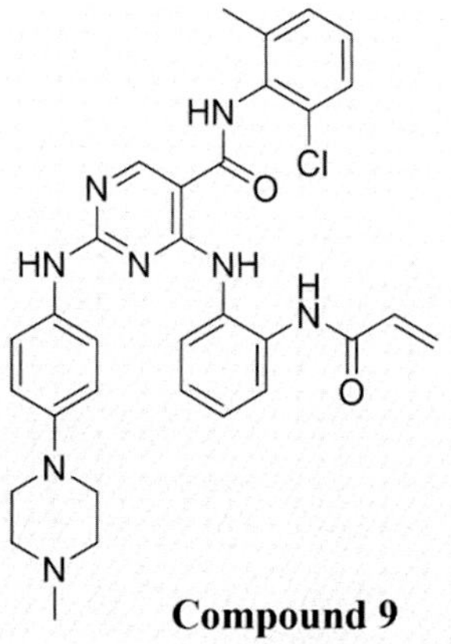

Compound 9
IC_{50} = 3 nM for c-Src

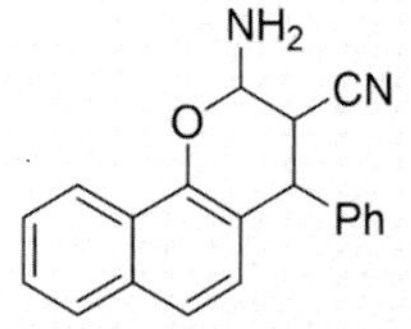

Compound 10
IC_{50} = 28.1 μM for c-Src

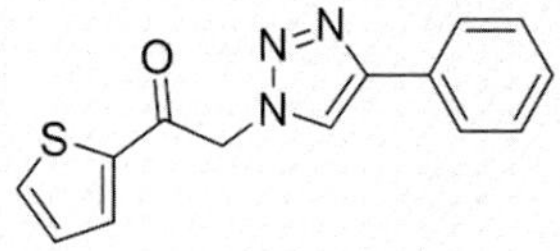

Compound 11
IC_{50} = 32.5 μM for c-Src

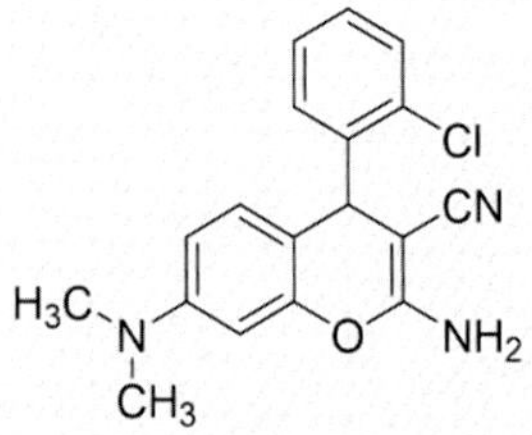

Compound 12
IC_{50} = 11.1 μM for c-Src

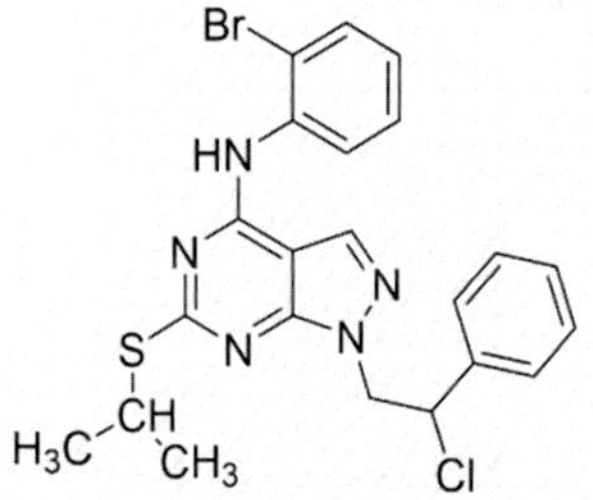

Compound 13
IC_{50} = 0.01 & 0.12 μM for c-Src & Abl

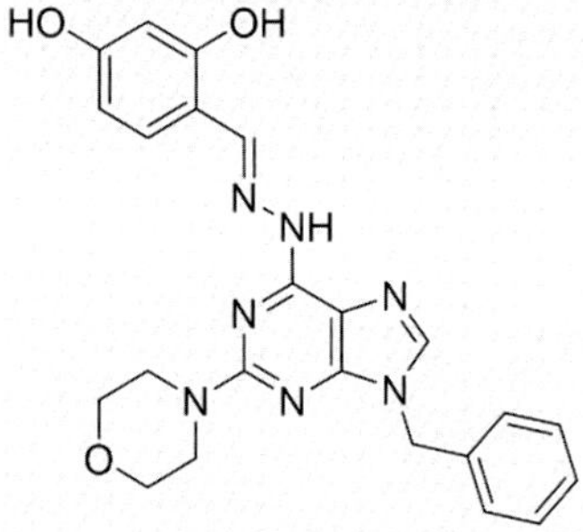

Compound 14
IC_{50} = 0.38 & 1.98 μM for c-Src & Abl

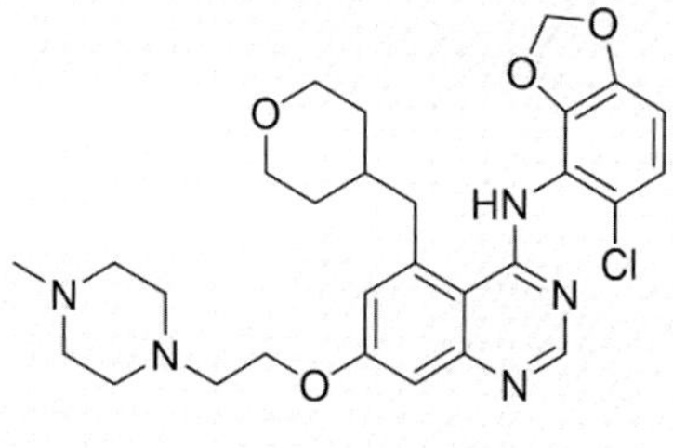

Compound 15
IC_{50} = 0.0027 μM for c-Src/Abl

FIGURE 5.5 Compounds 9–15 showing anticancer activity by inhibiting c-Src/Abl kinase inhibitor.

c-Src-mediated phosphorylation of intracellular substrates within intact cells. Furthermore, the introduction of polar substituents at the phenyl ring in position 7 of the compound 19 enhances the potency of c-Src inhibition in enzyme assays. Additionally, the incorporation of substituted ethylamine side chains improves cellular potency. Overall, this study underscores the potential of substituted compound 19 as a novel and highly potent class of inhibitors for the tyrosine kinase c-Src. These findings provide valuable insights for the development of targeted therapeutic strategies aimed at modulating c-Src-mediated signaling pathways in various disease contexts (Missbach et al., 2000).

Xin Cao et al. designed and synthesized 7-alkoxy-4-heteroarylamino-3-quinolinecarbonitriles as dual inhibitors of c-Src kinase and nitric oxide synthase (iNOS) in tumorigenesis. The compounds were assessed for their ability to inhibit both enzymes and block cancer-related signaling pathways. Most compounds demonstrated potent dual inhibition and displayed significant activity against various cancer cell lines. Notably, Compound 20 (CPU−Y020) exhibited remarkable efficacy, with IC50 values of 6.58 and 7.61 µM against HT-29 (colon cancer) and HepG2 (liver cancer) cell lines, respectively. This study highlights the potential of these compounds for targeted cancer therapy (Cao, You, Li, Guo, et al., 2008).

Eva Altmann et al. examined a new class of inhibitors known as 7-Heterocyclyl-5-aryl-pyrrolopyrimidines. These compounds demonstrate high potency and selectivity as inhibitors of the tyrosine kinase pp60c-Src. Specifically, compound 21 exhibits potent and selective inhibitory activity against pp60c-Src, making them promising candidates for targeted therapeutic interventions. This study contributes valuable insights into the development of potent and selective inhibitors for targeting c-Src and related signaling pathways (Altmann et al., 2001).

Alan J. Kraker et al. investigated the biochemical and cellular effects of c-Src kinase-selective pyridopyrimidine tyrosine kinase inhibitors. These compounds demonstrate potent inhibition of c-Src kinase, with IC50 values below 10 nM and selectivity ranging from 6 to 100-fold compared to other tyrosine kinases. They effectively inhibit the growth of human colon tumor cells, both in culture and in soft agar. The inhibitors also hinder the phosphorylation of c-Src cellular substrates, such as paxillin, p130cas, and Stat3. Importantly, the compounds do not inhibit the autophosphorylation of EGFr or PDGFr tyrosine kinases, indicating their selectivity in cellular environments. Overall, these findings demonstrate that the described compound 22 inhibitors are potent and selective inhibitors of c-Src tyrosine kinase. Their antiproliferative effects on tumor cells align with the inhibition of c-Src activity (Kraker et al., 2000).

The study conducted by Harunobu Mukaiyama et al. focuses on novel pyrazolo[1,5-a]pyrimidines as inhibitors of c-Src kinase. The aim was to enhance the potency of the c-Src inhibitor while addressing its hERG liability. By replacing the ethylenediamino group with an amino alcohol group at the 7-position, the blockade of the delayed cardiac current rectifier K+ (IKr) channel was successfully overcome. Additionally, modifications to the substituents at the 5-position and the side chain groups on the amino alcohols at the 7-position resulted in improved intracellular c-Src inhibitory activity and increased penetration into the central nervous system (CNS) of the compound 23 and make it more potent. Notably, compound 23 exhibited significant efficacy in vivo in a middle cerebral artery occlusion model (Mukaiyama et al., 2008) (Fig. 5.6).

Bernard Barlaam et al. designed and synthesized a novel series of new heterocyclic analogs of 4-(2-chloro-5-methoxyanilino) quinazolines as highly potent and selective c-Src kinase inhibitors. These compounds feature 5,7-disubstituted quinazoline structures with 4-heteroaryl substituents such as 2-pyridinylamine or 2-pyrazinylamine. Through their evaluation, compounds 24 emerged as remarkable inhibitors with sub-0.1 μM potency in a c-Src-driven cell proliferation assay. Moreover, these compounds exhibited favorable pharmacokinetic profiles suitable for oral dosing in rat models. This study highlights the potential of these novel analogs as effective c-Src kinase inhibitors (Barlaam et al., 2005).

Isabelle Pevet et al. developed and synthesized an innovative series of thieno[2,3-b]pyridine derivatives as novel c-Src inhibitors. With the aim of targeting the c-Src nonreceptor tyrosine kinase, known for its involvement in tumor progression, the researchers designed a series of compounds based on a 3-amino-thieno[2,3-b]pyridine identified during a high-throughput screening campaign. Out of which compound 25 was the led compound. Through molecular modeling and X-ray studies, they gained insights into the ligand orientation and interactions within the ATP hydrophobic pocket of c-Src. This knowledge guided the design and synthesis of new ligands with potent enzymatic and c-Src inhibitory activity. The findings provide valuable information about the impact of substituents on the thienopyridine ring and other aromatic moieties in their interaction with the enzyme (Pevet et al., 2011).

Xin Cao et al. designed and synthesized a novel series of 7-alkoxy-4-heteroarylamino-3-cyanoquinolines. The goal was to develop dual inhibitors targeting c-Src and iNOS, both crucial enzymes in tumorigenesis. Through comprehensive in vitro assays, the researchers assessed enzyme inhibition and antiproliferative activity. The results demonstrated significant inhibitory effects on both c-Src and iNOS, with compound 26 exhibiting the most potent inhibition, displaying IC50 values of 34.8 nM and 26.7 μM against the respective enzymes. Moreover, certain compounds displayed moderate antiproliferative activity against colon and liver cancer cell lines at 10 μM concentration (Cao, You, Li, Liu, et al., 2008).

Cao et al. designed and synthesized 7-alkoxy-4-heteroarylamino-3-quinolinecarbonitriles as dual inhibitors of c-Src kinase and nitric oxide synthase (iNOS). Both c-Src and iNOS are crucial regulatory enzymes in tumorigenesis, making them attractive targets for cancer therapy. The researchers designed and synthesized a series of compounds and evaluated their inhibitory effects on both enzymes through enzyme inhibition and antiproliferation assays in vitro. The results demonstrated that most of the compounds exhibited potent inhibition of c-Src and iNOS, with some showing significant activity against various cancer cell lines. Compound 27 (CPU—Y020) emerged as the most promising candidate, with impressive IC50 values of 6.58 and 7.61 μM against colon cancer (HT-29) and liver cancer (HepG2) cell

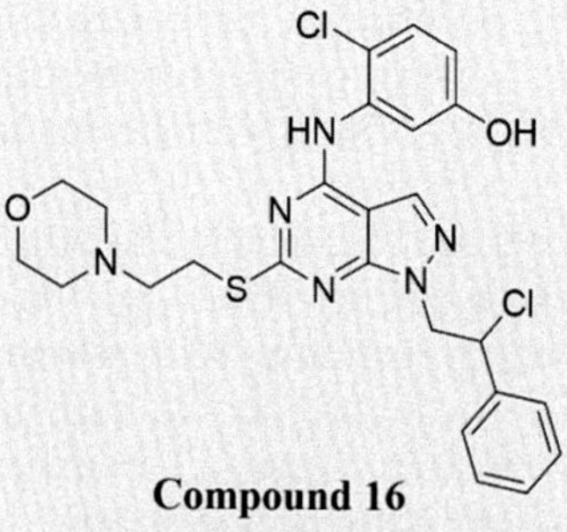

Compound 16
$IC_{50} = 0.0035 \ \mu M$ for c-Src

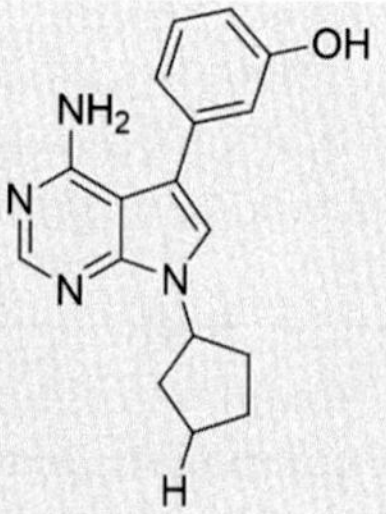

Compound 17
$IC_{50} = 0.001 \ \mu M$ for c-Src

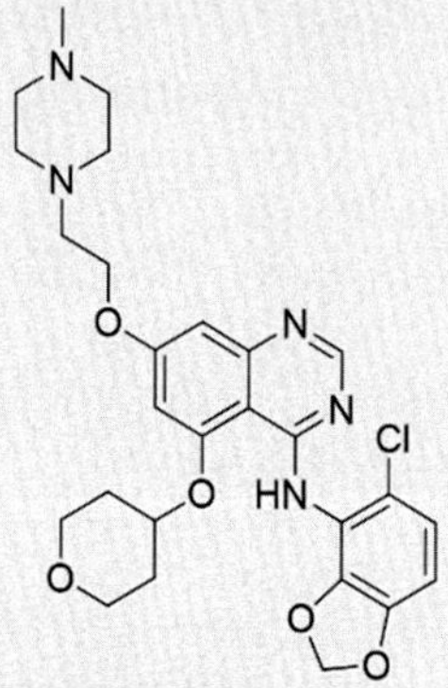

Compound 18
$IC_{50} = 0.18 \ \mu M$ for c-Src/Abl

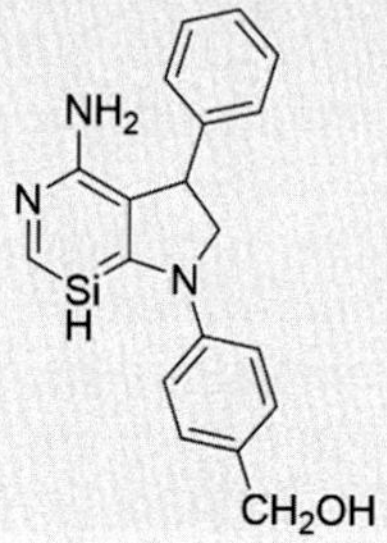

Compound 19
$IC_{50} = 0.02 \ \& 0.07 \ \mu M$ for c-Src/Abl

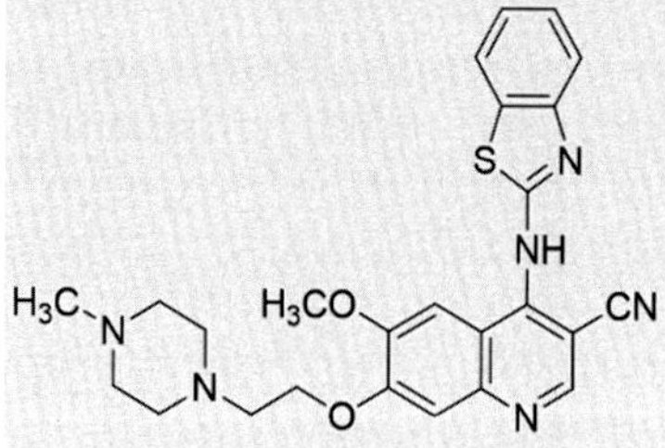

Compound 20
$IC_{50} = 9.23 \ M$ for c-Src

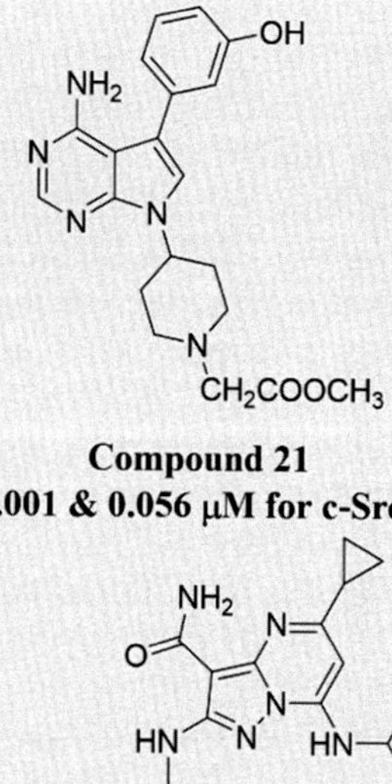

Compound 21
$IC_{50} = < 0.001 \ \& \ 0.056 \ \mu M$ for c-Src & Abl

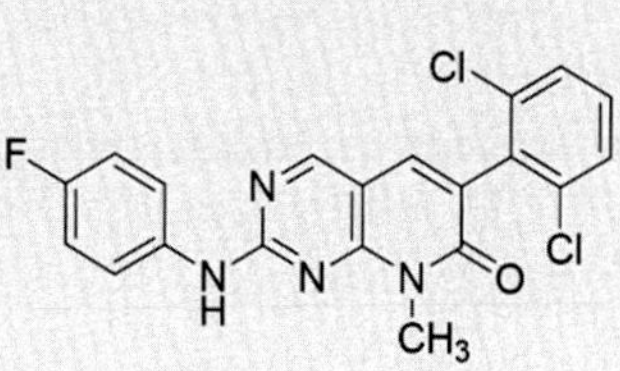

Compound 22
$IC_{50} = 32.9 \ \mu M$ for c-Src

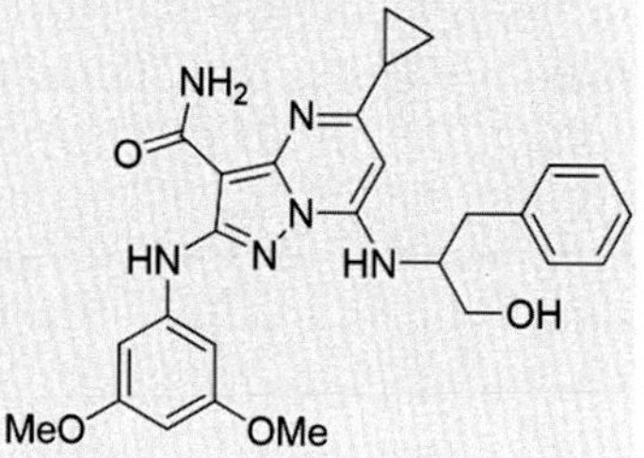

Compound 23
$IC_{50} = 0.003 \ \mu M$ for c-Src

FIGURE 5.6 Compounds 16–23 showing anticancer activity by inhibiting c-Src/Abl kinase inhibitor.

lines, respectively. These findings indicate the potential of these dual inhibitors for targeted cancer therapy (Cao, You, Li, Guo, et al., 2008).

Sebla Dincer et al. synthesized novel derivatives of Pyrrolo[2,3-d]pyrimidine and evaluated inhibitors of Src family-selective tyrosine kinases (SFKs), including Fyn, Lyn, Hck, and c-Src. The compounds displayed moderate inhibitory activity against the tested SFK enzymes, although their potency was lower compared to reference inhibitors such as PP2, A-419259, and CGP77675. Compound 5, specifically N-((2-amino-4-oxo-4,7-dihydro-3H-pyrrolo[2,3-d]pyrimidin-5-yl)methyl)-4-(3,4-dimethoxyphenyl)butanamide, exhibited slight inhibition against Fyn, Lyn, and c-Src, while no inhibitory effects were observed on Hck. Docking studies revealed favorable interactions between compound 28 and the active sites of Fyn and c-Src, surpassing the interactions observed with the reference compounds PP2 and CGP77675, respectively. These findings provide valuable insights into the binding mode of the compounds with SFK enzymes (Dincer et al., 2013).

Hany E. A. Ahmed et al. conducted a study in which they synthesized new derivatives of 1H-benzo[f]chromene using heterocyclocondensation methods under the influence of microwave irradiation. The chemical structures of these compounds were determined based on spectroscopic data such as IR, 1H NMR, 13C NMR, 13C NMR-DEPT/APT, and MS. The antiproliferative activity of the synthesized compounds was evaluated against three cancer cell lines: MCF-7, HCT-116, and HepG-2, with Vinblastine and Doxorubicin used as reference drugs. The results demonstrated significant and selective cytotoxic activity of the tested compounds against the cancer cell lines, while exhibiting weak cytotoxicity on the HFL-1 line. This suggests the potential of these compounds as effective candidates for anticancer treatment. Two specific compounds, 4c and compound 29, were further investigated for their ability to inhibit the invasiveness of the MDA-MB-231 breast cancer cell line but the compound 29 was more potent. These compounds showed a reduced metastatic effect compared to the reference drug. The study also examined the apoptotic mechanistic pathway of the compounds, revealing enhanced Caspase 3/7 activity, which further supports their potential as promising anticancer agents (Ahmed et al., 2018).

Guo Hua Zeng et al. carried out a study that aimed to theoretically investigate the potential of pyrazolo[3,4-d]pyrimidine derivatives as dual inhibitors for c-Src and Abl kinases. The research aimed to develop a comprehensive understanding of the structure-activity relationship through three-dimensional quantitative structure-activity relationship (3D-QSAR) and docking studies. By employing these approaches, the binding orientations and conformations of 87 compounds interacting with both kinases were analyzed. The generated CoMFA and CoMSIA models demonstrated high predictive power, with significant values for q2 and R2, indicating their reliability. External validations further confirmed the robustness of the models. Out of all 87 compound, the lead compound was compound 30 which having more capability for inhibiting c-Src/Abl kinase (Zeng et al., 2014) (Fig. 5.7).

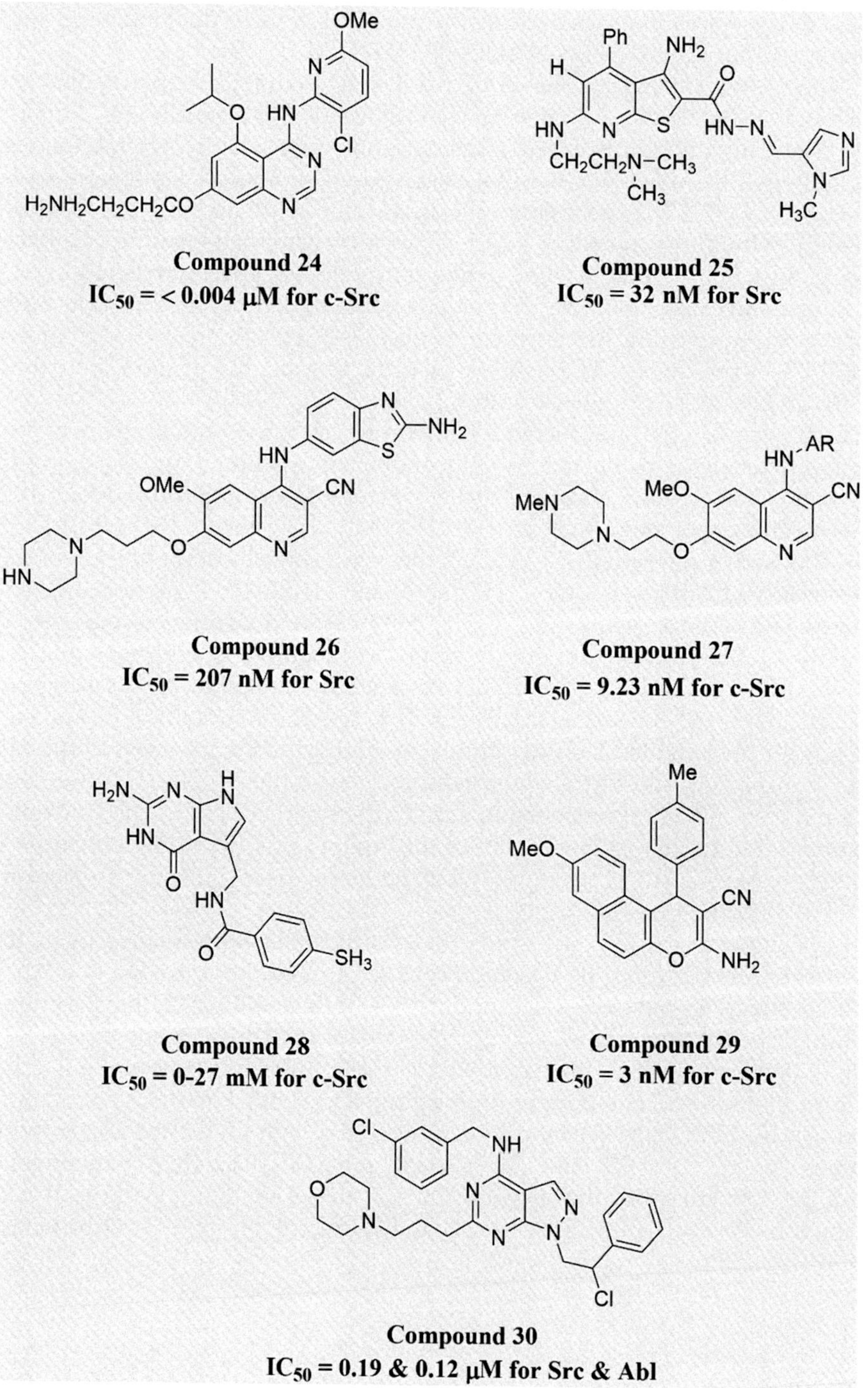

Compound 24
IC$_{50}$ = < 0.004 μM for c-Src

Compound 25
IC$_{50}$ = 32 nM for Src

Compound 26
IC$_{50}$ = 207 nM for Src

Compound 27
IC$_{50}$ = 9.23 nM for c-Src

Compound 28
IC$_{50}$ = 0-27 mM for c-Src

Compound 29
IC$_{50}$ = 3 nM for c-Src

Compound 30
IC$_{50}$ = 0.19 & 0.12 μM for Src & Abl

FIGURE 5.7   Compounds 24–30 showing anticancer activity by inhibiting c-Src/Abl kinase inhibitor.

References

Abdelall, E. K., Elshemy, H. A., Labib, M. B., & Mohamed, F. E. (2022). Characterization of novel heterocyclic compounds based on 4-aryl-4H-chromene scaffold as anticancer agents: Design, synthesis, antiprofilerative activity against resistant cancer cells, dual β-tubulin/c-Src inhibition, cell cycle arrest and apoptosis induction. *Bioorganic Chemistry, 120*, Article 105591.

Ahmed, H. E., El-Nassag, M. A., Hassan, A. H., Okasha, R. M., Ihmaid, S., Fouda, A. M., Afifi, T. H., Aljuhani, A., & El-Agrody, A. M. (2018). Introducing novel potent anticancer agents of 1H-benzo [f] chromene scaffolds, targeting c-Src kinase enzyme with MDA-MB-231 cell line anti-invasion effect. *Journal of Enzyme Inhibition and Medicinal Chemistry, 33*(1), 1074−1088.

Altmann, E., Missbach, M., Green, J., Šuša, M., Wagenknecht, H.-A., & Widler, L. (2001). 7-Pyrrolidinyl-and 7-piperidinyl-5-aryl-pyrrolo [2, 3-d] pyrimidines—potent inhibitors of the tyrosine kinase c-Src. *Bioorganic & Medicinal Chemistry Letters, 11*(6), 853−856.

Bapat, S., Viswanadh, N., Mujahid, M., Shirazi, A. N., Tiwari, R., Parang, K., Karthikeyan, M., Muthukrishnan, M., & Vyas, R. (2019). *Synthesis, biological evaluation and molecular modeling studies of novel chromone/aza-chromone fused α-aminophosphonates as src kinase inhibitors.*

Barlaam, B., Fennell, M., Germain, H., Green, T., Hennequin, L., Morgentin, R., Olivier, A., Plé, P., Vautier, M., & Costello, G. (2005). New heterocyclic analogues of 4-(2-chloro-5-methoxyanilino) quinazolines as potent and selective c-Src kinase inhibitors. *Bioorganic & Medicinal Chemistry Letters, 15*(24), 5446−5449.

Boczek, E. E., Luo, Q., Dehling, M., Röpke, M., Mader, S. L., Seidl, A., Kaila, V. R., & Buchner, J. (2019). Autophosphorylation activates c-Src kinase through global structural rearrangements. *Journal of Biological Chemistry, 294*(35), 13186−13197.

Brandvold, K. R., Steffey, M. E., Fox, C. C., & Soellner, M. B. (2012). Development of a highly selective c-Src kinase inhibitor. *ACS Chemical Biology, 7*(8), 1393−1398.

Brasher, B. B., Roumiantsev, S., & Van Etten, R. A. (2001). Mutational analysis of the regulatory function of the c-Abl Src homology 3 domain. *Oncogene, 20*(53), 7744−7752.

Cao, X., You, Q.-D., Li, Z.-Y., Guo, Q.-L., Shang, J., Yan, M., Chern, J.-W., & Chen, M.-L. (2008). Design and synthesis of 7-alkoxy-4-heteroarylamino-3-quinolinecarbonitriles as dual inhibitors of c-Src kinase and nitric oxide synthase. *Bioorganic & Medicinal Chemistry, 16*(11), 5890−5898.

Cao, X., You, Q.-D., Li, Z.-Y., Liu, X.-R., Xu, D., Guo, Q.-L., Shang, J., Chern, J.-W., & Chen, M.-L. (2008). The design, synthesis and biological evaluation of 7-alkoxy-4-heteroarylamino-3-cyanoquinolines as dual inhibitors of c-Src and iNOS. *Bioorganic & Medicinal Chemistry Letters, 18*(23), 6206−6209.

Chatain, N., Ziegler, P., Fahrenkamp, D., Jost, E., Moriggl, R., & Müller-Newen, G. (2013). Src family kinases mediate cytoplasmic retention of activated STAT5 in BCR−ABL-positive cells. *Oncogene, 32*(31), 3587−3597.

Chhikara, B. S., Ashraf, S., Mozaffari, S., St Jeans, N., Mandal, D., Tiwari, R. K., Ul-Haq, Z., & Parang, K. (2020). Phenylpyrazalopyrimidines as tyrosine kinase inhibitors: Synthesis, antiproliferative activity, and molecular simulations. *Molecules, 25*(9), 2135.

Cipak, L. (2022). Protein kinases: Function, substrates, and implication in diseases. *International Journal of Molecular Sciences, 23*, 3560.

Daday, C., de Buhr, S., Mercadante, D., & Gräter, F. (2022). Mechanical force can enhance c-Src kinase activity by impairing autoinhibition. *Biophysical Journal, 121*(5), 684−691.

Danson, S., Mulvey, M. R., Turner, L., Horsman, J., Escott, K., Coleman, R. E., Ahmedzai, S. H., Bennett, M. I., & Andrew, D. (2019). An exploratory randomized-controlled trial of the efficacy of the Src-kinase inhibitor saracatinib as a novel analgesic for cancer-induced bone pain. *Journal of Bone Oncology, 19*, Article 100261.

Daud, A. I., Krishnamurthi, S. S., Saleh, M. N., Gitlitz, B. J., Borad, M. J., Gold, P. J., Chiorean, E. G., Springett, G. M., Abbas, R., & Agarwal, S. (2012). Phase I study of bosutinib, a src/abl tyrosine kinase inhibitor, administered to patients with advanced solid TumorsPhase I study of bosutinib in advanced solid tumors. *Clinical Cancer Research, 18*(4), 1092−1100.

Decourtye-Espiard, L., & Guilford, P. (2023). The chemoprevention of hereditary diffuse gastric cancer. In *Hereditary gastric and breast cancer syndrome: CDH1: One genotype with multiple phenotypes* (pp. 321−341). Springer.

Dincer, S., Cetin, K. T., Onay-Besikci, A., & Ölgen, S. (2013). Synthesis, biological evaluation and docking studies of new pyrrolo [2, 3-d] pyrimidine derivatives as Src family-selective tyrosine kinase inhibitors. *Journal of Enzyme Inhibition and Medicinal Chemistry, 28*(5), 1080−1087.

Dölker, N., Gorna, M. W., Sutto, L., Torralba, A. S., Superti-Furga, G., & Gervasio, F. L. (2014). The SH2 domain regulates c-Abl kinase activation by a cyclin-like mechanism and remodulation of the hinge motion. *PLoS Computational Biology, 10*(10), Article e1003863.

Dorff, T. B., Quinn, D. I., Pinski, J. K., Goldkorn, A., Sadeghi, S., Tsao-Wei, D., Groshen, S., Kuhn, P., & Gross, M. E. (2019). Randomized phase II trial of abiraterone alone or with dasatinib in men with metastatic castration-resistant prostate cancer (mCRPC). *Clinical Genitourinary Cancer, 17*(4), 241–247.

Dosch, A. R., Dai, X., Gaidarski, A. A., III, Shi, C., Castellanos, J. A., VanSaun, M. N., Merchant, N. B., & Nagathihalli, N. S. (2019). Src kinase inhibition restores E-cadherin expression in dasatinib-sensitive pancreatic cancer cells. *Oncotarget, 10*(10), 1056.

Dottorando, F. C. & Di Maria, S. Development of novel pyrazolo [3, 4-d] pyrimidines as anticancer agents: Synthesis of potent c-src/abl inhibitors.

Du, G., Rao, S., Gurbani, D., Henning, N. J., Jiang, J., Che, J., Yang, A., Ficarro, S. B., Marto, J. A., & Aguirre, A. J. (2020). Structure-based design of a potent and selective covalent inhibitor for SRC kinase that targets a P-loop cysteine. *Journal of Medicinal Chemistry, 63*(4), 1624–1641.

Elaskalani, O., Gilmore, G., Hagger, M., Baker, R. I., & Metharom, P. (2022). Adenosine 2A receptor activation amplifies ibrutinib antiplatelet effect; implications in chronic lymphocytic leukemia. *Cancers, 14*(23), 5750.

Fallah-Tafti, A., Tiwari, R., Nasrolahi Shirazi, A., Akbarzadeh, T., Mandal, D., Shafiee, A., Parang, K., & Foroumadi, A. (2011). 4-Aryl-4H-chromene-3-carbonitrile derivatives: Evaluation of src kinase inhibitory and anticancer activities. *Medicinal Chemistry, 7*(5), 466–472.

Ferrero, G., Velazquez, F., & Caputto, B. (2012). The kinase c-Src and the phosphatase TC45 coordinately regulate c-Fos tyrosine phosphorylation and c-Fos phospholipid synthesis activation capacity. *Oncogene, 31*(28), 3381–3391.

Gilburt, J. A., Girvan, P., Blagg, J., Ying, L., & Dodson, C. A. (2019). Ligand discrimination between active and inactive activation loop conformations of Aurora-A kinase is unmodified by phosphorylation. *Chemical Science, 10*(14), 4069–4076.

Greuber, E. K., Smith-Pearson, P., Wang, J., & Pendergast, A. M. (2013). Role of ABL family kinases in cancer: From leukaemia to solid tumours. *Nature Reviews Cancer, 13*(8), 559–571.

Gul, M., Navid, A., Fakhar, M., & Rashid, S. (2023). SHP-1 tyrosine phosphatase binding to c-src kinase phosphor-dependent conformations: A comparative structural framework. *PLoS One, 18*(1), Article e0278448.

Hantschel, O., & Superti-Furga, G. (2004). Regulation of the c-Abl and Bcr–Abl tyrosine kinases. *Nature Reviews Molecular Cell Biology, 5*(1), 33–44.

Hennequin, L. F., Allen, J., Breed, J., Curwen, J., Fennell, M., Green, T. P., Lambert-van der Brempt, C., Morgentin, R., Norman, R. A., & Olivier, A. (2006). N-(5-Chloro-1, 3-benzodioxol-4-yl)-7-[2-(4-methylpiperazin-1-yl) ethoxy]-5-(tetrahydro-2 H-pyran-4-yloxy) quinazolin-4-amine, a novel, highly selective, orally available, dual-specific c-Src/Abl kinase inhibitor. *Journal of Medicinal Chemistry, 49*(22), 6465–6488.

Hermida-Prado, F., Villaronga, M.Á., Granda-Díaz, R., del-Río-Ibisate, N., Santos, L., Hermosilla, M. A., Oro, P., Allonca, E., Agorreta, J., & Garmendia, I. (2019). The SRC inhibitor dasatinib induces stem cell-like properties in head and neck cancer cells that are effectively counteracted by the mithralog EC-8042. *Journal of Clinical Medicine, 8*(8), 1157.

Jin, W. (2020). Regulation of Src family kinases during colorectal cancer development and its clinical implications. *Cancers, 12*(5), 1339.

Jones, R. J., Bahl, A., De Bono, J. S., Ralph, C., Elliott, T., Robinson, A., Westbury, C., Birtle, A. J., Staffurth, J. N., & Protheroe, A. (2021). SAPROCAN: Saracatinib (AZD0530) and docetaxel in metastatic, castrate-refractory prostate cancer (mCRPC)-A phase I/randomized phase II study by the United Kingdom National Cancer Research Institute Prostate Group. *American Society of Clinical Oncology, 39*, 107.

Karim, N. A., Ullah, A., Wang, H., Shoukier, M., Pulliam, S., Khaled, A., Patel, N., & Morris, J. C. (2022). A phase I study of the non-receptor kinase inhibitor bosutinib in combination with pemetrexed in patients with selected metastatic solid tumors. *Current Oncology, 29*(12), 9461–9473.

Karuppagounder, S. S., Wang, H., Kelly, T., Rush, R., Nguyen, R., Bisen, S., Yamashita, Y., Sloan, N., Dang, B., & Sigmon, A. (2023). The c-Abl inhibitor IkT-148009 suppresses neurodegeneration in mouse models of heritable and sporadic Parkinson's disease. *Science Translational Medicine, 15*(679), Article eabp9352.

Kasahara, K., Re, S., Nawrocki, G., Oshima, H., Mishima-Tsumagari, C., Miyata-Yabuki, Y., Kukimoto-Niino, M., Yu, I., Shirouzu, M., & Feig, M. (2021). Reduced efficacy of a Src kinase inhibitor in crowded protein solution. *Nature Communications, 12*(1), 4099.

Kato, S., Jardim, D. L., Johnson, F. M., Subbiah, V., Piha-Paul, S., Tsimberidou, A. M., Falchook, G. S., Karp, D., Zinner, R., & Wheler, J. (2018). Phase I study of the combination of crizotinib (as a MET inhibitor) and dasatinib (as a c-SRC inhibitor) in patients with advanced cancer. *Investigational New Drugs, 36*, 416−423.

Kennedy, L. C., & Gadi, V. (2018). Dasatinib in breast cancer: Src-ing for response in all the wrong kinases. *Annals of Translational Medicine, 6*(Suppl. 1).

Kraker, A. J., Hartl, B. G., Amar, A. M., Barvian, M. R., Showalter, H. H., & Moore, C. W. (2000). Biochemical and cellular effects of c-Src kinase-selective pyrido [2, 3-d] pyrimidine tyrosine kinase inhibitors. *Biochemical Pharmacology, 60*(7), 885−898.

Kruewel, T., Schenone, S., Radi, M., Maga, G., Rohrbeck, A., Botta, M., & Borlak, J. (2010). Molecular characterization of c-Abl/c-Src kinase inhibitors targeted against murine tumour progenitor cells that express stem cell markers. *PLoS One, 5*(11), Article e14143.

Kumar, D., Reddy, V. B., Kumar, A., Mandal, D., Tiwari, R., & Parang, K. (2011). Click chemistry inspired one-pot synthesis of 1, 4-disubstituted 1, 2, 3-triazoles and their Src kinase inhibitory activity. *Bioorganic & Medicinal Chemistry Letters, 21*(1), 449−452.

Lang, L., Shay, C., Zhao, X., Xiong, Y., Wang, X., & Teng, Y. (2019). Simultaneously inactivating Src and AKT by saracatinib/capivasertib co-delivery nanoparticles to improve the efficacy of anti-Src therapy in head and neck squamous cell carcinoma. *Journal of Hematology & Oncology, 12*, 1−14.

Leak, S., Horne, G. A., & Copland, M. (2023). Targeting BCR-ABL1-positive leukaemias, a review article. *Cambridge Prisms: Precision Medicine*, 1−15.

Lee, S., Park, S., Ryu, J.-S., Kang, J., Kim, I., Son, S., Lee, B.-S., Kim, C.-H., & Kim, Y. S. (2022). c-Src inhibitor PP2 inhibits head and neck cancer progression through regulation of the epithelial−mesenchymal transition. *Experimental Biology and Medicine, 248*, 492−500.

Levinson, N. M., Kuchment, O., Shen, K., Young, M. A., Koldobskiy, M., Karplus, M., Cole, P. A., & Kuriyan, J. (2006). A Src-like inactive conformation in the abl tyrosine kinase domain. *PLoS Biology, 4*(5), e144.

Li, X., Wang, F., Ren, M., Du, M., & Zhou, J. (2019). The effects of c-Src kinase on EMT signaling pathway in human lens epithelial cells associated with lens diseases. *BMC Ophthalmology, 19*(1), 1−10.

Lu, F.-T., Luo, F., Qiu, M.-Z., Cao, J.-X., Luo, Q.-Y., Yang, D.-J., & Zhao, H.-Y. (2022). SRC inhibitor saracatinib enhances efficacy of PD-1/PD-L1 immune checkpoint blockade in non-small cell lung cancer. *Cancer Research, 82*(12_Suppl. ment), 6094-6094.

Ma, J.-g., Huang, H., Chen, S.-m., Chen, Y., Xin, X.-l., Lin, L.-p., Ding, J., Liu, H., & Meng, L.-h. (2011). PH006, a novel and selective Src kinase inhibitor, suppresses human breast cancer growth and metastasis in vitro and in vivo. *Breast Cancer Research and Treatment, 130*, 85−96.

Mashimo, K., Tsubaki, M., Takeda, T., Asano, R., Jinushi, M., Imano, M., Satou, T., Sakaguchi, K., & Nishida, S. (2019). RANKL-induced c-Src activation contributes to conventional anti-cancer drug resistance and dasatinib overcomes this resistance in RANK-expressing multiple myeloma cells. *Clinical and Experimental Medicine, 19*, 133−141.

Matos, B., Howl, J., Jerónimo, C., & Fardilha, M. (2021). Modulation of serine/threonine-protein phosphatase 1 (PP1) complexes: A promising approach in cancer treatment. *Drug Discovery Today, 26*(11), 2680−2698.

McClendon, C. J., & Miller, W. T. (2020). Structure, function, and regulation of the SRMS tyrosine kinase. *International Journal of Molecular Sciences, 21*(12), 4233.

Mingione, V. R., Paung, Y., Outhwaite, I. R., & Seeliger, M. A. (2023). Allosteric regulation and inhibition of protein kinases. *Biochemical Society Transactions, 51*(1), 373−385.

Missbach, M., Altmann, E., Widler, L., Šuša, M., Buchdunger, E., Mett, H., Meyer, T., & Green, J. (2000). Substituted 5, 7-diphenyl-pyrrolo [2, 3d] pyrimidines: Potent inhibitors of the tyrosine kinase c-src. *Bioorganic & Medicinal Chemistry Letters, 10*(9), 945−949.

Molinari, A., Fallacara, A. L., Di Maria, S., Zamperini, C., Poggialini, F., Musumeci, F., Schenone, S., Angelucci, A., Colapietro, A., & Crespan, E. (2018). Efficient optimization of pyrazolo [3, 4-d] pyrimidines derivatives as c-Src kinase inhibitors in neuroblastoma treatment. *Bioorganic & Medicinal Chemistry Letters, 28*(21), 3454−3457.

Morris, P. G., Rota, S., Cadoo, K., Zamora, S., Patil, S., D'Andrea, G., Gilewski, T., Bromberg, J., Dang, C., & Dickler, M. (2018). Phase II study of paclitaxel and dasatinib in metastatic breast cancer. *Clinical Breast Cancer, 18*(5), 387−394.

Mukaiyama, H., Nishimura, T., Kobayashi, S., Komatsu, Y., Kikuchi, S., Ozawa, T., Kamada, N., & Ohnota, H. (2008). Novel pyrazolo [1, 5-a] pyrimidines as c-Src kinase inhibitors that reduce IKr channel blockade. *Bioorganic & Medicinal Chemistry, 16*(2), 909−921.

Musumeci, F., Schenone, S., Brullo, C., & Botta, M. (2012). An update on dual Src/Abl inhibitors. *Future Medicinal Chemistry, 4*(6), 799–822.

Nam, H.-J., Im, S.-A., Oh, D.-Y., Elvin, P., Kim, H.-P., Yoon, Y.-K., Min, A., Song, S.-H., Han, S.-W., & Kim, T.-Y. (2013). Antitumor activity of saracatinib (AZD0530), a c-src/abl kinase inhibitor, alone or in combination with chemotherapeutic agents in gastric CancerAntitumor effects of saracatinib in gastric cancer. *Molecular Cancer Therapeutics, 12*(1), 16–26.

Oswald, A. J., Symeonides, S. N., Wheatley, D., Chan, S., Brunt, A. M., McAdam, K., Schmid, P., Waters, S., Poole, C., & Twelves, C. (2023). Aromatase inhibition plus/minus src inhibitor saracatinib (AZD0530) in advanced breast cancer therapy (ARISTACAT): A randomised phase II study. *Breast Cancer Research and Treatment, 199*(1), 35–46.

Panjarian, S., Iacob, R. E., Chen, S., Engen, J. R., & Smithgall, T. E. (2013). Structure and dynamic regulation of Abl kinases. *Journal of Biological Chemistry, 288*(8), 5443–5450.

Patwardhan, P., & Resh, M. D. (2010). Myristoylation and membrane binding regulate c-Src stability and kinase activity. *Molecular and Cellular Biology, 30*(17), 4094–4107.

Peng, J., Zeng, Y., Hu, X., Huang, S., Gao, X., Tian, D., Tian, S., Qiu, L., Liu, J., & Dong, R. (2022). KC-180-2 exerts anti-SCLC effects via dual inhibition of tubulin polymerization and src signaling. *ACS Omega, 7*(36), 32164–32175.

Pevet, I., Brulé, C., Tizot, A., Gohier, A., Cruzalegui, F., Boutin, J. A., & Goldstein, S. (2011). Synthesis and pharmacological evaluation of thieno [2, 3-b] pyridine derivatives as novel c-Src inhibitors. *Bioorganic & Medicinal Chemistry, 19*(8), 2517–2528.

Poulin, B., Sekiya, F., & Rhee, S. G. (2005). Intramolecular interaction between phosphorylated tyrosine-783 and the C-terminal Src homology 2 domain activates phospholipase C-γ1. *Proceedings of the National Academy of Sciences, 102*(12), 4276–4281.

Qian, X.-L., Zhang, J., Li, P.-Z., Lang, R.-G., Li, W.-D., Sun, H., Liu, F.-F., Guo, X.-J., Gu, F., & Fu, L. (2017). Dasatinib inhibits c-src phosphorylation and prevents the proliferation of Triple-Negative Breast Cancer (TNBC) cells which overexpress Syndecan-Binding Protein (SDCBP). *PLoS One, 12*(1). e0171169.

Rafinejad, A., Fallah-Tafti, A., Tiwari, R., Shirazi, A. N., Mandal, D., Shafiee, A., Parang, K., Foroumadi, A., & Akbarzadeh, T. (2012). 4-Aryl-4 H-naphthopyrans derivatives: One-pot synthesis, evaluation of src kinase inhibitory and anti-proliferative activities. *Daru Journal of Pharmaceutical Sciences, 20*, 1–7.

Ramadan, M., Elshaier, Y, A. M. M., Aly, A. A., Abdel-Aziz, M., Fathy, H. M., Brown, A. B., Pridgen, J. R., Dalby, K. N., & Kaoud, T. S. (2021). Development of 2′-aminospiro [pyrano[3,2–c]quinoline]-3′-carbonitrile derivatives as non-ATP competitive Src kinase inhibitors that suppress breast cancer cell migration and proliferation. *Bioorganic Chemistry, 116*, Article 105344.

Roskoski, R., Jr. (2005). Src kinase regulation by phosphorylation and dephosphorylation. *Biochemical and Biophysical Research Communications, 331*(1), 1–14.

Roskoski, R., Jr. (2015). Src protein-tyrosine kinase structure, mechanism, and small molecule inhibitors. *Pharmacological Research, 94*, 9–25.

Seeliger, M. A., Ranjitkar, P., Kasap, C., Shan, Y., Shaw, D. E., Shah, N. P., Kuriyan, J., & Maly, D. J. (2009). Equally potent inhibition of c-Src and Abl by compounds that recognize inactive kinase conformations. *Cancer Research, 69*(6), 2384–2392.

Shaul, Y. (2000). c-Abl: Activation and nuclear targets. *Cell Death and Differentiation, 7*(1), 10–16.

Te Boekhorst, V., & Friedl, P. (2016). Plasticity of cancer cell invasion—mechanisms and implications for therapy. *Advances in Cancer Research, 132*, 209–264.

Tintori, C., Fallacara, A. L., Radi, M., Zamperini, C., Dreassi, E., Crespan, E., Maga, G., Schenone, S., Musumeci, F., & Brullo, C. (2015). Combining X-ray crystallography and molecular modeling toward the optimization of pyrazolo [3, 4-d] pyrimidines as potent c-Src inhibitors active in vivo against neuroblastoma. *Journal of Medicinal Chemistry, 58*(1), 347–361.

Wang, L., Zheng, Y., Li, D., Yang, J., Lei, L., Yan, W., Zheng, W., Tang, M., Shi, M., & Zhang, R. (2021). Design, synthesis, and bioactivity evaluation of dual-target inhibitors of tubulin and SRC kinase guided by crystal structure. *Journal of Medicinal Chemistry, 64*(12), 8127–8141.

Young, M. A., Gonfloni, S., Superti-Furga, G., Roux, B., & Kuriyan, J. (2001). Dynamic coupling between the SH2 and SH3 domains of c-Src and Hck underlies their inactivation by C-terminal tyrosine phosphorylation. *Cell, 105*(1), 115–126.

Yuan, M., Song, Z.-H., Ying, M.-D., Zhu, H., He, Q.-J., Yang, B., & Cao, J. (2020). N-Myristoylation: From cell biology to translational medicine. *Acta Pharmacologica Sinica, 41*(8), 1005–1015.

Zeng, G. H., Fang, D. Q., Wu, W. J., Wang, J. P., Xie, W. G., Ma, S. J., Wu, J. H., & Shen, Y. (2014). Theoretical studies on pyrazolo [3, 4-d] pyrimidine derivatives as potent dual c-src/abl inhibitors using 3D-QSAR and docking approaches. *Molecular Informatics, 33*(3), 183–200.

Zhou, Y., Xu, X., Wang, F., He, H., Gong, G., Xiong, L., & Qi, B. (2020). Identification of novel quinoline analogues bearing thiazolidinones as potent kinase inhibitors for the treatment of colorectal cancer. *European Journal of Medicinal Chemistry, 204*, Article 112643.

Cyclin-dependent kinase 4 and 6 in cancer: Exploration of CDK4/6 inhibitors as anticancer agents

Nilay Kumar Nandi[1], Chahat[2,5], Rohit Bhatia[2], Gaurav Chauhan[4], Sourav Kalra[3] and Bhupinder Kumar[5]

[1]Meerut Institute of Engineering and Technology, Department of Pharmaceutical Technology, Meerut, Uttar Pradesh, India; [2]Department of Pharmaceutical Chemistry, ISF College of Pharmacy Moga, Moga, Punjab, India; [3]School of Pharmacy, Chitkara University, Himachal Pradesh, India; [4]School of Engineering and Sciences, Tecnologico de Monterrey, Monterrey, Nuevo León, Mexico; [5]Department of Pharmaceutical Sciences, HNB Garhwal University, Srinagar, Uttarakhand, India

1. Introduction

The cell cycle and its regulatory system are remarkably maintained in eukaryotic creatures (Harashima et al., 2013). There is plethora of information available on how the cell cycle is regulated in vertebrates, which demonstrated that the sequential activation and subsequent inactivation of both cell cycle progression and cell division. The cyclins and cyclin-dependent kinases (CDKs) are two main types of regulatory molecules in cell cycle (Otto & Sicinski, 2017; Reinhardt & Yaffe, 2013). Cyclins and CDKs, which operate as governing components, form heterodimers and subsequently enzymatic components when their cyclin partners CDKs are absent (Liu et al., 2021). Cyclins are governing elements that go through a phase of production and destruction during each cell cycle. Cyclins are classified into four groups based on the period of their manifestation and distinct roles in the cell cycle (Martínez-Alonso & Malumbres, 2020). G1/S cyclins, S cyclins, and M cyclins are the three main types, which are directly responsible for the regulation of cell cycle activities, while the fourth class, G1 cyclins, monitors cell cycle entrance in response to a stimulus (Roskoski, 2019). Growth factors are required during the G1 phase to begin and sustain the appropriate transition to the S phase. Growth factors increase the formation of G1 cyclins, illustrated by the cyclin D group of cyclins, that interact with CDK4/6 to trigger the formation of downstream effectors, among which is cyclin E, initially in the G1 phase (Goel et al., 2022; Wang, 2021). The elevated quantities of cyclin E (a G1/S cyclin) and the functioning of its companion, CDK2, push the cell beyond a constriction threshold in the cell cycle, following which the cell is irrevocably resolved to continue with DNA formation even if growth factors are removed (Rubin et al., 2020). As a result, the S and M cyclins are essential for the beginning of DNA replication and entry into mitosis, respectively (Liu et al., 2021; Tchakarska & Sola, 2020; Wood & Endicott, 2018). Various cyclin-CDK dimer combinations function at different stages of the cell cycle (Fischer et al., 2022). After binding cyclin processing, it phosphorylates a number of downstream target proteins, by either switching on or switching off them, which subsequently orchestrates the synchronized entrance into the next stage of the cell cycle (Bertoli et al., 2013; Joshi et al., 2017).

Protein kinases CDKs are proline-directed serine or threonine play a key role in cell cycle regulation progressions in concatenation (Düster et al., 2022). CDKs phosphorylate a diverse collection of proteins that begin and control the processes that distinguish every period of the cell cycle (Hochegger et al., 2008). A complex network of proteins and enzymes regulate the cyclic activity of CDKs largely by the transitory interaction of CDKs with cyclins that trigger and guide CDKs on particular substrates in a responsible way (Dai et al., 2019; Matthews et al., 2022). In addition, the numbers of the individual CDKs remain relatively stable throughout the cell cycle, but the numbers of the several cyclins fluctuate owing to periodic production and regulated breakdown (Zheng, 2022). Different genes in the genetic material encode CDKs, CDK-like enzymes, and enzymes with a "cyclin box" and hence characterized as cyclins, whereas only a small number are responsible for cell cycle progression (Loyer & Trembley, 2020; Malumbres, 2014; Roskoski, 2019).

Cell-cycle CDKs influence various additional functions in addition to their principal involvement in cell cycle regulation including the following:

- Transcription of genes (CDK2 and CDK1 activate the function of the transcription factors FOXM1 and FOXM2) (Liu et al., 2008),
- DNA healing (Cyclin E locates and stabilizes stalled replication forks, as well as increases checkpoint kinase 1 (CHK1) stimulation) (Lu et al., 2009),
- Cyclin D1 builds at the region of double-strand breaks (DSB) and facilitates DNA repair through homologous recombination with some other components).
- Metabolic process (CDK5 umpire glycogen metabolism in liver),
- Self-renewal of stem cells (Oct-4 expression may be monitored by CDK1),
- Imprinting regulation (CDK1 and CDK2 phosphorylate and promote the mutant factors regulator of zester homolog 2 (EZH2) and DNA methyl-transferase 1 (Dnmt1)).
- T-cells expansion (CDK4 and CDK6 impact T-cell initiation by modulating the nuclear factor of activated T cells (NFAT) proteins)
- Sperm production and neural activities (Besson et al., 2008; Malumbres & Barbacid, 2009).

Furthermore, several members of the CDK family contain proteins with activities beyond cell cycle progression, most of which are linked to the modulation of basal transcription. CDK3 is associated with RB-dependent G0 cell cycle outflow while CDK5 is

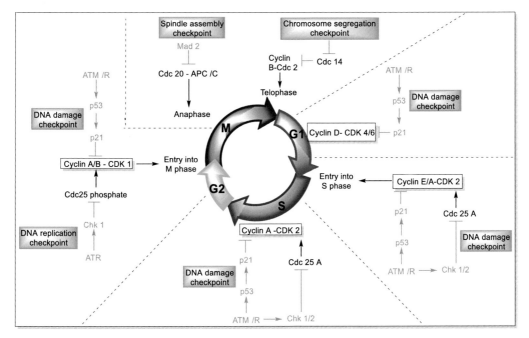

FIGURE 6.1 Function of CDKs and cyclins in cell cycle.

related to the control of various postmitotic occasions in specific cell types such as neurons. CDK7 is entangled in basal transcription regulation and is really a major aspect of the CAK complex, and CDK10 and CDK11 are concerned with transcription and splicing, as well as modulating G2/M transition. Lastly, CDK9 and CDK12 play key roles in the DNA injury response, which is connected to the cell cycle indirectly (Shen et al., 2019) (Fig. 6.1).

2. Different types of CDKs

The target protein identities are determined by the specific mix of cyclin-CDK groups. Unlike CDKs, which are generated continuously throughout the cell cycle; cyclins are generated and eliminated at certain periods of the cell cycle, which is frequently reliant on numerous signaling molecules. The cyclical nature of these molecules gives the expression to ensure the safeguards the orderly progression of the cell cycle.

CDK/Cyclin in cell cycle: CDKs may be divided into two distinct subgroups depending on their corollaries, see Table 6.1.

- CDKs involved in cell cycle (CDK1, CDK2, CDK4, CDK6)
- Transcriptional CDKs (mostly CDK7, CDK8, and CDK9).
- In terms of cyclins, components of the A (A1 and A2), B, D (D1, D2, and D3), and E (E1 and E2) categories of cyclins are fully engaged in the regulation of cell cycle progression.

TABLE 6.1 CDK with their biological role, its regulator cyclin, and its role in cancer.

CDK classes	Biological role	Cyclin partner	Function in type of cancer
CDK1	Control of the M phase of cell cycle (Chen et al., 2009)	Cyclin B/Cyclin A	Breast cancer, lung cancer, bladder cancer
CDK2	Control of G1-S phase of cell cycle (Russo et al., 1996)	Cyclin E	Breast cancer, melanoma
CDK2	Control of G1-S phase of cell cycle (Russo et al., 1996)	Cyclin A	Thymic carcinoma, lymphoma
CDK3	DNA damage Repair (Tomashevski et al., 2010)	Cyclin C	Renal cancer, lung cancer, liver cancer
CDK4	Control of G1 phase of cell cycle and Rb/E2F transcription (Aggarwal et al., 2010)	Cyclin D	Melanoma, breast cancer, osteosarcoma, skin cancer, bladder cancer, lung cancer
CDK5	Neuronal function (Lavoie & St-Pierre, 2011)	p35 and p39	Lung cancer, neuroblastoma
CDK6	Control of G1 phase of cell cycle and Rb/E2F transcription (Aggarwal et al., 2010)	Cyclin D	Breast cancer, skin cancer, bladder cancer, stomach cancer
CDK7	Activates CDKs kinase, involved in transcription (Fisher & Morgan, 1994)	Cyclin H	Breast cancer, lung cancer
CDK8	Role in Wnt/β-catenin pathway and RNAPII transcription (Dale et al., 2015; Firestein et al., 2008)	Cyclin C	—
CDK9	RNAPII transcription and repair DNA damage (David et al., 2010)	Cyclin T	Breast cancer, lung cancer, cervical cancer
CDK10	ETS2 transcription (Zhong et al., 2012)	Cyclin M	—
CDK11A	RNA splicing (Hu et al., 2003)	Cyclin L	Urothelial cancer, colorectal cancer, head and neck cancer
CDK11B	RNA splicing (Hu et al., 2003)	Cyclin L	Urothelial cancer, colorectal cancer, head and neck cancer
CDK12	RNAPII transcription and DNA damage (Blazek et al., 2011)	Cyclin K	Skin cancer, pancreatic cancer, melanoma, lymphoma, head and neck cancer, cervical cancer, carcinoid
CDK13	RNAPII transcription (Blazek et al., 2011; Cheng et al., 2012)	Cyclin K	Carcinoid, colorectal cancer
CDK14	Role in Wnt/β-catenin pathway (Davidson, 2010)	Cyclin Y	Prostate cancer
CDK15	Antiapoptotic protein (Park et al., 2014)	Cyclin Y	Renal cancer, pancreatic cancer
CDK16	Spermatogenesis (Mikolcevic et al., 2012)	Cyclin Y	Endometrial cancer, lymphoma, ovarian cancer

TABLE 6.1   CDK with their biological role, its regulator cyclin, and its role in cancer.—cont'd

CDK classes	Biological role	Cyclin partner	Function in type of cancer
CDK17	Phosphorylation of histone protein (Tan & Khachigian, 2009)	–	Carcinoid, colorectal cancer, melanoma, renal cancer, thyroid cancer
CDK18	Signal transduction cascade (Matsuda et al., 2017)	–	Melanoma, thyroid cancer, cervical cancer, glioma
CDK19	Transcriptional activity (Dale et al., 2015)	–	Head and neck cancer, melanoma, glioma, prostrate cancer
CDK20	Activates CDK2 (Liu et al., 2004).	–	–

Adopted and Modified from with permissiong Kalra, S., Joshi, G., Munshi, A., & Kumar, R. (2017). Structural insights of cyclin dependent kinases: Implications in design of selective inhibitors. European Journal of Medicinal Chemistry, 142, 424—458. https://doi.org/10.1016/j. ejmech.2017.08.071

3. Regulation by CDKs in cancer

CDKs are important regulators that allow cells to move between distinct stages during the cell cycle. Most of the genes taking part in the cell cycle progression are commonly altered, resulting in uncontrolled cell division, tumor development, and eventually causing human cancer (Fig. 6.2). In addition, multiple components of the CDK machinery are dysregulated in different malignancies (Zhang et al., 2021).

CDK4/CDK6 domains are implicated in cell attachment, transit, and cytoskeletal restructuring (Zhang et al., 2021). Cyclin D1 is involved in regulating the cell cycle via the interaction of CDK4 and CDK6 (Viallard et al., 2001), which phosphorylates and deactivates the retinoblastoma protein pRb, leading to the activation of a subgroup of E2F target genes linked with proliferation. Furthermore, the cell cycle progression is pRB-dependent. Tumor metastasis requires cellular migration (Leal-Esteban & Fajas, 2020). Depletion of cyclin D1 improves adhesion and decreases migration in macrophages, fibroblasts, and epithelial cells (Kalra et al., 2020; Montalto & De Amicis, 2020). As a result, cyclin D aids cellular migration by binding p27Kip1 and reducing Rho GTPase activity, as well as upregulating ROCKII as well as thrombospondin transcription (TSP-1). The overexpression and cyclin D enlargement in cancer cells, as well as its activation by mitogenic growth factors, cytokines, and other genes involved In carcinogenic growth, imply that cyclin D is important in cancer cell metastasis and invasion (Soleti, 2008).

Gene transcription and mRNA processing are also controlled by cyclins. Recruitment of Cyclin D1 to genomic DNA was also linked to the shuttling and regulating genes that control DNA damage repair signals. CDK9 and cyclin T create a complex that phosphorylates RNAPII's CTD S2 to control efficient elongation transcription (Egloff, 2021). The expression of cyclin T1 is controlled during T-cell activation. Overexpression of cyclin T is sufficient to cause tumor development, according to an in vivo investigation (Wang et al., 2019). Furthermore, cyclin L regulates splicing via binding to CDK11 and interacting with the splicing protein family. Cyclin L is an oncogene that causes head and neck cancer when it is overexpressed (Chou et al., 2020; Loyer & Trembley, 2020).

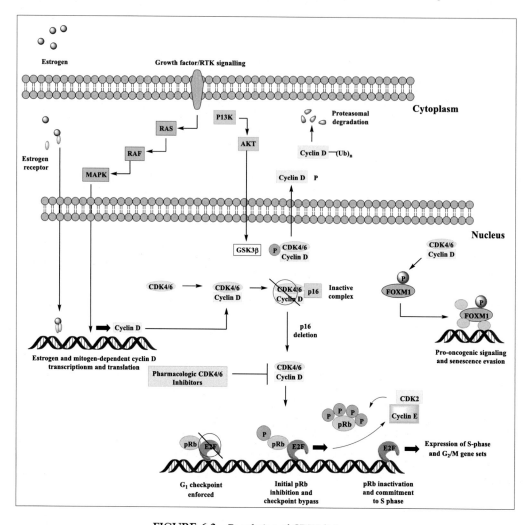

FIGURE 6.2   Regulation of CDK4/6 in cancer.

Cyclin D1 has recently been shown to be essential for tumor maintenance; loss of cyclin D1 led to decreased tumor-enhanced cellular aging and growth, implying as in breast carcinomas, cyclin D1 is necessary for tumor development (Montalto & De Amicis, 2020). Cyclin A is necessary for embryonic and hematopoietic stem cell functioning but is superfluous in fibroblast cell proliferation (Kreis et al., 2019). During the onset of the S-phase, levels of cyclin A increase. Overexpression of cyclin A leads to prostate cancer invasion and metastasis and may have a role in colorectal cancer development but correlates with poor prognosis in breast cancer. Cyclin A interacts with CDK1 and CDK2 as well as phosphorylates the DNA replication targets (Montalto & De Amicis, 2020).

Similarly in B-cell lymphoma, decreased or missing cyclin H expression corresponds with decreased growth, whereas increased cyclin H levels are associated with an extremely elevated danger of gastrointestinal stromal tumors (Peng et al., 2020). Reducing cyclin D1 concentrations in many kinds of human cancerous cells (mantle cell lymphoma, melanoma, squamous cell carcinoma, and colon cancers) resulted in poor adherence of RAD51 to the genomic Instability, making the cells more sensitive to radiation (Jirawatnotai et al., 2011; Su et al., 2016).

Reduced expression of the cyclin G2 transcript has been associated with malignancies of the thyroid and oral cavity (Kim et al., 2004) and Cyclin B1 upregulation has been seen in a variety of human cancers, including colon cancer or rectal cancer, nonsmall cell lung cancer, and squamous cell carcinoma of the head and neck (Soria et al., 2000), and its upregulation has been linked to a poor prognosis in breast cancer. Furthermore, aneuploidy and rapid pro-liferation of human breast carcinomas are linked to cyclin B1 overexpression (Diaz-Moralli et al., 2013; Klein et al., 2018; Wood & Endicott, 2018). This understanding justifies evaluating the cell cycle and its complicated regulatory system as prospective targets for future cancer treatment medication development (Ding et al., 2020).

3.1 CDK4

Structurally, cyclin-dependent kinase 4 (CDK4) is found on chromosome 12q14.1 (Kalra et al., 2017). It is a small band of about 3.2 kbp that runs from 58,142,307 to 58,145,500 on the chromosome. CDK4 crystal structures with no cocrystallized ligand have been observed in five cases. With the exception of dimer PDB ID: 3G33, all of the PDB IDs share the same 577 residues. CDK4's 3D crystal structure (PDB ID:2W9Z) (Yousuf et al., 2022).

Cyclin D/CDK4/CDKN1B is essential for nuclear translocation as well as the functionality of the cyclin D-CDK4 combination (Aboushousha et al., 2020). CDK4 aggregates have impor-tant roles in the integration of mitogenomic and antimitogenic signals. CDK4 complexes inhibit retinoblastoma proteins via phosphorylation including RB1 and regulate the G/S tran-sition during cell-cycle. Phosphorylation of retinoblastoma protein permits the transcription factor E2F to be released from the RB/E2F aggregates and the resultant transcription of E2F target genes, which are necessary for G1 advancement (Shirodkar et al., 1992). Activity regu-lation is through phosphorylation of both the THR172 and D-type cyclin interaction, which are important for catalase activity (Islam et al., 2021).

3.2 CDK6

Cyclin D proteins control CDK6. This gene encodes for a protein that is a member of the cyclin-dependent kinase family. It is located on the longer arm of chromosome 7q21-22 (Gao et al., 2020). About 11 of the 16 CDK6 crystal structures are reported to have cocrystallized ligands/inhibitors. Overall, 5 of the 16 PDB IDs are missing a cocrystallized ligand. In partic-ular, the CDK6 protein (PDB ID: 2EUF) engages with the inhibitors through hydrogen bonding (VAL101, ASP163) and hydrophobic interactions (LEU152, ILE19).

CDK6 is associated with the start and persistence of cell cycle outflow throughout cell dif-ferentiation; limits cell proliferation and adversely controls cell differentiation, but is required for the proliferation of select cell kinds (e.g., corpuscle and biological process cells) (Caron et al., 2018; Padgett & Santos, 2020). It is essential for cell proliferation within the lateral ven-tricle's subventricular zone as well as the hippocampus's dentate gyrus. It promotes the assembly of newborn neurons, in all probability by modulating G1 length. It is also needed during thymocyte development.

It promotes changes within the simple protein body structure together through cell differentiation. In this process, the tensed fibers are lost and movement increases. Apparently interfering with RUNX1 and lowering its transcriptional activation potential, this restricts myeloid differentiation while promoting the expansion of conventional myeloid progenitors (Abbastabar et al., 2018).

It enables β-cell development in hepatocellular islets of Langerhans and is involved in centrosome formation across cell cycle stages.

CDK6 could be a supermolecule enzyme activating cell proliferation, and it is concerned with the vital purpose of restricting the cell cycle. As a result, CDK6 and alternative uneven controllers of the G1 stage of the cell cycle are recognized in tumors. CDK6 is additionally overexpressed in tumors that exhibit drug resistance, to illustrate brain tumor cancers that demonstrate susceptibility to therapy exploitation TMZ (temozolomide) once they have a CDK6 upregulation variant. Similarly, CDK6 upregulation is harmful; additionally, related to opposition via endocrine treatment with the opposed steroid hormone of breast cancer, fulvestrant is used. The usual cell cycle management is harmed in that opening move resulting in different types of cancer; alterations of CDK6 can directly or indirectly have an effect on the subsequent cycle controls.

CDK6 instability is critical in lymphoid tumors via way of means of growing angiogenesis. These aptitudes are via CDK6 activation because of genome changes or mutational dysregulations. Furthermore, CDK6 is probably modified via mutator phenotype, a method of tumor suppressor gene dysregulation; this symbolizes any other emerging cancer characteristic.

Medulloblastoma represents the most frequent kind of childhood brain cancer. Upregulated CDK6 represents a predictor of a bad outcome for this condition. Because CDK6 mutations are so frequent in these cells, this became a quest for seeking approaches to precisely inhibit CDK6 development in certain cell lines. New developments that effectively inhibit xenograft tumor development in rat models were found.

These enzymes are vital for the functioning of the cell cycle, so immediate targeting of CDK6 and CDK4 should be utilized with care in cancer therapy. Moreover, tiny compounds that address these enzymes may exacerbate drug-resistant occurrences. Nevertheless, these kinases have been demonstrated to be beneficial as coadjuvants in treating breast cancer. An alternative technique for controlling CDK6/4 production involves the use of a mutant D-cyclin that connects to CDK6/4 with strong potential but does not stimulate its enzymatic activity. Furthermore, therapeutic consequences in healthy subjects have yet to be observed (Goel et al., 2020; Sánchez-Martínez et al., 2019).

4. Structure—activity relationship for the already reported CDK 4/6 inhibitors

In 2015, the existence of CDK4/6 inhibitors gained importance with the approval of palbociclib by the USFDA, and subsequently, the abemaciclib and ribociclib got approval in 2017. CDK4/6 is an important target for cancer, and various research groups are working on the new CDK4/6 inhibitors.

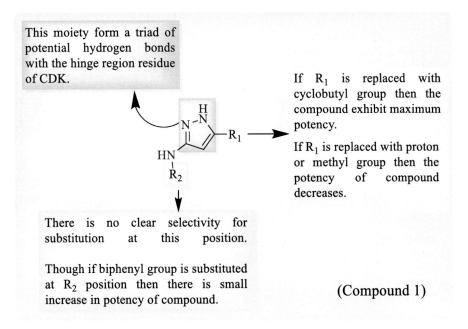

This moiety form a triad of potential hydrogen bonds with the hinge region residue of CDK.

If R_1 is replaced with cyclobutyl group then the compound exhibit maximum potency.

If R_1 is replaced with proton or methyl group then the potency of compound decreases.

There is no clear selectivity for substitution at this position.

Though if biphenyl group is substituted at R_2 position then there is small increase in potency of compound.

(Compound 1)

FIGURE 6.3   Amino-pyrazole derivatives designed by Rana et al.

Rana et al. developed a library of amino-pyrazole derivatives (compound 1); structure—activity relationship studies showed that an optimal substitution at the R_1 position yields compounds targeting the hydrophobic compartment and analogs as a powerful and particular CDK (Fig. 6.3). It was stated that the size of the R_1 substitution was gradually raised to investigate the hydrophobic pocket, while aryl substituents with and without oxygen atoms at the R_2 position were investigated to investigate the CDK area; therefore, the R_2 substituent will be exposed via the oxygen atoms to improve the potency for CDKs. However, there was no clear preference at the R_2 position for its effect on enzymatic activity. This suggests that the substituents at the R_2 position are not genuinely surface-revealed analogs, even as top results contained a cyclo-butyl substituent at the R1 site but no similar grouping was seen for the R_2 site. Amino-pyrazole analogs significantly improved caspase activation by at least twofold. Structure—activity relationship investigations found that a cyclo-butyl modification at the R_1 site was best for performance and that there was no evident preference for alteration at the R_2 site (Rana et al., 2018).

Ono et al. developed a novel series of fused tricyclic derivatives (compound 2) with different heterocycles on ring A, targeting dual CDK; docking models that were based on a collection of chemicals were used for structure-based medication design (Fig. 6.4). The docking model of the compound has been proposed that a nitrogen atom at the tricyclic scaffold's N-2 position creates a hydrogen bond with +NH3 of Lys52. As a result, using a collection of compounds to introduce alternative 5-membered heterocyclic rings in replacement of the A-ring showed activity. Changing the methyl group's location from N-1 to N-2 and removing the methyl group significantly reduced binding efficacy. In

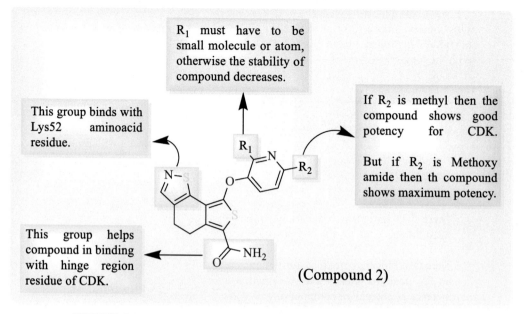

R_1 must have to be small molecule or atom, otherwise the stability of compound decreases.

This group binds with Lys52 aminoacid residue.

If R_2 is methyl then the compound shows good potency for CDK.

But if R_2 is Methoxy amide then th compound shows maximum potency.

This group helps compound in binding with hinge region residue of CDK.

(Compound 2)

FIGURE 6.4   Novel series of fused tricyclic derivatives developed by Ono et al.

comparison to imidazole, the binding potency of the isoxazole compound was marginally reduced. The introduction of the iso-thiazole compound showed dramatically increased binding activity against CDK. The insertion of an extra nitrogen atom at the 4-position, yielding the thia-diazole derivative, showed slightly reduced efficacy as well as enhanced hydrophilicities. Carboxamide moiety alterations such as a carboxyl group or nitrile alterations that led to reduced binding activity heavy groups are thought to be adverse for binding affinity. The addition of a 2-pyridyl group as the N-substituent, in contrast, resulted in limited binding activity. The 2-pyridyl ring was replaced with smaller 5-membered heteroaryl rings, such as N-methylimidazole or isoxazole, which culminated in a remarkable return in enzymatic power (Ono et al., 2017).

Wang et al. designed and synthesized a series of 4-(2,3-dihydro-1*H*-benzo[d]pyrrolo[1,2-a] imidazole-7-yl)-N-(5-(piperazin-1-ylmethyl)pyridine-2-yl)pyrimidin-2-amine (compound 3) for inhibitory activity against CDK (Fig. 6.5); structure—activity relationship showed that insertion of the pyridine ring enhances the CDK inhibitory activity as well as selectivity via association with the side chain of hinge residue His100. When R_1 or R_2 was substituted with hydrogen, it might impact the CDK4/6 activities. When a methyl group was added to the R_3, the activity reduced dramatically owing to steric hindrance. R-substituted drugs had no noticeable effect on CDK4/6 inhibitory potential. When group A was replaced by bigger aliphatic rings, such as cyclo-pentyl, cyclohexyl, or cyclo-heptyl, they had a noticeable influence on CDK4/6 action. When group A was changed by methyl cyclo-pentyl, ethyl cyclo-pentyl, or dimethyl cyclo-pentyl alternatives, they had a limited influence on CDK. It was found that dimethyl cyclo-pentyl group is responsible for tight entry into the catalytic site, contributing to the formation of a hydrogen bond between both the nitrogen atoms of

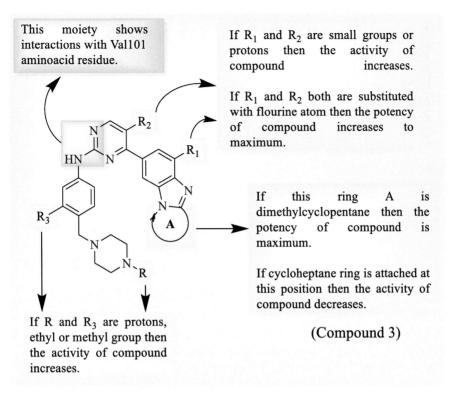

This moiety shows interactions with Val101 aminoacid residue.

If R_1 and R_2 are small groups or protons then the activity of compound increases.

If R_1 and R_2 both are substituted with flourine atom then the potency of compound increases to maximum.

If this ring A is dimethylcyclopentane then the potency of compound is maximum.

If cycloheptane ring is attached at this position then the activity of compound decreases.

If R and R_3 are protons, ethyl or methyl group then the activity of compound increases.

(Compound 3)

FIGURE 6.5 A series of 4-(2,3-dihydro-1H-benzo[d]pyrrolo[1,2-a]imidazole-7-yl)-N-(5-(piperazin-1-ylmethyl) pyridine-2-yl)pyrimidin-2-amine synthesized by Wang et al.

imidazole and the NH of Lys43. The heavier group cyclo-heptyl, on the other hand, is twisted in the cavity, resulting in a decrease of binding affinity to the kinase target, specifically, the loss of the hydrogen bond with Lys43 (Wang et al., 2018).

Zha et al. designed and synthesized a triple targeted inhibitor of novel tetrahydro-naphthyridine series (compound 4) (Fig. 6.6); structure–activity relationship stated that the benzo[d]imidazole moiety interacted in an edge-to-face connection with the phenylalanine gatekeeper residue, whereas the amino pyrimidine ring structure involved in two interactions through hydrogen bonds with hinge loop residues. Furthermore, ordered water facilitated a hydrogen bonding contact between the aromatic nitrogen in tetrahydro-naphthyridine and the residue His100. Secondly, there was a salt-bridge contact between the nitrogen in the saturated ring of tetrahydro-naphthyridine, which was protonated within physiological circumstances, and the threonine residue in the crystal structure with CDK6. Surprisingly, the substituents in tetrahydro-naphthyridine of nitrogen sit in a kinase pathway that opens toward the solvent and can tolerate a range of polar groups. SAR analyses of di-heteroaromatic amine derivatives as CDK4/6 inhibitors found that amino-pyrimidine and amino-pyridine frameworks were both preferred for preserving high enzymatic and cellular activity. However, removing the nitrogen in tetrahydro-naphthyridine/pyrimidine, as well

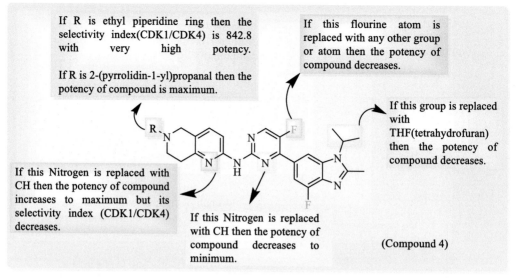

If R is ethyl piperidine ring then the selectivity index(CDK1/CDK4) is 842.8 with very high potency.

If R is 2-(pyrrolidin-1-yl)propanal then the potency of compound is maximum.

If this flourine atom is replaced with any other group or atom then the potency of compound decreases.

If this group is replaced with THF(tetrahydrofuran) then the potency of compound decreases.

If this Nitrogen is replaced with CH then the potency of compound increases to maximum but its selectivity index (CDK1/CDK4) decreases.

If this Nitrogen is replaced with CH then the potency of compound decreases to minimum.

(Compound 4)

FIGURE 6.6   A novel series of tetrahydronaphthyridine was designed by Zha et al.

as replacing 2,4-pyrimidine with 4,6-pyrimidine, resulted in a significant increase in CDK1 enzymatic activity, but these compounds could effectively sustain CDK4 enzymatic activity with IC50 ranging from 1.4 to 9.8 nM (Zha et al., 2018).

Zhao et al. reported a novel series of 4,5-dihydro-1H-pyrazolo[4,3-h] quinazoline derivatives (compound 5) as selective CDK4/6 inhibitors (Fig. 6.7). SAR suggested that pyridinyl-amine could be a good replacement for aniline in the matter of selectivity of the compound. Pyridine could increase the selectivity over kinase due to its interaction with His100. Replacing the benzene ring with a pyridine motif showed increased potency for CDK4/6 as well as improved selectivity over CDK2. The aniline counterparts of synthesized compounds are less selective CDK4/6 inhibitors, introducing the pyridine group that exhibited a 70-fold selectivity for CDK4 over CDK2. Removal of the piperazine resulted in a reduction in potency and selectivity. The piperazine moiety proved to be not only a solubilizing group but also an important selectivity determinant due to deleterious interactions unique to CDK4/6 (Zhao et al., 2018).

Alagoz et al. designed and synthesized a series of 5-((5-substituted-1H-indole-3-yl) methylene)-3-(2-oxo-2-(3/4-substituted phenylethyl)-thiazolidine- 2,4-dione (compound 6) as CDK6 inhibitors (Fig. 6.8). All of the synthesized compounds having an unsubstituted nitrogen atom in molecules promote the H-bonding at target site. The nitrogen of the thiazolidine ring was blocked, and the impact of inserting two extra oxo groups on the H-bonding characteristics was examined. A compound containing two chloro groups, one at the fifth position of the indole moiety and another at the terminal phenyl's para position, was examined. The p-chloro group of another molecule was replaced with an m-nitro group. However, docking data show that the latter has much higher H-bonding. In retrospect, these modifications might have enhanced cytotoxicity (Ates-Alagoz et al., 2021).

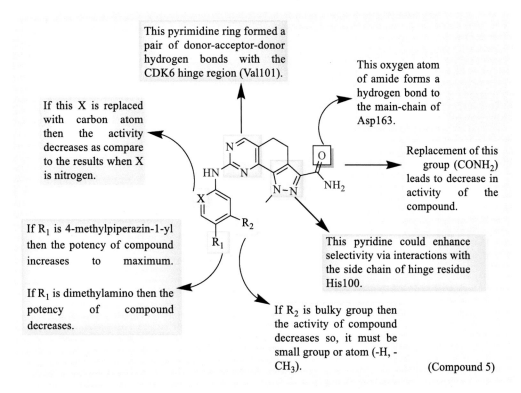

This pyrimidine ring formed a pair of donor-acceptor-donor hydrogen bonds with the CDK6 hinge region (Val101).

This oxygen atom of amide forms a hydrogen bond to the main-chain of Asp163.

If this X is replaced with carbon atom then the activity decreases as compare to the results when X is nitrogen.

Replacement of this group (CONH$_2$) leads to decrease in activity of the compound.

If R$_1$ is 4-methylpiperazin-1-yl then the potency of compound increases to maximum.

This pyridine could enhance selectivity via interactions with the side chain of hinge residue His100.

If R$_1$ is dimethylamino then the potency of compound decreases.

If R$_2$ is bulky group then the activity of compound decreases so, it must be small group or atom (-H, -CH$_3$).

(Compound 5)

FIGURE 6.7   A novel series of 4,5-dihydro-1H-pyrazolo[4,3-h] quinazoline derivatives synthesized by Zhao et al.

Zhi et al. designed and synthesized a series of 4-(heterocyclic substituted amino)-1H-pyrazole-3-carboxamide derivatives (compound 7) and their remarkable acute myeloid leukemia (AML) action (Fig. 6.9); the SAR study showed that the hydrophilic group was critical for CDK4 binding. Moreover, substituting piperidine for benzene and pyridine rings reduced their effectiveness toward CDK2/4 and FLT3. This demonstrated that the compound's inhibition of CDK2/4 and FLT3 required both a hydrophilic group and an aromatic ring structure. A number of modified benzene were inserted to determine the best groups in the hydrophilic area of the ATP-binding site. A reduction in kinase inhibition assay was detected after connecting N-methyl piperazine or morpholine to benzene by carbonyl group compared to FN-1501. Heavier moieties (such as homo-piperazine) showed no discernible effect on the activities of compounds toward CDK2/CDK4 and FLT3 when linked strongly to the benzene ring. Modifying the N-methyl homo-piperazine to meta-position in the benzene ring resulted in a significant reduction in the CDK4 inhibition effect and antiproliferative activity against MV4-11. Furthermore, replacing homo-piperazine with morpholine resulted in a 10-fold reduction in IC50 value against FLT3 when compared to FN-1501. The substitution of NH for S in the hydrophobic ring structure, on the other hand, has minimal influence on their kinase inhibitory function. Furthermore, compounds containing a single piperazine group inhibited CDK2 and FLT3, most likely as a result of the additional intermolecular contact

R_2 must be an electronegative atom or group.

If R_2 is -Cl atom then the activity of compound is higher as compare to compound with R_1 is -OCH_3 or -Br.

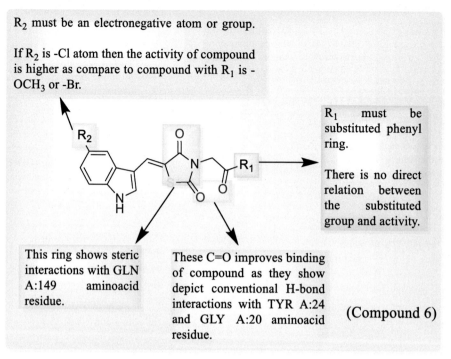

R_1 must be substituted phenyl ring.

There is no direct relation between the substituted group and activity.

This ring shows steric interactions with GLN A:149 aminoacid residue.

These C=O improves binding of compound as they show depict conventional H-bond interactions with TYR A:24 and GLY A:20 aminoacid residue.

(Compound 6)

FIGURE 6.8   A series of 5-((5-substituted-1H-indole-3-yl) methylene)-3-(2-oxo-2-(3/4-substituted phenylethyl)-thiazolidine-2,4-dione synthesized by Alagoz et al.

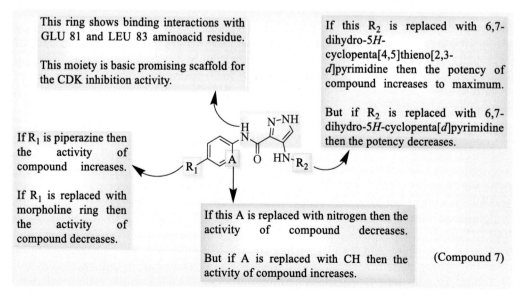

This ring shows binding interactions with GLU 81 and LEU 83 aminoacid residue.

This moiety is basic promising scaffold for the CDK inhibition activity.

If this R_2 is replaced with 6,7-dihydro-5H-cyclopenta[4,5]thieno[2,3-d]pyrimidine then the potency of compound increases to maximum.

But if R_2 is replaced with 6,7-dihydro-5H-cyclopenta[d]pyrimidine then the potency decreases.

If R_1 is piperazine then the activity of compound increases.

If R_1 is replaced with morpholine ring then the activity of compound decreases.

If this A is replaced with nitrogen then the activity of compound decreases.

But if A is replaced with CH then the activity of compound increases.

(Compound 7)

FIGURE 6.9   A series of 4-(heterocyclic substituted amino)-1H-pyrazole-3-carboxamide was designed by Zhi et al.

between both the secondary amine of piperazine and CDK2 (GLU8)/FLT3 (ASN701) (Zhi et al., 2019).

Shi et al. designed and synthesized a series of new 2,6,7-substituted pyrrolo[2,3-*d*] pyrimidine derivatives (compound 8) of CDK 4/6 inhibitor regarding their antiproliferative properties in pancreatic cancer cell cultures (Fig. 6.10). When compared to the parent medicine ribociclib, a series of six anilino-carbonyl-substituted derivatives inhibited the two growing cancer cells of MIA PaCa-2 and BxPC-3 by many to 10-fold. The structural—activity relationship stated that if the cyclopentane ring is replaced with a benzene ring then the activity of the compound decreases. If 1-(pyridin-3-yl) piperazine is replaced with cyclohexanamine then the potency of the compound reduces. Pyrrolo pyrimidine is the basic pharmacophore for the CDK inhibitory activity, any modification in this moiety leads to a decrease in activity. Further, if the secondary amine is replaced with a tertiary amine then the activity of the compound decreases. Lastly if R is replaced with methoxy at the C-2 position, then the potency of compound increases to maximum. But if methoxy is attached to the C-4 position then the compound becomes inactive (Kumar et al., 2021).

Park et al. synthesized and biologically evaluated a series of N9-cis-cyclobutylpurine derivatives (compound 9) for use as cyclin-dependent kinase (CDK) inhibitors (Fig. 6.11). All synthesized compounds were examined for CDK and CDK2/cyclin A inhibitory activities. The substituent impact of R1, pyridin-3-yl-methylamine in the 6-position of purine, was selected for this investigation. At a dose of 25 nM, most of the aliphatic amides inhibited CDK with fewer than 50% inhibition. At 25 nM, the benzamide analogs 2,6-difluoro and 2,6-dichloro demonstrated better than 50% inhibition. For the heteroaryl amides, 2-pyridyl showed substantial inhibition with IC50 values in the low double-digit nanomolar limits, while the other isomers displayed mild inhibition. In contrast to the methyl in pyridyl,

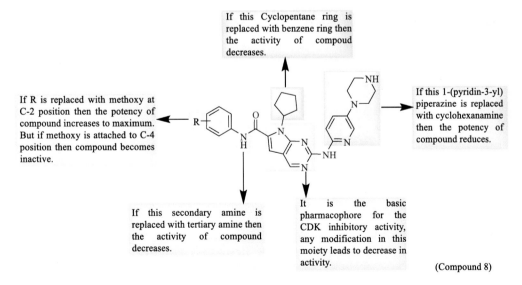

(Compound 8)

FIGURE 6.10   A class of new 2,6,7-substituted pyrrolo[2,3-*d*] pyrimidine series is synthesized by Shi et al.

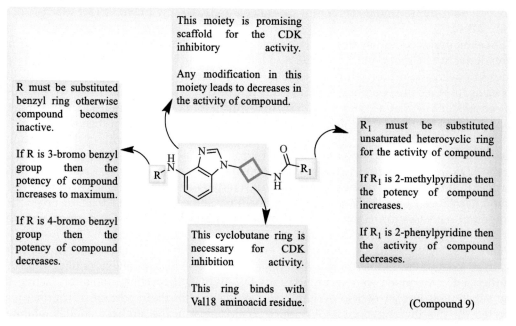

FIGURE 6.11   Park et al. synthesized and evaluated a series of N9-cis-cyclobutylpurine derivatives.

trifluoromethyl, and phenyl lowered anti-CDK activity marginally. At 25 nM, pyrazine inhibited the enzyme rather weakly. These findings showed that the nitrogen in the 2-position of the pyridyl moiety is required for CDK inhibition. The findings show that 2-pyridylmethyl and 4-pyridylmethyl, rather than 3-pyridylmethyl, demonstrated mild inhibitory action against CDK. For the benzyl amines, 3-chlorobenzyl amine and 3-bromobenzyl amine were inhibited with single-digit nanomolar activity (IC_{50} = 1.3–5.4 nM). Moreover, 3-substituted benzylamines were shown to be more active than 2- and 4-substituted benzylamines. These findings suggested that, like dinaciclib, a substitution in the 3-position of phenyl is required in connection with CDK. Therefore, in collections, no electron impact by substituents was detected. The anilines and alkyl amines had only little inhibitory activity (Park et al., 2017).

Li et al. designed, synthesized, and biologically assessed a novel CDK4 inhibitor with potent anticancer activity (compound 10) (Fig. 6.12). SAR study states that in comparison to ribociclib (IC_{50} = 13 nM), the X_1 location with fluorine substitution demonstrated greater efficacy targeting CDK4 (IC_{50} = 5.7 nM). Whenever X_1 has a fluorine atom, X_2 has a hydrogen atom, and L is used as a link, and the R group substituent is changed. The effectiveness was comparable when R was a methyl-piperazine group. Consequently, changing the R position of piperazine led to lower inhibitory efficacy toward CDK4. When R was altered to merely a hydrogen atom, the molecules were multiple times less effective than ribociclib (IC50:

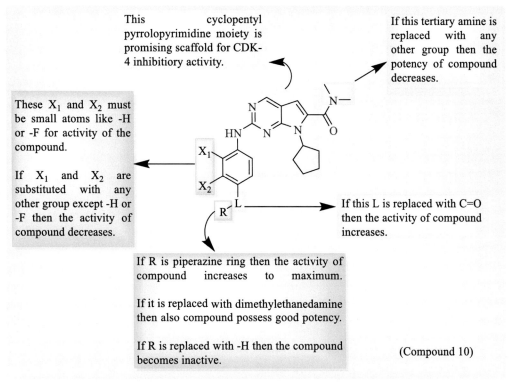

This cyclopentyl pyrrolopyrimidine moiety is promising scaffold for CDK-4 inhibitiory activity.

If this tertiary amine is replaced with any other group then the potency of compound decreases.

These X$_1$ and X$_2$ must be small atoms like -H or -F for activity of the compound.

If X$_1$ and X$_2$ are substituted with any other group except -H or -F then the activity of compound decreases.

If this L is replaced with C=O then the activity of compound increases.

If R is piperazine ring then the activity of compound increases to maximum.

If it is replaced with dimethylethanedamine then also compound possess good potency.

If R is replaced with -H then the compound becomes inactive.

(Compound 10)

FIGURE 6.12   Novel CDK4 inhibitor designed by Li et al.

2379 nM, 97 nM, and 2153 nM). The CDK performances were clearly restored when the R position was replaced by the piperazine group (IC$_{50}$: 3.9 nM, 0.92 nM, and 3.1 nM), indicating that the piperazine group at the R position may be a worthwhile substituent. As a result, it was discovered that X1 or X2 positions containing a fluorine atom may boost CDK4 inhibitory action. The activity was somewhat influenced by the L position with bond or carbamoyl. CDK4 activity was influenced by R position substitutions (Li et al., 2021).

Guo et al. designed and synthesized a series of novel LEE011 derivatives (compound11) containing pyridine N-oxide (Fig. 6.13). The structure–activity relationship study was as follows. It was evident that the N-oxide substituent of pyrrolo[2,3-d]pyrimidines-2-amine scaffold based on ribociclib demonstrated strong inhibitory efficacy targeting CDK4 at 1 μM. Keeping N-oxide substituent intact, the alterations at N-4 position of the piperazine ring of the molecule were employed using different substituents. The inactivation of CDK4 and CDK6 enzymes by these drugs at 1 M was investigated. Results showed that the compounds had relatively outstanding inhibition activities against CDK4. The hydrophobic methyl and isopropyl groups applied to the piperazine ring's N-4 position maintain the inhibition effect

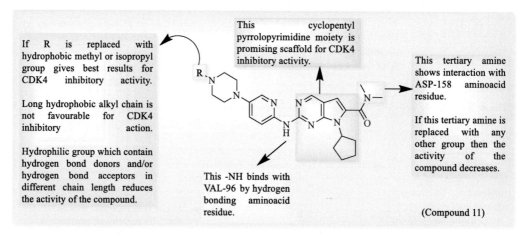

If R is replaced with hydrophobic methyl or isopropyl group gives best results for CDK4 inhibitory activity.

Long hydrophobic alkyl chain is not favourable for CDK4 inhibitory action.

Hydrophilic group which contain hydrogen bond donors and/or hydrogen bond acceptors in different chain length reduces the activity of the compound.

This cyclopentyl pyrrolopyrimidine moiety is promising scaffold for CDK4 inhibitory activity.

This tertiary amine shows interaction with ASP-158 aminoacid residue.

If this tertiary amine is replaced with any other group then the activity of the compound decreases.

This -NH binds with VAL-96 by hydrogen bonding aminoacid residue.

(Compound 11)

FIGURE 6.13   Guo et al. designed and synthesized a series of novel LEE011.

toward CDK4. When the alkyl chain was extended from acetyl to heptanoyl, the CDK4 inhibitory activity was reduced considerably, indicating that a length of the hydrocarbon alkyl chain is not conducive to CDK4 inhibition effect compounds were created to examine the effect of alterations on the piperazine N-4 position with hydrophilic groups including hydrogen bond donors and/or hydrogen bond acceptors in varied chain lengths on CDK4 inhibition effect. Evidently, the CDK4 inhibition effect of these drugs was determined to be significantly lower effective. This chemical was then used in further in vitro biological research. Significantly, all of the synthesized compounds displayed mild CDK6 inhibitory activity, indicating that the N-oxide substituent added to the N position on the pyridine ring may increase CDK4 selectivity over CDK6. CDK4 and CDK6 have overlapping roles in development due to their high homology, same substrate specificities, and enzymatic activity (Guo et al., 2018).

Warhi et al. synthesized a series of oxindole—indole conjugates (compound 12) as anticancer CDK inhibitors (Fig. 6.14). There SAR study demonstrated that having various substituents on the oxindole moiety's C-5 and C-7; R and R_1, as well as several substitutions on the N-1 of the oxindole moiety does not favour the activity. If R is methyl and R_1 is unsubstituted, the activity is maximum. In further studies, the oxindole moiety was substituted by indane and tetralin rings in molecules to investigate the oxindole moiety's advantage over all the other pharmacophoric groups. The IC_{50} values for the adducts examined were evaluated to get clarity into their antiproliferative efficacy. When the IC_{50} values for the investigated composites against MCF-7 breast cancer cells were analyzed, it was discovered that most composites with such a significant electron-withdrawing 5-NO_2 group and a 5,7-dimethyl substitution on the oxindole moiety appropriately doubled the inhibitory activity compared to staurosporine (Al-Warhi et al., 2020).

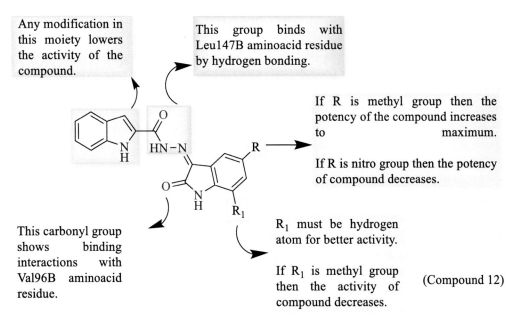

Any modification in this moiety lowers the activity of the compound.

This group binds with Leu147B aminoacid residue by hydrogen bonding.

If R is methyl group then the potency of the compound increases to maximum.

If R is nitro group then the potency of compound decreases.

This carbonyl group shows binding interactions with Val96B aminoacid residue.

R_1 must be hydrogen atom for better activity.

If R_1 is methyl group then the activity of compound decreases.

(Compound 12)

FIGURE 6.14 Warhi et al. synthesized a series of oxindole–indole conjugates as anticancer CDK inhibitors.

References

Abbastabar, M., Kheyrollah, M., Azizian, K., Bagherlou, N., Tehrani, S. S., Maniati, M., & Karimian, A. (2018). Multiple functions of p27 in cell cycle, apoptosis, epigenetic modification and transcriptional regulation for the control of cell growth: A double-edged sword protein. *DNA Repair, 69*, 63–72.

Aboushousha, T., Hammam, O., Aref, A., Kamel, A., Badawy, M., & Hamid, A. A. (2020). Tissue profile of CDK4 and STAT3 as possible innovative therapeutic targets in urinary bladder cancer. *Asian Pacific Journal of Cancer Prevention, 21*, 547.

Aggarwal, P., Vaites, L. P., Kim, J. K., Mellert, H., Gurung, B., Nakagawa, H., Herlyn, M., Hua, X., Rustgi, A. K., & McMahon, S. B. (2010). Nuclear cyclin D1/CDK4 kinase regulates CUL4 expression and triggers neoplastic growth via activation of the PRMT5 methyltransferase. *Cancer Cell, 18*, 329–340.

Al-Warhi, T., El Kerdawy, A. M., Aljaeed, N., Ismael, O. E., Ayyad, R. R., Eldehna, W. M., Abdel-Aziz, H. A., & Al-Ansary, G. H. (2020). Synthesis, biological evaluation and in silico studies of certain oxindole–indole conjugates as anticancer CDK inhibitors. *Molecules, 25*, 2031.

Ates-Alagoz, Z., Kisla, M. M., Karadayi, F. Z., Baran, S., Doğan, T. S., & Mutlu, P. (2021). Design, synthesis, molecular docking and ADME studies of novel indole-thiazolidinedione derivatives and their antineoplastic activity as CDK6 inhibitors. *New Journal of Chemistry, 45*, 18025–18038.

Bertoli, C., Skotheim, J. M., & De Bruin, R. A. (2013). Control of cell cycle transcription during G1 and S phases. *Nature Reviews Molecular Cell Biology, 14*, 518–528.

Besson, A., Dowdy, S. F., & Roberts, J. M. (2008). CDK inhibitors: Cell cycle regulators and beyond. *Developmental Cell, 14*, 159–169.

Blazek, D., Kohoutek, J., Bartholomeeusen, K., Johansen, E., Hulinkova, P., Luo, Z., Cimermancic, P., Ule, J., & Peterlin, B. M. (2011). The Cyclin K/Cdk12 complex maintains genomic stability via regulation of expression of DNA damage response genes. *Genes & Development, 25*, 2158–2172.

Caron, N., Genin, E. C., Marlier, Q., Verteneuil, S., Beukelaers, P., Morel, L., Hu, M. G., Hinds, P. W., Nguyen, L., & Vandenbosch, R. (2018). Proliferation of hippocampal progenitors relies on p27-dependent regulation of Cdk6 kinase activity. *Cellular and Molecular Life Sciences, 75*, 3817—3827.

Chen, Y.-J., Dominguez-Brauer, C., Wang, Z., Asara, J. M., Costa, R. H., Tyner, A. L., Lau, L. F., & Raychaudhuri, P. (2009). A conserved phosphorylation site within the forkhead domain of FoxM1B is required for its activation by cyclin-CDK1. *Journal of Biological Chemistry, 284*, 30695—30707.

Cheng, S.-W. G., Kuzyk, M. A., Moradian, A., Ichu, T.-A., Chang, V. C.-D., Tien, J. F., Vollett, S. E., Griffith, M., Marra, M. A., & Morin, G. B. (2012). Interaction of cyclin-dependent kinase 12/CrkRS with cyclin K1 is required for the phosphorylation of the C-terminal domain of RNA polymerase II. *Molecular and Cellular Biology, 32*, 4691—4704.

Chou, J., Quigley, D. A., Robinson, T. M., Feng, F. Y., & Ashworth, A. (2020). Transcription-associated cyclin-dependent kinases as targets and biomarkers for cancer TherapyTranscription-associated CDKs in cancer. *Cancer Discovery, 10*, 351—370.

Dai, Y., Jin, F., Wu, W., & Kumar, S. K. (2019). Cell cycle regulation and hematologic malignancies. *Blood Science, 1*, 34—43.

Dale, T., Clarke, P. A., Esdar, C., Waalboer, D., Adeniji-Popoola, O., Ortiz-Ruiz, M.-J., Mallinger, A., Samant, R. S., Czodrowski, P., & Musil, D. (2015). A selective chemical probe for exploring the role of CDK8 and CDK19 in human disease. *Nature Chemical Biology, 11*, 973—980.

David, S. Y., Zhao, R., Hsu, E. L., Cayer, J., Ye, F., Guo, Y., Shyr, Y., & Cortez, D. (2010). Cyclin-dependent kinase 9—cyclin K functions in the replication stress response. *EMBO Reports, 11*, 876—882.

Davidson, G. (2010). *The cell cycle and Wnt.* Taylor & Francis.

Diaz-Moralli, S., Tarrado-Castellarnau, M., Miranda, A., & Cascante, M. (2013). Targeting cell cycle regulation in cancer therapy. *Pharmacology & Therapeutics, 138*, 255—271.

Ding, L., Cao, J., Lin, W., Chen, H., Xiong, X., Ao, H., Yu, M., Lin, J., & Cui, Q. (2020). The roles of cyclin-dependent kinases in cell-cycle progression and therapeutic strategies in human breast cancer. *International Journal of Molecular Sciences, 21*, 1960.

Düster, R., Ji, Y., Pan, K.-T., Urlaub, H., & Geyer, M. (2022). Functional characterization of the human Cdk10/Cyclin Q complex. *Open Biology, 12*, Article 210381.

Egloff, S. (2021). CDK9 keeps RNA polymerase II on track. *Cellular and Molecular Life Sciences, 78*, 5543—5567.

Firestein, R., Bass, A. J., Kim, S. Y., Dunn, I. F., Silver, S. J., Guney, I., Freed, E., Ligon, A. H., Vena, N., & Ogino, S. (2008). CDK8 is a colorectal cancer oncogene that regulates β-catenin activity. *Nature, 455*, 547—551.

Fischer, M., Schade, A. E., Branigan, T. B., Müller, G. A., & DeCaprio, J. A. (2022). Coordinating gene expression during the cell cycle. *Trends in Biochemical Sciences, 47*(12).

Fisher, R. P., & Morgan, D. O. (1994). A novel cyclin associates with M015/CDK7 to form the CDK-activating kinase. *Cell, 78*, 713—724.

Gao, X., Leone, G. W., & Wang, H. (2020). Cyclin D-CDK4/6 functions in cancer. *Advances in Cancer Research, 148*, 147—169.

Goel, B., Tripathi, N., Bhardwaj, N., & Jain, S. K. (2020). Small molecule CDK inhibitors for the therapeutic management of cancer. *Current Topics in Medicinal Chemistry, 20*, 1535—1563.

Goel, S., Bergholz, J. S., & Zhao, J. J. (2022). Targeting CDK4 and CDK6 in cancer. *Nature Reviews Cancer, 22*, 356—372.

Guo, Q., Li, Y., Zhang, C., Huang, Z., Wang, X., Nie, Y., Li, Y., Liu, Y., Yang, S., & Xiang, R. (2018). Selective and novel cyclin-dependent kinases 4 inhibitor: Synthesis and biological evaluation. *Medicinal Chemistry Research, 27*, 1666—1678.

Harashima, H., Dissmeyer, N., & Schnittger, A. (2013). Cell cycle control across the eukaryotic kingdom. *Trends in Cell Biology, 23*, 345—356.

Hochegger, H., Takeda, S., & Hunt, T. (2008). Cyclin-dependent kinases and cell-cycle transitions: Does one fit all? *Nature Reviews Molecular Cell Biology, 9*, 910—916.

Hu, D., Mayeda, A., Trembley, J. H., Lahti, J. M., & Kidd, V. J. (2003). CDK11 complexes promote pre-mRNA splicing. *Journal of Biological Chemistry, 278*, 8623—8629.

Islam, R., Rahaman, M., Hoque, H., Hasan, N., Prodhan, S. H., Ruhama, A., & Jewel, N. A. (2021). Computational and structural based approach to identify malignant nonsynonymous single nucleotide polymorphisms associated with CDK4 gene. *PLoS One, 16*, Article e0259691.

Jirawatnotai, S., Hu, Y., Michowski, W., Elias, J. E., Becks, L., Bienvenu, F., Zagozdzon, A., Goswami, T., Wang, Y. E., & Clark, A. B. (2011). A function for cyclin D1 in DNA repair uncovered by protein interactome analyses in human cancers. *Nature, 474*, 230–234.

Joshi, G., Nayyar, H., Kalra, S., Sharma, P., Munshi, A., Singh, S., & Kumar, R. (2017). Pyrimidine containing epidermal growth factor receptor kinase inhibitors: Synthesis and biological evaluation. *Chemical Biology & Drug Design, 90*, 995–1006.

Kalra, S., Joshi, G., Kumar, M., Arora, S., Kaur, H., Singh, S., Munshi, A., & Kumar, R. (2020). Anticancer potential of some imidazole and fused imidazole derivatives: Exploring the mechanism via epidermal growth factor receptor (EGFR) inhibition. *RSC Medicinal Chemistry, 11*, 923–939.

Kalra, S., Joshi, G., Munshi, A., & Kumar, R. (2017). Structural insights of cyclin dependent kinases: Implications in design of selective inhibitors. *European Journal of Medicinal Chemistry, 142*, 424–458.

Kim, Y., Shintani, S., Kohno, Y., Zhang, R., & Wong, D. T. (2004). Cyclin G2 dysregulation in human oral cancer. *Cancer Research, 64*, 8980–8986.

Klein, M. E., Kovatcheva, M., Davis, L. E., Tap, W. D., & Koff, A. (2018). CDK4/6 inhibitors: The mechanism of action may not Be as simple as once thought. *Cancer Cell, 34*, 9–20.

Kreis, N.-N., Louwen, F., & Yuan, J. (2019). The multifaceted p21 (Cip1/Waf1/CDKN1A) in cell differentiation, migration and cancer therapy. *Cancers, 11*, 1220.

Kumar, R. R., Kumar, V., Kaur, D., Nandi, N. K., Dwivedi, A. R., Kumar, V., & Kumar, B. (2021). Investigation of indole-3-piperazinyl derivatives as potential antidepressants: Design, synthesis, in-vitro, in-vivo and in-silico analysis. *ChemistrySelect, 6*, 11276–11284.

Lavoie, G., & St-Pierre, Y. (2011). Phosphorylation of human DNMT1: Implication of cyclin-dependent kinases. *Biochemical and Biophysical Research Communications, 409*, 187–192.

Leal-Esteban, L. C., & Fajas, L. (2020). Cell cycle regulators in cancer cell metabolism. *Biochimica et Biophysica Acta, Molecular Basis of Disease, 1866*, Article 165715.

Li, Y., Du, R., Nie, Y., Wang, T., Ma, Y., & Fan, Y. (2021). Design, synthesis and biological assessment of novel CDK4 inhibitor with potent anticancer activity. *Bioorganic Chemistry, 109*, Article 104717.

Liu, P., Kao, T., & Huang, H. (2008). CDK1 promotes cell proliferation and survival via phosphorylation and inhibition of FOXO1 transcription factor. *Oncogene, 27*, 4733–4744.

Liu, Y., Fu, L., Wu, J., Liu, M., Wang, G., Liu, B., & Zhang, L. (2021). Transcriptional cyclin-dependent kinases: Potential drug targets in cancer therapy. *European Journal of Medicinal Chemistry, 229*, 114056.

Liu, Y., Wu, C., & Galaktionov, K. (2004). p42, a novel cyclin-dependent kinase-activating kinase in mammalian cells. *Journal of Biological Chemistry, 279*, 4507–4514.

Loyer, P., & Trembley, J. H. (2020). Roles of CDK/Cyclin complexes in transcription and pre-mRNA splicing: Cyclins L and CDK11 at the cross-roads of cell cycle and regulation of gene expression. In , *107. Paper presented at the seminars in cell & developmental biology*.

Lu, X., Liu, J., & Legerski, R. J. (2009). Cyclin E is stabilized in response to replication fork barriers leading to prolonged S phase arrest. *Journal of Biological Chemistry, 284*, 35325–35337.

Malumbres, M., & Barbacid, M. (2009). Cell cycle, CDKs and cancer: A changing paradigm. *Nature Reviews Cancer, 9*, 153–166.

Malumbres, M. (2014). Cyclin-dependent kinases. *Genome Biology, 15*, 1–10.

Martínez-Alonso, D., & Malumbres, M. (2020). Mammalian cell cycle cyclins. *Paper presented at the seminars in cell & developmental biology*.

Matsuda, S., Kawamoto, K., Miyamoto, K., Tsuji, A., & Yuasa, K. (2017). PCTK3/CDK18 regulates cell migration and adhesion by negatively modulating FAK activity. *Scientific Reports, 7*, 45545–45559.

Matthews, H. K., Bertoli, C., & de Bruin, R. A. (2022). Cell cycle control in cancer. *Nature Reviews Molecular Cell Biology, 23*, 74–88.

Mikolcevic, P., Sigl, R., Rauch, V., Hess, M. W., Pfaller, K., Barisic, M., Pelliniemi, L. J., Boesl, M., & Geley, S. (2012). Cyclin-dependent kinase 16/PCTAIRE kinase 1 is activated by cyclin Y and is essential for spermatogenesis. *Molecular and Cellular Biology, 32*, 868–879.

Montalto, F. I., & De Amicis, F. (2020). Cyclin D1 in cancer: A molecular connection for cell cycle control, adhesion and invasion in tumor and stroma. *Cells, 9*, 2648.

Ono, K., Banno, H., Okaniwa, M., Hirayama, T., Iwamura, N., Hikichi, Y., Murai, S., Hasegawa, M., Hasegawa, Y., & Yonemori, K. (2017). Design and synthesis of selective CDK8/19 dual inhibitors: Discovery of 4, 5-dihydrothieno [3', 4': 3, 4] benzo [1, 2-d] isothiazole derivatives. *Bioorganic & Medicinal Chemistry, 25*, 2336–2350.

Otto, T., & Sicinski, P. (2017). Cell cycle proteins as promising targets in cancer therapy. *Nature Reviews Cancer, 17*, 93–115.

Padgett, J., & Santos, S. D. (2020). From clocks to dominoes: Lessons on cell cycle remodelling from embryonic stem cells. *FEBS Letters, 594*, 2031–2045.

Park, M. H., Kim, S. Y., Kim, Y. J., & Chung, Y.-H. (2014). ALS2CR7 (CDK15) attenuates TRAIL induced apoptosis by inducing phosphorylation of survivin Thr34. *Biochemical and Biophysical Research Communications, 450*, 129–134.

Park, S. J., Kim, E., Yoo, M., Lee, J.-Y., Park, C. H., Hwang, J. Y., & Du Ha, J. (2017). Synthesis and biological evaluation of N9-cis-cyclobutylpurine derivatives for use as cyclin-dependent kinase (CDK) inhibitors. *Bioorganic & Medicinal Chemistry Letters, 27*, 4399–4404.

Peng, C., Yang, Y., Ji, L., Yang, P., Yang, X., & Zhang, Y. (2020). Cyclin H predicts the poor prognosis and promotes the proliferation of ovarian cancer. *Cancer Cell International, 20*, 1–10.

Rana, S., Sonawane, Y. A., Taylor, M. A., Kizhake, S., Zahid, M., & Natarajan, A. (2018). Synthesis of aminopyrazole analogs and their evaluation as CDK inhibitors for cancer therapy. *Bioorganic & Medicinal Chemistry Letters, 28*, 3736–3740.

Reinhardt, H. C., & Yaffe, M. B. (2013). Phospho-Ser/Thr-binding domains: Navigating the cell cycle and DNA damage response. *Nature Reviews Molecular Cell Biology, 14*, 563–580.

Roskoski, R., Jr. (2019). Cyclin-dependent protein serine/threonine kinase inhibitors as anticancer drugs. *Pharmacological Research, 139*, 471–488.

Rubin, S. M., Sage, J., & Skotheim, J. M. (2020). Integrating old and new paradigms of G1/S control. *Molecular Cell, 80*, 183–192.

Russo, A. A., Jeffrey, P. D., Patten, A. K., Massagué, J., & Pavletich, N. P. (1996). Crystal structure of the p27Kip1 cyclin-dependent-kinase inibitor bound to the cyclin A-Cdk2 complex. *Nature, 382*, 325.

Sánchez-Martínez, C., Lallena, M. J., Sanfeliciano, S. G., & de Dios, A. (2019). Cyclin dependent kinase (CDK) inhibitors as anticancer drugs: Recent advances (2015–2019). *Bioorganic & Medicinal Chemistry Letters, 29*, Article 126637.

Shen, S., Dean, D. C., Yu, Z., & Duan, Z. (2019). Role of cyclin-dependent kinases (CDKs) in hepatocellular carcinoma: Therapeutic potential of targeting the CDK signaling pathway. *Hepatology Research, 49*, 1097–1108.

Shirodkar, S., Ewen, M., DeCaprio, J. A., Morgan, J., Livingston, D. M., & Chittenden, T. (1992). The transcription factor E2F interacts with the retinoblastoma product and a p107-cyclin A complex in a cell cycle-regulated manner. *Cell, 68*, 157–166.

Soleti, R. (2008). *Role of membrane microparticles in angiogenesis*. Université d'Angers.

Soria, J.-C., Jang, S. J., Khuri, F. R., Hassan, K., Liu, D., Hong, W. K., & Mao, L. (2000). Overexpression of cyclin B1 in early-stage non-small cell lung cancer and its clinical implication. *Cancer Research, 60*, 4000–4004.

Su, H., Jin, X., Shen, L., Fang, Y., Fei, Z., Zhang, X., Xie, C., & Chen, X. (2016). Inhibition of cyclin D1 enhances sensitivity to radiotherapy and reverses epithelial to mesenchymal transition for esophageal cancer cells. *Tumor Biology, 37*, 5355–5363.

Tan, N. Y., & Khachigian, L. M. (2009). Sp1 phosphorylation and its regulation of gene transcription. *Molecular and Cellular Biology, 29*, 2483–2488.

Tchakarska, G., & Sola, B. (2020). The double dealing of cyclin D1. *Cell Cycle, 19*, 163–178.

Tomashevski, A., Webster, D., Grammas, P., Gorospe, M., & Kruman, I. (2010). Cyclin C-dependent cell cycle entry is required for activation of nonhomologous end joining DNA repair in postmitotic neurons. *Cell Death & Differentiation, 17*, 1189–1198.

Viallard, J. F., Lacombe, F., Belloc, F., Pellegrin, J. L., & Reiffers, J. (2001). Molecular mechanisms controlling the cell cycle: Fundamental aspects and implications for oncology. *Cancer Radiotherapie, 5*, 109–129.

Wang, J., Liu, J., Tian, F., Zhan, Y., & Kong, D. (2019). Cyclin-dependent kinase 9 expression and its association with CD8+ T cell infiltration in microsatellite-stable colorectal cancer. *Oncology Letters, 18*, 6046–6056.

Wang, Y., Liu, W.-J., Yin, L., Li, H., Chen, Z.-H., Zhu, D.-X., Song, X.-Q., Cheng, Z.-Z., Song, P., & Wang, Z. (2018). Design and synthesis of 4-(2, 3-dihydro-1H-benzo [d] pyrrolo [1, 2-a] imidazole-7-yl)-N-(5-(piperazin-1-ylmethyl) pyridine-2-yl) pyrimidin-2-amine as a highly potent and selective cyclin-dependent kinases 4 and 6 inhibitors and the discovery of structure-activity relationships. *Bioorganic & Medicinal Chemistry Letters, 28*, 974–978.

Wang, Z. (2021). Regulation of cell cycle progression by growth factor-induced cell signaling. *Cells, 10*, 3327.

Wood, D. J., & Endicott, J. A. (2018). Structural insights into the functional diversity of the CDK–cyclin family. *Open Biology, 8*, Article 180112.

Yousuf, M., Alam, M., Shamsi, A., Khan, P., Hasan, G. M., Haque, Q. M. R., & Hassan, M. I. (2022). Structure-guided design and development of cyclin-dependent kinase 4/6 inhibitors: A review on therapeutic implications. *International Journal of Biological Macromolecules, 218*, 394–408.

Zha, C., Deng, W., Fu, Y., Tang, S., Lan, X., Ye, Y., Su, Y., Jiang, L., Chen, Y., & Huang, Y. (2018). Design, synthesis and biological evaluation of tetrahydronaphthyridine derivatives as bioavailable CDK4/6 inhibitors for cancer therapy. *European Journal of Medicinal Chemistry, 148*, 140–153.

Zhang, L., Zhang, Y., & Hu, X. (2021). Targeting the transcription cycle and RNA processing in cancer treatment. *Current Opinion in Pharmacology, 58*, 69–75.

Zhao, H., Hu, X., Cao, K., Zhang, Y., Zhao, K., Tang, C., & Feng, B. (2018). Synthesis and SAR of 4, 5-dihydro-1H-pyrazolo [4, 3-h] quinazoline derivatives as potent and selective CDK4/6 inhibitors. *European Journal of Medicinal Chemistry, 157*, 935–945.

Zheng, Z.-L. (2022). Cyclin-dependent kinases and CTD phosphatases in cell cycle transcriptional control: Conservation across eukaryotic kingdoms and uniqueness to plants. *Cells, 11*, 279.

Zhi, Y., Wang, Z., Yao, C., Li, B., Heng, H., Cai, J., Xiang, L., Wang, Y., Lu, T., & Lu, S. (2019). Design and synthesis of 4-(heterocyclic substituted amino)-1H-Pyrazole-3-Carboxamide derivatives and their potent activity against Acute myeloid leukemia (AML). *International Journal of Molecular Sciences, 20*, 5739.

Zhong, X.-y., Xu, X.-x., Yu, J.-h., Jiang, G.-x., Yu, Y., Tai, S., Wang, Z.-D., & Cui, Y.-F. (2012). Clinical and biological significance of Cdk10 in hepatocellular carcinoma. *Gene, 498*, 68–74.

Impact of epidermal growth factor receptors as a key clinical target against cancer

Ankush Kumar[1], Raj Kumar Narang[2] and Rohit Kumar Bhatia[3]

[1]Institute of Pharmaceutical Sciences, IET Bhaddal Technical Campus, Ropar, Punjab, India; [2]Department of Pharmaceutics, ISF College of Pharmacy, Moga, Punjab, India; [3]Department of Pharmaceutical Chemistry, ISF College of Pharmacy, Moga, Punjab, India

1. Introduction

Cancer is the second biggest cause of mortality in the world, and it is a serious public health issue (Naujokas et al., 2013; Stewart et al., 2003; Torre et al., 2015). Cancer is a condition in which aberrant cells divide uncontrolled and cause tissue destruction (D'Arcy, 2019). According to recent research issued by the National Cancer Registry Program (NCRP), the number of cancer cases is expected to rise from 13.9 lakh in 2020 to 15.7 lakh by 2025, an almost 20% increase (Lath et al., 2022; Shafi et al., 2021, p. 45). One bright spot is that at least one-third of frequent cancers may be avoided (Montagna et al., 2003). Prostate cancer (43%), colorectal cancer (23%), and testicular cancer (23%) are the three most common malignancies in men. Skin, breast, lung, colorectal, and uterine cancers are the most frequent cancers among women in the United States. Cervical and ovarian cancers are only seen in women, although they are a leading cause of cancer globally (Rahib et al., 2014; Siegel et al., 2012; Sirovich et al., 2003). Breast cancer is the most frequent cancer on the list, with 284,200 new cases projected in the United States in 2021. Prostate cancer and lung cancer are the next most frequent cancers (Shaath et al., 2021). In India, breast cancer, which accounts for more than a fourth of all female malignancies, has become a serious public health problem in Indian cities, particularly in metropolitan areas such as Delhi, Bengaluru, and Chennai (Ali et al., 2011; Leong et al., 2010). Cancers are caused by a variety of variables, and most cancers, like many other illnesses, are the consequence of exposure to a variety of lifestyle factors (Breslow et al.,

Current Molecular Targets of Heterocyclic Compounds for Cancer Therapy
https://doi.org/10.1016/B978-0-323-96121-9.00007-3

1980). It is crucial to note that, while some of these factors are unavoidable, around one-third of breast cancer cases can be avoided by lowering dietary and behavioral hazards (Key et al., 2004). The independent development of cancer cells has been linked to many families of growth factors and growth factor receptors (Eswarakumar et al., 2005).

The epidermal growth factor receptor (EGFR) is one of them, and it plays a key role in the development and progression of many carcinoma types (Salomon et al., 1995). These receptors are also responsible for early embryonic development and renewal of stem cells in the liver and skin (Raggi et al., 2016). However, it is vital to note that the EGFR is part of a receptor family that includes three other proteins: ErbB-2, ErbB-3, and ErbB-4 (Graus-Porta et al., 1997; Suo et al., 2002; Tzahar et al., 1994). These proteins make a system in which a signal binds to a receptor and is frequently relayed to another receptor (Avraham et al., 2011). This mechanism made the initial signal to be amplified and diversified, which is necessary for cell proliferation (Yarden, 2001). As a result, it is impossible to analyze the impact of EGFR signaling without considering the complicated connections that occur among the ErbB and growth factors (Mitsudomi et al., 2007; Normanno et al., 2006; Samaga et al., 2009; Scagliotti et al., 2004). Such interactions may be necessary for the development of more effective treatment techniques to suppress EGFR signaling in cancer patients. The EGFR (also known as ErbB-1/HER1), ErbB-2 (HER2), ErbB-3 (HER3), and ErbB-4 receptors are all members of the ErbB family of receptor tyrosine kinases (RTK) (HER4) (Fig. 7.1) (Kim et al., 2016; Ribeiro et al., 2014). EGFR contains a hydrophobic transmembrane, ligand-binding site, and cytoplasmic TK site (Plowman et al., 1993). The intracellular TK-site of ErbB receptors is substantially conserved, while ErbB-3's kinase domain has significant amino acid changes. As a result, it is devoid of kinase activity (Bublil et al., 2010; Shi et al., 2010).

When the epidermal growth factor binds to the receptor, it activates the epidermal growth factor receptor. This receptor refreshes the metalloproteinase and causes the cross-phosphorylation of tyrosine kinase (Grandis et al., 2004; Gschwind et al., 2002; Vermeer et al., 2003). This activates two pathways RAS and PI3K. RAS activates the RAF, and further, it activates the MEK. PLCγ, Eps15, and Cbl are the different signaling molecules that bind to this TK (Chattopadhyay et al., 1999). By activating MEK, it causes cell proliferation. AKT is phosphorylated and activated by PI3K activation, which causes it to be localized in the plasma membrane (Hong et al., 2016). This enzyme belongs to the SH2 (Src homology 2-like) protein domain-containing AKT subfamily of serine/threonine kinases (McCubrey et al., 2007; Toker, 2000). Then, mTOR activates Akt signaling and helps in cell motility and cell survival, which also causes angiogenesis (Fig. 7.2). When there is overexpression of the cells and the number of cells increases in the body organs and other parts, EGFR inhibitors are used (Okawa et al., 2007; Verbeek et al., 1998). These are those substances that block the activity of EGF protein and decrease cell growth. Gefitinib and erlotinib (first-generation EGFR inhibitors) were the first-line EGFR inhibitors that are used in lung cancer (Herbst et al., 2003; Le et al., 2019). Gefitinib acts by inhibiting the phosphorylation of TK and stopping the further mechanism (Formisano et al., 2015; Höpfner et al., 2004). It decreases cell proliferation that causes angiogenesis (Huang et al., 2002).

El-Sayed and coworkers have designed and synthesized the 4,6-disubstituted 2-(4-(dimethylamino)styryl)quinolone derivatives and assessed them for anticancer activity. The anticancer activity of all the synthesized compounds was performed by using MTT assay on two cancer cell lines HepG2 and HCT116, which were hepatocellular and colon cancer cell

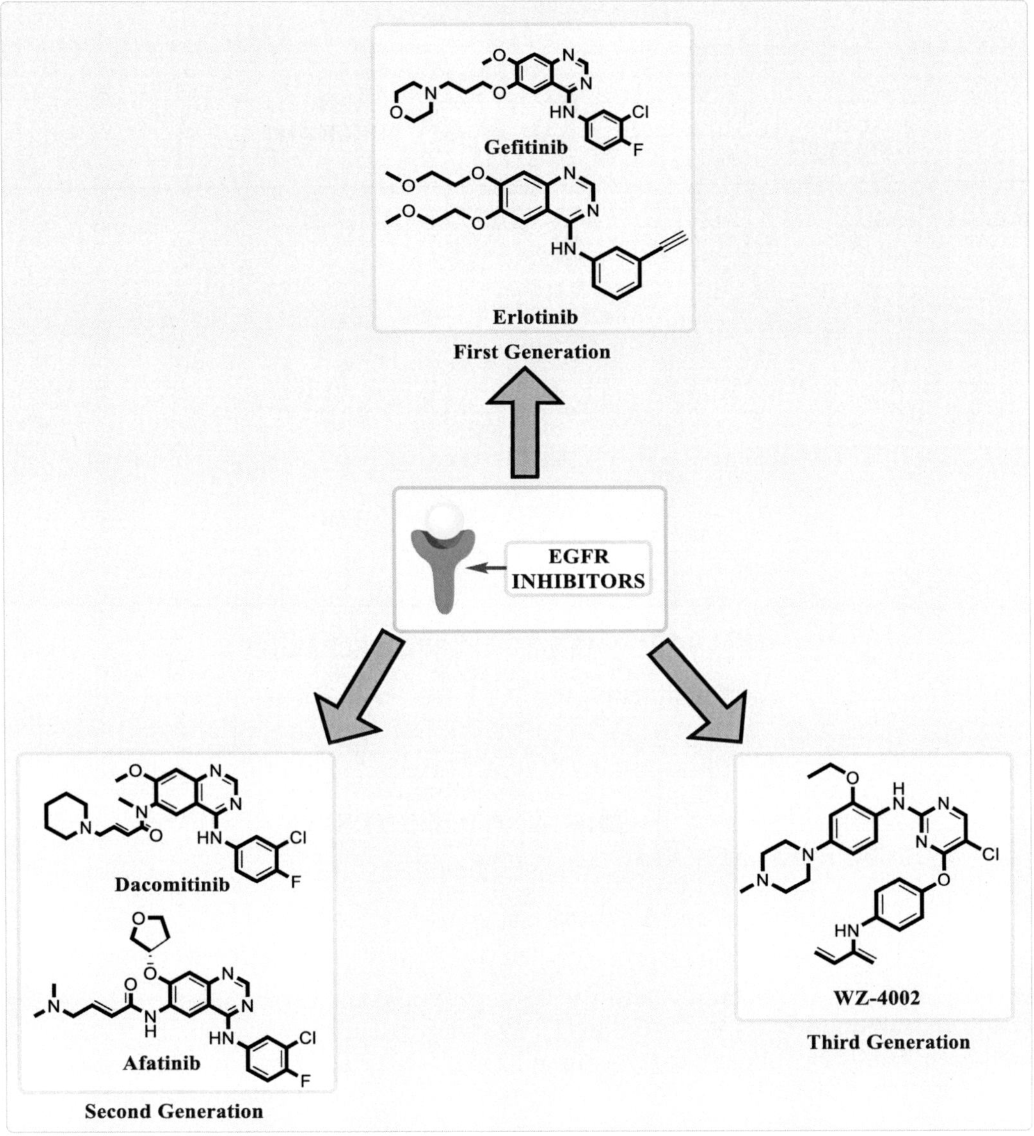

FIGURE 7.1 Types of EGFR inhibitors.

lines, respectively. Moreover, 5-fluorouracil and afatinib were taken as reference drugs. They found that compound **1** was most potent with IC$_{50}$ of 7.7 ± 0.1 μg/mL and 8.8 ± 0.26 μg/mL against HepG2 and HCT116 cell lines. IC$_{50}$ ranging between 1 and 10 μg/mL led to high inhibitory activity. The activity of the EGFR kinase was measured using an enzyme-linked immunosorbent assay. They performed docking studies of compound **1** by using MOE 2008.10 software. Docking studies showed that the quinoline ring present in compound **1**

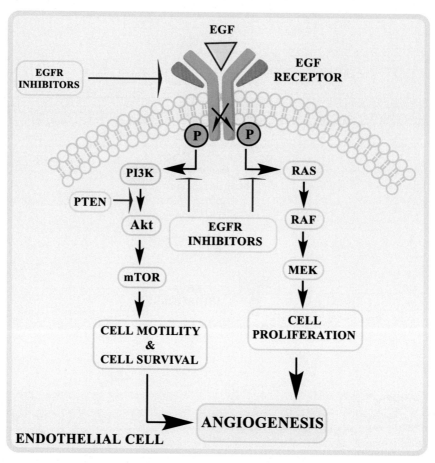

FIGURE 7.2   Signaling pathway of EGFR.

was surrounded hydrophobically with Val702, Leu694, and Leu820 amino acids. The 2-styryl moiety of compound **1** acts as a backbone like 6,7-dialkoxy present in erlotinib. The docking interaction energy of compound **1** was found to be -20.89 kcal/mol. It was revealed that compound **1** was perfectly docked in the assumed binding site of EGFR, which was similar to erlotinib (El-Sayed et al., 2018). SAR studies revealed that the methyl group on the quinoline ring was necessary for activity (Fig. 7.3). It was also found that if the bromine group was introduced at this position, the anticancer activity was slightly decreased. Moreover, 1,3,4-thiadiazol-2-amine moiety on the quinoline ring made the compound active. Replacement with the carboxylate group at this position decreased the anticancer activity 100 times to compound **1**.

Song et al. synthesized a series of morpholine-substituted diphenylpyrimidine derivatives as potent anticancer agents. The anticancer activity of synthesized compounds was evaluated on five cancer cell lines of the normal human bronchial epithelial cell line- H1975, A431, HCC827, A549, and HBE by using an MTT assay. Gefitinib and rociletinib were taken as +ve

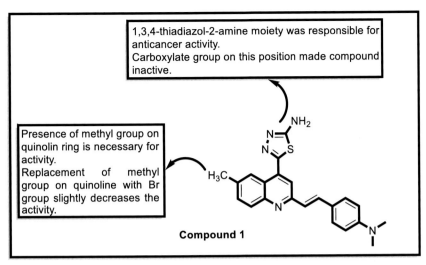

1,3,4-thiadiazol-2-amine moiety was responsible for anticancer activity.
Carboxylate group on this position made compound inactive.

Presence of methyl group on quinolin ring is necessary for activity.
Replacement of methyl group on quinoline with Br group slightly decreases the activity.

Compound 1

FIGURE 7.3   Structure and SAR of compound 1.

control. Compound **2** was found to be most potent with IC_{50} of 0.037 μM against the H1975 cell line. Kinase inhibitory activity was seen on T790M/L858R-mutated EGFR kinases by using the ADP-Glo kinase assay method. They found that compound **1** showed a high selectivity index of 631.9 for T790M mutants, which showed that it causes fewer side effects. They also found that compound **2** showed 28 times higher potency than rociletinib, which has IC_{50} of 20.0 nM. They also performed Western blot analysis, which showed that compound **2** showed their inhibitory potential by inhibiting the phosphorylation step. In vivo studies showed that compound **2** also inhibits the growth of cancer likely rociletinib, which is 70.15% (50 mg). Three doses 50, 20, and 10 mg/kg/day were found to be mostly tolerated doses without any loss in body weight. They performed docking by using Autodock 4.2 to determine the interactions of synthesized compounds with the $EGFR^{T790M}$ enzyme. Docking studies showed that nitrogen of the pyrimidine ring showed hydrogen bonding interactions with Leu792 amino acid. The acrylamide formed a covalent bond with the Cys797 amino acid. SAR studies showed that if the NH group was replaced with O, the compound became inactive. The chlorine group on pyrimidinyl moiety was responsible for anticancer activity. If the chlorine group was replaced with fluorine, the IC_{50} of the compound increased 10 times, and cytotoxicity increased (Fig. 7.4). Acrylamide moiety on C-3 of the terminal benzene ring showed the highest anticancer activity. If this moiety is replaced at the C-2 position, the compound becomes inactive (Song et al., 2017).

Joshi et al. synthesized and evaluated pyrimidine derivatives for their selectivity toward lung, colon, and breast cancer cell lines. Four compounds were found as EGFR inhibitors. Among these, compound **3** was found to be most potent with IC_{50} values of 5.3 ± 0.74 μM, 4.9 ± 0.89 μM, and 3.9 ± 0.65 μM against three cancer cell lines HCT-116, MCF-7, and A549, respectively. They performed an EGFR inhibitory assay to check the phosphorylation inhibition of EGFR. Erlotinib was taken as +ve control. Results showed that compound **3** showed inhibitory activity at 740 ± 0.6 nM. RT-PCR assay was also performed to check the

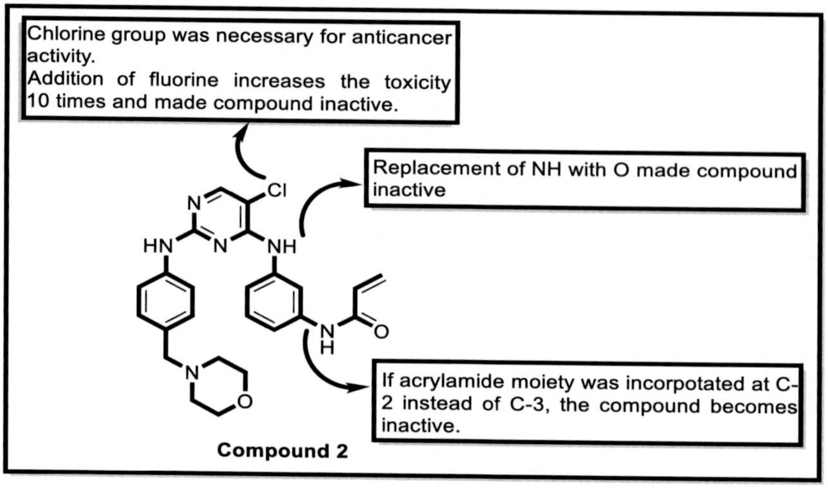

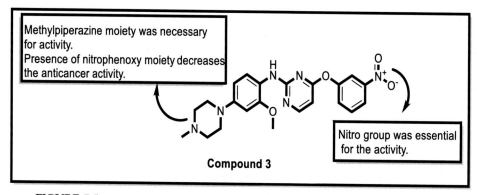

FIGURE 7.4   SAR of compound 2.

DNA replication of cancerous cells. Results showed that compound **3** mainly inhibits EGFR, which causes downregulation of twist. Docking studies were also performed on the ATP binding site of the epidermal growth factor receptor (PDB: 1M17). The docking score of compound **3** was −8.09, which was quite close to erlotinib (−9.02). Docking results showed that compound **3** has higher EGFR inhibitory activity. They found that the nitro group of compound **3** aligned with THR766. H-bonding interactions were also seen with GLU738, THR766 CYS773, and ASP831. The antiproliferative potential was also performed by using an MTT assay on three cell lines namely MCF-7, HCT-116, and A549. Results also showed that compound **3** mainly inhibits the A549 cell line. DHE-based ROS assay was also performed on the lung cell line (A549). Results showed that there is little change in ROS levels at three different concentrations—1, 5, and 25 μM. Cell cycle analysis revealed that compound **3** mainly showed an effect at the sub-G1 phase (0%—30%). No change has been seen in the G1, S, and G2-M phases. SAR studies showed that methylpiperazine moiety was responsible for anticancer activity (Fig. 7.5). If the nitrophenoxy group was introduced, the activity decreased. Nitro group was also essential for activity (Joshi et al., 2017).

FIGURE 7.5   Structure and structure—activity relationship of most potent compound 3.

Fukuda and coworkers have reported the synthesis of A-ring-modified lamellarin N analogs and evaluated them as EGFR inhibitors. Compound **4** was found to be most potent against T790M/L858R mutants with an IC$_{50}$ value of 8.9 nM. Docking studies were carried out using MOE software by taking PDB ID: 4I22 in ATP binding sites of EGFR T790M/L858R/V948R. Results showed that the lactone ring formed H-bonding with NH of Met793 and OH with the carboxylate of Asp855. Another hydrogen bond interaction was also seen between OH at C13 with the carbonyl group of Arg841. Compound **4** also showed hydrogen bond interaction with Asp800, which was responsible for high activity. Docking results also showed that interactions of ring A with Phe795, Asp800, and Asp804 were responsible for the increase in anticancer activity. The structure—activity relationship revealed that a propylene linker was necessary for the optimum activity (Fig. 7.6). If this propylene linker was replaced with an ethylene linker, the anticancer activity of compound **4** decreased. They also explained that the hydroxyl group at C-21 was important for kinase inhibitory activity. Replacement of OH with methoxy decreased the activity (Fukuda et al., 2017).

To develop potent anticancer agents, Abdelazeem et al. synthesized a series of novel diphenylthiazole derivatives. They selected the epidermal growth factor receptor as a target for anticancer activity. The synthesized compounds were evaluated for growth inhibition potential against three cancer cell lines such as MCF-7, HT-29, and A549. The structure—activity relationship revealed that methyl-substituted Schiff base derivatives showed better anticancer activity. They found that substitution with maleic moiety also showed some activity. Bulky groups on terminal phenyl rings were optimum for activity. If there is no substitution on the phenyl ring, the compound becomes inactive. It was evaluated by the SAR study that compound **5** was the most active among all synthesized compounds Fig. 7.7. The IC$_{50}$ value of compound **5** was 6.25, 5.21, and 8.32 μM against three cell lines MCF-7, HT-29, and A549, respectively. Doxorubicin was taken as a reference drug. A docking simulation was

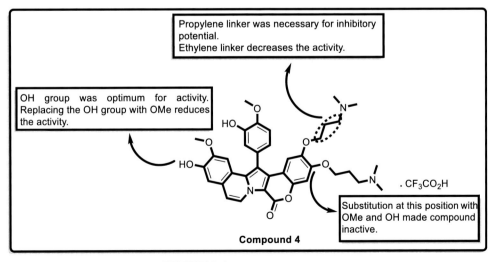

FIGURE 7.6   SAR of compound 4.

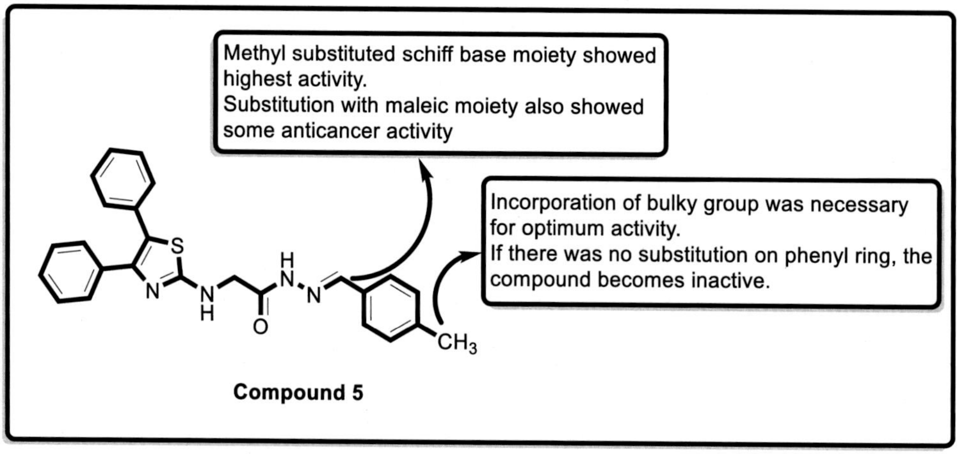

Methyl substituted schiff base moiety showed highest activity.
Substitution with maleic moiety also showed some anticancer activity

Incorporation of bulky group was necessary for optimum activity.
If there was no substitution on phenyl ring, the compound becomes inactive.

Compound 5

FIGURE 7.7   SAR of compound 5.

performed to determine the binding modes of compounds within the ATP-active site of BRAF and EGFR. It was investigated by docking simulation that diphenylthiazole moiety formed hydrophobic interactions with Leu694, Pro770, Gly722, and Asp776. Some $\pi-\pi$ interactions were also seen between p-tolyl moiety and Phe699 (Abdelazeem et al., 2017).

Novel chalcone derivatives endowed with triazolo[4,3-a]- quinoxaline moieties were synthesized in 2017 by Alswah et al. Compounds were screened for their anticancer property toward some cell lines such as MCF-7, HCT-116, and HEPG-2. Among all the synthesized compounds, only compound **6** was found to be most potent with IC_{50} of 3.61, 1.65, and 8.58 µM against MCF-7, HCT-116, and HEPG-2, respectively. It was also reported that compound **6** was also a potent target-specific antitumor agent. To check EGFR inhibitory activity, staurosporine was taken as a reference drug. Results showed that compound **6** showed EGFR inhibition of 0.039 µM. SAR studies showed that triazoloquinoxaline moiety was responsible for anticancer activity (Fig. 7.8). Quinoxaline ring plays an important role in EGFR inhibition. They also revealed that the methoxy group at the third and fourth position of the terminal phenyl ring of chalcone was necessary for optimum activity. Docking studies were performed

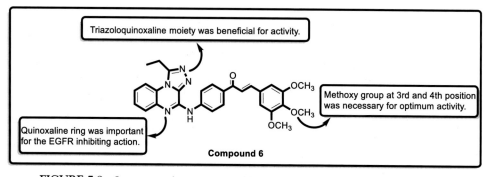

FIGURE 7.8   Structure and structure–activity relationship of most potent compound 6.

on the ATP pocket of EGFR TK targets. Results showed that compound **6** showed a higher binding energy of −15.5 kcal/mol. They also found that the methoxy group and carbonyl formed hydrogen bonding interactions with Lys721 and Met769. Triazoloquinoxaline moiety also formed aromatic hydrophobic interactions with Lys704. The chalcone moiety was surrounded hydrophobically by Leu248, Ala315 Ile378, and Leu255 residues in the β-subunit (Alswah et al., 2018).

Novel 1,2,4-triazole derivatives that act as EGFR inhibitors were developed by El-Sherief et al. El-Sherief et al. prepared 1,2,4-triazole derivatives as potential EGFR inhibitors and also investigated their antiproliferative activity against the NCI 60 cell line. Among all 1,2,4-triazole derivatives, compound **7** was found to possess high antiproliferative and EGFR inhibitory activity against human tumor cell lines such as Panc-1, PaCa-2 HT-29, and H-460. The IC$_{50}$ of compound **7** was found to be 2.8, 2.6, 2.4, and 1.6 μM against Panc-1, PaCa-2 HT-29, and H-460, respectively. Cell cycle analysis and apoptosis detection assay were carried out. It was found that compound **7** mainly causes preapoptosis in the G1 phase and causes cell cycle arrest at the G2/M phase. Researchers group has performed docking at the ATP binding site of EGFR. Compound **7** displayed a couple of hydrogen bonds between trimethoxyphenyl or monomethoxy moieties and Thr830. Hydrophobic interactions were also seen between phenyl ring and Ala719, thr766, and Leu764. Compound **7** also formed π stacking with Phe771 and π−cation with Lys721. Thus, seven was found to have the highest docking score −90.41. SAR exploration demonstrated that chlorophenyl moiety exhibited the highest EGFR inhibition activity. They found that para-substituted compounds showed higher activity than meta-substituted Fig. 7.9. Terminal methoxy group was necessary for anticancer activity (El-Sherief et al., 2018).

George et al., in 2018, accomplished in vitro cytotoxic screening against MCF-7, HeLa, DLD1, and WI38 cell lines and illustrated an SAR study of quinoline-based 4,5-dihydropyrazoles and their thiazole hybrids as EGFR inhibitors. Among all compounds, **8** was found as a potent EGFR inhibitor. IC$_{50}$ of compound **8** was 0.064 μM against the DLD1 cell line. As a positive control, CHS 828 was employed. EGFR inhibitory activity was determined by using gefitinib as reference drug. The IC$_{50}$ of compound **8** was 42.52 nM. SAR exploration verified that quinolinyl pyrazoline hybrids led to increased

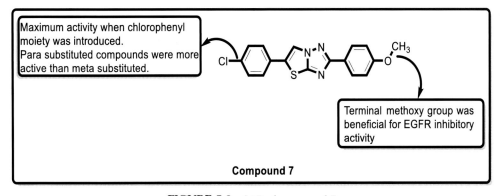

FIGURE 7.9   SAR of compound 7.

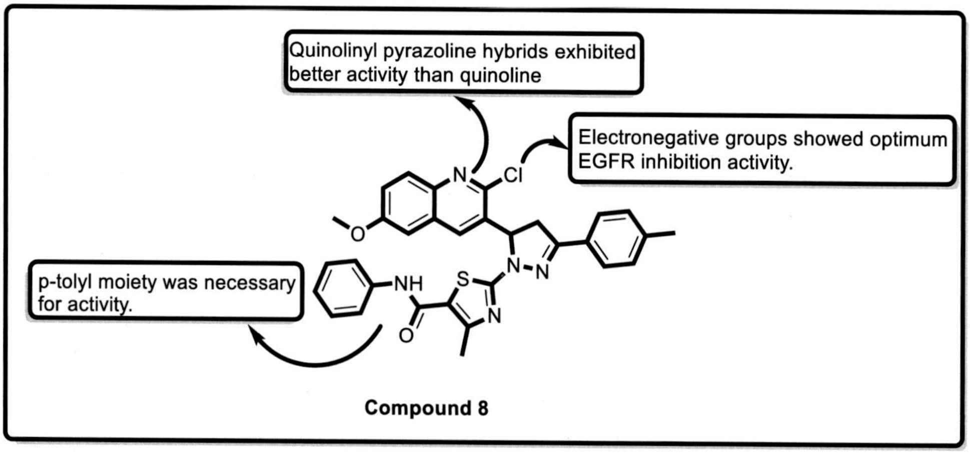

FIGURE 7.10 SAR of potent compound 8.

activity with high efficacy. Electronegative groups on quinolinyl such as F, Cl showed optimum EGFR inhibition activity than electropositive groups Fig. 7.10. Molecular docking of **8** on the binding site of EGFR was done to prepare a binding model. It formed hydrogen bonding interactions with Met769 and also exhibited cation−π interaction with Lys721. The docking score of compound **8** was found to be −12.94 kcal/mol. Other interactions were also formed hydrophobically with Leu694. The 2D structure was more stable by the hydrophobic−hydrophobic interaction with 4,5-dihydropyrazoles moiety at the other end of the ATP binding pockets (George et al., 2019).

In 2019, novel 1H-pyrazolo[3,4-d] pyrimidine derivatives were prepared by Gaber et al., which were later biologically appraised to explore anticancer activity against five cancer cell lines, which included MCF7, HepG2, A549, H1975, and HCC827. In vitro antiproliferative activities have been explored in comparison with reference drugs Lapatinib, Sorafenib, Erlotinib, and Osimertinib by using MTT assay. Results showed that compound **9** have better inhibitory potential which was found to be 0.50 ± 1.90 μM, 0.01 ± 0.71 μM, 0.62 ± 1.70 μM, 0.04 ± 0.33 μM, and 0.12 ± 0.07 μM against MCF7, A549, HepG2, H1975, and HCC827 cell lines, respectively. They also evaluated the in vitro enzymatic inhibitory of synthesized compounds against EGFR^{WT} and EGFR^{790M}. The IC$_{50}$ value of potent compound **9** was found to be 0.09 ± 0.11 nM and 5.30 ± 0.52 nM against EGFR^{WT} and EGFR^{790M} enzymes, respectively. They also performed in vitro DNA-flow cytometric analysis against the HepG2 cell line to determine that, in which phase of the cell cycle, compound **9** causes cell arrest. Their findings showed that compound **9** mainly stops the G$_0$/G$_1$ and G$_2$/M stages of the cell cycle. Annexin V-FITC apoptosis assay proposed that compound **9** causes apoptosis in HepG2 cells. Early apoptosis was increased from 0.21% to 15.61% and late apoptosis from 0.12% to 45.45%. They found that compound **9** showed better apoptotic activity than others. SAR results illuminated that antiproliferative activity was increased upon the introduction of fluorophenyl moiety (Fig. 7.11). The presence of ketohydrazinyl linker was responsible for maximum activity. It was investigated by docking that 1H-pyrazolo [3,4-d]pyrimidine moiety of compound **9** has shown hydrogen bonding with Lys721 amino acid. Researchers also reported that

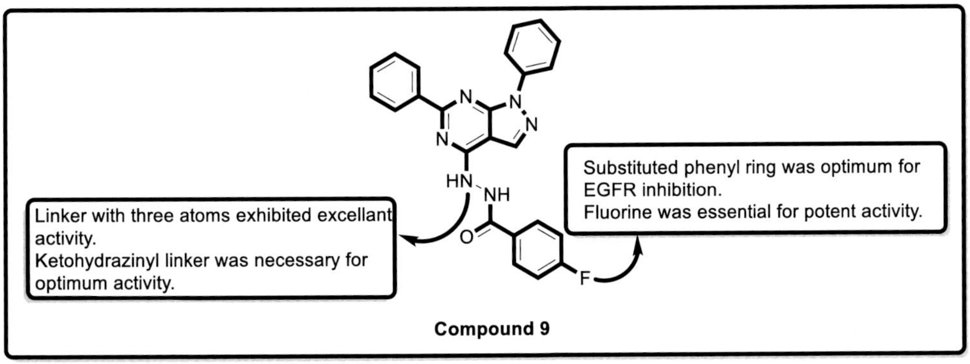

FIGURE 7.11 Structure and SAR of compound 9.

ketohydrazinyl moiety also formed a couple of hydrogen bonds with Asp831 and Thr830. Phe832, Lue843, Lue764, Lue753, and Thr766 residues formed hydrophobic interactions with the fluoro phenyl molecule. The docking energy of compound **9** was -24.89 kcal/mol and -26.68 kcal/mol against $EGFR^{WT}$ and $EGFR^{790M}$ (Gaber et al., 2018).

In 2018, Zhang et al. developed a series of 6,7-dimorpholinoalkoxy quinazoline derivatives, which were found to have EGFR inhibitory activity. These compounds were later used to explore antiproliferative activity by using an MTT assay against five cancer cell lines which included A431 (human epidermoid cell), SW480 (colon cancer cells), A549, HCC827, and NCI−H1975 (NSCLC cell lines). They found that compound **10** was found to be most potent with IC_{50} of $1.31 \pm 0.55 \, \mu M$. $1.65 \pm 0.29 \, \mu M$, $0.37 \pm 0.06 \, \mu M$, $4.87 \pm 0.68 \, \mu M$, $3.27 \pm 1.25 \, \mu M$ against A431, SW480, A549, HCC827, and NCI−H1975, respectively. EGFR inhibitory activity of compound **10** was found to be 7.0 ± 1.4 nM against $EGFR^{wt}$-TK and 9.3 ± 0.9 nM against $EGFR^{T790M}$-TK. SAR studies authenticated that the three-carbon spacer exhibited excellent inhibitory activity. If the spacer decreased, the EGFR inhibitory activity decreased. They also found that 3-chloro-4-(3-fluorobenzyloxy)aniline substitution was necessary for optimum activity Fig. 7.12. Molecular modeling studies revealed that nitrogen of the quinazoline ring formed hydrogen bonding with NH of Met793 amino acid. Some other H-bondings were also seen between the oxygen of morpholine and Lys745 amino acid, and also between fluorine of fluorocenzyloxy of compound 10 with Asp855 and Phe856 amino acid. They found that compound **10** mainly decreased the level of p-Tyr and p-EGFR, which showed that compound **10** stopped phosphorylation and made EGFR inactive. Compound 10 also caused cell cycle arrest in the G0/G1 phase of the cell cycle in A549 cells (Zhang et al., 2018).

To develop potent anticancer agents, Abdelatef et al. (2018) synthesized novel spirobenzo[h]chromene and spirochromane derivatives. It was inspected that compound **11** was found to be the most potent EGFR inhibitor. The anticancer activity was evaluated against MCF-7, HT-29, and A549 cell lines. They found that a compound containing hydrazine derivative was the most effective EGFR inhibitor. The IC_{50} of compound **11** was $4.09 \pm 0.21 \, \mu M$, $1.78 \pm 0.24 \, \mu M$, and $4.45 \pm 0.54 \, \mu M$ against MCF-7, HT-29, and A549 cell lines, respectively. They also checked the effect of some compounds on normal cells such as fibroblast (F180) by using an MTT assay. Results exhibited that compound **11** displayed

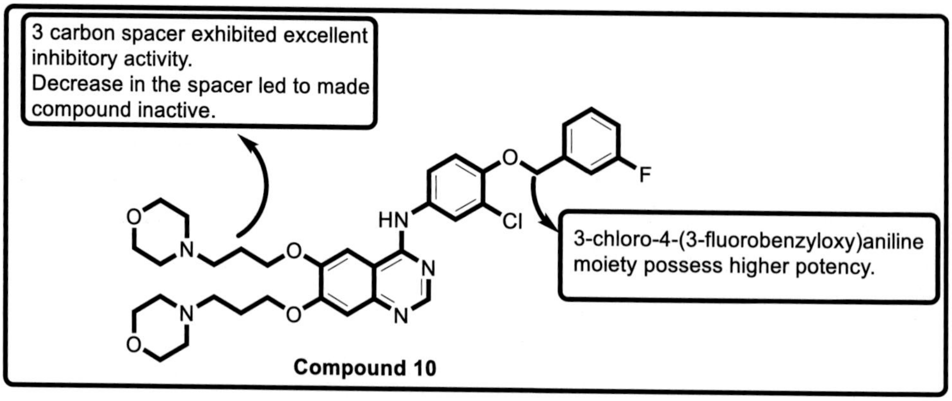

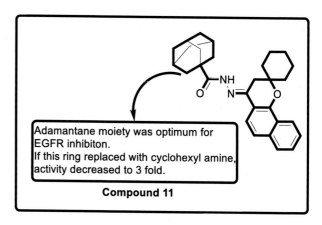

> 3 carbon spacer exhibited excellent inhibitory activity.
> Decrease in the spacer led to made compound inactive.

> 3-chloro-4-(3-fluorobenzyloxy)aniline moiety possess higher potency.

Compound 10

FIGURE 7.12   SAR of compound 10.

good safety toward F180 with IC$_{50}$ more than 40 µM. Researchers also assessed their EGFR inhibitory activity. Results illustrated that compound **11** showed better EGFR inhibitory potential than other compounds with IC$_{50}$ of 1.2 ± 0.4 µM among other compounds. SAR studies illustrated that an adamantine ring was necessary for optimum activity (Fig. 7.13). If this ring was replaced with a cyclohexyl amine, the EGFR inhibition decreased threefold. Docking studies of compound **11** were performed on ATP binding sites of EGFR kinase (PDB ID: 1M17). Various hydrophobic interactions were formed between spirochromane and Leu694, Leu768, Asp776, and Leu820. They also found that adamantyl moiety in compound **11** formed hydrophobic interactions with Ala719, Met742, and leu764 (Abdelatef et al., 2018).

Novel indole-2-carboxamides and pyrazino[1,2-a]indol1(2H)-ones derivatives were synthesized by Youssif and coworkers. The anticancer activity was assessed against five cancer cell lines such as PC-3, A-549, MCF-7, PaCa-2, and HT-29. They found that compound 12 was found to be the most potent antiproliferative agent, which has IC$_{50}$ of 0.9 ± 0.2 µM,

FIGURE 7.13   SAR of compound 11.

> Adamantane moiety was optimum for EGFR inhibiton.
> If this ring replaced with cyclohexyl amine, activity decreased to 3 fold.

Compound 11

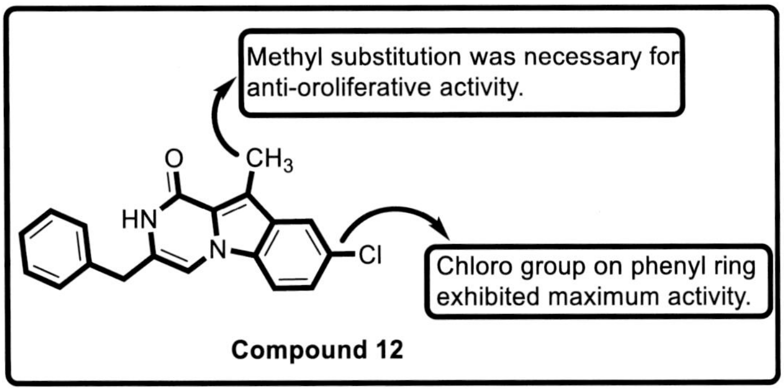

FIGURE 7.14   SAR of compound 12.

$0.8 \pm 0.5\,\mu\text{M}$, $0.1 \pm 0.08\,\mu\text{M}$, $0.3 \pm 0.2\,\mu\text{M}$, and $0.6 \pm 0.2\,\mu\text{M}$ against PC-3, A-549, MCF-7, PaCa-2, and HT-29 cell lines. Compound **12** was found to be a potent EGFR inhibitor with IC_{50} $1.7 \pm 0.5\,\mu\text{M}$ EGFR inhibition by taking Erlotinib as a reference. They found that compound **12** inhibits the phosphorylation step. SAR illustrated that methyl substitution on the indole ring exhibited optimum activity. They also found that substituted phenyl ring showed higher EGFR inhibition than unsubstituted. Chloro moiety on the phenyl ring showed the highest anticancer activity (Fig. 7.14). Docking studies resulted that benzyl moiety of compound 12 formed cation—π interaction with Lys721. Other π—π interactions were also seen between benzyl moiety and Phe699 residue (Youssif et al., 2018).

Elmetwally and coworkers designed a new series of thieno[2,3-d]pyrimidine derivatives as dual EGFR and HER2 inhibitors. All the synthesized compounds were accessed for EGFR and HER2 inhibition assay and compound **13** was found to be the most potent inhibitor toward both enzymes. The IC_{50} of compound **13** was 0.278, 0.352, and 0.415 μM against $EGFR^{WT}$, $EGFR^{T790M}$, and HER2, respectively. All the synthesized compounds were tested for their antiproliferative activity against HepG2 HCT-116 MCF-7 A431 cell lines by applying the MTT colorimetric assay. Compound **13** exhibited excellent antiproliferative activity against the MCF-7 cell line. The IC_{50} of compound **13** was found to be $7.592 \pm 0.32\,\mu\text{M}$ against the MCF-7 cell line. They also performed in vitro DNA-flow cytometric analysis. Results illustrated that compound **13** mainly inhibits the G2/M phase of the cell cycle. They found that there was 10.66% cell arrest in the G2/M phase when the cells were treated with DMSO. However, by treating compound **13** with MCF-7, the cell cycle arrest increased to 49.82%. Annexin V/PI assay was performed to check that the cells died with apoptosis or necrosis. Results showed that compound **13** mainly caused an increase in early apoptosis (0.72%—7.92%) and late apoptosis (0.27%—12.47%). They found that cells mainly died due to apoptosis not by necrosis. A small change was also seen from 0.45% to 3.08% in necrosis, which was negligible. Structure—activity relationships showed that the NH linker was necessary for optimum activity. They found that if the NH linker was replaced with (NHPhNH-) linker, the EGFR inhibition decreased. The presence of substituted phenyl decreased the anticancer inhibition (Fig. 7.15). Molecular docking studies were performed to check the perfect orientation of compounds at the ATP binding site of EGFR. Results exhibited that the quinazoline ring of compound **13** formed hydrogen bonding with Met769. Another pie—sigma

FIGURE 7.15 SAR of thieno[2,3-d]pyrimidine derivative 13.

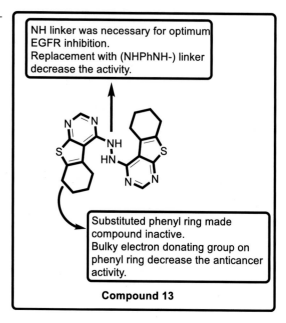

NH linker was necessary for optimum EGFR inhibition.
Replacement with (NHPhNH-) linker decrease the activity.

Substituted phenyl ring made compound inactive.
Bulky electron donating group on phenyl ring decrease the anticancer activity.

Compound 13

interaction was also formed between the phenyl ring with Leu694. The binding energy of compound **13** was −28.56 kcal/mol (Elmetwally et al., 2019).

Sever and coworkers have reported the synthesis of a new series of thiazolyl-pyrazolines as dual EGFR and HER2 inhibitors. All the synthesized compounds were accessed for enzyme and EGFR inhibition. They found that compound **14** was active against EGFR and HER2 enzyme with IC$_{50}$ of 4.34 ± 0.66 µM and 2.28 ± 0.53 µM, respectively. The antiproliferative activity was determined by using an MTT assay on A549, MCF-7, and A375 cell lines. They found that compound **14** is mainly effective against A549 and MCF-7 cell lines with high potency. The IC$_{50}$ was found to be 10.76 ± 1.81 µM 8.05 ± 1.47 µM against A549 and MCF-7 cell lines, respectively. Sever and coworkers also found that most of the synthesized compounds were found to be inactive against A375 cells, which have more than 100 µM inhibitory potential. SAR studies illustrated that the morpholine ring was necessary for anticancer activity. If the morpholine ring is replaced with a piperidine ring, the EGFR inhibitory potential decreases. They also found that the addition of a cyanophenyl ring on the thiazole ring exhibited optimum activity. If the cyanophenyl ring was replaced with 4-nitrophenyl and 4-methylphenyl, the anticancer activity reduced (Fig. 7.16). Docking studies were performed against the ATP-binding site of EGFR by taking erlotinib (PDB ID: 4HJO) as a reference and also on the HER2 binding site (PDB ID: 3RCD). They found that the cyano group on the phenyl ring made H−π interaction with Lys721. Another H−π interaction was also seen between the thiazole of compound **14** and Val702 (Sever et al., 2019).

George and coworkers have reported the synthesis of 1,3,5-trisubstituted pyrazoline derivatives as EGFR inhibitors. All the synthesized compounds were assessed against two cancer cell lines- MCF-7 and WI38 for antiproliferative activity. Compound **15** was found to be most

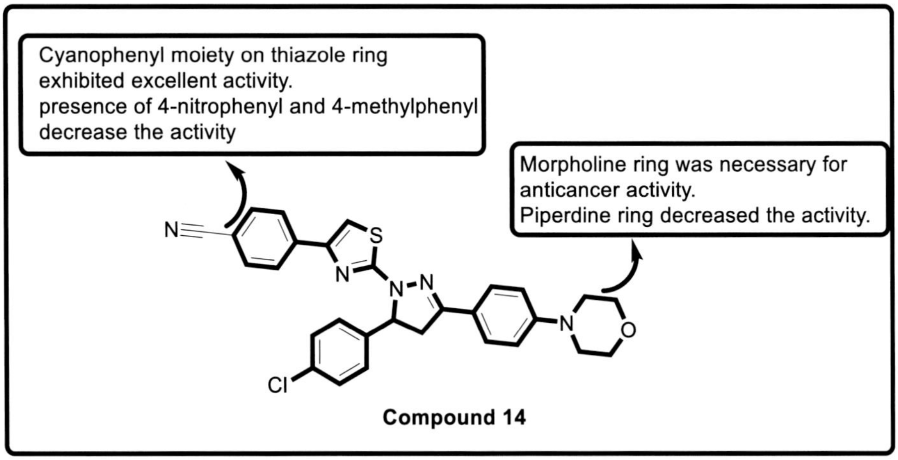

Cyanophenyl moiety on thiazole ring exhibited excellent activity.
presence of 4-nitrophenyl and 4-methylphenyl decrease the activity

Morpholine ring was necessary for anticancer activity.
Piperdine ring decreased the activity.

Compound 14

FIGURE 7.16   Structure and SAR of thiazolyl-pyrazolines derivative 14.

active against the MCF-7 cell line which has IC$_{50}$ of $3.93 \pm 0.07 \, \mu$M. Compound **15** also showed 1.39 μM (IC$_{50}$) EGFR inhibitions. SAR studies showed that the chloro group on the phenyl ring was necessary for anticancer activity. They found that if the chloro group was replaced with the methoxy group, the activity decreased. SAR studies also revealed that styryl moiety was necessary for optimum activity (Fig. 7.17). Docking studies were also performed on the EGFR active site. They found H-bonding interactions with Met769. Some hydrophobic interactions were also formed between the phenyl moiety of compound **15** with Val702, Ala719, Met742, and Leu764. They also found hydrophobic interactions between 4-chlorophenyl of pyrazoline and leu820 amino acid. The binding score of compound **15** was −9.55 kcal/mol (George et al., 2020).

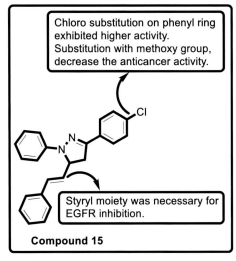

Chloro substitution on phenyl ring exhibited higher activity.
Substitution with methoxy group, decrease the anticancer activity.

Styryl moiety was necessary for EGFR inhibition.

Compound 15

FIGURE 7.17   SAR of compound 15.

Abou-Zied and coworkers have synthesized xanthine derivatives containing chalcone moiety as EGFR inhibitors and apoptotic inducers. All the synthesized compounds were evaluated for anticancer agents on three cancer cell lines such as Panc-1 MCF-7 HT-29 and A-549. Compound **16** was found to be most potent against these cell lines. The IC_{50} was found to be 1.3, 1.0, 1.2, and 1.5 µM. EGFR-TK assay revealed that compound **16** inhibits the autophosphorylation step with IC_{50} of 0.3 µM. Caspase-3-activation assay was performed on pancreas cell lines. Results of the caspase-3-activation assay showed that compound **16** causes apoptosis in overexpressive cells (Conc. = 532.20 Pg/mL). Flow cytometric cell cycle analysis was carried out on Panc-1 to determine that, in which phase of the cell cycle, compound 16 exhibits cell arrest. Results showed that compound **16** decreased the % from 53.64% to 26.67%. Doxorubicin was taken as a standard drug which explained that compound **16** exhibited cell arrest in the G2/M phase. SAR studies showed that 1,3-dimethyl groups on xanthine exhibited the most potent activity. If the 1-Cl group was added, the activity decreased to sevenfold. They also found that chlorophenyl moiety was necessary for EGFR inhibition (Fig. 7.18). A docking study was performed by taking the EGFR crystal structure from a protein data bank which has a PDB ID of 1M17. Results showed that chalcone made H-bonding with Arg817 and Asp831. Xanthine moiety in compound **16** also made H-bonding with Pro770 and His871 (Abou-Zied et al., 2019).

Xiao et al. synthesized and executed docking simulation of some innovative thiophene-pyrimidine derivatives as EGFR inhibitors. The synthesized compounds were screened for anticancer evaluation on four cancer cell lines such as A549, A431, Hela, and MCF-7. Researchers found that compound **17** was the most potent anticancer agent against these cell lines. The observed IC_{50} value was found to be 4.34 ± 0.60 µM, 3.79 ± 0.57 µM, 6.39 ± 0.94 µM, and 18.99 ± 1.71 µM against A549, A431, Hela, and MCF-7, respectively, by taking olmutinib as reference drug. In vitro H1975 cell viability assay was carried out on different compounds, which showed that by treating cells with compound **17**, there was 44.31% inhibition at 1 µM. Compound **17** also showed kinase inhibitory activity. Results showed that compound **17** causes 95.9% $EGFR^{T790M}$ inhibition with IC_{50} of 65.0 nM. SAR studies revealed that anisidine moiety played an important role in EGFR inhibition. They also found that conjugation of side chains was necessary for anticancer activity.

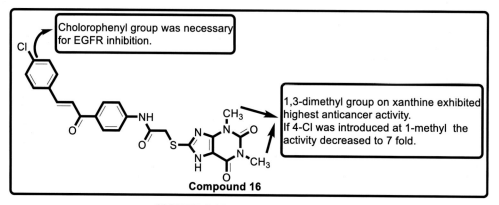

FIGURE 7.18   SAR of compound 16.

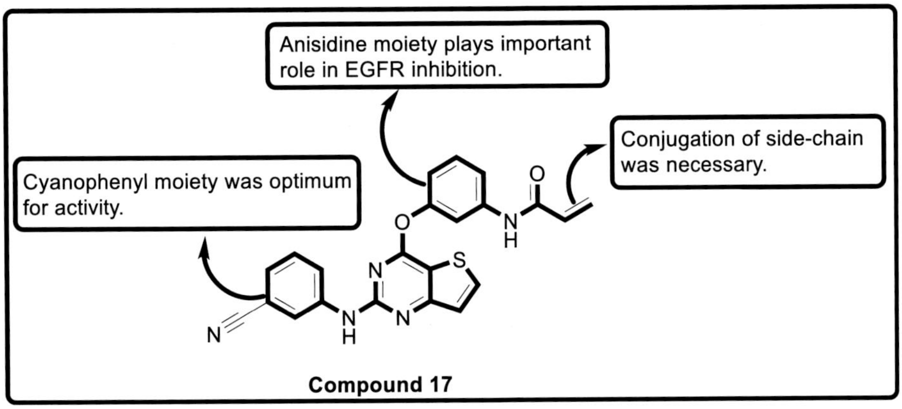

Anisidine moiety plays important role in EGFR inhibition.

Cyanophenyl moiety was optimum for activity.

Conjugation of side-chain was necessary.

Compound 17

FIGURE 7.19   Structure and SAR of thiophene-pyrimidine derivative 17.

The cyanophenyl ring was optimum for activity (Fig. 7.19). Docking studies (PDB 2ID: 31 KA) showed that the aminopyrimidine group of compound **17** forms an H-bond with Met790 amino acid. In most cases, the amide group interacts with Cys797. But, in this, the amide group formed interactions with Arg841 (Xiao et al., 2020).

Alam and coworkers have synthesized 1,3,4-oxadiazole derivatives as EGFR inhibitors. They designed these derivatives based on the naproxen ring by attaching a linker. Because naproxen derivatives such as propanamide exhibited excellent anticancer activity. Among all the synthesized compounds, compound **18** was found to be the most potent anticancer agent and also found to be the most potent EGFR inhibitor. The anticancer activity was evaluated on three cancer cells named as MCF-7, HepG2, and HCT-116. They found that compound **18** was highly effective against two cell lines, MCF-7 and HepG2, which have IC_{50} of 2.13 and 1.63 µg/mL, respectively. ELISA test was performed to check the EGFR inhibitory activity. EGFR inhibition of compound **18** was found to be 0.41 µM. The number of cell deaths caused by compound **18** was the highest among all compounds. Structure–activity relationship illustrated that the 1,3,4-oxadiazol ring exhibited excellent activity (Fig. 7.20).

FIGURE 7.20   SAR of 1,3,4-oxadiazole derivative 18.

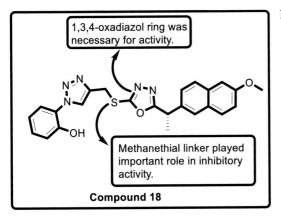

1,3,4-oxadiazol ring was necessary for activity.

Methanethial linker played important role in inhibitory activity.

Compound 18

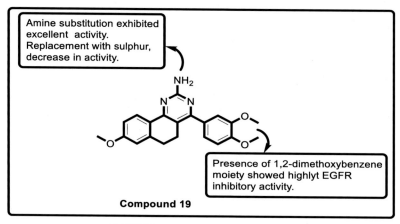

Amine substitution exhibited excellent activity. Replacement with sulphur, decrease in activity.

Presence of 1,2-dimethoxybenzene moiety showed highlyt EGFR inhibitory activity.

Compound 19

FIGURE 7.21   SAR of compound 19.

They found that methanethiol linker played an important role in EGFR inhibition. Docking was performed to find the best binding interactions of the compound with its protein epidermal growth factor receptor. Compound **18** formed H-interactions with Asn818 (Alam et al., 2021).

Abdelsalam and coworkers have synthesized fused indazoles, quinazolines, and quinoline derivatives as potent EGFR inhibitors. The anticancer activity was appraised on three cancer cell lines namely HepG2, MCF-7, and HCT116 and Caco-2. They found compound **19** as a potent anticancer agent against the MCF-7 cell line. The obtained IC_{50} was 7.21 μM against the MCF-7 cell line. EGFR inhibitory activity was determined by ADP-Glo kinase assay. Results showed that compound **19** was a potent EGFR inhibitor with IC_{50} of 0.13 ± 0.01 μM. SAR illustrated that the compound containing amine substitution on the quinazoline ring exhibited excellent activity. If the amine group was replaced with sulfur, the activity decreased to twofold (Fig. 7.21). Compound **19**, containing 1,2-dimethoxybenzene moiety, showed the most potent anticancer activity. Docking studies were performed on the ATP binding site of EGFR. Results showed that N1 of quinazoline ring forms an H-bonding with Met769, and N3 of quinazoline with Thr766 (Abdelsalam et al., 2019).

2. Conclusion

Cancer prognosis has been associated with an aberrant EGFR signaling cascade. Tyrosine kinase is activated by EGFR amplification, deletion mutations, and overexpressions, which ultimately aid in the growth of malignant cancer. The crucial cell survival downregulated EGFR is in charge of a complex network of signaling processes that results in cell growth and proliferation. Because of this, EGFR has been researched as a potential target of cancer treatment. EGFR flagging alone is not adequate to keep up with cell endurance endlessly; however, it may act as one of the sensors controlling the level of apoptotic motioning inside a cell. The way to create powerful anti-EGFR remedial techniques lies in the comprehension of what kind of blend of designated machines will render the EGFR endurance flagging pathway inadequate for recuperating and how to coordinate these new natural specialists with standard accessible treatments.

References

Abdelatef, S. A., et al. (2018). Design, synthesis and anticancer evaluation of novel spirobenzo [h] chromene and spirochromane derivatives with dual EGFR and B-RAF inhibitory activities. *European Journal of Medicinal Chemistry, 150*, 567–578.

Abdelazeem, A. H., et al. (2017). Novel diphenylthiazole derivatives with multi-target mechanism: Synthesis, docking study, anticancer and anti-inflammatory activities. *Bioorganic Chemistry, 75*, 127–138.

Abdelsalam, E. A., et al. (2019). Synthesis and in vitro anticancer evaluation of some fused indazoles, quinazolines and quinolines as potential EGFR inhibitors. *Bioorganic Chemistry, 89*, Article 102985.

Abou-Zied, H. A., et al. (2019). EGFR inhibitors and apoptotic inducers: Design, synthesis, anticancer activity and docking studies of novel xanthine derivatives carrying chalcone moiety as hybrid molecules. *Bioorganic Chemistry, 89*, Article 102997.

Alam, M. M., et al. (2021). Naproxen based 1, 3, 4-oxadiazole derivatives as EGFR inhibitors: Design, synthesis, anticancer, and computational studies. *Pharmaceuticals, 14*(9), 870.

Ali, I., Wani, W. A., & Saleem, K. (2011). Cancer scenario in India with future perspectives. *Cancer Therapy, 8*.

Alswah, M., et al. (2018). Design, synthesis and cytotoxic evaluation of novel chalcone derivatives bearing triazolo [4, 3-a]-quinoxaline moieties as potent anticancer agents with dual EGFR kinase and tubulin polymerization inhibitory effects. *Molecules, 23*(1), 48.

Avraham, R., & Yarden, Y. (2011). Feedback regulation of EGFR signalling: Decision making by early and delayed loops. *Nature Reviews Molecular Cell Biology, 12*(2), 104–117.

Breslow, N. E., Day, N. E., & Heseltine, E. (1980). *Statistical methods in cancer research. Vol. 1*. International Agency for Research on Cancer Lyon.

Bublil, E. M., et al. (2010). Kinase-mediated quasi-dimers of EGFR. *The FASEB Journal, 24*(12), 4744–4755.

Chattopadhyay, A., et al. (1999). The role of individual SH2 domains in mediating association of phospholipase C-γ1 with the activated EGF receptor. *Journal of Biological Chemistry, 274*(37), 26091–26097.

D'Arcy, M. S. (2019). Cell death: A review of the major forms of apoptosis, necrosis and autophagy. *Cell Biology International, 43*(6), 582–592.

El-Sayed, M. A.-A., et al. (2018). Synthesis and biological evaluation of 2-styrylquinolines as antitumour agents and EGFR kinase inhibitors: Molecular docking study. *Journal of Enzyme Inhibition and Medicinal Chemistry, 33*(1), 199–209.

El-Sherief, H. A., et al. (2018). Synthesis, anticancer activity and molecular modeling studies of 1, 2, 4-triazole derivatives as EGFR inhibitors. *European Journal of Medicinal Chemistry, 156*, 774–789.

Elmetwally, S. A., et al. (2019). Design, synthesis and anticancer evaluation of thieno [2, 3-d] pyrimidine derivatives as dual EGFR/HER2 inhibitors and apoptosis inducers. *Bioorganic Chemistry, 88*, Article 102944.

Eswarakumar, V., Lax, I., & Schlessinger, J. (2005). Cellular signaling by fibroblast growth factor receptors. *Cytokine & Growth Factor Reviews, 16*(2), 139–149.

Formisano, L., et al. (2015). Src inhibitors act through different mechanisms in Non-Small Cell Lung Cancer models depending on EGFR and RAS mutational status. *Oncotarget, 6*(28), Article 26090.

Fukuda, T., et al. (2017). Design, synthesis, and evaluation of A-ring-modified lamellarin N analogues as noncovalent inhibitors of the EGFR T790M/L858R mutant. *Bioorganic & Medicinal Chemistry, 25*(24), 6563–6580.

Gaber, A. A., et al. (2018). Design, synthesis and anticancer evaluation of 1H-pyrazolo [3, 4-d] pyrimidine derivatives as potent EGFRWT and EGFRT790M inhibitors and apoptosis inducers. *Bioorganic Chemistry, 80*, 375–395.

George, R. F., et al. (2020). Some 1, 3, 5-trisubstituted pyrazoline derivatives targeting breast cancer: Design, synthesis, cytotoxic activity, EGFR inhibition and molecular docking. *Bioorganic Chemistry, 99*, Article 103780.

George, R. F., et al. (2019). Synthesis and anti-proliferative activity of some new quinoline based 4, 5-dihydropyrazoles and their thiazole hybrids as EGFR inhibitors. *Bioorganic Chemistry, 83*, 186–197.

Grandis, J. R., & Sok, J. C. (2004). Signaling through the epidermal growth factor receptor during the development of malignancy. *Pharmacology & Therapeutics, 102*(1), 37–46.

Graus-Porta, D., et al. (1997). ErbB-2, the preferred heterodimerization partner of all ErbB receptors, is a mediator of lateral signaling. *The EMBO Journal, 16*(7), 1647–1655.

Gschwind, A., Prenzel, N., & Ullrich, A. (2002). Lysophosphatidic acid-induced squamous cell carcinoma cell proliferation and motility involves epidermal growth factor receptor signal transactivation. *Cancer Research, 62*(21), 6329–6336.

Herbst, R. S., & Bunn, P. A. (2003). Targeting the epidermal growth factor receptor in non-small cell lung cancer. *Clinical Cancer Research, 9*(16), 5813–5824.

Höpfner, M., et al. (2004). Targeting the epidermal growth factor receptor by gefitinib for treatment of hepatocellular carcinoma. *Journal of Hepatology, 41*(6), 1008–1016.

Hong, S. Y., et al. (2016). Oncogenic activation of the PI3K/Akt pathway promotes cellular glucose uptake by down-regulating the expression of thioredoxin-interacting protein. *Cellular Signalling, 28*(5), 377–383.

Huang, S.-M., et al. (2002). Modulation of radiation response and tumor-induced angiogenesis after epidermal growth factor receptor inhibition by ZD1839 (Iressa). *Cancer Research, 62*(15), 4300–4306.

Joshi, G., et al. (2017). Pyrimidine containing epidermal growth factor receptor kinase inhibitors: Synthesis and biological evaluation. *Chemical Biology & Drug Design, 90*(5), 995–1006.

Key, T. J., et al. (2004). Diet, nutrition and the prevention of cancer. *Public Health Nutrition, 7*(1a), 187–200.

Kim, J., et al. (2016). Anti-cancer effect of metformin by suppressing signaling pathway of HER2 and HER3 in tamoxifen-resistant breast cancer cells. *Tumor Biology, 37*(5), 5811–5819.

Lath, A., et al. (2022). Anti-cancer peptides: Their current trends in the development of peptide-based therapy and anti-tumor drugs. *Biotechnology & Genetic Engineering Reviews*, 1–40.

Le, T., & Gerber, D. E. (2019). Newer-generation EGFR inhibitors in lung cancer: How are they best used? *Cancers, 11*(3), 366.

Leong, S. P., et al. (2010). Is breast cancer the same disease in Asian and Western countries? *World Journal of Surgery, 34*(10), 2308–2324.

McCubrey, J. A., et al. (2007). Targeting the RAF/MEK/ERK, PI3K/AKT and p53 pathways in hematopoietic drug resistance. *Advances in Enzyme Regulation, 47*, 64.

Mitsudomi, T., & Yatabe, Y. (2007). Mutations of the epidermal growth factor receptor gene and related genes as determinants of epidermal growth factor receptor tyrosine kinase inhibitors sensitivity in lung cancer. *Cancer Science, 98*(12), 1817–1824.

Montagna, M., et al. (2003). Genomic rearrangements account for more than one-third of the BRCA1 mutations in northern Italian breast/ovarian cancer families. *Human Molecular Genetics, 12*(9), 1055–1061.

Naujokas, M. F., et al. (2013). The broad scope of health effects from chronic arsenic exposure: Update on a worldwide public health problem. *Environmental Health Perspectives, 121*(3), 295–302.

Normanno, N., et al. (2006). Epidermal growth factor receptor (EGFR) signaling in cancer. *Gene, 366*(1), 2–16.

Okawa, T., et al. (2007). The functional interplay between EGFR overexpression, hTERT activation, and p53 mutation in esophageal epithelial cells with activation of stromal fibroblasts induces tumor development, invasion, and differentiation. *Genes & Development, 21*(21), 2788–2803.

Plowman, G. D., et al. (1993). Ligand-specific activation of HER4/p180erbB4, a fourth member of the epidermal growth factor receptor family. *Proceedings of the National Academy of Sciences, 90*(5), 1746–1750.

Raggi, C., et al. (2016). Cancer stem cells and tumor-associated macrophages: A roadmap for multitargeting strategies. *Oncogene, 35*(6), 671–682.

Rahib, L., et al. (2014). Projecting cancer incidence and deaths to 2030: The unexpected burden of thyroid, liver, and pancreas cancers in the United States. *Cancer Research, 74*(11), 2913–2921.

Ribeiro, F. A. P., et al. (2014). Effective targeting of the epidermal growth factor receptor (EGFR) for treating oral cancer: A promising approach. *Anticancer Research, 34*(4), 1547–1552.

Salomon, D. S., et al. (1995). Epidermal growth factor-related peptides and their receptors in human malignancies. *Critical Reviews in Oncology-Hematology, 19*(3), 183–232.

Samaga, R., et al. (2009). The logic of EGFR/ErbB signaling: Theoretical properties and analysis of high-throughput data. *PLoS Computational Biology, 5*(8), e1000438.

Scagliotti, G. V., et al. (2004). The biology of epidermal growth factor receptor in lung cancer. *Clinical Cancer Research, 10*(12), 4227s–4232s.

Sever, B., et al. (2019). Design, synthesis and biological evaluation of a new series of thiazolyl-pyrazolines as dual EGFR and HER2 inhibitors. *European Journal of Medicinal Chemistry, 182*, Article 111648.

Shaath, H., Elango, R., & Alajez, N. M. (2021). Molecular classification of breast cancer utilizing long non-coding RNA (lncRNA) transcriptomes identifies novel diagnostic lncRNA panel for triple-negative breast cancer. *Cancers, 13*(21), 5350.

Shafi, L., Iqbal, P., & Khaliq, R. (2021). *An overview of cancer burden in North and South (India).* India: Cape Comorin Trust.

Shi, F., et al. (2010). ErbB3/HER3 intracellular domain is competent to bind ATP and catalyze autophosphorylation. *Proceedings of the National Academy of Sciences, 107*(17), 7692–7697.

Siegel, R., et al. (2012). Cancer treatment and survivorship statistics, 2012. *CA: A Cancer Journal for Clinicians, 62*(4), 220–241.

Sirovich, B. E., Schwartz, L. M., & Woloshin, S. (2003). Screening men for prostate and colorectal cancer in the United States: Does practice reflect the evidence? *JAMA, 289*(11), 1414–1420.

Song, Z., et al. (2017). Synthesis and biological evaluation of morpholine-substituted diphenylpyrimidine derivatives (Mor-DPPYs) as potent EGFR T790M inhibitors with improved activity toward the gefitinib-resistant non-small cell lung cancers (NSCLC). *European Journal of Medicinal Chemistry, 133*, 329–339.

Stewart, B. W., & Kleihues, P. (2003). *World cancer report.*

Suo, Z., et al. (2002). EGFR family expression in breast carcinomas. c-erbB-2 and c-erbB-4 receptors have different effects on survival. *The Journal of Pathology: A Journal of the Pathological Society of Great Britain and Ireland, 196*(1), 17–25.

Toker, A. (2000). Protein kinases as mediators of phosphoinositide 3-kinase signaling. *Molecular Pharmacology, 57*(4), 652–658.

Torre, L. A., et al. (2015). Global cancer statistics, 2012. *CA: A Cancer Journal for Clinicians, 65*(2), 87–108.

Tzahar, E., et al. (1994). ErbB-3 and ErbB-4 function as the respective low and high affinity receptors of all Neu differentiation factor/heregulin isoforms. *Journal of Biological Chemistry, 269*(40), 25226–25233.

Verbeek, B. S., et al. (1998). Overexpression of EGFR and c-erbB2 causes enhanced cell migration in human breast cancer cells and NIH3T3 fibroblasts. *FEBS Letters, 425*(1), 145–150.

Vermeer, P. D., et al. (2003). Segregation of receptor and ligand regulates activation of epithelial growth factor receptor. *Nature, 422*(6929), 322–326.

Xiao, Z., et al. (2020). Design, synthesis and antitumor activity of novel thiophene-pyrimidine derivatives as EGFR inhibitors overcoming T790M and L858R/T790M mutations. *European Journal of Medicinal Chemistry, 203*, Article 112511.

Yarden, Y. (2001). The EGFR family and its ligands in human cancer: Signalling mechanisms and therapeutic opportunities. *European Journal of Cancer, 37*, 3–8.

Youssif, B. G., et al. (2018). Design, synthesis, mechanistic and histopathological studies of small-molecules of novel indole-2-carboxamides and pyrazino [1, 2-a] indol-1 (2H)-ones as potential anticancer agents effecting the reactive oxygen species production. *European Journal of Medicinal Chemistry, 146*, 260–273.

Zhang, Y., et al. (2018). 6, 7-Dimorpholinoalkoxy quinazoline derivatives as potent EGFR inhibitors with enhanced antiproliferative activities against tumor cells. *European Journal of Medicinal Chemistry, 147*, 77–89.

Cancer and insulin-like growth factor inhibitors: Recent advancements and SAR analysis

Diksha Choudhary[1,a], Bhupinder Kumar[2] and Amandeep Thakur[3,a]

[1]Chitkara College of Pharmacy, Chitkara University, Rajpura, Punjab, India; [2]Department of Pharmaceutical Sciences, HNB Garhwal University, Srinagar, Uttarakhand, India; [3]School of Pharmacy, College of Pharmacy, Taipei Medical University, Taipei, Taiwan

1. Introduction

Cancer is a highly malignant disease characterized by the uncontrolled growth of cells that caused around 10 million deaths in the year 2020 (World Heath Organization, 2022). Due to the solemnity of the disease, researchers have made substantial efforts to develop effective therapy against cancer. Currently, various local such as surgery and radiation, and systemic treatments, including chemotherapy, immunotherapy, and targeted therapy, are being clinically used for the treatment of various cancer types; however, the effectiveness of the therapies is hurdled by various factors, including resistance (Vasan et al., 2019), selectivity (Atkins & Gershell, 2002), and side effects during therapies including anemia, appetite loss, bleeding and bruising (Thrombocytopenia), constipation, immunotherapy, and organ-related inflammation, hair loss (Alopecia), nerve problems (Peripheral neuropathy), nausea, and vomiting (Treatment Types in American Cancer Society, 2022; Abu El-Kass et al., 2021). Additionally, the emergence of resistance in the cancer cells and nonselective characteristics of the therapies are directed toward the identification of new targets or the development of new or novel treatments against cancer (Ward et al., 2021; Zhong et al., 2021).

In chemotherapy, various proteins/enzymes were identified as potential targets, and drugs were developed for subsequent targeting of the receptors (Dang et al., 2017; Zhong

---

[a] Both authors have equal contribution.

et al., 2021). In this context, insulin-like growth factors have emerged as a promising target whose role has been extensively known for the tumorigenesis, antiapoptotic, and growth of cancer cells (Chen & Sharon, 2013; Pollak, 2000) Conservatively, the insulin-like growth factors regulate the growth hormone (GH)-stimulated somatic growth, GH-independent anabolic responses in many cells and tissues, and development of the fetus and other organs (Kleinberg, 1998). However, numerous studies suggest that the aberrance in the insulin-like growth factor (IGF) signaling pathway attributes to the progression of cancer by following the various cellular pathways, including PI3K and MEK pathways (Grimberg, 2003). Considering the genesis of cancer through IGF signaling persuaded researchers to develop effective therapeutics and to provide the proof of concept that IGF signaling inhibition could be developed as an effective strategy against cancer.

Delightedly, the indefatigable efforts of the researchers developed various therapeutics, including monoclonal antibodies, small molecules, and antibody-drug conjugate against the IGF signaling, which showed promising results in the preclinical and clinical studies (Janssen & Varewijck, 2014). Ganitumab (AMG-479), a monoclonal antibody, and Linsitinib, a small molecule IGF-1R inhibitors, are in the most advanced phase (Phase 3) of the clinical trials and showed promising results in the preclinical and clinical stages. Apart from the developed therapeutics, efforts of the researchers are also being directed toward the development of new/novel promising small molecules to make effective and expedient therapeutic. In this context, newly introduced scaffolds such as Imidazo[5,1-f]-[1,2,4] triazine, substituted diarylureas, 2,3-dihydroimidazo[2,1-b]thiazoles, and imidazo[1,5-a]pyrazines were developed as promising scaffolds that were found to be a putative inhibitor of the IGF-R. Moreover, the utilization of overexpressed IGF-R in cancer cells to develop a bioimaging agent as a diagnostic and visualizing agent during surgical retraction provides hope to employ IGF as a promising therapeutic target. This chapter will provide insights into IGF singling, the mechanism of singling in cancer, drugs under clinical trials, and recent efforts of researchers to develop new/novel scaffolds against IGF-R singling. We are hopeful that the presented compilation will help to understand the IGF singling forms basics to the recent advancements.

2. Insulin-like growth factors

IGFs are the essential mediators responsible for development, survival, and aging (Moschos & Mantzoros, 2002). The first report on IGFs was published in 1957, where Daughaday and Salmon revealed a serum factor (sulfation factor) that promotes the uptake of 35S-sulfate through hormonal control. The identification of the sulfation factor was carried out by incorporating the 35S-sulfate through cartilage in vitro in the rat serum, and the activity was compared with the untreated rats (Salmon & Daughaday, 1957; Yakar et al., 2018). Later, it was found that the described sulfation factor affects the metabolism of adipose tissue by showing the nonsuppressible insulin-like activity (NSILA) correspondingly to crystalline insulin and was named "somatomedin"(Daughaday et al., 1972; Froesch et al., 1963; Van Wyk et al., 1971). In 1976, the further structural disclosure of somatomedin was led to the identification of two polypeptides (NSILA I and II), which shares ~ 50% homological similarities to proinsulin and designated as insulin-like growth factor 1 and 2 (Rinderknecht & Humbel, 1976, 1978). IGF-1 and IGF-2 consist of various peptide regions and have high structural similarities. Briefly, IGF-1 is composed of A, B, C, and D peptide regions where A and B

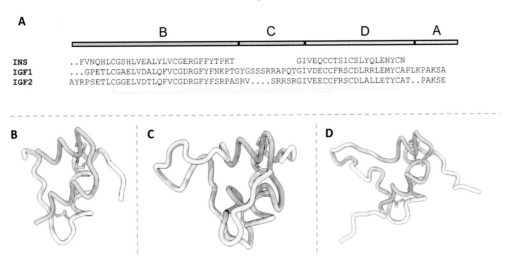

A

	B	C	D	A

INS   ..FVNQHLCGSHLVEALYLVCGERGFFYTPKT   GIVEQCCTSICSLYQLENYCN
IGF1   ...GPETLCGAELVDALQFVCGDRGFYNKPTGYGSSSRRAPQTGIVDECCFRSCDLRRLEMYCAPLKPAKSA
IGF2   AYRPSETLCGGELVDTLQFVCGDRGFYFSRPASRV....SRRSRGIVEECCFRSCDLALLETYCAT..PAKSE

B   C   D

FIGURE 8.1 (A) Sequence of the free insulin, IGF 1, and IGF2. (B) Structure of free insulin. (C) Structure of IGF1. (D) Structure of IGF 2. The domains are depicted as follows: A = orange, B = purple, C = pink, D = cyan, and disulfide bond = yellow. *Adapted from under Creative Commons Attribution 3.0 Unported Licence of Royal Society of Chemistry). From Turvey, S. J., McPhillie, M. J., Kearney, M. T., Muench, S. P., Simmons, K. J., & Fishwick, C. W. G. (2022). Recent developments in the structural characterization of the IR and IGF1R: implications for the design of IR-IGF1R hybrid receptor modulators. RSC Medicinal Chemistry, 13(4), 360–374. https://doi.org/10.1039/d1md00300c*

chains are connected with a disulfide bond with an overall molecular weight of 7649 Da and 70 amino acids in the structure (Laron, 2001). However, the IGF-2 is composed of 67 amino acids and accommodates A–E domains with an overall molecular weight of 7.5 kDa (Livingstone, 2013). The structure of the free insulin, IGF1, and IGF2 are shown in Fig. 8.1.

Despite high homological resemblance, IGF1 and IGF-2 processes have divergent biological functioning and have different pharmacological effects in the various development and functioning processes. The IGFs regulate the development and metabolic processes through IGF receptors named as IGF1R and IGF2R. The IGF1 receptor controls the cellular processes via the downstream PI3K/Akt pathway, whereas IGF2R involvement is focused on the capturing and degradation of extracellular IGF2 and IGF1 during the development stages (Suh et al., 2013). Notably, the oscillation in the level of the expression of IGFs is also observed throughout the lifespan where elevated IGF1 expression is observed in the adult stage while IGF2 expression is higher in the fetal stage as the functions of IGF2 are mainly replaced by IGF1 (Bergman et al., 2013). Additionally, a recent study demonstrated that IGF-1 and IGF-2 have different effects on the human mesenchymal stem cell's myogenic differentiation indicating the divergent functioning of the mediators (Aboalola & Han, 2017). Moreover, IGFs regulate the normal functioning of various organ development and cellular processes including the development of the digestive system, and male and female fetuses (White et al., 2018), neuroendocrine growth (Al-Samerria & Radovick, 2021), etc. The distinct effect of IGF-1 and IGF-2 on body functioning and development is summarized in Fig. 8.2.

Conservatively, insulin/IGFs regulate the various cellular and metabolic processes by following ATK/PI3K and ERK/MAPK pathways. The binding of insulin/IGF1 to the receptor initiates the signaling of the IGFR pathways resulting in the autophosphorylation of the β subunits. The subsequent activation results in the phosphorylation of the tyrosine residues of the IRS proteins and the reorganization site for the mediators SH2 domains. The SH2 domain

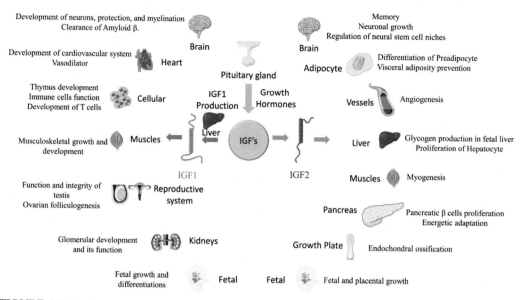

FIGURE 8.2   Role of IGF-1 and IGF-2 in the development and functioning (Puche & Castilla-Cortázar, 2012; Sélénou et al., 2022).

activates the subunits such as p85 followed by PDK and AKT and subsequently embarks the metabolic processes of insulin/IGF1. Conversely, the activation of the IGFR receptor regulates the GRB2 subunit that processes various cellular processes, including cell growth and differentiation. Moreover, the activation of the other mediating substrates, such as SHC and GAB1, revivifies various cellular processes that activate biological effects, including glucose transport and glycogen synthesis (Fig. 8.3) (Griffeth et al., 2014).

3. Involvement of IGFs/IGFR in various diseases

The involvement of IGFs has been widely explicated for various diseases and is considered as a predictive biomarker (Frenkel et al., 2013; Monzavi & Cohen, 2002). Studies have revealed that the aberrant expression of IGFs results in critical illness, which induces severe body dysfunctions, including skeletal muscle loss, impaired recovery of organ systems, and retarded wound healing (Elijah et al., 2011). Additionally, the divergence in the expression of the IGFs has been proven to be a causative factor for the development of metabolic disorders and cardiovascular disorders and found to be a biomarker in various cancer types (Asghari-Hanjani & Vafa, 2019; Holly et al., 2019). Moreover, the emergence of reports on the embroilment of IGFs/IGFR in neurological disorders, COVID-19, and other diseases proved it to be a biomarker for the prediction and therapeutic target against various diseases (Hazrati et al., 2022; Shi et al., 2022) (Fig. 8.3).

4. Role of IGF in cancer

IGF's role in cancer development has been extensively studied for various cancers including breast cancer, ovarian cancer, prostate cancer, lung cancer, hematologic

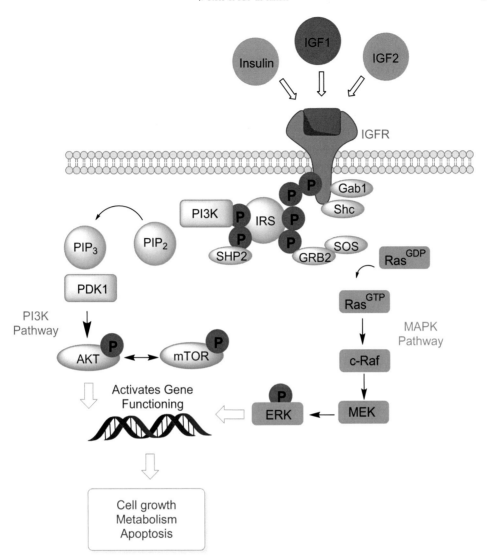

FIGURE 8.3 IGF pathway regulation in the body.

malignancies, central nervous system (CNS) tumors, gastrointestinal cancers, head and neck cancers, and bone and soft tissue tumors (Denduluri et al., 2015). The initial involvement of IGFs in the development has been studied in cell culture experiments (Fürstenberger & Senn, 2002). Further, it was found that the IGF's involvement is not limited to the regulation; however, the interaction of the IGFs with other oncogenes promotes the regulation and progression of cancer (Yu & Rohan, 2000). Later, the literature preceding revealed the molecular mechanisms of the involvement of IGF1 mediation through PI3K/Akt and MAPK/ERK1/2 pathways in the progression of various cancer types (Christopoulos et al., 2015; Shelton et al., 2004; Zhu et al., 2011). The activation of the IGF-mediated PI3K pathway by HOXB13 and NUCKS1 promotes invasive behavior of gastric cancer cells (Guo et al., 2021; Huang et al., 2019). The PI3K pathway was identified as a protective shield in cancer cells, and it showed antiapoptotic properties through IGF-1 mediation and promoted the survival of the cancer cells (Zhang et al., 2018). The further activation of AKT and mTOR stimulates the various cellular mediators' glycogen synthase kinase-3 β, p21, p27, and cyclin-D that promote the cell cycle progression (Simpson et al., 2017). Simultaneously, the stimulation of mitogen-activated protein kinase (MAPK) pathways activates the cyclin D/cyclin-dependent kinase 4 (CDK4), which leads to the E2F-dependent transcription (Zhang et al., 1999). The activation of the transcription factor results in the antiapoptotic effect, which leads to cancer cell progression (Peruzzi et al., 1999). Moreover, it was found that IGF-1 maintains the cancer cell stemness and drug resistance, which makes it a prudent target against cancer (Ngo et al., 2021) (Fig. 8.4).

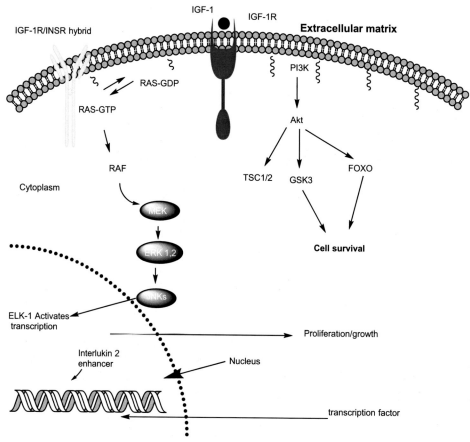

FIGURE 8.4   Involvement of molecular pathways associated with IGF signaling.

5. Clinical developments for IGFs

The monumental literature and findings on the involvement of the IGF in cancer progression and maintenance constrained the researchers to develop a promising therapeutic strategy against IGFs and IGFRs. Delightedly, the indefatigable efforts of the researchers expedited the development of various strategies, including monoclonal antibodies, ligand neutralization, receptor down-regulators, and antisense oligonucleotides, that have shown promising therapeutic effects in preclinical and clinical stages. Moreover, the introduction of small molecules, including tyrosine kinase inhibitors and peptide-based inhibitors, has established an excellent progression against the IGF pathway which enlightened optimism toward the development of promising new/novel therapeutics (Cao & Yee, 2021; Wang et al., 2022). Among all, the monoclonal antibodies were found to be a promising therapeutic in various clinical trials. Ganitumab (AMG-479), a monoclonal antibody that inhibits the interaction of IGF1 and IGF2 with IGFR, is in the most advanced phase (Phase 3) in combination with or without promising anticancer agents such as vincristine, doxorubicin, cyclophosphamide, ifosfamide, and etoposide for the treatment newly diagnosed metastatic Ewing sarcoma (NCT02306161). The other monoclonal antibodies including Figitumumab (CP-751,871), Dalotuzumab (MK-0646), Cixutumumab (IMC-A12), and Robatumumab (MK-7454) have completed the Phase 2 of the clinical trials and some of the studies are in Phase 1. Moreover, Cixutumumab (IMC-A12), Istiratumab (MM-141), BIIB022, and Xentuzumab (BI 836845) have accomplished Phase 1, where all showed promising results in the studies. Apart from the clinical success, the journey of the monoclonal antibodies against IGFR has seen a fall back in 2010 as Pfizer discontinued a Phase 3 trial of Figitumumab in combination with erlotinib against previously treated patients with advanced nonsmall cell lung cancer owing to the ineffectiveness of the Figitumumab with erlotinib; however, other monoclonal antibodies are found to be promising in the clinical trials (Pfizer Discontinues A Phase 3 Study Of Figitumumab In Previously Treated Patients With Advanced Non-Small Cell Lung Cancer, 2010).

Besides monoclonal antibodies, small molecules have significantly progressed in clinical trials. Linsitinib, an IGF-1R inhibitor, has progressed to Phase 3 of the clinical trials (NCT00924989). In the primary analysis of the study, it was found that Linsitinib could not produce a significant implication on the overall survival of the patients (Fassnacht et al., 2015). However, another phase 2 study of Linsitinib over patients with gastrointestinal stromal tumors has revealed the acceptable tolerance of Linsitinib in patients with wild-type gastrointestinal stromal tumors indicating that further evaluation may reveal promising results (Von Mehren et al., 2020). Another IGFR inhibitor named BMS-754807 has completed Phase 2 of the clinical trial in combination with Herceptin (NCT00788333) and some other studies have completed Phase 1 of the clinical trial (NCT00569036, NCT00898716). Moreover, Picropodophyllin has completed Phase 2 and Phase 1 for the treatment of various cancerous malignancies (NCT01561456, NCT01725555).

Apart from small molecules, antibody-drug conjugates have unfailingly produced a significant impact on the developing therapeutics list. W0101 is the first-in-class antibody-drug conjugate that targets the IGFRs. In preclinical studies, W0101 showed promising antitumor activity against solid tumors with high expressions of the IGFR where a single dose of 3 mg/

kg significantly inhibited the growth of MCF-7 breast cancer cells with high IGFR (Akla et al., 2020). Currently, W0101 is in Phase 2 clinical trials for the treatment of advanced or metastatic solid tumors with study identification number NCT03316638. IGF-MTX, a conjugate of the IGF and methotrexate accomplished to target IGFR has emerged as a promising therapeutic against various cancer malignancies. IGF-MTX has completed Phase 1 of the clinical trials (NCT02045368) and results indicate that IGF-MTX is well tolerated by patients with advanced tumors expressing IGF-1 receptors (Venepalli et al., 2019). Overall, the emerging therapeutics have shown encouraging results in the initial phases, and further evaluation may lead to the development of a promising drug against the IGF signing pathway. The various therapeutics targeting the IGFR under clinical evaluation for the treatment of cancer are compiled in Table 8.1.

6. Recent development targeting IGFR

The quest to develop an effective treatment against cancer persuades researchers to identify novel and new biological targets in cancer cells. In this context, biologists have made great efforts to identify the biological relevance of IGF signaling in cancer cells and designate it as a promising target against cancer. Elicited from the biologist's imperative revelations, Medicinal chemists have capitalized on the comprehension of the biologist and developed various chemical architectures against IGF signaling that showed promising results in preliminary studies. This section deals with the efforts of the chemist in the development of new/novel scaffolds against IGF singling.

Cheng et al. have conducted a medicinal chemistry campaign to develop an effective anticancer agent by modifying the unexplored 5′- and 3′-positions of Indirubin (1) (a potent kinase inhibitor). A series of compounds was synthesized by substituting 5′- and 3′-positions of the Indirubin, and synthesized compounds were evaluated against various tumor cell lines. In preliminary screening, it was found that the modification at the 5′-position did not favor the activity, while substitution at 3′-showed a promising effect against cancer cell lines. In series, compound 3 was found to be most potent against LXFL and MCF7 cells line with an IC_{50} value of 1.1 and 0.85 μM, respectively. Later, the most potent compound, 3, was screened over a panel of 22 kinases where it predominantly inhibited the expression of IGF-1R with an IC_{50} value of 169 nM without affecting the expression of other kinases, including CDKs and GSK3β, and produced a similar effect in IGF overexpressed cancer cells. Moreover, compound 3 arrested the cancer cell growth at the G2/M phase and effectively inhibited the growth of a panel of NCL-60 cell line in the range of 3.19—0.08 μM (Fig. 8.5) (Cheng et al., 2017).

Degorce et al. optimized a series of 2-anilino-pyrimidine (4) to introduce a drugable IGF-1R inhibitor. Various chemical modifications were carried out in the chemical architectures, and various pharmacokinetic properties were evaluated. In modifications, it is noteworthy to mention that replacing imidazopyridines with pyrazolopyridines improves activity and lipophilicity and promotes other drug-able properties. Among the series, compound 5 was found to be the most promising compound, which selectively inhibited the IGF-1R against a panel of 60 protein kinases with an IC_{50} value of 0.014 μM. Moreover, the efficacy of

TABLE 8.1 Various therapeutics under clinical trials.

S. No.	Therapeutics	Mechanism of action	Clinical progress	Identification number
		Monoclonal antibodies		
1.	Cixutumumab (IMC-A12)	It targets the human IGF-IR1 (Fouladi et al., 2015).	Phase 1, Completed	NCT00785538
2.	Ganitumab (AMG-479)	It inhibited the interaction of IGF1 and IGF2 with IGFR (Calzone et al., 2013).	Phase 3 (in combination), Active, not recruiting Phase 2, Completed	NCT02306161 NCT01024387
3.	Figitumumab (CP-751,871)	It targets the IGF-1R (Zhang et al., 2014).	Phase 2, Completed Phase 1, Completed	NCT00560560 NCT00474760
4.	Dalotuzumab (MK-0646)	It is a monoclonal antibody that targets the IGF-1 receptor (Doi et al., 2013).	Phase 2, Completed Phase 1, Completed Phase 1, Completed Phase 1, Completed	NCT00610129 NCT00759785 NCT00635778 NCT00694356
5.	Cixutumumab (IMC-A12)	It targets the IGF-1R (Naing et al., 2013).	Phase 2, Completed Phase 2, Completed Phase 2, Completed Phase 1, Completed Phase 1, Completed	NCT01160458 NCT00520481 NCT00781911 NCT00785538 NCT01007032
6.	Robatumumab (MK-7454)	It binds to IGFs-1R and inhibits the binding of IGFs (Anderson et al., 2016).	Phase 2, Completed	NCT00551213
7.	Istiratumab (MM-141)	It inhibits the IGF-1R and ErbB3 (Baum et al., 2012).	Phase 1, Completed	NCT01733004
8.	BIIB022	It inhibits the IGF-1 receptor (Dong et al., 2008).	Phase 1, Completed	NCT00555724
9.	Xentuzumab (BI 836845)	It neutralizes the IGF-1 and IGF-2 (de Bono et al., 2020).	Phase 1, Active, not recruiting Early Phase 1, Recruiting	NCT02145741 NCT05110495
		Small molecules		
10.	Linsitinib	It is an oral tyrosine kinase inhibitor (IGF-1R inhibitor) (Von Mehren et al., 2020).	Phase 3, Completed Phase 2, Completed	NCT00924989 NCT01560260
11.	BMS-754807	It is a small molecule that inhibits IGF-1R (Carboni et al., 2009).	Phase 2, Completed Phase 1, Completed Phase 1, Completed	NCT00788333 NCT00569036 NCT00898716
12.	Picropodophyllin	It is an IGF-1R inhibitor that causes mitotic arrest and catastrophe by depolymerizing the microtubules through IGF-1R mediation (Waraky et al., 2014).	Phase 2, Completed Phase 1, Completed	NCT01561456 NCT01725555

(Continued)

TABLE 8.1   Various therapeutics under clinical trials.—cont'd

S. No.	Therapeutics	Mechanism of action	Clinical progress	Identification number
		Antibody-drug conjugates/conjugates		
13.	W0101	It is an antibody-drug conjugate (ADC) targeting the IGF-1R (Venepalli et al., 2019).	Phase 2, Recruiting	NCT03316638
14.	IGF-MTX	It specifically binds to the IGF-1 receptor (McTavish et al., 2009).	Phase 1, Completed	NCT02045368

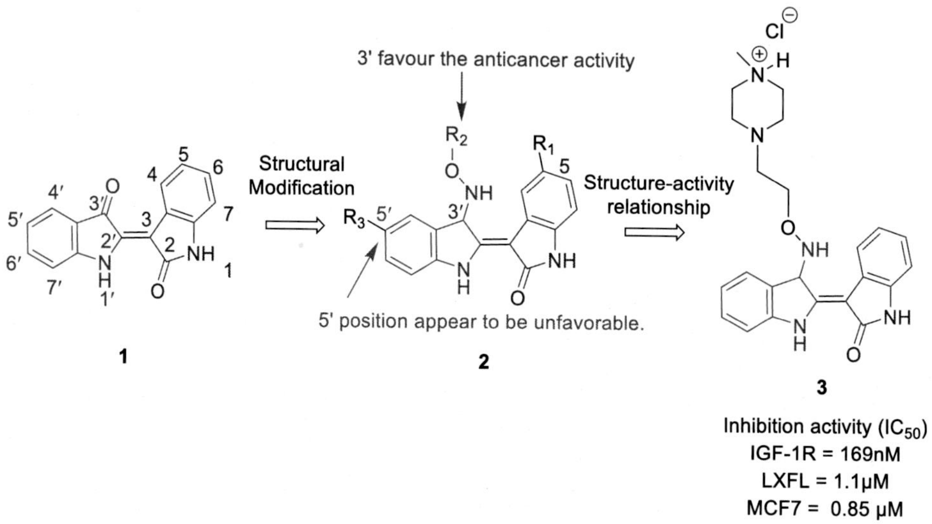

FIGURE 8.5   Indirubin-derived IGF-1R inhibitors.

compound **5** was evaluated over the Colo-205 human tumor xenograft model, which efficiently reduced the volume as compared to the drug Gemcitabine. The results of compound **5** over various parameters are shown in Fig. 8.6 (Degorce et al., 2016).

Jin et al. revealed a potent imidazo[5,1-f]-[1,2,4] triazine (6)-based dual inhibitor of the IGF and IGF-1R. A series of 5,7-disubstituted imidazo[5,1-f][1,2,4]triazine inhibitors were synthesized and evaluated against IGF-1R and IGF, where compound **7** was found to be most potent in series with the IC$_{50}$ value of 0.017 and 0.076 μM, respectively. Further, compound **7** was evaluated in vivo in multiple species including mice, rhesus monkeys, and rats where it showed promising pharmacokinetic properties. Interestingly, the bioavailability (F %) reached 100% in monkeys. Additionally, the compound was evaluated over the GEO colon carcinoma xenograft model, which reduced the tumor volume to 70% at the dose of 10 mg/kg. Moreover, the selectivity profile of compound **7** was screened over a panel of 167 kinases using an in-house Caliper EZ Reader mobility shift assay where compound **7**

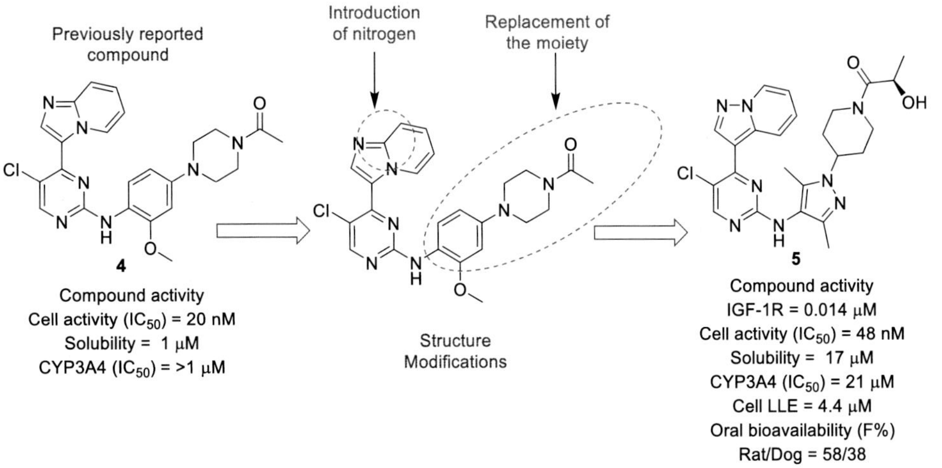

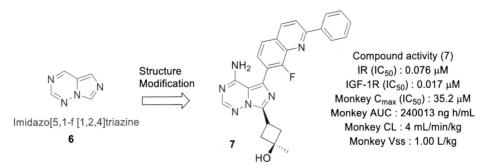

FIGURE 8.6   (Pyrazol-4-ylamino)-pyrimidines as potential IGF-1R inhibitors.

significantly displayed >50% inhibition at the concentration of 1 μM against IGF-1R and IR. Overall, imidazo[5,1-f]-[1,2,4]triazine scaffold was found to be a promising chemical framework for the development of potential anti-IGF-1R agents (Fig. 8.7) (Jin et al., 2010).

Liu et al. introduced thiazolidine-2,4-dione as a deliberated scaffold against IGF and IGF-R by screening the library of the 202328 compounds. Various screening methodologies, including receptor-based pharmacophore modeling, glide XP docking, and IGF-1R assay, were utilized, which led to the identification of two potent compounds, namely **8** and **9**. Further, a medicinal chemistry campaign was carried out over both potent compounds and synthesized a series of compounds. The synthesized series was evaluated over the MCF-7 cell line, where compound **10** was found to be the most promising compound with the IC_{50} value of 14.8 μM. Further analysis of compound **10** over IGF-R and IR was screened, where it potentially showed dual inhibition for both receptors with an IC_{50} value of 2.9 and 57.6 μM, respectively. Overall, the modified thiazolidine-2,4-dione displayed promising results against the IGF-R receptor (Fig. 8.8) (Liu et al., 2010).

FIGURE 8.7   Imidazo[5,1-f]-[1,2,4] triazine-based dual inhibitor of the IGF and IGF-1R.

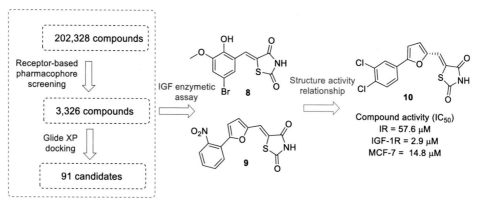

FIGURE 8.8   Thiazolidine-2,4-dione as a potential scaffold against IGF and IGF-R.

In a quest to identify a new scaffold against IGF signaling, Qvit et al. attempted to introduce macrocyclic new scaffolds that were found to be promising scaffolds. A series of 34 compounds were screened against the MCF-7 cell lines. In series, compound **11** was found to be most potent with an IC$_{50}$ value of 6 μM. Further, studies indicate that compound **11** reduced the expression of IGF-1-induced ERK phosphorylation and inhibited the expression of phosphorylated IGF-1R. Conclusively, the monocyclic scaffolds can also be developed as promising therapeutics against IGF signaling (Fig. 8.9) (Qvit et al., 2008).

Aware et al. developed a series of 2-amino-4-pyrazole-cyclopentyl pyrimidines, which displayed potential IGF activity. A structure–activity relationship was generated by synthesizing a series of substituted 2-amino-4-pyrazole-cyclopentyl pyrimidines, and activity was evaluated over IGF-R. In series, compound **12** was found to be the most promising compound with an IC$_{50}$ value of 0.02 μM (Fig. 8.10A). The docking studies of compound **12** with the IGF-R revealed that compound **12** well fitted to the binding pocket and formed key interactions with the Met1052, Leu1051, and Glu 1050 (Fig. 8.10B). Further, the antiproliferative activity of the compound was evaluated over various cell lines, which is shown in Fig. 8.10A. Moreover, the bioavailability studies of the compound were carried out over Sprague Dawley rats, where it displayed low oral bioavailability of 11.3% and a high clearance rate of 3548 mL/h/kg, indicating that further modification is required to attain drug-

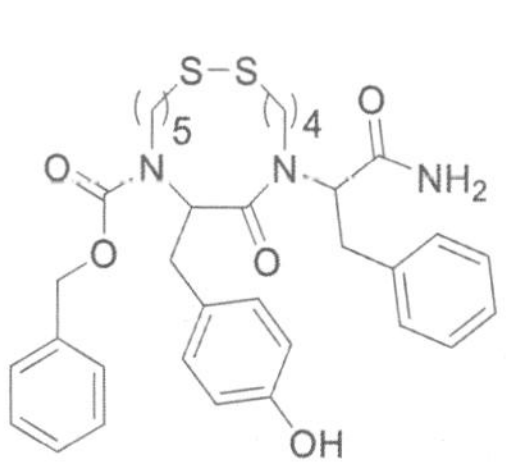

11
Compound activity (IC$_{50}$)
MCF-7 = 6 μM

FIGURE 8.9   Macrocyclic scaffold as anti-IGF-R agent.

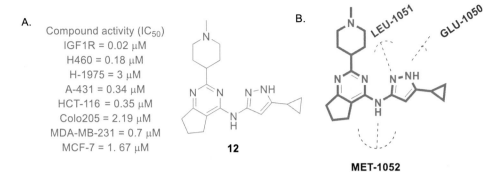

A.

Compound activity (IC$_{50}$)
IGF1R = 0.02 μM
H460 = 0.18 μM
H-1975 = 3 μM
A-431 = 0.34 μM
HCT-116 = 0.35 μM
Colo205 = 2.19 μM
MDA-MB-231 = 0.7 μM
MCF-7 = 1. 67 μM

12

B.

MET-1052

FIGURE 8.10 (A) Most potent compound from series of 2-amino-4-pyrazole-cyclopentyl pyrimidines. (B) Key interactions of 12 with amino acids of IGF-1R.

able properties. Overall, the results from the series indicate that 2-amino-4-pyrazole-cyclo-pentyl pyrimidines can serve as a promising scaffold in the development of putative anti-IGF drugs (Aware et al., 2015).

The dual inhibitors are considered potential therapeutics against cancer. Schmidt et al. developed an N'-aroyl-2-(1H-indol-3-yl)-2-oxoacetohydrazide-based dual inhibitor of IGF-1R and SRC. A commercially available compound was screened to identify the initial lead, and further structural diversification in the architecture of compound 13 led to the development of a series of compounds. Further, the developed series was screened against IGF-1R and SRC, where compound 14 was found to be most potent in series with an IC$_{50}$ value of 0.67 and 0.52 μM, respectively. Later, compound 14 was evaluated over A549ATCC, NCI—H522 (both nonsmall cell lung cancer cell lines), and OVCAR-8 (ovarian cancer), where it significantly inhibited the growth of the cells with an average inhibition of 81.05%. Moreover, the dual targeting potential of the compounds was supported by docking studies where compounds well fitted in both pockets, indicating that the N'-aroyl-2-(1H-indol-3-yl)-2-oxoacetohydrazide modifications can lead to potential IGF-1R or dual inhibitors of IGF-1R (Fig. 8.11) (Schmidt et al., 2011).

Gadekar et al. introduced a series of 2,3-dihydroimidazo[2,1-b]thiazoles, which acted as potential dual inhibitors of IGF-1R and EGRF inhibitors. Initially, the compound ITI (15) was utilized as a lead, and further modification led to the compound series. In series, compound 16 was found to be the most potent against IGF-1R and EGFR kinases with an IC$_{50}$ value of 16 and 4 nM, respectively. Additionally, the antiproliferative profile of compound

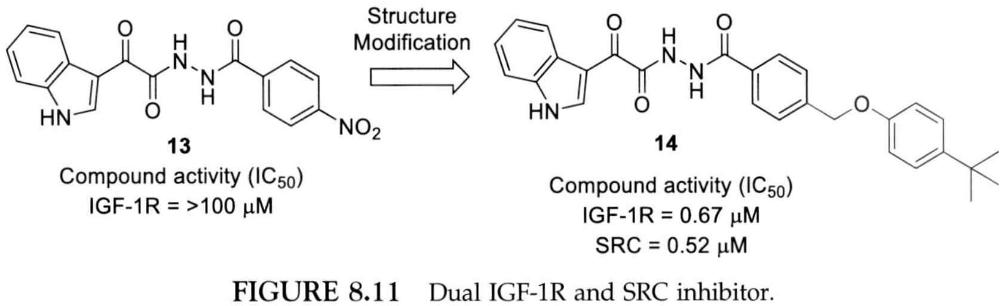

13
Compound activity (IC$_{50}$)
IGF-1R = >100 μM

Structure
Modification

14
Compound activity (IC$_{50}$)
IGF-1R = 0.67 μM
SRC = 0.52 μM

FIGURE 8.11 Dual IGF-1R and SRC inhibitor.

16 was evaluated over H460, H-1975 (EGFR Mutant), A-431, HCT-116, COLO-205, and MDA-MB-231 cell line, where it significantly inhibited the growth of cells with an IC$_{50}$ value of 2.1 µM, 3 µM, 1 µM, 1.8 µM, 3.94 µM, and 1.2 µM, respectively. Further, the oral pharmacokinetic study of compound **16** was evaluated over swiss; however, compound **16** had disappointedly poor PK properties (results are shown in Fig. 8.12). To attain drugable properties, the **16** was further modified, and a series of the compounds were synthesized by utilizing multistep synthesis. In the synthesized series, compound **17** displayed promising activity against IGFR and EGFR with IC$_{50}$ values of 52 and 36 nM, respectively. Moreover, the PK profile of compound **17** was evaluated, where it showed a promising PK profile, and the results are displayed in Fig. 8.12. Overall, the utilization of 2,3-dihydroimidazo [2,1-b]thiazoles opens the doors to the design of structurally diverse dual inhibitors of IGFR (Gadekar et al., 2021).

Tumor resection is commonly utilized as the first-line effective strategy for the treatment of various cancers; however, complete removal of the tumor cells is highly strenuous. During surgical procedures, the visualizing probes are used to stain the infective cells; however, no effective probe has been developed for breast cancer for long surgical procedures. To develop an effective visualizing probe against breast cancer, Xu et al. introduced near-infrared fluorescent dyes with the capability of binding to the highly expressed IGF-R in breast cancer. A series of compounds were synthesized by merging the fluorescent probes with the bindable chemical architecture. The binding affinity of the probe was evaluated by utilizing inverted fluorescence microscopy on IGF1R-expressed MCF-7 cells. In the results, it was found that the developed probes bound to the IGF-R-expressed cells; however, compound **18** showed promising results and was designated for further evaluation. Further, tumor targeting ability (in vivo) was determined over Balb/C nude mice bearing MCF-7, and PC3 tumors and expressions were monitored by the near-infrared optical imaging system. In the assay, it was found that compound **18** was highly uptaken by the tumor cells and

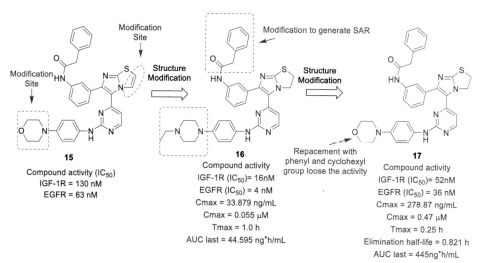

FIGURE 8.12   2,3-Dihydroimidazo[2,1-b]thiazoles as potential dual inhibitors of IGF-1R and EGFR.

displayed significant serum stability in rat plasma for 24 h, indicating that **18** can recognize and stabilize in the highly expressed IGF-R cells. Moreover, the safety study of compound **18** was carried out over a group of mice where **18** did not produce any significant toxicity. Conclusively, the developed agents can be utilized as promising tools for diagnosing and treating cancer (Fig. 8.13) (Xu et al., 2021).

Anderson et al. utilized the parallel synthesis of diarylureas (**19**) and introduced a new series of compounds that were found to be promising anti-IGFR inhibitors. Variously substituted compounds were attempted by combining various substitutions. In series, compound **20** was the most promising compound with an IC_{50} value of 9.7 µM (Anderson et al., 2006). Later, the group utilized the previously reported compounds as a lead and extended the library of the compounds by diversifying the substitution at both R1 and R2. Gratefully, the substitutions led to the identification of a compound with the 2-trifluoromethyl group, and 3-chloro-5-methoxyphenyl substitution (**21**) was found to be most potent in series with an IC_{50} value of 3.5 µM. Further, the docking study of the compound revealed that it binds to the TP-binding site of IGF-1 and formed key interactions with the Val1023, Val983, Ser979, and Thr112 amino acids of the binding pockets. Overall, the developed series of compounds with aminoquinoline can be utilized as a lead for the development of new IGF-R inhibitors (Fig. 8.14) (Engen et al., 2010).

Mulvihill et al. introduced 2-phenylquinolin-7-yl-derived imidazo[1,5-a]pyrazines a potent IGF-1R inhibitor. Initially, the imidazopyrazine derivative (**22**) was modified, which led to the identification of compound **23**. Compound **23** was further modified and synthesized a series of compounds, which were evaluated against a panel of kinase 28 kinases. In series, compound **24** was found to be most promising in series with an IC_{50} value of 20 nM, and displayed adequate microsomal stability of 0.28 in humans. Further, the antiproliferative activity of the compound was evaluated over H292, H358, HT29, GEO, and Coco 205 cell lines where it displayed significant inhibition with an IC_{50} value of 1.95 µM, 0.69 µM, 2.98 µM, 1.26 µM, 0.27 µM, and 0.93 µM, respectively. Moreover, compound **24** was evaluated over a 3T3/huIGFIR xenograft mouse model where it potentially inhibited the tumor volume and displayed promising pharmacokinetic properties (Fig. 8.15) (Mulvihill et al., 2008).

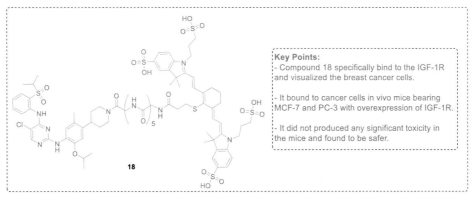

FIGURE 8.13   Bioimaging tool targeting IGF-1R.

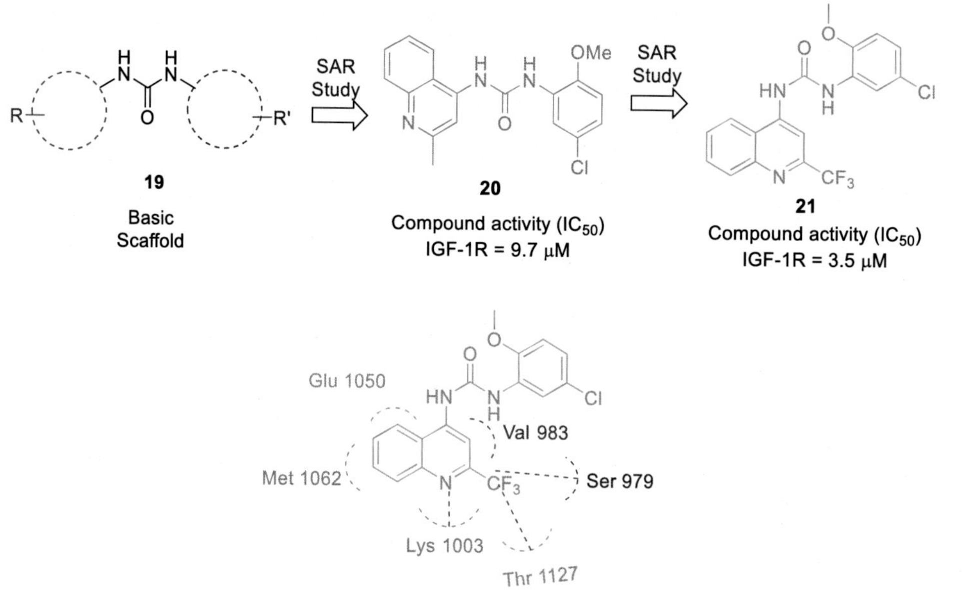

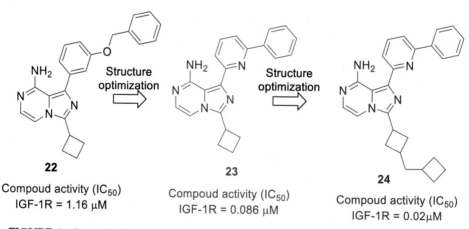

Key interaction of compound 21 with IGF-1R

FIGURE 8.14   Substituted diarylureas as lead compounds for IGF-R

22
Compoud activity (IC$_{50}$)
IGF-1R = 1.16 μM

23
Compoud activity (IC$_{50}$)
IGF-1R = 0.086 μM

24
Compoud activity (IC$_{50}$)
IGF-1R = 0.02 μM

FIGURE 8.15   2-Phenylquinolin-7-yl-derived imidazo[1,5-a]pyrazines a potent IGF-1R inhibitor.

7. Conclusion

Cancer is a devastating disease that causes millions of deaths worldwide. Researchers have made substantial efforts to develop effective treatment options; however, the notorious nature of the cancer cells makes the therapy ineffective owing to the mutations at the various target sites. In this context, IGF singling has emerged as a fascinating target against cancer, and various developed therapeutics are in the advanced clinical stages. The success of Ganitumab (AMG-479), a monoclonal antibody, and Linsitinib, a small molecule IGF-1R inhibitor, at the initial clinical trials, enlightened a hope of the approval of effective therapeutics against IGF-R singling. Additionally, the continued efforts of the researchers led to the introduction of new/novel therapeutics that can be developed as promising therapeutics against IGF-R signaling. It is noteworthy to mention that introduced scaffolds, namely imidazo[5,1-f]-[1,2,4] triazine, substituted diarylureas, 2,3-dihydroimidazo[2,1-b]thiazoles, and imidazo [1,5-a]pyrazines, have shown promising results in the preclinical stages, and further optimization may lead to the development of a potential drug candidate. Moreover, the overexpression of IGF galvanized the researcher to develop an effective bio-imaging tool that can sense the IGF-overexpressed cancer cells in mice models. Further evaluation and developments might open the doors to make it an effective diagnostic and imaging tool for surgical retractions.

References

Aboalola, D., & Han, V. K. M. (2017). Different effects of insulin-like growth factor-1 and insulin-like growth factor-2 on myogenic differentiation of human mesenchymal stem cells. *Stem Cells International, 2017*. https://doi.org/10.1155/2017/8286248

Abu El-Kass, S., Ragheb, M. M., Hamed, S. M., Turkman, A. M., & Zaki, A. T. (2021). Needs and self-care efficacy for cancer patients suffering from side effects of chemotherapy. *Journal of Oncology, 2021*. https://doi.org/10.1155/2021/8880366

Akla, B., Broussas, M., Loukili, N., Robert, A., Beau-Larvor, C., Malissard, M., Boute, N., Champion, T., Haeuw, J. F., Beck, A., Perez, M., Dreyfus, C., Pavlyuk, M., Chetaille, E., & Corvaia, N. (2020). Efficacy of the antibody—drug conjugate W0101 in preclinical models of IGF-1 receptor overexpressing solid tumors. *Molecular Cancer Therapeutics, 19*(1), 168—177. https://doi.org/10.1158/1535-7163.MCT-19-0219

Al-Samerria, S., & Radovick, S. (2021). The role of insulin-like growth factor-1 (IGF-1) in the control of neuroendocrine regulation of growth. *Cells, 10*(10), 2664. https://doi.org/10.3390/cells10102664

Anderson, M. O., Yu, H., Penaranda, C., Maddux, B. A., Goldfine, I. D., Youngren, J. F., & Guy, R. K. (2006). Parallel synthesis of diarylureas and their evaluation as inhibitors of insulin-like growth factor receptor. *Journal of Combinatorial Chemistry, 8*(5), 784—790. https://doi.org/10.1021/cc050136z

Anderson, P. M., Bielack, S. S., Gorlick, R. G., Skubitz, K., Daw, N. C., Herzog, C. E., Monge, O. R., Lassaletta, A., Boldrini, E., Pápai, Z., Rubino, J., Pathiraja, K., Hille, D. A., Ayers, M., Yao, S. L., Nebozhyn, M., Lu, B., & Mauro, D. (2016). A phase II study of clinical activity of SCH 717454 (robatumumab) in patients with relapsed osteosarcoma and Ewing sarcoma. *Pediatric Blood and Cancer, 63*(10), 1761—1770. https://doi.org/10.1002/pbc.26087

AsghariHanjani, N., & Vafa, M. (2019). The role of IGF-1 in obesity, cardiovascular disease, and cancer. *Medical Journal of the Islamic Republic of Iran, 33*(1). https://doi.org/10.34171/mjiri.33.56

Atkins, J. H., & Gershell, L. J. (2002). Selective anticancer drugs. *Nature Reviews Cancer, 2*(9), 645—646. https://doi.org/10.1038/nrc900

Aware, V., Gaikwad, N., Chavan, S., Manohar, S., Bose, J., Khanna, S., B-Rao, C., Dixit, N., Singh, K. S., Damre, A., Sharma, R., Patil, S., & Roychowdhury, A. (2015). Cyclopentyl-pyrimidine based analogues as novel and potent IGF-1R inhibitor. *European Journal of Medicinal Chemistry, 92*, 246—256. https://doi.org/10.1016/j.ejmech.2014.12.053

Baum, J., Johnson, B., Adams, S., Tang, J., Kohli, N., Rennard, R., Sundararajan, P., Xu, L., Jiao, Y., Schoeberl, B., Nielsen, U., Fitzgerald, J., & Lugovskoy, A. (2012). Abstract 2719: MM-141, a novel bispecific antibody co-targeting IGF-1R and ErbB3, blocks ligand-induced signaling and demonstrates antitumor activity. *Cancer Research, 72*(8_Suppl. ment). https://doi.org/10.1158/1538-7445.am2012-2719

Bergman, D., Halje, M., Nordin, M., & Engström, W. (2013). Insulin-like growth factor 2 in development and disease: A mini-review. *Gerontology, 59*(3), 240—249. https://doi.org/10.1159/000343995

de Bono, J., Lin, C. C., Chen, L. T., Corral, J., Michalarea, V., Rihawi, K., Ong, M., Lee, J. H., Hsu, C. H., Yang, J. C. H., Shiah, H. S., Yen, C. J., Anthoney, A., Jove, M., Buschke, S., Fuertig, R., Schmid, U., Goeldner, R. G., Strelkowa, N., … Cheng, A. L. (2020). Two first-in-human studies of xentuzumab, a humanised insulin-like growth factor (IGF)-neutralising antibody, in patients with advanced solid tumours. British Journal of Cancer, 122(9), 1324–1332. https://doi.org/10.1038/s41416-020-0774-1

Calzone, F. J., Cajulis, E., Chung, Y. A., Tsai, M. M., Mitchell, P., Lu, J., Chen, C., Sun, J., Radinsky, R., Kendall, R., & Beltran, P. J. (2013). Epitope-Specific mechanisms of IGF1R inhibition by Ganitumab. PLoS One, 8(2). https://doi.org/10.1371/journal.pone.0055135

Cao, J., & Yee, D. (2021). Disrupting insulin and IGF receptor function in cancer. International Journal of Molecular Sciences, 22(2), 555. https://doi.org/10.3390/ijms22020555

Carboni, J. M., Wittman, M., Yang, Z., Lee, F., Greer, A., Hurlburt, W., Hillerman, S., Cao, C., Cantor, G. H., Dell-John, J., Chen, C., Discenza, L., Menard, K., Li, A., Trainor, G., Vyas, D., Kramer, R., Attar, R. M., & Gottardis, M. M. (2009). BMS-754807, a small molecule inhibitor of insulin-like growth factor-1R/IR. Molecular Cancer Therapeutics, 8(12), 3341–3349. https://doi.org/10.1158/1535-7163.MCT-09-0499

Chen, H. X., & Sharon, E. (2013). IGF-1R as an anti-cancer target-trials and tribulation. Chinese Journal of Cancer, 32(5), 242–252. https://doi.org/10.5732/cjc.012.10263

Cheng, X., Merz, K. H., Vatter, S., Zeller, J., Muehlbeyer, S., Thommet, A., Christ, J., Wölfl, S., & Eisenbrand, G. (2017). Identification of a water-soluble Indirubin derivative as potent inhibitor of insulin-like growth factor 1 receptor through structural modification of the parent natural molecule. Journal of Medicinal Chemistry, 60(12), 4949–4962. https://doi.org/10.1021/acs.jmedchem.7b00324

Christopoulos, P. F., Msaouel, P., & Koutsilieris, M. (2015). The role of the insulin-like growth factor-1 system in breast cancer. Molecular Cancer, 14(1). https://doi.org/10.1186/s12943-015-0291-7

Dang, C. V., Reddy, E. P., Shokat, K. M., & Soucek, L. (2017). Drugging the 'undruggable' cancer targets. Nature Reviews Cancer, 17(8), 502–508. https://doi.org/10.1038/nrc.2017.36

Daughaday, W. H., Hall, K., Raben, M. S., Salmon, W. D., Leo Van Den Brande, J., & Van Wyk, J. J. (1972). Somatomedin: Proposed designation for sulphation factor [7]. Nature, 235(5333), 107. https://doi.org/10.1038/235107a0

Degorce, S. L., Boyd, S., Curwen, J. O., Ducray, R., Halsall, C. T., Jones, C. D., Lach, F., Lenz, E. M., Pass, M., Pass, S., & Trigwell, C. (2016). Discovery of a potent, selective, orally bioavailable, and efficacious novel 2-(Pyrazol-4-ylamino)-pyrimidine inhibitor of the insulin-like growth factor-1 receptor (IGF-1R). Journal of Medicinal Chemistry, 59(10), 4859–4866. https://doi.org/10.1021/acs.jmedchem.6b00203

Denduluri, S. K., Idowu, O., Wang, Z., Liao, Z., Yan, Z., Mohammed, M. K., Ye, J., Wei, Q., Wang, J., Zhao, L., & Luu, H. H. (2015). Insulin-like growth factor (IGF) signaling intumorigenesis and the development ofcancer drug resistance. Genes and Diseases, 2(1), 13–25. https://doi.org/10.1016/j.gendis.2014.10.004

Doi, T., Muro, K., Yoshino, T., Fuse, N., Ura, T., Takahari, D., Feng, H. P., Shimamoto, T., Noguchi, K., & Ohtsu, A. (2013). Phase 1 pharmacokinetic study of MK-0646 (dalotuzumab), an anti-insulin-like growth factor-1 receptor monoclonal antibody, in combination with cetuximab and irinotecan in Japanese patients with advanced colorectal cancer. Cancer Chemotherapy and Pharmacology, 72(3), 643–652. https://doi.org/10.1007/s00280-013-2240-8

Dong, J., Tamraz, S., Berquist, L., Boccia, A., Sereno, A., Chu, P., Ho, S., Joseph, I., Reff, M., & Hariharan, K. (2008). BIIB022, a human antibody targeting human insulin-like growth factor-1 receptor (IGF-1R), enhances the antitumor activities of Tarceva in non-small cell lung carcinoma (NSCLC) and Rapamycin in sarcoma cell lines. Cancer Research, 68.

Elijah, I. E., Branski, L. K., Finnerty, C. C., & Herndon, D. N. (2011). The GH/IGF-1 system in critical illness. Best Practice & Research Clinical Endocrinology & Metabolism, 25(5), 759–767. https://doi.org/10.1016/j.beem.2011.06.002

Engen, W., O'Brien, T. E., Kelly, B., Do, J., Rillera, L., Stapleton, L. K., Youngren, J. F., & Anderson, M. O. (2010). Synthesis of aryl-heteroaryl ureas (AHUs) based on 4-aminoquinoline and their evaluation against the insulin-like growth factor receptor (IGF-1R). Bioorganic & Medicinal Chemistry, 18(16), 5995–6005. https://doi.org/10.1016/j.bmc.2010.06.071

Fassnacht, M., Berruti, A., Baudin, E., Demeure, M. J., Gilbert, J., Haak, H., Kroiss, M., Quinn, D. I., Hesseltine, E., Ronchi, C. L., Terzolo, M., Choueiri, T. K., Poondru, S., Fleege, T., Rorig, R., Chen, J., Stephens, A. W., Worden, F., & Hammer, G. D. (2015). Linsitinib (OSI-906) versus placebo for patients with locally advanced or metastatic adrenocortical carcinoma: A double-blind, randomised, phase 3 study. The Lancet Oncology, 16(4), 426–435. https://doi.org/10.1016/S1470-2045(15)70081-1

Fürstenberger, G., & Senn, H. J. (2002). Insulin-like growth factors and cancer. *The Lancet Oncology, 3*(5), 298–302. https://doi.org/10.1016/S1470-2045(02)00731-3

Fouladi, M., Perentesis, J. P., Wagner, L. M., Vinks, A. A., Reid, J. M., Ahern, C., Thomas, G., Mercer, C. A., Krueger, D. A., Houghton, P. J., Doyle, L. A., Chen, H., Weigel, B., & Blaney, S. M. (2015). A phase I study of cixutumumab (IMC-A12) in combination with temsirolimus (CCI-779) in children with recurrent solid tumors: A children's oncology group phase I consortium report. *Clinical Cancer Research, 21*(7), 1558–1565. https://doi.org/10.1158/1078-0432.CCR-14-0595

Frenkel, S., Zloto, O., Pe'er, J., & Barak, V. (2013). Insulin-like growth factor-1 as a predictive biomarker for metastatic uveal melanoma in humans. *Investigative Ophthalmology & Visual Science, 54*(1), 490–493. https://doi.org/10.1167/iovs.12-10228

Froesch, E. R., Bürgi, H., Ramseier, E. B., Bally, P., & Labhart, A. (1963). Antibody-suppressible and nonsuppressible insulin-like activities in human serum and their physiologic significance. An insulin assay with adipose tissue of increased precision and specificity. *Journal of Clinical Investigation, 42*(11), 1816–1834. https://doi.org/10.1172/JCI104866

Gadekar, P. K., Urunkar, G., Roychowdhury, A., Sharma, R., Bose, J., Khanna, S., Damre, A., & Sarveswari, S. (2021). Design, synthesis and biological evaluation of 2,3-dihydroimidazo[2,1-b]thiazoles as dual EGFR and IGF1R inhibitors. *Bioorganic Chemistry, 115*, 105151. https://doi.org/10.1016/j.bioorg.2021.105151

Griffeth, R. J., Bianda, V., & Nef, S. (2014). The emerging role of insulin-like growth factors in testis development and function. *Basic and Clinical Andrology, 24*(1). https://doi.org/10.1186/2051-4190-24-12

Grimberg, A. (2003). Mechanisms by which IGF-I may promote cancer. *Cancer Biology & Therapy, 2*(6), 630–635. https://doi.org/10.4161/cbt.2.6.678

Guo, C., Chu, H., Gong, Z., Zhang, B., Li, C., Chen, J., & Huang, L. (2021). HOXB13 promotes gastric cancer cell migration and invasion via IGF-1R upregulation and subsequent activation of PI3K/AKT/mTOR signaling pathway. *Life Sciences, 278*. https://doi.org/10.1016/j.lfs.2021.119522

Hazrati, E., Gholami, M., Farahani, R. H., Ghorban, K., Ghayomzadeh, M., & Rouzbahani, N. H. (2022). The effect of IGF-1 plasma concentration on COVID-19 severity. *Microbial Pathogenesis, 164*, 105416. https://doi.org/10.1016/j.micpath.2022.105416

Holly, J. M. P., Biernacka, K., & Perks, C. M. (2019). The neglected insulin: IGF-II, a metabolic regulator with implications for diabetes, obesity, and cancer. *Cells, 8*(10), 1207. https://doi.org/10.3390/cells8101207

Huang, Y. K., Kang, W. M., Ma, Z. Q., Liu, Y. Q., Zhou, L., & Yu, J. C. (2019). NUCKS1 promotes gastric cancer cell aggressiveness by upregulating IGF-1R and subsequently activating the PI3K/Akt/mTOR signaling pathway. *Carcinogenesis, 40*(2), 370–379. https://doi.org/10.1093/carcin/bgy142

Janssen, J. A. M. J. L., & Varewijck, A. J. (2014). IGF-IR targeted therapy: Past, present and future. *Frontiers in Endocrinology, 5*. https://doi.org/10.3389/fendo.2014.00224

Jin, M., Gokhale, P. C., Cooke, A., Foreman, K., Buck, E., May, E. W., Feng, L., Bittner, M. A., Kadalbajoo, M., Landfair, D., Siu, K. W., Stolz, K. M., Werner, D. S., Laufer, R. S., Li, A. H., Dong, H., Steinig, A. G., Kleinberg, A., Yao, Y., … Mulvihill, M. J. (2010). Discovery of an orally efficacious imidazo[5, 1-f]-[1,2,4]triazine dual inhibitor of IGF-1R and IR. *ACS Medicinal Chemistry Letters, 1*(9), 510–515. https://doi.org/10.1021/ml100178g

Kleinberg, D. L. (1998). Role of IGF-I in normal mammary development. *Breast Cancer Research and Treatment, 47*(3), 201–208. https://doi.org/10.1023/A:1005998832636

Laron, Z. (2001). Insulin-like growth factor 1 (IGF-1): A growth hormone. *Journal of Clinical Pathology - Molecular Pathology, 54*(5), 311–316. https://doi.org/10.1136/mp.54.5.311

Liu, X., Xie, H., Luo, C., Tong, L., Wang, Y., Peng, T., Ding, J., Jiang, H., & Li, H. (2010). Discovery and SAR of thiazolidine-2,4-dione analogues as insulin-like growth factor-1 receptor (IGF-IR) inhibitors via hierarchical virtual screening. *Journal of Medicinal Chemistry, 53*(6), 2661–2665. https://doi.org/10.1021/jm901798e

Livingstone, C. (2013). IGF2 and cancer. *Endocrine-Related Cancer, 20*(6), R321–R339. https://doi.org/10.1530/ERC-13-0231

McTavish, H., Griffin, R. J., Terai, K., & Dudek, A. Z. (2009). Novel insulin-like growth factor-methotrexate covalent conjugate inhibits tumor growth in vivo at lower dosage than methotrexate alone. *Translational Research, 153*(6), 275–282. https://doi.org/10.1016/j.trsl.2009.02.005

Monzavi, R., & Cohen, P. (2002). IGFs and IGFBPs: Role in health and disease. *Best Practice & Research Clinical Endocrinology & Metabolism, 16*(3), 433–447. https://doi.org/10.1053/beem.2002.0212

Moschos, S. J., & Mantzoros, C. S. (2002). The role of the IGF system in cancer: From basic to clinical studies and clinical applications. *Oncology, 63*(4), 317–332. https://doi.org/10.1159/000066230

Mulvihill, M. J., Ji, Q. S., Coate, H. R., Cooke, A., Dong, H., Feng, L., Foreman, K., Rosenfeld-Franklin, M., Honda, A., Mak, G., Mulvihill, K. M., Nigro, A. I., O'Connor, M., Pirrit, C., Steinig, A. G., Siu, K., Stolz, K. M., Sun, Y., Tavares, P. A. R., Yao, Y., & Gibson, N. W. (2008). Novel 2-phenylquinolin-7-yl-derived imidazo[1,5-a]pyrazines as potent insulin-like growth factor-I receptor (IGF-IR) inhibitors. *Bioorganic & Medicinal Chemistry, 16*(3), 1359–1375. https://doi.org/10.1016/j.bmc.2007.10.061

Naing, A., LoRusso, P., Fu, S., Hong, D., Chen, H. X., Doyle, L. A., Phan, A. T., Habra, M. A., & Kurzrock, R. (2013). Insulin growth factor receptor (IGF-1R) antibody cixutumumab combined with the mTOR inhibitor temsirolimus in patients with metastatic adrenocortical carcinoma. *British Journal of Cancer, 108*(4), 826–830. https://doi.org/10.1038/bjc.2013.46

Ngo, M. H. T., Jeng, H. Y., Kuo, Y. C., Nanda, J. D., Brahmadhi, A., Ling, T. Y., Chang, T. S., & Huang, Y. H. (2021). The role of igf/igf-1r signaling in hepatocellular carcinomas: Stemness-related properties and drug resistance. *International Journal of Molecular Sciences, 22*(4), 1–34. https://doi.org/10.3390/ijms22041931

Peruzzi, F., Prisco, M., Dews, M., Salomoni, P., Grassilli, E., Romano, G., Calabretta, B., & Baserga, R. (1999). Multiple signaling pathways of the insulin-like growth factor 1 receptor in protection from apoptosis. *Molecular and Cellular Biology, 19*(10), 7203–7215. https://doi.org/10.1128/MCB.19.10.7203

Pfizer discontinues a phase 3 study of figitumumab in previously treated patients with advanced non-small cell lung cancer. 2010.

Pollak, M. (2000). Insulin-like growth factor physiology and cancer risk. *European Journal of Cancer, 36*(10), 1224–1228. https://doi.org/10.1016/S0959-8049(00)00102-7

Puche, J. E., & Castilla-Cortázar, I. (2012). Human conditions of insulin-like growth factor-I (IGF-I) deficiency. *Journal of Translational Medicine, 10*, 1–29.

Qvit, N., Reuveni, H., Gazal, S., Zundelevich, A., Blum, G., Niv, M. Y., Feldstein, A., Meushar, S., Shalev, D. E., Friedler, A., & Gilon, C. (2008). Synthesis of a novel macrocyclic library: Discovery of an IGF-1R inhibitor. *Journal of Combinatorial Chemistry, 10*(2), 256–266. https://doi.org/10.1021/cc700113c

Rinderknecht, E., & Humbel, R. E. (1976). Amino-terminal sequences of two polypeptides from human serum with nonsuppressible insulin-like and cell-growth-promoting activities: Evidence for structural homology with insulin B chain. *Proceedings of the National Academy of Sciences, 73*(12), 4379–4381. https://doi.org/10.1073/pnas.73.12.4379

Rinderknecht, E., & Humbel, R. E. (1978). Primary structure of human insulin-like growth factor II. *FEBS Letters, 89*(2), 283–286. https://doi.org/10.1016/0014-5793(78)80237-3

Salmon, W. D., & Daughaday, W. H. (1957). A hormonally controlled serum factor which stimulates sulfate incorporation by cartilage in vitro. *The Journal of Laboratory and Clinical Medicine, 49*(6), 825–836.

Schmidt, S., Preu, L., Lemcke, T., Totzke, F., Schächtele, C., Kubbutat, M. H. G., & Kunick, C. (2011). Dual IGF-1R/SRC inhibitors based on a N'-aroyl-2-(1H-indol-3-yl)-2-oxoacetohydrazide structure. *European Journal of Medicinal Chemistry, 46*(7), 2759–2769. https://doi.org/10.1016/j.ejmech.2011.03.065

Sélénou, C., Brioude, F., Giabicani, E., Sobrier, M. L., & Netchine, I. (2022). IGF2: Development, genetic and epigenetic abnormalities. *Cells, 11*, 1886.

Shelton, J. G., Steelman, L. S., White, E. R., & McCubrey, J. A. (2004). Synergy between PI3K/Akt and Raf/MEK/ERK pathways in IGF-1R mediated cell cycle progression and prevention of apoptosis in hematopoietic cells. *Cell Cycle, 3*(3), 370–377. https://doi.org/10.4161/cc.3.3.747

Shi, X., Zheng, J., Ma, J., Wang, Z., Sun, W., Li, M., Huang, S., & Hu, S. (2022). Insulin-like growth factor in Parkinson's disease is related to nonmotor symptoms and the volume of specific brain areas. *Neuroscience Letters, 783*, 136735. https://doi.org/10.1016/j.neulet.2022.136735

Simpson, A., Petnga, W., Macaulay, V. M., Weyer-Czernilofsky, U., & Bogenrieder, T. (2017). Insulin-like growth factor (IGF) pathway targeting in cancer: Role of the IGF Axis and opportunities for future combination studies. *Targeted Oncology, 12*(5), 571–597. https://doi.org/10.1007/s11523-017-0514-5

Suh, H. S., Zhao, M. L., Derico, L., Choi, N., & Lee, S. C. (2013). Insulin-like growth factor 1 and 2 (IGF1, IGF2) expression in human microglia: Differential regulation by inflammatory mediators. *Journal of Neuroinflammation, 10*. https://doi.org/10.1186/1742-2094-10-37

Treatment Types in American Cancer Society. (2022). https://www.cancer.org/treatment/treatments-and-side-effects/treatment-types.html.

Van Wyk, J. J., Hall, K., Van Den Brande, J. L., & Weaver, R. P. (1971). Further purification and characterization of sulfation factor and thymidine factor from acromegalic plasma. *Journal of Clinical Endocrinology and Metabolism, 32*(3), 389–403. https://doi.org/10.1210/jcem-32-3-389

Vasan, N., Baselga, J., & Hyman, D. M. (2019). A view on drug resistance in cancer. *Nature, 575*(7782), 299–309. https://doi.org/10.1038/s41586-019-1730-1

Venepalli, N. K., Emmadi, R., Danciu, O. C., Chowdhery, R., Cabay, R. J., Gaitonde, S., Aardsma, N., Kothari, R., Liu, L. C., Fischer, J. H., Zaidi, A., Russell, M. J., & Dudek, A. Z. (2019). Phase i study of IGF-methotrexate conjugate in the treatment of advanced tumors expressing IGF-1R. *American Journal of Clinical Oncology: Cancer Clinical Trials, 42*(11), 862–869. https://doi.org/10.1097/COC.0000000000000611

Von Mehren, M., George, S., Heinrich, M. C., Schuetze, S. M., Yap, J. T., Yu, J. Q., Abbott, A., Litwin, S., Crowley, J., Belinsky, M., Janeway, K. A., Hornick, J. L., Flieder, D. B., Chugh, R., Rink, L., & Van Den Abbeele, A. D. (2020). Linsitinib (OSI-906) for the treatment of adult and pediatric wild-type gastrointestinal stromal tumors, a SARC phase II study. *Clinical Cancer Research, 26*(8), 1837–1845. https://doi.org/10.1158/1078-0432.CCR-19-1069

Wang, P., Mak, V. C., & Cheung, L. W. (2022). Drugging IGF-1R in cancer: New insights and emerging opportunities. *Genes and Diseases, 10*, 199–211. https://doi.org/10.1016/j.gendis.2022.03.002

Waraky, A., Akopyan, K., Parrow, V., Strömberg, T., Axelson, M., Abrahmsén, L., Lindqvist, A., Larsson, O., & Aleem, E. (2014). Picropodophyllin causes mitotic arrest and catastrophe by depolymerizing microtubules via Insulin-like growth factor-1 receptor-independent mechanism. *Oncotarget, 5*(18), 8379–8392. https://doi.org/10.18632/oncotarget.2292

Ward, R. A., Fawell, S., Floc'H, N., Flemington, V., McKerrecher, D., & Smith, P. D. (2021). Challenges and opportunities in cancer drug resistance. *Chemical Reviews, 121*(6), 3297–3351. https://doi.org/10.1021/acs.chemrev.0c00383

White, V., Jawerbaum, A., Mazzucco, M. B., Gauster, M., Desoye, G., & Hiden, U. (2018). IGF2 stimulates fetal growth in a sex- and organ-dependent manner. *Pediatric Research, 83*(1), 183–189. https://doi.org/10.1038/pr.2017.221

World Heath Organization. (2022). *Cancer*. https://www.who.int/news-room/fact-sheets/detail/cancer.

Xu, H., Zhao, Y., Gao, X., Wang, F., & Gu, Y. (2021). An innovative fluorescent probe targeting IGF1R for breast cancer diagnosis. *European Journal of Medicinal Chemistry, 219*, 113440. https://doi.org/10.1016/j.ejmech.2021.113440

Yakar, S., Werner, H., & Rosen, C. J. (2018). 40 years of IGF1: Insulin-like growth factors: Actions on the skeleton. *Journal of Molecular Endocrinology, 61*(1), T115–T137. https://doi.org/10.1530/JME-17-0298

Yu, H., & Rohan, T. (2000). Role of the insulin-like growth factor family in cancer development and progression. *Journal of the National Cancer Institute, 92*(18), 1472–1489. https://doi.org/10.1093/jnci/92.18.1472

Zhang, M., Liu, J., Li, M., Zhang, S., Lu, Y., Liang, Y., Zhao, K., & Li, Y. (2018). Insulin-like growth factor 1/insulin-like growth factor 1 receptor signaling protects against cell apoptosis through the PI3K/AKT pathway in glioblastoma cells. *Experimental and Therapeutic Medicine, 16*(2), 1477–1482. https://doi.org/10.3892/etm.2018.6336

Zhang, T., Shen, H., Dong, W., Qu, X., Liu, Q., & Du, J. (2014). Antitumor effects and molecular mechanisms of figitumumab, a humanized monoclonal antibody to IGF-1 receptor, in esophageal carcinoma. *Scientific Reports, 4*. https://doi.org/10.1038/srep06855

Zhang, W., Lee, J. C., Kumar, S., & Gowen, M. (1999). ERK pathway mediates the activation of Cdk2 in IGF-1-induced proliferation of human osteosarcoma MG-63 cells. *Journal of Bone and Mineral Research, 14*(4), 528–535. https://doi.org/10.1359/jbmr.1999.14.4.528

Zhong, L., Li, Y., Xiong, L., Wang, W., Wu, M., Yuan, T., Yang, W., Tian, C., Miao, Z., Wang, T., & Yang, S. (2021). Small molecules in targeted cancer therapy: Advances, challenges, and future perspectives. *Signal Transduction and Targeted Therapy, 6*(1). https://doi.org/10.1038/s41392-021-00572-w

Zhu, C., Qi, X., Chen, Y., Sun, B., Dai, Y., & Gu, Y. (2011). PI3K/Akt and MAPK/ERK1/2 signaling pathways are involved in IGF-1-induced VEGF-C upregulation in breast cancer. *Journal of Cancer Research and Clinical Oncology, 137*(11), 1587–1594. https://doi.org/10.1007/s00432-011-1049-2

Mitotic kinesin spindle protein (KSP/Eg5 ATPase) inhibitors

Ravindra Kumar Chourasiya[1], Wafa Hourani[2], Pran Kishore Deb[3] and Katharigatta N. Venugopala[4,5]

[1]SVN Institute of Pharmaceutical Sciences, Swami Vivekanand University, Sagar, Madhya Pradesh, India; [2]Department of Pharmaceutical Sciences, Faculty of Pharmacy, Philadelphia University, Amman, Jordan; [3]Department of Pharmaceutical Sciences and Technology, Birla Institute of Technology (BIT), Mesra, Jharkhand, India; [4]Department of Biotechnology and Food Science, Faculty of Applied Sciences, Durban University of Technology, Durban, South Africa; [5]Department of Pharmaceutical Sciences, College of Clinical Pharmacy, King Faisal University, Al-Ahsa, Saudi Arabia

1. Introduction

Cancer cells are frequently targeted during mitosis for various therapeutic interventions. A number of classical mitotic spindle poisons/inhibitors continued to be used in medical practice for decades, including vinca alkaloids and taxanes (Haschka et al., 2018; Wood et al., 2001). Multiple processes must cooperate to confirm correct mitotic spindle construction and control during mitosis (Gadde & Heald, 2004). Cell motility plays a vital role in physiological processes, whereas cell adhesion plays a major role in tissue development and maintenance; furthermore, the cell polarity plays a critical role in creating a barrier for pathogens (Ong & Torres, 2019).

Moreover, there are a number of logical relations between mitosis and other pathways crucial for the development and endurance of cancer, including cell death, checkpoint activation, and DNA (Deoxyribonucleic acid) damage (Jackson et al., 2007; Venugopala, 2022). Antimitotic medications are being developed to target nonstructural mitotic components like mitotic kinesins, aurora kinases, and polo-like kinases (Garber, 2005).

The movement of the spindle and chromosomes during mitosis is governed by a family of 11 proteins called mitotic kinesins (Bergnes et al., 2005). As mitotic kinesins play a special role in cell division, they have been proven to be fascinating drug targets for cancer therapy (Lee et al., 2007).

For the construction of a bipolar spindle and to guarantee that sister chromatids are segregated equally, mitosis-specific kinesin spindle protein (KSP, Eg5) is crucial. The mitotic spindle meeting checkpoint (SAC) is activated when the kinesin spindle protein is inhibited, ensuing in the development of a monopolar spindle and the arrest of metaphase due to the maintenance of cdc2/cyclin B activity. Cellular death and drug-induced increase of mitotic cells are intimately related. The selective KSP inhibitor ARRY-520 is active in a varied choice of tumor xenograft models and has low nanomolar efficacy in solid and hematologic tumor cell lines (Tunquist et al., 2010).

1.1 Mitotic kinesin biology

In mitosis, spindle fibers are extremely long structures consisting of microtubules, expanding from sister chromatids to the centrosomes on each pole. Microtubules are essential components of mitotic spindles, a sophisticated cytoskeleton machine inside our body that functions as moving parts; for instance, when chromosomes begin to fold back in telophase, that occurs as a result of mitotic kinesin (Chaffey et al., 2003). However, chromosomes are heavily dependent upon the disintegration of microtubules to fold back into their original form. Mitotic kinesin is located within mitotic spindles and is crucial for the protection, maintenance, and regulation of the cell (Wordeman, 2010). There are 14 different subfamilies within the mitotic kinesin superfamily primarily classified according to their motility, affinity, and function, including the kinesins that travel to the positive end of the microtubules and those having more affinity toward the negative end of the microtubules and the kinesins that depolymerize microtubules. Most kinesins are attracted toward the positive end, including Eg5; ATPase is necessary for the movement of kinesins along the microtubules (Wordeman, 2010).

KSP works in cell division on the stage(s) between prophase and prometaphase, as well as on telophase and cytokinesis. There are different types of kinesin proteins, also known as kinesins, such as KIF11 (Eg5) and KIF15 (HKLP-2) (Joseph et al., 2021). KSP plays a major role in cell division, including chromosome repositioning, centrosome separation, microtubule positioning, and spindle polarization. Mitotic spindle dysfunction during anaphase, telophase, or cytokinesis can result in mis-segregation and multinucleation (Moreno-Andrés et al., 2023). These kinesins were missing in postmitotic neurons and more abundant in tumor tissues than in surrounding normal tissues. Similar expression profiles were seen in a variety of uncharacterized mitotic kinesins, including Kif15/HKIp2, KinI3, Kip3a, and Kip3d (Tham, 2019).

Thus, once a mutation occurs, it could cause diseases, such as microcephaly, lymphedema, mental retardation, or autosomal recessive in KIF11 (Ostergaard et al., 2012); and Braddock—Carey Syndrome and microdeletion syndrome in KIF15 (Joseph et al., 2021). The human genome project is all about comparing the genetic code of "irregular" proteins and a "healthy" genetic code, which is an intriguing technique to explore the many causes of illnesses.

Eg5, a kinesin protein with affinity for the positive terminal end of microtubules, is responsible for a number of processes including the establishment, upkeep, and control of mitotic spindles. The protein Eg5, also known as KIF11, can either be the cause of some diseases or as a prognostic indicator for other diseases. For example, the inverse relationship between Eg5 and hepatocellular carcinoma can serve as a prognostic indicator because the more the cancer worsens, the more the protein upregulates (Shao et al., 2021).

ATPase aids the movement of the motor proteins along the microtubules. Mitotic slippage is when a cell prematurely exits cell division and either continues or bypasses cytokinesis. The depletion of adenosine triphosphate (ADP) can either delay but complete cell division or lead to mitotic arrest. The "powerhouse" of ATP is the mitochondria, and mitochondrial disorders have been found to affect the major organs in the body, including the brain, skeletal muscle, liver, heart, and kidneys (Park et al., 2018). Diseases, including ataxia, retinitis pigmentosa, and neuropathy, can be brought on by the depletion of ATP. Retinitis pigmentosa is a genetic congenital condition that mostly causes vision loss as people age, whereas ataxia is a disorder that affects coordination, speech, and balance. Damage to the nerves that results in asthenia, paresthesia, neuropathy, pain, malignancy, and maybe even death is known as neuropathy (Johnson et al., 2019).

1.2 Kinesin structure and function

As a subset of the large superfamily of motor proteins, mitotic kinesins are also involved in cargo transport, spindle and chromosome movement, and microtubule dynamics (Mann & Wadsworth, 2019). While they fluctuate broadly in function and intracellular localization, all of them possess microtubule-stimulated ATPase activity. When ATP is hydrolyzed, chemical energy is released that is used either to move microtubules in a directional manner or to depolymerize microtubules. These proteins function well when ATP hydrolysis is tightly coupled with microtubule association and conformational movement.

Mitotic spindle motor proteins serve as transporters along microtubules and are the primary cytoskeleton machine in the cell, while kinesins are ATP-dependent motor proteins that are important in cell division. Myosin moves on actin filaments, whereas dynein and kinesin both move along microtubules, but one typically goes toward the negative end (dynein) and the other toward the positive end. There are three separate primary proteins: myosin, kinesin, and dynein, however, we will only be focused on kinesins (kinesin) (Abraham et al., 2018).

The three major regions of kinesins are as follows: the head (for movement), and the stalk and tail (for interaction with chromosomes and vesicles); the combination of all three regions together will lead to the termination of the cell cycle resulting in apoptosis (Ali & Yang, 2020). Kinesins have a lighter tail-end that connects to the vesicles (or cargo), and it uses ATPase to hydrolyze ATP for movement. It simultaneously moves the vesicles along the microtubules. This movement of the vesicles along the microtubules has been compared to "human walking." The head that is attached to the microtubule is the one that is bound to ATP while the other head remains stationary until abruptly switching. The vesicles move along the microtubule with the constant movement of receiving ATP and releasing ADP as a result of the rapid switching between both heads. Since they require ATP to work, motor proteins serve a variety of vital transporter functions in the body, including transporting "cell life" up axons to neuron terminals (Gennerich & Vale, 2009). A conventional kinesin is a double-headed enzyme with heavy and light chains that are identical (Li et al., 2021). The heavy chains are made up of three distinct domains: an N-terminal motor domain, a stalk region, and a C-terminal tail domain as depicted in Fig. 9.1 (Wojcik et al., 2013). In the motor domain, consisting of the catalytic core and neck linker, microtubules and ATP are bound, allowing movement along the microtubule. During dimerization, coiled structures are formed in the stalk region (Qin et al., 2020), while the C-terminal tail domain facilitates protein—protein

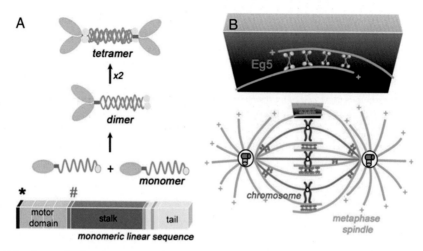

FIGURE 9.1   Sequence, function, and structure of kinesin-5 proteins. (A) Linear sequence organization and general structure of the domains within one kinesin molecule are shown at the bottom of the panel. The asterisk and pound signs highlight the position of the cover neck and the neck linker, respectively. Dimer and tetrameric organization of the kinesin-5 proteins is also drawn. (B) Cartoon representation of the mitotic spindle and the tetrameric Eg5 molecules cross-bridging spindle microtubules. *This figure is adapted with permission from Wojcik et al. (2013).*

interactions necessary to attach cargo to the kinesin. Polypeptide units recognized as light chains are also associated with the tail domain, which may bind to the membranes of cellular vesicles or organelles (Jeong et al., 2020). It has been demonstrated that when conventional kinesin is fully functional, it has the ability to walk along a microtubule in 80Å long steps before dissociating from it (Jeong et al., 2020).

2. Kinesin spindle protein inhibitors

A mitotic kinesin called KSP, often referred to as Hs (*Homo sapiens*) Eg5, is found in the mitotic spindle and is necessary for the early stages of mitosis to produce a bipolar mitotic spindle (Garcia-Saez & Skoufias, 2021). As a homotetramer, this protein can bind the oppositely polarized microtubules originating from the distinct spindle poles. Following ATP hydrolysis, KSP is capable to move processivity along with microtubules due to the coordinated activity of matching motor domains arranged at either end of the homotetramer. To form a bipolar mitotic spindle, KSP is bound to two microtubules, forcing spindle poles apart in the direction away from the centrosome (Kim et al., 2019). Mitotic arrest results from inhibiting KSP, which leads to monopolar mitotic spindles formed when centrosomes do not separate. By acting on a different protein rather than the microtubule cytoskeleton itself, medications that target KSP may prevent peripheral neuropathies associated with antimicrotubule drugs (Shi et al., 2022). Small molecule inhibitors have been demonstrated to cause mitotic arrest in a variety of tumor cell lines both in vitro and in vivo, and this, together with the anticipated reduction in brain toxicity, has aided in the development of numerous active antimitotic drug discovery initiatives (Arnst et al., 2019).

KSPs are crucial transporters for vesicles and other "cell life" along the microtubules to their destination; therefore, if kinesins are overexpressed, illnesses and other issues may result. KSP movement depends on ATP, and human disorders may be brought on by ATP depletion. Therefore, it is essential to control the KSP movement. Unfortunately, it is possible for proteins to be upregulated and ATP to be depleted; hence, kinesin spindle protein inhibitors were developed to stop cellular damage (Johnson et al., 2019). Kinesins can be inhibited by KSP inhibitors (mainly kinesin-binding protein) in a variety of ways, including by altering their motility through ADP and/or ATP, cellular function, or even just by preventing them from connecting to the microtubule (Johnson et al., 2019).

2.1 Monastrol

Monastrol was the first known selective inhibitor of KSP. Monastrol is a cell-permeable allosteric inhibitor, it primarily works on ADP-release from Eg5 weakening the kinesin and preventing the collapse (and death) of the cell, but it does not directly inhibit ATP. Monastrol is an enantiomer and it has an R- and S-enantiomer. The R-enantiomer has been found to be more active than the S-enantiomer of monastrol (Maliga et al., 2002).

In both the presence and absence of microtubules, the drug has been shown to block ADP release. The IC_{50} was in the range of 88 to more than 500 µg/mL against HeLa (cervical cancer) and MCF-7 (breast cancer) cell lines (Bidram et al., 2020). Recent structural insights into the function of this inhibitor were disclosed by the X-ray crystal structure of the KSP-ADP complex with monastrol (Happy, 2019). It was found that monastrol causes a dramatic change in conformations in helices α2 and α3 as well as the insertion of the loop (L5), leading to the construction of an induced-fit pocket, which is not observable in the KSP-ADP structure as depicted in Fig. 9.2 (Seneci, 2018). Based on consequent kinetic and thermodynamic studies, it was suggested that monastrol binds weakly to nucleotide-free states and/or KSP−ATP collision complexes with open loops (Chen, 2018). In response to tight ATP binding, a

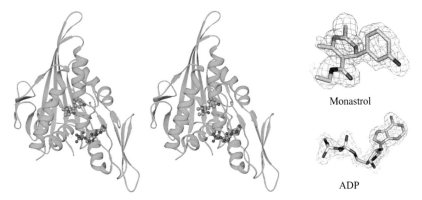

Monastrol

ADP

FIGURE 9.2   Ribbon stereo diagram of KSP displaying the two binding pockets spaced around 12 Å apart when Mg^{2+}. ADP and monastrol are present. The "balls and sticks" model is represented by monastrol and ADP. The Mg^{2+} is shown as a white ball next to the ADP phosphate molecule. On the right side of the figure, both of the structures' expanded electron density maps are shown separately. *This figure is adapted with permission from Yan et al. (2004).*

conformational change is proposed that closes the inhibitor pocket, increasing monastrol's affinity for KSP. The process of structural changes in solution was explained using spectroscopic probes, and the findings supported the crystallographic predictions (Sarabi et al., 2022). The activity was lowered by substituting the phenyl ring or 3-hydroxy group, the same way it was lowered by substituting the sulfur in thiourea with oxygen. The potency of analogs with fused bicyclic cores was increased. Monastrol (1) was 10 times less potent than compound (2), which had an IC_{50} of 2 mM. The potency was further boosted to 200 nM by adding a gem-dimethyl group in the compound (3). Both compounds (2) and (3) were also shown to enhance cellular potency with the desired phenotype in Fig. 9.3.

Kinetic analysis and crystallization of Eg5-ADP monastrol complexes have been used to investigate monastrol's mechanism of inhibiting Eg5 as depicted in Fig. 9.4 (Cochran et al., 2005). There is no competition between monastrol and ATP since it is a noncompetitive reversible inhibitor. The binding arises by induced fit in a pocket 12 Å away from the nucleotide-binding site. To develop the inhibitor binding site, local and distal conformational changes are required that permit ATP binding but lock Eg5 in a conformation not appropriate for releasing ADP. The interaction between Eg5 and MTs is not disrupted by monastrol

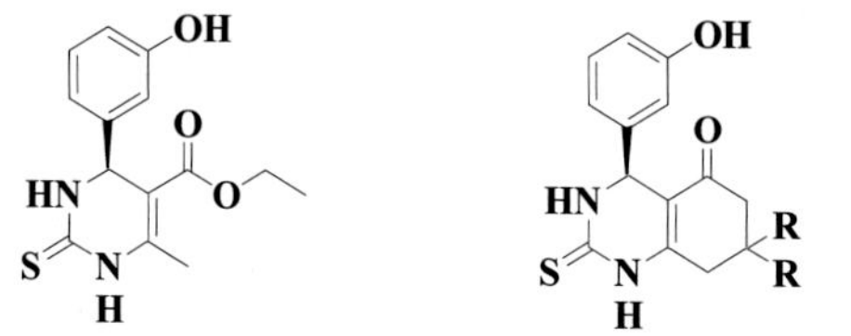

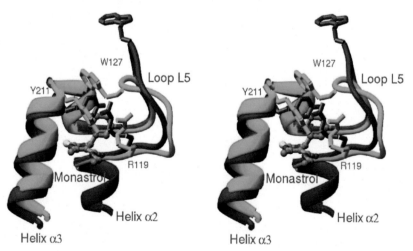

FIGURE 9.3   Structure of compounds (1−3).

FIGURE 9.4   Structural comparison of the Mg^{2+}. ADP dual complex of KSP's monastrol binding pocket in stereo before (*red*) and after (*green*), side-chains of R119, W127, and Y211 are depicted to indicate their positions before and following monastrol binding (PDB ID 1I6). *This figure is adapted with permission from Yan et al. (2004).*

(Fang et al., 2020). Eg5-ADP-monastrol complexes bind MTs in low-friction modes without ATP hydrolysis and conformational variations (Mousavi & Fatemi, 2019).

2.2 S-trityl-L-cysteine

S-trityl-L-cysteine (STLC, **4**) is a potent Eg5 inhibitor with antimitotic properties. As noted in KSP inhibitors, reversible noncompetitive inhibitors bind noncovalently near the active site but do not prevent the substrate (ADP) from locking onto the enzyme or protein (Eg5) in this case. STLC binds to Eg5 through its amino and carboxyl group forming an ADP-STLC-Eg5 complex; thus, STLC can be seen as a cytostatic drug that stops the growth of damaged cells but does not kill them (Radwan et al., 2019).

In the NCI 60 tumor cell line screen, this molecule showed greater tumor growth inhibition activity in vitro and in cell-based assays as compared to monastrol. Both basal and microtubule-stimulated ATPases are inhibited by STLC (**4**) (Fig. 9.5), a reversible tight-binding inhibitor (Fig. 9.6). There is a common binding region between STLC and monastrol on Eg5 designed by loop L5/helix α2 and helix α3/strand β5. Both inhibitors may cause parallel local conformational deviations within the interaction site according to hydrogen/deuterium conversation mass spectrometry experiments (H/D-MS) (Fukai et al., 2021).

2.3 Beta carboline

The Eg5 IC_{50} for tetrahydro-β-carboline (TH-β carboline, **5**) was 2.5 M. Compound (**6**) quickly showed a decimal increase in Eg5 binding affinity with a single methyl group added to the aryl ring in Fig. 9.7. A cocrystal structure **7** of ligands (**3**) by combining Eg5 cocrystallography efforts was created, which, like the pyrimidinone series, induces a new pocket (Fig. 9.8). It is in line with every cocrystal structure in the PDB (Protein Data Bank) that exhibits comparable structural alterations in the protein when ligands bind to the same allosteric site (Chourasiya et al., 2013a, 2013b, 2016). Phenolic −OH group forms a strong hydrogen bond with the carbonyl backbone of Glu118, which is about 10 times as potent as −H or 100 times as potent as−Me. The carboline-NH and amide carbonyl hydrogen bonds exhibit less than ideal geometries, which may indicate that most of the binding is hydrophobic. It is noteworthy to observe that the protein prefers the R enantiomer even though compound (**6**) was saturated into the crystal as a racemic mixture. After modeling overlays with potent in-house pyrimidinone series Eg5 inhibitors, an amino functionality was introduced to open up additional hydrogen bonds to Glu215 or Tyr211. As a result, the acetyl entity was chain stretched to terminate with a basic primary amine, resulting in the TH-β-carboline (**7**) showing better binding affinity to Eg5 (Barsanti et al., 2010).

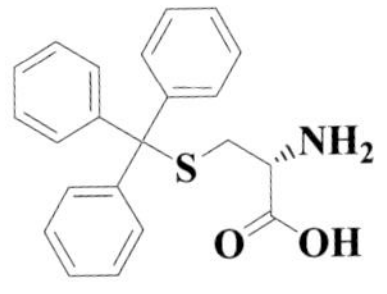

4 (STLC)

FIGURE 9.5 Structure of compound **4**.

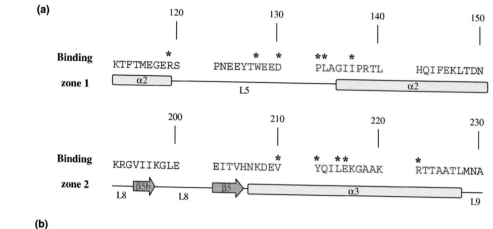

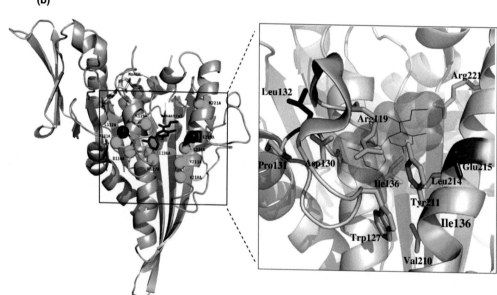

FIGURE 9.6   (A) The locations of the 11 residues in the Eg5 main sequence that will undergo mutation (*black symbols*). *Red* highlights indicate the two peptide sequences that the H/D exchange tests identified as representing the inhibitor-binding pocket. Below the sequence are exposed secondary ligand elements determined by X-ray crystallography. (B) Ribbon diagram displaying the 11 residues identified for mutagenesis in the ternary Eg5-ADP-monastrol complex. The control residues are shown in *blue*, whereas the other residues are shown in *green*. Ball and stick models of ADP and monastrol (*red*) are displayed. *This figure is adapted with permission from Brier et al. (2006).*

2.3.1 Tetrahydro-β-carbolines

According to a cell-based screen, compound (**8**), or HR22C16, is an inhibitor of KSP (IC$_{50}$ 0.65 μM). More refinement produced stronger compounds, including (**9**) (IC$_{50}$ 90 nM) (Luo & Song, 2021). A study on the synthesis and biological assessment of 60 analogs with both cis- and trans-isomers and various R groups was carried out (Wang et al., 2021). In general,

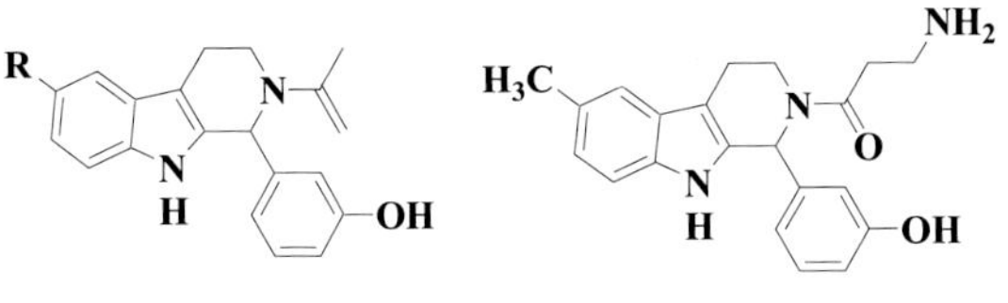

FIGURE 9.7   Structure of compounds (5–7).

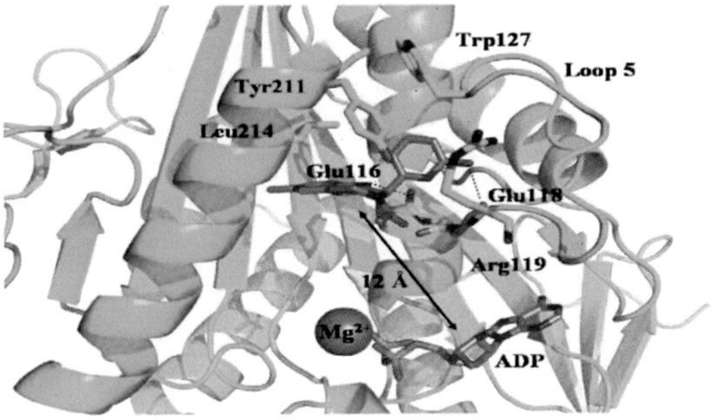

5: R = H, IC$_{50}$ = 2.5 μM
6: R = CH$_3$, IC$_{50}$ = 0.2 μM

7: IC$_{50}$ = nM

FIGURE 9.8   Cocrystal ligands of (3) attached to Eg5; Tyr211 sidechain is moved by the carboline phenol to a new position. The top of the pocket is formed by Loop 5 translocating about 10 Å *This figure is adapted with permission from Barsanti et al. (2010).*

absolute stereochemistry was favored, with trans-isomers being more active than cis-isomers. The IC$_{50}$ of compound (**10**) against KSP was 650 nM, making it the most potent analog among the others. In paclitaxel-sensitive (1A9) and paclitaxel-resistant (PTX10) ovarian cell lines, HR22C16 and its homolog (**11**) both exhibited activities (Fig. 9.9). The IC$_{50}$ values of compound (**11**) in 1A9 and PTX10 cells were 0.8 and 2.3 mM, respectively. Compound (**11**) exhibits antiproliferative activity through intrinsic apoptotic pathways associated with mitotic arrest and cell death. There was an interesting finding that compound (**11**) was antagonistic to paclitaxel. Whether compound (**11**) (1 mM) was given concurrently with paclitaxel (5 nM) or paclitaxel was given first (24 h), the monopolar spindle phenotype predominated (Marcus et al., 2005).

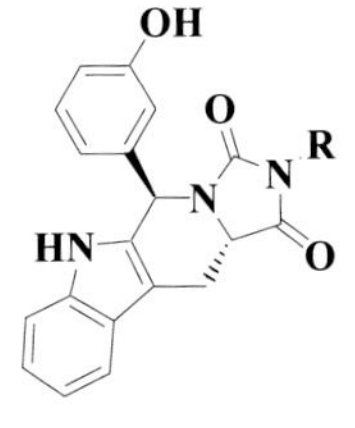

8: R= n-Bu; **9**: R= CH$_2$CH$_2$NH$_2$; **10**: R= Bn; **11**: R= n-Pr

FIGURE 9.9   Structure of compounds (8–11).

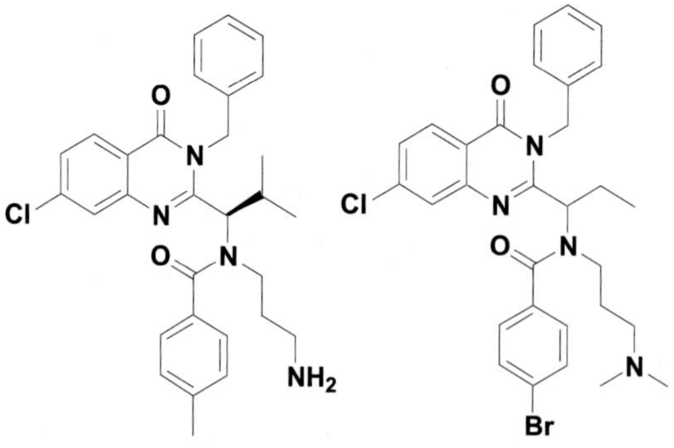

FIGURE 9.10   Structure of compounds (12) and (13).

2.4 Ispinesib and related compounds

Ispinesib (SB-715992/CK0238273, 12) is the first mitotic kinesin inhibitor with a quinazo-linone core to reach clinical development (Fig. 9.10). Similar to its previously reported coun-terpart (13), Ispinesib (12) binds to the motor domain and inhibits KSP ATPase activity in an ATP noncompetitive method. Additionally, it was discovered to be 470,000 times more KSP-selective than other kinesins. In various phase I/II clinical trials, Ispinesib was tested against several cancer diseases including recurrent renal cell cancer, breast cancer, recurrent or met-astatic head and neck cancer, and liver and colorectal cancer. A total of 16 clinical trials were conducted on Ispinesib, without any conclusive evidence of the beneficial effect of Ispinesib (Novais et al., 2021; Škubník et al., 2020). The combination of Ispinesib with Docetaxel (clin-ical trial number NCT00119171), Capecitabine (clinical trial number NCT00119171), and Car-boplatin (clinical trial no.: NCT0011136578) has also been evaluated in different clinical trials. Among these combination trials, the best results were evident to be a steady state response with capecitabine and carboplatin (Hawkins et al., 2008; Knox et al., 2008; Tang et al., 2008).

2.4.1 Quinazolinone core replacement

Attention has been paid to the potent pharmacophore represented by Ispinesib, especially with regard to replacing the quinazolinone moiety. Compounds (14−19), which had both a 6,6 and a 6,5 ring structure, were the first to emerge as one of the fused bicyclic examples (Fig. 9.11) (Aquila et al., 2004; Coleman et al., 2004; Coleman & Fraley, 2004; Lombardo et al., 2003; McDonald et al., 2003; Wang et al., 2004, 2005). It has been reported that BMS-601027 has an IC_{50} of 86 nM for KSP ATPase and a 317 nM IC_{50} for cells (Wang et al., 2004). There have also been examples of compounds (20−24) that substitute 6- and 5-membered analogs for the original core of pyrimidinone (Coleman et al., 2003).

2.5 Chromen-4-one derivatives

Lead optimization study on Ispinesib (12) by replacing its quinazolinone core with a chro-men-4-one ring resulted in the discovery of the compound (25) (SB-743921) (Fig. 9.12) by

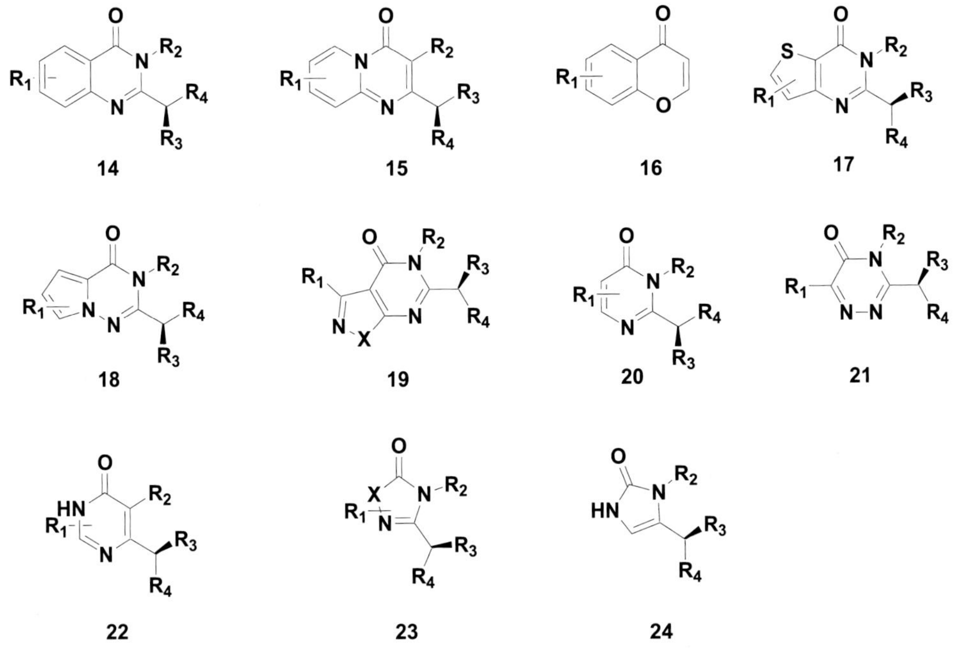

FIGURE 9.11   Structure of compounds (14–24).

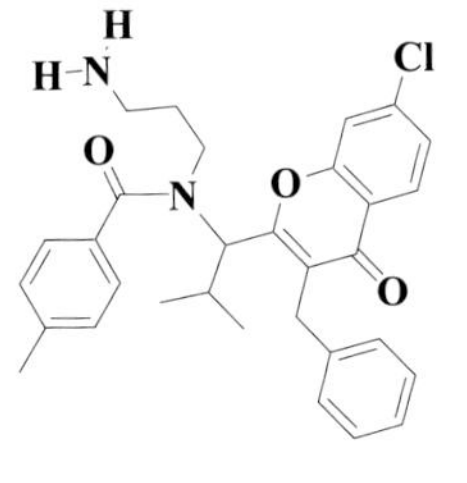

SB-743921 (25)

FIGURE 9.12   Structure of compound (25).

Merck in 2006. SB-743921 exhibited fivefold increase in potency against KSP as compared to the Ispinesib (12) with an ATPase IC_{50} activity of 0.1 nM. This compound was investigated in several phase I/II clinical trials against various cancer diseases including cholangiocarcinoma and metastatic or recurrent head and neck squamous cell carcinoma. However, the best partial response was observed in non-Hodgkin lymphoma patients (Novais et al., 2021).

2.6 Dihydropyrrole and dihydropyrazole derivatives

The 3,5-dialyl-4,5-dihydropyrazoles (Fig. 9.13), (26) and (27), were discovered to have ATPase IC_{50} values of 3.6 and 6.9 mM, respectively (Cox et al., 2005). Combination of chloro

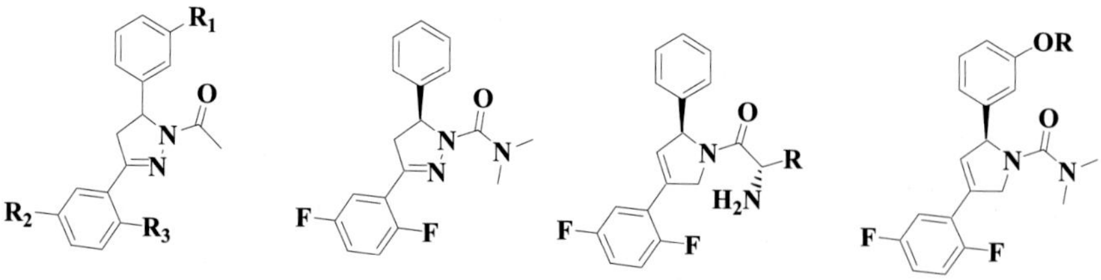

26: R_1 = H; R_2 = H; R_3 = Cl
27: R_1 = OH; R_2 = H; R_3 = H
28: R_1 = OH; R_2 = H; R_3 = Cl
29: R_1 = OH; R_2 = R_3 = F

30

31: R = i-Pr
32: R = c-Pr

33: R = H
34: R = $PO(OH)_2$

FIGURE 9.13   Structure of compounds (26−34).

and hydroxy substituents in a similar molecule (28) resulted in an IC_{50} of 450 nM. It was discovered that compound (29) (IC_{50} 51 nM) was more effective and tolerable for 3-phenyl substitution but virtually completely intolerable for variation on the 5-phenyl ring (Lerchen et al., 2018). When compound (30) with dimethyl urea underwent N^1-substitution with bigger acyl or alkyl groups, it demonstrated potency comparable to compound (29). The (S)-antipode of compound (29) was isolated by chiral phase HPLC (High-performance liquid chromatography) having an ATPase IC_{50} of 26 nM. In A2780 human ovarian carcinoma cells with an IC_{50} of 15 nM, it also caused caspase-3 induction, a well-authorized marker of apoptosis. To create a scaffold that preserved the hybridization of the carbon atoms containing aryls, the dihydropyrazole core was changed to a dihydropyrrole. The dihydropyrrole core was modified by adding basic amide and urea groups to increase the potency. Compounds (31) and (32) had ATPase IC_{50} values of 3.6 and 2.0 nM, respectively. Both the compounds triggered mitotic arrest in A2780 cells with IC_{50} values of 12 and 8.6 nM, respectively. Based on the X-ray crystal structures, it was discovered that KSP interacted with inhibitors (S)-(29), (30), and (32) bound to a similar allosteric pocket as monastrol (Qian et al., 2006). In cancer cell lines, compound (31) induction of apoptosis and the spindle checkpoint were studied. Spindle assembly checkpoint activation and mitotic slippage are both necessary for the induction of apoptosis. Therefore, in cancer cells with competent spindle checkpoints, drugs that encourage mitotic slippage may work in concert with KSP inhibitors (Tao et al., 2005). Compound (31) has a half-life of 1−4 h in rats, dogs, and monkeys and is highly soluble in aqueous solutions (410 mg/mL) and has a moderate clearance (21−40 mL/min/kg). Additionally, hERG potassium channel binding was moderate for this dihydropyrrole family. Compounds (31) and (32) had hERG IC_{50} values of 2.4 and 3.5 mM, respectively, which led to efforts to reduce hERG binding in this series (Garbaccio et al., 2006). hERG binding was decreased while efficacy was preserved when the phenyl ring was refunctionalized with a 3-OH group and neutral N^1-acyl groups. The ATPase IC_{50} of compound (33) was 7 nM, the mitotic EC_{50} was 22 nM, and the hERG IC_{50} was 33 mM. To improve solubility, phosphate prodrugs of (33) were made to replace the basic amino group. The solubility of the prodrug (34) at pH 7 was enhanced to 420 mg/mL, while it was inactive against KSP (IC_{50} 41 mM). Parent (**33**) was produced quickly by cleavage in blood. Tetrahydropyridine (Fraley et al., 2004), dihydroisoxazole (Fraley et al., 2006; Qian et al., 2006), and dihydrooxadiazole (Cox et al., 2006) groups were substituted for the central dihydropyrrole and dihydropyrazole groups in some more closely related KSP inhibitors.

2.7 Tetrahydroisoquinoline compounds

A brand-new class of tetrahydroisoquinolines (Fig. 9.14) was discovered using high-throughput screening. The IC_{50} of compound (**35**) was 9.7 mM in an ATPase experiment, while its IC_{50} in a proliferation study using A2780 human ovarian cancer cells was 2.4 mM. A nuclear magnetic resonance (NMR) experiment revealed that compound (**35**) binds to a similar allosteric site as monastrol. Based on NMR and crystallographic data of KSP monastrol and KSP-HR2216 cocrystal structures, a binding model was developed that guided the structure—activity relationships (SAR) for the series. An optimization study concluded that 7,8-dimethyl groups could replace the fused dihydrofuran ring (**35**) without sacrificing effectiveness. Analogs with amino groups added to chains of 2—4 carbon atoms exhibited activity comparable to that of compound (**35**) when N was substituted with alkyl groups bigger than methyl. As a result, the charged side chain can perhaps point toward the direction of a solvent that can be facilitated by the products of N-acylation, such as amides, sulfonamides, carbamates, and primary urea. A slightly higher ATPase IC_{50} (IC_{50} 2.75 mM) was observed for the compound (**36**) (racemic) containing an N,N-dimethyl urea as compared to the compound (**35**). To summarize the H-bond between the carbonyl group in the backbone amide Glu118 of KSP and the phenol-OH group in monastrol, a hydroxyl group has been added to the 3-position of compound (**36**). As a result, the ATPase assay showed an eightfold increase in efficacy (IC_{50} 306 nM) and threefold in the cellular assay (IC_{50} 376 nM). The 4-OH counterpart, in contrast, exhibited no action (Tarby et al., 2006). The (R)-antipode of compound (**36**) cocrystalized with KSP as predicted, and it is likely to bind to KSP at its recognized allosteric location. It was clear that there existed an H-bond between the phenol's oxygen and the carbonyl oxygen of Arg119 and Glu118. Furthermore, tetrahydroisoquinoline, dimethyl urea, and the phenyl ring were found to interact with the protein via Van der Waals interactions as well (Qian et al., 2006).

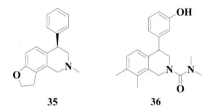

FIGURE 9.14   Structure of compounds (**35**) and (**36**).

3. Conclusion

As proteins essential to the development of the kinetocore, centrosome, and mitotic spindle have been identified, there has been a boost in the number of focused antimitotic drug development initiatives in recent years. The quick development of mitotic kinesin inhibitors and their entrance into proof-of-concept clinical trials can be used as a standard for the viability of this sector of anticancer drug research. Ispinesib has shown anticancer activity and is currently being tested in Phase II clinical trials for the treatment of locally advanced or metastatic breast cancer (NCT00607841), nonsmall cell lung cancer that is platinum-resistant, ovarian cancer (NCT00097409), hepatocellular cancer (NCT00095992), colorectal cancer, head and neck carcinoma, and for prostate cancer (NCT00096499) that is hormone-resistant (Khalaf et al., 2020). It is also reported that SB-743921 is entering Phase I studies as a second KSP inhibitor with non-Hodgkin lymphoma and Hodgkin lymphoma patients (NCT00343564) (Chamariya & Suvarna, 2022). The bulk of these drugs bind with the similar induced-fit, in the allosteric pocket as monastrol and are anticipated to have similar effects. In fact, a number of other potent and structurally diverse molecules are also currently being developed in preclinical studies. In addition to the 13 mitotic kinesins already identified, researchers are still in the early stages of their research against this class of targets. To advance the investigation of these special proteins as anticancer targets in the future, the clinical development of KSP-targeting medicines must continue.

4. Summary and future outlook

In the modern world, cancer is an illness of great relevance. Over the past 10 years, attempts to discover innovative anticancer drugs have been continuously centered on cell cycle targets, with antimitotic techniques having the greatest impact. Specific small molecule kinesin inhibitors can provide new insight into the roles that kinesins play in dynamic processes and their functions. As seen by an increase in papers in the chemistry and biology literature, the entry of phase I and II clinical candidates against the mitotic kinesin KSP has only served to fuel interest in this unique family of proteins. A number of chemical entities have now been identified as mitotic kinesin protein (KSP) inhibitors, as discussed in this chapter. There are still some mitotic kinesins that need further research such as KIF11/KIF2A/KIF3B/KIF20B/KIF23. It will be possible to test the hypothesis that inhibiting particular mitotic kinesins will be a useful method for treating human cancer when the biology relating to these notable proteins is understood. We believe that using small molecule inhibitors as kinesin probes is only getting started. In addition to those drugs being investigated for potential cancer treatments, there is potential for the use of selective kinesin inhibitors as anticancer therapeutics.

It is possible to envision the use of specific kinesin inhibitors in combination with other drugs that target the cell cycle as a potentially successful approach in both chemical genetics and therapy. Further understanding of the temporal and dynamic roles of kinesins within cellular processes, particularly for those engaged in cell proliferation, is almost certain to reveal new therapeutic prospects. The neck linker region, the nucleotide-binding pocket, and MT interaction areas, in addition to the motor domain, have all been implicated in inhibition processes, each with varied degrees of target specificity. In the future, we anticipate finding many more hotspots. The biggest obstacle in making many of the discussed inhibitors available will be translational and collaborative research. Further exploration of the variety of inhibitors that are currently on the market and clinical research will fuel the subsequent research.

Abbreviation

ADP adenosine diphosphate
ATP adenosine triphosphate
DNA seoxyribonucleic acid
HPLC high-performance liquid chromatography
KSP kinesin spindle protein
SAC spindle meeting checkpoint
STLC S-trityl-L-cysteine

References

Abraham, Z., Hawley, E., Hayosh, D., Webster-Wood, V. A., & Akkus, O. (2018). Kinesin and dynein mechanics: Measurement methods and research applications. *Journal of Biomechanical Engineering, 140*, 020805.

Ali, I., & Yang, W.-C. (2020). The functions of kinesin and kinesin-related proteins in eukaryotes. *Cell Adhesion & Migration, 14*, 139−152.

Aquila, B., Block, M. H., Davies, A., Ezhuthachan, J., Filla, S., Luke, R. W., Pontz, T., Theoclitou, M.-E., & Zheng, X. (2004). *WO Patent 04078758-A1.*

Arnst, K. E., Banerjee, S., Chen, H., Deng, S., Hwang, D. J., Li, W., & Miller, D. D. (2019). Current advances of tubulin inhibitors as dual acting small molecules for cancer therapy. *Medicinal Research Reviews, 39*, 1398−1426.

Barsanti, P. A., Wang, W., Ni, Z.-J., Duhl, D., Brammeier, N., Martin, E., Bussiere, D., & Walter, A. O. (2010). The discovery of tetrahydro-β-carbolines as inhibitors of the kinesin Eg5. *Bioorganic & Medicinal Chemistry Letters, 20*, 157−160.

Bergnes, G., Brejc, K., & Belmont, L. (2005). Mitotic kinesins: Prospects for antimitotic drug discovery. *Current Topics in Medicinal Chemistry, 5*, 127−145.

Bidram, Z., Sirous, H., Khodarahmi, G. A., Hassanzadeh, F., Dana, N., Hariri, A. A., & Rostami, M. (2020). Monastrol derivatives: In silico and in vitro cytotoxicity assessments. *Research in Pharmaceutical Sciences, 15*, 249−262.

Brier, S., Lemaire, D., Debonis, S., Forest, E., & Kozielski, F. (2006). Molecular dissection of the inhibitor binding pocket of mitotic kinesin Eg5 reveals mutants that confer resistance to antimitotic agents. *Journal of Molecular Biology, 360*, 360−376.

Chaffey, N., Alberts, B., Johnson, A., Lewis, J., Raff, M., Roberts, K., & Walter, P. (2003). *Molecular biology of the cell* (4th ed.). Oxford University Press.

Chamariya, R., & Suvarna, V. (2022). Role of KSP inhibitors as anti-cancer therapeutics: An update. *Anti-Cancer Agents in Medicinal Chemistry (Formerly Current Medicinal Chemistry-Anti-Cancer Agents), 22*, 2517−2538.

Chen, G.-Y. (2018). *Contribution of EG5-mediated microtubule dynamics to the regulation of mitotic spindle stability: Molecular mechanism of kinesin-microtubule interaction.* The Pennsylvania State University.

Chourasiya, R., Akkinepally, R. R., & Agrawal, R. (2013). Pharmacophore modeling and QSAR analysis of novel β-carboline derivatives as antitumor agents. *Letters in Drug Design and Discovery, 10*, 572−584.

Chourasiya, R. K., Mourya, V., & Agrawal, R. K. (2016). QSAR analysis for some β-carboline derivatives as antitumor. *Journal of Saudi Chemical Society, 20*, 536−542.

Chourasiya, R. K., Rao, A. R., & Agrawal, R. K. (2013). QSAR and docking studies of novel β-carboline derivatives as anticancer. *Medicinal Chemistry Research, 22*, 2991−3001.

Cochran, J. C., Gatial, J. E., 3rd, Kapoor, T. M., & Gilbert, S. P. (2005). Monastrol inhibition of the mitotic kinesin Eg5. *Journal of Biological Chemistry, 280*, 12658—12667.

Coleman, P. J., Fraley, M. E., & Hoffman, W. F. (2004). *WO Patent 04039774-A2.*

Coleman, P. J., & Fraley, M. E. (2004). Inhibitors of the mitotic kinesin spindle protein. *Expert Opinion on Therapeutic Patents, 14*, 1659—1667.

Coleman, P. J., Hartman, G. D., & Neilson, L. A. (2003). *WO Patent 03099211-A2.*

Cox, C. D., Breslin, M. J., Mariano, B. J., Coleman, P. J., Buser, C. A., Walsh, E. S., Hamilton, K., Huber, H. E., Kohl, N. E., Torrent, M., Yan, Y., Kuo, L. C., & Hartman, G. D. (2005). Kinesin spindle protein (KSP) inhibitors. Part 1: The discovery of 3,5-diaryl-4,5-dihydropyrazoles as potent and selective inhibitors of the mitotic kinesin KSP. *Bioorganic & Medicinal Chemistry Letters, 15*, 2041—2045.

Cox, C. D., Fraley, M. E., & Garbaccio, R. M. (2006). *WO Patent 06031348-A2.*

Fang, C.-T., Kuo, H.-H., Hsu, S.-C., & Yih, L.-H. (2020). HSP70 regulates Eg5 distribution within the mitotic spindle and modulates the cytotoxicity of Eg5 inhibitors. *Cell Death & Disease, 11*, 1—18.

Fraley, M. E., Garbaccio, R. M., & Hartman, G. D. (2006). *WO Patent 06023440-A2.*

Fraley, M. E., Garbaccio, R. M., Olson, C. M., & Tasber, E. S. (2004). *WO Patent 2004058700-A2.*

Fukai, R., Ogo, N., Ichida, T., Yamane, M., Sawada, J.-I., Miyoshi, N., Murakami, H., & Asai, A. (2021). Design, synthesis, and evaluation of a novel prodrug, a S-trityl-L-cysteine derivative targeting kinesin spindle protein. *European Journal of Medicinal Chemistry, 215*, Article 113288.

Gadde, S., & Heald, R. (2004). Mechanisms and molecules of the mitotic spindle. *Current Biology, 14*, R797—R805.

Garbaccio, R. M., Fraley, M. E., Tasber, E. S., Olson, C. M., Hoffman, W. F., Arrington, K. L., Torrent, M., Buser, C. A., Walsh, E. S., Hamilton, K., Schaber, M. D., Fernandes, C., Lobell, R. B., Tao, W., South, V. J., Yan, Y., Kuo, L. C., Prueksaritanont, T., Slaughter, D. E., … Hartman, G. D. (2006). Kinesin spindle protein (KSP) inhibitors. Part 3: Synthesis and evaluation of phenolic 2,4-diaryl-2,5-dihydropyrroles with reduced hERG binding and employment of a phosphate prodrug strategy for aqueous solubility. *Bioorganic & Medicinal Chemistry Letters, 16*, 1780—1783.

Garber, K. (2005). Divide and conquer: New generation of drugs targets mitosis. *JNCI: Journal of the National Cancer Institute, 97*, 874—876.

Garcia-Saez, I., & Skoufias, D. A. (2021). Eg5 targeting agents: From new anti-mitotic based inhibitor discovery to cancer therapy and resistance. *Biochemical Pharmacology, 184*, Article 114364.

Gennerich, A., & Vale, R. D. (2009). Walking the walk: How kinesin and dynein coordinate their steps. *Current Opinion in Cell Biology, 21*, 59—67.

Happy, O. T. (2019). *Studies on novel inhibitor of mitotic kinesin Eg5: A validated chemotherapeutic target.* Japan: Nagasaki University.

Haschka, M., Karbon, G., Fava, L. L., & Villunger, A. (2018). Perturbing mitosis for anti-cancer therapy: Is cell death the only answer? *EMBO Reports, 19*, e45440.

Hawkins, M. M., Lancashire, E. R., Winter, D. L., Frobisher, C., Reulen, R. C., Taylor, A. J., Stevens, M. C., & Jenney, M. (2008). The British Childhood Cancer Survivor Study: Objectives, methods, population structure, response rates and initial descriptive information. *Pediatric Blood and Cancer, 50*, 1018—1025.

Jackson, J. R., Patrick, D. R., Dar, M. M., & Huang, P. S. (2007). Targeted anti-mitotic therapies: Can we improve on tubulin agents? *Nature Reviews Cancer, 7*, 107—117.

Jeong, Y. J., Park, S. W., Kim, S.-J., Kim, M., Urm, S.-H., Lee, J. G., & Seog, D.-H. (2020). Rab effector EHBP1L1 associates with the tetratricopeptide repeat domain of kinesin light chain 1. *Journal of Life Science, 30*, 10—17.

Johnson, T. A., Jinnah, H., & Kamatani, N. (2019). Shortage of cellular ATP as a cause of diseases and strategies to enhance ATP. *Frontiers in Pharmacology, 98*, 10.

Joseph, N. F., Swarnkar, S., & Puthanveettil, S. V. (2021). Double duty: Mitotic kinesins and their post-mitotic functions in neurons. *Cells, 10*, 136.

Khalaf, K., Janowicz, K., Dyszkiewicz-Konwińska, M., Hutchings, G., Dompe, C., Moncrieff, L., Jankowski, M., Machnik, M., Oleksiewicz, U., & Kocherova, I. (2020). CRISPR/Cas9 in cancer immunotherapy: Animal models and human clinical trials. *Genes, 11*, 921.

Kim, C. D., Kim, E. D., Liu, L., Buckley, R. S., Parameswaran, S., Kim, S., & Wojcik, E. J. (2019). Small molecule allosteric uncoupling of microtubule depolymerase activity from motility in human Kinesin-5 during mitotic spindle assembly. *Scientific Reports, 9*, 1—13.

Knox, J. J., Gill, S., Synold, T. W., Biagi, J. J., Major, P., Feld, R., Cripps, C., Wainman, N., Eisenhauer, E., & Seymour, L. (2008). A phase II and pharmacokinetic study of SB-715992, in patients with metastatic hepatocellular carcinoma: A study of the National Cancer Institute of Canada Clinical Trials Group (NCIC CTG IND.168). *Investigational New Drugs, 26*, 265—272.

Lee, M. S., Johansen, L., Zhang, Y., Wilson, A., Keegan, M., Avery, W., Elliott, P., Borisy, A. A., & Keith, C. T. (2007). The novel combination of chlorpromazine and pentamidine exerts synergistic antiproliferative effects through dual mitotic action. *Cancer Research, 67*, 11359—11367.

Lerchen, H. G., Wittrock, S., Stelte-Ludwig, B., Sommer, A., Berndt, S., Griebenow, N., Rebstock, A. S., Johannes, S., Cancho-Grande, Y., & Mahlert, C. (2018). Antibody—drug conjugates with pyrrole-based KSP inhibitors as the payload class. *Angewandte Chemie International Edition, 57*, 15243—15247.

Li, M., Li, Y., Jia, L., Li, S., Li, M., Yang, G., Liu, N., Ren, H., Mou, M., & Zheng, A. (2021). The classification and therapeutic applications of molecular motors. *European Journal of Medicinal Chemistry Reports, 3*, Article 100009.

Lombardo, L. J., Bhide, R. S., Kim, K. S., & Lu, S. (2003). *WO Patent 03099286-A1.*

Luo, B., & Song, X. (2021). A comprehensive overview of β-carbolines and its derivatives as anticancer agents. *European Journal of Medicinal Chemistry, 224*, Article 113688.

Maliga, Z., Kapoor, T. M., & Mitchison, T. J. (2002). Evidence that monastrol is an allosteric inhibitor of the mitotic kinesin Eg5. *Chemistry & Biology, 9*, 989—996.

Mann, B. J., & Wadsworth, P. (2019). Kinesin-5 regulation and function in mitosis. *Trends in Cell Biology, 29*, 66—79.

Marcus, A. I., Peters, U., Thomas, S. L., Garrett, S., Zelnak, A., Kapoor, T. M., & Giannakakou, P. (2005). Mitotic kinesin inhibitors induce mitotic arrest and cell death in Taxol-resistant and -sensitive cancer cells. *Journal of Biological Chemistry, 280*, 11569—11577.

Mcdonald, A. I., Bergnes, G., Feng, B., Morgans, D. J., Knight, S. D., Newlander, K. A., Dhanak, D., & Brook, C. S. (2003). *WO Patent 03088903-A2.*

Moreno-Andrés, D., Holl, K., & Antonin, W. (2023). The second half of mitosis and its implications in cancer biology. In *Seminars in cancer biology* (Vol. 88, pp. 1—17). Academic Press. https://doi.org/10.1016/j.semcancer.2022.11.013

Mousavi, S. F., & Fatemi, M. H. (2019). A combination of molecular docking, receptor-guided QSAR, and molecular dynamics simulation studies of S-trityl-l-cysteine analogues as kinesin Eg5 inhibitors. *Structural Chemistry, 30*, 115—126.

Novais, P., Silva, P. M. A., Amorim, I., & Bousbaa, H. (2021). Second-generation antimitotics in cancer clinical trials. *Pharmaceutics, 13*, 1011.

Ong, J. Y., & Torres, J. Z. (2019). Dissecting the mechanisms of cell division. *Journal of Biological Chemistry, 294*, 11382—11390.

Ostergaard, P., Simpson, M. A., Mendola, A., Vasudevan, P., Connell, F. C., Van Impel, A., Moore, A. T., Loeys, B. L., Ghalamkarpour, A., & Onoufriadis, A. (2012). Mutations in KIF11 cause autosomal-dominant microcephaly variably associated with congenital lymphedema and chorioretinopathy. *The American Journal of Human Genetics, 90*, 356—362.

Park, Y. Y., Ahn, J.-H., Cho, M.-G., & Lee, J.-H. (2018). ATP depletion during mitotic arrest induces mitotic slippage and APC/CCdh1-dependent cyclin B1 degradation. *Experimental & Molecular Medicine, 50*, 1—14.

Qian, X., Wolff, A. A., & Bergnes, G. (2006). Progress on mitotic kinesin inhibitors as anti-cancer therapeutics. In A. Wood (Ed.), *Annual reports in medicinal chemistry*. Academic Press.

Qin, J., Zhang, H., Geng, Y., & Ji, Q. (2020). How kinesin-1 utilize the energy of nucleotide: The conformational changes and mechanochemical coupling in the unidirectional motion of kinesin-1. *International Journal of Molecular Sciences, 21*, 6977.

Radwan, M. O., Ciftci, H. I., Ali, T. F., Ellakwa, D. E., Koga, R., Tateishi, H., Nakata, A., Ito, A., Yoshida, M., & Okamoto, Y. (2019). Antiproliferative S-trityl-L-cysteine-derived compounds as SIRT2 inhibitors: Repurposing and solubility enhancement. *Molecules, 24*, 3295.

Sarabi, D., Ostojić, L., Bosman, R., Vallejos, A., Linse, J.-B., Wulff, M., Levantino, M., & Neutze, R. (2022). Modeling difference x-ray scattering observations from an integral membrane protein within a detergent micelle. *Structural Dynamics, 9*, Article 054102.

Seneci, P. (2018). *Chemical sciences in early drug discovery: Medicinal chemistry 2.0.* Elsevier.

Shao, Y.-Y., Sun, N.-Y., Jeng, Y.-M., Wu, Y.-M., Hsu, C., Hsu, C.-H., Hsu, H.-C., Cheng, A.-L., & Lin, Z.-Z. (2021). Eg5 as a prognostic biomarker and potential therapeutic target for hepatocellular carcinoma. *Cells, 10*, 1698.

Shi, Y., Cui, X., Jiang, T., Pan, Y., Lin, Y., Feng, X., Ding, Z., Yang, C., Tan, Y., & Wang, H. (2022). The therapeutic effect of KSP inhibitors in preclinical models of cholangiocarcinoma. *Cell Death & Disease, 13*, 1—13.

Škubník, J., Jurášek, M., Ruml, T., & Rimpelová, S. (2020). Mitotic poisons in research and medicine. *Molecules, 25,* 4632.

Tang, P. A., Siu, L. L., Chen, E. X., Hotte, S. J., Chia, S., Schwarz, J. K., Pond, G. R., Johnson, C., Colevas, A. D., Synold, T. W., Vasist, L. S., & Winquist, E. (2008). Phase II study of ispinesib in recurrent or metastatic squamous cell carcinoma of the head and neck. *Invest New Drugs, 26,* 257–264.

Tao, W., South, V. J., Zhang, Y., Davide, J. P., Farrell, L., Kohl, N. E., Sepp-Lorenzino, L., & Lobell, R. B. (2005). Induction of apoptosis by an inhibitor of the mitotic kinesin KSP requires both activation of the spindle assembly checkpoint and mitotic slippage. *Cancer Cell, 8,* 49–59.

Tarby, C. M., Kaltenbach, R. F., Huynh, T., Pudzianowski, A., Shen, H., Ortega-Nanos, M., Sheriff, S., Newitt, J. A., Mcdonnell, P. A., Burford, N., Fairchild, C. R., Vaccaro, W., Chen, Z., Borzilleri, R. M., Naglich, J., Lombardo, L. J., Gottardis, M., Trainor, G. L., & Roussell, D. L. (2006). Inhibitors of human mitotic kinesin Eg5: Characterization of the 4-phenyl-tetrahydroisoquinoline lead series. *Bioorganic & Medicinal Chemistry Letters, 16,* 2095–2100.

Tham, C. L. (2019). *Biochemical characterisation of human KifC1 and Eg5, two potential targets for drug development in cancer chemotherapy.* UCL (University College London).

Tunquist, B. J., Woessner, R. D., & Walker, D. H. (2010). Mcl-1 stability determines mitotic cell fate of human multiple myeloma tumor cells treated with the kinesin spindle protein inhibitor ARRY-520. *Molecular Cancer Therapeutics, 9,* 2046–2056.

Venugopala, K. N. (2022). Targeting the DNA damage response machinery for lung cancer treatment. *Pharmaceuticals, 15,* 1475.

Wang, J., Gong, F., Liang, T., Xie, Z., Yang, Y., Cao, C., Gao, J., Lu, T., & Chen, X. (2021). A review of synthetic bioactive tetrahydro-β-carbolines: A medicinal chemistry perspective. *European Journal of Medicinal Chemistry, 225,* Article 113815.

Wang, W., Constantine, R. N., Lagniton, L. M., Pecchi, S., Burger, M. T., & Desai, M. C. (2005). *US Patent 0085490-A1.*

Wang, W., Lagniton, L. M., Constantine, R. N., & Burger, M. T. (2004). *WO Patent 04111058-A1.*

Wojcik, E. J., Buckley, R. S., Richard, J., Liu, L., Huckaba, T. M., & Kim, S. (2013). Kinesin-5: Cross-bridging mechanism to targeted clinical therapy. *Gene, 531,* 133–149.

Wood, K. W., Cornwell, W. D., & Jackson, J. R. (2001). Past and future of the mitotic spindle as an oncology target. *Current Opinion in Pharmacology, 1,* 370–377.

Wordeman, L. (2010). How kinesin motor proteins drive mitotic spindle function: Lessons from molecular assays. In *Seminars in cell & developmental biology* (pp. 260–268). Elsevier.

Yan, Y., Sardana, V., Xu, B., Homnick, C., Halczenko, W., Buser, C. A., Schaber, M., Hartman, G. D., Huber, H. E., & Kuo, L. C. (2004). Inhibition of a mitotic motor protein: Where, how, and conformational consequences. *Journal of Molecular Biology, 335,* 547–554.

p21-Activated kinase 1 inhibitors

Ravichandran Veerasamy[1] and Rohini Karunakaran[2]

[1]Pharmaceutical Chemistry Unit, Faculty of Pharmacy, AIMST University, Semeling, Bedong, Kedah, Malaysia; [2]Unit of Biochemistry, Faculty of Medicine, AIMST University, Semeling, Bedong, Kedah, Malaysia

1. Introduction

p21-Activated kinases (PAKs) are members of the serine/threonine kinase family and are involved in cell signaling, proliferation, survival, and the actin cytoskeleton because they are located at the crossroads of multiple signaling pathways. PAKs are divided into two groups based on sequence and structural homology (Fig. 10.1): group I (PAK1, PAK2, and PAK3) (Bagrodia & Cerione, 1999; Bagrodia et al., 1995) and group II (PAK4, PAK5, and PAK6) (Jaffer & Chernoff, 2002). PAK1, also known as p65PAK, was identified in the rat brain in 1994 as a binding partner and target of the RAC and CDC42 GTPases. The structural similarity of p65PAK to the yeast protein Ste20 was discovered through sequencing analysis (Manser et al., 1994). Group 2's actions should ideally be based on CDC42 (Rane & Minden, 2014). Despite the fact that PAK isoforms have similar kinase domains, they differ in substrate specificity and cellular activity due to structural and metabolic variations (Kichina et al., 2010). PAK levels that are out of whack have been linked to various ailments and infections. In cancer and hyperpigmentation, PAK1 and PAK4 are overexpressed or unregulated (Maruta, 2014; Sampat & Minden, 2018). Because PAK1 and PAK4 have different physiological activities, PAK1 could be a safer pharmacological target than PAK4 (Maruta, 2014).

PAK1 has also been linked to neurofibromatosis, Alzheimer's disease, type 2 diabetes, hypertension, infectious and inflammatory diseases, epilepsy, schizophrenia, depression, autism, and obesity (Biswal et al., 2020; Maruta, 2014). PAK1 is now thought to be a major therapeutic target for treating various types of cancers because it enhances cell survival and tumorigenesis by activating several downstream substrates in oncogenic signaling, including BAD, CRAF, caspase 7, caspase 8, merlin, estrogen receptor, beta-catenin, aurora A, histone 3, and Ras-related nuclear protein 1 (Biswal et al., 2020; Radu et al., 2014). In this chapter, the usefulness of PAK1 as a cancer therapeutic target and recent advances in the development of PAK1 inhibitors as anticancer medications are discussed.

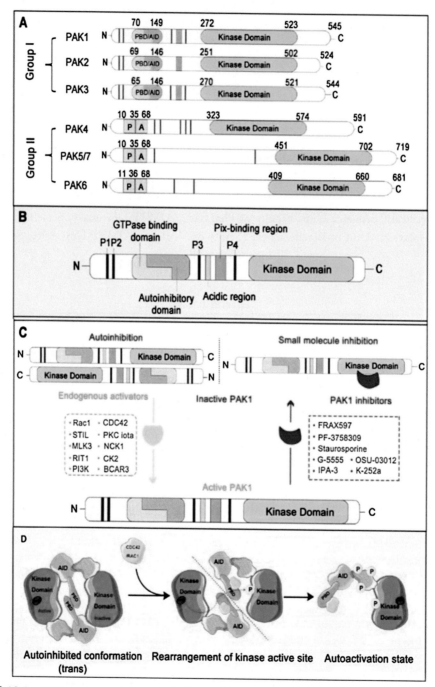

FIGURE 10.1 PAK1 structure and the autoactivation mechanism. (A) schematic representation of the P21-activated kinases including Group I PAKs and Group II PAKs. Of them, PAK1−3 are allotted to Group I PAKs, and PAK4−7 are allotted to Group II PAKs. (B) PAK1 contains a p21-binding domain (PBD) at the N-terminus for GTPase association, an auto-inhibitory domain (AID), and a C-terminal kinase domain. (C) PAK1 can be activated or inhibited by numerous regulators and inhibitors. (D) The autoactivation mechanism of PAK1 which mainly dependent on phosphorylation. *Adopted without any change from Yao, D., Li, C., Rajoka, M. S. R., He, Z., Huang, J., Wang, J., & Zhang, J. (2020). P21-activated kinase 1: Emerging biological functions and potential therapeutic targets in Cancer.* Theranostics, 10(21), 9741−9766. https://doi.org/10.7150/thno.46913, CC-BY-4.0.

2. PAK1 structure and regulation

PAK1 is a 545-amino-acid multidomain protein containing an N-terminal regulatory domain and a C-terminal kinase (catalytic) domain (Fig. 10.1). In the year 2000, its crystal structure in an autoinhibited conformation was discovered (Lei et al., 2000; Shen & Manser, 2012). The catalytic domain is a two-lobe kinase with a single phosphorylation site (Thr423), and many sequence motifs for interacting with associate proteins at the N-terminal end. At the N-terminal end, the catalytic domain is a two-lobe kinase with a single phosphorylation site (Thr423) and several sequence motifs for interacting with related proteins. The interactive-binding (CRIB) domain of CDC42/RAC1 largely overlaps the AID residues 83−149. Three Pro-rich N-terminal motifs interact with SH3-domain-containing adaptor proteins: GRB2 (residues 12−18), NCK (residues 40−45), and the exchange factor PIX (residues 186−203) (Shen & Manser, 2012). PAK1 binding to cell membrane phosphoinositides is dependent on the basic region next to the CRIB domain, which has a positive charge (Strochlic et al., 2010). The regulatory region's phosphorylation sites play a role in enabling and stabilizing PAK1's active conformation (Fig. 10.1) (Pirruccello et al., 2006).

The widely recognized mechanism of group I PAK activation is that Cdc42 or Rac binding to the PBD domain breaks PAK−PAK dimerization, causing the two PAK molecules to dissociate (Lei et al., 2000). Sequential autophosphorylation can fully activate individual PAK molecules. PAK1 contains seven autophosphorylation sites (Manser et al., 1997), and a transautoinhibitory mechanism regulates its activity (Parrini et al., 2002). Furthermore, cross-phosphorylation by other kinases, as well as binding to phospholipids and SH3-containing proteins, can all be used to modify PAK1 activity in a GTPase-independent manner (Shin et al., 2013). The tiny molecule interacts with crucial conformational regions but does not target the catalytic site, which could be advantageous in the development of PAK1 inhibitors with lower off-target toxicity and higher specificity (Rudolph et al., 2015). "Inhibitor targeting PAK1 activation3 (IPA3)" is an allosteric small-molecule inhibitor of group I PAKs (Deacon et al., 2008).

3. PAK1 role in cancer

In practically all cancer types, PAK1 is typically overexpressed or overactivated, and it is particularly pronounced in malignancies. PAK1 had a higher number of DNA copy increases, according to studies using a comparative genomic hybridization array and tumor tissue microarrays. According to the 11q13-q14amplicon, PAK1 gene copy number gains were observed in 30% of ovarian carcinomas, and PAK1 protein was expressed in 85% of the tumors (Schraml et al., 2003). Increased PAK1 expression improved cyclin D1 promoter activity, cyclin D1 mRNA and protein levels, and cyclin D1 nuclear accumulation in breast cancer cells (Balasenthil et al., 2004). The growth and progression of tumors are inextricably tied to the process of angiogenesis.

PAK1 signaling is necessary for the expression, function, and angiogenesis of vascular endothelial growth factors. By upregulating vascular endothelial growth factors, Heregulin promotes PAK1 and controls angiogenesis (Bagheri-Yarmand et al., 2000). PAK1 is also a potent regulator of endothelial cell migration (Kiosses et al., 2002). Ras, an oncogene that is activated in 30% of human cancers, is involved in PAK1 activation during cellular transformation. The activation of PI 3-kinase, a second Ras effector that triggers PAK-mediated regulatory phosphorylation of Raf-1, appears to be one way Ras activates Raf-1 kinase (Sun et al., 2000). In breast cancers, the PI-3 kinase—PAK1—p38MAPK pathway has been found to be hyperactive. Furthermore, PAK1 activity is higher in grade II breast cancers (Salh et al., 2002). Tyrosine phosphorylation stimulates the catalytic activity of the PAK family of serine/threonine kinases (McManus et al., 2000). The phosphorylation and inactivation of NF2 by Pak1 may contribute to tumor cell spread and metastasis (Sells et al., 2000).

Anomalies in the expression and signaling pathways downstream of the epidermal growth factor receptor (EGFR) facilitate malignant transformation in human cancers (Adam et al., 1998). The Cdc42/Rac-regulated PAK is activated and translocated to membrane ruffles by hepatocyte growth factor, and it has been shown to play a role in epithelial cell spreading (Royal et al., 2000). Platelet-derived growth factor (PDGF)-mediated activation of PAK1 family kinases and fibroblast cell migration need EGFR transactivation (He et al., 2001). PDGF-induced chemotactic cell migration was reduced by overexpression of mutant PAK1, showing that PDGF signaling via PAK1 to the p38MAPK and other pathways is necessary (Dechert et al., 2001). Among other things, tumor development necessitates greater transformation, directed migration, and cell survival. In human cancer cells with these growth factor receptor pathways disturbed, the EGFR-tyrosine kinase inhibitor ZD1839 may cause considerable suppression of the EGFR and PAK1 pathways, resulting in decreased aberrant cell morphologies and enhanced differentiation (Barnes et al., 2003).

3.1 PAK1 in cancer drug resistance

The most difficult aspect of cancer treatment is drug resistance. Many drugs with good initial effects have swiftly lost their therapeutic efficacy due to resistance-related mutations, activation of compensatory pathways, and the influence of other unknown reasons. Suppression of PAK1 in combination with inhibition of other cancer regulatory pathways has always been beneficial to tumor treatment (Fig. 10.2). Because both EGFR and PAK1 activate the Ras-MAPK and PI3K-AKT signaling pathways, EGFR inhibitors showed limited impact in EGFR-mutated lung cancer due to unique location mutations. PAK1 inhibitors can considerably improve the therapeutic impact of EGFR-TKI inhibitors in EGFR-TKI-resistant nonsmall cell lung cancer and lung adenocarcinoma (Ito et al., 2019; Wu et al., 2016). Furthermore, PAK1 inhibition has a synergistic impact with TKIs in chronic myeloid leukemia (CML) (Flis et al., 2019). PAK1 suppression can enhance the responsiveness of resistant and nonresistant cells to gemcitabine because PAK1 activation stimulates the Wnt/-catenin signaling, remodeling cascade, which is responsible for gemcitabine resistance (Wang et al., 2019). In addition, in nonsmall cell lung cancer, blocking the PAK1-regulated Wnt/-catenin pathway can enhance cancer cell susceptibility to cisplatin (Chen et al., 2016). As a result, PAK1 has been identified as a promising cancer therapeutic target.

4. PAK1 inhibitors

Many PAK1-targeting drugs, such as ATP-competitive inhibitors, allosteric inhibitors, and peptide inhibitors, have been created as preclinical medicines based on the diverse binding modes in

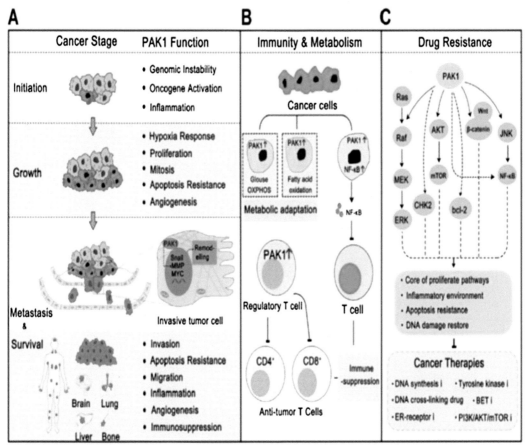

FIGURE 10.2   PAK1 in cancer progression, immunity, metabolism, and drug resistance. (A) in different cancer stages, PAK1 functions properly to promote cancer progression, including regulation of cancer-related pathways, angiogenesis, tumor microenvironment remodeling, immune evasion, and apoptosis inhibition. Similarly, these effects also contribute to drug resistance in cancer therapies. (B) PAK1 can help cancer cells change their metabolic pattern to adapt to a new survival environment. In addition, PAK1 can affect the vitality of immune cells and help cancer cells' immune escape. (C) PAK1 promotes the resistance of cancer cells to various antitumor drugs through the PAK1 PPI network. *Adopted without any change from Yao, D., Li, C., Rajoka, M. S. R., He, Z., Huang, J., Wang, J., & Zhang, J. (2020). P21-activated kinase 1: Emerging biological functions and potential therapeutic targets in Cancer. Theranostics, 10(21), 9741−9766. https://doi.org/10.7150/thno. 46913, CC-BY-4.0.*

the kinase domain, and one has even been tested in a clinical trial. The above PAK1 inhibitors' different biochemical and pharmacokinetic features could lead to interesting therapeutic medicines.

4.1 ATP competitive PAK1 inhibitors

4.1.1 *Oxindole/maleimide derivatives*

With a Ki value of 2.4 nM and limited anticancer activity in vitro, K-252a (**1**, Fig. 10.3), an indolocarbazole alkaloid, was the first chemical to be identified as a PAK1 inhibitor

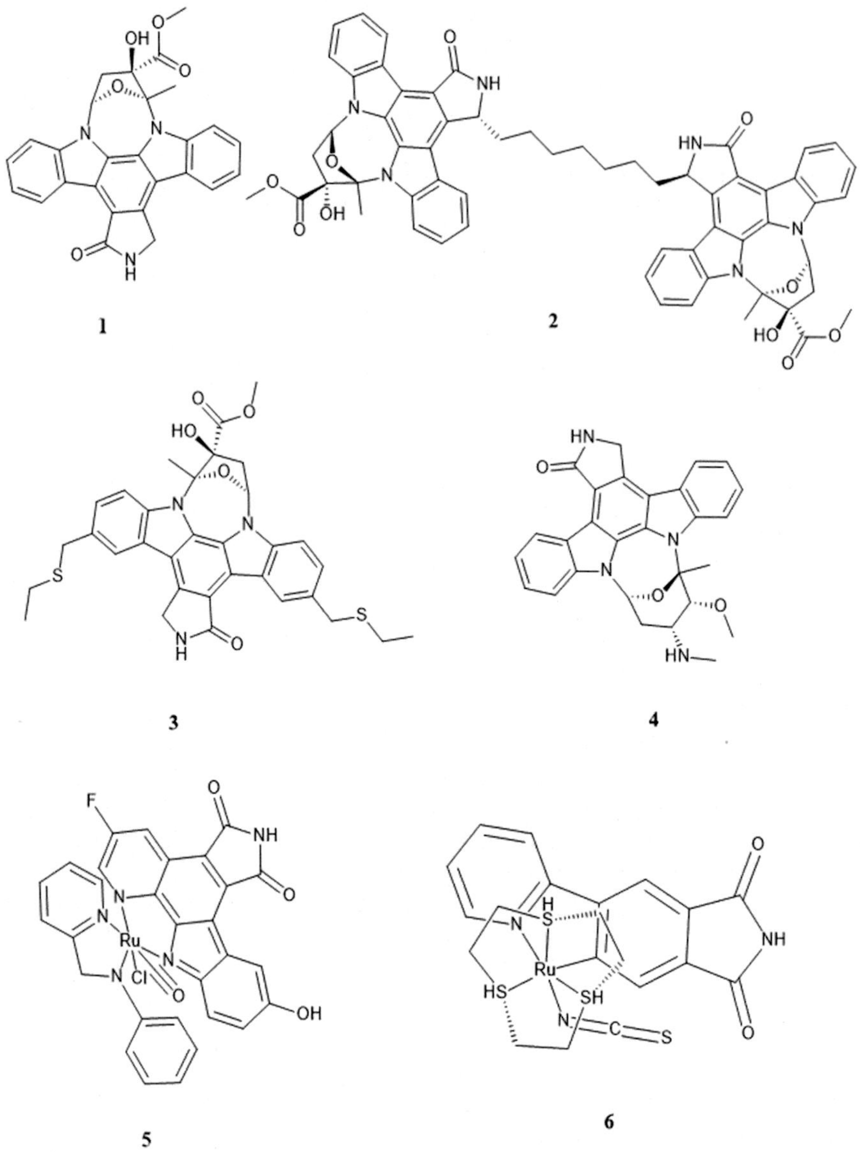

FIGURE 10.3   Structure of compounds 1–6.

(Kase et al., 1987). The K-252a scaffold has been used to create a few K-252a derivatives, including the well-known KTD606 (a K252a dimer) (**2**, Fig. 10.3) and CEP1347 (**3**, Fig. 10.3), which have been tested for antiproliferative activity (Nheu et al., 2002). The natural substance staurosporine (**4**, Fig. 10.3), which is based on indolocarbazole, is a prototype ATP-competitive kinase inhibitor that inhibits PAK proteins and other kinases in the Sterile 20 (STE20) family. With a PAK1 IC_{50} of 0.75 nM, it is one of the most powerful PAK1 inhibitors

(Karaman et al., 2008). Due to its lack of selectivity and undesired side effects, the therapeutic application of staurosporine has been limited. With an IC_{50} of 130 nM, FL172 (**5**, Fig. 10.3), one of the analogs of staurosporine, showed that it was more selective for PAK1 but less effective. Among the 264 kinases studied, only 15 demonstrated inhibition of >80%. However, there is little information on cell activity or pharmacokinetics, therefore it is unknown whether this technique will provide clinically relevant inhibitors if pursued further (Maksimoska et al., 2008). Later, the same group of writers modified the structure of -FL172 by moving the metal atom within the active site to other places, yielding (R)-1 (**6**, Fig. 10.3), which has a better affinity (IC_{50} of 83 nM) but less kinase selectivity since the reduced steric bulkiness may account for the reduction (Blanck et al., 2012).

4.1.2 Pyrazoles

Scientists from Pfizer were among the first to search for PAK inhibitors. Pyrolopyrazole and aminopyrazole, which are kinase inhibitor scaffolds with pyrazole cores fused into a bicyclic structure, can establish hydrogen bond interactions within the PAK kinase hinge region (Tonani et al., 2004). After being discovered as a potent, orally available PAK1 inhibitor with a Ki value of 14 nM, PF-3758309 (**7**, Fig. 10.4) has moved to Phase I clinical trials as an anticancer therapy in patients with advanced/metastatic solid tumors (Campbell et al., 2014; Rosen et al., 2011). This is a pan-PAK inhibitor with poor selectivity for other kinases such as AKT and CHK2. In a single person, PF-3758309 was later shown to be clinically unsuccessful. PF-3758309 was taken out of clinical trials due to its low oral bioavailability (1% in humans), gastrointestinal toxicity, and lack of tumor response (Mileshkin et al., 2011).

Genentech announced the development of novel aminopyrazole-based PAK1 inhibitors in 2013 for the treatment of cancer and hyperproliferative diseases. II-11 (**8**, Fig. 10.4) has the greatest PAK1 inhibitory activity among these compounds, with a Ki of 1.6 nM and a cellular IC_{50} of 43 nM (Aliagas-Martin, Crawford, et al., 2013). Genentech reported aza-bicyclic heterocycles at the pyrimidine 2-position in a separate filing, with the aminopyrazole substituent nearly primarily cyclopropyl or fluorocyclopropyl, implying that this is significant for binding affinity (**9**, Fig. 10.4, PAK1 Ki = 8 nM) (Aliagas-Martin, Mathieu, et al., 2013).

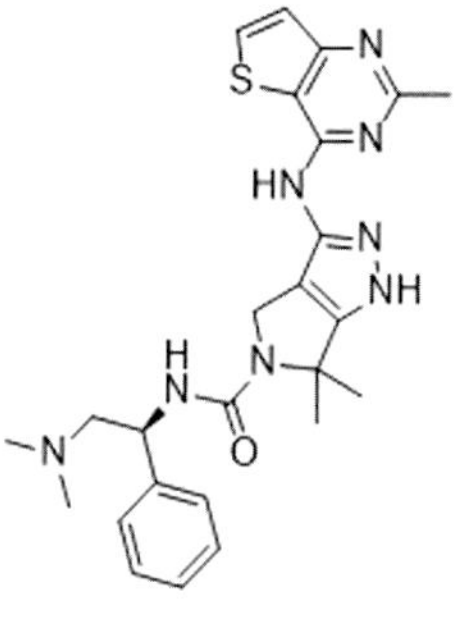

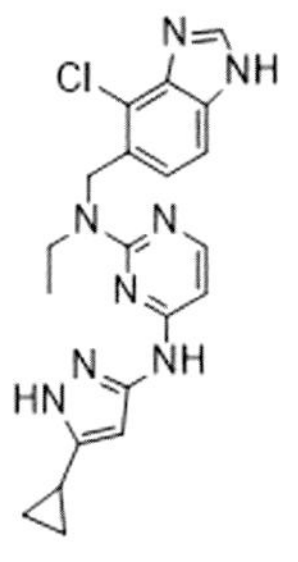

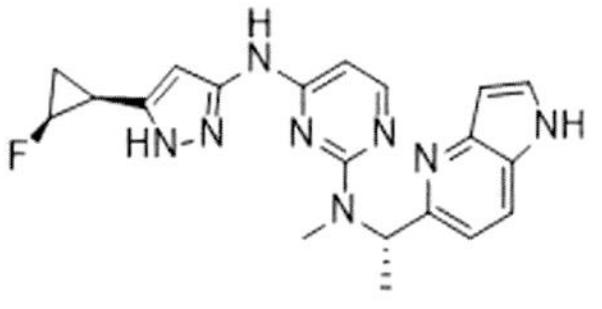

FIGURE 10.4   Structure of compounds 7–9.

4.1.3 Pyrimidines

In a series of patent filings for PAK inhibitors based on a pyrido[2,3-d]pyrimidine-7-one core, Campbell et al. (2014) highlighted Afraxis, a biotechnology company founded in 2007. As a result, several different variations have been revealed in a series of patents (McKew et al., 2015; Vollrath et al., 2013). FRAX414 (**10**, Fig. 10.5) has a 20-fold increase in PAK1 activity without impacting PAK4 activity after a 2,4-di-Cl-phenyl ring is added to the 6-position of the core of FRAX019 (**11**, Fig. 10.5). FRAX597 (**12**, Fig. 10.5) was created by replacing the p-Cl group of FRAX414 with a heterocycle, resulting in a strong PAK1inhibitor with an IC_{50} value

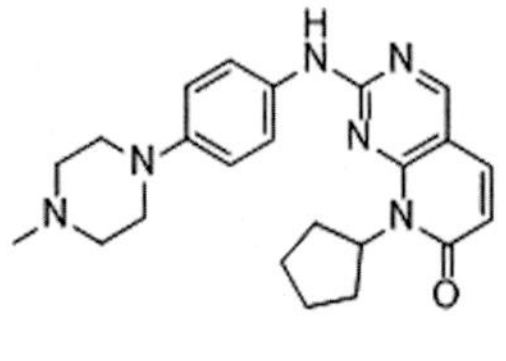

10

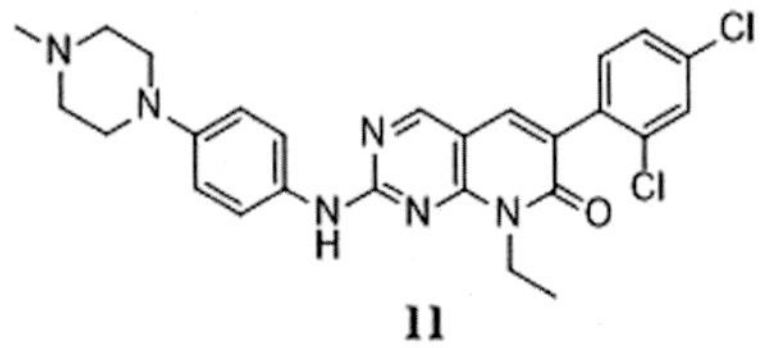

11

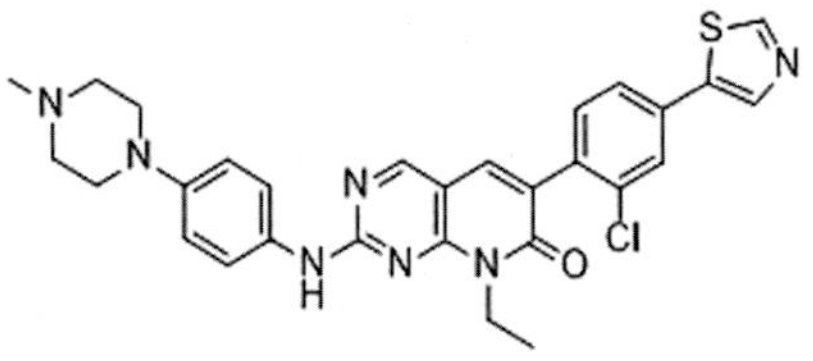

12

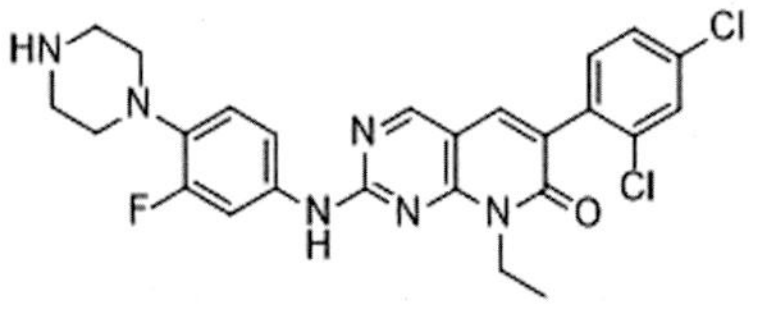

13

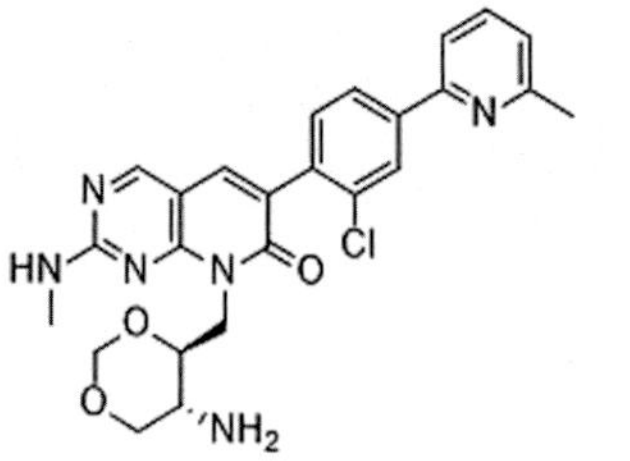

14

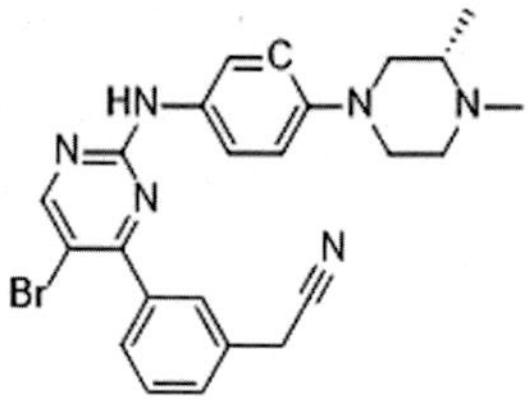

15

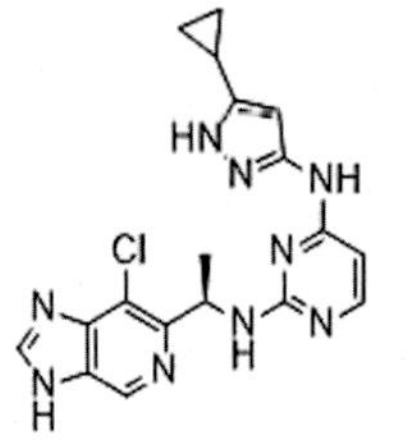

16

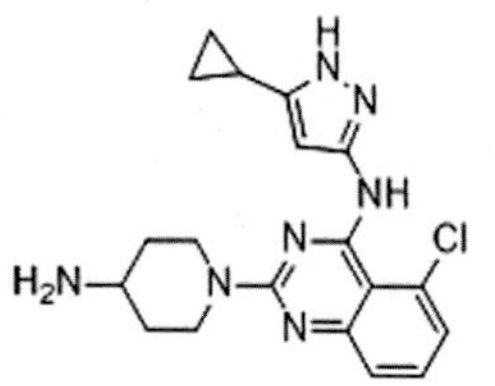

17

FIGURE 10.5 Structure of compounds 10–19.

of 7.7 nM, which is >130-fold more powerful than its PAK4 inhibition. In an orthotopic model of NF2, substantial antiproliferative and anticancer activity was established against NF2-deficient schwannoma cells (Licciulli et al., 2013). FRAX486 (**13**, Fig. 10.5), a derivative of FRAX597, has been proven to suppress prostate stromal cell formation and possesses a potent PAK1 inhibitor with an IC_{50} of 8.3 nM. It was created to treat Fragile X syndrome (Dolan et al., 2013). G5555 (**14**, Fig. 10.5) is a selective PAK1 inhibitor with an IC_{50} of 3.7 nM, and it was synthesized using an unusual LowpKa polar moiety (Ndubaku et al., 2015).

Aminopyrimidine-based drugs have also been found as potent PAK1 inhibitors. 2-Arylamino-4-aryl-pyrimidines were discovered by Xu et al. (2013) as powerful PAK1 inhibitors, with compound **15** (Fig. 10.5) demonstrating potent inhibitory efficacy of 65 nm against PAK1 (Xu et al., 2013). To increase selectivity against PAK1, compounds **8** (Fig. 10.4), **16**, and **17** (Fig. 10.5) were developed with a 5-cyclopropyl-1Hpyrazolegroup inserted at the 4-site of the aminopyrimidine core for targeting the ribose pocket (Crawford et al., 2015; Hao et al., 2018; Lee et al., 2016). G-9791 (**18**, Fig. 10.6), a pyridone side-chain analog, has been discovered to be a selective PAK1 inhibitor with low toxicity (Rudolph et al., 2016). A high throughput virtual filtering method led to the discovery of Compound **19** (Fig. 10.6), a strong PAK1 inhibitor (Ferenc et al., 2010). Ferenc et al. (2010) described the in silico design of ATP-competitive PAK1 inhibitors with proven aminopyrimidine hinge-binding cores. The authors created several analogs having primarily primary amine side chains, including compounds **20** and **21** (Fig. 10.6), which are illustrated below. Compound **21**, with an IC_{50} of 650 nM, is the most potent of the 10 compounds provided, whereas **20** had an IC_{50} of 1400 nM (Ferenc et al., 2010).

4.1.4 Azaindole

The 7-azaindole has been identified as a PAK1 inhibitor, according to AstraZeneca. A 7-azaindole derivative PAK1 inhibitor **22** (Fig. 10.7, IC_{50} = 18 nM) prefers PAK1 kinase activity

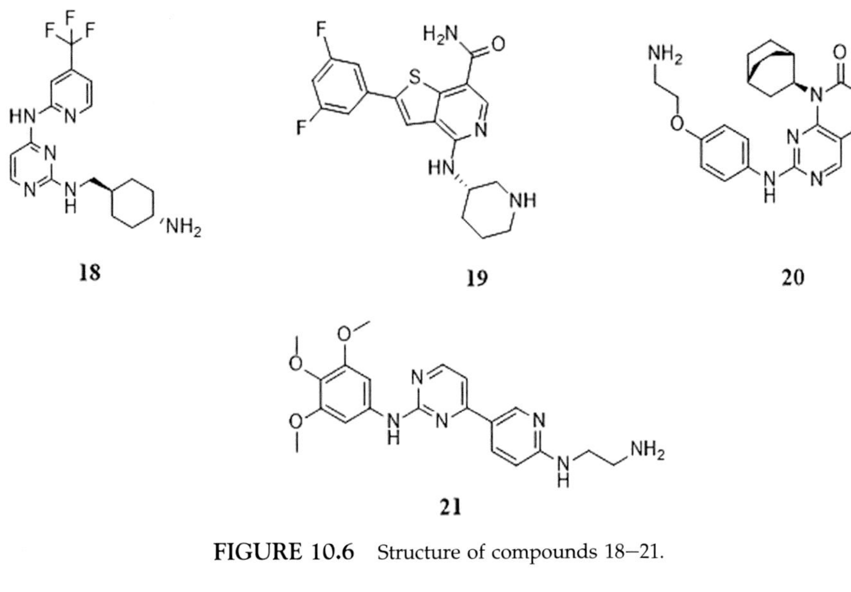

FIGURE 10.6 Structure of compounds 18−21.

FIGURE 10.7 Structure of compounds 22 and 23.

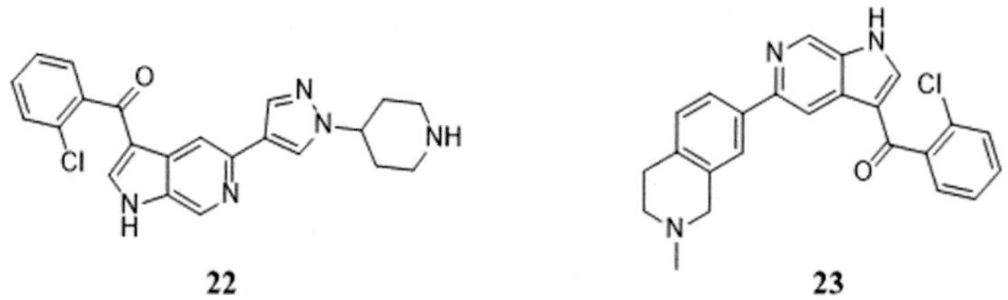

22

23

over PAK4 kinase activity ($IC_{50} = 550$ nM). Compound **23** (Fig. 10.7, AZ-PAK-36) is a more powerful analog (PAK1 $IC_{50} = 1$ nM) with superior cell permeability than compound **22** and a cellular EC_{50} of 140 nM (phos-PAK1 assay). However, there are no more in vitro or in vivo efficacy or pharmacological studies available (McCoull et al., 2014).

4.1.5 Other ATP-competitive inhibitors

The PDK1 inhibitor OSU-03012 (**24**, Fig. 10.8), derived from celecoxib, inhibited PAK1 with an IC_{50} value of 7.7 nM, allowing motile NPA thyroid carcinoma cells to migrate (Porchia et al., 2007). AK963 (**25**, Fig. 10.8), a simple urea derivative, displayed PAK1 inhibitory effectiveness and suppressed the growth of gastric cancer cells by downregulating the PAK1-NF-B-cyclinB1 pathway (Zhou et al., 2019). Recently, ZMF-10 (**26**, Fig. 10.8), with an IC_{50} of 174 nM and high selectivity for PAK1, was discovered. ZMF-10 generated ER stress and inhibited migration by activating FOXO3 and inhibiting JNK1/2, ERK1/2, and AKT signaling (Zhang et al., 2020).

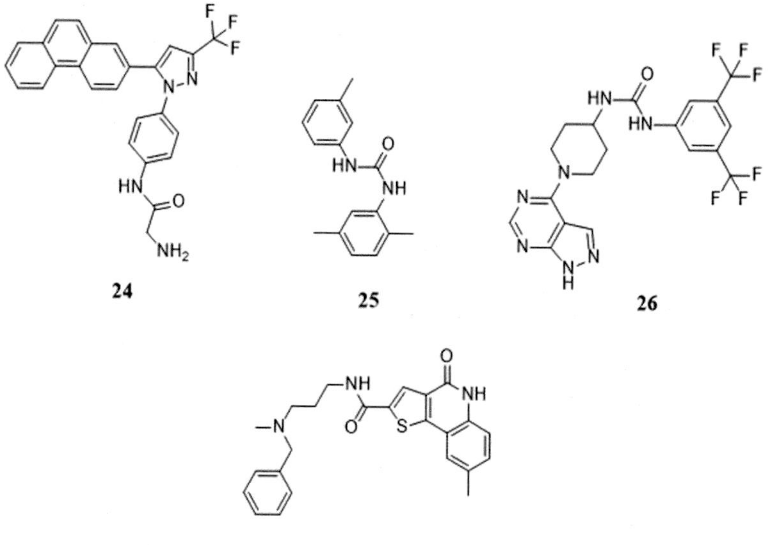

24

25

26

27

FIGURE 10.8 Structure of compounds 24–27.

CP734 (**27**, Fig. 10.8) was discovered as a strong inhibitor of PAK1 by Wang et al. (2020) using a structure-based virtual screening technique. *N*-[3-(benzyl-methylamino)propyl]-8-methyl-4-oxo-5H-thieno[4,5-c] CP734 is also known as quinoline-2-carboxamide. PAK1 kinase activity was suppressed in vitro with an IC50 value of 15.27 mol/L, but it did not affect PAK2, PAK3, or PAK6, and only weak inhibitory effects on PAK4 and PAK7. They also found that at 20 mol/L, CP734 stimulation significantly reduced intracellular PAK1 activity in BxPC-3 cells. They also claimed that CP734 slowed cell proliferation in a dose- and time-dependent way. PAK1 inhibitor CP734 was discovered to be ATP-competitive (Wang et al., 2020).

4.2 Allosteric PAK1 inhibitors

Deacon et al. (2008) used a PAK1 activation assay to improve the selectivity of PAK1 inhibitors. This test evaluates the quantity of ATP that remained after Cdc42-activated PAK1 phosphorylates the substrate, myelin basic protein (MBP). The compound IPA-3 (**28**, Fig. 10.9) is described in this work as a novel medication that covalently binds to PAK1-Cysteine 360 and inhibits PAK1 in its inactive form. IPA-3 can no longer bind to PAK1 and limit its activity if Cdc42 preactivates it. This action inhibits only Group I remodeling PAKs, with very no effect on Group II PAKs (Viaud & Peterson, 2009). Despite these promising results, the metabolic instability of IPA-3 precludes its usage in humans, making future research on this chemical extremely difficult. Novartis reported a dibenzodiazepine derivative Group I PAK allosteric inhibitor, although its optimization of the single-agent, in vivo, and animal stability have not been studied yet (Rudolph et al., 2015). Allosterically decreasing PAK activity by interfering with their regulatory domains (PBDs) rather than their ATP-binding sites, Kim et al. (2016) found tiny compounds comprising 1,4-naphthohydroquinone and 1,4-naphthoquinone in vitro and in live cells. Inhibitors identified for Group I PAKs, particularly PAK1 and PAK3, selectively inhibited PAK1 and PAK3 (Kim et al., 2016).

4.3 Treatment combinations with PAK inhibitors

Gemcitabine was coupled with the natural substance glaucarubinone (**29**, Fig. 10.9) in one research. Glaucarubinone is derived from the Simarouba glauca tree's seeds (Pierré et al., 1980; Yeo et al., 2014). The phosphorylation of PAK1 and PAK4 is reduced in pancreatic

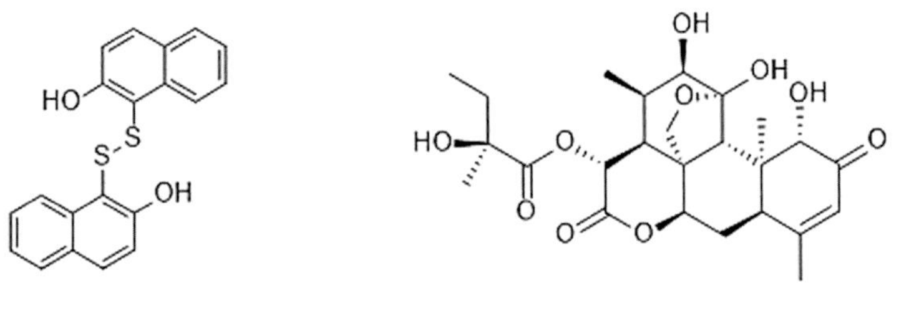

FIGURE 10.9 Structure of compounds 28 and 29.

28   29

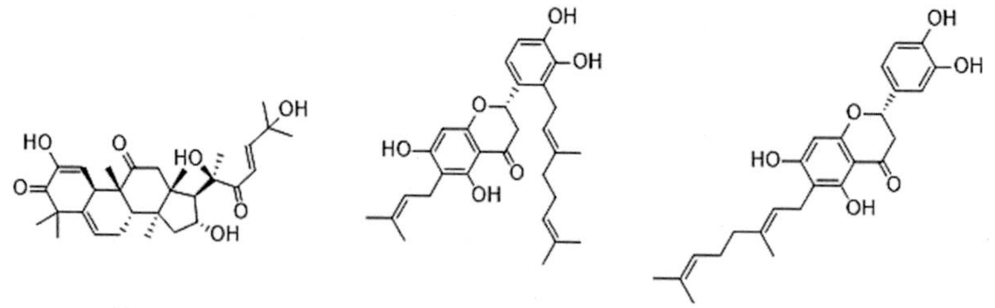

FIGURE 10.10   Structure of compounds 30–32.

cell lines treated with glaucarubinone alone. When glaucarubinone is paired with gemcitabine, the reduction is even greater. Furthermore, by inhibiting PAK1 and PAK4 activity in the in vivo pancreatic models, the two drugs had a synergistic effect (Yeo et al., 2014). For the treatment of pancreatic cancer, glaucarubinone alone has little effect and the selectivity of PAK inhibitors is unsure, therefore it would be interesting to examine the use of gemcitabine in combination with more powerful PAK inhibitors. Gemcitabine and a PAK inhibitor may be useful in treating a wide range of cancers, according to a new study that focuses on colorectal cancer and the glaucarubinone-inhibiting impact of PAK1/-catenin (Huynh et al., 2015).

4.4 Natural products

Shahinozzaman et al. (2020) used AutoDock Vina with the PAK1 catalytic domain in the hinge region to investigate drug-like characteristics and docking of 37 natural compounds. The binding energies of the compounds ranged from −4.5 to −9.6 kcal/mol. Cucurbitacin I (30, Fig. 10.10) and staurosporine (4, Fig. 10.3) had the highest binding energy (−9.6 kcal/mol) of the 37 herbal compounds tested. Nymphaeol C (31, Fig. 10.10) and nymphaeol A (32, Fig. 10.10), two additional compounds, exhibited binding energies of −9.0 kcal/mol. This research shows that they have the potential to be effective PAK1 inhibitors. They also have lower inhibition constants, ranging from 0.25 to 0.009 mM, than other drugs (Shahinozzaman et al., 2020).

Even though a variety of effective PAK1 inhibitors, including ATP competitive and allosteric inhibitors, have been discovered, the development of PAK1 inhibitors still confronts considerable hurdles. To begin, these inhibitors' selectivity, particularly toward ATP competitive inhibition, must be enhanced. The druggability of most PAK1 inhibitors must then be assessed further to ensure that they can be used in clinical trials.

5. Conclusion

Increased interest in PAK1 as a druggable therapeutic target for diseases involving elevated levels of PAK1 or unregulated PAK upstream/downstream signaling has occurred recently. Proliferation, metabolism reprogramming, mitosis, invasion, metastasis, and treatment resistance are all controlled by PAK1. EGFR/HER2/MAPK, Wnt/-catenin, JNK/c-jun, NF−B, cell cycle, apoptosis, autophagy, and others, such as TGF- and STAT5 signaling, are all pathways in which PAK1 is implicated. For the most part, inhibitors of PAK1 also bind to the group I-related PAK2 and/or PAK3 proteins. It is expected that PAK1's role in cancer progression, from tumor formation to increased motor capacity, will lead to the development of more PAK inhibitors.

References

Adam, L., Vadlamudi, R., Kondapaka, S. B., Chernoff, J., Mendelsohn, J., & Kumar, R. (1998). Heregulin regulates cytoskeletal reorganization and cell migration through the p21-activated kinase-1 via phosphatidylinositol-3 kinase. *Journal of Biological Chemistry, 273*(43), 28238−28246. https://doi.org/10.1074/jbc.273.43.28238

Aliagas-Martin, I., Crawford, J., Lee, W., Mathieu, S., & Rudolph, J. (2013). *Serine/threonine pak1 inhibitors*. WO2013026914A1.

Aliagas-Martin, I., Mathieu, S., Rudolph, J., & Lee, W. (2013). *4-diamine-pyrimidine derivative as serine/threonine kinase inhibitors*. WO2013092940A1.

Bagheri-Yarmand, R., Vadlamudi, R. K., Wang, R. A., Mendelsohn, J., & Kumar, R. (2000). Vascular endothelial growth factor up-regulation via p21-activated kinase-1 signaling regulates heregulin-β1-mediated angiogenesis. *Journal of Biological Chemistry, 275*(50), 39451−39457. https://doi.org/10.1074/jbc.M006150200

Bagrodia, S., & Cerione, R. A. (1999). PAK to the future. *Trends in Cell Biology, 9*(9), 350−355. https://doi.org/10.1016/S0962-8924(99)01618-9

Bagrodia, S., Taylor, S. J., Creasy, C. L., Chernoff, J., & Cerione, R. A. (1995). Identification of a mouse p21(Cdc42/Rac) activated kinase. *Journal of Biological Chemistry, 270*(39), 22731−22737. https://doi.org/10.1074/jbc.270.39.22731

Balasenthil, S., Sahin, A. A., Barnes, C. J., Wang, R. A., Pestell, R. G., Vadlamudi, R. K., & Kumar, R. (2004). p21-activated kinase-1 signaling mediates cyclin D1 expression in mammary epithelial and cancer cells. *Journal of Biological Chemistry, 279*(2), 1422−1428. https://doi.org/10.1074/jbc.M309937200

Barnes, C. J., Bagheri-Yarmand, R., Mandal, M., Yang, Z., Clayman, G. L., Hong, W. K., & Kumar, R. (2003). Suppression of epidermal growth factor receptor, mitogen-activated protein kinase, and Pak1 pathways and invasiveness of human cutaneous squamous cancer cells by the tyrosine kinase inhibitor ZD1839 (Iressa). *Molecular Cancer Therapeutics, 2*(4), 345−351.

Biswal, J., Jayaprakash, P., Suresh Kumar, R., Venkatraman, G., Poopandi, S., Rangasamy, R., & Jeyaraman, J. (2020). Identification of Pak1 inhibitors using water thermodynamic analysis. *Journal of Biomolecular Structure and Dynamics, 38*(1), 13−31. https://doi.org/10.1080/07391102.2019.1567393

Blanck, S., Maksimoska, J., Baumeister, J., Harms, K., Marmorstein, R., & Meggers, E. (2012). The art of filling protein pockets efficiently with octahedral metal complexes. *Angewandte Chemie - International Edition, 51*(21), 5244−5246. https://doi.org/10.1002/anie.201108865

Campbell, D., Durón, Vollrath, B., & Wade, W. (2014). *Compounds for treating neuropsychiatric conditions*. US8674095B2.

Chen, M. J., Wu, D. W., Wang, Y. C., Chen, C. Y., & Lee, H. (2016). PAK1 confers chemoresistance and poor outcome in non-small cell lung cancer via β-catenin-mediated stemness. *Scientific Reports, 6*. https://doi.org/10.1038/srep34933

Crawford, J. J., Lee, W., Aliagas, I., Mathieu, S., Hoeflich, K. P., Zhou, W., Wang, W., Rouge, L., Murray, L., La, H., Liu, N., Fan, P. W., Cheong, J., Heise, C. E., Ramaswamy, S., Mintzer, R., Liu, Y., Chao, Q., & Rudolph, J. (2015). Structure-guided design of group i selective p21-activated kinase inhibitors. *Journal of Medicinal Chemistry, 58*(12), 5121−5136. https://doi.org/10.1021/acs.jmedchem.5b00572

Deacon, S. W., Beeser, A., Fukui, J. A., Rennefahrt, U. E. E., Myers, C., Chernoff, J., & Peterson, J. R. (2008). An isoform-selective, small-molecule inhibitor targets the autoregulatory mechanism of p21-activated kinase. *Chemistry & Biology, 15*(4), 322−331. https://doi.org/10.1016/j.chembiol.2008.03.005

Dechert, M. A., Holder, J. M., & Gerthoffer, W. T. (2001). p21-activated kinase 1 participates in tracheal smooth muscle cell migration by signaling to p38 MAPK. *American Journal of Physiology - Cell Physiology, 281*(1), C123−C132. https://doi.org/10.1152/ajpcell.2001.281.1.c123

Dolan, B. M., Duron, S. G., Campbell, D. A., Vollrath, B., Shankaranarayana Rao, B. S., Ko, H. Y., Lin, G. G., Govindarajan, A., Choi, S. Y., & Tonegawa, S. (2013). Rescue of fragile X syndrome phenotypes in Fmr1 KO mice by the small-molecule PAK inhibitor FRAX486. *Proceedings of the National Academy of Sciences of the United States of America, 110*(14), 5671–5676. https://doi.org/10.1073/pnas.1219383110

Ferenc, B., Csaba, S. K., Zoltán, G., Jeno, M., Zoltán, V., György, K., & László, O. (2010). P21-aktivált kináz gátlók vizsgálata \in silico\ módszerek felhasználásával. *Acta Pharmaceutica Hungarica, 80*(4), 155–161.

Flis, S., Bratek, E., Chojnacki, T., Piskorek, M., & Skorski, T. (2019). Simultaneous inhibition of BCR-ABL1 tyrosine kinase and PAK1/2 serine/threonine kinase exerts synergistic effect against chronic myeloid leukemia cells. *Cancers, 11*(10). https://doi.org/10.3390/cancers11101544

Hao, C., Zhao, F., Song, H., Guo, J., Li, X., Jiang, X., Huan, R., Song, S., Zhang, Q., Wang, R., Wang, K., Pang, Y., Liu, T., Lu, T., Huang, W., Wang, J., Lin, B., He, Z., Li, H., … Cheng, M. (2018). Structure-based design of 6-Chloro-4-aminoquinazoline-2-carboxamide derivatives as potent and selective p21-activated kinase 4 (PAK4) inhibitors. *Journal of Medicinal Chemistry, 61*(1), 265–285. https://doi.org/10.1021/acs.jmedchem.7b01342

He, H., Levitzki, A., Zhu, H. J., Walker, F., Burgess, A., & Maruta, H. (2001). Platelet-derived growth factor requires epidermal growth factor receptor to activate p21-activated kinase family kinases. *Journal of Biological Chemistry, 276*(29), 26741–26744. https://doi.org/10.1074/jbc.C100229200

Huynh, N., Beutler, J. A., Shulkes, A., Baldwin, G. S., & He, H. (2015). Glaucarubinone inhibits colorectal cancer growth by suppression of hypoxia-inducible factor 1α and β-catenin via a p-21 activated kinase 1-dependent pathway. *Biochimica et Biophysica Acta - Molecular Cell Research, 1853*(1), 157–165. https://doi.org/10.1016/j.bbamcr.2014.10.013

Ito, M., Codony-Servat, C., Karachaliou, N., & Rosell, R. (2019). Targeting PKCι-PAK1 in EGFR-mutation positive non-small cell lung cancer. *Translational Lung Cancer Research, 8*(5), 667–673. https://doi.org/10.21037/tlcr.2019.08.25

Jaffer, Z. M., & Chernoff, J. (2002). p21-Activated kinases: Three more join the Pak. *The International Journal of Biochemistry & Cell Biology, 34*(7), 713–717. https://doi.org/10.1016/S1357-2725(01)00158-3

Karaman, M. W., Herrgard, S., Treiber, D. K., Gallant, P., Atteridge, C. E., Campbell, B. T., Chan, K. W., Ciceri, P., Davis, M. I., Edeen, P. T., Faraoni, R., Floyd, M., Hunt, J. P., Lockhart, D. J., Milanov, Z. V., Morrison, M. J., Pallares, G., Patel, H. K., Pritchard, S., Wodicka, L. M., & Zarrinkar, P. P. (2008). A quantitative analysis of kinase inhibitor selectivity. *Nature Biotechnology, 26*(1), 127–132. https://doi.org/10.1038/nbt1358

Kase, H., Iwahashi, K., Nakanishi, S., Matsuda, Y., Yamada, K., Takahashi, M., Murakata, C., Sato, A., & Kaneko, M. (1987). K-252 compounds, novel and potent inhibitors of protein kinase C and cyclic nucleotide-dependent protein kinases. *Biochemical and Biophysical Research Communications, 142*(2), 436–440. https://doi.org/10.1016/0006-291X(87)90293-2

Kichina, J. V., Goc, A., Al-Husein, B., Somanath, P. R., & Kandel, E. S. (2010). PAK1 as a therapeutic target. *Expert Opinion on Therapeutic Targets, 14*(7), 703–725. https://doi.org/10.1517/14728222.2010.492779

Kim, D. J., Choi, C. K., Lee, C. S., Park, M. H., Tian, X., Kim, N. D., Lee, K. I., Choi, J. K., Ahn, J. H., Shin, E. Y., Shin, I., & Kim, E. G. (2016). Small molecules that allosterically inhibit p21-activated kinase activity by binding to the regulatory p21-binding domain. *Experimental & molecular medicine, 48*, e229. https://doi.org/10.1038/emm.2016.13

Kiosses, W. B., Hood, J., Yang, S., Gerritsen, M. E., Cheresh, D. A., Alderson, N., & Schwartz, M. A. (2002). A dominant-negative p65 PAK peptide inhibits angiogenesis. *Circulation Research, 90*(6), 697–702. https://doi.org/10.1161/01.RES.0000014227.76102.5D

Lee, W., Crawford, J. J., Aliagas, I., Murray, L. J., Tay, S., Wang, W., Heise, C. E., Hoeflich, K. P., La, H., Mathieu, S., Mintzer, R., Ramaswamy, S., Rouge, L., & Rudolph, J. (2016). Synthesis and evaluation of a series of 4-azaindole-containing p21-activated kinase-1 inhibitors. *Bioorganic & Medicinal Chemistry Letters, 26*(15), 3518–3524. https://doi.org/10.1016/j.bmcl.2016.06.031

Lei, M., Lu, W., Meng, W., Parrini, M. C., Eck, M. J., Mayer, B. J., & Harrison, S. C. (2000). Structure of PAK1 in an autoinhibited conformation reveals a multistage activation switch. *Cell, 102*(3), 387–397. https://doi.org/10.1016/S0092-8674(00)00043-X

Licciulli, S., Maksimoska, J., Zhou, C., Troutman, S., Kota, S., Liu, Q., Duron, S., Campbell, D., Chernoff, J., Field, J., Marmorstein, R., & Kissil, J. L. (2013). FRAX597, a small molecule inhibitor of the p21-activated kinases, inhibits tumorigenesis of neurofibromatosis type 2 (NF2)-associated schwannomas. *Journal of Biological Chemistry, 288*(40), 29105–29114. https://doi.org/10.1074/jbc.M113.510933

Maksimoska, J., Feng, L., Harms, K., Yi, C., Kissil, J., Marmorstein, R., & Meggers, E. (2008). Targeting large kinase active site with rigid, bulky octahedral ruthenium complexes. *Journal of the American Chemical Society, 130*(47), 15764–15765. https://doi.org/10.1021/ja805555a

Manser, E., Huang, H. Y., Loo, T. H., Chen, X. Q., Dong, J. M., Leung, T., & Lim, L. (1997). Expression of constitutively active α-PAK reveals effects of the kinase on actin and focal complexes. *Molecular and Cellular Biology, 17*(3), 1129–1143. https://doi.org/10.1128/mcb.17.3.1129

Manser, E., Leung, T., Salihuddin, H., Zhao, Z. S., & Lim, L. (1994). A brain serine/threonine protein kinase activated by Cdc42 and Rac1. *Nature, 367*(6458), 40–46. https://doi.org/10.1038/367040a0

Maruta, H. (2014). Herbal therapeutics that block the oncogenic kinase PAK1: A practical approach towards PAK1-dependent diseases and longevity. *Phytotherapy Research, 28*(5), 656–672. https://doi.org/10.1002/ptr.5054

McCoull, W., Hennessy, E. J., Blades, K., Box, M. R., Chuaqui, C., Dowling, J. E., Davies, C. D., Ferguson, A. D., Goldberg, F. W., Howe, N. J., Kemmitt, P. D., Lamont, G. M., Madden, K., McWhirter, C., Varnes, J. G., Ward, R. A., Williams, J. D., & Yang, B. (2014). Identification and optimisation of 7-azaindole PAK1 inhibitors with improved potency and kinase selectivity. *MedChemComm, 5*(10), 1533–1539. https://doi.org/10.1039/c4md00280f

McKew, J., Huang, W., Campbell, D., Durön, Behnke, M., & Shen. (2015). *Pak inhibitors for the treatment of fragile x syndrome.* US20150031693A1.

McManus, M. J., Boerner, J. L., Danielsen, A. J., Wang, Z., Matsumura, F., & Maihle, N. J. (2000). An oncogenic epidermal growth factor receptor signals via a p21-activated kinase-caldesmon-myosin phosphotyrosine complex. *Journal of Biological Chemistry, 275*(45), 35328–35334. https://doi.org/10.1074/jbc.M005399200

Mileshkin, L. R., Rosen, L. S., Blumenkopf, T., Breazna, A., Darang, S., Davison, J., Gallo, J., Goldman, J. W., Wang, D. D., Zhang, S., & Eckhardt, S. G. (2011). Phase I, dose-escalation, safety, pharmacokinetic, and pharmacodynamic study of single-agent PF-03758309, an oral PAK inhibitor, in patients with advanced solid tumors. *Journal of Clinical Oncology, 29*(15_Suppl. l). https://doi.org/10.1200/jco.2011.29.15_suppl.e13607. e13607-e13607.

Ndubaku, C. O., Crawford, J. J., Drobnick, J., Aliagas, I., Campbell, D., Dong, P., Dornan, L. M., Duron, S., Epler, J., Gazzard, L., Heise, C. E., Hoeflich, K. P., Jakubiak, D., La, H., Lee, W., Lin, B., Lyssikatos, J. P., Maksimoska, J., Marmorstein, R., … Rudolph, J. (2015). Design of selective PAK1 inhibitor G-5555: Improving properties by employing an unorthodox low-pKa polar moiety. *ACS Medicinal Chemistry Letters, 6*(12), 1241–1246. https://doi.org/10.1021/acsmedchemlett.5b00398

Nheu, T. V., He, H., Hirokawa, Y., Tamaki, K., Florin, L., Schmitz, M. L., Suzuki-Takahashi, I., Jorissen, R. N., Burgess, A. W., Nishimura, S., Wood, J., & Maruta, H. (2002). The K252a derivatives, inhibitors for the PAK/MLK kinase family, selectively block the growth of RAS transformants. *Cancer Journal, 8*(4), 328–336. https://doi.org/10.1097/00130404-200207000-00009

Parrini, M. C., Lei, M., Harrison, S. C., & Mayer, B. J. (2002). Pak1 kinase homodimers are autoinhibited in trans and dissociated upon activation by Cdc42 and Rac1. *Molecular Cell, 9*(1), 73–83. https://doi.org/10.1016/S1097-2765(01)00428-2

Pierré, A., Robert-Géro, M., Tempête, C., & Polonsky, J. (1980). Structural requirements of quassinoids for the inhibition of cell transformation. *Biochemical and Biophysical Research Communications, 93*(3), 675–686. https://doi.org/10.1016/0006-291X(80)91131-6

Pirruccello, M., Sondermann, H., Pelton, J. G., Pellicena, P., Hoelz, A., Chernoff, J., Wemmer, D. E., & Kuriyan, J. (2006). A dimeric kinase assembly underlying autophosphorylation in the p21 activated kinases. *Journal of Molecular Biology, 361*(2), 312–326. https://doi.org/10.1016/j.jmb.2006.06.017

Porchia, L. M., Guerra, M., Wang, Y. C., Zhang, Y., Espinosa, A. V., Shinohara, M., Kulp, S. K., Kirschner, L. S., Saji, M., Chen, C. S., & Ringel, M. D. (2007). 2-Amino-N-{4-[5-(2-phenanthrenyl)-3-(trifluoromethyl)-1H-pyrazol-1-yl]-phenyl} acetamide (OSU-03012), a celecoxib derivative, directly targets p21-activated kinase. *Molecular Pharmacology, 72*(5), 1124–1131. https://doi.org/10.1124/mol.107.037556

Radu, M., Semenova, G., Kosoff, R., & Chernoff, J. (2014). PAK signalling during the development and progression of cancer. *Nature Reviews Cancer, 14*(1), 13–25. https://doi.org/10.1038/nrc3645

Rane, C. K., & Minden, A. (2014). P21 activated kinases: Structure, regulation, and functions. *Small GTPases, 5.* https://doi.org/10.4161/sgtp.28003

Rosen, L. S., Blumenkopf, T. A., Breazna, A., Darang, S., Gallo, J. D., Goldman, J., Wang, D., Mileshkin, Linda, & Eckhardt, S. Gail (2011). Abstract A177: Phase 1, dose-escalation, safety, pharmacokinetic and pharmacodynamic study of single agent PF-03758309, an oral PAK inhibitor, in patients with advanced solid tumors. *Molecular Cancer Therapeutics, 10*(11_Suppl.). https://doi.org/10.1158/1535-7163.targ-11-a177. A177–A177.

Royal, I., Lamarche-Vane, N., Lamorte, L., Kaibuchi, K., & Park, M. (2000). Activation of Cdc42, Rac, PAK, and Rho-kinase in response to hepatocyte growth factor differentially regulates epithelial cell colony spreading and disso-ciation. *Molecular Biology of the Cell, 11*(5), 1709–1725. https://doi.org/10.1091/mbc.11.5.1709

Rudolph, J., Crawford, J. J., Hoeflich, K. P., & Wang, W. (2015). Inhibitors of p21-activated kinases (PAKs). *Journal of Medicinal Chemistry, 58*(1), 111–129. https://doi.org/10.1021/jm501613q

Rudolph, J., Murray, L. J., Ndubaku, C. O., O'Brien, T., Blackwood, E., Wang, W., Aliagas, I., Gazzard, L., Crawford, J. J., Drobnick, J., Lee, W., Zhao, X., Hoeflich, K. P., Favor, D. A., Dong, P., Zhang, H., Heise, C. E., Oh, A., Ong, C. C., … Zhong, Y. (2016). Chemically diverse group i p21-activated kinase (PAK) inhibitors impart acute cardiovascular toxicity with a narrow therapeutic window. *Journal of Medicinal Chemistry, 59*(11), 5520–5541. https://doi.org/10.1021/acs.jmedchem.6b00638

Salh, B., Marotta, A., Wagey, R., Sayed, M., & Pelech, S. (2002). Dysregulation of phosphatidylinositol 3-kinase and downstream effectors in human breast cancer. *International Journal of Cancer, 98*(1), 148–154. https://doi.org/10.1002/ijc.10147

Sampat, N., & Minden, A. (2018). Inhibitors of the p21 activated kinases. *Current Pharmacology Reports, 4*(3), 238–249. https://doi.org/10.1007/s40495-018-0132-7

Schraml, P., Schwerdtfeger, G., Burkhalter, F., Raggi, A., Schmidt, D., Ruffalo, T., King, W., Wilber, K., Mihatsch, M. J., & Moch, H. (2003). Combined array comparative genomic hybridization and tissue microarray analysis suggest PAK1 at 11q13.5-q14 as a critical oncogene target in ovarian carcinoma. *American Journal of Pathology, 163*(3), 985–992. https://doi.org/10.1016/S0002-9440(10)63458-X

Sells, M. A., Pfaff, A., & Chernoff, J. (2000). Temporal and spatial distribution of activated Pak1 in fibroblasts. *Journal of Cell Biology, 151*(7), 1449–1458. https://doi.org/10.1083/jcb.151.7.1449

Shahinozzaman, M., Ishii, T., Ahmed, S., Halim, M. A., & Tawata, S. (2020). A computational approach to explore and identify potential herbal inhibitors for the p21-activated kinase 1 (PAK1). *Journal of Biomolecular Structure and Dynamics, 38*(12), 3514–3526. https://doi.org/10.1080/07391102.2019.1659855

Shen, Z. Z., & Manser, E. (2012). PAK family kinases: Physiological roles and regulation. *Cellular Logistics, 2*, 59–68.

Shin, Y. J., Kim, Y. B., & Kim, J. H. (2013). Protein kinase CK2 phosphorylates and activates p21-activated kinase 1. *Molecular Biology of the Cell, 24*(18), 2990–2999. https://doi.org/10.1091/mbc.E13-04-0204

Strochlic, T. I., Viaud, J., Rennefahrt, U. E. E., Anastassiadis, T., & Peterson, J. R. (2010). Phosphoinositides are essential coactivators for p21-activated kinase 1. *Molecular Cell, 40*(3), 493–500. https://doi.org/10.1016/j.molcel.2010.10.015

Sun, H., King, A. J., Diaz, H. B., & Marshall, M. S. (2000). Regulation of the protein kinase Raf-1 by oncogenic Ras through phosphatidylinositol 3-kinase, cdc42/rac and Pak. *Current Biology, 10*(5), 281–284. https://doi.org/10.1016/S0960-9822(00)00359-6

Tonani, R., Bindi, Fancelli, D., & Pittala, ' V (2004). *Heterobicyclic pyrazole derivatives as kinase inhibitors.* WO2004007504A1.

Viaud, J., & Peterson, J. R. (2009). An allosteric kinase inhibitor binds the p21-activated kinase autoregulatory domain covalently. *Molecular Cancer Therapeutics, 8*(9), 2559–2565. https://doi.org/10.1158/1535-7163.MCT-09-0102

Vollrath, B., Campbell, D., Durón, & Wade, W. (2013). *8-ethyl-6-(aryl)pyrido[2,3-D]pyrimidin-7(8H)-ones for the treatment of CNS disorders.* US8372970B2.

Wang, J., Zhu, Y., Chen, J., Yang, Y., Zhu, L., Zhao, J., Yang, Y., Cai, X., Hu, C., Rosell, R., Sun, X., & Cao, P. (2020). Identification of a novel PAK1 inhibitor to treat pancreatic cancer. *Acta Pharmaceutica Sinica B, 10*(4), 603–614. https://doi.org/10.1016/j.apsb.2019.11.015

Wang, K., Baldwin, G. S., Nikfarjam, M., & He, H. (2019). Antitumor effects of all-trans retinoic acid and its synergism with gemcitabine are associated with downregulation of p21-activated kinases in pancreatic cancer. *American Journal of Physiology - Gastrointestinal and Liver Physiology, 316*(5), G632–G640. https://doi.org/10.1152/ajpgi.00344.2018

Wu, D. W., Wu, T. C., Chen, C. Y., & Lee, H. (2016). PAK1 is a novel therapeutic target in tyrosine kinase inhibitor-resistant lung adenocarcinoma activated by the PI3K/AKT signaling regardless of EGFR mutation. *Clinical Cancer Research, 22*(21), 5370–5382. https://doi.org/10.1158/1078-0432.CCR-15-2724

Xu, Y., Foulks, J. M., Clifford, A., Brenning, B., Lai, S., Luo, B., Parnell, K. M., Merx, S., McCullar, M. V., Kanner, S. B., & Ho, K. K. (2013). Synthesis and structure-activity relationship of 2-arylamino-4-aryl- pyrimidines as potent PAK1 inhibitors. *Bioorganic & Medicinal Chemistry Letters, 23*(14), 4072–4075. https://doi.org/10.1016/j.bmcl.2013.05.059

Yeo, D., Huynh, N., Beutler, J. A., Christophi, C., Shulkes, A., Baldwin, G. S., Nikfarjam, M., & He, H. (2014). Glaucarubinone and gemcitabine synergistically reduce pancreatic cancer growth via down-regulation of P21-activated kinases. *Cancer Letters, 346*(2), 264–272. https://doi.org/10.1016/j.canlet.2014.01.001

Zhang, J., Zou, L., Tang, P., Pan, D., He, Z., & Yao, D. (2020). Design, synthesis and biological evaluation of 1H-pyrazolo [3,4-d]pyrimidine derivatives as PAK1 inhibitors that trigger apoptosis, ER stress and anti-migration effect in MDA-MB-231 cells. *European Journal of Medicinal Chemistry, 194,* 112220. https://doi.org/10.1016/j.ejmech.2020.112220

Zhou, Y., Zhang, J., Wang, J., Cheng, M. S., Zhao, D. M., & Li, F. (2019). Targeting PAK1 with the small molecule drug AK963/40708899 suppresses gastric cancer cell proliferation and invasion by downregulation of PAK1 activity and PAK1-related signaling pathways. *The Anatomical Record, 302*(9), 1571–1579. https://doi.org/10.1002/ar.24095

p38 mitogen-activated protein kinase inhibitors

Ashraf K. El-Damasy[1,2], *Mohamed S.H. Salem*[3,4], *Mahmoud M. Sebaiy*[5] *and Mohamed Saleh Elgawish*[6,7]

[1]Department of Medicinal Chemistry, Faculty of Pharmacy, Mansoura University, Mansoura, Egypt; [2]Brain Science Institute, Korea Institute of Science and Technology (KIST), Seoul, Republic of Korea; [3]SANKEN (The Institute of Scientific and Industrial Research), Osaka University, Osaka, Japan; [4]Pharmaceutical Organic Chemistry Department, Faculty of Pharmacy, Suez Canal University, Ismailia, Egypt; [5]Medicinal Chemistry Department, Faculty of Pharmacy, Zagazig University, Sharkia, Egypt; [6]Department of Medicinal Chemistry, Faculty of Pharmacy, Suez Canal University, Ismailia, Egypt; [7]Department of Chemistry, Korea University, Seoul, Republic of Korea

1. Introduction

Kinases are a wide family of enzymes with over 500 members that catalyze the transfer of phosphate from high-energy phosphate donor molecules such as ATP to its specific substrates. Kinases are extensively utilized in cells to transmit signals and control complex activities. The mitogen-activating protein kinases (MAPK) pathway, which is also named the RAS/RAF/MEK/ERK pathway, is a key channel between extracellular signals and their consequential intracellular responses. Through multistage phosphorylation, MAPK delivers mitogenic signals from outside the cell to the nucleus (Fig. 11.1). Various cellular processes depend on this MAPK signaling pathway such as cell proliferation, differentiation, survival, and even apoptosis (Braicu et al., 2019). Cancer and other human diseases are attributed to gain-of-function or loss-of-function mutations in kinases. At least 30% of all tumors are characterized by a defect in the MAPK pathway that causes the downregulation of some antiproliferative genes and loss of control over cell growth (Chambard et al., 2007; Cheng & Tian, 2017). Mutations in Ras and/or Raf proteins are primarily responsible for promoting these malignancies due to their contribution not only to the MAPK pathway but also to many other pathways that play a similar role in controlling cell growth such as PI3K/AKT (Mahapatra

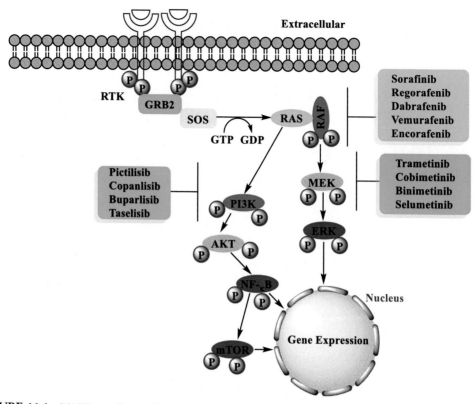

FIGURE 11.1 MAPK signaling pathway and approved MAPK inhibitor. *AKT*, protein kinase B; *ERK*, extracellular signal-regulated kinase; *GDP*, guanosine diphosphate; *GRB*, growth factor receptor bound protein; *GTP*, guanosine triphosphate; *MEK*, mitogen-activated protein kinase; mTOR, mammalian target of rapamycin; *NF-kB*, nuclear factor-kB; *PI3K*, phosphatidylinositol 3-kinase; *RAF*, v-raf murine sarcoma viral oncogene; *RAS*, rat sarcoma viral oncogene; *RTK*, receptor tyrosine kinase; *SOS*, son of sevenless homolog.

et al., 2017; Mendoza et al., 2011). Since realizing the critical role of this MAPK pathway in cancer, researchers have tended to target it as a potential therapy. In 1995, the first MAPK inhibitor appeared, which in turn works on the allosteric site of MEK 1/2 proteins. Later, more efforts were exerted and a series of other MAPK inhibitors (Fig. 11.1) were discovered, which target most of the MAPK proteins like KRAS/BRAF/MEK/and ERK (Dudley et al., 1995; Sebolt-Leopold, 2008). In this chapter, we will shed light on the types of MAPK and their roles in various biological processes. Then, we specify a large area to extensively review the FDA-approved drugs MAPK inhibitors, their synthetic pathways, the rationales beyond their discovery, and the binding modes to their receptors. Among all MAPK inhibitors, MEK inhibitors are still considered the most common. However, in most cases, it is not administered as a single therapy, but as a combination with either BRAF inhibitors or other inhibitors that target various pathways and receptors as will be discussed in this chapter. Most MAPK inhibitors activate different compensatory feedback responses in the cancerous microenvironment, the thing that triggers adaptive resistance to these MAPK inhibitors (Caunt et al., 2015; Turke et al., 2012). These combinations were implemented to restrict the resistance possibility based on the integration in various translational studies (Kozar et al., 2019). In the fourth and fifth parts, we will discuss the different mechanisms responsible for MAPK-inhibitors' resistance and show the various tactics to obstacle this resistance. Finally, we will aim to highlight examples of the future of MAPK inhibitors therapeutic out of oncology and how the inhibition of MAPK pathway could manage many diseases like pulmonary disease, inflammation, rheumatic arthritis, pain, cardiovascular diseases, Alzheimer's, and viral infections.

2. MAPK types and signal transduction

Most of the classical MAPKs have some similar characteristics, like the activation based on dual phosphorylation sites, an architecture of a three-tiered pathway, and other similar recognition sites of the substrate. However, there are also old types that lack such dual phosphorylation sites, instead, they form only two-tiered pathways and do not have the required features by other MAPKs for substrate binding. These types are usually known as "atypical" MAPKs (Coulombe & Meloche, 2007).

There are three subfamilies of the mammalian MAPK family of kinase:

1. Extracellular signal-regulated kinases (ERKs)
2. c-Jun N-terminal kinases (JNKs)
3. p38 mitogen-activated protein kinases (p38s)

Generally, ERKs are being activated by mitogens and growth factors, while inflammatory cytokines and cellular stresses activate JNKs and p38s (Yu et al., 2020).

2.1 Extracellular signal-regulated kinases

In molecular biology, ERKs, also known as classical MAP kinases, are widely expressed intracellular protein kinase signaling molecules that play an important role in mitosis regulation, meiosis, and postmitotic functions in newly differentiated cells. Many variant stimuli activate the ERK pathway such as growth factors, virus infection, cytokines, carcinogens, transforming agents, and ligands for heterotrimeric G protein-coupled receptors. The term, extracellular signal-regulated kinases, was used as a MAPK synonym, but recently, it is being adopted for a specific category of the mammalian MAPK family.

In MAPK/ERK pathway, the c-Raf is activated by Ras, followed by mitogen-activated protein kinase (also abbreviated as MKK, MEK, or MAP2K) and then MAPK1/2. Ras is activated typically by growth hormones by GRB2/SOS and receptor tyrosine kinases (RTKs) but may receive also other signals. ERKs are commonly known to activate many transcription factors, like ELK1, and other downstream protein kinases. ERK pathway disruption is common in different cancer types, especially c-Raf, Ras, and some receptors such as HER2 (Rao & Reddy, 1994).

2.2 c-Jun N-terminal kinases

JNKs, are identified originally as kinases that bind and phosphorylate the c-Jun on both Ser-63 and Ser-73 moieties incorporated in its transcriptional domain of activation. These kinases belong to MAPK family and rapidly respond to stress stimuli, like UV irradiation, cytokines, osmotic shock, and heat shock. JNKs play also an important role in the differentiation of T cells and the cellular pathway of apoptosis. JNKs are activated when their threonine (Thr) and tyrosine (Tyr) residues in a Thr-Pro-Tyr motif are dually phosphorylated within kinase subdomain VIII. Activation is processed by two main MAP kinase kinases, which are MKK4 and MKK7; however, on the other hand, Ser/Thr and Tyr protein phosphatases can inactivate JNKs. It is being suggested that this signaling pathway can lead to inflammation responses in mammals and even insects (Ip & Davis, 1998).

2.3 p38 mitogen-activated protein kinases

p38 mitogen-activated protein kinases are another MAPK class that is also responsive to some stress stimuli that affect JNKs such as UV irradiation, cytokines, osmotic shock, and heat shock. These kinases are involved in cell differentiation, autophagy, and apoptosis. p38 MAPK pathway persistent activation due to aging in muscle satellite cells (muscle stem cells) can lead to impairment of muscle regeneration (Cosgrove et al., 2014; Segalés et al., 2016).

p38 MAP kinase is also known as cytokinin specific binding protein, and it is the mammalian ortholog of the yeast Hog1p MAP kinase, which plays an important role in a signaling cascade that controls cellular responses to stress and cytokines. Four p38 MAP kinases, which are p38-α (MAPK14), p38-β (MAPK11), p38-γ (MAPK12/ERK6), and p38-δ (MAPK13/SAPK4), have been identified. In a similar way to the SAPK/JNK pathway, p38 MAP kinase is activated through various cellular stresses such as inflammatory cytokines, osmotic shock, UV light, lipopolysaccharides (LPS), and growth factors (Han et al., 1994). p38 MAP kinase is activated by MKK3 and SEK through phosphorylation at Thr-180 and Tyr-182. Activated p38 MAP kinase can then phosphorylate and activate MAPKAP kinase 2 and then phosphorylate the transcription factors Mac, MEF2, ATF2, and p53 (She et al., 2000). p38 MAP kinase can also phosphorylate posttranscriptional regulating factors such as TTP, and also in fruit flies, it participates in circadian clock regulation (Dusik et al., 2014; Tudor et al., 2009).

3. FDA-approved MAPK inhibitors

3.1 FDA-approved BRAF inhibitors

To date, five drugs including sorafenib, regorafenib, vemurafenib, dabrafenib, and encorafenib were approved by the FDA as BRAF inhibitors for the treatment of cancers overexpressing the oncogenic BRAF, including metastatic colorectal cancer (mCRC), renal cell carcinoma (RCC), and/or metastatic melanoma harboring $BRAF^{V600E/K}$ mutations (Fig. 11.2).

3.1.1 Sorafenib

Sorafenib (BAY43-9006, Nexavar) is an orally active multikinase inhibitor, which was initially discovered as an RAF inhibitor with potent nanomolar activity against wild-type BRAF, BRAFV600E mutant, as well as C-RAF (Wilhelm et al., 2004). Moreover, sorafenib directly suppresses the autophosphorylation of multiple RTKs including VEGFR1, 2, and3,

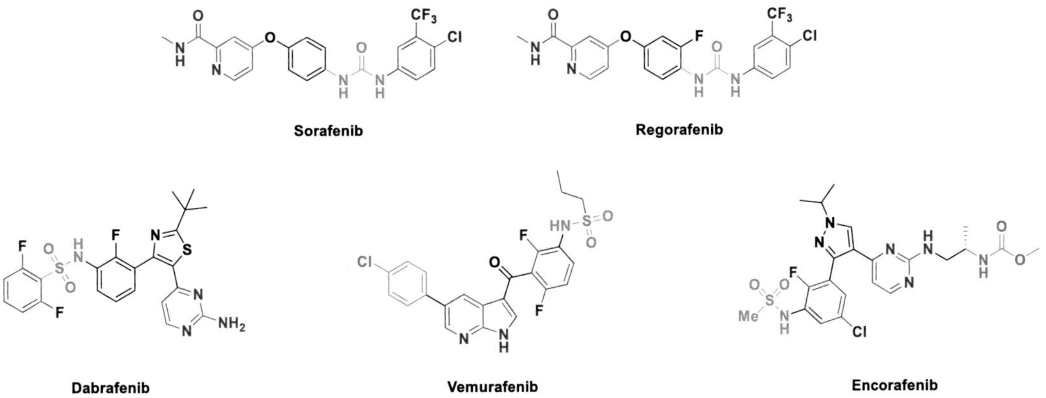

Sorafenib

Regorafenib

Dabrafenib

Vemurafenib

Encorafenib

FIGURE 11.2 FDA-approved BRAF inhibitors. For only the electronic version of this chapter, the color of the drug moieties refers to their binding role; *red color* for hinge binding motifs, *green* for front pocket region binders, *orange* for DFG binding motifs, and *blue* for hydrophobic fragments.

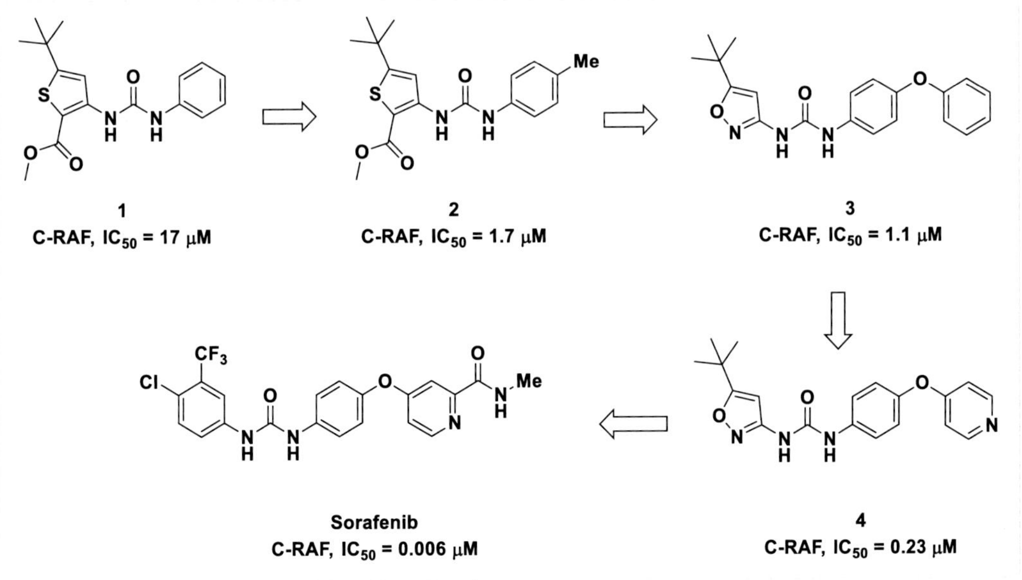

1
C-RAF, IC_{50} = 17 μM

2
C-RAF, IC_{50} = 1.7 μM

3
C-RAF, IC_{50} = 1.1 μM

Sorafenib
C-RAF, IC_{50} = 0.006 μM

4
C-RAF, IC_{50} = 0.23 μM

FIGURE 11.3 Summary of the structural optimization leading to the discovery of sorafenib as a C-RAF inhibitor.

PDGFRβ, RET, and c-Kit (Carlomagno et al., 2006; Wilhelm et al., 2004), which render it an optimal choice for treatment of advanced RCC, where C-RAF and VEGFR are overexpressed. Sorafenib was approved by the FDA in 2005 for RCC management (Wilhelm et al., 2006). The discovery of sorafenib was the outcome of extensive lead optimization endeavors and high throughput screening of more than 200,000 compounds to target the Ras-Raf-MEK-ERK (MAPK) signaling pathway (Fig. 11.3) (Smith et al., 2001; Wilhelm et al., 2004). Starting

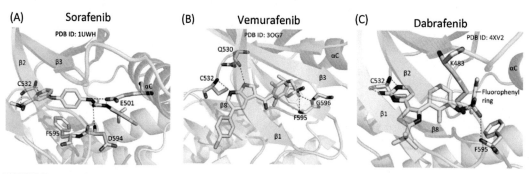

FIGURE 11.4   The binding mode of FDA-approved BRAF inhibitors. (A) Sorafenib complex with BRAF wild type, (B) vemurafenib bound to BRAF^V600E, and (C) Dabrafenib bound to BRAF^V600E. For only the electronic version of this chapter, the carbon atoms of the drugs are presented in *yellow color. CL*, catalytic loop; *GRL*, glycine-rich loop. The dotted lines indicate hydrogen bonds. *Reproduced from Roskoski (2018) with permission.*

from 3-thienyl urea 1 as a promising lead (C-RAF; IC50 = 17 μM), various structural alterations were adopted and eventually resulted in the identification of sorafenib, a pyridylamide based diaryl urea, as a potent C-RAF inhibitor with single digit nanomolar IC50 value. The privileged picolinamide moiety of sorafenib occupies the ATP binding pocket of BRAF through three fundamental interactions with aromatic residues: Trp530 of the hinge region, Phe582 at the end of the catalytic loop, and Phe594 of the DFG motif. The pyridine ring nitrogen atom is engaged in a critical hydrogen bond (HB) with Cys531 of the hinge region, while the methyl amide moiety engages the carbonyl of Cys531. Moreover, the urea functionality of sorafenib forms two HBs with the catalytic Glu500 residue and Asp593 of the DFG motif. Most importantly, the hydrophobic trifluoromethyl phenyl ring is buried deep into a hydrophobic pocket created between the αC and αE helices and N-terminal regions of the DFG motif and catalytic loop (Fig. 11.4A). Such a pattern of interactions traps the DFG motif in an inactive conformation, therefore sorafenib is categorized as a type II tyrosine kinase inhibitor (Wan et al., 2004). The main pharmacologic properties of sorafenib include its variable oral bioavailability, tight binding to plasma proteins (~99.5%), and its hepatic mediated metabolism via CYP3A4 and glucuronidation-assisted by UGT1A9 (Tlemsani et al., 2015). Among the various metabolites of sorafenib, the pyridine-N-oxide derivative stood out as the major active metabolite. Hypertension, diarrhea, skin rash, hand-foot syndrome, and fatigue are the most common adverse effects of sorafenib, which may stem from its multiple kinase inhibitory action (Hasskarl, 2014).

3.1.2 Regorafenib

Regorafenib (BAY73-4506, Stivarga) was approved by the FDA for the treatment of mCRC in 2012. Regorafenib is the fluoro congener of sorafenib, where a fluorine atom is added in the central phenyl ring leading to a distinct biochemical profile, improved potency, and increased patient survival compared with sorafenib (Wilhelm et al., 2014). Similar to sorafenib, regorafenib is an oral multikinase inhibitor of BRAF (wild-type and its V600E mutant), C-RAF, FGFR, VEGFR1/-2/-3, PDGFR, TIE2 and KIT, and RET (Wilhelm et al., 2011). Despite the lack of X-ray crystal structure of regorafenib with any of its target kinases, it has been categorized as a type II kinase inhibitor based on its high structural similarities to sorafenib

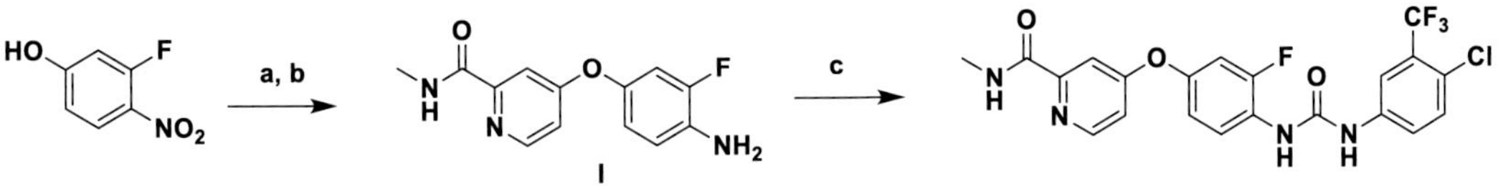

SCHEME 11.1 Synthesis of regorafenib. Reagents and conditions: (A) 10% Pd/C, ethyl acetate, H_2 atmosphere, rt, 4 h; (B) t-BuOK, 0°C, 25 min, 4-chloro-N-methyl-2-pyridinecarboxamide, DMA, 100°C, 16 h; (C) 4-chloro-3-(trifluoromethyl)phenyl isocyanate, toluene, rt, 72 h.

(Roskoski, 2016). Pharmacologically, regorafenib is metabolized by hepatic routes, and its pyridine-N-oxide and pyridine-N-oxide-N-desmethyl metabolites are the main active metabolites (Tlemsani et al., 2015). The safety profile of regorafenib was typical for an angiokinase inhibitor, and the most common side effects observed with regorafenib were rash, hypertension, hand-foot skin reaction, and diarrhea. The rare serious adverse effects associated with regorafenib are gastrointestinal perforation, hypertensive crisis, liver injury, and reversible posterior leukoencephalopathy (Dhillon, 2017). The synthetic approach of regorafenib comprises three main steps (Scheme 11.1). Reduction of 3-fluoro-4-nitrophenol under H_2 atmosphere in the presence of Pd/C affords the relevant aniline. Next, selective O-arylation of aniline with 4-chloro-N-methyl-2-pyridinecarboxamide was performed under potassium t-butoxide catalyzed conditions to yield the ether-tethered bicyclic derivative. Finally, the coupling of the free amine with 4-chloro-3-trifluoromethyl)phenyl isocyanate furnished the fluorinated ureide regorafenib.

3.1.3 Vemurafenib

Vemurafenib (PLX4032, Zelboraf) was granted FDA approval in 2011 as a first-in-class suppressor of cancer-relevant BRAF for the treatment of patients with metastatic or unresectable melanoma harboring the BRAFV600E mutation. In contrast to the broad-spectrum kinase inhibitory profile of sorafenib and regorafenib, vemurafenib elicits high selectivity toward the oncogenic BRAFV600E and C-RAF kinases with IC50 values of 31 and 48 nM (Bollag et al., 2012). The favorable biochemical selectivity of vemurafenib is reflected on the cellular level, where potent inhibition of MEK1/2 and/or ERK1/2 phosphorylation and proliferation occurs exclusively in melanoma cell lines harboring BRAF-V600 mutants, including V600E, V600D, V600K, and V600R (Yang et al., 2010). Despite the efficacy of vemurafenib in the treatment of BRAFV600E-driven melanoma, it shows limited effect in patients with colon cancer carrying BRAFV600E oncoprotein. This is because of the occurrence of rapid feedback EGFR activation in colon cancer cells upon inhibition of BRAFV600E by vemurafenib, which ultimately counteracts the ability of vemurafenib to inhibit cell proliferation (Prahallad et al., 2012). In the same line, vemurafenib triggers a paradoxical activation of the MAP kinase cascade in wild-type BRAF cells, which results in certain adverse effects like keratoacanthoma, alopecia, and arthralgias. These adverse events are significantly minimized upon the combination of vemurafenib with cobimetinib as an MEK inhibitor (Larkin et al., 2014). Vemurafenib, a 7-azaindole derivative, is a type I1/2A inhibitor of BRAF, where it occupies the ATP adenine pocket with a DFG-in conformation, forming a unique HB through its sulfonamide nitrogen and the backbone NH of D594 (Bollag et al., 2012). In addition, vemurafenib mimics the adenine core of ATP by being engaged in two crucial HB interactions; one is formed between the NH group of the 7-azaindole skeleton and the carbonyl

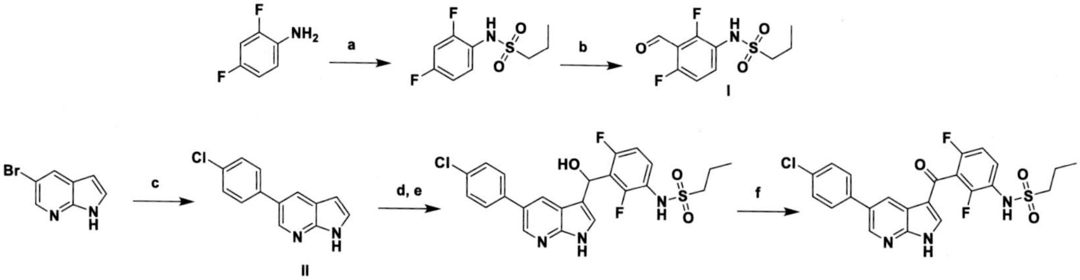

SCHEME 11.2 Synthesis of vemurafenib. Reagents and conditions: (A) Propane 1-sulfonyl chloride, Et₃N, THF, rt, overnight (o/n); (B) LDA, THF, −78°C, DMF, −78°C to rt, 40 min; (C) K₂CO₃, H₂O, CH₃CN, tetrakis(-triphenylphosphine)palladium, 170°C, o/n; (D) Compound I, KOH, MeOH, rt, 72 h; (E) 8% HBr, rt, o/n; (F) DDQ, 1,4-dioxane, H₂O, rt, 2 h.

functionality of the hinge residue Q530, and the second is noticed between the pyrrole ring nitrogen and the amino group of the C532 hinge residue (Fig. 11.4B). While the proximal 4-chlorophenyl motif is oriented to the solvent region, the terminal 2,4-difluorophenyl sulfonamide induces an exterior shift of the regulatory αC-helix (Bollag et al., 2012). Moreover, vemurafenib makes van der Waals interactions with D594 (in DFG region), along with multiple hydrophobic contacts with the I463 (β1-strand), V471 after the G-rich loop, A481, L505, L514 (αC-β4 loop), the T529 gatekeeper, W531 (hinge region), and DFG-F595 (Roskoski, 2016). The synthetic outline for vemurafenib commences with the coupling of the 2,4-difluoroaniline with sulfonyl chloride, followed by aromatic ring formylation in the presence of lithium diisoproylamide to afford the intermediate I (Scheme 11.2) (Babcock et al., 2013). 5-Bromoazaindole was subjected to Suzuki coupling with 4-chlorophenylboronic acid to produce intermediate II. Aldol coupling of I and II, followed by hydrobromic acid-catalyzed demethylation and oxidation by 2,3-dichloro-5,6-dicyanobenzoquinone yields vemurafenib.

3.1.4 Dabrafenib

Dabrafenib (GSK2118436, Tafinlar) is the second clinically available BRAF inhibitor, which received accelerated approval by the FDA in 2013 as a therapy for patients with unresectable or metastatic melanoma carrying the BRAF^V600E mutation. In 2014, dabrafenib was approved in combination with trametinib, an MEK inhibitor, for the management of metastatic melanoma harboring BRAF^V600E or BRAF^V600K mutations. Also, this combination was clinically approved for the treatment of patients with metastatic nonsmall cell lung cancer (NSCLC) driven by BRAF^V600E mutation. Compared to the previously described BRAF inhibitors, dabrafenib exhibits the highest potency with an IC₅₀ value of 0.7 nM against BRAF^V600E. Moreover, dabrafenib is highly selective toward BRAF^V600E, wild-type BRAF, and CRAF rather than other oncogenic kinases (Rheault et al., 2013).

The discovery of dabrafenib was a result of systemic structural modifications of thiazole compound **III** as one of the GSK candidates targeting BRAF^V600E (Fig. 11.5) (Rheault et al., 2013). Despite the potent in vitro kinase inhibitory effect of thiazole **III** against the BRAF^V600E in cell-free and cell-based (SKMEL28 melanoma) assays, its low clearance, and favorable oral systemic exposure in rats, compound **III** showed very high clearance, low bioavailability in nonrodent species as well as increased metabolic liabilities. Truncation of the tail in **III** by

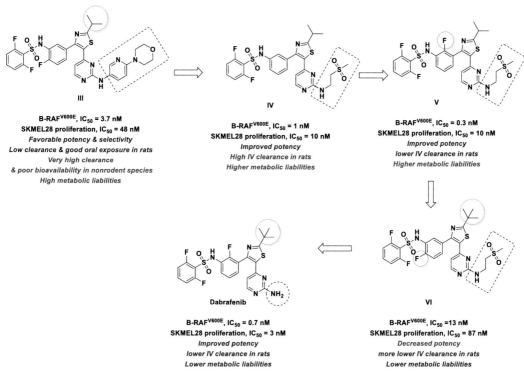

FIGURE 11.5 Illustration of the structural optimization leading to the discovery of dabrafenib as BRAF^{V600E} inhibitor.

replacing its aminopyridine with a polar sulfonamide moiety **IV** improved both enzyme potency as well as inhibition of cell growth in BRAF^{V600E}-dependent SKMEL28, yet led to remarkably higher clearance in rats. Further extensive SAR exploration on this scaffold revealed that fluorination at the *ortho*-position of the central phenyl ring (**V**) augmented the enzyme potency, maintained cellular activity, and resulted in an improved pharmacokinetic profile. Changing the isopropyl thiazole with the bulkier *tert*-butyl thiazole core (**VI**) along with shifting the fluorine atom from *ortho*-to *para*-position of thiazole led to better clearance and improved metabolic stability, however, the potency was decreased. Ultimately, combining the structural amendments of fluorination at *ortho*-position like **V**, replacing the isopropyl thiazole core with the corresponding *tert*-butyl derivative, and utilizing the simplified aminopyrimidine tail resulted in the identification of dabrafenib with optimized pharmacokinetic profile, minimized metabolic liability, and improved biochemical and cellular potency (Rheault et al., 2013).

Similar to vemurafenib, dabrafenib is categorized as an ATP-competitive type I$_{1/2}$A inhibitor, since it binds BRAF$_{V600E}$ in its inactive DFG-in, *C*-helix-out conformation. Dabrafenib is tightly bound to BRAF^{V600E} (PDB ID: 4XV2) (Zhang et al., 2015) through four crucial HBs as follows; the *N1* of the pyrimidine hinge binding motif with the −NH group of Cys532 residue, the 2-amino group of pyrimidine with the −CO group of Cys532, one of the

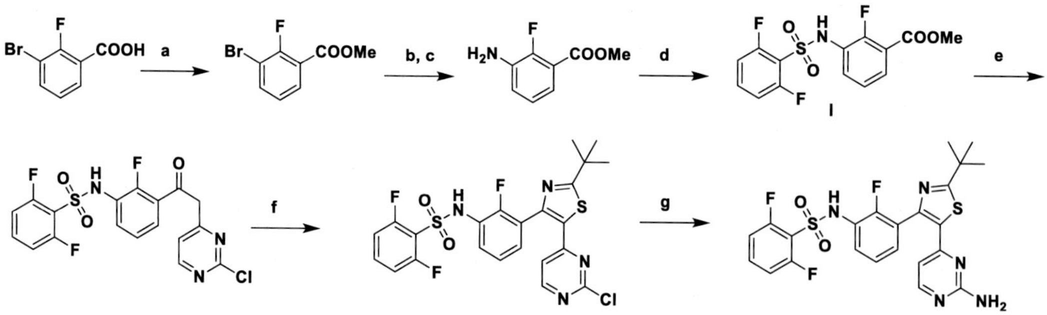

SCHEME 11.3 Synthesis of dabrafenib. Reagents and conditions: (A) H_2SO_4, MeOH, reflux, 1 h; (B) 1,1-Dimethylethyl carbamate, $Pd_2(dba)_3 \cdot CHCl_3$, xantphos, Cs_2CO_3, toluene, 90°C, o/n; (C) TFA, DCM, rt, 1 h; (D) 2,6-difluorobenzenesulfonyl chloride, pyridine, DCM, rt, o/n; (E) LiHMDS, THF, 0°C, then 2-chloro-4-methylpyrimidine, 20°C, 1 h; (F) NBS, DMA, 15 min, rt, then 2,2,2-trimethylthioacetamide, 80°C, 3 h; (G) 7N methanolic NH_3, 90°C, 24 h.

sulfonamide oxygens with the K483 at β3-strand, and the other sulfonamide oxygen with the −NH group of Phe595 at DFG motif (Fig. 11.4C). Moreover, dabrafenib is engaged in van der Waals contact with DFG-D594 as well as various hydrophobic interactions with β1-strand I463, F468 in the G-rich loop, β2-strand V471, the β3-strand A481 and K483, αC-helix L505, L514, L515, and F516 in the αC-β4 loop, β5-strand I527, the hinge region Q530 and W531, the β8-strand F583. The synthetic route for dabrafenib begins with Fischer esterification of 3-bromo-2-fluorobenzoic acid, followed by a Buchwald−Hartwig amination to afford the corresponding aniline ester (Scheme 11.3). Treatment of the aniline derivative with 2,6-difluorobenzenesulfonyl chloride produced the diaryl sulfonamide ester **I**. Base catalyzed deprotonation of 2-chloro-4-methylpyrimidine with lithium bis(trimethylsilyl)amide (LHMDS) then addition to ester **I** furnished the chloropyrimidine. Bromination of the keto group mediated by NBS along with thiazole ring formation cyclization with 2,2-dimethylpropanethioamide achieved the *ter*-butyl thiazole scaffold, which was subjected to S_NAr displacement with ammonium hydroxide to yield dabrafenib (Ding et al., 2015).

3.1.5 Encorafenib

Encorafenib (LGX818, Braftovi) is a superb potent and selective imidazolyl-pyrimidine-based RAF suppressor with differential antiproliferative and apoptotic effects in cancer cells expressing BRAF[V600E]. FDA approval was granted to encorafenib in 2018 in combination with the MEK inhibitor binimetinib for the treatment of BRAF[V600E/K]-mutant melanoma. Later on, in 2020, the FDA approved encorafenib in combination with cetuximab, a monoclonal antibody EGFR inhibitor, for the treatment of metastatic CRC overexpressing BRAF[V600E]. Encorafenib strongly suppresses phospho-ERK ($EC_{50} = 3$ nM) in A375 human melanoma cell, which leads to potent inhibition of cell growth with EC_{50} of 4 nM as well as inducing cellular senescence and autophagy (Li et al., 2016; Stuart et al., 2012). Being exceptional among other RAF inhibitors, encorafenib did not suppress the proliferation of more than 400 cell lines harboring wild-type BRAF. Moreover, it showed extremely slow dissociation from BRAF[V600E], which resulted in sustained MAPK pathway inhibition (Stuart et al., 2012). In view of the cellular profile, encorafenib might act as αC_{out} BRAF inhibitor;

however, this notion is not yet confirmed because of the lack of its X-ray crystal (Roskoski, 2020).

Encorafenib was developed as one of the dabrafenib congeners, where both drugs share a common construction with an isosteric scaffold derived from a pyrimidine amine directly attached to a five-membered ring (*tert*-butyl thiazole in dabrafenib and isopropyl pyrazole in encorafenib), which in turn is linked directly to a fluorophenyl fragment (with an extra chlorine in encorafenib) that bears a sulfonamide group. While dabrafenib has no substituent on its aminopyrimidine moiety, encorafenib is characterized by the existence of a chlorine atom on its central phenyl ring and a polar extension on the aminopyrimidine. Also, the terminal difluorophenyl attached to sulfonamide in dabrafenib is replaced by a small methyl group in encorafenib. Interestingly, such a set of structural modifications on dabrafenib resulted in encorafenib, which promotes a weaker paradoxical effect and possesses a lower affinity for pregnane X receptor than dabrafenib.

The preparation of encorafenib adopts a convergent synthetic pathway that necessitates the synthesis of three key building blocks: carbamate **I**, aryl boronic ester **II**, and the trisubstituted pyrazole scaffold **III** (Scheme 11.4) (Flick et al., 2020). The synthesis of **I** involves Cbz protection of the primary amine of (*S*)-(−)-1,2-diaminopropane salt, followed by the formation of methylcarbamate on the NH. Elimination of the Cbz group by hydrogenation, and acid treatment provides the chiral carbamate salt **I**. The synthesis of **II** commences with the formylation of 2-bromo-4-chloro-1-fluorobenzene afford the benzaldehyde derivative. Oxidation to carboxylic acid followed by Curtius rearrangement produces the Boc-aniline, which is then subjected to Miyaura conditions to afford the boronic ester **II**. Synthesis of **III** involves the benzyl protection of isopropylhydrazine followed by alkylation with 2-(1-ethoxyethylidene)propanedinitrile. Acid-catalyzed cyclization constructs the aminopyrazole scaffold. Next, two functional group transformations are involved, the conversion of the cyano group into the corresponding methyl ketone along with a Sandmeyer conversion of the amine into iodine. α-Enamination of the ketone paves the cyclization with guanidine to yield the 2-aminopyrimidine ring (**III**). Next, a Sandmeyer transformation of the arylamine into hydroxyl followed by chlorination allows the appendage of intermediate **I**. Then, the arylboronic ester **II** is introduced on the pyrazole ring via Suzuki cross-coupling. Boc deprotection produces the aniline, which underwent treatment with mesyl chloride to produce a bismesylated intermediate that, after treatment with NaOH and subsequent acidification, leads to differential monosulfonyl deprotection furnishing encorafenib.

3.2 FDA-approved MEK inhibitors

Currently, four drugs, trametinib, cobimetinib, binimetinib, and selumetinib, were granted approval by the FDA as MEK inhibitors for the treatment of patients carrying BRAF$^{V600E/K}$ mutations either as monotherapy or in a combination of BRAF inhibitors to suppress the paradoxical activation of the MAPK pathway upon BRAF inhibition. Such combinations reduce the potential of adverse events like arthralgia and hyperkeratosis (Fig. 11.6).

3.2.1 *Trametinib*

Trametinib (GSK1120212, Mekinist) is a highly potent and selective MEK1/2 inhibitor, which received FDA approval in 2013 for the treatment of patients with unresectable/

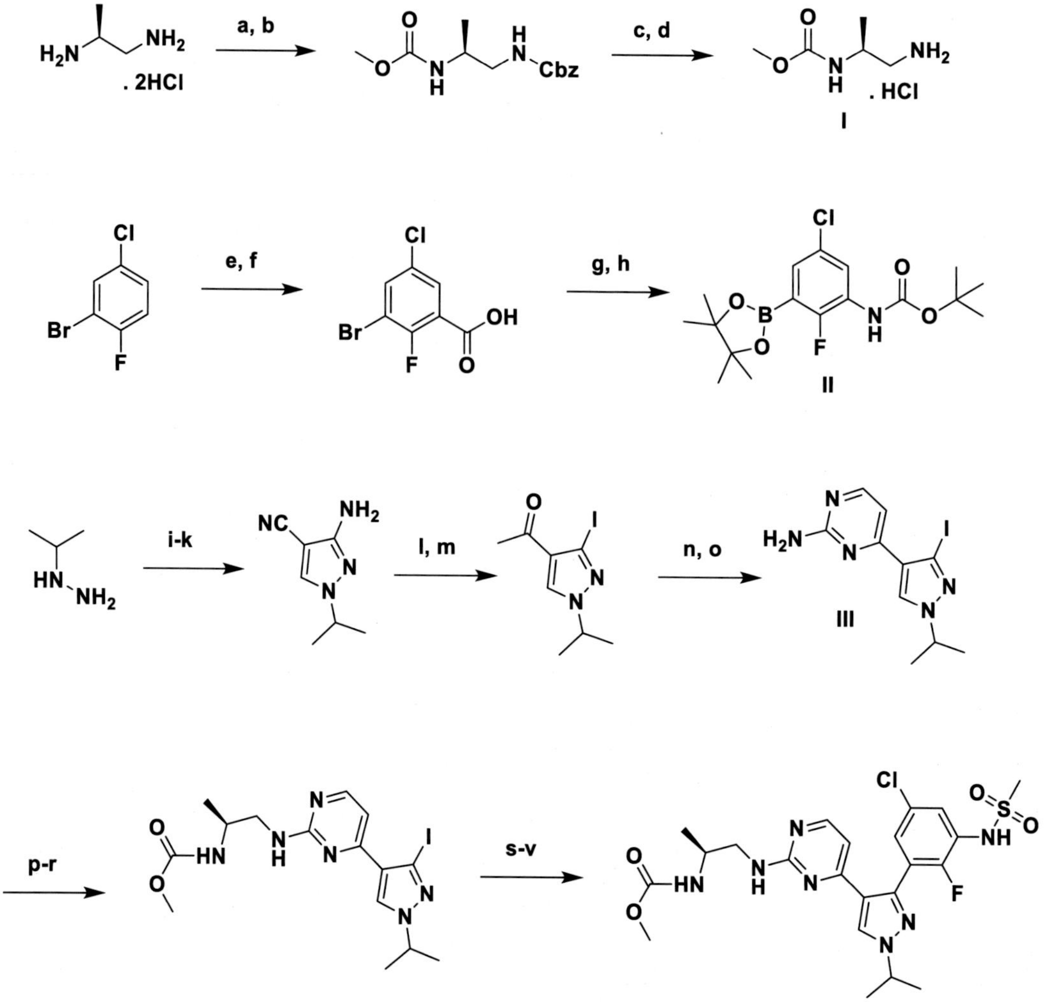

SCHEME 11.4 Synthesis of encorafenib. Reagents and conditions: (A) Benzyl chloroformate, K_2CO_3, DCM, 5°C, 3 h; then rt, o/n; (B) methyl chloroformate, Et_3N, DCM, 5°C; then rt, on; (C) H_2, Pd/C, MeOH, rt; (D) HCl, DCM, 0–5°C, 30 min; (E) TMP, N-butyllithium, THF, −75°C, 1.5 h; then 2-bromo-4-chloro- 1-fluorobenzene, −72°C, 1 h; then DMF, −70°C, 1 h; (F) $KMnO_4$, t-BuOH, H_2O, 30–60°C, 2.5 h; (G) diphenyl phosphoryl azide, Et_3N, t-BuOH, toluene, 75–84°C, 2.5 h; (H) B_2Pin_2, KOAc, toluene, $PdCl_2$(dppf), 108°C, 15 h; (I) benzaldehyde, NaOAc, EtOH, rt, 20 h; (J) (ethoxyethylidene)malononitrile, DMAP, EtOH, 50°C, 30 min; (K) HCl (12 N), MeOH, 63°C, 30 min; (L) MeLi·LiBr, cyclopentyl methyl ether, −10°C, 2.5 h; then 10°C, 1 h; (M) BF_3·OEt_2, isoamylnitrite, −20 to 10°C, 30 min; then I_2, KI, MeCN, rt, 30 min; (N) Bredereck's reagent, DMF, 120°C, 20 min; (O) guanidine carbonate, NMP, 130°C, 5 h; (P) $NaNO_2$, TFA, DCM, 27°C, 5 h; then K_2CO_3, H_2O; (Q) $POCl_3$, DIPEA, MeCN, DMF, 80°C, 3 h; (R) I, Na_2CO_3, DMSO, 90°C, 18 h; (S) II, Na_2CO_3, $PdCl_2$(dppf), toluene, H_2O, 80°C, 2 h; (T) HCl (12 N), toluene, rt,1 h; (U) MsCl, Et_3N, MeTHF, 0–20°C, 40 min; (V) NaOH, MeTHF, H_2O, 30 min; then HCl.

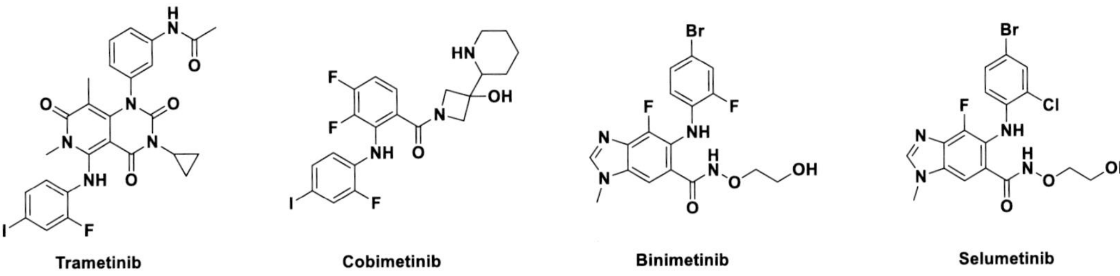

FIGURE 11.6 FDA-approved MEK inhibitors.

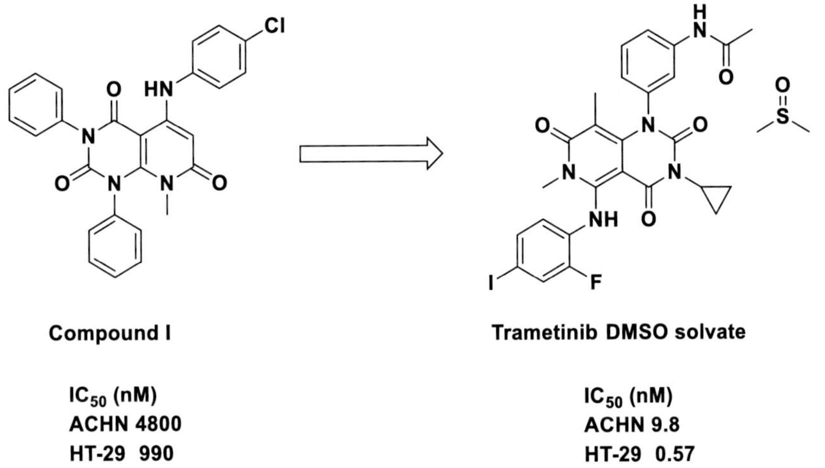

FIGURE 11.7 Development of trametinib from its lead I.

metastatic melanoma carrying BRAF$^{V600E/K}$ mutations. Being clinically efficacious with a favorable toxicity profile than monotherapy, trametinib in combination with dabrafenib was approved by the FDA for the therapy of melanoma overexpressing BRAF$^{V600E/K}$. The discovery of trametinib was a result of an extensive medicinal chemistry campaign, by Japan Tobacco, conducted on compound I (Fig. 11.7) guided by the growth inhibitory activity against ACHN and HT-29 cancer cell lines (Abe et al., 2011). Trametinib potently suppresses RAF-catalyzed MEK1 and MEK2 phosphorylation with nanomolar affinity in biochemical assays along with its ability to suppress the growth of different solid cancer cells harboring BRAF and KRAS mutants with nanomolar potency (Abe et al., 2011; Gilmartin et al., 2011).

Trametinib is classified as a type III allosteric MEK1/2 inhibitor since it binds to MEK1/2 kinases at a region that is close to the ATP-binding site. It forms a HB with a conserved b3-lysine in addition to multiple hydrophobic interactions with backbone residues within the aC-helix, the activation segment, and the b5 strand (Fig. 11.8A) (Roskoski, 2017). Such an allosteric binding mode of trametinib makes it unnecessary to compete with millimolar concentrations of cellular ATP, which the majority of FDA-approved competitive kinase inhibitors must do. Interestingly, it was recently found that trametinib directly engages the kinase

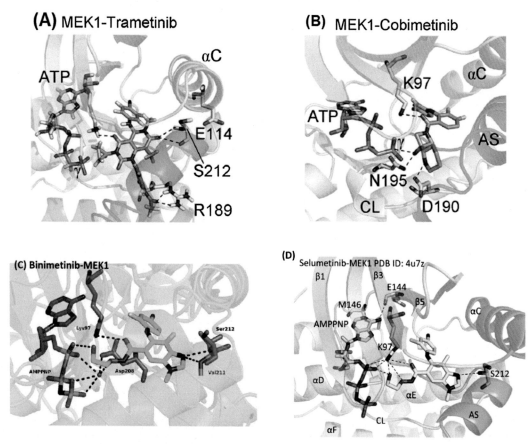

FIGURE 11.8   The binding mode of FDA-approved MEK inhibitors. (A) Trametinib complex with MEK1, (B) Cobimetinib bound to MEK1, (C) Structure of binimetinib in complex with BRAF:MEK1 kinases and AMP-PNP (PDB ID: 7M0U), and (D) Selumetinib complex with MEK1. Key H-bond interactions are depicted as black dashes. *A and B were reproduced from Ref. Roskoski (2017). with permission, and C and D were reproduced from Ref. Ayala-Aguilera et al. (2022); Roskoski (2021), respectively with permission.*

suppressor of RAS (KSR) at the MEK interface and binds KSR—MEK while disrupting the related RAF—MEK complex (Khan et al., 2020).

3.2.2 Cobimetinib

Cobimetinib (GDC-0973, XL518, Cotellic), a diphenylamine-based potent and selective MEK inhibitor, was approved by the FDA in 2015 to be clinically used in combination with vemurafenib for the treatment of BRAF (V600 E/K) mutant melanoma. The discovery story of cobimetinib commenced with the identification of PD0325901 as a highly potent MEK1 inhibitor (IC50 = 0.6 nM) with remarkable cellular potency against MDA-MB-231T breast cancer cells (IC50 = 0.9 nM), in which harbor both KRAS G13D and BRAF G464V mutations. Despite the elicited efficacy of PD0325901 against malignant tumors in preclinical models, it suffered from metabolic instability due to its carbamate ester. In addition, certain

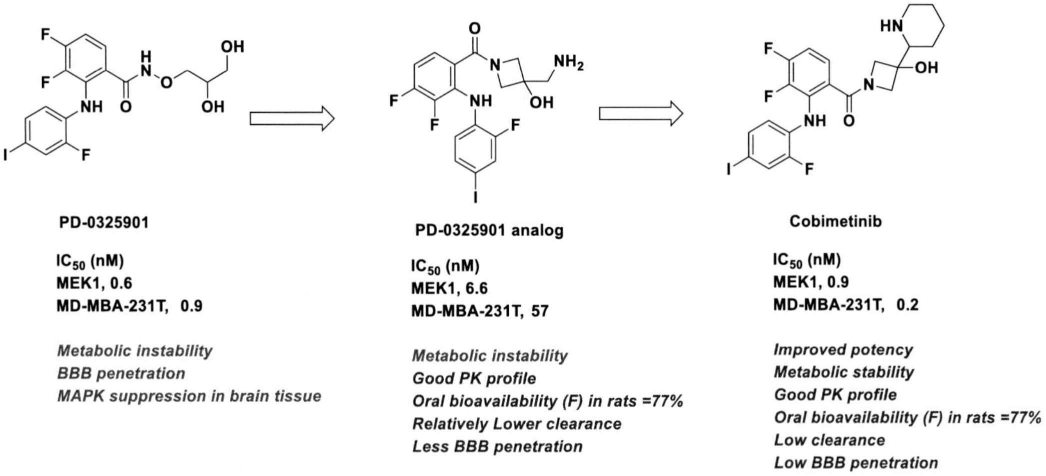

PD-0325901

IC$_{50}$ (nM)
MEK1, 0.6
MD-MBA-231T, 0.9

Metabolic instability
BBB penetration
MAPK suppression in brain tissue

PD-0325901 analog

IC$_{50}$ (nM)
MEK1, 6.6
MD-MBA-231T, 57

Metabolic instability
Good PK profile
Oral bioavailability (F) in rats =77%
Relatively Lower clearance
Less BBB penetration

Cobimetinib

IC$_{50}$ (nM)
MEK1, 0.9
MD-MBA-231T, 0.2

Improved potency
Metabolic stability
Good PK profile
Oral bioavailability (F) in rats =77%
Low clearance
Low BBB penetration

FIGURE 11.9   Development of cobimetinib from PD-0325901 and its analog.

neurological manifestations like ataxia and syncope were noticed in patients receiving PD-0325901, probably due to the BBB penetration and MAPK pathway knockout in brain tissue (Rice et al., 2012). A campaign of structural modifications based on PD-0325901 was investigated to improve its metabolic stability and safety profile as well as achieve a sustained duration of efficacy that enables once-daily dosing, which ultimately culminated in the development of cobimetinib. It displayed excellent pharmacokinetics in preclinical species, low BBB penetration, and a good safety profile tolerating dose increments. The azetidinyl carboxamide moiety in cobimetinib rendered the molecule metabolically stable (Fig. 11.9) (Rice et al., 2012). Administration of cobimetinib in combination with vemurafenib showed remarkable efficacy and tolerable safety profile with lower incidence of adverse events, including stomatitis, fatigue, arthralgia, and prolongation of the QT interval than those seen on monotherapy with vemurafenib (Keating, 2016).

Similar to trametinib, cobimetinib binds proximal to the ATP site of MEK1/2, therefore referred to as an allosteric type III inhibitor (Roskoski, 2018). Besides engaging in an H-bond with β3-Lys97, the cyclic constraint of the cobimetinib resides in the amide adjacent to the catalytic loop, allowing H-bonding between the azetidinyl moiety and Asp190, Asn195, and the γ-phosphoryl oxygen of ATP (Fig. 11.8B) (Rice et al., 2012). Such a highly complex network of interactions enabled cobimetinib to stabilize the inactive conformation of MEK1/2, leading to the misconfiguration of catalytic residues and consequently occlusion of the peptide–protein binding pocket (Roskoski, 2018).

3.2.3 Binimetinib

Binimetinib (MEK162, ARRY-438162, Mektovi) is an aniline-benzimidazole-based potent MEK1/2 inhibitor that received—in combination with encorafenib—approval by the FDA in 2018 for the treatment of melanoma patients carrying BRAFV600 E/K. Similar to trametinib and cobimetinib, binimetinib exhibits high selectivity toward MEK, with no significant inhibitory effect over other protein kinases up to 20 μM. Also, binimetinib inhibits both basal

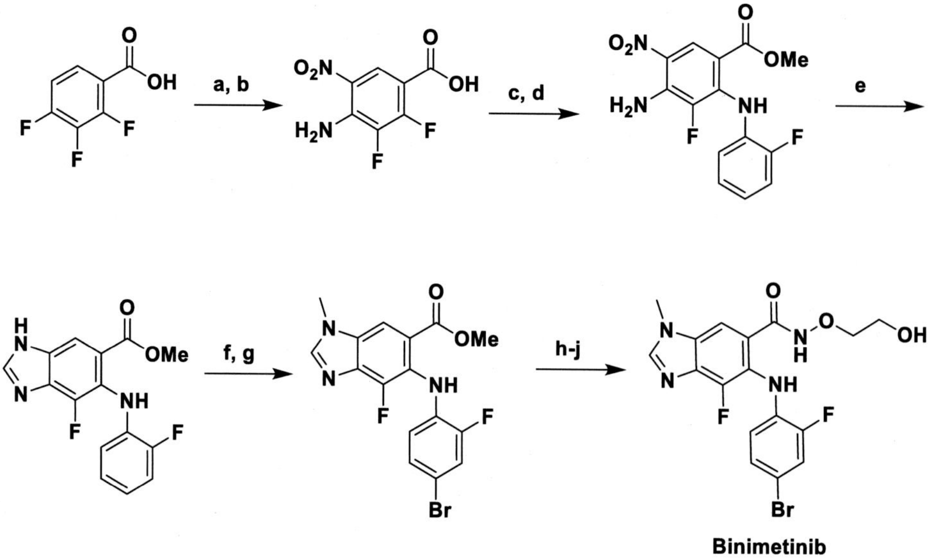

SCHEME 11.5 Synthesis of binimetinib. Reagents and conditions: (A) 2,3,4-trifluorobenzoic acid, H_2SO_4, conc. HNO_3, rt, 2.5 h; (B) NH_4OH, 0°C to rt, 2.5 h; then HCl, 0°C; (C) (diazomethyl)trimethylsilane, THF:MeOH (4:1), 0°C to rt, 0.5 h; then AcOH; (D) 2-fluorophenylamine, xylene, 140°C, 6 days; (E) formic acid, $Pd(OH)_2/C$, EtOH, 40°C, 2 h; then 95°C, o/n; (F) NBS, DMF, 30 min, rt; (G) iodomethane, K_2CO_3, DMF, 75°C, 1 h; (H) NaOH, THF:H_2O (2:1), rt, 2 h; (I) O-(2-ethenoxyethyl)-hydroxylamine, HOBt, EDCI, Et3N, DMF, rt, 48 h; (J) HCl, EtOH, 24 h.

and induced ERK phosphorylation—in two-digits nanomolar range—in BRAF mutant-depending cancer cells (Lee et al., 2010). Among MEK inhibitors, binimetinib is classified as a non-ATP-competitive type III inhibitor, where it forms H-bonds with Val211, Ser212, and Lys97, while the distal OH is engaged in an H-bond with adenylyl imidodiphosphate (AMPPNP). In addition, water-mediated H-bonds are established between binimetinib, AMP-PNP, and Asp208 (PDB ID: 7M0U) (Fig. 11.8C). The synthetic route for binimetinib includes 10 steps (Scheme 11.5) and commences with the nitration of 2,3,4-trifluorobenzoic acid at position 5, followed by substitution of p-fluorine with an amine group. Next is Fischer's esterification of the acid moiety, followed by SNAr of o-fluorine with 2-fluorophenylamine to generate the diarylamine core. Further, the nitro group is reduced by $Pd(OH)_2/C$ and treated with formic acid to construct the benzimidazole scaffold. Incorporation of bromine at the p-position of fluoroaniline was achieved by N-bromosuccinimide (NBS), followed by methylation of imidazole-NH, and then alkaline hydrolysis of the ester. The generated acid is then coupled with O-(2-ethenoxyethyl)-hydroxylamine to yield the required hydroxymate. Finally, acidic hydrolysis of the vinyl ether furnishes binimetinib.

3.2.4 Selumetinib

Selumetinib being closely related to binimetinib, selumetinib (AZD-6244, ARRY-142886, Koselugo) shares all structural features of binimetinib except that the bromine atom is replaced by chlorine. Selumetinib elicits potent inhibitory activity against MEK1/2 (IC50 = 8 nM) along with suppression of ERK phosphorylation and growth inhibitory activity against cancer cells harboring BRAF and RAS mutations (Markham & Keam, 2020). FDA approval was granted to selumetinib in 2020 for the treatment of type 1 neurofibromatosis (NF1) in pediatric patients with incurable plexiform neurofibromas (PNs). Transcription of the NF1 gene produces neurofibromin which stimulates the GTPase activity of Ras. However, the mutated gene product of NF1 is inactive, leading to dysregulation of MAPK signaling and uncontrolled growth of cells. The most prevalent side events associated with selumetinib therapy include gastrointestinal symptoms, creatine phosphokinase elevation, acneiform rash, and paronychia (Gross et al., 2020). Selumetinib is a type III allosteric inhibitor, binding adjacent to the ATP pocket of the inactive MEK1 (Chelix-out) -in a similar fashion to binimetinib- and a closed activation segment (pdb ID: 4u7z). The cocrystal structure of selumetinib in complex with MEK1 and AMPPNP revealed its engagement in crucial H-bonds with Lys97 and Ser212 of MEK1, and with AMPPNP via its hydroxyl group, in addition to various hydrophobic interactions with numerous residues located at different regions (Fig. 11.8D). Selumetinib is synthesized in a similar approach to that described earlier for binimetinib.

4. Mechanisms of resistance

Various mechanisms have been discovered and observed in either pre- or posttreatment with MAPK inhibitors. These mechanisms can be classified as either primary/intrinsic when there is no clinical value is accomplished, and secondary/acquired when it is observed following a clinical benefit.

4.1 Mechanisms of primary resistance

Many mechanisms are involved as primary reasons for MAPK-inhibitors' resistance. This kind of primary resistance is more common in some diseases, that need to be treated with MAPK inhibitors, like melanoma (Manzano et al., 2016). Up to 35% of melanoma cases show resistance after BRAF inhibition as a result of PTEN loss, which serves as a major regulator and suppressor of cancer via the PI3K pathway that plays the same role as the MAPK pathway (Paraiso et al., 2011; Xing et al., 2012). As a result of CD1 or CDK4 mutations, PTEN is lost, which develops resistance to BRAF inhibitors in melanoma cases (Smalley et al., 2008). Moreover, resistance to MAPK inhibitors especially BRAF inhibitors can arise as a result of several factors such as c-MET, that can activate tumor cell growth (Straussman et al., 2012). Generally, mutations to MAPK pathway proteins in many cases affect negatively on the binding of their inhibitors (Caunt et al., 2015; Kozar et al., 2019). One of the common examples of this primary resistance to MAPK inhibitors especially BRAF and KRAS inhibitors is the inactivation of NF1 due to its mutation. NF1 is a tumor suppressor present in around 14% of melanoma cases, and its deactivation leads to the reactivation of both PI3K/AKT/mTOR and MAPK pathways (Gibney & Smalley, 2013). These examples do not cover all the published reports, but they give an idea of the nature of this kind of primary resistance.

4.2 Mechanisms of secondary resistance

4.2.1 MAPK-pathway reactivation

The mechanisms of acquired resistance are related principally to the recurrence of the MAPK signaling pathway (>70%) (Manzano et al., 2016). For example, MEK-inhibitor treatment renders the inhibitors unable to bind to MEK protein (Caunt et al., 2015; Emery et al., 2009; Wagle et al., 2014). Similarly, amplification of BRAF was identified in more than 20% of melanoma cases following the treatment with BRAF inhibitors, Hence, BRAF protein will be amplified leading to the recurrence of the MAPK pathway. Some reports show that MAPK reactivation could be blocked with the grouping of BRAF-inhibitor and MEK-inhibitor (Poulikakos et al., 2011). Similarly, ERK2 overexpression was identified as a mechanism of resistance to ERK inhibitors. However, MEK inhibitors showed a superior therapeutic effect in these situations suggesting that ERK-inhibitor/MEK-inhibitor combination therapy may restrict this acquired resistance (Jaiswal et al., 2018). Some clinical trials show that both BRAF-inhibitors and MEK-inhibitor cause NRAS mutation, which activates transduction signals via CRAF. NRAS mutation affects MAPK reactivation and also the PI3K pathway representing the second most occurring mutation in melanoma (20%) (Ascierto et al., 2013; Heidorn et al., 2010). KRAS inhibitors also show acquired mutation, most notably at codons 12, 13, 61, 68, 95, and 96, which prevent the binding of KRAS inhibitors like adagrasib (Awad et al., 2021).

4.2.2 RTKS hyperactivation

One of the primary mechanisms responsible for acquired resistance to MAPK inhibitors is the activation of an alternative pathway through the hyperactivation of RTKs. Positioned upstream of MAPK, RTKs, when hyperactivated, instigate a signaling pathway that governs cellular proliferation, thereby contributing to adaptive resistance (Schlessinger, 2000). RTKs including EGFR, ERBB3, c-KIT, IGF-1R, and PDGFR can push cell signaling and boost cellular growth through a variety of signaling pathways (Duncan et al., 2012; Kauko et al., 2018; Nazarian et al., 2010). Upon the inhibition of MAPK with ERK 1/2, RTKs develop an adaptive response and are rapidly reactivated to compensate for this suppression (Arozarena & Wellbrock, 2017; Awad et al., 2021; Caunt et al., 2015; Villanueva et al., 2010).

4.2.3 Analogous signaling pathways (PI3K/STAT/Hippo) activation

Parallel mechanisms for cell proliferation and growth exist in addition to the MAPK pathway. The signaling pathways PI3K, STAT, and Hippo are among these (Balmanno et al., 2009; Dai et al., 2011; Lin et al., 2015). Cancer cells can switch to these mechanisms for the essential signals to drive growth when the MAPK pathway is blocked, leading to MAPK-inhibitor adaptive resistance. PI3K stands out as one of the key mechanisms for MAPK inhibition resistance. This route has already been recognized as a driving mechanism of carcinogenesis in a variety of malignancies, and it is a viable therapeutic target (Fruman & Rommel, 2014). Various reports demonstrated PI3K activation following the induction of MAPK inhibitor therapy, revealing how tumor cells respond (Irvine et al., 2018; Turke et al., 2012). Similarly, one study combining a STAT3 inhibitor with an MEK inhibitor (selumetinib) as an efficient protocol to overcome resistance in an astrocytoma xenograft model confirmed that the STAT pathway is another parallel possibility for the adaptive resistance to MAPK inhibitors (Bid et al., 2013). The Hippo pathway effector YAP1 has also been found to enhance the adaptive resistance to MEK inhibitors. A recent study showed that combining MEK inhibitors with YAP inhibitors can overcome the adaptive resistance in human NSCLC cells, resulting in tumor cell death (Lin et al., 2015).

4.2.4 Cellular transformation and transcriptional factors

4.2.4.1 MITF

Another potential resistance mechanism is tumor cells' capacity to switch phenotypic states and rewire the different metabolic pathways. It was observed that melanoma cells with elevated MITF expression had more "proliferative" profiles, whereas cells with truncated MITF expression had more "invasive" profiles. MITF plays a key role as a transcription factor to regulate the development of melanocytes and depending on its level, the sensitivity to MEK inhibitors can be discussed. Melanoma cell lines with a higher expression of MITF were more sensitive to MEK inhibition, whereas cell lines with low MITF were resistant (Kemper et al., 2014). The invasive phenotype that can be induced upon MAPK-inhibitor treatment was characterized by greater motility and migration, as well as a higher potential for metastatic spread (Zipser et al., 2011). The capacity of melanoma cells to flip between a proliferative and invasive cell type has been established, but a further sign of this ability seems to be the inductive resistance to MEK and/or BRAF inhibitors (Kozar et al., 2019). In a study of KRAS-mutant lung cancer cell lines, epithelial-mesenchymal transition (EMT) was linked to MEK treatment resistance. This behavior is comparable to melanoma phenotypic flipping as EMT has been shown to rewire cells in previous lung cancer investigations, leading to a distinct feedback mechanism (Kitai et al., 2016). After an MEK inhibitor, ERBB3 reactivated epithelial phenotypic cells, while fibroblast growth factor receptor 1 reactivated mesenchymal-like KRAS-mutant cells (FGFR1) (Kitai et al., 2016).

4.2.4.2 ZEB1 (zinc finger E-box binding homeobox 1)

ZEB1 is a critical transcription factor in EMT regulation side by side with microRNA-200 as shown in some models of KRAS mutated lung cancer. ZEB1 overexpression in cells resulted in MAPK-independent tumor development and greater resistance to MEK inhibitors because of EMT upregulation (Lee et al., 2010). High levels of ZEB1 can inhibit MAPK in epithelial cells of lung cancer by inhibiting interleukin (IL17TH), which is required for MAPK signaling. KRAS inhibitors have been found to cause two types of mutations: One within the drug-binding pocket, which prevents drug binding, and another at oncogenic hotspots, which causes decreased GTP hydrolysis (e.g., G13D and Q61R) or increased GDP-to-GTP nucleotide exchange (e.g., G13D, A59S, and A146P). As a result of these resistance mutations, the fraction of KRAS protein in the active GTP-bound form that does not bind to the medication is likely to grow (Awad et al., 2021; Lito et al., 2016).

5. Therapeutic strategies to overcome MAPK resistance

5.1 Combination therapy for targeting many proteins/pathways

Many of the causes of MAPK inhibitor resistance involve the activation of other parallel pathways: PI3K, AKT, mTOR, or Hippo pathways. Various reports have utilized the combination therapy blocking numerous routes at the same time to bypass these limitations. FDA has established that the combination therapy of both BRAF-inhibitors (e.g., encorafenib) and MEK-inhibitors (e.g., binimetinib) in mutant melanoma cases showed higher potency when compared to single treatments (Kakadia et al., 2018; Kozar et al., 2019). This combination can be considered the most common in all MAPK inhibitors that postpone the acquired resistance and enhance overall survival (Shirley, 2018).

5.1.1 Targeting parallel pathways (PI3K/AKT/mTOR/Hippo)

Preclinical data from research combining PI3K inhibitors or mTOR/PI3K dual inhibitors with MAPK inhibitors showed a promising preliminary effect on suppressing MAPK resistance (Arozarena & Wellbrock, 2017). In the same way, combining AKT/PI3K dual inhibitors with MAPK inhibitors switched the MAPK-acquired resistance leading finally to apoptosis of various BRAF inhibitor/MEK inhibitor-resistant melanoma cell lines (Atefi et al., 2011; Greger et al., 2012; Tsubaki et al., 2019). Various studies demonstrated the synergistic effect of PI3K inhibitors on MAPK inhibitors, which opened the gate for a lot of clinical trials of this promising combination on many cancer types. The results of these studies showed a higher value of the combinations compared to single therapy (Turke et al., 2012). However, many of these clinical trials have been terminated due to the toxic effects of long administration (Arend et al., 2020; Bardia et al., 2020; Bedard et al., 2015). The combination of both YAP inhibitors with MAPK inhibitors showed a promising result as well, in BRAF-mutant tumor cell lines (Lin et al., 2015).

5.1.2 Targeting RTKs

Hyperactivation of RTKs emerges as one of the major reasons behind MAPK resistance. Consequently, it is reasonable to start studying the effect of combination therapy with RTK inhibitors like EGFR, ERBB2, or FGFR1 inhibitors as a tactic for tackling MAPK inhibitors' resistance. Many studies reported the synergistic effect of such combinations (MAPK and RTK inhibitors) when taken together compared to the single MAPK-inhibitors therapy (Fernandez et al., 2019; Sun et al., 2014; Tan et al., 2013).

5.1.3 Targeting ZEB1 with MAPK

Previously, we showed that ZEB1 has a key role as a transcription factor in developing MAPK adaptive resistance, which is always linked with its high expression. Hence, the inhibition of ZEB1 either using mocetinostat or miR-200 can be an effective strategy to recover this kind of adaptive resistance to MAPK inhibitors. ZEB1 inhibitors showed a synergistic effect when combined with MAPK inhibitors in many cases especially those characterized by a high level of ZEB1 expression (Peng et al., 2019).

5.1.4 Targeting BCL-XL with MAPK

According to recent studies, combining BCL-XL with MEK inhibitors showed a better result on ovarian cancer xenograft models produced from patients, as well as lung and pancreatic tumor cell lines compared to single therapy (Iavarone et al., 2019; Tan et al., 2013). As previously mentioned, BCL-XL inhibits BIM, a critical proapoptotic protein, lowering the efficacy of MEK inhibitors and leading to adaptive resistance. Consequently,

BCL-XL has emerged as a therapeutic target for MAPK inhibitors, particularly MEK inhibitors, in combination therapy (Faber et al., 2014).

5.2 Single inhibitor to block multiple pathways

Some proteins (e.g., SHP-2, and SCHOC-2) can be considered as a bridge between MAPK and other signaling pathways making a single inhibitor work as a blocker for various signaling pathways (Ran et al., 2016). This feature can be utilized as a weapon against MAPK adaptive resistance mimicking the role of combination therapy. In numerous cancer models, inhibiting SHP-2 was able to prevent adaptive resistance by blocking ERK reactivation after MEK inhibition (Fedele et al., 2018). Also, the crucial role of SHOC-2 reduction, a key protein for RAF activation, was realized in sensitizing RAS-driven malignancies to MAPK-inhibitors similar to the role of SHP-2 with RTKs (Sulahian et al., 2019).

5.3 Combining immunotherapeutic agents with MAPK-inhibitors

MAPK-inhibitors such as trametinib show a positive effect on the tumor immune environment via T-cell infiltration. Trametinib at low doses reduced tumor burden through apoptosis and increased the number of tumor antigens available for T-cell identification. Some studies attenuate this effect for their inhibition of the defense mechanism of the tumor against T-cell response known as myeloid-derived suppressor cells (Lee et al., 2019). As a result, combining both immunotherapeutic agents side by side with MAPK inhibitors emerged as an effective tactic to tackle the adaptive resistance to MAPK inhibitors through their synergistic effect. In comparison with monotherapy, combining immunotherapeutic agents for instance (anti-PD-1), or (anti-PD-L1) with MEK inhibitors showed synergism and enhanced the outcome in vivo. Furthermore, in BRAF-mutant melanoma, a clinical trial combining BRAF inhibitors, MEK inhibitors, and anti-PD-1 revealed good patient objective response (Ribas et al., 2019) Table 11.1 shows the clinical trials of some different therapeutic combinations to stand against the MAPK.

6. The future of MAPK inhibitors therapeutics

Protein kinases are important regulatory proteins that use phosphorylation to control intracellular communication networks. They can be found in almost every biological activity. However, only a small percentage of the kinome has been successfully addressed with pharmaceutical therapy, and our knowledge of kinase biology is constantly growing. Many of the first kinase inhibitors were developed for use in oncology. Today, because of the widespread availability of kinase profiling services, there is a new trend aimed at utilizing kinases for therapeutic development outside of oncology. FDA approved Tofacitinib (Fig. 11.10), a Janus kinase (JAK) inhibitor, as the first nononcology kinase inhibitor for the treatment of rheumatoid arthritis (RA) in 2012. Additionally, the FDA has also launched Abrocitinib (Fig. 11.10) as a second JAK inhibitor for the treatment of atopic dermatitis (Bieber et al., 2021; Dhillon,

TABLE 11.1 The clinical trials of some different therapeutic combinations to stand against the MAPK resistance in different cancer types and at different levels of completion.

Drug	Combination drug	Drug target	Conditions	NCT number	Trial phase	Status
Trametinib (MEK inhibitor)	GSK2141795	Akt inhibitor	Melanoma	NCT01941927	2	Completed (Lin et al., 2015)
	Erlotinib	EGFR inhibitor	Lung adenocarcinoma	NCT03076164	2	Completed
	Dabrafenib	BRAF inhibitor	Stage III/IV melanoma	NCT04059224	2	Recruiting (Eng et al., 2019)
				NCT04666272		
	Durvalumab	(Anti-PD-L1)	Colorectal and colon cancer	NCT03428126	2	Active, not recruiting
	Nazartinib	EGFR inhibitor	Bronchial neoplasms	NCT03516214	1	Completed
	Pembrolizumab	(Anti-PD-L1)	NSCLC	NCT03299088	1	Active, not recruiting
	Ceritinib	ALK inhibitor	NSCLC	NCT03501368	1	Recruiting
	GSK2256098	FAK inhibitor	Pancreatic cancer	NCT02428270	2	Active, not recruiting
	Everolimus Lenvatinib	mTOR inhibitor RTK inhibitor	Solid tumor Hepatocellular carcinoma	NCT04803318	2	Recruiting
	Sorafenib	RTK inhibitor	Hepatocellular cancer	NCT02292173	1	Completed
Selumetinib (MEK inhibitor)	Sirolimus	mTOR inhibitor	Neurofibromatosis	NCT03433183	2	Recruiting
	Vistusertib	mTOR inhibitor	Breast and lung cancer	NCT02583542	1/2	Active, not recruiting
	Osimertinib	EGFR inhibitor	NSCLC	NCT03392246	2	Recruiting
	Pembrolizumab	(Anti-PD-L1)	Metastatic solid tumors	NCT03833427	1	Active, not recruiting
	Durvalumab Tremelimumab	(Anti-PD-L1) Anti-CTLA-4	Stage IV NSCLC	NCT03581487	1/2	Recruiting
	Temsirolimus	mTOR inhibitor	S-III soft tissue sarcoma	NCT01206140	2	Completed
Cobimetinib (MEK inhibitor)	Vemurafenib	BRAF inhibitor	Malignant melanoma	NCT02537600	2	Completed (Ascierto et al., 2016)
			Melanoma	NCT03139513	2	Completed

6. The future of MAPK inhibitors therapeutics

			NCT number	Phase	Status
Atezolizumab	(Anti-PD-L1)	Colorectal cancer	NCT02788279	3	Completed(Eng et al., 2019)
MEHD7945A	EGFR/HER3	Neoplasms	NCT01986166	1	Completed
Venetoclax Atezolizumab	BCL-2 (Anti-PD-L1)	Multiple myeloma	NCT03312530	1/2	Completed
Bevacizumab Atezolizumab	VEGF inhibitor (Anti-PD-L1)	Colorectal cancer	NCT02876224	1	Completed
Ipatasertib	Akt inhibitor	Neoplasms	NCT01562275	1	Completed
GDC-0994	ERK-inhibitor	NSCLC	NCT02457793	1	Completed
Mirdametinib (MEK inhibitor) Fulvestrant	AF2 inhibitor	Breast cancer	NCT05054374	1/2	Recruiting
Lifirafenib	BRAF/EGFR	Solid tumors, adult	NCT03905148	1/2	Recruiting
Binimetinib (MEK inhibitor) Futibatinib	FGFR1-4	Solid tumors/NSCLC	NCT04965818	1/2	Recruiting
Palbociclib	Anti-CDK4/6	Lung cancer	NCT03170206	1/2	Recruiting
Pexidartinib	CSF1R inhibitor	Gastrointestinal stromal tumor (GIST)	NCT03158103		Completed
Nivolumab Ipilimumab	(Anti-PD-L1) CTLA-4 inhibitor	(MSS) Metastatic colorectal cancer with RAS mutation	NCT03271047	2	Completed
Alpelisib	PI3K inhibitor	AML/solid tumors	NCT01449058	1	Completed
Ribociclib	Anti-CDK4/6	NRAS mutant melanoma	NCT01781572	1/2	Completed
Pimasertib (MEK inhibitor) Temsirolimus	mTOR inhibitor	Advanced solid tumor	NCT01378377	1	Terminated due to toxicity of the combination
Gemcitabine		Pancreatic adenocarcinoma	NCT01016483	2	Completed (Van Cutsem et al., 2018)
SAR245409	(PI3K and mTOR inhibitor)	Solid tumors Breast cancer	NCT01390818	1	Completed
M7824	(Anti-PD-L1)	Stage IV breast cancer	NCT04789668	1/2	Recruiting
SAR405838	MDM2 inhibitor	Neoplasm malignant	NCT01985191	1	Completed

(Continued)

TABLE 11.1 The clinical trials of some different therapeutic combinations to stand against the MAPK resistance in different cancer types and at different levels of completion.—cont'd

Drug	Combination drug	Drug target	Conditions	NCT number	Trial phase	Status
Dabrafenib (BRAF inhibitor)	Trametinib Ipilimumab	MEK-inhibitor CTLA-4 inhibitor	Solid tumors	NCT01767454	1	Completed
	Pazopanib	VEGFR/PDGFR	Adult solid tumors	NCT01713972	1	Completed
	Vemurafenib Trametinib	BRAF inhibitor MEK-inhibitor	Melanoma	NCT01597908	3	Completed
	Midazolam	GABA	Solid tumors	NCT00880321	1	Completed
Temuterkib (BRAF inhibitor)	Abemaciclib	CDK inhibitor	NSCLC	NCT04956640	1	Recruiting
	Erlotinib	EGFR inhibitor	Colorectal neoplasms			
	Sintilimab LY3295668 Cetuximab LY3537982	(Anti-PD-L1) Aurora A EGFR inhibitor KRAS-G12C inhibitor				
Belvarafenib (BRAF inhibitor)	Cobimetinib Atezolizumab	MEK-inhibitor (Anti-PD-L1)	Melanoma	NCT04835805	1	Recruiting
	Entrectinib Alectinib Atezolizumab Ipatasertib Pralsetinib Inavolisib Idasanutlin Trastuzumab	RTK inhibitor ALK inhibitor (Anti-PD-L1) Akt inhibitor RET inhibitor PI3Kα inhibitor MDM2 inhibitor HER2 inhibitor	Solid tumors	NCT04589845	2	Recruiting
	Cetuximab Cobimetinib	EGFR inhibitor MEK-inhibitor	Advanced solid tumor	NCT03284502	1	Recruiting
MK-8353 (ERK inhibitor)	Selumetinib	MEK-inhibitor	Solid tumors	NCT03745989	1	Completed
	Pembrolizumab (Anti-PD-L1)		Colorectal cancer	NCT02972034	1	Active, not recruiting

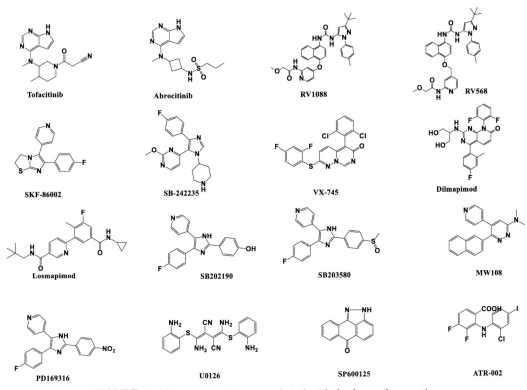

FIGURE 11.10 MAPK inhibitors in clinical trials for future therapeutics.

2017). The next section will focus on MAPK inhibitor therapeutic research and development, as well as pharmacological activity outside of oncology.

There are numerous protein kinases are implicated in signaling pathways that tether in-flammatory mediators to airway hypercontractility, hypersecretion of mucus, and airway remodeling, all of which contribute to the devastating lung function seen in chronic pulmo-nary diseases (COPD) (Kropski et al., 2018). One of these kinases is MAPK, which promotes cell proliferation and consequent airway remodeling in asthmatic airway smooth muscle cells. On one hand, targeted suppression of the proinflammatory p38 MAP kinase could help patients with COPD avoid the side effects of p38 inhibitors. Knobloch et al. investigated a narrow-spectrum protein kinase inhibitor, RV1088 (Fig. 11.10), that inhibits p38 MAPK, the c-Src, and JAK tyrosine kinases to attenuate inflammatory signals (Knobloch et al., 2018). The efficacy and safety of another narrow-spectrum protein kinase (RV568) (Fig. 11.10) that inhibit both p38 MAPK and c-Src have yet to be published in phase II clinical trial for the treatment of moderate to severe COPD. On another hand, the widespread roles of protein ki-nases in various cells have motivated innovative techniques to administer inhibitors via inha-lation, reducing systemic off-target effects when the medications are given orally. Using this approach, p38 MAP kinase inhibitors that prevent proinflammatory signals from causing tis-sue damage and remodeling but maintain beneficial antiinflammatory signals are currently being developed (Defnet et al., 2020).

Understanding the role of p38 MAPK in signal transduction and the control of a variety of cellular responses has been made easier by the introduction of inhibitors that are both potent and selective. SKF-86002 (Fig. 11.10), the pyridinyl imidazole class of compounds, was the first known molecular target of the human p38 MAPK which inhibits the biosynthesis of inflammatory cytokines such as interleukin-1 (IL-1) and tumor-necrosis factor (TNF) in human monocytes stimulated with LPS. The production of IL-1, TNF, and other cytokines has been demonstrated to be inhibited by several p38 MAPK inhibitors (Lee et al., 1994). Several of the more promising drugs have recently entered human clinical trials, demonstrating favorable pharmacokinetic and pharmacodynamic features. P38 MAPK inhibitors are expected to be effective in arthritic and inflammatory illnesses, and some drugs (SB-242235, VX-745) (Fig. 11.10) have already completed Phase II and III trials. Clinical studies have been halted on many occasions due to safety concerns (Cirillo et al., 2005; Lee et al., 1994). It is believed that employing p38 MAPK inhibitors in illnesses where inflammatory cytokines are high could be helpful because they restrict the manufacture and impact of inflammatory cytokines. Patients with inflammatory bowel illness have also demonstrated increased p38 MAPK activation (Kumar et al., 1999).

Under certain pain situations, p38 MAPK can be activated in neurons and glia, contributing to the onset and/or maintenance of pain. Although clinical trials targeting the p38 MAPK pathway do not appear to provide us with evidence for treating pain in patients, p38 MAPK plays a crucial role in the control of pain in a number of animal models, and a p38 MAPK inhibitor shows antinoceptive effects. SCIO-469, a selective p38 MAPK inhibitor, was demonstrated to have an antinociceptive impact in patients with acute postsurgical tooth pain in an early clinical trial (Peng et al., 2019). In a placebo-controlled cross-over experiment, the p38 MAPK kinase inhibitor dilmapimod (Fig. 11.10) was reported to lower the average daily pain score in those with neuropathic pain following nerve injury (Anand et al., 2011). Losmapimod (Fig. 11.10), a p38/MAPK inhibitor, was used to treat a group of individuals with persistent pain owing to lumbosacral radiculopathy, but it failed to show any analgesic efficacy. Clinical investigations are yet insufficient to provide a clearer picture (Ostenfeld et al., 2015). As a result, more research will be required to identify the specifics of p38 MAPK's upstream and downstream pathways.

There is some evidence that p38 MAPK has a role in Alzheimer's disease (AD). Several studies have suggested that p38 MAPK plays a significant role in vascular injury in rabbits and ischemia-reperfusion injury in the liver and lungs of rats. Amyloid beta (Aβ) toxicity can be induced by activating MAPK, which increases RAGE expression, tau hyperphosphorylation, and apoptosis, all of which contribute to AD pathogenesis. NF−B activation, glutamate excitotoxicity, and impairment of synaptic plasticity are additional consequences that all qualify the p38 MAPK as a possible target to end the vicious toxicity loop. The effectiveness of p38 MAPK inhibitors in treating AD has been recently the subject of numerous in vivo and in vitro studies (Ostenfeld et al., 2015). SB202190 and SB203580 (Fig. 11.10), two pyridinyl imidazole compounds, have exhibited promising antiapoptotic properties in vivo (Fernandez et al., 2019; Hensley et al., 1999; Kumar et al., 1999). In animal experiments, MW108 (Fig. 11.10) reduces p38 activation and can delay cognitive deterioration (Maphis et al., 2016). In vivo, the antiinflammatory, antioxidative, and antiapoptotic properties of PD169316 (Fig. 11.10) improved spatial memory (Kheiri et al., 2019). Natural substances from Camellia sinensis (green tea), olive oil polyphenols, propolis pinocembrin, and periwinkle extract have demonstrated strong antiapoptotic effects, which are mediated by p38 MAPK inhibition. These therapeutic targets are rarely used because of adverse effects on the central nervous system or cross-reactivity with other kinases, suggesting poor effectiveness in clinical research (Kheiri et al., 2019).

Noncardiovascular and nonrespiratory indications have had less good data available in the public domain to date. However, published phase I/II data on the impact of p38 MAPK inhibition on biomarkers, safety, tolerability, and pharmacokinetics/pharmacodynamics in cardiovascular disease have been promising so far. Only outcome-driven phase III trials will be able to assess if the therapeutic potential of p38 MAPK inhibition in cardiovascular disease can be translated into secure, efficient clinical benefits for patients beyond what is now available (Fisk et al., 2014).

Some DNA and RNA viruses were discovered to activate the MAPK cascade in infected cells in the late 1990s (Cargnello & Roux, 2011). Inhibiting the RAF/MEK/ERK signaling pathway, which appears to be significant for virus production and ribonucleoprotein (RNP) released from the nucleus during the viral life cycle, inhibited Influenza A virus IAV proliferation, according to Stephan Ludwig and colleagues. The same group demonstrated that U0126 (Fig. 11.10) as MEK1/2 inhibitor exhibited promising antiviral activity against IAV, IBV, H1N1, and astrovirus (Droebner et al., 2011). Recently, SB203580 (Fig. 11.10), a JNK-1 inhibitor, has been reported, as a possible therapeutic solution for Japanese encephalitis virus infection (Kindrachuk et al., 2015). Kinome analysis has also confirmed the pivotal role of the MAPK pathway in the infection by Middle East respiratory syndrome coronavirus (MERS-CoV). At micromolar concentration, both SB203580 and U0126 can prevent infection by (MERS-CoV) at 45% and 51%, respectively. Importantly, the authorized MAPK pathway inhibitors selumetinib and trametinib showed remarkable inhibitory effects (>95%), indicating that repurposing existing drugs to treat MERS-CoV infection could be a realistic tactic (Droebner et al., 2011; Kindrachuk et al., 2015). Additionally, compound ATR-002 was discovered to have broad antiviral efficacy against multiple influenza virus strains in both a mouse model and cell culture. It has already completed a Phase I clinical trial with healthy volunteers. In particular, Atriva Therapeutics is currently conducting a randomized, double-blind Phase II trial to assess ATR-002 (Fig. 11.10) as a treatment for COVID-19 (http://www.clinicaltrials.gov/).

7. Summary and future outlook

Understanding the behavior of MAPK in signal transduction and the regulation of a variety of cellular processes has improved with the introduction of selective and potent MAPK inhibitors. Active MAPKs cause downstream proteins to be activated, which amplifies vital molecules (mainly transcription factors) involved in critical biological processes including metabolism, motility, survival, mitosis, differentiation, and apoptosis. MAPK inhibitors might succeed in the management of various diseases besides cancer such as COPD, rheumatic arthritis, inflammatory diseases, cardiovascular diseases, Alzheimer's, and viral infection, and some of the drug-like molecules have entered Phase II and III trials. However, clinical studies have been halted on many occasions due to safety concerns. Cross-reactivities against other kinases or cellular signaling molecules as a result of ATP competition may be one of the underlying causes of these adverse effects. In this situation, novel inhibitors with a higher selectivity profile that are not ATP-competitive and do not target other kinases may be the destination. Allosteric inhibition, which involves binding to a pocket that does not overlap with the highly conserved ATP-binding site, is gaining traction as a new way to study the kinome, with the potential to broaden the therapeutic application profiles of MAPK inhibitors. The discovery of BRAF and MEK allosteric inhibitors for metastatic melanoma with the ^{V600E}-BRAF mutation marked a significant advancement in the treatment of this lethal disease. Unfortunately, within months, the majority of patients relapse and become refractory to further treatment. Fortunately, combining anti-BRAF/MEK targeted therapy has resulted in significant increases in melanoma responses when compared to the two modalities separately. Patient's prognosis and survival are being improved in ongoing clinical trials combining MAPK-pathway inhibitors with immunotherapies and other targeted medicines. Moreover, the ubiquitous nature of protein kinases in various cell types has motivated innovative techniques to administer inhibitors via inhalation, reducing systemic off-target effects when the medications are given orally. The success of MAPK kinase inhibitors might be enhanced by delivery techniques that minimize off-target effects.

References

Abe, H., Kikuchi, S., Hayakawa, K., Iida, T., Nagahashi, N., Maeda, K., Sakamoto, J., Matsumoto, M., Miura, T., Matsumura, K., Seki, N., Inaba, T., Kawasaki, H., Yamaguchi, T., Kakefuda, R., Nanayama, T., Kurachi, H., Hori, Y., Yoshida, T., … Laquerre, S. (2011). Discovery of a highly potent and selective MEK inhibitor: GSK1120212 (JTP-74057 DMSO solvate). *ACS Medicinal Chemistry Letters, 2*(4), 320–324. https://doi.org/10.1021/ml200004g

Anand, P., Shenoy, R., Palmer, J. E., Baines, A. J., Lai, R. Y. K., Robertson, J., Bird, N., Ostenfeld, T., & Chizh, B. A. (2011). Clinical trial of the P38 MAP kinase inhibitor dilmapimod in neuropathic pain following nerve injury. *European Journal of Pain, 15*(10), 1040–1048. https://doi.org/10.1016/j.ejpain.2011.04.005

Arend, R. C., Davis, A. M., Chimiczewski, P., O'Malley, D. M., Provencher, D., Vergote, I., Ghamande, S., & Michael, J. (2020). Emr 20006-012: A phase II randomized double-blind placebo controlled trial comparing the combination of pimasertib (MEK inhibitor) with SAR245409 (PI3K inhibitor) to pimasertib alone in patients with previously treated unresectable borderline or low grade ovarian cancer. *Gynecologic Oncology, 156*(2), 301–307. https://doi.org/10.1016/j.ygyno.2019.12.002

Arozarena, I., & Wellbrock, C. (2017). Overcoming resistance to BRAF inhibitors. *Annals of Translational Medicine, 5*(19), 387. https://doi.org/10.21037/atm.2017.06.09

Ascierto, P. A., McArthur, G. A., Dréno, B., Atkinson, V., Liszkay, G., Di Giacomo, A. M., Mandalà, M., Demidov, L., Stroyakovskiy, D., Thomas, L., de la Cruz-Merino, L., Dutriaux, C., Garbe, C., Yan, Y., Wongchenko, M., Chang, I., Hsu, J. J., Koralek, D. O., Rooney, I., Ribas, A., & Larkin, J. (2016). Cobimetinib combined with vemurafenib in advanced BRAFV600-mutant melanoma (CoBRIM): Updated efficacy results from a randomised, double-blind, phase 3 trial. *The Lancet Oncology, 17*(9), 1248–1260. https://doi.org/10.1016/S1470-2045(16)30122-X

Ascierto, P. A., Schadendorf, D., Berking, C., Agarwala, S. S., van Herpen, C. M. L., Queirolo, P., Blank, C. U., Hauschild, A., Beck, T., St-Pierre, A., Niazi, F., Wandel, S., Peters, M., Zubel, A., & Dummer, R. (2013). MEK162 for patients with advanced melanoma harbouring NRAS or Val600 BRAF mutations: A non-randomised, open-label phase 2 study. *The Lancet Oncology, 14*(3), 249–256. https://doi.org/10.1016/S1470-2045(13)70024-X

Atefi, M., von Euw, E., Attar, N., Ng, C., Chu, C., Guo, D., Nazarian, R., Chmielowski, B., Glaspy, J., Comin-Anduix, B., Mischel, P., Lo, R., & Ribas, A. (2011). Reversing melanoma cross-resistance to BRAF and MEK inhibitors by co-targeting the AKT/MTOR pathway. *PLoS One, 6*(12). https://doi.org/10.1371/journal.pone.0028973

Awad, M., Liu, S., Arbour, K., Zhu, V., Johnson, M., Heist, R., Patil, T., Riely, G., Jacobson, J., Dilly, J., Yang, X., Persky, N., Root, D., Sholl, L., Lee, L., Garg, K., Li, M., Engstrom, L., Waters, L., … Aguirre, A. (2021). Abstract

LB002: Mechanisms of acquired resistance to KRAS G12C inhibition in cancer. *Cancer Research, 81*, 81. https://doi.org/10.1158/1538-7445.am2021-lb002

Ayala-Aguilera, C. C., Valero, T., Lorente-Macías, Á., Baillache, D. J., Stephen, C., & Unciti-Broceta, A. (2022). Small molecule kinase inhibitor drugs (1995–2021): Medical indication, pharmacology, and synthesis. *Journal of Medicinal Chemistry*, 1047–1131. https://doi.org/10.1021/acs.jmedchem.1c00963

Babcock, H. P., Moffitt, J. R., Cao, Y., & Zhuang, X. (2013). Fast compressed sensing analysis for super-resolution imaging using L1-homotopy. *Proceedings of National Acadamic Science United States of America Optics Express Review*, (20), 28583–28596. Article 10921.

Balmanno, K., Chell, S. D., Gillings, A. S., Hayat, S., & Cook, S. J. (2009). Intrinsic resistance to the MEK1/2 inhibitor AZD6244 (ARRY-142886) is associated with weak ERK1/2 signalling and/or strong PI3K signalling in colorectal cancer cell lines. *International Journal of Cancer, 125*(10), 2332–2341. https://doi.org/10.1002/ijc.24604

Bardia, A., Gounder, M., Rodon, J., Filip, J., Lolkema, M. P., Stephenson, J. J., Bedard, P. L., Schuler, M., Sessa, C., LoRusso, P., Thomas, M., Maacke, H., Evans, H., Sun, Y., & Tan, D. (2020). Phase Ib study of combination therapy with MEK inhibitor binimetinib and phosphatidylinositol 3-kinase inhibitor Buparlisib in patients with advanced solid tumors with RAS/RAF alterations. *The Oncologist, 25*(1), e160–e169. https://doi.org/10.1634/theoncologist.2019-0297

Bedard, P. L., Tabernero, J., Filip, J., Wainberg, Z. A., Paz-Ares, L., Vansteenkiste, J., Van Cutsem, E., Pérez-García, J., Stathis, A., Britten, C., Le, N., Carter, K., Demanse, D., Csonka, D., Peters, M., Zubel, A., Nauwelaerts, H., & Sessa, C. (2015). A phase Ib dose-escalation study of the oral pan-PI3K inhibitor buparlisib (BKM120) in combination with the oral MEK1/2 inhibitor trametinib (GSK1120212) in patients with selected advanced solid tumors. *Clinical Cancer Research, 21*(4), 730–738. https://doi.org/10.1158/1078-0432.CCR-14-1814

Bid, H. K., Kibler, A., Phelps, D. A., Manap, S., Xiao, L., Lin, J., Capper, D., Oswald, D., Geier, B., DeWire, M., Smith, P., Kurmasheva, R., Mo, X., Fernandez, S., & Houghton, P. (2013). Development, characterization, and reversal of acquired resistance to the MEK1 inhibitor selumetinib (AZD6244) in an in vivo model of childhood astrocytoma. *Clinical Cancer Research, 19*(24), 6716–6729. https://doi.org/10.1158/1078-0432.CCR-13-0842

Bieber, T., Simpson, E. L., Silverberg, J. I., Thaçi, D., Paul, C., Pink, A. E., Kataoka, Y., Chu, C., DiBonaventura, M., Rojo, R., Antinew, J., Ionita, I., Sinclair, R., Forman, S., Zdybski, J., Biswas, P., Malhotra, B., Zhang, F., & Valdez, H. (2021). Abrocitinib versus placebo or dupilumab for atopic dermatitis. *New England Journal of Medicine, 384*(12), 1101–1112. https://doi.org/10.1056/nejmoa2019380

Bollag, G., Tsai, J., Zhang, J., Zhang, C., Ibrahim, P., Keith, N., & Hirth, P. (2012). Vemurafenib: The first drug approved for BRAF-mutant cancer. *Nature Reviews Drug Discovery*, 873–886. https://doi.org/10.1038/nrd3847

Braicu, C., Buse, M., Busuioc, C., Drula, R., Gulei, D., Raduly, L., Rusu, A., Irimie, A., Atanasov, A., Slaby, O., Ionescu, C., & Berindan-Neagoe, I. (2019). A comprehensive review on MAPK: A promising therapeutic target in cancer. *Cancers, 11*, 1618. https://doi.org/10.3390/cancers11101618

Cargnello, M., & Roux, P. P. (2011). Activation and function of the MAPKs and their substrates, the MAPK-activated protein kinases. *Microbiology and Molecular Biology Reviews, 75*(1), 50–83. https://doi.org/10.1128/mmbr.00031-10

Carlomagno, F., Suresh, A., Guida, T., Salvatore, G., Troncone, G., Wilhelm, S. M., & Santoro, M. (2006). BAY 43-9006 inhibition of oncogenic RET mutants. *Journal of the National Cancer Institute, 98*(5), 326–334. https://doi.org/10.1093/jnci/djj069

Caunt, C. J., Sale, M. J., Smith, P. D., & Cook, S. J. (2015). MEK1 and MEK2 inhibitors and cancer therapy: The long and winding road. *Nature Reviews Cancer*, 577–592. https://doi.org/10.1038/nrc4000

Chambard, J. C., Renaud, L., Pouysségur, J., & Lenormand, P. (2007). ERK implication in cell cycle regulation. *Biochimica et Biophysica Acta - Molecular Cell Research*, 1299–1310. https://doi.org/10.1016/j.bbamcr.2006.11.010

Cheng, Y., & Tian, H. (2017). Current development status of MEK inhibitors. *Molecules, 22*(10), 1551. https://doi.org/10.3390/molecules22101551

Cirillo, P., Pargellis, C., & Regan, J. (2005). The non-diaryl heterocycle classes of P38 MAP kinase inhibitors. *Current Topics in Medicinal Chemistry, 2*(9), 1021–1035. https://doi.org/10.2174/1568026023393390

Cosgrove, B. D., Gilbert, P. M., Porpiglia, E., Mourkioti, F., Lee, S. P., Corbel, S. Y., Llewellyn, M. E., Delp, S. L., & Blau, H. M. (2014). Rejuvenation of the muscle stem cell population restores strength to injured aged muscles. *Nature Medicine, 20*(3), 255–264. https://doi.org/10.1038/nm.3464

Coulombe, P., & Meloche, S. (2007). Atypical mitogen-activated protein kinases: Structure, regulation and functions. *Biochimica et Biophysica Acta - Molecular Cell Research*, 1376–1387. https://doi.org/10.1016/j.bbamcr.2006.11.001

Dai, B., Meng, J., Peyton, M., Girard, L., Bornmann, W. G., Lin, J., Minna, J. D., Fang, B., & Roth, J. A. (2011). STAT3 mediates resistance to MEK inhibitor through microRNA MiR-17. *Cancer Research, 71*(10), 3658–3668. https://doi.org/10.1158/0008-5472.CAN-10-3647

Defnet, A. E., Hasday, J. D., & Paul, S. (2020). Kinase inhibitors in the treatment of Obstructive pulmonary diseases. *Current Opinion in Pharmacology*, 11–18. https://doi.org/10.1016/j.coph.2020.03.005

Dhillon, S. (2017). Tofacitinib: A review in rheumatoid arthritis. *Drugs, 77*(18), 1987–2001. https://doi.org/10.1007/s40265-017-0835-9

Ding, H. X., Leverett, C. A., Kyne, R. E., Liu, K. K. C., Fink, S. J., Flick, A. C., & O'Donnell, C. J. (2015). Synthetic approaches to the 2013 new drugs. *Bioorganic and Medicinal Chemistry*, 1895–1922. https://doi.org/10.1016/j.bmc.2015.02.056

Droebner, K., Pleschka, S., Ludwig, S., & Oliver, P. (2011). Antiviral activity of the MEK-inhibitor U0126 against pandemic H1N1v and highly pathogenic avian influenza virus in vitro and in vivo. *Antiviral Research, 92*(2), 195–203. https://doi.org/10.1016/j.antiviral.2011.08.002

Dudley, D. T., Pang, L., Decker, S. J., Bridges, A. J., & Saltiel, A. R. (1995). A synthetic inhibitor of the mitogen-activated protein kinase cascade. *Proceedings of the National Academy of Sciences of the United States of America, 92*(17), 7686–7694. https://doi.org/10.1073/pnas.92.17.7686

Duncan, J. S., Whittle, M. C., Nakamura, K., Abell, A. N., Midland, A. A., Zawistowski, J. S., Johnson, N. L., Granger, D., Jordan, N., Darr, D., Usary, J., Kuan, P., Smalley, D., Major, B., He, X., Hoadley, K., Zhou, B., Sharpless, N., Perou, C., … Johnson, G. (2012). Dynamic Reprogramming of the kinome in response to targeted MEK inhibition in triple-negative breast cancer. *Cell, 149*(2), 307–321. https://doi.org/10.1016/j.cell.2012.02.053

Dusik, V., Senthilan, P. R., Mentzel, B., Hartlieb, H., Wülbeck, C., Yoshii, T., Raabe, T., & Helfrich-Förster, C. (2014). The MAP kinase P38 is part of drosophila melanogaster's circadian clock. *PLoS Genetics, 10*(8), e1004565. https://doi.org/10.1371/journal.pgen.1004565

Emery, C. M., Vijayendran, K. G., Zipser, M. C., Sawyer, A. M., Niu, L., Kim, J. J., Hatton, C., Chopra, R., Oberholzer, P., Karpova, M., MacConaill, L., Zhang, J., Gray, N., Sellers, W., Dummer, R., & Garraway, L. (2009). MEK1 mutations confer resistance to MEK and B-RAF inhibition. *Proceedings of the National Academy of Sciences of the United States of America, 106*(48), 20411–20416. https://doi.org/10.1073/pnas.0905833106

Eng, C., Kim, T. W., Bendell, J., Argilés, G., Tebbutt, N. C., Di Bartolomeo, M., Falcone, A., Fakih, M., Kozloff, M., Segal, N., Sobrero, A., Yan, Y., Chang, I., Uyei, A., Roberts, L., & Ciardiello, F. (2019). Atezolizumab with or without cobimetinib versus regorafenib in previously treated metastatic colorectal cancer (IMblaze370): A multicentre, open-label, phase 3, randomised, controlled trial. *The Lancet Oncology, 20*(6), 849–861. https://doi.org/10.1016/S1470-2045(19)30027-0

Faber, A. C., Coffee, E. M., Costa, C., Dastur, A., Ebi, H., Hata, A. N., Yeo, A. T., Edelman, E., Song, Y., Tam, A., Boisvert, J., Milano, R., Roper, J., Kodack, D., Jain, R., Corcoran, R., Rivera, M., Ramaswamy, S., Hung, K., Benes, C., & Engelman, J. (2014). MTOR inhibition specifically sensitizes colorectal cancers with KRAS or BRAF mutations to BCL-2/BCL-XL inhibition by suppressing MCL-1. *Cancer Discovery, 4*(1), 42–52. https://doi.org/10.1158/2159-8290.cd-13-0315

Fedele, C., Ran, H., Wei, W., Jen, J., Geer, M. J., Araki, K., Ozerdem, U., Simeone, D., Miller, G., Neel, B., & Tang, K. (2018). Shp2 inhibition prevents adaptive resistance to mek inhibitors in multiple cancer models. *Cancer Discovery*, 1237–1249. https://doi.org/10.1158/2159-8290.CD-18-0444

Fernandez, M. L., Dawson, A., Hoenisch, J., Kim, H., Bamford, S., Salamanca, C., Gabriel, D., Shepherd, T., Cremona, M., Hennessy, B., Anderson, S., Volik, S., Collins, C., Huntsman, D., & Carey, M. (2019). Markers of MEK inhibitor resistance in low-grade serous ovarian cancer: EGFR is a potential therapeutic target. *Cancer Cell International, 19*(1). https://doi.org/10.1186/s12935-019-0725-1

Fisk, M., Gajendragadkar, P. R., Mäki-Petäjä, K. M., Wilkinson, I. B., & Joseph, C. (2014). Therapeutic potential of P38 MAP kinase inhibition in the management of cardiovascular disease. *American Journal of Cardiovascular Drugs, 14*(3), 155–165. https://doi.org/10.1007/s40256-014-0063-6

Flick, A. C., Leverett, C. A., Ding, H. X., McInturff, E., Fink, S. J., Helal, C. J., Deforest, J. C., Morse, P. D., Mahapatra, S., & O'Donnell, C. J. (2020). Synthetic approaches to new drugs approved during 2018. *Journal of Medicinal Chemistry*, 10652–10704. https://doi.org/10.1021/acs.jmedchem.0c00345

Fruman, D. A., & Rommel, C. (2014). PI3K and cancer: Lessons, challenges and opportunities. *Nature Reviews Drug Discovery, 13*(2), 140–156. https://doi.org/10.1038/nrd4204

Gibney, G. T., & Smalley, K. S. M. (2013). An unholy alliance: cooperation between BRAF and NF1 in melanoma development and BRAF inhibitor resistance. *Cancer Discovery, 3*(3), 260–263. https://doi.org/10.1158/2159-8290.CD-13-0017

Gilmartin, A. G., Bleam, M. R., Groy, A., Moss, K. G., Minthorn, E. A., Kulkarni, S. G., Rominger, C. M., Erskine, S., Fisher, K., Yang, J., Zappacosta, F., Annan, R., Sutton, D., & Laquerre, S. (2011). GSK1120212 (JTP-74057) is an inhibitor of MEK activity and activation with favorable pharmacokinetic properties for sustained in vivo pathway inhibition. *Clinical Cancer Research, 17*(5), 989–1000. https://doi.org/10.1158/1078-0432.CCR-10-2200

Greger, J. G., Eastman, S. D., Zhang, V., Bleam, M. R., Hughes, A. M., Smitheman, K. N., Dickerson, S. H., Laquerre, S. G., Liu, L., & Gilmer, T. M. (2012). Combinations of BRAF, MEK, and PI3K/MTOR inhibitors overcome acquired resistance to the BRAF inhibitor GSK2118436 dabrafenib, mediated by NRAS or MEK mutations. *Molecular Cancer Therapeutics, 11*(4), 909–920. https://doi.org/10.1158/1535-7163.MCT-11-0989

Gross, A. M., Wolters, P. L., Dombi, E., Baldwin, A., Whitcomb, P., Fisher, M. J., Weiss, B., Kim, A., Bornhorst, M., Shah, A., Martin, S., Roderick, M., Pichard, D., Carbonell, A., Paul, S., Therrien, J., Kapustina, O., Heisey, K., Clapp, D. W., … Widemann, B. C. (2020). Selumetinib in children with inoperable plexiform neurofibromas. *New England Journal of Medicine, 382*(15), 1430–1442. https://doi.org/10.1056/nejmoa1912735

Han, J., Lee, J. D., Bibbs, L., & Ulevitch, R. J. (1994). A MAP kinase targeted by endotoxin and hyperosmolarity in mammalian cells. *Science, 265*(5173), 808–811. https://doi.org/10.1126/science.7914033

Hasskarl, J. (2014). Sorafenib: Targeting multiple tyrosine kinases in cancer. *Small Molecules in Oncology, 201*, 145–164. https://doi.org/10.1007/978-3-642-54490-3_8

Heidorn, S. J., Milagre, C., Whittaker, S., Nourry, A., Niculescu-Duvas, I., Dhomen, N., Hussain, J., Reis-Filho, J., Springer, C., Pritchard, C., & Marais, R. (2010). Kinase-dead BRAF and oncogenic RAS cooperate to drive tumor progression through CRAF. *Cell, 140*(2), 209–221. https://doi.org/10.1016/j.cell.2009.12.040

Hensley, K., Floyd, R. A., Zheng, N. Y., Nael, R., Robinson, K. A., Nguyen, X., Pye, Q. N., Stewart, C., Geddes, J., Markesbery, W., Patel, E., Johnson, G., & Bing, G. (1999). P38 kinase is activated in the alzheimer's disease brain. *Journal of Neurochemistry, 72*(5), 2053–2058. https://doi.org/10.1046/j.1471-4159.1999.0722053.x

Iavarone, C., Zervantonakis, I. K., Selfors, L. M., Palakurthi, S., Liu, J. F., Drapkin, R., Matulonis, U. A., Hallberg, D., Velculescu, V., Leverson, J., Sampath, D., Mills, G., & Brugge, J. (2019). Combined MEK and Bcl-2/XL inhibition is effective in high-grade serous ovarian cancer patient–derived xenograft models and BIM levels are predictive of responsiveness. *Molecular Cancer Therapeutics, 18*(3), 642–655. https://doi.org/10.1158/1535-7163.MCT-18-0413

Ip, Y. T., & Davis, R. J. (1998). Signal transduction by the C-jun N-terminal kinase (JNK) - from inflammation to development. *Current Opinion in Cell Biology, 10*(2), 205–219. https://doi.org/10.1016/S0955-0674(98)80143-9

Irvine, M., Stewart, A., Pedersen, B., Boyd, S., Kefford, R., & Rizos, H. (2018). Oncogenic PI3K/AKT promotes the step-wise evolution of combination BRAF/MEK inhibitor resistance in melanoma. *Oncogenesis, 7*(9), 72. https://doi.org/10.1038/s41389-018-0081-3

Jaiswal, B. S., Durinck, S., Stawiski, E. W., Yin, J., Wang, W., Lin, E., Moffat, J., Martin, S. E., Modrusan, Z., & Seshagiri, S. (2018). ERK mutations and amplification confer resistance to ERK-inhibitor therapy. *Clinical Cancer Research, 24*(16), 4044–4055. https://doi.org/10.1158/1078-0432.CCR-17-3674

Kakadia, S., Yarlagadda, N., Awad, R., Kundranda, M., Niu, J., Naraev, B., Mina, L., Dragovich, T., Gimbel, M., & Mahmoud, F. (2018). Mechanisms of resistance to BRAF and MEK inhibitors and clinical update of us food and drug administration-approved targeted therapy in advanced melanoma. *OncoTargets and Therapy, 7095–7107.* https://doi.org/10.2147/OTT.S182721

Kauko, O., O'Connor, C. M., Kulesskiy, E., Sangodkar, J., Anna, A., Izadmehr, S., Yetukuri, L., Yadav, B., Padzik, A., Laajala, T., Haapaniemi, P., Momeny, M., Varila, T., Ohlmeyer, M., Aittokallio, T., Wennberg, K., Narla, G., & Westermarck, J. (2018). PP2A inhibition is a druggable MEK inhibitor resistance mechanism in KRAS-mutant lung cancer cells. *Science Translational Medicine, 10*(450), eaaq1093. https://doi.org/10.1126/scitranslmed.aaq1093

Keating, G. M. (2016). Cobimetinib plus vemurafenib: A review in BRAF V600 mutation-positive unresectable or metastatic melanoma. *Drugs, 76*(5), 605–615. https://doi.org/10.1007/s40265-016-0562-7

Kemper, K., De Goeje, P. L., Peeper, D. S., & Van Amerongen, R. (2014). Phenotype switching: Tumor cell plasticity as a resistance mechanism and target for therapy. *Cancer Research, 74*(21), 5937–5941. https://doi.org/10.1158/0008-5472.CAN-14-1174

Khan, Z. M., Real, A. M., Marsiglia, W. M., Chow, A., Duffy, M. E., Yerabolu, J. R., Scopton, A. P., & Dar, A. C. (2020). Structural basis for the action of the drug trametinib at KSR-bound MEK. *Nature, 588*(7838), 509–514. https://doi.org/10.1038/s41586-020-2760-4

Kheiri, G., Dolatshahi, M., Rahmani, F., & Rezaei, N. (2019). Role of P38/MAPKs in alzheimer's disease: Implications for amyloid beta toxicity targeted therapy. *Reviews in the Neurosciences, 30*(1), 9–30. https://doi.org/10.1515/revneuro-2018-0008

Kindrachuk, J., Ork, B., Hart, B. J., Mazur, S., Holbrook, M. R., Frieman, M. B., Traynor, D., Johnson, R., Dyall, J., Kuhn, J., Olinger, G., Hensley, L., & Jahrling, P. (2015). Antiviral potential of ERK/MAPK and PI3K/AKT/MTOR signaling modulation for middle east respiratory syndrome coronavirus infection as identified by temporal kinome analysis. *Antimicrobial Agents and Chemotherapy, 59*(2), 1088–1099. https://doi.org/10.1128/AAC.03659-14

Kitai, H., Ebi, H., Tomida, S., Floros, K. V., Kotani, H., Adachi, Y., Oizumi, S., Nishimura, M., Faber, A. C., & Yano, S. (2016). Epithelial-to-mesenchymal transition defines feedback activation of receptor tyrosine kinase signaling induced by MEK inhibition in KRAS-mutant lung cancer. *Cancer Discovery, 6*(7), 754–769. https://doi.org/10.1158/2159-8290.CD-15-1377

Knobloch, J., Jungck, D., Charron, C., Stoelben, E., Ito, K., & Koch, A. (2018). Superior anti-inflammatory effects of narrow-spectrum kinase inhibitors in airway smooth muscle cells from subjects with chronic obstructive pulmonary disease. *Journal of Allergy and Clinical Immunology, 141*(3), 1122–1124. https://doi.org/10.1016/j.jaci.2017.09.026

Kozar, I., Margue, C., Rothengatter, S., Haan, C., & Kreis, S. (2019). Many ways to resistance: How melanoma cells evade targeted therapies. *Biochimica et Biophysica Acta - Reviews on Cancer, 1871*(2), 313–322. https://doi.org/10.1016/j.bbcan.2019.02.002

Kropski, J. A., Richmond, B. W., Gaskill, C. F., Foronjy, R. F., & Majka, S. M. (2018). Eregulated angiogenesis in chronic lung diseases: A possible role for lung mesenchymal progenitor cells (2017 grover conference series). *Pulmonary Circulation, 8*(1), 2045893217739807. https://doi.org/10.1177/2045893217739807.

Kumar, S., Jiang, M. S., Adams, J. L., & Lee, J. C. (1999). Pyridinylimidazole compound SB 203580 inhibits the activity but not the activation of P38 mitogen-activated protein kinase. *Biochemical and Biophysical Research Communications, 263*(3), 825–831. https://doi.org/10.1006/bbrc.1999.1454

Lee, P. A., Wallace, E., Marlow, A., Yeh, T., Marsh, V., Anderson, D., Woessner, R., Hurley, B., Lyssikatos, J., Poch, G., Gross, S., Rana, S., Winski, S., & Koch, K. (2010). Abstract 2515: Preclinical development of ARRY-162, a potent and selective MEK 1/2 inhibitor. *Cancer Research, 70*(8), 2515. https://doi.org/10.1158/1538-7445.am10-2515

Larkin, J., Ascierto, P. A., Dréno, B., Atkinson, V., Liszkay, G., Maio, M., Mandalà, M., Demidov, L., Stroyakovskiy, D., Thomas, L., de la Cruz-Merino, L., Dutriaux, C., Garbe, C., Sovak, M. A., Chang, I., Choong, N., Hack, S. P., McArthur, G. A., & Ribas, A. (2014). Combined vemurafenib and cobimetinib in BRAF -mutated melanoma. *New England Journal of Medicine, 371*(20), 1867–1876. https://doi.org/10.1056/nejmoa1408868

Lee, J. C., Laydon, J. T., McDonnell, P. C., Gallagher, T. F., Kumar, S., Green, D., McNulty, D., Blumenthal, M., Heys, J., Landvatter, S., Strickler, J., McLaughlin, M., Siemens, I., Fisher, S., Livi, G., White, J., Adams, J., & Young, P. (1994). A protein kinase involved in the regulation of inflammatory cytokine biosynthesis. *Nature, 372*(6508), 739–746. https://doi.org/10.1038/372739a0

Lee, J. W., Zhang, Y., Eoh, K. J., Sharma, R., Sanmamed, M. F., Wu, J., Choi, J., Park, H., Iwasaki, A., Kaftan, E., Chen, L., Papadimitrakopoulou, V., Herbst, R., & Koo, J. (2019). The combination of MEK inhibitor with immunomodulatory antibodies targeting programmed death 1 and programmed death ligand 1 results in prolonged survival in kras/P53-driven lung cancer. *Journal of Thoracic Oncology, 14*(6), 1046–1060. https://doi.org/10.1016/j.jtho.2019.02.004

Li, Z., Jiang, K., Zhu, X., Lin, G., Song, F., Zhao, Y., Piao, Y., Liu, J., Cheng, W., Bi, X., Gong, P., Song, Z., & Meng, S. (2016). Encorafenib (LGX818), a potent BRAF inhibitor, induces senescence accompanied by autophagy in BRAFV600E melanoma cells. *Cancer Letters, 370*(2), 332–344. https://doi.org/10.1016/j.canlet.2015.11.015

Lin, L., Sabnis, A. J., Chan, E., Olivas, V., Cade, L., Pazarentzos, E., Asthana, S., Neel, D., Yan, J., Lu, X., Pham, L., Wang, M., Karachaliou, N., Cao, M., Manzano, J., Ramirez, J., Torres, J., Buttitta, F., Rudin, C., & Bivona, T. G. (2015). The Hippo effector YAP promotes resistance to RAF- and MEK-targeted cancer therapies. *Nature Genetics, 47*(3), 250–256. https://doi.org/10.1038/ng.3218

Lito, P., Solomon, M., Li, L. S., Hansen, R., & Rosen, N. (2016). Cancer therapeutics: Allele-specific inhibitors inactivate mutant KRAS G12C by a trapping mechanism. *Science, 351*(6273), 604–608. https://doi.org/10.1126/science.aad6204

Mahapatra, D. K., Asati, V., & Kumar Bharti, S. (2017). MEK inhibitors in oncology: A patent review (2015-present). *Expert Opinion on Therapeutic Patents*, 887–906. https://doi.org/10.1080/13543776.2017.1339688

Manzano, J. L., Layos, L., Bugés, C., De los Llanos, M., Vila, L., Martínez-Balibrea, E., & Martínez-Cardús, A. (2016). Resistant mechanisms to BRAF inhibitors in melanoma. *Annals of Translational Medicine*, 4(12), 237. https://doi.org/10.21037/atm.2016.06.07

Maphis, N., Jiang, S., Xu, G., Kokiko-Cochran, O.N., Roy, S.M., Van Eldik, L.J., Martin Watterson, D., Lamb, B.T., & Bhaskar, K. (2016). Selective suppression of the α isoform of P38 MAPK rescues late-stage tau pathology. *Alzheimer's Research and Therapy* 8(1). https://doi.org/10.1186/s13195-016-0221-y.

Markham, A., & Keam, S.J. (2020). Selumetinib: First approval. *Drugs* 80(9). https://doi.org/10.1007/s40265-020-01331-x.

Mendoza, M.C., Emrah E., & Blenis, J. (2011). The Ras-ERK and PI3K-MTOR pathways: Cross-talk and compensation. *Trends in Biochemical Sciences*. https://doi.org/10.1016/j.tibs.2011.03.006.

Nazarian, R., Shi, H., Wang, Q., Kong, X., Koya, R. C., Lee, H., Chen, Z., Lee, M., Attar, N., Sazegar, H., Chodon, T., Nelson, S., McArthur, G., Sosman, J., Ribas, A., & Lo, R. (2010). Melanomas acquire resistance to B-RAF(V600E) inhibition by RTK or N-RAS upregulation. *Nature*, 468(7326), 973–977. https://doi.org/10.1038/nature09626

Ostenfeld, T., Krishen, A., Lai, R. Y., Bullman, J., Green, J., Anand, P., Scholz, J., & Kelly, M. (2015). A randomized, placebo-controlled trial of the analgesic efficacy and safety of the P38 MAP kinase inhibitor, losmapimod, in patients with neuropathic pain from lumbosacral radiculopathy. *The Clinical Journal of Pain*, 31(4), 283–293. https://doi.org/10.1097/AJP.0000000000000122

Paraiso, K. H. T., Xiang, Y., Rebecca, V. W., Abel, E. V., Ann Chen, Y., Cecilia Munko, A., Wood, E., Fedorenko, I., Sondak, V., Anderson, A., Ribas, A., Palma, M., Nathanson, K., Koomen, K., Messina, J., & Smalley, K. (2011). PTEN loss confers BRAF inhibitor resistance to melanoma cells through the suppression of BIM expression. *Cancer Research*, 71(7), 2750–2760. https://doi.org/10.1158/0008-5472.CAN-10-2954

Peng, D. H., Kundu, S. T., Fradette, J. J., Diao, L., Pan, T., Byers, L. A., Wang, J., Canales, J., Villalobos, P., Mino, B., Yang, Y., Minelli, R., Peoples, M., Bristow, C., Heffernan, T., Carugo, A., Wistuba, I., & Gibbons, D. (2019). ZEB1 suppression sensitizes KRAS mutant cancers to MEK inhibition by an IL17RD-dependent mechanism. *Science Translational Medicine*, 11(483), eaaq1238. https://doi.org/10.1126/scitranslmed.aaq1238

Poulikakos, P. I., Persaud, Y., Janakiraman, M., Kong, X., Ng, C., Moriceau, G., Shi, H., Atefi, M., Titz,, B., Gabay, M. T., Salton, M., Dahlman, K. B., Tadi, M., Wargo, J. A., Flaherty, K. T., Kelley, M. C., Misteli, T., Chapman, P. B., Sosman, J. A., … Solit, D. B. (2011). RAF inhibitor resistance is mediated by dimerization of aberrantly spliced BRAF(V600E). *Nature*, 480(7377), 387–390. https://doi.org/10.1038/nature10662

Prahallad, A., Sun, C., Huang, S., Salazar, R., Zecchin, D., Beijersbergen, R. L., Bardelli, A., & Bernards, R. (2012). Unresponsiveness of colon cancer to BRAF(V600E) inhibition through feedback activation of EGFR. *Nature*, 483(7387), 100–103. https://doi.org/10.1038/nature10868

Ran, H., Tsutsumi, R., Araki, T., & Neel, B. G. (2016). Sticking it to cancer with molecular glue for SHP2. *Cancer Cell*, 194–196. https://doi.org/10.1016/j.ccell.2016.07.010

Rao, V. N., & Reddy, E. P. (1994). Elk-1 proteins interact with MAP kinases. *Oncogene*, 9(7).

Rheault, T. R., Stellwagen, J. C., Adjabeng, G. M., Hornberger, K. R., Petrov, K. G., Waterson, A. G., Dickerson, S. H., Mook Jr, R., Laquerre, S., King, A., Rossanese, O., Arnone, M., Smitheman, K., Kane-Carson, L., Han, C., Moorthy, G., Moss, K., & Uehling, D. (2013). Discovery of dabrafenib: A selective inhibitor of raf kinases with antitumor activity against B-Raf-driven tumors. *ACS Medicinal Chemistry Letters*, 4(3), 358–362. https://doi.org/10.1021/ml4000063

Ribas, A., Lawrence, D., Atkinson, V., Agarwal, S., Miller, W. H., Carlino, M. S., Fisher, R., Long, G., Hodi, F., Tsoi, J., Grasso, C., Mookerjee, B., Zhao, Q., Ghori, R., Moreno, B., Ibrahim, N., & Hamid, O. (2019). Combined BRAF and MEK inhibition with PD-1 blockade immunotherapy in BRAF-mutant melanoma. *Nature Medicine*, 25(6), 936–940. https://doi.org/10.1038/s41591-019-0476-5

Roskoski, R. (2017). Allosteric MEK1/2 inhibitors including cobimetanib and trametinib in the treatment of cutaneous melanomas. *Pharmacological Research*. https://doi.org/10.1016/j.phrs.2016.12.009

Rice, K. D., Aay, N., Anand, N. K., Blazey, C. M., Bowles, O. J., Bussenius, J., Costanzo, S., Curtis, J., Defina, S., Dubenko, L., Engst, S., Joshi, A., Kennedy, A., Kim, A., Koltun, E., Lougheed, J., Manalo, J., Martini, J., Nuss, J., Peto, C., Tsang, T., Yu, P., & Johnston, S. (2012). Novel carboxamide-based allosteric MEK inhibitors: Discovery and optimization efforts toward XL518 (GDC-0973). *ACS Medicinal Chemistry Letters*, 3(5), 416–421. https://doi.org/10.1021/ml300049d

Roskoski, R. (2016). Classification of small molecule protein kinase inhibitors based upon the structures of their drug-enzyme complexes. *Pharmacological Research, 103*, 26–48. https://doi.org/10.1016/j.phrs.2015.10.021

Roskoski, R. (2020). Properties of FDA-approved small molecule protein kinase inhibitors: A 2020 update. *Pharmacological Research, 152*, 104609. https://doi.org/10.1016/j.phrs.2019.104609

Roskoski, R. (2021). Properties of FDA-approved small molecule protein kinase inhibitors: A 2021 update. *Pharmacological Research, 165*, 105463. https://doi.org/10.1016/j.phrs.2021.105463

Roskoski, R. (2018). Targeting oncogenic raf protein-serine/threonine kinases in human cancers. *Pharmacological Research, 135*, 238–258. https://doi.org/10.1016/j.phrs.2018.08.013

Schlessinger, J. (2000). Cell signaling by receptor tyrosine kinases. *Cell, 141*(7), 1117–1134. https://doi.org/10.1016/S0092-8674(00)00114-8

Sebolt-Leopold, J. S. (2008). Advances in the development of cancer therapeutics directed against the RAS-mitogen-activated protein kinase pathway. *Clinical Cancer Research, 14*(12), 3651–3656. https://doi.org/10.1158/1078-0432.CCR-08-0333

Segalés, J., Perdiguero, E., & Muñoz-Cánoves, P. (2016). Regulation of muscle stem cell functions: A focus on the P38 MAPK signaling pathway. *Frontiers in Cell and Developmental Biology, 30*(4), 91. https://doi.org/10.3389/fcell.2016.00091

She, Q. B., Chen, N., & Dong, Z. (2000). ERKs and P38 kinase phosphorylate P53 protein at serine 15 in response to UV radiation. *Journal of Biological Chemistry, 275*(27), 20444–20449. https://doi.org/10.1074/jbc.M001020200

Shirley, M. (2018). Encorafenib and binimetinib: First global approvals. *Drugs, 78*(12), 1277–1284. https://doi.org/10.1007/s40265-018-0963-x

Smalley, K. S. M., Lioni, M., Dalla Palma, M., Xiao, M., Desai, B., Egyhazi, S., Hansson, J., Wu, H., King, A., Van Belle, P., Elder, D., Flaherty, K., Herlyn, M., & Nathanson, K. (2008). Increased cyclin D1 expression can mediate BRAF inhibitor resistance in BRAF V600E-mutated melanomas. *Molecular Cancer Therapeutics, 7*(9), 2876–2883. https://doi.org/10.1158/1535-7163.MCT-08-0431

Smith, R. A., Barbosa, J., Blum, C. L., Bobko, M. A., Caringal, Y. V., Dally, R., Johnson, J. S., Katz, M., Kennure, N., Kingery-Wood, J., Lee, W., Lowinger, T., Lyons, J., Marsh, V., Rogers, D., Swartz, S., Walling, T., & Wild, H. (2001). Discovery of heterocyclic ureas as a new class of raf kinase inhibitors: identification of a second generation lead by a combinatorial chemistry approach. *Bioorganic and Medicinal Chemistry Letters, 11*(20), 2775–2778. https://doi.org/10.1016/S0960-894X(01)00571-6

Straussman, R., Morikawa, T., Kevin, S., Barzily-Rokni, M., Qian, Z. R., Du, J., Davis, A., Mongare, M., Gould, J., Frederick, D., Cooper, Z., Chapman, P., Solit, D., Ribas, A., Lo, R., Flaherty, K., Ogino, S., Wargo, J., & Golub, T. (2012). Tumour micro-environment elicits innate resistance to RAF inhibitors through HGF secretion. *Nature, 487*(7408), 500–504. https://doi.org/10.1038/nature11183

Stuart, D. D., Li, N., Poon, D. J., Aardalen, K., Kaufman, S., Merritt, H., Salangsang, F., Lorenzana, E., Li, A., Ghoddusi, M., Caponigro, G., Sun, F., Kulkarni, S., Kakar, S., Turner, N., Zang, R., Tellew, J., & Pryer, N. (2012). Abstract 3790: Preclinical profile of LGX818: A potent and selective RAF kinase inhibitor. *Cancer Research, 72*(8), 3790. https://doi.org/10.1158/1538-7445.am2012-3790

Sulahian, R., Kwon, J. J., Walsh, K. H., Pailler, E., Bosse, T. L., Thaker, M., Almanza, D., Dempster, J., Pan, J., Piccioni, F., Dumont, N., Gonzalez, A., Rennhack, J., Nabet, B., Bachman, J., Goodale, A., Lee, Y., Bagul, M., Liao, R., Navarro, A., & Yuan, T. (2019). Synthetic lethal interaction of SHOC2 depletion with MEK inhibition in RAS-driven cancers. *Cell Reports, 29*(1), 118–134. https://doi.org/10.1016/j.celrep.2019.08.090

Sun, C., Hobor, S., Bertotti, A., Zecchin, D., Huang, S., Galimi, F., Cottino, F., Prahallad, N., Grernrum, W., Tzani, A., Schlicker, A., Wessels, L., Smit, E., Thunnissen, E., Halonen, P., Lieftink, C., Beijersbergen, R., Nicolantonio, F., Bardelli, A., Trusolino, L., & Bernards, R. (2014). Intrinsic resistance to MEK inhibition in kras mutant lung and colon cancer through transcriptional induction of ERBB3. *Cell Reports, 7*(1), 86–93. https://doi.org/10.1016/j.celrep.2014.02.045

Tan, N., Wong, M., Nannini, M. A., Hong, R., Lee, L. B., Price, S., Williams, K., Savy, P., Sampath, D., Settleman, J., Fairbrother, W., & Belmont, L. (2013). Bcl-2/Bcl-XL inhibition increases the efficacy of MEK inhibition alone and in combination with PI3 kinase inhibition in lung and pancreatic tumor models. *Molecular Cancer Therapeutics, 12*(6), 853–864. https://doi.org/10.1158/1535-7163.MCT-12-0949

Tlemsani, C., Olivier, H., Arrondeau, J., Boudou-Rouquette, P., Cessot, A., Blanchet, B., Thomas-Schoemann, A., Coriat, R., Durand, J., Giroux, J., Alexandre, J., & Goldwasser, F. (2015). Effect of glucuronidation on transport and tissue accumulation of tyrosine kinase inhibitors: Consequences for the clinical management of sorafenib and regorafenib. *Expert Opinion on Drug Metabolism and Toxicology, 11*(5), 785−794. https://doi.org/10.1517/17425255.2015.1030392

Tsubaki, M., Takeda, T., Noguchi, M., Jinushi, M., Seki, S., Morii, Y., Shimomura, K., Imano, M., Takao, S., & Nishida, S. (2019). Overactivation of akt contributes to MEK inhibitor primary and acquired resistance in colorectal cancer cells. *Cancers, 11*(12), 1866. https://doi.org/10.3390/cancers11121866

Tudor, C., Marchese, F. P., Hitti, E., Anna, A., Rawlinson, L., Gaestel, M., Blackshear, P. J., Clark, A. R., Saklatvala, J., & Dean, J. L. E. (2009). The P38 MAPK pathway inhibits tristetraprolin-directed decay of interleukin-10 and proinflammatory mediator MRNAs in murine macrophages. *FEBS Letters, 583*(12), 1933−1940. https://doi.org/10.1016/j.febslet.2009.04.039

Turke, A. B., Song, Y., Costa, C., Cook, R., Arteaga, C. L., Asara, J. M., & Engelman, J. A. (2012). MEK inhibition leads to PI3K/AKT activation by relieving a negative feedback on ERBB receptors. *Cancer Research, 72*(13), 3228−3237. https://doi.org/10.1158/0008-5472.CAN-11-3747

Van Cutsem, E., Hidalgo, M., Canon, J. L., Macarulla, T., Bazin, I., Elena, P., Manojlovic, N., Radenkovic, D, Verslype, C, Raymond, E, Cubillo, A, Schueler, A, Zhao, C, & Hammel, P (2018). Phase I/II trial of pimasertib plus gemcitabine in patients with metastatic pancreatic cancer. *International Journal of Cancer, 143*(8), 2053−2064. https://doi.org/10.1002/ijc.31603

Villanueva, J., Vultur, A., Lee, J. T., Somasundaram, R., Fukunaga-Kalabis, M., Cipolla, A. K., Bradley, W., Xu, X., Gimotty, P., Kee, D., Santiago-Walker, A., Letrero, R, D'Andrea, K., Pushparajan, A., Hayden, J., Brown, K, Laquerre, S., McArthur, G., Sosman, J., Nathanson, K., & Herlyn, M. (2010). Acquired resistance to BRAF inhibitors mediated by a RAF kinase switch in melanoma can be overcome by cotargeting MEK and IGF-1R/PI3K. *Cancer Cell, 18*(6), 683−695. https://doi.org/10.1016/j.ccr.2010.11.023

Wagle, N., Van Allen, E. M., Treacy, D. J., Frederick, D. T., Cooper, Z. A., Taylor-Weiner, A., Rosenberg, M., Goetz, E., Sullivan, R., Farlow, D., Friedrich, D., Anderka, K., Perrin, D., Johannessen, C., McKenna, A., Cibulskis, K., Kryukov, G., Hodis, E., Lawrence, D., … Garraway, L. A. (2014). MAP kinase pathway alterations in BRAF-mutant melanoma patients with acquired resistance to combined RAF/MEK inhibition. *Cancer Discovery, 4*(1), 61−68. https://doi.org/10.1158/2159-8290.CD-13-0631

Wilhelm, S., Carter, C., Lynch, M., Lowinger, T., Dumas, J., Smith, R. A., Schwartz, B., Simantov, R., & Kelley, S. (2006). Discovery and development of sorafenib: A multikinase inhibitor for treating cancer. *Nature Reviews Drug Discovery, 5*(10), 835−844. https://doi.org/10.1038/nrd2130

Wilhelm, S. M., Carter, C., Tang, L., Wilkie, D., McNabola, A., Rong, H., Chen, C., Zhang, X., Vincent, P., McHugh, M., Cao, Y., Shujath, J., Gawlak, S., Eveleigh, D., Rowley, B., Liu, L., Adnane, L., Lynch, M., Auclair, D., … Trail, P. A. (2004). BAY 43-9006 exhibits broad spectrum oral antitumor activity and targets the RAF/MEK/ERK pathway and receptor tyrosine kinases involved in tumor progression and angiogenesis. *Cancer Research, 64*(19), 7099−7109.

Wilhelm, S. M., Dumas, J., Adnane, L., Lynch, M., Carter, C. A., Schütz, G., Heinz Thierauch, K., & Zopf, D. (2011). Regorafenib (BAY 73-4506): A new oral multikinase inhibitor of angiogenic, stromal and oncogenic receptor tyrosine kinases with potent preclinical antitumor activity. *International Journal of Cancer, 129*(1), 245−255. https://doi.org/10.1002/ijc.25864

Wan, P. T. C., Garnett, M. J., Mark Roe, S., Lee, S., Niculescu-Duvaz, D., Good, V. M., Jones, C., Marshall, C., Springer, C., Barford, D., & Marais, R. (2004). Mechanism of activation of the RAF-ERK signaling pathway by oncogenic mutations of B-RAF. *Cell, 116*(6), 855−867. https://doi.org/10.1016/S0092-8674(04)00215-6

Wilhelm, S., Adnane, L., Hirth-Dietrich, C., Ehrlich, P., & Lynch, M. (2014). Preclinical characterization of BAY 73-4506: A kinase inhibitor with broad spectrum antitumor activity targeting oncogenic and angiogenic kinases. *Molecular Cancer Therapeutics, 6*(11 Suppl. ment), B260.

Xing, F., Persaud, Y., Pratilas, C. A., Taylor, B. S., Janakiraman, M., She, Q. B., Gallardo, H., Hefter, B., Dolgalev, I., Viale, A., Heguy, A., De Stanchina, E., Cobrinik, D., Bollag, J., Wolchok, G., Houghton, A., & Solit, D. (2012). Concurrent loss of the PTEN and RB1 tumor suppressors attenuates RAF dependence in melanomas harboring V600E BRAF. *Oncogene, 31*(4), 446−457. https://doi.org/10.1038/onc.2011.250

Yang, H., Higgins, B., Kolinsky, K., Packman, K., Go, Z., Iyer, R., Stanley, K., Zhao, S., Lee, R., Grippo, J., Schostack, K., Simcox, M., Heimbrook, D., Bollag, G., & Su, F. (2010). RG7204 (PLX4032), a selective BRAFV600E inhibitor, displays potent antitumor activity in preclinical melanoma models. *Cancer Research, 70*(13), 5518−5527. https://doi.org/10.1158/0008-5472.CAN-10-0646

Yu, J., Sun, X., Goie, J. Y. G., & Zhang, Y. (2020). Regulation of host immune responses against influenza a virus infection by mitogen-activated protein kinases (Mapks). *Microorganisms, 8*(7), 1067. https://doi.org/10.3390/microorganisms8071067

Zhang, C., Spevak, W., Zhang, Y., Burton, E. A., Ma, Y., Habets, G., Zhang, J., Lin, J., Ewing, T., Matusow, B., Tsang, G., Marimuthu, A., Cho, H., Wu, G., Wang, W., Fong, D., Nguyen, H., Shi, C., Womack, P., ... Bollag, G. (2015). RAF inhibitors that evade paradoxical MAPK pathway activation. *Nature, 526*(7574), 583–587. https://doi.org/10.1038/nature14982

Zipser, M. C., Eichhoff, O. M., Widmer, D. S., Schlegel, N. C., Schoenewolf, N. L., Stuart, D., Liu, W., Gardner, C., Smith, P., Nuciforo, P., Dummer, R., & Hoek, K. (2011). A proliferative melanoma cell phenotype is responsive to RAF/MEK inhibition independent of BRAF mutation status. *Pigment Cell and Melanoma Research, 24*(2), 326–333. https://doi.org/10.1111/j.1755-148X.2010.00823.x

12

Proviral integration site for Moloney murine leukemia virus-1 (PIM-1) kinase inhibitors

Vinod Kumar Gurjar[1], Vivek Shrivastava[1], Shweta Jain[2], Rakesh Chawla[3] and Ankur Vaidya[4]

[1]School of Pharmacy, Faculty of Pharmacy, Parul University, Vadodara, Gujarat, India; [2]Sir Madanlal Institute of Pharmacy, Etawah, Uttar Pradesh, India; [3]University Institute of Pharmaceutical Sciences & Research, Baba Farid University of Health Sciences, Faridkot, Punjab, India; [4]Faculty of Pharmacy, Uttar Pradesh University of Medical Sciences, Saifai, Uttar Pradesh, India

1. Introduction

Pim-1, a carcinogenic threonine and serine kinase, promotes cell cycle progression and suppresses apoptosis. It is upregulated in numerous human malignancies. Pim-1 is the proviral integration site for Moloney murine leukemia virus 1. Prior research has indicated that the Pim-1 3′-UTR is crucial for controlling Pim-1 mRNA stability. The serine and threonine recognized as the proto-oncogene, Pim-1 Kinase Pim-1 participates in a number of biological processes, including apoptosis, cell division, proliferation, and cancer. Pim-1 kinase carries out its physiological action by phosphorylating many different cellular substrates, such as Myc, p21$^{Cip1/WAF1}$, and p27^{KIP1}. Pim-1 and c-Myc work together to promote cell development and alteration.

Through the Jak/STAT pathway involving STAT3 and/or STAT5, some interleukins (ILs) and growth factors (GFs) can regulate Pim-1 expression at the transcriptional level (Chang et al., 2010). Additionally, under conditions of cellular stress like hypoxia or shear stress, its expression may be increased. Pim-1 is posttranscriptionally regulated by microRNAs (miRNAs), according to studies that have just confirmed Pim-1 as a miR-33a target. Pim-1's stability is controlled by the ubiquitin-proteasome route, Hsp90, and Hsp70 at the protein level (Weirauch et al., 2013).

Several cytokines that such as SCF, and interleukins like, IL-2, IL-3, IL-6, IL-7, G-CSF, IFN-α, GM-CSF, and prolactin, activate the JAK/STAT signaling pathways and cause Pim-1 to express. This shows that Pim-1 induction is caused by alterations in the signal conduction route through these receptors. According to reports, Pim-1 is increased in cells that express mutant FLT3 or STAT5 that are constitutively active. Numerous cancers, such as lymphoid and hematopoietic carcinomas, such as prostate carcinomas of squamous cells, colorectal tumors, gastric and, pancreatic ductal adenocarcinomas, and bladder cancer, are associated with the onset and progression of excessive expression of Pim-1. Recent research has shown that Pim-1 kinase inhibitors, Pim-1 knockdown, and reducing Pim-1 levels with a monoclonal antibody all cause antiproliferative activity in tumor cells, confirming the notion that Pim-1 is a probable tumor target for the creation of medicinal agents. Initially, Pim-1 was discovered to be a PIM-1 favorable proviral inclusion site. The amount of Pim-1 mRNA is markedly raised by proviral insertion in the 3'-UTR of Pim-1. According to reports, the AUUUA destabilizing motif is present in the Pim-1 transcript and contributes to its short half-life. It is thought that ARE-binding proteins control the AU-rich element (AREs)'s destabilizing activity. An ARE-binding protein called tristetraprolin (TTP) can recognize AREs and encourage the degradation of the transcripts. Many cancers have decreased TTP expression, which could be a factor in the rise in the number of transcripts with AUUUA elements in their 3'-UTRs (Kim et al., 2012).

Pim-1 kinase's physiological and pathological functions comparatively to other STPKs, including mitogen-activated protein kinases and protein kinases A, B, and C, Pim-1 does not require activation by other protein kinases. Although phosphorylation stabilizes the protein kinase, which is constitutively active, it is not necessary for the control of the enzyme's catalytic activity. Phosphatase 2A is a negative regulator of Pim stability, suggesting that autophosphorylation and/or phosphorylation by unidentified entities may be significant regulators of PIM activities. Pim-1 is mostly expressed in the thymus, bone marrow, spleen, fetal liver, and other hematopoietic organs, while it is not expressed in mature tissue. Recent research has demonstrated that Pim-1 kinase is a downstream effector molecule of numerous cytokines signaling pathways and can phosphorylate a wide range of protein substrates. The PIM proteins' proven relevance in oncology is paralleled by their pro-survival activity in immunology. Whereby aberrant expression of these kinases has been connected to several human malignancies, including multiple myeloma, chronic lymphocytic leukemia, and pancreatic, and prostate cancers. Pim-1 has significance for the development of neo-intima in the wall of the aorta, pulmonary arterial hypertension, and other vascular disorders that involve the proliferation of cells in the arterial wall. Additionally, Pim-1's function in the vascular proliferation of smooth muscle cells mediated by high glucose (HG) has been investigated. It has been demonstrated that hypoxia stimulates Pim-1 expression, which encourages the formation of solid tumors. Antitumor medications occasionally cause stress in addition to hypoxia and oxidative stress, which improves tumor survival. For the anticancer drug docetaxel, such a response has a mechanism that has been discovered (Bogusz et al., 2017).

2. Structure of PIM-1

A classic bi-lobed kinase fold is adopted by PIM-1. A solitary helix and mostly strands make up the N-terminal domain (residues from 37 to 122). Most of the residues in the

C-terminal domain (residues from 126 to 305) are helical. The residues from 123 to 125 form a hinge region that joins the domains together. The Pim-1 kinase's ATP-binding site is surrounded by two loops: a glycine-rich loop (G-loop; residues from 44 to 52) and a stimulating loop (residues from 185 to 204), as well as a hinge region. It is situated between the two domains. Interactions at the hinge region show the distinctiveness of ATP binding in PIM1. The hinge region of Pim-1 deficiencies of one of the traditional hydrogen bond donors inside the support and in its place has a proline residue (Pro123) at an analogous position 7. The majority of protein kinases interact with ATP by creating two hydrogen bonds within this area. This unique characteristic made the PIM1 protein kinase an appealing target for drug development (Bogusz et al., 2017).

3. Physiological functions of PIM-1

Pim kinases have a role in several physiological processes, including the regulation of transcription and the proliferation and endurance of leukocytes. Although Pim-1 and 2 are expressed at low levels in a variety of tissues, cytokine-driven activation (including ILs 2, 3, 7, GM-CSF, INF-α and γ), which is mediated by the JAK/STAT pathway, causes a strong leukocytic induction (Fig. 12.1). Pim-1 participates in the stabilization of Socs1, a JAK/STAT pathway suppressor, as part of a negative response loop in the JAK/STAT pathway. In actuality, IL-4 stimulation causes extended JAK/STAT signaling in Socs1 and Pim-1,2 knockout mice. Pim-1 knockout mice have a very modest phenotype, whereas

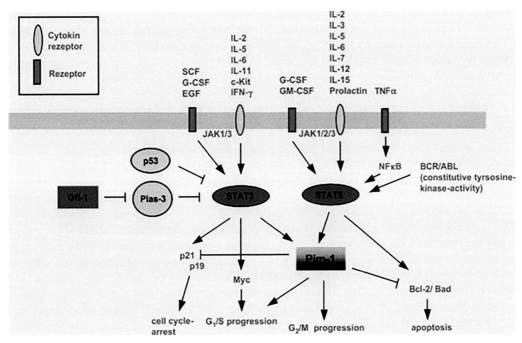

FIGURE 12.1 Signal transduction pathways in which Pim-1 is involved (Bachmann & Möröy, 2005).

triple knockout animals for all Pim genes show a lifetime reduction in body size due to impaired cellular proliferation. Furthermore, Pim triple knockout mice display a reduced sensitivity to hematopoietic growth regulators. Pim kinases share many same substrates with Akt/PKB and other AGC kinases, including BAD, p21WAF1/CIP1, and Cot/Tp1-2 substrates, suggesting that they regulate hematopoietic cell proliferation and survival redundantly.

Nuclear transcription protein (p100), cell cycle regulators (p21, Cdc25A phosphatase, and C-TAK1/MARK3/Par1A), proapoptotic proteins (BAD on Ser-112), and other proteins are all phosphorylated by Pim kinases. All of these proteins play a part in controlling nuclear transcription and the cell cycle. The suppression of chromatin and mRNA splicing control, as well as processes that are significant elements of the nuclear transcription control mechanisms, is carried out by heterochromatin protein 1 (HP1) and Pim-1 family protein. The NFATc1 protein relays signals from T-cell receptors while the co-activator p100 activates c-Myb. Upon the removal of growth factors, pim kinases can cause apoptotic resistance. Pim kinases play crucial functions in cell growth and survival, therefore they have a clear survival advantage throughout tumor development (Ouhtit et al., 2015).

4. Functional relevance of PIM-1 in carcinomas

Tumors that overexpress the Pim-1 kinase provirus integration site have a bad prognosis. The basis for Pim-1's role as a proto-oncogene is provided by several of its target proteins that are involved in crucial cellular functions. The promotion of early transformation, cell proliferation, and cell survival is known to be facilitated by Pim kinases. Pim-1 kinase has been discovered to play a role in the growth of many tumors, most notably cancer of the prostate, oral cancer, Burkitt's lymphoma (BL), and different hematological lymphomas. Pim-1 may function as a downstream effector of the VEGF-A/Flk1 pathway and contribute to angiogenesis and vasculogenesis.

4.1 Colon carcinoma

Pim-1 is essential for many signaling pathways that are related to tumors, and its functional importance in colon cancer is established. In addition to tumor cells, colon cancer–associated stroma and tumor-adjacent mucosa also affect colon cancer prognostic variables when it comes to disease-free survival. Because of this, the activation of the proto-oncogene pim-1 in a variety of tumor components, including tumor cells, cancer-associated stroma, and tumor-adjacent mucosa, may be essential for deciding a patient's prognosis. Pim-1-negative immune inflammatory cells and pim-1-positive immune inflammatory cells that follow cancer-related fibroblasts were associated with improved disease-free survival (DFS) and overall survival (OS), indicating that these immune cell subclasses may serve as tumor-killing immune cells. This finding suggests that pim-1 may serve as a possible marker to distinguish between immune inflammatory cells that promote tumors and those that destroy them (Peng et al., 2013).

4.2 Bladder cancer

Multiple investigations have shown that Pim-1 kinase contributes to the development of various cancers, yet little has been known about Pim-1's impact on bladder cancer. Shengjie Guo et al. speculate that Pim-1 may contribute to the initiation and progression of bladder cancer. Pim-1 is a viable option for targeted therapy in cancer of the bladder due to its role in drug resistance and bladder cancer cell proliferation (Guo et al., 2010).

4.3 Cervical cancer

PIM-1 expression in cervical cancer patients is positively correlated with tumor growth and metastasis. Cervical cancer tissue exhibits much higher levels of PIM-1 than surrounding tissue. Based on a receiver operating characteristic (ROC) analysis, Pim-1 is a sensitive biomarker for the identification of cervical cancer. Additionally, the levels of EGFR and Pim-1 in cervical cancer tissue were positively associated, and EGFR was overexpressed in the tumor tissues of cervical cancer patients (Yang et al., 2020).

Both SACC-83 and SACC-LM cell lines depend on Pim-1 for cell proliferation, apoptosis, cell cycle, and invasion. In the tissues of adenoid cystic carcinoma (ACC), Pim-1 and RUNX3 levels were negatively pertinent and strongly correlated with T-stage and nerve invasion. This study supports Pim-1's oncogenic function in ACC. Additionally, the results indicated that Pim-1 might be a novel therapeutic target and possible prognostic indicator for ACC malignancy (Zhu et al., 2014).

4.4 Pancreatic cancer

Pim-1 aids in tumorigenesis and aids in the diagnosis and prognosis of pancreatic cancer. In pancreatic cancer cells, Pim-1 knockdown reduced cell growth, induced cell cycle arrest, increased apoptosis, resensitized cells to gemcitabine and erlotinib therapy, and inhibited the expression of ABCG2 and enhancer of zeste homolog 2 (EZH2) mRNA. A positive feedback loop was generated by Pim-1kinase and the EGFR pathway. The Pim-1 expression is considerably elevated in pancreatic cancer tissues, and high levels of expression are detrimental to prognosis ($P = .025$, hazard ratio $= 2.113$, 95% confidence interval: $1.046-4.266$) (Xu et al., 2016).

4.5 Prostate cancers

Pim-1 kinase was first associated with pancreatic cancer (PC) by Dhanasekaran et al., who demonstrated its considerably abnormal expression in pancreatic cancer (Guo et al., 2010). According to studies, interleukin-6 activates JAK-STAT as well as other signaling transcription factors involved in the start of pancreatic cancer, hence promoting Pim-1 kinase activation. Pim-1 is recognized as a pancreatic cancer biomarker because Pim-1 overexpression in high-grade prostatic intraepithelial neoplasia (HG-PIN) is regarded as a beginning event in pancreatic cancer progression. Strong Pim-1 expression has been associated with aberrant mitotic spindles, chromosomal disaggregation, and expanded centrosomes, which are the traits that cause androgen-dependent cells in the prostate to change into androgen-independent prostate cancer cells. Because Pim-1 and Myc's expression levels were co-regulated in pancreatic cancer, a synergism between them was also proposed. Additionally, Pim-1's downregulation is strongly linked with poor prognosis outcomes for the disease because of the amount of PSA repetition, even though Pim-1 was typically overexpressed in prostatic neoplasia. Pim-1 controlled the activity of androgen receptors (AR), important pancreatic cancer players that are phosphorylated by several kinases. Through Ser-213 and Thr-850 phosphorylation, the Pim-1 kinase isoforms Pim-1S and Pim-1L play a critical role in preserving AR stability and transcriptional activity throughout pancreatic cancer. While only the long isoform can phosphorylate AR at Thr-850, stabilizing it, only the short isoform can speed up AR breakdown by phosphorylating it at Ser-213 (Ouhtit et al., 2015).

5. PIM-1 kinase inhibitors

Numerous inhibitors have been suggested as potential therapeutics, and current active drug research and development initiatives are focused on using small-molecule modulators to inhibit Pim kinase. The development of inhibitors placed a particular emphasis on the simultaneous negative control of all three isoforms to enable more effective cancer treatment because Pim-1/2/3 isoforms share cellular compensatory mechanisms that sustain one another's functioning. Because the Pan-Pim kinase domain has a proline amino acid residue and a tertiary amine in the hinge region, it differs from those of other protein kinases (Fig. 12.2). This structural characteristic made it possible to create selective Pim kinase inhibitors without off-target effects on other kinases (Alnabulsi & Al-Hurani, 2020).

The analysis of crystal structures for reported pan-Pim kinase inhibitors (ATP-competitive) revealed the significance of polar contacts with catalytic Lys67 as a crucial factor in determining their inhibition potential. Additionally, the potency of inhibitors can be increased by their capacity to interact hydrophobically with the G-loop and polarly with either the

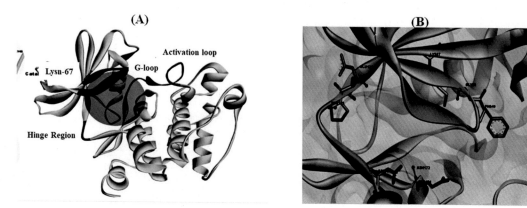

FIGURE 12.2   (A) The G-loop and hinge region amino acid residues are highlighted in the Pim-1 kinase's solid ribbon presentation of its ATP-binding site (PDB ID: 1YXT); (B) A crucial amino acid residue is present in the ATP-binding site (Alnabulsi & Al-Hurani, 2020).

hinge region or/and the acidic patch (Asp128, Asn172, and Glu171) in the C terminus of the ATP-binding site (Alnabulsi & Al-Hurani, 2020).

Pim-1 has been related to several proteins target that are involved in transcriptional control, signal transduction pathways, cell cycle regulation, apoptosis, and other processes that regulate cell survival. Additionally, Pim-1 has been shown to cooperate with the cancer-causing transcription factor c-Myc, phosphorylating and regulating it as well as engaging with it on the chromatin level to boost the expression of c-Myc target genes. Since Pim-1 can significantly contribute to the malignant transformation of cells during carcinogenesis, it is currently recognized as a proto-oncogene. Many tumor types, including prostate cancer, B-cell lymphoma, colorectal cancer, and pancreatic cancer, have an overexpression of Pim-1 that has been linked to a poor prognosis. Prostate cancer and hematological malignancies are known to have increased tumor start and development when Pim-1 is suppressed or inhibited, and these conditions have cancer-preventing qualities (Weirauch et al., 2013).

5.1 Natural compounds

Pim kinases marker have been linked to the emergence of resistance to rapamycin, an mTOR inhibitor, and tyrosine kinase inhibitors. These findings suggest that Pim kinases may be useful therapeutic targets for the treatment of cancer and support the synthesis of Pim antagonists as an exciting field of chemical biology. There have only been a few selective Pim kinase inhibitors documented in the literature so far, most of which target Pim-1 and 2, but an increase in recent studies documenting the development of new and selective Pim kinase inhibitors implies a growing interest in this area.

Effective chemical probes for understanding protein kinases are small-molecule inhibitors. Additionally, they might be used as prototype therapeutic drugs to address conditions brought on by uncontrolled kinase activity. The function of Pim-1 can be inhibited in vitro by recognized, promiscuous kinase inhibitors, according to three prior publications. Jacobs et al. demonstrated that the morpholino-substituted chromone LY294002 and several staurosporine and bisindoyl-maleimide analogs may suppress Pim-1 activity in vitro (Jacobs et al., 2005). Then, Fabian et al. (2005) developed an interaction map involving 20 small-molecule kinase inhibitors that are currently being studied in clinical settings and 113 kinases (Jacobs et al., 2005). Only three compounds—two staurosporine analogs and flavopiridol (semisynthetic flavonoid)—being tested as a cyclin-dependent kinase (CDKs 1, 2, and 4) inhibitor had measurable binding to Pim-1.

5.2 Quercetagetin

A flavonoid with submicromolar inhibitory action against Pim-1 is quercetagetin (Fig. 12.3). A moderately effective, ATP-competitive inhibitor known as flavonol quercetagetin (3,3′,4′,5,6,7-Hexahydroxyflavone) was discovered (IC_{50}, 0.34 Mmol/L). In intact RWPE2 prostate cancer cells, quercetagetin can also suppress Pim-1 activity that is depending on dosage (ED_{50}, 5.5 Mmol/L). Additionally, different prostate epithelial cell lines' susceptibilities to quercetagetin's growth-inhibiting effects varied in direct proportion to their Pim-1 protein concentrations. Quercetagetin may be helpful for clinical trials designed to

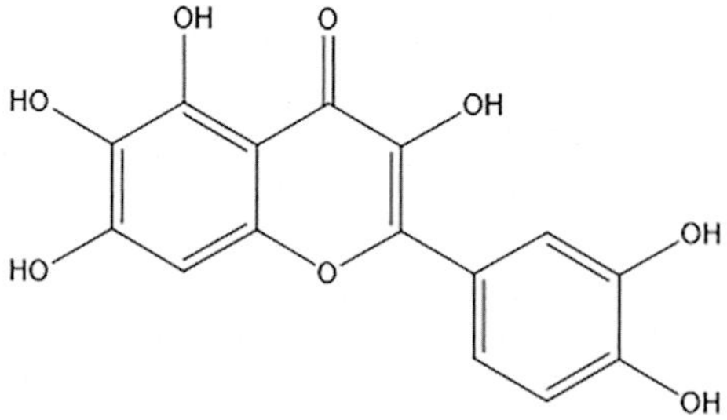

FIGURE 12.3   Structure of quercetagetin.

promote the development of therapeutically viable Pim-1 inhibitors since it can act as an abstemiously powerful and selective, cell-permeable pim-1 kinase inhibitor (Holder et al., 2007).

Cinnamon, one of the oldest and most popular spices, has been used as a flavor and preservative by numerous cultures around the world for beverages, baked items, and candies. The proliferation of lymphoma, melanoma, hepatocellular carcinoma, colon cancer, and cervical cancer cells in vitro and melanoma in vivo has been found to be inhibited by cinnamon extracts. According to reports, these extracts also inhibit angiogenesis by specifically targeting VEGFR2. 2'-Hydroxycinnamicaldehyde (2'-HCA) is an important phytoconstituent of cinnamon essential oil and may be found in amounts ranging from 0.01 to 0.8 mg/g in commercial cinnamon powder. It is recognized as a key bioactive ingredient in cinnamon and is thought to stop the growth of many human cancer cell lines, including those that are lung, breast, colon, leukemia, ovarian, and leukemia-related. Additionally, 20-HCA inhibits both the allograft growth of oral RK3E-ras-Fluc cancer cells and the in vivo xenograft growth of colon HCT116 cancer cells. The growth of animal xenografts that mimicked human leukemia or skin cancer was significantly inhibited by 2'-HCA. 2'-HCA's potential as an anticancer agent stemming by specifically targeting the Pim-1 kinase has been demonstrated in preclinical studies (Kim et al., 2015) (Fig. 12.4).

5.3 Hispidulin

Pim-1 can be inhibited by the natural flavonoid hispidulin (Fig. 12.5) at a dose of 2.71 mM. The co-crystal structure (PDB ID: 4XH6) demonstrated its capacity to form H-bonds with Lys67 and lpophilic interactions with the residue (Leu120) (Fig. 12.6). In addition to HB with Lys67 and the absence of a OH group at ring C, hispidulin was disposed into the ATP-active site without interacting with the residues in the hinge region. Pim-1, an oncogenic

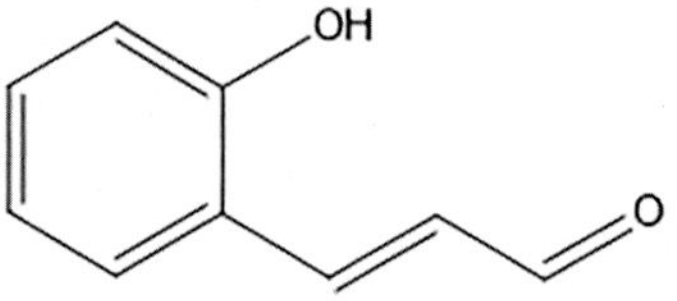

FIGURE 12.4   Structure of 2'-HCA.

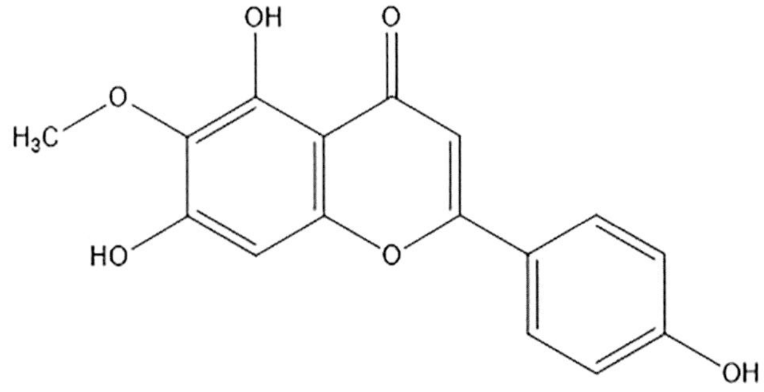

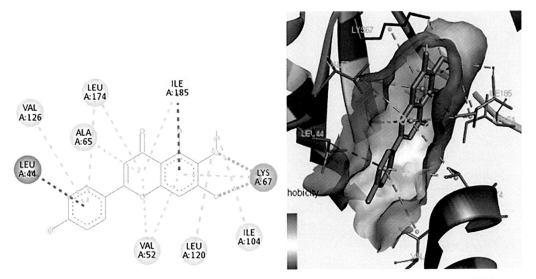

FIGURE 12.5   Structure of hispidulin.

FIGURE 12.6   2D and 3D co-crystal structure of kinase Pim-1 bound to hispidulin (PDB ID: 4XH6).

protein kinase, is inhibited by hispidulin. The binding mechanism of Pim-1 bound to hispidulin is different from quercetin's, according to crystallographic research, which suggests that flavonoids' ability to bind is influenced by hydrogen-bonding interactions with the kinase's hinge region (Chao et al., 2015; Liu et al., 2018).

5.4 Tetrazine derivatives

The National Cancer Institute (NCI) is currently looking at 1,2,4,5-Tetrazine molecules to see how efficient they are at preventing cancer. 1,2,4,5-Tetrazine is a prominent class of heterocyclic scaffold that has a broad range of natural products and bioactive chemicals as well as many practical and synthetic applications. The biological features of 1,2,4,5-Tetrazine and its derivatives, which include antiinflammatory, antiviral, and antibacterial activities, as well as anticancer activity, have been determined to have a high potential.

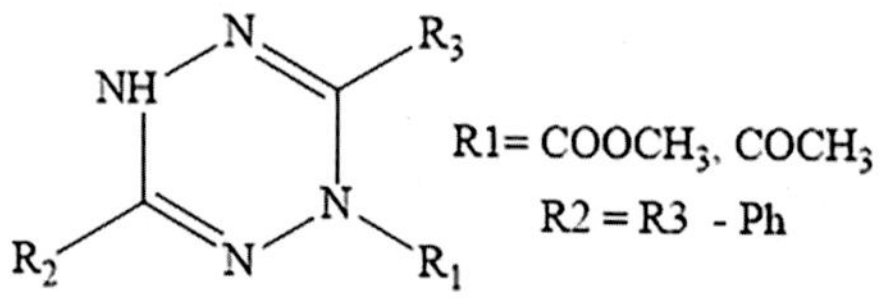

(1)

FIGURE 12.7   Structure of 1,2,4,5-Tetrazine derivatives **(1)**.

Halima Hazhazi and colleagues use the computational methods of molecular docking and QSAR to evaluate a series of 1,2,4,5-Tetrazine derivatives **(1)**. QSAR models of 1,2,4,5-Tetrazine derivative anticancer activity in gas and solvent phases showed good statistical values in both phases (Hazhazi et al., 2019) (Fig. 12.7).

5.5 Pyrazole derivatives

Aromatic heterocyclic nitrogen-containing systems are of interest for developing protein kinase inhibitors. A well-known heterocyclic component with nitrogen that finds widespread use in medicine is called pyrazole. The literature has indicated that the pyrazole derivatives have antitumor and kinase-inhibitory properties. Using cyclohexane-1,3-dione, Mohareb et al. synthesize and test thiophene, pyrazole, and pyran derivatives. Chemical **(2)** was the most active chemical, having an IC_{50} value of 0.28 μM, according to the Pim-1 kinase assay. It is possible to infer that the presence of aromatic rings in the compound's structure enhances its cytotoxic activity (Mohareb, Hilmy, & Elshehawy, 2018). Compounds **(3)**, **(4)**, and **(5)** are the most effective inhibitors of kinase, while chemicals also demonstrated substantial inhibitions toward the tyrosine kinases (Mohareb & Mikhail, 2020) (Fig. 12.8).

5.6 Diaminopyrazole

A study aimed to find new Pim-1 kinase inhibitors that might have anticancer effects that target multiple myeloma was started by Wang, Blackaby, et al. (2019). Burger et al. report an inhibitor with a diamino pyridine scaffold **(6)** (Burger et al., 2013), which served as the basis for the research. First, the idea of replacing the 5-aminothiazole group with the 3-aminopyridine **(7)** isostere to find a novel scaffold of Pim kinase inhibitors. Although the 5-Aminobenzothiazole bioisostere **(8)** is a poor PK profile concerning oral bioavailability (F% = 23%) compared with 54% for compound **(7)** and hERG inhibition (IC_{50} = 0.11 mM) prompted efforts toward its optimization, it nonetheless maintained good enzymatic activity and demonstrated s1uperior cellular activity. Given the crucial hydrogen link that must exist within the catalytic Lys67 residue and the pyridine-N of the 4-aminopyridine moiety **(7)**, a second bioisosteric replacement was carried out, substituting pyrazole for pyridine. Additionally, piperidine ring extension into azepane revealed lead **(8)** as a new Pim kinase inhibitor. Further optimization was necessary due to compound **(8)** is low oral bioavailability (F% = 8%) (Alnabulsi & Al-Hurani, 2020).

To examine the structural requirements of diamino pyrazole prototypes that enable favorable enzymatic and subcellular Pim kinase inhibitory activity together with good PK profiles,

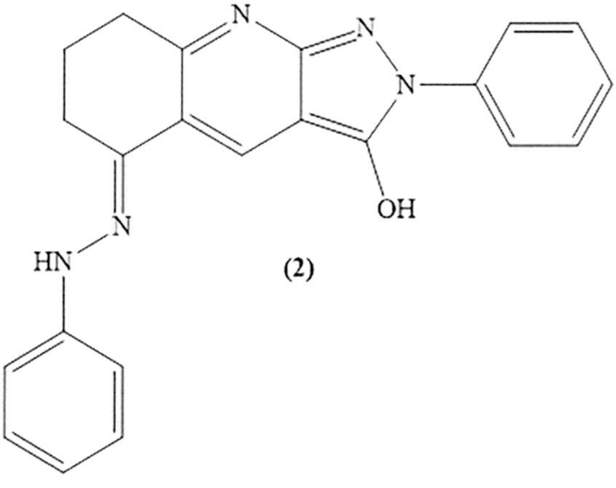

FIGURE 12.8 Structure of compounds (3–5).

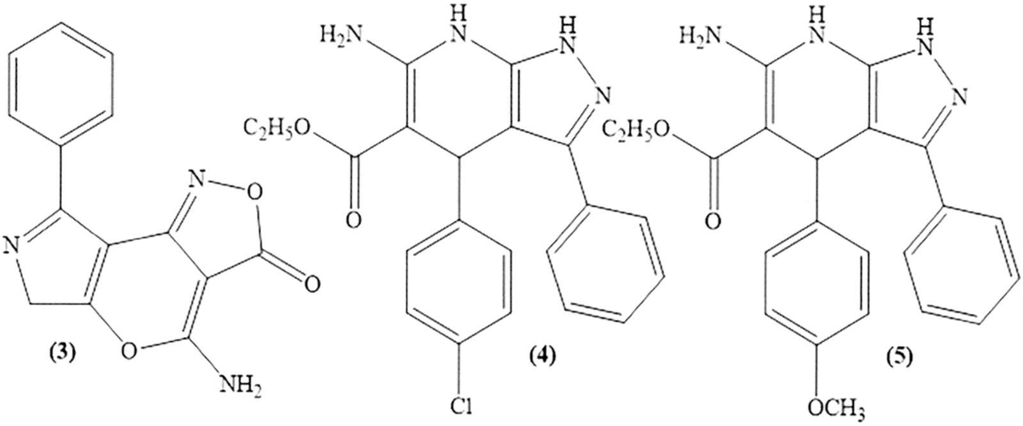

several analogues were synthesized. It was discovered that the activity, permeability, and oral bioavailability of aminothiazole depended on an amino group at position C5. Additionally, the permeability and oral bioavailability of the molecule were significantly impacted by the basicity of the primary amine on the azepine ring, which could not be replaced by alcohol or a secondary amine. The decrease in primary amine basicity, achieved either by direct replacement of the primary amine with fluoroalkyl molecules or by replacement of the azepine ring with various EWGs at different positions, had varying effects on pharmacokinetics in addition to enzymatic and cellular activity. After ensuring the ideal balance between biochemical assay and cellular potency, kinase selectivity, and a good PK profile, the optimized analogue **GDC-0339** was discovered as a novel oral Pim kinase clinical candidate with a potential anticancer activity that could be investigated for use against multiple myeloma (Suchaud et al., 2013) (Fig. 12.9).

Suchaud et al. created novel 1,6-dihydropyrazolo and 3,6-dihydropyrazolo carbazoles and tested them for their ability to inhibit Pim kinase as well as their ability to suppress the proliferation of two different prostate cancer cell lines. Except for the chlorinated analogue **(9)**,

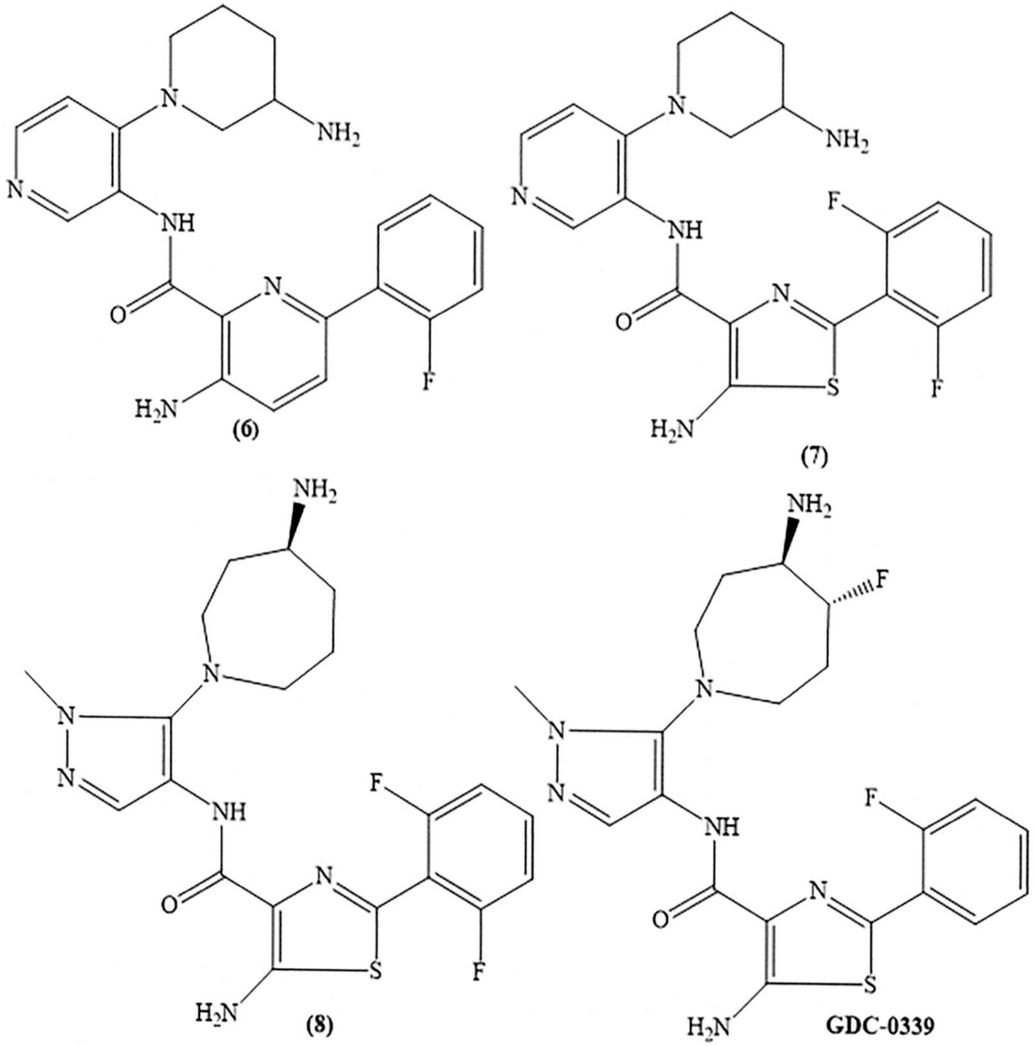

FIGURE 12.9   Structure of compounds (6–8 and GDC-0339).

nitro derivatives in both series were more effective Pim inhibitors than their amino equivalents. Another substance greatly inhibited Pim-3 while having a weaker effect on Pim-1 and Pim-2, and might therefore be utilized as an intriguing molecular tool to research the biological activities of Pim-3 kinase (Suchaud et al., 2013) (Fig. 12.10).

5.7 Phenanthridines derivatives

Suchaud et al. developed a new class of nitro or amino-substituted pyrazolo[4,3-a]phenanthridines from 5-bromo-6-nitroindazole (10). The nitro series can be thought of as an

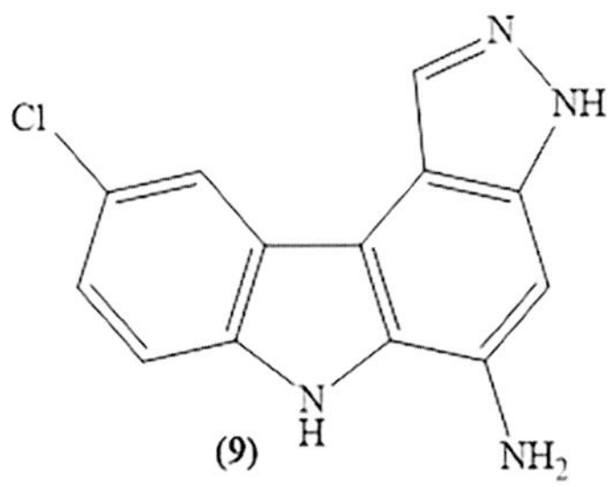

FIGURE 12.10   Structure of compounds **(9)**.

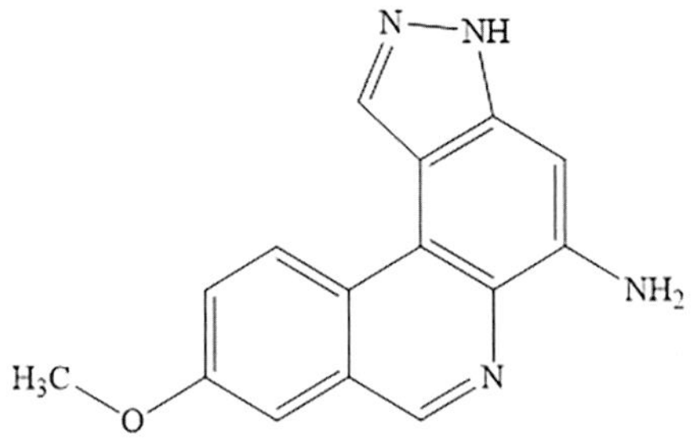

FIGURE 12.11   Structure of compounds **(10)**.

intriguing place to start when creating new Pim kinase inhibitors, as evidenced by the examination of their inhibitory activity toward Pim kinases (Suchaud et al., 2014) (Fig. 12.11).

5.8 Pyridine derivatives

Pyridine is a common heterocyclic compound in nature that has an atom of nitrogen. It performs a crucial role in many enzymes of the living system as a prosthetic group participating in redox activities in the biological system. Because of its capacity to interact with major receptors, pyridine is a crucial pharmacophore, privileged nucleus, and excellent heterocyclic system in drug design and development, with wide applications in anticancer research. It serves as the foundation for many of the drugs that are currently on the market. In the fight against cancer, a number of pyridine derivatives have been shown to inhibit kinases, tubulin polymerization, androgen receptors, human carbonic anhydrase, topoisomerase enzyme, and a number of other targets (Narasimhamurthy et al., 2022).

To explore the pim-1 inhibitory effect of these compounds, Naguib and colleagues construct a series of 5-bromo-thieno-pyridines containing amide or benzoyl groups at position C2. The ability of each synthesized chemical to inhibit the pim-1 enzyme was evaluated. The pim-1 kinas inhibitory activity of two compounds **(11)** and **(12)** was modest, with IC_{50} values of 35.7 and 12.71 mM, respectively (Naguib & El-Nassan, 2016) (Fig. 12.12).

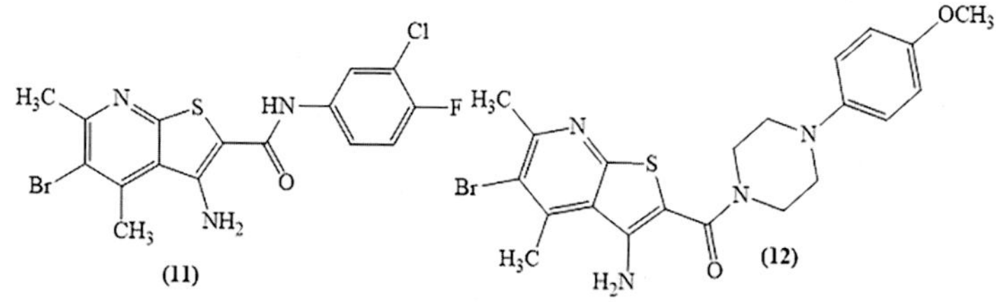

FIGURE 12.12   Structure of compounds (11–12).

Pyridothienopyrimidin-4-one derivatives (13) have been identified by Naguib and colleagues as powerful pim-1 inhibitors. These derivatives were created using a structural rigidification technique by closing the rings of their thieno[2,3-b]pyridine precursors (14), ensuring that the carbonyl group was present and oriented correctly for enzyme interaction. Both the cytotoxic and enzyme-inhibitory activities significantly improved as a result of our efforts. The 2-aryl-2,3-dihydro derivatives (15a–c), which showed pim-1 inhibition between 1.18 and 1.97 mM, were the most effective inhibitors (El-Nassan et al., 2018) (Fig. 12.13).

Thieno[2,3-b]pyridines' ring closure-based structure rigidification turned out to be a successful method for increasing both their cytotoxic and pim-1 inhibitory activities. As pim-1 inhibitors, a group of pyridothienopyrimidin-4-one compounds were created and produced.

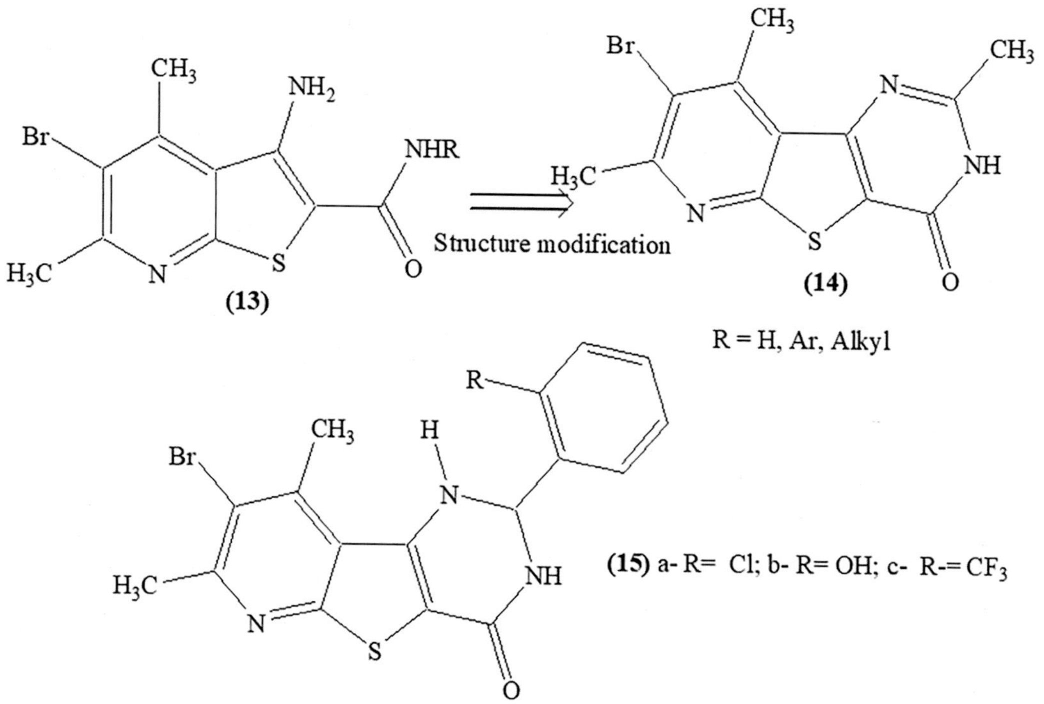

FIGURE 12.13   Structure of compounds (13–15abc).

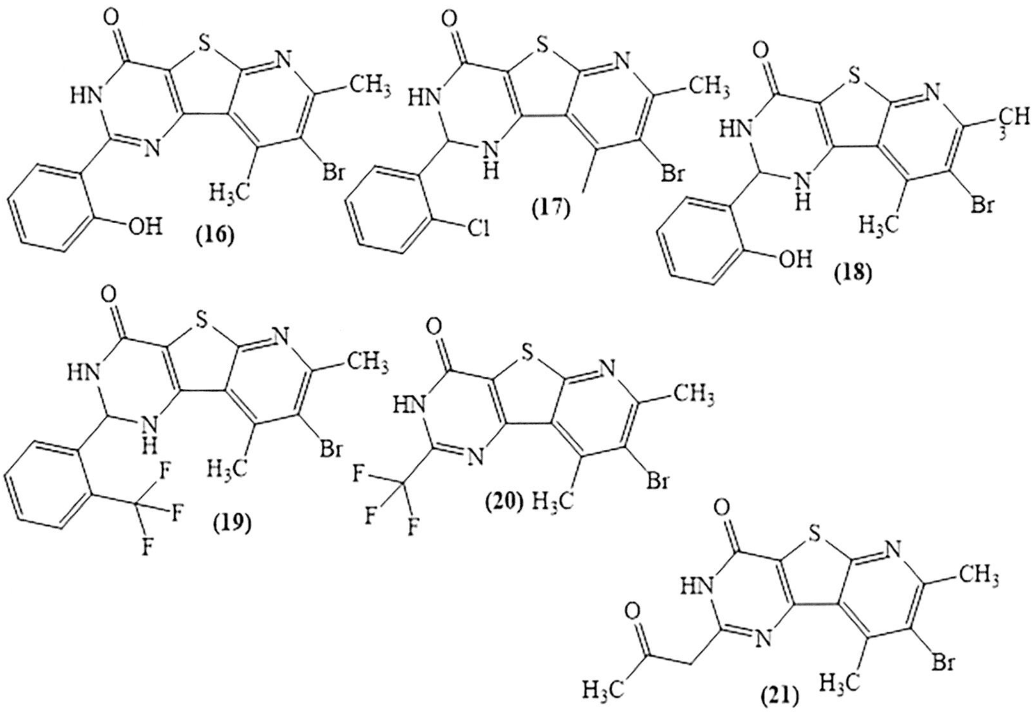

FIGURE 12.14 Structure of compounds (16—21).

Six pyridothienopyrimidin-4-ones (16—21) showed highly effective pim-1 inhibitory activity with IC_{50} values of 4.62, 1.18, 1.38, 1.97, 8.83, and 4.18 µM, respectively. Only one thieno-pyridine derivative displayed potent pim-1 inhibition with IC_{50} of 12.71 mM. The most effective pim-1 inhibitors, according to a SAR investigation of pyridothienopyrimidin-4-ones, were provided by the 2-(2-substituted phenyl)-2,3-dihydro family (17—19) (Naguib et al., 2017) (Fig. 12.14).

Two new series of 2-amino cyano pyridine and 2-oxo cyanopyridine were synthesized for a study, and their effectiveness against the HepG2 liver cancer cell line, the HCT-116 colon cancer cell line, and the MCF-7 breast cancer cell line was assessed. Human prototype kinase Pim-1 was used to assess Pim kinase inhibitory activity. Quantikine-Human active Caspase-3 Immunoassay was used to quantify the active caspase-3 level. Compound (22) displayed strong Pim-1 kinase inhibitory activity, with an IC_{50} value of 0.94 µM (Abouzid et al., 2017) (Fig. 12.15).

Multiple Myeloma is significantly influenced by the kinase, Pim-2. Since Pim-2 kinase has a high affinity for ATP, inhibiting it can be difficult. In a study, it was discovered that the indazole core binds to the PIM kinase's ATP binding site. Hu et al. proved that the development of pan-Pim inhibitors uses 1H-pyrazolo-pyridine (23) (6-aza indazole) (with Ki value of 14.0 nM). When a hydrophobic group (fluorophenyl) was added to 6-aza indazole at the C3 position, more active molecules were created. The improvement of activity has been further attributed to the incorporation of an oxygen spacer. In compound (24) (Ki value of 0.041 nM),

FIGURE 12.15   Structure of compounds (22).

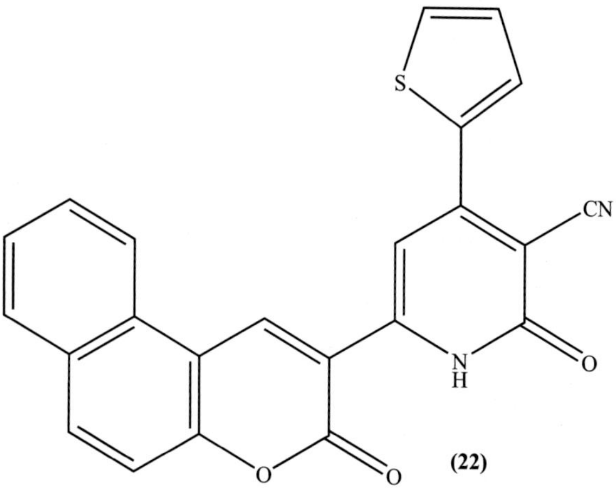

(22)

the substituent at C5 of the 5-pyridine ring were equivalent to those in compound (25) (Ki value of 0.00004 µM). The second N of the pyrazole main group, which contains a range of substituents, was discovered to be crucial for modifying the compounds' physicochemical properties. In compound (26) (Ki value of 171.0 nM), the aliphatic amide group on R was substituted, resulting in molecules with decreased potency. The urea derivative has also been discovered to be effective at nanomolar concentrations. Potency may be improved by substituents at the R position such as piperazinone, morpholine, tetrahydrofuran, or tetrahydropyran. Although the homopiperazine derivative (27), which had a slightly higher Ki value of 0.020 nM, had a lower hydrophobic efficiency value, the improvement in potency was most likely caused by greater hydrophobicity. Compound (28) (Ki value of 0.013 nM) has a methyl group substituted at the C4 position of the pyridine ring to further impose an orthogonal orientation of the piperidine ring, leading to a 2- to 4-fold increase in activity (Hu et al., 2015) (Fig. 12.16).

Several substituted pyridine derivatives have been synthesized to find novel anti-Pim kinase drugs. The inhibitory potential of these molecules is influenced by the catalytic core, two water molecules, the primary carbonyl chain of the Pim-1 kinase, and a putative weak hydrogen bond between the aromatic hydrogen on the phenyl ring. Histone proteins were used as the Pim-1 kinase substrate in the radioactive filter-plate test to determine the associated IC_{50} values. The efficacy of compound (29) was reduced 35-fold when pyridone carbonyl was converted to a ring-closer compound (IC_{50} value: 0.05 µM). The O group at X position compounds were more potent than those with other heteroatom substitutions. Compounds having potential activity were generated by using a halogen instead of the phenyl ring. The synthetic results are further supported by molecular modeling investigations, which demonstrated that the carbonyl group on the pyridone ring binds to both the Lys67 residue side chain and the Pim-1 kinase, which is required for activity (Cheney et al., 2007) (Fig. 12.17).

To test the in vitro effectiveness against Pim-1 kinase, 1, 2-dihydropyridine-3-carbonitrile analogs were synthesized in a study using the Cyclex Pim-1 kinase assay/inhibitor screening kit. The HT-29 cell line was used for the MTT assay. Since the substituents are present like methylthio imidazole at the C3 position and benzodioxole at the C6 position, the 3-

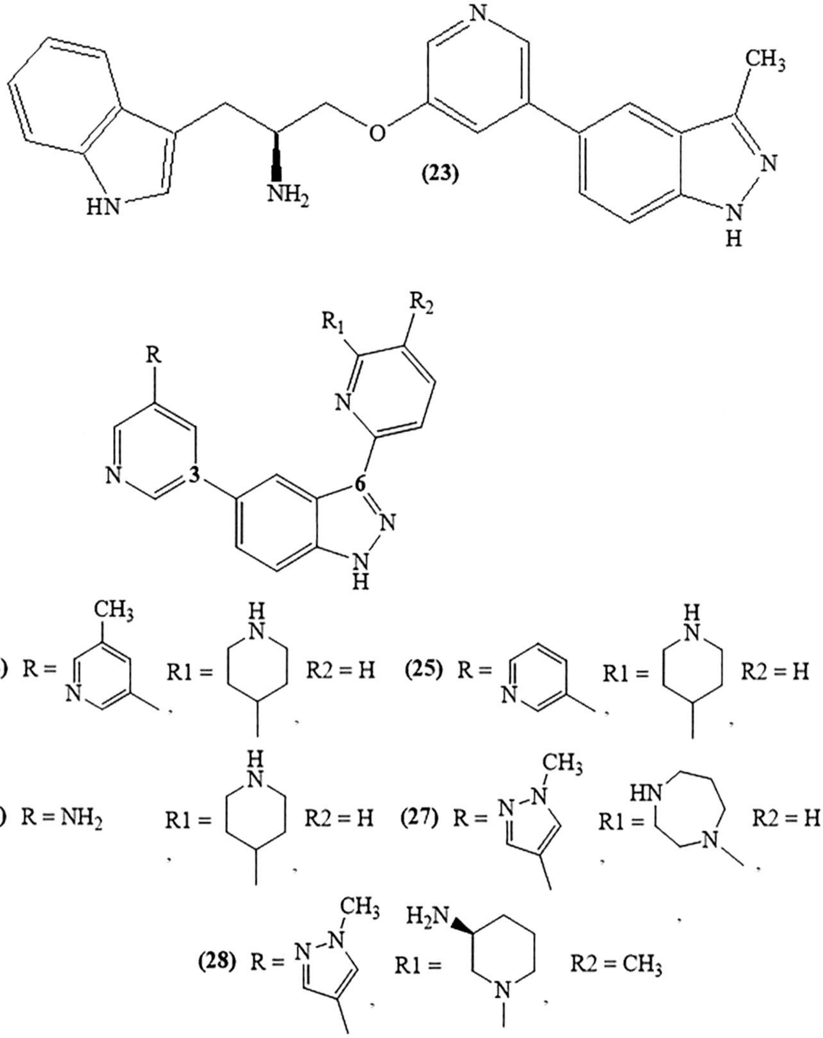

FIGURE 12.16 Structure of compounds (23–28).

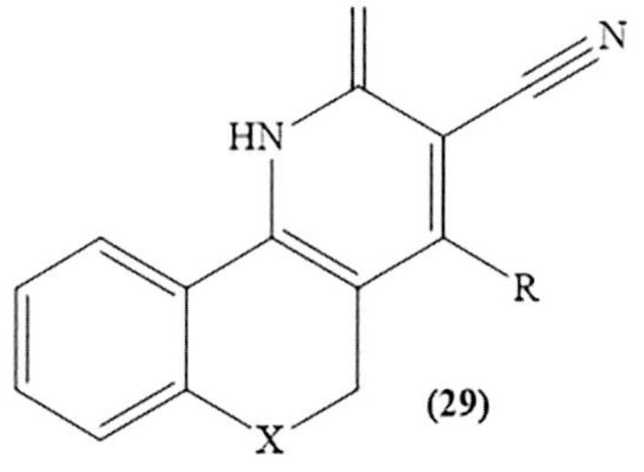

FIGURE 12.17 Structure of compound (29).

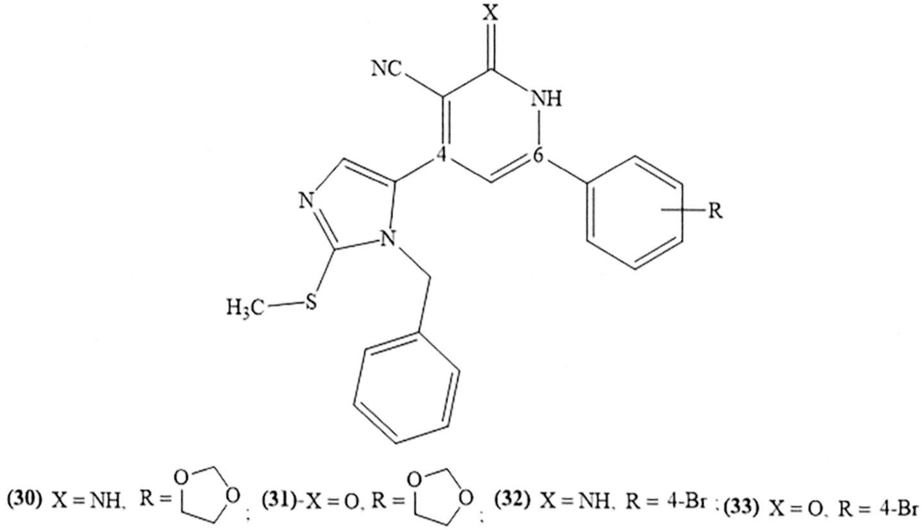

(30) X = NH, R = [benzodioxole] : (31)-X = O, R = [benzodioxole] : (32) X = NH, R = 4-Br : (33) X = O, R = 4-Br

FIGURE 12.18   Structure of compounds (30—33).

carbonitrile (30) exhibited strong activity (IC$_{50}$ = 111.01 nM). Since the existence of the methylthio imidazole and benzodioxole substituents at the C4 and C6 positions on 2-oxo-3-carbonitrile, compound (31) displayed the lowest inhibitory activity (IC$_{50}$ = 433.71 nM). The PIM-1 inhibitory potencies of all the compounds in the series are at submicromolar concentrations (IC$_{50}$ 150 nM), compared to the cytotoxicity on the HT-29 cell line, which possesses an IC$_{50}$ of above 130 μM. The Pim-1 kinase cavity is where these inhibitors bind, as shown by the docking studies. The molecules displayed HB interactions with residue Lys-169 and Lys-67, which are important for inhibiting Pim-1 kinase. It was further demonstrated by the series that compounds (30—33) had nontoxic Pim-1 inhibitory action (Abnous et al., 2017) (Fig. 12.18).

Quinoline derivatives (34—38) exhibited strong Pim-1 kinase inhibitory action on par with quercetin, the standard. Quercetin and the other compounds (34—38) acted as good inhibitors of Pim-1 kinase, according to kinetic experiments utilizing the Lineweaver—Burk double-reciprocal plot for the most potent derivatives on Pim-1 kinase. While compound (37) inhibited the Pim-1 kinase enzyme in a competitive and noncompetitive manner. Furthermore, according to molecular modeling research, compounds (34) and (35) met the requirements for hydrophobic and ligand effectiveness to be lead-like compounds (El-Miligy et al., 2023) (Fig. 12.19).

The execution stage of cell apoptosis revolves around the activation of caspases. Apoptosis to be induced in response to chemotherapeutic drugs such as taxanes, 5-fluorouracil, and doxorubicin, caspase 3 activation is necessary. The B-cell lymphoma-2 (Bcl-2) family, which includes Bcl-2, Bcl-xL, and MCL-1, is one of the primary controllers of cell survival. Farrag et al. developed and created two novel series of 6-(4-benzamido)-3-cyanopyridine 6-(4-phthalimido)-3-cyanopyridine derivatives, which were then tested for their inhibitory activity against Pim-1 kinase. Compounds with a 6-phthalimidophenyl side chain are preferred over those with a 6-benzamidophenyl side chain for PIM-1 inhibition. The most active

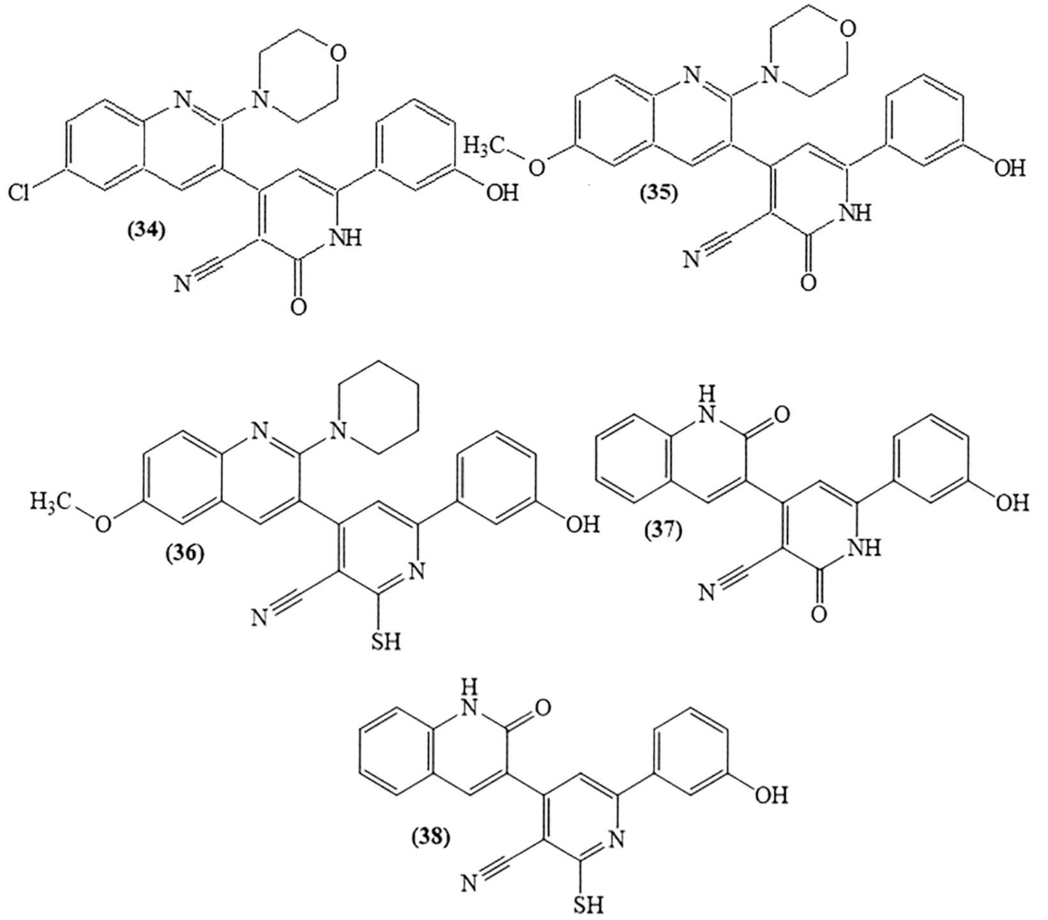

FIGURE 12.19 Structure of compounds (34–38).

cyanopyridines **(39–41)** were more active than 5-FU, while the remaining substances exhibited good to moderate cytotoxicity (Farrag et al., 2020) (Fig. 12.20).

5.9 Pyridinamines derivatives

The amino-thiazole hit I (Fig. 12.21), which had modest action against Pim-1 and 3, served as the foundation for the clinical candidate **PIM447**. There were no intermolecular HB interactions with the hydrophilic residues of Pim-1 as evidenced by the crystallization of I into the Pim-1 active site. Therefore, with the implementation of significant structural alterations that concentrated on enhancing structure bulkiness and adding nitrogen atoms at various skeleton places C2 greatly increased the potency. As a result of the high lipophilicity, attempts to enhance drug-like qualities were concentrated, and **LGB321** was discovered to be a picomolar pan-Pim inhibitor with good cellular activity (Garcia et al., 2014; Keane et al., 2015).

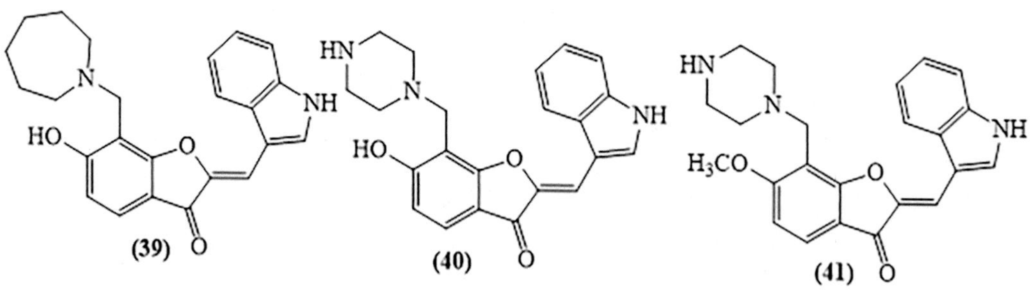

FIGURE 12.20   Structure of compounds (39—41).

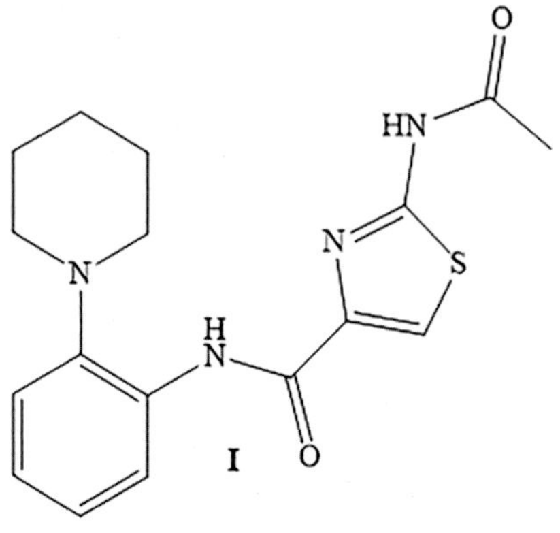

FIGURE 12.21   Structure of amino-thiazole hit (I).

Despite the possibility of using **LGB321** as an in vitro and in vivo Pim target validation probe, its metabolic instability prevented further research and development. According to structure—stability investigations, activity loss from piperidine oxidation and subsequent ring opening was prevented by substituting cyclohexane. Additionally, preclinical studies showed that **INCB053914** can be effective as a chemotherapeutic against hematological tumors when used alone or in combination with other anticancer medications. In light of this, **NCB053914** is currently being assessed in Phase I clinical research as a monotherapy in patients with advanced hematological malignancies and Phase II trials when paired with intermediate-dose zacytidine, cytarabine, or ruxolitinib (Alnabulsi & Al-Hurani, 2020) (Fig. 12.22).

5.10 Imidazo[1,2-b]pyridazines

A novel Pim-1 and 2 inhibitor, imidazo-pyridazine, was discovered from early research on the crystal structures of Pim-1 in association with ATP-mimetic—based inhibitors. The three hit inhibitors with an activity range between 0.04 and 0.12 mM against Pim-1 were found in initial SAR studies that focused on the modification of groups at C3 and C6. In the Supergen patent (WO 2008/058126 A2), which also disclosed the chemical structure of the therapeutic

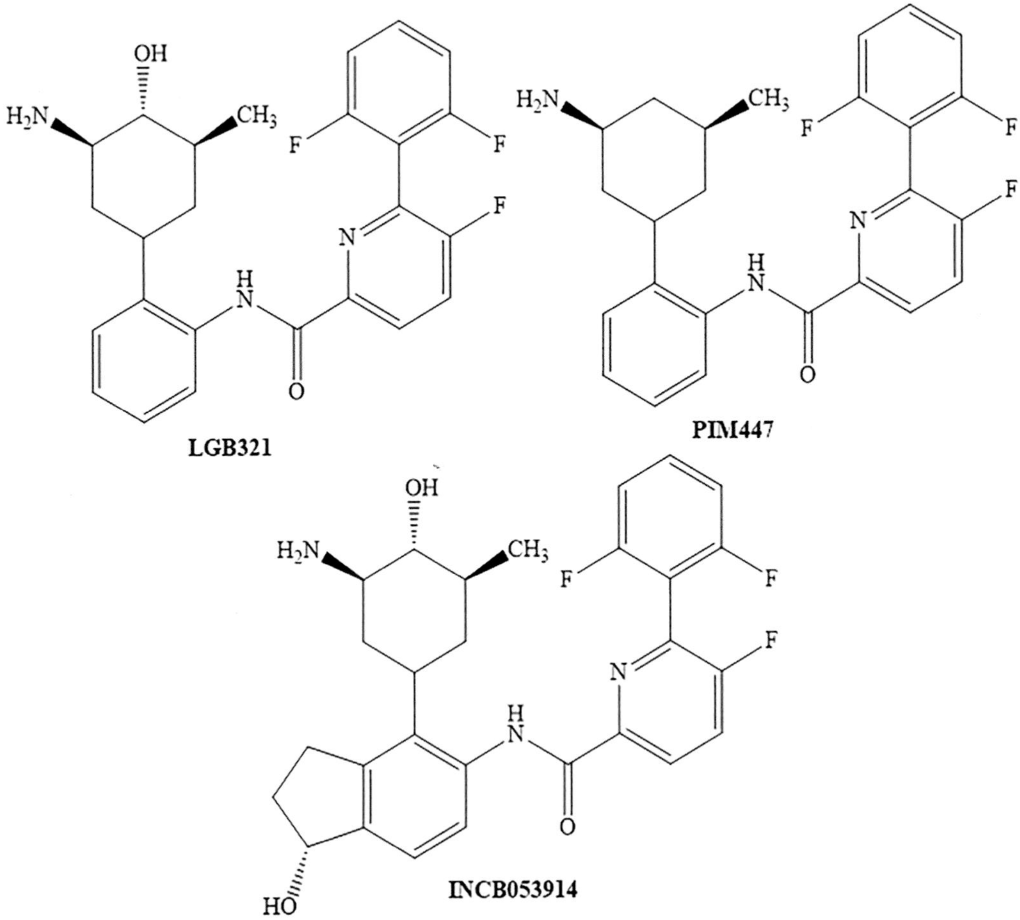

FIGURE 12.22 Structure of Pyridinamines derivatives (**LGB321, INCB053914 & NCB053914**) *Imidazo[1,2-b] pyridazines.*

candidate **SGI-1776**. In patients with relapsed and/or refractory leukemias, **SGI-1776** was the first Pim inhibitor to undergo clinical testing. P-glycoprotein (ABCB1) and breast cancer resistance protein (ABCG2) cell surface expression as well as drug transport are decreased by the SGI-1776 through both Pim-1-dependent and -independent processes (Natarajan et al., 2013). However, due to its capacity to block the ether-ago-go-related gene (hERG) channel and the resulting cardiac damage, its clinical evaluation was stopped. However, efforts to create imidazo-pyridazine Pim inhibitors persisted, leading to the discovery of the powerful and specific Pim-1 blocker **TP-3654** that lacked hERG or cytochrome P450 inhibition characteristics. The TP-**3654** is now being evaluated clinically in individuals with advanced solid tumors (Fig. 12.23).

Wurtz et al. prepared several imidazopyridazine compounds and assessed their capacity to block Pim kinase. Compound **(42)** in this series showed potential effects in the nanomolar range toward Pim-1 and 2 kinase isotypes with IC_{50} values of 0.024 and 0.095 nM,

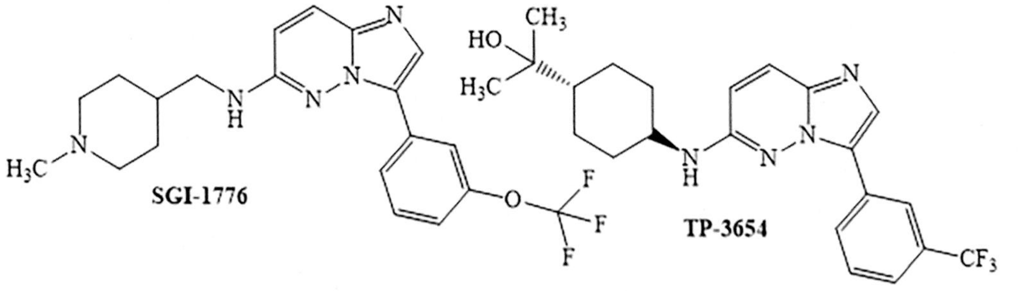

FIGURE 12.23   Structure of **SGI-1776 and TP-3654**.

accordingly. According to the SAR study, the piperidine ring's 5-position methyl group **(42)** showed a notable increase in efficacy when compared to the amino group **(42)**. On the other hand, the activity of a cis-fluoro-substitution at the same location of the piperidine ring was poorer. In the cellular experiment, the trans-5-methyl-piperidine analogue showed rather a robust action. However, compared to the cis analogue, the molecule had a 20-fold lower efficacy (Wurz et al., 2016) (Fig. 12.24).

5.11 Pyrimidine derivatives

To inhibit pan-Pim, several substituted benzofuropyrimidinones have been created. The substances **(43−46)** have demonstrated strong antikinase activity against the Pim-1 kinase (with IC_{50} values of 17.0, 7.0, and 27.0 nM, respectively). The SAR investigations showed that the alkyl benzofuropyrimidinone **(46)** exhibited good oral activities, permeability, and Pim inhibitory activity (with an IC_{50} value of 5.0 nM). After structural features were optimized, it was discovered that the 8-bromo group was crucial for activity because the des-

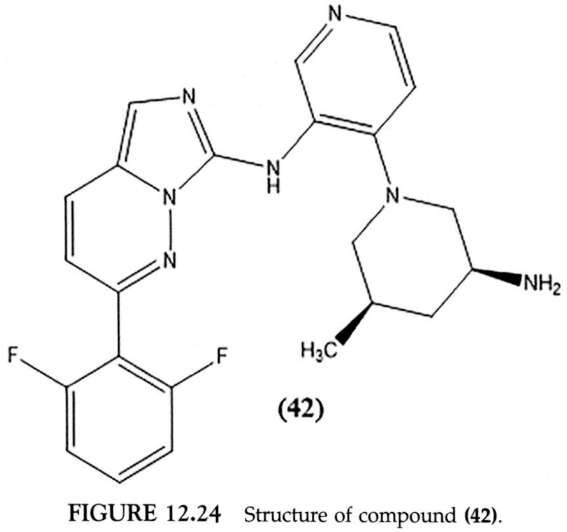

FIGURE 12.24   Structure of compound **(42)**.

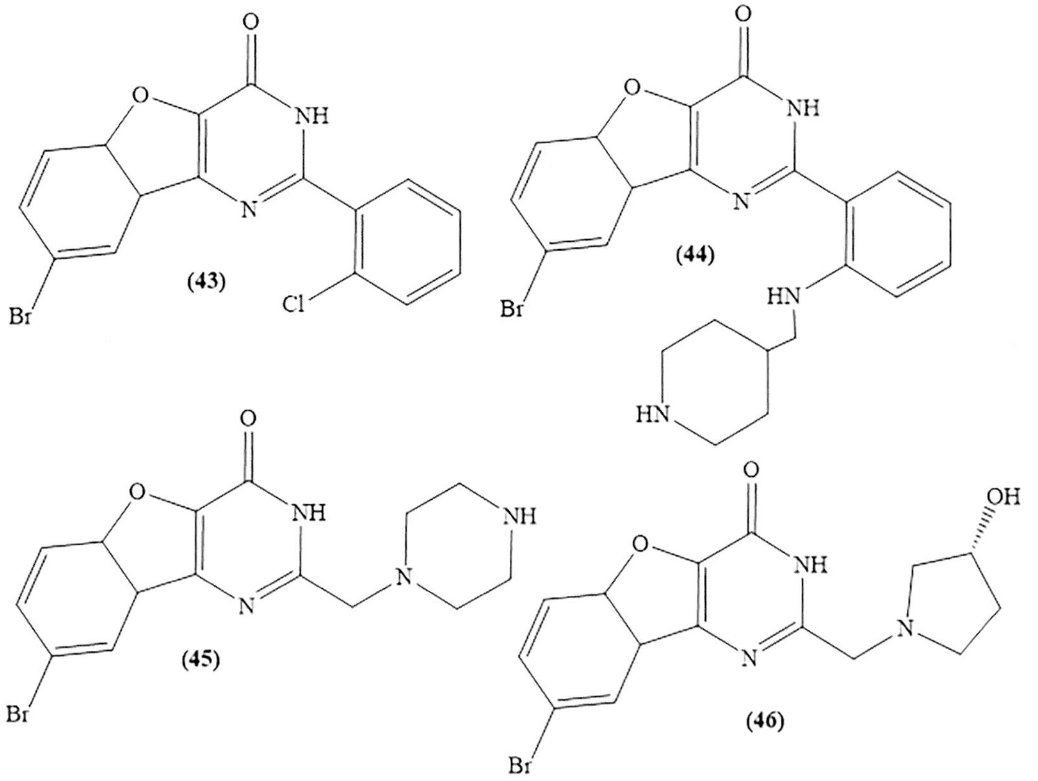

FIGURE 12.25 Structure of compound (43–46).

Br analogue was inactive. Chloride was substituted for the Bromo group at position C8 to make compounds with good inhibitory action, whereas cyano (CN) or phenyl (Ph) was substituted instead to produce compounds with lesser inhibitory activity. The results of the in vivo investigation were corroborated by molecular modeling studies, which also discovered an 8-Bromo group in the Pim kinase's hinge region. Comparing compounds with the incorporation of halogen group on the 8-position to that of nonhalogenated 8-methyl analogs revealed molecules with increased activity, suggesting that the ligand and dipole's interaction and the target protein are important for biological activity (Tsuhako et al., 2012) (Fig. 12.25).

   In comparison to the lead compound, the 8-position hydrogen bonding participation was not significant (43). However, Pim-1's crystal structure showed that if a hydroxyl group was positioned in the C7 position rather than the C8 position of the benzo-furopyrimidinone, the carbonyl backbone of the residue Glu121 in the linker region was reachable for HB. Unfortunately, the lead molecule was more powerful than the 7-OH analogue (44). Analogs with enhanced Pim-1 kinase activities related to the parent ring (piperazine) analogue were developed by expanding the steric mass surrounding the piperazine to maximize Van der Waals interaction with the larger DFG out pocket, however, this did not increase Pim-2 or Pim-3 properties. At the Pim kinase-specific site S112, compound (44) inhibits the phosphorylation

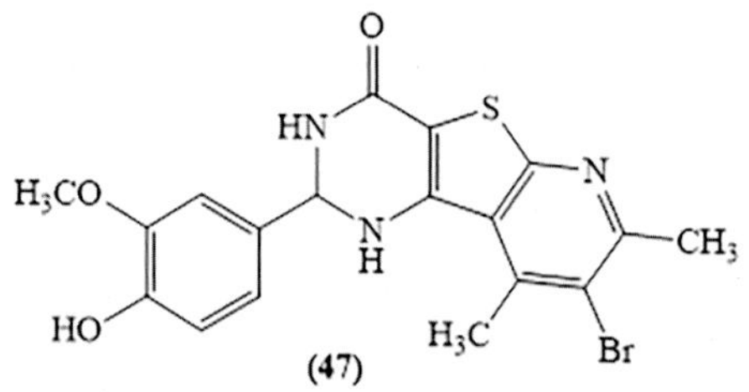

FIGURE 12.26   Structure of compounds (47–48).

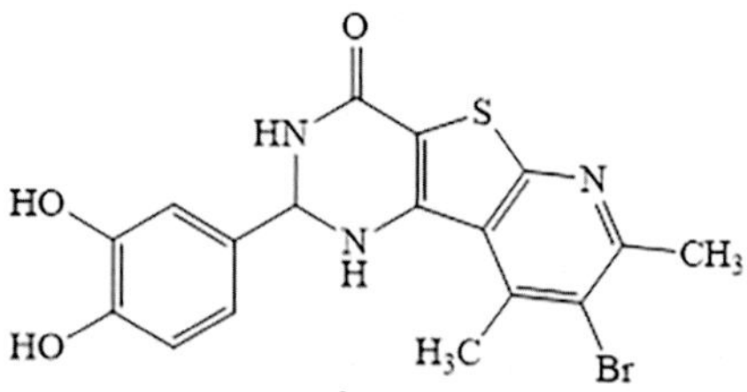

of BAD depending on the dose. Since compound **(46)** is not bioactively effective against JAK2/FLT-3 (with IC$_{50}$ > 3600 nM), it is thought that this inhibitory action in cells is caused by Pim activity (Tsuhako et al., 2012).

To increase the Pim1 kinase inhibitory action, a variety of 2-arylpyridothieno-pyrimidin-4-ones, pyridothieno-triazolopyrimidines, and 4-imino-pyridothieno-pyrimidines were synthesized. A human proto-oncogene Pim-1 ELISA Kit was used to test the kinase inhibitory activity of these synthesized derivatives. The MTT assay method was used to assess the cytotoxic activity of the most potent Pim-1 inhibitors against the HCT116 and MCF7 cell lines. All of the compounds in this series displayed IC$_{50}$ values between 0.06 and 1.76 µM. There was no discernible difference between the molecules with the 4-pyrimidinone, 4-imino (=NH), or the cyclized tri-azolopyrimidine ring. The most effective Pim-1 inhibitors have been discovered to be compounds **(47)** (3-OCH$_3$-4-OH) and **(48)** (3,4-dihydroxy) derivative, with IC$_{50}$ values of 0.08 and 0.06 µM, respectively (Mohareb, Hilmy, & Elshehawy, 2018) (Fig. 12.26).

5.12 Pyrazolopyrimidine derivatives

Pyrazole scaffold was recently studied for its significant biological and therapeutic properties. One of the most significant pyrazoles is 5-amino pyrazole, which reacts with various electrophilic compounds, such as diketones and αβ-ketoesters, to produce several heterocycles, including pyrazolo[1,5-]pyrimidines. Additionally, it was shown that pyrazolo[1,5-] pyrimidines have a broad spectrum of significant structural templates for drug discovery, including antibacterial, histamine releaser, antidiabetic, and anticancer activities. Their cytotoxic properties result from a chemical structure that resembles a purine base (Philoppes et al., 2020).

To improve its inhibitory efficacy and PK profile, Wang et al. study hit compound **(49)** and evaluate as a possible Pim-1 inhibitor. Initially, the piperidine ring was modified with a substituent 4-cyanobenzyl **(50)** to reduce the likelihood of physiological pH 7.4 initiation, where zwitterion is the main form. The important HB interaction with catalytic residue Lys67 was conserved in both compounds, as evidenced by the X-ray co-crystal structures of **(49)** (PDB ID: 4K0Y) and **(50)** (PDB ID: 4K18) in the Pim-1 active site. The phenol group of **(49)** and N6 of **(50)** were engaged in this connection. In addition, compared to **(49)**, piperidine to 4-cyanobenzyl group change favorably brought 4-fluoro aniline **(50)** closer to the hinge area. Later, to confirm intermolecular interactions with the hinge region **(51)**, the 4-fluoro aniline

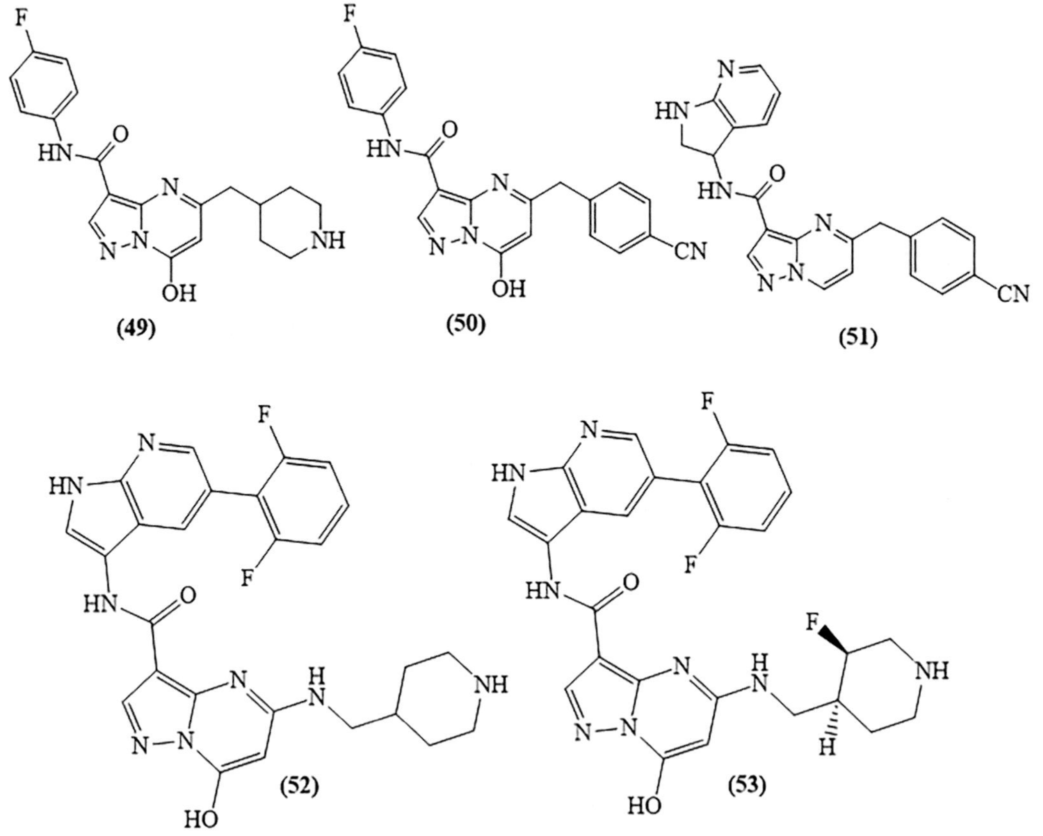

FIGURE 12.27 Structure of compounds (49–53).

ring was switched out for pyrrolopyridine. This enhances the inhibitory activity. Furthermore, SAR study to improve biological efficacy of compound (52) found it to be an intriguing lead with picomolar potency, however, its low potency cytotoxicity required further optimization. When a fluorine atom was added to the piperidine ring, the high piperidine N basicity that caused the low cellular potency was allegedly lowered (53). As a result, compound (53) was recognized as a promising lead Pim inhibitor with a unique structure, good biological potency, and potent cellular activity deserving of more research (Wang et al., 2013) (Fig. 12.27).

A powerful inhibitor of pan-Pim kinase was discovered to be the pyrazolo-pyrimidine derivative (54), with an IC_{50} value of 87.0 nM, and its derivative (55), with an IC_{50} value of 1.3 nM. The activity and relative selectivity against PIM kinase was determined by the C3 and C5 locations. Compound (56), with an IC_{50} value of 1.5 nM, was created by extending the C3 portion, particularly around the bicyclic and biaryl moiety. While maintaining the Pim-1 efficacy, molecules with functional groups like benzothiophene or benzothiazole improved their potency against PIM-2 by a factor of four. In comparison to ortho- and para-substituted derivatives, the meta-substituted compounds demonstrated higher activity.

The Pim inhibitory effectiveness decreased when rings with O-tethered activity or heteroatom-linked rings were substituted (Dwyer et al., 2013). Compound (57) shows strong action against Pim-2 in this instance. The activity of the 5-position of the 7-azaindole moiety depends on its replacement with a lipophilic group, which led to the production of compounds with a hundredfold rise in inhibitory activity against the Pim-2 kinase. Activity dropped off dramatically when the 7-azaindole moiety was swapped out for an indole moiety or when the nitrogen was moved from the 7-position to 5-position. In compound (58) the −NH group was swapped out for a −CH$_2$ group, which reduced the inhibitory action. Compound (59) showed the strongest activity in this series and discovered a possible lead for each of the three Pim kinase isotypes (Wang et al., 2013) (Fig. 12.28).

Pyridyl carboxamide derivatives, which demonstrated greater metabolic stability, have been synthesized and tested in the hunt for new pan-PIM inhibitors. Each Pim isoform was screened using the compounds in Pim-1, 2, and 3 biochemical experiments, where ATP numbers at or below their respective ATP Ki and Km values were recorded. Instead of the aminopiperidine substituted molecule (60) (Ki value of 0.001 μM), modification on

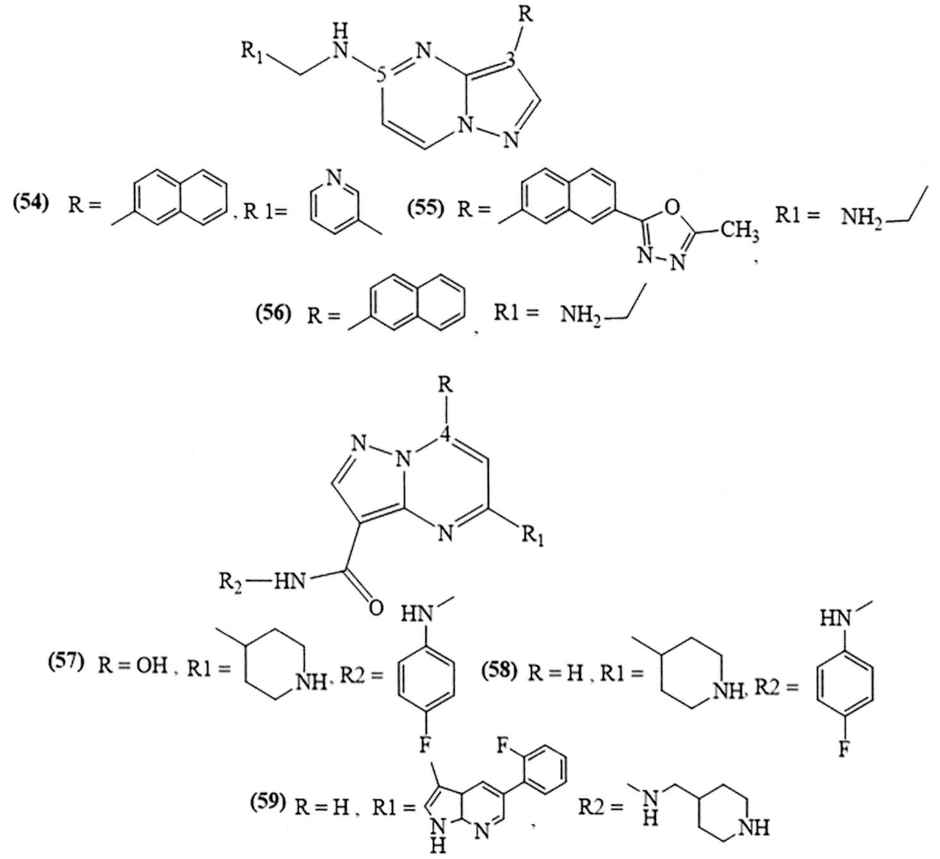

FIGURE 12.28   Structure of compounds (54−59).

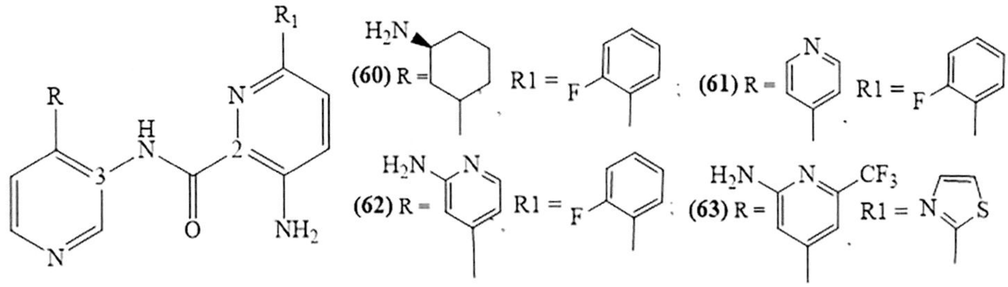

FIGURE 12.29 Structure of compounds (60−63).

the A-ring with 4-pyridine moiety gives compound (61) with a considerable drop-in activity (with Ki value of 0.008 µM). In the ribose-binding region (Glu171 and/or Asp128) of the kinase (Pim-2), the amino group substitution at the C2-position of the pyridine derivative (62) (with Ki value of 0.001 µM) synthesized derivative with HB interactions. Substitution of a difluorophenyl substituent on the B-ring resulted in molecules with considerably higher activity. The activity decreased when the amino group was relocated to the heterocyclic ring. A thiazole ring was used to replace the difluorophenyl moiety in the compound (63), which had improved inhibitory efficacy (Ki value: 0.001 µM) (Nishiguchi et al., 2016) (Fig. 12.29).

5.13 Pyrazolopyridines

Recent research has shown that targeting Pim-1 kinase is a key aspect of breast cancer treatment. The development of pyrazolo-pyridine ring system-based analogs that target Pim-1 kinase as anticancer drugs for breast cancer, is reported by Nafie and coworker. The in vitro cytotoxic activity of every freshly synthesized substance was tested against the noncancerous MCF-10A cells and the MCF-7 and MDA-MB-231 two breast cancer cell lines. To clarify the Pim-1 kinase antagonistic property as the molecular method of activity, Pim-1 kinase was used to test the most active compound discovered by in vitro drug screening. When compared to 5-FU, which had an IC$_{50}$ value of 17 nM, Compounds (64) and (65) had the strongest inhibitory action among the evaluated derivatives (Nafie et al., 2020) (Fig. 12.30).

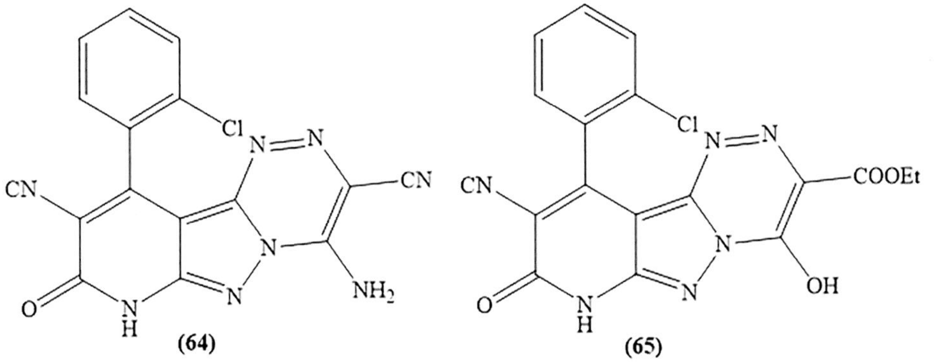

FIGURE 12.30 Structure of compounds (64−65).

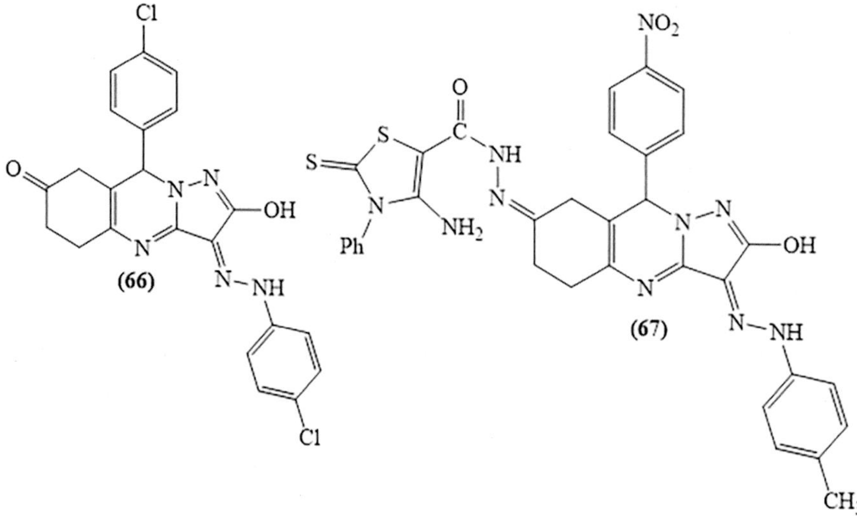

FIGURE 12.31   Structure of compounds (66–67).

5.14 Pyrazolo quinazoline derivatives

Heterocyclic compounds of five and six members, such as pyrimidines, substituted pyrazoles, and quinolines, have attracted a lot of attention recently due to their biological and pharmacological properties. In addition, numerous pyrazole-containing natural and synthetic compounds have been demonstrated to have a range of pharmacological and biological effects. Prostate cancer cell lines, as well as other common cancer cell lines, were the targets of in vitro biological activities and were assessed for a range of new quinazolines and their fused derivatives. Compounds (66) and (67) were the most potent at inhibiting Pim-1 activity, with IC_{50} values of 0.53 and 0.38 µM, respectively (Mohareb et al., 2017) (Fig. 12.31).

5.15 Pyran derivatives

In particular, fused pyrans are significant core components of many natural products. Pyran analogs are a well-known and significant class of naturally occurring chemicals that have numerous pharmacological uses. Pyrans and their fused derivatives have garnered interest recently because of their numerous biological functions. According to reports, benzo[b]pyran derivatives are potent anticancer agents that work well even at very low doses. By utilizing β-diketones, Mohareb et al. synthesize fused pyran derivatives. The generated compounds exhibited strong antiproliferative effects against various cancer cell lines together with strong tyrosine kinase inhibitory effects, with compounds (68–72) showing the strongest inhibitory effects against Pim-1 kinase (Mohareb et al., 2021) (Fig. 12.32).

The Pim kinase was effectively inhibited by the quinoline derivatives. Many analogs have been created in this direction for antitumor efficacy toward the prostate cancer PC-3 cell line. The inhibitory activity of Pim-1 kinase has been measured using the Ser/Thr KinEase assay kit (CisBio). Compounds (73–75) in this series, with GI_{50} values of

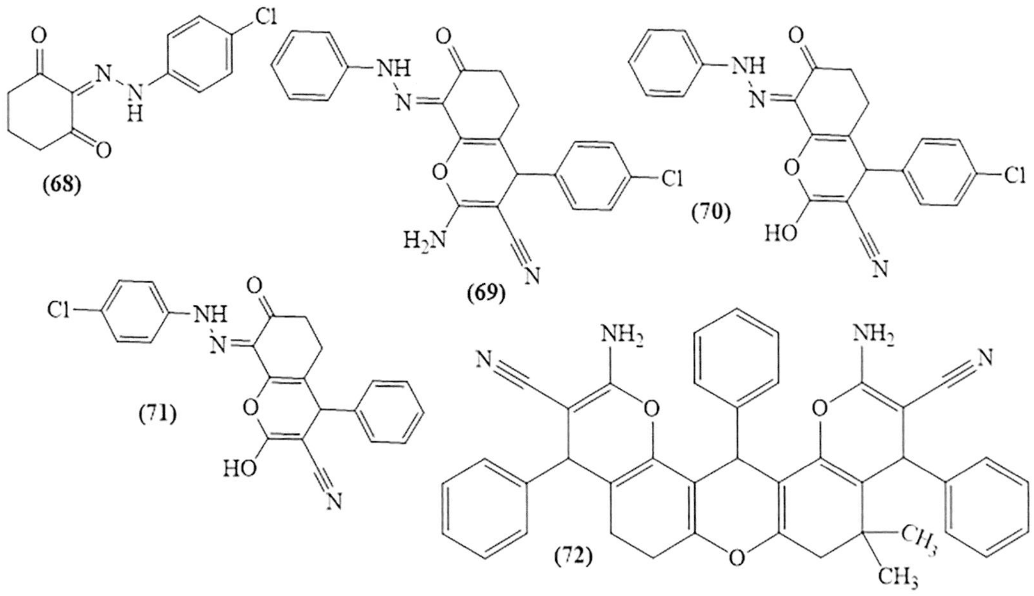

FIGURE 12.32   Structure of compounds (68–72).

2.60 μM, 2.81 μM, and 1.29 M, respectively, showed potential activity against the Pim-1 kinase. The SAR investigation demonstrated that the secondary amine coupled with pyridine and a quinoline ring is necessary for the compounds' antiproliferative effect. Compound (75) has the potential to be a PIM-1 kinase inhibitor due to its capacity to cause apoptosis and halt the cell cycle. Consider using these substances to treat prostate cancer (Li et al., 2016) (Fig. 12.33).

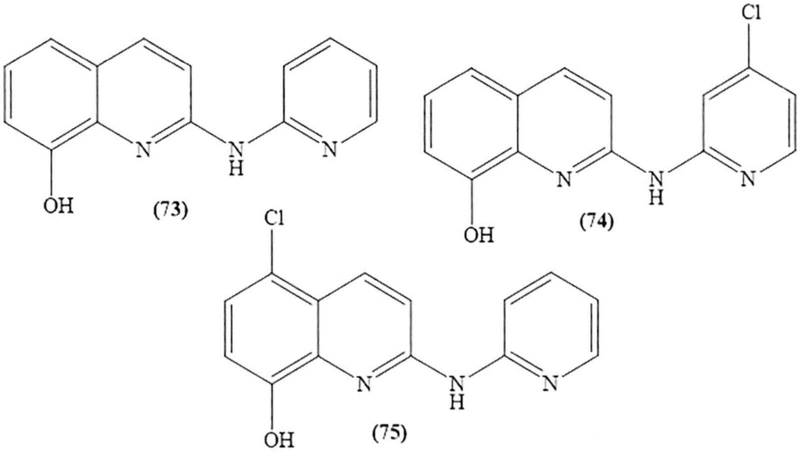

FIGURE 12.33   Structure of compounds (73–75).

5.16 Quinoline derivatives

Pim-1 kinase, a cytoplasmic serine/threonine kinase, regulates programmed cell death by using substrates that regulate apoptosis and cellular metabolism. In a series of quinoline-2-carboxamides and 2-styrylquinolines. Sliman et al. discovered compounds that may act as Pim-1 kinase inhibitors. An important pharmacophore for action was found to be the 8-hydroxyquinoline 7-carboxylic acid moiety. The kinase inhibitory potency may be caused by this scaffold's interaction with Asp186 and Lys67 residues in the ATP-binding site, according to a molecular modeling study (Sliman et al., 2010).

Mohareb et al. develop the reaction of cyclohexan-1,3-dione with dimeric cyanomethylene and trichloroacetonitrile along with the use of the resulting compound as an appropriate starting material for subsequent hetero-cyclization to produce several fused ring analogs like 2,3,6,7-tetrahydro quinazoline, dihydrothieno-isoquinoline, isoquinoline. These compounds were examined for five tyrosine kinases: c-Kit, Flt-3, VEGFR-2, EGFR, PDGFR, and Pim-1 kinase. The most potent Pim-1 kinase inhibitors were substances (76—80) (Mohareb et al., 2022) (Fig. 12.34).

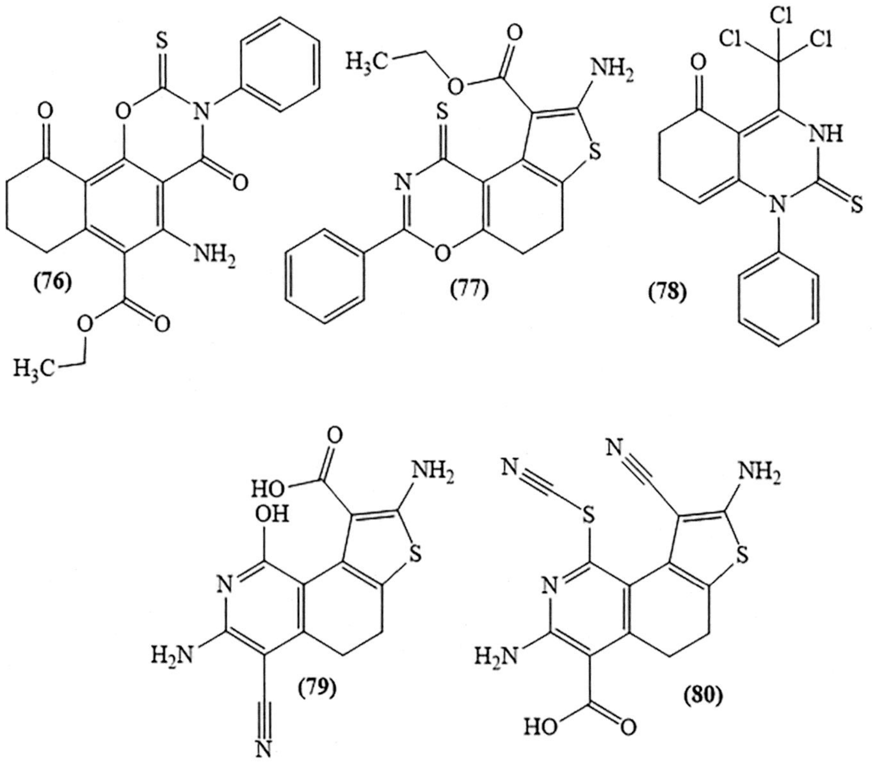

FIGURE 12.34   Structure of compounds (76—80).

5.17 Quinoxaline derivatives

From nonmacrocyclic starting materials, Victor and colleagues created several macrocyclic Pim-1/2 kinase inhibitors. In both Pim-1/2 both in cellular as well as cell-free enzyme tests evaluating Pim-1/2 based phosphorylation of BAD, some of the macrocycles show significant increases in potency. The binding conformation was stabilized, and there were more positive van der Waals contacts among the macrocyclic linker and the Pim protein, which increased efficacy. The macrocycle **(81)** with the (Z) configuration and allylic-methyl substitution was shown to have the best pharmacokinetics, solubility, and enzyme activity. The maximum dose examined (100 mg/kg) gave a higher than 50% reduction of AD phosphorylation for at least 16 h in a KMS-12- BM tumor xenograft model. The oral dose of compound **(81)** was capable of reducing Pim-based phosphorylation of BAD with an EC_{50} of 3.6 μM. In a 16-day efficacy model, a daily oral dose of 100 mg/kg was well tolerated and capable of totally suppressing the growth of KMS-12-BM xenografts. It has been established that compound **(81)** possesses features fit for the in vivo research of Pim kinase inhibitory action, and compound **(81)** is the first illustration of a macrocyclization method that improves Pim kinase inhibitors (Cee et al., 2016).

Clinical trials are now being conducted for the most promising Pim-1 kinase inhibitors, several of which showed considerable in vitro anticancer activity on cancer cell lines and in various in vivo tumor xenograft models. In contrast to other protein kinases, Pim-1's active site is unique in that it contains a hinge region with backbone peptide atoms that forms hydrogen bonds (H-bonds) with the adenine moiety of ATP. There is a proline residue (Pro123) in this region that cannot donate an H-bond and hinders the formation of the conserved H-bond that connects the hinge backbone to the ATP adenine ring as found in other kinases. The carbonyl backbone of glutamate 121 (Glu121) and the adenine amino group of ATP must therefore form just one hinge H-bond for Pim-1 to bind ATP. Additionally, the hinge is altered by the insertion of a valine (Val126), which is lacking in other kinases, increasing the catalytic pocket (Fig. 12.35). Selective inhibitors can be created by taking advantage of this special property.

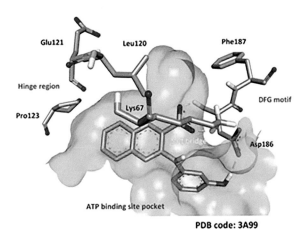

PDB code: 3A99

FIGURE 12.35   Binding pose for compound (81) into the ATP pocket of Pim-1 (PDB ID: 3A99).

A large number of Pim-1 inhibitors work primarily as ATP competitive inhibitors by targeting the ATP-binding pocket. They can be divided into two groups: those that mimic ATP and bind to the hinge region's Glu121 residue and those that don't and interact with the ATP binding site differently. Oyallon and colleagues discovered several quinoxaline-2-carboxylic acid derivatives that specifically target the Moloney murine leukemia virus-1 (HsPim-1) kinase human proviral integration site. To better understand the SAR under investigation, many analogs were synthesized. Docking experiments carried out in the ATP pocket of HsPim-1 support an unconventional method of binding for these inhibitors. The lead compound **(82)**, with a strong selectivity profile against a group of mammalian protein kinases, was able to block HsPim-1 enzymatic activity at nanomolar concentrations (IC$_{50}$ of 74 nM) (Oyallon et al., 2018).

In addition, they discuss the development, synthesis, SAR, and in vitro assessments of fresh quinoxaline analogs that function as dual Pim-1 and 2 inhibitors. Effective submicromolar Pim-1/2 inhibitors were found in two lead compounds, **(83)** and **(84)**. These compounds can also stop the growth of two human cell lines that express large levels of Pim-1/2 kinases endogenously, MV4-11 acute myeloid leukemia (AML) and colorectal cancer cell line, HCT-116 (Oyallon et al., 2021) (Figs. 12.36 and 12.37).

5.18 Oxazine derivatives

Numerous Pim-1 inhibitors, including mitoxantrone, thioridazine, 10-DEBC12, and its derivative molecule, have been discovered recently by using structure-based drug design

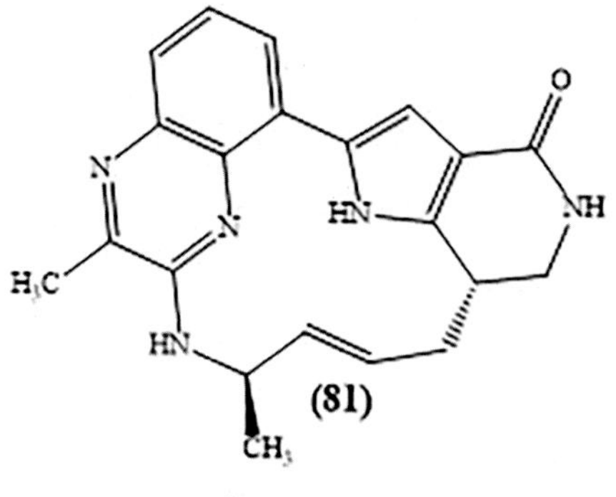

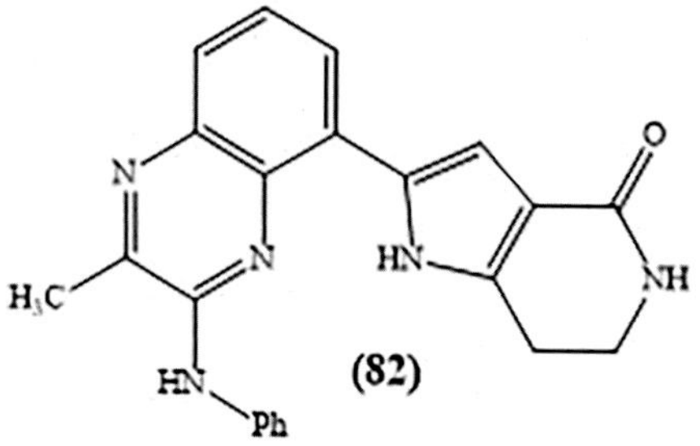

FIGURE 12.36   Structure of compounds (81–82).

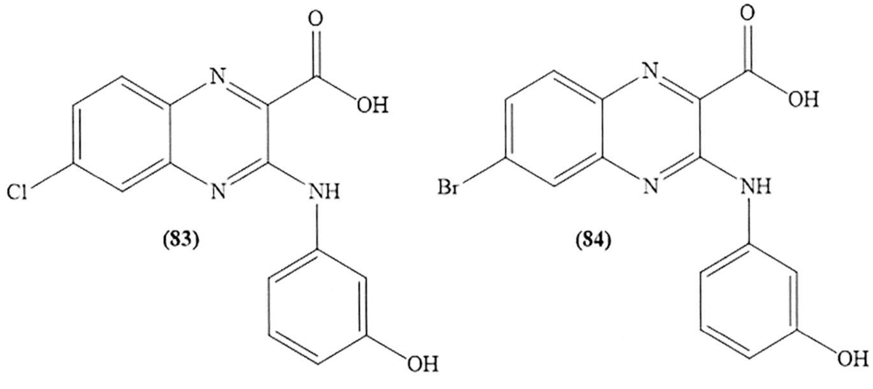

FIGURE 12.37 Structure of compounds (83–84).

approaches. It is possible to determine the complex crystal structures of these inhibitors with Pim-1 kinase, and they offered a structural basis for comprehension of interactions between the ligands and the target. Additionally, it would be advantageous to develop effective inhibitors with new scaffolds and acceptable physicochemical characteristics like permeability of the membrane. The study of small-molecule medications has focused a lot of attention on macrocycles, which are compounds with enormous rings of more than 12 atoms. Macrocyclization significantly affects target selectivity, potency, and PK/PD. As a result, it was extremely desirable to use them in numerous medication design initiatives. Three forms of pyridine-containing benzo-pyridines were developed by using linkers of various lengths and types. By placing oxygen at different positions along the aliphatic chain of macrocyclic compounds, the 1,4-oxazine macrocyclic derivatives (85), (86), and (87) were developed to study how the aliphatic chain changes conformation and to increase solubility. These developed compounds were investigated for their potential to inhibit Pim-1. Compound (86) demonstrated the strongest inhibitory activity ($IC_{50} = 35$ nM) for Pim-1 kinase in in vitro study, all other compounds demonstrated significant inhibitory activities (with IC_{50} 100 nM) (Xu et al., 2022) (Fig. 12.38).

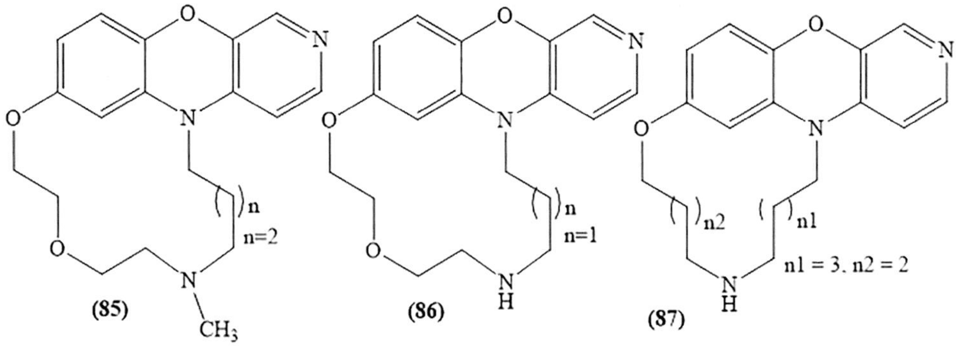

FIGURE 12.38 Structure of compounds (85–87).

5.19 Oxindole derivative

The Cylene pharmaceutical library's high-throughput screening revealed oxindole to be a brand-new Pim-1 inhibitor. The significance of the oxindole scaffold with an unsubstituted lactam NH as the core for inhibitory activity was underlined by SAR analyses. Additionally, the alicyclic amide's ability to isosterically substitute carboxylic acid while maintaining the coplanarity of the furan and phenyl rings and possessing basic nitrogen was essential to the compound's inhibitory function. The MV-4-11 acute myeloid leukemia cell line, which is particularly susceptible to **CX-6258**, was found in SAR tests as a novel, potent pan-Pim inhibitor with cellular antiproliferative action. Pim kinase inhibition is anticipated to be effective in the treatment of cancer, and compound **CX-6258** is presently undergoing additional preclinical research to assess its potential for use in human clinical trials (Haddach et al., 2012) (Fig. 12.39).

The C3-functionalized oxindole, which lies at the basis of many natural compounds, is now being recognized as a promising novel drug development scaffold with potential anticancer and other biological actions. A unique set of C3-functionalized oxindoles called 3-(2-oxo-4-phenylbut-3-en-1-ylidene) indolin-2-ones were developed by Sun and coworkers, and they were screened for their capacity to prevent cell proliferation against various human cancer cell lines, including SW620, HeLa, and A549. This biological investigation found that these substances with indole and aromatic, unsaturated ketone as their scaffolds demonstrated mild to 10 detectable anticancer effects. Additionally, the Pim kinase inhibition results showed that compound **(88)** has effective and selective anti-Pim-1 kinase activity ($IC_{50} = 5\ \mu M$). Additionally, compound **(88)** demonstrated a significant reduction of tubulin polymerization, which may have resulted from blocking Pim-1 (Sun et al., 2015) (Fig. 12.40).

5.20 2-Azaindole (indazole) derivatives

After the virtual screening of combined commercial databases and in vitro biochemical experiments, indole was found to be a promising Pim-1 hit inhibitor (Sun et al., 2015). A structure-based optimization process was prompted by insufficient kinase selectivity and the subpar pharmacokinetic profile. The skeleton of **(89)** was separated into three sections

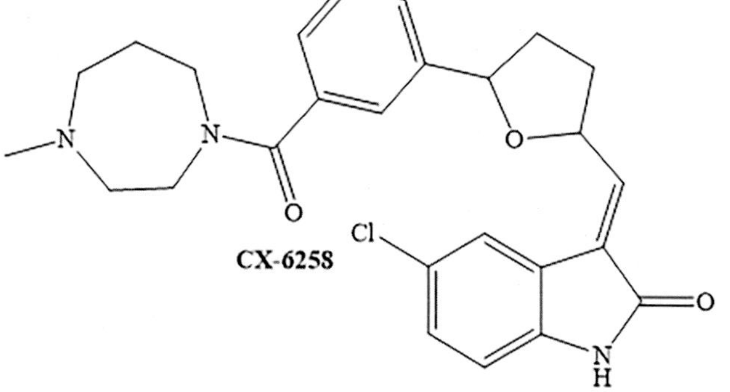

FIGURE 12.39 Structure of compounds **(CX-6258)**.

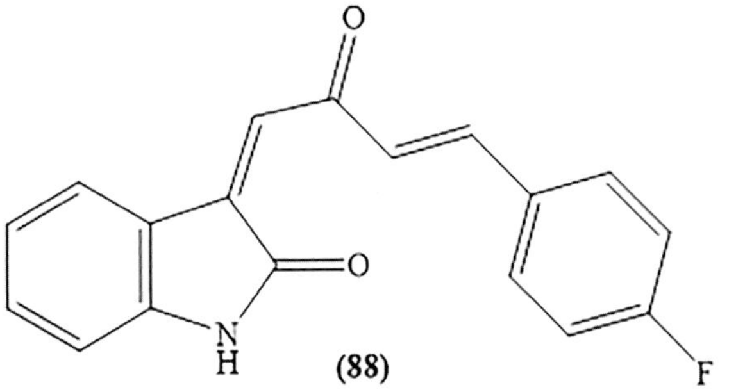

FIGURE 12.40   Structure of oxindole derivative (88).

for potency optimization, and SAR investigations were carried out for each section in turn, commencing at the top and moving down the left and right sides.

The capacity of indole to interact with the ATP-binding site, where its top moiety (at C7) inhabited the pocket facing the acidic region, was shown by X-ray crystallography of the Pim-1 active site. A nitrogen atom was added to (90) to ensure that it could form a hydrogen bond with either Glu171 or Asp128, enhancing its effectiveness. In addition, because it is prone to metabolism and does not interact in any way with the active site residues, the left-hand side phenolic hydroxy group, which is in the direction of the G-loop, was chosen to undergo additional modification. While the activity was unaffected by the elimination of phenolic-OH, methylation (91) increased the activity by interacting hydrophobically with the G-loop. The right-hand side, on the other hand, did not permit significant structural modification because, between its indole-NH and Glu121 of the hinge region, essential HBs were formed. Consequently, the best isosteres of indole with enhanced potency and lower cLog P were 7-azaindole (92) and 2-azaindole (93). Given the kinase selectivity, compound (93) was chosen for additional preclinical study; however, compound (92) had a better in vitro PK profile and had its kinase selectivity further enhanced (Tsuganezawa et al., 2012) (Fig. 12.41).

The formation of hydrogen bonds between the amino acids in the hinge region of various kinases and the N7 of the 7-azaindole ring was cited as the cause of the low kinase selectivity of the compound (92). By sterically blocking hydrogen bond formation by adding an alkyl or minor halogen group at position C6. However, when the bulk of the substituent increased, the inhibitory effectiveness dropped; this was turned around when OCH3 was swapped

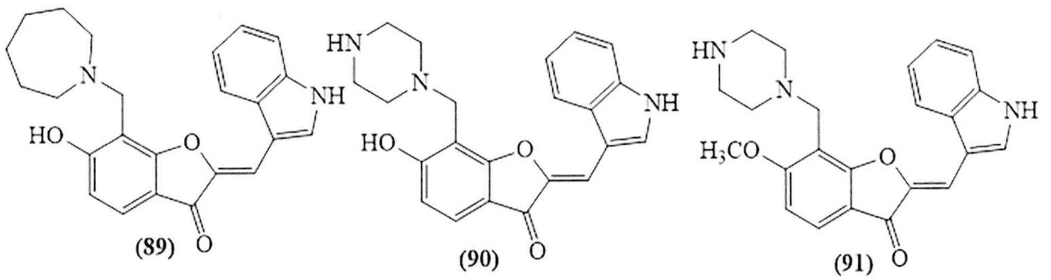

FIGURE 12.41   Structure of oxindole derivative (89-91).

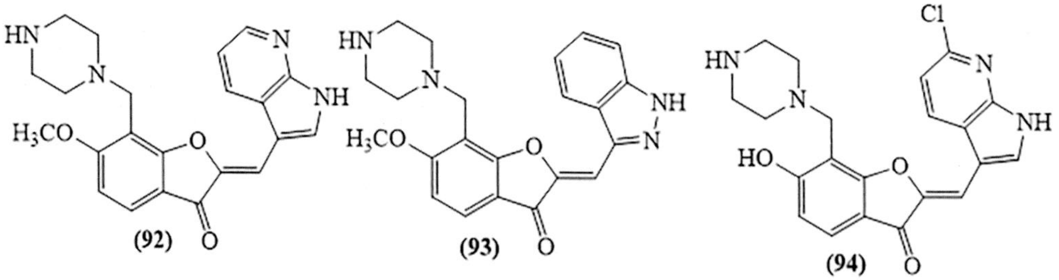

FIGURE 12.42   Structure of compounds (82–94).

out for an OH group. With these changes, compound (94) was discovered as selective Pim-1 kinase inhibitor with increased Pim-2 inhibition efficacy (Nakano et al., 2012, 2017) (Fig. 12.42).

5.21 3,5-disubstituted 6-azaindazoles

Hu et al. discovered a new Pim inhibitor with a 6-aza-indazole chemotype after studying SAR of the Akt inhibitor (95). In the beginning, an extension approach at three specific sites (C3, C5, or C6) was used to ensure intermolecular interactions with the acidic area. Pim kinase inhibition was associated with a 5-pyridyl-6-azaindazole core (96). As a result, a subnanomolar inhibitor (97) was discovered. The interaction of this inhibitor with the catalytic Lys67 was further investigated by adding various polar ends to the C6 of the aza indazole core ring. Due to its balanced biochemical and cellular efficacy profiles, the 3,5-disubstituted 6-aza indazole derivative (97) was selected as a Pim kinase lead inhibitor (Fig. 12.43).

The inferior pharmacokinetic profile of the compound (98), in particular its incredibly low oral bioavailability in rats, is required for further optimization. The reasons for this restricted bioavailability were looked into by looking at its hepatic and GI metabolic stability and in-vitro permeability. Focusing on intestinal metabolism is a result of the many analogs' diverse

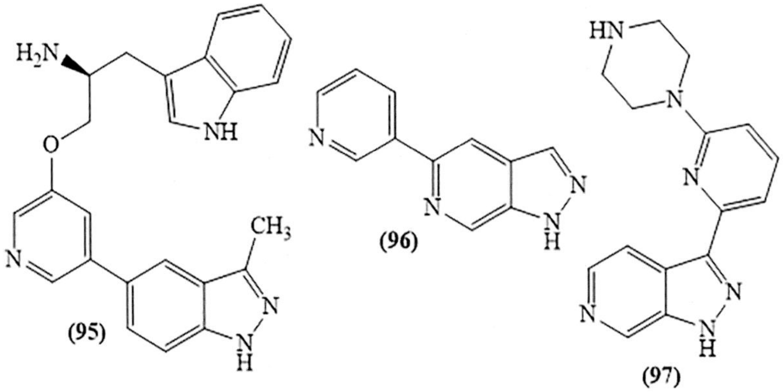

FIGURE 12.43   Structure of compounds (95–97).

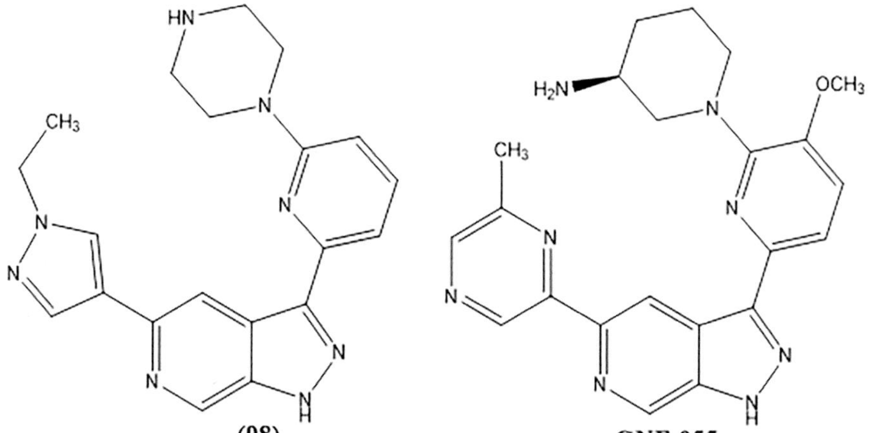

FIGURE 12.44 Structure of compounds (98 and GNE 955).

metabolic and permeability profiles. When substances were incubated with rat intestinal microsomes, it became clear that any activity was stopped by glucuronidation at the 6-aza indazole core. Because the 6-aza indazole ring is essential for any inhibitory activity, it was challenging to increase metabolic stability without surrendering any inhibitory effects. Several heteroaromatic ring isosteres were proposed and investigated to accomplish the goal, and 5-aza indazole GNE 955 emerged as a promising drug candidate with excellent in vivo stability characteristics. Nevertheless, Wang et al.'s discovery of a substitute scaffold with improved pharmacodynamic and pharmacokinetic profiles led to the termination of further development of 5-aza indazole as a Pim kinase inhibitor (Hu et al., 2015; Wang et al., 2017) (Fig. 12.44).

5.22 Quinazolinone-pyrrolopyrrolones

As a potential Pim kinase inhibitor, the macrocyclic optimization method of (99), which led to methyl quinoxaline (100), showed potential Pim kinase inhibitory activity. Compound (100), when used in a murine KMS-12 BM multiple myeloma xenograft model, demonstrated good biochemical and cellular Pim-1/2 inhibitory activity as well as good effectiveness. On the other hand, due to the poor pharmacokinetic properties in dogs, SAR studies led to the discovery of more metabolically stable substances with retained biochemical and cellular Pim kinase inhibitory action, which resulted in the development of an orally active Pim kinase inhibitor (101). However, because of its limited water solubility, (101) has undergone additional optimization to improve its drug-like characteristics (Pettus et al., 2016) (Fig. 12.45).

The co-planarity between the quinazolinone and pyrrolopyrrolone rings is important for binding to the ATP pocket, as shown by the co-crystal structure of compound (101) into the Pim-1 active site (PDB ID: 5IPJ). Low water solubility is caused by this co-planarity because it makes it easier for molecules to form a crystal lattice. Since N-alkyl and N-methyl substituents are located at the N2 and C3 of the quinazolinone ring, respectively,

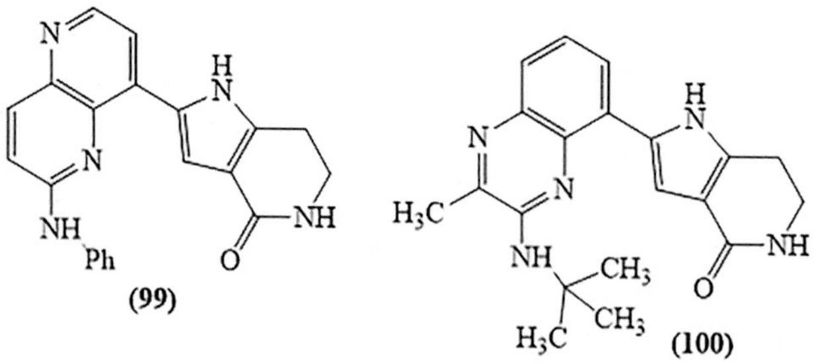

FIGURE 12.45   Structure of compounds **(99 and 100)**.

drug-likeness-driven optimization of several concentrated on their variation. It was discovered by SAR study and pharmacokinetic profiling, a potential medication for hematological cancers is 2-((1-methylcy-clopropyl)amino)quinazolin-4(3H)-one **(102)**. Compound **(102)**, in comparison to **(101)**, demonstrated enhanced biological and cellular activity, high solubility, and a comparable method of interaction with the binding site of Pim-1 (PDB ID: 6MT0) (Wang, Andrews, et al., 2019) (Fig. 12.46).

5.23 Quinoxaline-pyrrolodihdropiperidinones

To find prospective therapeutic candidates with anticancer action, it was decided to further optimize the reported naphthyridine pyrrolodihydropiperidinone hit **(103)**. First, the Pim kinase selectivity of **(103)** was improved through structure-based optimization in comparison to other kinases. When rationalizing the optimization, consideration was given to the ability of naphthyridine nitrogen at position C5 to form favorable hydrogen bonds with the backbone NH group of the kinase hinge region. The Methylquinoxaline **(104)**, an isosteric substitute for naphthyridine, considerably increased the kinase selectivity and also increased the inhibitory potency of the Pim-1 kinase. Further structural modifications that substituted large alkyl groups for the phenyl substituent connected to the secondary amine did not improve effectiveness in biochemical tests. Later, it was proposed that adding an alkyl group to pyrrolodihydropiperidinone's secondary amine may preserve the overall U-shape conformer of the hit inhibitor **(97)** and improve lipophilic interactions with the residues in the G-loop (Fig. 12.47).

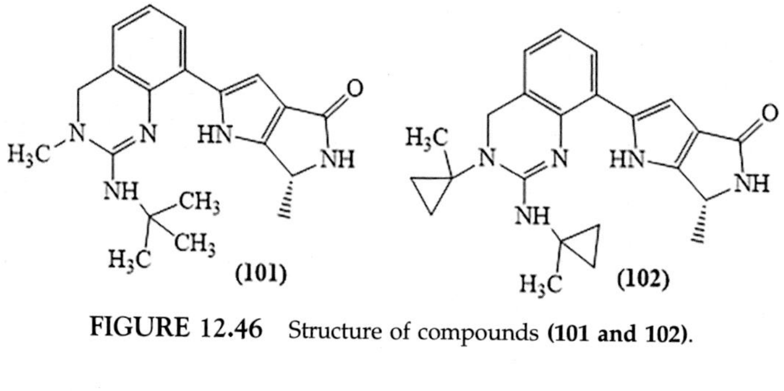

FIGURE 12.46   Structure of compounds **(101 and 102)**.

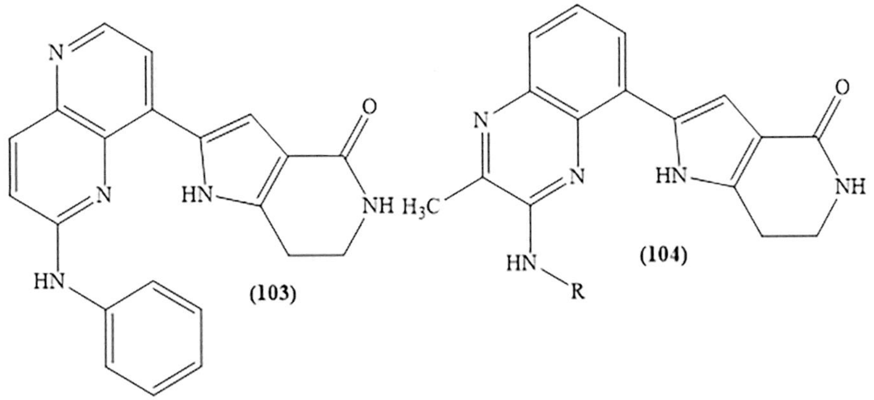

FIGURE 12.47 Structure of compounds **(103 and 104)**.

The quinazoline and pyrrolodihydropiperidinone rings were connected by a link made of five atoms with various alkyl substituents, as well as a variety of saturated and unsaturated bonds with various arrangements **(105)**. This created a 13-membered macrocyclic structure. Considering the excellent PK profile, solubility, and therapeutic potency, the (Z)-configured, allylic methyl substituted macrocycle **(105)** was selected for further investigation. In a KMS-12 BM tumor xenograft model, the oral activity and effectiveness of **(106)** (EC$_{50}$ = 30 nM) revealed the successful macrocyclization optimization technique that produced a drug with features suited for in vivo Pim kinase inhibition study (Cee et al., 2016) (Fig. 12.48).

5.24 Thiazole derivative

Important five-member heterocyclic derivatives known as thiazole derivatives have an aromatic structure, a nitrogen atom, a sulfur atom, and a thiazole functional group. Because of the broad spectrum of biological activities of thiazole derivatives, synthetic organic chemists

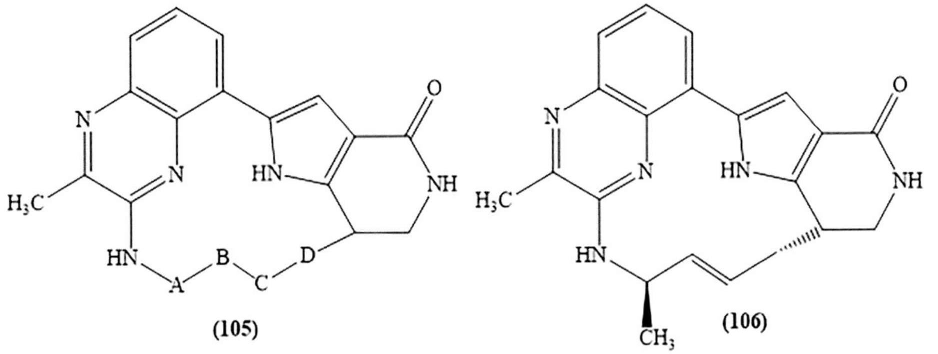

FIGURE 12.48 Structure of compounds **(105 and 106)**.

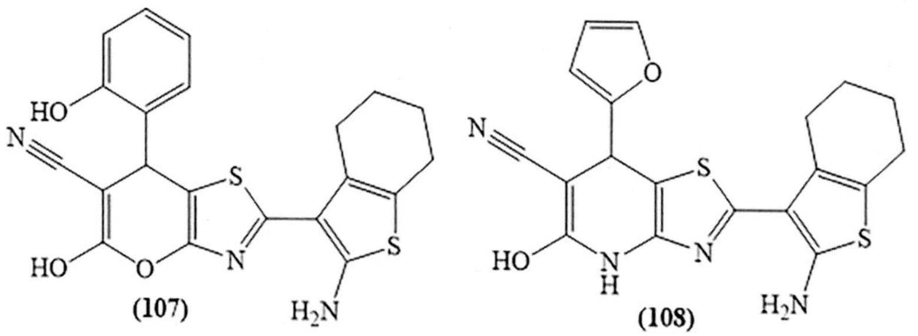

FIGURE 12.49   Structure of compounds (107 and 108).

have focused a lot of their research in the past few decades on developing these compounds for the synthesis of novel heterocyclic compounds from straightforward and easily accessible substrates. Abdallah and co-workers synthesize pyrano-thiazole and thiazolo-pyridine derivatives through multicomponent reactions by the reaction of thiazol one with several active methylene reagents such as alkyl cyanoacetate or nitrile in basic conditions and evaluate for their anticancer activity against six cancer cell lines. Three compounds were selected to examine their anti-Pim-1 kinase activity out of three compounds (107) and (108) exhibited the maximum inhibitions with IC_{50} values of 0.39 and 0.26 μM, respectively (Abdallah et al., 2019) (Fig. 12.49).

For the development of biologically active compounds, several 2-aminothiophene and thiophene derivatives were exposed to chemical changes using ions and other reagents. By combining cyclohexan-1,4-dione with sulfur and cyanoacetylhydrazine. Mohareb et al. showed how to develop a thiophene derivative with various active centers that improve its suitability for various hetero-cyclization procedures. Five tyrosine kinases, Pim 1 kinase, and various cancer cell lines were used to analyze the synthesized products. Thiophene-3-carbohydrazide derivatives (109) showed the strongest inhibition of Pim-1 kinase with an IC_{50} of 0.06 μM (Mohareb, Wardakhan, & Abbas, 2019) (Fig. 12.50).

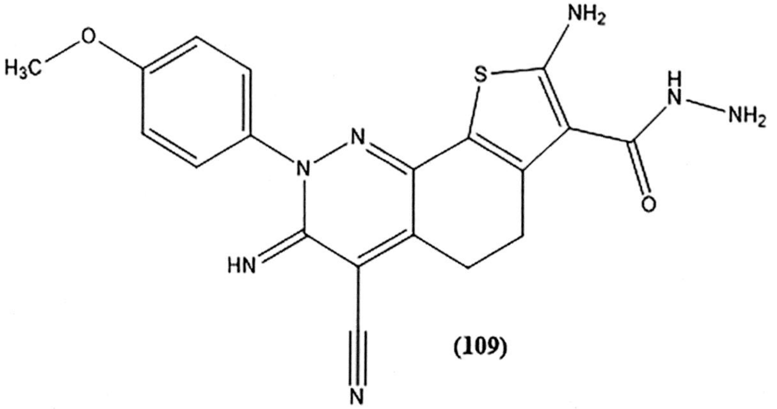

FIGURE 12.50   Structure of compound (109).

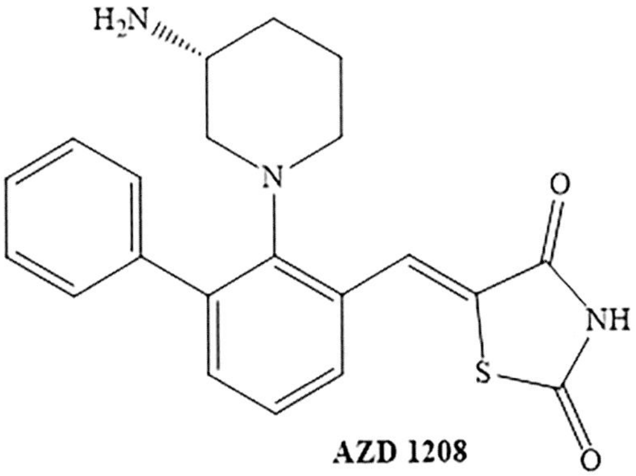

FIGURE 12.51   Structure of compound (AZD 1208).

5.25 Thiazolidine-2,4-dione

Dakin et al. discovered thiazolidine-2,4-dione as a powerful and focused pan-Pim kinase inhibitor with potent anticancer activity. Initial SAR study showed that while removing phenolic hydroxy group preserved activity, adding cyclic amines at ortho to the thiazolidine-2,4-dione moiety increased potency by a factor of more than 10. Furthermore, the efficacy of the cyclic amine was increased by the addition of a lipophilic group (phenyl ring in **AZD1208**) at ortho, because this group can interact hydrophobically with hydrophobic amino acids at position 126. Prior to its clinical assessment in patients with solid and hematological malignancies, preclinical research on the therapeutic candidate **AZD1208** was carried out. Unfortunately, research on **AZD1208** was halted since it failed to show any therapeutic utility and increased CYP3A4 activity in participants (Lee et al., 2019) (Fig. 12.51).

Another substance, **SMI-4a**, may have inhibited the cell cycle and proliferation of non-small cell lung cancer (NSCLC) cells in in vitro study, while inducing apoptosis. In addition, **SMI-4a** also suppresses cancer cell growth in mouse models with NSCLC cell. PI3K/AKT/mTOR pathway which is involved in the antitumor process induced by SMI-4a. The **(Z)-SMI-4a** is a potent, selective, cell-permeable, and ATP-competitive Pim-1 inhibitor with an IC_{50} of 24 μM and a Ki of 0.6 μM. **(Z)-SMI-4a** also inhibits Pim-2 (IC_{50} of 100 μM) and has little effect on the other serine/threonine- or tyrosine-kinases. **(Z)-SMI-4a** having anticancer activity, Pim-1 inhibitor may serve as a new molecular targeted drug for NSCLC patients (Jiang et al., 2019) (Fig. 12.52).

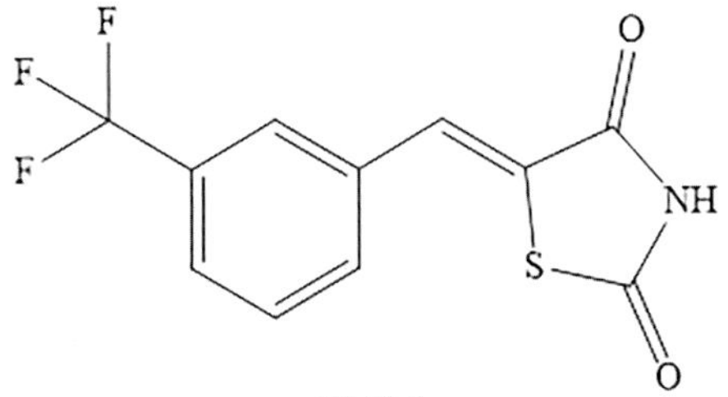

SMI-4a

FIGURE 12.52   Structure of compound (SMI-4a).

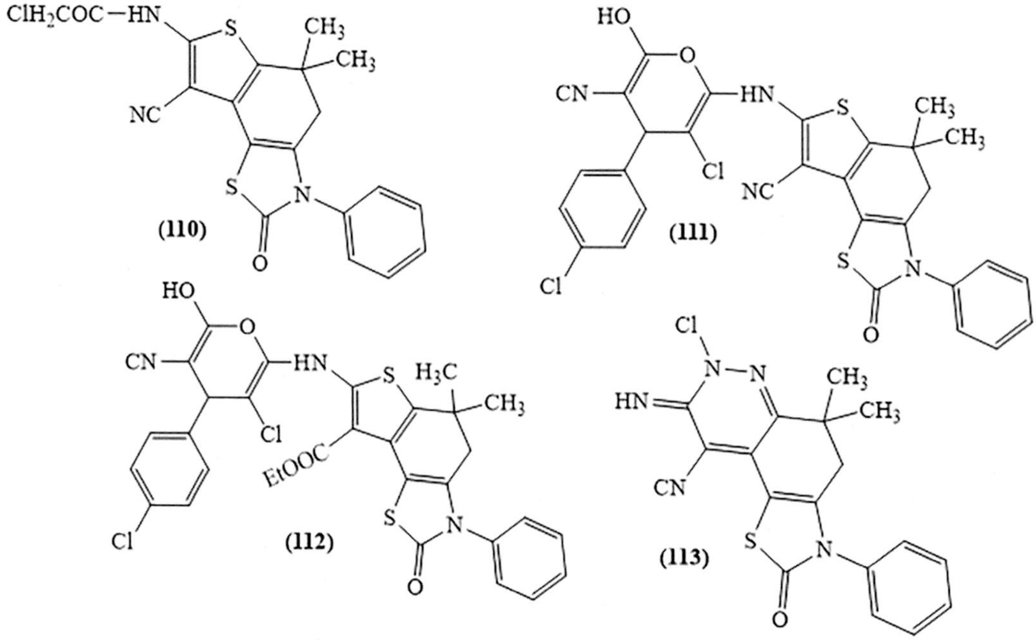

FIGURE 12.53   Structure of thiophene derivatives (110–113).

Considering the basic principles of drugs design, adding thiophene rings to the thiazole nucleus would likely result in the production of more bioactive molecules due to the wide range of applications that these types of compounds have.

Mohareb and colleagues investigated the formation of thiophene and pyran derivatives conjugated to the thiazole moiety through additional hetero-cyclization beginning with dimedone. Tyrosine kinase and Pim1 kinase were used to synthesize the compounds through several cancer cell lines. Compounds (110–113) were shown to be quite effective at inhibiting the Pim-1 kinase enzyme when substances were tested for this ability (Mohareb, Klapötke, & Reinhardt, 2018) (Fig. 12.53).

Flanders et al. recently showed screening for the (Z)-thiazolidine-2,4-diones' Pim kinase inhibitory activity. The most active compound (114) demonstrated notable activity with a Ki of 7.7 nM against various cancer-related kinases and the ability to suppress the development of cancer cells in solid tumors and hematologic malignancies. When the NH-group at the α-position of the pyrimidine ring was first attached, there was no discernible increase in potency. Pyrimidine's attached NH group demonstrated a crucial involvement in the establishment of an HB with the Pim kinase target. This NH group's substitution with a $CONH_2$ (amide group) resulted in decreased activity, further demonstrating how important the terminal NH group is for Pim inhibitory function (Flanders et al., 2015) (Fig. 12.54).

The 5-(1H-indol-5-yl)-1,3,4-thiadiazol-2-amines, a new family of Pim inhibitors, demonstrated outstanding activity toward all three Pim isoforms. The KINOME profiling assay was used to carry out the kinase profiling investigation. According to the SAR analysis, compounds (115) and (116) had 100-fold more activity against three Pim isoforms (IC_{50} values of

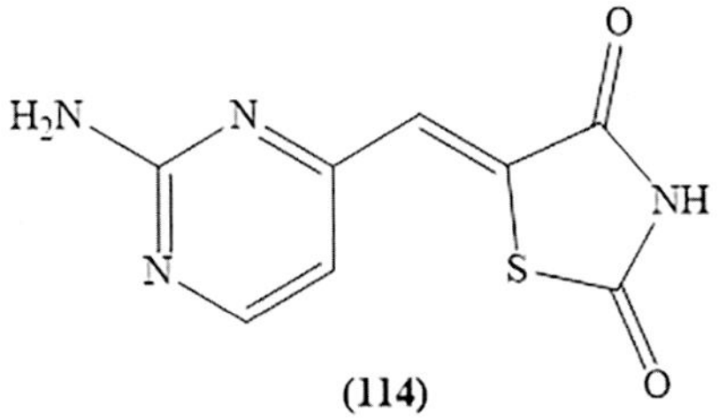

FIGURE 12.54   Structure of compound (114).

0.002 and 0.007 µM, respectively). While the aromatic group at position C3 was removed, molecules with a potential action that interacts with the glycine-rich helix of receptor molecules were developed. The substituted phenyl derivatives and quinoline exhibited only mild activity, however, the compounds with the 6-position replaced with 2-pyridyl groups were found to be the most promising. Only submicromolar amounts of the 6-aminopyridine analogue were active against Pim kinases. When pyrrolidine was added to the pyridine ring's sixth position, a potency improvement of ninefold was noticed. Improvements in activity were seen with the 6-membered ring substituted morpholino analogue, as shown by IC_{50} values of 151 nM in the Pim-1 cell assay and detectable Pim-2 cell growth (7.57 µM) (Wu et al., 2015) (Fig. 12.55).

When primary alkylamines were added to the pyridine's 6-position, the Pim-2 cell assay's potency increased; in contrast, the activity of the cyclohexylamine analogue was reduced. The new class of Pim inhibitors, 5-(1H-indol-5-yl)-1,3,4-thiadiazol-2-amines (117), demonstrated potential inhibitory activity against Pim kinases. The screened drug (118) employing HTRF assays showed excellent inhibitory action against all three PIM kinase isoforms (PIM-1: 0.017 µM, PIM-2: 0.031 µM, and PIM-3: 0.007 µM) using high-throughput screening tests. The 2-pyridyl group substitution at the C6 position with bulky groups showed promising activity, according to the SAR investigations, whereas substituted phenyl analogs and quinoline displayed only modest activity. An analogue of 6-aminopyridine exhibited submicromolar

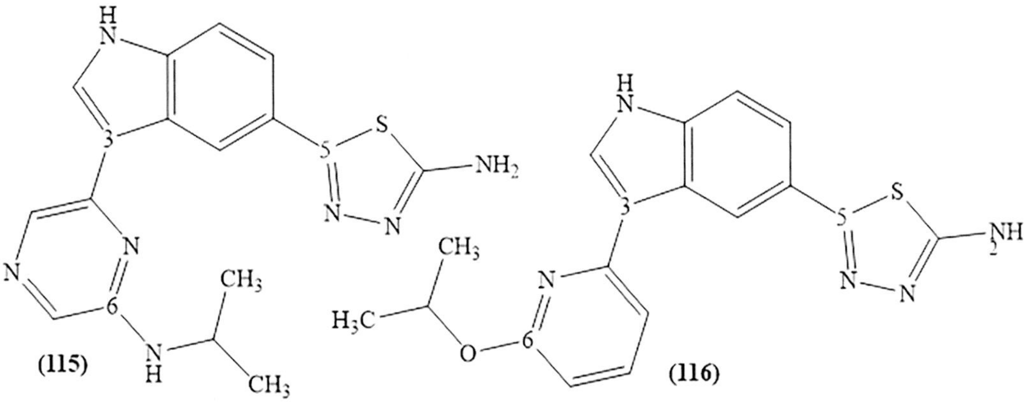

FIGURE 12.55   Structure of compounds (115–116).

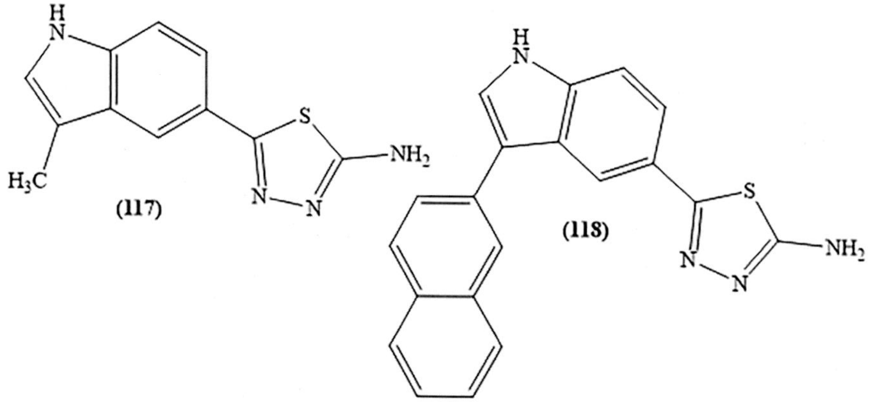

FIGURE 12.56   Structure of compounds (117–118).

activity. The potency increased nine times after a 6-pyrrolidine was added to the pyridine ring. The 6-membered ring of the morpholino analogue, which has an IC_{50} of 152 nM against Pim-1 and 7.57 μM for Pim-2 kinase, demonstrated promising activity. The substitution of bigger groups (cyclopentoxy) or smaller groups (methoxy and ethoxy) led to compounds with the least amount of Pim kinase inhibitory activity. The molecules formed by the modification at the C5 pyrazine position have decreased activity. Furthermore, the three PIM isoforms were effectively inhibited by the 5-(1H-indol-5-yl)-1,3,4-thiadiazol-2-amine derivatives that were developed (Wu et al., 2015) (Fig. 12.56).

According to the SAR analysis, substitution at the 2-pyridine ring's C-3 position is crucial for activity. This C-3 position demonstrated mild activity (119) (with IC_{50} value of 0.177 μM) when quinoline and phenyl rings were replaced. The most potent activity (120) (IC_{50} value of 0.865 μM) was achieved by substituting a 2-pyridyl ring with bulky groups at position C6. The 6-aminopyridine analogue exhibited submicromolar activity, while the potency was at least nine times higher after the C6 position (121) pyrrolidine group was inserted, with an IC_{50} value of 0.048 μM. The 6-position morpholino ring substitution resulted in an increase in activity against the Pim-1 kinase (IC_{50} value of 152 nM). Primary alkylamine substitution at the 6-position of pyridine has been observed to increase potency against Pim-2 kinase, but the cyclohexylamine counterpart has demonstrated lower potency (Wu et al., 2015) (Fig. 12.57).

Prostate cancer, several types of leukemia, and lymphoma all frequently overexpress the Pim kinases. The Pim-1 kinase may be inhibited by 5-(3-trifluoromethylbenzylidene)thiazolidine-2,4-dione (122), which has an IC_{50} value of 3 μM and operates as a competitive inhibitor concerning ATP. ATP-depletion assays have been used for PIM protein kinase tests. A group of thiazolidine-diones were synthesized based on compound (122), with the most effective compounds showing IC_{50} values of 13 nM for Pim-1 and 2.3 μM for Pim-2, respectively. While the thiazolidine nitrogen is important for activity, substituting it in this position led to molecules with 1000-fold lower activity. The activity of the benzylidene analogs with 4-substituted fluoro and chloro group was 10 times more than that of the comparable 3-substitution. The 3-bromo substituted drugs' ability to inhibit Pim-2 was low. Compounds

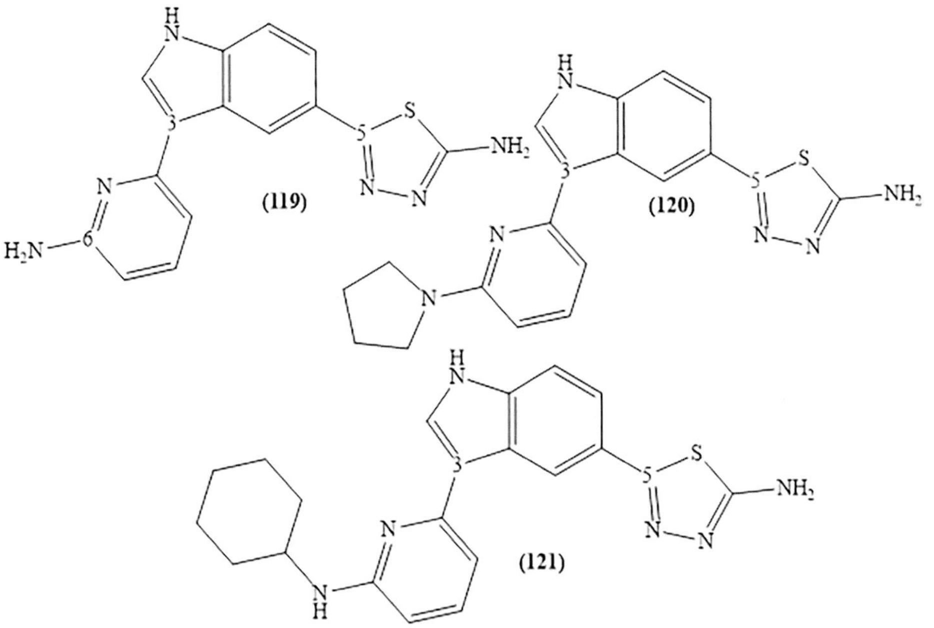

FIGURE 12.57 Structure of compounds (119–121).

with a trifluoromethoxy group were 10–15 times more active than counterparts with a methoxy group (Xia et al., 2009) (Fig. 12.58).

Potential Pim kinase inhibitors with scaffolds made of substituted benzylidene-thiazolidine-dione (TZD) were created in a study. With GI_{50} values below 100 nM, these inhibitors demonstrated strong antiproliferative action in the megakaryoblastic leukemia (AMKL) cell line MOLM-16. The SAR study showed that compound (123) had a rise in activity against each of the three Pim kinases when a basic amine group, such as dimethylpyrrolidin-3-amine, was introduced at the R1 position. The series' Boc-protected derivatives showed less activity than their unprotected counterparts. Molecules lacking a basic amine group decreased in activity. A few cyclic amines had demonstrated potential activity, such as (3S)-pyrrolidin-3-amine (124) and (3R)-piperidin-3-amine (125). Pim kinase inhibitory activity was induced by several groups, including phenyl at the meta-position of the phenyl ring, alkoxy, chlorine (126), and bromine (Dakin et al., 2012) (Fig. 12.59).

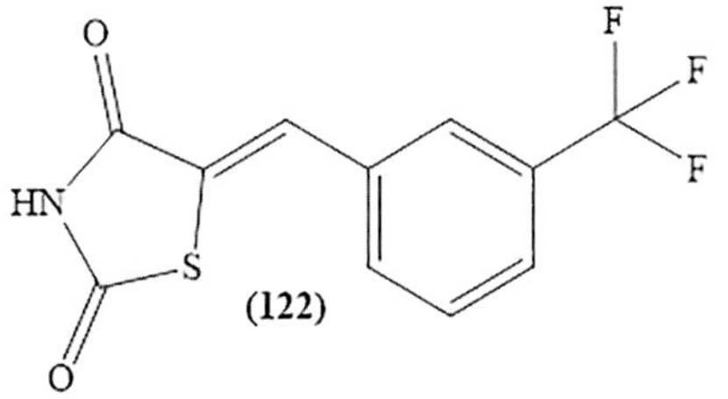

FIGURE 12.58 Structure of compound (122).

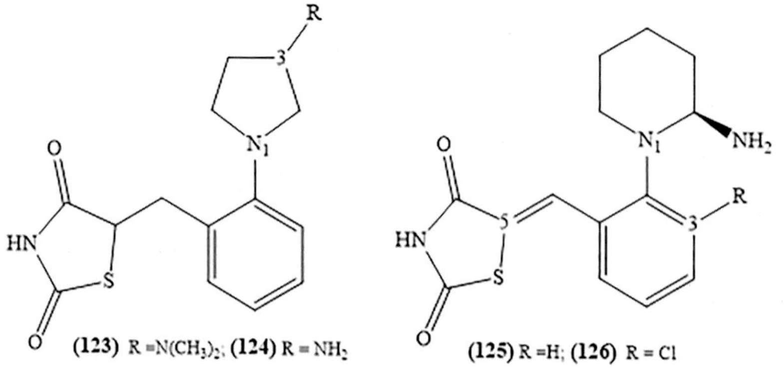

(123) R =N(CH$_3$)$_2$; **(124)** R = NH$_2$ **(125)** R =H; **(126)** R = Cl

FIGURE 12.59 Structure of compounds **(123–126)**.

In a different study, isoxazolo-quinoline-3,4-diones were synthesized and found to be effective inhibitors of Pim-1/2 kinases. The hydroxyl group substitution on the benzene ring is shown to be essential in the HB interaction in the hinge expanse of Pim kinases by molecular modeling and SAR studies. The most active derivative **(127)**, with Ki values of 2.5 and 43.5 nM against Pim-1 and 2, respectively, demonstrated potential activity. The carbonyl group of the isoxazolone and the charged amino group of Lys67 formed an HB at a distance of around 3.0 Å, which was discovered to be the mechanism by which the ligand and protein interacted. Additionally, Lys67 was linked to the oxygen on the quinolinone ring of the inhibitor by a water molecule. This behavior was similarly displayed by other Pim-1 inhibitors (Tong et al., 2008) (Fig. 12.60).

Ishchenko et al. have screened several Pim kinase inhibitors with nanomolar potency based on SBDD approach. The key amino acids needed for the activity, aside from those found only in the acidic ribose pocket, were revealed by the binding interaction of the co-crystal ligand with Pim-1 kinase active site. The product **(128)** that resulted from compound **(129)** demonstrated the significance of the amide group's interaction with K67. Similar to the micromolar range of chemical **(130)**,compound **(128)** showed Pim-1 inhibitory activity (Ishchenko et al., 2015) (Fig. 12.61).

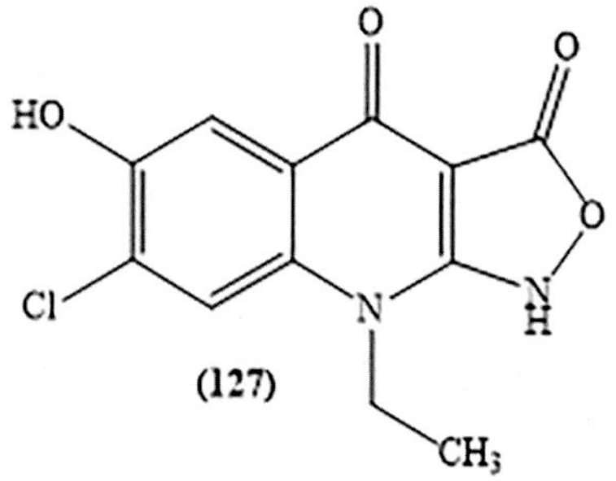

(127)

FIGURE 12.60 Structure of compound **(127)**.

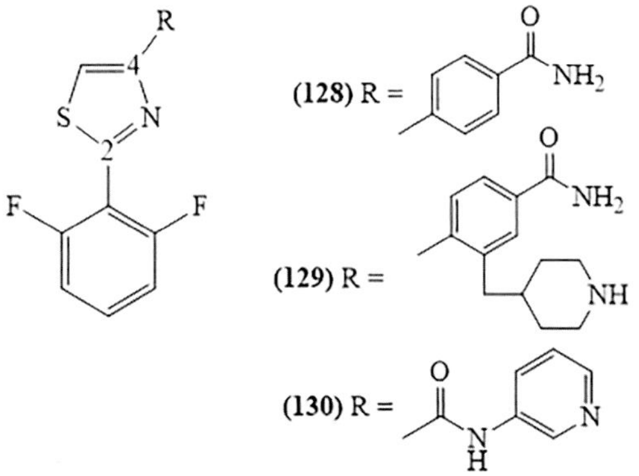

FIGURE 12.61   Structure of compounds (128–130).

Bataille et al. have found novel compounds against the Pim kinase using a high throughput screening technique. The intrinsic features of the compounds were ascertained using molecular modeling and optimization approaches, and these compounds showed high Pim kinase selectivity. To assess the antiproliferative abilities of certain inhibitors, two leukemia cancer cell lines K562 and MV4-11 have been used. With an IC_{50} of 0.75 µM, the inhibitor (131) had the strongest action against the Pim-expressing leukemic cancer cell line K562. The SAR analyses proved that the hit molecule contains a thiazole core as the series' B-ring, an important element for the best possible balance of characteristics. The third-ring extension from the second ring significantly increased Pim kinase activity. Improvement in potency and the addition of other physical features are caused by the addition of a functional group to the C-ring (Bataille et al., 2017) (Fig. 12.62).

The potential anticancer activity of a number of new thiazolidine-2,4-dione derivatives has been developed, synthesized, and tested. Using the sulforhodamine B technique, the anticancer efficacy of synthetic drugs has been assessed against a subset of human breast cancer cell lines (MCF-7). A large amount of cytotoxic activity, comparable to that of the conventional anticancer medication adriamycin, was demonstrated by compound (132) with a 2-cyano phenyl group among the synthesized compounds. The thiazolidine-2,4-dione moiety connected to the substituted phenyl group on the oxadiazole ring showed considerable growth inhibitory efficacy against the MCF-7 cell line, according to the SAR investigation (Asati & Bharti, 2018) (Fig. 12.63).

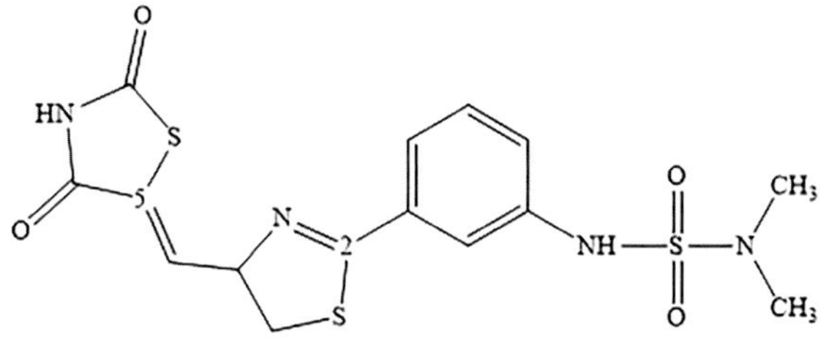

(131)

FIGURE 12.62   Structure of compound (131).

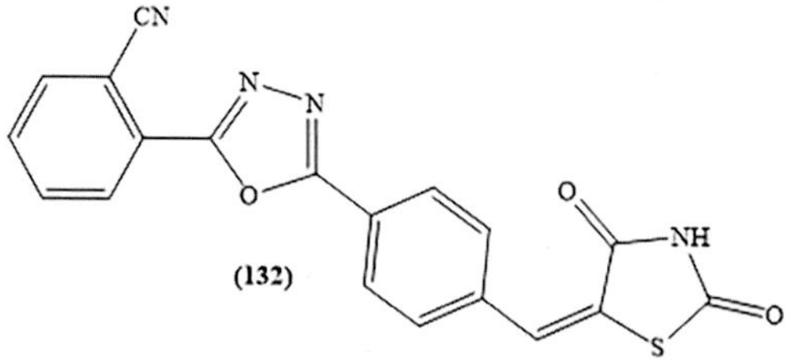

FIGURE 12.63   Structure of compound **(132)**.

5.26 Thiophenes derivatives

Wherever ring D in steroidal nucleus alteration occurred, hetero-cyclization of steroids was observed to generate physiologically active compounds. To create novel heterocyclic compounds, estrone is employed as a model. The steroid D-ring can be chemically modified to change its functional groups, sizes, and stereochemistry. Numerous structure—activity connections have been identified as a result of these synthetic alterations. Pharmaceutical corporations have expressed interest in steroid compounds with heterocyclic fused rings to the D-ring of the steroid nucleus. According to Mohareb et al., by interacting with other chemical agents, the reaction product of cyanoacetylhydrazine and elemental sulfur with estrone underwent hetero-cyclization. The newly synthesized compounds' biological activities were investigated for c-Met kinase, antiproliferative activities against six common cancer cell lines, and the Pim-1 kinase inhibitory activity. Compounds **(133)** and **(134)** were the most effective compounds when chemicals were chosen to investigate their Pim-1 kinase inhibitory ability (Mohareb, Samir, & Halim, 2019) (Fig. 12.64).

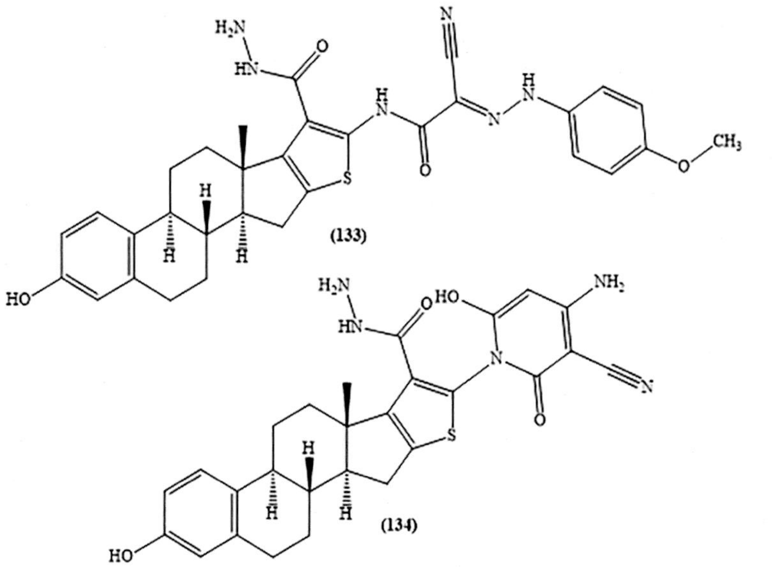

FIGURE 12.64   Structure of compounds **(133 and 134)**.

5.27 Thienopyridines

The significant heterocyclic compounds thienopyridines, tetrahydrothieno-pyridines, and their derivatives are of great interest. Several molecules with a tetrahydrothienopyridine structure are known to be nonpeptide GPIIb/IIIa antagonists with antibacterial properties. When benzylic or substituted, benzylic moiety is added to the nitrogen of the thienopyridine ring, the pharmacological activities of the parent molecule can undergo significant structural alteration. The parent moiety's improved biological activity was one of the substitutions that took place at the thienopyridine moiety's nitrogen. The most potent compounds were tested as Pim-1 kinase inhibitors. Mohareb et al. synthesized a series of tetrahydro-benzothieno-pyridine derivatives from the reaction of 2-amino-3-benzoyl-4,5-dihydrobenzo[b]thiophen-6-one along with studying their cytotoxic evaluations. Compounds (135−138) were chosen to investigate their Pim-1 kinase inhibitory ability because, across a range of 10 concentrations, they exhibited strong inhibition of the C-Met kinase and the tested cancer cell lines. The IC_{50} values for these compounds were also determined. Compounds (136) and (137), had an IC_{50} value of 0.28 and 0.32 μM, respectively, and were more active at inhibiting Pim-1 activity than (135) and (138) ($IC_{50} > 10$ M). SGI-1776 was employed as a positive control in the test, with an IC_{50} of 0.048 μM (Mohareb, Abdo, & El-Sharkawy, 2018) (Fig. 12.65).

5.28 Triazine derivatives

As Pim-1 inhibitors, the substituted pyrido-triazines were synthesized by using scaffold hopping methods. These chemicals showed both Pim-1 kinase inhibitory action and antiproliferative effects for prostate cancer cells. With IC_{50} values ranging from 0.69 to 0.80 μM, several compounds from series (138−140), have demonstrated their micromolar inhibitory actions. The pyrido-triazine moity at the C6 position was significant for activity, according to the SAR research. Instead of 4-O, this position's substituent(s) with a 4-NH group showed significance for activity. On this piperazine ring, the alkyl group replacements harm activity. Furthermore, molecules with a single heteroatom showed less activity than those with two heteroatoms. The results of the docking study revealed that the aromatic 4-aniline form a crucial p-p stack interaction or stack interaction with Phe49 of Pim-1 kinase, whereas the 3-N of the pyrido-triazine ring produced an HB with residue Lys67 (Fan et al., 2016) (Fig. 12.66).

5.29 Triazole derivatives

A novel family of pan-Pim kinase inhibitors (142) synthesized, based on the CK2 inhibitor CX-4945. Compounds with potential action were generated by substituting secondary amide or triazole groups at the C7 position and halogenoanilines at the C-5 position. These compounds typically interact with Serine 112 of Pim kinase, which is part of the enzyme that has an antiproliferative effect. The addition of 2-chlorine, fluorine, and methyl groups at the C5 substituted phenyl ring resulted in an overall increase in potency. Additionally, comparable changes at the phenyl ring's para position have demonstrated less efficacy. The main cause of the drop-in biological activity was the alkylation of the C5 amine group. When the big solubilizing group was added to the aniline's fourth position, compounds with preserved

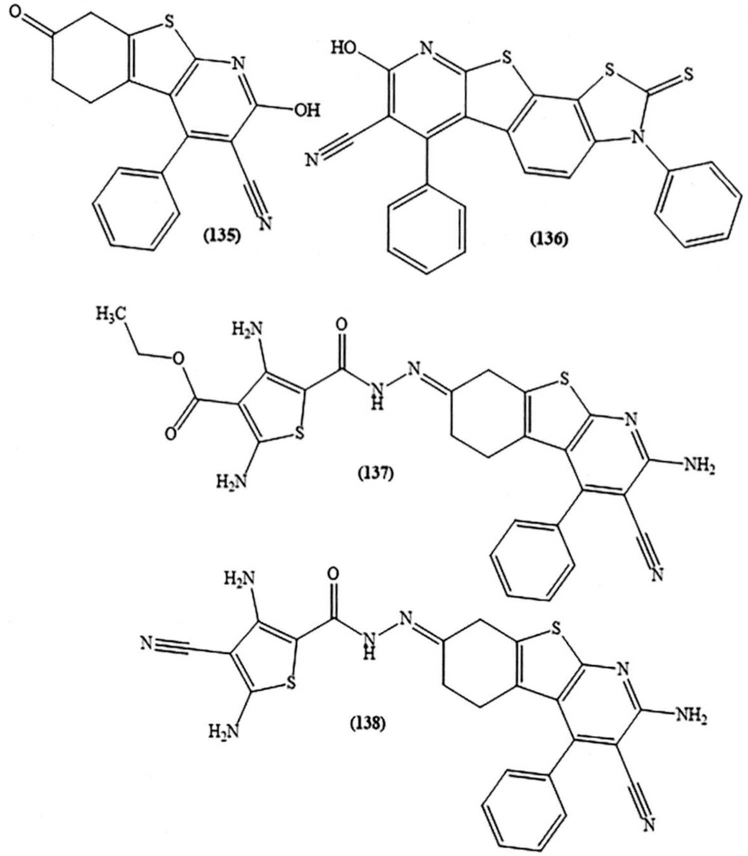

FIGURE 12.65   Structure of compounds **(135–138)**.

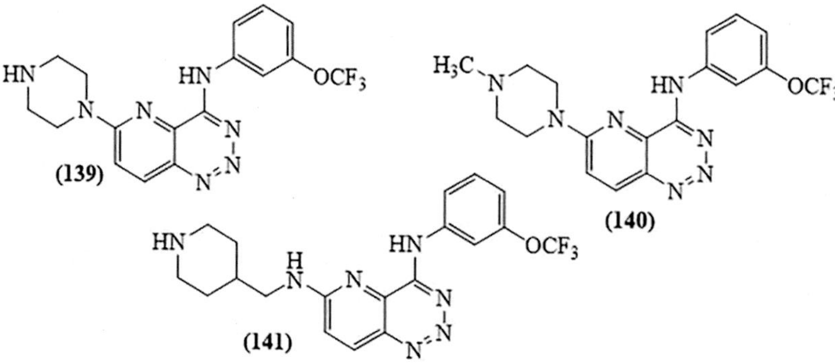

FIGURE 12.66   Structure of compounds **(139–141)**.

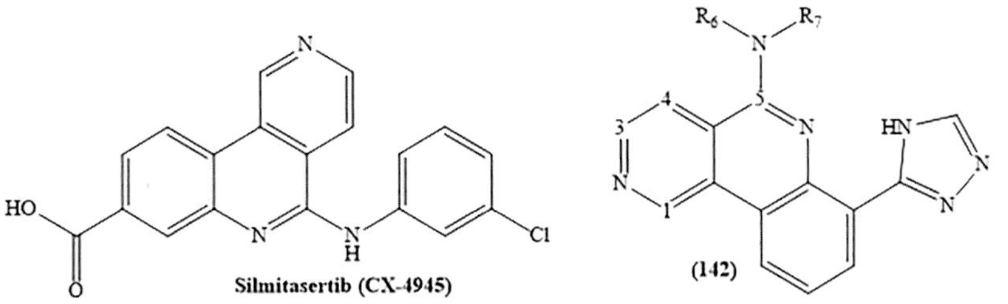

FIGURE 12.67   Structure of compounds silmitasertib **(CX-4945)** and **(142)**.

potency were created. The lowered activity was brought on by the addition of groups like alkyl sulfone, fluorine, and trifluoromethoxy at the C4-position of aniline. Compounds with a methoxy group at C3-position and fluorine or methyl at C2-position are more effective against Pim kinase. For Pim-1 and 2 kinases, the compounds with two fluorine atoms at the ortho position of the aniline displayed IC_{50} values of 0.002 and 0.001 μM, respectively (Pierre et al., 2011) (Fig. 12.67).

A variety of triazolo-pyridines synthesized and tested against Pim kinase with the introduction of many novel approaches. In this experiment, the majority of the compounds showed activity of 0.5 μM, whereas the most powerful molecule **(143)** showed an IC_{50} value of 69 nM. As the lead molecule for additional compound optimization, compound **(144)** has been chosen. The p-hydroxy group is important for activity, and replacing it with a methoxy group resulted in molecules that lost their activity, according to the SAR study. Similar suppression was seen when piperidinyl methyl amines were used in place of the imidazopyridazine compounds. The most effective activity was shown by the second triazolopyridine series, with compound **(145)** having an IC_{50} value of 6 nM. The potency of this series slightly decreased when the piperidine NH group was replaced with an alkyl chain. The decrease in activity against Pim-1 kinase was caused by groups like fluorine, methoxy, amide, or keto. The activity of the piperazine derivative was decreased. The compounds with fewer methylene units than the parent molecule had nanomolar-level activity (Pastor et al., 2012) (Fig. 12.68).

5.30 Imidazo[1,2-b]pyridazine

The imidazo[1,2-b]pyridazine scaffold **(SGI-1776)** is associated with hERG inhibition, and subsequent attempts to counteract this inhibition used a scaffold-hopping approach starting with a varied fragment database and **SGI-1776** structure. This was successful in locating a novel triazolo-pyridazine scaffold for the Pim lead inhibitor **(146)**. The space of inhibitors inside the Pim-1 catalytic region was demonstrated by docking and simulation studies of compound **(147)** and structurally similar compounds after the G-loop was dislocated with substituents at C6 and C7 positions. Then, the introduction of a third ring connecting C6 and C7 led to the development of a brand-new tricyclic trizolopyridazine scaffold. Using a human nonsmall cell lung carcinoma cell line (NSCLC) A549, overexpressing Pim-1 kinase activity, SAR studies of the tricyclic trizolopyridazine identified compound **(147)** as a potential Pim inhibitor lack of hERG inhibitory activity and deserving of further development to

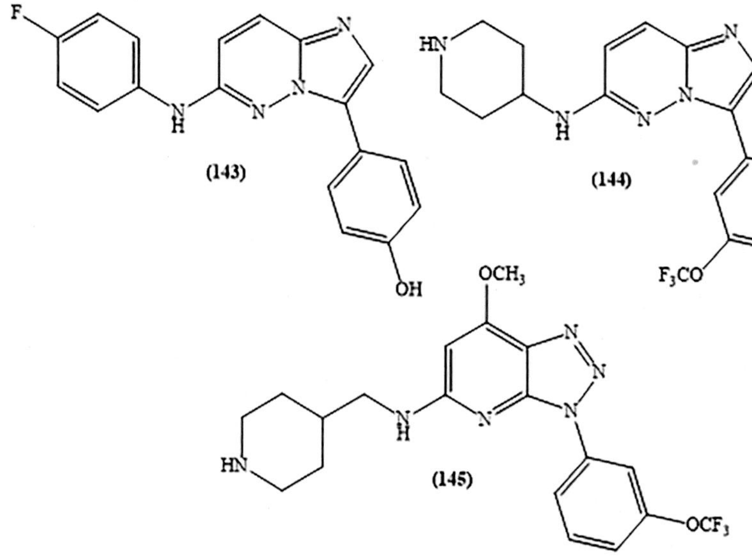

FIGURE 12.68   Structure of compounds (143–145).

improve its biochemical Pim-2 inhibitory activity and cellular Pim inhibition ability (Martinez-Gonzalez et al., 2019) (Fig. 12.69).

5.31 Triazolo[4,5-b]pyridines

The use of the fragment-hopping technique offers a great foundation for ongoing drug discovery studies. Saluste et al. used a scaffold-hopping technique based on a chemically viable

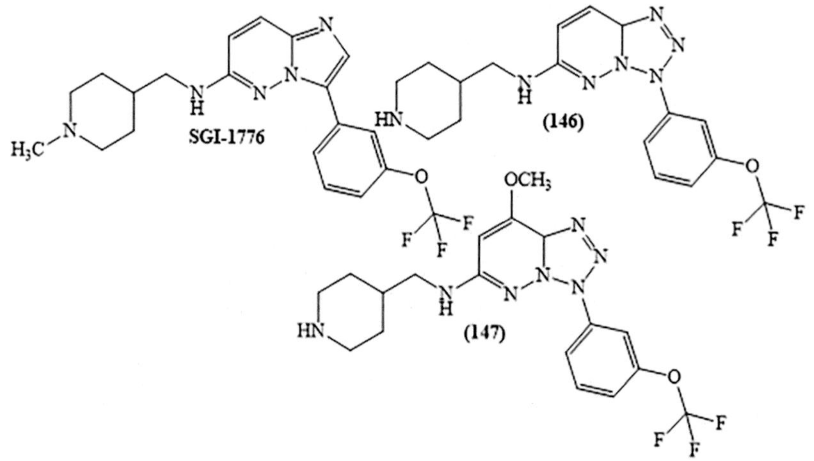

FIGURE 12.69   Structure of compounds (SGI-1776, 146 and 147).

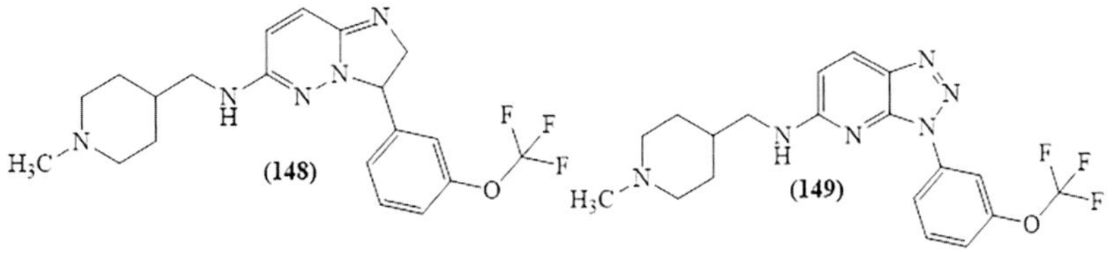

FIGURE 12.70 Structure of compounds (148 and 149).

fragment database called Benzofuran derivatives to discover a novel chemical class known as triazolo-pyridines as a Pim-1 inhibitor. Compound (148), which was recently withdrawn from Phase-I clinical trials, and compound (149), which carries the selected new scaffold, share similar primary activities (IC_{50} in the $20-150$ nM range) (Saluste et al., 2012) (Fig. 12.70).

As Pim-1 kinase inhibitors, several benzofuran-2-carboxylic acids have recently been produced. In kinase tests, the compounds (150–152) showed strong action against Pim-1 and Pim. The Pim-1 binding complex's X-ray structures revealed crucial HB interactions and salt bridge (SB) formation, which were facilitated by the compound's amino groups and carboxylic acid. The SAR of these complexes' binding to the receptor molecule revealed important factors like (a) The lipophilic binding site of the Pim-1 hinge area and the lipophilic interactions of the substituents at the C5-position of the benzofuran are responsible for interaction; (b) The salt-bridge contact, which is mediated by HB interactions with residues E89, D186, and 2-carboxylic acid group to residue K67, defines another crucial binding site. (c) A minimal acceptance of additional replacements nearby the gatekeeper site; and (d) The ribose binding area may have space for structural growth (Xiang et al., 2011) (Fig. 12.71).

5.32 Benzofuropyrimidinones derivatives

A novel family of benzofuropyrimidinones for Pim kinase inhibitors is studied by Tsuhako et al. (2012). Compound (153) was discovered to be an ATP-competitive inhibitor in studies on ATP competition. Additionally, co-crystalize structure of the compound (153) with Pim-1

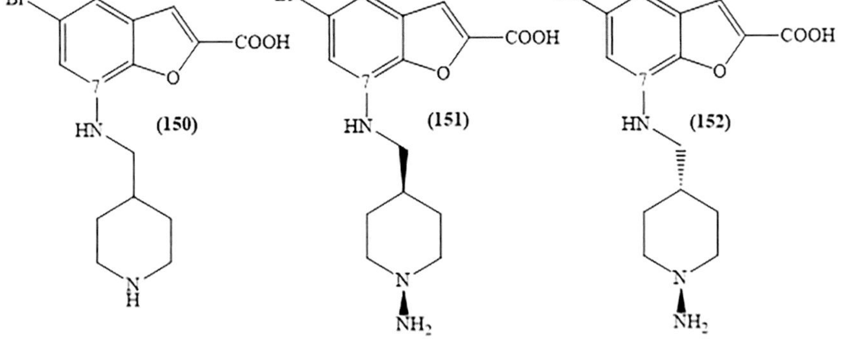

FIGURE 12.71 Structure of compounds (150–152).

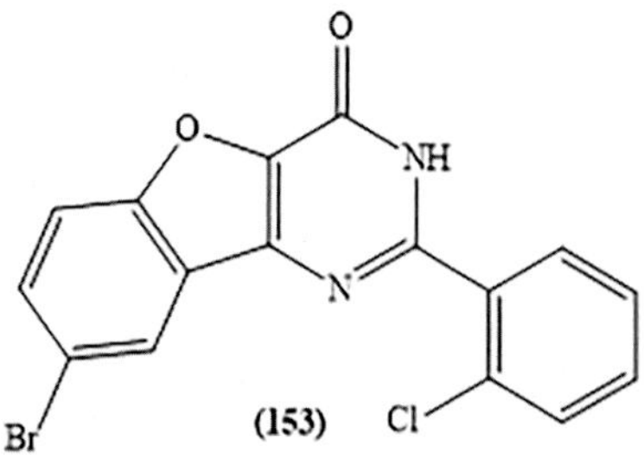

FIGURE 12.72   Structure of compound (153).

showed interactions in the ATP-binding active site, there are no HB interactions with the hinge, in contrast to normal kinase inhibitors that form bonds in this region. This is a distinctive characteristic of Pim inhibitors because Pim's hinge sequence has an insertion of a proline, causing the hinge region to protrude up to four from the ATP-binding site (Fig. 12.72).

Wurz and colleagues created a new series of Pim-1,2 inhibitors with an amino oxadiazole motif after examining the significant levels of Pim expression in numerous solid tumor and hematological malignancies. According to the research, patients might benefit from a small molecule Pim-1,2 inhibitor that inhibits Pim signaling. They outline how they got from the very Pim-selective indole-thiadiazole molecule to the final product. The Pim-1 and 2 isoforms of cyclopropane (154) were discovered to have outstanding enzymatic potency (with Ki values of 0.55 and 0.28 nM, respectively) and to be able to prevent the phosphorylation of BAD in the Pim-overexpressing KMS-12 cell line ($IC_{50} = 150$ nM) (Wurz et al., 2015) (Fig. 12.73).

5.33 Pyrrolo-carbazole derivatives

Quercetagetin is a flavonoid that inhibits Pim-1 at submicromolar concentrations. The substituted imidazo[1,2-b]- pyridazines and triazolo[4,3-b]-pyridazines class were shown to have a powerful and selective Pim-1 inhibitory action of nanomolar potency, in contrast to the modest inhibitory activity of quercetagetin. Specifically, Rufine et al. synthesized pyrrolo[2,3-a]- and [3,2-a]carbazole derivatives and reported on their efforts to use the pyrrolo [2,3-a]carbazole scaffold for the development of effective and novel Pim kinase inhibitor

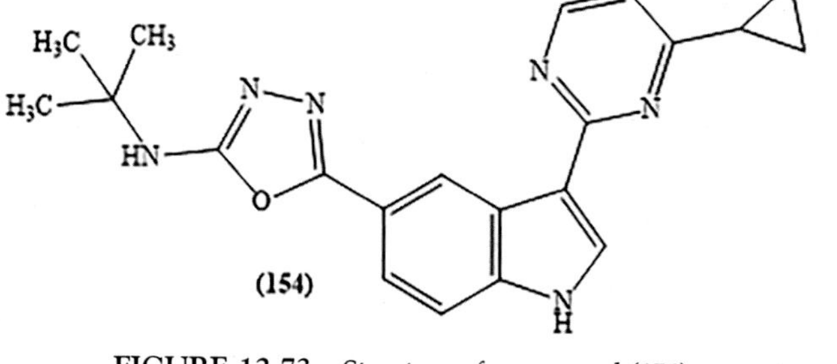

FIGURE 12.73   Structure of compound (154).

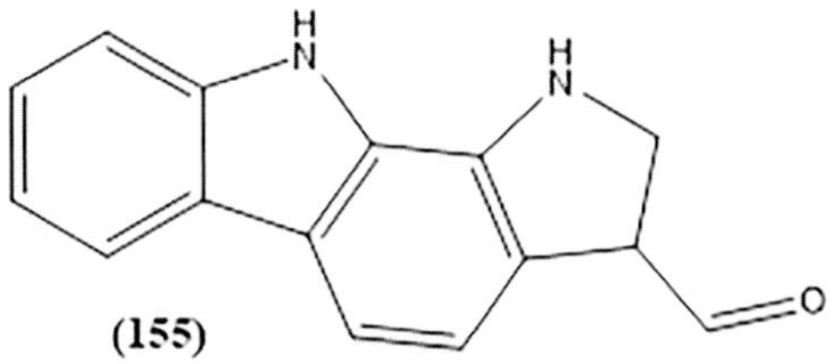

FIGURE 12.74   Structure of compound (155).

(155). The X-ray cocrystal structure of the lead molecule finally reveals the ATP competitive but not imitative binding mechanism of Pim-1 (Akué-Gédu et al., 2009) (Fig. 12.74).

5.34 Benzodiazocine derivative

Akué-Gédu et al. developed several pyrrolo[2,3-a]carbazole compounds that, at submicromolar doses, dramatically inhibited Pim protein kinases. In vitro, kinase experiments revealed that the benzodiazocine derivative (156) specifically potently inhibited Pim-1 and 3 isoforms (with IC$_{50}$ values 8 and 13 nM, respectively). Compound (156), which has a planar pyrrolocarbazole scaffold, did not exhibit any substantial DNA binding and was not a powerful topoisomerase I inhibitor, indicating that 1 is probably very selective for Pim-1 and Pim-3. The study's findings strongly imply that (156) is a promising option for an anticancer medication because of its selectivity for certain Pim protein kinases and capacity to boost the effectiveness of traditional chemotherapeutic agents. Additionally, the compound demonstrated greater inhibitory action against Pim-1 compared to the reference molecule (156). Due to the compound's significant biological potential, researchers examined its chemical interactions with Pim-1, its capacity to specifically inhibit a wider variety of protein kinases, and its potential for cytotoxicity (Akué-Gédu et al., 2009) (Fig. 12.75).

5.35 Indole derivatives

Various 3,5-disubstituted indole derivatives were logically developed as Pim kinase inhibitors. The most effective inhibitor showed IC$_{50}$ values of 6.2 nM against Pim-1 and 6.1 nM against Pim-3 respectively. In this series, cyclic analogs having potential activity against Pim-1 and Pim-3 as well as modest activity against Pim-2 were studied. Examples of

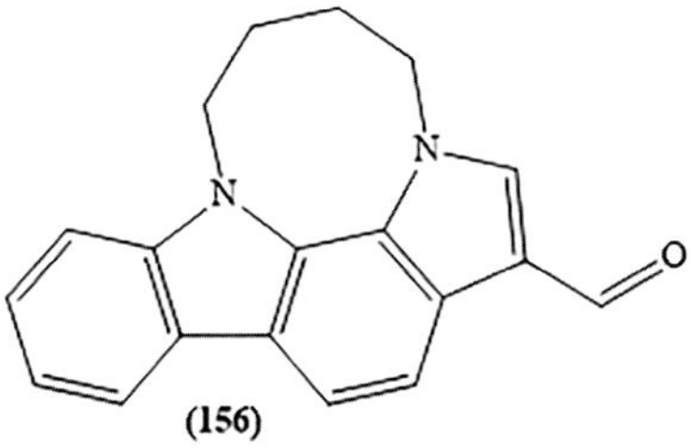

FIGURE 12.75   Structure of compound (156).

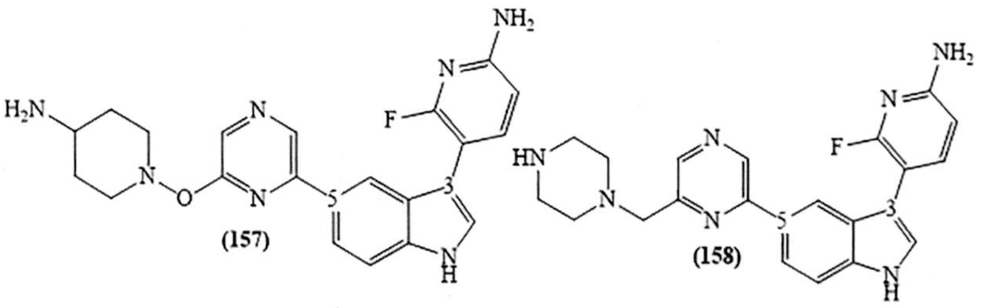

FIGURE 12.76   Structure of compound (157 and 158).

compounds from this class include compounds (156) and (157). A hydrophobic group was added close to the basic amino group, and it showed same effectiveness as the heterocyclic analogs (More et al., 2014) (Fig. 12.76).

Tests have been conducted on several human leukemia cell lines, including MV4-11, Jurkat clone E6-1, and K562 as well as an assessment of the inhibitory potential of the novel chemical meridian C (159). The SAR study showed that a series with an indole substitution at the C-3 and C-5 locations had increased potency, which further contributed to a better understanding of the process. The strongest member of the group, compound (160), showed remarkable selectivity and a nanomolar IC_{50} value for the Pim-1. Insertion of the 2-aminoethyl group via an amine bond markedly improved activity against the Pim-1 kinase. When a substituted ketone group was used in place of the 2-aminopyrimidine ring at the C3 position of indole, Pim-1 potency was seen to increase by 50-fold. Docking studies results showed that the indole protein's Lys67 residue interacts with the pyrazine-2-yl group at the C5 position (Nishiguchi et al., 2011; Wang et al., 2015) (Fig. 12.77).

The discovery of a hit compound (161), led to the synthesis of several 3-(2-pyrazinyl)-1H-indazoles. Compound (162) in this series demonstrated strong activity with IC_{50} value of 1400 nM. The compound displayed notable inhibition as a result of the lipophilic groups that were affixed to the ring. The findings of the study demonstrated that the reduced lipophilicity is caused by one or more C5 substituents. The loss of one fluorine atom from an aromatic ring might not have an impact on potency, but the loss of both fluorine atoms led to a reduction in cellular potency. When compared to other analogs, the assimilation of various substituents such as NH_2, OH, R—$CONH_2$, methanesulfonamide, and methylsulfonyl groups at C4 of the 2-fluorophenyl ring may be the reason for the equivalent enzyme activity and higher pharmacological activity (Wang et al., 2015) (Fig. 12.78).

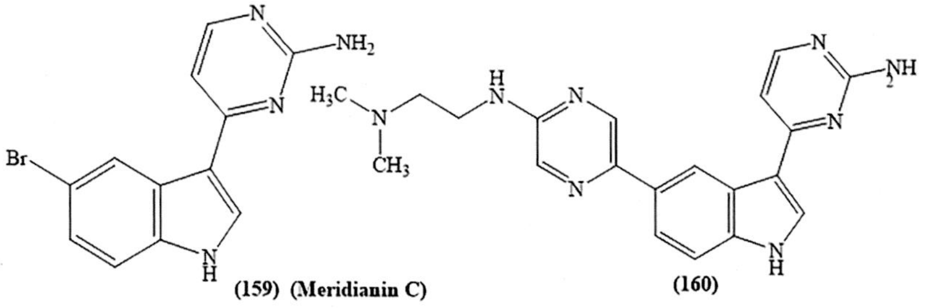

FIGURE 12.77   Structure of compounds (159 and 160).

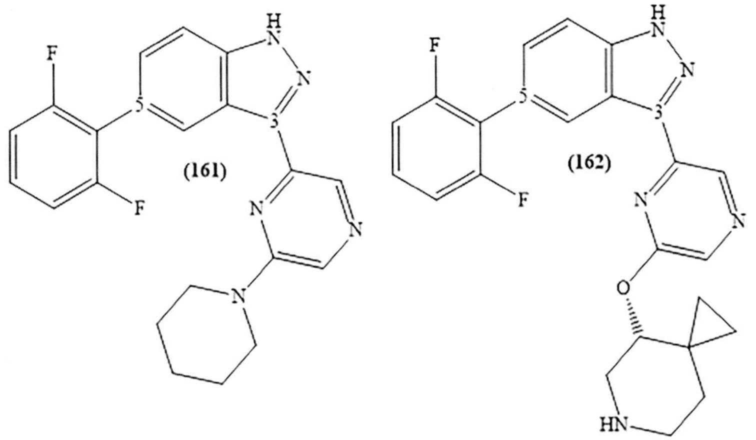

FIGURE 12.78   Structure of compounds **(161 and 162)**.

Nakano et al. employed novel techniques to enhance selectivity over Pim kinase. They produced the 7-azaindole derivative **(163)** by focusing on a unique bulge in the ATP-binding pocket of Pim kinase, which has shown intriguing ADMET properties. The 6-chlorinated derivatives **(164)**, in particular, among the 6-substituted 7-azaindoles showed to be a powerful and selective Pim inhibitor and suggested to be a promising lead molecule for subsequent drug research (Nakano et al., 2017) (Fig. 12.79).

5.36 Oxadiazole derivatives

In a study, the compound **(165)** generated from oxadiazole showed strong Pim-1/2 inhibitory activity with Ki values of 0.55 and 0.28 nM, respectively. The phosphorylation of BAD was inhibited by Pim overexpression in KMS-12 cells ($IC_{50} = 150$ nM). According to a SAR investigation, adding amino-oxadiazole resulted in a compound's potency being increased when the amino-thiadiazole moiety is removed from previously synthesized compounds. The indole ring's 3-position replacement was crucial for the activity **(166)**.

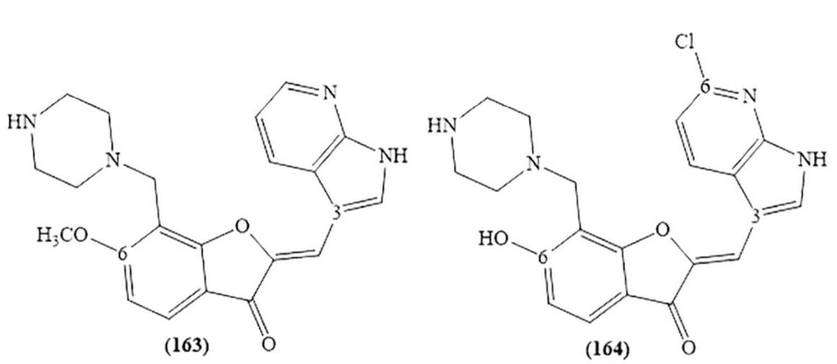

FIGURE 12.79   Structure of compounds **(163 and 164)**.

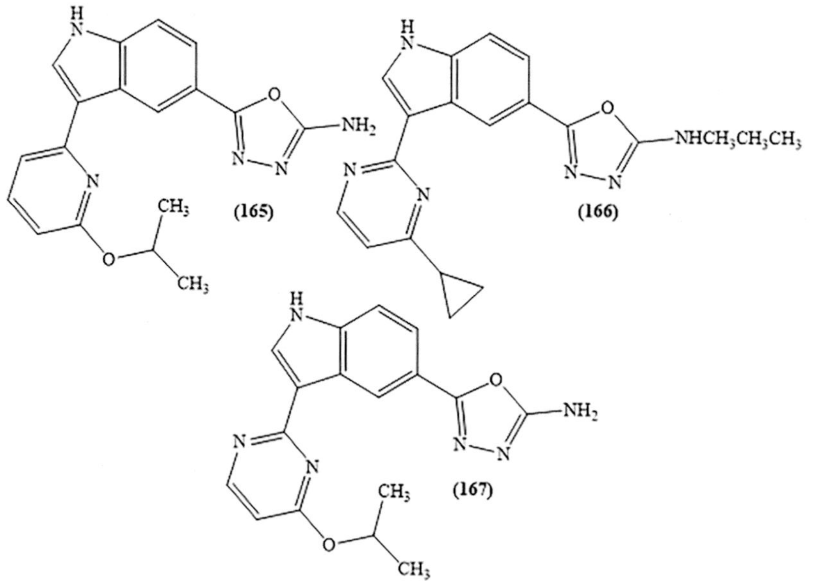

FIGURE 12.80   Structure of compounds (165–167).

The activity was reduced by removing the pyridine nitrogen. The enzymatic and cellular potential was reduced when morpholine was substituted at the indole ring. On the indole ring (167), the addition of the pyrazine ring instead of isopropoxy group produced positive action. An increase in potency was observed when the isopropoxy group was swapped out for a difluoropiperidine or a difluoropyrrolidine. In comparison to compound (165), the substitution with the 4-cyclopropylpyrimidin-2-yl group improved the action against Pim-2 and increased potency by a factor of two ($IC_{50} = 319$ nM) (Wurz et al., 2015) (Fig. 12.80).

5.37 Pyrazine derivatives

Numerous 2,6-disubstituted pyrazine derivatives have been developed as CK2 kinase inhibitors. Lead compound (168) was developed by structure-guided optimization of a 5-substituted-3-thiophene carboxylic acid screening hit which found inhibitory activity in both enzymatic and cellular assays. A set of 70 kinases was screened using an inhibitory concentration of 1.0 μM to evaluate the selectivity profile of the compound (168); calculations of the biological IC_{50} value were then performed on those kinases with percent inhibition values higher than 70%. Analogs with strong PIM kinase activity were also found thanks to later design and hybridization efforts (169). The potency of CK2 was dramatically reduced when the 2-thienyl-5-carboxylate was substituted with 3-substituted benzoic acid, whereas the addition of isomeric 4-benzoic acid (168) increased the potency of CK2 threefold and improved the enzyme's affinity for Pim-1/2. The deacylated analogue (168) showed a 100-fold increase in activity with submicromolar efficacy against Pim-2 (IC_{50} value: 0.14 μM) (Gingipalli et al., 2018) (Fig. 12.81).

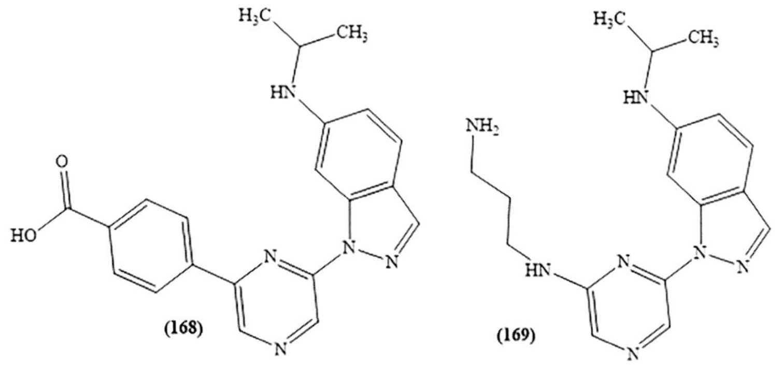

FIGURE 12.81   Structure of compounds (168 and 169).

5.38 Chalcones derivatives

One of the most significant families of natural compounds in the plant world is the 1,3-diphenyl-2E-propene-1-one, which serves as the scaffold for the benzylidene acetophenone. A three-carbon, αβ-unsaturated carbonyl bridge connects the two aromatic nuclei that make up its structure. Chalcones are often produced synthetically by reacting aryl ketones with aromatic aldehydes while the reaction is being catalyzed or assisted by condensing agents. To create a range of biologically active target molecules, chalcone compounds were utilized in numerous heterocyclic processes. The compounds that were created displayed biological actions against cancer as well as antiinflammatory and other biological impacts. Megally and coworkers investigate several hetero-cyclization processes of some chalcones (170) that produce pyrazole and thiophene rings and assess how effective these compounds are against tumors (Megally Abdo et al., 2020) (Fig. 12.82).

5.39 Thioridazine derivatives

The N- and C-terminal domains of Pim-1 kinase form a hinge region that connects them in a conventional kinase fold. However, residue P123 at the hinge region disrupts the typical HB arrangement with the adenine moiety of ATP or associated inhibitors because there isn't an HB donor present. Due to their distinctive hinge region topology, Pim-1 kinase inhibitors may be structurally distinct from many other traditional kinase inhibitors. A structure-based hierarchical virtual screening method revealed thioridazine to be a low micromolar inhibitor of Pim-1, which is a selective dopamine receptor antagonist. A new series of Pim-1 inhibitors is the thioridazine derivatives (Li et al., 2014) (Fig. 12.83).

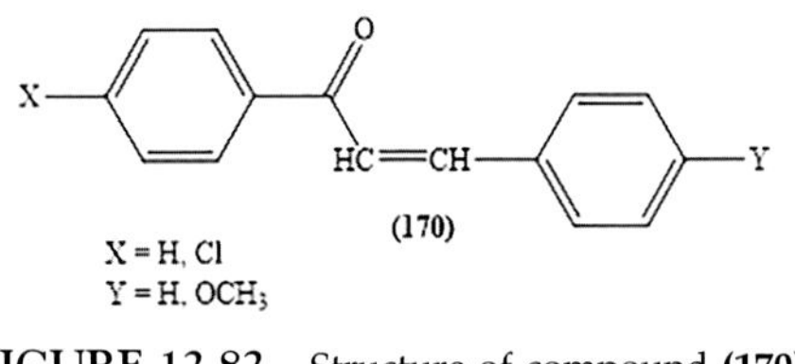

X = H, Cl
Y = H, OCH$_3$

FIGURE 12.82   Structure of compound (170).

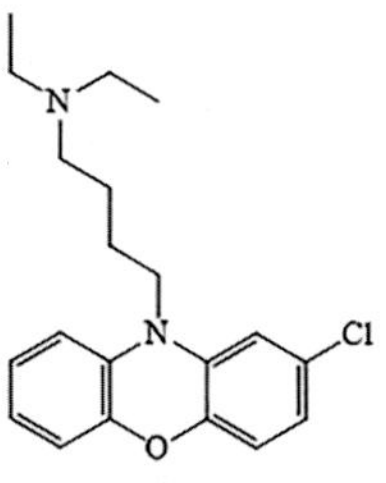

(10-DEBC)

10-[4'-(N,N-Diethylamino)butyl]-2-chlorophenoxazine

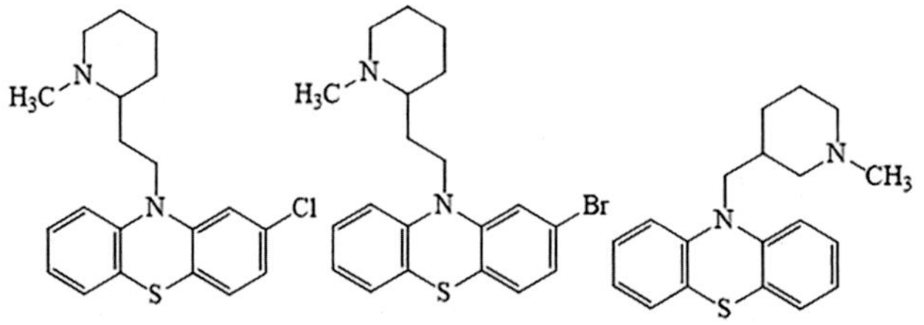

NC1186055   NC1186058   NC164076

FIGURE 12.83   Structure of compound **(10-DEBC, NC1186055, NC1186058, and NC164076)**.

As effective and specific Pim-1 kinase inhibitors, Li et al. explain the synthesis and design of **10-DEBC** and its analogs **(NC1186055, NC1186058,** and **NC164076).** Through these efforts, several 10-DEBC compounds with enhanced Pim-1 inhibitory action were discovered. The most active compounds in our series are compound **(171)** and compound **(172)**, which exhibit around a 1000-time increase in activity over the original lead molecule **10-DEBC** (Li et al., 2020) (Fig. 12.84).

5.40 Cyanopyridine derivatives

Abouzid designed and synthesized two novel series of 2-amino and 2-oxocyanopyridine and evaluated as Pim-1 kinase inhibitors. A set of three cancer cell lines, MCF-7, HCT-116,

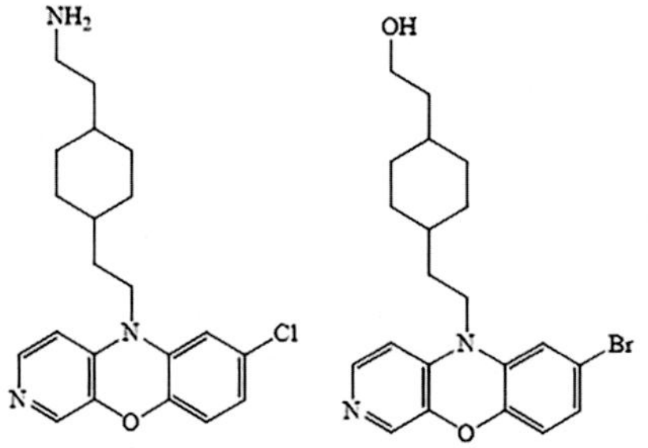

(171)   **(172)**

FIGURE 12.84   Structure of compounds **(171 and 172)**.

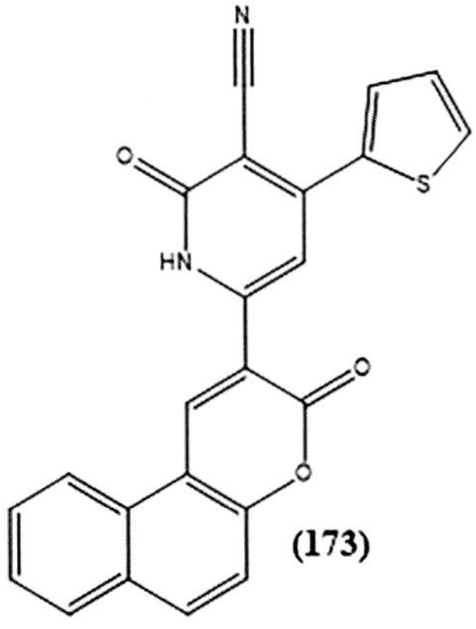

FIGURE 12.85   Structure of compound **(173)**.

and HepG2 used to test each newly synthesized compounds for in vitro anticancer activity. The Pim-1 kinase inhibitory activity of the two series was also evaluated, and the majority of the examined compounds (26%−89%) exhibited considerable Pim-1 kinase inhibitory activity. The IC_{50} values also revealed extremely powerful compounds in the submicromolar range, with compound **(173)** having an IC_{50} value of 0.94 mM (Abouzid et al., 2017) (Fig. 12.85).

5.41 2-Aminobenzothiazole derivatives

Harshita et al. developed and evaluated a novel series of derivatives that contain a dithiocarbamate molecule as a side chain at the second position of the 2-amino benzothiazole nucleus. According to the results of the 3-(4,5-dimethylthiazol-2-yl)-2,5-diphenyl tetrazolium bromide assay, compounds **(174−176)** of the series were found to be powerful anticancer agents against the human ovarian cancer cell line SK-OV-3, with IC_{50} values of 34.52 0.5, 34.28 0.06, and 29.17 0.6 µM (Harshita et al., 2020) (Fig. 12.86).

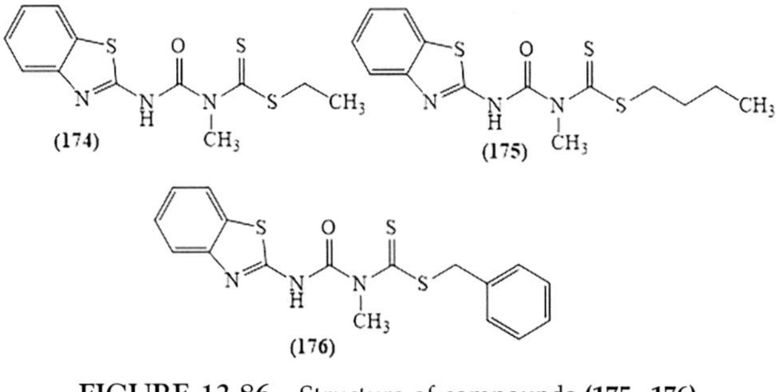

FIGURE 12.86   Structure of compounds **(175−176)**.

6. Summary

Pim-1 kinase is a crucial enzyme that plays a role in drug resistance, apoptosis, senescence, cell proliferation, differentiation, and survival. Pim-1 is one of the key anticancer targets due to its interactions with many proteins and affiliations with numerous signaling pathways. Various Pim-1 inhibitors are undergoing preclinical or clinical testing. Preclinical research is still being done on a growing number of novel Pim-1 inhibitors. These initiatives further imply that Pim-1 is thought to be a principal therapeutic target in a number of cancers. Additionally, Pim-1 interacts with and phosphorylates Pgp, BCRP, and FLT3-ITD, which links Pim-1 as an effective targeted treatment for cancer stem cells. Drug resistance is a characteristic of cancer stem cells. The latest research on Pim-1's function in cellular senescence in various cancer microenvironments enables us to be cautious while treating cancer patients individually. For the future generation of precision medicine in cancer, targeting Pim-1 in immunotherapy and individualized therapy would be of utmost importance because Pim-1 is a potential prostate cancer biomarker and interacts with numerous signaling pathways.

References

Abdallah, A. E., Mohareb, R. M., & Ahmed, E. A. (November 2019). Novel pyrano [2, 3-d] thiazole and thiazolo [4, 5-b] pyridine derivatives: One-pot three-component synthesis and biological evaluation as anticancer agents, c-met, and pim-1 kinase inhibitors. *Journal of Heterocyclic Chemistry, 56*(11), 3017–3029.

Abnous, K., Manavi, H., Mehri, S., Alibolandi, M., Kamali, H., Ghandadi, M., & Hadizadeh, F. (June 2017). In vitro evaluation of dihydropyridine-3-carbonitriles as potential cytotoxic agents through PIM-1 protein kinase inhibition. *Research in Pharmaceutical Sciences, 12*(3), 196.

Abouzid, K. A. M., Al-Ansary, G. H., & El-Naggar, A. M. (2017). Eco-friendly synthesis of novel cyanopyridine derivatives and their anticancer and PIM-1 kinase inhibitory activities. *European Journal of Medicinal Chemistry, 134,* 357–365.

Akué-Gédu, R., Rossignol, E., Azzaro, S., Knapp, S., Filippakopoulos, P., Bullock, A. N., Bain, J., Cohen, P., Prudhomme, M., Anizon, F., & Moreau, P. (October 22, 2009). Synthesis, kinase inhibitory potencies, and in vitro antiproliferative evaluation of new Pim kinase inhibitors. *Journal of Medicinal Chemistry, 52*(20), 6369–6381.

Alnabulsi, S., & Al-Hurani, E. A. (November 1, 2020). Pim kinase inhibitors in cancer: Medicinal chemistry insights into their activity and selectivity. *Drug Discovery Today, 25*(11), 2062–2069.

Asati, V., & Bharti, S. K. (February 15, 2018). Design, synthesis and molecular modeling studies of novel thiazolidine-2, 4-dione derivatives as potential anti-cancer agents. *Journal of Molecular Structure, 1154,* 406–417.

Bachmann, M., & Möröy, T. (April 1, 2005). The serine/threonine kinase Pim-1. *The International Journal of Biochemistry & Cell Biology, 37*(4), 726–730.

Bataille, C. J., Brennan, M. B., Byrne, S., Davies, S. G., Durbin, M., Fedorov, O., Huber, K. V., Jones, A. M., Knapp, S., Liu, G., & Nadali, A. (May 1, 2017). Thiazolidine derivatives as potent and selective inhibitors of the PIM kinase family. *Bioorganic & Medicinal Chemistry, 25*(9), 2657–2665.

Bogusz, J., Zrubek, K., Rembacz, K. P., Grudnik, P., Golik, P., Romanowska, M., Wladyka, B., & Dubin, G. (October 17, 2017). Structural analysis of PIM1 kinase complexes with ATP-competitive inhibitors. *Scientific Reports, 7*(1), Article 13399.

Burger, M. T., Han, W., Lan, J., Nishiguchi, G., Bellamacina, C., Lindval, M., Atallah, G., Ding, Y., Mathur, M., McBride, C., & Beans, E. L. (December 12, 2013). Structure guided optimization, in vitro activity, and in vivo activity of pan-PIM kinase inhibitors. *ACS Medicinal Chemistry Letters, 4*(12), 1193–1197.

Cee, V. J., Chavez, F., Jr., Herberich, B., Lanman, B. A., Pettus, L. H., Reed, A. B., Wu, B., Wurz, R. P., Andrews, K. L., Chen, J., & Hickman, D. (April 14, 2016). Discovery and optimization of macrocyclic quinoxaline-pyrrolo-dihydro-piperidinones as potent pim-1/2 kinase inhibitors. *ACS Medicinal Chemistry Letters, 7*(4), 408–412.

Chang, M., Kanwar, N., Feng, E., Siu, A., Liu, X., Ma, D., & Jongstra, J. (September 1, 2010). PIM kinase inhibitors downregulate STAT3Tyr705 phosphorylation inhibition of STAT3 activation. *Molecular Cancer Therapeutics, 9*(9), 2478–2487.

Chao, S. W., Su, M. Y., Chiou, L. C., Chen, L. C., Chang, C. I., & Huang, W. J. (August 28, 2015). Total synthesis of hispidulin and the structural basis for its inhibition of proto-oncogene kinase Pim-1. *Journal of Natural Products, 78*(8), 1969–1976.

Cheney, I. W., Yan, S., Appleby, T., Walker, H., Vo, T., Yao, N., Hamatake, R., Hong, Z., & Wu, J. Z. (March 15, 2007). Identification and structure–activity relationships of substituted pyridones as inhibitors of Pim-1 kinase. *Bioorganic & Medicinal Chemistry Letters, 17*(6), 1679–1683.

Dakin, L. A., Block, M. H., Chen, H., Code, E., Dowling, J. E., Feng, X., Ferguson, A. D., Green, I., Hird, A. W., Howard, T., & Keeton, E. K. (July 15, 2012). Discovery of novel benzylidene-1, 3-thiazolidine-2, 4-diones as potent and selective inhibitors of the PIM-1, PIM-2, and PIM-3 protein kinases. *Bioorganic & Medicinal Chemistry Letters, 22*(14), 4599–4604.

Dwyer, M. P., Keertikar, K., Paruch, K., Alvarez, C., Labroli, M., Poker, C., Fischmann, T. O., Mayer-Ezell, R., Bond, R., Wang, Y., & Azevedo, R. (November 15, 2013). Discovery of pyrazolo [1, 5-a] pyrimidine-based pim inhibitors: A template-based approach. *Bioorganic & Medicinal Chemistry Letters, 23*(22), 6178–6182.

El-Miligy, M. M., Abdelaziz, M. E., Fahmy, S. M., Ibrahim, T. M., Abu-Serie, M. M., Mahran, M. A., & Hazzaa, A. A. (December 31, 2023). Discovery of new pyridine-quinoline hybrids as competitive and non-competitive PIM-1 kinase inhibitors with apoptosis induction and caspase 3/7 activation capabilities. *Journal of Enzyme Inhibition and Medicinal Chemistry, 38*(1), Article 2152810.

El-Nassan, H. B., Naguib, B. H., & Beshay, E. A. (January 1, 2018). Synthesis of new pyridothienopyrimidinone and pyridothienotriazolopyrimidine derivatives as pim-1 inhibitors. *Journal of Enzyme Inhibition and Medicinal Chemistry, 33*(1), 58–66.

Fabian, M. A., Biggs, W. H., III, Treiber, D. K., Atteridge, C. E., Azimioara, M. D., Benedetti, M. G., Carter, T. A., Ciceri, P., Edeen, P. T., Floyd, M., Ford, J. M., Galvin, M., Gerlach, J. L., Grotzfeld, R. M., Herrgard, S., Insko, D. E., Insko, M. A., Lai, A. G., Lélias, J. M., ... Lockhart, D. J. (2005). A small molecule-kinase interaction map for clinical kinase inhibitors. *Nature Biotechnology, 23*(3), 329–336.

Fan, Y. B., Li, K., Huang, M., Cao, Y., Li, Y., Jin, S. Y., Liu, W. B., Wen, J. C., Liu, D., & Zhao, L. X. (February 15, 2016). Design and synthesis of substituted pyrido [3, 2-d]-1, 2, 3-triazines as potential Pim-1 inhibitors. *Bioorganic & Medicinal Chemistry Letters, 26*(4), 1224–1228.

Farrag, A. M., Ibrahim, M. H., Mehany, A. B., & Ismail, M. M. (December 1, 2020). New cyanopyridine-based scaffold as PIM-1 inhibitors and apoptotic inducers: Synthesis and SARs study. *Bioorganic Chemistry, 105*, Article 104378.

Flanders, Y., Dumas, S., Caserta, J., Nicewonger, R., Baldino, M., Lee, C. S., & Baldino, C. M. (June 3, 2015). A versatile synthesis of novel pan-PIM kinase inhibitors with initial SAR study. *Tetrahedron Letters, 56*(23), 3186–3190.

Garcia, P. D., Langowski, J. L., Wang, Y., Chen, M., Castillo, J., Fanton, C., Ison, M., Zavorotinskaya, T., Dai, Y., Lu, J., & Niu, X. H. (April 1, 2014). Pan-PIM kinase inhibition provides a novel therapy for treating hematologic cancers pan-PIM kinase inhibition in hematologic cancers. *Clinical Cancer Research, 20*(7), 1834–1845.

Gingipalli, L., Block, M. H., Bao, L., Cooke, E., Dakin, L. A., Denz, C. R., Ferguson, A. D., Johannes, J. W., Larsen, N. A., Lyne, P. D., & Pontz, T. W. (May 1, 2018). Discovery of 2, 6-disubstituted pyrazine derivatives as inhibitors of CK2 and PIM kinases. *Bioorganic & Medicinal Chemistry Letters, 28*(8), 1336–1341.

Guo, S., Mao, X., Chen, J., Huang, B., Jin, C., Xu, Z., & Qiu, S. (December 2010). Overexpression of Pim-1 in bladder cancer. *Journal of Experimental & Clinical Cancer Research, 29*, 1–7.

Haddach, M., Michaux, J., Schwaebe, M. K., Pierre, F., O'Brien, S. E., Borsan, C., Tran, J., Raffaele, N., Ravula, S., Drygin, D., & Siddiqui-Jain, A. (February 9, 2012). Discovery of CX-6258. A potent, selective, and orally efficacious pan-Pim kinases inhibitor. *ACS Medicinal Chemistry Letters, 3*(2), 135–139.

Harshita, P. S., Supriya, C. H., Sravanthi, S., Jyothi, V., Peddi, S. R., Manga, V., Saddanapu, V., & Jyostna, T. S. (December 31, 2020). Design synthesis and biological evaluation of dithiocarbamate substituted 2-aminobenzothiazole derivatives as proviral integration site of Moloney murine leukaemia virus 1 kinase inhibitors. *Indian Journal of Pharmaceutical Sciences, 82*(6), 1015–1024.

Hazhazi, H., Melkemi, N., Salah, T., & Bouachrine, M. (September 1, 2019). DFT-based reactivity and combined QSAR, molecular docking of 1, 2, 4, 5-Tetrazine derivatives as inhibitors of Pim-1 kinase. *Heliyon, 5*(9), Article e02451.

Hu, H., Wang, X., Chan, G. K. Y., Chang, J. H., Do, S., Drummond, J., Ebens, A., Lee, W., Ly, J., Lyssikatos, J. P., Murray, J., Moffat, J. G., Chao, Q., Tsui, V., Wallweber, H., & Kolesnikov, A. (November 15, 2015). Discovery of 3,5-substituted 6-azaindazoles as potent pan-PIM inhibitors. *Bioorganic & Medicinal Chemistry Letters, 25*(22), 5258–5264.

Holder, S., Zemskova, M., Zhang, C., Tabrizizad, M., Bremer, R., Neidigh, J. W., & Lilly, M. B. (2007). Characterization of a potent and selective small-molecule inhibitor of the PIM1 kinase. *Molecular Cancer Therapeutics, 6,* 163–172.

Ishchenko, A., Zhang, L., Le Brazidec, J. Y., Fan, J., Chong, J. H., Hingway, A., Raditsis, A., Singh, L., Elenbaas, B., Hong, V. S., & Marcotte, D. (February 1, 2015). Structure-based design of low-nanomolar PIM kinase inhibitors. *Bioorganic & Medicinal Chemistry Letters, 25*(3), 474–480.

Jacobs, M. D., Black, J., Futer, O., Swenson, L., Hare, B., Fleming, M., & Saxena, K. (April 8, 2005). PIM1 ligand-bound structures reveal the mechanism of serine/threonine kinase inhibition by LY294002. *Journal of Biological Chemistry, 280*(14), 13728–13734.

Jiang, W., Chen, Y., Song, X., Shao, Y., Ning, Z., & Gu, W. (2019). Pim-1 inhibitor SMI-4a suppresses tumor growth in non-small cell lung cancer via PI3K/AKT/mTOR pathway. *OncoTargets and Therapy, 12*, 3043.

Keane, N. A., Reidy, M., Natoni, A., Raab, M. S., & O'dwyer, M. (July 2015). Targeting the Pim kinases in multiple myeloma. *Blood Cancer Journal, 5*(7), e325.

Kim, H. K., Kim, C. W., Vo, M. T., Lee, H. H., Lee, J. Y., Yoon, N. A., Lee, C. Y., Moon, C. H., Min, Y. J., Park, J. W., & Cho, W. J. (August 17, 2012). Expression of proviral integration site for Moloney murine leukemia virus 1 (Pim-1) is post-transcriptionally regulated by tristetraprolin in cancer cells. *Journal of Biological Chemistry, 287*(34), 28770–28778.

Kim, J. E., Son, J. E., Jeong, H., Kim, D. J., Seo, S. G., Lee, E., Lim, T. G., Kim, J. R., Kimbung, Y. R., Chen, H., & Bode, A. M. (July 1, 2015). A novel cinnamon-related natural product with pim-1 inhibitory activity inhibits leukemia and skin cancer cinnamon inhibits pim-1 in leukemia and skin cancer. *Cancer Research, 75*(13), 2716–2728.

Lee, M., Lee, K. H., Min, A., Kim, J., Kim, S., Jang, H., Lim, J. M., Kim, S. H., Ha, D. H., Jeong, W. J., & Suh, K. J. (April 1, 2019). Pan-Pim kinase inhibitor AZD1208 suppresses tumor growth and synergistically interacts with Akt inhibition in gastric cancer cells. Cancer Research and Treatment. *Official Journal of Korean Cancer Association, 51*(2), 451–463.

Li, G., Zhang, W., Xie, Y., Li, Y., Cao, R., Zheng, G., Huang, N., & Zhou, Y. (May 14, 2020). Structure-based optimization of 10-DEBC derivatives as potent and selective Pim-1 kinase inhibitors. *Journal of Chemical Information and Modeling, 60*(6), 3287–3294.

Li, K., Li, Y., Zhou, D., Fan, Y., Guo, H., Ma, T., Wen, J., Liu, D., & Zhao, L. (April 15, 2016). Synthesis and biological evaluation of quinoline derivatives as potential anti-prostate cancer agents and Pim-1 kinase inhibitors. *Bioorganic & Medicinal Chemistry, 24*(8), 1889–1897.

Li, W., Wan, X., Zeng, F., Xie, Y., Wang, Y., Zhang, W., Li, L., & Huang, N. (2014). More than just a GPCR ligand: Structure-based discovery of thioridazine derivatives as pim-1 kinase inhibitors. *MedChemComm, 5*(4), 507–511.

Liu, K., Gao, H., Wang, Q., Wang, L., Zhang, B., Han, Z., Chen, X., Han, M., & Gao, M. (May 2018). Retracted: Hispidulin suppresses cell growth and metastasis by targeting PIM 1 through JAK 2/STAT 3 signaling in colorectal cancer. *Cancer Science, 109*(5), 1369–1381.

Martinez-Gonzalez, S., Rodriguez-Aristegui, S., de la Oliva, C. A., Hernández, A. I., Cantalapiedra, E. G., Varela, C., García, A. B., Rabal, O., Oyarzabal, J., Bischoff, J. R., & Klett, J. (April 15, 2019). Discovery of novel triazolo [4, 3-b] pyridazin-3-yl-quinoline derivatives as PIM inhibitors. *European Journal of Medicinal Chemistry, 168*, 87–109.

Megally Abdo, N. Y., Samir, E. M., & Mohareb, R. M. (April 2020). Synthesis and evaluation of novel 4 H-pyrazole and thiophene derivatives derived from chalcone as potential anti-proliferative agents, Pim-1 kinase inhibitors, and PAINS. *Journal of Heterocyclic Chemistry, 57*(4), 1993–2009.

Mohareb, R. M., Abdo, N. Y., & Wardakhan, W. W. (October 2017). Synthesis and evaluation of pyrazolo [5, 1-b] quinazoline-2-carboxylate, and its thiazole derivatives as potential antiproliferative agents and Pim-1 kinase inhibitors. *Medicinal Chemistry Research, 26*, 2520–2537.

Mohareb, R. M., Hilmy, K. M., & Elshehawy, Y. A. (2018). Discovery of new thiophene, pyrazole, isoxazole derivatives as antitumor, c-Met, tyrosine kinase and Pim-1 kinase inhibitors. *Bulletin of the Chemical Society of Ethiopia, 32*(2), 285–308.

Mohareb, R. M., Ibrahim, R. A., & Alwan, E. S. (March 20, 2021). Multi-component reactions of cyclohexan-1, 3-diketones to produce fused pyran derivatives with antiproliferative activities and tyrosine kinases and pim-1 kinase inhibitions. *Acta Chimica Slovenica, 68*(1), 51−64.

Mohareb, R. M., Ibrahim, R. A., Elmetwally, A. M., & Gamaan, M. S. (March 15, 2022). Synthesis of fused quinoline derivatives with antiproliferative activities and tyrosine kinases, pim-1 kinase inhibitions. *Acta Chimica Slovenica, 69*(1), 13−29.

Mohareb, R. M., Klapötke, T. M., & Reinhardt, E. (2018). Uses of dimedone for the synthesis of thiazole derivatives as new anti-tumor, c-Met, tyrosine kinase, and Pim-1 inhibitions. *Medicinal Chemistry Research, 27*, 2494−2511.

Mohareb, R. M., & Mikhail, I. R. (April 1, 2020). Synthesis of Thiazole, Thiophene, pyran and pyridine derivatives derived from 3-phenyl-1H-pyrazol-5 (4H)-one with anti-proliferative, tyrosine kinase and PIM-1 kinase inhibitions. *Letters in Drug Design and Discovery, 17*(4), 485−501.

Mohareb, R. M., Samir, E. M., & Halim, P. A. (2019). Synthesis, and anti-proliferative, Pim-1 kinase inhibitors and molecular docking of thiophenes derived from estrone. *Bioorganic Chemistry, 83*, 402−413.

Mohareb, R. M., Wardakhan, W. W., & Abbas, N. S. (2019). Synthesis of tetrahydrobenzo [b] thiophene-3-carbohydrazide derivatives as potential anti-cancer agents and Pim-1 kinase Inhibitors. *Anti-Cancer Agents in Medicinal Chemistry, 19*(14), 1737−1753.

Mohareb, R. M., Abdo, N. Y. M., & El-Sharkawy, K. A. (2018). New approaches for the uses of cyclohexan-1, 4-dione for the synthesis of 5, 6, 7, 8-tetrahydrobenzo [4, 5] thieno [2, 3-b] pyridine derivatives used as potential anti-prostate cancer agents and pim-1 kinase inhibitors. *Anti-Cancer Agents in Medicinal Chemistry, 18*(12), 1736−1749.

More, K. N., Jang, H. W., Hong, V. S., & Lee, J. (June 1, 2014). Pim kinase inhibitory and antiproliferative activity of a novel series of meridianin C derivatives. *Bioorganic & Medicinal Chemistry Letters, 24*(11), 2424−2428.

Nafie, M. S., Amer, A. M., Mohamed, A. K., & Tantawy, E. S. (December 15, 2020). Discovery of novel pyrazolo [3, 4-b] pyridine scaffold-based derivatives as potential PIM-1 kinase inhibitors in breast cancer MCF-7 cells. *Bioorganic & Medicinal Chemistry, 28*(24), Article 115828.

Naguib, B. H., El-Nassan, H. B., & Abdelghany, T. M. (January 1, 2017). Synthesis of new pyridothienopyrimidinone derivatives as Pim-1 inhibitors. *Journal of Enzyme Inhibition and Medicinal Chemistry, 32*(1), 457−467.

Naguib, B. H., & El-Nassan, H. B. (November 1, 2016). Synthesis of new thieno [2, 3-b] pyridine derivatives as pim-1 inhibitors. *Journal of Enzyme Inhibition and Medicinal Chemistry, 31*(6), 1718−7825.

Nakano, H., Hasegawa, T., Kojima, H., Okabe, T., & Nagano, T. (May 11, 2017). Design and synthesis of potent and selective PIM kinase inhibitors by targeting unique structure of ATP-binding pocket. *ACS Medicinal Chemistry Letters, 8*(5), 504−509.

Nakano, H., Saito, N., Parker, L., Tada, Y., Abe, M., Tsuganezawa, K., Yokoyama, S., Tanaka, A., Kojima, H., Okabe, T., & Nagano, T. (June 14, 2012). Rational evolution of a novel type of potent and selective proviral integration site in Moloney murine leukemia virus kinase 1 (PIM1) inhibitor from a screening-hit compound. *Journal of Medicinal Chemistry, 55*(11), 5151−5164.

Narasimhamurthy, K. H., Kallesha, N., Mohan, C. D., & Rangappa, K. S. (September 19, 2022). Anticancer functions of pyridine heterocycles. In *Cytotoxicity*. IntechOpen.

Natarajan, K., Bhullar, J., Shukla, S., Burcu, M., Chen, Z. S., Ambudkar, S. V., & Baer, M. R. (February 15, 2013). The Pim kinase inhibitor SGI-1776 decreases cell surface expression of P-glycoprotein (ABCB1) and breast cancer resistance protein (ABCG2) and drug transport by Pim-1-dependent and-independent mechanisms. *Biochemical Pharmacology, 85*(4), 514−524.

Nishiguchi, G. A., Atallah, G., Bellamacina, C., Burger, M. T., Ding, Y., Feucht, P. H., Garcia, P. D., Han, W., Klivansky, L., & Lindvall, M. (November 1, 2011). Discovery of novel 3, 5-disubstituted indole derivatives as potent inhibitors of Pim-1, Pim-2, and Pim-3 protein kinases. *Bioorganic & Medicinal Chemistry Letters, 21*(21), 6366−6369.

Nishiguchi, G. A., Burger, M. T., Han, W., Lan, J., Atallah, G., Tamez, V., Lindvall, M., Bellamacina, C., Garcia, P., Feucht, P., & Zavorotinskaya, T. (May 1, 2016). Design, synthesis and structure activity relationship of potent pan-PIM kinase inhibitors derived from the pyridyl carboxamide scaffold. *Bioorganic & Medicinal Chemistry Letters, 26*(9), 2328−2332.

Ouhtit, A., Muzumdar, S., Gupta, I., Shanmuganathan, S., & Tamimi, Y. (January 1, 2015). Understanding the functional discrepancy of Pim-1 in cancer. *Nucleus, 5*(6), 7.

Oyallon, B., Brachet-Botineau, M., Logé, C., Bonnet, P., Souab, M., Robert, T., Ruchaud, S., Bach, S., Berthelot, P., Gouilleux, F., & Viaud-Massuard, M. C. (June 25, 2018). Structure-based design of novel quinoxaline-2-carboxylic acids and analogues as Pim-1 inhibitors. *European Journal of Medicinal Chemistry, 154*, 101−109.

Oyallon, B., Brachet-Botineau, M., Logé, C., Robert, T., Bach, S., Ibrahim, S., Raoul, W., Croix, C., Berthelot, P., Guillon, J., & Pinaud, N. (February 6, 2021). New quinoxaline derivatives as dual Pim-1/2 kinase inhibitors: Design, synthesis and biological evaluation. *Molecules, 26*(4), 867.

Pastor, J., Oyarzabal, J., Saluste, G., Alvarez, R. M., Rivero, V., Ramos, F., Cendón, E., Blanco-Aparicio, C., Ajenjo, N., Cebriá, A., & Albarrán, M. I. (February 15, 2012). Hit to lead evaluation of 1, 2, 3-triazolo [4, 5-b] pyridines as PIM kinase inhibitors. *Bioorganic & Medicinal Chemistry Letters, 22*(4), 1591−1597.

Peng, Y. H., Li, J. J., Xie, F. W., Chen, J. F., Yu, Y. H., Ouyang, X. N., & Liang, H. J. (October 7, 2013). Expression of pim-1 in tumors, tumor stroma and tumor-adjacent mucosa co-determines the prognosis of colon cancer patients. *PLoS One, 8*(10), Article e76693.

Pettus, L. H., Andrews, K. L., Booker, S. K., Chen, J., Cee, V. J., Chavez, F., Jr., Chen, Y., Eastwood, H., Guerrero, N., Herberich, B., & Hickman, D. (July 14, 2016). Discovery and optimization of quinazolinone-pyrrolopyrrolones as potent and orally bioavailable pan-pim kinase inhibitors. *Journal of Medicinal Chemistry, 59*(13), 6407−6430.

Philoppes, J. N., Khedr, M. A., Hassan, M. H., Kamel, G., & Lamie, P. F. (July 1, 2020). New pyrazolopyrimidine derivatives with anticancer activity: Design, synthesis, PIM-1 inhibition, molecular docking study and molecular dynamics. *Bioorganic Chemistry, 100*, Article 103944.

Pierre, F., Stefan, E., Nédellec, A. S., Chevrel, M. C., Regan, C. F., Siddiqui-Jain, A., Macalino, D., Streiner, N., Drygin, D., Haddach, M., & O'Brien, S. E. (November 15, 2011). 7-(4H-1, 2, 4-Triazol-3-yl) benzo [c][2, 6] naphthyridines: A novel class of pim kinase inhibitors with potent cell antiproliferative activity. *Bioorganic & Medicinal Chemistry Letters, 21*(22), 6687−6692.

Saluste, G., Albarran, M. I., Alvarez, R. M., Rabal, O., Ortega, M. A., Blanco, C., Kurz, G., Salgado, A., Pevarello, P., Bischoff, J. R., & Pastor, J. (October 24, 2012). Fragment-hopping-based discovery of a novel chemical series of proto-oncogene PIM-1 kinase inhibitors. *PLoS One, 7*(10), Article e45964.

Sliman, F., Blairvacq, M., Durieu, E., Meijer, L., Rodrigo, J., & Desmaële, D. (May 1, 2010). Identification and structure−activity relationship of 8-hydroxy-quinoline-7-carboxylic acid derivatives as inhibitors of Pim-1 kinase. *Bioorganic & Medicinal Chemistry Letters, 20*(9), 2801−2805.

Suchaud, V., Gavara, L., Giraud, F., Nauton, L., Théry, V., Anizon, F., & Moreau, P. (September 1, 2014). Synthesis of pyrazolo [4, 3-a] phenanthridines, a new scaffold for Pim kinase inhibition. *Bioorganic & Medicinal Chemistry, 22*(17), 4704−4710.

Suchaud, V., Gavara, L., Saugues, E., Nauton, L., Théry, V., Anizon, F., & Moreau, P. (July 15, 2013). Identification of 1, 6-dihydropyrazolo [4, 3-c] carbazoles and 3, 6-dihydropyrazolo [3, 4-c] carbazoles as new Pim kinase inhibitors. *Bioorganic & Medicinal Chemistry, 21*(14), 4102−4111.

Sun, H. B., Wang, X. Y., Li, G. B., Zhang, L. D., Liu, J., & Zhao, L. F. (2015). Design, synthesis and biological evaluation of novel C3-functionalized oxindoles as potential Pim-1 kinase inhibitors. *Rsc Advances, 5*(37), 29456−29466.

Tong, Y., Stewart, K. D., Thomas, S., Przytulinska, M., Johnson, E. F., Klinghofer, V., Leverson, J., McCall, O., Soni, N. B., Luo, Y., & Lin, N. H. (October 1, 2008). Isoxazolo [3, 4-b] quinoline-3, 4 (1H, 9H)-diones as unique, potent and selective inhibitors for Pim-1 and Pim-2 kinases: Chemistry, biological activities, and molecular modeling. *Bioorganic & Medicinal Chemistry Letters, 18*(19), 5206−5208.

Tsuganezawa, K., Watanabe, H., Parker, L., Yuki, H., Taruya, S., Nakagawa, Y., Kamei, D., Mori, M., Ogawa, N., Tomabechi, Y., & Handa, N. (March 30, 2012). A novel Pim-1 kinase inhibitor targeting residues that bind the substrate peptide. *Journal of Molecular Biology, 417*(3), 240−252.

Tsuhako, A. L., Brown, D. S., Koltun, E. S., Aay, N., Arcalas, A., Chan, V., Du, H., Engst, S., Franzini, M., Galan, A., & Huang, P. (June 1, 2012). The design, synthesis, and biological evaluation of PIM kinase inhibitors. *Bioorganic & Medicinal Chemistry Letters, 22*(11), 3732−3738.

Wang, H. L., Andrews, K. L., Booker, S. K., Canon, J., Cee, V. J., Chavez, F., Jr., Chen, Y., Eastwood, H., Guerrero, N., Herberich, B., & Hickman, D. (2019). Discovery of (R)-8-(6-Methyl-4-oxo-1, 4, 5, 6-tetrahydropyrrolo [3, 4-b] pyrrol-2-yl)-3-(1-methylcyclopropyl)-2-((1-methylcyclopropyl) amino) quinazolin-4 (3 H)-one, a potent and selective Pim-1/2 kinase inhibitor for hematological malignancies. *Journal of Medicinal Chemistry, 62*(3), 1523−1540.

Wang, H. L., Cee, V. J., Chavez, F., Jr., Lanman, B. A., Reed, A. B., Wu, B., Guerrero, N., Lipford, J. R., Sastri, C., Winston, J., & Andrews, K. L. (February 15, 2015). The discovery of novel 3-(pyrazin-2-yl)-1H-indazoles as potent pan-Pim kinase inhibitors. *Bioorganic & Medicinal Chemistry Letters, 25*(4), 834−840.

Wang, X., Blackaby, W., Allen, V., Chan, G. K., Chang, J. H., Chiang, P. C., Diene, C., Drummond, J., Do, S., Fan, E., & Harstad, E. B. (2019). Optimization of pan-Pim kinase activity and oral bioavailability leading to diaminopyrazole (GDC-0339) for the treatment of multiple myeloma. *Journal of Medicinal Chemistry, 62*(4), 2140–2153.

Wang, X., Kolesnikov, A., Tay, S., Chan, G., Chao, Q., Do, S., Drummond, J., Ebens, A. J., Liu, N., Ly, J., & Harstad, E. (May 25, 2017). Discovery of 5-azaindazole (GNE-955) as a potent pan-Pim inhibitor with optimized bioavailability. *Journal of Medicinal Chemistry, 60*(10), 4458–4473.

Wang, X., Magnuson, S., Pastor, R., Fan, E., Hu, H., Tsui, V., Deng, W., Murray, J., Steffek, M., Wallweber, H., & Moffat, J. (June 1, 2013). Discovery of novel pyrazolo [1, 5-a] pyrimidines as potent pan-Pim inhibitors by structure-and property-based drug design. *Bioorganic & Medicinal Chemistry Letters, 23*(11), 3149–3153.

Weirauch, U., Beckmann, N., Thomas, M., Grünweller, A., Huber, K., Bracher, F., Hartmann, R. K., & Aigner, A. (July 1, 2013). Functional role and therapeutic potential of the pim-1 kinase in colon carcinoma. *Neoplasia, 15*(7). 783–IN28.

Wu, B., Wang, H. L., Cee, V. J., Lanman, B. A., Nixey, T., Pettus, L., Reed, A. B., Wurz, R. P., Guerrero, N., Sastri, C., & Winston, J. (February 15, 2015). Discovery of 5-(1H-indol-5-yl)-1, 3, 4-thiadiazol-2-amines as potent PIM inhibitors. *Bioorganic & Medicinal Chemistry Letters, 25*(4), 775–780.

Wurz, R. P., Pettus, L. H., Jackson, C., Wu, B., Wang, H. L., Herberich, B., Cee, V., Lanman, B. A., Reed, A. B., Chavez, F., Jr., & Nixey, T. (February 15, 2015). The discovery and optimization of aminooxadiazoles as potent Pim kinase inhibitors. *Bioorganic & Medicinal Chemistry Letters, 25*(4), 847–855.

Wurz, R. P., Sastri, C., D'Amico, D. C., Herberich, B., Jackson, C. L., Pettus, L. H., Tasker, A. S., Wu, B., Guerrero, N., Lipford, J. R., & Winston, J. T. (November 15, 2016). Discovery of imidazopyridazines as potent Pim-1/2 kinase inhibitors. *Bioorganic & Medicinal Chemistry Letters, 26*(22), 5580–5590.

Xia, Z., Knaak, C., Ma, J., Beharry, Z. M., McInnes, C., Wang, W., Kraft, A. S., & Smith, C. D. (January 8, 2009). Synthesis and evaluation of novel inhibitors of Pim-1 and Pim-2 protein kinases. *Journal of Medicinal Chemistry, 52*(1), 74–86.

Xiang, Y., Hirth, B., Asmussen, G., Biemann, H. P., Bishop, K. A., Good, A., Fitzgerald, M., Gladysheva, T., Jain, A., Jancsics, K., & Liu, J. (May 15, 2011). The discovery of novel benzofuran-2-carboxylic acids as potent Pim-1 inhibitors. *Bioorganic & Medicinal Chemistry Letters, 21*(10), 3050–3056.

Xu, J., Shen, C., Xie, Y., Qiu, B., Ren, X., Zhou, Y., Li, G., Zheng, G., & Huang, N. (September 15, 2022). Design, synthesis, and bioactivity evaluation of macrocyclic benzo [b] pyrido [4, 3-e][1, 4] oxazine derivatives as novel Pim-1 kinase inhibitors. *Bioorganic & Medicinal Chemistry Letters, 72*, Article 128874.

Xu, J., Xiong, G., Cao, Z., Huang, H., Wang, T., You, L., Zhou, L., Zheng, L., Hu, Y., Zhang, T., & Zhao, Y. (December 2016). PIM-1 contributes to the malignancy of pancreatic cancer and displays diagnostic and prognostic value. *Journal of Experimental & Clinical Cancer Research, 35*(1), 1–2.

Yang, H., He, K., Dong, W., Fang, J., Zhong, S., Tang, L., & Long, L. (September 2020). PIM-1 may function as an oncogene in cervical cancer via activating the EGFR signaling. *The International Journal of Biological Markers, 35*(3), 67–73.

Zhu, X., Xu, J. J., Hu, S. S., Feng, J. G., Jiang, L. H., Hou, X. X., Cao, J., Han, J., Ling, Z. Q., & Ge, M. H. (December 2014). Pim-1 acts as an oncogene in human salivary gland adenoid cystic carcinoma. *Journal of Experimental & Clinical Cancer Research, 33*(1), 1–2.

Rearranged during transfection (RET) inhibitors

Vivek Shrivastava[1], Vinod Kumar Gurjar[1], Shweta Jain[2], Ankur Vaidya[3] and Ankur Sharma[4]

[1]School of Pharmacy, Faculty of Pharmacy, Parul University, Vadodara, Gujarat, India; [2]Sir Madanlal Institute of Pharmacy, Etawah, Uttar Pradesh, India; [3]Faculty of Pharmacy, Uttar Pradesh University of Medical Sciences, Saifai, Uttar Pradesh, India; [4]Department of Medicine and Rheumatology, The University of Oklahoma Health Sciences Centre, Oklahoma City, OK, United States

1. Introduction

Since the initial identification of the first tyrosine kinase in the early 1980s, the scientific community has recognized that tumors displaying abnormal tyrosine kinase activity hold significant promise as potential targets for therapeutic intervention in carcinogenic diseases. Among these receptor tyrosine kinases, RET stands out as a crucial player. Its discovery dates back to 1985 when researchers identified it as a novel transforming gene in NIH3T3 cells. This transformation occurred after the introduction of DNA derived from human lymphoma cells (Takahashi et al., 1985), leading to uncontrolled cell growth and the development of cancerous characteristics in these cells. This groundbreaking finding opened up new avenues for understanding the role of tyrosine kinases in cancer and paved the way for potential treatment approaches in related disorders.

Takahashi and colleagues used Southern blot analysis to show that the potential transforming gene was created by the recombination of two DNA sequences that were more than 25 kb apart on the human genome. This resulted in a transcriptionally functioning unit. The method by which this unique transforming gene was found led to its later naming. Since its discovery, RET has been shown to be important for a variety of developmental processes, including the growth of the kidney and the enteric nervous system in the embryo (Chi et al., 2009; Schuchardt et al., 1994). As a result, many disease phenotypes, including Hirschsprung's disease and cancer, are associated with RET changes (Jain et al., 2004; Tomuschat & Puri, 2015).

The RET has undergone a number of alterations over the past 3 decades that cause its kinase activity to become constitutively active. Numerous cancer subtypes are thought to be caused by this process (Iwashita et al., 1996; Mulligan et al., 1993; Smith et al., 1997; Wagner et al., 2012). It is thought that aberrant RET activity is a prime candidate for targeted treatment methods due to its role as an oncogenic driver in many malignancies. Initially, the medical community utilized multi-kinase inhibitors in their efforts to combat aberrant tyrosine kinase activity. As research progressed, a significant milestone was achieved with the development of the first generation of selective RET inhibitors. This marked a crucial advancement in targeting specific pathways associated with RET, offering a more focused and potentially effective approach to treating related disorders (Bhattacharya et al., 2022).

This chapter provides a comprehensive overview of canonical RET signaling biology, highlighting its crucial role in significant developmental processes. Additionally, it delves into the potential oncogenic implications resulting from aberrant RET activity observed in various cancer types. This chapter will also explore specific modifications to RET that lead to its constitutive activation, causing cancer, and discuss the limitations of therapeutic approaches using repurposed multi-kinase inhibitors to suppress RET. Furthermore, it will examine the development of medications precisely targeting RET kinase activity, aiming to address these therapeutic challenges (Takahashi et al., 1985).

1.1 Structure and canonical RET signaling

RET, a transmembrane receptor tyrosine kinase (RTK), possesses a distinctive extracellular domain characterized by 16 cysteine residues and four cadherin-like domains encompassed in a 120 amino acid sequence (Ibáñez, 2013). Under specific conditions, including Ca^{2+} ion binding to RET's cadherin-like domains and the binding of GDNF family ligands to the co-receptor GDNF family receptor-a (GFRa1-4), two RET receptors come together, facilitating dimerization and subsequent autophosphorylation of numerous tyrosine residues on their cytoplasmic tails (Li et al., 2019a; Li et al., 2019b).

Phosphorylation of the cytoplasmic tyrosine residues of RET plays a critical role in facilitating the recruitment and binding of various adaptor proteins. These proteins are essential for mediating the signaling of external stimuli and triggering downstream signaling cascades, including the PI3K/AKT, RAS/RAF/MEK/ERK, JAK2/STAT3, and PLCg pathways (Fig. 13.1).

RET-Y687 recruits and binds to SHP2 phosphatase, resulting in the activation of the PI3K/AKT pathway, which, in turn, promotes cell survival (Perrinjaquet et al., 2010). For signal transducer and activator of transcription 3 (STAT3) to undergo phosphorylation, activation, and subsequent translocation into the nuclear envelope for STAT3 target gene transcription, docking sites RETY752 and Y928 are required (Schuringa et al., 2001). Additionally, RET-Y981 plays a crucial role in binding and activating Src kinase (Encinas et al., 2004). Furthermore, phosphorylation of RET-Y905 serves to stabilize RET's active conformation and is essential for the binding of adaptor proteins Grb7/10 (Iwashita et al., 1996; Kawamoto et al., 2004).

Following the phosphorylation of phospho-RET (Y1015), phospholipase C-g binds and triggers the activation of the protein kinase C (PKC) pathway (Borrello et al., 1996). Moreover,

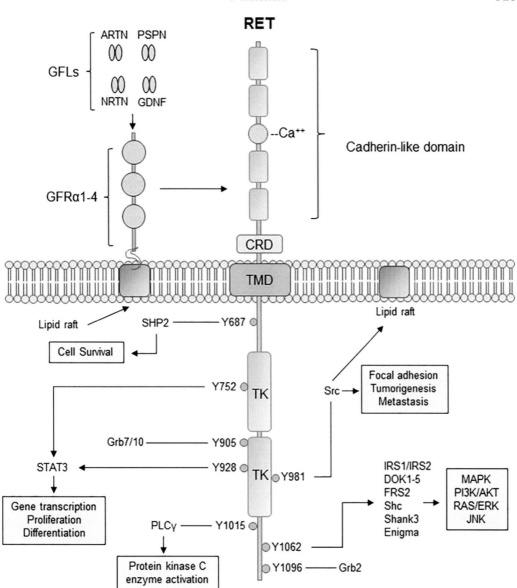

FIGURE 13.1 Canonical RET signaling [22 open access].

RET-Y1062 phosphorylation facilitates the recruitment of a diverse array of adaptor proteins necessary for the activation of the PI3K/AKT, RAS/RAF/MEK/ERK, and MAPK pathways (Asai et al., 1996). Additionally, Grb2 binds to phospho-RET (Y1096) and engages in another interaction that enables RET to activate the RAS/RAF/MEK/ERK pathway, stimulating cell proliferation and differentiation (Alberti et al., 1998; Liu et al., 1996). The structure of the RET protein encompasses several distinct domains, including an extracellular region with a ligand-binding domain, a transmembrane region anchoring the protein to the cell membrane, and an intracellular region housing the tyrosine kinase domain responsible for signal transduction (Ibáñez, 2013).

1.2 Ligands and activation

RET can be activated by binding to specific ligands belonging to the glial cell line-derived neurotrophic factor (GDNF) family. These ligands include GDNF, neurturin, persephin, and artemin. Upon binding of these ligands to the extracellular region of RET, it triggers receptor dimerization, leading to the autophosphorylation of specific tyrosine residues within the intracellular domain (Ibáñez, 2013).

1.3 Downstream signaling pathways

Following autophosphorylation, RET initiates the activation of multiple intracellular signaling pathways, including the mitogen-activated protein kinase/extracellular signal-regulated kinase (MAPK/ERK), phosphoinositide 3-kinase/protein kinase B (PI3K/AKT), and phospholipase Cγ (PLCγ) pathways. These pathways play crucial roles in regulating various cellular processes, such as cell survival, proliferation, and differentiation (Ibáñez, 2013).

1.4 Role in neural development

The neural crest cells' ability to differentiate into other cell types, such as neurons and glial cells, during embryonic development depends on RET signaling. RET is essential for the growth of particular neuronal populations, like the enteric neurons in the gastrointestinal tract (Li et al., 2006).

1.5 Role in tissue homeostasis

Apart from its role in neural development, RET plays a crucial role in maintaining tissue homeostasis in different organs. Notably, in the kidneys, RET signaling is indispensable for the development and preservation of the ureteric bud and the branching morphogenesis of the nephron. Additionally, RET is involved in the development and maintenance of the lungs, thyroid, and parathyroid glands (Branzk et al., 2018).

1.6 RET mutations and disease

Aberrant RET signaling caused by genetic mutations in the RET gene is linked to various diseases. Among these, multiple endocrine neoplasia type 2 (MEN2) stands out as a hereditary cancer syndrome characterized by the formation of tumors in endocrine organs, primarily affecting the thyroid gland. Additionally, RET mutations are associated with congenital disorders like Hirschsprung's disease, which impacts the enteric nervous system (Asai et al., 1995; Martínez-Jiménez et al., 2020). Understanding the normal cellular functions and signaling pathways regulated by RET is crucial for unraveling its role in disease development and for the development of targeted therapies. Further research continues to shed light on RET biology and its implications in various physiological and pathological processes (Asai et al., 1995).

2. Aberrant activation of RET in cancer and other diseases

The RET gene encodes for RTKs, which play a vital role in facilitating optimal cellular function, particularly in the growth of the nervous system and tissue homeostasis. Nevertheless, abnormal activation of RET signaling pathways has been associated with diverse diseases, ranging from cancer to congenital disorders (see Table 13.1). This essay delves into the implications of aberrant RET activation in cancer and other diseases, emphasizing its significance in the development of these conditions and exploring potential therapeutic implications (Asai et al., 1995). RET has been implicated in proto-oncogenic roles in various cancer types, such as lung, thyroid, and breast cancers. While only a small percentage, less than 5%, of cancer patients exhibit RET abnormalities (Cerami et al., 2012; Gao et al., 2013; Subbiah & Cote, 2020), certain cancer types are witnessing an increase in the occurrence of activating RET alterations, including genetic amplifications and chromosomal reorganizations. This section of the review will delve into the consequences of oncogenic RET modifications in cancers with altered RET, elucidating their significance in disease progression.

TABLE 13.1   Aberrant activation of RET in cancer and other diseases.

1. RET mutations in cancer	Aberrant activation of RET in cancer and other diseases
a. Multiple endocrine neoplasia type 2 (MEN2)	RET gene mutations cause MEN2, a hereditary cancer-causing thyroid gland tumor growth.
b. Medullary thyroid cancer (MTC)	Thyroid gland parafollicular C cells cause MTC, caused by RET mutations promoting unchecked cell proliferation and tumor formation.
c. Nonsmall cell lung cancer (NSCLC)	A subset of NSCLC patients, especially those with lung adenocarcinoma, harbor activating RET gene fusions. RET fusions result from chromosomal rearrangements, leading to constitutive activation of the RET kinase domain. RET fusions represent a targetable alteration in NSCLC. Clinical trials using RET inhibitors have shown promising results.
2. Aberrant activation of RET in congenital disorders	
a. Hirschsprung's disease	A congenital illness known as Hirschsprung's disease is characterized by the lack of ganglion cells in the enteric nervous system. RET loss-of-function mutations are the major cause, disrupting normal development and migration of enteric neural crest cells.
b. Hypoventilation syndrome (CCHS)	CCHS is a rare disorder affecting autonomic control of breathing. Most cases of CCHS are associated with mutations in the RET gene, impairing development and function of neural crest−derived cells in the autonomic nervous system.

2.1 Oncogenic RET alterations and RET fusions

In the late 1980s, the identification of an oncogenic RET fusion in papillary thyroid cancers (PTCs) marked the first significant discovery of RET alterations (Grieco et al., 1990; Takahashi et al., 2020). Since then, other teams have found additional RET rearrangements in a variety of solid tumors (Ou & Zhu, 2020). Transcriptional sequencing of neighboring genes is affected by topological rearrangements, such as inversions or translocations (Kim et al., 2014), or Pre-mRNA motifs are spliced, two normally separate genes are brought together to form oncogenic gene fusions (Jividen & Li, 2014). The majority of RET fusions are transmembrane domain-deficient, resulting in chimeric, cytosolic proteins that operate as oncogenes by constitutively activating the RET kinase domain (Fig. 13.1A). Since the initial discovery of the first RET fusion in thyroid malignancies, at least 13 fusion partners have been identified in PTCs. Among them, the most prevalent are coiled-coil domain containing 6 (CCDC6-RET) and nuclear receptor co-activator 4 (NCOA4)-RET (Li, McCusker et al., 2019; Li, Shang, et al., 2019). Similarly, in lung tumors, at least 45 RET fusion partners have been found, with KIF5B-RET (70%–90%) and CCDC6-RET (10%–25%) being the most common ones (Fig. 13.2).

Although RET fusions have been found in other malignancies, such as salivary gland carcinomas and breast cancer, they are significantly less common in these cancer types (0.16% and 3.2%, respectively) (Kato et al., 2017). Therefore, in many different tumor types, RET fusions pose a clinical and therapeutic difficulty (Table 13.1).

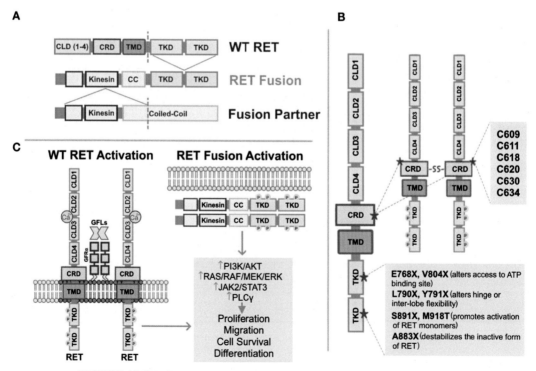

FIGURE 13.2	Altered RET and their mechanisms of activation [22 open access].

In addition to carcinogenic fusions, germline mutations in RET can contribute to carcinogenesis and tumorigenesis, particularly in MEN2. For instance, mutations in RET's extracellular domain affecting cysteine residues (C609, C611, C618, C620, C630, C634) promote the formation of intermolecular disulfide bonds. Consequently, this leads to constitutive dimerization and activation of RET independent of GDNF (Glial cell line—derived neurotrophic factor) stimulation (Fig. 13.1B) (Arlt et al., 2000). Moreover, alterations in the RET tyrosine kinase domain cause changes in hinge or inter-lobe flexibility (Y791X, L790X), leading to the activation of RET monomers (M918T, S891X), or destabilization of the inactive form of RET (A883X). All these changes result in various levels of basal activation (Liu et al., 2018) (Table 13.1). Together, oncogenic RET changes might encourage RET signaling's constitutive activation, which fuels the development of tumors in the tissues affected (Fig. 13.1C).

2.2 RET mutations in cancer

2.2.1 Multiple endocrine neoplasia type 2 (MEN2)

MEN2 is a hereditary cancer syndrome caused by activating germline mutations in the RET gene. These mutations result in the continuous activation of the RET receptor, leading to the development of tumors in endocrine organs, particularly the thyroid gland. MEN2 is classified into three subgroups: MEN2A, MEN2B, and familial medullary thyroid carcinoma (FMTC). The syndrome primarily affects four tissues: (i) the thyroid C cells, responsible for producing the hormone calcitonin; (ii) the adrenal medulla; (iii) the parathyroid; and (iv) the enteric autonomic nerve plexuses (Ponder & Smith, 1996). The thyroid C cells, enteric nerve plexuses, and adrenal medulla all have their origins in the neural ectoderm. The precursor cells responsible for the development of thyroid C cells originate from the vagal neural crest and migrate to the caudal portion of the fourth branchial arch, which corresponds to the location of the ultimobranchial body in birds. Subsequently, these cells migrate into the central portion of each thyroid lobe to form the C cells. They are close to the pharyngeal endoderm, which gives rise to the parathyroids, while they are in the branchial arch. Both migrating neural crest cells and the pharyngeal endoderm express RET throughout mouse development (Avantaggiato et al., 1994; Pachnis et al., 1993). The expression of RET in the endoderm could elucidate the involvement of the parathyroids in MEN 2 disease. The enteric autonomic nervous system originates from RET-expressing cells derived from the hindbrain neural crest. These cells migrate alongside the vagus nerve, while the adrenal medulla is derived from the trunk neural crest, along with other components of the sympathoadrenal chain, which are occasionally implicated in MEN 2 (Anderson, 1993). It is clear how RET loss of function mutations cause HSCR based on in vitro evidence that it functions as a survival factor for growing intestinal neuroblasts (Durbec et al., 1996). From the in vitro research, it is unclear how RET signaling affects the growth of thyroid C cells, the adrenal medulla, and the parathyroids. Unknown is the exact mechanism through which ret mutations cause tumor development in MEN 2 syndrome.

2.2.2 Papillary thyroid cancers

PTCs (papillary thyroid cancers) account for approximately 85% of all thyroid cancer cases and are the most common type of differentiated thyroid cancer, often associated with radiation exposure (Cabanillas et al., 2016). Initially, PTC incidence was linked to RAS-activating mutations and subsequent activation of the RAS/MAPK/ERK pathway (Lemoine et al., 1988, 1989; Suarez et al., 1988). While analyzing oncogenes for homology with known kinase genes, including RET, the true nature of this novel gene remained unclear, leading to its designation as "PTC." Subsequently, Fusco et al. (1987) identified cancer-causing RET as an unidentified transforming gene in metastatic PTC. It was revealed that PTC represents a rearranged version of RET, and rearranged RET DNA sequences were readily detected in PTC-positive papillary thyroid tumors, as reported in a follow-up investigation by the same research group (Grieco et al., 1990). The research conducted by Ishizaka et al., 1989b provided evidence of abnormal RET transcripts in PTC tumor samples, further supporting the findings. Subsequently, Lanzi et al. identified two more constitutively active and tyrosine phosphorylated RET rearrangements in PTC, known as RET/PTC1 and RET/PTC2. Interestingly, these rearrangements did not seem to be associated with the cell membrane (Lanzi et al., 1992). Santoro et al. also discovered another RET rearrangement designated as RET/PTC3, where retinoic acid (RET) fuses with the N-terminus of Riα (PRKAR1A) (Bongarzone et al., 1993; Sozzi et al., 1994). Additionally, nuclear receptor coactivator 4 (NCoA4/ELE1) was found to be involved in RET/PTC2, and RET/PTC3 results from the fusion of the RET kinase domain with the N-terminus of these oncogenes, respectively (Fig. 13.3).

The RET/PTC1-3 fusions are distinct but share several common characteristics. These include the widespread expression of the 5′ fusion partner (Jhiang et al., 1994; Tong et al., 1995), altered subcellular localization of RET kinase function, and crucial activation of RET kinase due to ligand-independent dimerization of the receptor (Fusco et al., 1994; Ishizaka et al., 1992). Carcinogenic properties of RET/PTC1 have been established through transgenic overexpression experiments, leading to the development of spontaneous and metastatic

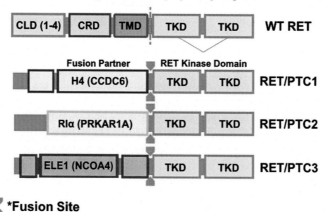

FIGURE 13.3   RET/PTC reorganizations in papillary thyroid carcinomas (PTCs) [22 open access].

thyroid carcinomas in mice. These tumors exhibit a histological resemblance to human papillary thyroid carcinoma (PTC) tumors (Jhiang et al., 1996; Santoro et al., 1996). However, it remains uncertain whether RET/PTC1 overexpression serves as a precursor to thyroid tumorigenesis in humans. Nevertheless, RET/PTC activation was identified in 42% (11/26) of the studied occult thyroid carcinomas, suggesting that RET/PTC activity may indeed play a role in the development of papillary thyroid carcinogenesis (Viglietto et al., 1995).

These SPCs often have clinically evident node metastases but are frequently microscopic or not detected by ultrasonograms. Importantly, subsequent research revealed a frequent occurrence of RET rearrangements in individuals exposed to radiation (Ito et al., 1993), including children affected by the Chernobyl nuclear plant accident (Bounacer et al., 1997). This suggests a link between radiation exposure and the development of RET alterations. To date, at least 12 oncogenic RET fusions have been identified in PTC, indicating that RET alterations play a significant role in the initiation and progression of PTC. Further analysis of PTC tumors revealed that the PTC subclass of thyroid malignancies has the highest levels of RET proto-oncogene expression (Santoro et al., 1992). It is important to acknowledge that clonal RET/PTC alterations can occur in 10%—20% of PTC patients and can be triggered by various factors (Nikiforov & Nikiforova, 2011). For example, in regions with significant exposure to radioisotopes, RET/PTC alterations can be found in up to 70% of pediatric PTC cases (Zhu et al., 2006). Fortunately, Rhoden and colleagues demonstrated that more than 25%—30% of spontaneous PTC cases contain RET/PTC rearrangements (Rhoden et al., 2004, 2006). Moreover, a comparative study conducted by Zhu and colleagues revealed that the method used to assess RET/PTC rearrangements could impact the reported frequency within the sample cohort. Therefore, when estimating the occurrence of RET/PTC rearrangements in samples from patients with PTC, it is essential to exercise caution and consider these variations in evaluation approaches.

2.2.3 Medullary thyroid cancer

MTC (medullary thyroid cancer) is a malignant tumor that originates from the parafollicular C cells of the thyroid gland. About 25%—30% of sporadic MTC cases and almost all cases in patients with MEN2 are caused by RET mutations. The aberrant activation of RET signaling in MTC results in uncontrolled cell proliferation and tumor growth (Tomuschat & Puri, 2015).

The MTCs are a rare type of thyroid tumor that originates in the parafollicular C cells, accounting for only 2%—4% of malignant thyroid neoplasms. Approximately 30% of MTC cases have a hereditary basis, while the majority occur spontaneously. MTCs are categorized into several primary clinical subtypes, including Familial Medullary Thyroid Carcinoma (FMTC), Multiple Endocrine Neoplasia Type 2B (MEN2B), MEN2A with Hirschsprung disease, MEN2A with cutaneous lichen amyloidosis (CLA), and classical MEN2A. Among these, FMTC displays a relatively delayed latency and a milder clinical course compared to MEN2A and MEN2B (Jin & Moley, 2016). After discovering a link between the development of a thyroid cancer and the presence of pheochromocytoma, J.H. Sipple initially identified MEN2A in 1961 (Sipple, 1961). MTC, pheochromocytoma, and/or primary hyperparathyroidism are all present in the MEN2A subtype, which accounts for 70%—80% of hereditary MTC cases (and may also contain Hirschsprung's disease or CLA) (Verga et al., 2003).

Aggressive MTC, pheochromocytoma, intestinal tumors, neuromas, and Marfanoid body habitus are all co-present in the MEN2B subtype.

Santoro et al. (1990) were the first to associate RET rearrangements with MTC when they discovered RET fusion products in pheochromocytomas and MTC samples. Subsequently, Yamamoto and colleagues conducted a study that revealed the close proximity of the MEN2A gene locus and the chromosomal location of RET (Yamamoto et al., 1991), suggesting a potential genetic link between RET expression and the presence of MEN2A. However, it was noted that these mutations were specifically found in families with MEN2A and FMTC, not in those with MEN2B. Based on this observation, Donis-Keller and colleagues proposed a strong correlation between exon 7/8-specific RET mutations and the prevalence of MEN2A and FMTC (Donis-Keller et al., 1993). Mulligan et al. conducted a study and confirmed their previous findings, demonstrating the presence of germline missense mutations within the RET proto-oncogene in 87% (20/23 cases) of the MEN2A families. Notably, these mutations were not detected in families without MEN2A, providing further evidence for the association between the identified mutations and MEN2A. Additionally, Mulligan et al. discovered that 19 out of the 20 groups with germline missense RET mutations shared a mutation in a cysteine residue within the RET extracellular domain. This observation suggests that patients with this specific mutation may have an increased likelihood of developing MEN2A or FMTC. In a subsequent investigation, 118 families not associated with MEN2A, MEN2B, or FMTC were examined. It was discovered that the RET-C634 mutation, located close to the transmembrane domain, was present in 86% of the FMTC families and over 95% of the MEN2A families (Mulligan et al., 1994a). However, Mulligan et al. (1994b) did not find the RET-C634 mutation in the MEN2B families examined in this study, consistent with their previous research (Mulligan et al., 1993). Interestingly, the frequency of the RET-C634 mutation was significantly higher in MEN2A families (84%) compared to FMTC families (50%). These findings suggest that the RET-C634 mutation is associated with a higher predisposition to develop MEN2A, likely due to increased RET activity. This is supported by the fact that MEN2A patients often experience hyperparathyroidism and/or pheochromocytoma, conditions that are not commonly observed in FMTC. While RET-C634 mutations are commonly associated with MEN2A cases, it's important to note that MEN2B families also frequently carry RET mutations. In a separate study, the RET-C634 mutation was identified in 34 unrelated MEN2B patients (Carlson et al., 1994). Furthermore, the 1994 discovery of RET-M918T was confirmed in nine unrelated MEN2B patients through DNA sequence analysis (Hofstra et al., 1994). The RET-M918T mutation induces oncogenic signaling by stabilizing monomeric RET, leading to increased binding with ATP and activation even in the absence of GDNF ligand (Dixit et al., 2009; Gujral et al., 2006; Iwashita et al., 1996). This particular mutation is observed in 95% of MEN2B patients (Mulligan et al., 1995). Additionally, the RET-A883F mutation, which is highly activating (Gimm et al., 1997; Iwashita et al., 1999; Smith et al., 1997), is believed to destabilize RET's inactive conformation by altering the local structure of the protein (Wagner et al., 2012).

2.2.4 Nonsmall cell lung cancer

In some patients with nonsmall cell lung cancer (NSCLC), particularly those diagnosed with lung adenocarcinoma, activating RET gene fusions are present. These fusions arise from chromosomal rearrangements, resulting in continuous activation of the RET kinase domain. Targeting RET fusions has emerged as a promising treatment approach for NSCLC, and encouraging results have been observed in clinical trials utilizing RET inhibitors. Lung cancer ranks as the second most frequently diagnosed cancer and remains a leading cause of cancer-related deaths among both men and women in the United States (Siegel et al., 2020). The NSCLC represents the majority of lung cancer cases, making up 80%−85% of all diagnoses, and it can be classified into three major subtypes: adenocarcinoma, squamous cell carcinoma, and large cell carcinoma. Despite the differences in subtypes, NSCLC is often treated using similar therapeutic approaches, such as surgical resection, neoadjuvant or adjuvant chemotherapy, and immunotherapy, which accounts for their common categorization (Cascetta et al., 2021).

In approximately 1%−2% of nonsmall cell lung cancer (NSCLC) cases, RET rearrangements have been identified (Takeuchi et al., 2012; Tsuta et al., 2014; Wang et al., 2012a, 2012b). Since the discovery of the first RET fusion (KIF5B-RET) in lung cancer (Ju et al., 2012; Lipson et al., 2012), significant efforts have been made to identify new RET fusions in NSCLC. Notably, Ou and Zhou have documented at least 48 distinct RET fusion partners found in NSCLC (Ou & Zhu, 2020). Among these, the most common are KIF5B-RET and CCDC6-RET, found in 1%−2% of NSCLC patients. While the majority of NSCLC cases do not exhibit other driver mutations, an extensive study conducted by Kato and colleagues involving over 4871 samples revealed that RET fusions can co-occur with other genetic changes, such as those in PI3K-associated genes or MAPK effector genes, in up to 82% (72/88) of NSCLC patients (Kato et al., 2017). Consequently, NSCLC cases positive for RET fusions may exhibit distinct clinical and pathological characteristics compared to NSCLC cases with alternative oncogenic abnormalities.

Indeed, Wang and colleagues' analysis revealed that lung carcinomas with RET fusions exhibit more poorly differentiated tumors compared to those with ALK or EGFR alterations. This finding indicates that RET fusions define a distinct molecular and clinicopathological subtype of nonsmall cell lung cancer (NSCLC) (Wang et al., 2012a,b). In NSCLC, the occurrence of distant metastases is a significant concern, with approximately 30%−40% of cases spreading to sites such as the bone, lungs, brain, and adrenal glands (Tamura et al., 2015). Of particular concern are brain metastases, as 10% of NSCLC patients present with brain metastases at the time of diagnosis, and throughout the disease course, approximately 30% of NSCLC patients eventually develop brain metastases (Waqar et al., 2018). The baseline incidence of brain metastases in RET fusion-positive nonsmall cell lung cancer (NSCLC) is 27%, and this occurrence is not influenced by age, smoking status, or the 5′ fusion partner status. Throughout the course of the disease, this proportion increases to 49%. Consequently, ongoing research efforts are focused on identifying biological targets in brain-metastatic NSCLC and developing therapeutic agents that can effectively cross the blood−brain barrier (BBB).

In this pursuit, multikinase inhibitors (MKIs) initially designed to target frequently altered oncogenic drivers like EGFR, MET, KIT, and VEGFR2 were repurposed as RET inhibitors due to their moderate selectivity against altered RET in NSCLC (Horiike et al., 2016; Takeuchi et al., 2021). Many of these inhibitors have demonstrated activity against brain metastases (Klempner et al., 2017; Zou et al., 2022). However, a multiinstitutional research study led by Drilon and colleagues revealed that less than 20% of patients with stage IV lung cancer and brain metastases at the time of diagnosis, who were treated with RET-targeting MKIs, showed an intracranial response. This indicates that while MKIs are effective against RET, they may not be sufficient for treating lung cancers with brain metastases (Drilon et al., 2018a).

2.2.5 Alterations in other tumor types

While faulty RET signaling is observed in other tumor types, albeit at a lower frequency, aberrant RET activity is primarily associated with thyroid carcinomas and NSCLC. The importance of RET signaling in various solid tumor types and the implications of RET inhibition in these cancers will be briefly discussed below.

2.2.5.1 Breast cancers

Around 1.2% of breast cancer cases show alterations in the RET gene. Among these changes, RET amplifications make up 66% of the cases, while activating fusions account for 7% (Paratala et al., 2018). The most frequent RET fusions observed in breast cancer are CCDC6-RET and NCOA4-RET, similar to those found in other solid tumor types discussed earlier. These fusions result in the continuous activation of RET, promoting increased cell proliferation and survival, ultimately contributing to carcinogenesis development (Li et al., 2012; Tsuta et al., 2014).

In a subgroup of estrogen receptor-alpha positive (ER+) breast cancers, RET and its co-receptor, GFRa1, are often co-overexpressed. Consequently, early research on RET in breast cancer primarily focused on cases of ER + breast cancer (Mechera et al., 2019). It is noteworthy that the co-overexpression of RET-GFRa1 was associated with enhanced cell proliferation and survival in ER + cells and demonstrated a negative correlation with baseline marker expression (Esseghir et al., 2007). These findings imply that targeting the RET pathway could present a promising approach to addressing this specific subgroup of breast cancer. A study by Gattelli et al. (2013) revealed that RET activation stimulates the growth, proliferation, and migration of estrogen receptor-alpha positive (ER+) breast cancer cells in both in vitro and in vivo settings. These findings strongly suggest that RET actively contributes to ER + breast malignancies. In the standard-care therapy for ER + breast tumors, ERα antagonists like tamoxifen and fulvestrant are commonly used (Ignatiadis & Sotiriou, 2013). These antagonists function by inhibiting the interaction between estradiol (E2) and ERα, effectively blocking ERα signaling (Shiau et al., 1998). Endocrine resistance occurs in up to 50% of breast cancer patients either initially or during prolonged therapy (Clarke et al., 2015). Interestingly, a study by Plaza-Menacho et al. revealed that activated RET promotes estrogen-independent stimulation of ERα (Plaza-Menacho et al., 2010). This suggests an interaction between the RET and ERα pathways in endocrine-resistant breast cancers, indicating that RET plays a role in influencing the response of ER + breast cancer cells to endocrine treatments.

Another therapeutic approach for the therapy of ER + breast tumors is aromatase inhibition (Sood et al., 2021). As an essential enzyme for the manufacturing of estrogen, aromatase also known as estrogen synthase can promote the production of estrogen and support the growth of ER + breast tumors (Zhao et al., 2016). Similar to what has been shown using tamoxifen, several ER + breast cancer cases have breast tumors that are aromatase-resistant at the time of identification or acquire this type of resistance as a result of continued therapy (Hanamura & Hayashi, 2018). Isacke and colleagues made the discovery that aromatase-resistant estrogen receptor-positive (ER+) breast cancer displays hyperactive RET signaling (Morandi et al., 2013). Furthermore, they discovered that pharmacological inhibition of RET reduces the susceptibility of these breast cancer cells to aromatase inhibitors in the presence of glial cell line-derived neurotrophic factor (GDNF). Additionally, RET has been identified as an estrogen receptor (ER) target gene, and both RET and ERα stimulate distinct metabolic processes in luminal breast cancers. These findings provide insight into how RET-mediated mechanisms contribute to endocrine resistance in ER + breast cancer cells. Consequently, there is a physiological rationale for the multifaceted targeting of both RET and ERα receptors to combat hormone resistance in luminal breast cancers (Boulay et al., 2008; Wang et al., 2012a,b). In endocrine-resistant estrogen receptor-positive (ER+) breast tumors, targeting RET could be a potential therapeutic strategy with potential benefits for patients. However, research conducted by Andreucci and colleagues revealed that when both RET and aromatase are targeted simultaneously, the translational impact is comparable to that of single therapy using either RET or aromatase inhibitors (Andreucci et al., 2016). Additionally, while RET expression is closely linked to ER expression in luminal breast cancers, it does not hold predictive value as a standalone biomarker in breast cancer tissue (Mechera et al., 2019). Therefore, further investigation is required to determine whether targeting RET will have a positive clinical impact on patients with luminal breast cancer.

HER2-enriched and triple-negative breast cancers (TNBCs) are breast cancer subtypes known for their aggressiveness and high metastatic potential (Chen et al., 2018). Among these subtypes, both triple-negative and HER2-enriched breast tumors express the RET protein (Boulay et al., 2008). Patients diagnosed with TNBC typically receive preoperative or adjuvant treatment, along with surgical resection. Trastuzumab is one of the leading treatments administered to breast tumors that are HER2-enriched (Waks & Winer, 2019). However, despite initial improvements seen in HER2-positive breast cancer patients treated with trastuzumab, they eventually develop challenging-to-treat trastuzumab resistance (Gardaneh et al., 2017; Pohlmann et al., 2009). Trastuzumab resistance in HER2-enriched breast cancers, which also exhibit RET activation, may be attributed to SRC-independent signaling. A recent study has linked trastuzumab resistance with the activation of the RET-HER2 signaling axis, whereas trastuzumab-naive cells rely on the RET-SRC-HER2 signaling pathway (Gardaneh et al., 2017). Similar to TNBCs, no long-lasting clinically beneficial therapies have been established for HER2-enriched breast cancers. Several studies have demonstrated the efficacy of MKIs in targeting RET to reduce TNBC proliferation and tumor growth in both in vitro and in vivo experiments. Surprisingly, although RET activation has not been specifically identified as a pro-tumorigenic kinase in TNBC, MKIs have shown promising outcomes in targeting RET in this particular subtype of breast cancer. For example, vandetanib, which targets RET, VEGFR-2, and EGFR, exhibits potent antitumor effects against xenografts derived from TNBC patients with hyperactive RET (Hatem et al., 2016), suggesting that RET inhibition could be a novel therapeutic option for TNBC patients. Moreover, recent data suggests that RET may play a role in controlling breast cancer metastasis. Breast cancer brain metastases (BCBM) were found to express RET more frequently compared to their corresponding primary breast tumors. Treatment of these BCBM tissues with the MKI cabozantinib resulted in reduced RET activation, inhibition of BCBM growth, and induction of apoptosis. These findings highlight the potential therapeutic significance of targeting RET to combat breast cancer metastasis (Varešlija et al., 2019).

Breast carcinogenesis may arise from the co-overexpression of wild-type RET and its co-receptor, GFRα1, along with oncogenic RET alterations. The overexpression of RET and GFRα1 is observed in 25%–75% of breast cancer patients (Morandi et al., 2011). Esseghir and colleagues demonstrated that the co-overexpression of RET and GFRα1 in luminal MCF7 cells, in response to GDNF stimulation, supports cell proliferation and survival. Additionally, stromal cells overexpress GDNF in response to proinflammatory signals in the tumor microenvironment (Esseghir et al., 2007). Subsequent research by Boulay and co-workers revealed functional interactions between the RET and ERα pathways in luminal breast cancer cells. Furthermore, stimulation of the ERα pathway can increase RET expression (Boulay et al., 2008). These findings suggest that luminal breast tumors positive for RET may benefit from RET suppression. As a result, RET-targeted therapy could be advantageous for breast cancer patients who overexpress RET-GFRα1, in addition to the approximately 1.2% of breast cancer cases that have RET mutations (Paratala et al., 2018).

2.2.5.2 Salivary gland cancer

The World Health Organization classifies salivary gland tumors into over 30 malignant and benign categories based on cytology rather than the location of the starting tumor (Seethala & Stenman, 2017). Among these tumors, salivary duct carcinomas (SDCs) frequently exhibit changes in the RET gene, as identified through genomic profiling. Notably, three clinical cases displayed RET fusion products, specifically CCDC6-RET or NCOA4-RET fusions. Although the analysis was conducted retrospectively, researchers observed that individuals with SDC tumors harboring the NCOA4-RET fusion showed a favorable response to treatment with cabozantinib. These patients experienced a decrease in chest wall lesions and an improvement in visible neck recurrence (Wang et al., 2016). These findings indicate the potential therapeutic relevance of targeting RET in certain cases of salivary duct carcinomas.

It is debatable whether or not SDCs and intraductal salivary gland carcinomas (ISGCs) should be categorized as two distinct kinds of cancer. In contrast to the infiltrating salivary duct carcinomas, which were initially identified in the late 1960s (Delgado et al., 1993), intraductal salivary gland carcinomas (ISGCs) were first described in 1983 as benign masses composed entirely of intraductal components. Low-grade intraductal carcinomas (LG-ICs) were first reported by Delgado and colleagues in 1996 and are histologically distinct from ISGCs. LG-ICs present as benign lumps resembling mammary ductal hyperplasia (Delgado et al., 1996). They are considered a rare type of salivary gland tumor, primarily originating in the parotid gland and more commonly found in the female population. Moreover, LG-ICs are generally asymptomatic (Giovacchini et al., 2019). By utilizing next-generation RNA sequencing, researchers examined 23 samples of low-grade intraductal carcinomas (LG-ICs) and identified one case with NCOA4-RET fusion. In total, 47% of ICs showed some form of RET rearrangement, indicating that RET may act as an early driver in the process of salivary gland carcinogenesis (Weinreb et al., 2018). Another study, similar in nature, reported that 8 out of 17 cases (47%) of salivary gland ICs had RET rearrangements (Skálová et al., 2019). Furthermore, various studies have identified oncogenic RET fusions in different subtypes of salivary gland carcinomas. These include ETV6-RET fusions in mammary analogue secretory carcinomas, NCOA4-RET in intercalated duct-line salivary duct carcinomas, TRIM27-RET fusions in mixed intercalated duct-like and apocrine types of salivary duct carcinomas, and recently TRIM33-RET fusions were detected in oncocytic intraductal carcinoma (Bishop et al., 2021; Fisch et al., 2021; Petersson et al., 2020; Skálová et al., 2018a,b).

2.2.5.3 Prostate cancer

Cancer of the prostate is the most frequently diagnosed cancer and the second-leading cause of cancer-related fatalities worldwide, with over 1.4 million new cases expected by 2020 (Wang et al., 2022). In their early stages, prostate tumors are frequently asymptomatic, but indications can involve urinary retention, hematuria, dysuria, fatigue, and bone discomfort (Langan, 2019). Prostatic intraepithelial neoplasia (PIN) refers to prostate cancers in their early stages characterized by an increase in epithelial cell proliferation within benign prostatic acini (Kim & Yang, 2002). High-grade PIN is classified as a precursor to prostate cancer because it satisfies multiple criteria for a precancerous condition (Bostwick & Qian, 2004). Prostatic adenocarcinoma and metastatic prostate cancer are the advanced stages of castration-resistant or castration-susceptible malignant prostate cancer progression (Wang et al., 2018) resulting from PIN. Prostate examinations and blood tests for prostate-specific antigen (PSA) are used for prostate cancer screening (Kim & Yang, 2002). Uncertainty persists, however, as to whether PSA testing affects the progression of the disease.

In a prostate cancer xenograft model, Robinson et al. presented initial evidence indicating the overexpression of wild-type RET in prostate cancer (Robinson et al., 1996). Their study revealed significantly higher levels of RET protein expression in high-grade prostatic intraepithelial neoplasia (PIN) and prostate cancer tissues when compared to benign prostatic tissue. Moreover, they observed a positive correlation between RET expression and the Gleason score of tumors, suggesting a potential role of RET overexpression in the progression from benign to malignant prostate tumors (Dawson et al., 1998). Simultaneously, Ban et al. conducted research that further supported the significance of RET expression in prostate cancer growth in vivo. Their investigation found that 19% (61 out of 325) of the analyzed prostate cancer tissues exhibited specific overexpression of RET in tumor cells (Ban et al., 2017). These findings underscore the potential importance of RET as a molecular target in understanding and treating prostate cancer.

The results mentioned above offer additional evidence supporting the role of RET overexpression in the development and progression of prostate cancer. Interestingly, the increase in GDNF (glial cell line–derived neurotrophic factor) or GFRa1 (GDNF family receptor alpha 1) secretion by peripheral nerves within the prostate (He et al., 2014) may be a contributing factor to the heightened RET activity observed in prostate malignancies. This elevated RET activity could potentially promote perineural invasion of the disease, wherein cancer cells invade nerves surrounding the prostate, facilitating tumor spread and metastasis. The interaction between RET and the GDNF/GFRa1 signaling pathway may thus play a crucial role in the aggressive behavior of prostate cancer and warrants further investigation for potential therapeutic interventions.

2.2.5.4 Colorectal cancers

Colorectal cancer (CRC) is a significant global health concern, ranking as the third most prevalent cancer worldwide, with approximately 1.1 million new cases reported annually.

Tragically, it stands as the second leading cause of cancer-related deaths (Cervantes et al., 2023). The disease originates in the epithelial cells lining the colon and gastrointestinal tract. Typically, CRC begins as benign polyps, which can then progress into larger polyps, followed by adenomas, and ultimately develop into carcinoma (Jänne & Mayer, 2000). As CRC advances, it has the potential to metastasize to various organs, such as the liver, peritoneum, lungs, bones, and brain, presenting further challenges in treatment and management (Riihimäki et al., 2016). The complexity of CRC underscores the need for continued research and improved strategies to combat its impact on public health.

In human sigmoid colon cancer, Ishizaka et al. made an intriguing discovery of ret-II, which represents a second form of active RET lacking the coding sequence for the transmembrane region found in wildtype RET (Ishizaka et al., 1988). The specific origin of the sequences preceding the kinase domain of ret-II remains unknown, prompting subsequent research to propose that ret-II may result from a gene fusion event (Ishizaki et al., 1989a). Through extensive genome investigations, it has been revealed that RET fusions, including CCDC6-RET and NCOA4-RET, are present in a small subset (0.2%) of colorectal cancer (CRC) cases, accounting for 6 out of 3117 cases studied (Le Rolle et al., 2015). Additionally, analyses of metastatic CRCs (mCRCs) with RET rearrangements indicate that these cases exhibit worse survival rates, raising the possibility of using pharmaceutical RET inhibition as a potential treatment strategy (Pietrantonio et al., 2018). In the context of treating CRC tumor cells carrying the NCOA4-RET fusion, vandetanib, a multi-kinase inhibitor with nonselective RET action, has shown effectiveness (Kim et al., 2018). These findings open up new avenues for targeted therapies in CRC cases involving RET rearrangements, offering potential hope for improved treatment outcomes for patients with this particular molecular subtype of colorectal cancer. However, further research is needed to fully understand the molecular mechanisms and clinical implications of RET fusions in CRC and to optimize the use of RET-targeted therapies in the management of this disease.

The role of RET in colorectal cancer (CRC) remains a topic of ongoing debate, as different studies have yielded conflicting results regarding its involvement in the disease. Some data suggest that RET mutations may have an oncogenic role in CRC. However, there are also studies that propose a tumor-suppressive role for RET in CRC.

For instance, a study conducted by Luo et al., (2013) observed increased methylation of the RET gene and subsequent downregulation of RET in CRC samples, suggesting that RET might act as a tumor suppressor in the examined CRC cases (Luo et al., 2013). On the other hand, a more recent investigation in 2021 found that immunohistochemical analyses revealed a decrease in RET protein expression in CRC tissue compared to nearby normal tissue (Ashkboos et al., 2021). This decrease in RET expression indicates an inverse relationship between RET expression and the development of CRC, potentially suggesting an oncogenic role for RET in some contexts. These conflicting findings have created uncertainties regarding the precise roles of RET in different subpopulations of CRC tumors. The complexity in understanding the exact function of RET in CRC may pose challenges in effectively treating CRC tumors with alterations in the RET gene. Further research is necessary to elucidate the context-specific effects of RET alterations in CRC and to determine the potential implications for targeted therapies. By gaining a better understanding of the role of RET in CRC, researchers may be able to develop more tailored and effective treatment strategies for patients with CRC tumors harboring RET alterations.

2.2.5.5 Pancreatic and epithelial ovarian cancers

The expression of RET has been found to have significant associations with lymphatic invasion, survival rates after tumor resection, and the degree of tumor cell differentiation in pancreatic cancer. These findings suggest that the glial cell line-derived neurotrophic factor (GDNF) may play a crucial role in promoting pancreatic cancer proliferation and metastasis, particularly in patients with perineural invasion. Notably, a strongly positive expression of GDNF could potentially serve as an indication for early intensified radiotherapy in these cases. Furthermore, RET expression in pancreatic cancer tissues may serve as a valuable prognostic marker, aiding in the assessment of disease outcomes and patient prognosis.

Epithelial ovarian cancer (EOC) is a highly aggressive and deadly malignancy, presenting challenges with cancer recurrence and drug resistance. To address these limitations of current treatments, it is essential to enhance the genetic characterization of EOC patients and identify new potential targets for therapeutic intervention. Targeted therapies, particularly those directed at protein tyrosine kinases (PTKs), show promise in offering improved efficacy and reduced toxicity compared to standard treatments. However, there is a need for further investigation to better understand the role of PTKs in EOC and to identify specific actionable targets that can be exploited to develop more effective treatment strategies. By advancing our knowledge of the genetic and molecular characteristics of EOC, we can pave the way for more personalized and targeted approaches to tackle this challenging cancer.

In various other solid tumor types, altered RET is present, albeit at a low frequency. In pancreatic cancer cases, there is a notable occurrence of overexpression of wild-type RET, coreceptor GFRa1, and GDNF in approximately 50%–70% of cases (Amit et al., 2019; Zeng et al., 2008). However, RET mutations are observed in only a small subset, accounting for approximately 1.9% of pancreatic malignancies (Kato et al., 2017). Interestingly, research conducted by Ceyhan et al. demonstrated that activating RET with another glial cell line-derived neurotrophic factor (GFL) called Artemin can promote the invasion and migration of pancreatic cancer cells (Ceyhan et al., 2006). This finding suggests that alterations in the RET signaling pathway, driven by the interaction with different GFLs like GDNF and Artemin, may play a role in the aggressive behavior of pancreatic cancer, contributing to its invasive and migratory properties. Understanding these molecular mechanisms could potentially pave the way for targeted therapeutic approaches that aim to inhibit RET signaling and its interactions with specific GFLs to impede the progression and metastasis of pancreatic cancer.

Subsequently, a study using a transgenic mouse model of pancreatic cancer, aimed at enhancing RET overexpression, further confirmed the role of increased wild-type RET activity in promoting pancreatic tumorigenesis and perineural invasion, supporting the conclusion that heightened RET activity can foster the development of metastatic pancreatic malignancy. In the context of the pancreatic tumor microenvironment, there is an intriguing phenomenon where surrounding cells increase the production of GDNF, leading to enhanced RET activity in pancreatic tumor cells. This paracrine effect promotes perineural invasion, contributing to the aggressive nature of pancreatic cancer (Amit et al., 2017; Cavel et al., 2012). Despite the infrequency of RET alterations in pancreatic malignancies, patients with abnormal RET pathway activity may still find benefit from RET-targeted therapy. This is exemplified by the identification of the first pancreatic cancer patient with a RET fusion-

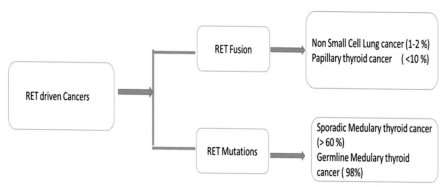

FIGURE 13.4   RET mutations and disease.

positive tumor in 2021 (Ma et al., 2021), indicating that specific subsets of pancreatic cancer cases may be driven by oncogenic RET alterations.

In addition to its involvement in pancreatic malignancies, RET mutations are also found in approximately 1.2% of ovarian tumors (Kato et al., 2017). Notably, vandetanib, a multi-kinase inhibitor with nonselective RET action, has demonstrated efficacy in treating epithelial ovarian carcinomas that harbor oncogenic RET mutations (Guan et al., 2020). These discoveries highlight the potential significance of RET as a therapeutic target in both pancreatic and ovarian cancers, particularly in cases with identified RET alterations. Further research and clinical studies are warranted to better understand the relevance of RET-targeted therapies in managing these specific subtypes of cancer and to determine the most effective treatment approaches for patients with abnormal RET pathway activity.

2.3 Mechanisms of RET activation

Mechanisms of RET activation involve gene fusions, point mutations, SNPs, and ligand-mediated activation (Fig. 13.4). These mechanisms play significant roles in the development and progression of various diseases, including cancer (Table 13.2). Understanding the underlying mechanisms of RET activation is essential for unraveling disease pathogenesis, identifying therapeutic targets, and developing targeted therapies. Further research into the complex regulatory mechanisms of RET activation will contribute to advancements in precision medicine and the development of novel therapeutic interventions for RET-associated disorders (Mulligan et al., 1994b; Santoro et al., 2002; Wagner et al., 2012).

3. Classes of RET inhibitors

The development of RET inhibitors represents a significant advancement in targeted therapy for RET-driven diseases, including cancer. Tyrosine kinase inhibitors, multi-kinase inhibitors, and selective RET inhibitors offer diverse strategies to inhibit RET activity and disrupt downstream signaling pathways. With ongoing research and clinical trials, the continued identification and optimization of RET inhibitors hold the promise of improved treatment

TABLE 13.2 Mechanisms of RET activation.

	Mechanisms of RET activation
Gene fusions involving RET	Gene fusions involving RET occur when the RET gene becomes juxtaposed with a different gene due to chromosomal rearrangements, resulting in constitutive activation of RET kinase activity.
Point mutations and single nucleotide polymorphisms (SNPs)	Point mutations and SNPs within the RET gene can lead to activation or alteration of RET function. Certain mutations result in constitutive activation of RET kinase activity, contributing to the development of hereditary cancer syndromes.
Ligand-mediated activation of RET	When GDNF family ligands bind to the extracellular domain of RET, RET is activated through ligand-mediated activation. This causes receptor dimerization, which then triggers autophosphorylation and the start of further signaling pathways.

outcomes and personalized medicine approaches for patients with RET-altered malignancies and other diseases (Klohs et al., 1997; Regua et al., 2022).

RET (rearranged during transfection) inhibitors represent a specialized family of medications designed to target and suppress the activity of the RET receptor tyrosine kinase. These inhibitors have emerged as a promising therapeutic strategy due to the association of aberrant RET activation with various diseases, including cancer. This essay explores the different classes of RET inhibitors and their mechanisms of action, with a particular focus on tyrosine kinase inhibitors (TKIs), which have been extensively studied in this context (Mulligan, 2014).

TKIs function by binding to the ATP-binding pocket of the RET kinase domain, effectively blocking the binding of ATP and thereby preventing the autophosphorylation and activation of the RET receptor. Several examples of TKIs that specifically target RET include the following:

Vandetanib: Vandetanib is a multi-targeted TKI that effectively inhibits not only RET but also other important receptors, including VEGFR (vascular endothelial growth factor receptor) and EGFR (epidermal growth factor receptor). Its ability to target multiple receptors makes it a valuable therapeutic option in various cancers. Vandetanib has demonstrated notable efficacy in the treatment of advanced MTC and has been approved for this specific indication. Its ability to inhibit RET signaling is particularly crucial in MTC, as this type of thyroid cancer is often driven by RET mutations or rearrangements. By targeting RET, Vandetanib can disrupt the aberrant signaling pathways that contribute to the growth and spread of MTC tumors, leading to improved outcomes for patients with this condition.

Cabozantinib: Cabozantinib is another multitargeted TKI that effectively inhibits multiple receptors, including RET, MET, and VEGFR. Its broad spectrum of target inhibition makes it a promising therapeutic option for various malignancies.

Cabozantinib has shown clinical activity in patients with RET fusion-positive nonsmall cell lung cancer (NSCLC). RET fusions, which result from genetic rearrangements involving the RET gene, are a specific molecular subtype of NSCLC. In these cases, the RET fusion protein becomes constitutively active, driving cancer cell growth and survival. By inhibiting RET, along with MET and VEGFR, Cabozantinib can disrupt the signaling pathways that contribute to tumor growth and spread in RET fusion-positive NSCLC. By targeting MET, it can further impede cancer cell proliferation, as MET plays a role in promoting cell growth and survival. Additionally, inhibition of VEGFR hinders the formation of new blood vessels that supply nutrients to tumors, thereby inhibiting tumor growth and angiogenesis. Due to its demonstrated efficacy in RET fusion-positive NSCLC, Cabozantinib has gained approval for this indication. It represents a promising targeted treatment option for patients with this specific molecular subtype of nonsmall cell lung cancer, offering potential benefits in terms of disease control and improved patient outcomes.

3.1 Multikinase inhibitors/nonselective RET inhibitors

Some RET inhibitors belong to the class of multikinase inhibitors, which target multiple receptor tyrosine kinases simultaneously. While they inhibit RET, they also affect other kinases, which may broaden their therapeutic effects (Garuti et al., 2015). Examples of multikinase inhibitors with RET-inhibitory activity include the following:

3.1.1 Sorafenib

Sorafenib (Fig. 13.5) is a notable multi-kinase inhibitor that targets several key kinases, including RET, VEGFR, and RAF. Developed initially as an RAF inhibitor, Sorafenib has demonstrated additional inhibitory activity against RET, making it a potential therapeutic option for cancers driven by abnormal RET signaling. This broad-spectrum kinase inhibition allows it to have multiple mechanisms of action, offering promise in the treatment of various cancers. Sorafenib is administered orally and acts as an ATP-competitive Raf kinase inhibitor (Lyons et al., 2001). It has exhibited efficacy against several other kinases, such as BRAF, VEGFR-2, and VEGFR-3, as well as PDGFRβ, effectively reducing tumor growth and angiogenesis in preclinical studies (Wilhelm et al., 2004). Further investigations have revealed that Sorafenib can block the action of both wild-type RET and oncogenic-altered RET, displaying some degree of selectivity (Henderson et al., 2008; Plaza-Menacho et al., 2007). This inhibition of RET signaling proves beneficial in halting the proliferation and growth of tumor cells driven by RET alterations, such as in PTC, both in laboratory studies (in vitro) and in animal models (in vivo).

The ability of Sorafenib to target multiple kinases, including RET, has broadened its potential application as a targeted therapy for RET-driven cancers. Its oral administration and

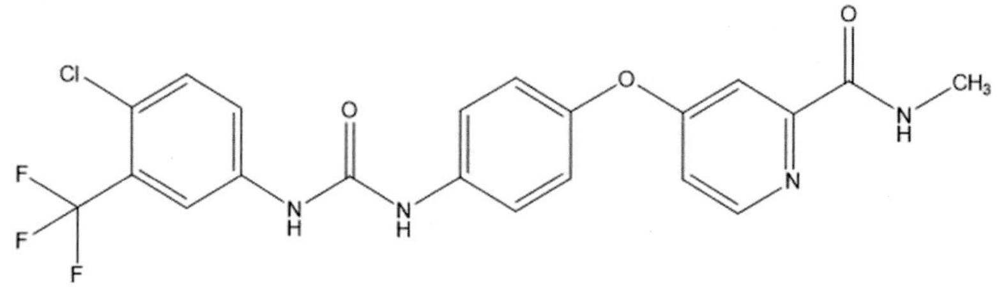

FIGURE 13.5   Structure of sorafenib.

demonstrated efficacy in preclinical studies make it a promising candidate for clinical investigations and potential use in patients with cancers exhibiting RET dysregulation. Furthermore, research has indicated that the RET-V804M gatekeeper mutation, which is associated with resistance to some targeted therapies, does not impact the inhibition of RET by sorafenib. This suggests that sorafenib may still offer clinical benefits to patients with MTC who have this specific RET mutation.

Plaza-Menacho and colleagues found that sorafenib treatment leads to the degradation of RET protein independently of proteosomal targeting, indicating that sorafenib functions as an ATP-competitive inhibitor. This novel finding reveals an additional mechanism through which sorafenib reduces RET activity upon treatment, potentially contributing to its efficacy as a therapeutic option for RET-driven cancers like MTC. Interestingly, a study conducted by Mao and colleagues supported the observation that sorafenib not only influences RET expression but also alters VEGFR2 expression. However, the specific effects of sorafenib on RET and VEGFR2 expression appear to be dependent on the particular cell line used in the study. Further mechanistic studies are needed to fully understand these complex effects, especially considering that different cellular contexts may yield diverse outcomes (Mao et al., 2012).

The diverse effects of sorafenib on various cellular contexts highlight the complexity of its interactions with RET and VEGFR2 signaling pathways. These complexities underscore the need for further investigation to better understand the potential clinical applications of sorafenib in targeting RET-driven cancers and its broader implications for VEGFR2-related pathways. Such studies could pave the way for optimizing the use of sorafenib as a therapeutic agent in specific cancer subtypes and identifying potential combinations with other targeted therapies for improved patient outcomes.

In 2005, the FDA granted approval for sorafenib's use in the treatment of advanced renal cell carcinoma (Kane et al., 2006). Since then, it has received additional approvals for managing unresectable hepatocellular carcinomas (Lang, 2008) and iodine-refractory, metastatic differentiated thyroid tumors (McFarland & Misiukiewicz, 2014). These approvals highlight the promising applications of sorafenib in different cancer types. However, despite its success in certain cancer indications, a study by Horiike and colleagues found that sorafenib did not produce a positive response in patients with nonsmall cell lung cancer (NSCLC) (Horiike et al., 2016). This finding raises questions regarding the potential clinical benefits of sorafenib for patients with RET fusion-positive NSCLC, given its role as a RET inhibitor. To determine the efficacy of sorafenib in this specific patient population and in other cancers with RET alterations, further research is essential (Thein et al., 2021). Additional studies are necessary to understand how sorafenib can be optimized as a treatment option for patients with RET-altered NSCLC and other cancers driven by RET dysregulation. These investigations will help to identify potential combination therapies and patient selection criteria, ultimately improving the clinical outcomes of patients with RET-driven malignancies.

3.1.2 SU5416 (Semaxanib)

Mologni et al. studied the small-molecule inhibitor SU5416 (Semaxanib) (Fig. 13.6) that inhibits the activity of RET kinase. SU5416 is a member of the class 3-substituted indolin-2-one tyrosine kinase inhibitors. This substance was initially identified as a selective VEGFR2 (Flk-1/KDR) inhibitor, however, it has now been discovered to also inhibit Kit, Met, and FLT-3. SU5416 has entered clinical development because of outstanding pharmacokinetics; it is

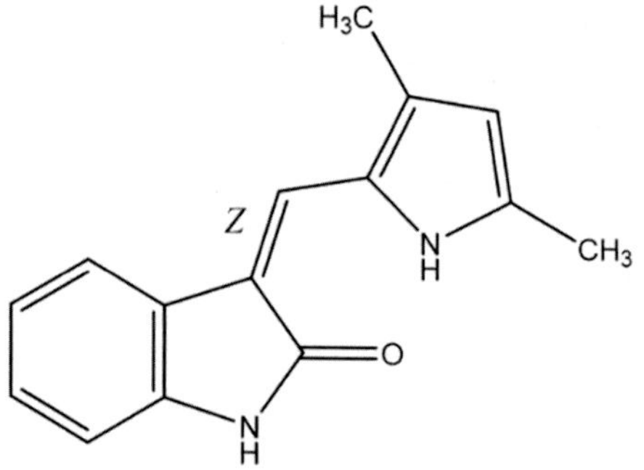

FIGURE 13.6   Structure of SU5416 (Semaxanib).

primarily being used as an antiangiogenic medication. Due to its ability to inhibit c-Kit and Flt-3, SU5416 has more recently been tested as an experimental treatment for acute myeloid leukemia (Mologni et al., 2006).

3.1.3 Ponatinib

Ponatinib (Fig. 13.7) is an MKI permitted for the treatment of certain types of leukemia. It inhibits RET, as well as other kinases such as BCR-ABL and FGFR. Its inhibitory activity against RET suggests potential utility in RET-altered malignancies.

The main target of Ponatinib is BCR-ABL, an aberrant tyrosine kinase that characterizes CML and Ph + ALL. Due to a genetic anomaly that results in the BCR-ABL protein being produced, CML is characterized by the bone marrow producing an excessive and uncontrolled amount of white blood cells. CML often progresses to more aggressive phases like accelerated or blast crises after a chronic phase of excessive white blood cell production. A form of acute lymphoblastic leukemia known as Ph + ALL is capable of producing the BCR-ABL gene.

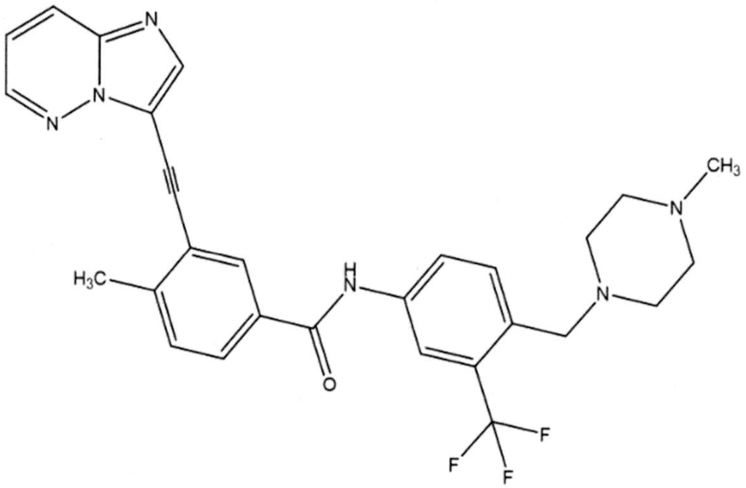

FIGURE 13.7   Structure of ponatinib.

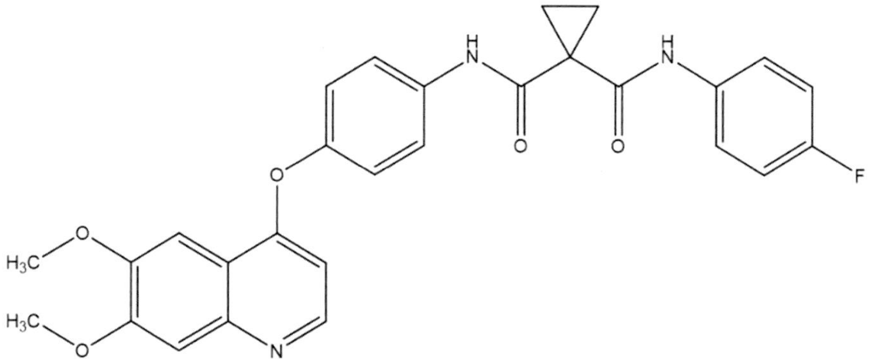

FIGURE 13.8 Structure of cabozantinib.

Tyrosine kinase inhibitors are frequently used in conjunction with chemotherapy to treat it since it has a more aggressive course than CML. Both of these conditions could potentially respond to ponatinib therapy because they both express the BCR-ABL protein. In 95% of CML patients, BCR-ABL is found (Tan et al., 2019).

3.1.4 Cabozantinib

Cabozantinib (Fig. 13.8) is an ATP-competitive MKI that can be taken orally and inhibits a variety of kinases, including RET, FLT3, TRK, KIT, c-MET, and VEGFR2. In vitro, cabozantinib efficiently reduces cell division, growth, migration, and invasion. In vivo, it increases tumor cell and endothelial cell apoptosis. In several clinical trials, such as those for MTC and renal cell carcinoma, Cabozantinib was tolerated well (Choueiri et al., 2014; Kurzrock et al., 2011; Yakes et al., 2011).

Indeed, Cabozantinib has gained significant FDA approvals for the treatment of various cancer types. In 2012, it was approved for managing MTC, renal cell carcinoma (RCC), and hepatocellular carcinoma (HCC). Subsequently, in 2016 and 2017, it received further approvals as a second-line therapy for kidney cancer. Notably, Cabozantinib has also shown promising results in a phase II clinical trial (NCT01639508) involving patients with RET-fusion-positive lung cancer. In this study, patients were administered Cabozantinib at a daily dose of 60 mg orally. The trial demonstrated a partial response in 28% of patients (7 out of 25 patients), providing strong evidence for the effectiveness of Cabozantinib in treating RET-fusion-positive lung tumors (Drilon et al., 2013, 2016). These findings highlight the potential for Cabozantinib to be a valuable therapeutic option for lung cancer patients with specific RET alterations. The approval of Cabozantinib in various cancer indications and its demonstrated efficacy in treating RET-driven lung cancer emphasize its role as a targeted therapy with broad applications in oncology. As research in precision medicine continues to progress, Cabozantinib's potential as a treatment for specific molecular subtypes of cancer, such as those with RET alterations, offers hope for improved outcomes in patients with these challenging malignancies.

Indeed, a phase III clinical trial (NCT00704730) focusing on the treatment of metastatic MTC cases harboring the specific RET-M918T mutation demonstrated compelling results for Cabozantinib. In this trial, patients received daily oral administration of Cabozantinib at a dose of 140 mg. The study revealed that Cabozantinib significantly improved overall survival, with patients in the treatment group having a median overall survival of 26.6 months compared to 21.1 months in the placebo group. Moreover, Cabozantinib also significantly improved progression-free survival (Schlumberger et al., 2017; Sherman et al., 2016). These findings highlight the potential efficacy of Cabozantinib as a targeted therapy for cancers with RET alterations, particularly in cases with the RET-M918T mutation. This highlights its promising role in managing such malignancies and suggests that it could be a valuable treatment option for patients with RET-altered cancers.

Furthermore, when evaluating only individuals with RET-M918T mutations, the overall response rate (ORR) for patients who received Cabozantinib rose to 34%. This indicates a substantial proportion of patients experiencing a positive response to Cabozantinib therapy (Schlumberger et al., 2017). Such outcomes further emphasize the potential benefits of Cabozantinib in managing specific molecular subtypes of cancer driven by RET alterations. Overall, the results from these clinical trials underscore the significant potential of Cabozantinib as a targeted therapy for RET-altered cancers, providing encouraging evidence for its efficacy and offering hope for improved outcomes in patients with these challenging malignancies.

3.1.5 Lenvatinib

Lenvatinib (Fig. 13.9) is an orally administered ATP-competitive multi-kinase inhibitor (MKI) that has demonstrated efficacy against various kinases, including FLT-1, FLT-4, KIT, FGFR1, PDGFR, and VEGFR1-3. Extensive research has shown that lenvatinib has the ability to reduce angiogenesis and proliferation of both small cell lung cancer (SCLC) and breast cancer cells in laboratory studies (in vitro) and animal models (in vivo) (Glen et al., 2011; Matsui et al., 2008a,b; Yamamoto et al., 2014). Importantly, lenvatinib has also shown promising results in inhibiting RET fusion kinases and RET pathway activity in preclinical models with RET fusion-positive tumors. This is a significant finding as RET fusions drive the development and progression of certain cancers. Lenvatinib has effectively suppressed the growth of tumor cells harboring RET fusions in animal models (in vivo), as confirmed by further studies (Okamoto et al., 2013; Tohyama et al., 2014). These preclinical findings highlight the potential of lenvatinib as a targeted therapeutic option for cancers with alterations in the RET pathway.

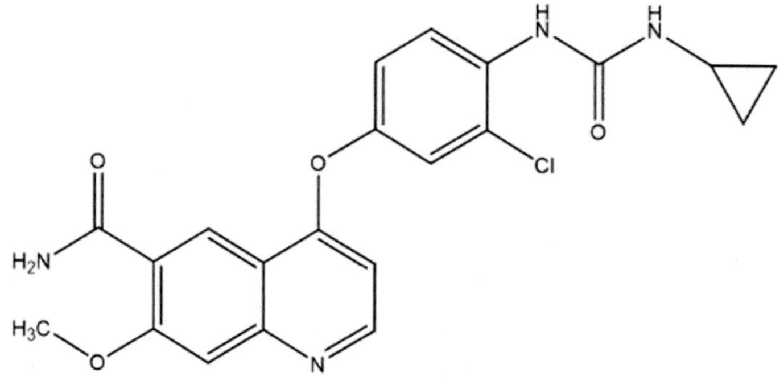

FIGURE 13.9   Structure of lenvatinib.

In patients with RET fusion-positive nonsmall cell lung cancer (NSCLC), oral administration of lenvatinib once daily at a dosage of 24 mg resulted in a relatively low response rate, with only 16% of patients showing an objective response (4 out of 25 patients). Despite this modest response, the treatment with lenvatinib was effective in increasing the median progression-free survival (Kodama et al., 2014). While the response rate may be modest, the improvement in progression-free survival is a positive outcome, indicating that lenvatinib could still be beneficial for some patients with RET fusion-positive NSCLC. Lenvatinib has garnered FDA approvals for the treatment of differentiated thyroid cancer in 2015 (Hewett et al., 2018) and for managing unresectable hepatocellular carcinoma in 2018 (Nair et al., 2021). These approvals highlight its established efficacy in treating these specific cancer types. Additionally, the FDA has granted approval for the use of lenvatinib in combination therapy for endometrial cancer and renal cell carcinoma (Arora et al., 2020). This indicates the growing recognition of lenvatinib's potential in combination treatments for these cancer types. These approvals underscore the significant potential of lenvatinib in addressing various cancer types and its valuable role as a targeted therapy option for patients with RET-altered malignancies.

3.1.6 Vandetanib

Vandetanib is a multi-kinase inhibitor that primarily targets the RET-tyrosine kinase, in addition to inhibiting other important receptors such as the vascular endothelial growth factor receptor (VEGFR) and the epidermal growth factor receptor (EGFR). It is administered orally and acts as a tyrosine kinase inhibitor, with a specific focus on inhibiting KDR/VEGFR-2, with moderate activity against FLT-1/VEGFR-1, EGFR, and PDGFRβ (Ciardiello et al., 2004; Hennequin et al., 2002). One of Vandetanib's notable characteristics is its ability to suppress VEGF signaling and angiogenesis effectively. As a result, it can reduce the growth of various tumor cell xenografts derived from human lung, prostate, breast, ovarian, and colon cancer cells. Indeed, the preclinical studies showcasing Vandetanib's potent antiangiogenic and antitumor effects provide strong evidence supporting its potential as a targeted therapy for a broad spectrum of cancers. Additionally, a study conducted by Carlomagno et al. in the same year further supports Vandetanib's promising therapeutic potential. In this study, Vandetanib effectively inhibited the kinase activity of various RET fusion proteins, including RET/PTC, RET/MEN2A, and RET/EGFR, in transformed NIH3T3 cells. Notably, it not only restored the morphological phenotype of these transformed cells to that of parental cells but also prevented their anchorage-independent growth. These findings underscore Vandetanib's ability to target and inhibit key signaling pathways, highlighting its potential as a promising therapeutic agent for targeting cancers driven by RET alterations and other malignancies associated with the pathways it modulates (Fig. 13.10).

The specificity of Vandetanib for RET was further confirmed through a *Drosophila melanogaster* model of papillary thyroid carcinomas and multiple endocrine neoplasia type 2 (MEN2) syndromes. This validation affirmed Vandetanib's potential to inhibit various RET isoforms, indicating its effectiveness in treating RET-dependent carcinomas (Vidal et al., 2005). The study provided additional evidence supporting Vandetanib's role as a targeted therapy for cancers with RET alterations. However, a subsequent study conducted by Carlomagno and colleagues (Carlomagno et al., 2004) revealed important findings regarding the clinical efficacy of Vandetanib in cases with specific RET gatekeeper mutations. The research

FIGURE 13.10   Structure of vandetanib.

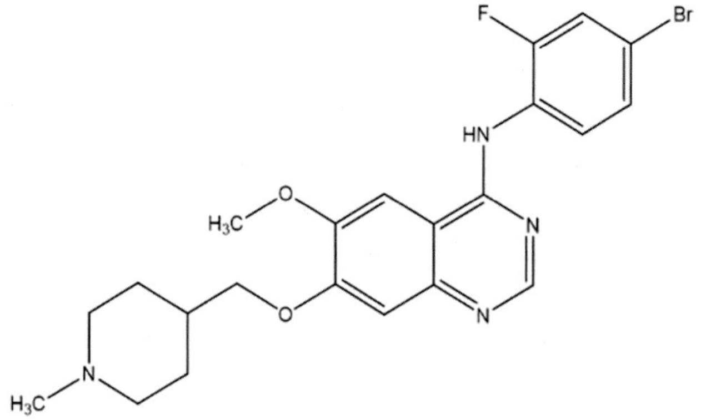

identified RET-V804L or RET-V804M gatekeeper variants that confer resistance to the drug, limiting its effectiveness in these particular cases. This underscores the importance of understanding the molecular profiles of individual patients when considering Vandetanib as a treatment option, as the presence of certain mutations can impact its therapeutic response.

In clinical trials involving patients with advanced or metastatic hereditary MTC, Vandetanib was well-tolerated when administered once daily at a dosage of 300 mg orally (Robinson et al., 2010; Wells et al., 2010). This favorable safety profile is an important consideration for its potential use as a therapeutic agent in clinical settings.

In clinical trials involving patients with advanced MTC, Vandetanib demonstrated enhanced therapeutic efficacy, leading to improved progression-free survival (PFS) compared to the placebo group. The median PFS in the Vandetanib treatment group was significantly longer (30.5 months) compared to the placebo group (19.3 months) (Wells et al., 2012). These results provide strong evidence for Vandetanib's clinical effectiveness in managing RET-related malignancies, particularly in patients with advanced MTC. Vandetanib is a multi-kinase inhibitor (MKI) that can target various kinases, and one of its targets is the RET kinase, which is involved in the development and progression of MTC. However, the observed anti-tumor effects of vandetanib in MTC may not be solely attributed to inhibiting RET kinase activity. There might be other mechanisms through which vandetanib exerts its therapeutic effects in MTC.

3.1.7 Regorafenib

Regorafenib (depicted in Fig. 13.11) is a potent compound known for its remarkable anti-angiogenic, antitumorigenic, and pro-apoptotic properties. It effectively targets several kinases, including VEGFR1-3, TIE2, PDGFRb, KIT, and RET, both in laboratory studies (in vitro) and animal models (in vivo) (Wilhelm et al., 2011). This orally available drug acts as an ATP-competitive inhibitor (Knowles et al., 2006) and has shown promising outcomes when used as a standalone therapy, leading to partial response or stable disease in individuals with advanced or incurable solid tumors (George et al., 2012; Mross et al., 2012; Strumberg et al., 2012). While regorafenib has proven to be a valuable option in managing certain cancers due to its favorable tolerability and potential clinical benefits, it's essential

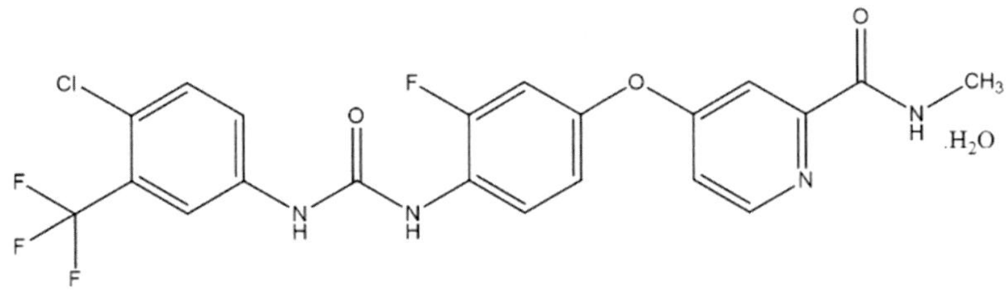

FIGURE 13.11 Structure of regorafenib.

to consider possible side effects. For instance, in patients with renal cell carcinoma who underwent prolonged treatment, some adverse effects were observed (Eisen et al., 2012). Despite this, its overall efficacy and safety profile make it a crucial treatment choice for certain malignancies, offering hope to patients in need of effective therapeutic options.

Researchers led by Chen and their team have demonstrated the effectiveness of regorafenib in inhibiting the growth of neuroblastoma cells in both laboratory and animal models. This potent inhibition is achieved by targeting the activity of RET and the RET-mediated PI3K/AKT signaling pathway (Chen et al., 2017). Moreover, regorafenib exhibits additional beneficial effects, such as reducing PD-L1 expression and blocking the RET-Src signaling axis. This dual action leads to the inhibition of JAK1/2-STAT1 and MAPK signaling, suggesting that blocking the RET-Src axis may also have a positive impact on the immune response against tumor cells in vivo (Wu et al., 2019). As the understanding of regorafenib's mechanisms grows, it is currently under investigation in various clinical trials for different types of cancer. While its potential efficacy in RET-altered tumors has not been studied yet, ongoing research on regorafenib shows promise for the development of targeted therapies catering to a wide range of cancer patients, including those with RET alterations. These findings hold the potential to advance the field of cancer treatment and provide new hope for patients with specific molecular alterations like RET abnormalities.

3.1.8 Sunitinib

Sunitinib (Fig. 13.12) was developed in 2003 as an orally available ATP-competitive inhibitor with a specific focus on VEGFR, PDGFR, KIT, and FLT3 receptor tyrosine kinases. As a monotherapy administered on a daily basis, sunitinib has demonstrated impressive results in inhibiting tumor growth across various cancer cell types, including breast, NSCLC, colon cancer, glioma, and melanoma. Its effectiveness in impeding tumor progression can be attributed

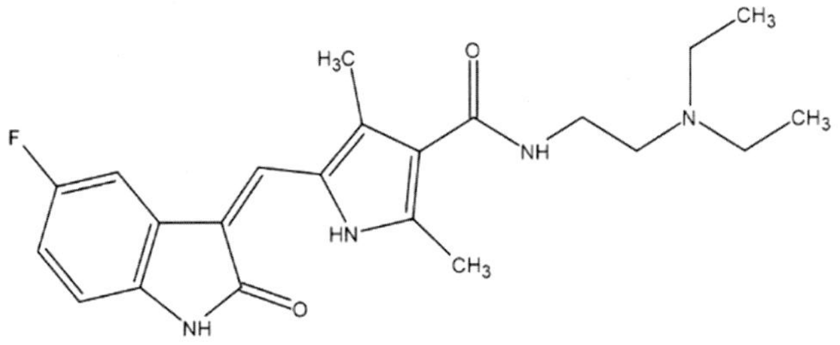

FIGURE 13.12 Structure of sunitinib.

<cimg src="./.png"/>

to its potent inhibition of tumor cell angiogenesis, as well as its ability to reduce endothelial cell migration and prevent tubule formation in vivo. These actions highlight sunitinib's role as a significant VEGF inhibitor (Osusky et al., 2004).

Sunitinib has demonstrated its effectiveness in inhibiting downstream MAPK signaling in PTC tumors that carry RET/PTC3 fusions (Jeong et al., 2014). The FDA approved sunitinib in 2006 for the treatment of GI stromal tumors and advanced renal cell carcinomas. However, a pilot clinical trial (NCT02450123) that was assessing the safety and efficacy of sunitinib (50 mg, p.o. daily) in solid tumors with RET fusion was placed on hold in 2020, and its current status remains undisclosed (Deeks & Keating, 2006).

3.1.9 Alectinib

Alectinib (Fig. 13.13) is an orally available ATP inhibitor with a specific focus on ALK alterations and gatekeeper mutations, while still preserving MET activity (Sakamoto et al., 2011). Notably, alectinib has demonstrated the ability to effectively inhibit ALK-L1196M, a gatekeeper mutation that had previously shown resistance to earlier generations of ALK inhibitors. Through both in vitro and in vivo studies, alectinib has shown its efficacy in suppressing ALK activation, blocking the activation of STAT3, PI3K/AKT, and MAPK pathways, and effectively inhibiting tumor growth in cases where ALK alterations are present (Lu et al., 2009).

Alectinib has shown positive responses and good tolerance in patients with ALK mutations in nonsmall cell lung cancer (NSCLC) (Seto et al., 2013). Notably, alectinib also demonstrates specificity against RET with gatekeeper mutations (V804L and V804M), as observed in Kodama et al.'s study (Kodama et al., 2014). Both in vitro and in vivo experiments have provided evidence of its effective inhibition of both wild-type RET and constitutively active RET-M918T NSCLC cells. When clinically evaluated in treatment-naive patients, alectinib showed good tolerability. However, in patients with RET fusion-positive NSCLC, twice-daily oral administration of alectinib at a dose of 600 mg resulted in limited activity, with an overall response rate (ORR) of 4% (1 out of 25 patients) and a progression-free survival (PFS) of 3.4 months (Takeuchi et al., 2021).

Developing new and highly specific RET inhibitors (RETi) is of paramount importance to address V804 gatekeeper alterations, overcome resistance to MKIs, and achieve selective inhibition of KDR (kinase insert domain receptor). However, the precise mechanisms

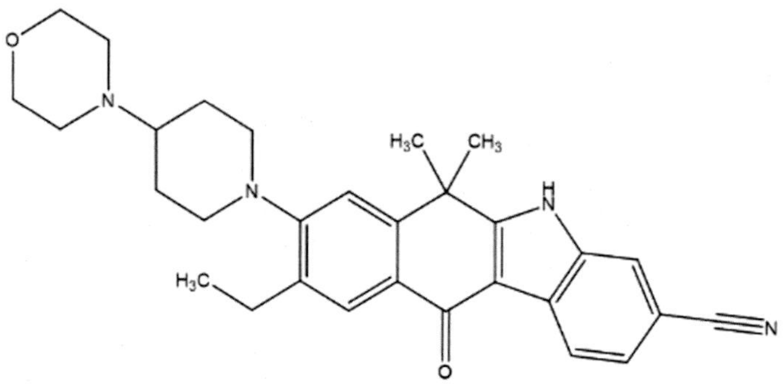

FIGURE 13.13   Structure of alectinib.

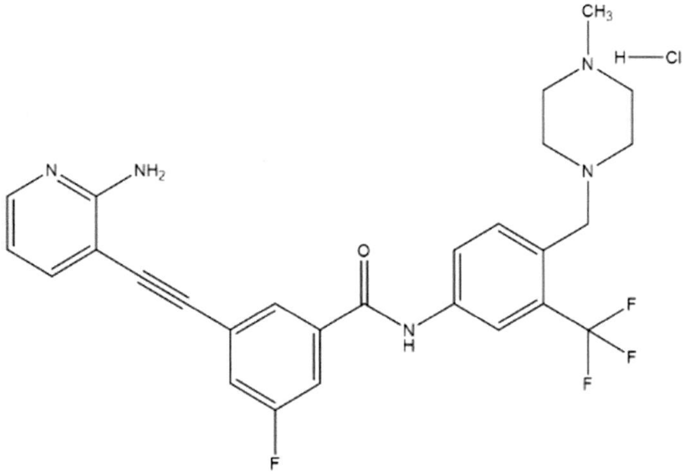

FIGURE 13.14   Structure of SYHA1815.

underlying the antiproliferative effects of RET inhibition in RET-dependent settings are not yet fully elucidated. In this study, researchers introduced a novel selective RETi named SYHA1815 (depicted in Fig. 13.14). Notably, SYHA1815 demonstrated a significant reduction in the kinase activity of both RET wild type and the V804 mutant, with an IC50 falling in the subnanomolar to nanomolar range. Remarkably, SYHA1815 exhibited approximately 20 times greater selectivity for RET over KDR when compared to the recently released selective inhibitor, pralsetinib. Furthermore, at a high dosage (200 nmol/L), SYHA1815 had only a minimal inhibitory effect on cellular KDR signaling, thus confirming its specificity for RET over KDR (Jiang et al., 2021).

3.1.10 Advantages

1. Broad Spectrum of Activity: Multi-kinase inhibitors target multiple kinases simultaneously, allowing for a broader spectrum of activity. This can be advantageous in cases where multiple signaling pathways are dysregulated or when targeting multiple kinases is desirable for therapeutic efficacy.
2. Potential Synergistic Effects: In some cases, the simultaneous inhibition of multiple kinases can lead to synergistic effects, enhancing the overall therapeutic response. This can be beneficial when the dysregulation of multiple kinases contributes to disease progression.
3. Established Clinical Use: Several MKIs have been approved for the treatment of various cancers and other diseases. Their clinical use and safety profiles have been extensively studied, providing a solid foundation for their use in clinical practice (Garuti et al., 2015; Krug & Hilgeroth, 2008).

3.1.11 Disadvantages

1. Off-Target Effects: Multi-kinase inhibitors can inhibit multiple kinases, including those that are not directly involved in the targeted disease. This can lead to off-target effects

and potential toxicity. Balancing the desired target inhibition with unwanted off-target effects is a critical challenge.

2. Lack of Specificity: The lack of specificity of multi-kinase inhibitors can limit their efficacy and potentially lead to suboptimal outcomes. In some cases, specific targeting of a single kinase may be more desirable to achieve optimal therapeutic response and minimize adverse effects.

3. Resistance Development: The broad spectrum of activity of multi-kinase inhibitors may increase the likelihood of resistance development. The simultaneous inhibition of multiple kinases can create selective pressure, leading to the emergence of resistant clones that circumvent the drug's inhibitory effects.

4. Dose-Limiting Toxicity: The potential for off-target effects and the need for higher doses to achieve sufficient inhibition of multiple kinases can increase the risk of dose-limiting toxicities, impacting the tolerability of these inhibitors.

3.2 Selective RET inhibitors

A more recent class of medications called selective RET inhibitors was created particularly to target RET kinase activity with excellent selectivity. They are designed to reduce the effects they have on unintended kinases. Preclinical and clinical trials on a few selective RET inhibitors are currently being conducted, and the results are encouraging (Garuti et al., 2015). The last 5 years have seen a rise in efforts to create RET-specific medicines. Targeting the RET oncoprotein through pharmacological modulation has proven to be effective in treating RET-driven malignancies. In a significant milestone, the first kinase inhibitors designed specifically to target RET, pralsetinib, and selpercatinib, received clinical approval in 2020 (Saha et al., 2021). These RET-selective medications mark a crucial advancement in the management of RET-altered cancers, offering new hope and potential therapeutic options for patients with these types of malignancies.

3.2.1 Pralsetinib

Pralsetinib, also known as BLU-667 (Fig. 13.15), stands out as a highly selective RET inhibitor, displaying remarkable effectiveness in treating RET fusion-positive NSCLC and RET-mutated MTC. Due to its promising outcomes in these indications, pralsetinib has earned accelerated approval (Markham, 2020). As a targeted therapy, it holds significant potential in the management of diverse cancers driven by RET gene alterations. This assessment delves into the mechanism of action of BLU-667, its regulatory approvals, and its wide-ranging

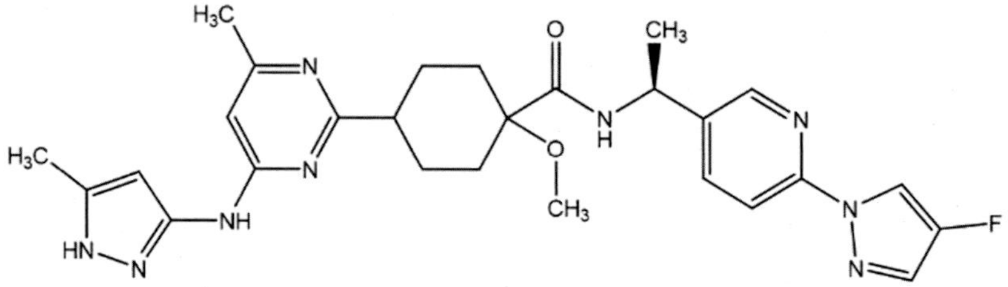

FIGURE 13.15   Structure of pralsetinib.

therapeutic applications in cancer treatment. Pralsetinib, a highly selective RET kinase inhibitor, has a well-defined mechanism of action. It has received regulatory approvals for the treatment of metastatic RET fusion-positive NSCLC and advanced or metastatic RET-mutant MTC, validating its efficacy in these specific cancer types. With its targeted approach, BLU-667 provides a valuable treatment option for patients with RET-altered cancers, showcasing impressive response rates and durable outcomes (Zhang et al., 2022).

Ongoing research and clinical trials continue to explore the potential of BLU-667 in addressing other cancers with RET alterations, contributing significantly to the advancement of precision medicine in oncology. BLU-667 is a potent and highly selective RET kinase inhibitor, effectively hindering the phosphorylation and activation of the RET receptor tyrosine kinase by binding to the ATP binding pocket of the RET kinase domain. By blocking RET signaling, BLU-667 suppresses tumor growth and also impacts downstream pathways involved in cell growth, survival, and proliferation. The phase I clinical trial, known as ARROW, involved adults with advanced solid tumors like MTC and nonsmall cell lung cancer (NSCLC), among others. This trial evaluated the safety, tolerability, and efficacy of BLU-667, concluding that the optimal phase II dose is 400 mg/day. Encouraging results were presented at the 2019 American Society of Clinical Oncology meeting, demonstrating a significant 90% tumor reduction, 60% objective response rate, and 100% disease control rate in 48 patients with RET-fusion NSCLC. These findings highlight the promise of BLU-667 as a potential therapeutic option for a range of RET-altered cancers, offering hope for improved outcomes for patients in the future. The drug, pralsetinib, showed an effect regardless of RET fusion partner. Pralsetinib was granted two FDA breakthrough designations for MTC and NSCLC as a result of these encouraging findings. Furthermore, partial responses were seen in gastrointestinal malignancies with RET fusions, such as pancreatic cancer and cholangiocarcinoma, and the ORR was 83% (5 out of 6 patients) in patients with RET fusion-positive PTC (Krug & Hilgeroth, 2008).

3.2.2 LOXO-292 (selpercatinib)

Selpercatinib (Fig. 13.16) stands out as a highly selective RET inhibitor, obtaining approval for treating RET fusion-positive NSCLC, RET-mutated MTC, and RET fusion-positive thyroid

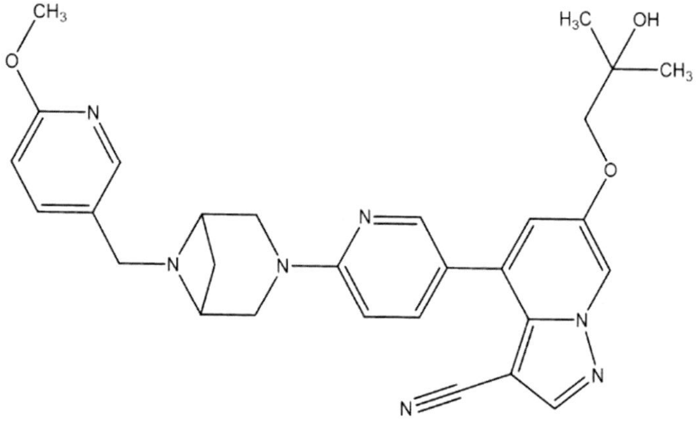

FIGURE 13.16 Structure of selpercatinib.

cancer (Bradford et al., 2021). Its remarkable clinical activity led to accelerated approvals. Also known as LOXO-292, Selpercatinib represents a targeted therapy that exhibits significant clinical efficacy in addressing various cancers driven by RET alterations. Functioning as a potent RET kinase inhibitor, Selpercatinib attaches to ATP-binding sites, effectively blocking RET signaling. By doing so, it hinders cell growth, proliferation, and survival in cancers where RET aberrations lead to abnormal activation (Grüllich, 2018). The approval and positive clinical results of Selpercatinib offer hope for improved treatment options and outcomes for patients with these specific types of cancers.

Selpercatinib is an exceptionally selective inhibitor of the RET kinase, displaying impressive effectiveness in the treatment of cancers with RET alterations, notably advanced or metastatic RET fusion-positive NSCLC and RET-mutant MTC. By targeting the RET kinase domain, it effectively suppresses RET signaling, resulting in the inhibition of tumor growth and progression. The promising mechanism of action of Selpercatinib offers hope for patients with these specific types of cancers, providing a potential avenue for improved treatment outcomes. The regulatory approvals of selpercatinib by the FDA, EMA, and other health authorities have provided patients with RET-altered cancers a targeted therapeutic option that has demonstrated substantial clinical benefits. Continued research and clinical investigations will further refine the use of selpercatinib and expand its applications in other RET-altered solid tumors, contributing to improved outcomes and quality of life for patients affected by these diseases (Gouda & Subbiah, 2023; Wirth et al., 2020).

3.2.3 Agerafenib

Agerafenib (Fig. 13.17) is an orally available, ATP-competitive, and highly selective inhibitor of both RET and BRAF, aiming to enhance the clinical benefits of MKIs in cancers with RET alterations. In preclinical studies involving various RET-altered cancer types, RXDX-105 demonstrated superior and selective inhibition of both wild-type and transformed RET, outperforming MKIs with nonselective RET activity. Notably, it exhibited rapid response capabilities in the primary tumor and brain metastases of a patient with RET fusion-positive lung cancer (Li et al., 2017). The preclinical findings were promising, indicating that RXDX-105 could serve as a highly effective and innovative anticancer drug, with the potential to cross the blood–brain barrier (BBB). However, in the phase I/Ib trial (NCT01877811) evaluating daily oral administration of Agerafenib (275 mg) to patients with RET fusion-positive

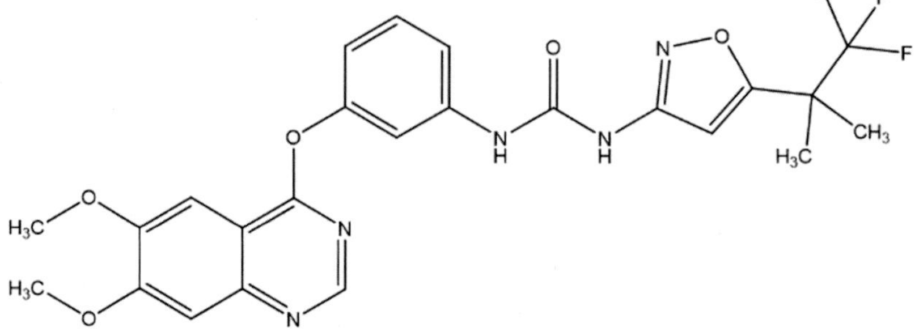

FIGURE 13.17 Structure of Agerafenib.

NSCLC, the outcomes were disappointing. The treatment did not produce any response in the 20 patients enrolled, and it led to several treatment-related side effects, including diarrhea, fatigue, and hypophosphatemia. As a result of the lack of clinical response, this clinical trial was ultimately terminated (Drilon et al., 2019).

3.2.4 Advantages

1. High Selectivity:
   Selective RET inhibitors are designed to specifically target the RET kinase, minimizing off-target effects on other kinases. This high selectivity allows for a more precise and focused inhibition of the RET signaling pathway, reducing the potential for off-target toxicity and adverse effects.
2. Enhanced Therapeutic Efficacy:
   By specifically targeting RET, selective inhibitors can achieve a higher degree of target inhibition, resulting in enhanced therapeutic efficacy. This can lead to improved clinical outcomes, such as tumor regression and prolonged progression-free survival, in patients with RET-driven diseases.
3. Reduced Side Effects:
   The selectivity of these inhibitors for RET can potentially reduce the incidence and severity of side effects compared to nonselective kinase inhibitors. By minimizing off-target effects, selective RET inhibitors may provide a better safety profile and improved tolerability for patients.
4. Personalized Medicine:
   Selective RET inhibitors offer the potential for personalized medicine approaches, particularly in the context of RET-driven cancers. With the availability of genetic testing, patients with specific RET alterations can be identified and targeted with the appropriate selective inhibitor, maximizing the therapeutic benefit for individual patients (Grüllich, 2018).

3.2.5 Disadvantages

1. Limited Target Range:
   Selective RET inhibitors, by design, only target the RET kinase and may not have activity against other relevant kinases or alternative signaling pathways that contribute to disease progression. This limited target range may reduce the overall effectiveness of selective inhibitors in cases where RET activation is influenced by other factors.
2. Resistance Development:
   Similar to other targeted therapies, the development of resistance can limit the long-term effectiveness of selective RET inhibitors. Despite their high selectivity, resistant clones may emerge due to acquired mutations or alternative signaling pathways, leading to treatment failure.
3. Lack of Established Clinical Use:
   Compared to nonselective multi-kinase inhibitors, selective RET inhibitors are a relatively newer class of drugs. Consequently, their clinical use and long-term safety profiles may be less established, requiring ongoing monitoring and further research to understand their efficacy and potential limitations (Grüllich, 2018).

4. Mechanisms of action

RET inhibitors exert their therapeutic effects through various mechanisms, including ATP competitive inhibition, allosteric inhibition, blockade of downstream signaling pathways, induction of apoptosis, and antiangiogenic effects. These mechanisms collectively lead to the inhibition of aberrantly activated RET signaling, thereby suppressing cell survival, proliferation, and migration in RET-driven diseases, particularly cancer. Understanding the diverse mechanisms of action employed by RET inhibitors is crucial for the development of effective targeted therapies and the advancement of precision medicine approaches for patients with RET-altered malignancies and other diseases (Table 13.3) (Grüllich, 2018; Subbiah et al., 2020a,b; Subbiah & Cote, 2020).

5. Therapeutic applications of RET inhibitors

RET inhibitors demonstrate significant therapeutic potential in various diseases driven by RET alterations. The targeted inhibition of RET signaling offers new avenues for precision medicine and personalized treatment approaches. Ongoing research, clinical trials, and the development of novel RET inhibitors will continue to expand the therapeutic applications of these agents, bringing hope to patients with RET-driven malignancies and other disorders (Andreev-Drakhlin et al., 2020; Kohno et al., 2012).

5.1 RET-driven cancers

One of the primary therapeutic applications of RET inhibitors is in the treatment of RET-driven cancers. Several cancer types exhibit RET alterations, such as gene fusions, point

TABLE 13.3 A concise overview of the different ways RET inhibitors exert their therapeutic effects.

Mechanisms of action of RET inhibitors		
ATP competitive inhibition	RET inhibitors bind to the ATP-binding pocket within the catalytic domain of RET, preventing ATP binding and inhibiting autophosphorylation and activation of RET.	Vandetanib, cabozantinib
Allosteric inhibition	Some RET inhibitors bind to distinct sites outside the ATP-binding pocket, inducing conformational changes that impair RET autophosphorylation and downstream signaling.	BLU-667 (pralsetinib), LOXO-292 (selpercatinib)
Blockade of downstream signaling pathways	RET inhibitors inhibit downstream signaling pathways by reducing phosphorylation.	Vandetanib, cabozantinib
Induction of apoptosis	RET inhibitors cause cancer cell apoptosis by inhibiting aberrant signaling pathways.	BLU-667 (pralsetinib), LOXO-292 (selpercatinib)
Antiangiogenic effects	RET inhibitors inhibit blood vessel formation, preventing tumor angiogenesis and growth.	Vandetanib, cabozantinib

mutations, and amplifications, which result in constitutive activation of RET signaling (Huang et al., 2020; Kannaiyan & Mahadevan, 2018; Mologni, 2011). RET inhibitors have shown promising results in the following cancers:

Medullary Thyroid Cancer (MTC): RET inhibitors, such as vandetanib and cabozantinib, have demonstrated efficacy in advanced or metastatic MTC by inhibiting RET kinase activity and suppressing tumor growth (Santoro et al., 2020).

Nonsmall Cell Lung Cancer (NSCLC): Indeed, RET fusions have been found in a subgroup of patients with nonsmall cell lung cancer (NSCLC). The emergence of RET inhibitors, such as selpercatinib and pralsetinib, has demonstrated considerable clinical effectiveness in treating NSCLC patients with RET fusions. These targeted therapies have led to long-lasting and positive responses, offering new hope for patients with RET fusion-positive NSCLC.

Colorectal Cancer (CRC): RET alterations have been observed in a subset of CRC patients. RET inhibitors are being explored as a potential targeted therapy for this subgroup of patients, offering a new treatment option.

Neuroendocrine Tumors (NETs):

RET alterations, particularly gene fusions, have been identified in neuroendocrine tumors (NETs) arising in various organs. RET inhibitors have shown promise in the treatment of RET-altered NETs, providing a targeted therapeutic approach to inhibit RET-driven signaling and control tumor growth (Drilon et al., 2018b; Santoro et al., 2020).

5.2 Other RET-driven diseases

Beyond cancer, RET inhibitors hold potential therapeutic applications in other RET-driven diseases, including the following:

The MEN2 is a hereditary cancer syndrome caused by germline mutations in the RET gene. Specifically concerning MEN2-associated medullary thyroid carcinoma, RET inhibitors show promise as both preventive measures and treatment options. By directly targeting the abnormal RET signaling at the root of the condition, these inhibitors hold significant potential in effectively managing and controlling the development of medullary thyroid carcinoma in individuals with MEN2. This approach presents a valuable and hopeful therapeutic strategy for affected patients.

Familial Medullary Thyroid Carcinoma (FMTC): FMTC is another hereditary condition resulting from RET gene mutations. RET inhibitors offer targeted treatment options for FMTC patients with RET kinase-activating mutations (Drilon et al., 2018b; Santoro et al., 2020).

6. Resistance mechanisms and overcoming resistance to RET inhibitors

6.1 Resistance mechanisms

Treatment of RET-driven illnesses is still complicated by resistance to RET inhibitors. Optimizing the therapeutic potential of RET inhibitors requires a thorough understanding of the mechanisms behind resistance and the creation of countermeasures. Promising techniques to combat resistance, enhance treatment results, and extend the clinical benefits of RET inhibitors for patients include ongoing research, the development of next-generation inhibitors, rational medication combinations, and combinatorial approaches with immunotherapies (Lu & Zhou, 2021; Lin et al., 2020; Roskoski & Sadeghi-Nejad, 2018).

6.1.1 Secondary mutations in the RET kinase domain

Secondary mutations within the RET kinase domain can impair the binding of RET inhibitors, rendering them less effective. These mutations can alter the conformation of the kinase domain, preventing inhibitor binding or reducing the affinity of the inhibitor for the mutated RET protein (Knowles et al., 2006).

6.1.2 Activation of bypass pathways

Cancer cells can activate alternative signaling pathways to bypass the inhibition of RET. By utilizing parallel or compensatory signaling pathways, such as other receptor tyrosine kinases or downstream effectors, cancer cells can maintain survival and growth despite RET inhibition (Román-Gil et al., 2022).

6.1.3 Upregulation of efflux pumps

Cancer cells may upregulate ATP-binding cassette (ABC) transporters, such as P-glycoprotein, to actively pump out the RET inhibitors, thereby reducing intracellular drug concentration and limiting their efficacy.

6.1.4 Activation of survival pathways

In response to RET inhibition, cancer cells may adaptively activate survival pathways, such as the PI3K/AKT or MAPK/ERK pathways, to counteract the effects of RET inhibition and promote cell survival and proliferation. This adaptive activation of alternative pathways can lead to resistance by bypassing the inhibited RET signaling and sustaining cell growth (Román-Gil et al., 2022). Understanding and addressing these resistance mechanisms are crucial for improving the effectiveness of RET-targeted therapies in the treatment of RET-altered cancers.

6.2 Overcoming resistance

6.2.1 Development of next-generation RET inhibitors

Ongoing research and development endeavors are focused on the creation of next-generation RET inhibitors that can offer enhanced efficacy against resistant mutations. These advanced inhibitors are designed to tackle primary and secondary resistance mutations by targeting specific regions within the RET kinase domain, displaying superior potency compared to earlier inhibitors (Das et al., 2021; Du et al., 2021; Russo et al., 2020). These efforts represent a significant stride toward addressing the challenges of resistance and elevating the potential of RET-targeted therapies in the clinical management of various RET-altered cancers.

6.2.2 Combination therapies

Combining RET inhibitors with other targeted therapies or chemotherapy agents can help overcome resistance. Rational drug combinations that target alternative signaling pathways or downstream effectors can disrupt compensatory pathways and enhance therapeutic response (Chong & Jänne, 2013; Fürstenau & Eichhorst, 2021; Keller et al., 2017; Nijenhuis et al., 2013).

6.2.3 Dual inhibition of RET and bypass pathways

Combining RET inhibition with the simultaneous targeting of identified bypass pathways presents a promising strategy to prevent or overcome resistance in cancer treatment. This approach aims to disrupt multiple nodes within the signaling network, effectively blocking the escape routes that cancer cells may utilize to evade therapy. By deploying combination therapies, we can enhance the overall treatment response and potentially achieve more robust and sustained outcomes (Ezzat et al., 2005; Gild et al., 2023; Jin et al., 2009).

6.2.4 Combinatorial approaches with immunotherapies

The combination of RET inhibitors with immunotherapies, such as immune checkpoint inhibitors, holds the potential to boost the immune response against cancer cells. This strategy aims to leverage the immune system's capabilities to target and eliminate cancer cells that might evade the direct effects of RET inhibitors (Adashek et al., 2021; French, 2020; Galon & Bruni, 2019; Ott et al., 2017). By synergistically targeting both the molecular pathways and the immune response, this approach offers a promising avenue for enhancing the effectiveness of treatment in RET-altered cancers.

7. Future perspectives and challenges of RET inhibitors

The future of RET inhibitors holds significant promise in the treatment of various RET-altered diseases. Overcoming resistance, advancing precision medicine approaches, exploring combinatorial strategies, and addressing challenges related to safety, access, and affordability are key areas of focus. Continued research, collaboration among researchers and pharmaceutical companies, and the integration of emerging technologies will drive advancements in RET inhibitor therapy, ultimately improving patient outcomes and quality of life.

RET inhibitors have emerged as promising targeted therapies for various diseases driven by aberrant RET activation. As research and clinical experience with RET inhibitors continue to grow, several future perspectives and challenges are worth considering. This essay explores the potential future directions of RET inhibitors and highlights the challenges that need to be addressed for their widespread use and continued improvement.

7.1 Targeting resistance mechanisms

Overcoming resistance to RET inhibitors remains a significant challenge. Future research should focus on identifying and targeting specific resistance mechanisms, including secondary mutations, bypass pathways, and upregulated efflux pumps. Understanding the molecular basis of resistance will guide the development of novel inhibitors and combination therapies to enhance treatment response and extend patient survival (Chong & Jänne, 2013; Scalvini et al., 2021).

7.2 Precision medicine approaches

As our understanding of RET alterations expands, incorporating precision medicine approaches will become increasingly important. Genetic testing for RET alterations in patients will allow for personalized treatment strategies, enabling the selection of the most appropriate RET inhibitor based on the specific genetic profile of the patient's tumor. This approach can improve treatment outcomes and minimize unnecessary side effects (Fordham et al., 2021; Miyabayashi et al., 2021).

7.3 Combinatorial strategies

Combination therapies with RET inhibitors hold promise for maximizing treatment efficacy. Combinations with other targeted therapies, immunotherapies, or chemotherapy agents can enhance response rates and overcome resistance mechanisms. Identifying the optimal combinations and understanding their mechanisms of action will be key to developing effective treatment strategies (Boch et al., 2022; Lamberti et al., 2020; Zhong et al., 2021).

7.4 Pediatric applications

RET alterations are also significant in pediatric cancers, including MTC and neuroblastoma. To harness the therapeutic potential of RET inhibitors in pediatric patients, further investigations should be conducted. These studies should focus on optimizing dosing regimens and evaluating the long-term safety profiles of RET inhibitors in this specific population (Boch et al., 2022; Kiriakopoulos et al., 2022). By doing so, we can pave the way for more effective and safe treatments for young patients affected by these malignancies.

7.5 Biomarker discovery

Identification of reliable biomarkers for predicting response to RET inhibitors is essential. Biomarkers can aid in patient selection, treatment monitoring, and assessing treatment response. Exploring potential biomarkers, such as RET mutation status, gene expression signatures, or circulating tumor DNA, will enhance the precision and effectiveness of RET inhibitor therapy.

7.6 Resistance development

The development of acquired resistance remains a challenge in the long-term use of RET inhibitors. Continued research into resistance mechanisms and the development of strategies to overcome resistance are critical for maintaining treatment efficacy and extending patient survival (Hu et al., 2023).

7.7 Safety and tolerability

While RET inhibitors have shown clinical benefits, their safety profiles need to be further characterized. Monitoring and managing adverse effects, such as gastrointestinal toxicities or cardiovascular events, are essential to ensure the overall safety and tolerability of RET inhibitor therapy (Lin & Gainor, 2021).

7.8 Access and affordability

Ensuring equitable access to RET inhibitors for patients worldwide remains a challenge. Issues related to drug affordability, availability in certain regions, and reimbursement policies need to be addressed to maximize patient access to these potentially life-saving therapies (Lin & Gainor, 2021).

8. Conclusion

RET inhibitors have emerged as valuable targeted therapies for diseases driven by aberrant activation of the RET receptor tyrosine kinase. Through extensive research and clinical trials, these inhibitors have shown promising results in various cancers and other RET-altered diseases. Selective RET inhibitors offer advantages such as high selectivity, enhanced therapeutic efficacy, and reduced side effects compared to nonselective kinase inhibitors. They have demonstrated therapeutic applications in RET-driven cancers, including medullary thyroid carcinoma, nonsmall cell lung cancer, and colorectal cancer, as well as other RET-altered diseases such as neuroendocrine tumors and familial cancer syndromes. The future of RET inhibitors lies in targeting resistance mechanisms, advancing precision medicine approaches, exploring combinatorial strategies, and addressing challenges related to safety, access, and affordability. Continued research and collaboration among scientists, clinicians, and pharmaceutical companies are vital for further improving the efficacy, safety, and availability of RET inhibitors. Additionally, ongoing efforts to identify biomarkers, optimize dosing regimens, and expand applications to pediatric patients will contribute to the continued progress in this field. In conclusion, RET inhibitors represent a significant advancement in targeted therapy for RET-altered diseases, holding great potential to transform the treatment landscape and improve outcomes for affected patients.

References

Adashek, J. J., Desai, A. P., Andreev-Drakhlin, A. Y., Roszik, J., Cote, G. J., & Subbiah, V. (2021). Hallmarks of RET and co-occurring genomic alterations in RET-aberrant cancers. *Molecular Cancer Therapeutics, 20*(10), 1769–1776. https://doi.org/10.1158/1535-7163.MCT-21-0329

Alberti, L., Borrello, M. G., Ghizzoni, S., Torriti, F., Rizzetti, M. G., & Pierotti, M. A. (1998). Grb2 binding to the different isoforms of Ret tyrosine kinase. *Oncogene, 17*(9), 1079–1087. https://doi.org/10.1038/sj.onc.1202046

Amit, M., Na'ara, S., Fridman, E., Vladovski, E., Wasserman, T., Milman, N., & Gil, Z. (2019). RET, a targetable driver of pancreatic adenocarcinoma. *International Journal of Cancer, 144*(12), 3014–3022. https://doi.org/10.1002/ijc.32040

Amit, M., Na'Ara, S., Leider-Trejo, L., Binenbaum, Y., Kulish, N., Fridman, E., Shabtai-Orbach, A., Wong, R. J., & Gil, Z. (2017). Upregulation of RET induces perineurial invasion of pancreatic adenocarcinoma. *Oncogene, 36*(23), 3232–3239. https://doi.org/10.1038/onc.2016.483

Anderson, D. J. (1993). Molecular control of cell fate in the neural crest: The sympathoadrenal lineage. *Annual Review of Neuroscience, 16*(1), 129–158. https://doi.org/10.1146/annurev.ne.16.030193.001021

Andreev-Drakhlin, A., Cabanillas, M., Amini, B., & Subbiah, V. (2020). Systemic and CNS activity of selective RET inhibition with selpercatinib (LOXO-292) in a patient with RET-mutant medullary thyroid cancer with extensive CNS metastases. *JCO Precision Oncology, 4*(4), 1302–1306. https://doi.org/10.1200/po.20.00096

Andreucci, E., Francica, P., Fearns, A., Martin, L. A., Chiarugi, P., Isacke, C. M., & Morandi, A. (2016). Targeting the receptor tyrosine kinase RET in combination with aromatase inhibitors in ER positive breast cancer xenografts. *Oncotarget, 7*(49), 80543–80553. https://doi.org/10.18632/oncotarget.11826

Arlt, D. H., Baur, B., Wagner, B., & Höppner, W. (2000). A novel type of mutation in the cysteine rich domain of the RET receptor causes ligand independent activation. *Oncogene, 19*(30), 3445–3448. https://doi.org/10.1038/sj.onc.1203688

Arora, S., Balasubramaniam, S., Zhang, W., Zhang, L., Sridhara, R., Spillman, D., Mathai, J. P., Scott, B., Golding, S. J., Coory, M., Pazdur, R., & Beaver, J. A. (2020). FDA approval summary: Pembrolizumab plus lenvatinib for endometrial carcinoma, a collaborative international review under project orbis. *Clinical Cancer Research, 26*(19), 5062–5067. https://doi.org/10.1158/1078-0432.CCR-19-3979

Asai, N., Iwashita, T., Matsuyama, M., & Takahashi, M. (1995). Mechanism of activation of the ret proto-oncogene by multiple endocrine neoplasia 2A mutations. *Molecular and Cellular Biology, 15*(3), 1613–1619. https://doi.org/10.1128/mcb.15.3.1613

Asai, N., Murakami, H., Iwashita, T., & Takahashi, M. (1996). A mutation at tyrosine 1062 in MEN2A-ret and MEN2B-ret impairs their transforming activity and association with shc adaptor proteins. *Journal of Biological Chemistry, 271*(30), 17644–17649. https://doi.org/10.1074/jbc.271.30.17644

Ashkboos, M., Nikbakht, M., Zarinfard, G., & Soleimani, M. (2021). Ret protein expression in colorectal cancer; an immunohistochemical assessment. *Asian Pacific Journal of Cancer Prevention, 22*(4), 1019–1023. https://doi.org/10.31557/APJCP.2021.22.4.1019

Avantaggiato, V., Dathan, N. A., Grieco, M., Fabien, N., Lazzaro, D., Fusco, A., Simeone, A., & Santoro, M. (1994). Developmental expression of the RET protooncogene. *Cell Growth & Differentiation, 5*(3), 305–311.

Ban, K., Feng, S., Shao, L., & Ittmann, M. (2017). RET signaling in prostate cancer. *Clinical Cancer Research, 23*(16), 4885–4896. https://doi.org/10.1158/1078-0432.CCR-17-0528

Bhattacharya, S., Asati, V., Ali, A., Ali, A., & Gupta, G. D. (2022). In-silico studies for the development of novel RET inhibitors for cancer treatment. *Journal of Molecular Structure, 1251*. https://doi.org/10.1016/j.molstruc.2021.132040

Bishop, J. A., Nakaguro, M., Whaley, R. D., Ogura, K., Imai, H., Laklouk, I., Faquin, W. C., Sadow, P. M., Gagan, J., & Nagao, T. (2021). Oncocytic intraductal carcinoma of salivary glands: A distinct variant with TRIM33–RET fusions and BRAF V600E mutations. *Histopathology, 79*(3), 338–346. https://doi.org/10.1111/his.14296

Boch, T., Köhler, J., Janning, M., & Loges, S. (2022). Targeting the EGF receptor family in non-small cell lung cancer— increased complexity and future perspectives. *Cancer Biology & Medicine, 19*(11), 1543–1564. https://doi.org/10.20892/j.issn.2095-3941.2022.0540

Bongarzone, I., Monzini, N., Borrello, M. G., Carcano, C., Ferraresi, G., Arighi, E., Mondellini, P., Della Porta, G., & Pierotti, M. A. (1993). Molecular characterization of a thyroid tumor-specific transforming sequence formed by the fusion of ret tyrosine kinase and the regulatory subunit RI alpha of cyclic AMP-dependent protein kinase A. *Molecular and Cellular Biology, 13*(1), 358–366. https://doi.org/10.1128/MCB.13.1.358

Borrello, M. G., Alberti, L., Arighi, E., Bongarzone, I., Battistini, C., Bardelli, A., Pasini, B., Piutti, C., Rizzetti, M. G., Mondellini, P., Radice, M. T., & Pierotti, M. A. (1996). The full oncogenic activity of Ret/ptc2 depends on tyrosine 539, a docking site for phospholipase Cγ. *Molecular and Cellular Biology, 16*(5), 2151–2163. https://doi.org/10.1128/mcb.16.5.2151

Bostwick, D. G., & Qian, J. (2004). High-grade prostatic intraepithelial neoplasia. *Modern Pathology, 17*(3), 360–379. https://doi.org/10.1038/modpathol.3800053

Boulay, A., Breuleux, M., Stephan, C., Fux, C., Brisken, C., Fiche, M., Wartmann, M., Stumm, M., Lane, H. A., & Hynes, N. E. (2008). The ret receptor tyrosine kinase pathway functionally interacts with the ERα pathway in breast cancer. *Cancer Research, 68*(10), 3743–3751. https://doi.org/10.1158/0008-5472.CAN-07-5100

Bounacer, A., Wicker, R., Caillou, B., Cailleux, A. F., Sarasin, A., Schlumberger, M., & Suárez, H. G. (1997). High prevalence of activating ret proto-oncogene rearrangements, in thyroid tumors from patients who had received external radiation. *Oncogene, 15*(11), 1263–1273. https://doi.org/10.1038/sj.onc.1200206

Bradford, D., Larkins, E., Mushti, S. L., Rodriguez, L., Skinner, A. M., Helms, W. S., Lauren, S. L. P., Zirkelbach, J. F., Li, Y., Liu, J., Charlab, R., Turcu, F. R., Liang, D., Ghosh, S., Roscoe, D., Philip, R., Zack-Taylor, A., Tang, S.,

Kluetz, P. G., … Singh, H. (2021). Fda approval summary: Selpercatinib for the treatment of lung and thyroid cancers with ret gene mutations or fusions. *Clinical Cancer Research, 27*(8), 2130–2135. https://doi.org/10.1158/1078-0432.CCR-20-3558

Branzk, N., Gronke, K., & Diefenbach, A. (2018). Innate lymphoid cells, mediators of tissue homeostasis, adaptation and disease tolerance. *Immunological Reviews, 286*(1), 86–101. https://doi.org/10.1111/imr.12718

Cabanillas, M. E., McFadden, D. G., & Durante, C. (2016). Thyroid cancer. *The Lancet, 388*(10061), 2783–2795. https://doi.org/10.1016/S0140-6736(16)30172-6

Carlomagno, F., Guida, T., Anaganti, S., Vecchio, G., Fusco, A., Ryan, A. J., Billaud, M., & Santoro, M. (2004). Disease associated mutations at valine 804 in the RET receptor tyrosine kinase confer resistance to selective kinase inhibitors. *Oncogene, 23*(36), 6056–6063. https://doi.org/10.1038/sj.onc.1207810

Carlson, K. M., Dou, S., Chi, D., Scavarda, N., Toshima, K., Jackson, C. E., Wells, S. A., Goodfellow, P. J., & Donis-Keller, H. (1994). Single missense mutation in the tyrosine kinasecatalytic domain of the RET protooncogene is associated with multiple endocrineneoplasia type 2B. *Proceedings of the National Academy of Sciences, 91*(4), 1579–1583. https://doi.org/10.1073/pnas.91.4.1579

Cascetta, P., Sforza, V., Manzo, A., Carillio, G., Palumbo, G., Esposito, G., Montanino, A., Costanzo, R., Sandomenico, C., De Cecio, R., Piccirillo, M. C., La Manna, C., Totaro, G., Muto, P., Picone, C., Bianco, R., Normanno, N., & Morabito, A. (2021). RET inhibitors in non-small-cell lung cancer. *Cancers, 13*(17). https://doi.org/10.3390/cancers13174415

Cavel, O., Shomron, O., Shabtay, A., Vital, J., Trejo-Leider, L., Weizman, N., Krelin, Y., Fong, Y., Wong, R. J., Amit, M., & Gil, Z. (2012). Endoneurial macrophages induce perineural invasion of pancreatic cancer cells by secretion of GDNF and activation of RET tyrosine kinase receptor. *Cancer Research, 72*(22), 5733–5743. https://doi.org/10.1158/0008-5472.CAN-12-0764

Cerami, E., Gao, J., Dogrusoz, U., Gross, B. E., Sumer, S. O., Aksoy, B. A., Jacobsen, A., Byrne, C. J., Heuer, M. L., Larsson, E., Antipin, Y., Reva, B., Goldberg, A. P., Sander, C., & Schultz, N. (2012). The cBio Cancer Genomics Portal: An open platform for exploring multidimensional cancer genomics data. *Cancer Discovery, 2*(5), 401–404. https://doi.org/10.1158/2159-8290.CD-12-0095

Cervantes, A., Adam, R., Roselló, S., Arnold, D., Normanno, N., Taïeb, J., Seligmann, J., De Baere, T., Osterlund, P., Yoshino, T., & Martinelli, E. (2023). Metastatic colorectal cancer: ESMO clinical practice guideline for diagnosis, treatment and follow-up ☆. *Annals of Oncology, 34*(1), 10–32. https://doi.org/10.1016/j.annonc.2022.10.003

Ceyhan, G. O., Giese, N. A., Erkan, M., Kerscher, A. G., Wente, M. N., Giese, T., Büchler, M. W., & Friess, H. (2006). The neurotrophic factor artemin promotes pancreatic cancer invasion. *Annals of Surgery, 244*(2), 274–281. https://doi.org/10.1097/01.sla.0000217642.68697.55

Chen, W., Hoffmann, A. D., Liu, H., & Liu, X. (2018). Organotropism: New insights into molecular mechanisms of breast cancer metastasis. *Npj Precision Oncology, 2*(1). https://doi.org/10.1038/s41698-018-0047-0

Chen, Z., Zhao, Y., Yu, Y., Pang, J. C., Woodfield, S. E., Tao, L., Guan, S., Zhang, H., Bieerkehazhi, S., Shi, Y., Patel, R., Vasudevan, S. A., Yi, J. S., Muscal, J. A., Xu, G. T., & Yang, J. (2017). Small molecule inhibitor regorafenib inhibits RET signaling in neuroblastoma cells and effectively suppresses tumor growth in vivo. *Oncotarget, 8*(61), 104090–104103. https://doi.org/10.18632/oncotarget.22011

Chi, X., Michos, O., Shakya, R., Riccio, P., Enomoto, H., Licht, J. D., Asai, N., Takahashi, M., Ohgami, N., Kato, M., Mendelsohn, C., & Costantini, F. (2009). Ret-dependent cell rearrangements in the Wolffian duct epithelium initiate ureteric bud morphogenesis. *Developmental Cell, 17*(2), 199–209. https://doi.org/10.1016/j.devcel.2009.07.013

Chong, C. R., & Jänne, P. A. (2013). The quest to overcome resistance to EGFR-targeted therapies in cancer. *Nature Medicine, 19*(11), 1389–1400. https://doi.org/10.1038/nm.3388

Choueiri, T. K., Pal, S. K., McDermott, D. F., Morrissey, S., Ferguson, K. C., Holland, J., Kaelin, W. G., & Dutcher, J. P. (2014). A phase I study of cabozantinib (XL184) in patients with renal cell cancer. *Annals of Oncology, 25*(8), 1603–1608. https://doi.org/10.1093/annonc/mdu184

Ciardiello, F., Bianco, R., Caputo, R., Caputo, R., Damiano, V., Troiani, T., Melisi, D., De Vita, F., De Placido, S., Bianco, A. R., & Tortora, G. (2004). Antitumor activity of ZD6474, a vascular endothelial growth factor receptor tyrosine kinase inhibitor, in human cancer cells with acquired resistance to Antiepidermal growth factor receptor therapy. *Clinical Cancer Research, 10*(2), 784–793. https://doi.org/10.1158/1078-0432.CCR-1100-03

Clarke, R., Tyson, J. J., & Dixon, J. M. (2015). Endocrine resistance in breast cancer—an overview and update. *Molecular and Cellular Endocrinology, 418*, 220–234. https://doi.org/10.1016/j.mce.2015.09.035

Das, D., Wang, J., & Hong, J. (2021). Next-generation kinase inhibitors targeting specific biomarkers in non-small cell lung cancer (NSCLC): A recent overview. *ChemMedChem, 16*(16), 2459–2479. https://doi.org/10.1002/cmdc.202100166

Dawson, D. M., Lawrence, E. G., MacLennan, G. T., Amini, S. B., Kung, H. J., Robinson, D., Resnick, M. I., Kursh, E. D., Pretlow, T. P., & Pretlow, T. G. (1998). Altered expression of RET proto-oncogene product in prostatic intraepithelial neoplasia and prostate cancer. *Journal of the National Cancer Institute, 90*(7), 519–523. https://doi.org/10.1093/jnci/90.7.519

Deeks, E. D., & Keating, G. M. (2006). Sunitinib. *Drugs, 66*(17), 2255–2266. https://doi.org/10.2165/00003495-200666170-00007

Delgado, R., Klimstra, D., & Albores-Saavedra, J. (1996). Low grade salivary duct carcinoma: A distinctive variant with a low grade histology and a predominant intraductal growth pattern. *Cancer, 78*(5), 958–967. https://doi.org/10.1002/(SICI)1097-0142(19960901)78:5<958::AID-CNCR4>3.0.CO;2-8

Delgado, R., Vuitch, F., & Albores-Saavedra, J. (1993). Salivary duct carcinoma. *Cancer, 72*(5), 1503–1512. https://doi.org/10.1002/1097-0142(19930901)72:5<1503::aid-cncr2820720503>3.0.co;2-k

Dixit, A., Torkamani, A., Schork, N. J., & Verkhivker, G. (2009). Computational modeling of structurally conserved cancer mutations in the RET and MET kinases: The impact on protein structure, dynamics, and stability. *Biophysical Journal, 96*(3), 858–874. https://doi.org/10.1016/j.bpj.2008.10.041

Donis-keller, H., Dou, S., Chi, D., Carlson, K. M., Toshima, K., Lairmore, T. C., Howe, J. R., Moley, J. F., Goodfellow, P., & Wells, S. A. (1993). Mutations in the RET proto-oncogene are associated with MEN 2a and FMTC. *Human Molecular Genetics, 2*(7), 851–856. https://doi.org/10.1093/hmg/2.7.851

Drilon, A., Fu, S., Patel, M. R., Fakih, M., Wang, D., Olszanski, A. J., Morgensztern, D., Liu, S. V., Cho, B. C., Bazhenova, L., Rodriguez, C. P., Doebele, R. C., Wozniak, A., Reckamp, K. L., Seery, T., Nikolinakos, P., Hu, Z., Oliver, J. W., Trone, D., … Ahn, M. J. (2019). A phase I/IB trial of the vegfr-sparing multikinase ret inhibitor RXDX-105. *Cancer Discovery, 9*(3), 384–395. https://doi.org/10.1158/2159-8290.CD-18-0839

Drilon, A., Lin, J. J., Filleron, T., Ni, A., Milia, J., Bergagnini, I., Hatzoglou, V., Velcheti, V., Offin, M., Li, B., Carbone, D. P., Besse, B., Mok, T., Awad, M. M., Wolf, J., Owen, D., Camidge, D. R., Riely, G. J., Peled, N., & Gautschi, O. (2018a). Frequency of brain metastases and multikinase inhibitor outcomes in patients with RET–rearranged lung cancers. *Journal of Thoracic Oncology, 13*(10), 1595–1601. https://doi.org/10.1016/j.jtho.2018.07.004

Drilon, A., Hu, Z. I., Lai, G. G. Y., & Tan, D. S. W. (2018b). Targeting ret-driven cancers: Lessons from evolving preclinical and clinical landscapes. *Nature Reviews Clinical Oncology, 15*(3), 151–167. https://doi.org/10.1038/nrclinonc.2017.175

Drilon, A., Rekhtman, N., Arcila, M., Wang, L., Ni, A., Albano, M., Van Voorthuysen, M., Somwar, R., Smith, R. S., Montecalvo, J., Plodkowski, A., Ginsberg, M. S., Riely, G. J., Rudin, C. M., Ladanyi, M., & Kris, M. G. (2016). Cabozantinib in patients with advanced RET-rearranged non-small-cell lung cancer: An open-label, single-centre, phase 2, single-arm trial. *The Lancet Oncology, 17*(12), 1653–1660. https://doi.org/10.1016/S1470-2045(16)30562-9

Drilon, A., Wang, L., Hasanovic, A., Suehara, Y., Lipson, D., Stephens, P., Ross, J., Miller, V., Ginsberg, M., Zakowski, M. F., Kris, M. G., Ladanyi, M., & Rizvi, N. (2013). Response to cabozantinib in patients with RET fusion-positive lung adenocarcinomas. *Cancer Discovery, 3*(6), 630–635. https://doi.org/10.1158/2159-8290.CD-13-0035

Du, X., Yang, B., An, Q., Assaraf, Y. G., Cao, X., & Xia, J. (2021). Acquired resistance to third-generation EGFR-TKIs and emerging next-generation EGFR inhibitors. *Innovation, 2*(2). https://doi.org/10.1016/j.xinn.2021.100103

Durbec, P. L., Larsson-Blomberg, L. B., Schuchardt, A., Costantini, F., & Pachnis, V. (1996). Common origin and developmental dependence on c-ret of subsets of enteric and sympathetic neuroblasts. *Development, 122*(1), 349–358.

Eisen, T., Joensuu, H., Nathan, P. D., Harper, P. G., Wojtukiewicz, M. Z., Nicholson, S., Bahl, A., Tomczak, P., Pyrhonen, S., Fife, K., Bono, P., Boxall, J., Wagner, A., Jeffers, M., Lin, T., & Quinn, D. I. (2012). Regorafenib for patients with previously untreated metastatic or unresectable renal-cell carcinoma: A single-group phase 2 trial. *The Lancet Oncology, 13*(10), 1055–1062. https://doi.org/10.1016/S1470-2045(12)70364-9

Encinas, M., Crowder, R. J., Milbrandt, J., & Johnson, E. M. (2004). Tyrosine 981, a novel ret autophosphorylation site, binds c-src to mediate neuronal survival. *Journal of Biological Chemistry, 279*(18), 18262–18269. https://doi.org/10.1074/jbc.M400505200

Esseghir, S., Todd, S. K., Hunt, T., Poulsom, R., Plaza-Menacho, I., Reis-Filho, J. S., & Isacke, C. M. (2007). A role for glial cell-derived neurotrophic factor-induced expression by inflammatory cytokines and RET/GFRα1 receptor up-regulation in breast cancer. *Cancer Research, 67*(24), 11732–11741. https://doi.org/10.1158/0008-5472.CAN-07-2343

Ezzat, S., Huang, P., Dackiw, A., & Asa, S. L. (2005). Dual inhibition of RET and FGFR4 restrains medullary thyroid cancer cell growth. *Clinical Cancer Research, 11*(3), 1336–1341.

Fisch, A. S., Laklouk, I., Nakaguro, M., Nosé, V., Wirth, L. J., Deschler, D. G., Faquin, W. C., Dias-Santagata, D., & Sadow, P. M. (2021). Intraductal carcinoma of the salivary gland with NCOA4-RET: Expanding the morphologic spectrum and an algorithmic diagnostic approach. *Human Pathology, 114*, 74–89. https://doi.org/10.1016/j.humpath.2021.05.004

Fürstenau, M., & Eichhorst, B. (2021). Novel agents in chronic Lymphocytic leukemia: New combination therapies and strategies to overcome resistance. *Cancers, 13*(6). https://doi.org/10.3390/cancers13061336

Fordham, A. M., Ekert, P. G., & Fleuren, E. D. G. (2021). Precision medicine and phosphoproteomics for the identification of novel targeted therapeutic avenues in sarcomas. *Biochimica et Biophysica Acta - Reviews on Cancer, 1876*(2). https://doi.org/10.1016/j.bbcan.2021.188613

French, J. D. (2020). Immunotherapy for advanced thyroid cancers—rationale, current advances and future strategies. *Nature Reviews Endocrinology, 16*(11), 629–641. https://doi.org/10.1038/s41574-020-0398-9

Fusco, A., Butti, M. G., Coronelli, S., Borrello, M. G., Mondellini, P., Porta, G. D., & Pierotti, M. A. (1994). Frequent activation of ret protooncogene by fusion with a new activating gene in papillary thyroid carcinomas. *Cancer Research, 54*(11), 2979–2985.

Fusco, A., Grieco, M., Santoro, M., Berlingieri, M. T., Pilotti, S., Pierotti, M. A., Porta, G. D., & Vecchio, G. (1987). A new oncogene in human thyroid papillary carcinomas and their lymph-nodal metastases. *Nature, 328*(6126), 170–172. https://doi.org/10.1038/328170a0

Galon, J., & Bruni, D. (2019). Approaches to treat immune hot, altered and cold tumours with combination immunotherapies. *Nature Reviews Drug Discovery, 18*(3), 197–218. https://doi.org/10.1038/s41573-018-0007-y

Gao, J., Aksoy, B. A., Dogrusoz, U., Dresdner, G., Gross, B., Sumer, S. O., Sun, Y., Jacobsen, A., Sinha, R., Larsson, E., Cerami, E., Sander, C., & Schultz, N. (2013). Integrative analysis of complex cancer genomics and clinical profiles using the cBioPortal. *Science Signaling, 6*(269). https://doi.org/10.1126/scisignal.2004088

Gardaneh, M., Shojaei, S., Kaviani, A., & Behnam, B. (2017). GDNF induces RET–SRC–HER2-dependent growth in trastuzumab-sensitive but SRC-independent growth in resistant breast tumor cells. *Breast Cancer Research and Treatment, 162*(2), 231–241. https://doi.org/10.1007/s10549-016-4078-3

Garuti, L., Roberti, M., & Bottegoni, G. (2015). Multi-kinase inhibitors. *Current Medicinal Chemistry, 22*(6), 695–712. https://doi.org/10.2174/0929867321666141216125528

Gattelli, A., Nalvarte, I., Boulay, A., Roloff, T. C., Schreiber, M., Carragher, N., Macleod, K. K., Schlederer, M., Lienhard, S., Kenner, L., Torres-Arzayus, M. I., & Hynes, N. E. (2013). Ret inhibition decreases growth and metastatic potential of estrogen receptor positive breast cancer cells. *EMBO Molecular Medicine, 5*(9), 1335–1350. https://doi.org/10.1002/emmm.201302625

George, S., Wang, Q., Heinrich, M. C., Corless, C. L., Zhu, M., Butrynski, J. E., Morgan, J. A., Wagner, A. J., Choy, E., Tap, W. D., Yap, J. T., Van Den Abbeele, A. D., Manola, J. B., Solomon, S. M., Fletcher, J. A., Von Mehren, M., & Demetri, G. D. (2012). Efficacy and safety of regorafenib in patients with metastatic and/or unresectable GI stromal tumor after failure of imatinib and sunitinib: A multicenter phase II trial. *Journal of Clinical Oncology, 30*(19), 2401–2407. https://doi.org/10.1200/JCO.2011.39.9394

Gild, M. L., Bullock, M., Tsang, V., Clifton-Bligh, R. J., Robinson, B. G., & Wirth, L. J. (2023). Challenges and strategies to combat resistance mechanisms in thyroid cancer therapeutics. *Thyroid, 33*(6), 682–690. https://doi.org/10.1089/thy.2022.0704

Gimm, O., Marsh, D. J., Andrew, S. D., Frilling, A., Dahia, P. L. M., Mulligan, L. M., Zajac, J. D., Robinson, B. G., & Eng, C. (1997). Germline dinucleotide mutation in codon 883 of the RET proto-oncogene in multiple endocrine neoplasia type 2B without codon 918 mutation. *Journal of Clinical Endocrinology and Metabolism, 82*(11), 3902–3904. https://doi.org/10.1210/jcem.82.11.4508

Giovacchini, F., Bensi, C., Belli, S., Laurenti, M. E., Mandarano, M., Paradiso, D., Giansanti, M., & Tullio, A. (2019). Low-grade intraductal carcinoma of salivary glands: A systematic review of this rare entity. *Journal of Oral Biology and Craniofacial Research, 9*(1), 96–110. https://doi.org/10.1016/j.jobcr.2018.11.003

Glen, H., Mason, S., Patel, H., Macleod, K., & Brunton, V. G. (2011). E7080, a multi-targeted tyrosine kinase inhibitor suppresses tumor cell migration and invasion. *BMC Cancer, 11.* https://doi.org/10.1186/1471-2407-11-309

Gouda, M. A., & Subbiah, V. (2023). Precision oncology with selective RET inhibitor selpercatinib in RET-rearranged cancers. *Therapeutic Advances in Medical Oncology, 15.* https://doi.org/10.1177/17588359231177015

Grüllich, C. (2018). Cabozantinib: Multi-kinase inhibitor of MET, AXL, RET, and VEGFR2. *Recent Results in Cancer Research, 211,* 67–75. https://doi.org/10.1007/978-3-319-91442-8_5

Grieco, M., Santoro, M., Berlingieri, M. T., Melillo, R. M., Donghi, R., Bongarzone, I., Pierotti, M. A., Della Ports, G., Fusco, A., & Vecchiot, G. (1990). PTC is a novel rearranged form of the ret proto-oncogene and is frequently detected in vivo in human thyroid papillary carcinomas. *Cell, 60*(4), 557–563. https://doi.org/10.1016/0092-8674(90)90659-3

Guan, L., Li, Z., Xie, F., Pang, Y., Zhang, C., Tang, H., Zhang, H., Chen, C., Zhan, Y., Zhao, T., Jiang, H., Jia, X., Wang, Y., & Lu, Y. (2020). Oncogenic and drug-sensitive RET mutations in human epithelial ovarian cancer. *Journal of Experimental & Clinical Cancer Research, 39*(1). https://doi.org/10.1186/s13046-020-01557-3

Gujral, T. S., Singh, V. K., Jia, Z., & Mulligan, L. M. (2006). Molecular mechanisms of RET receptor-mediated oncogenesis in multiple endocrine neoplasia 2B. *Cancer Research, 66*(22), 10741–10749. https://doi.org/10.1158/0008-5472.CAN-06-3329

Hanamura, T., & Hayashi, S.i. (2018). Overcoming aromatase inhibitor resistance in breast cancer: Possible mechanisms and clinical applications. *Breast Cancer, 25*(4), 379–391. https://doi.org/10.1007/s12282-017-0772-1

Hatem, R., Labiod, D., Château-Joubert, S., De Plater, L., El Botty, R., Vacher, S., Bonin, F., Servely, J. L., Dieras, V., Bièche, I., & Marangoni, E. (2016). Vandetanib as a potential new treatment for estrogen receptor-negative breast cancers. *International Journal of Cancer, 138*(10), 2510–2521. https://doi.org/10.1002/ijc.29974

He, S., Chen, C.-H., Chernichenko, N., He, S., Bakst, R. L., Barajas, F., Deborde, S., Allen, P. J., Vakiani, E., Yu, Z., & Wong, R. J. (2014). GFRα1 released by nerves enhances cancer cell perineural invasion through GDNF-RET signaling. *Proceedings of the National Academy of Sciences, 111*(19). https://doi.org/10.1073/pnas.1402944111

Henderson, Y. C., Ann, S. H., Kang, Y., & Clayman, G. L. (2008). Sorafenib potently inhibits papillary thyroid carcinomas harboring RET/PTC1 rearrangement. *Clinical Cancer Research, 14*(15). https://doi.org/10.1158/1078-0432.CCR-07-1772

Hennequin, L. F., Stokes, E. S. E., Thomas, A. P., Johnstone, C., Plé, P. A., Ogilvie, D. J., Dukes, M., Wedge, S. R., Kendrew, J., & Curwen, J. O. (2002). Novel 4-anilinoquinazolines with C-7 basic side chains: Design and structure activity relationship of a series of potent, orally active, VEGF receptor tyrosine kinase inhibitors. *Journal of Medicinal Chemistry, 45*(6), 1300–1312. https://doi.org/10.1021/jm011022e

Hewett, Y., Ghimire, S., Farooqi, B., & Shah, B. K. (2018). Lenvatinib—a multikinase inhibitor for radioiodine-refractory differentiated thyroid cancer. *Journal of Oncology Pharmacy Practice, 24*(1), 28–32. https://doi.org/10.1177/1078155216680119

Hofstra, R. M. W., Landsvater, R. M., Ceccherini, I., Stulp, R. P., Stelwagen, T., Luo, Y., Pasini, B., Hoppener, J. W. M., Van Amstel, H. K. P., Romeo, G., Lips, C. J. M., & Buys, C. H. C. M. (1994). A mutation in the RET proto-oncogene associated with multiple endocrine neoplasia type 2B and sporadic medullary thyroid carcinoma. *Nature, 367*(6461), 375–376. https://doi.org/10.1038/367375a0

Horiike, A., Takeuchi, K., Uenami, T., Kawano, Y., Tanimoto, A., Kaburaki, K., Tambo, Y., Kudo, K., Yanagitani, N., Ohyanagi, F., Motoi, N., Ishikawa, Y., Horai, T., & Nishio, M. (2016). Sorafenib treatment for patients with RET fusion-positive non-small cell lung cancer. *Lung Cancer, 93,* 43–46. https://doi.org/10.1016/j.lungcan.2015.12.011

Hu, X., Khatri, U., Shen, T., & Wu, J. (2023). Progress and challenges in RET-targeted cancer therapy. *Frontiers of Medicine, 17*(2), 207–219. https://doi.org/10.1007/s11684-023-0985-y

Huang, L., Jiang, S., & Shi, Y. (2020). Tyrosine kinase inhibitors for solid tumors in the past 20 years (2001–2020). *Journal of Hematology & Oncology, 13*(1). https://doi.org/10.1186/s13045-020-00977-0

Ibáñez, C. F. (2013). Structure and physiology of the RET receptor tyrosine kinase. *Cold Spring Harbor Perspectives in Biology, 5*(2). https://doi.org/10.1101/cshperspect.a009134

Ignatiadis, M., & Sotiriou, C. (2013). Luminal breast cancer: From biology to treatment. *Nature Reviews Clinical Oncology, 10*(9), 494–506. https://doi.org/10.1038/nrclinonc.2013.124

Ishizaka, Y., Shima, H., Sugimura, T., & Nagao, M. (1992). Detection of phosphorylated ret(TPC) oncogene product in cytoplasm. *Oncogene, 7*(7), 1441–1444.

Ishizaka, Y., Tahira, T., Ochiai, M., Ikeda, I., Sugimura, T., & Nagao, M. (1988). Molecular cloning and characterization of human ret-II oncogene. *Oncogene Research, 3*(2), 193–197.

Ishizaki, Y., Ochiai, M., Tahira, T., Sugimura, T., & Nagao, M. (1989a). Activation of the ret-II oncogene without a sequence encoding a transmembrane domain and transforming activity of two ret-II oncogene products differing in carboxy-termini due to alternative splicing. *Oncogene, 4*(6), 789−794.

Ishizaka, Y., Itoh, F., Tahira, T., Ikeda, I., Ogura, T., Sugimura, T., & Nagao, M. (1989b). Presence of aberrant transcripts of ret proto-oncogene in a human papillary thyroid carcinoma cell line. *Japanese Journal of Cancer Research, 80*(12), 1149−1152. https://doi.org/10.1111/j.1349-7006.1989.tb01645.x

Ito, T., Seyama, T., Iwamoto, K. S., Hayashi, T., Mizuno, T., Tsuyama, N., Dohi, K., Nakamura, N., & Akiyama, M. (1993). In vitro irradiation is able to cause RET oncogene rearrangement. *Cancer Research, 53*(13), 2940−2943.

Iwashita, T., Asai, N., Murakami, H., Matsuyama, M., & Takahashi, M. (1996). Identification of tyrosine residues that are essential for transforming activity of the ret proto-oncogene with MEN2A or MEN2B mutation. *Oncogene, 12*(3), 481−487.

Iwashita, T., Kato, M., Murakami, H., Asai, N., Ishiguro, Y., Ito, S., Iwata, Y., Kawai, K., Asai, M., Kurokawa, K., Kajita, H., & Takahashi, M. (1999). Biological and biochemical properties of Ret with kinase domain mutations identified in multiple endocrine neoplasia type 2B and familial medullary thyroid carcinoma. *Oncogene, 18*(26), 3919−3922. https://doi.org/10.1038/sj.onc.1202742

Jain, S., Naughton, C. K., Yang, M., Strickland, A., Vij, K., Encinas, M., Golden, J., Gupta, A., Heuckeroth, R., Johnson, E. M., & Milbrandt, J. (2004). Mice expressing a dominant-negative Ret mutation phenocopy human Hirschsprung disease and delineate a direct role of Ret in spermatogenesis. *Development, 131*(21), 5503−5513. https://doi.org/10.1242/dev.01421

Jeong, W.-J., Mo, J.-H., Park, M. W., Choi, I. J., An, S.-Y., Jeon, E.-H., & Ahn, S.-H. (2014). Sunitinib inhibits papillary thyroid carcinoma with RET/PTC rearrangement but not BRAF mutation. *Cancer Biology & Therapy, 12*(5), 458−465. https://doi.org/10.4161/cbt.12.5.16303

Jhiang, S. M., Sagartz, J. E., Tong, Q., Parker-thornburg, J., Capen, C. C., Cho, J. Y., Xing, S., & Ledent, C. (1996). Targeted expression of the ret/PTC1 oncogene induces papillary thyroid carcinomas. *Endocrinology, 137*(1), 375−378. https://doi.org/10.1210/endo.137.1.8536638

Jhiang, S. M., Smanik, P. A., & Mazzaferri, E. L. (1994). Development of a single-step duplex RT-PCR detecting different forms of ret activation, and identification of the third form of in vivo ret activation in human papillary thyroid carcinoma. *Cancer Letters, 78*(1−3), 69−76. https://doi.org/10.1016/0304-3835(94)90033-7

Jiang, Y., Peng, X., Ji, Y., Dai, Y., Fang, Y., Xiong, B., Ren, W., Hu, Y., Chen, Y., & Ai, J. (2021). The novel RET inhibitor SYHA1815 inhibits RET-driven cancers and overcomes gatekeeper mutations by inducing G1 cell-cycle arrest through c-Myc downregulation. *Molecular Cancer Therapeutics, 20*(11), 2198−2206. https://doi.org/10.1158/1535-7163.MCT-21-0127

Jin, L. X., & Moley, J. F. (2016). Surgery for lymph node metastases of medullary thyroid carcinoma: A review. *Cancer, 122*(3), 358−366. https://doi.org/10.1002/cncr.29761

Jin, N., Jiang, T., Rosen, D. M., Nelkin, B. D., & Ball, D. W. (2009). Dual inhibition of mitogen-activated protein kinase kinase and mammalian target of rapamycin in differentiated and anaplastic thyroid cancer. *Journal of Clinical Endocrinology and Metabolism, 94*(10), 4107−4112. https://doi.org/10.1210/jc.2009-0662

Jividen, K., & Li, H. (2014). Chimeric RNAs generated by intergenic splicing in normal and cancer cells. *Genes, Chromosomes and Cancer, 53*(12), 963−971. https://doi.org/10.1002/gcc.22207

Jänne, P. A., & Mayer, R. J. (2000). Chemoprevention of colorectal cancer. *New England Journal of Medicine, 342*(26), 1960−1968. https://doi.org/10.1056/NEJM200006293422606

Ju, Y. S., Lee, W. C., Shin, J. Y., Lee, S., Bleazard, T., Won, J. K., Kim, Y. T., Kim, J. I., Kang, J. H., & Seo, J. S. (2012). A transforming KIF5B and RET gene fusion in lung adenocarcinoma revealed from whole-genome and transcriptome sequencing. *Genome Research, 22*(3), 436−445. https://doi.org/10.1101/gr.133645.111

Kane, R. C., Farrell, A. T., Saber, H., Tang, S., Williams, G., Jee, J. M., Liang, C., Booth, B., Chidambaram, N., Morse, D., Sridhara, R., Garvey, P., Justice, R., & Pazdur, R. (2006). Sorafenib for the treatment of advanced renal cell carcinoma. *Clinical Cancer Research, 12*(24), 7271−7278. https://doi.org/10.1158/1078-0432.CCR-06-1249

Kannaiyan, R., & Mahadevan, D. (2018). A comprehensive review of protein kinase inhibitors for cancer therapy. *Expert Review of Anticancer Therapy, 18*(12), 1249−1270. https://doi.org/10.1080/14737140.2018.1527688

Kato, S., Subbiah, V., Marchlik, E., Elkin, S. K., Carter, J. L., & Kurzrock, R. (2017). RET aberrations in diverse cancers: Next-generation sequencing of 4,871 patients. *Clinical Cancer Research, 23*(8), 1988−1997. https://doi.org/10.1158/1078-0432.CCR-16-1679

Kawamoto, Y., Takeda, K., Okuno, Y., Yamakawa, Y., Ito, Y., Taguchi, R., Kato, M., Suzuki, H., Takahashi, M., & Nakashima, I. (2004). Identification of RET autophosphorylation sites by mass spectrometry. *Journal of Biological Chemistry, 279*(14), 14213−14224. https://doi.org/10.1074/jbc.M312600200

Keller, H. R., Zhang, X., Li, L., Schaider, H., & Wells, J. W. (2017). Overcoming resistance to targeted therapy with immunotherapy and combination therapy for metastatic melanoma. *Oncotarget, 8*(43).

Kim, H. L., & Yang, X. J. (2002). Prevalence of high-grade prostatic intraepithelial neoplasia and its relationship to serum prostate specific antigen. *International Brazilian Journal of Urology, 28*(5), 413−417.

Kim, H. P., Cho, G. A., Han, S. W., Shin, J. Y., Jeong, E. G., Song, S. H., Lee, W. C., Lee, K. H., Bang, D., Seo, J. S., Kim, J. I., & Kim, T. Y. (2014). Novel fusion transcripts in human gastric cancer revealed by transcriptome analysis. *Oncogene, 33*(47), 5434−5441. https://doi.org/10.1038/onc.2013.490

Kim, S. Y., Oh, S. O., Kim, K., Lee, J., Kang, S. Y., Kim, K. M., Lee, W. Y., Kim, S. T., & Nam, D. N. (2018). NCOA4-RET fusion in colorectal cancer: Therapeutic challenge using patient-derived tumor cell lines. *Journal of Cancer, 9*(17), 3032−3037. https://doi.org/10.7150/jca.26256

Kiriakopoulos, A., Dimopoulou, A., Nastos, C., Dimopoulou, D., Dimopoulou, K., Menenakos, E., & Zavras, N. (2022). Medullary thyroid carcinoma in children: Current state of the art and future perspectives. *Journal of Pediatric Endocrinology & Metabolism, 35*(1), 1−10. https://doi.org/10.1515/jpem-2021-0502

Klempner, S. J., Borghei, A., Hakimian, B., Ali, S. M., & Ou, S. H. I. (2017). Intracranial activity of cabozantinib in MET exon 14−positive NSCLC with brain metastases. *Journal of Thoracic Oncology, 12*(1), 152−156. https://doi.org/10.1016/j.jtho.2016.09.127

Klohs, W. D., Fry, D. W., & Kraker, A. J. (1997). Inhibitors of tyrosine kinase. *Current Opinion in Oncology, 9*(6), 562−568. https://doi.org/10.1097/00001622-199711000-00012

Knowles, P. P., Murray-Rust, J., Kjær, S., Scott, R. P., Hanrahan, S., Santoro, M., Ibáñez, C. F., & McDonald, N. Q. (2006). Structure and chemical inhibition of the RET tyrosine kinase domain. *Journal of Biological Chemistry, 281*(44), 33577−33587. https://doi.org/10.1074/jbc.M605604200

Kodama, T., Tsukaguchi, T., Satoh, Y., Yoshida, M., Watanabe, Y., Kondoh, O., & Sakamoto, H. (2014). Alectinib shows potent antitumor activity against RET-rearranged non-small cell lung cancer. *Molecular Cancer Therapeutics, 13*(12), 2910−2918. https://doi.org/10.1158/1535-7163.MCT-14-0274

Kohno, T., Ichikawa, H., Totoki, Y., Yasuda, K., Hiramoto, M., Nammo, T., Sakamoto, H., Tsuta, K., Furuta, K., Shimada, Y., Iwakawa, R., Ogiwara, H., Oike, T., Enari, M., Schetter, A. J., Okayama, H., Haugen, A., Skaug, V., Chiku, S., … Shibata, T. (2012). KIF5B-RET fusions in lung adenocarcinoma. *Nature Medicine, 18*(3), 375−377. https://doi.org/10.1038/nm.2644

Krug, M., & Hilgeroth, A. (2008). Recent advances in the development of multi-kinase inhibitors. *Mini-Reviews in Medicinal Chemistry, 8*(13), 1312−1327. https://doi.org/10.2174/138955708786369591

Kurzrock, R., Sherman, S. I., Ball, D. W., Forastiere, A. A., Cohen, R. B., Mehra, R., Pfister, D. G., Cohen, E. E. W., Janisch, L., Nauling, F., Hong, D. S., Ng, C. S., Ye, L., Gagel, R. F., Frye, J., Müller, T., Ratain, M. J., & Salgia, R. (2011). Activity of XL184 (cabozantinib), an oral tyrosine kinase inhibitor, in patients with medullary thyroid cancer. *Journal of Clinical Oncology, 29*(19), 2660−2666. https://doi.org/10.1200/JCO.2010.32.4145

Lamberti, G., Andrini, E., Sisi, M., Rizzo, A., Parisi, C., Di Federico, A., Gelsomino, F., & Ardizzoni, A. (2020). Beyond EGFR, ALK and ROS1: Current evidence and future perspectives on newly targetable oncogenic drivers in lung adenocarcinoma. *Critical Reviews in Oncology, 156*. https://doi.org/10.1016/j.critrevonc.2020.103119

Lang, L. (2008). FDA approves sorafenib for patients with inoperable liver cancer. *Gastroenterology, 134*(2). https://doi.org/10.1053/j.gastro.2007.12.037

Langan, R. C. (2019). Benign prostatic hyperplasia. *Primary Care: Clinics in Office Practice, 46*(2), 223−232. https://doi.org/10.1016/j.pop.2019.02.003

Lanzi, C., Borrello, M. G., Bongarzone, I., Migliazza, A., Fusco, A., Grieco, M., Santoro, M., Gambetta, R. A., Zunino, F., Della Porta, G., & Pierotti, M. A. (1992). Identification of the product of two oncogenic rearranged forms of the RET proto-oncogene in papillary thyroid carcinomas. *Oncogene, 7*(11), 2189−2194.

Le Rolle, A. F., Klempner, S. J., Garrett, C. R., Seery, T., Sanford, E. M., Balasubramanian, S., Ross, J. S., Stephens, P. J., Miller, V. A., Ali, S. M., & Chiu, V. K. (2015). Identification and characterization of RET fusions in advanced colorectal cancer. *Oncotarget, 6*(30), 28929−28937. https://doi.org/10.18632/oncotarget.4325

Lemoine, N. R., Mayall, E. S., Wyllie, F., Farr, C. J., Hughes, D., Padua, R. A., Thurston, V., Williams, E. D., & Wynford-Thomas, D. (1988). Activated ras oncogenes in human thyroid cancers. *Cancer Research, 48*(16), 4459−4463.

Lemoine, N. R., Mayall, E. S., Wyllie, F. S., Williams, E. D., Goyns, M., Stringer, B., & Wynford-Thomas, D. (1989). High frequency of ras oncogene activation in all stages of human thyroid tumorigenesis. *Oncogene, 4*(2), 159—164.

Li, A. Y., McCusker, M. G., Russo, A., Scilla, K. A., Gittens, A., Arensmeyer, K., Mehra, R., Adamo, V., & Rolfo, C. (2019a). RET fusions in solid tumors. *Cancer Treatment Reviews, 81*. https://doi.org/10.1016/j.ctrv.2019.101911

Li, F., Feng, Y., Fang, R., Fang, Z., Xia, J., Han, X., Liu, X. Y., Chen, H., Liu, H., & Ji, H. (2012). Identification of RET gene fusion by exon array analyses in "pan-negative" lung cancer from never smokers. *Cell Research, 22*(5), 928—931. https://doi.org/10.1038/cr.2012.27

Li, G. G., Somwar, R., Joseph, J., Smith, R. S., Hayashi, T., Martin, L., Franovic, A., Schairer, A., Martin, E., Riely, G. J., Harris, J., Yan, S., Wei, G., Oliver, J. W., Patel, R., Multani, P., Ladanyi, M., & Drilon, A. (2017). Antitumor activity of RXDX-105 in multiple cancer types with RET rearrangements or mutations. *Clinical Cancer Research, 23*(12), 2981—2990. https://doi.org/10.1158/1078-0432.CCR-16-1887

Li, J., Shang, G., Chen, Y. J., Brautigam, C. A., Liou, J., Zhang, X., & Bai, X. C. (2019b). Cryo-EM analyses reveal the common mechanism and diversification in the activation of RET by different ligands. *Elife, 8*. https://doi.org/10.7554/eLife.47650.001

Li, L., Su, Y., Zhao, C., Zhao, H., Liu, G., Wang, J., & Xu, Q. (2006). The role of Ret receptor tyrosine kinase in dopaminergic neuron development. *Neuroscience, 142*(2), 391—400. https://doi.org/10.1016/j.neuroscience.2006.06.018

Lin, J. J., & Gainor, J. F. (2021). An early look at selective RET inhibitor resistance: New challenges and opportunities. *British Journal of Cancer, 124*(11), 1757—1758. https://doi.org/10.1038/s41416-021-01344-7

Lin, J. J., Liu, S. V., McCoach, C. E., Zhu, V. W., Tan, A. C., Yoda, S., Peterson, J., Do, A., Prutisto-Chang, K., Dagogo-Jack, I., Sequist, L. V., Wirth, L. J., Lennerz, J. K., Hata, A. N., Mino-Kenudson, M., Nardi, V., Ou, S. H. I., Tan, D. S. W., & Gainor, J. F. (2020). Mechanisms of resistance to selective RET tyrosine kinase inhibitors in RET fusion-positive non-small-cell lung cancer. *Annals of Oncology, 31*(12), 1725—1733. https://doi.org/10.1016/j.annonc.2020.09.015

Lipson, D., Capelletti, M., Yelensky, R., Otto, G., Parker, A., Jarosz, M., Curran, J. A., Balasubramanian, S., Bloom, T., Brennan, K. W., Donahue, A., Downing, S. R., Frampton, G. M., Garcia, L., Juhn, F., Mitchell, K. C., White, E., White, J., Zwirko, Z., … Stephens, P. J. (2012). Identification of new ALK and RET gene fusions from colorectal and lung cancer biopsies. *Nature Medicine, 18*(3), 382—384. https://doi.org/10.1038/nm.2673

Liu, X., Shen, T., Mooers, B. H. M., Hilberg, F., & Wu, J. (2018). Drug resistance profiles of mutations in the RET kinase domain. *British Journal of Pharmacology, 175*(17), 3504—3515. https://doi.org/10.1111/bph.14395

Liu, X., Vega, Q. C., Decker, R. A., Pandey, A., Worby, C. A., & Dixon, J. E. (1996). Oncogenic RET receptors display different autophosphorylation sites and substrate binding specificities. *Journal of Biological Chemistry, 271*(10), 5309—5312. https://doi.org/10.1074/jbc.271.10.5309

Lu, C., & Zhou, Q. (2021). Diagnostics, therapeutics and RET inhibitor resistance for RET fusion—positive non-small cell lung cancers and future perspectives. *Cancer Treatment Reviews, 96*. https://doi.org/10.1016/j.ctrv.2021.102153

Lu, L., Ghose, A. K., Quail, M. R., Albom, M. S., Durkin, J. T., Holskin, B. P., Angeles, T. S., Meyer, S. L., Ruggeri, B. A., & Cheng, M. (2009). ALK mutants in the kinase domain exhibit altered kinase activity and differential sensitivity to small molecule ALK inhibitors. *Biochemistry, 48*(16), 3600—3609. https://doi.org/10.1021/bi8020923

Luo, Y., Tsuchiya, K. D., Il Park, D., Fausel, R., Kanngurn, S., Welcsh, P., Dzieciatkowski, S., Wang, J., & Grady, W. M. (2013). RET is a potential tumor suppressor gene in colorectal cancer. *Oncogene, 32*(16), 2037—2047. https://doi.org/10.1038/onc.2012.225

Lyons, J. F., Wilhelm, S., Hibner, B., & Bollag, G. (2001). Discovery of a novel Raf kinase inhibitor. *Endocrine-Related Cancer, 8*(3), 219—225. https://doi.org/10.1677/erc.0.0080219

Ma, J., Wang, B., Meng, E., & Meng, X. (2021). Case report: Identification of ERC1-RET fusion in a patient with pancreatic ductal adenocarcinoma. *Gland Surgery, 10*(9), 2874—2879. https://doi.org/10.21037/gs-21-469

Mao, W. F., Shao, M. H., Gao, P. T., Ma, J., Li, H. J., Li, G. L., Han, B. H., & Yuan, C. G. (2012). The important roles of RET, VEGFR2 and the RAF/MEK/ERK pathway in cancer treatment with sorafenib. *Acta Pharmacologica Sinica, 33*(10), 1311—1318. https://doi.org/10.1038/aps.2012.76

Markham, A. (2020). Pralsetinib: First approval. *Drugs, 80*(17), 1865—1870. https://doi.org/10.1007/s40265-020-01427-4

Martínez-Jiménez, F., Muiños, F., Sentís, I., Deu-Pons, J., Reyes-Salazar, I., Arnedo-Pac, C., Mularoni, L., Pich, O., Bonet, J., Kranas, H., Gonzalez-Perez, A., & Lopez-Bigas, N. (2020). A compendium of mutational cancer driver genes. *Nature Reviews Cancer, 20*(10), 555−572. https://doi.org/10.1038/s41568-020-0290-x

Matsui, J., Funahashi, Y., Uenaka, T., Watanabe, T., Tsuruoka, A., & Asada, M. (2008a). Multi-kinase inhibitor E7080 suppresses lymph node and lung metastasis of human mammary breast tumor MDA-MB-231 via inhibition of vascular endothelial growth factor-receptor (VEGF-R) 2 and VEGF-R3 kinase. *Clinical Cancer Research, 14*(17), 5459−5465. https://doi.org/10.1158/1078-0432.CCR-07-5270

Matsui, J., Yamamoto, Y., Funahashi, Y., Tsuruoka, A., Watanabe, T., Wakabayashi, T., Uenaka, T., & Asada, M. (2008b). E7080, a novel inhibitor that targets multiple kinases, has potent antitumor activities against stem cell factor producing human small cell lung cancer H146, based on angiogenesis inhibition. *International Journal of Cancer, 122*(3), 664−671. https://doi.org/10.1002/ijc.23131

McFarland, D. C., & Misiukiewicz, K. J. (2014). Sorafenib in radioactive iodine-refractory well-differentiated metastatic thyroid cancer. *OncoTargets and Therapy, 7*, 1291−1299. https://doi.org/10.2147/OTT.S49430

Mechera, R., Soysal, S. D., Piscuoglio, S., Ng, C. K. Y., Zeindler, J., Mujagic, E., Däster, S., Glauser, P., Hoffmann, H., Kilic, E., Droeser, R. A., Weber, W. P., & Muenst, S. (2019). Expression of RET is associated with Oestrogen receptor expression but lacks prognostic significance in breast cancer. *BMC Cancer, 19*(1). https://doi.org/10.1186/s12885-018-5262-0

Miyabayashi, K., Nakagawa, H., & Koike, K. (2021). Molecular and phenotypic profiling for precision medicine in pancreatic cancer: Current advances and future perspectives. *Frontiers in Oncology, 11*. https://doi.org/10.3389/fonc.2021.682872

Mologni, L. (2011). Development of RET kinase inhibitors for targeted cancer therapy. *Current Medicinal Chemistry, 18*(2), 162−175. https://doi.org/10.2174/092986711794088308

Mologni, L., Sala, E., Cazzaniga, S., Rostagno, R., Kuoni, T., Puttini, M., Bain, J., Cleris, L., Redaelli, S., Riva, B., Formelli, F., Scapozza, L., & Gambacorti-Passerini, C. (2006). Inhibition of RET tyrosine kinase by SU5416. *Journal of Molecular Endocrinology, 37*(2), 199−212. https://doi.org/10.1677/jme.1.01999

Morandi, A., Martin, L. A., Gao, Q., Pancholi, S., Mackay, A., Robertson, D., Zvelebil, M., Dowsett, M., Plaza-Menacho, I., & Isacke, C. M. (2013). GDNF-RET signaling in ER-positive breast cancers is a key determinant of response and resistance to aromatase inhibitors. *Cancer Research, 73*(12), 3783−3795. https://doi.org/10.1158/0008-5472.CAN-12-4265

Morandi, A., Plaza-Menacho, I., & Isacke, C. M. (2011). RET in breast cancer: Functional and therapeutic implications. *Trends in Molecular Medicine, 17*(3), 149−157. https://doi.org/10.1016/j.molmed.2010.12.007

Mross, K., Frost, A., Steinbild, S., Hedbom, S., Büchert, M., Fasol, U., Unger, C., Krätzschmar, J., Heinig, R., Boix, O., & Christensen, O. (2012). A phase I dose-escalation study of regorafenib (BAY 73-4506), an inhibitor of oncogenic, angiogenic, and stromal kinases, in patients with advanced solid tumors. *Clinical Cancer Research, 18*(9), 2658−2667. https://doi.org/10.1158/1078-0432.CCR-11-1900

Mulligan, L. M., Eng, C., Healey, C. S., Clayton, D., Kwok, J. B. J., Gardner, E., Ponder, M. A., Frilling, A., Jackson, C. E., Lehnert, H., Neumann, H. P. H., Thibodeau, S. N., & Ponder, B. A. J. (1994a). Specific mutations of the RET proto-oncogene are related to disease phenotype in MEN 2A and FMTC. *Nature Genetics, 6*(1), 70−74. https://doi.org/10.1038/ng0194-70

Mulligan, L. M., Eng, C., Attlé, T., Lyonnet, S., Marsh, D. J., Hyland, V. J., Robinson, B. G., Frilling, A., Verellen-dumoulln, C., Safar, A., Venter, D. J., Munnich, A., & Ponder, B. A. J. (1994b). Diverse phenotypes associated with exon 10 mutations of the RET proto-oncogene. *Human Molecular Genetics, 3*(12), 2163−2168. https://doi.org/10.1093/hmg/3.12.2163

Mulligan, L. M., Kwok, J. B. J., Healey, C. S., Elsdon, M. J., Eng, C., Gardner, E., Love, D. R., Mole, S. E., Moore, J. K., Papi, L., Ponder, M. A., Telenius, H., Tunnacliffe, A., & Ponder, B. A. J. (1993). Germ-line mutations of the RET proto-oncogene in multiple endocrine neoplasia type 2A. *Nature, 363*(6428), 458−460. https://doi.org/10.1038/363458a0

Mulligan, L. M., Marsh, D. J., Robinson, B. G., Schuffenecker, I., Zedenius, J., Lips, C. J. M., Gagel, R. F., Takai, S. I., Noll, W. W., Fink, M., Raue, F., Lacroix, A., Thibodeau, S. N., Frilling, A., Ponder, B. A. J., & Eng, C. (1995). Genotype-phenotype correlation in multiple endocrine neoplasia type 2: Report of the nternational RET Mutation Consortium. *Journal of Internal Medicine, 238*(4), 343−346. https://doi.org/10.1111/j.1365-2796.1995.tb01208.x

Mulligan, L. M. (2014). RET revisited: Expanding the oncogenic portfolio. *Nature Reviews Cancer, 14*(3), 173−186. https://doi.org/10.1038/nrc3680

Nair, A., Reece, K., Donoghue, M. B., Yuan, W., Rodriguez, L., Keegan, P., & Pazdur, R. (2021). FDA supplemental approval summary: Lenvatinib for the treatment of unresectable hepatocellular carcinoma. *The Oncologist, 26*(3), e484−e491. https://doi.org/10.1002/onco.13566

Nijenhuis, C. M., Haanen, J. B. A. G., Schellens, J. H. M., & Beijnen, J. H. (2013). Is combination therapy the next step to overcome resistance and reduce toxicities in melanoma? *Cancer Treatment Reviews, 39*(4), 305−312. https://doi.org/10.1016/j.ctrv.2012.10.006

Nikiforov, Y. E., & Nikiforova, M. N. (2011). Molecular genetics and diagnosis of thyroid cancer. *Nature Reviews Endocrinology, 7*(10), 569−580. https://doi.org/10.1038/nrendo.2011.142

Okamoto, K., Kodama, K., Takase, K., Sugi, N. H., Yamamoto, Y., Iwata, M., & Tsuruoka, A. (2013). Antitumor activities of the targeted multi-tyrosine kinase inhibitor lenvatinib (E7080) against RET gene fusion-driven tumor models. *Cancer Letters, 340*(1), 97−103. https://doi.org/10.1016/j.canlet.2013.07.007

Osusky, K. L., Hallahan, D. E., Fu, A., Ye, F., Shyr, Y., & Geng, L. (2004). The receptor tyrosine kinase inhibitor SU11248 impedes endothelial cell migration, tubule formation, and blood vessel formation in vivo, but has little effect on existing tumor vessels. *Angiogenesis, 7*(3), 225−233. https://doi.org/10.1007/s10456-004-3149-y

Ott, P. A., Hodi, F. S., Kaufman, H. L., Wigginton, J. M., & Wolchok, J. D. (2017). Combination immunotherapy: A road map. *Journal for ImmunoTherapy of Cancer, 5*(1). https://doi.org/10.1186/s40425-017-0218-5

Ou, S.-H. I., & Zhu, V. W. (2020). Catalog of 5′ fusion partners in RET+ NSCLC circa 2020. *JTO Clinical and Research Reports, 1*(2). https://doi.org/10.1016/j.jtocrr.2020.100037

Pachnis, V., Mankoo, B., & Costantini, F. (1993). Expression of the c-ret proto-oncogene during mouse embryogenesis. *Development, 119*(4), 1005−1017. https://doi.org/10.1242/dev.119.4.1005

Paratala, B. S., Chung, J. H., Williams, C. B., Yilmazel, B., Petrosky, W., Williams, K., Schrock, A. B., Gay, L. M., Lee, E., Dolfi, S. C., Pham, K., Lin, S., Yao, M., Kulkarni, A., DiClemente, F., Liu, C., Rodriguez-Rodriguez, L., Ganesan, S., Ross, J. S., … Hirshfield, K. M. (2018). RET rearrangements are actionable alterations in breast cancer. *Nature Communications, 9*(1). https://doi.org/10.1038/s41467-018-07341-4

Perrinjaquet, M., Vilar, M., & Ibáñez, C. F. (2010). Protein-tyrosine phosphatase SHP2 contributes to GDNF neurotrophic activity through direct binding to phospho-Tyr687 in the RET receptor tyrosine kinase. *Journal of Biological Chemistry, 285*(41), 31867−31875. https://doi.org/10.1074/jbc.M110.144923

Petersson, F., Michal, M., Ptáková, N., Skalova, A., & Michal, M. (2020). Salivary gland mucinous adenocarcinoma with minor (mammary analogue) secretory and low-grade in situ carcinoma components sharing the same ETV6-RET translocation and with no other molecular genetic aberrations detected on NGS analysis. *Applied Immunohistochemistry and Molecular Morphology, 28*(6), E54−E57. https://doi.org/10.1097/PAI.0000000000000806

Pietrantonio, F., Di Nicolantonio, F., Schrock, A. B., Lee, J., Morano, F., Fucà, G., Nikolinakos, P., Drilon, A., Hechtman, J. F., Christiansen, J., Gowen, K., Frampton, G. M., Gasparini, P., Rossini, D., Gigliotti, C., Kim, S. T., Prisciandaro, M., Hodgson, J., Zaniboni, A., … Cremolini, C. (2018). RET fusions in a small subset of advanced colorectal cancers at risk of being neglected. *Annals of Oncology, 29*(6), 1394−1401. https://doi.org/10.1093/annonc/mdy090

Plaza-Menacho, I., Mologni, L., Sala, E., Gambacorti-Passerini, C., Magee, A. I., Links, T. P., Hofstra, R. M. W., Barford, D., & Isacke, C. M. (2007). Sorafenib functions to potently suppress RET tyrosine kinase activity by direct enzymatic inhibition and promoting RET lysosomal degradation independent of proteasomal targeting. *Journal of Biological Chemistry, 282*(40), 29230−29240. https://doi.org/10.1074/jbc.M703461200

Plaza-Menacho, I., Morandi, A., Robertson, D., Pancholi, S., Drury, S., Dowsett, M., Martin, L. A., & Isacke, C. M. (2010). Targeting the receptor tyrosine kinase RET sensitizes breast cancer cells to tamoxifen treatment and reveals a role for RET in endocrine resistance. *Oncogene, 29*(33), 4648−4657. https://doi.org/10.1038/onc.2010.209

Pohlmann, P. R., Mayer, I. A., & Mernaugh, R. (2009). Resistance to trastuzumab in breast cancer. *Clinical Cancer Research, 15*(24), 7479−7491. https://doi.org/10.1158/1078-0432.CCR-09-0636

Ponder, B. A. J., & Smith, D. (1996). The MEN II syndromes and the role of the ret proto-oncogene. *Advances in Cancer Research, 70*, 179−222. https://doi.org/10.1016/s0065-230x(08)60875-1

Regua, A. T., Najjar, M., & Lo, H. W. (2022). RET signaling pathway and RET inhibitors in human cancer. *Frontiers in Oncology, 12*. https://doi.org/10.3389/fonc.2022.932353

Rhoden, K. J., Johnson, C., Brandao, G., Howe, J. G., Smith, B. R., & Tallini, G. (2004). Real-time quantitative RT-PCR identifies distinct c-RET, RET/PTC1 and RET/PTC3 expression patterns in papillary thyroid carcinoma. *Laboratory Investigation, 84*(12), 1557−1570. https://doi.org/10.1038/labinvest.3700198

Rhoden, K. J., Unger, K., Salvatore, G., Yilmaz, Y., Vovk, V., Chiappetta, G., Qumsiyeh, M. B., Rothstein, J. L., Fusco, A., Santoro, M., Zitzelsberger, H., & Tallini, G. (2006). RET/papillary thyroid cancer rearrangement in non-neoplastic thyrocytes: Follicular cells of Hashimoto's thyroiditis share low-level recombination events with a subset of papillary carcinoma. *Journal of Clinical Endocrinology and Metabolism, 91*(6), 2414–2423. https://doi.org/10.1210/jc.2006-0240

Riihimäki, M., Hemminki, A., Sundquist, J., & Hemminki, K. (2016). Patterns of metastasis in colon and rectal cancer. *Scientific Reports, 6*(1). https://doi.org/10.1038/srep29765

Robinson, B. G., Paz-Ares, L., Krebs, A., Vasselli, J., & Haddad, R. (2010). Vandetanib (100 mg) in patients with locally advanced or metastatic hereditary medullary thyroid cancer. *The Journal of Clinical Endocrinology & Metabolism, 95*(6), 2664–2671. https://doi.org/10.1210/jc.2009-2461

Robinson, D., He, F., Pretlow, T., & Kung, H. J. (1996). A tyrosine kinase profile of prostate carcinoma. *Proceedings of the National Academy of Sciences, 93*(12), 5958–5962. https://doi.org/10.1073/pnas.93.12.5958

Román-Gil, M. S., Pozas, J., Rosero-Rodríguez, D., Chamorro-Pérez, J., Ruiz-Granados, Á., Caracuel, I. R., Grande, E., Molina-Cerrillo, J., & Alonso-Gordoa, T. (2022). Resistance to RET targeted therapy in thyroid cancer: Molecular basis and overcoming strategies. *Cancer Treatment Reviews, 105.* https://doi.org/10.1016/j.ctrv.2022.102372

Roskoski, R., & Sadeghi-Nejad, A. (2018). Role of RET protein-tyrosine kinase inhibitors in the treatment RET-driven thyroid and lung cancers. *Pharmacological Research, 128,* 1–17. https://doi.org/10.1016/j.phrs.2017.12.021

Russo, A., Cardona, A. F., Caglevic, C., Manca, P., Ruiz-Patiño, A., Arrieta, O., & Rolfo, C. (2020). Overcoming TKI resistance in fusion-driven NSCLC: New generation inhibitors and rationale for combination strategies. *Translational Lung Cancer Research, 9*(6), 2581–2598. https://doi.org/10.21037/tlcr-2019-cnsclc-06

Saha, D., Ryan, K. R., Lakkaniga, N. R., Acharya, B., Garcia, N. G., Smith, E. L., & Frett, B. (2021). Targeting rearranged during transfection in cancer: A perspective on small-molecule inhibitors and their clinical development. *Journal of Medicinal Chemistry, 64*(16), 11747–11773. https://doi.org/10.1021/acs.jmedchem.0c02167

Sakamoto, H., Tsukaguchi, T., Hiroshima, S., Kodama, T., Kobayashi, T., Fukami, T. A., Oikawa, N., Tsukuda, T., Ishii, N., & Aoki, Y. (2011). CH5424802, a selective ALK inhibitor capable of blocking the resistant gatekeeper mutant. *Cancer Cell, 19*(5), 679–690. https://doi.org/10.1016/j.ccr.2011.04.004

Santoro, M., Carlomagno, F., Hay, I. D., Herrmann, M. A., Grieco, M., Melillo, R., Pierotti, M. A., Bongarzone, I., Della Porta, G., & Berger, N. (1992). Ret oncogene activation in human thyroid neoplasms is restricted to the papillary cancer subtype. *Journal of Clinical Investigation, 89*(5), 1517–1522. https://doi.org/10.1172/JCI115743

Santoro, M., Moccia, M., Federico, G., & Carlomagno, F. (2020). RET gene fusions in malignancies of the thyroid and other tissues. *Genes, 11*(4). https://doi.org/10.3390/genes11040424

Santoro, M., Chiappetta, G., Cerrato, A., Salvatore, D., Zhang, L., Manzo, G., Picone, A., Portella, G., Santelli, G., Vecchio, G., & Fusco, A. (1996). Development of thyroid papillary carcinomas secondary to tissue-specific expression of the RET/PTC1 oncogene in transgenic mice. *Oncogene, 12*(8), 1821–1826.

Santoro, M., Melillo, R. M., Carlomagno, F., Fusco, A., & Vecchio, G. (2002). Molecular mechanisms of RET activation in human cancer. *Annals of the New York Academy of Sciences, 963,* 116–121. https://doi.org/10.1111/j.1749-6632.2002.tb04102.x

Santoro, M., Rosati, R., Grieco, M., Berlingieri, M. T., Luca-Colucci D'Amato, G., De Franciscis, V., & Fusco, A. (1990). The ret proto-oncogene is consistently expressed in human pheochromocytomas and thyroid medullary carcinomas. *Oncogene, 5*(10), 1595–1598.

Scalvini, L., Castelli, R., La Monica, S., Tiseo, M., & Alfieri, R. (2021). Fighting tertiary mutations in EGFR-driven lung-cancers: Current advances and future perspectives in medicinal chemistry. *Biochemical Pharmacology, 190.* https://doi.org/10.1016/j.bcp.2021.114643

Schlumberger, M., Elisei, R., Müller, S., Schöffski, P., Brose, M., Shah, M., Licitra, L., Krajewska, J., Kreissl, M. C., Niederle, B., Cohen, E. E. W., Wirth, L., Ali, H., Clary, D. O., Yaron, Y., Mangeshkar, M., Ball, D., Nelkin, B., & Sherman, S. (2017). Overall survival analysis of EXAM, a phase III trial of cabozantinib in patients with radiographically progressive medullary thyroid carcinoma. *Annals of Oncology, 28*(11), 2813–2819. https://doi.org/10.1093/annonc/mdx479

Schuchardt, A., D'Agati, V., Larsson-Blomberg, L., Costantini, F., & Pachnis, V. (1994). Defects in the kidney and enteric nervous system of mice lacking the tyrosine kinase receptor Ret. *Nature, 367*(6461), 380–383. https://doi.org/10.1038/367380a0

Schuringa, J. J., Wojtachnio, K., Hagens, W., Vellenga, E., Buys, C. H. C. M., Hofstra, R., & Kruijer, W. (2001). MEN2A-RET-induced cellular transformation by activation of STAT3. *Oncogene, 20*(38), 5350–5358. https://doi.org/10.1038/sj.onc.1204715

Seethala, R. R., & Stenman, G. (2017). Update from the 4th edition of the world health organization classification of head and neck tumours: Tumors of the salivary gland. *Head and Neck Pathology, 11*(1), 55–67. https://doi.org/10.1007/s12105-017-0795-0

Seto, T., Kiura, K., Nishio, M., Nakagawa, K., Maemondo, M., Inoue, A., Hida, T., Yamamoto, N., Yoshioka, H., Harada, M., Ohe, Y., Nogami, N., Takeuchi, K., Shimada, T., Tanaka, T., & Tamura, T. (2013). CH5424802 (RO5424802) for patients with ALK-rearranged advanced non-small-cell lung cancer (AF-001JP study): A single-arm, open-label, phase 1-2 study. *The Lancet Oncology, 14*(7), 590–598. https://doi.org/10.1016/S1470-2045(13)70142-6

Sherman, S. I., Clary, D. O., Elisei, R., Schlumberger, M. J., Cohen, E. E. W., Schöffski, P., Wirth, L. J., Mangeshkar, M., Aftab, D. T., & Brose, M. S. (2016). Correlative analyses of RET and RAS mutations in a phase 3 trial of cabozantinib in patients with progressive, metastatic medullary thyroid cancer. *Cancer, 122*(24), 3856–3864. https://doi.org/10.1002/cncr.30252

Shiau, A. K., Barstad, D., Loria, P. M., Cheng, L., Kushner, P. J., Agard, D. A., & Greene, G. L. (1998). The structural basis of estrogen receptor/coactivator recognition and the antagonism of this interaction by tamoxifen. *Cell, 95*(7), 927–937. https://doi.org/10.1016/S0092-8674(00)81717-1

Siegel, r J., Miller, K. D., Fuchs, H. E., & Jemal, A. (2020). Stinchcombe TE. Current management of RET rearranged non-small cell lung cancer. *Therapeutic Advances in Medical Oncology, 71.*

Sipple, J. H. (1961). The association of pheochromocytoma with carcinoma of the thyroid gland. *The American Journal of Medicine, 31*(1), 163–166. https://doi.org/10.1016/0002-9343(61)90234-0

Skálová, A., Ptáková, N., Santana, T., Agaimy, A., Ihrler, S., Uro-Coste, E., Thompson, L. D. R., Bishop, J. A., Baněčkova, M., Rupp, N. J., Morbini, P., de Sanctis, S., Schiavo-Lena, M., Vanecek, T., Michal, M., & Leivo, I. (2019). NCOA4-RET and TRIM27-RET are characteristic gene fusions in salivary intraductal carcinoma, including invasive and metastatic tumors. *The American Journal of Surgical Pathology, 43*(10), 1303–1313. https://doi.org/10.1097/pas.0000000000001301

Skálová, A., Vanecek, T., Martinek, P., Weinreb, I., Stevens, T. M., Simpson, R. H. W., Hyrcza, M., Rupp, N. J., Baneckova, M., Michal, M., Slouka, D., Svoboda, T., Metelkova, A., Etebarian, A., Pavelka, J., Potts, S. J., Christiansen, J., Steiner, P., & Michal, M. (2018a). Molecular profiling of mammary analog secretory carcinoma revealed a subset of tumors harboring a novel ETV6-RET translocation. *The American Journal of Surgical Pathology, 42*(2), 234–246. https://doi.org/10.1097/pas.0000000000000972

Skálová, A., Vanecek, T., Uro-Coste, E., Bishop, J. A., Weinreb, I., Thompson, L. D. R., De Sanctis, S., Schiavo-Lena, M., Laco, J., Badoual, C., Santana Conceiçao, T., Ptáková, N., Baněčkova, M., Miesbauerová, M., & Michal, M. (2018b). Molecular profiling of salivary gland intraductal carcinoma revealed a subset of tumors harboring NCOA4-RET and novel TRIM27-RET fusions. *The American Journal of Surgical Pathology, 42*(11), 1445–1455. https://doi.org/10.1097/PAS.0000000000001133

Smith, D. P., Houghton, C., & Ponder, B. A. J. (1997). Germline mutation of RET codon 883 in two cases of de novo MEN 2B. *Oncogene, 15*(10), 1213–1217. https://doi.org/10.1038/sj.onc.1201481

Sood, A., Lang, D. K., Kaur, R., Saini, B., & Arora, S. (2021). Relevance of aromatase inhibitors in breast cancer treatment. *Current Topics in Medicinal Chemistry, 21*(15), 1319–1336. https://doi.org/10.2174/1568026621666210701143445

Sozzi, G., Bongarzone, L., Miouo, M., Borrello, M. G., Butti, M. G., Porta, G. D., Pierotti, M. A., & Pilotti, S. (1994). A t(10; 17) translocation creates the RET/PTC2 chimeric transforming sequence in papillary thyroid carcinoma. *Genes, Chromosomes and Cancer, 9*(4), 244–250. https://doi.org/10.1002/gcc.2870090404

Strumberg, D., Scheulen, M. E., Schultheis, B., Richly, H., Frost, A., Büchert, M., Christensen, O., Jeffers, M., Heinig, R., Boix, O., & Mross, K. (2012). Regorafenib (BAY 73-4506) in advanced colorectal cancer: A phase I study. *British Journal of Cancer, 106*(11), 1722–1727. https://doi.org/10.1038/bjc.2012.153

Suarez, H. G., Du Villard, J. A., Caillou, B., Schlumberger, M., Tubiana, M., Parmentier, C., & Monier, R. (1988). Detection of activated ras oncogenes in human thyroid carcinomas. *Oncogene, 2*(4), 403–406.

Subbiah, V., & Cote, G. J. (2020). Advances in targeting RET-dependent cancers. *Cancer Discovery, 10*(4), 498–505. https://doi.org/10.1158/2159-8290.CD-19-1116

Subbiah, V., Hu, M. I.-N., Gainor, J. F., Mansfield, A. S., Alonso, G., Taylor, M. H., Zhu, V. W., Garrido Lopez, P., Amatu, A., Doebele, R. C., Cassier, P. A., Keam, B., Schuler, M. H., Zhang, H., Clifford, C., Palmer, M., Green, J., Turner, C. D., & Curigliano, G. (2020a). Clinical activity of the RET inhibitor pralsetinib (BLU-667) in patients with RET fusion+ solid tumors. *Journal of Clinical Oncology, 38*(15_Suppl. l). https://doi.org/10.1200/jco.2020.38.15_suppl.109

Subbiah, V., Yang, D., Velcheti, V., Drilon, A., & Meric-Bernstam, F. (2020b). State-of-the-art strategies for targeting RET-dependent cancers. *Journal of Clinical Oncology, 38*(11), 1209–1221. https://doi.org/10.1200/JCO.19.02551

Takahashi, M., Kawai, K., & Asai, N. (2020). Roles of the RET proto-oncogene in cancer and development. *JMA Journal, 3*(3), 175–181. https://doi.org/10.31662/jmaj.2020-0021

Takahashi, M., Ritz, J., & Cooper, G. M. (1985). Activation of a novel human transforming gene, ret, by DNA rearrangement. *Cell, 42*(2), 581–588. https://doi.org/10.1016/0092-8674(85)90115-1

Takeuchi, K., Soda, M., Togashi, Y., Suzuki, R., Sakata, S., Hatano, S., Asaka, R., Hamanaka, W., Ninomiya, H., Uehara, H., Lim Choi, Y., Satoh, Y., Okumura, S., Nakagawa, K., Mano, H., & Ishikawa, Y. (2012). RET, ROS1 and ALK fusions in lung cancer. *Nature Medicine, 18*(3), 378–381. https://doi.org/10.1038/nm.2658

Takeuchi, S., Yanagitani, N., Seto, T., Hattori, Y., Ohashi, K., Morise, M., Matsumoto, S., Yoh, K., Goto, K., Nishio, M., Takahara, S., Kawakami, T., Imai, Y., Yoshimura, K., Tanimoto, A., Nishiyama, A., Murayama, T., & Yano, S. (2021). Phase 1/2 study of alectinib in RET-rearranged previously-treated non-small cell lung cancer (ALL-RET). *Translational Lung Cancer Research, 10*(1), 314–325. https://doi.org/10.21037/tlcr-20-549

Tamura, T., Kurishima, K., Nakazawa, K., Kagohashi, K., Ishikawa, H., Satoh, H., & Hizawa, N. (2015). Specific organ metastases and survival in metastatic non-small-cell lung cancer. *Molecular and Clinical Oncology, 3*(1), 217–221. https://doi.org/10.3892/mco.2014.410

Tan, F. H., Putoczki, T. L., Stylli, S. S., & Luwor, R. B. (2019). Ponatinib: A novel multi-tyrosine kinase inhibitor against human malignancies. *OncoTargets and Therapy, 12*, 635–645. https://doi.org/10.2147/OTT.S189391

Thein, K. Z., Velcheti, V., Mooers, B. H. M., Wu, J., & Subbiah, V. (2021). Precision therapy for RET-altered cancers with RET inhibitors. *Trends in Cancer, 7*(12), 1074–1088. https://doi.org/10.1016/j.trecan.2021.07.003

Tohyama, O., Matsui, J., Kodama, K., Hata-Sugi, N., Kimura, T., Okamoto, K., Minoshima, Y., Iwata, M., & Funahashi, Y. (2014). Antitumor activity of lenvatinib (E7080): An angiogenesis inhibitor that targets multiple receptor tyrosine kinases in preclinical human thyroid cancer models. *Journal of Thyroid Research, 2014*, 1–13. https://doi.org/10.1155/2014/638747

Tomuschat, C., & Puri, P. (2015). RET gene is a major risk factor for hirschsprung's disease: A meta-analysis. *Pediatric Surgery International, 31*(8), 701–710. https://doi.org/10.1007/s00383-015-3731-y

Tong, Q., Li, Y., Smanik, P. A., Fithian, L. J., Xing, S., Mazzaferri, E. L., & Jhiang, S. M. (1995). Characterization of the promoter region and oligomerization domain of H4 (D10S170), a gene frequently rearranged with the ret proto-oncogene. *Oncogene, 10*(9), 1781–1787.

Tsuta, K., Kohno, T., Yoshida, A., Shimada, Y., Asamura, H., Furuta, K., & Kushima, R. (2014). RET-rearranged non-small-cell lung carcinoma: A clinicopathological and molecular analysis. *British Journal of Cancer, 110*(6), 1571–1578. https://doi.org/10.1038/bjc.2014.36

Varešlija, D., Priedigkeit, N., Fagan, A., Purcell, S., Cosgrove, N., O'Halloran, P. J., Ward, E., Cocchiglia, S., Hartmaier, R., Castro, C. A., Zhu, L., Tseng, G. C., Lucas, P. C., Puhalla, S. L., Brufsky, A. M., Hamilton, R. L., Mathew, A., Leone, J. P., Basudan, A., … Young, L. S. (2019). Transcriptome characterization of matched primary breast and brain metastatic tumors to detect novel actionable targets. *Journal of the National Cancer Institute, 111*(4), 388–398. https://doi.org/10.1093/jnci/djy110

Verga, U., Fugazzola, L., Cambiaghi, S., Pritelli, C., Alessi, E., Cortelazzi, D., Gangi, E., & Beck-Peccoz, P. (2003). Frequent association between MEN 2A and cutaneous lichen amyloidosis. *Clinical Endocrinology, 59*(2), 156–161. https://doi.org/10.1046/j.1365-2265.2003.01782.x

Vidal, M., Wells, S., Ryan, A., & Cagan, R. (2005). ZD6474 suppresses oncogenic RET isoforms in a Drosophila model for type 2 multiple endocrine neoplasia syndromes and papillary thyroid carcinoma. *Cancer Research, 65*(9), 3538–3541. https://doi.org/10.1158/0008-5472.CAN-04-4561

Viglietto, G., Chiappetta, G., Martinez-Tello, F. J., Fukunaga, F. H., Tallini, G., Rigopoulou, D., Visconti, R., Mastro, A., Santoro, M., & Fusco, A. (1995). RET/PTC oncogene activation is an early event in thyroid carcinogenesis. *Oncogene, 11*(6), 1207–1210.

Wagner, S. M., Zhu, S., Nicolescu, A. C., & Mulligan, L. M. (2012). Molecular mechanisms of RET receptor-mediated oncogenesis in multiple endocrine neoplasia 2. *Clinics, 67*(S1), 77–84. https://doi.org/10.6061/clinics/2012(Sup01)14

Waks, A. G., & Winer, E. P. (2019). Breast cancer treatment: A review. *JAMA, the Journal of the American Medical Association, 321*(3), 288–300. https://doi.org/10.1001/jama.2018.19323

Wang, G., Zhao, D., Spring, D. J., & Depinho, R. A. (2018). Genetics and biology of prostate cancer. *Genes & Development, 32*(17–18), 1105–1140. https://doi.org/10.1101/gad.315739.118

Wang, C., Mayer, J. A., Mazumdar, A., & Brown, P. H. (2012a). The rearranged during transfection/papillary thyroid carcinoma tyrosine kinase is an estrogen-dependent gene required for the growth of estrogen receptor positive breast cancer cells. *Breast Cancer Research and Treatment, 133*(2), 487–500. https://doi.org/10.1007/s10549-011-1775-9

Wang, R., Hu, H., Pan, Y., Li, Y., Ye, T., Li, C., Luo, X., Wang, L., Li, H., Zhang, Y., Li, F., Lu, Y., Lu, Q., Xu, J., Garfield, D., Shen, L., Ji, H., Pao, W., Sun, Y., & Chen, H. (2012b). RET fusions define a unique molecular and clinicopathologic subtype of non-small-cell lung cancer. *Journal of Clinical Oncology, 30*(35), 4352–4359. https://doi.org/10.1200/JCO.2012.44.1477

Wang, K., Russell, J. S., McDermott, J. D., Elvin, J. A., Khaira, D., Johnson, A., Jennings, T. A., Ali, S. M., Murray, M., Marshall, C., Oldham, D. S., Washburn, D., Wong, S. J., Chmielecki, J., Yelensky, R., Lipson, D., Miller, V. A., Stephens, P. J., Serracino, H. S., Ross, J. S., & Bowles, D. W. (2016). Profiling of 149 salivary duct carcinomas, carcinoma ex pleomorphic adenomas, and adenocarcinomas, not otherwise specified reveals actionable genomic alterations. *Clinical Cancer Research, 22*(24), 6061–6068. https://doi.org/10.1158/1078-0432.CCR-15-2568

Wang, L., Lu, B., He, M., Wang, Y., Wang, Z., & Du, L. (2022). Prostate cancer incidence and mortality: Global status and temporal trends in 89 countries from 2000 to 2019. *Frontiers in Public Health, 10.* https://doi.org/10.3389/fpubh.2022.811044

Waqar, S. N., Samson, P. P., Robinson, C. G., Bradley, J., Devarakonda, S., Du, L., Govindan, R., Puri, V., & Morgensztern, D. (2018). Non–small-cell lung cancer with brain metastasis at presentation. *Clinical Lung Cancer, 19*, 373–379.

Weinreb, I., Bishop, J. A., Chiosea, S. I., Seethala, R. R., Perez-Ordonez, B., Zhang, L., Sung, Y. S., Chen, C. L., Assaad, A., Oliai, B. R., & Antonescu, C. R. (2018). Recurrent RET gene rearrangements in intraductal carcinomas of salivary gland. *The American Journal of Surgical Pathology, 42*(4), 442–452. https://doi.org/10.1097/PAS.0000000000000952

Wells, S. A., Gosnell, J. E., Gagel, R. F., Moley, J., Pfister, D., Sosa, J. A., Skinner, M., Krebs, A., Vasselli, J., & Schlumberger, M. (2010). Vandetanib for the treatment of patients with locally advanced or metastatic hereditary medullary thyroid cancer. *Journal of Clinical Oncology, 28*(5). https://doi.org/10.1200/JCO.2009.23.6604

Wells, S. A., Robinson, B. G., Gagel, R. F., Dralle, H., Fagin, J. A., Santoro, M., Baudin, E., Elisei, R., Jarzab, B., Vasselli, J. R., Read, J., Langmuir, P., Ryan, A. J., & Schlumberger, M. J. (2012). Vandetanib in patients with locally advanced or metastatic medullary thyroid cancer: A randomized, double-blind phase III trial. *Journal of Clinical Oncology, 30*(2), 134–141. https://doi.org/10.1200/JCO.2011.35.5040

Wilhelm, S. M., Carter, C., Tang, L. Y., Wilkie, D., McNabola, A., Rong, H., Chen, C., Zhang, X., Vincent, P., McHugh, M., Cao, Y., Shujath, J., Gawlak, S., Eveleigh, D., Rowley, B., Liu, L., Adnane, L., Lynch, M., Auclair, D., … Trail, P. A. (2004). BAY 43-9006 exhibits broad spectrum oral antitumor activity and targets the RAF/MEK/ERK pathway and receptor tyrosine kinases involved in tumor progression and angiogenesis. *Cancer Research, 64*(19), 7099–7109. https://doi.org/10.1158/0008-5472.CAN-04-1443

Wilhelm, S. M., Dumas, J., Adnane, L., Lynch, M., Carter, C. A., Schütz, G., Thierauch, K. H., & Zopf, D. (2011). Regorafenib (BAY 73-4506): A new oral multikinase inhibitor of angiogenic, stromal and oncogenic receptor tyrosine kinases with potent preclinical antitumor activity. *International Journal of Cancer, 129*(1), 245–255. https://doi.org/10.1002/ijc.25864

Wirth, L. J., Sherman, E., Robinson, B., Solomon, B., Kang, H., Lorch, J., Worden, F., Brose, M., Patel, J., Leboulleux, S., Godbert, Y., Barlesi, F., Morris, J. C., Owonikoko, T. K., Tan, D. S. W., Gautschi, O., Weiss, J., De La Fouchardière, C., Burkard, M. E., … Wirth, L. J. (2020). Efficacy of selpercatinib in RET-altered thyroid cancers. *New England Journal of Medicine, 383*(9), 825–835. https://doi.org/10.1056/NEJMoa2005651

Wu, R. Y., Kong, P. F., Xia, L. P., Huang, Y., Li, Z. L., Tang, Y. Y., Chen, Y. H., Li, X., Senthilkumar, R., Zhang, H. L., Sun, T., Xu, X. L., Yu, Y., Mai, J., Peng, X. D., Yang, D., Zhou, L. H., Feng, G. K., Deng, R., & Zhu, X. F. (2019).

Regorafenib promotes antitumor immunity via inhibiting PD-L1 and Ido1 expression in melanoma. *Clinical Cancer Research, 25*(14), 4530–4541. https://doi.org/10.1158/1078-0432.CCR-18-2840

Yakes, F. M., Chen, J., Tan, J., Yamaguchi, K., Shi, Y., Yu, P., Qian, F., Chu, F., Bentzien, F., Cancilla, B., Orf, J., You, A., Laird, A. D., Engst, S., Lee, L., Lesch, J., Chou, Y. C., & Joly, A. H. (2011). Cabozantinib (XL184), a novel MET and VEGFR2 inhibitor, simultaneously suppresses metastasis, angiogenesis, and tumor growth. *Molecular Cancer Therapeutics, 10*(12), 2298–2308. https://doi.org/10.1158/1535-7163.MCT-11-0264

Yamamoto, M., Miki, T., Tanaka, N., Miya, A., Shin, E., Karakawa, K., Kobayashi, T., Tahira, T., Ishizaka, Y., Itoh, F., Nagao, M., Mori, T., & Takai, S. I. (1991). Tight linkage of the ret proto-oncogene with the multiple endocrine neoplasia type 2A locus. *Japanese Journal of Clinical Oncology, 21*(3), 149–152.

Yamamoto, Y., Matsui, J., Matsushima, T., Obaishi, H., Miyazaki, K., Nakamura, K., Tohyama, O., Semba, T., Yamaguchi, A., Hoshi, S., Mimura, F., Haneda, T., Fukuda, Y., Kamata, J.-I., Takahashi, K., Matsukura, M., Wakabayashi, T., Asada, M., Nomoto, K.-I., … Tsuruoka, A. (2014). Lenvatinib, an angiogenesis inhibitor targeting VEGFR/FGFR, shows broad antitumor activity in human tumor xenograft models associated with microvessel density and pericyte coverage. *Vascular Cell, 6*(1). https://doi.org/10.1186/2045-824X-6-18

Zeng, Q., Cheng, Y., Zhu, Q., Yu, Z., Wu, X., Huang, K., Zhou, M., Han, S., & Zhang, Q. (2008). The relationship between over-expression of glial cell-derived neurotrophic factor and its RET receptor with progression and prognosis of human pancreatic cancer. *Journal of International Medical Research, 36*(4), 656–664. https://doi.org/10.1177/147323000803600406

Zhang, L., Moccia, M., Briggs, D. C., Bharate, J. B., Lakkaniga, N. R., Knowles, P., Yan, W., Tran, P., Kharbanda, A., Wang, X., Leung, Y. K., Frett, B., Santoro, M., McDonald, N. Q., Carlomagno, F., & Li, H. Y. (2022). Discovery of N-trisubstituted pyrimidine derivatives as type I RET and RET gatekeeper mutant inhibitors with a novel kinase binding pose. *Journal of Medicinal Chemistry, 65*(2), 1536–1551. https://doi.org/10.1021/acs.jmedchem.1c01280

Zhao, H., Zhou, L., Shangguan, A. J., & Bulun, S. E. (2016). Aromatase expression and regulation in breast and endometrial cancer. *Journal of Molecular Endocrinology, 57*(1), R19–R33. https://doi.org/10.1530/JME-15-0310

Zhong, L., Li, Y., Xiong, L., Wang, W., Wu, M., Yuan, T., Yang, W., Tian, C., Miao, Z., Wang, T., & Yang, S. (2021). Small molecules in targeted cancer therapy: Advances, challenges, and future perspectives. *Signal Transduction and Targeted Therapy, 6*(1). https://doi.org/10.1038/s41392-021-00572-w

Zhu, Z., Ciampi, R., Nikiforova, M. N., Gandhi, M., & Nikiforov, Y. E. (2006). Prevalence of RET/PTC rearrangements in thyroid papillary carcinomas: Effects of the detection methods and genetic heterogeneity. *Journal of Clinical Endocrinology and Metabolism, 91*(9), 3603–3610. https://doi.org/10.1210/jc.2006-1006

Zou, Z., Xing, P., Hao, X., Wang, Y., Song, X., Shan, L., Zhang, C., Liu, Z., Ma, K., Dong, G., & Li, J. (2022). Intracranial efficacy of alectinib in ALK-positive NSCLC patients with CNS metastases—a multicenter retrospective study. *BMC Medicine, 20*(1). https://doi.org/10.1186/s12916-021-02207-x

14

Serine/threonine-protein kinase B-Raf inhibitors

Rohini Karunakaran[1], Ravindra Kumar Chourasiya[2], Ankur Vaidya[3] and Ravichandran Veerasamy[4]

[1]Unit of Biochemistry, Faculty of Medicine, AIMST University, Semeling, Bedong, Kedah, Malaysia; [2]SVN Institute of Pharmaceutical Sciences, Swami Vivekanand University, Sagar, Madhya Pradesh, India; [3]Pharmacy College, Uttar Pradesh University of Medical Sciences, Etawah, Uttar Pradesh, India; [4]Pharmaceutical Chemistry Unit, Faculty of Pharmacy, AIMST University, Semeling, Bedong, Kedah, Malaysia

1. Introduction

B-Raf is a serine-threonine protein kinase that belongs to the Raf family. A conserved protein kinase signaling cascade that controls several vitally important physiological activities includes the B-Raf kinase (Pollock & Meltzer, 2002). The RAF—RAS—MEK—ERK signaling cascade includes this RAF isoform, one of three RAF paralogs in humans. Around 8% of all malignancies have been shown to have a B-Raf mutation, with the most significant incidence being seen in melanomas (66%). It is commonly accepted that mutant B-RAF plays a significant part in melanoma's expansion and spread (Roskoski, 2010). This gene contributes to several characteristics that distinguish the growth of malignancies, such as cell proliferation, survival, and resistance to apoptosis. B-RAF mutations are prevalent in melanocytic skin lesions and continue to be present in malignant melanoma. Direct suppression of B-RAF has demonstrated modest therapeutic efficacy in treating melanoma, which may be attributed to the intricacy of the RAF—RAS—MEK—ERK circuit (Mark & Rapp, 1984).

Further studies on alternative therapy options are needed to cure melanomas caused by oncogenic B-RAF. The discovery of a highly effective Raf inhibitor might significantly impact cancer therapy that relies on the Raf survival and proliferation signaling pathway (Zebisch & Troppmair, 2006). The novel drugs vemurafenib and dabrafenib, which block mutant serine/threonine protein kinase B-raf, have been proven efficient in clinical trials. Through carefully planned clinical studies, patients with BRAF mutant melanoma have been especially helpful in examining the complexity of the MAP kinase and PI3K/Akt/mT or signaling pathways (Fedorenko et al., 2011; Mitsiades & Fagin, 2010).

2. Mitogen-activated protein kinases

The serine/threonine kinases family, which includes mitogen-activated protein kinases (MAPKs), is essential for regulating cell growth, differentiation, and survival (Fedorenko et al., 2011; Mark & Rapp, 1984; Zebisch & Troppmair, 2006). Current studies have also shown that specific MAP kinases, with p38 MAP kinase, stress-activated protein kinase (SAPK), c-Jun N terminal protein kinase (JNK), and p42/p44 extracellular signal-related kinase (ERK 1 and 2), have significant independent signaling pathways to effect pleiotropic functions (Fig. 14.1). As regulators of transcription factor activity, MAPK signaling pathways are crucial (Mitsiades & Fagin, 2010). The apoptotic cascade involves serine/threonine kinase signaling pathways, leading to the initiation of JNK and p38 MAPK and effector caspases. Caspase 9 (a cytosolic downstream caspase) is activated by the release of cytochrome C, activating caspase 3. Pro-apoptosis genes are induced when JNK is activated (Kumar et al., 2003).

3. RAF—RAS—MEK—ERK (MAP kinase) signaling paths

Raf gene (v-Raf) was first discovered in 1983 by Mark and Rap and was characterized by murine sarcoma virus 3611. Raf-1, commonly referred to as C-Raf-1, has an 80,626 base pair

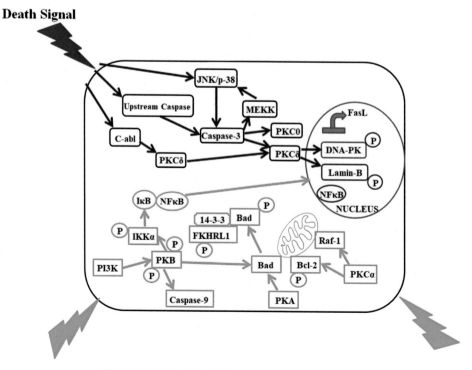

FIGURE 14.1　Serine/threonine signaling pathways.

structure and codes for a 3291nucleotide mRNA and a 648 amino acid peptide (Fedorenko et al., 2011; Wan et al., 2004). The human B-Raf gene, which has 18 exons and encodes mRNA with a length of 2949 base pairs, is found on chromosome 7q34. The Raf isoform consists of three domains: the Ras-binding and cystine-rich CR1 N-terminal domain; the serine/threonine-rich CR2 domain; and the protein kinase-active CR3 C-terminal domain. The protein-serine/threonine kinase family members A Raf, B Raf, and C Raf and MEK and ERK form the traditional mitogen-activated protein kinase signaling path (Garnett & Marais, 2004). The proliferation, differentiation, and tumors are all heavily influenced by the RAF/MEK/ERK kinase signaling path, as depicted in Fig. 14.1 (Hsueh et al., 2013; Michaloglou et al., 2008).

Protein kinases control several cellular processes, including proliferation, metabolism, nervous system activity, gene transcription, and immunological response. Cancer, diabetes, and inflammatory illnesses all have protein kinase signaling dysregulation (Kumar et al., 2003). The RAF/RAS/MEK/ERK path, which is important in several forms of cancer, is present in about 30% of human malignancies. The transfer of proliferative signals from cell surface receptors to the cell nucleus is mediated by the Raf family's intracellular serine/threonine protein kinases. Numerous tumor types have been found to harbor activating mutations of B-Raf (Wan et al., 2004). This includes melanoma, papillary thyroid cancer, and colon carcinoma. Hence, B-Raf continues to be a promising target for cancer treatment, thanks to the progress in creating small molecule B-Raf inhibitors. Small chemical B-Raf inhibitors specific to the V600E variant of the kinase have been discovered. Discussions will center on attempts to optimize the pharmacokinetic profile and studies into the series' structure-activity relationship (SAR). Drugs that show substantial selectivity in a kinase selectivity profile against other tyrosine and serine/threonine kinases inhibit mutant B Raf (V600E) preferentially in vitro at low nanomolar potencies in the biochemical, phenotypic, and cellular modes of active study (Garnett & Marais, 2004; Michaloglou et al., 2008). We will also show that medicines in this series, when given at safe doses with an optimal pharmacokinetic/pharmacodynamic (PK/PD) profile, inhibit the growth of A375 xenografts in vivo. Last but not least, we discovered and created a brand-novel class of powerful B-Raf (V600E) kinase inhibitors (Hsueh et al., 2013).

The RAF—RAS—MEK—ERK oncogenic path is frequently used in human malignancies. Through a complicated mechanism, Ras-GTP facilitates the synthesis of active homo- or heterodimers of A Raf, B Raf, and C Raf. The MAP kinases MEK1 and MEK2 phosphorylate and stimulate the protein serine/threonine kinases ERK1 and ERK2 (Furqan et al., 2013). The latter is responsible for many cytosolic and nuclear proteins' regulation phosphorylation. In the X-ray structure of a face-to-face dimer, the activation regions of B-Raf and MEK1 interact, with B Raf in an active form and MEK1 in an inactive one. The interaction of the four traditional parts of the RAF—RAS—MEK—ERK signaling module is facilitated by scaffolding proteins like the Kinase Suppressor of Ras (KSR1/2), a critical component in this signaling cascade. RAS mutations are responsible for about 30% of human malignancies (Huang et al., 2013; Lee, Mukhi, et al, 2012; Zhao et al., 2012). There are more than 70 distinct B-Raf mutations. Studies demonstrate that B-Raf correlates with human melanoma development and that the appearance of mutant B Raf causes the development of benign melanocytic hyperplasia (Cross et al., 2000; Fiskus & Mitsiades, 2016) (Fig. 14.2).

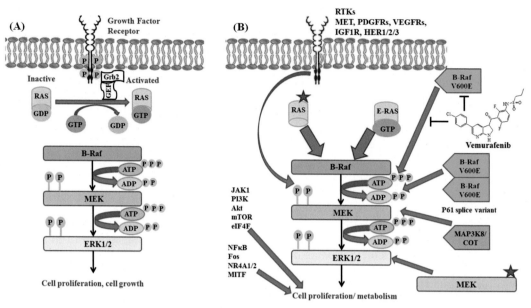

FIGURE 14.2   (A) RAF—RAS—MEK—ERK/MAPK cascade expresses mitogenic and other stimulatory signals from cell membrane receptors to the nucleus, phosphorylating transcription factors such as Myc and Elk-1. (B) Somatic B RAF alterations lead to constitutive kinase activity.

B-Raf is also specifically involved in carcinogenesis. The B-Raf protein and the associated signaling system have demonstrated potential as therapeutic targets for several illnesses. The cascade also phosphorylates many cytoplasmic proteins to control important cell fate decisions and activities, including proliferation, differentiation, and gene expression (Davies et al., 2002). A potent oncogene and potential therapeutic target are BRAF. BRAF inhibitors are clinically effective against melanomas based on BRAF mutations. The US Food and Drug Administration has approved the combination of a B Raf inhibitor and a MEK inhibitor (Cross et al., 2000). It has been suggested to use several ways to verify the clinical effectiveness of B Raf inhibitors. The RAF/RAS/MAPK path's activation is vital to malignancy growth. Interference with this route can potentially have antitumor effects, and clinical specimens, xenograft tumor models, and cell culture experiments have all shown this to be at least partially true. Inhibitors of Raf and MEK can reduce this signaling pathway, which can have clinical implications (Eisen et al., 2006; Fiskus & Mitsiades, 2016; Lee, Kim, et al., 2012; Shinozaki et al., 2007). According to studies, Raf inhibitor dramatically boosted cancer's CD4 and CD8 lymphocyte infiltration. A decrease in tumor volume and an increase in necrosis were associated with increased CD8 cells (Hauschild et al., 2009; Kudo & Ueshima, 2010).

4. BRAF as therapeutic target

Researchers have shown that altered B RAF is a potent oncogene of melanoma phenotype and is a crucial therapeutic target since BRAF-activating mutations are common in melanoma and malignancies. RNA interference suppresses the expression of BRAF-V600E and inhibits the MEK/MAPK pathway, arrests cell growth, apoptosis, and reduces invasive capacity. Suppression of BRAF-V600E induces tumor regression (Kudo & Ueshima, 2010; Stenner et al., 2012; Wu & Zhu, 2011). Extensive research has led to the clinical advancement and B RAF inhibitors in clinical progress (Poulikakos et al., 2010).

5. B-RAF inhibitors

Developments in targeting B-Raf have several advancements in treating oncological conditions (Yang et al., 2012). Due to its anti-angiogenesis properties, the FDA has approved sorafenib **(1)** (BAY 43−9006 OR Nexavar), a first-generation multi-target kinase inhibitor, for the action of melanoma, renal, hepatocellular carcinoma, and thyroid cancer. The efficacy of second-generation RAF inhibitors has significantly increased (Fig. 14.1. By targeting the B-Raf V600 E mutation, vemurafenib **(2)** (PLX4032, RG7204) functionality has proven to be incredibly effective for the treatment of melanoma (Fig. 14.3). This Raf inhibitor interacts with the mutant B-Raf monomer ATP binding domain (Andrulis et al., 2013). These medicines promote cell cycle arrest, death, and potent inhibition of MAPK/ERK proliferation. According to recent clinical findings, Vemurafenib's effectiveness against melanoma is restricted to the expression of mutant B-Raf. In patients with papillary thyroid carcinoma, vemurafenib

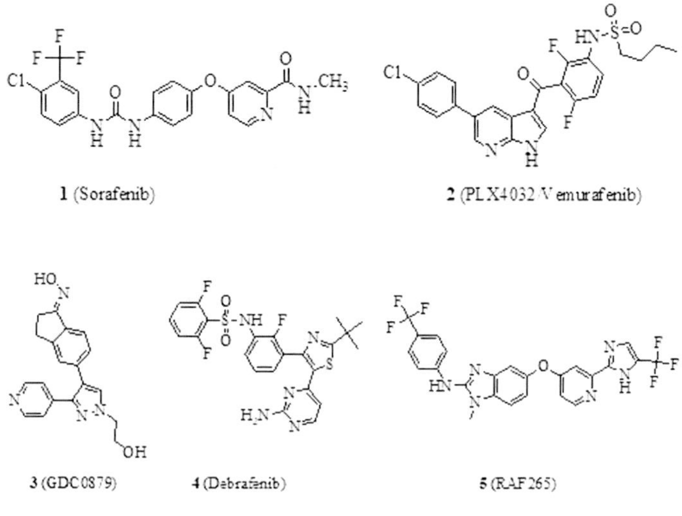

FIGURE 14.3 Structure of compounds sorafenib **(1)**, vemurafenib **(2)**, GDC0879 **(3)**, Debrafenib **(4)** and RAF265 **(5)**.

is also efficacious and has demonstrated excellent clinical outcomes. The therapy of thyroid cancer cells is linked to the binding of MAPK/ERK signaling (Bhatt et al., 2005; Boni et al., 2010; Kono et al., 2006; Nazarian et al., 2010) (Fig. 14.3).

Small new compounds that target mutant B-Raf have been actively used in the treatment of melanoma, according to several clinical studies incorporating preclinical models and clinical trials. When examined in mice, GDC0879 (3) has demonstrated that the inhibitory action is related to the cell's B-Raf V600E state (Curtin et al., 2005). It has been demonstrated that LGX818 functions as a potent and specific RAF kinase inhibitor with minimal efficacy against wild-type B RAF. In clinical trials, XL281 demonstrated antitumor activity as a selective RAF kinase inhibitor and has been used to treat papillary thyroid disease and colorectal melanoma. A powerful inhibitor of melanoma and wild-type B RAF, mutant and thyroid cell carcinoma, ARQ-736 is an ATP-competitive pan RAF kinase (Cruz et al., 2003; Landi et al., 2006; Sosman et al., 2012) (Table 14.1).

Saturable radiotracer binding to A375 melanoma cells was shown by an in vitro cellular binding assay. A powerful and extremely selective B-Raf inhibitor called encorafenib treats melanoma clinically. Its B-Raf dissociation half-life is substantially longer (T1/2 > 30 h) than that of vemurafenib (0.5 h), dabrafenib (4) (2 h), and Encorafenib's (6) half-maximal inhibitory concentration (IC50) for both wild type and V600E B Raf in biochemical experiments are the same (0.47 and 0.35 nM, respectively) (Dornan et al., 2020).

Because the RAF pathway is vital in cell cycle progression and apoptosis, B Raf, the major isoform in the brain, has been considered a potential target for stroke treatment. The SAR for SB-699393 (7) was developed from an earlier described powerful and selective B Raf inhibitor and concentrated on enhancing brain penetration by lowering HBD and tPSA, then optimizing physicochemical characteristics for ADME performance while retaining brain penetration (Yuan & Mary, 2018) (Fig. 14.4).

TABLE 14.1   B-Raf inhibitors in clinical trials.

B-Raf inhibitors/drugs	Diseases
Sorafenib	Renal cell carcinoma
Vemurafenib	Advanced melanoma
Dabrafenib (4) Trametinib	Advanced melanoma; solid tumors
ARQ-736	Advanced solid tumors
RAF265 (5)	Advanced melanoma
LGX818	Advanced melanoma
PLX3603	Advanced solid tumors
Multiple combinations of drugs	Pancreatic cancer; acute myeloid leukemia; hepatocellular carcinoma; renal cell carcinoma

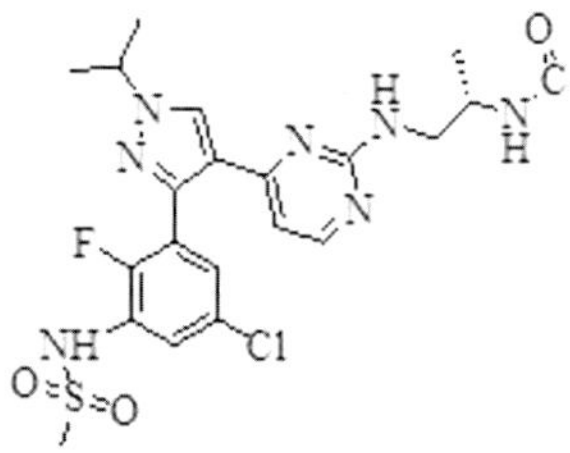

FIGURE 14.4 Structure of compounds Encorafenib (6) and SB-699393 (7).

6 (Encorafenib)   7 (SB-699393)

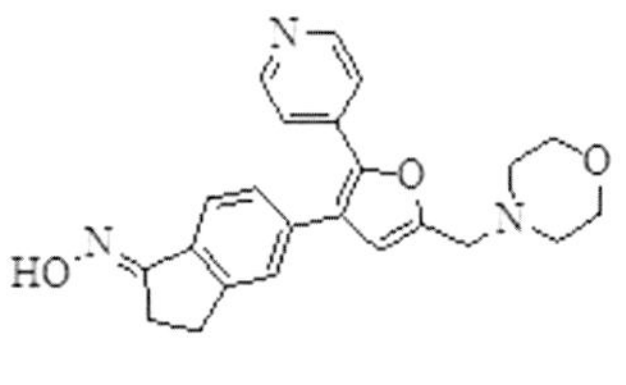

6. MEK inhibitors

The Ras/Raf pathway's downstream signaling mediator is MEK. MEK is a small molecule inhibitor that has received much attention as a potential cancer treatment (Chourasiya et al., 2013a, 2013b, 2016). The BRAF mutant cells were MEK-dependent and notably more responsive to MEK inhibition, according to clinical research (Hauschild et al., 2012; Ponti et al., 2012). As another method of treating BRAF-mutant tumors, MEK inhibitors have demonstrated that they stop tumor growth in BRAF mutants (Falchook et al., 2012; Long et al., 2012; Su et al., 2012). Studies have also demonstrated the effectiveness of MEK inhibitors in treating metastatic melanoma, and it appears that these inhibitors are most effective and provide the most therapeutic benefit when combined with other treatments (Joseph et al., 2010; Rubinstein et al., 2010; Solit et al., 2006). Several studies have been initiated for treatment measures, and another attractive combination of inhibitors is B-Rafis with MEK (Wu et al., 2013). Research has shown that combined treatment is successful; clinical study has shown that dabrafenib and trametinib are effective in treating melanoma patients (Johannessen et al., 2010; Nazarian et al., 2010; Villanueva et al., 2010). Studies have also indicated that B-Rafis resistance may confer MEK resistance (Akinleye et al., 2013; Poulikakos et al., 2011).

The allosteric inhibitor of mitogen activated protein kinase (MAPK), extracellular signal regulated kinase (ERK), and MEK, trametinib, is exceedingly potent. In patients with confirmed BRAF V600 E/K mutations, it has been approved for treating metastatic melanoma and anaplastic thyroid carcinoma. Trametinib is quite effective; however, some adverse side effects are dose-limiting and may require stopping the medication. These include cutaneous, gastrointestinal, and liver toxicity. The authors created a radio-labeled trametinib and assessed its in vitro and in vivo features to solve these problems.

In conclusion, [124]I-trametinib (8) absorption may be prevented by cold trametinib in several cancer cell lines, proving the radiotracer's specificity both in vitro and in vivo. KRAS and BRAF mutant cell lines took up [124]I-trametinib more readily than KRAS cancer cell lines with wild-type KRAS. Instead of utilizing the existing single fixed-dosage strategy, [124]I-trametinib can personalize the dose in vivo. When paired with radiomic data, it can also be used to track the development of therapeutic resistance. Furthermore, creating iodinated trametinib allows for the measurement of drug distribution for better drug delivery studies. In conjunction with other BRAF inhibitors, trametinib is frequently used to treat metastatic melanoma, although the medication has many side effects that limit its use. Cold trametinib significantly inhibited the overall absorption of [124]I-trametinib in vitro, which was reported to

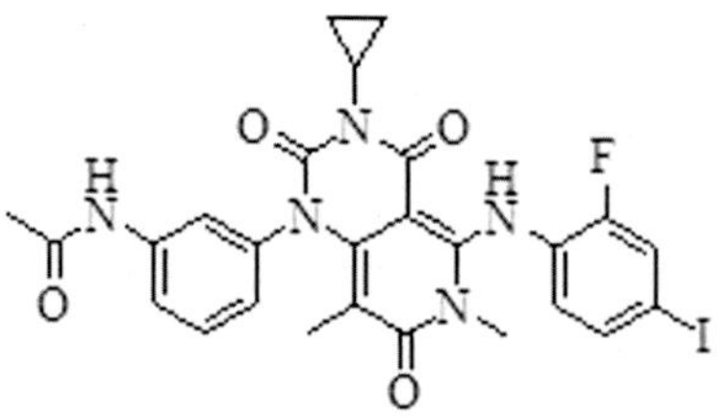

8 (^{124}I-Trametinib)

FIGURE 14.5 Structure of compound Trametinib (8).

be more avidly absorbed in KRAS and B RAF-altered cancer lines than in wild-type mela-noma cells (Pratt et al., 2020) (Fig. 14.5).

6.1 Others derivatives

6.1.1 Imidazo [2, 1-b] thiazole derivatives

The design and synthesis of a novel series of imidazo [2, 1-b] thiazoles were completed. The novel compounds have a pyrimidine ring at site five and a 3-fluorophenyl group at place 6 of the imidazo [2, 1-b] thiazole (9). The amide or sulfonamide moiety of the pyrimidine ring is joined to an ethyl or propyl linker at location 2 of the pyrimidine ring. Most of the series derivatives exhibited cytotoxic action against melanoma and colon tumor cell lines. With an IC50 value of 9.3 nM, compound 1 demonstrated potential inhibitory activity on ^{V600E}BRAF (Fig. 14.6).

Utilizing the Molecular Operating Environment (MOE) program, the docking study of the target compounds of the series with the B RAF kinase enzyme domain (PDB ID: 5CSW) (Wai-zenegger et al., 2016) was examined. According to the docking study, the majority of the target substances interact chemically with the amino acids Phe 595, Trp 531, Leu 514, Gly 534, Cys 532, Lys 578, Asp 594, Asn 580, Phe 583, and Lys 483. All of the target molecules also had similar binding groups with the B RAF kinase active site, including arene—arene and arene—cation in-teractions (naphthyl, phenyl, pyrimidinyl, and imidazolyl rings), as well as H-bonding interac-tions (sulfonamide, amide, and N pyrimidine chemical moieties). Analysis of the docking results revealed that most target compounds showed higher molecular interactions with the B RAF active site than the natural ligand. The target compounds with sulfonamide chemical moiety demonstrated more molecular interactions with the B RAF active site than those with the amide group, it was discovered (Mohammed, Usama, & Chang, 2019).

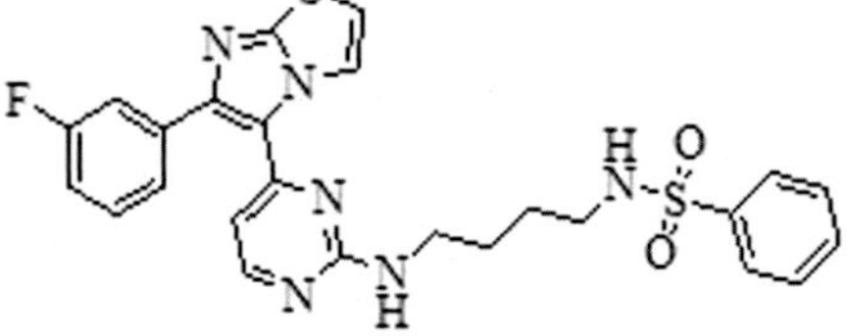

9 (Imidazo[2,1-b]thiazole derivatives)

FIGURE 14.6 Structure of imidazo [2, 1-b] thiazole derivatives.

6.2 Benzoylimidazole derivatives

In recent research, the histone deacetylase (HDAC) inhibitor and kinase inhibitor combos demonstrated additive and synergistic effects. With IC50 values of 9.11 and 5.40 M, respectively, the representative dual Raf/HDAC inhibitor compound (10) demonstrated superior antiproliferative activity against A549 (nonsmall cell lung carcinoma) and SK—Mel—2 (malignant tumor) in the cellular experiment to sorafenib (Chen et al., 2019). The study proposes a novel design strategy by combining the pharmacophores of the BRafV600E inhibitor and HDACs inhibitor in one molecule (Fig. 14.7).

6.3 Triarylimidazole bearing a phenylpyrazole group

The serine/threonine-specific protein kinase V RAF murine sarcoma viral oncogene homolog B1 (B RAF) is frequently altered in cutaneous melanoma and many other malignancies. A capable therapeutic approach for treating melanoma is the inhibition of mutant BRAF. A triarylimidazole BRAF inhibitor (dimethyl-[2-(4-5-[4-(1H-pyrazol-3-yl)-phenyl]-4-pyridin-4-yl-1H-imidazole-2-yl-phenoxy)-ethyl] amine) was discovered to be a functional BRAF inhibitor. Authors created analogs based on this starting point, eventually discovering 6-2-[4-(4-methyl-piperazine-1-yl)-phenyl] (11). The substance (11) has nanomolar activity in three assays: inhibition of purified mutant B RAF activity in vitro, inhibition of oncogenic B RAF-driven activation of extracellular regulated kinase (ERK) in B RAF altered melanoma cell lines, and inhibition of proliferation in these cells.

Triarylimidazoles have been described as inhibitor molecules for p388 and RAF, two examples of active kinase conformation kinases. The general structure of these latter kinase inhibitors consists of a hinge binding assembly, typically pyrimidine or pyridine, a central imidazole molecule that binds to the ribose position in the ATP binding pocket, and a substituted aromatic group that interacts with the hydrophobic pocket next to the gatekeeper residue. In the direction of the solvent, the third aryl ring extends beyond the ATP pocket. The described binding mode is supported by the co-crystal ligands of BRAF and SB-590,885 (12), a triarylimidazole BRAF inhibitor, which shows binding mode to the active conformation of BRAF. These substances are, therefore, BRAF type I inhibitors. SB-590885 and L-779450 (13) are two instances of triarylimidazole BRAF inhibitors described as active. These BRAF inhibitors have a phenol or oxime ring that functions as an H-bond donor and is necessary for their activity (Niculescu-Duvaz et al., 2010) (Fig. 14.8).

6.4 Imidazo [2, 1-b] oxazole derivatives

In the experiments now being discussed, a novel family of B RAF kinase inhibitors with an imidazo [2, 1-b] oxazole scaffold was designed and synthesized based on the structures of the well-

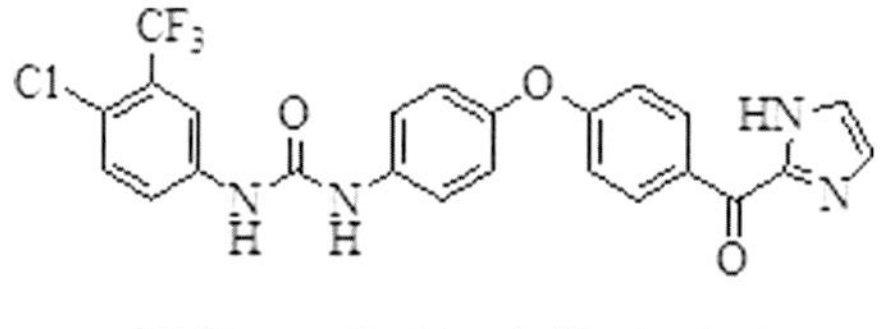

10 (Benzoylimidazole Derivative)

FIGURE 14.7   Structure of compound Benzoylimidazole Derivatives (10).

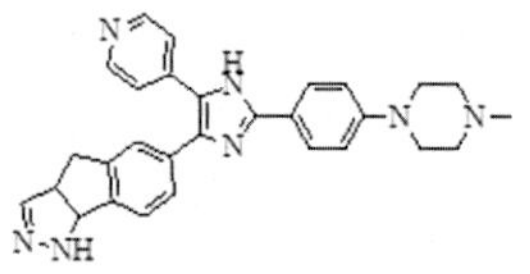

11 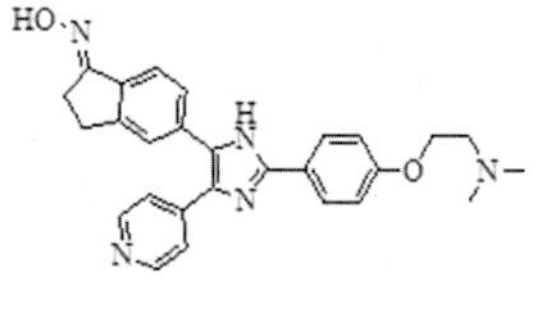   12 (SB-590885)

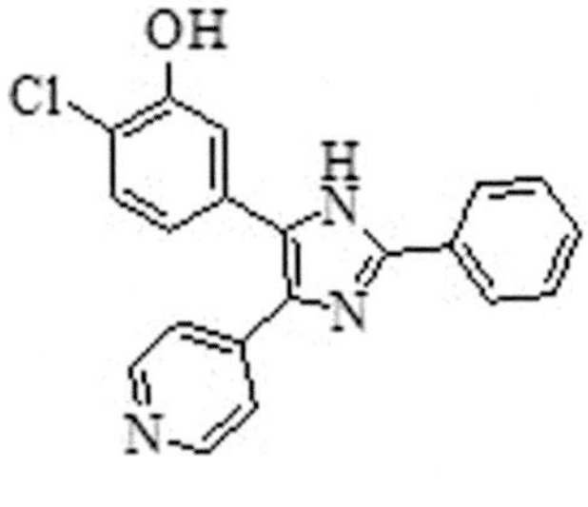

13 (L-779450)

FIGURE 14.8 Structure of compounds (4- methyl- piperazine-1-yl) —phenyl **(11)** derivative, SB-590,885 **(12)** and L-779450 **(13)**.

known B RAF inhibitors. The primary cytotoxic activity of the 22 selected compounds was evaluated against the A375 and SKMEL28 cell lines, and their activities were compared to those of sorafenib as a reference molecule. Additionally, the target molecules' anticancer properties were examined using the NCI-60 cell line assay. Compound **(14)** has an IC50 of 34 nM, making it the most effective against ^{V600E} B-RAF (Mohammed, Usama, Mohammed, et al., 2019) (Fig. 14.9).

6.5 Pyrazol derivatives

Cell cycle progression and apoptosis seem tightly regulated by the MEK—RAF—ERK cascade. The ERK path is constitutively activated by the BRAFV600E mutation, which can cause dysregulation of cellular growth. The biological activities of several 5-phenyl-1H-pyrazol derivatives have been developed and created, and their potential as BRAF^{V600E} inhibitors have been assessed. All of the compounds were previously unreported, although compound **(15)** showed the most significant inhibitory action (BRAF^{V600E} IC50 = 0.19 M): 1-(4-bromo-2-hydroxybenzyl)-3-phenyl-1-(5-phenyl-1H-pyrazol-3-yl) urea. The results of the antiproliferative assay showed that compound **(15)** had strong antiproliferative activity against the tumor cell lines A375 and WM266.4 in vitro, with IC50 values of 1.50 and 1.32 M, respectively. These values were similar to the positive control vemurafenib (Dong et al., 2013) (Fig. 14.10).

6.6 Pyrido [2, 3-b] pyrazinone derivatives

This study recognized the synthesis of novel pyrido [2, 3-b] pyrazinone derivatives. Investigations were made into the synthetic compound's in vitro cancer activities against the

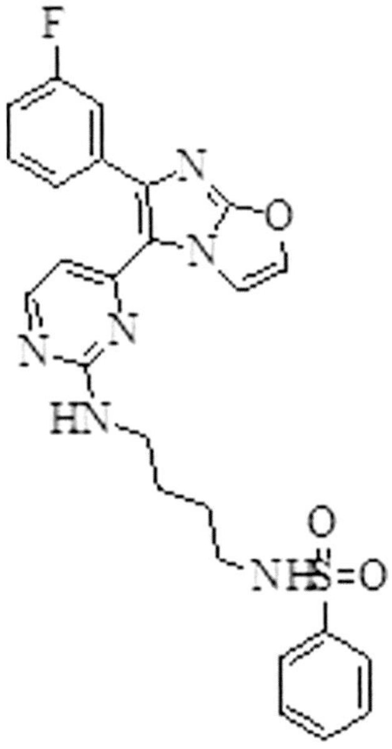

14

FIGURE 14.9 Structure of Imidazo [2, 1-b] oxazole derivative **(14)**.

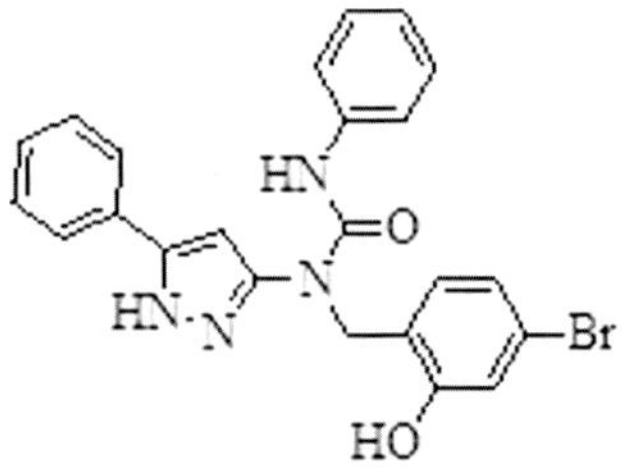

15

FIGURE 14.10 Structure of compound 1-(4-bromo-2-hydroxy-benzyl)-3-phenyl-1-(5-phenyl-1H-pyrazol-3-yl) urea **(15)**.

human colon cancer cell line (HCT 116) and kinase assay (^{V600E}BRAF). The outcomes showed that among the synthetic derivatives, molecule 6 (4-methoxy benzylidene acid hydrazide replacement) was the utmost active (IC50 13.103 M). They showed inhibitory action against V600EBRAF (81.33% inhibition). Additionally, utilizing an appropriate molecular docking procedure, the developed derivatives were put through simulations with the dynamic site of the mutant B RAF kinase domain. Docking studies indicated a high docking score with B RAF protein kinase domain 21.85,171 kcal/mol better than natural ligands, consistent with the compound **(16)** strong activity (Amin et al., 2019) (Fig. 14.11).

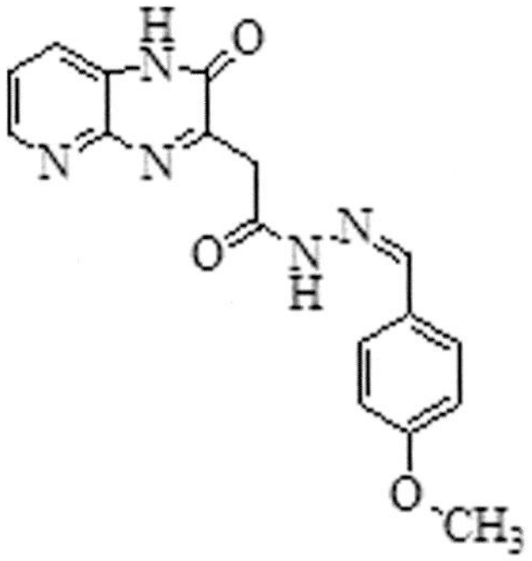

16

FIGURE 14.11   Structure of Pyrido [2, 3-b] pyrazinone derivative **(16)**.

6.7 N-hydroxyalkanamide derivatives

It has been demonstrated that combining a BRAF inhibitor with a histone deacetylase inhibitor (BRAFi) will increase the antitumor activity and slow the development of BRAFi resistance. This study designed and synthesized a series of (thiazol-5-yl) pyrimidin-2-yl) amino)-N-hydroxyalkanamide derivatives as novel dual inhibitors of B RAF and HDACs. Compound **(17)**, in particular, exhibited potent inhibitory effects on the BRAF, HDAC1, and HDAC6 enzymes. HCT116 cells with wild-type B RAF and HT-29 cells with the BRAF^{V600E} mutant had reduced their growth. Both cells demonstrated double inhibition against downstream HDAC and BRAF proteins. Considering the data, compound 7 is recommended as a probable lead compound for further research and as a supportive tool for inspecting the effects of B RAF/HDAC dual inhibitors (Li et al., 2022) (Fig. 14.12).

6.8 7-Azaindole derivative

The most typical known oncogenic protein kinase mutation is BRAFV600E. Additionally, inhibitors that specifically target "active" protein kinases have been confirmed to be highly effective in treating cancer. As a result, authors worked to create kinase inhibitors that specifically target the V600E variant of B-Raf. Compounds **(18)** and **(19)** are potent and specific inhibitors of active B-Raf that were found utilizing a structure-guided discovery methodology. The 7-azaindole derivative PLX4720 **(20)** creates a family of kinase inhibitors with

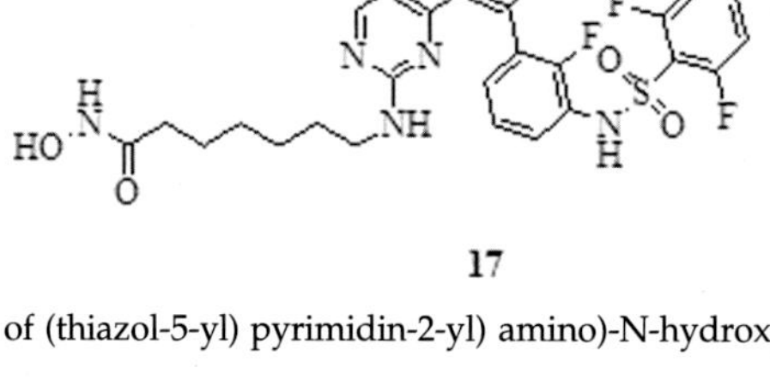

17

FIGURE 14.12   Structure of (thiazol-5-yl) pyrimidin-2-yl) amino)-N-hydroxyalkanamide derivative **(17)**.

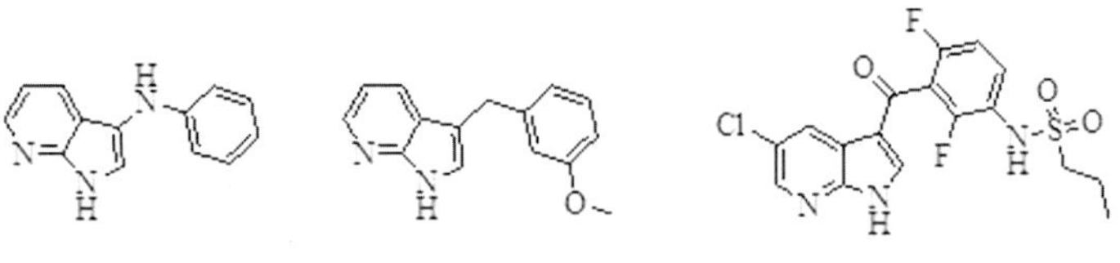

FIGURE 14.13   Structure of 7-Azaindole derivatives (18–20).

noteworthy discrimination in biochemical and cellular studies by inhibiting B-Raf^{V600E} with an IC50 of 13 nM. PLX4720 selectively inhibits the active B Raf^{V600E} kinase, unlike a wide variety of other kinases, and its potentially fatal effects are also limited to cells with the V600E genotype. The high degree of selectivity is supported by the fact that PLX4720 significantly reduces ERK phosphorylation in cancer cell lines that express B Raf^{V600E} but not in cells that do not express oncogenic B Raf. In melanoma models, PLX4720 only causes B-RafV600E-positive cells to experience cell cycle arrest and death. Orally administered PLX4720 causes considerable tumor development delays, including tumor regressions, in B Raf^{V600E}-dependent tumor xenograft models, without showing any toxicity. The study described here covers the entire discovery process, from initial identification through structural and biological studies in animal models to a potential therapeutic for testing in cancer patients with B Raf^{V600E}-driven tumors (Tsai et al., 2008) (Fig. 14.13).

7. Conclusion

B-Raf is a common target of oncogenic mutations in human tumors. The most frequent kind of BRAF mutation results in constitutive kinase activity. The B-Raf kinase activation region has a valine to glutamate (V600E) substitution that acts as a phosphomimetic mutation to simulate the occurrence of a negative charge. A recognized oncogene and possible therapeutic target are the BRAF V600E mutation. B-Raf inhibition has been the "poster child" of the accuracy medicine pattern with respect to molecularly targeted therapies in solid malignancies, and it is crucial in the case of cutaneous melanoma. In the clinic, Rafis that are small enough to be taken orally have shown therapeutic efficacy against BRAF-mutant melanomas. Additionally, B-Rafis have the unintended side effect of paradoxically accelerating the growth of people with BRAF-wild-type cancers, which limits their therapeutic benefit for patients without BRAF mutations.

Similar to how B-Rafis may cause gastrointestinal polyps, bladder cancer, leukemia, and cutaneous squamous-cell carcinomas (typically keratoacanthomas), they can also cause additional B RAF wild type, RAS-altered malignancies. Rafis' clinical activity has been less than melanoma in solid nonmelanoma cancers with B RAF alterations (such as thyroid and colon tumors). The de novo presence of bypass signaling pathways necessitates the development of more combinatorial approaches to get around this limitation. Raf inhibitor development, mutation detection, and understanding of the function of this crucial signaling protein in the growth of cancer have all advanced significantly.

8. Summary and future outlook

The need for combination regimens (to simultaneously inhibit MEK, PI3K/AKT/mT, etc.) is self-evident given that the duration of response to B-Rafis is frequently relatively brief and that various mechanisms of resistance/survival/escape may develop (Rubinstein et al., 2010; Solit et al., 2006; Wu et al., 2013). Anti-HIV or antituberculosis multidrug regimens can contain three, four, or even more drugs due to the wide variety of potential resistance mechanisms and the possibility for intratumoral, intrapatient, and interpatient heterogeneity, which has both advantages and disadvantages (Nazarian et al., 2010). The obvious promise of combining immunotherapies with B-Rafis, initially for melanoma and thereafter for other cancers, has been highlighted by the recent successes of immunotherapy methods against cutaneous melanoma. According to evidence acquired before clinical trials, B-Rafis may increase the immunogenicity of melanoma cells with a B RAF mutation (by derepressing the expression of melanocytic differentiation markers) (Johannessen et al., 2010; Nazarian et al., 2010; Villanueva et al., 2010).

Abbreviation

BRAF v-raf murine sarcoma viral oncogene homolog B
ERK Extracellular signal-regulated kinase
FDA Food and Drug Administration
MAPK Mitogen-activated protein kinase
MEK Mitogen-activated protein kinase
RAF Rapidly accelerated fibrosarcoma or rapidly growing fibrosarcoma
RET Rearranged during transfection
VEGFR Vascular endothelial growth factor receptor

References

Akinleye, A., Furqan, M., Mukhi, N., Ravella, P., & Liu, D. (2013). MEK and the inhibitors: From bench to bedside. *Journal of Hematology & Oncology, 6*(1), 27.

Amin, K., El-Badry, O., Rahman, D. A., & Ammar, U. (2019). Synthesis and in vitro biological evaluation of new pyrido [2,3-b] pyrazinone-based cytotoxic agents and molecular docking as BRAF inhibitors. *Chemistry Select, 4*, 8882–8885.

Andrulis, M., Lehners, N., & Capper, D. (2013). Targeting the BRAF V600E mutation in multiple myeloma. *Cancer Discovery, 3*, 862–869.

Bhatt, K. V., Spofford, L. S., & Aram, G. (2005). Adhesion control of cyclin D1 and p27Kip1 levels is deregulated in melanoma cells through BRAF-MEK-ERK signalling. *Oncogene, 24*, 3459–3471.

Boni, A., Cogdill, A. P., & Dang, P. (2010). Selective BRAFV600E inhibition enhances T-cell recognition of melanoma without affecting lymphocyte function. *Cancer Research, 70*, 5213–5219.

Chen, X., Gong, G., Chen, X., Song, R., Duan, M., Qiao, R., Jiao, Y., Qi, J., Chen, Y., & Zhu, Y. (2019). Design, synthesis and biological evaluation of novel benzoylimidazole derivatives as Raf and histone deacetylases dual inhibitors. *Chemical and Pharmaceutical Bulletin, 67*, 1116–1122.

Chourasiya, R. K., Akkinepally, R. R., & Agrawal, R. K. (2013a). Pharmacophore modeling and QSAR analysis of novel β-carboline derivatives as antitumor agents. *Letters in Drug Design and Discovery, 10*, 572–584.

Chourasiya, R. K., Akkinepally, R. R., & Agrawal, R. K. (2013b). QSAR and docking studies of novel β-carboline derivatives as anticancer. *Medicinal Chemistry Research, 22*, 2991–3001.

Chourasiya, R. K., Mourya, V. K., & Agrawal, R. K. (2016). QSAR analysis for some β-carboline derivatives as anti-tumor. *Journal of Saudi Chemical Society, 20*, 536–542.

Cross, T., Sheel-Toellner, D., Henriquez Nick, V., Deacon, E., Salmon, M., & Lord, J. M. (2000). Serine/threonine protein kinases and apoptosis. *Experimental Cell Research, 256*, 34–41.

Cruz, F., 3rd, Rubin, B. P., & Wilson, D. (2003). Absence of BRAF and NRAS mutations in uveal melanoma. *Cancer Research, 63*, 5761–5766.

Curtin, J. A., Fridlyand, J., & Kageshita, T. (2005). Distinct sets of genetic alterations in melanoma. *New England Journal of Medicine, 353*, 2135–2147.

Davies, H., Bignell, G. R., Cox, C., Stephens, P., Edkins, S., Clegg, S., Teague, J., Woffendin, H., Garnett, M. J., Bottomley, W., Davis, N., Dicks, E., Ewing, R., Floyd, Y., Gray, K., Hall, S., Hawes, R., Hughes, J., Kosmidou, V., … Futreal, P. A. (2002). Mutations of the BRAF gene in human cancer. *Nature, 417*(6892), 949–954.

Dong, J. J., Li, Q. S., Wang, S. F., Li, C. Y., Zhao, X., Qiu, H. Y., Zhao, M. Y., & Zhu, H. L. (2013). Synthesis, biological evaluation and molecular docking of novel 5-phenyl-1H-pyrazol derivatives as potential BRAF^{V600E} inhibitors. *Organic & Biomolecular Chemistry, 11*, 6328–6337.

Dornan, M. H., Petrenyov, D., Simard, J. M., Boudjemeline, M., Mititelu, R., DaSilva, J. N., & Belanger, A. P. (2020). Synthesis of a 11C-isotopologue of the B-Raf-selective inhibitor encorafenib using in-loop [11C] CO2 fixation. *ACS Omega, 5*, 20960–20966.

Eisen, T., Ahmad, T., Flaherty, K. T., Gore, M., Kaye, S., Marais, R., Gibbens, I., Hackett, S., James, M., Schuchter, L. M., Nathanson, K. L., Xia, C., Simantov, R., Schwartz, B., Poulin-Costello, M., O'Dwyer, P. J., & Ratain, M. J. (2006). Sorafenib in advanced melanoma: A Phase II randomised discontinuation trial analysis. *British Journal of Cancer, 95*(5), 581–586.

Falchook, G. S., Long, G. V., Kurzrock, R., Kim, K. B., Arkenau, T. H., Brown, M. P., Hamid, O., Infante, J. R., Millward, M., Pavlick, A. C., O'Day, S. J., Blackman, S. C., Curtis, C. M., Lebowitz, P., Ma, B., Ouellet, D., & Kefford, R. F. (2012). Dabrafenib in patients with melanoma, untreated brain metastases, and other solid tumours: A phase 1 dose-escalation trial. *Lancet, 379*(9829), 1893–1901.

Fedorenko, I. V., Paraiso, K. H., & Smalley, K. S. (2011). Acquired and intrinsic BRAF inhibitor resistance in BRAF V600E mutant melanoma. *Biochemical Pharmacology, 82*, 201–209.

Fiskus, W., & Mitsiades, N. (2016). B-Raf inhibition in the clinic: Present and future. *Annual Review of Medicine, 67*, 29–43.

Furqan, M., Mukhi, N., Lee, B., & Liu, D. (2013). Dysregulation of JAK-STAT pathway in hematological malignancies and JAK inhibitors for clinical application. *Biomarker Research, 1*(1), 5.

Garnett, M. J., & Marais, R. (2004). Guilty as charged: B-RAF is a human oncogene. *Cancer Cell, 6*, 313–319.

Hauschild, A., Agarwala, S. S., Trefzer, U., Hogg, D., Robert, C., Hersey, P., Eggermont, A., Grabbe, S., Gonzalez, R., Gille, J., Peschel, C., Schadendorf, D., Garbe, C., O'Day, S., Daud, A., White, J. M., Xia, C., Patel, K., Kirkwood, J. M., & Keilholz, U. (2009). Results of a phase III, randomised, placebo-controlled study of sorafenib in combination with carboplatin and paclitaxel as second-line treatment in patients with unresectable stage III or stage IV melanoma. *Journal of Clinical Oncology, 27*(17), 2823–2830.

Hauschild, A., Grob, J. J., Demidov, L. V., Jouary, T., Gutzmer, R., Millward, M., Rutkowski, P., Blank, C. U., Kaempgen, E., Martín-Algarra, S., Karaszewska, B., Mauch, C., Chiarion-Sileni, V., Martin, A. M., Swann, S., Haney, P., Mirakhur, B., Guckert, M. E., … Chapman, P. B. (2012). Dabrafenib in BRAF-mutated metastatic melanoma: A multicentre, open-label, phase 3 randomised controlled trial. *Lancet, 380*(9839), 358–365.

Hsueh, C.-T., Liu, D., & Wang, H. (2013). Novel biomarkers for diagnosis, prognosis, targeted therapy, and clinical trials. *Biomarker Research, 1*(1), 1.

Huang, T., Zhuge, J., & Zhang, W. (2013). Sensitive detection of BRAF V600E mutation by amplification refractory mutation system (ARMS)-PCR. *Biomarker Research, 1*(1), 3.

Johannessen, C. M., Boehm, J. S., Kim, S. Y., Thomas, S. R., Wardwell, L., Johnson, L. A., Emery, C. M., Stransky, N., Cogdill, A. P., Barretina, J., Caponigro, G., Hieronymus, H., Murray, R. R., Salehi-Ashtiani, K., Hill, D. E., Vidal, M., Zhao, J. J., Yang, X., Alkan, O., … Garraway, L. A. (2010). COT drives resistance to RAF inhibition through MAP kinase pathway reactivation. *Nature, 468*(7326), 968–972.

Joseph, E. W., Pratilas, C. A., Poulikakos, P. I., Tadi, M., Wang, W., Taylor, B. S., Halilovic, E., Persaud, Y., Xing, F., Viale, A., Tsai, J., Chapman, P. B., Bollag, G., Solit, D. B., & Rosen, N. (2010). The RAF inhibitor PLX4032 inhibits ERK signaling and tumor cell proliferation in a V600E BRAF-selective manner. *Proceedings of the National Academy of Sciences, 107*(33), 14903–14908.

Kono, M., Dunn, I. S., & Durda, P. J. (2006). Role of the mitogen-activated protein kinase signalling pathway in the regulation of human melanocytic antigen expression. *Molecular Cancer Research, 4*, 779–792.

Kudo, M., & Ueshima, K. (2010). Positioning of a molecular-targeted agent, sorafenib, in the treatment algorithm for hepatocellular carcinoma and implication of many complete remission cases in Japan. *Oncology, 78*(Suppl 1), 154–166.

Kumar, R., Angelini, S., Czene, K., Sauroja, I., Hahka-Kemppinen, M., Pyrhönen, S., & Hemminki, K. (2003). BRAF mutations in metastatic melanoma: A possible association with clinical outcome. *Clinical Cancer Research, 9*, 3362–3368.

Landi, M. T., Bauer, J., & Pfeiffer, R. M. (2006). MC1R germline variants confer risk for BRAF-mutant melanoma. *Science, 313*, 521–522.

Lee, B., Mukhi, N., & Liu, D. (2012a). Current management and novel agents for malignant melanoma. *Journal of Hematology & Oncology, 5*(1), 3.

Lee, S. T., Kim, S. W., Ki, C. S., Jang, J. H., Shin, J. H., Oh, Y. L., Kim, J. W., & Chung, J. H. (2012b). Clinical implication of highly sensitive detection of the BRAF V600Emutation in fine-needle aspirations of thyroid nodules: A comparative analysis of three molecular assays in 4585 consecutive cases in a BRAF V600E mutation-prevalent area. *Journal of Clinical Endocrinology & Metabolism, 97*(7), 2299–2306.

Li, Y., Huang, Y., Cheng, H., Xu, F., Qi, R., Dai, B., Yang, Y., Tu, Z., Peng, L., & Zhang, Z. (2022). Discovery of BRAF/HDAC dual inhibitors suppressing proliferation of human colorectal cancer cells. *Frontiers in Chemistry, 10*, 353. https://doi.org/10.3389/fchem.2022.910353

Long, G. V., Trefzer, U., Davies, M. A., Kefford, R. F., Ascierto, P. A., Chapman, P. B., Puzanov, I., Hauschild, A., Robert, C., Algazi, A., Mortier, L., Tawbi, H., Wilhelm, T., Zimmer, L., Switzky, J., Swann, S., Martin, A. M., Guckert, M., Goodman, V., … Schadendorf, D. (2012). Dabrafenib in patients with Val600Glu or Val600Lys BRAF-mutant melanoma metastatic to the brain (BREAK-MB): A multicentre, open-label, phase 2 trial. *Lancet Oncology, 13*(11), 1087–1095.

Mark, G. E., & Rapp, U. R. (1984). Primary structure of v-raf: Relatedness to the src family of oncogenes. *Science, 224*(4646), 285–289.

Michaloglou, C., Vredeveld, L. C., Mooi, W. J., & Peeper, D. S. (2008). BRAF(E600) in benign and malignant human tumours. *Oncogene, 27*, 877–895.

Mitsiades, N., & Fagin, J. A. (2010). Molecular genetics of thyroid cancer: Pathogenetic significance and clinical applications. In R. E. W. Refetoff (Ed.), *Genetic diagnosis of endocrine disorders* (pp. 117–138). San Diego, CA: Academic.

Mohammed, S. A., Usama, M. A., & Chang, H. O. (2019a). Anticancer profile of newly synthesised BRAF inhibitors possess 5- (pyrimidin-4-yl) imidazo[2,1-b] thiazole scaffold. *Bioorganic & Medicinal Chemistry, 27*, 2041–2051.

Mohammed, S. A., Usama, M. A., Mohammed, I. E., Mahmoud, M. G. E., Karim, I. M., Ali, E. M. H., Yoo, K. H., Lee, K. T., & Oh, C. H. (2019b). Synthesis, and anticancer activity of imidazo[2,1-b] oxazole-based RAF kinase inhibitors. *Bioorganic Chemistry, 93*, Article 103349.

Nazarian, R., Shi, H., Wang, Q., Kong, X., Koya, R. C., Lee, H., Chen, Z., Lee, M. K., Attar, N., Sazegar, H., Chodon, T., Nelson, S. F., McArthur, G., Sosman, J. A., Ribas, A., & Lo, R. S. (2010). Melanomas acquire resistance to B-RAF(V600E) inhibition by RTK or N-RAS upregulation. *Nature, 468*(7326), 973–977.

Niculescu-Duvaz, D., Niculescu-Duvaz, I., Suijkerbuijk, B. M. J. M., Ménard, D., Zambon, A., Nourry, A., Davies, L., Manne, H. A., Friedlos, F., Ogilvie, L., Hedley, D., Takle, A. K., Wilson, D. M., Pons, J. F., Coulter, T., Kirk, R., Cantarino, N., Whittaker, S., Marais, R., & Springer, C. J. (2010). Novel tricyclic pyrazole BRAF inhibitors with imidazole or furan central scaffolds. *Bioorganic & Medicinal Chemistry, 18*, 6934–6952.

Pollock, P. M., & Meltzer, P. S. (2002). A genome-based strategy uncovers frequent BRAF mutations in melanoma. *Cancer Cell, 2*, 5–7.

Ponti, G., Tomasi, A., & Pellacani, G. (2012). Overwhelming response to Dabrafenib in a patient with double BRAF mutation (V600E; V600M) metastatic malignant melanoma. *Journal of Hematology & Oncology, 5*(1), 60.

Poulikakos, P. I., Persaud, Y., Janakiraman, M., Kong, X., Ng, C., Moriceau, G., Shi, H., Atefi, A., Titz, B., Gabay, M. T., Salton, M., Dahlman, K. B., Tadi, M., Wargo, J. A., Flaherty, K. T., Kelley, M. C., Misteli, T., Chapman, P. B., Sosman, J. A., … Solit, D. B. (2011). RAF inhibitor resistance is mediated by dimerization of aberrantly spliced BRAF(V600E). *Nature, 480*(7377), 387–390.

Poulikakos, P. I., Zhang, C., Bollag, G., Shokat, K. M., & Rosen, N. (2010). RAF inhibitors transactivate RAF dimers and ERK signalling in cells with wild-type BRAF. *Nature, 464*(7287), 427–430.

Pratt, E. C., Isaac, E., Stater, E. P., Yang, G., Ouerfelli, O., Pillarsetty, N., & Grimm, J. (2020). Synthesis of the PET tracer 124I-trametinib for MAPK/ERK kinase distribution and resistance monitoring. *Journal of Nuclear Medicine, 61*, 1845–1850.

Roskoski, R. J. (2010). RAF protein-serine/threonine kinases: Structure and regulation. *Biochemical and Biophysical Research Communications, 399*(3), 313–317.

Rubinstein, J. C., Sznol, M., & Pavlick, A. C. (2010). Incidence of the V600K mutation among melanoma patients with BRAF mutations, and potential therapeutic response to the specific BRAF inhibitor PLX4032. *Journal of Translational Medicine, 8*, 67.

Shinozaki, M., O'Day, S. J., Kitago, M., Amersi, F., Kuo, C., Kim, J., et al. (2007). Utility of circulating B-RAF DNA mutation in serum for monitoring melanoma patients receiving biochemotherapy. *Clinical Cancer Research, 13*(7), 2068–2074.

Solit, D. B., Garraway, L. A., Pratilas, C. A., Sawai, A., Getz, G., Basso, A., Ye, Q., Lobo, J. M., She, Y., Osman, I., Golub, T. R., Sebolt-Leopold, J., Sellers, W. R., & Rosen, N. (2006). BRAF mutation predicts sensitivity to MEK inhibition. *Nature, 439*(7074), 358–362.

Sosman, J. A., Kim, K. B., Schuchter, L., Gonzalez, R., Pavlick, A. C., Weber, J. S., McArthur, G. A., Hutson, T. E., Moschos, S. J., Flaherty, K. T., Hersey, P., Kefford, R., Lawrence, D., Puzanov, I., Lewis, K. D., Amaravadi, R. K., Chmielowski, B., Lawrence, H. J., Shyr, Y., … Ribas, A. (2012). Survival in BRAF V600-mutant advanced melanoma treated with vemurafenib. *New England Journal of Medicine, 366*(8), 707–714.

Stenner, F., Chastonay, R., Liewen, H., Haile, S. R., Cathomas, R., Rothermundt, C., Siciliano, R. D., Stoll, S., Knuth, A., Buchler, T., Porta, C., Renner, C., & Samaras, P. (2012). A pooled analysis of sequential therapies with sorafenib and sunitinib in metastatic renal cell carcinoma. *Oncology, 82*(6), 333–340.

Su, F., Viros, A., Milagre, C., Trunzer, K., Bollag, G., Spleiss, O., Reis-Filho, J. S., Kong, X., Koya, R. C., Flaherty, K. T., Chapman, P. B., Kim, M. J., Hayward, R., Martin, M., Yang, H., Wang, Q., Hilton, H., Hang, J. S., Noe, J., … Marais, R. (2012). RAS mutations in cutaneous squamous-cell carcinomas in patients treated with BRAF inhibitors. *New England Journal of Medicine, 366*(3), 207–215.

Tsai, J., Lee, J. T., Wang, W., Zhang, J., Cho, H., Mamo, S., Bremer, R., Gillette, S., Kong, J., Haass, N. K., Sproesser, K., Li, L., Smalley, K. S. M., Fong, D., Zhu, Y. L., Marimuthu, A., Nguyen, H., Lam, B., Liu, J., … Bollag, G. (2008). Discovery of a selective inhibitor of oncogenic B-Raf kinase with potent antimelanoma activity. *PNAS, 105*(8), 3041–3046.

Villanueva, J., Vultur, A., Lee, J. T., Somasundaram, R., Fukunaga-Kalabis, M., Cipolla, A. K., Wubbenhorst, B., Xu, X., Gimotty, P. A., Kee, D., Santiago-Walker, A. E., Letrero, R., D'Andrea, K., Pushparajan, A., Hayden, J. E., Brown, K. D., Laquerre, S., McArthur, G. A., Sosman, J. A., … Herlyn, M. (2010). Acquired resistance to BRAF inhibitors mediated by a RAF kinase switch in melanoma can be overcome by co targeting MEK and IGF-1R/PI3K. *Cancer Cell, 18*(6), 683–695.

Waizenegger, I. C., Baum, A., & Steurer, S. (2016). A Novel RAF kinase inhibitor with DFGout–binding mode: High efficacy in BRAF-mutant tumor xenograft models in the absence of normal tissue hyperproliferation. *Molecular Cancer Therapeutics, 15*, 354–365.

Wan, P. T., Garnett, M. J., Roe, S. M., Lee, S., Niculescu-Duvaz, D., Good, V. M., Jones, C. M., Marshall, C. J., Springer, C. J., Barford, D., & Marais, R. (2004). Mechanism of activation of the RAF-ERK signaling pathway by oncogenic mutations of B-RAF. *Cell, 116*, 855–867.

Wu, C. P., Sim, H. M., Huang, Y. H., Liu, Y. C., Hsiao, S. H., & Cheng, H. W. (2013). Overexpression of ATP-binding cassette transporter ABCG2 as a potential mechanism of acquired resistance to vemurafenib in BRAF (V600E) mutant cancer cells. *Biochemical Pharmacology, 85*(3), 325–334.

Wu, J., & Zhu, A. (2011). Targeting insulin-like growth factor axis in hepatocellular carcinoma. *Journal of Hematology & Oncology, 4*(1), 30.

Yang, H., Higgins, B., Kolinsky, K., Packman, K., Bradley, W. D., Lee, R. J., Schostack, K., Simcox, M. E., Kopetz, S., Heimbrook, D., Lestini, B., Bollag, G., & Su, F. (2012). Anti-tumor activity of BRAF inhibitor vemurafenib in preclinical models of BRAF-mutant colorectal cancer. *Cancer Research, 72*(3), 779–789.

Yuan, S., & Mary, M. (2018). Brain penetrant kinase inhibitors: Learning from kinase neuroscience discovery. *Bioorganic & Medicinal Chemistry Letters, 28*, 1981–1991.

Zebisch, A., & Troppmair, J. (2006). Back to the roots: The remarkable RAF oncogene story. *Cellular and Molecular Life Sciences CMLS, 63*(11), 1314–1330.

Zhao, W., Du, Y., Ho, W., Fu, X., & Zhao, Z. (2012). JAK2V617F and p53 mutations coexist in erythroleukemia and megakaryoblastic leukemic cell lines. *Experimental Hematology & Oncology, 1*(1), 15.

15

Tubulin polymerization inhibitors

Sanjeev Kumar Sahu[1], Manish Chaudhary[1], Shweta Jain[2] and Kuldeep Kumar Bansal[3]

[1]School of Pharmaceutical Sciences, Lovely Professional University, Phagwara, Punjab, India; [2]Sir Madanlal Institute of Pharmacy, Etawah, Uttar Pradesh, India; [3]Pharmaceutical Sciences Laboratory, Faculty of Science and Engineering Abo Akademi University, Turku, Finland

1. Introduction

During the mitosis process (cell division), daughter nuclei or cells are formed by the division of single parent nuclei or cells and this requires efficient mitotic spindle assembly for the whole mitosis process. These spindles are a bunch of microtubules (originating from the centrosome) that guide the chromosome movements during mitosis. These spindle units generally separate sister chromatids and allow them to move in the opposite direction during cell division (Ems-McClung & Walczak, 2010; Honore et al., 2005).

Tubulin is a macromolecule (protein) generally found in protozoan class kinetoplastid. Here, it has five different forms namely alpha (α), beta (β), gamma (γ), delta (δ), epsilon (ϵ), and zeta (ζ) tubulin. Out of these five, α and β help in microtubule formation by polymerizing into protofilament. Moreover, 10–15 units of protofilaments in lateral form form a microtubule. Like other processes, critical concentrations of dimmers are required for the polymerization process, and the rate can be enhanced by the addition of dimer units. Arrangement of these α and β units should be done carefully to achieve specific polarity of microtubule. For this, one end of each tubulin unit needs to be exposed and can be termed as α and β end, respectively (Akhmanova & Steinmetz, 2008; Pellegrini & Budman, 2005).

Microtubules are dimmers of tubulin and are hollow and long in nature as shown in Fig. 15.1. Generally, these dimmers are stable due to complex formation, but due to the presence of GTP binding sites (two sites), these are vulnerable to hydrolysis. The GTP binding site of α-tubulin present at the interface of two monomers does not hydrolyze with irreversible binding with GTP, whereas the GTP binding site of β-tubulin present at the surface hydrolyzes with reversible binding into GDP. α-tubulin site attached with GTP plays a structural function, while β-tubulin with GTP and after hydrolysis helps in the attachment of new dimmers. GTP-bound and GDP-bound tubulins have different kinetics. GDP ones that are

TUBULIN STRUCTURE AND MICROTUBULE METRICS

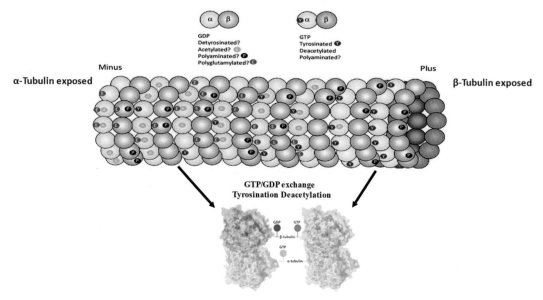

FIGURE 15.1   Tubulin structure and microtubule metrics.

generally present at the tip of the microtubule are more prone to depolymerization, while the ones in the middle did not depolymerize instantly. Disassembly can be protected by GTP tubulins when they are at the tip of the microtubule (rescue). Microtubule continuously undergoes growing and shrinking (catastrophe) (Howard & Hyman, 2003; Kirschner, 1980; Sontag et al., 2005).

Microtubules are present and are an essential part or component of cells and cytoskeletons. These help in cell structure maintenance along with micro- and intermediate-like filaments, and these also make up the structure of mobile parts of microorganisms like cilia and flagella. Along with this, these help in intracellular transport (ex. Organelle, other intracellular substances). Their extensive role in cell division makes them the perfect target for cancer treatment (Howard & Hyman, 2003; MacNeal & Purich, 1978).

1.1 Mechanism of action of microtubule targeting drugs

The anticancer effect of drugs targeting microtubules shows their effect by microtubule disruption producing abnormal spindles in the mitosis process, which in turn affects the cell cycle (G2/M phase). These drugs are also called antimitotic drugs. These drugs (at high concentrations) act via two mechanisms.

1. Inhibiting microtubule formation—polymerization inhibition, destabilization of tubules, decreasing polymer mass
2. Stabilizing microtubule formation—enhances polymerization, stabilization of tubules, increasing polymer mass

Based on this mechanism, these are classified into two categories: (1) microtubule destabilizing agents like vinca alkaloids and colchicine, and (2) microtubule stabilizing agents like taxanes. At low concentrations, these functions are the same except for interference in polymer mass. In turn, these halt the mitotic process and increase apoptosis (Pellegrini & Budman, 2005).

1.2 Binding sites on microtubule

Currently, there are three microtubule binding sites.

- Vinca site: present toward the end on the GTP binding site of β-tubulin (Gigant et al., 2005).
- Taxane site: present in the lateral interface (lumen of tubule-hydrophobic) in between the protofilaments (Seidman et al., 2001).
- Colchicine site: present in between the dimer space of α-tubulin and β-tubulin (Ravelli et al., 2004).

There are other sites as well that are still unknown (specific position and function of the site) till date, for instance, the site of binding of laulimalide. Vinca and colchicines inhibit tubulin polymerization, which in turn leads to microtubule polymerization inhibition and cell proliferation in cell division (mitosis). The taxanes promote polymerization, which leads to stable microtubules and disrupts the microtubule depolymerization process (Jordan et al., 1993; Li et al., 1999, pp. 139–148).

Antimitotic drugs with different molecular structures are there that might bind to the same binding site of tubulin (Fig. 15.2). These are natural (from organisms, plants, and other sources), synthetic analogs as well as semisynthetic derivatives. Currently, molecules that bind with tubulin are of utmost interest as anticancer agents, along with this for resistant or refractory cancer patients or for synergistic effects of molecules for cancer treatment. These effects are studied extensively by various scholars. These molecules are also useful for treating parasitic diseases like Mediterranean fever and inflammation caused by microorganisms (Ben-Chetrit & Levy, 1998; Giannakakou et al., 1998; Martello et al., 2000).

2. Induction of tubulin assembly—binding at taxoid and laulimalide site

Presently, antimitotic agents bind tubulin by at least five different modes, out of which two modes have a high affinity toward polymerized tubulin in comparison to tubulin heterodimer. For the induction of tubulin assembly, there are two binding sites: here, natural compounds with cytotoxicity (IC_{50}) less than 50 nM have been discussed.

There are various natural derivatives that bind with taxoid sites. These include paclitaxel, epothilones A and B, discodermolide, eleutherobin, cyclostreptin (FR182877), and dictyostatin 1 (Fig. 15.3). Initially, the binding of paclitaxel to the taxoid site for induction of tubulin assembly was reported in 1979. Similarly, for epothilones A and B, binding at the taxoid site for induction of assembly was reported in 1995 (Edler et al., 2005; Kowalski, Giannakakou, Gunasekera, et al., 1997; Kowalski, Giannakakou, & Hamel, 1997; Madiraju et al., 2005; Parness & Horwitz, 1981).

FIGURE 15.2   Binding sites on microtubule (Zhang & Kanakkanthara, 2020).

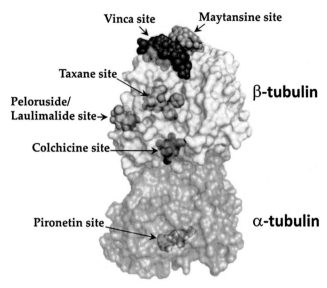

Laulimalide that binds on a different site than taxoid while inducing tubulin assembly was first reported in 1999. Binding at a different site than the taxoid site led to the failure of laulimalide as it cannot inhibit or synergize other drugs like paclitaxel in promoting tubulin assembly. In addition to this, peloruside A, which binds to the laulimalide site, cannot inhibit the taxoid site, but this can inhibit laulimalide binding (Gaitanos et al., 2004; Gapud et al., 2004; Hood et al., 2002; Pryor et al., 2002).

These molecules lead to hyperassembly and increase the stability of the cell division process. These reactions mostly proceed in various conditions like no or decreased polymerization process, at low temperatures in GTP deficiency, in cells with deficiency of microtubule-associated proteins or associated components (for instance glycerol), and decreased tubulin amount. These need to be monitored and allowed naturally (without drug administration) to form microtubules as these drugs alter the disassembly process. Like in cold temperature conditions, increased Ca^{2+} levels cause disassembly of tubulin while in the presence of these drugs, disassembly does not occur.

Studies indicated that these drugs bind stereometrically to tubulin, which in turn causes abnormal or more spindle formation that disrupts ongoing mitotic cell division. Consecutively, in interphase, there are misorganized microtubules (appropriate length is not attained for all tubules), leading these cells toward apoptosis and decreasing cancerous cell formation (Pryor et al., 2002).

3. Inhibition of tubulin assembly via β-tubulin alkylation or binding with colchicine or vinca domains

The other three modes by which drugs act on tubulin polymerization assembly come under inhibition of assembly. Generally, these include β-tubulin alkylation, binding with

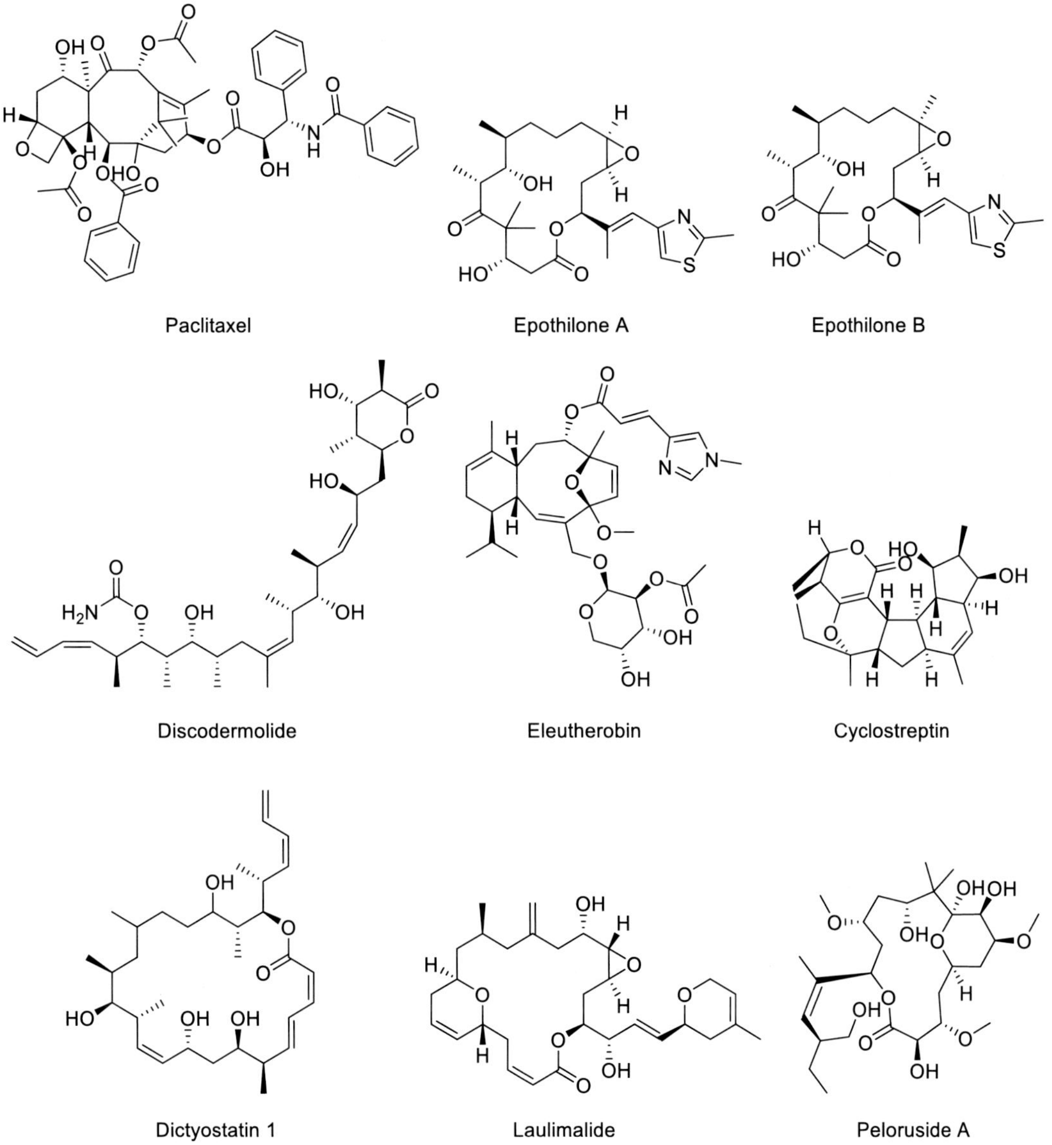

Paclitaxel   Epothilone A   Epothilone B

Discodermolide   Eleutherobin   Cyclostreptin

Dictyostatin 1   Laulimalide   Peloruside A

FIGURE 15.3   Structures of compounds that induce microtubule assembly.

colchicines, or vinca domains (Fig. 15.4). Due to these mechanisms, tubulin assembly is disrupted, which leads to the disappearance of microtubules. Concentration plays an important role here; at high concentrations, no spindle formation takes place, whereas at low concentrations, these are disrupted or abnormal spindle formations. Also, during interphase, the microtubule network is weakened, while at higher concentrations it disappears.

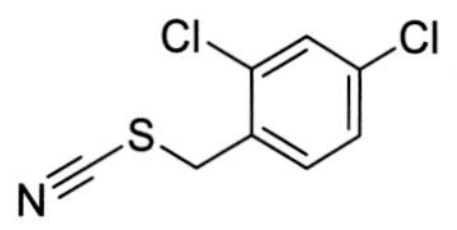

2,4-dichlorobenzyl thiocyanate

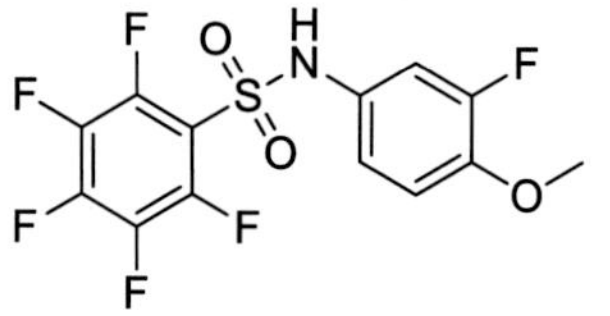

2-fluoro-1-methoxy-4-pentafluorophenylsulfonamidobenzene

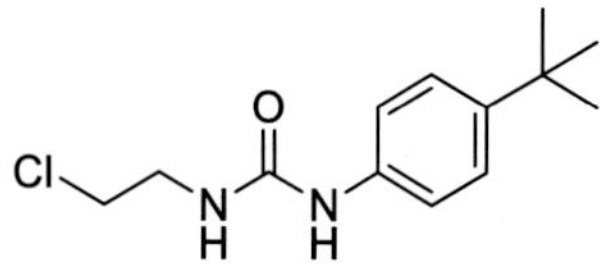

4-tert-butyl-[3-(2-chloroethyl)ureido]benzene

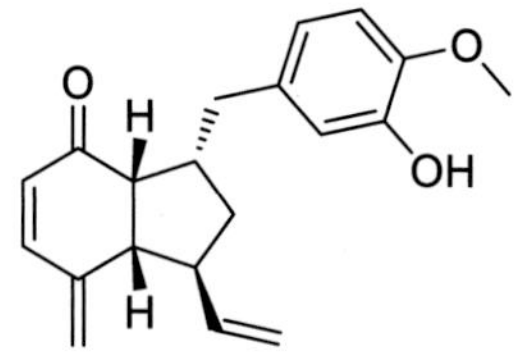

Ottelione A

FIGURE 15.4   Structures of antimitotic compounds that alkylate tubulin.

Certain derivatives that form covalent bonds with amino acid residues of tubulin, generally cysteine amino acid residue, lead to mitosis process disruption. This process (alkylation) of Cys causes loss in the polymerization potential of tubulin. For instance, the covalent bond between cysteine residues and 2,4-dichlorobenzyl thiocyanate (inhibits in 200—500 nM concentrations) within tubulin inhibits mitosis, and interaction of Cys-239 is most effective among all residues. While doing so, it does not affect the binding capacity for colchicine or GTP (Abraham et al., 1986; Bai et al., 1989). Similarly, 2-fluoro-1-methoxy-4-pentafluorophenylsulfonamidobenzene (T138067) also inhibits polymerization by binding to Cys-239 residue and is an analog of colchicine (also inhibits colchicines binding domain). Colchicine also interferes with the binding of T138067 with tubulin. In addition to this, T138067 has an IC_{50} value of 10—50 nM. Initially, aryl chloroethyl urea derivative 4-tert-butyl-[3-(2-chloroethyl)ureido]benzene, was supposed to interact with Cys-239 also it was effective against cancer cell line in micromolar concentrations. Various analogs were synthesized to improve cytotoxicity and to be more effective. Additionally, with Cys-239, Glu-198 of β-tubulin has been studied for alkylation inhibition of tubulin assembly (Bouchon et al., 2005; Mounetou et al., 2003; Shan et al., 1999).

Then, ottelione A (RPR112378) natural derivative was identified to inhibit the polymerization process by interacting with Cys residue. RPR112378 (structural analog of colchicine domain inhibitors) interacts with the colchicine domain and inhibits tubulin. It was most effective with IC_{50} 20 pM (Combeau et al., 2000).

Most colchicine domain binding drugs do not tend to do alkylation except for T138067 and ottelione A. These generally interact with the β-tubulin site near the interface of α- and β-tubulins. Apart from this, chloroacetyl containing colchicine derivative contain two cysteine units (Cys-239 and Cys-354) of β-tubulin (Bai et al., 2000; Beutler et al., 1993; Lin et al., 1988; Ravelli et al., 2004; Shi et al., 1995).

These derivatives are less complicated in comparison to derivatives that interact with the vinca domain while having different structures. Some reported colchicine domain interacting derivatives include natural derivatives like podophyllotoxin, steganacin, combretastatins,

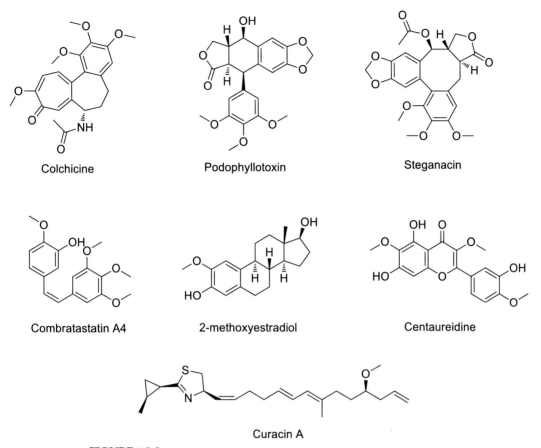

Colchicine   Podophyllotoxin   Steganacin

Combratastatin A4   2-methoxyestradiol   Centaureidine

Curacin A

FIGURE 15.5   Structures of natural products that bind in the colchicine site.

2-methoxyestradiol, flavones, and curacins, and some synthetic includes carbamates, heterocyclic ketones, and benzoylphenyl ureas (Fig. 15.5). The synthetic derivatives are also used for the same purposes (Fig. 15.6). Most of these have low IC_{50} values in the range of nM–μM (Blokhin et al., 1995; Hoebeke et al., 1976; Li et al., 1994; Paull et al., 1992).

However, these derivatives have less permeability to microtubules as these mostly bind with free tubulin to form tubulin-colchicine complexes and they remain bound to microtubules. It shows that the colchicine site on tubulin is not entirely covered in the polymer. The available ligand sites are radiolabeled with colchicine itself. Colchicine binding in comparison with other drugs had different properties like interactions do not occur at temperature 0–10°C while increasing temperature up to 40°C enhances interactions. Also, dissociation of colchicines is slow after interaction with tubulin, sometimes described as irreversible. Whereas, other drugs (other than colchicine) interacted easily at low temperatures and were easily dissociated. These factors can lead to variations in the inhibition power, not only due to temperature and time but also interactions (binding capacity) and dissociation that are essential for an inhibitor. Due to these reaction conditions and unfavorable modifications, derivatives generally fail to inhibit the site and have worse results. (Batra et al., 1986; Hastie, 1991; Jiang et al., 1990; Lin et al., 1991; Sternlicht et al., 1980).

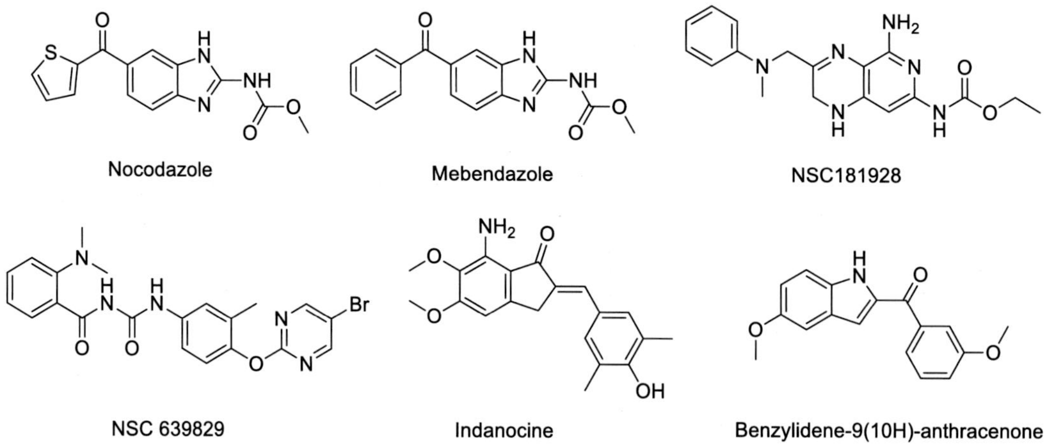

Nocodazole   Mebendazole   NSC181928

NSC 639829   Indanocine   Benzylidene-9(10H)-anthracenone

FIGURE 15.6   Structures of synthetic derivatives that bind in the colchicine site.

The last mechanism for tubulin polymerization inhibition is interaction with vinca domain of tubulin. Almost all the drugs in this category bind to site like interaction sites of vinca alkaloids in the tubulin, while there are different patterns of binding when these are evaluated by various methods like Lineweaver—Burk and Hanes analyses. Competitive as well as noncompetitive patterns were observed. It was proposed that the vinca site contains competitive and noncompetitive inhibitor (nearby sites to vinca) modes or binding sites. Noncompetitive inhibitors were observed due to steric interference by the drug molecules nearby to vinca-binding sites (Bai et al., 1990). Drugs that interact with vinca include vinblastine, vincristine (also competitive inhibitors); the maytansinoids (plant product maytansine); the ansamitocins P-3 and P-4 (fermented); macrolide rhizoxin; and myxobacterial macrocycle disorazol A1 (Fig. 15.7). In a study, competitive inhibition was observed with the drugs maytansine, rhizoxin, vincristine, or vinblastine. It was stated that maytansine and rhizoxin interacted at the same site but not at the vinca binding site. This indicates that like colchicines binding site, vinca also has a limited extent in microtubules both in length as well as at ends. IC_{50} of these derivatives against cell lines range from 0.5 to 1 nM for maytansine and 20—40 nM for vinblastine. Interaction of vinblastine in microtubules occurs mostly at αβ-tubulin dimmers in the tubulin (Bai et al., 1991, 1995; Elnakady et al., 2004; Gigant et al., 2005; Irschik et al., 1995; Jordan et al., 1986; Takahashi et al., 1987).

Noncompetitive inhibitors are classified into two categories including macrocyclic polyethers and peptides/depsipeptides. Macrocyclic polyethers further consist of two categories namely halichondrins and spongistatins (altohytrins) (Fig. 15.8). The most studied derivatives of tubulin inhibitors out of all noncompetitive inhibitors are halichondrin B and spongistatin. These inhibit the binding of radiolabeled vinblastin in noncompetitive mode. Additionally, analog of halichondrin B, eribulin mesylate, was approved by the FDA in 2010 for metastatic breast cancer. In addition, spongistatin 1 is a noncompetitive inhibitor of the peptide antimitotics, dolastatin 10. As dolastatin 10 (a noncompetitive inhibitor) blocks vinca alkaloids, this can be concluded that vinca might contain three binding regions. Macrocyclic polyethers are most effective as they have IC_{50} values in the pM range along with spongistatins to be the

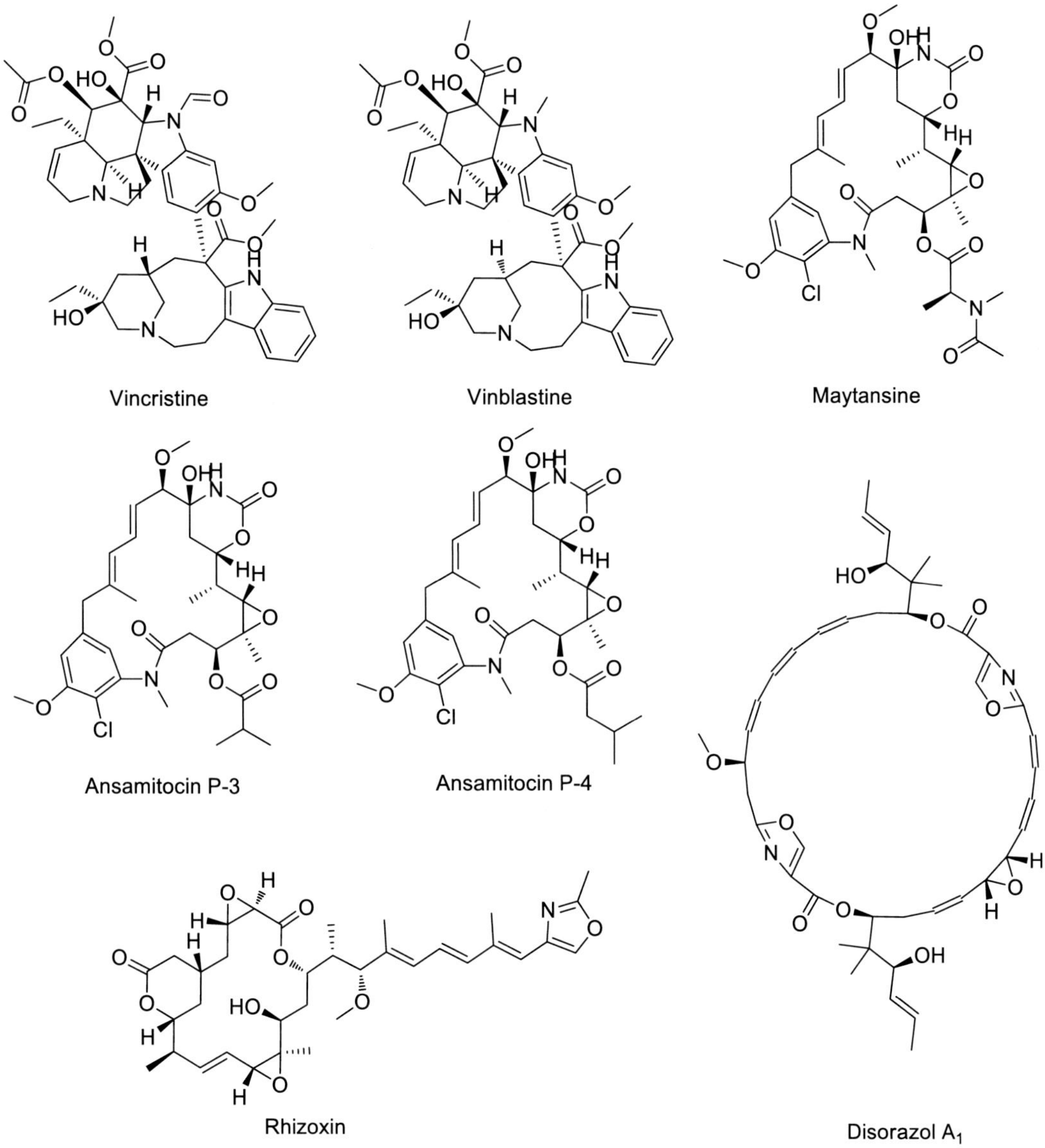

Vincristine   Vinblastine   Maytansine

Ansamitocin P-3   Ansamitocin P-4

Rhizoxin   Disorazol A$_1$

FIGURE 15.7   Structures of competitive natural inhibitors of vinca site.

most potent out of these (Bai et al., 1990, 1993, 1995; Dybdal-Hargreaves et al., 2015; Towle et al., 2001).

Structures of the molecules affect the binding with the vinca domain for instance peptides and depsipeptides bind differently. These are natural molecules containing modified amino acid residues (a common feature of peptides and depsipeptides) (Fig. 15.9). These are generally obtained from various organisms and have varied ranges of activity. Based on their

FIGURE 15.8 Structures of macrocyclic polyethers.

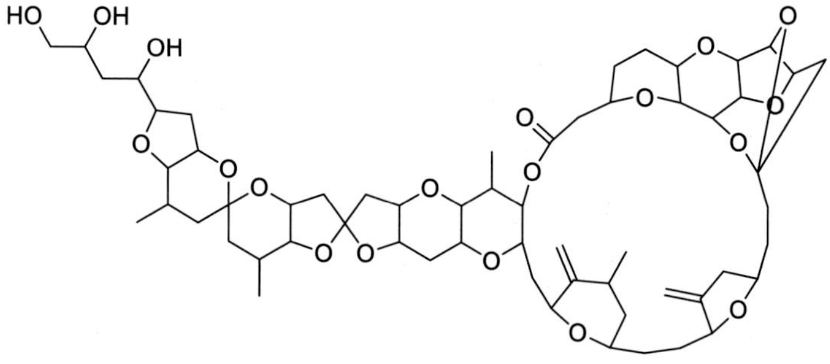

Halichondrin B

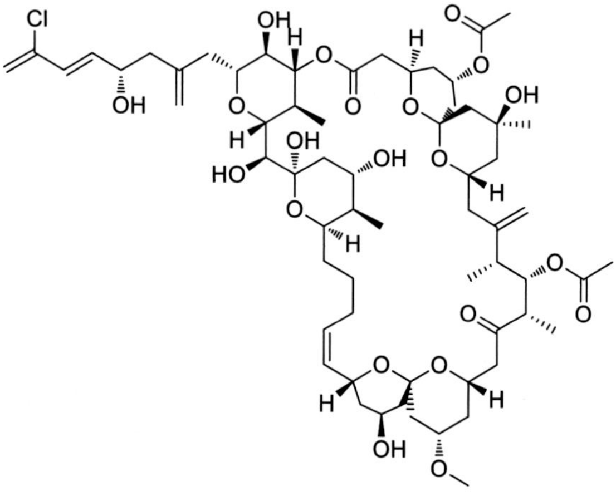

Spongistatin 1

inhibition at the alkaloid interaction site, these are divided into two: one that binds at the site and inhibits and another that does not inhibit (Hamel & Covell, 2002).

    Various agents like phomopsin A, ustiloxin A (fungus derived) (Li et al., 1995), dolastatin 10 (Bai et al., 1999), hemiasterlin, vitilevuamide (marine drugs) (Edler et al., 2002), cryptophycin 1 (cyanobacterial agent) (Bai et al., 1996), and tubulysin A (myxobacterial agent) (Höfle et al., 2003) inhibited vinblastine, vincristine, and rhizoxin binding strongly to tubulin assembly. Various studies like synthesis of radiolabeled dolastin 10 and noncompetitive inhibition of spongistatin 1 and others led to the discovery of various analogs; for instance, a derivative of dolastatin 10, cryptophycin 1, hemiasterlin, and phomopsin A are competitive in nature. Dolastatin 15 (Bai et al., 1992) and diazonamide A (Cruz-Monserrate et al., 2003) were studied for interaction at the vinca binding site. It was found that dolastatin 15 interacted less with the site and was replaced by dolastatin 10, cryptophycin 1, hemiasterlin, and phomopsin A, while results for diazonamide A were not clear. Celogentin C, a peptide, inhibited microtubule assembly and was a potent derivative. However, there was no data for this interacting with the vinca alkaloid binding site (Kobayashi et al., 2001).

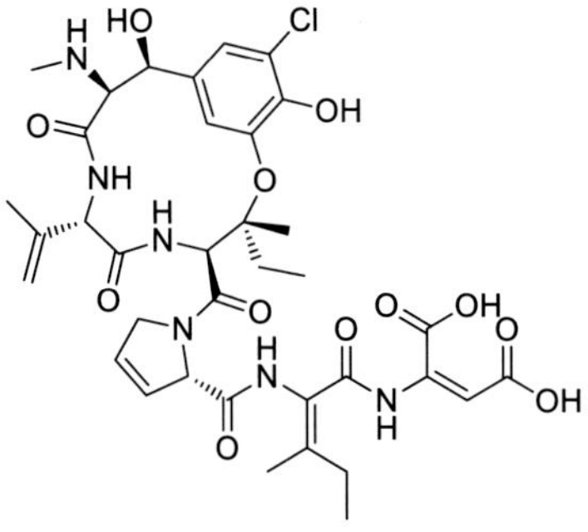

Phomopsin A

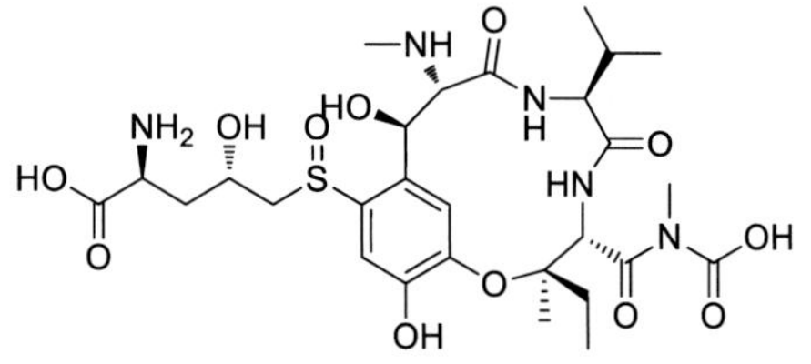

Ustiloxin A

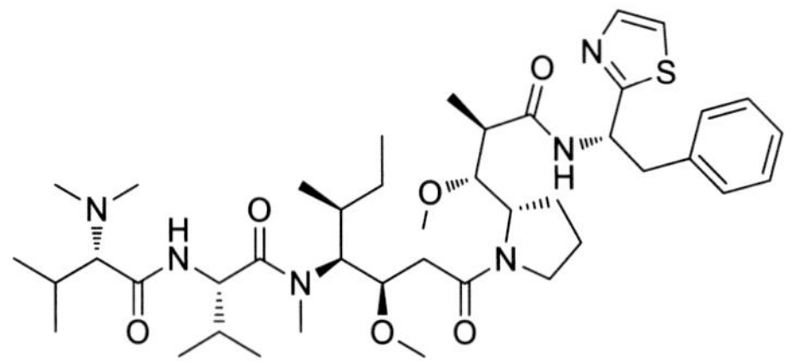

Dolastatin 10

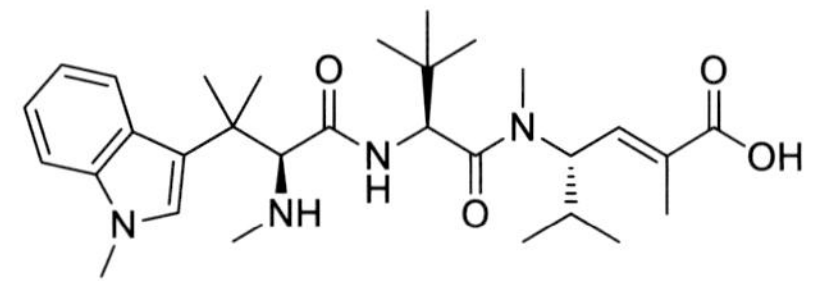

Hemiasterlin

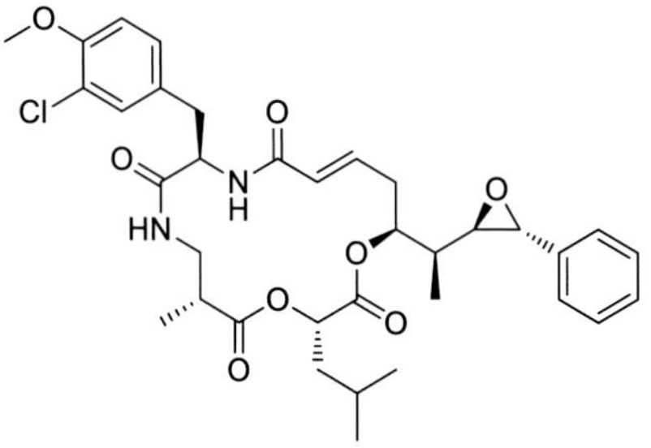

Cryptophycin 1

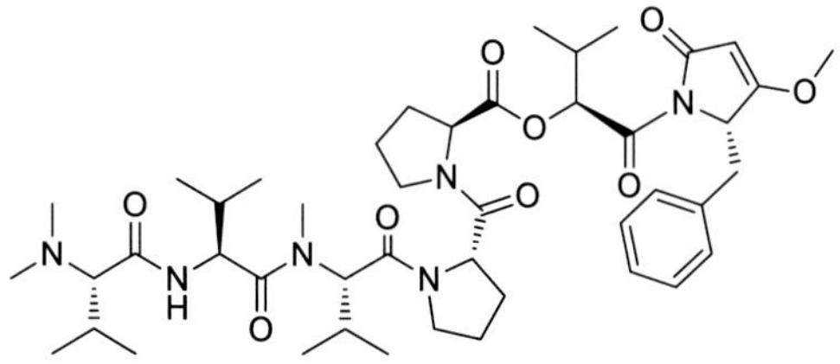

Dolastatin 15

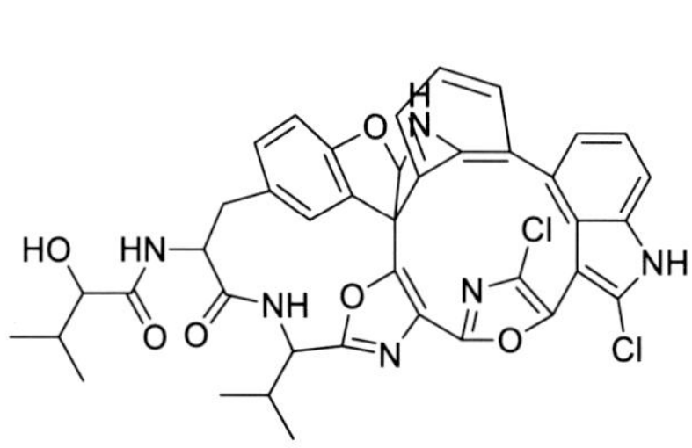

Diazonamide A

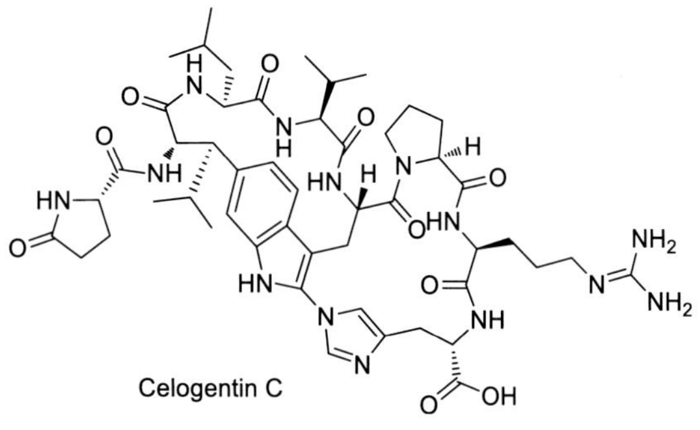

Celogentin C

FIGURE 15.9 Structures of peptides and depsipeptides.

Nowadays, there are various heterocyclic molecules that are being designed and tested for their tubulin polymerization inhibitory activity like stilbene and chalcone derivatives, carbocyclic analogs, fused ring systems and their analogs, and heterocyclic analogs with different membered rings. Colchicine 1, vincristine, vinblastine, and eribulin are some FDA-approved drugs (Kaur et al., 2014).

4. Recent developments in tubulin polymerization inhibitors

Wang et al. (2019) designed and synthesized 25 benzimidazole-pyrazole derivatives, and their evaluation was performed against A549, Hela, HepG2, and MCF-7 cancer cell lines. Among all synthesized compounds, compound **1** was the most potent anticancer agent. SAR studies indicated that p-CF_3 at A-ring and $-OCH_3$ and $-CH_3$ substitutions at B-ring increase the anticancer activity. Compound **1** with IC_{50} 0.15—0.33 µM was the most potent among all synthesized derivatives. Compound **1** with IC_{50} 1.52 µM against tubulin was the most potent. These results indicated that benzenesulfonamide-pyrazole compounds can be utilized for the development of promising anticancer agents (tubulin polymerization inhibitors) (Wang, Shi, et al., 2019).

(1)

Li et al. (2019) synthesized indole quinoline hybrid compounds and evaluated anticancer and antitubulin activity against HepG2, KB, HCT-8, MDA-MB-231, H22, and LO2 cancer cell lines. Compounds **2** and **3** were more potent than other synthesized compounds against all cell lines specifically the K562 cell line with IC_{50} values 5—11 µM, comparable to the CA-4 activity. Compounds **2** with CH_3 and **3** with CH_2OH had the best tubulin polymerization inhibition with IC_{50} 2.54 and 2.09 µM, respectively, while CA-4 had inhibition at IC_{50} 2.12 µM. It was indicated from the results that compound **3** arrests the G2/M phase of the cell cycle and also induces apoptosis of K562 cell lines in a dose-dependent manner (Li et al., 2019).

(2)   (3)

Wang et al. (2019) synthesized chalcone containing naphthalene and indole derivatives. The fifth position was essential for activity having α,β-unsaturated ketone substitution as changing the position of the group decreased anticancer activity. Compound **4** with IC_{50} values 0.65, 1.13, and 0.82 μM was most potent against HepG2, HCT116, and MCF-7 cancer cell lines, respectively. Meanwhile, the substitution of benzyl or bulk alkyl groups at the first position of the indole nucleus increases anticancer activity. Further investigation of the anti-tubulin activity of compound **4** was performed and the result indicated tubulin polymerization inhibition at IC_{50} 3.9 μM while colchicines inhibited at IC_{50} 13 μM. Compound **4** arrested the G2/M phase in a dose-dependent manner(Wang, Peng, & Li, 2019).

(4)

Yin et al. (2019) synthesized and evaluated resveratrol−cinnamoyl hybrids as tubulin polymerization inhibitors. Compound **5** with IC_{50} 0.12, 0.016, 0.44, 0.37, and 0.78 μM against A549, MCF-7, HepG2, HeLa, and MDA-231 cell lines, respectively, was the most potent among synthesized compounds. Compound **5** inhibited tubulin polymerization with IC_{50} 1.03 μM while standard CA-4 at IC_{50} 1.32 μM. Molecular docking indicated that compound **5** and colchicine had similar binding toward the colchicine binding site. The trimethoxy phenyl group of **5** had a hydrogen bond with Cys241, which is a major interaction for CBS inhibitors. In addition, the acyl ester group increased the flexibility, which allows compound **5** to bind with specified conformation. Compound **5** functions by disrupting microtubules similar to colchicines (Yin et al., 2019).

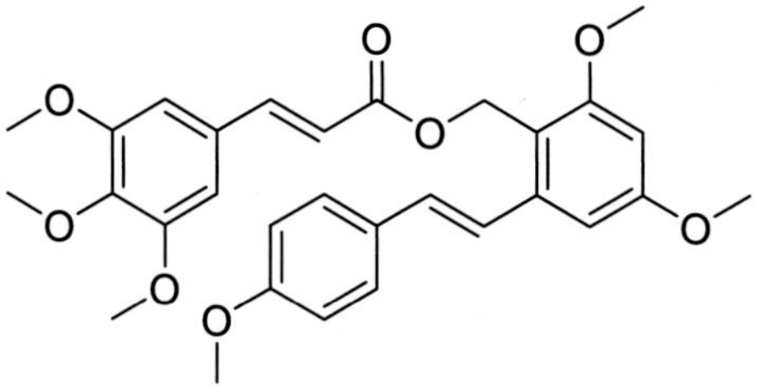

(5)

Xu et al. (2019) synthesized and evaluated pyridine-chalcone derivatives as potential antitubulin agents. Compound **6** was most potent with the IC$_{50}$ 0.023–0.047 µM against four cancer cell lines and one normal cell line. Compound **6** had IC$_{50}$ 0.023 µM against K562 cell lines. Methyl substitutions at the α-position of the unsaturated carbonyl group were favorable for tubulin inhibitory activity. Meanwhile, at B-ring, hydroxyl was essential for tubulin inhibition. Compound **6** with IC$_{50}$ 2.08 µM inhibited tubulin polymerization, while CA-4 at IC$_{50}$ 2.17 µM. Compound **6** arrested the G2/M phase, induced cell apoptosis, and microtubule assembly disintegrated. Compound **6** decreased the tumor weight by 65.8% at 20 mg/kg per day (i.v.), while referencing CA-41 50.9% at 20 mg/kg or CA-4P 62.7% at 20 mg/kg (Xu et al., 2019).

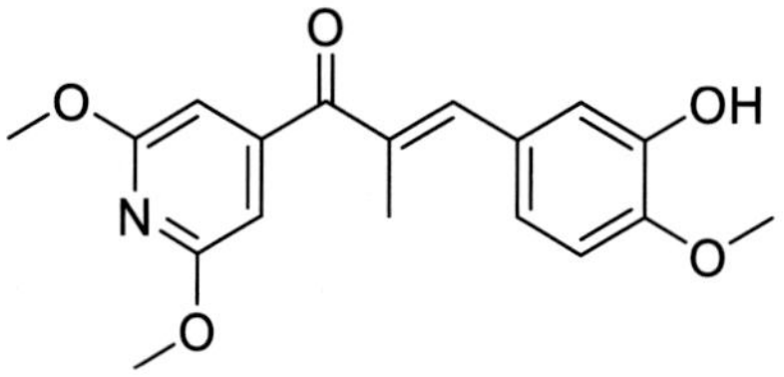

(6)

Govindaiah et al. (2019) synthesized 40,7-dihydroxycoumarin containing cyanohydrazone derivatives and evaluated them against A549, HeLa, SKNSH, and MCF7 cancer cell lines. Among synthesized compounds, compound **7** was the most potent with IC$_{50}$ 4.31, 5.14, 6.09, and 3.42 µM against A549, HeLa, SKNSH, and MCF7, respectively. Further evaluation of the pharmacological activity of compound **7** on cell cycle progression was studied and tubulin polymerization inhibition assays were also performed. The results showed that compound **7** arrested the G2/M phase and inhibited tubulin polymerization at an IC$_{50}$ value of 6.19 µM. The docking studies indicated that hydrazide–hydrazone derivatives are more active when the cyano group is linked to the hydrazone moiety improving the activity of the compound (Govindaiah et al., 2019).

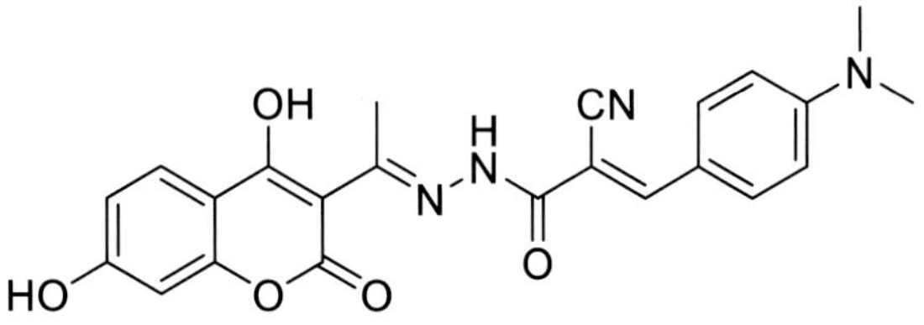

(7)

Manasa et al. (2020) synthesized 1,2,3-triazole and sulfonamide derivatives and evaluated against BT-474, HeLa, MCF-7, NCI—H460, and HaCaT using the MTT assay. Compound **8** with IC$_{50}$ 0.99 ± 0.01 μM was most potent against the BT-474 cancer cell line. Compound **8** inhibited tubulin polymerization, arrested the G2/M phase, and induced apoptosis to prevent cell proliferation. Molecular modeling studies indicated the binding of compound **8** at the colchicines binding site. The sulfonyl group had strong H-bond interaction with Ser178, and the triazole had two H-bond interactions with Ala250 and Lys254 (Manasa et al., 2020).

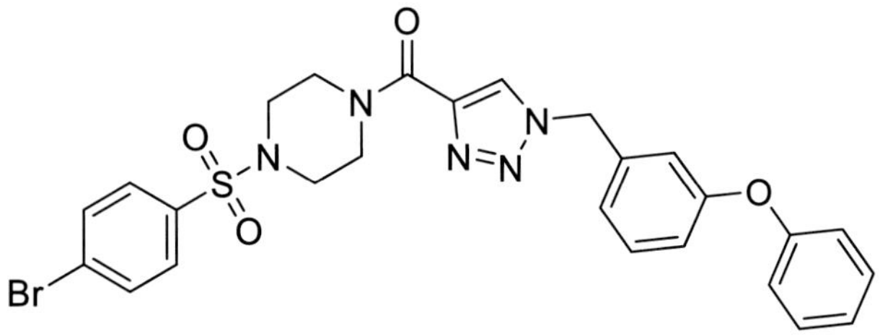

(8)

Qi et al. (2020) synthesized benzo[b]furan and triazole derivatives and evaluated them against HCT116, HepG2, HeLa, and A549. Compound **9** was the most potent with IC$_{50}$ 0.87, 0.73, 5.74, and 0.57 μM, against HCT116, HeLa, HepG2, and A549, respectively. SAR indicated that ethoxy and isopropyl substitution at the R2 position decreases anticancer activity also displacement of aniline by other heterocyclic rings like piperidine at R2 decreases cytotoxic activity. Compound **9** led to tubulin polymerization inhibition with an IC$_{50}$ value of 4.1 μM, in comparison with CA-4 (1.0 μM). Compound **9** arrested the G2/M phase by disrupting microtubules which led to cell apoptosis. Molecular modeling indicated that 3,4,5-trimethoxybenzene attaches with β-tubulin and forms a hydrophobic interaction with Cys241 residue, while the benzo[b]furan ring attaches with α-tubulin (Qi et al., 2020).

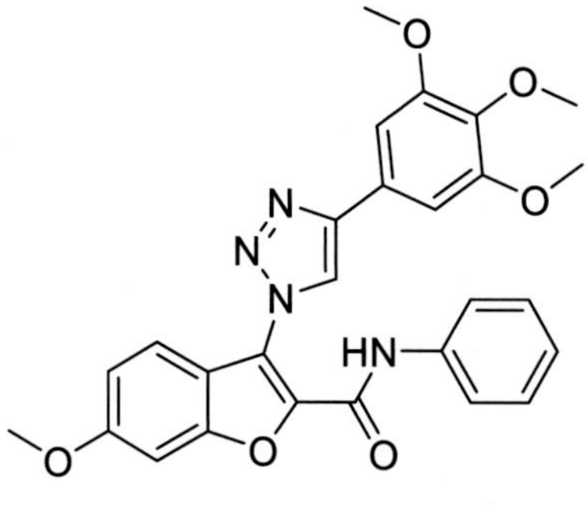

(9)

Donthiboina et al. (2020) synthesized benzimidazole-cinnamic acid hybrids and evaluated their cytotoxic activity. Among the synthesized compounds, **10** with IC$_{50}$ 0.29 μM was the most potent against the lung cancer cell line and had less cytotoxicity against NRK-52E with an IC$_{50}$ value of 1.58 μM. SAR indicated less substitution on the phenyl ring of cinnamic acid had less cytotoxicity. Substitution with electron-withdrawing groups on the phenyl ring led to a decrease or loss in activity. However, electron-donating substitutions on either ring had moderate or good activity. Compound **10** led to induction of apoptosis by increasing ROS, and tubulin polymerization was inhibited at IC$_{50}$ 4.64 μM, and also blocked cell proliferation at the G2/M phase (Donthiboina et al., 2020). Compound **10** is synthetic compound, whose structure is given below.

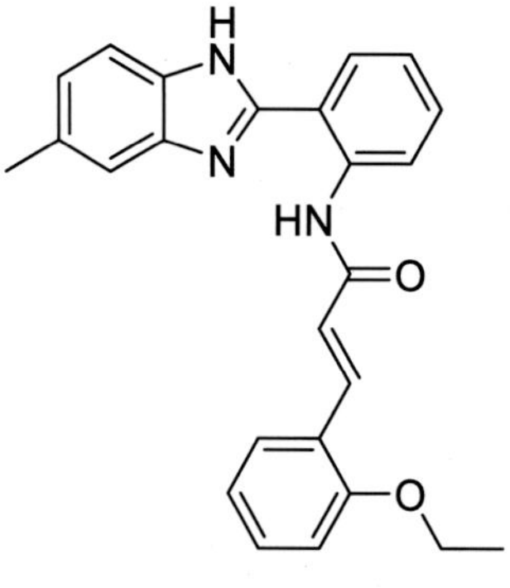

(10)

Wang et al. (2020) synthesized pyrazole-naphthalene derivatives as anticancer agents. Introduction of electron-withdrawing groups on phenyl ring enhanced inhibitory activity of derivatives. Compound **11** with IC$_{50}$ 2.78 μM with 4-C$_2$H$_5$O of the phenyl ring, was fivefold more potent than standard drug cisplatin IC$_{50}$ 15.24 μM. Compound **11** with IC$_{50}$ 4.6 μM was also a potent inhibitor of tubulin assembly, which inhibited tubulin polymerization (Wang et al., 2020).

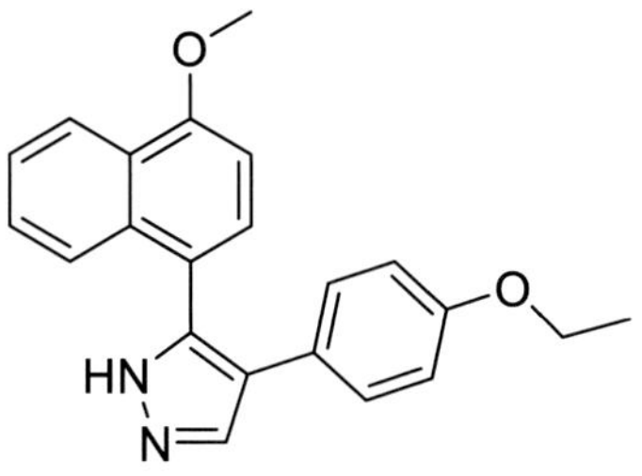

(11)

Jian et al. (2020) synthesized pyrazolo[3,4-b]pyridines and evaluated their antiproliferative activity. Compound **12** with IC$_{50}$ 27.22, 27.04, 18.08, and 62.82 µM against MCF-7, MDA-MB-231, HeLa, and Kyse150, respectively, was the most potent. Electron-withdrawing group substitutions at phenyl moiety decreased antiproliferative activity. Compound **12** arrested HeLa cells in the G2/M phase. Compound **12** had antitubulin action with 31% at 10 µM tubulin polymerization inhibition. Molecular docking indicated that **12** binds with the colchicine binding site (Jian et al., 2020).

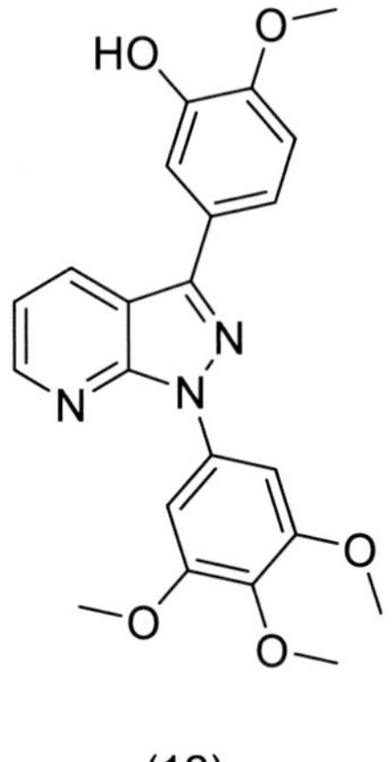

(12)

Wu et al. (2021) designed and synthesized indole-1,2,4-triazole derivatives and evaluated tubulin polymerization inhibitors. Synthesized compounds were evaluated against HepG2, HeLa, MCF-7, and A549. Out of all compounds, compound **13** with IC$_{50}$ values 0.23, 0.15, 0.38, and 0.30 µM, respectively, was the most potent. Tubulin polymerization assay indicated that compound **13** with IC$_{50}$ 2.1 µM was the most potent inhibitor, while colchicines with IC$_{50}$ 2.52 µM had inhibitory activity. Compound **13** had G2/M phase arrest leads to the decrement of mitotic cells. It also binds at the colchicine binding site, which was revealed by a docking study (Wu et al., 2021).

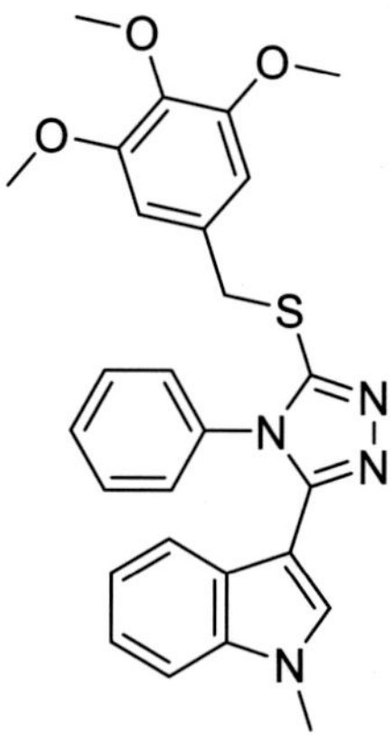

(13)

Wang et al. (2021) synthesized XRP44X analogs with replacement of the pyrazole ring of XRP44X with tetrazole and evaluated for antiproliferative activity and antitubulin activity. Among synthesized compounds, compound **14** with IC_{50} 0.090, 0.650, and 0.268 μM had potent activity against SGC-7901, A549, and HeLa, respectively. The O-substitutions at the phenyl ring increased the antiproliferative activity. Further, compound **14** had tubulin polymerization inhibition by disrupting microtubules in SGC-7901 cells. The cell cycle analysis showed that **14** arrested G2/M phase and induced apoptosis in SGC-7901 cells. A molecular dockings study indicated that compound **14** interacted with Ala*b*31. H-bonding was also there between tetrazole moiety and Asn*b*258, Lys*b*352 (Wang et al., 2021).

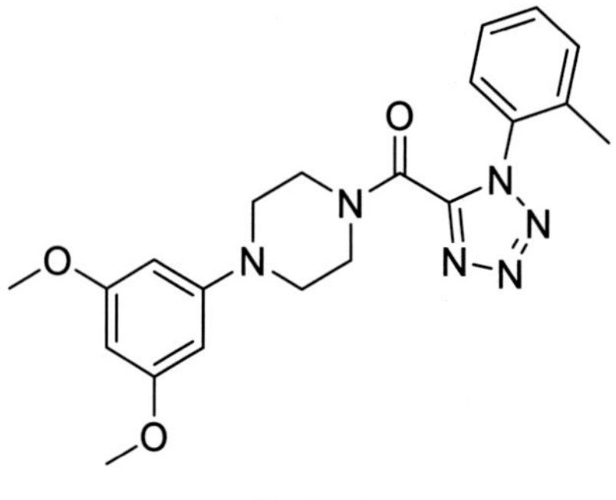

(13)

Oskuei et al. (2021) designed and synthesized imidazole-chalcone analogs. These compounds were evaluated as antitubulin and anticancer agents against MCF7, A549, HepG2, and MCF7/MX. Compounds **14** and **15** with IC_{50} values 7.05−63.43 μM were potent among synthesized compounds. Substituting Br at R2 increased the cytotoxic activity against A549 cancer cells while Cl and F substitution decreased activity. Compounds **14** and **15** inhibited tubulin polymerizations at 50 and 100 μM with inhibition (42.85% and 25%) and (55.71% and 60.71%), respectively. These compounds arrested the G2/M phase (at low conc) and increased apoptosis (at higher conc). Molecular docking indicated that **14** had binding at hydrophobic pocket (with Glu183α, Thr224α, Lys254β, Asn101α, Val351β, Lys352β, and Leu 248β). In addition, compound **14** had H-bonded with Ser178α and Ala316β (Oskuei et al., 2021).

(14) (15)

5. Summary and future outlook

Tubulin polymerization inhibition is one of the targets for anticancer drugs as reported in various literature. There are various examples of active molecules like Colchicine 1, vincristine, and vinblastine from different chemical classes that have shown tubulin polymerization inhibitory potential and are being approved for clinical use. In addition, different modifications can be done to existing drug moieties like cyclic or heterocyclic that might improve the biological profile of the developed molecules. Various analogs of important classes like combretastatin derivatives and indole derivatives may serve as a potential lead for the synthesis of more efficient and potent biologically active molecules.

References

Abraham, I., Dion, R. L., Chi, D., Gottesman, M. M., & Hamel, E. (1986). 2, 4-Dichlorobenzyl thiocyanate, an antimitotic agent that alters microtubule morphology. *Proceedings of the National Academy of Sciences, 83*, 6839–6843.

Akhmanova, A., & Steinmetz, M. O. (2008). Tracking the ends: A dynamic protein network controls the fate of microtubule tips. *Nature Reviews Molecular Cell Biology, 9*, 309–322.

Bai, R., Cichacz, Z. A., Herald, C. L., Pettit, G. R., & Hamel, E. (1993). Spongistatin 1, a highly cytotoxic, sponge-derived, marine natural product that inhibits mitosis, microtubule assembly, and the binding of vinblastine to tubulin. *Molecular Pharmacology, 44*, 757–766.

Bai, R., Covell, D. G., Pei, X.-F., Ewell, J. B., Nguyen, N. Y., Brossi, A., & Hamel, E. (2000). Mapping the binding site of colchicinoids on β-tubulin: 2-chloroacetyl-2-demethylthiocolchicine covalently reacts predominantly with cysteine 239 and secondarily with cysteine 354. *Journal of Biological Chemistry, 275*, 40443–40452.

Bai, R., Durso, N. A., Sackett, D. L., & Hamel, E. (1999). Interactions of the sponge-derived antimitotic tripeptide hemiasterlin with tubulin: Comparison with dolastatin 10 and cryptophycin 1. *Biochemistry, 38*, 14302–14310.

Bai, R., Friedman, S. J., Pettit, G. R., & Hamel, E. (1992). Dolastatin 15, a potent antimitotic depsipeptide derived from dolabella auricularia: Interaction with tubulin and effects on cellular microtubules. *Biochemical Pharmacology, 43,* 2637–2645.

Bai, R. L., Lin, C. M., Yen, N. N., Liu, T. Y., & Hamel, E. (1989). Identification of the cysteine residue of. beta.-tubulin alkylated by the antimitotic agent 2, 4-dichlorobenzyl thiocyanate, facilitated by separatio of the protein subunits of tubulin by hydrophobic column chromatography. *Biochemistry, 28,* 5606–5612.

Bai, R., Paull, K. D., Herald, C. L., Malspeis, L., Pettit, G. R., & Hamel, E. (1991). Halichondrin B and homohalichondrin B, marine natural products binding in the vinca domain of tubulin. Discovery of tubulin-based mechanism of action by analysis of differential cytotoxicity data. *Journal of Biological Chemistry, 266,* 15882–15889.

Bai, R., Pettit, G. R., & Hamel, E. (1990). Binding of dolastatin 10 to tubulin at a distinct site for peptide antimitotic agents near the exchangeable nucleotide and vinca alkaloid sites. *Journal of Biological Chemistry, 265,* 17141–17149.

Bai, R., Schwartz, R. E., Kepler, J. A., Pettit, G. R., & Hamel, E. (1996). Characterization of the interaction of cryptophycin 1 with tubulin: Binding in the Vinca domain, competitive inhibition of dolastatin 10 binding, and an unusual aggregation reaction. *Cancer Research, 56,* 4398–4406.

Bai, R., Taylor, G. F., Cichacz, Z. A., Herald, C. L., Kepler, J. A., Pettit, G. R., & Hamel, E. (1995). The spongistatins, potently cytotoxic inhibitors of tubulin polymerization, bind in a distinct region of the vinca domain. *Biochemistry, 34,* 9714–9721.

Batra, J. K., Powers, L., Hess, F. D., & Hamel, E. (1986). Derivatives of 5, 6-diphenylpyridazin-3-one: Synthetic antimitotic agents which interact with plant and mammalian tubulin at a new drug-binding site. *Cancer Research, 46,* 1889–1893.

Ben-Chetrit, E., & Levy, M. (1998). Colchicine: 1998 update. *Seminars in Arthritis and Rheumatism,* 48–59. Elsevier.

Beutler, J. A., Cardellina, J. H., II, Lin, C. M., Hamel, E., Cragg, G. M., & Boyd, M. R. (1993). Centaureidin, a cytotoxic flavone from Polymnia fruticosa, inhibits tubulin polymerization. *Bioorganic & Medicinal Chemistry Letters, 3,* 581–584.

Blokhin, A. V., Yoo, H.-D., Geralds, R. S., Nagle, D. G., Gerwick, W. H., & Hamel, E. (1995). Characterization of the interaction of the marine cyanobacterial natural product curacin A with the colchicine site of tubulin and initial structure-activity studies with analogues. *Molecular Pharmacology, 48,* 523–531.

Bouchon, B., Chambon, C., Mounetou, E., Papon, J., Miot-Noirault, E., Gaudreault, R. C., Madelmont, J.-C., & Degoul, F. (2005). Alkylation of β-tubulin on Glu 198 by a microtubule disrupter. *Molecular Pharmacology, 68,* 1415–1422.

Combeau, C., Provost, J., Lancelin, F., Tournoux, Y., Prod'homme, F., Herman, F., Lavelle, F., Leboul, J., & Vuilhorgne, M. (2000). RPR112378 and RPR115781: Two representatives of a new family of microtubule assembly inhibitors. *Molecular Pharmacology, 57,* 553–563.

Cruz-Monserrate, Z., Vervoort, H. C., Bai, R., Newman, D. J., Howell, S. B., Los, G., Mullaney, J. T., Williams, M. D., Pettit, G. R., & Fenical, W. (2003). Diazonamide A and a synthetic structural analog: Disruptive effects on mitosis and cellular microtubules and analysis of their interactions with tubulin. *Molecular Pharmacology, 63,* 1273–1280.

Donthiboina, K., Anchi, P., Gurram, S., Mani, G. S., Uppu, J. L., Godugu, C., Shankaraiah, N., & Kamal, A. (2020). Synthesis and biological evaluation of substituted N-(2-(1H-benzo [d] imidazole-2-yl) phenyl) cinnamides as tubulin polymerization inhibitors. *Bioorganic Chemistry, 103,* Article 104191.

Dybdal-Hargreaves, N. F., Risinger, A. L., & Mooberry, S. L. (2015). Eribulin mesylate: Mechanism of action of a unique microtubule-targeting AgentEribulin: A unique microtubule-targeting agent. *Clinical Cancer Research, 21,* 2445–2452.

Edler, M. C., Buey, R. M., Gussio, R., Marcus, A. I., Vanderwal, C. D., Sorensen, E. J., Díaz, J. F., Giannakakou, P., & Hamel, E. (2005). Cyclostreptin (FR182877), an antitumor tubulin-polymerizing agent deficient in enhancing tubulin assembly despite its high affinity for the taxoid site. *Biochemistry, 44,* 11525–11538.

Edler, M. C., Fernandez, A. M., Lassota, P., Ireland, C. M., & Barrows, L. R. (2002). Inhibition of tubulin polymerization by vitilevuamide, a bicyclic marine peptide, at a site distinct from colchicine, the vinca alkaloids, and dolastatin 10. *Biochemical Pharmacology, 63,* 707–715.

Elnakady, Y. A., Sasse, F., Lünsdorf, H., & Reichenbach, H. (2004). Disorazol A1, a highly effective antimitotic agent acting on tubulin polymerization and inducing apoptosis in mammalian cells. *Biochemical Pharmacology, 67,* 927–935.

Ems-McClung, S. C., & Walczak, C. E. (2010). Kinesin-13s in mitosis: Key players in the spatial and temporal organization of spindle microtubules. *Seminars in Cell & Developmental Biology,* 276–282. Elsevier.

Gaitanos, T. N., Buey, R. M., Díaz, J. F., Northcote, P. T., Teesdale-Spittle, P., Andreu, J. M., & Miller, J. H. (2004). Peloruside A does not bind to the taxoid site on β-tubulin and retains its activity in multidrug-resistant cell lines. *Cancer Research, 64*, 5063–5067.

Gapud, E. J., Bai, R., Ghosh, A. K., & Hamel, E. (2004). Laulimalide and paclitaxel: A comparison of their effects on tubulin assembly and their synergistic action when present simultaneously. *Molecular Pharmacology, 66*, 113–121.

Giannakakou, P., Villalba, L., Li, H., Poruchynsky, M., & Fojo, T. (1998). Combinations of pacliatxel and vinblastine and their effects on tublin polymerization and cellular cytotoxicity: Characterization of a synergistic schedule. *International Journal of Cancer, 75*, 57–63.

Gigant, B., Wang, C., Ravelli, R. B., Roussi, F., Steinmetz, M. O., Curmi, P. A., Sobel, A., & Knossow, M. (2005). Structural basis for the regulation of tubulin by vinblastine. *Nature, 435*, 519–522.

Govindaiah, P., Dumala, N., Grover, P., & Prakash, M. J. (2019). Synthesis and biological evaluation of novel 4, 7-dihydroxycoumarin derivatives as anticancer agents. *Bioorganic & Medicinal Chemistry Letters, 29*, 1819–1824.

Hamel, E., & Covell, D. G. (2002). Antimitotic peptides and depsipeptides. *Current Medicinal Chemistry-Anti-Cancer Agents, 2*, 19–53.

Hastie, S. B. (1991). Interactions of colchicine with tubulin. *Pharmacology & Therapeutics, 51*, 377–401.

Höfle, G., Glaser, N., Leibold, T., Karama, U., Sasse, F., & Steinmetz, H. (2003). Semisynthesis and degradation of the tubulin inhibitors epothilone and tubulysin. *Pure and Applied Chemistry, 75*, 167–178.

Hoebeke, J., Van Nijen, G., & De Brabander, M. (1976). Interaction of oncodazole (R 17934), a new anti-tumoral drug, with rat brain tubulin. *Biochemical and Biophysical Research Communications, 69*, 319–324.

Honore, S., Pasquier, E., & Braguer, D. (2005). Understanding microtubule dynamics for improved cancer therapy. *Cellular and Molecular Life Sciences CMLS, 62*, 3039–3056.

Hood, K. A., West, L. M., Rouwé, B., Northcote, P. T., Berridge, M. V., Wakefield, S. J., & Miller, J. H. (2002). Peloruside A, a novel antimitotic agent with paclitaxel-like microtubule-stabilizing activity. *Cancer Research, 62*, 3356–3360.

Howard, J., & Hyman, A. A. (2003). Dynamics and mechanics of the microtubule plus end. *Nature, 422*, 753–758.

Irschik, H., Jansen, R., Gerth, K., Höfle, G., & Reichenbach, H. (1995). Disorazol A, an efficient inhibitor of eukaryotic organisms isolated from myxobacteria. *Journal of Antibiotics, 48*, 31–35.

Jian, X.-E., Yang, F., Jiang, C.-S., You, W.-W., & Zhao, P.-L. (2020). Synthesis and biological evaluation of novel pyrazolo [3, 4-b] pyridines as cis-restricted combretastatin A-4 analogues. *Bioorganic & Medicinal Chemistry Letters, 30*, Article 127025.

Jiang, J. B., Hesson, D., Dusak, B., Dexter, D., Kang, G., & Hamel, E. (1990). Synthesis and biological evaluation of 2-styrylquinazolin-4 (3H)-ones, a new class of antimitotic anticancer agents which inhibit tubulin polymerization. *Journal of Medicinal Chemistry, 33*, 1721–1728.

Jordan, M. A., Toso, R. J., Thrower, D., & Wilson, L. (1993). Mechanism of mitotic block and inhibition of cell proliferation by taxol at low concentrations. *Proceedings of the National Academy of Sciences, 90*, 9552–9556.

Jordan, M., Margolis, R., Himes, R., & Wilson, L. (1986). Identification of a distinct class of vinblastine binding sites on microtubules. *Journal of Molecular Biology, 187*, 61–73.

Kaur, R., Kaur, G., Gill, R. K., Soni, R., & Bariwal, J. (2014). Recent developments in tubulin polymerization inhibitors: An overview. *European Journal of Medicinal Chemistry, 87*, 89–124.

Kirschner, M. W. (1980). Implications of treadmilling for the stability and polarity of actin and tubulin polymers in vivo. *The Journal of Cell Biology, 86*, 330–334.

Kobayashi, J.i., Suzuki, H., Shimbo, K., Takeya, K., & Morita, H. (2001). Celogentins A– C, new antimitotic bicyclic peptides from the seeds of celosia rgentea. *Journal of Organic Chemistry, 66*, 6626–6633.

Kowalski, R. J., Giannakakou, P., Gunasekera, S. P., Longley, R. E., Day, B. W., & Hamel, E. (1997). The microtubule-stabilizing agent discodermolide competitively inhibits the binding of paclitaxel (Taxol) to tubulin polymers, enhances tubulin nucleation reactions more potently than paclitaxel, and inhibits the growth of paclitaxel-resistant cells. *Molecular Pharmacology, 52*, 613–622.

Kowalski, R. J., Giannakakou, P., & Hamel, E. (1997). Activities of the microtubule-stabilizing agents epothilones A and B with purified tubulin and in cells resistant to paclitaxel (Taxol®). *Journal of Biological Chemistry, 272*, 2534–2541.

Li, L., Wang, H.-K., Kuo, S.-C., Wu, T.-S., Mauger, A., Lin, C. M., Hamel, E., & Lee, K.-H. (1994). Antitumor agents 155. Synthesis and biological evaluation of 3′, 6, 7-substituted 2-phenyl-4-quinolones as antimicrotubule agents. *Journal of Medicinal Chemistry, 37*, 3400–3407.

Li, Q., Sham, H. L., & Rosenberg, S. H. (1999). *Antimitotic agents, annual reports in medicinal chemistry*. Elsevier.

Li, W., Shuai, W., Sun, H., Xu, F., Bi, Y., Xu, J., Ma, C., Yao, H., Zhu, Z., & Xu, S. (2019). Design, synthesis and biological evaluation of quinoline-indole derivatives as anti-tubulin agents targeting the colchicine binding site. *European Journal of Medicinal Chemistry, 163*, 428–442.

Li, Y., Koiso, Y., Kobayashi, H., Hashimoto, Y., & Iwasaki, S. (1995). Ustiloxins, new antimitotic cyclic peptides: Interaction with porcine brain tubulin. *Biochemical Pharmacology, 49*, 1367–1372.

Lin, C. M., Kang, G., Roach, M., Jiang, J., Hesson, D., Luduena, R., & Hamel, E. (1991). Investigation of the mechanism of the interaction of tubulin with derivatives of 2-styrylquinazolin-4 (3H)-one. *Molecular Pharmacology, 40*, 827–832.

Lin, C. M., Singh, S., Chu, P., Dempcy, R., Schmidt, J., Pettit, G., & Hamel, E. (1988). Interactions of tubulin with potent natural and synthetic analogs of the antimitotic agent combretastatin: A structure-activity study. *Molecular Pharmacology, 34*, 200–208.

MacNeal, R. K., & Purich, D. (1978). Stoichiometry and role of GTP hydrolysis in bovine neurotubule assembly. *Journal of Biological Chemistry, 253*, 4683–4687.

Madiraju, C., Edler, M. C., Hamel, E., Raccor, B. S., Balachandran, R., Zhu, G., Giuliano, K. A., Vogt, A., Shin, Y., & Fournier, J.-H. (2005). Tubulin assembly, taxoid site binding, and cellular effects of the microtubule-stabilizing agent dictyostatin. *Biochemistry, 44*, 15053–15063.

Manasa, K. L., Thatikonda, S., Sigalapalli, D. K., Vuppaladadium, S., Devi, G. P., Godugu, C., Alvala, M., Nagesh, N., & Babu, B. N. (2020). Design and synthesis of substituted (1-(benzyl)-1 H-1, 2, 3-triazol-4-yl)(piperazin-1-yl) methanone conjugates: Study on their apoptosis inducing ability and tubulin polymerization inhibition. *RSC Medicinal Chemistry, 11*, 1295–1302.

Martello, L. A., McDaid, H. M., Regl, D. L., Yang, C.-P. H., Meng, D., Pettus, T. R., Kaufman, M. D., Arimoto, H., Danishefsky, S. J., & Smith, A. B., III (2000). Taxol and discodermolide represent a synergistic drug combination in human carcinoma cell lines. *Clinical Cancer Research, 6*, 1978–1987.

Mounetou, E., Legault, J., Lacroix, J., & C.-Gaudreault, R. (2003). A new generation of N-Aryl-N '-(1-alkyl-2-chloroethyl) ureas as microtubule disrupters: Synthesis, antiproliferative activity, and β-tubulin alkylation kinetics. *Journal of Medicinal Chemistry, 46*, 5055–5063.

Oskuei, S. R., Mirzaei, S., Jafari-Nik, M. R., Hadizadeh, F., Eisvand, F., Mosaffa, F., & Ghodsi, R. (2021). Design, synthesis and biological evaluation of novel imidazole-chalcone derivatives as potential anticancer agents and tubulin polymerization inhibitors. *Bioorganic Chemistry, 112*, Article 104904.

Parness, J., & Horwitz, S. B. (1981). Taxol binds to polymerized tubulin in vitro. *The Journal of Cell Biology, 91*, 479–487.

Paull, K. D., Lin, C. M., Malspeis, L., & Hamel, E. (1992). Identification of novel antimitotic agents acting at the tubulin level by computer-assisted evaluation of differential cytotoxicity data. *Cancer Research, 52*, 3892–3900.

Pellegrini, F., & Budman, D. R. (2005). Tubulin function, action of antitubulin drugs, and new drug development. *Cancer Investigation, 23*, 264–273.

Pryor, D. E., O'Brate, A., Bilcer, G., Díaz, J. F., Wang, Y., Wang, Y., Kabaki, M., Jung, M. K., Andreu, J. M., & Ghosh, A. K. (2002). The microtubule stabilizing agent laulimalide does not bind in the taxoid site, kills cells resistant to paclitaxel and epothilones, and may not require its epoxide moiety for activity. *Biochemistry, 41*, 9109–9115.

Qi, Z.-Y., Hao, S.-Y., Tian, H.-Z., Bian, H.-L., Hui, L., & Chen, S.-W. (2020). Synthesis and biological evaluation of 1-(benzofuran-3-yl)-4-(3, 4, 5-trimethoxyphenyl)-1H-1, 2, 3-triazole derivatives as tubulin polymerization inhibitors. *Bioorganic Chemistry, 94*, Article 103392.

Ravelli, R. B., Gigant, B., Curmi, P. A., Jourdain, I., Lachkar, S., Sobel, A., & Knossow, M. (2004). Insight into tubulin regulation from a complex with colchicine and a stathmin-like domain. *Nature, 428*, 198–202.

Seidman, R., Gitelman, I., Sagi, O., Horwitz, S. B., & Wolfson, M. (2001). The role of ERK 1/2 and p38 MAP-kinase pathways in taxol-induced apoptosis in human ovarian carcinoma cells. *Experimental Cell Research, 268*, 84–92.

Shan, B., Medina, J. C., Santha, E., Frankmoelle, W. P., Chou, T.-C., Learned, R. M., Narbut, M. R., Stott, D., Wu, P., & Jaen, J. C. (1999). Selective, covalent modification of β-tubulin residue Cys-239 by T138067, an antitumor agent with in vivo efficacy against multidrug-resistant tumors. *Proceedings of the National Academy of Sciences, 96*, 5686–5691.

Shi, Q., Chen, K., Li, L., Chang, J.-J., Autry, C., Kozuka, M., Konoshima, T., Estes, J. R., Lin, C. M., & Hamel, E. (1995). Antitumor agents, 154. Cytotoxic and antimitotic flavonols from Polanisia dodecandra. *Journal of Natural Products, 58*, 475–482.

Sontag, C. A., Staley, J. T., & Erickson, H. P. (2005). In vitro assembly and GTP hydrolysis by bacterial tubulins BtubA and BtubB. *The Journal of Cell Biology, 169,* 233–238.

Sternlicht, H., Ringel, I., & Szasz, J. (1980). The co-polymerization of tubulin and tubulin chochicine complex in the absence and presence of associated proteins. *Journal of Biological Chemistry, 255,* 9138–9148.

Takahashi, M., Iwasaki, S., Kobayashi, H., Okuda, S., Murai, T., & Sato, Y. (1987). Rhizoxin binding to tubulin at the maytansine-binding site. *Biochimica et Biophysica Acta (BBA)-General Subjects, 926,* 215–223.

Towle, M. J., Salvato, K. A., Budrow, J., Wels, B. F., Kuznetsov, G., Aalfs, K. K., Welsh, S., Zheng, W., Seletsky, B. M., & Palme, M. H. (2001). In vitro and in vivo anticancer activities of synthetic macrocyclic ketone analogues of halichondrin B. *Cancer Research, 61,* 1013–1021.

Wang, C., Li, Y., Liu, Z., Wang, Z., Liu, Z., Man, S., Zhang, Y., Bao, K., Wu, Y., & Guan, Q. (2021). Design, synthesis and biological evaluation of 1-Aryl-5-(4-arylpiperazine-1-carbonyl)-1 H-tetrazols as novel microtubule destabilizers. *Journal of Enzyme Inhibition and Medicinal Chemistry, 36,* 549–560.

Wang, G., Liu, W., Peng, Z., Huang, Y., Gong, Z., & Li, Y. (2020). Design, synthesis, molecular modeling, and biological evaluation of pyrazole-naphthalene derivatives as potential anticancer agents on MCF-7 breast cancer cells by inhibiting tubulin polymerization. *Bioorganic Chemistry, 103,* Article 104141.

Wang, G., Peng, Z., & Li, Y. (2019). Synthesis, anticancer activity and molecular modeling studies of novel chalcone derivatives containing indole and naphthalene moieties as tubulin polymerization inhibitors. *Chemical and Pharmaceutical Bulletin, 67,* 725–728. c19-00217.

Wang, Y.-T., Shi, T.-Q., Zhu, H.-L., & Liu, C.-H. (2019). Synthesis, biological evaluation and molecular docking of benzimidazole grafted benzsulfamide-containing pyrazole ring derivatives as novel tubulin polymerization inhibitors. *Bioorganic & Medicinal Chemistry, 27,* 502–515.

Wu, M. K., Man, R. J., Liao, Y. J., Zhu, H. L., & Zhou, Z. G. (2021). Discovery of novel indole-1, 2, 4-triazole derivatives as tubulin polymerization inhibitors. *Drug Development Research, 82,* 1008–1020.

Xu, F., Li, W., Shuai, W., Yang, L., Bi, Y., Ma, C., Yao, H., Xu, S., Zhu, Z., & Xu, J. (2019). Design, synthesis and biological evaluation of pyridine-chalcone derivatives as novel microtubule-destabilizing agents. *European Journal of Medicinal Chemistry, 173,* 1–14.

Yin, Y., Lian, B.-P., Xia, Y.-Z., Shao, Y.-Y., & Kong, L.-Y. (2019). Design, synthesis and biological evaluation of resveratrol-cinnamoyl derivates as tubulin polymerization inhibitors targeting the colchicine binding site. *Bioorganic Chemistry, 93,* Article 103319.

Zhang, D., & Kanakkanthara, A. (2020). Beyond the paclitaxel and vinca alkaloids: Next generation of plant-derived microtubule-targeting agents with potential anticancer activity. *Cancers, 12,* 1721.

Tumor necrosis factor receptor–associated protein 1 (TRAP1) inhibitors

Sanjeev Kumar Sahu[1], Charanjit Kaur[1], Shweta Jain[2], Pushpendra Kumar[3] and Ankur Vaidya[3]

[1]School of Pharmaceutical Sciences, Lovely Professional University, Phagwara, Punjab, India;
[2]Sir Madanlal Institute of Pharmacy, Etawah, Uttar Pradesh, India; [3]Faculty of Pharmacy,
Uttar Pradesh University of Medical Sciences, Saifai, Uttar Pradesh, India

1. Introduction

Tumor necrosis factor receptor–associated protein 1 (TRAP1) belongs to the HSP90 chaperone family found in the matrix of mitochondria. It is essential for preserving intracellular homeostasis and mitochondrial integrity. It prevents the opening of the mitochondrial permeability transition pore (mPTP) by antagonizing the pro-apoptotic action of cyclophilin D. Along with regulating mitochondrial bioenergetics, endoplasmic reticulum stress, and succinate dehydrogenase inhibition, it also guards the cells by decreasing reactive oxygen species (ROS) formation against oxidative stress (Clerkin et al., 2008). In a yeast two-hybrid screen, it interacts with the type I TNF receptor's intracellular domain and is intimately connected to apoptosis.

These death receptors trigger signaling cascades that result in apoptosis and the activation of caspases. Recently, it was found that this family of cytoplasmic proteins can both encourage the production of genes that support cell survival and negatively regulate apoptotic pathways. Members of this family, responsible for the transmission of signal molecules, were given the moniker TNF receptor-associated factors (TRAFs) due to their proclivity to bind to tumor necrosis factor receptor II (TNFR II) (Ware et al., 1996). Further research has shown the crucial roles of TRAFs in controlling apoptosis as well as stress responses, by acting as cytoplasmic adapter proteins, different receptors on the cell surface.

Latent membrane protein 1 (LMP1) from the Epstein—Barr virus, IL-1R (interleukin-1 receptor), and members of the TNFR superfamily are a few receptors known to recruit TRAF proteins. There are currently six unique TRAF molecules known to exist in mammalian species. The retinoblastoma protein and the tumor suppressors EXT1 (exostosis 1) and EXT2 (exostosin 2) are among those with which TRAP1 is known to interact, but the consequences of these interactions in terms of their functional significance are still unknown.

In order to influence N-cadherin's expression (cell adhesion molecule) and alter of neuronal intercellular adhesion, TRAP1 works in conjunction with TNFR1. In cultured hippocampus neurons, TRAP1 also affects the shape of dendritic spines (Xie et al., 2021).

2. Role of TRAP1 in cancers

Cancer is a group of complicated ailments where the survival of cancer cells depends on metabolic reprogramming. In human malignant tumors, the mitochondrial chaperone TRAP1 controls the development of the cancer by either acting as an oncogene or a tumor suppressor. TRAP1 participates in metabolism regulation and influences the transition from aerobic glycolysis to oxidative phosphorylation (OXPHOS). Furthermore, it controls the cell cycle to regulate cell division, increases tumors spread by triggering the fission of mitochondria, and disruption in its activity can lead to apoptosis yet possesses no impact on healthy cells (Fig. 16.1). Consequently, a method that specifically involves TRAP1, maybe a potential plan to design anticancer therapeutics. This chapter examines the connection of TRAP1's aberrant expression and carcinogenesis, as well as the processes at the molecular level, by which TRAP1 controls tumor growth, evaluates TRAP1's function in apoptosis, and assesses TRAP1's potential therapeutic relevance in tumors (Liu et al., 2010).

2.1 Over expression of TRAP1 in tumors

For many years, it has been noted that the expression of TRAP1 is closely connected to the onset and growth of tumors. It is well known that heat shock proteins (HSPs) play a crucial role in keeping oncogenes in an active conformation and that their levels rise in tumors in response to a variety of stimuli to re-establish protein-folding in a normal state. "Non-oncogenic addiction" is the phrase that has lately been used to describe how cancer cells become dependent on normal cell processes such as an increase in HSP levels. Neoplastic cells utilize this approach to endure and even thrive in the acidic, hypoxic, and nutrient-deficient tumor microenvironment.

TRAP1 expression is elevated in different human cancers, like breast, nonsmall cell lung cancer, prostate, and nasopharyngeal cancer. For instance, a statistically significant positive correlation between the pathological T stage and TRAP1 expression was found in the first extensive analysis of human colorectal cancer tissues. Additionally, it was suggested in the study that TRAP1 triggers the epithelial-mesenchymal transition (EMT), which has a role in the metastasis of primary tumors, causing tumor cells to enter stromal tissue (Zhang et al., 2021). As demonstrated in a study by Tian et al. (2014), TRAP1 expression is negatively correlated with the degree of ESCC differentiation and is expressed at much greater levels in

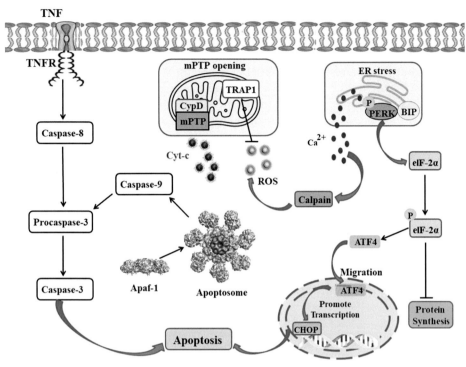

FIGURE 16.1   Role of tumor necrosis factor receptor–associated protein 1 (TRAP1) in cancer.

esophageal squamous cell carcinoma (ESCC) tissues in comparison to healthy cells. In ESCC cells, TRAP1 knockdown induces G2/M arrest, which leads to cell cycle dysregulation, and significantly raises the fraction of apoptotic cells (Tian et al., 2014).

Si et al. (2015) found that metastases of the lymph nodes, patient prognosis, and clinical stage were all strongly associated with a significant rise in the expression of TRAP1 in the cancer tissues of the kidney compared to normal cells. Patients who expressed high levels of TRAP1 had a bad prognosis (Si et al., 2015). Furthermore, Wu et al. (2016) demonstrated that through its control over metabolic reprogramming, TRAP1 knockout significantly reduced the spread of glioblastoma multiforme cells, stimulated G2/M arrest, apoptosis, prevented primary neurosphere recovery, and the formation of neurospheres (Wu et al., 2016). These findings suggest that the TRAP1 protein may have oncogenic effects that influence the cancer patient's prognosis by encouraging the spread, invasion, and resistance to apoptosis in human malignant tumor cells.

But in some tumor cells, TRAP1 could potentially act as a tumor suppressor. TRAP1 expression and tumor stage were shown to be significantly inversely correlated in individuals with clear cell renal cell carcinoma, bladder cancer, and cervical cancer, according to Yoshida et al. (2013). Additionally, it was shown that TRAP1 knockdown increased the levels of reactive oxygen species (ROS), encouraged the activation of mitochondrial c-Src, and markedly increased invasion and cell motility (Yoshida et al., 2013), indicating the larger tendency of tumors with low TRAP1 expression to disseminate and expand from the initial location (Yoshida et al., 2013).

Additionally, Aust et al. (2012) investigated ovarian cancer cells identified as estrogen receptor—positive and found that there were favorable connections between estrogen receptor positivity and high expression of TRAP1 and overall survival as well as a chemotherapeutic response (Aust et al., 2012). Furthermore, an elevated prevalence of gene deletion in TRAP1 in cases of high-grade severe ovarian cancer, and the amount of its expression being related to the number of gene copies, which could describe its reduced expression in ovarian cancer patients were discovered by Amoroso et al. (2016). Thus, the involvement of TRAP1 in various tumors is connected to the prognosis of patients, implying that it is a potential target for the treatment of tumor.

Recent research suggests that TRAP1 is a prosurvival protein with heat shock protein (HSP)-like properties. It protects cells against oxidative stress and apoptosis induced by various inducers such as b-HIVS (b-hydroxyisovaleryl shikonin), chemotherapeutic drugs, and granzyme M, by inhibiting ROS formation. TRAP1 differs from the other HSP90 family members and does not bind HOP (HSP90-organizing protein) or HSP90 co-chaperone p23. Furthermore, it contains a distinct LxCxE motif, which permits its attachment to retinoblastoma protein (Rb) following heat shock and during mitosis, when it transfers from its mitochondrial position to the nucleus and helps in the refolding of denatured Rb (Chen et al., 1996).

Liu et al. (2010) discovered that TRAP1 reduces apoptosis induced by high glucose, improves renal function, mitigates mitochondrial damage, and increases cell viability in diabetic mice. On the basis of these findings, TRAP1 inhibits CypD's proapoptotic action on mPTP opening, performing an antiapoptotic role (Liu et al., 2010).

When exposed to oxidative stress, intracellular redox equilibrium is compromised, resulting in ROS build up and cellular damage. TRAP1 inhibits succinate dehydrogenase (SDH), which lowers the formation of superoxide anions, ROS, and modifies redox balance to protect malignant cells from oxidative stress. TRAP1 inhibition causes ROS build-up, whereas its overexpression inhibits ROS generation. The production of ROS is linked to mitochondrial Ca^{2+} excess and the release of Cyt-c, which leads to the opening of mPTP followed by apoptosis (Clerkin et al., 2008).

2.2 As regulators of survival or programmed cell death

The TNFR superfamily plays a vital role in the survival of cells. In some cases, receptors with a death domain in their cytoplasmic tail, such as Transgenic Adenocarcinoma Mouse Prostate (TRAMP), Death Receptor (DR3), CD95, and TNFRI, may stimulate complex pathways of proteases and kinases that trigger apoptosis. But the transmission of signals across such receptors can also result in JNK and NF-κB activation, which is suggested to be important for the activation of lymphocytes and the elicitation of their signaling activities. The binding of functional Fas-associated protein with death domain (FADD) protein to death domains harboring TNFR-related receptors causes cell death, and a dominant-negative deletion mutant of it, which prevents apoptosis, has no impact on JNK or NF-kB activation. While suppressing the activation of NF-kB enhances apoptosis, inhibiting JNK via dominant-negative MEKK1 reduces programmed cell death in HeLa cells but displays a weaker effect in MCF7 cells (Wang et al., 2002).

RIP, a death domain-containing threonine/serine kinase, has also been found to associate with the TRAF protein's subset and get drawn to TRAF-dependent signaling ensembles. While its carboxy-terminal death domain is required for RIP-induced cell death, the elimination of the amino end which comprises the kinase region of RIP reduces the stimulation of JNK. The domain of RIP bridging the domains of death and kinase, is proven to be crucial to RIP's stimulation of NF-kB activation. These findings imply that receptors containing a death domain can induce either cell death or a stress response, depending on the adaptor molecules linked to the receptor (Meylan et al., 2004).

Under certain circumstances, both CD40 and CD30 have been demonstrated to stimulate apoptosis, despite the absence of a death domain in their cytoplasmic tails. The carboxyl terminus of CD30, which contains the receptor's TRAF binding domain, is required for CD30 to induce programmed cell death. It is unknown if the entire process is related to the TRAF proteins' capacity to recruit and bind proteins containing death domains to the CD30 signaling complex. In a study conducted by Speiser et al. (1997), unexpectedly, TRAF1 expression was elevated in T-cell hybridomas after TCR cross-linking, although TRAF2 expression was not affected. TRAF1 overexpression in transgenic animals, on the other hand, indicates an inhibitory function of TRAF1 on the death of CD8+ cells induced by antigen (Speiser et al., 1997). Therefore, it seems to be an ensemble of signaling pathways that use TRAF1 through different routes depending on the framework of cells and are controlled by TRAF, cell surface receptors, and ligand expression levels.

2.3 In apoptosis induced by β-Hydroxyisovalerylshikonin

b-Hydroxyisovalerylshikonin (β-HIVS), a phytoconstituent obtained from *Lithospermum radix*, is an ATP inhibitor of protein-tyrosine kinases (non-competitive), such as EGFR and v-Src, and promotes cell death in numerous human cancer cell lines. In this investigation, cDNA array analysis revealed that b-HIVS inhibited the expression of the gene encoding TRAP1, and its level in mitochondria reduced with time during apoptosis in human lung cancer DMS114 cells and leukemia HL60 cells. When cells were exposed to VP16, they showed a similar decrease in TRAP1 levels. DMS114 cells were sensitized to β-HIV-induced cell death after being treated with TRAP1-specific siRNA. Furthermore, when DMS114 cells showed a reduction in TRAP1 expression by TRAP1-specific siRNA, it increased cytochrome c release from mitochondria. N-acetylcysteine inhibited the inhibition of TRAP1 expression by VP16 or β-HIVS, showing the role of ROS in the expression of TRAP1. These findings imply the role of suppressing TRAP1 expression in mitochondria in the activation of apoptosis caused by ROS (Masuda et al., 2004).

2.4 Dual role as an oncogene or tumor suppressor

TRAP1 is a regulatory adaptogen that regulates energy metabolism in tumor cells. This protein is strongly expressed in a variety of tumors, including breast, colon, lung, prostate, and glioblastoma, and it is frequently linked to drug resistance. But TRAP1 expression declines in certain cancers, such as bladder, renal, and ovarian cancers, where it is related to poor prognoses and resistance to chemotherapy. It is the only mitochondrial member among the HSP90 family that interacts with respiratory complexes directly, adding to their integrity and function (Arch et al., 1998).

3. TNF-α and cancer

A significant amount of epidemiological and clinical evidence has developed over the past 10 years to support the idea that persistent inflammation might enhance or hasten the formation and progression of tumors. TNF-α, vascular endothelial growth factors (VEGFs), and interleukin (IL)-6, whose production is primarily controlled by the transcription nuclear factor (NF)-κB, are among the proinflammatory gene products engaged in such interactions. Clinical studies have found unusually high amounts of circulating cytokines in cancer patients, and researchers are now looking at using inflammation as a target for cancer treatments. Tyrosine kinase (TK) inhibitors (mostly VEGFR inhibitors), VEGF inhibitors, and medications that suppress angiogenesis are the three main categories of antiangiogenic medicines that have been authorized for clinical use and research so far. TNF-a antagonists have become more widely accessible recently. The first clinical studies on anti-TNF-α medication demonstrated the safety and efficacy of this medication when administered to cancer patients. Further research is required to determine whether anti-TNF-α or NF-κB inhibitors truly offer a unique method of treating cancer, most likely when used in conjunction with other medicines like antiangiogenic or cytotoxic drugs (Guadagni et al., 2007).

TNF-α elicits multiple effects in a variety of cells by connecting to and stimulating two cell-surface receptors known as TNF-R1 and TNF-R2. TNF-α is known to promote transplanted tumor necrosis in mice, an action that is primarily mediated by enhanced vascular permeability and consequent vascular collapse. It shows a strong anticancer effect when injected locally at high concentrations, according to subsequent clinical trials, due to the selective destruction of intratumoral blood vessels. However, evidence has suggested that it stimulates anchorage-independent growth and possesses mitogenic action, which increases tumor cells' ability to spread. Moreover, TNF-α mice deficient are immune to skin tumors and its antibodies inhibit their development. Thus, tumors can be regressed by its high-dose local delivery, but its continuous release might enhance cancer development and spread endogenously. Its binding to TNF-R complexes (preassembled) causes a shift in the various TNF-R chain's orientation, initiating transduction of the signal via the sudden mobilization of three types of subsequent molecules: c-inhibitors of apoptosis (c-IAP), TNF-R-associated factors (TRAF), and proteins with death domains (DD) (Chauhan et al., 2022).

NF-κB may be one of the significant constituents of the mechanism promoting the tumor among all the numerous signaling pathways activated by inflammation and infection. This notion is based on the discovery that NF-κB is a key stimulator of antiapoptotic gene expression, which was first described in the context of TNF-a signaling. Despite having several death domains (DDs) in the intracellular component of its principal receptor, TNF-R1, TNF-a does not induce programmed cell death except when paired with protein or RNA synthesis inhibitors. The need for these inhibitors can be reduced by inactivating NF-κB by either deleting its RelA subunit or expressing NF-κB (IκB)-super repressor (IκB-SR), the inhibitor. Numerous genes stimulated by cytokines and producing angiogenic peptides or cellular adhesion molecules, are transcriptionally controlled by NF-κB family transcription factors. NF-κB members are normally restricted to the cytoplasm by interaction with inhibitory proteins of the IκB family. IκB proteins are phosphorylated and degraded by TNF-α, causing the production, nuclear translocation, and binding of DNA with NF-κB, followed by responsive gene activation (Karin, 2006).

4. TRAP1 as a target of oncotherapy

TRAP1 is a crucial governing component of metabolic reprogramming in cancer cells, favoring the Warburg phenotype. It is also engaged in the dual control of the antiapoptotic and apoptotic pathways in cancer cells. Through interrupting the cell cycle, enhancing motility, and encouraging cancer cell metastasis and invasion, it is engaged in several biological processes. Thus, it is a potential pharmacological target, and treatment with its inhibitors in combination with chemotherapy might evolve into a new cancer treatment approach (Masgras et al., 2021).

5. TRAP1 inhibitors

TRAP1 inhibitors have been developed, including honokiol bis-dichloroacetate (HDCA), shepherding, DN401, and gamitrinibs. However, no TRAP1-targeted inhibitors have been approved as anticancer drugs (Xie et al., 2021).

5.1 Inhibitors simultaneously acting on both Hsp90 and TRAP1

Because there are no pharmacologic tools for targeting TRAP1 and Hsp90, current drugs act on both TRAP1 and Hsp90, with lesser selectivity for TRAP1. Shepherdin and geldanamycin are TRAP1 and Hsp90 inhibitors that do not increase the expression of Hsp70; these drugs cause apoptosis through the opening of CyD-dependent mPTP (Siegelin, 2013). There are two major regions of gamitrinibs: a 17-AAG region and a mitochondrial targeting sequence consisting of one to four tandem repeats of triphenylphosphonium (gamitrinib-TPP) or cyclic guanidinium (gamitrinib-(G1-G4)). The latter inhibits the growth of localized and metastatic prostate cancer in the case of transgenic adenocarcinoma of the prostate (TRAMP) and shows tolerance in a mouse model. It was reported as a safe and effective for long-term systemic treatment in TRAMP mice without any instance of organ toxicity, weight loss, inflammation, or prostatic intraepithelial neoplasia (Kang et al., 2011).

Shepherdin, a peptidomimetic, inhibits the Hsp90-Survivin connection, irreversibly breaks mitochondria, causes cytoplasmic Hsp90 client protein degradation, and ultimately tumor cell death via apoptosis and autophagy in glioblastoma cells (Siegelin et al., 2010). In a similar way, shepherdin administration to retinoblastoma cells decreases Survivin stability, decreases MMP-2 activity, and enhances the proapoptotic proteins Bax, Bim, and caspase-9 expression, which trigger autophagy and caspase-dependent death (Venkatesan et al., 2016).

Furthermore, DN401 is a purine scaffold analogue of BIIB-02112 (an Hsp90 inhibitor) with a high binding affinity toward TRAP1 but lower affinity toward Hsp90 (Park et al., 2017). This molecule destroys Hsp90 and TRAP1 client proteins in cancer cells without increasing Hsp70; this process causes fragmentation of mitochondria and programmed cell death, boosting the anticancer potential of the drug (Park et al., 2020).

5.2 TRAP1-specific inhibitors

Several studies are currently underway on inhibitors that act specifically on TRAP1 and not Hsp90 to improve the treatment of TRAP1-dependent disorders and anticancer therapeutics. HDCA is a new TRAP1 inhibitor with anticancer efficacy that does not affect Hsp90 ATPase activity in a dose-dependent manner to increase SDH activity, lowering the tumor cell number and cancerous progression (Sanchez-Martin et al., 2021). Costantino et al. (2009) proposed a possible approach for triggering apoptosis by targeting the TRAP1 ATPase domain, with cationic appendages chosen as drug delivery vehicles to the mitochondria. This study found that the buildup of guanidine-based chemicals in mitochondria hindered the production of recombinant TRAP1 ATPase, restricting colon cancer cell proliferation and triggering apoptosis (Costantino et al., 2009). According to Sanchez-Martin et al. (2020), structure- and dynamics-based allosteric ligands can be a potential cancer treatment option via selective targeting of TRAP1 (Sanchez-Martin et al., 2020). Rondanin et al. (2018) reported a few compounds (Fig. 16.2) having both Hsp90 and TRAP1 inhibitory activity (Rondanin et al., 2018).

5.3 TRAP1 inhibitors and chemotherapeutics

Upregulation of TRAP1 provides protection against DNA damage and apoptosis caused by oxidative stress and cisplatin (Gesualdi et al., 2007). Overexpression of TRAP1 protects HT-29 colorectal cancer cells from cell death triggered by irinotecan, 5-fluorouracil, and oxaliplatin, whereas shepherdin blocks ATPase in TRAP1 and counters the resistance to these chemotherapeutic agents (Costantino et al., 2009). According to a study conducted by Kuchitsu et al. (2020), the inhibition of TRAP1 further inhibits the lung adenocarcinoma cells proliferation while increasing their sensitivity to cisplatin, implying that the expression of TRAP1 may influence relapse and resistance to chemotherapy in lung adenocarcinoma patients (Kuchitsu et al., 2020). These findings suggest that it promotes tumor resistance to chemotherapy treatments. Due to its role in developing a phenotype resistant to multiple drug treatments, combined TRAP1 targeting and chemotherapeutic drug treatment may have synergistic anticancer action against numerous malignant tumors in humans (Al-Lazikani et al., 2012). Apart from the studies done so far on the combination of Hsp90 inhibitors and chemotherapy medicines, more research is required to prove the synergistic effect of chemotherapy and TRAP1-specific inhibitors (Davenport et al., 2010; Park et al., 2014; Stuhmer et al., 2012).

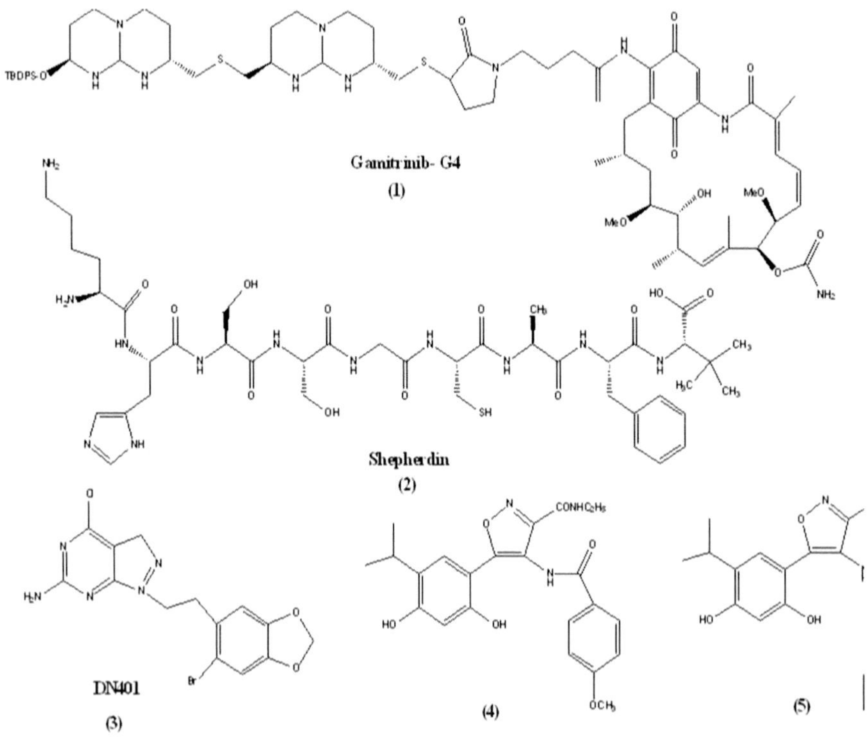

G amitrinib- G4
(1)

Shepherdin
(2)

DN401
(3)

(4)

(5)

Dual Inhibitors of Hsp90 and TRAP1

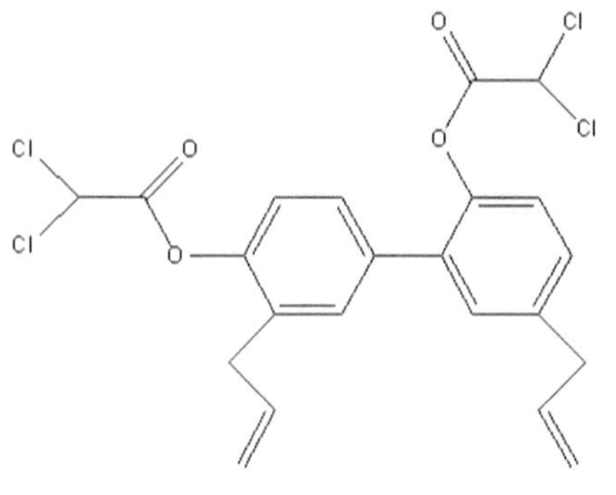

Honokiol bis-dichloroacetate (HDCA)

Specific TRAP1 Inhibitors

FIGURE 16.2 Examples of dual and specific TRAP1 inhibitors.

5.4 Role of glycoprotein IIb/IIIa (aIIbb3)

May et al. (2002) investigated the impact of glycoproteins (GP) IIb/IIIa (aIIbb3) on platelet surface exposure and the onset of proteolysis in HUVECs (human umbilical vein endothelial cells) during platelet—endothelial interactions (May et al., 2002).

They discovered that thrombin-stimulated platelets' transitory (60 min adherence increased the expression of membrane type-1 matrix metalloproteinase (MT1-MMP) (reverse transcriptase—polymerase chain reaction), urokinase-type plasminogen activator receptor, secretion of urokinase-type plasminogen activator, MMP-1 (ELISA), tissue-type plasminogen activator, as well as MMP-2 and MMP-9-induced proteolytic activity (gelatin zymography) in HUVECs. These effects were abolished by preventing physical platelet-endothelial interactions with transwell systems or by mAbs anti-GP IIb/IIIa (7E3), anti-CD40L (TRAP1), GRGDSP, or anti-$a_v b_3$ (LM609). Furthermore, the antagonists of GP IIb/IIIa like integrelin, tirofiban, and lamifiban inhibited MMP-9 and -2. The proteolysis is initiated with activation of platelets on endothelial cells and is mimicked by CD40 interaction using soluble CD40L but is not influenced by antibody clustering of CD40L, $a_v b_3$, and CD62P exposure on platelets. It is elevated by adherence to HUVECs or immobilized fibrinogen and is inhibited by GRGDSP or LM609. Cross-linking GP IIb/IIIa in suspension with secondary mAb and fibrinogen increased CD40L surface exposure. Bivalent mAb 7E3 consistently increased CD40L expression, but GP IIb/IIIa ligation with monovalent Fab fragment c7E3 or soluble fibrinogen alone had no impact. Platelet adherence via GP IIb/IIIa promotes CD40L and CD62P surface exposure. HUVEC proteolytic activity is produced by the coordinated action of β3-integrin-mediated platelet attachment and subsequent CD40L-triggered signals. Effective anti-CD40L or anti-GP IIb/IIIa treatments may thus aid in plaque stabilization (May et al., 2002) (Fig. 16.3).

5.5 HSP90-related inhibitors

It has been reported that the human TRAP1 and hsp75 sequences are similar, and a comparable protein from Drosophila was cloned. According to immunofluorescence investigations, human TRAP1 is in mitochondria. This localization is corroborated by the presence of mitochondrial localization regions in both the human and Drosophila proteins' amino termini. They examined TRAP1's ability to function as a hsp90-like chaperone due to its strong homology to hsp90. It was not able to form stable complexes with the traditional Hop (p60), p23, and hsp90 co-chaperones. In vitro, studies showed no influence on the reconstitution of hsp90-dependent hormone, its binding to the progesterone receptor, and in replacement of hsp90 to drive receptor maturation in its hormone-binding state. But TRAP1 has enough in common with hsp90 to bind ATP, which is sensitive to the hsp90 inhibitor geldanamycin. TRAP1 also demonstrated ATPase activity, which was reduced by both radicicol and geldanamycin. As a result, TRAP1 acts differently than hsp90 (Felts et al., 2000) (Fig. 16.4).

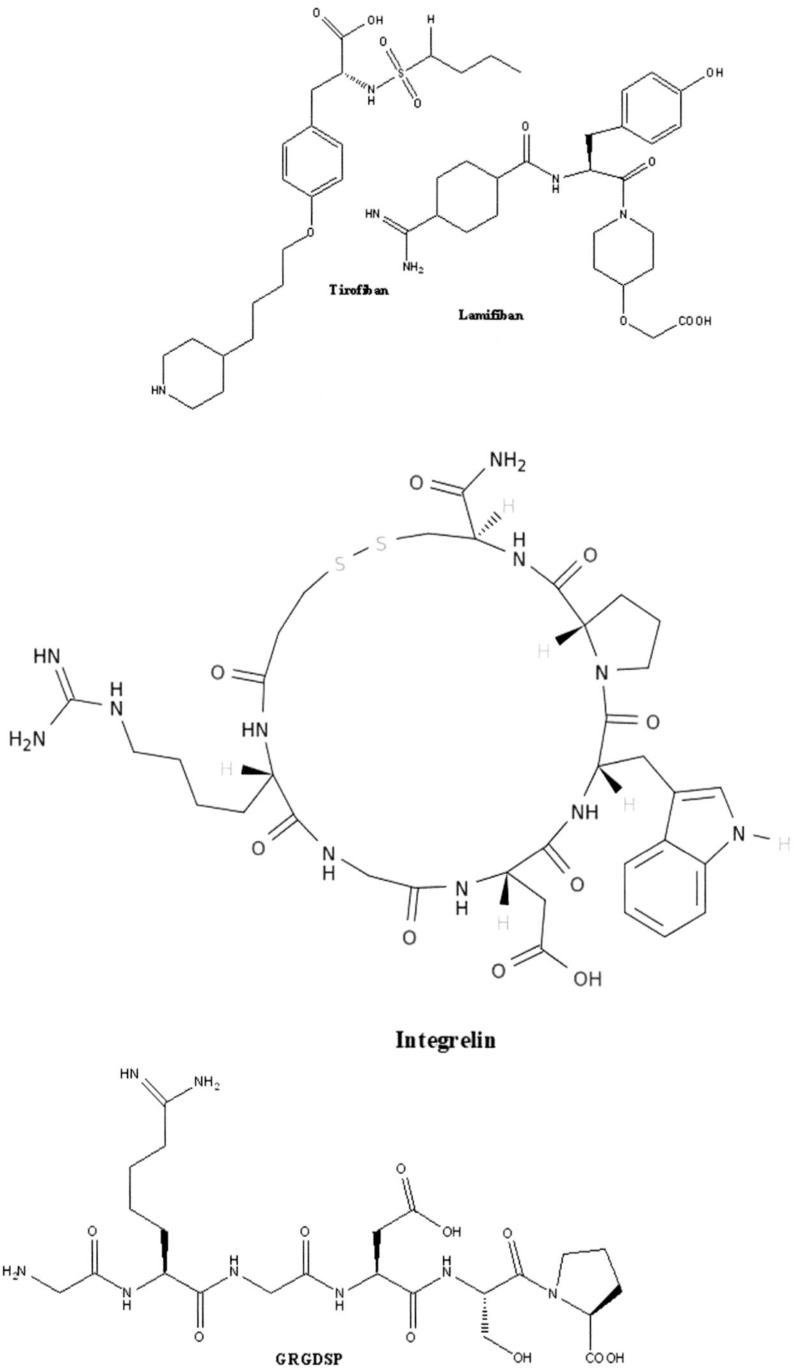

Tirofiban

Lamifiban

Integrelin

GRGDSP

FIGURE 16.3 Glycopeptides as TRAP1 inhibitors.

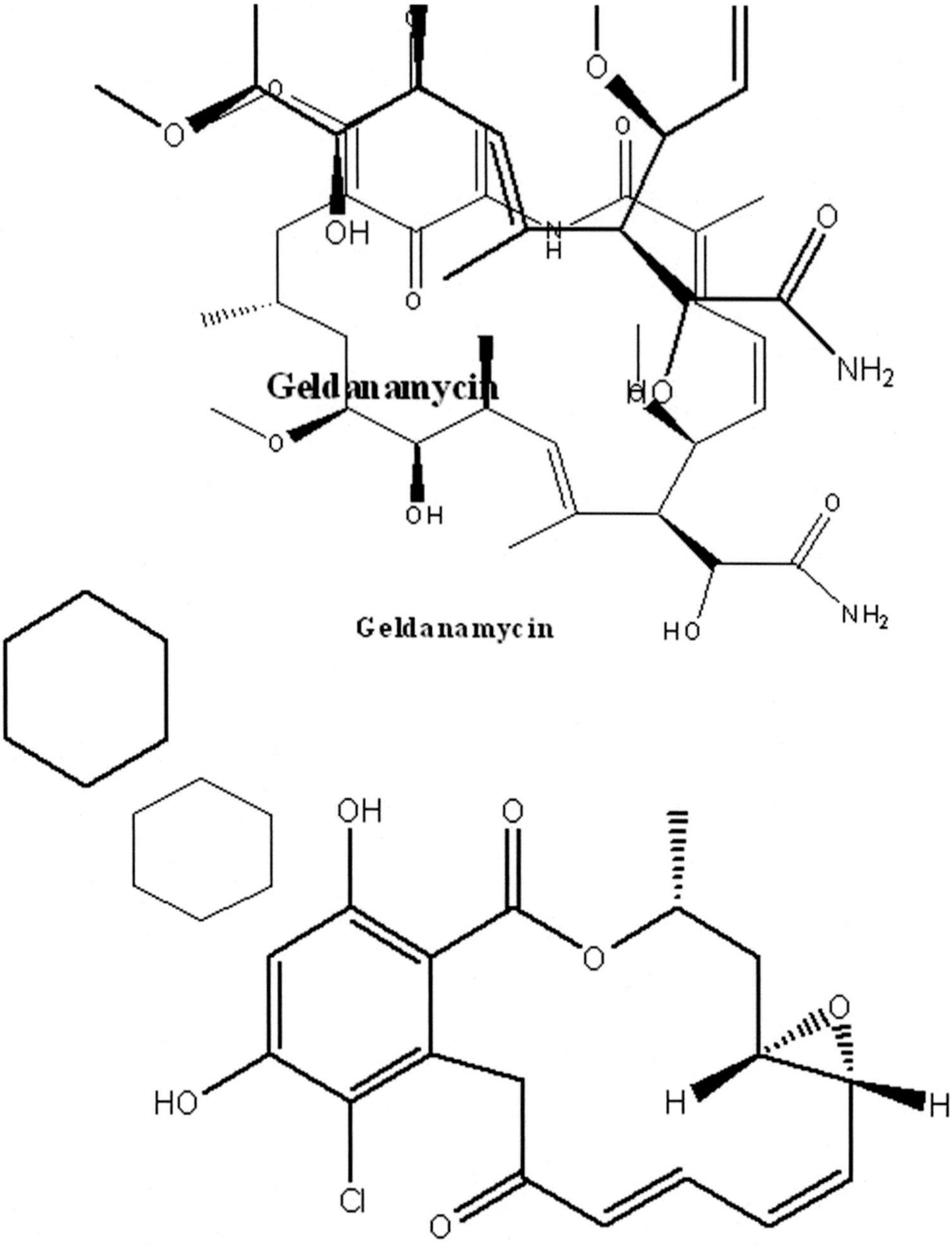

Geldanamycin

Radicicol

FIGURE 16.4 HSP90-related inhibitors.

5.6 Gamitrinib triphenyl phosphonium (G-TPP)

A new signaling network mediated via TRAP1 by creating Drosophila TRAP1 mutants that grew into adults and produced viable offspring, suggesting that TRAP1 is not essential for growth or reproduction. Under oxidative stress, its mutation or knockdown significantly improved the survival of Drosophila. This mutation alleviated dopaminergic (DA) neuron loss and mitochondrial dysfunction caused by deletion of the familial Parkinson disease gene PINK1 (Pten-induced kinase 1).

Gamitrinib-triphenyl phosphonium, an Hsp90 inhibitor that increases cell death in HeLa and MCF7 cells, consistently inhibited oxidative stress-induced cell death and mitochondrial dysfunction caused by PINK1 mutation in mouse embryonic fibroblast cells and DA cell models such as SH-SY5Y and SN4741 cells. Furthermore, gamitrinib-triphenyl phosphonium inhibited poor locomotor activity and DA neuron loss in Drosophila PINK1 null mutants. Further genetic studies revealed that TRAP1 mutants have increased expression of Thor, a downstream target gene of the transcription factor FOXO. However, the elimination of FOXO almost eliminated the protective functions of TRAP1 and PINK1 mutations against oxidative stress. These findings strongly show that inhibiting the mitochondrial chaperone TRAP1 provides a FOXO-dependent retrograde cell protection signal from the mitochondria to the nucleus (Kim et al., 2016) (Fig. 16.5).

5.7 Role of acetylcysteine

Acetylcysteine is a synthetic N-acetyl derivative and prodrug of the endogenous amino acid L-cysteine, a precursor of the antioxidant glutathione (GSH), with mucolytic, antioxidant, and potential cytoprotective, cancer-preventive, and antiinflammatory activities. It may inhibit tumor cell proliferation, progression, and survival, in susceptible tumor cells that rely on ROS-mediated signaling for their proliferation and malignant behavior. Under certain circumstances, acetylcysteine can induce apoptosis in susceptible cells, including certain tumor cells, via the intrinsic mitochondria-dependent pathway without involving endoplasmic reticulum stress. Also, acetylcysteine may be able to degrade Notch2, thereby preventing proliferation, migration, and invasion in Notch2-overexpressing glioblastoma cells.

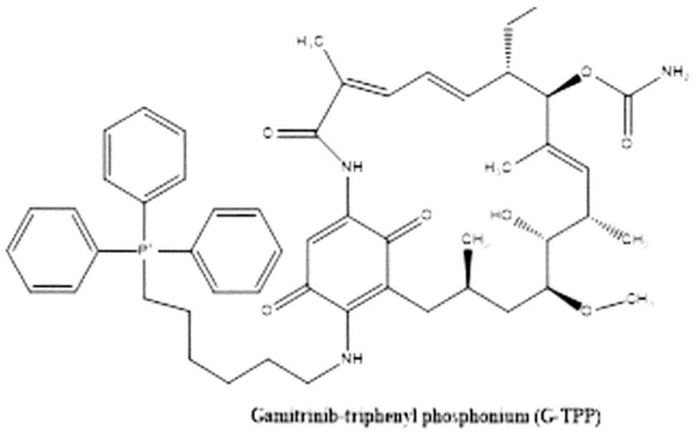

FIGURE 16.5 Gamitrinib triphenyl phosphonium as TRAP1 inhibitors.

Gamitrinib-triphenyl phosphonium (G-TPP)

Acetylcysteine also possesses antiinflammatory activity through the modulation of the nuclear factor-kappa B (NF-kB) pathway and the modulation of cytokine synthesis (https://pubchem.ncbi.nlm.nih.gov/#query=acetyl%20cysteine).

5.8 SPD-304 analogs

SPD-304 is a small molecule inhibitor that has shown promising results in preclinical studies as a TRAP1 inhibitor (Papaneophytou et al., 2015).

Recent advancements in the development of SPD-304 analogs as TRAP1 inhibitors have focused on improving the potency and selectivity of the molecule. One such analogue is SPD-827, which has been shown to have increased potency compared to SPD-304. In vitro studies have demonstrated that SPD-827 is able to inhibit TRAP1 activity in cancer cells, leading to reduced cell viability and increased apoptosis.

Another SPD-304 analogue that has shown promise as a TRAP1 inhibitor is CKD-516. In a recent study, CKD-516 was found to have potent anticancer activity in vitro and in vivo. Treatment with CKD-516 resulted in decreased cell viability and increased apoptosis in multiple cancer cell lines. In a mouse xenograft model of lung cancer, CKD-516 significantly reduced tumor growth and increased survival.

In addition to improving the potency and selectivity of SPD-304 analogs, researchers are also exploring the use of these molecules in combination with other cancer therapies. For example, a recent study found that combining SPD-827 with the chemotherapy drug gemcitabine resulted in enhanced anticancer activity in pancreatic cancer cells. The combination treatment resulted in increased apoptosis and decreased cell proliferation compared to either treatment alone (Rinotas et al., 2020).

Overall, recent advancements in the development of SPD-304 analogs as TRAP1 inhibitors hold promise for the development of new cancer therapies. These molecules have shown potent anticancer activity in preclinical studies and may be effective in combination with other cancer treatments. Further research is needed to fully understand the potential of these molecules as TRAP1 inhibitors in cancer therapy (Fig. 16.6).

5.9 Cyclopeptide

Cyclopeptides are a class of compounds that have received significant attention in recent years as potential therapeutics for a wide range of diseases. One area of research where cyclopeptides are showing particular promise is in the development of tumor necrosis factor receptor—associated protein 1 (TRAP1) inhibitors (Nakamoto et al., 2021).

Recent research has focused on the development of cyclopeptide-based TRAP1 inhibitors as a potential new class of cancer therapeutics. These compounds are designed to specifically target TRAP1 and disrupt its function, leading to the death of cancer cells.

One promising example is a cyclopeptide called Gamitrinib, which was developed by a team of researchers at the University of California, San Diego. This compound was designed to target the mitochondrial form of TRAP1 and has been shown to induce apoptosis (cell death) in cancer cells both in vitro and in vivo.

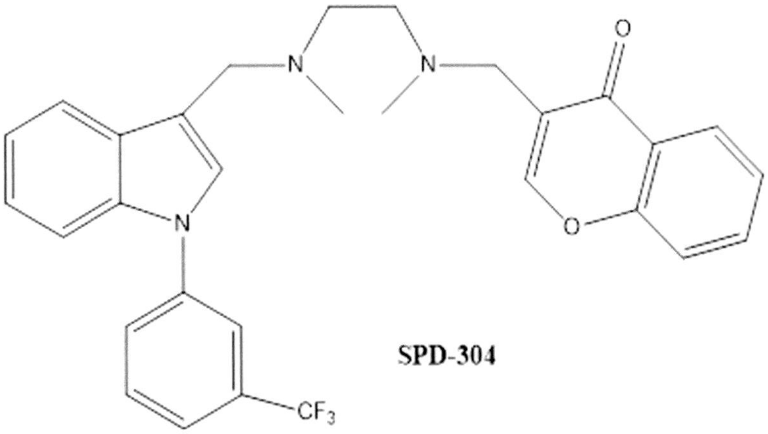

SPD-304

FIGURE 16.6 SPD-304 as TRAP1 inhibitors.

Another recent advancement in the field of cyclopeptides as TRAP1 inhibitors is the development of a new class of compounds called macrocyclic peptides. These compounds are larger than traditional cyclopeptides and are designed to bind to TRAP1 and disrupt its function more effectively. A recent study published in the Journal of Medicinal Chemistry described the development of a macrocyclic peptide called CTPI-2, which was shown to be a potent TRAP1 inhibitor and to induce apoptosis in cancer cells in vitro (Bruno et al., 2022).

The recent study in the development of cyclopeptides and macrocyclic peptides as TRAP1 inhibitors represents a promising new approach to cancer therapy. While more research is needed to fully understand the potential of these compounds, early results suggest that they could provide a new avenue for the development of more effective and targeted cancer treatments.

5.10 EF24 and EF31 analogs

EF24 and EF31 are analogs of curcumin, a natural compound found in turmeric that has been shown to possess anticancer properties. One of the key targets of EF24 and EF31 is TRAP1, which is a mitochondrial chaperone protein that plays a key role in cell survival and has been implicated in the development of various types of cancer (Mistretta et al., 2014).

Recent studies have shown promising results in the development of EF24 and EF31 as TRAP1 inhibitors for cancer therapy. Studies showed that EF24 inhibited TRAP1 activity in breast cancer cells, leading to decreased cell proliferation and increased apoptosis (cell death). Furthermore, studies demonstrated that EF31 inhibited TRAP1 expression in ovarian cancer cells, leading to decreased cell proliferation and migration.

In addition to their potential as TRAP1 inhibitors, EF24 and EF31 have also been shown to possess other anticancer properties. For example, EF24 has been shown to inhibit the growth of pancreatic cancer cells by inducing apoptosis and inhibiting cell migration, while EF31 has been shown to inhibit the growth of glioblastoma cells by inducing cell cycle arrest and apoptosis (Baldwin, 2014).

Despite these promising results, there are still challenges to developing EF24 and EF31 as effective anticancer drugs. One challenge is the low bioavailability of these compounds, which limits their effectiveness in vivo. Researchers are exploring various strategies to improve the bioavailability of these compounds, including the use of nanoparticles and other delivery systems.

The development of EF24 and EF31 as TRAP1 inhibitors holds great promise for the development of new cancer therapies. Further research is needed to fully understand the mechanisms underlying the anticancer properties of these compounds and to optimize their efficacy and safety for clinical use (Fig. 16.7)

5.11 ZINC05848961, ZINC09402309, ZINC04502991

These are small-molecule compounds that have been identified through virtual screening of compound libraries. These compounds have been shown to bind to TRAP1 and inhibit its activity in vitro. Studies have also demonstrated that these compounds can induce cell death in cancer cells, while having little to no effect on normal cells. This selectivity makes them promising candidates for the development of targeted cancer therapies. Further preclinical and clinical studies are needed to fully evaluate the potential of ZINC05848961, ZINC09402309, and ZINC04502991 as TRAP1 inhibitors for cancer therapy. However, their initial identification as TRAP1 inhibitors represents an important step toward the development of novel and effective cancer treatments (Qaiser et al., 2021) (Fig. 16.8).

5.12 Macrocyclic hydroxamic acids

Macrocyclic hydroxamic acids (MHAs) have emerged as a promising class of inhibitors for various targets, including TRAP1 which plays a crucial role in regulating cellular homeostasis and has been implicated in various diseases, including cancer (Janin, 2005).

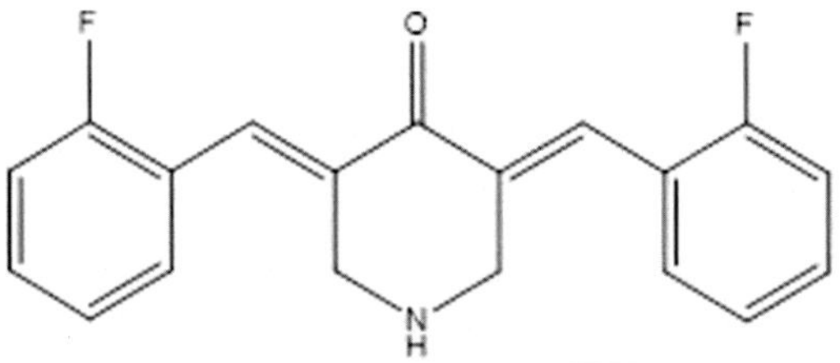

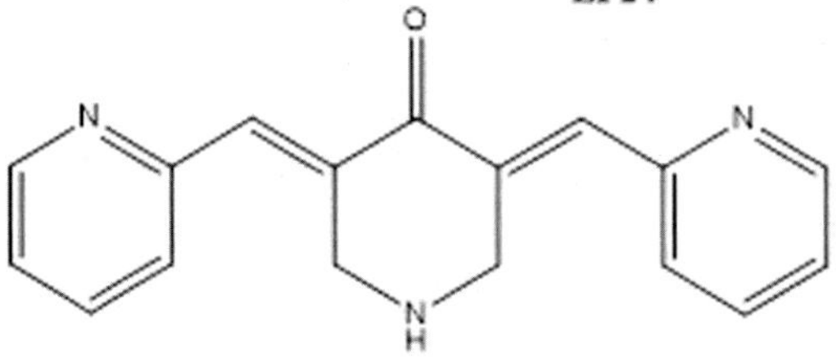

FIGURE 16.7   EF24 and EF31 as TRAP1 inhibitors.

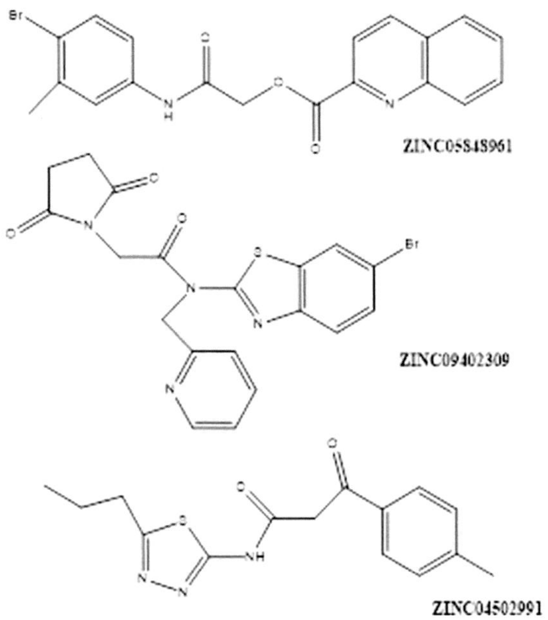

FIGURE 16.8   ZINC05848961, ZINC09402309, and ZINC04502991 as TRAP1 inhibitors.

Recently, there have been several advancements in the development of MHAs as TRAP1 inhibitors. Liang et al. (2022) reported the medicinal chemistry perspective of macrocyclic derivatives with antitumor activity that showed potent TRAP1 inhibition in both enzymatic and cellular assays. They were found to have antiproliferative activity in several cancer cell lines, suggesting their potential as an anticancer agent (Liang et al., 2022).

Another study published in the same journal reported the development of a new series of MHAs that exhibited high TRAP1 inhibitory activity and selectivity over other heat shock protein 90 (HSP90) isoforms. The lead compound was shown to induce apoptosis in cancer cells, suggesting its potential as a therapeutic agent for cancer treatment (Liang et al., 2022).

Furthermore, a recent study reported the discovery of a natural product, called trisporic acid, that acts as a potent TRAP1 inhibitor. The researchers demonstrated that trisporic acid can inhibit the growth of cancer cells and enhance the efficacy of chemotherapy in a mouse model of breast cancer (Loizzo et al., 2021).

These recent advancements in the development of MHAs as TRAP1 inhibitors hold great promise for the development of novel anticancer therapies. However, further studies are needed to optimize the potency, selectivity, and pharmacokinetic properties of these compounds for clinical use (Fig. 16.9).

5.13 SH-130

In recent years, there have been significant advancements in the development of TRAP1 inhibitors, particularly in the context of SH-130. SH-130 is a small molecule TRAP1 inhibitor

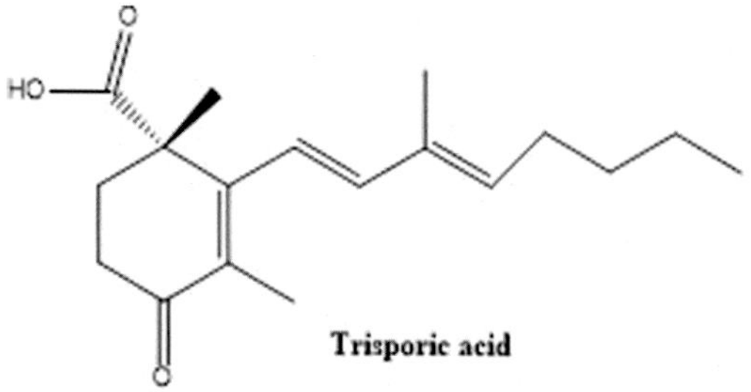

FIGURE 16.9   Trisporic acid as TRAP1 inhibitors.

that has shown promising preclinical results in various cancer models, including pancreatic, lung, and breast cancer.

One recent study published in the *Journal of Medicinal Chemistry* in 2021 reported the development of a series of novel SH-130 analogs with improved TRAP1 inhibitory activity and selectivity. The researchers used a structure-based design approach to optimize the binding affinity of the analogs to TRAP1 while minimizing off-target effects. The most promising analogs showed potent TRAP1 inhibition in vitro and in vivo and exhibited significant antitumor activity in mouse models of pancreatic and breast cancer (Dai et al., 2008).

Another study published in Cancer Research in 2020 demonstrated the potential of SH-130 as a sensitizer for radiotherapy in lung cancer. The researchers found that SH-130 treatment increased the sensitivity of lung cancer cells to radiation therapy by suppressing the DNA damage response and promoting apoptosis. Furthermore, SH-130 treatment enhanced the therapeutic efficacy of radiation therapy in mouse models of lung cancer (Xu et al., 2007).

The development of TRAP1 inhibitors, particularly SH-130, has demonstrated the potential of targeting TRAP1 as a novel therapeutic strategy for the treatment of various human diseases, particularly cancer. Further preclinical and clinical studies are warranted to validate the efficacy and safety of TRAP1 inhibitors in humans (Fig. 16.10).

FIGURE   16.10   SH-130   as   TRAP1 inhibitors.

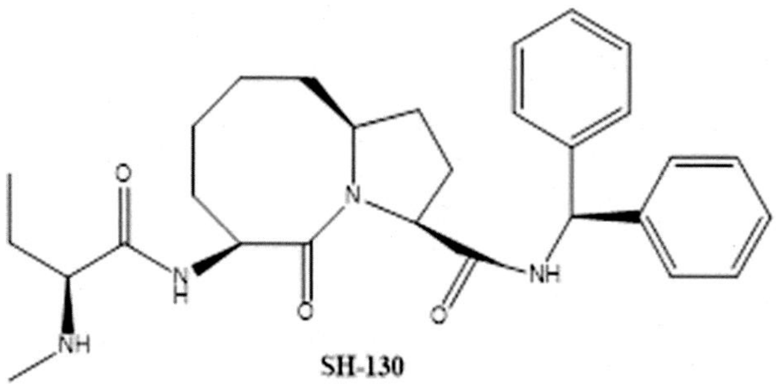

SH-130

5.14 Pyrimidine-5-carbonitrile

Pyrimidine-5-carbonitrile derivatives have recently gained attention as potential inhibitors of TRAP1. In a recent study, Vyas et al. (2022) reported the synthesis and evaluation of a series of pyrimidine-5-carbonitrile derivatives as TRAP1 inhibitors. The researchers used a structure-based drug design approach to identify compounds that could bind to the ATP-binding site of TRAP1 (Vyas et al., 2022).

The study found that several of the pyrimidine-5-carbonitrile derivatives exhibited potent inhibitory activity against TRAP1, with IC_{50} values in the low nanomolar range. Additionally, the compounds showed selectivity for TRAP1 over other heat shock protein 90 (Hsp90) family members, indicating that they may have a favorable therapeutic index.

El-Dydamony et al. (2022) reported the synthesis and biological evaluation of a series of pyrimidine-5-carbonitrile derivatives as potential TRAP1 inhibitors. The researchers used a combination of molecular docking, molecular dynamics simulations, and in vitro assays to identify compounds that could bind to the ATP-binding site of TRAP1 and inhibit its activity (El-Dydamony et al., 2022).

The study found that several of the pyrimidine-5-carbonitrile derivatives exhibited potent inhibitory activity against TRAP1, with IC_{50} values in the low micromolar range. Additionally, the compounds showed selectivity for TRAP1 over other Hsp90 family members, indicating that they may have a favorable therapeutic index.

These studies suggest that pyrimidine-5-carbonitrile derivatives have potential as TRAP1 inhibitors for the treatment of cancer. Further studies are needed to optimize the potency and selectivity of these compounds and evaluate their efficacy in animal models of cancer (Fig. 16.11).

5.15 Monoclonal antibodies

Several monoclonal antibodies targeting TRAP1 are currently in development for the treatment of cancer, which have been shown to inhibit the growth of cancer cells in *in vitro* models. Clinical trials are currently underway to evaluate the safety and efficacy of TRAP1-targeting mAbs in humans.

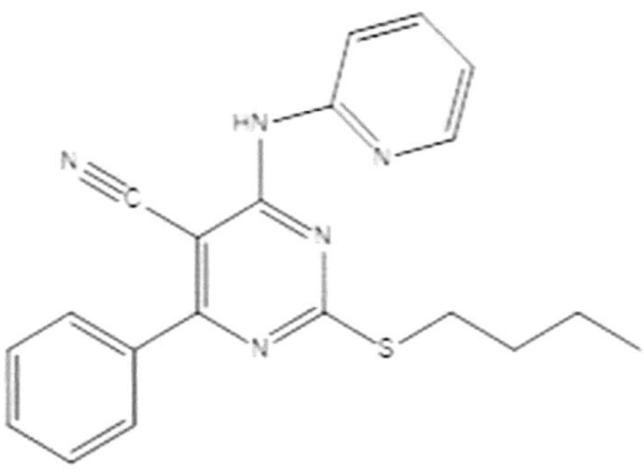

FIGURE 16.11 Pyrimidine-5-carbonitrile analogs as TRAP1 inhibitors.

Pyrimidine-5-carbonitrile analogues with In vitro anti- proliferative activity

Monoclonal antibodies have several potential benefits as cancer therapeutics, including high specificity for their targets, low toxicity, and the ability to be modified for improved pharmacokinetics and efficacy. Additionally, TRAP1 inhibitors have been shown to synergize with other cancer therapies, such as chemotherapy and radiation, making them a promising option for combination therapy. Despite their promise, there are also several challenges associated with the development of monoclonal antibodies as cancer therapeutics. These include high development costs, the potential for immunogenicity (i.e., an immune response against the mAb), and the difficulty of delivering mAbs to tumors that are located deep within the body (Goodin, 2008; Lu et al., 2020).

5.16 Risks of TNF inhibitors with TRAP1

Tumor necrosis factor (TNF) inhibitors are a class of drugs that are commonly used to treat a range of inflammatory conditions such as rheumatoid arthritis, psoriasis, and inflammatory bowel disease. However, recent studies have shown that TNF inhibitors may pose a risk for patients with a genetic variant in the tumor necrosis factor receptor—associated protein 1 (TRAP1) gene (Yao et al., 2023).

Recent studies have shown that TNF inhibitors may interact with TRAP1, leading to an increased risk of adverse effects in patients with TRAP1 mutations. Ajith and Jayakumar (2014) reported that TNF inhibitors increased the risk of cardiovascular disease in patients with TRAP1 mutations and increased the risk of cancer cell growth in TRAP1-deficient cells (Ajith & Jayakumar, 2014).

In addition to the increased risk of adverse effects in patients with TRAP1 mutations, TNF inhibitors may also increase the risk of infections, including tuberculosis and other opportunistic infections. Patients taking TNF inhibitors are advised to undergo regular screening for tuberculosis and other infections, and to report any signs of infection to their healthcare provider immediately (Park et al., 2022).

While TNF inhibitors are a valuable treatment option for patients with inflammatory conditions, it is important for healthcare providers to consider the potential risks associated with TRAP1 mutations and to monitor patients closely for adverse effects. Patients with TRAP1 mutations may benefit from alternative treatment options, and genetic testing may be useful in identifying individuals at increased risk.

6. Conclusion and future prospects

TRAP1 is an important molecular chaperone that plays a crucial role in regulating cellular processes such as apoptosis, metabolism, and signal transduction. The overexpression of TRAP1 has been linked to the development and progression of various types of cancer, making it an attractive target for the development of cancer therapies. Therefore, tumor necrosis factor receptor-associated protein 1 (TRAP1) is a promising therapeutic target for cancer treatment.

TRAP1 inhibitors have shown promising results in preclinical studies, demonstrating the potential for targeting TRAP1 in cancer treatment. These inhibitors have been shown to induce cell death in cancer cells, suppress tumor growth, and increase the efficacy of existing chemotherapeutic agents. However, more research is needed to fully understand the mechanisms of action of TRAP1 inhibitors and to determine their safety and efficacy in human clinical trials. Overall, TRAP1 inhibitors hold great promise as a novel approach to cancer treatment, and further research in this field could potentially lead to the development of more effective and targeted therapies for patients with cancer.

References

Ajith, T. A., & Jayakumar, T. G. (October 10, 2014). Mitochondria-targeted agents: Future perspectives of mitochondrial pharmaceutics in cardiovascular diseases. *World Journal of Cardiology, 6*(10), 1091.

Al-Lazikani, B., Banerji, U., & Workman, P. (2012). Combinatorial drug therapy for cancer in the post-genomic era. *Nature Biotechnology, 30*(7), 679—691. https://doi.org/10.1038/nbt.2284

Amoroso, M. R., Matassa, D. S., Agliarulo, I., Avolio, R., Lu, H., Sisinni, L., Lettini, G., Gabra, H., Landriscina, M., & Esposito, F. (2016). TRAP1 downregulation in human ovarian cancer enhances invasion and epithelial- mesenchymal transition. *Cell Death and Disease, 7*(12), Article e2522. https://doi.org/10.1038/cddis.2016.400

Arch, R. H., Gedrich, R. W., & Thompson, C. B. (September 15, 1998). Tumor necrosis factor receptor-associated factors (TRAFs)—A family of adapter proteins that regulates life and death. *Genes and development, 12*(18), 2821—2830.

Aust, S., Bachmayr-Heyda, A., Pateisky, P., Tong, D., Darb-Esfahani, S., Denkert, C., Chekerov, R., Sehouli, J., Mahner, S., Van Gorp, T., & Vergote, I. (2012). Role of TRAP1 and estrogen receptor alpha in patients with ovarian cancer -A study of the OVCAD consortium. *Molecular Cancer, 11*, 69. https://doi.org/10.1186/1476-4598-11-69

Bruno, G., Li Bergolis, V., Piscazzi, A., Crispo, F., Condelli, V., Zoppoli, P., Maddalena, F., Pietrafesa, M., Giordano, G., Matassa, D. S., & Esposito, F. (June 1, 2022). TRAP1 regulates the response of colorectal cancer cells to hypoxia and inhibits ribosome biogenesis under conditions of oxygen deprivation. *International Journal of Oncology, 60*(6), 1—2.

Chauhan, A., Islam, A. U., Prakash, H., & Singh, S. (June 1, 2022). Phytochemicals targeting NF-κB signaling: Potential anti-cancer interventions. *Journal of Pharmaceutical Analysis, 12*(3), 394—405.

Chen, C. F., Chen, Y., Dai, K., Chen, P. L., Riley, D. J., & Lee, W. H. (September 1996). A new member of the hsp90 family of molecular chaperones interacts with the retinoblastoma protein during mitosis and after heat shock. *Molecular and cellular biology, 16*(9), 4691—4699.

Clerkin, J. S., Naughton, R., Quiney, C., & Cotter, T. G. (July 18, 2008). Mechanisms of ROS modulated cell survival during carcinogenesis. *Cancer letters, 266*(1), 30—36.

Costantino, E., Maddalena, F., Calise, S., Piscazzi, A., Tirino, V., Fersini, A., Ambrosi, A., Neri, V., Esposito, F., & Landriscina, M. (June 28, 2009). TRAP1, a novel mitochondrial chaperone responsible for multi-drug resistance and protection from apoptotis in human colorectal carcinoma cells. *Cancer letters, 279*(1), 39—46. https://doi.org/10.1016/j.canlet.2009.01.018

Dai, Y., Liu, M., Tang, W., DeSano, J., Burstein, E., Davis, M., Pienta, K., Lawrence, T., & Xu, L. (December 1, 2008). Molecularly targeted radiosensitization of human prostate cancer by modulating inhibitor of apoptosis. *Clinical Cancer Research, 14*(23), 7701—7710.

Davenport, E. L., Zeisig, A., Aronson, L. I., Moore, H. E., Hockley, S., Gonzalez, D., Smith, E. M., Powers, M. V., Sharp, S. Y., Workman, P., & Morgan, G. J. (2010). Targeting heat shock protein 72 enhances Hsp90 inhibitor-induced apoptosis in myeloma. *Leukemia, 24*(10), 1804—1807. https://doi.org/10.1038/leu.2010.168

El-Dydamony, N. M., Abdelnaby, R. M., Abdelhady, R., Ali, O., Fahmy, M. I., Fakhr Eldeen, R. R., & Helwa, A. A. (December 31, 2022). Pyrimidine-5-carbonitrile based potential anticancer agents as apoptosis inducers through PI3K/AKT axis inhibition in leukaemia K562. *Journal of Enzyme Inhibition and Medicinal Chemistry, 37*(1), 895—911.

Felts, S. J., Owen, B. A., Nguyen, P., Trepel, J., Donner, D. B., & Toft, D. O. (February 4, 2000). The hsp90-related protein TRAP1 is a mitochondrial protein with distinct functional properties. *Journal of Biological Chemistry, 275*(5), 3305—3312.

Gesualdi, N. M., Chirico, G., Pirozzi, G., Costantino, E., Landriscina, M., & Esposito, F. (2007). Tumor necrosis factor-associated protein 1 (TRAP-1) protects cells from oxidative stress and apoptosis. *Stress: The International Journal on the Biology of Stress, 10*(4), 342—350. https://doi.org/10.1080/10253890701314863

Goodin, S. (June 1, 2008). Development of monoclonal antibodies for the treatment of colorectal cancer. *American Journal of Health-System Pharmacy, 65*(11_Suppl._4), S3—S7.

Guadagni, F., Ferroni, P., Palmirotta, R., Portarena, I., Formica, V., & Roselli, M. (2007). TNF/VEGF cross-talk in chronic inflammation-related cancer initiation and progression: An early target in anticancer therapeutic strategy. *In Vivo, 21*(2), 147—161.

Baldwin, P. R. (2014). *Development of monocarbonyl curcumin analogues towards treating tuberculosis and cancer* (Doctoral dissertation, Emory University).

https://pubchem.ncbi.nlm.nih.gov/#query=acetyl%20cysteine.

Janin, Y. L. (December 1, 2005). Heat shock protein 90 inhibitors. A text book example of medicinal chemistry? *Journal of Medicinal Chemistry, 48*(24), 7503—7512.

Kang, B. H., Tavecchio, M., Goel, H. L., Hsieh, C. C., Garlick, D. S., Raskett, C. M., Lian, J. B., Stein, G. S., Languino, L. R., & Altieri, D. C. (2011). Targeted inhibition of mitochondrial Hsp90 suppresses localised and metastatic prostate cancer growth in a genetic mouse model of disease. *British Journal of Cancer, 104*(4), 629—634. https://doi.org/10.1038/bjc.2011.9

Karin, M. (June 2006). NF-κB and cancer: Mechanisms and targets. *Molecular Carcinogenesis, 45*(6), 355—361. Published in cooperation with the University of Texas MD Anderson Cancer Center.

Kim, H., Yang, J., Kim, M. J., Choi, S., Chung, J. R., Kim, J. M., Yoo, Y. H., Chung, J., & Koh, H. (January 22, 2016). Tumor necrosis factor receptor-associated protein 1 (TRAP1) mutation and TRAP1 inhibitor gamitrinib-triphenylphosphonium (G-TPP) induce a forkhead box O (FOXO)-dependent cell protective signal from mitochondria. *Journal of Biological Chemistry, 291*(4), 1841—1853.

Kuchitsu, Y., Nagashio, R., Igawa, S., Kusuhara, S., Tsuchiya, B., Ichinoe, M., Satoh, Y., Naoki, K., Murakumo, Y., Saegusa, M., & Sato, Y. (2020). TRAP1 is a predictive biomarker of platinum-based adjuvant chemotherapy benefits in patients with resected lung adenocarcinoma. *BioMed Res-Tokyo, 41*(1), 53—65. https://doi.org/10.2220/biomedres.41.53

Liang, Y., Fang, R., & Rao, Q. (April 29, 2022). An insight into the medicinal chemistry perspective of macrocyclic derivatives with antitumor activity: A systematic review. *Molecules, 27*(9), 2837.

Liu, D., Hu, J., Agorreta, J., Cesario, A., Zhang, Y., Harris, A. L., Gatter, K., & Pezzella, F. (October 28, 2010). Tumor necrosis factor receptor-associated protein 1 (TRAP1) regulates genes involved in cell cycle and metastases. *Cancer Letters, 296*(2), 194—205.

Loizzo, M. R., Malfa, G. A., Acquaviva, R., Tundis, R., & Bonesi, M. (January 1 2021). Carotenoids as tools in breast cancer therapy. In *Discovery and development of anti-breast cancer agents from natural products* (pp. 123—146). Elsevier.

Lu, R. M., Hwang, Y. C., Liu, I. J., Lee, C. C., Tsai, H. Z., Li, H. J., & Wu, H. C. (December 2020). Development of therapeutic antibodies for the treatment of diseases. *Journal of Biomedical Science, 27*(1), 1—30.

Masgras, I., Laquatra, C., Cannino, G., Serapian, S. A., Colombo, G., & Rasola, A. (November 1, 2021). The molecular chaperone TRAP1 in cancer: From the basics of biology to pharmacological targeting. In *Seminars in cancer biology* (Vol 76, pp. 45—53). Academic Press.

Masuda, Y., Shima, G., Aiuchi, T., Horie, M., Hori, K., Nakajo, S., Kajimoto, S., Shibayama-Imazu, T., & Nakaya, K. (October 8, 2004). Involvement of tumor necrosis factor receptor-associated protein 1 (TRAP1) in apoptosis induced by β-hydroxyisovalerylshikonin. *Journal of Biological Chemistry, 279*(41), 42503—42515.

May, A. E., Kälsch, T., Massberg, S., Herouy, Y., Schmidt, R., & Gawaz, M. (October 15, 2002). Engagement of glycoprotein IIb/IIIa (αIIbβ3) on platelets upregulates CD40L and triggers CD40L-dependent matrix degradation by endothelial cells. *Circulation, 106*(16), 2111—2117.

Meylan, E., Burns, K., Hofmann, K., Blancheteau, V., Martinon, F., Kelliher, M., & Tschopp, J. (May 1, 2004). RIP1 is an essential mediator of Toll-like receptor 3—induced NF-κB activation. *Nature Immunology, 5*(5), 503—507.

Mistretta, F., Buffi, N. M., Lughezzani, G., Lista, G., Larcher, A., Fossati, N., Abrate, A., Dell'Oglio, P., Montorsi, F., Guazzoni, G., & Lazzeri, M. (January 1, 2014). Bladder cancer and urothelial impairment: The role of TRPV1 as potential drug target. *BioMed Research International, 2014*.

Nakamoto, H., Yokoyama, Y., Suzuki, T., Miyamoto, Y., Fujishiro, T., Morikawa, M., & Miyata, Y. (August 2021). A cyclic lipopeptide surfactin is a species-selective Hsp90 inhibitor that suppresses cyanobacterial growth. *The Journal of Biochemistry, 170*(2), 255—264.

Papaneophytou, C., Alexiou, P., Papakyriakou, A., Ntougkos, E., Tsiliouka, K., Maranti, A., Liepouri, F., Strongilos, A., Mettou, A., Couladouros, E., & Eliopoulos, E. (2015). Synthesis and biological evaluation of potential small molecule inhibitors of tumor necrosis factor. *MedChemComm, 6*(6), 1196—1209.

Park, H. K., Jeong, H., Ko, E., Lee, G., Lee, J. E., Lee, S. K., Lee, A. J., Im, J. Y., Hu, S., Kim, H. S., & Lee, J. H. (2017). Paralog specificity determines subcellular distribution, action mechanism, and anticancer activity of TRAP1 inhibitors. *Journal of Medicinal Chemistry, 60*(17), 7569−7578. https://doi.org/10.1021/acs.jmedchem.7b00978

Park, D. W., Kim, Y. J., Sung, Y. K., Chung, S. J., Yeo, Y., Park, T. S., Lee, H., Moon, J. Y., Kim, S. H., Kim, T. H., & Yoon, H. J. (March 7, 2022). TNF inhibitors increase the risk of nontuberculous mycobacteria in patients with seropositive rheumatoid arthritis in a mycobacterium tuberculosis endemic area. *Scientific Reports, 12*(1), 4003.

Park, H. K., Lee, J. E., Lim, J., Jo, D. E., Park, S. A., Suh, P. G., & Kang, B. H. (2014). Combination treatment with doxorubicin and gamitrinib synergistically augments anticancer activity through enhanced activation of bim. *BMC Cancer, 14*, 431. https://doi.org/10.1186/1471-2407-14-431

Park, H. K., Yoon, N. G., Lee, J. E., Hu, S., Yoon, S., Kim, S. Y., Hong, J. H., Nam, D., Chae, Y. C., Park, J. B., & Kang, B. H. (2020). Unleashing the full potential of Hsp90 inhibitors as cancer therapeutics through simultaneous inactivation of Hsp90, Grp94, and TRAP1. *Experimental and Molecular Medicine, 52*(1), 79−91. https://doi.org/10.1038/s12276-019-0360-x

Qaiser, H., Saeed, M., Nerukh, D., & Ul-Haq, Z. (November 2, 2021). Structural insight into TNF-α inhibitors through combining pharmacophore-based virtual screening and molecular dynamic simulation. *Journal of Biomolecular Structure and Dynamics, 39*(16), 5920−5939.

Rinotas, V., Papakyriakou, A., Violitzi, F., Papaneophytou, C., Ouzouni, M. D., Alexiou, P., Strongilos, A., Couladouros, E., Kontopidis, G., Eliopoulos, E., & Douni, E. (September 21, 2020). Discovery of small-molecule inhibitors of receptor activator of nuclear factor-κB ligand with a superior therapeutic index. *Journal of Medicinal Chemistry, 63*(20), 12043−12059.

Rondanin, R., Lettini, G., Oliva, P., Baruchello, R., Costantini, C., Trapella, C., Simoni, D., Bernardi, T., Sisinni, L., Pietrafesa, M., & Ponterini, G. (July 15, 2018). New TRAP1 and Hsp90 chaperone inhibitors with cationic components: Preliminary studies on mitochondrial targeting. *Bioorganic and Medicinal Chemistry Letters, 28*(13), 2289−2293. https://doi.org/10.1016/j.bmcl.2018.05.031

Sanchez-Martin, C., Menon, D., Moroni, E., Ferraro, M., Ferraro, M., Masgras, I., Elsey, J., Arbiser, J. L., Colombo, G., & Rasola, A. (2021). Honokiol bis-dichloroacetate is a selective allosteric inhibitor of the mitochondrial chaperone TRAP1. *Antioxid Redox Sign, 34*(7), 505−516. https://doi.org/10.1089/ars.2019.7972

Sanchez-Martin, C., Moroni, E., Ferraro, M., Laquatra, C., Cannino, G., Masgras, I., Negro, A., Quadrelli, P., Rasola, A., & Colombo, G. (2020). Rational design of allosteric and selective inhibitors of the molecular chaperone TRAP1. *Cell Reports, 31*(3). https://doi.org/10.1016/j.celrep. 2020.107531

Si, T., Yang, G., Qiu, X., Luo, Y., Liu, B., & Wang, B. (2015). Expression of tumor necrosis factor receptor-associated protein 1 and its clinical significance in kidney cancer. *International Journal of Clinical and Experimental Pathology, 8*(10), Article 13090.

Siegelin, M. D. (2013). Inhibition of the mitochondrial Hsp90 chaperone network: A novel, efficient treatment strategy for cancer? *Cancer Letters, 333*(2), 133−146. https://doi.org/10.1016/j.canlet.2013.01.045

Siegelin, M. D., Plescia, J., Raskett, C. M., Gilbert, C. A., Ross, A. H., & Altieri, D. C. (2010). Global targeting of subcellular heat shock protein-90 networks for therapy of glioblastoma. *Molecular Cancer Therapeutics, 9*(6), 1638−1646. https://doi.org/10.1158/1535-7163.Mct-10-0097

Speiser, D. E., Lee, S. Y., Wong, B., Arron, J., Santana, A., Kong, Y. Y., Ohashi, P. S., & Choi, Y. (May 19, 1997). A regulatory role for TRAF1 in antigen-induced apoptosis of T cells. *Journal of Experimental Medicine, 185*(10), 1777−1783.

Stuhmer, T., Iskandarov, K., Gao, Z. H., Bumm, T., Grella, E., Jensen, M. R., Einsele, H., Chatterjee, M., & Bargou, R. C. (2012). Preclinical activity of the novel orally bioavailable HSP90 inhibitor NVP- HSP990 against multiple myeloma cells. *Anticancer Research, 32*(2), 453−462.

Tian, X., Ma, P., Sui, C. G., Meng, F. D., Li, Y., Fu, L. Y., Jiang, T., Wang, Y., & Jiang, Y. H. (2014). Suppression of tumor necrosis factor receptor-associated protein 1 expression induces inhibition of cell proliferation and tumor growth in human esophageal cancer cells. *FEBS Journal, 281*(12), 2805−2819. https://doi.org/10.1111/febs.12822

Venkatesan, N., Kanwar, J. R., Deepa, P. R., Navaneethakrishnan, S., Joseph, C., & Krishnakumar, S. (2016). Targeting HSP90/survivin using a cell permeable structure based peptido-mimetic shepherdin in retinoblastoma. *Chemico-Biological Interactions, 252*, 141−149. https://doi.org/10.1016/j.cbi.2016.04.011

Vyas, A., Sahu, B., Pathania, S., Nandi, N. K., Chauhan, G., Asati, V., & Kumar, B. (November 1, 2022). An insight on medicinal attributes of pyrimidine scaffold: An updated review. *Journal of Heterocyclic Chemistry, 126*.

Wang, T., Zhang, X., & Li, J. J. (October 1, 2002). The role of NF-κB in the regulation of cell stress responses. *International Immunopharmacology, 2*(11), 1509–1520.

Ware, C. F., VanArsdale, S., & VanArsdale, T. L. (January 1, 1996). Apoptosis mediated by the TNF-related cytokine and receptor families. *Journal of Cellular Biochemistry, 60*(1), 47–55.

Wu, J., Liu, Y., Cho, K., Dong, X., Teng, L., Han, D., Liu, H., Chen, X., Chen, X., Hou, X., & Peng, F. (2016). Down-regulation of TRAP1 sensitizes glioblastoma cells to temozolomide chemotherapy through regulating metabolic reprogramming. *NeuroReport, 27*(3), 136–144. https://doi.org/10.1097/WNR.0000000000000513

Xie, S., Wang, X., Gan, S., Tang, X., Kang, X., & Zhu, S. (January 26, 2021). The mitochondrial chaperone TRAP1 as a candidate target of oncotherapy. *Frontiers in Oncology, 10*, Article 585047.

Xu, L., Dai, Y., Meng, Y., Liu, M., Pienta, K., & Lawrence, T. (May 1, 2007). Molecularly targeted cancer chemo/radiosensitization in vitro and in vivo by modulating apoptotic pathways. *Cancer Research, 67*(9_Suppl.), 5052.

Yao, K., Dou, B., Zhang, Y., Chen, Z., Li, Y., Fan, Z., Ma, Y., Du, S., Wang, J., Xu, Z., & Liu, Y. (February 16, 2023). Inflammation—The role of TRPA1 channel. *Frontiers in Physiology, 14*, 258.

Yoshida, S., Tsutsumi, S., Muhlebach, G., Sourbier, C., Lee, M. J., Lee, S., Vartholomaiou, E., Tatokoro, M., Beebe, K., Miyajima, N., & Mohney, R. P. (2013). Molecular chaperone TRAP1 regulates a metabolic switch between mitochondrial respiration and aerobic glycolysis. *Proceedings of the National Academy of Sciences of the United States of America, 110*(17), E1604–E1612. https://doi.org/10.1073/pnas.1220659110

Zhang, H., Steed, A., Co, M., & Chen, X. (2021). Cancer stem cells, epithelial-mesenchymal transition, ATP and their roles in drug resistance in cancer. *Cancer Drug Resistance, 4*(3), 684.

17

Vascular endothelial growth factor receptors (VEGFR/PDGFR) inhibitors

Mohamed Saleh Elgawish[1,2] *and Eman Abdeldayem*[2]

[1]Department of Medicinal Chemistry, Faculty of Pharmacy, Suez Canal University, Ismailia, Egypt; [2]Department of Chemistry, Korea University, Seoul, Republic of Korea

1. Introduction

Since the 1980s, oncogenes like SRC5 and improvements in the molecular understanding of cancer have led to the recognition of protein kinases as prospective therapeutic targets. The high concentration of cellular ATP, however, was once thought to be an insurmountable obstacle in the creation of protein kinase inhibitors that bind to the hinge region where ATP is binding (Attwood et al., 2021). This cleared the way for the discovery and development of small-molecule synthetic inhibitors (SMKIs) targeting kinase with appropriate drug-like characteristics, selectivity, and potency by the end of the 1980s. Currently, the FDA has approved 73 SMKIs, and 16 more SMKIs have received approval from other regulatory bodies (Laufer & Bajorath, 2022). Approximately, 110 new kinases are being studied as targets for SMKI in clinical trials, which, when added to the roughly 45 targets of licensed kinase inhibitors, only account for about 30% of the human kinome (Roskoski, 2021). This finding indicates that there are still unrealized potential opportunities for this class of vital drugs. In many diseases, including cancer, the generation of new blood vessels from already-existing ones and vascular endothelial cells is of substantial necessity. Although the function of the capillary network in tumors was first identified in 1863 and shown to be originated from the host vascular bed, it was not until 1971 that the idea of employing angiogenesis-targeting drugs to treat cancer was first proposed. The mammalian platelet-derived growth factor (PDGF) supergene family is composed of five prototypes namely VEGFA, VEGFB, VEGFC, VEGF-D, and placental growth factor. The highly conserved glycoprotein VEGF is a potent multifunctional cytokine that has significant effects on the vascular endothelium and is likely essential for tumor-induced Novo vascular development. As a result, tumor growth can be slowed down by using particular angiogenesis inhibitors that target the vascular compartment (Ivy et al., 2009). An important anticancer technique is targeting tumor angiogenesis.

With seven FDA-approved SMKIs (Sunitinib, Pazopanib, Lenvatinib, Axitinib, Nintedanib, Vandetanib, and Tivozanib) and one mAb (Trastuzumab), the vascular endothelial growth factor receptor (VEGFR) family of receptor tyrosine kinases (RTKs) is among the most often targeted kinases. The angiogenic pathways controlled by VEGFR, PDGFR, KIT, fibroblast growth factor receptors (FGFRs), and MET have been successfully addressed by a large number of approved kinase inhibitors for a variety of indications (Attwood et al., 2021). Five SMKIs for renal cell carcinoma are FDA-approved and inhibit VEGFR as well as other RTKs. The FDA-approved mAb ramucirumab and the Chinese-approved SMKI fruquintinib have both been used to treat metastatic colorectal cancer (CRC) by inhibiting VEGFR. Vandetanib, cabozantinib, and lenvatinib are VEGFR inhibitors that have been used to treat medullary thyroid cancer. Imatinib inhibits PDGFR and KIT, and because of this effect, the FDA approved it for use in treating gastrointestinal stromal tumors (GISTs) in 2002. Avapritinib and ripretinib are designed to particularly target PDGFR and KIT activation loop mutants responsible for the relapse of up to 85%—90% of GIST patients and were approved for this case in 2020. Additional SMKIs have been developed for this tumor as well as others to boost activity and/or address first-generation drug resistance (Attwood et al., 2021).

With the exception of three rapalogues, four MEK inhibitors, and the dual SRC and tubulin polymerization inhibitor tirbanibulin, nearly all the FDA-approved SMKIs target the VEGFR/PDGFR at ATP-binding site (Smet et al., 2014). The ATP-binding site is conserved in the human kinome, and thus "ATP mimetics" frequently interact with a wide variety of other kinases, producing substances with promiscuous profiles. Multikinase inhibitors are promiscuous chemicals with the potential for toxicological risks, such as dasatinib or sunitinib. These substances have been linked to off-target adverse effects, but they also frequently produce predictable on-target adverse outcomes. However, there may be some possible benefits to this cross-reactivity. For example, imatinib's efficacy against various kinases has allowed for its use in a variety of diseases (Attwood et al., 2021).

An important aspect of kinase drug discovery, such as the targeted pathways and protein families (Huang et al., 2020), pharmacology and/or mechanism of action of the kinase (Wu et al., 2016), FDA-only approved SMKIs (Roskoski, 2021), linked clinical indications, or structural components (Roskoski, 2016), have been discussed in recent studies on kinase inhibitors. In this chapter, we shed light on not only FDA-approved VEGFR/PDGFR drugs but also all drugs in clinical trials covering drug development, synthetic pathway, and drug—receptor interaction. We also considered the physicochemical and ADME properties, adverse effects, and main structural criteria to design VEGFR inhibitors. As the chemical aspect of kinase inhibitors is the main goal of this book, we discuss the structural requirements for VEGFR/PDGFR inhibitors.

2. Molecular mechanisms and clinical applications of angiogenesis

Blood vessels evolved to allow hematopoietic cells to patrol the organism for immunological monitoring, give oxygen and nutrition, and eliminate waste. In a perfusion-independent manner, vessels also produce instructional signals for organogenesis. Despite the fact that arteries are essential for regenerating and proliferating various tissues, they can also fuel inflammatory and malignant disorders, and tumor cells could use the arteries to metastasize and terminate the life of cancer patients. Deviations from normal vessel growth can cause various disorders since vessels nourish practically every organ in the body. Inadequate artery growth or maintenance can lead to stroke, myocardial infarction, ulcerative disorders, and neurodegeneration, while aberrant vessel growth or remodeling can cause cancer, inflammatory disorders, pulmonary hypertension, and blinding eye illnesses. Because the current book focuses on cancer mechanisms and management, the next section will discuss angiogenesis and its function in cancer progression, as well as how preventing angiogenesis may be beneficial to cancer patients (Carmeliet, 2000; Folkman, 2007).

Several different types of vessel formation have been discovered. Angioblasts differentiate into endothelial cells in the developing mammalian embryo, which assemble into a vascular labyrinth—a process known as vasculogenesis. Different signals can distinguish between venous and arterial differentiation. Angiogenesis, or the expansion of the vessel's network, is ensured by subsequent sprouting. Arteriogenesis occurs when endothelial cell channels are covered by pericytes or vascular smooth muscle cells (VSMCs) to provide stability and control perfusion (Swift & Brant, 2009).

Autocrine signals including VEGF, fibroblast growth factors (FGFs), angiopoietin-1 (ANG-1), and NOTCH can provide protection for the healthy adult quiescent endothelium cells enduring their survival. Endothelial cells carry both oxygen sensors and hypoxia-inducible factors, and these sensors/factors enable the vasculature to modify its form to improve blood flow. A streamlined monolayer of phalanx cells made up of dormant endothelial cells is connected by junctional molecules. These endothelial cells are surrounded by pericytes that inhibit the development of the endothelial cells and release two cell-survival signals, VEGF and ANG-1. Endothelial and pericyte cells form a common basement membrane when at rest (Ferrara, 2009; Nagy et al., 2007). When a dormant vessel detects an angiogenic signal emitted by hypoxia, inflammation, or a tumor cell, pericytes separate from the vessel wall and liberate themselves from the basement membrane via proteolytic degradation carried out by matrix metalloproteinases (MMPs). Once the endothelial cells loosen their bonds, the new vessel is expanded. VEGF causes plasma proteins to extravasate and forms a temporary extracellular matrix (ECM) scaffold by increasing the permeability of the endothelial cell layer. A vessel must mature and stabilize to become functional. Signals such as platelet-derived growth factor B (PDGF-B), NOTCH, ANG-1, transforming growth factors (TGF), and ephrin-B2 drive endothelial cells to regain their quiescent phalanx state (Ferrara, 2009; Nagy et al., 2007). Because this chapter aims to explain the significance of VEGFR and PDGFR inhibition in cancer treatment, the following phrases will focus on these two kinase receptors.

Only a few members make up the VEGF family, which differs from other angiogenic superfamilies in that its members mostly perform nonredundant roles. The main component is VEGF (also known as VEGF-A), which signals through the VEGF receptor-2 to stimulate angiogenesis in both healthy and diseased conditions (Fig. 17.1). Soluble VEGF isoforms encourage vessel expansion, whereas matrix-bound isoforms encourage vessel branching (Stockmann et al., 2008). Endothelial cells emit autocrine VEGF that keep vascular homeostasis, while tumor, myeloid, and other stromal cells secrete paracrine VEGF that induces vessel branching and abnormalities in tumor vasculature. According to new findings, the biological function of VEGFR-2 signaling (Fig. 17.1) is dependent on its subcellular distribution—for

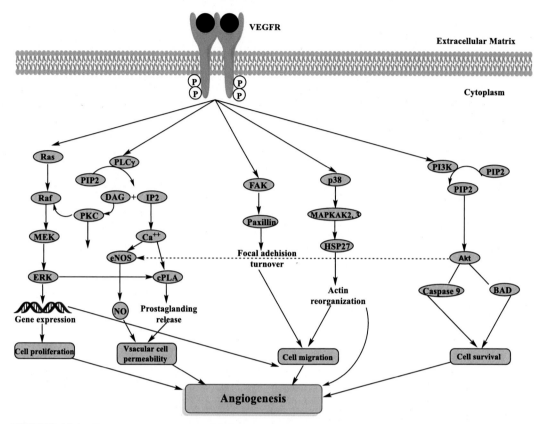

FIGURE 17.1   Tumor angiogenesis via VEGFR signaling pathway. VEGFR activation promotes angiogenesis by mediating proliferation, vascular permeability, cell migration, and cell survival.

example, VEGF must communicate from intracellular compartments for VEGFR-2 to trigger arterial morphogenesis. Human cancer and ophthalmic diseases can both be treated by blocking VEGF signaling, and pathological angiogenesis is also influenced by genetic differences in VEGF and/or its receptors (Lanahan et al., 2010; Lee et al., 2007). On one hand, blood-vessel tip cells are activated by VEGF-C, a ligand for the VEGFR-2 and VEGFR-3 receptors. As a result, anti-VEGFR-3 antibodies that impair receptor dimerization and/or ligand binding limit tumor growth in concert with VEGFR-2 suppression, making VEGFR-3 a promising antiangiogenic candidate. On another hand, the exact function of the VEGFR-1 receptor in angiogenesis is unknown. However, VEGFR-1 may operate as a VEGF decoy, decreasing the amount of free VEGF available to activate VEGFR-2 and explaining why VEGFR-1 deletion results in vessel overgrowth (Jain et al., 2009; Tvorogov et al., 2010).

Vessels must be developed and coated by mural cells to operate effectively. This process is aided by numerous growth-factor families like PDGFs, TGFs, and angiopoietins. Angiogenic endothelial cells emit PDGF-B to chemoattract PDGF receptor-positive (PDGFR-β^{+}) pericytes to stabilize endothelial cell channels (Jain, 2003). As a result, vascular leakage, tortuosity, microaneurysm development, and bleeding occur as a result of pericyte shortage following

PDGF-B ablation (Gaengel et al., 2009; Tomaso et al., 2009). Inhibition of PDGFR slows tumor overgrowth by triggering pericyte separation, which results in immature vasculature. Surprisingly, overexpression of PDGF-β reduces tumor growth in mice by boosting pericyte recruitment and causing endothelial cell growth to halt. Pericytes shield endothelial cells from VEGF withdrawal and give resistance to VEGF blockage because endothelial cells rely on pericyte VEGF synthesis for survival and this function necessitates a close endothelial-cell—pericyte connection. Therefore PDGF-β inhibition might modulate this relationship by affecting pericyte coverage and vessel number, particularly when VEGF is produced by pericytes rather than distant tumor cells (Nisancioglu et al., 2010; Sennino et al., 2009). Blocking PDGF-β renders mature arteries more vulnerable to VEGF inhibition by depleting the vasculature of pericytes, according to early investigations using multitarget receptor tyrosine kinase inhibitors (TKIs) (Nisancioglu et al., 2010). PDGF-β blockage may be utilized to treat nonmalignant vascular disorders including pulmonary hypertension, while the activation of PDGF-β may provide treatment options for vascular malformation stabilization (Gerhardt & Semb., 2008).

3. Inhibition of VEGFR and PDGFR signaling by small molecule drugs

Tyrosine kinases are responsible for transferring the γ-phosphate group to target proteins from ATP. RTKs are a class of transmembrane proteins composed of two domains, intracellular kinase domains, and extracellular ligand-binding domains. RTKs dimerize and autophosphorylate after tethering to their specific extracellular growth factors, inducing a cascade of downstream signaling pathways. VEGF, basic fibroblast growth factor, and PDGF are ligands for specific RTKs involved in intracellular signal transduction and generation of angiogenesis (Fujio & Walsh, 1999; Meadows et al., 2001).

The structural properties of extracellular domains of RTK have traditionally been used to classify them into seven classes namely class I to class VII. Each domain interacts with the corresponding ligands performing a specific function (Hennequin et al., 2000). RTKs have structural similarities in their cytoplasmic regions, which include kinase domains with an ATP-binding site, an activation loop that formed of one to three tyrosine residues, and carboxy-terminal lobes that bind tyrosine-containing peptide substrates and facilitate signal transmission. There are several RTK families with kinase insert domains that are quite similar, including class II (PDGFR, c-Kit, CsF-1R, and tyrosine-protein kinase Flt3) and class V (VEGFR1, VEGFR2, and VEGFR3) (Boyer, 2005; Hennequin et al., 2000).

To inhibit VEGFR2, numerous ATP-competitive small-molecule inhibitors attach to the highly conserved kinase domain of the ATP-binding pocket (Fig. 17.2 and Table 17.1) (Boyer, 2005). The ATP binding pocket is located between the amino-terminal and carboxy-terminal lobes, which are connected by critical residues capable of establishing hydrogen bonds with ATP. Because the ATP-binding sites in protein kinases are structurally conserved, small-molecule medications frequently exhibit high affinity for numerous RTK family members, including PDGFR, RAF, EGFR, and other targets (Table 17.1 and Fig. 17.2) (Clifford & Maher, 2001). Some small-molecule inhibitors have a multikinase inhibitor profile (Table.17.1), which means they have the ability to disrupt various biological processes involved in tumor growth and metastasis. Angiogenesis is upregulated in several pathological situations. Both VEGF

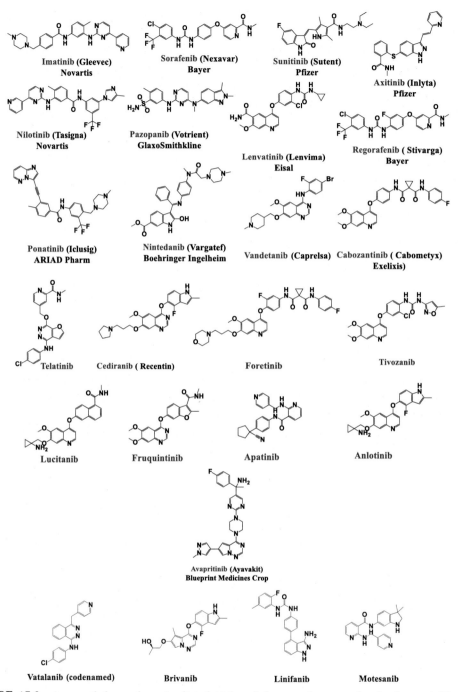

FIGURE 17.2   Approved drugs, drugs in clinical trial, and drugs no longer under development (*blue color*). Tyrosine kinase inhibitors targeting VEGFR and PDGFR.

TABLE 17.1 Tyrosine kinase inhibitors targeting VEGFR and PDGFR.

	Molecular target											
	VEGFR-1	VEGFR-2	VEGFR-3	PDGFRα	PDGFRβ	c-KIT	FLT3	RET	RAF-1	BRAF	TIE2	FGFR1
Sunitinib	*	*	*	*	*	*	*	*				
Sorafenib		*	*	*	*	*	*		*	*		
Regorafenib	*	*	*		*	*		*	*	*	*	*
Axitinib	*	*	*									
Nintedanib	*	*	*	*	*		*	*				*
Vandetanib	*	*	*	*	*			*				
Pazopanib	*	*	*	*	*	*						*
Vatalanib	*	*	*	*		*						
Cediranib	*	*	*	*	*	*						*
Cabozantinib	*	*	*			*	*	*			*	
Lenvatinib	*	*	*	*		*		*				*
Linifanib	*	*	*	*								
Telatinib		*	*		*							
Brivanib	*	*	*									*
Foretinib	*	*	*	*	*	*	*				*	
Motesanib	*	*	*	*	*	*						
Lucitanib	*	*	*	*	*							*
Fruquintinib	*	*	*									
Tivozanib	*	*	*									
Apatinib		*										

and VEGFR/PDGFR have been reported to be overexpressed in a large number of clinically relevant human solid tumors. A promising method for reducing aberrant angiogenesis is to modify VEGF and/or VEGFR/PDGFR signaling (Manley et al., 2002).

The currently FDA-approved VEGFR2 TKIs bind to the ATP-binding site. According to cocrystal structure studies, they are classified as type I or type II inhibitors depending on the conformation of VEGFR2 in connection with them. The orientation of the conserved triad Asp-Phe-Gly (DFG) at the start of the activation loop gives this conformation either the name "DFG-in or DFG-out." Type I inhibitors are designed to block the active version of VEGFR2 in an open activation loop conformation, DFG-In orientation. Type II inhibitors are those that target the inactive, DFG-out conformation, in which the DFG motif is flipped out relative to its active orientation (Liu & Gray., 2006). In addition to type, I and type II inhibitors, two

TABLE 17.2   General properties of kinase inhibitors (Okamato et al., 2015).

	Type I	Type II	Type III	Type IV	Type V
DFG conformation	In	Out	Out	ND	In
Binding region	ATP-binding site	ATP-binding site and neighboring region	Neighboring region	Allosteric site not adjacent to ATP-binding site	ATP-binding site and neighboring region
Selectivity	Low	High	High	High	High
ATP competitive	Yes	Yes	No	No	Yes
Association kinetic	Rapid	Slow	Slow	ND	Rapid
Dissociation kinetic	Rapid	Slow	Slow	ND	Slow

ND, not determined.

other categories of kinase inhibitors have been proposed based on how they interact with VEGFR2. Type III inhibitors bind to a location close to the ATP-binding site, but not to the hinge region; whereas, type IV inhibitors bind to a location that is distal to the ATP-binding site and cause conformational changes in the kinase, rendering it inactive (Elgawish et al., 2022). Type V inhibitor represented by Lenvatinib can bind both the hinge region and the neighboring allosteric region in VEGFR with DFG-in conformation. Table 17.2 can summarize the characteristics of various VEGFR2 inhibitors.

Fig. 17.3 depicts the difference in a binding manner between type I and type II inhibitors. The front cleft of the catalytic domain has the ATP binding site (composed of the adenine, phosphate, and sugar portions), but the back cleft contains a different location for the phosphorylation process. A gate between the front and back clefts of the receptor is created by Val-916 (a gatekeeper amino acid), making it possible for inhibitors to go readily from the front to the back cleft paving the way for the creation of VEGFR-2-specific inhibitors. The hydrophobic area (HYD-I and HYD-II), the hinge region, and the DFG motif region make up the active site of VEGFR-2. The HYD-I region is surrounded by the three amino acids Leu840, Gly992, and Phe918, while the HYD-II region is surrounded by the four amino acid residues Leu889, Ile892, Val898, and Ile1044 (Huang et al., 2012). Fig. 17.4 can summarize the drugs' moieties of the reported and approved drugs mentioned in Fig. 17.2 and Tables 17.1 and 17.3, which are organized according to their binding to four regions of VEGFR (hinge region, hydrophobic region I, hydrogen-bonding rich region, and hydrophobic region II).

4. The physicochemical properties of orally effective drugs

Both pharmacologists and medicinal chemists should consider the chemical features of new molecules when constructing orally active medications. Lipinski's "rule of five" is an experimental and computational method for calculating membrane permeability, solubility,

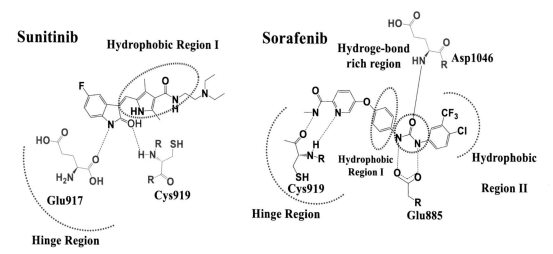

FIGURE 17.3   The difference between the binding mode of type I and type II inhibitors.

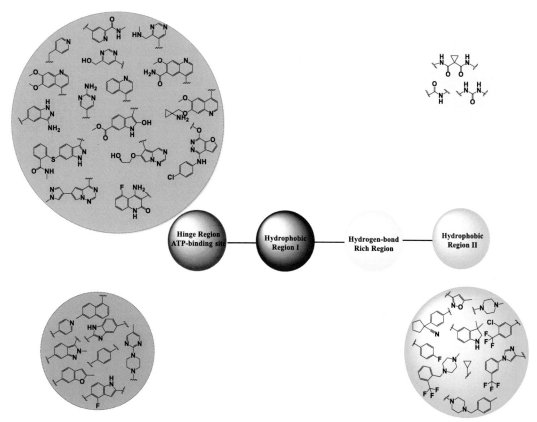

FIGURE 17.4   The approved and in-clinical trial drug moieties divided according to the site of interaction.

TABLE 17.3 In silico ADME prediction parameters of VEGFR and PDGFR inhibitors.

Title	mol MW[a]	donorHB[b]	acceptHB[c]	QPlogPo/w[d]	QPPCaco[e]	QPlogBB[f]	QPPMDCK[g]	#metab[h]	QPlogKhsa[i]	Percent human oral absorption[j]	Rule of Five[k]
Sorafenib	464.831	3	6	4.121	323.377	−0.98	1715.781	2	0.331	95.997	0
Regorafenib	464.831	3	6	4.109	320.768	−0.983	1702.714	2	0.328	95.861	0
Axitinib	386.47	2	4.5	4.711	808.06	−0.917	564.781	1	0.732	100	0
Nintedanib	539.633	1	11.5	2.555	11.067	−1.074	4.655	4	0.297	47.631	1
Vandetanib	475.36	1	6	5.123	1001.187	0.42	2382.541	4	0.823	100	1
Pazopanib	437.518	3	8.5	2.993	212.61	−1.759	94.534	5	0.267	86.127	0
Pazopanib	437.518	3	8.5	2.923	170.339	−1.876	74.518	6	0.272	83.997	0
Vatalanib	346.818	1	4	4.77	2735.192	−0.086	3618.418	3	0.606	100	0
Sunitinib	398.479	2	6	4.026	234.296	−0.593	205.93	3	0.642	92.933	0
Cediranib	450.512	1	6	5.39	701.671	−0.116	582.81	5	1.023	96.485	1
Cabozantinib	501.513	0	6	6.485	1634.312	−0.809	1518.554	3	1.118	96.512	2
Lenvatinib	426.858	4	6.75	2.529	117.602	−1.654	177.018	3	−0.015	78.812	0
Linifanib	375.404	5	3.5	3.026	163.819	−1.423	195.145	3	0.147	84.299	0
Telatinib	409.831	2	6.5	4.068	863.148	−0.857	1040.096	4	0.373	100	0
Brivanib	441.461	3	6.75	3.762	81.342	−1.227	57.204	7	0.647	83.166	0
Foretinib	632.663	0	9.7	6.632	370.516	−0.707	536.185	5	1.035	85.84	2
Motesanib	373.457	2	5.5	3.745	276.38	−0.406	136.321	5	0.647	92.571	0
Lucitinib	443.501	3	6.5	4	165.801	−0.866	78.469	3	0.679	90.094	0
Fruquintinib	393.398	1	7	3.687	1870.508	−0.551	973.433	5	0.297	100	0
Tivozanib	454.869	2	6.5	3.918	391.572	−1.159	641.716	4	0.348	96.292	0
Apatinib	397.479	1	6	4.577	466.629	−1.357	217.044	5	0.763	100	0

Acceptable ranges: (a) <500 amu; (b) <5; (c) <10; (d) <5; (e) >500 great; (f) (−3 to −1.2); (g) >500 great; (h) (1–8); (i) (−1.5 to 1.5), (j) >80% great; (k) maximum is 4. *metab*, number of likely metabolic reactions; *QPlogBB*, predicted brain/blood partition coefficient; *QPlogKhsa*, prediction of binding to human serum albumin; *QPPCaco*, predicted apparent Caco-2 cell permeability in nm/sec; *QPPMDCK*, predicted apparent MDCK cell permeability in nm/sec.

and efficacy in the context of drug development. The Lipinski criteria were developed after it was discovered that the majority of orally effective drugs are tiny, moderately lipophilic molecules. The Ro5 criteria are used when pharmacologically active lead compounds are serially enhanced to increase selectivity and activity while maintaining drug-like physicochemical characteristics (Roskoski, 2020): (i) the calculated Log P (cLogP) is greater than 5, (ii) there are more than five hydrogen-bond donors, (iii) there are more than 10 hydrogen-bond acceptors, and (iv) the molecular weight is greater than 500, the Ro5 predicts that less than ideal oral effectiveness will be observed. The average molecular weight (MW) of the VEGFR/PDGFR inhibitor, is 440.7, ranging from 346.8 (Vatalanib) to 632.6 (Foretinib) as shown in Table 17.3. Only Foretinib, Nintedanib, and Cabozantinib have shown MW higher than 500 Da. Cediranib, Vandetanib, Cabozantinib, and Foretinib are with a cLogP of greater than 5. Only Nintedanib contains a total of more than 10 hydrogen bond acceptors. Thus, Lipinski's Ro5 is not violated by VEGFR/PDGFR inhibitors. Other ADME functions such as permeability, binding to plasma protein, and oral absorption are described in Table 17.3.

5. Adverse effect of VEGFR/PDGFR TKIs

The adverse event profiles of small molecule TKIs are often tolerable. These substances have been linked to off-target adverse effects, but they also frequently lead to certain expected on-target adverse events. On-target negative effects are those brought on by the suppression of VEGF signaling whereas off-target adverse outcomes are those that cannot be clearly linked to the reduction of VEGF signaling. The off-target events are frequently the same across the agents, but these events are more closely linked to patient- or agent-specific factors than on-target events (Ivy et al., 2009). The common adverse effects are summarized in Table 17.4.

6. FDA-approved VEGFR/PDGFR TKIs

6.1 Sorafenib

The core scaffold of Sorafenib, a 4-pyridyl ring, is occupied the hinge region trapping the DFG motif in an inactive "out" configuration, classifying Sorafenib as a Type II tyrosine kinase inhibitor (Fig. 17.5A). Sorafenib creates H-bonds with the catalytic Glu885 residue, the DGF-Asp1046, and the Cys919 of the hinge region of VEGFR2, in addition to the dominant van der Waals and hydrophobic interactions (Fig. 17.5B). FDA has approved Sorafenib in 2005 for the treatment of advanced renal cell carcinoma (RCC) (https://www.fda.gov). Sorafenib also suppresses BRAF, VEGFR1, and -3, PDGFR, KIT, and RET in the nanomolar range, making it ideal for treating a variety of solids in combination with bevacizumab, erlotinib, carboplatin, paclitaxel, interferon, temsirolimus, and cetuximab as shown in various clinical trials (Wilhelm et al., 2006). Sorafenib was licensed by the FDA in 2007 and 2013 for the treatment of unresectable hepatocellular carcinoma (HCC) and metastatic differentiated thyroid cancer, respectively, due to its ability to target multiple kinases (https://www.fda.gov).

TABLE 17.4 On- and off-target adverse events associated with VEGFR/PDGFR TKIs.

On-target adverse events associated with VEGFR TKIs		Off-target adverse events associated with VEGFR TKIs	
Adverse effect	Frequency of event (%) ? SD	Adverse effect	Frequency of event (%) ? SD
Hypertension	32.80 ± 26	Fatigue	62.5 ± 27
Proteinuria	9.80 ± 15	Diarrhea	46.8 ± 18
Pulmonary hemorrhage	7.70 ± 8	Anorexia	32.9 ± 16
Hemorrhage (bleeding)	5.80 ± 5	Increased hemoglobin levels	26.1 ± 16
Hypothyroidism	5.10 ± 11	Hair loss (alopecia)	17.4 ± 9
Fistula	0.60 ± 1	Weight loss	16.8 ± 8
Reversible posterior leukoencephalopathy syndrome	0.56 ± 0	Lymphopenia	15.5 ± 15

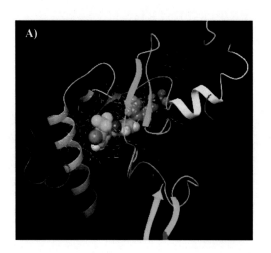

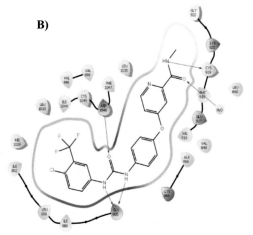

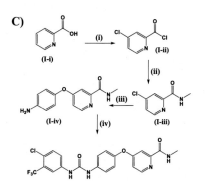

FIGURE 17.5 (A) 3D interaction poses of Sorafenib with VEGFR-2 (PDB ID 3WZE), (B) 2D interaction of sorafenib with same protein, (C) synthetic pathway for synthesis of Sorafenib (Ayala-Aguilera et al., 2022), and (D) summary of the structural optimization leading to the discovery of sorafenib as VEGFR inhibitor.

Sorafenib is manufactured in four steps (Fig. 17.5C) (Ayala-Aguilera et al., 2022; Riedl et al., 2012) (i) Picolinic acid (I-i) is reacted with thionyl chloride to activate the carboxylic acid while also introducing a chlorine atom at the para position of the pyridine ring. (ii) Intermediate (I-iii) is obtained via nucleophilic replacement of acyl chloride with methylamine (I-ii). (iii) An SNAr reaction with 4-aminophenol is then utilized to produce the suitable ether intermediate (I-iv), which is subsequently activated with potassium tert-butoxide. (iv) When the aniline moiety reacts with the 4-chloro-3-(trifluoromethyl)phenyl isocyanate, the urea derivative, Sorafenib, is created (Motzer et al., 2006). The first lead compound, the phenyl-urea thiophene ester (I-A), was discovered in a high-throughput screen against the c-RAF/MEK/ERK kinase cascade in 1995. The following optimization was performed with the goal of increasing c-RAF activity. This hit exhibited moderate activity against c-RAF (IC_{50} 17 µM); however, 4-methyl modification on the phenyl ring (I-B) resulted in a 10-fold improvement. The structure—activity relationship (SAR) of the series was further explored by creating a library of bis-aryl urea analogs of the lead molecule, which identified the 3-amino-isoxazole (I-C) with a c-RAF kinase inhibitor IC_{50} of 1.1 µM. By replacing the distal ring of c-RAF with a 4-pyridine, researchers were able to obtain a fivefold increase in activity while also lowering lipophilicity, improving water solubility, and imparting considerable inhibitory effect against human colon cancer HCT116 cell growth (I-D). Further SAR tests were carried out, including the examination of aromatic isoxazole moiety replacements, which revealed that the para-choro-meta-trifuroromethylphenyl ring was the most potent. The addition of a carboxamide functionality to the pyridyl ring enhanced potency even further, with tiny groups like methyl demonstrating the best action (Huang et al., 2012) (Fig. 17.5D).

6.2 Sunitinib

Sunitinib is a CDK2 Type I1/2B ATP-competitive inhibitor. KIT mutation in GIST patients induces resistance to Imatinib and promotes the medicinal chemist to develop Sunitinib (https://www.fda.gov). Sunitinib and its major/active metabolite (SU012662) inhibit KIT (Type IIB inhibition), VEGFR2 (Type IVb inhibition), PDGFR, and FLT3 at nanomolar potencies. Within the VEGFR2, the medication creates a hydrogen bonding with Ile10, Lue81, and Asp86, in addition to ionic bonding with Asp86 (Fig. 17.6A and B). Sunitinib was originally synthesized in nine convergent steps as a consequence of lead optimization to improve solubility, protein binding, efficacy, and selectivity toward VEGFR2 and PDGFR-β (Fig. 17.6C) (Ayala-Aguilera et al., 2022). The Wolff—Kishner reduction of 5-fluoroisatin (II-i) with hydrazine hydrate is the first step in the synthetic process, which results in ring opening (II-ii). The resulting acyl hydrazine is intramolecularly acylated in the presence of HCl to provide the oxindole intermediate (II-iii). The second significant intermediate, (II-vi), is produced by the Knorr pyrrole synthesis. When commercially available tert-butyl acetoacetate is condensed with sodium nitrite, an oxime intermediate is formed (II-iv). The oxime is reductively cyclized using 3-oxobutyrate ethyl ester, then hydrolytically decarboxylated and formylated with a Vilsmeier reagent made from DMF and $POCl_3$ (II-viii). The crucial intermediate II-ix is produced by combining the carboxylic acid produced by the base hydrolysis of the intermediate ethyl ester with 2-(diethylamino)ethylamine. The result of the condensation of II-x and III-iii is Sunitinib (Kassem et al., 2012; Tang et al., 2001).

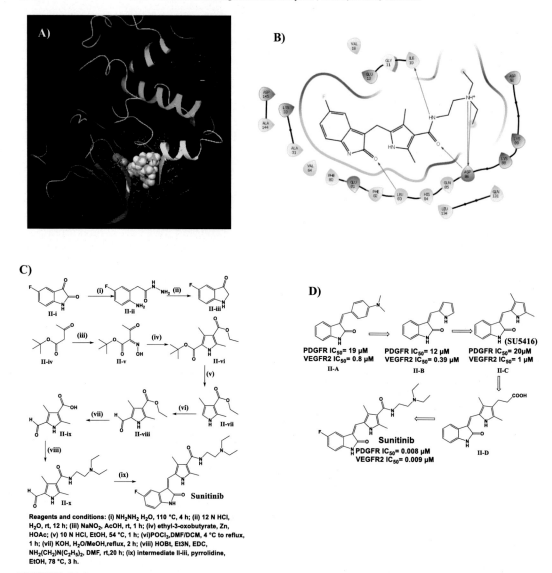

FIGURE 17.6 (A) 3D interaction poses of Sunitinib with VEGFR-2 (PDB ID 4AGD), (B) 2D interaction of Sunitinib with same protein, (C) synthetic pathway for synthesis of Sunitinib (Ayala-Aguilera et al., 2022), and (D) summary of the structural optimization leading to the discovery of Sunitinib as VEGFR inhibitor.

Sunitinib was discovered in a high-throughput screen of PDGFR kinase in 1994 at Sugen, which found the indolin-2-ones 6 and 7 (II-A), shown in Fig. 17.6D, as having moderate efficacy against PDGFR and enhanced potency against VEFGR-2. The expansion of this series' SAR resulted in the discovery of new species (SU5416). Despite in vitro assay of SU5416 (II-C) on tumor cell lines demonstrating no direct lethal effects, SU5416 reduced tumor vascular density and vascular leakage, suggesting that its anticancer efficacy is mediated through an antiangiogenesis mechanism. The first tiny molecule with antiangiogenic activity has reached the clinical trials was SU5416, which was dispensed intravenously. Despite clinical indications of antiangiogenesis efficacy, the drug's development was constrained by its pharmacokinetics and solubility profile. A series of water solubility and oral bioavailability molecules were investigated as well as their action against PDGFR was enhanced via the incorporation of the propionic acid group, as denoted by II-D. Additional optimization at the dimethylpyrrole led to the discovery of sunitinib, which improved the developability profile even more (Sun et al., 2009). Sunitinib was approved in 2006 for patients with advanced RCC and imatinib-resistant/intolerant GIST malignancies, and then in 2011 for patients with neuroendocrine pancreatic tumors (https://www.fda.gov; Ayala-Aguilera et al., 2022).

6.3 Pazopanib

Pazopanib has received FDA approval for the treatment of advanced RCC since 2009. It was created by GlaxoSmithKline (GW786034), and Novartis is now marketing it as Votrient. In 2012, the FDA approved Pazopanib for people with advanced soft tissue sarcoma who had previous chemotherapy (https://www.fda.gov). At nanomolar concentrations, pazopanib inhibits VEGFR1, -2, and -3. While, at somewhat greater concentrations, PDGFR, FGFR-1 and -3, ITK, KIT, LCK, and FMS are all inhibited. Pazopanib suppressed cell growth via inhibition of the VEGF-induced phosphorylation of VEGFR2 with nanomolar efficacy in cellular tests, whereas preclinical testing demonstrated antiangiogenic activity and a favorable pharmacokinetic profile (Mendel et al., 2003). Pazopanib is a pan-VEGFR inhibitor that competes with ATP. McTigue et al. revealed the X-ray crystal structure of Pazopanib in complex with a nonphosphorylated VEGFR2 confirmation that included the catalytic and juxta-membrane (JM). As a Type IIA inhibitor, pazopanib binds to its target, where the main amine of Asp1046 creates an H-bond with the dimethyl indazole headgroup, stabilizing the DFG-out conformation (McTigue et al., 2012).

The starting material, nitroindazole derivative, is synthesized by nitration of ethyl aniline (III-i) to yield 2-ethyl-5-nitroaniline (III-ii), which is then cyclized with isoamyl nitrite in acetic acid to provide a nitroindazole derivative (III-iii). The N-methylation of indazole in the presence of trimethyloxonium tetrafluoroborate yielded the aniline intermediate (III-v), after the reduction with tin(II). Intermediate III-vi is obtained by condensing aniline with 2,4-dichloropyrimidine under basic circumstances. The product, III-vii, is obtained by methylating the secondary amine with methyl iodide and then condensation with 5-amino-2-methylbenzenesulfonamide (Ayala-Aguilera et al., 2022; Harris et al., 2008) (Fig. 17.7A).

Fig. 17.7B shows the optimization steps for Pazopanib development which started using two different screening hits: the moderately potent dianilino-2,4-pyrimidine III-A (VEGFR-2 IC_{50} 0.4 μM) and the more potent 4-anilino-6,7-dimethoxyquinazoline III-B (VEGFR-2 IC_{50} 0.006 μM) to generate the first lead scaffold in the late 1990s. The key structural properties of the synthesized N-(3-bromoanilino)-N0-(4-methyl-3-hydroxyanilino)-2,4-pyrimidines (III-C) (VEGFR-2 IC_{50} 0.006 μM) were combined with a cellular potency inhibitory v-HUVEC cells of IC_{50} 0.54 μM. The pharmacokinetic profile of III-C and comparable analogs was poor, owing to the phenolic group which is quickly metabolized via phase II glucuronidation or sulfonation. To improve the pharmacokinetic properties of phenolic derivative, the indazolylpyrimidine III-C was synthesized by introducing a 3-methylindazole heterocycle in

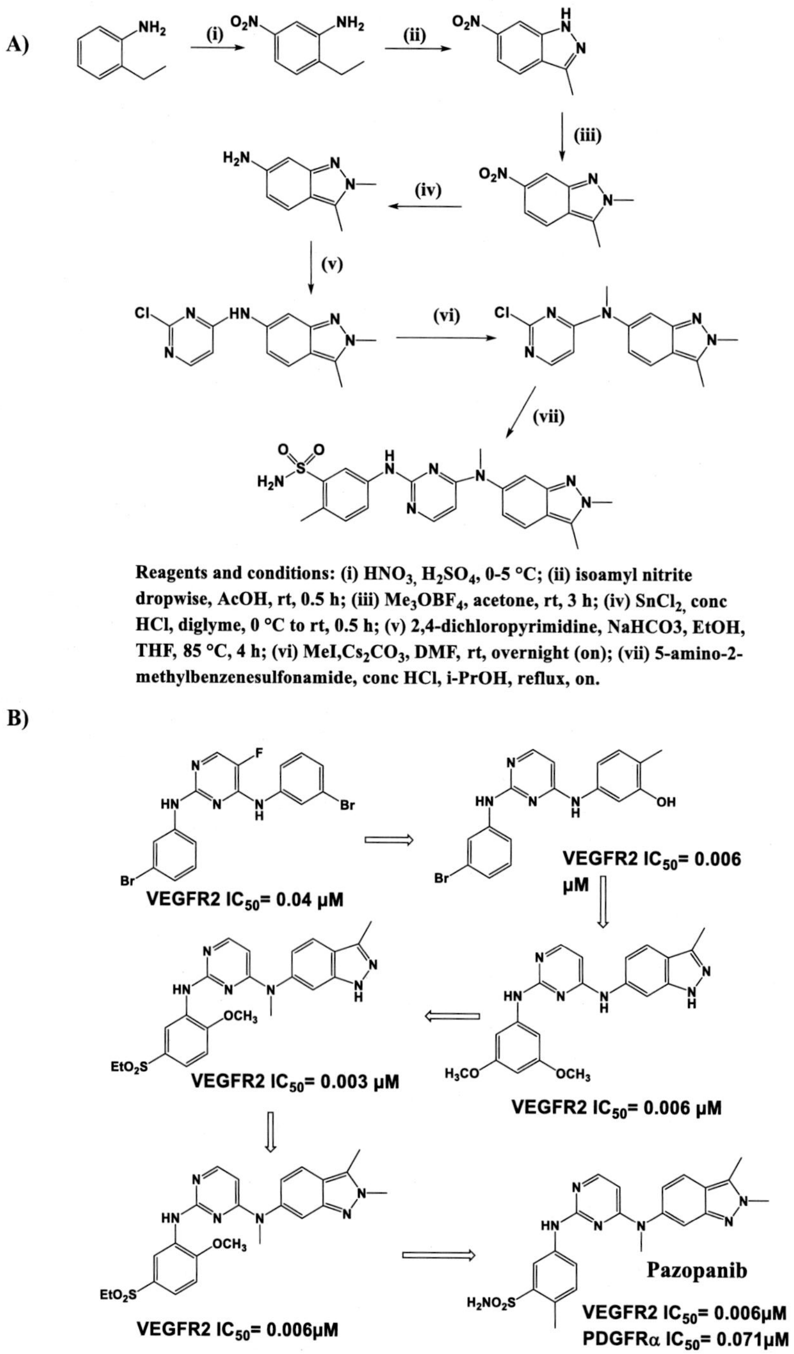
A)
(i)
(ii)
(iii)
(iv)
(v)
(vi)
(vii)
Reagents and conditions: (i) HNO3, H2SO4, 0-5 °C; (ii) isoamyl nitrite dropwise, AcOH, rt, 0.5 h; (iii) Me3OBF4, acetone, rt, 3 h; (iv) SnCl2, conc HCl, diglyme, 0 °C to rt, 0.5 h; (v) 2,4-dichloropyrimidine, NaHCO3, EtOH, THF, 85 °C, 4 h; (vi) MeI,Cs2CO3, DMF, rt, overnight (on); (vii) 5-amino-2-methylbenzenesulfonamide, conc HCl, i-PrOH, reflux, on.
B)
VEGFR2 IC50= 0.04 μM
VEGFR2 IC50= 0.006 μM
VEGFR2 IC50= 0.003 μM
VEGFR2 IC50= 0.006 μM
VEGFR2 IC50= 0.006μM
Pazopanib
VEGFR2 IC50= 0.006μM
PDGFRα IC50= 0.071μM

FIGURE 17.7 (A) Synthetic pathway for synthesis of Pazopanib (Ayala-Aguilera et al., 2022), and (B) summary of the structural optimization leading to the discovery of Sunitinib as VEGFR inhibitor.

lieu of phenolic functionality, a step showed a good potency against VEGFR-2 (IC_{50} 0.006 μM) and v-HUVECs (IC_{50} 0.18 μM). The more improvement of pharmacokinetic profile in rodent, the N-methylated pyrimidine III-D was generated, which not only improved the oral bioavailability by 65% but also reduced the clearance to 10 mL/min/kg). At this point, substituted pyrimidines with the 3-methylindazole heterocycle and the methylation of C-4 amino nitrogen showed good in vitro and cross-species pharmacokinetic characteristics. A variety of cytochrome P450 (CYP) isozymes, particularly 2C9, showed considerable inhibition (IC_{50} 10 μM). This is thought to be due to the indazole nitrogen attaching to the heme iron of the CYP enzyme. The methylation of the indazole at position 2 reduced this activity, resulting in the favorable heterocyclic scaffold 2,3-dimethylindazole (III-E). After a last adjustment of the aniline ring, pazopanib was identified as having the best combination of in vitro potency and pharmacokinetic developability characteristics (Harris et al., 2008) (Fig. 17.7B).

6.4 Axitinib

Pfizer (AG013736) developed Axitinib and marketed it as Inlyta. In 2012, FDA has approved Axitinib for use as a treatment for advanced RCC in patients who failed one of the prior systemic therapies. Resistance to VEGFR inhibitors in RCC metastatic patients led to the combined therapy of immunological checkpoint inhibitors (anti-PD-1) such as avelumab or pembrolizumab beside Axitinib. The approval of these combinations in 2019 was based on positive clinical trial results (https://www.fda.gov). Axitinib is also active against PDGFR and KIT29 at >10-fold greater concentrations and is a potent inhibitor in BCR-ABL-driven leukemia owing to the mutation in the T315I (https://www.fda.gov).

Axitinib is a subnanomolar potent and selective inhibitor of Type IIA VEGFR. The efficacy and selective antiangiogenic activity are attributable to two unique H-bonds deep within the ATP binding pocket of VEGFR2. The benzamide group penetrates the juxta-membrane region, creating H-bonds with the C-Glu885 and the Asp1046 of the DFG loop, cementing the inactive DFG-out conformation (Figs. 17.7A and 17.8B) (McTigue et al., 2012). The synthesis of Axitinib is quite complicated where there are 13 convergent stages in the synthesis of Axitinib (Fig. 17.8C) starting with commercially available 6-nitroindazole (IV-i) which, is iodinated at the C3 position and followed by the protection of N1 position with 3,4-dihydro-2H-pyran and methanesulfonic acid yielding (IV-ii). With 2-vinylpyridine, the protected nitroindazole can undergo a Heck reaction (IV-iii). The nitro group is reduced by iron, yielding the equivalent aniline. Under acidic circumstances, the aniline is diazotized with sodium nitrite, and the iodination of the C6 position is facilitated by the addition of potassium iodide (IV-iv). The thioether (IV-v) is produced by palladium-catalyzed cross-coupling of the C6-iodinated derivatives and the thiol intermediate (IV-vi). Axitinib is obtained via deprotecting the C3 site with tosylic acid (Ayala-Aguilera et al., 2022; Pemovska et al., 2015).

The discovery and optimization of Axitinib proceeded according to the next steps. The pyrazole IV-A with a mild efficacy toward VEFGR-2 was chosen among other hits for optimization because of its greater ligand efficiency (Fig. 17.8D). The primary objectives were to increase permeability, boost potency, and modify the metabolically susceptible aryl hydroxy and methoxy groups. First, the molecule was truncated to identify the essential features that

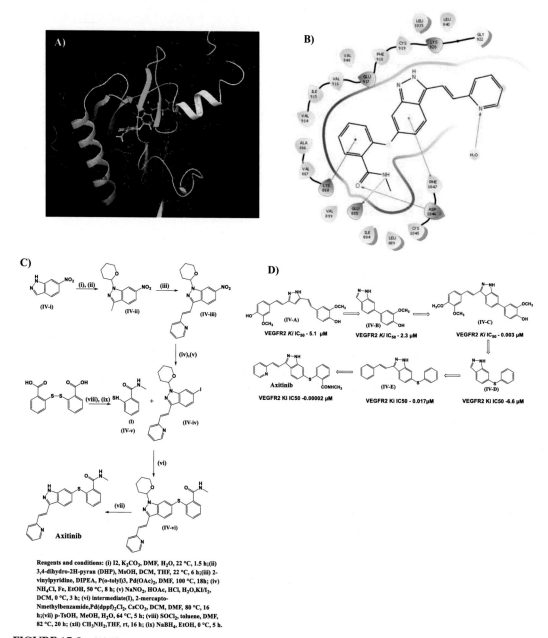

FIGURE 17.8 (A) 3D interaction poses of Axitinib with (juxta membrane and kinase domains (PDB ID 4AGC), (B) 2D interaction of Axitinib with same protein, (C) synthetic pathway for synthesis of Axitinib (Ayala-Aguilera et al., 2022), and (D) summary of the structural optimization leading to the discovery of Axitinib as VEGFR inhibitor.

showed high efficiency, followed by conformational restrictions to lock the hit into the desired bound shape. These steps resulted in the discovery of indazole IV-B, which evolved into the primary pharmacophore. After restoring styrene functioning, it was revealed that full-length indazole in mice showed excellent potency and ligand efficiency, but low kinase selectivity and oral bioavailability. To target the DFG-out conformation of VEGFR, a phenyl thiol moiety was introduced to the 6-position of the indazole ring denoting by IV-D. This modification not only improved the affinity but also reduced the metabolic liability of aryl hydroxy and methoxy functionalities. The potency of IV-E was significantly boosted once the styrene functionality was restored. Although IV-E is less powerful than IV-C, it has a higher kinase selectivity and a similar overall ligand efficiency. Axitinib with pico-molar potency and low lipophilicity was created by introducing ortho-pyridine in lieu of the terminal phenyl and adding an N-methyl carboxamide to position two of the phenyl thiol, which improves the affinity and stability to kinase domain via introducing two crucial H-bonding interactions trapping the DFG-loop to out conformation (Kania, 2009) (Fig. 17.8D).

6.5 Lenvatinib

Eisai Inc manufactured Lenvatinib (E7080) and marketed it as Lenvima (DTC). Primarily, FDA has approved Lenvatinib for treating patients with locally recurrent or metastatic, progressive, radioactive iodine-refractory differentiated thyroid cancer. Since then, Lenvatinib has received approval by the FDA to use it in two more indications. On the basis of the phase III trial REFLECT, in 2016, Lenvatinib was approved as a combination therapy with Everolimus for the treatment of patients with advanced RCC who had previously received antiangiogenic therapy, and 2 years later, Lenvatinib was licensed as a first-line treatment for patients with unresectable HCC (https://www.fda.gov).

Lenvatinib has a multikinase inhibitory activity via targeting VEGFR2/-3, PDGFR, RET, and KIT9 with a nanomolar efficacy in biochemical experiments. Lenvatinib is classified as a Type I1/2A VEGFR2 inhibitor; it occupied The ATP binding site and neighboring regions of the VEGFR2 kinase domain forming H-bonds with Glu885 at gatekeeper, Cys919 in the active site, and Asp1046 of DFG loop. Additionally, two possible water-mediated interactions between the 6-carbamoyl moiety of Lenvatinib and Asn923. An additional hydrophobic and Van der Wall interactions between the cyclopropane ring and Phe1047 in the neighboring allosteric regions orient the activation loop of the enzyme to be DFG-in conformation, while the C-helix-out (Okamoto et al., 2015) (Fig. 17.9A and B).

Lenvatinib is synthesized in nine steps according to its original scheme (Fig. 17.9C). First, 4-amino-2-chlorobenzonitrile (V-i) is undergoing an SNAr with sodium methoxide. To create the 1,4-dihydroquinoline ring (V-iii), Meldrum acid ethoxy methylene derivative is combined with a thermally induced cyclo-condensation. Under the basic circumstances, the nitrile group is transformed to the equivalent carboxylic acid followed by the generation of acyl chloride derivatives where the quinolone core is converted into a 4-chloroquinoline derivative using thionyl chloride. In aqueous ammonia, the acyl chloride functionality is converted to a carboxamide, yielding an intermediate (V-iv). Another connection with the anilino group is formed by an SNAr with 4-amino-3-chlorophenol, which yields the matching carbamate in the presence of phenyl chloroformate. Finally, cyclopropylamine treatment produces Lenvatinib (Okamoto et al., 2015).

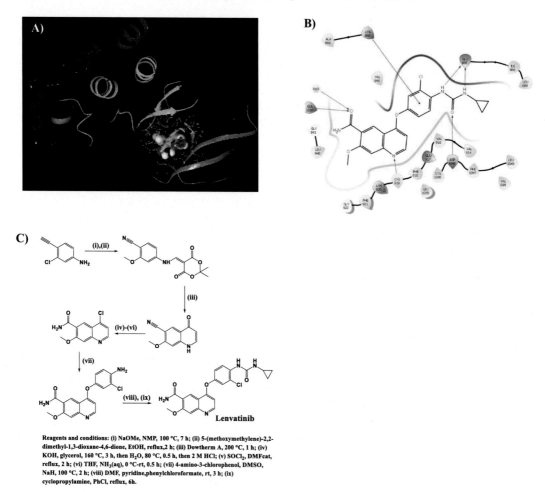

FIGURE 17.9 (A) 3D interaction poses of Lenvatinib with VEGFR-2 (PDB ID 3WZD), (B) 2D interaction of Lenvatinib with same protein, and (C) synthetic pathway for synthesis of Lenvatinib (Ayala-Aguilera et al., 2022).

6.6 Nintedanib

Nintedanib was first authorized in 2014 by the European Medicines Agency (EMA) in combination with docetaxel for the treatment of adult patients with locally progressed, metastatic, or locally recurrent nonsmall cell lung cancer (NSCLC) with an adenocarcinoma tumor histology (Huang et al., 2012). The FDA and the EMA in 2014 and 2015, respectively, licensed Nintedanib for the treatment of idiopathic pulmonary fibrosis (IPF) where it is marketed as Ofev (European Medicines Agency, European Union; Www.Ema.Europa.Eu (Accessed May 20, 2021). The mode of action of Nintedanib is to prevent the growth of endothelial cells, smooth muscle cells, and pericytes at nanomolar concentrations by acting on FGFR types 1, 2, and 3, as well as on PDGFR-α and-β, which supports its antiangiogenic activity. Nintedanib can also suppress LCK, SRC, FLT3, and LYN at similar doses (Dai et al., 2011).

The synthetic scheme of Nintedanib is based on a process that needs first to create the intermediates VI-ii and VI-v before proceeding. Intermediate VI-ii was released via nucleophilic substitution of 2-bromo-N-methyl-N-(4-nitrophenyl)-acetamide with 1-methyl piperazine (Fig. 17.10A). After that, the amino group is generated by the reduction of the nitro group, yielding intermediate VI-ii. Simultaneously, intermediate VI-v is created by the addition of methyl acetate to the para position of methyl 3-nitrobenzoat. The nitro group is then reduced to amino, which then undergoes cyclo-condensation with the neighboring ester group to

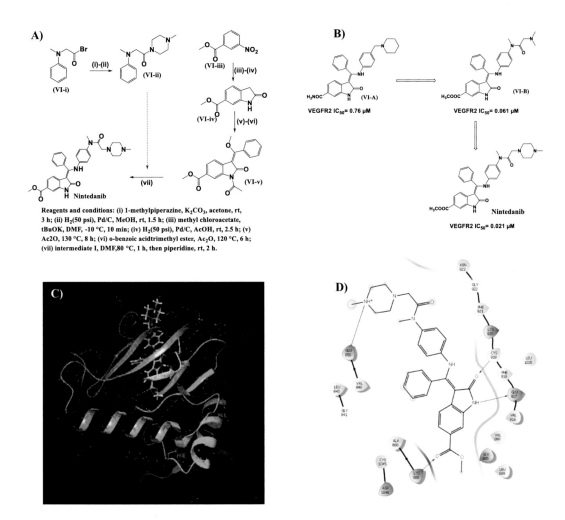

Reagents and conditions: (i) 1-methylpiperazine, K₂CO₃, acetone, rt, 3 h; (ii) H₂(50 psi), Pd/C, MeOH, rt, 1.5 h; (iii) methyl chloroacetate, tBuOK, DMF, -10 °C, 10 min; (iv) H₂(50 psi), Pd/C, AcOH, rt, 2.5 h; (v) Ac2O, 130 °C, 8 h; (vi) o-benzoic acidtrimethyl ester, Ac₂O, 120 °C, 6 h; (vii) intermediate I, DMF,80 °C, 1 h, then piperidine, rt, 2 h.

FIGURE 17.10   (A) Synthetic pathway for synthesis of Nintedanib (Ayala-Aguilera et al., 2022), (B) summary of the structural optimization leading to the discovery of Nintedanib as VEGFR inhibitor, (C) 3D interaction poses of Nintedanib with VEGFR-2 (PDB ID 3C7Q), and (D) 2D interaction of Nintedanib with same protein.

generate the indolinone core in a one-pot synthesis (VI-iv). N-acetylation of the C3 using acetic anhydride facilitates condensation with O-benzoic acid trimethyl ester, resulting in an intermediate VI-v. Finally, the interaction of the two intermediates produces Nintedanib (Fig. 17.10A) (Ayala-Aguilera et al., 2022; Ding et al., 2015). Nintedanib is the product of an antiangiogenic lead optimization method. It was discovered by cross-screening compounds created for a CDK4 program at Boehringer Ingelheim, which found the 6-amidosubstituted indolinone VI-A (Fig. 17.10B) as a VEGFR-2 submicromolar inhibitor. VI-A is wandering and exhibited a little CDK4 activity and an excellent kinase selectivity profile. The chemical stability was harmed when the core aryl group was substituted with smaller alkyl substituents. This is most likely happened because the phenyl group assumes a strain-free conformation perpendicular to the rest of the molecule (as shown in Fig. 17.10C for the Nintedanib cocrystal structure in VEGFR-2). The 6-position substitution of oxindole core had a major impact on the kinase efficacy and overall selectivity profile. Although 6-chloro-substitution proved beneficial effect, it resulted in lower selectivity profiles. 6-Methyl ester substituted oxindoles, VI-B, showed good potency and kinase selectivity, as well as reasonable bioavailability in rodents. The basic amine group added to the anilino moiety at the other end of the molecule not only caused a flat SAR profile since it is oriented toward the solvent front of the kinase pocket but also functioned as a useful tool to modify cell selectivity and solubility. In 2001, Nintedanib was chosen for preclinical development after being evaluated in xenograft studies (Roth et al., 2015).

As illustrated in Fig. 17.10C and D, Nintedanib competes with the ATP at its binding site in the hinge region with the oxindole moiety forming two H-bonding with both Cys-919 backbone nitrogen and Glu-917 backbone carbonyl oxygen at active site and gatekeeper, respectively. This oxindole binding mode is quite similar to Sunitinib binding mode (Fig. 17.7A and B). The 4-nitrogen atom of methyl piperidine forms a bidentate ionic contact with the carboxylate oxygens of Glu-850, directing it toward the solvent area. The carbonyl group of the methyl acetate at the 6-position of the oxindole forms an extrahydrogen bond with Lys-808 giving Nintedanib a high affinity to VEGFR.

6.7 Imatinib

Imatinib was the first medicine to target a molecular structure found exclusively in cancer cells (Ayala-Aguilera et al., 2022). Imatinib is a phenylamino-pyrimidine derivative which classified as a Type II (DFG-out) tyrosine kinase inhibitor. Imatinib has received approval in 2001 for treating all phases of Philadelphia chromosome-positive (Ph+) chronic myeloid leukemia (CML). In 2002, the benefit of Imatinib was expanded to include therapy for GISTs based on a phase I-II clinical trial (https://www.fda.gov). Additionally, Imatinib was the first drug to specifically target a molecular structure identified only in cancer cells. Imatinib is a selective inhibitor of Bcr-Abl, a hybrid tyrosine kinase that is overexpressed in some cancer cells (https://www.fda.gov).

Imatinib is a highly selective molecule with a nanomolar potency. Imatinib binds to the ABL domain of the BCR-ATP binding site, trapping the chimeric protein in an inactive conformation. Imatinib can create H-bonds with Met-318 at the hinge region, with Thr-315 and the C-Glu-286 at the gatekeeper, the DFG-Asp-381, as well as a bidentate linkage with His-361 and Ile-360 (Figs. 17.11A and B) (Roskoski, 2016). The synthetic scheme of Imatinib

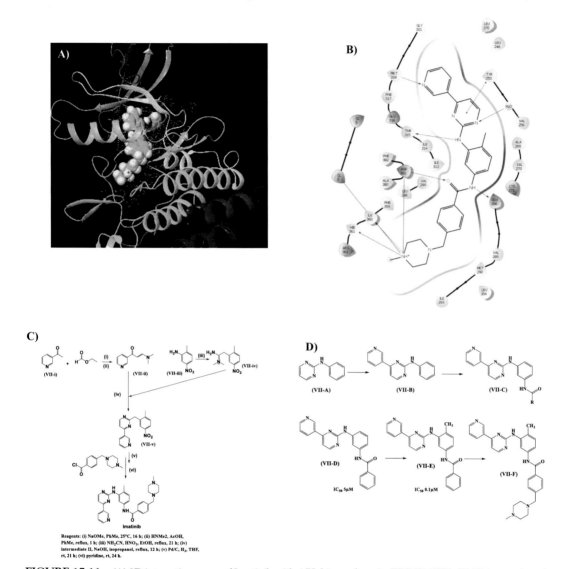

FIGURE 17.11 (A) 3D interaction poses of Imatinib with ABL kinase domain (PDB ID 1IEP), (B) 2D interaction of Imatinib with same protein, (C) synthetic pathway for synthesis of Imatinib (Ayala-Aguilera et al., 2022), and (D) summary of the structural optimization leading to the discovery of Imatinib as PDGFR inhibitor.

was started with a commercially available 3-acetylpyridine (VII-i), which undergoes an aldol condensation reaction with ethyl formate. the crucial intermediate VII-ii is generated by transforming the end product of aldol condensation to an enaminone using N, N-dimethylformamide. The core scaffold, aminopyrimidine, is formed by a reaction of cyanamide and 2-methyl-5-nitroaniline to produce a guanidinium salt derivative (VII-iv), which is subsequently treated with VII-ii. The nitro group (VII-v) is reduced to provide the equivalent aniline, which can then be acylated with an acid chloride to give Imatinib (Fig. 17.11C) (Deadman et al., 2013; Zimmermann, 1993).

Imatinib was developed using a phenylamino-pyrimidine as a core structure (VII-A) that was found by a chance screening of huge compound libraries. The primary goal of this study was to identify an inhibitor to serine—threonine kinase, protein kinase C (PKC), (Patrick, 2021). By substituting position 4 of pyrimidine with a pyridyl group, PKC was strongly inhibited (VII-B). The aromatic ring was subsequently modified by an amide group giving a (VII-C) structure that also has tyrosine kinase inhibitory action. PKC-like serine—threonine protein kinases were inhibited by structure VII-D, which also showed a mild inhibitor of tyrosine kinases. SAR was then tested against a variety of protein kinases and optimized for activity against tyrosine kinases using a series of chemically similar compounds. CGP 53,716 (VII-E), which was produced by adding an Ortho methyl group as a conformational blocker, had enhanced the activity and selectivity against tyrosine kinases while showing no activity against serine—threonine kinases. The *Ortho* methyl group might force the molecule to adopt a conformation suitable for binding to tyrosine kinase. The conformational blocker prevents the rotation of the Ar—N bond (Fig. 17.11D), leaving the pyridine and pyrimidine rings away. Additional modifications to improve activity and selectivity were achieved by inserting a piperazine ring (VII-F). The basic nitrogen of the piperazine ring enables the creation of water-soluble salts essential for aqueous solubility. A one-carbon spacer was added between the aromatic and the piperazine rings to abolish the mutagenicity of aniline moiety (Patrick, 2021).

6.8 Apatinib

Apatinib is the first tyrosine kinase inhibitor to get approval from the NMPA in China in 2014 for the treatment of gastric adenocarcinoma in patients with advanced or metastatic carcinoma. Apatinib was created by Advenchen Laboratories (YN968D1) and then sold to HLB Life Science (Elevar Therapeutics) and commercialized as Aitan. In 2021, Apatinib was classified as an orphan drug in the United States for the treatment of adenoid cystic carcinoma. Apatinib reduces tumor microvascular density via inhibition of VEGF-stimulated endothelial cell proliferation and migration (Hu et al., 2014). Apatinib is an orally active VEGFR2 inhibitor with a nanomolar efficacy. Apatinib is more selective for VEGFR than sunitinib, however; Apatinib can also inhibit other kinases including, RET, KIT, and SRC. The manner by which Apatinib binds to its target has not yet been determined because Apatinib does not currently share a crystal structure. Apatinib was first synthesized by Advenchen using four chemical steps (Fig. 17.12). The 1-phenylcyclopentanecarbonitrile is aromatically nitrated to produce the aniline derivative after the reduction by Pd-catalyzed hydrogenation, followed by linking with 2-chloronicotinoyl chloride. Apatinib is obtained by combining SNAr with 4-pyridylmethylamine (Ayala-Aguilera et al., 2022; Chen, 2004).

6.9 Tivozanib

Tivozanib is a VEGFR Type II inhibitor that is orally active with low-nanomolar potency and belongs to the ATP-competitive category. Tivozanib can also inhibit VEGFR1 and

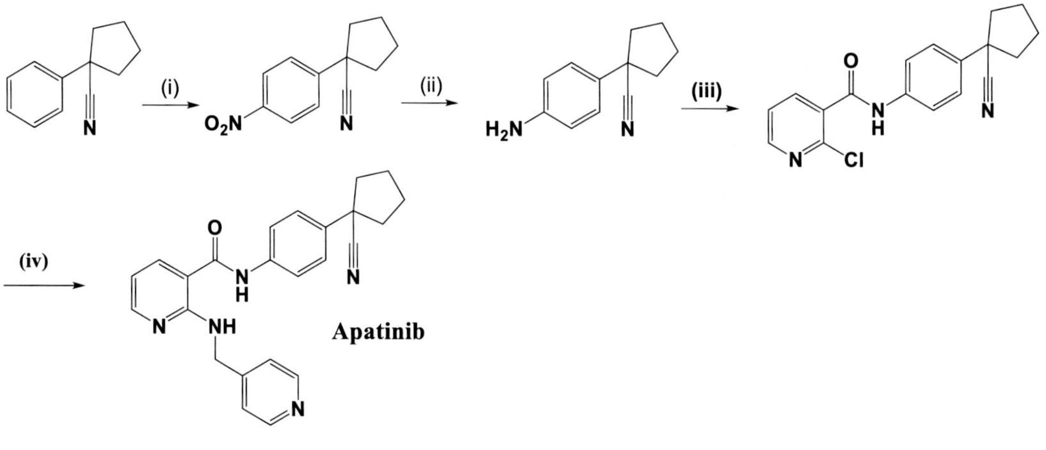

Reagents and conditions: (i) KNO$_3$, H$_2$SO$_4$, AcOH, 0°C, 20 min; then rt, 2 h; (ii) Pd/C (10%), H$_2$ (1 atm), EtOH, rt, 1 h; (iii) 2-chloronicotinoyl chloride, K$_2$CO$_3$, DCM, rt, 30 min; (iv) 4-pyridylmethylamine, pentanol, 120 °C, 4 h.

FIGURE 17.12 Synthetic pathway for synthesis of Apatinib (Ayala-Aguilera et al., 2022).

VEGFR3 (Chang et al., 2022) besides other tyrosine kinases including, PDGFRA, PDGFRH, EphB2, KIT, and TIE2, in the nanomolar range, according to biochemical screening (Nakamura et al., 2006). In 2017, Tivozanib has received approval from the European Medicines Agency (EMA) as the first line for treating adult patients with advanced RCC who had failed to respond to one prior cytokine therapy. The FDA authorized Tivozanib at the beginning of 2021 for the treatment of relapsed or refractory advanced RCC in adult patients who had not responded to two or more prior systemic treatments. The cocrystal structure of Tivozanib with VEGFR2 exhibited that Tivozanib resides in the ATP site and the regulatory domain pocket (RDP) located proximal to the ATP-binding pocket, establishing four H-bonding with Cys-919, Glu-885, and Asp-1046 (Fig. 17.13A and B) (McTigue et al., 2012). There are four chemical stages in the initial synthesis of Tivozanib: in the beginning, the 4-quinolone scaffold is created by adding ethyl formate and sodium methoxide to 2-amino-4,5-dimethoxyacetophenone. Chlorination of quinolone with POCl$_3$ produces a 4-chloroquinoline derivative. The reaction of 4-chloroquinoline derivative with 4-amino-3-chlorophenol yielding aniline analog. The urea motif is formed by the interaction of aniline derivative with triphosgene and 3-amino-5-methylisoxazole to finally give Tivozanib (Kubo et al., 2005) (Fig. 17.13C).

6.10 Anlotinib

Anlotinib was licensed by the Chinese NMPA in 2018 for treating a locally advanced or metastatic NSCLC in adult patients who have experienced a recurrence after two rounds of systemic chemotherapy. The biochemical assay revealed the mode of action of Anlotinib

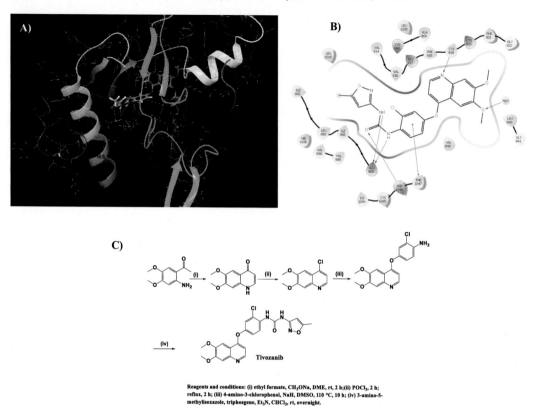

FIGURE 17.13 (A) 3D interaction poses of Tivozanib with juxtamembrane and kinase domains (PDB ID 4ASE), (B) 2D interaction of Tivozanib with same protein, and (C) synthetic pathway for synthesis of Tivozanib (Ayala-Aguilera et al., 2022).

through inhibition of the VEGFR phosphorylation by VEGF and the downstream effectors by impeding migration and tube formation. Anlotinib is a subnanomolar potent antiangiogenic VEGFR2 inhibitor (Xie et al., 2018). Although molecular docking studies indicate a deep engagement of Anlotinib into the hinge region to quench its activity via ATP competition, Anlotinib has not been categorized since it does not have a cocrystal structure with target kinase. Additionally, Anlotinib can inhibit PDGFRβ, KIT, and VEGFR1/-3 at nM doses (Xie et al., 2018). The functionalization of the quinolone core is the key step in the convergent synthesis of Anlotinib. N-Cbzamino-1-(hydroxymethyl)cyclopropane is mesylate to produce intermediate X-i. To enhance the SNAr interaction with 2-methyl-4-fluoro-5-hydroxyindole, a chloroquinazoline derivative is first prepared with POCl₃ to begin the synthesis of X-ii. Intermediates X-i and X-ii are coupled then the benzyl-protecting group is removed via hydrogenation to finally generate the Anlotinib (Ayala-Aguilera et al., 2022; Chen, 2008) (Fig. 17.14A).

6.11 Avapritinib

Avapritinib is a pyrrolotriazine derivative provisionally categorized as a Type I KIT and PDGFRA kinase inhibitor (https://www.fda.gov). Avapritinib received permission in 2020 to treat GIST patients suffering from a metastatic or incurable disease and have PDGFRA exon 18 mutations, including the common PDGFRA-D842V variant. Avapritinib has been given numerous distinct FDA designations, such as an orphan drug, breakthrough therapy, and fast track. Avapritinib has a strong antiactivation loop effect on KIT and PDGFRA mutants. Compared to wild-type kinases, Avapritinib exhibits increased activity against mutant proteins. Avapritinib displays low-cellular nanomolar efficacy and subnanomolar range of IC50 in all activation loop mutant forms including PDGFRA-D842V and KIT-D816V (Evans et al., 2017).

The synthetic pathway for Avapritinib using a convergent approach that begins with the creation of the intermediates XI-iii and XI-viii (Fig. 17.14B). In four steps, 4-bromo-1*H*-pyrrole-2-carboxylic acid methyl ester (XI-i) is converted into intermediate XI-iii. The pyrrole is N-aminated using *O*-(diphenylphosphinyl)hydroxylamine to generate the pyrrolotriazinone ring, which is then combined with formamide in a cycloaddition reaction to yield (XI-ii). Following a Pd-catalyzed Suzuki coupling, this core is cross-coupled with 4-pyrazoleboronic acid pinacol ester to produce *P*-choro-pyrrolotriazinone derivative XI-iii. The initial step in the synthesis of XI-viii is a nucleophilic substitution between the protected piperazine and ethyl 2-chloropyrimidine-5-carboxylate derivatives (XI-iv). A carboxylic acid derivative (XI-v) produced by basic ester hydrolysis is combined with *O*-dimethylhydroxylamine. The fluorophenyl ketone is then produced by reacting the resultant Weinreb amide with a phenyl Grignard, which is subsequently followed by an amine deprotection to produce (XI-viii). The XI-iii and XI-viii are brought together through an SNAr reaction between the 6-chloro of pyrrolotriazine XI-iii and the secondary amine of piperazine XI-viii. The intermediate (XI-ix) is created by the condensation of the ketone group with (S)-2-methylpropane-2-sulfinamide. The resulting N-sulfinyl imine is then alkylated by nucleophilic addition to methyl magnesium bromide. Finally, enantiopure Avapritinib is purified via chiral SFC after acidic cleavage of the N-sulfinyl group of the racemic mixture (Zhan et al., 2015) (Fig. 17.14B).

7. Summary and future outlook

VEGFR is a well-known modulator of tumor angiogenesis, growth, and metastasis among the known angiogenic factors. In a number of malignancies, aberrant angiogenesis has been attributed to VEGF production. VEGF controls a number of angiogenic processes, including capillary tube development and permeability, endothelial cell proliferation and migration as well as neovascular survival, and other physiological processes. Among the VEGFR, VEGFR2 is the most crucial receptor for regulating angiogenesis. Inhibiting the VEGF/VEGFR signaling pathway has been proposed as a promising therapeutic strategy for solid tumors. Bevacizumab (anti-VEGF) and ramucirumab (anti-VEGFR2) as monoclonal antibodies have recently been licensed for cancer therapy because of their high specificity. Although monoclonal antibodies have displayed a prolonged target inhibition and well safety profiles, monoclonal antibodies have their own drawbacks that shortage their clinical application, such as

Reagents and conditions: (i) MsCl, DIPEA, DCM, 0 °C, 30 min; (ii) POCl$_3$, reflux, 3 h; (iii) 2-methyl-4-fluoro-5-hydroxyindole, DMAP, 1,4-dioxane, reflux 3 days; (iv) Pd/C, HCONH4, EtOH, reflux, 1 h; (v)Cs$_2$CO$_3$, DMA, 100 °C, 10 h; (vi) H$_2$(50 psi), Pd/C, EtOH, 12 h.

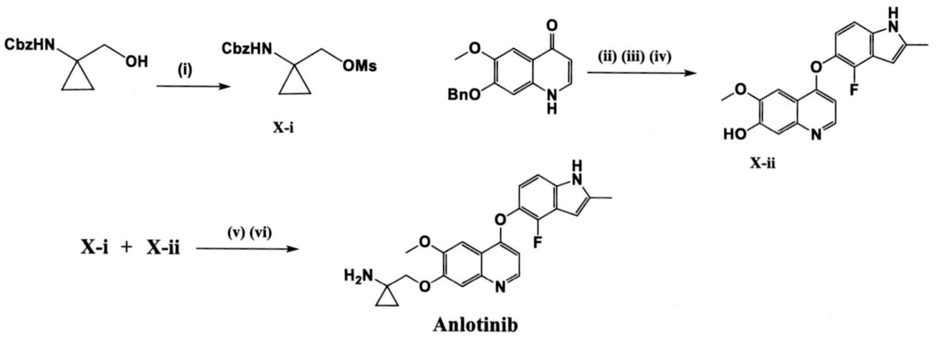

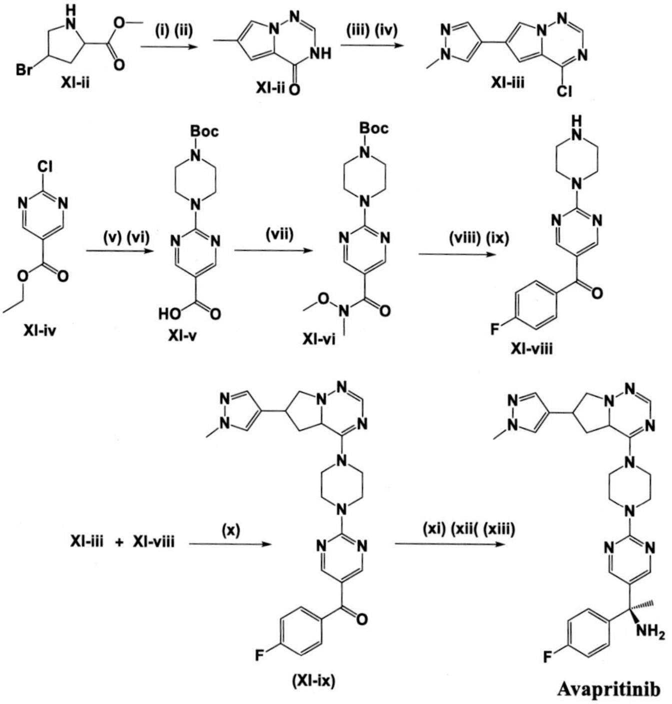

Reagents and conditions:(i) o-(diphenylphosphinyl)hydroxylamine, NaH, DMF, 0°C; (ii) formamide, 180°C; (iii) 4-pyrazoleboronic acid pinacol ester, Cs$_2$CO$_3$, PdCl$_2$dppf, H$_2$O, EtOH, 1,4-dioxane, 120°C; (iv) POCl$_3$, reflux; (v) tert-butylpiperazine-l-carboxylate, DIPEA, 1,4-dioxane, rt; (vi) NaOH, THF, MeOH, H$_2$O, 70°C; (vii) N,O-dimethylhydroxylamine, EDCI, HOBT, DCM, Et3N, rt; (viii) 4-fluorobenzenemagnesium bromide, THF, 0°C to rt; (ix) HCl, 1,4-dioxane, rt; (x) LIXa, DIPEA, 1,4-dioxane; (xi) (S)-2-methylpropane-2-sulfinamide, Ti(OEt)$_4$, THF, 70°C; (xii) MeMgBr, THF, 0°C; (xiii) 4 M HCl, 1,4-dioxane, rt.

FIGURE 17.14   (A) Synthetic pathway for synthesis of Anlotinib, (B) synthetic pathway for synthesis of Avapritinib (Ayala-Aguilera et al., 2022).

high cost, the need for intravenous dosing, the immunogenicity and the potential to cause autoimmune disorders following long-term therapy (Xie et al., 2018). In the last 2 decades, a growing number of approved small-molecule VEGFR TKIs, such as sorafenib, sunitinib, and pazopanib, and others mentioned in this chapter have been developed and showed a considerable improvement in patient quality of life and/or life expectancy. Even though there are a dozen VEGFR/PDGFR inhibitors on the market and several more in clinical trials, poor inhibitor selectivity, and efficacy, as well as drug resistance evolution, remain major barriers to developing long-term therapy. This is because most of VEGFR/PDGFR inhibitors target the ATP binding pocket, and there is thus an urgent need to develop advanced strategies for designing novel inhibitors to target kinases for which previous techniques have failed (Smet et al., 2014).

Allosteric inhibition, which involves binding to a pocket rather than the highly conserved ATP-binding site, is gaining popularity as a new method of studying the kinome, with the potential to broaden the therapeutic application profiles of kinase inhibitors (Smet et al., 2014). Most small VEGFR/PDGFR inhibitors discovered are either type I or type II ATP-competitive inhibitors. In type I inhibitors, the TKI binds to active kinases' ATP pockets with an "in" conformation of the conserved Asp-Phe-Glu motif (DFG), whereas type II inhibitors bind to inactive kinases with an "out" conformation of the DFG. Type II inhibitors solidify this inactive conformation and have advanced pharmacological features such as delayed dissociation rates, which prolong drug-target residence duration and result in significantly higher affinities than type I inhibitors. Contrary to popular belief, type II VEGFR/PDGFR inhibitors do not appear to be more selective than type I inhibitors. This nicely reflects many kinases' ability to adopt DFG-out conformations. Type III inhibitors bind to allosteric sites that are proximal to but not overlapping with the ATP-binding pocket, whereas type IV inhibitors bind to allosteric sites that are distal from the ATP-binding pocket (Cowan-Jacob et al., 2014; Pan & Mader, 2022; Smet et al., 2014).

Despite decades of effort, the number of FDA-approved TKIs targeting allosteric sites is limited, indicating the challenges in discovering and validating allosteric inhibitors. Only four type III MEK1/2 inhibitors (binimetinib, cobimetinib, trametinib, and selumetinib) and a type IV BCR-ABL1 inhibitor (Asciminib) have been licensed since 2013, demonstrating that the diversity of targets and the number of approvals are both underrepresentative of the allosteric mode of action. Allosteric ligands can increase kinome selectivity profiles while also showing promise in terms of pharmacology and in vivo tolerability; however, the FDA has not yet approved any type III or IV agents as VEGFR/PDGFR inhibitors. Better selectivity profiles and new opportunities for therapeutic development could result from drugs that bind to less conserved sites beyond the ATP pocket (Pan & Mader, 2022).

The development and clinical use of novel VEGFR/PDGFR candidates face significant challenges due to drug-induced toxicity and a lack of clinical safety. The majority of newly discovered VEGFR/PDGFR inhibitors have such severe side effects that their therapeutic benefit cannot even be tested in human patients. Some of the early VEGFR/PDGFR inhibitors may have been successful due to their broad kinase inhibition profiles (Morgan et al., 2018). For kinase inhibitors designed for extended treatment, both in combination therapies for precise targeted treatments in cancer and for innovative approaches to less urgent medical conditions, it is essential to have satisfactory selectivity and an associated safety profile.

References

Attwood, M. M., Fabbro, D., Sokolov, A. V., Knapp, S., & Schiöth, H. B. (2021). Trends in kinase drug discovery: Targets, indications and inhibitor design. *Nature Reviews Drug Discovery, 20*(11), 839–861. https://doi.org/10.1038/s41573-021-00252-y

Ayala-Aguilera, C. C., Valero, T., Lorente-Macías, Á., Baillache, D. J., Stephen, C., & Unciti-Broceta, A. (2022). Small molecule kinase inhibitor drugs (1995–2021): Medical indication, pharmacology, and synthesis. *Journal of Medicinal Chemistry, 65*(2), 1047–1131. https://doi.org/10.1021/acs.jmedchem.1c00963

Boyer, S. (2005). Small molecule inhibitors of KDR (VEGFR-2) kinase: An overview of structure activity relationships. *Current Topics in Medicinal Chemistry, 2*(9), 973–1000. https://doi.org/10.2174/1568026023393273

Carmeliet, P. (2000). Mechanisms of angiogenesis and arteriogenesis. *Nature Medicine, 6*(4), 389–395. https://doi.org/10.1038/74651

Chang, E., Weinstock, C., Zhang, L., Fiero, M. H., Zhao, M., Zahalka, E., Ricks, T. K., Fourie Zirkelbach, J., Qiu, J., Yu, J., Chen, X. H., Bhatnagar, V., Goldberg, K. B., Tang, S., Kluetz, P. G., Pazdur, R., Ibrahim, A., Beaver, J. A., & Amiri-Kordestani, L. (2022). FDA approval summary: Tivozanib for relapsed or refractory renal cell carcinoma. *Clinical Cancer Research, 28*(3), 441–445. https://doi.org/10.1158/1078-0432.CCR-21-2334

Chen, G. P. (2004). *Six membered amino-amide derivatives an angiogenesis inhibitors.* U.S. Pat. US20040259916A1.

Chen, G. P. (2008). *Spiro substituted compounds as angiogenesis inhibitors.* U.S.Pat. US8148532B2, 2008.

Clifford, S. C., & Maher, E. R. (2001). Von Hippel-Lindau disease: Clinical and molecular perspectives. *Advances in Cancer Research, 82*, 85–105. https://doi.org/10.1016/S0065-230X(01)82003-0

Cowan-Jacob, S. W., Jahnke, W., & Knapp, S. (2014). Novel approaches for targeting kinases: Allosteric inhibition, allosteric activation and pseudokinases. *Future Medicinal Chemistry, 6*, 541–561. https://doi.org/10.4155/fmc.13.216

Dai, B., Meng, J., Peyton, M., Girard, L., Bornmann, W. G., Lin, J., Minna, J. D., Fang, B., & Roth, J. A. (2011). STAT3 mediates resistance to MEK inhibitor through MicroRNA MiR-17. *Cancer Research, 71*(10). https://doi.org/10.1158/0008-5472.CAN-10-3647

Deadman, B. J., Hopkin, M. D., Baxendale, I. R., & Ley, S. V. (2013). The synthesis of bcr-abl inhibiting anticancer pharmaceutical agents imatinib, nilotinib and dasatinib. *Organic and Biomolecular Chemistry, 11*(11), 1766–1800. https://doi.org/10.1039/c2ob27003j

Ding, H. X., Leverett, C. A., Kyne, R. E., Liu, K. K. C., Fink, S. J., Flick, A. C., & O'Donnell, C. J. (2015). Synthetic approaches to the 2013 new drugs. *Bioorganic & Medicinal Chemistry, 23*(9), 1895–1922. https://doi.org/10.1016/j.bmc.2015.02.056

Elgawish, M. S., Nafie, M. S., Yassen, A. S. A., Yamada, K., & Ghareb, N. (2022). The design and synthesis of potent benzimidazole derivatives via scaffold hybridization and evaluating their antiproliferative and proapoptotic activity against breast and lung cancer cell lines. *New Journal of Chemistry, 46*(9), 4239–4256. https://doi.org/10.1039/d1nj05655g

Evans, E. K., Gardino, A. K., Kim, J. L., Hodous, B. L., Adam, S., Davis, A., Zhu, X. J., Schmidt-Kittler, O., Wilson, D., Wilson, D., DiPietro, L., Zhang, Y., Brooijmans, N., LaBranche, T. P., Wozniak, A., Gebreyohannes, Y. K., Schöffski, P., Heinrich, M. C., DeAngelo, D. J., & Lengauer, C. (2017). A precision therapy against cancers driven by KIT/PDGFRA mutations. *Science Translational Medicine, 9*(414), eaao1690. https://doi.org/10.1126/scitranslmed.aao1690

Ferrara, N. (2009). VEGF-A: A critical regulator of blood vessel growth. *European Cytokine Network, 20*(4), 158–163. https://doi.org/10.1684/ecn.2009.0170

Folkman, J. (2007). Angiogenesis: An organizing principle for drug discovery? *Nature Reviews Drug Discovery, 6*(4), 273–286. https://doi.org/10.1038/nrd2115

Fujio, Y., & Walsh, K. (1999). Akt mediates cytoprotection of endothelial cells by vascular endothelial growth factor in an anchorage-dependent manner. *Journal of Biological Chemistry, 274*(23), 16349–16354. https://doi.org/10.1074/jbc.274.23.16349

Gaengel, K., Genové, G., Armulik, A., & Betsholtz, C. (2009). Endothelial-mural cell signaling in vascular development and angiogenesis. *Arteriosclerosis, Thrombosis, and Vascular Biology, 29*(5), 630–638. https://doi.org/10.1161/ATVBAHA.107.161521

Gerhardt, H., & Semb, H. (2008). Pericytes: Gatekeepers in tumour cell metastasis? *Journal of Molecular Medicine, 86*(2), 135–144. https://doi.org/10.1007/s00109-007-0258-2

Harris, P. A., Boloor, A., Cheung, M., Kumar, R., Crosby, R. M., Ronda, G., Davis-Ward, Epperly, A. H., Hinkle, K. W., Hunter 3rd, R. N., Johnson, J. H., Knick, V. B., Laudeman, C. P., Luttrell, D. K., Mook, R. A., Nolte, R. T., Rudolph, S. K., Szewczyk, J. R., Truesdale, A. T., & Stafford, J. A. (2008). Discovery of 5-[[4-[(2,3-dimethyl-2H-indazol-6-Yl)methylamino]-2- pyrimidinyl]amino]-2-methyl-benzenesulfonamide (pazopanib), a novel and potent vascular endothelial growth factor receptor inhibitor. *Journal of Medicinal Chemistry, 51*(15), 4632−4640. https://doi.org/10.1021/jm800566m

Hennequin, L., Ple, P., Stokes, E., & McKerrecher, D. (2000). *No title.* https://patentscope.wipo.int/search/en/detail.jsf?docId=WO2000047212.

Huang, L., Jiang, S., & Shi, Y. (2020). Tyrosine kinase inhibitors for solid tumors in the past 20 years (2001−2020). *Journal of Hematology & Oncology, 13.* https://doi.org/10.1186/s13045-020-00977-0

Hu, X., Zhang, J., Xu, B., Jiang, Z., Joseph, R., Tong, Z., Zhang, Q., Wang, X., Feng, J., Pang, D., Fan, M., Li, J., Wang, B., Wang, Z., Zhang, Q., Sun, S., & Lioa, C. (2014). Multicenter phase II study of Apatinib, a novel VEGFR inhibitor in heavily pretreated patients with metastatic triple-negative breast cancer. *International Journal of Cancer, 135*(8), 1961−1969. https://doi.org/10.1002/ijc.28829

Huang, L., Huang, Z., Bai, Z., Xie, R., Sun, L., & Lin, K. (2012). Development and strategies of VEGFR-2/KDR inhibitors. *Future Medicinal Chemistry, 4*(14), 1839−1852. https://doi.org/10.4155/fmc.12.121

Ivy, S. P., Wick, J. Y., & Kaufman, B. M. (2009). An overview of small-molecule inhibitors of VEGFR signaling. *Nature Reviews Clinical Oncology, 6*(10), 569−579. https://doi.org/10.1038/nrclinonc.2009.130

Jain, R. K. (2003). Molecular regulation of vessel maturation. *Nature Medicine, 9*(6), 685−693. https://doi.org/10.1038/nm0603-685

Jain, R. K., Duda, D. G., Willett, C. G., Sahani, D. V., Zhu, A. X., Loeffler, J. S., Batchelor, T. T., & Sorensen, A. G. (2009). Biomarkers of response and resistance to antiangiogenic therapy. *Nature Reviews Clinical Oncology, 6*(6), 327−338. https://doi.org/10.1038/nrclinonc.2009.63

Kania, R. S. (2009). Structure-based design and characterization of Axitinib. In *Kinase inhibitor drugs* (pp. 167−201). Wiley Series in Drug Discovery and Development.

Kassem, M. G., Rahman, A. F. M. M., & Korashy, H. M. (2012). Sunitinib malate. In *Profiles of drug substances, excipients and related methodology* (Vol 37, pp. 363−388). Elsevier.

Kubo, K., Shimizu, T., Ohyama, S. I., Murooka, H., Iwai, A., Nakamura, K., Hasegawa, K., Kobayashi, Y., Takahashi, N., Takahashi, K., Kato, S., Izawa, T., & Isoe, T. (2005). Novel potent orally active selective VEGFR-2 tyrosine kinase inhibitors: Synthesis, structure-activity relationships, and antitumor activities of N-phenyl-N'-{4-(4-quinolyloxy)phenyl}ureas. *Journal of Medicinal Chemistry, 48*(5), 1359−1366. https://doi.org/10.1021/jm030427r

Lanahan, A. A., Hermans, K., Claes, F., Kerley-Hamilton, J. S., Zhuang, Z. W., Giordano, F. J., Carmeliet, P., & Simons, M. (2010). VEGF receptor 2 endocytic trafficking regulates arterial morphogenesis. *Developmental Cell, 18*(5), 713−724. https://doi.org/10.1016/j.devcel.2010.02.016

Laufer, S., & Bajorath, J. (2022). New Horizons in drug discovery − Understanding and advancing different types of kinase inhibitors: Seven years in kinase inhibitor research with impressive achievements and new future prospects. *Journal of Medicinal Chemistry, 65*(2), 891−892. https://doi.org/10.1021/acs.jmedchem.1c02126

Lee, S., Chen, T. T., Barber, C. L., Jordan, M. C., Murdock, J., Desai, S., Ferrara, N., Nagy, A., Roos, K. P., & Luisa Iruela-Arispe, M. (2007). Autocrine VEGF signaling is required for vascular homeostasis. *Cell, 130*(4), 691−703. https://doi.org/10.1016/j.cell.2007.06.054

Liu, Yi, & Gray, N. S. (2006). Rational design of inhibitors that bind to inactive kinase conformations. *Nature Chemical Biology, 2*(7), 358−364. https://doi.org/10.1038/nchembio799

Manley, P. W., Furet, P., Guido, B., Brüggen, J., Mestan, J., Meyer, T., Schnell, C. R., Wood, J., Haberey, M., Huth, A., Krüger, M., Menrad, A., Ottow, E., Seidelmann, D., Siemeister, G., & Thierauch, K. (2002). Anthranilic acid amides: A novel class of antiangiogenic VEGF receptor kinase inhibitors. *Journal of Medicinal Chemistry, 45*(26), 5687−5693. https://doi.org/10.1021/jm020899q

McTigue, M., Murray, B. W., Chen, J. H., Deng, Y. L., James, S., & Kania, R. S. (2012). Molecular conformations, interactions, and properties associated with drug efficiency and clinical performance among VEGFR TK inhibitors. *Proceedings of the National Academy of Sciences of the United States of America, 109*(45), 18281−18289. https://doi.org/10.1073/pnas.1207759109

Meadows, K. N., Bryant, P., & Kevin, P. (2001). Vascular endothelial growth factor induction of the angiogenic phenotype requires ras activation. *Journal of Biological Chemistry, 276*(52), 49289−49298. https://doi.org/10.1074/jbc.M108069200

Mendel, D. B., Douglas Laird, A., Xin, X., Louie, S. G., Christensen, J. G., Li, G., Schreck, R. E., Abrams, T. J., Ngai, T. J., Lee, L. B., Murray, L. J., Carver, J., Chan, E., Moss, K. G., Haznedar, J. O., Sukbuntherng, J., Blake, R. A., Sun, L., Tang, C., & Cherrington, J. M. (2003). In vivo antitumor activity of SU11248, a novel tyrosine kinase inhibitor targeting vascular endothelial growth factor and platelet-derived growth factor receptors: Determination of a pharmacokinetic/pharmacodynamic relationship. *Clinical Cancer Research, 9*(1 I), 327−337.

Morgan, P., Brown, D. G., Lennard, S., Anderton, M. J., Carl Barrett, J., Eriksson, U., Fidock, M., Hamrén, M., Johnson, A., March, R. E., Matcham, J., Mettetal, J., Nicholls, D. J., Platz, S., Rees, S., Snowden, M. A., & Pangalos, M. N. (2018). Impact of a five-dimensional framework on R&D productivity at AstraZeneca. *Nature Reviews Drug Discovery, 17*(3), 167−181. https://doi.org/10.1038/nrd.2017.244

Motzer, R. J., Dror Michaelson, M., Redman, B. G., Hudes, G. R., George, W., Figlin, R. A., Ginsberg, M. S., Kim, S. T., Baum, C. M., DePrimo, S. E., Li, J. Z., Bello, C. L., Theuer, C. P., George, D. J., & Rini, B. I. (2006). Activity of SU11248, a multitargeted inhibitor of vascular endothelial growth factor receptor and platelet-derived growth factor receptor, in patients with metastatic renal cell carcinoma. *Journal of Clinical Oncology, 24*(1), 16−24. https://doi.org/10.1200/JCO.2005.02.2574

Nagy, J. A., Dvorak, A. M., & Dvorak, H. F. (2007). VEGF-A and the induction of pathological angiogenesis. *Annual Review of Pathology, 2*, 251−275. https://doi.org/10.1146/annurev.pathol.2.010506.134925

Nakamura, K., Taguchi, E., Miura, T., Yamamoto, A., Takahashi, K., Bichat, F., Guilbaud, N., Hasegawa, K., Kubo, K., Fujiwara, Y., Suzuki, R., Kubo, K., Shibuya, M., & Isae, T. (2006). KRN951, a highly potent inhibitor of vascular endothelial growth factor receptor tyrosine kinases, has antitumor activities and affects functional vascular properties. *Cancer Research, 66*(18), 9134−9142. https://doi.org/10.1158/0008-5472.CAN-05-4290

Nisancioglu, M. H., Betsholtz, C., & Genové, G. (2010). The absence of pericytes does not increase the sensitivity of tumor vasculature to vascular endothelial growth factor-A blockade. *Cancer Research, 70*(12). https://doi.org/10.1158/0008-5472.CAN-09-4245

Okamoto, K., Ikemori-Kawada, M., Jestel, A., Von König, K., Funahashi, Y., Matsushima, T., Tsuruoka, A., Inoue, A., & Matsui, J. (2015). Distinct binding mode of multikinase inhibitor lenvatinib revealed by biochemical characterization. *ACS Medicinal Chemistry Letters, 6*(1), 89−94. https://doi.org/10.1021/ml500394m

Pan, Y., & Mader, M. M. (2022). Principles of kinase allosteric inhibition and pocket validation. *Journal of Medicinal Chemistry, 65*(7), 5288−5299. https://doi.org/10.1021/acs.jmedchem.2c00073

Patrick, G. L. (2021). *An introduction to medicinal chemistry* (5th ed.). Nuevos Sistemas de Comunicación e Información.

Pemovska, T., Johnson, E., Kontro, M., Repasky, G. A., Chen, J., Wells, P., Cronin, C. N., McTigue, M., Kallioniemi, O., Porkka, K., Murray, B. W., & Wennerberg, K. (2015). Axitinib effectively inhibits BCR-ABL1(t315I) with a distinct binding conformation. *Nature, 519*(7541), 102−105. https://doi.org/10.1038/nature14119

Riedl, B., Dumas, B. J., Khire, U., Lowinger, T. B., Scott, W. J., Smith, R. A., Wood, J. E., Monahan, M.-K., Natero, R., Renick, J., & Sibley, R. N. (2012). *φ-Carboxyaryl substituted diphenyl ureas as Raf kinase inhibitors*. https://patents.google.com/patent/US7351834B1/en.

Roskoski, R. (2016). Classification of small molecule protein kinase inhibitors based upon the structures of their drug-enzyme complexes. *Pharmacological Research, 103*, 26−48. https://doi.org/10.1016/j.phrs.2015.10.021

Roskoski, R., Jr. (2020). Properties of FDA-approved small molecule protein kinase inhibitors: A 2020 update. *Pharmacological Research, 152*, 104609. https://doi.org/10.1016/j.phrs.2019.104609

Roskoski, R., Jr. (2021). Properties of FDA-approved small molecule protein kinase inhibitors: A 2021 update. *Pharmacological Research, 165*, 105463. https://doi.org/10.1016/j.phrs.2021.105463

Roth, G. J., Binder, R., Colbatzky, F., Dallinger, C., Schlenker-Herceg, R., Hilberg, F., Wollin, S. L., & Kaiser, R. (2015). Nintedanib: From discovery to the clinic. *Journal of Medicinal Chemistry, 58*(3), 1053−1063. https://doi.org/10.1021/jm501562a

Sennino, B., Frank, K., Tabruyn, S. P., Mancuso, M. R., Hu-Lowe, D. D., Kuo, C. J., & McDonald, D. M. (2009). Cellular source and amount of vascular endothelial growth factor and platelet-derived growth factor in tumors determine response to angiogenesis inhibitors. *Cancer Research, 69*(10), 4527−4536. https://doi.org/10.1158/0008-5472.CAN-08-3779

Smet, F. D., Arthur, C., & Carmeliet, P. (2014). Allosteric targeting of receptor tyrosine kinases. *Nature Biotechnology, 32*(11), 1113−1120. https://doi.org/10.1038/nbt.3028

Stockmann, C., Doedens, A., Alexander, W., Zhang, N., Takeda, N., Joshua, I., Greenberg, D. A. C., & Johnson, R. S. (2008). Deletion of vascular endothelial growth factor in myeloid cells accelerates tumorigenesis. *Nature, 456*(7223), 814–818. https://doi.org/10.1038/nature07445

Sun, C. L., Christensen, J. G., & McMahon, G. (2009). Discovery and development of sunitinib (SU11248): A multi-target tyrosine kinase inhibitor of tumor growth, survival, and angiogenesis. In *Kinase inhibitor drugs* (pp. 1–39). Wiley.

Swift, M. R., & Brant, M. W. (2009). Arterial-venous specification during development. *Circulation Research, 104*(5), 576–588. https://doi.org/10.1161/CIRCRESAHA.108.188805

Tang, P. C., Miller, T., Li, X., Sun, L., Wei, C. C., Shirazian, S., Liang, C., Vojkovsky, T., & Nematalla, A. (2001). *Pyrrole substituted 2-indolinone protein kinase inhibitors.* https://patents.google.com/patent/CA2399358A1/en.

Tomaso, E. di, London, N., Fuja, D., James, L., Tyrrell, J. A., Kamoun, W., Munn, L. L., & Jain, R. K. (2009). PDGF-C induces maturation of blood vessels in a model of glioblastoma and attenuates the response to anti-VEGF treatment. *PLoS One, 4*(4), e5123. https://doi.org/10.1371/journal.pone.0005123

Tvorogov, D., Anisimov, A., Zheng, W., Leppänen, V. M., Tammela, T., Laurinavicius, S., Holnthoner, W., Heloterä, H., Holopainen, T., Jeltsch, M., Kalkkinen, N., Lankinen, H., Ojala, P. M., & Alitalo, K. (2010). Effective suppression of vascular network formation by combination of antibodies blocking VEGFR ligand binding and receptor dimerization. *Cancer Cell, 18*(6), 630–640. https://doi.org/10.1016/j.ccr.2010.11.001

Wilhelm, S., Carter, C., Lynch, M., Lowinger, T., Dumas, J., Smith, R. A., Schwartz, B., Simantov, R., & Kelley, S. (2006). Discovery and development of sorafenib: A multikinase inhibitor for treating cancer. *Nature Reviews Drug Discovery, 5*(10), 835–844. https://doi.org/10.1038/nrd2130

Wu, P., Nielsen, T. E., & Clausen, M. H. (2016). Small-molecule kinase inhibitors: An analysis of FDA-approved drugs. *Drug Discovery Today, 21*(1), 5–10. https://doi.org/10.1016/j.drudis.2015.07.008

Xie, C., Wan, X., Quan, H., Zheng, M., Fu, Li, Li, Y., & Lou, L. (2018). Preclinical characterization of anlotinib, a highly potent and selective vascular endothelial growth factor receptor-2 inhibitor. *Cancer Science, 109*(4), 1207–1219. https://doi.org/10.1111/cas.13536

Zhan, Y., Hodous, B., Kim, J., Wilson, K., & Wilson, D. (2015). *Compositions useful for treating disorders related to kit.* issued 2015. WO Pat.%0AWO2015057873, 2015.

Zimmermann, J. (1993). *Pyrimidin derivatives and process for their preparation.* European Patent Office, Article EP0564409A1. European Patent. Applications, issued 1993.

Index

'*Note:* Page numbers followed by "f" indicate figures and "t" indicate tables.'

A

Acetylcysteine, 431–432
Activin receptor-like kinase-2 (ALK2)
  disorders associated, 3–4
  inhibitors
    2-aminopyrazine-3-carboxamide derivatives, 4, 5f
    aminopyrimidine, 4–6, 5f
    7-aryl-imidazo[1,2-a]pyridine-3-ylquinolines, 7, 8f
    bicyclic pyrazoles, 6, 6f
    bis-heteroaryl pyrazole-based inhibitors, 8–9, 8f, 10f
    3,5-diaryl-2-aminopyridine ALK2 inhibitors, 12, 12f
    dorsomorphin, 4
    3D-QSAR study, 6
    2-fluoro-6-methoxybenzamide derivative, 7f
    LDN-214117, 6–7
    macrocyclic inhibitors OD36 and OD52, 9, 9f
    molecular docking experiment, 6
    pharmacophore hypothesis, 6
    5-[1-(piperidin-4-yl)-1H-pyrazol-4-yl]pyridine-2-amine scaffold, 11–12, 11f
    quinazolinone-based inhibitors, 9–10, 10f
    quinoline fused pyrazolo[1,5-a]pyrimidine derivatives, 12, 13f
    simulations analysis, 9
    3-(4-sulfamoylnaphthyl) substituted pyrazolo[1,5-a]pyrimidines, 10–11, 11f
  physiological role, 3
  signal transduction, 2–3
  structure and types, 1–2, 2f
Agerafenib, 354–355, 354f
Alectinib, 350–351, 350f
Allosteric inhibitors, 93–95
Allosteric PAK1 inhibitors, 211
2-Amino and 2-oxocyanopyridine, 314–315
2-Amino aromatic heterocyclic derivatives, 65
2-Amino-4-aryl-4H-benzo[h or f]chromene-3-carbonitrile derivatives, 99
2-Aminobenzothiazole derivatives, 315, 315f
2-Aminopyrazine-3-carboxamide derivatives, 4, 5f
2-Amino-4-pyrazole-cyclopentyl pyrimidines, 172–173, 173f

Amino-pyrazole derivatives, 123, 123f
Aminopyrimidine-based drugs, 209
Angiogenesis
  autocrine signals, 445
  organogenesis, 444–445
  vessel formation, 445
Anlotinib, 467–468, 470f
Anthraquinone and coumarin derivatives, 64–65
Antimitotic drugs, 397
Apatinib, 466, 467f
2-Arylamino-4-aryl-pyrimidines, 209
7-Aryl-imidazo[1,2-a]pyridine-3-ylquinolines, 7, 8f
Asciminib, 41, 42f
Ataxia telangiectasia (AT), 17
  genetic predisposition, 17
  management, 18
Ataxia telangiectasia-mutated (ATM) and Rad3-related (ATR) inhibitors
  checkpoints, 18–23
  clinical trial
    BAY1895344, 30
    berzosertib, 28–29
    camnosertib, 28f, 31–32
    ceralasertib, 30
    M6620, 29–30
  DNA damage response, 18, 19f
  heterocyclics
    AZ20, 27
    azabenzimidazole, 27–28
    caffeine, 23–25
    NU6027, 25
    NVP-BEZ235 and ETP-46464, 26
    Schisandrin B, 25
    torin-2, 26
    VE-821, 27
    wortmannin, 25
  human ATR-ATRIP complex, 20–21, 20f
  kinases, 19f
  in precipitating cancer, 23
  signaling pathways, 21–23, 22f
  structure, 21, 21f
  synthesis, 24f
Ataxia telangiectasia mutated (ATM) kinase, 18

Ataxia telangiectasia Rad3-related (ATR) inhibitors.
    See Ataxia telangiectasia-mutated (ATM) and
    Rad3-related (ATR) inhibitors
ATP competitive p21-Activated kinase 1 (PAK1)
    inhibitors
  AK963, 210
  azaindole, 209—210, 210f
  CP734, 211
  oxindole/maleimide derivatives, 205—207, 206f
  PDK1 inhibitor OSU-03012, 210
  pyrazoles, 207, 207f
  ZMF-10, 210
Autocrine signals, 445
Avapritinib, 469
Axitinib, 459—461, 460f
AZ20, 27
Azabenzimidazole, 27—28
Azaindole, 209—210, 210f
7-Azaindole derivative, 311, 311f, 388—389
2-Azaindole (indazole) derivatives, 288—290

B
BAY1895344, 28f, 30
Belvarafenib, 240t—242t
Benzimidazole-cinnamic acid hybrids, 410
Benzodiazocine derivative, 309, 309f
Benzofuropyrimidinones derivatives, 307—308
Benzoylimidazole derivatives, 384f, 385
Berzosertib, 28—29
Beta carboline, 189—191
Beta-hydroxyisovalerylshikonin (β-HIVS), 423
Bicyclic scaffold inhibitors
  protein kinase CK1
    benzimidazole and indazole derivatives, 47—50
    benzothiazole derivatives, 50
    isoquinoline and indolinone derivatives, 48f
    purine and purine-like derivatives, 50—51
  protein kinase CK2
    benzotriazole derivatives, 57—59
    flavonoid derivatives, 61—62
    polyhalogenated benzimidazole, 57—59
    pyrazolo-triazine and pyrazolo-pyrimidine
      derivatives, 60—61, 61f
Binimetinib, 233—234, 240t—242t
Bis-heteroaryl pyrazole-based ALK2 inhibitors, 9, 10f
Bis-heteroaryl pyrazole-based inhibitors, 8, 8f
Bladder cancer, Moloney murine leukemia virus-1
    (PIM-1) kinase, 259
Bosutinib, 40—41, 40f, 93
BRAF inhibitors, 223f, 381
  dabrafenib, 226—228
  encorafenib, 228—229
  regorafenib, 224—225

  sorafenib, 222—224
  vemurafenib, 225—226
B-Raf kinase, 377
Breakpoint cluster region-Abelson (BCR-AbL)
  inhibitors
    first-generation, 38—39
    second-generation, 39—41
    third generation, 41
  structure and function, 37—38, 38f
Breast cancer, 139—140, 334—336
Bruton's tyrosine kinase (BTK) inhibitors, 96

C
Cabozantinib, 341—342, 345—346, 345f
Caffeine, 23—25, 24f
Camnosertib, 28f, 31—32
Casein kinase (CK)
  protein kinase CK1
    inhibitors, 47—56
    sequence alignment, 46f
    structures and function, 45—47
  protein kinase CK2
    inhibitors, 57—70
    structures and function, 56—57
  protein kinase Fam20C, 70—72
Casein kinase 1 (CK1) inhibitors
  bicyclic scaffold inhibitors, 47—51
  monocyclic scaffold inhibitors, 51—54
  sequence alignment, 46f
  structures and function, 45—47
  tricyclic scaffold inhibitors, 54—56, 55f
Casein kinase 2 (CK2) inhibitors
  bicyclic scaffold inhibitors, 57—62
  monocyclic scaffold inhibitors, 65—69
  tetracyclic scaffold inhibitors, 69—70
  tricyclic scaffold inhibitors, 62—65
Caspase-3-activation assay, 154
Celogentin C, 404
Ceralasertib, 28f, 30
Cervical cancer, proviral integration site for Moloney
    murine leukemia virus-1 (PIM-1) kinase, 259
Chalcones derivatives, 313, 313f
6-Chlorinated derivatives, 311, 311f
Chromen-4-one derivatives, 192—193,
    193f
Chronic lymphocytic leukemia (CLL), 96
Chronic myeloid leukemia (CML), breakpoint cluster
    region-Abelson
  inhibitors, 38—41
  structure, 37—38, 38f
Cinnamon, 262
c-Jun N-terminal kinases, 221—222
Cobimetinib, 232—233, 233f, 240t—242t

Colon carcinoma, Moloney murine leukemia virus-1 (PIM-1) kinase, 258
Colorectal cancer (CRC)
    potent kinase inhibitors for, 98
    rearranged during transfection (RET)
        inhibitor, 357
        mutation, 337—338
Covalent inhibitors, 95—96
CP734, 211
c-Src kinase
    cellular signaling, 88—89, 89f
    conserved domain structure, 84—85, 85f
    dephosphorylation, 88
    N-terminal myristoylation site, 84—85
    phosphorylation, 87—88
    SH2 domain, 84, 86
    SH3 domain, 84—86
    structural features, 84—87
    tyrosine kinase domain, 84—87
Cucurbitacin, 212, 212f
Cyanopyridine derivatives, 314—315, 315f
Cyclin-dependent kinase 4/6 (CDK4/6) inhibitors
    amino-pyrazole derivatives, 123, 123f
    4-(2,3-dihydro-1H-benzo[d]pyrrolo[1,2-a]imidazole-7-yl)-N-(5-(piperazin-1-ylmethyl) pyridine-2-yl) pyrimidin-2-amine, 124—125, 125f
    4,5-dihydro-1H-pyrazolo[4,3-h] quinazoline derivatives, 126, 127f
    fused tricyclic derivatives, 123—124, 124f
    4-(heterocyclic substituted amino)-1H-pyrazole-3-carboxamide, 127, 128f
    LEE011 derivatives, 131—132, 132f
    N9-cis-cyclobutylpurine derivatives, 129—130, 130f
    oxindole—indole conjugates, 132, 133f
    5-((5-substituted-1H-indole-3-yl) methylene)-3-(2-oxo-2-(3/4-substituted phenylethyl)-thiazolidine-2,4-dione, 126, 128f
    2,6,7-substituted pyrrolo[2,3-d] pyrimidine, 129, 129f
    tetrahydronaphthyridine, 125—126, 126f
Cyclin-dependent kinases (CDKs)
    cell cycle, 117f
    cyclic activity, 116
    regulation, cancer
        CDK6, 121—122
        CDK9 and cyclin T, 119
        cell cycle progression, 119
        cyclin B1 overexpression, 121
        cyclin D1, 119—120
        cyclin H expression, 120—121
    types, 117, 118t—119t
Cyclins, 115—116
    cell cycle, 117f
    cell cycle regulation, 116

classification, 115—116
Cyclopeptides, 432—433

D
Dabrafenib, 226—228, 227f, 240t—242t
Dasatinib, 40, 40f
Diaminopyrazole, 264—266, 266f
3,5-Diaryl-2-aminopyridine ALK2 inhibitors, 12, 12f
Diffuse idiopathic skeletal hyperostosis (DISH), activin receptor-like kinase-2 (ALK2), 3—4
Diffuse intrinsic pontine glioma (DIPG), activin receptor-like kinase-2 (ALK2), 3
4,5-Dihydro-1H-pyrazolo[4,3-h] quinazoline derivatives, 126, 127f
2,3-Dihydroimidazo[2,1-b]thiazoles, 173—174, 174f
Dihydropyrrole and dihydropyrazole derivatives, 193—195, 194f
6,7-Dimorpholinoalkoxy quinazoline derivatives, 149, 150f
3,5-Disubstituted 6-azaindazoles, 290—291
1,4-Disubstituted 1,2,3-triazoles, 99—101
DN401, 426
Dolastatin 10, 402—403
Dorsomorphin, 4

E
Eg5 protein, 184
Encorafenib, 228—230
Epidermal growth factor receptor (EGFR) inhibitors
    docking studies, 140—142
    proteins, 140
    signaling pathway, 142f
    structure—activity relationship (SAR) studies
        acrylamide moiety, 142—143, 144f
        A-ring-modified lamellarin N analogs, 145, 145f
        chalcone derivatives, 146—147, 146f
        1,2-dimethoxybenzene moiety, 156
        6,7-dimorpholinoalkoxy quinazoline derivatives, 149, 150f
        diphenylthiazole derivatives, 145—146, 146f
        1H-pyrazolo[3,4-d] pyrimidine derivatives, 148—149
        indole-2-carboxamides and pyrazino[1,2-a] indol1(2H)-ones derivatives, 150—151
        morpholine-substituted diphenylpyrimidine derivatives, 142—143
        1,3,4-oxadiazole derivatives, 155—156, 155f
        pyrimidine derivatives, 143—144, 144f
        quinoline-based 4,5-dihydropyrazoles, 147—148, 148f
        spirobenzo[h]chromene and spirochromane derivatives, 149—150, 150f
        styryl moiety, 152—153

Epidermal growth factor receptor (EGFR) inhibitors
(*Continued*)
thiazolyl-pyrazolines, 152
thieno[2,3-d]pyrimidine derivatives, 151–152
thiophene-pyrimidine derivatives, 154–155, 155f
T790M mutants, 142–143
1,2,4-triazole derivatives, 147, 147f
1,3,5-trisubstituted pyrazoline derivatives,
152–153
xanthine derivatives, 154
types, 141f
Epithelial ovarian cancer (EOC), 339–340
Erlotinib, 140
Extracellular signal-regulated kinases (ERKs), 221

F
Fam20C
inhibitors, 71–72, 71f
structures and function, 70–71, 71f
Fibrodysplasia ossificans progressiva (FOP), activin
receptor-like kinase-2 (ALK2), 3
2-Fluoro-6-methoxybenzamide derivative, 7f
2-Fluoro-1-methoxy-4-
pentafluorophenylsulfonamidobenzene
(T138067), 400

G
Gamitrinib triphenyl phosphonium (G-TPP), 431,
431f
Ganitumab, 167
Ganoderma microsporum immunomodulatory
protein, 94
Gefitinib, 140
Glaucarubinone, 211–212
Glial cell line-derived neurotrophic factor (GDNF),
339
Glycopeptides, 429f
Glycoprotein IIb/IIIa (aIIbb3), 428

H
Head and neck squamous cell carcinomas (HNSCC)
dasatinib, 91
serine/threonine-protein phosphatase 2 (PP2), 95
Heat shock proteins (HSPs), 420
Hispidulin, 262–263, 263f
Homopiperazine derivative, 269–270
HSP90-related inhibitors, 428, 430f
2'-Hydroxycinnamicaldehyde (2'-HCA), 262

I
Imatinib, 37–39
2D and 3D interaction, 464–466, 465f
N-methylpiperazine addition, 38–39

resistance mechanisms, 39
structural optimization, 466
Imidazo [2, 1-b] oxazole derivatives, 385–386
Imidazo[1,2-b]pyridazines, 274–276
Imidazo [2, 1-b] thiazoles derivatives, 384
Imidazo[5,1-f]-[1,2,4] triazine-based dual inhibitor,
170–171, 171f
Immunotherapies
MAPK-inhibitors, 239
rearranged during transfection (RET) inhibitors, 359
INCB053914, 274
Indirubin, 168
Indirubin-derived insulin-like growth factor
inhibitors (IGFR), 170f
Indole-2-carboxamides, 150–151
Indole derivatives, 309–311
Indole-1,2,4-triazole derivatives, 411–412
Inhibitors of Wnt production (IWPs), 50
Insulin-like growth factor (IGF)
cancer development, 164–166
cellular and metabolic process regulation, 163–164
development and functioning, 164f
diseases, 164
molecular pathways, 166f
pathway regulation, 165f
structure, 163f
sulfation factor, 162–163
Insulin-like growth factor inhibitors (IGFR)
bioimaging tool targeting, 174–175, 175f
clinical developments, 167–168
diseases, 164
therapeutics targeting
2-amino-4-pyrazole-cyclopentyl pyrimidines,
172–173, 173f
2-anilino-pyrimidine, 168–170
clinical trials, 169t–170t
diarylureas, 175, 176f
2,3-dihydroimidazo[2,1-b]thiazoles, 173–174, 174f
dual IGF-1R and SRC inhibitor, 173, 173f
imidazo[5,1-f]-[1,2,4] triazine-based dual inhibitor,
170–171, 171f
indirubin, 168, 170f
macrocyclic scaffold, 172, 172f
2-phenylquinolin-7-yl-derived imidazo[1,5-a]
pyrazines, 175, 176f
(pyrazol-4-ylamino)-pyrimidines, 168–170, 171f
thiazolidine-2,4-dione, 171, 172f
Ispinesib and related compounds, 192, 192f

K
Kinases, 219–221
Kinesin, 185–186, 186f
Kinesin spindle protein (KSP), 184, 187
Klisyri (KX01), 99

L

Latent membrane protein 1 (LMP1), 420
Laulimalide, 398
LDN-214117, 6–7
LEE011 derivatives, 131–132, 132f
Lenvatinib, 346–347, 346f, 461
    FDA approval, 461
    multikinase inhibitory activity, 461
    synthesis, 461, 462f
    VEGFR-2, 3D interaction, 462f
LGB321, 274
Linsitinib, 167
Louis–Bar Syndrome, 17

M

M6620, 29–30
Macrocyclic hydroxamic acids (MHAs), 434–435, 436f
Macrocyclic polyethers, 402–403
Medullary thyroid carcinoma (MTC)
    rearranged during transfection (RET) inhibitor, 357
    rearranged during transfection (RET) mutation, 331–332
Medulloblastoma, 122
MEK inhibitors, 232f
    binimetinib, 233–234
    cobimetinib, 232–233, 233f
    trametinib, 229–232
Membrane type-1 matrix metalloproteinase (MT1-MMP), 428
Metastatic castration-resistant prostate cancer (mCRPC)
    dasatinib, 92
    saracatinib (AZD0530) and docetaxel, 94–95
Methylquinoxaline, 292
Microtubules, 184
    assembly inhibition, 399f
    binding sites, 397, 398f
    functions, 396
    metrics, 396f
    structure, 395–396
    targeting drugs, 396–397
Middle East respiratory syndrome coronavirus (MERS-CoV), 245
Mirdametinib, 240t–242t
MITF, 237
Mitogen-activating protein kinases (MAPK), 378
    c-Jun N-terminal kinases, 221–222
    extracellular signal-regulated kinases (ERKs), 221
    p38 mitogen-activated protein kinases, 222
    signaling pathway, 219–221, 220f
Mitogen-activating protein kinases (MAPK) inhibitors
    Alzheimer's disease (AD), 244–245

BRAF inhibitors, 222–229
chronic pulmonary diseases (COPD), 243
clinical trials, 243f
MEK inhibitors, 229–235
primary resistance, 235
resistance and therapeutic strategies
    multiple pathway inhibition, 239
    PI3K/AKT/mTOR/Hippo pathways, 238
    therapeutic combinations, 239, 240t–242t
secondary resistance, 236–237
Mitotic kinesin biology, 184–185
Mitotic kinesin spindle protein (KSP/Eg5 ATPase) inhibitors
    beta carboline, 189–191
    chromen-4-one derivatives, 192–193
    dihydropyrrole and dihydropyrazole derivatives, 193–195, 194f
    ispinesib and related compounds, 192
    mitotic arrest, 186
    monastrol, 187–189
    S-trityl-L-cysteine (STLC), 189, 189f
    tetrahydroisoquinolines, 195, 195f
Mitotic slippage, 185
MK-8353, 240t–242t
Monastrol
    Eg5-ADP monastrol complexes, 188–189
    enantiomer, 187
    structural insights, 187–188
    structure, 188f
Monoclonal antibodies, 437–438
Monocyclic scaffold inhibitors
    casein kinase 1 (CK1)
        imidazole and isoxazole derivatives, 51–53, 52f
        pyrazole derivatives, 53–54, 54f
    casein kinase 2 (CK2), 66f
        2-amino aromatic heterocyclic derivatives, 65
        phenyl-based derivatives, 65–69
Multiple endocrine neoplasia type 2 (MEN2), rearranged during transfection (RET) mutation, 329
Multiple myeloma, 269–270

N

N-benzyl-2-(5-phenylpyridin-2-yl) acetamide-based derivatives, 98
NCB053914, 274
N9-cis-cyclobutylpurine derivatives, 129–130, 130f
Neuroendocrine tumors (NETs), rearranged during transfection (RET) inhibitor, 357
N-hydroxyalkanamide derivatives, 388
Nilotinib, 39–40, 39f
Nintedanib
    2D and 3D interaction, 464

Nintedanib (*Continued*)
    mode of action, 462–463
    synthetic pathway, 463–464, 463f
N-methyl-D-aspartate (NMDA) glutamate receptors, 94
Nonsmall cell lung cancer (NSCLC)
    rearranged during transfection (RET) inhibitor, 357
    rearranged during transfection (RET) mutation, 332–334
Nonsuppressible insulin-like activity (NSILA), 162–163
NU6027, 24f, 25
Nuclear factor (NF)-κB, 424–425
NVP-BEZ235 and ETP-46464, 26
Nymphaeol C and A, 212, 212f

O

Ottelione A, 400
Oxadiazole derivatives, 311–312, 312f
1,3,4-Oxadiazole derivatives, 155–156, 155f
Oxazine derivatives, 286–287, 287f
Oxindole–indole conjugates, 132, 133f

P

p21-Activated kinase 1 (PAK1)
    autoactivation mechanism, 201
    cancer drug resistance, 204, 205f
    inhibitors
        allosteric PAK1 inhibitors, 211
        ATP competitive, 205–211
        natural products, 212
        treatment combinations, 211–212
    regulation, 203
    structure, 201, 202f, 203
    tyrosine phosphorylation, 203–204
Pancreatic cancer
    proviral integration site for Moloney murine leukemia virus-1 (PIM-1) kinase, 259
    rearranged during transfection (RET) mutation, 339–340
Pancreatic ductal adenocarcinoma (PDAC), 92
Papillary thyroid carcinomas (PTCs), κrearranged during transfection (RET) mutation, 330–331
Pazopanib, 457–459, 458f
Peptide substrate-based inhibitors, 95
Phenanthridines derivatives, 266–267, 267f
2-Phenylquinolin-7-yl-derived imidazo[1,5-a] pyrazines, 175, 176f
Pimasertib, 240t–242t
5-[1-(piperidin-4-yl)-1H-pyrazol-4-yl]pyridine-2-amine-based ALK2 inhibitors, 11–12, 11f
Platelet-derived growth factor (PDGF), 443–444, 446–447

tyrosine kinase inhibitors targeting, 447–450, 448f, 449t
PLX4720, 388–389
p38 mitogen-activated protein kinases, 222
Polyhalogenated phenyl carboxylic acids, 65–67
Ponatinib, 41, 41f, 344–345, 344f
Pralsetinib, 352–353, 352f
Prostate cancer, 139–140
    proviral integration site for Moloney murine leukemia virus-1 (PIM-1) kinase, 259–260
    rearranged during transfection (RET) mutation, 337
Proviral integration site for Moloney murine leukemia virus-1 (PIM-1) kinase
    biological process, 255
    inhibitors
        2-aminobenzothiazole derivatives, 315, 315f
        2-azaindole (indazole) derivatives, 288–290
        benzodiazocine derivative, 309, 309f
        benzofuropyrimidinones derivatives, 307–308
        chalcones derivatives, 313
        cyanopyridine derivatives, 314–315, 315f
        diaminopyrazole, 264–266, 266f
        3,5-disubstituted 6-azaindazoles, 290–291
        hispidulin, 262–263, 263f
        imidazo[1,2-b]pyridazines, 274–276
        indole derivatives, 309–311
        natural compounds, 261
        oxadiazole derivatives, 311–312
        oxazine derivatives, 286–287, 287f
        oxindole derivative, 288, 288f
        pyran derivatives, 282–283, 283f
        pyrazine derivatives, 312
        pyrazole derivatives, 264, 265f
        pyrazolopyridines, 281, 281f
        pyrazolopyrimidine derivatives, 278–281, 279f
        pyrazolo quinazoline derivatives, 282, 282f
        pyridinamines derivatives, 273–274
        pyridine derivatives, 267–273, 268f
        pyrimidine derivatives, 276–278, 277f
        pyrrolo-carbazole derivatives, 308–309
        quercetagetin, 261–262, 262f
        quinazolinone-pyrrolopyrrolones, 291–292, 292f
        quinoline derivatives, 284, 284f
        quinoxaline derivatives, 285–286, 285f
        quinoxaline-pyrrolodihydropiperidinones, 292–293
        tetrazine derivatives, 263–264, 264f
        thiazole derivative, 293–294
        thiazolidine-2,4-dione, 295–301
        thienopyridines, 303, 304f
        thiophenes derivatives, 302, 302f
        thioridazine derivatives, 313–314
        triazine derivatives, 303, 304f
        triazole derivatives, 303–305

triazolo[4,5-b]pyridines, 306–307
overexpression
    bladder cancer, 259
    cervical cancer, 259
    colon carcinoma, 258
    pancreatic cancer, 259
    prostate cancer, 259–260
physiological functions, 256–258
regulation, 255
signal transduction pathways, 257f
structure, 256–257
Pyran derivatives, 282–283, 283f
Pyrazine derivatives, 312, 313f
Pyrazino[1,2-a]indol1(2H)-ones derivatives, 150–151
Pyrazol derivatives, 386
Pyrazole derivatives, 264, 265f
Pyrazole-naphthalene derivatives, 410–411
Pyrazolo[3,4-b]pyridines, 411
Pyrazolopyridines, 281, 281f
Pyrazolopyrimidine derivatives, 278–281, 279f
Pyrazolo quinazoline derivatives, 282, 282f
Pyridinamines derivatives, 273–274, 274f–275f
Pyrido [2, 3-b] pyrazinone derivatives, 386–387
Pyridothienopyrimidin-4-one derivatives, 268,
    268f–269f
Pyrimidine-5-carbonitrile, 437, 437f
Pyrrolo-carbazole derivatives, 308–309

Q

Quercetagetin, 261–262, 262f, 308–309
Quinazolinone-based inhibitors, 9–10, 10f
Quinazolinone-pyrrolopyrrolones, 291–292, 292f
Quinoline-based 4,5-dihydropyrazoles, 148f
Quinoline derivatives, 272, 273f, 284, 284f
Quinoline fused pyrazolo[1,5-a]pyrimidine
    derivatives, 12, 13f
Quinoxaline derivatives, 285–286, 285f
Quinoxaline-pyrrolodihdropiperidinones, 292–293

R

RAF-RAS-MEK-ERK (MAP kinase) oncogenic paths,
    379
Rearranged during transfection (RET)
    activation
        aberrant, 327t
        mechanisms, 340, 341t
    canonical signaling, 324, 325f
    downstream signaling pathways, 326
    inhibitors
        access and affordability, 361
        biomarker discovery, 360
        combinatorial strategies, 360
        mechanisms of action, 356

multikinase inhibitors/nonselective, 342–352
pediatric applications, 360
precision medicine approaches, 360
resistance development, 360
resistance mechanisms, 357–359
safety and tolerability, 360–361
selective, 352–355
therapeutic applications, 356–357
tyrosine kinase inhibitors (TKIs) targeting, 341
ligands and activation, 326
mutations, 326–329, 340f
    breast cancer, 334–336
    colorectal cancer (CRC), 337–338
    medullary thyroid carcinoma (MTC), 331–332
    multiple endocrine neoplasia type 2 (MEN2), 329
    nonsmall cell lung cancer (NSCLC), 332–334
    pancreatic and epithelial ovarian cancers, 339–340
    papillary thyroid carcinomas (PTCs), 330–331
    prostate cancer, 337
    salivary gland cancer, 336–337
neural development, 326
oncogenic alterations and fusions, 328–329
structure, 340–355
tissue homeostasis, 326
Rearranged during transfection (RET) inhibitors,
    340–355
Receptor activator of NF-κB ligand (RANKL), 92
Receptor tyrosine kinases (RTKs), 447
    hyperactivation, 236
Regorafenib, 224–225, 348–349, 349f
Retinitis pigmentosa, 185

S

Salivary gland cancer, rearranged during transfection
    (RET) mutation, 336–337
Saracatinib, 93–94
SB202190 and SB203580, 244–245
Schisandrin, 24f
Schisandrin B, 25
SCIO-469, 244
Selpercatinib, 353–354, 353f
Selumetinib, 234–235, 240t–242t
Semaxanib, 343–344, 344f
Serine/threonine-protein kinase B-RAF inhibitors
    clinical development, 381f
    clinical trials, 381–382, 382t
    encorafenib, 382, 383f
    GDC0879, 382
    mitogen-activated protein kinase (MEK) inhibitors
        7-azaindole derivative, 388–389
        benzoylimidazole derivatives, 385
        imidazo [2, 1-b] oxazole derivatives, 385–386
        imidazo [2, 1-b] thiazoles derivatives, 384

Serine/threonine-protein kinase B-RAF inhibitors
(*Continued*)
N-hydroxyalkanamide derivatives, 388
pyrazol derivatives, 386
pyrido [2, 3-b] pyrazinone derivatives, 386–387
triarylimidazole with phenylpyrazole group, 385
SB-699393, 382, 383f
vemurafenib, 381–382
Serine/threonine signaling pathways, 378f
SH-130, 435–436, 436f
Shepherdin, 425–426
SKF-86002, 244
Small molecule inhibitors, 186
Small-molecule synthetic inhibitors (SMKIs), 443–444
Sorafenib, 222–224, 342–343, 342f, 453–455, 454f
SPD-304 analogs, 432, 433f
Spirobenzo[h]chromene and spirochromane
derivatives, 149–150, 150f
Src-Abl nonreceptor tyrosine kinases inhibitors
7-alkoxy-4-heteroarylamino-3-cyanoquinolines, 105
7-alkoxy-4-heteroarylamino-3-quinolinecarbonitriles,
104–107
allosteric inhibitors, 93–95
2-amino-4-aryl-4H-benzo[h or f]chromene-3-
carbonitrile derivatives, 99
2-amino-7-dimethylamino-4H-chromene-3-
carbonitrile, 101
2′-aminospiro[pyrano[3,2-c] quinoline]-3′-carbonitrile
derivatives, 96–97
4-aryl-4H-chromene scaffold, 96
ATP-competitive inhibitors, 90–93
AZD0530, 101–102
4-(2-chloro-5-methoxyanilino) quinazolines, 105
conserved domain structure, 85f
covalent inhibitors, 95–96
Ð5,7-diphenyl-pyrrolopyrimidines, 102–104
1,4-disubstituted 1,2,3-triazoles, 99–101
1H-benzo[f]chromene, 107
7-heterocyclyl-5-aryl-pyrrolopyrimidines, 104
Klisyri (KX01), 99
N-benzyl-2-(5-phenylpyridin-2-yl) acetamide-based
derivatives, 98
peptide substrate-based inhibitors, 95
pyrazolo[1,5-a]pyrimidines, 104–105
pyrazolo[3,4-d]pyrimidine derivatives, 96, 101, 107
pyrazolopyrimidine derivatives, 102
pyridopyrimidine tyrosine kinase inhibitors, 104
pyrrolo[2,3-d]pyrimidine, 107
saracatinib, 102
structural features, 84–87
thieno[2,3-b]pyridine derivatives, 105
tyrosine kinases, 98
Staurosporine, 212, 212f

S-trityl-L-cysteine (STLC), 189, 189f
3-(4-Sulfamoylnaphthyl) substituted pyrazolo[1,5-a]
pyrimidines, 10–11, 11f
Sunitinib, 349–350, 349f, 455–457, 456f
SYHA1815, 351f
Syndecan-Binding Protein (SDCBP), 92

T
Temuterkib, 240t–242t
Tetracyclic scaffold inhibitors, CK2 inhibitors, 69–70
Tetrahydro-β-carbolines, 190–191, 191f
Tetrahydroisoquinolines, 195, 195f
Tetrahydronaphthyridine, 125–126, 126f
Tetrazine derivatives, 263–264, 264f
Thiazolidine-2,4-dione, 171, 172f, 295–301
Thiazolyl-pyrazolines, 152–153
Thieno[2,3-b]pyridine derivatives, 105
Thieno[2,3-d]pyrimidine derivatives, 151–152, 152f
Thienopyridines, 303, 304f
Thiophenes derivatives, 302, 302f
Thioridazine derivatives, 313–314, 314f
Tivozanib, 466–467, 468f
Torin-2, 26, 29f
Trametinib, 229–232, 231f, 239, 240t–242t
Triarylimidazoles, 385
Triazine derivatives, 303, 304f
Triazole derivatives, 303–305
Triazolo[4,5-b]pyridines, 306–307
Tricyclic scaffold CK2 inhibitors, 63f
anthraquinone and coumarin derivatives, 64–65
benzonaphthyridine derivatives, 62–64
Triple-negative breast cancer (TNBC), 92
Trisporic acid, 436f
Tristetraprolin (TTP), 256
1,3,5-Trisubstituted pyrazoline derivatives, 152–153
Tubulin, 395
assembly, 397–398
inhibition, 399f
structure, 396f
Tubulin polymerization inhibitors
benzenesulfonamide-pyrazole compounds, 406
benzimidazole-cinnamic acid hybrids, 410
benzo[b]furan and triazole derivatives, 409–410
chalcone, 407
colchicine binding site, 401, 401f
Cys-239 alkylation, 400
40,7-dihydroxycoumarin, 408–409
imidazole-chalcone analogs, 412–413
indole quinoline hybrid compounds, 406–407
indole-1,2,4-triazole derivatives, 411–412
macrocyclic polyethers, 402–403
ottelione A, 400
peptides and depsipeptides, 405f

pyrazole-naphthalene derivatives, 410–411
pyrazolo[3,4-b]pyridines, 411
pyridine-chalcone derivatives, 408
resveratrol-cinnamoyl hybrids, 407–408
1,2,3-triazole and sulfonamide derivatives, 409
tubulin assembly, 398–399
vinca domain, 402, 403f
XRP44X analogs, 412
Tumor necrosis factor alpha (TNF-α)
    and cancer, 424–425
    as oncogene, 423–424
Tumor necrosis factor receptor-associated protein 1
        (TRAP1)
    cancers, 421f
        apoptosis, 422–423
        esophageal squamous cell carcinoma (ESCC)
            tissues, 420–421
        kidney, 421
        ovarian cancer, 422
        TRAP1 over expression, 420–422
    inhibitors
        acetylcysteine, 431–432
        ATPase domain, 426
        and chemotherapeutics, 426
        cyclopeptide, 432–433
        EF24 and EF31 analogs, 433–434, 434f
        gamitrinib triphenyl phosphonium (G-TPP), 431
        glycoprotein IIb/IIIa (aIIbb3), 428
        Hsp90 and TRAP1, 425–426, 427f
        HSP90-related inhibitors, 428, 430f
        macrocyclic hydroxamic acids (MHAs), 434–435,
            436f
        monoclonal antibodies, 437–438
        pyrimidine-5-carbonitrile, 437
        SH-130, 435–436, 436f
        SPD-304 analogs, 432
        TNF inhibitors risk, 438
        ZINC05848961, ZINC09402309, ZINC04502991,
            434, 435f
    as oncogene, 423–424
    oncotherapy target, 425
    programmed cell death regulation, 422–423
    yeast two-hybrid screen, 419

V
Vandetanib, 341, 347–348, 348f
Vascular endothelial growth factor (VEGF),
        445–446
Vascular endothelial growth factor receptors
        (VEGFR/PDGFR) inhibitors
    allosteric inhibition, 471
    properties, 450t
    in silico ADME prediction parameters, 452t
    tumor angiogenesis, 446f
    type I and type II inhibitors, 450, 451f
    tyrosine kinase inhibitors
        adverse effect, 453, 454t
        FDA-approved, 453–469
        targeting, 447–450, 448f, 449t
VE-821, 27
Vemurafenib, 225–226, 381–382, 381f
VX970, 28f

W
Wortmannin, 24f, 25

Z
Zinc finger E-box binding homeobox 1 (ZEB1), 237

Printed in the United States
by Baker & Taylor Publisher Services